VALUING A BUSINESS

The Analysis and Appraisal of
Closely Held Companies

VALUING A BUSINESS

The Analysis and Appraisal of Closely Held Companies

Third Edition

Shannon P. Pratt, DBA, CFA, FASA
Managing Director
Willamette Management Associates

Robert F. Reilly, CPA, CFA, ASA
Managing Director
Willamette Management Associates

Robert P. Schweihs, ASA
Managing Director
Willamette Management Associates

IRWIN
Professional Publishing
Chicago • Bogotá • Boston • Buenos Aires • Caracas
London • Madrid • Mexico City • Sydney • Toronto

Irwin Professional Book Group

Senior sponsoring editor:	Amy Hollands Gaber
Project editor:	Karen J. Nelson
Production supervisor:	Laurie Kersch
Assistant manager, desktop services:	Jon Christopher
Designer:	Matthew Baldwin
Compositor:	Electronic Publishing Services, Inc.
Typeface:	11/13 Times Roman
Printer:	The Maple-Vail Book Manufacturing Group

Times Mirror
Higher Education Group

Library of Congress Cataloging-in-Publication Data

Pratt, Shannon P.
    Valuing a business: the analysis and appraisal of closely held companies/Shannon P. Pratt, Robert F. Reilly, Robert P. Schweihs.
-- 3rd ed.
    p. cm.
    Includes bibliographical references and index.
    ISBN 1-55623-971-8
    1. Corporations--Valuation. 2. Corporations--Valuation--Law and legislation--United States. I. Reilly, Robert F. II. Schweihs.
Robert P. III. Title.
HG4028.V3P7 1996
658.8'1--dc20   95-33137

Printed in the United States of America
1 2 3 4 5 6 7 8 9 0 MP 2 1 0 9 8 7 6 5

To Charlene

whose voice you hear when you call Shannon's office

who sets Shannon's schedule and sees that he gets there

and who produced this manuscript,
integrated the many editorial changes,
and proofed virtually every page of the final typeset text

With grateful appreciation

About the Authors

Dr. Shannon P. Pratt is a managing director and one of the founders of Willamette Management Associates. Founded in the 1960s, Willamette Management Associates is one of the oldest and largest independent valuation consulting, economic analysis, and financial advisory firms in the country. It is has regional offices in Atlanta, Georgia; McLean, Virginia; Chicago, Illinois; and Portland, Oregon. Willamette Management Associates is well known for its extensive research library, with a constantly updated collection of books, articles, transaction data sources, and court cases involving business valuation issues. This book draws heavily on that resource.

In addition to this book, Dr. Pratt is the author of *Valuing Small Businesses and Professional Practices,* second edition, with Robert Reilly and Robert Schweihs (Irwin Professional Publishing, 1993), and the co-author of *Guide to Business Valuations,* fifth edition (Practitioners Publishing Company, 1995).

Dr. Pratt holds a doctorate in finance from Indiana University and a bachelor of arts in business administration from the University of Washington. He is a chartered financial analyst and an accredited senior appraiser (certified in business valuation) and fellow of the American Society of Appraisers (the highest designation awarded by that society). Dr. Pratt has held many offices of the various professional societies and has served on numerous committees. Currently, he is a life member emeritus of the Business Valuation Committee of the American Society of Appraisers, a life member emeritus of the Valuation Advisory Committee of The ESOP Association, and a trustee of The Appraisal Foundation. He is frequently called upon to testify in disputed business valuation matters.

Robert F. Reilly is a managing director of Willamette Management Associates. He holds a master of business administration degree in finance from the Columbia University Graduate School of Business and a bachelor of arts degree in economics from Columbia College. He is an accredited senior appraiser of the American Society of Appraisers (certified in business valuation), a chartered financial analyst, a certified public accountant, a certified management accountant, an accredited tax advisor, a certified general appraiser, and a state certified affiliate of the Appraisal Institute. Mr. Reilly currently serves in an editorial capacity for—and is a regular contributor to—such professional journals as *The American Bankruptcy Institute Journal and The Journal of Property Tax Administration.* As an appraiser and economist, he has testified both in domestic and international courts on substantially over 100 occasions regarding the valuation of assets, properties, and business interests and regarding various economic damages issues.

Robert P. Schweihs is a managing director of Willamette Management Associates. He holds a master of business administration degree in economics and finance from the University of Chicago and a bachelor of science degree in mechanical engineering from the University of Notre Dame. He is an accredited senior appraiser of the American Society of Appraisers (certified in business valuation). Mr. Schweihs is a frequent speaker to professional societies and an author of articles on various aspects of business valuation. He is often called upon to testify in court on contested business valuation matters.

Preface

The book is designed to serve three purposes:

- A comprehensive and updated reference for currently active business appraisers.
- An introductory text on business appraisal for both academic courses and beginning practitioners.
- A reference for nonappraisers who use and/or evaluate business appraisals.

The authors have endeavored to present the current state of the art, thinking, and practice of the business valuation profession, which has progressed significantly since the second edition in 1989. Where clear consensus on positions exist, such consensus is presented. Where there are differing opinions, we try to present the issues clearly and fairly, reflecting extensive outside review (see Acknowledgments). We also present considerable documentation of various courts' positions on controversial issues.

More Emphasis on *Users* of Business Valuations

There is more emphasis in this edition on guidance for *users* of valuation work products, such as:

- Attorneys.
- Judges.
- Business owners, directors, and officers.
- Federal and state taxation and other regulatory authorities.
- CPAs.
- Investment bankers, merger and acquisition specialists, and business brokers.
- Bank trust officers and other trustees and fiduciaries.
- Commercial bankers.
- Financial and estate planners and other consultants to businesses and business owners.

Such people are increasingly aware that, even if they rely on a qualified appraisal, they should understand *why* the stock is worth, say, $10 per share rather than some higher or lower value. All the chapters have been written and edited with the user as well as the preparer of the valuation work product in mind, and material to this end has been added, most noticeably the chapter on Reviewing a Business Valuation Report.

Changes Since the Second Edition

The very substantial changes in this third edition reflect the impressive evolution and increased sophistication achieved by the business valuation profession since the second edition seven years ago. The changes also reflect input from hundreds of users of the book in every kind of business appraisal application, for which we are grateful.

General improvements in this edition include:

* Reorganized for a better information flow.
* A greatly expanded treatment of valuation approaches and methods.
* Hundreds of new bibliographical and information source references, conveniently placed at the end of most chapters.
* More comprehensive indexing, including a separate index to court cases referenced by type of case.
* A new and easier-to-follow notation system for formulas.

New material in this edition includes:

* **Discounts and premiums.** A new chapter on minority discount and control premium issues plus updated and expanded data on discounts for lack of marketability.
* **Reviewing a business valuation report.** An entirely new chapter in "checklist" format and cross-referenced to coverage of each topic elsewhere in the book.
* **Intangible asset valuation.** An entirely new three-chapter section.
* **Limited liability corporations and partnerships, S corporations, and other pass-through entities.** An entirely new chapter.
* **Ad valorem taxes.** An entirely new chapter.
* **Income tax planning and compliance.** An entirely new chapter.
* **IRS authority.** A new appendix indexing IRS Revenue Rulings and the *IRS Valuation Guide for Income, Estate and Gift Taxes* by subject matter.
* **Court case references.** Many new references throughout the book.

International Recognition of U.S. Business Valuation Leadership

It is gratifying to note that U.S. business appraisal leadership in general, and this book in particular, have gained a position of international acceptance in business valuation. The second edition has been used for business valuation education in several English-speaking countries and translated into several languages. This should be helpful to those involved in both international transactions and valuations within other countries.

Rapid Evolution of Business Valuation Practice

Don't throw away your second edition. There is so much new material in this third edition that we had to drop chapters and portions from the second edition to make it manageable. Much of the material not carried forward is still valid and useful for reference. Also, with hundreds of new bibliographical references, we had to drop many of the older ones, some of which are still valid and of interest.

Business and intangible asset valuation as a cohesive discipline is still at a relatively young stage of development in the United States. We will reflect these ongoing developments in future editions, and we solicit readers' critiques, comments, and suggestions. Please address your observations to any one of us at the addresses shown below.

In the meantime, Shannon Pratt plans to provide our readers with updates on information sources, bibliographical references, regulatory pronouncements, court decision citations, professional association news, and other timely information through a new newsletter, *Shannon Pratt's Business Valuation*. For information on this newsletter, or a complimentary sample copy, please contact Shannon Pratt.

Shannon P. Pratt
Willamette Management Associates
111 S.W. Fifth Avenue, Suite 2150
Portland, Oregon 97204
(503) 222-0577
(503) 222-7392 (FAX)

Robert F. Reilly
Willamette Management Associates
7918 Jones Branch Drive, Suite 210
McLean, Virginia 22102
(703) 556-6600
(703) 893-6078 (FAX)

Robert P. Schweihs
Willamette Management Associates
8600 West Bryn Mawr Avenue, Suite 950
Chicago, Illinois 60631
(312) 399-4300
(312) 399-4310 (FAX)

Acknowledgments

This third edition has benefitted immeasurably from the most extensive professional peer review of any of our books to date. All or parts of the manuscript have been reviewed and improved by a broad representation of the business valuation and investment banking community.

The following people from outside our firm reviewed the entire manuscript and provided the authors with very valuable comments and suggestions:

Joseph A. Agiato, Jr.
Goodman, Rakower & Agiato

M. Mark Lee
Bear, Stearns & Co. Inc.

Gregory J. Cowhey
Financial Research, Inc.

Gilbert E. Matthews
Bear, Stearns & Co. Inc.

Jay E. Fishman
Financial Research, Inc.

James S. Rigby, Jr.
The Financial Valuation Group

John A. Carrick
College Park, MD

Portions of the manuscript were also reviewed by the following individuals:

Michael Annin
Ibbotson Associates

Richard C. May
Valuemetrics, Inc.

Michael Mattson
Ibbotson Associates

Z. Christopher Mercer
Mercer Capital Management, Inc.

Erich Z. Sylvester
The Financial Valuation Group

Chapter 27, "Taxation Planning and Compliance—Gift and Estate," and Chapter 28, "Buy–Sell Agreements," were written by Curtis R. Kimball, the national director of estate and gift tax services and director of the Atlanta, Georgia, office of Willamette Management Associates. "A Sample Report," Chapter 18, was written by James R. Rabe, co-director of the Portland, Oregon, office of Willamette Management Associates. Chapter 20, "Debt Securities," was updated from the second edition by Scott L. Beauchene, a senior associate in our firm's Portland, Oregon, office.

Jeff Tarbell, a senior associate in our Chicago, Illinois, office, reviewed the entire manuscript to ensure the accuracy of the mathematical formulas and calculations. Karin Zamba, an associate in our Portland, Oregon, office, applied the ratio analysis discussed in Chapter 8 to the Sample Report from Chapter 18 and prepared exhibits for Chapter 21.

Pam Mastroleo served as the project manager for this undertaking, a job she performed superbly. This included acting as a liaison and coordinating with the authors, the publisher, and the many outside reviewers. She wrote the first draft of Chapter 6, "Researching Economic and Industry Information." She was also responsible for the bibliographies for each chapter and the general bibliography in Appendix D. Pam also proofread the manuscript.

Charlene Blalock was responsible for typing the entire manuscript, including many drafts of some of the chapters reflecting new materials and the many substantive outside reviewers comments and contributions. This was a monumental task. Charlene was also responsible for the final proofing of the entire book and for obtaining permission for using material reprinted in this book from other sources.

For permission to use material, we especially wish to thank:

- The Appraisal Foundation
- The American Society of Appraisers
- Practitioners Publishing Company
- Ibbotson Associates
- Prentice Hall
- Robert Morris Associates
- Standard & Poor's
- Merrill Lynch Business Valuation Services

Our gratitude goes to all the people singled out above as well as all those unnamed but not forgotten people who wrote letters and had discussions with us about many conceptual and technical points since the last edition. As always, of course, final responsibility for all content and judgments rests with the authors.

Shannon Pratt
Portland, Oregon

Robert Schweihs
Chicago, Illinois

Robert Reilly
McLean, Virginia

Contents

Relevant Time Period. Levels of Financial Statement Preparation. Impact of Enterprise Legal Structure. Federal Income Tax Returns. Interim Statements. Other Financial Schedules. *Current Assets and Liabilities. Plant and Equipment. Officers' and Directors' Compensation Schedule. Distribution of Ownership. Dividend or Partnership Withdrawal Schedule. Schedule of Key-Person Life Insurance. Off-Balance-Sheet Assets or Liabilities. Related Party Transaction Information.* Operating Information. *Company History. Brochures, Catalogs, and Price Lists. Key Personnel. Customer and Supplier Base. Contractual Agreements and Obligations. Industry and Trade Association Information.* List of Past Transactions in the Stock or Offers to Buy. Budgets and Forecasts. Capital Requirements. *Capital Expenditures. Deferred Maintenance. Working Capital Requirements.* Company Documents Relating to the Rights of Owners. *Corporate or Partnership Records. Buy–Sell and ESOP Agreements. Employment and Noncompete Agreements.* Summary.

Value per Share. Adjusting the Balance Sheet to Current Values.
Summary. Bibliography.

List of Exhibits

Notation System Used in This Book

A source of confusion for those trying to understand financial theory and methods is the fact that financial writers have not adopted a standard system of notation. For this edition, we have studied dozens of financial texts and have developed a system of notation that reflects either the most commonly used conventions or ones that seem intuitively easy to correctly understand. If other financial writers adopt this standardized system of notation, we believe it will go a long way toward removing ambiguity, clarifying communication, and making it easier for readers to absorb financial articles and texts.

Value at a point in time:

$$PV = \text{Present value}$$
$$FV = \text{Future value}$$
$$MVIC = \text{Market value of invested capital}$$

Cost of capital and rate of return variables:

k = Discount rate (generalized)

k_e = Discount rate for common equity capital (cost of common equity capital). Unless otherwise stated, it generally is assumed that this discount rate is applicable to net cash flow available to common equity.

k_p = Discount rate for preferred equity capital

k_d = Discount rate for debt (Note: for complex capital structures there could be more than one class of capital in any of the above categories, requiring expanded subscripts.)

k_{ni} = Discount rate for equity capital when net income rather than net cash flow is the measure of economic income being discounted

c = Capitalization rate

c_e = Capitalization rate for common equity capital (cost of common equity capital). Unless otherwise stated, it generally is assumed that this capitalization rate is applicable to net cash flow available to common equity.

c_{ni} = Capitalization rate for net income

c_p = Capitalization rate for preferred equity capital

c_d = Capitalization rate for debt (Note: for complex capital structures there could be more than one class of capital in any of the above categories, requiring expanded subscripts.)

t = Tax rate (expressed as a percentage of pretax income)

R = Rate of return

R_f = Rate of return on a risk-free security

$E(R)$ = Expected rate of return

$E(R_m)$ = Expected rate of return on the "market" (usually used in the context of a market for equity securities, such as the NYSE or S&P 500)

$E(R_i)$ = Expected rate of return on security i

B = Beta (a coefficient, usually used to modify a rate of return variable)

B_L = Levered beta

B_U = Unlevered beta

RP = Risk premium

RP_m = Risk premium for the "market" (usually used in the context of a market for equity securities, such as the NYSE or S&P 500)

RP_s = Risk premium for size

RP_u = Risk premium for unsystematic risk attributable to the specific company

RP_i = Risk premium for the ith security

$K_1 \ldots K_n$ = Risk premium associated with risk factor 1 through n for the average asset in the market (used in conjunction with Arbitrage Pricing Theory)

WACC = Weighted average cost of capital

Income variables:

E = Expected economic income (in a generalized sense, i.e., could be dividends, any of several possible definitions of cash flows, net income, and so on)

NI = Net income (after entity-level taxes)

NCF_e = Net cash flow to equity

NCF_f = Net cash flow to the firm (to overall invested capital, or entire capital structure, including all equity and long-term debt)

PMT = Payment (interest and principal payment on debt security)

D = Dividends

GCF = Gross cash flow (usually net income plus noncash charges)

EBIT = Earnings before interest and taxes

EBDIT = Earnings before depreciation, interest, and taxes ("Depreciation" in this context usually includes amortization. Some writers use "EBDITA" to specifically indicate that amortization is included.)

Periods or variables in a series:

i = The ith period, or the ith variable in a series (may be extended to the jth variable, the kth variable, and so on)

n = The number of periods or variables in the series, or the last number in the series

∞ = Infinity

$_o$ = Period$_o$, the base period, usually the latest year immediately preceding the valuation date

Weightings:

W = Weight

W_e = Weight of common equity in capital structure

W_p = Weight of preferred equity in capital structure
W_d = Weight of debt in capital structure

NOTE: For purposes of computing a weighted average cost of capital (WACC), it is assumed that above weightings are at market value.

Growth:

g = Rate of growth

Mathematical functions:

Σ = Sum of (add up all the variables that follow)
Π = Product of (multiply together all the variables that follow)
$\overline{x}$ = Mean average (the sum of the values of the variables divided by the number of variables)
G = Geometric mean (the product of the values of the variables taken to the root of the number of variables)

Part I

Introduction to Business Valuation

Chapter 1

Business Valuation Professional Standards

There are available substantive aids and/or methods which are generally recognized and accepted by the appraisal profession and the Courts.[1]

The most significant achievement in the discipline of business appraisal since the second edition of this book in 1989 is the development of professional standards with regard to business valuations. Finally, after over half a century, business valuation has evolved from the much used and abused Appeals and Review Memorandum (ARM) 34 published in 1920[2] to a profession with promulgated standards in 1995. Meaningful business valuation standards started with the first draft of the Uniform Standards of Professional Appraisal Practice in 1988 and continued with updates of that and the American Society of Appraisers Business Valuation Standards in the mid-1990s.

Anyone performing, or in any way using, a business appraisal should be aware of these standards. This chapter summarizes the sources of and status of these and other standards. The bibliography at the end of the chapter details sources for complete, current information and updating of future developments. This chapter also discusses briefly certain professional and governmental bodies that have addressed business valuation issues in various ways, although without necessarily setting standards.

The Appraisal Foundation

Background and Organization

The Appraisal Foundation was established in 1987 by nine appraisal organizations constituting the North American Council of Appraisal Organizations (NACAO) and six nonappraiser members including the American Bankers Association and the U.S. League of Savings Institutions. Eight of the nine appraisal organizations were composed entirely of real estate appraisers. One, the American Society of Appraisers, is multidisciplinary. The American Society of Appraisers awards certification in real estate, machinery and equipment, personal property, business valuation, and technical valuation.

The Board of Trustees of The Appraisal Foundation consists of representatives of the sponsor organizations plus 14 trustees-at-large. The board of trustees appoints two independent boards:

1. The **Appraisal Standards Board** promulgates the Uniform Standards of Professional Appraisal Practice (see below).
2. The **Appraisal Qualifications Board** promulgates appraiser qualifications. So far, it has done so only for real estate appraisers, but as of this writing, the board of trustees has recommended development of qualifications both for personal property appraisers and for business appraisers.

---

[1]Internal Revenue Service, *Course Book on Valuation Training for Appeals Officers,* 1993, Lesson 1, p. 10.

[2]ARM 34 was issued by the U.S. Treasury Department in 1920 as a formula to compute the value of goodwill to compensate distilling companies put out of business by Prohibition.

Exhibit 1–1
1995 Uniform Standards of Professional Appraisal Practice

Introduction

Preamble
Ethics Provision
Competency Provision
Departure Provision
Jurisdictional Exception
Supplemental Standards
Definitions

Standards and Standards Rules

Standard 1   Real Property Appraisal
Standard 2   Real Property Appraisal, Reporting
Standard 3   Review Appraisal and Reporting
Standard 4   Real Estate/Real Property Consulting
Standard 5   Real Estate/Real Property Consulting, Reporting
Standard 6   Mass Appraisal and Reporting
Standard 7   Personal Property Appraisal
Standard 8   Personal Property Appraisal, Reporting
Standard 9   Business Appraisal
Standard 10 Business Appraisal, Reporting

Statements on Appraisal Standards

SMT-1   Standards Rule 3-1(f) (Review Appraisal)

SMT-2   Discounted Cash Flow Analysis
SMT-3   Retrospective Value Estimates
SMT-4   Prospective Value Estimates
SMT-5   Confidentiality Rule of the Ethics Provision
SMT-6   Reasonable Exposure Time in Market Value Estimates
SMT-7   Permitted Departure from Specific Guidelines for Real Property Appraisals (Effective July 1, 1994)

Advisory Opinions

G-1   Sales History
G-2   Inspection of Subject Property Real Estate
G-3   Update of an Appraisal
G-4   Standards Rule 1-5(b)
G-5   Assistance in the Preparation of an Appraisal
G-6   The Review Appraisal Function
G-7   Marketing Time Estimates
G-8   Market Value vs. Fair Value in Real Property Appraisals
G-9   Responsibility of Appraisers Concerning Toxic or Hazardous Substance Contamination
G-10   The Appraiser-Client Relationship
G-11   Content of the Appraisal Report Options of Standard 2
G-12   Use of the Appraisal Report Options of Standard 2

SOURCE: *Uniform Standards of Professional Appraisal Practice* (Washington, DC: The Appraisal Foundation, 1995). USPAP is available from The Appraisal Foundation, 1029 Vermont Avenue N.W., Suite 900, Washington, DC 20005, (202) 347-7722.

Uniform Standards of Professional Appraisal Practice (USPAP)

The Financial Institution Reform, Recovery, and Enforcement Act (FIRREA) makes compliance with USPAP mandatory for all federally related real estate transactions. Although not yet mandatory as of this writing for most federally related transactions involving personal property and business appraisals, USPAP has been adopted by major appraisal organizations in North America and has become widely recognized as the generally accepted standards of appraisal practice.

The content of USPAP is summarized in Exhibit 1–1. The Standards themselves and the Statements on Appraisal Standards, are mandatory for members of professional appraisal organizations that have adopted USPAP (including the American Society of Appraisers). Advisory opinions are illustrative and offer advice, but they are not mandatory.

USPAP is published annually in November (see bibliography at end of chapter for details).

American Society of Appraisers

Background and Activities

The American Society of Appraisers (ASA) is a long-standing, multidisciplinary organization that offers education and professional accreditation in many appraisal disciplines, including real property, machinery and equipment, personal property, and a number of technical valuation specialties, as well as in business valuation. From 1984 through 1994, the business valuation discipline was the ASA's fastest growing area of accreditation.

The professional designation ASA stands for *Accredited Senior Appraiser.* To acquire this designation, one needs to do the following: demonstrate five years of full-time equivalent experience in the discipline in which the designation is granted; pass the relevant examinations (a one-hour ethics exam and comprehensive technical exams); and submit two appraisal reports that meet the examining committee's standards. The American Society of Appraisers also awards the professional designation AM, Accredited Member, which has all the same requirements as the ASA except for only a two-year full-time equivalent experience requirement. The "full-time equivalent" experience requirement can be met on a part-time basis—that is, two years of doing business appraisal work half-time equals one year full-time equivalent, and so on.

The American Society of Appraisers offers a series of four three-day basic courses in business valuation, each presented several times per year at various locations around the United States. The society also offers several one- to three-day courses and seminars on specific valuation topics, such as small business valuation, intangible asset valuation, and litigation support. In addition, the ASA holds an annual meeting for members from all appraisal disciplines. In recent years, this event has included two days of educational meetings on business appraisal topics. Also, the Business Valuation Committee sponsors a two-day advanced business valuation seminar each fall. Local ASA chapters or regional groups of chapters occasionally sponsor educational programs.

The Business Valuation Committee also publishes a quarterly journal, *Business Valuation Review,* and the ASA publishes a multidisciplinary appraisal journal, *Valuation.* Addresses for ASA publications and information are included in the bibliography at the end of this chapter.

ASA Business Appraisal Standards

The American Society of Appraisers, through its Business Valuation Committee, completed a set of business valuation standards. These are reprinted in full as Appendix C at the back of this book.

The ASA fully embraces USPAP, and compliance with USPAP is mandatory for all accredited members of ASA. Also, the ASA Business Valuation Standards provide more detail on implementation of business valuation approaches and methods, and compliance with the ASA Business Valuation Standards is mandatory for all ASA member business valuations. The Business Valuation Committee of the ASA also has recognized certain books as "authoritative references," and these are noted in the bibliography at the end of this chapter. The purpose of this recognition is to call attention to treatises that provide professional depth in research and presentation, but not necessarily to endorse all positions taken by each such reference.

Institute of Business Appraisers

The Institute of Business Appraisers (IBA), founded in 1978, offers seminars on business appraisal topics and grants the professional designation CBA, Certified Business Appraiser. The CBA designation requires an examination and the approval of appraisal reports, but has no experience requirement.

The IBA publishes a code of ethics and, in 1993, completed a set of business appraisal standards. As with the ASA standards, the IBA standards fully embrace USPAP and provide additional detailed guidance. The address for IBA materials is presented in the bibliography at the end of the chapter.

Canadian Institute of Chartered Business Valuators

The Canadian Institute of Chartered Business Valuators (CICBV), founded in 1971, provides educational meetings and the professional designation CBV, Chartered Business Valuator. The CBV designation requires an examination and three years of full-time experience, five years of part-time experience, or two years of experience and a required course of study.

The CICBV publishes the proceedings of its biennial professional meetings in *The Journal of Business Valuation.* It also publishes a code of ethics and CICBV Practice Standards. The address for CICBV materials and information is presented in the bibliography at the end of the chapter.

Other Organizations that Have Addressed Business Valuation Issues

The ESOP Association

The ESOP Association is an organization of companies that have employee stock ownership plans (ESOPs) and companies that provide professional advisory services to ESOP companies. One of the association's committees is the Valuation Advisory Committee, composed of 25 professional practitioner members of leading companies regularly performing ESOP valuations.

The ESOP Association Valuation Advisory Committee meets twice a year to discuss issues concerning the valuation of ESOP shares, primarily those in closely held companies. The ESOP Association neither certifies nor endorses business appraisers or any other specialists, nor does it issue standards as such. However, it publishes a very useful book, *Valuing ESOP Shares,* reflecting the deliberations and views of the Valuation Advisory Committee on many issues affecting the valuation of ESOP shares. The address to obtain this book and other ESOP Association information is presented in the bibliography at the end of this chapter.

American Institute of Certified Public Accountants (AICPA)

The Management Consulting Services Division of the AICPA issues Management Consulting Standards that apply generally to consulting engagements. Some such engagements may involve a business valuation, but the standards do not specifically address business valuation as such.

There is nothing in the uniform CPA examination that addresses the subject of business appraisal. However, many CPAs who are active in business appraisal have also achieved certification as business appraisers by the ASA and/or IBA. In Canada, most chartered accountants who are active in business appraisal are certified by the CICBV and/or the ASA.

The AICPA has a provision for testing and conferring an accreditation designation related to the practice of accounting called the Personal Financial Specialist (PFS) offered through the Personal Financial Planning Division. The Management Consulting Services Division of the AICPA is considering development of a business valuation accreditation designation, tentatively to be known as Business Valuation Specialist. The AICPA also has a Business Valuation Task Force, which is studying this issue, as well as AICPA education programs in business valuation.

In the meantime, the AICPA has issued a 2½-hour videotape, *Business Valuation Videocourse,* and Small Business Consulting Practice Aid 93-3, *Conducting a Valuation of a Closely Held Business.* See the bibliography at the end of this chapter for details. The AICPA, through its Continuing Professional Education Division (CPE), offers both group-study and self-study CPE courses in business valuation. The AICPA also offers a certificate of educational achievement program (CEA) in business valuation. It is an eight-module program covering valuation concepts, methodology, and report writing. The CEA program does not confer an accreditation at the program's conclusion, and the certificate is not considered a professional designation.

Association for Investment Management and Research

The Association for Investment Management and Research (AIMR) publishes educational materials, conducts seminars, and confers the professional designation CFA, Chartered Financial Analyst. Achievement of the CFA designation requires passing three rigorous all-day examinations, given annually. Each exam must be passed sequentially, so it is a minimum three-year program.

AIMR materials and the CFA exams are oriented primarily to the analysis of publicly traded securities and the management of investment portfolios. As the interaction between publicly traded and closely held companies (mergers, acquisitions, leveraged buyouts, spin-offs, and so on) has accelerated in recent years, the AIMR has given increasing attention to analysis and appraisal of closely held companies. In 1990, the Institute of Chartered Financial Analysts published a monograph titled *Valuation of Closely Held Companies and Inactively Traded Securities* (see bibliography) based on a seminar by the same name.

An increasing number of business appraisers (primarily those valuing medium to larger companies) hold both the ASA and CFA professional designations.

Internal Revenue Service

Congress directs the U.S. Treasury Department to issue regulations to provide structure for the tax laws it passes. These regulations do not have the force of law, but present the position of the IRS on various tax matters, including the valuation of businesses, business interests, and related intangible assets. Regulations are actually formulated by the IRS, but they are approved by the Secretary of the Treasury or his delegate. As an example, the regulations for Chapter 14 of the estate and gift tax laws require appraisers to use a special valuation methodology in certain circumstances with regard to family-owned businesses.

The IRS issues "Pronouncements" representing administrative (as opposed to legislative) tax authority. The pronouncements include: Revenue Rulings, Revenue Procedures, Letter Rulings, Technical Advice Memorandums, and General Counsel Memorandums. These pronouncements illustrate the treatment of certain issues not clearly addressed in the regulations. Over time, many of the positions espoused by the IRS through regulations and Revenue Rulings come up in court disputes. The resolution of these issues by the courts establishes case law precedent. Much, but by no means all, of the case law has been supportive of positions taken in the regulations and Revenue Rulings. The most important of the Revenue Rulings that relate to business valuation are:

59-60	Discusses valuing closely held stock.
65-193	Deletes the final §4.02(f) of Revenue Ruling 59-60 dealing with the valuation of intangibles.
68-609	Discusses "formula method" for determining fair market value of intangible assets of a business. Supersedes ARM 34. Theory in Revenue Ruling 59-60 applies to income and other taxes as well as to estate and gift taxes, and to business interests of any type, including partnerships and proprietorships, and to intangible assets for all tax purposes.
77-287	Recognizes relevance of restricted stock studies (see Chapter 15) in determining discounts for lack of marketability.
83-120	Discusses valuing preferred stock.
93-12	Allows the application of minority discounts to partial interest transfers even when a family owns overall control of a closely held business. Supersedes and reverses Revenue Ruling 81-253, which disallowed such discounts, but was overturned by case law.

Representing less authority than the Revenue Rulings, the Private Letter Rulings, Technical Advice Memorandums, and General Counsel Memorandums issued by the IRS are responses to specific inquiries from taxpayers (and/or from IRS field offices) and may not be cited as precedent. Nevertheless, these can be helpful in understanding the Service's likely position on emerging issues for tax-related appraisals.

IRS internal publications and other official materials also provide useful insights. The January 1994 *Course Book on Valuation Training for Appeals Officers* is available through Commerce Clearing House or on-line (see bibliography).

To provide a convenient reference tool for both users and preparers of business and intangible asset appraisals, we have indexed the Revenue Rulings listed in this section and also the chapters of the IRS *Course Book on Valuation Training for Appeals Officers* dealing with valuation of businesses and intangible assets. This index is included as Appendix A at the back of the book.

Revenue Rulings and other IRS pronouncements often are cited for valuation guidance for purposes other than taxes. This can be useful to the extent that the material contains general valuation guidance. However, as discussed extensively in this book, valuation methods may differ for different purposes, and all aspects of Revenue Rulings may not be appropriate for nontax purposes.

Department of Labor

Like the IRS Revenue Rulings, regulations issued by the Department of Labor (DOL) do not have the force of law. They represent the department's position with respect to interpretation of the law as it applies to certain issues.

In May 1988, the DOL issued a proposed draft of a Regulation Relating to the Definition of Adequate Consideration (for ESOP stock). Hearings have been held and written comments have been received. The complete text of the 1988 proposed regulation was included as Exhibit 23–2 in Chapter 23 on ESOPs in the second edition of this book. On May 8, 1995, the DOL announced that it had withdrawn the proposed regulations, effective February 1, 1995.

Recognition of Professional Standards by Courts

Most business valuations have the potential for a legal challenge. Courts like to have professionally accepted standards to rely on for guidance in deciding disputed issues. Courts may suspect poor appraisal work, but it helps them tremendously to be able to cite authority for rejection of work that fails to meet professional standards. The authors, and many other business appraisers, have brought the authority of the standards and other professional guidance discussed in this chapter to bear very fruitfully in court on numerous occasions.

One result of previous editions of this book, and the development of the standards and other professional guidance discussed in this chapter, is an increased consensus and consistency in the resolution of business valuation issues, both in the courts and elsewhere. There have been numerous references to this book in reported decisions quoting testimony that ultimately assisted the court in reaching its decision. We believe this has contributed to the consistency of judicial decisions. The standards and other guidance discussed in this chapter continue to build consensus and consistency on business valuation issues. As these materials are more widely disseminated and recognized, undoubtedly they will significantly impact court decisions in the future.

International Acceptance of U.S. Standards and Practices

The United States is by far the world leader in both markets for and analysis of securities, companies, and business interests. This is true for both publicly traded securities and also closely held businesses and business interests.

Two factors have combined to accelerate the spread of U.S. technology in financial appraisals and markets throughout the world:

1. Rapidly increasing international flow of capital.
2. Growing privatization of formerly socially owned businesses in almost every country of every continent.

The standards and guidance in this chapter and throughout this book are becoming increasingly applicable to international as well as domestic transactions as the world financial markets become more homogenous.

Parts or all of the second edition of this book already have been translated into several foreign languages. Several governments have adopted USPAP and the ASA Business Valuation Standards as mandatory criteria for business valuations for transactions involving privatization. The authors, and other ASA members, have taught material from this book, USPAP, and ASA Business Valuation Standards in many countries throughout the world. Such presentations have been made under the varied auspices of private business organizations, local professional appraisal societies, local governments, academic institutions, the United Nations, and the World Bank.

Most meetings of the professional organizations listed in this chapter are attended by representatives of many foreign countries. The worldwide appetite for translations and teachers of U.S. business appraisal standards and practices is challenging our professionals' ability to fill such demand. We believe this growing global homogeneity of business appraisal standards and practices will contribute positively to successful privatization, worldwide capital flows, and economic growth.

Summary

The first half of the 1990s marked the culmination of longtime efforts to develop business valuation standards on which the professional business valuation community could achieve general consensus. These standards are rapidly being disseminated and recognized, not only throughout the professional business appraisal community and the courts in the United States, but also worldwide.

We believe these developments have already had some positive impact on the average quality of business valuation work. Business valuation practitioners are becoming more knowledgeable and rigorous in their practices. The standards also provide attorneys, CPAs, business owners, courts, and others who rely on business appraisals some widely accepted criteria by which to judge the quality of a business valuation. Chapter 19 of this book, "Reviewing a Business Valuation Report," will be helpful in evaluating a business valuation product against the background of these standards.

The standards will continue to undergo refinement, but a solid foundation is finally in place.

Bibliography

American Institute of Certified Public Accountants, Harborside Financial Center, 201 Plaza III, Jersey City, NJ 07311-3881, (800) 862-4272.

- *Business Valuation Videocourse,* moderated by Shannon P. Pratt (Jersey City, NJ: American Society of Certified Public Accountants, 1993). The objective of this videocourse is to provide practitioners with an overview of the essentials of business valuation. Joining Dr. Pratt in the 2½-hour video presentation are Robert F. Reilly, Robert P. Schweihs, and Jay E. Fishman. The videocourse and accompanying course handbook are available from the AICPA, P.O. Box 2209, Jersey City, NJ 07303-2209, (800) 862-4272. The course code number is 350115.

- *Conducting a Valuation of a Closely Held Business,* by Gary R. Trugman (Jersey City, NJ: AICPA, Management Consulting Services Division, 1993). A consulting service practice aid available from the AICPA.

American Society of Appraisers, P.O. Box 17265, Washington, DC 20041, (703) 478-2228.

- Principles of Appraisal Practice and Code of Ethics—available free from the ASA.
- Standards for Business Valuation—single copies available free from the publisher of *Business Valuation Review.*
- *Business Valuation Review*, a quarterly publication of the Business Valuation Committee of the American Society of Appraisers. Subscriptions are available by calling or writing the publisher: P.O. Box 24222, Denver, CO 80224, (303) 758-6148. Back issues are also available.
- *Valuation,* published periodically by the ASA, is multidisciplinary.
- Books recognized as "authoritative references" by the American Society of Appraisers Business Valuation Committee:
  — Campbell, Ian R. *The Valuation and Pricing of Privately-Held Business Interests.* Toronto: The Canadian Institute of Chartered Accountants, 1990.
  — Fishman, Jay E., and Shannon P. Pratt, et al. *Guide to Business Valuations,* 5th ed. Fort Worth: Practitioners Publishing Company, 1995.
  — Mercer, Z. Christopher. *Valuing Financial Institutions.* Burr Ridge, IL: Irwin Professional Publishing, 1992.
  — Pratt, Shannon P. *Valuing a Business: The Analysis and Appraisal of Closely Held Companies,* 2nd ed. Burr Ridge, IL: Irwin Professional Publishing, 1989.
  — Pratt, Shannon P. *Valuing Small Businesses and Professional Practices,* 2nd ed. Burr Ridge, IL: Irwin Professional Publishing, 1993.
  — Smith, Gordon V., and Russell L. Parr. *Valuation of Intellectual Property and Intangible Assets,* 2nd ed. New York: John Wiley & Sons, 1994.
  — Zukin, James H., and John G. Mavredakis, eds. *Financial Valuation: Businesses and Business Interests.* New York: Maxwell Macmillan, 1990, updated annually.

The Appraisal Foundation, 1029 Vermont Avenue, N.W., Suite 900, Washington, DC 20005, (202) 347-7722.

- *Uniform Standards of Professional Appraisal Practice,* issued annually in November.
- Information Service. The Information Service is designed to provide summary-oriented information to appraisers, users of appraisal services, and others who have an interest in remaining current on the activities of The Appraisal Foundation, the Appraisal Standards Board (ASB), and the Appraiser Qualifications Board (AQB).
- Subscription Service. The Subscription Service is the complete source of information for appraisers, users of appraisal services, and others on the activities of The Appraisal Foundation, the Appraisal Standards Board (ASB), and the Appraiser Qualifications Board (AQB).

Association for Investment Management and Research, 5 Boar's Head Lane, P.O. Box 3668, Charlottesville, VA 22903, (804) 977-6600.

- *Financial Analysts Journal*, published bimonthly.
- *Valuation of Closely Held Companies and Inactively Traded Securities,* edited by E. Theodore Veit, 1990 (monograph).

Canadian Institute of Chartered Business Valuators, 277 Wellington Street, W., 5th floor, Toronto, Ontario, Canada M5V 3H2, (416) 204-3396.

- CICBV Practice Standards–all have been officially ratified by their members.

The ESOP Association, 1100 17th Street, N.W., Suite 210, Washington, DC 20036, (202) 293-2971.

- *Valuing ESOP Shares,* revised edition, 1994.

Internal Revenue Service, 1111 Constitution Avenue, N.W., Washington, DC 20224, (202) 566-5000.

- *IRS Valuation Guide for Income, Estate, and Gift Taxes* (*Course Book on Valuation Training for Appeals Officers)* (1994). Available through Commerce Clearing House Publishers, (800) 248-3248.

Chapter 2

Defining the Appraisal Assignment

It is impossible to intelligently discuss methods of valuation without reference to some assumed definition of value.[1]

Many people hold the mistaken notion that there can be only one "value." As we will see in this chapter, there are many definitions of value, and the purpose of the appraisal usually determines the appropriate definition of value.

This chapter is designed to help the appraiser and the client (or the client's legal and other advisors) to focus together on all the elements that need to be specified in the appraisal assignment, so that appropriate methodology will be employed to accomplish the objective of the specific engagement.

Identifying and clearly defining the purpose and objective of the business valuation assignment goes a long way toward eliminating many of the problems that occur with the conclusions of business valuation projects. While it seems simple, and should be simple to understand, failure to clearly define the elements of the appraisal assignment *at the outset of the business appraisal* is one of the greatest sources of errors, delays, excess costs, and misunderstandings between client and appraiser in a business valuation.

Defining the valuation assignment is the logical beginning of the valuation process, providing focus for all the valuation considerations and efforts to be undertaken. Inadequate specification of the appraisal assignment often results in misdirected efforts and invalid conclusions.

It may seem obvious that the first step is to define the task. However, when asked to participate in finding a solution to a client's problem, the client often does not know how to define the appraiser's assignment, and communication to agree on and mutually understand the assignment is often the most critical step. In fact, valuation assignments that have turned out poorly are often due to a failure to carefully define the assignment at the outset.

The reason for this failure may be that the client lacks sufficient experience to realize all the details that should be included in the appraisal assignment or has not thought through the implications of some aspects of the appraisal. People who do not engage in business appraisals on a regular basis are unlikely to consider all the key elements of an appraisal assignment. The professional appraiser should help the client (and/or the client's attorney) in these details. However, appraisers are not lawyers and do not practice law. When legal issues are involved, it is the ultimate responsibility of the attorney, not the appraiser, to frame those issues.

Regardless of why the shortcomings occur, time spent at the outset in being thorough and explicit in defining the appraisal assignment is time well spent.

Basic Elements of the Appraisal Assignment

The basic elements of the appraisal assignment include:

1. Name of the client and of the appraiser.
2. Definition of the legal interest or interests to be appraised.

---

[1] James C. Bonbright, *The Valuation of Property*, Vol. I (Charlottesville, VA: The Michie Company, 1965 [reprint of 1937 ed.]), p. 128.

3. Date or dates of the valuation (the date as of which the appraiser's opinion of value applies).
4. Purpose or purposes of the appraisal (the use to which the valuation exercise is expected to be put).
5. Applicable standard (or definition) of value.
6. Going-concern versus liquidation premise of value.
7. Description of the specific ownership characteristics:
    a. Size of interest relative to total.
    b. Degree of marketability (e.g., public, private, and related matters).
8. Form and extent of written and/or oral report.
9. Special requirements, limitations, or special instructions for the professional appraiser.

Often, it is impossible to define at the outset all the relevant details of the appraisal assignment. In those cases, it may be helpful for the appraiser to list the elements that are understood and the elements remaining to be understood. The appraiser then can follow up to try to resolve such questions. Exhibit 2–1 presents a general checklist for defining the appraisal assignment.

Writing valuation objectives and requirements forces those responsible for the valuation to think carefully through all of its essential elements. It also helps prevent misdirecting the valuation process and helps the various parties involved, such as the principals, brokers, attorneys, and professional appraisers, avoid misunderstandings that otherwise might arise.

Exhibit 2–1
Valuation Assignment Checklist

Name of entity _____

Form of ownership
   ☐ Regular corporation   ☐ Limited partnership
   ☐ Subchapter S corporation   ☐ Sole proprietorship
   ☐ General partnership   ☐ Other (please specify)

State in which incorporated or registered

Valuation being done on   ☐ stock basis, or   ☐ asset basis
   (If asset basis, list assets to be included and liabilities to be assumed, if any)

Are there other classes of equity interests outstanding?   ☐ Yes   ☐ No
   (If yes, please specify)

Proportion of total entity being valued
Any restrictions on transfer?
Purpose or purposes of the valuation

Applicable standard of value (If pursuant to a federal or state statute, corporate bylaw or other governing law or document, so indicate)
Appraisal date
Is covenant not to compete involved?   ☐ Yes   ☐ No
Is employment agreement(s) involved?   ☐ Yes   ☐ No
If independent appraiser is retained:
   Name of appraiser
   Name of client
   Form and extent of appraisal report
   Expected completion date (specify due date of various phases)
   Fee arrangement

SOURCE: Willamette Management Associates.

As the appraisal assignment develops, the file containing information on it will grow. As the missing details from the original appraisal assignment are changed or filled in, the appraiser typically notes them by memorandums to the file as they are discovered.

Definition of Who Made and Who Accepted the Assignment

The most obvious reason for clearly defining the client and the appraiser is to know who is responsible for providing the services and who is responsible for paying for the services.

Another reason is that the appraiser has a responsibility to release confidential information about the appraisal only to the client. Others receive confidential information about the appraisal only with the client's permission, or if required by law.

If the case involves pending or potential litigation, the attorney may prefer to have his law firm retain the appraiser, rather than have the client retain the appraiser directly. This relationship may protect the appraiser's work and files from subpoena by the opposing attorney, although the effectiveness of such protection varies greatly from one situation to another.

Even when a business transaction is likely to be the ultimate outcome, it is important to specify by whom the appraiser is engaged. The appraiser may be engaged by the board of directors of the buying or selling company, the employee stock ownership plan trustee, or one or more individual shareholders of the buying or selling company, for example. The appraiser's relationship to the parties involved should be clear.

When specifying who is to provide the appraisal services, the important distinction is whether the client is retaining the appraisal firm itself or the individual appraiser employed by the firm. The common practice is to retain the firm rather than the individual appraiser. This practice protects the client, since the firm is responsible for completing the assignment regardless of impairments to the individual's capability to perform the work. This practice also tends to provide continuity in retention of the working papers and related records, making them accessible if they are needed months or even years later, as they frequently are.

Description of the Legal Interest or Interests to Be Appraised

To determine the applicable valuation approach and analytical steps to be taken, *exactly* what is to be appraised must be made clear. Much of the confusion and disagreement among appraisers and appraisal writings arises simply because it is not clear exactly what asset, property, or business interest is to be valued.

Description of the Business Entity

If the entity at issue is incorporated, both the official name and the state of incorporation are necessary for an adequate definition of it. The state of incorporation is necessary because two or more corporations that are incorporated in different states may have identical names. Furthermore, the laws of the state of incorporation may have a bearing on the value of a particular business.

If, on the other hand, the business is not a corporation but some other structure, the form as well as the name must be specified. Some of the most common forms of business organization are sole proprietorships, general and limited partnerships, and cooperatives. By the same token, if the entity's structure gives rise to special legal or tax considerations, that structure should be specified. Some of these forms include S corporations, limited liability corporations, limited liability partnerships, family limited partnerships, professional corporations, real estate investment trusts, investment companies registered under the Investment Company Act of 1940, and personal holding companies.

Description of the Specific Business Interest

The definition of the specific business interest can be broken into two broad questions:

1. Is the appraisal to be an appraisal of assets or an appraisal of securities?
2. In either case, exactly *what* assets or *what* securities are subject to appraisal?

By *securities* in the above context, we mean ownership interests such as stock, debt, and partnership interests, as opposed to direct ownership of underlying assets of the subject business entity.

Assets versus Securities. Stock or a partnership interest represents an indirect ownership interest in whatever bundle of assets and liabilities (actual and contingent) exists in the business enterprise. Stock or partnership ownership is quite different from direct ownership of assets and direct obligation for liabilities. If stock or a partnership interest is to be valued, it must be identified in the appraisal assignment. If assets are to be valued, those assets (and any liabilities to be assumed) must be specified. For example, the assignment might include language such as "...engaged to estimate the fair market value of the fixed assets, inventory, and goodwill, on a going-concern basis, of..." In the analysis of the stock or a partnership interest in a business as compared to the assets of a business, noteworthy tax, legal, and financial characteristics come into play. These may have a significant impact on the valuation.[2]

And, typically, the valuation methods (and, certainly, the individual valuation procedures and variables) that are appropriate in the valuation of business securities—such as debt and equity instruments—are not appropriate in the valuation of business assets such as tangible and intangible assets. This is true even when both the business securities and the business assets are valued under the same appraisal premise such as value in continued use as a going concern.

Partial Interests. If a partial interest in an entity is to be valued, the proportionate relationship of the partial interest to the whole is obviously important. If there is more than one class of stock, such as preferred and common, or voting and nonvoting common, then the appraisal assignment should indicate which class of

---

[2]See, for example, *Edwin A. Gallun* v. *Comm.*, 33 T.C.M. 284 (1974).

stock is being appraised. If the business to be appraised is only a portion of the entire entity, such as a division or branch, it is necessary to state explicitly which aspects are included in the project.

Equity or Invested Capital. The *value of the business* is an ambiguous term until it is clear exactly what elements of equity and debt are to be included in that value.

Equity means the ownership interest. In a corporation, equity is represented by stock. If there is more than one class of stock, the term *equity* by itself usually means the combined value of all classes of stock. If it is intended that the value represents only one class of stock in a multiclass capital structure, there should be a statement as to which class of equity the value purports to represent.

In a partnership, equity is represented by partners' capital. If it is a multiclass partnership (such as a limited partnership), there should be a statement as to which class or classes of partnership interests the value purports to represent.

In a sole proprietorship, equity is the owner's interest.

Invested capital is not always as clearly defined. Therefore, if the term is used, it should be supplemented by a definition of exactly what it means in the given valuation context.

Usually, invested capital means all equity and interest-bearing debt, whether short-term or long-term. Also, invested capital commonly means all equity and only long-term debt. Investment bankers often do not include the company's cash among the assets when assessing the value of "invested capital." There are so many variations that it is essential to pin down *exactly* what is and is not to be included on both the left and right sides of the valuation balance sheet.

Enterprise Value. The term *enterprise value* unfortunately is used at best very ambiguously and at worst very carelessly. It means different things to different people, each of whom may believe that their definition is the right definition.

It is generally used to represent some sort of aggregate value of the company. However, that could mean aggregate value of minority stock, value of either all common equity or all equity on a control basis, value of all invested capital, value of some portion (or all) of the assets, or something else.

Both the Uniform Standards of Professional Appraisal Practice and the American Society of Appraisers define a *business enterprise* as "a commercial, industrial, or service organization pursuing an economic activity." However, neither USPAP nor ASA offers a definition of *enterprise value.* The ASA Business Valuation Standards Committee has discussed this term since 1985 and thus far has failed to find a consensus as to its definition.

If one encounters the term *enterprise value,* it is best not to assume any definition, but to make an attempt to identify the definition intended in its use. If one uses the term, it is important to spell out the intended definition, or the reader might infer an unintended definition. Because of the ambiguity, we have generally avoided using the term in this book.

Interests Other than Direct Fee Simple Ownership

If the ownership is something other than direct fee simple ownership of the stock, partnership interest, or other interest, the ownership interest needs to be specified. For example, the interest being appraised could be a life or term estate or a reversionary or remainder estate.

Ownership is, in effect, a bundle of rights. If the bundle of rights is anything less than a direct, unencumbered, simple ownership, the exact specification of the bundle of rights being appraised may have a significant bearing on value.

Description of the Specific Ownership Interest Characteristics

The description of the specific ownership interest subject to appraisal—and the particular investment attributes with regard to that ownership interest—can have a material impact on the appropriate valuation methodology and ultimate conclusion.

The primary ownership interest characteristics that need to be addressed in almost every business valuation are the following:

1. Control or minority valuation basis (not necessarily a black and white issue; there may be elements of control without absolute control).
2. Degree of marketability.

As such, the descriptions of the specific ownership interest characteristics are often in the nature of modifiers (adjectives) to the standard of value, such as "fair market value on a nonmarketable, minority ownership interest basis."

Sometimes the characteristics of the specific ownership interest subject to appraisal can be imposed artificially in a particular legal context. To give an example, under California Corporations Code Section 2000 (the California corporate dissolution statute), the case law is generally interpreted to mean that a minority interest is valued *as if* it were a proportional share of the value of 100 percent of the company taken as a whole.[3]

To the extent that ownership interest characteristics are legally mandated or have been agreed on between the parties, they should be specified in the appraisal assignment, with documentation as to their source. In many cases, the appraiser must consult with counsel to determine which ownership interest characteristics are appropriate. Also, the ownership interest characteristics may not be totally black or white issues, but in some cases may be matters of degree. *The descriptions of ownership interests often are major issues in disputed business valuation cases.* Consultation with the attorney involved and careful consideration of the implications of the purpose of the valuation can help to clarify issues related to choosing the appropriate description of the ownership interest for the situation.

Control versus Minority

As discussed in considerable detail in later chapters, the rights of control add value to shares of stock, typically making them worth considerably more than minority shares.

The degree of control versus minority represented by the interest being valued often is not necessarily a clear-cut issue. The degree of control or lack of it may fall anywhere across a broad spectrum, depending on the percentage owner-

---

[3]See, for example, *Ronald* v. *4-Cs Electronic Packaging,* 168 Cal. App. 3d 290 (1985) and *Brown* v. *Allied Corrugated Box Co.,* 91 Cal. App. 3d 477 (1979).

ship, the distribution of other ownership interests, and state laws governing rights of various percentage ownership interests in circumstances pertinent to the valuation situation at hand.

In most valuation situations, the degree of control can be stated clearly and unequivocally at the outset. In some cases, however, the degree of control represented in the interest being valued is a matter of controversy.

Degree of Marketability

For the purpose of this book, we define *marketability* as the ability to convert the asset to cash very quickly, at minimal cost, and with a high degree of certainty of realizing the anticipated amount of proceeds.

The benchmark usually used to represent full marketability is an actively traded stock of a public company, which the owner can sell at or very near the last reported transaction price, less a very modest commission, merely by a phone call to a broker, receiving cash within three business days. The premise as to the extent to which the entity or business being valued is marketable is usually considered in relation to this benchmark.

All other things being equal, investors prefer to own something they can liquidate immediately without any depressing effect on value rather than something that is difficult, time consuming, and/or costly to liquidate. As will be seen in Chapter 15 on this subject, the degree of marketability or lack of it has a much greater impact on value than most people realize. It is not uncommon for discounts to run as high as 50 percent, and, in many instances higher!

The impact of the issue of marketability may be legally mandated or may be agreed between the parties. More often than not, however, this issue is an important subject of the appraiser's analysis. To the extent that matters affecting marketability are known (e.g., rights or restrictions regarding transfer of the ownership interest), it generally is desirable to note them in the engagement letter.

Date of the Valuation

The date, or dates, at which the business is being valued is critically important because circumstances can cause values to vary materially from one date to another, and the valuation date directly influences data available for the valuation. Every day, observers of the public stock markets see sudden and substantial changes in the value of a particular company's stock. In many court cases, especially those involving tax litigation, significant changes in value over very short time spans have been justified because of changes in relevant circumstances.[4]

Many internal and external factors can cause changes in the value of an interest in a company. Obviously, a sudden change in a company's earnings, especially if unanticipated, can have a substantial effect on value. Also, the value of a business interest varies with the cost of capital, a factor over which individual businesses have little control. Major events, such as the signing or termination of a major customer contract, can also have a dramatic, immediate impact on value.

---

[4]See, for example, *Morris M. Messing*, 48 T.C. 502 (1967), acq. 1968-1 C.B. 2. Even though the company made a public offering at over $36 shortly after a gift of stock, the court upheld a value of $13 for gift tax purposes as of the date of the gift.

In most business valuations, the opinion of value will be based at least partly on other, similar transactions, such as the prices at which stocks in the same or a related industry are trading in the public market relative to their earnings, assets, dividends, or other relevant variables, if such data are available. It is important to know the valuation date when using guideline companies in the appraisal so that the guideline transaction data can be compiled as of the valuation date, or as near to it as is practically possible.

Sometimes there is more than one valuation date. For example, in a marital dissolution, the parties may be concerned with the change in value that occurred during the marriage. In estate tax cases, the trustee, executor, or personal representative will consider adopting the "alternative valuation date" (currently six months after the date of death) to determine which is more advantageous and thus would be interested in the value of the estate's property on two dates six months apart.

In some litigated cases, the valuation date itself is an issue to be resolved by the court. In such situations, the appraiser must be prepared to address the valuation as of several dates, sometimes without knowing until after the judgment is rendered which date the court determined to be relevant. Since the choice of valuation date in such cases will be a legal matter, the attorney for whom the expert appraiser will be testifying should take the responsibility, as part of defining the assignment, of considering all the potentially applicable valuation dates and instructing the appraiser to be prepared to address the value as of each date.

Purpose of the Appraisal

No single valuation method is universally applicable to all appraisal purposes. The context in which the appraisal is to be used is a critical factor.

Different statutory, regulatory, and case precedent standards govern valuations of businesses and business interests under various jurisdictions for diverse purposes. *Many business appraisals fail to reach a number representing the appropriate definition of value because the appraiser failed to match the valuation methods to the purpose for which it was being performed. The result of a particular appraisal can also be inappropriate if the client attempts to use the valuation conclusion for some purpose other than the intended one.*

Valuation reports should contain a set of limiting conditions, and one of the typical limiting conditions is as follows:

> This appraisal is valid only for the appraisal date or dates specified herein and this appraisal is valid only for the appraisal purpose or purposes specified herein. No other purpose is intended or should be inferred.

Litigation over business valuation is common. Much of this litigation arises because the parties fail to match the valuation method to the appraisal's intended purpose.

The purpose of the valuation encompasses the use to which the valuation exercise is expected to be put. Subsequent chapters of this book explore how valuation methods are impacted by special and specific purposes to which the valuation analysis may be put (Part VII). Valuations for each of these different purposes are often affected by a mass of complex federal and state statutes and legal precedents.

A valuation conclusion prepared for one purpose may not be the appropriate valuation conclusion for another purpose. The purpose of the valuation often determines the applicable standard of value—that is, the definition of value being sought—and almost always influences it. Standards of value are discussed in the next section, and an exhibit following that section illustrates the matching of certain valuation purposes with applicable standards of value.

Standards of Value

The word *value* means different things to different people. Even to the same person, *value* means different things in different contexts, as we discussed in the previous section.

Without carefully defining the term *value*, the conclusions reached in the valuation report have no meaning.

Is the objective of the appraisal to estimate fair market value, market value, fair value, true value, investment value, intrinsic value, fundamental value, insurance value, book value, use value, collateral value, ad valorem value, or some other value?

Clients rarely give it much thought. Many don't have enough technical background in business valuation to raise the right questions. One of the professional appraiser's most important tasks is to work carefully and thoroughly with the client and/or attorney to arrive at a definition of value that is appropriate to the specific purpose of the valuation engagement.

In this book, a *standard of value* is a definition of the type of value being sought. A *premise of value* is an assumption as to the set of actual or hypothetical transactional circumstances applicable to the subject valuation.

For many situations, the standard of value is legally mandated, whether by law or by binding legal documents or contracts. In other cases, it is a function of the wishes of the parties involved. The standard of value usually reflects an assumption as to who will be the buyer and who will be the seller in the hypothetical or actual sales transaction regarding the subject assets, properties, or business interests. It defines or specifies the parties to the actual or hypothetical transaction. In other words, the standard of value addresses the question: "value to whom?" The standard of value, either directly by statute or (more often) as interpreted in case law, often addresses what valuation methods are appropriate and what factors should or should not be considered.

Fair Market Value

In the United States, the most widely recognized and accepted standard of value related to business valuations is *fair market value*. With regard to business valuations, it is the standard that applies to virtually all federal and state tax matters, such as estate taxes, gift taxes, inheritance taxes, income taxes, and ad valorem taxes. It is also the legal standard of value in many other—though not all—valuation situations.

Fair market value is defined by the ASA as "the amount at which property would change hands between a willing seller and a willing buyer when neither is acting under compulsion and when both have reasonable knowledge of the relevant facts."[4] This definition comports to that found in the U.S. Tax Code and in Revenue Ruling 59-60.

In most interpretations of fair market value, the willing buyer and willing seller are hypothetical persons dealing at arm's length, rather than any particular buyer or seller. In other words, a price would not be considered representative of fair market value if influenced by special motivations not characteristic of a typical buyer or seller.

There is also general agreement that the definition implies the parties have the ability as well as the willingness to buy or to sell. The *market* in this definition can be thought of as all the potential buyers and sellers of like businesses or practices.

The concept of fair market value also assumes prevalent economic and market conditions at the date of the particular valuation. You have probably heard someone say, "I couldn't get anywhere near the value of my house if I put it on the market today," or, "The value of XYZ Company stock is really much more (or less) than the price it's selling for on the New York Stock Exchange today." The standard of value that such a person has in mind is some standard *other than* fair market value, since the concept of fair market value means the price at which a transaction could be expected to take place under *conditions existing at the valuation date.*

The terms *market value* and *cash value* are sometimes used interchangeably with the term *fair market value.* The use of these essentially synonymous standard of value terms is often influenced by the type of asset, property, or business interest subject to appraisal.

In the United States, the most widely recognized and accepted standard of value related to real estate appraisals is market value. The Appraisal Foundation defines *market value* as follows:

> MARKET VALUE: Market value is the major focus of most real property appraisal assignments. Both economic and legal definitions of market value have been developed and refined. A current economic definition agreed upon by agencies that regulate federal financial institutions in the United States of America is:
>
> > The most probable price which a property should bring in a competitive and open market under all conditions requisite to a fair sale, the buyer and seller each acting prudently and knowledgeably, and assuming the price is not affected by undue stimulus. Implicit in this definition is the consummation of a sale as of a specified date and the passing of title from seller to buyer under conditions whereby:
> >
> > 1. buyer and seller are typically motivated;
> > 2. both parties are well informed or well advised, and acting in what they consider their best interests;
> > 3. a reasonable time is allowed for exposure in the open market;
> > 4. payment is made in terms of cash in United States dollars or in terms of financial arrangements comparable thereto; and
> > 5. the price represents the normal consideration for the property sold unaffected by special or creative financing or sales concessions granted by anyone associated with the sale.

---

[4]American Society of Appraisers, Business Valuation Standards—Definitions.

Substitution of another currency for United States dollars in the fourth condition is appropriate in other countries or in reports addressed to clients from other countries. Persons performing appraisal services that may be subject to litigation are cautioned to seek the exact legal definition of market value in the jurisdiction in which the services are being performed.[5]

The most salient change in the above definition of market value compared to definitions widely accepted a few years ago is the phrase "the most probable price" in substitution for "the highest price."

Business appraisers should be cognizant of the subtle, but important, differences between the fair market value standard (as defined by the ASA, for example) and the market value standard (as defined by the Appraisal Institute, for example).

Investment Value

In real estate terminology, investment value is defined as "value to a particular investor based on individual investment requirements, as distinguished from the concept of market value, which is impersonal and detached."[6] Fortunately, business appraisal terminology embraces the same distinction in most contexts.

One of the leading real estate appraisal texts makes the following comments regarding the distinction between market value and investment value:

> Market value can be called "the value of the marketplace"; *investment value is the specific value of goods or services to a particular investor (or class of investors) based on individual investment requirements.* Market value and investment value are different concepts; the values estimated for each may or may not be numerically equal depending on the circumstances. Moreover, market value estimates are commonly made without reference to investment value, but investment value estimates are frequently accompanied by a market value estimate to facilitate decision making.
>
> Market value estimates assume no specific buyer or seller. Rather, the appraiser considers a hypothetical transaction in which both the buyer and the seller have the understanding, perceptions, and motivations that are typical of the market for the property or interests being valued. Appraisers must distinguish between their own knowledge, perceptions, and attitudes and those of the market or markets for the property in question. The special requirements of a given client are irrelevant to a market value estimate.[7]

The distinctions noted in the above quote can be carried over to business appraisal. There can be many valid reasons for the *investment value* to one particular owner or prospective owner to differ from the fair market value. Among these reasons are:

1. Differences in estimates of future earning power.
2. Differences in perception of the degree of risk.
3. Differences in tax status.
4. Synergies with other operations owned or controlled.

---

[5]*Uniform Standards of Professional Appraisal Practice* (Washington, DC: The Appraisal Foundation, 1995).

[6]*The Dictionary of Real Estate Appraisal*, 3rd ed. (Chicago: Appraisal Institute, 1993).

[7]*The Appraisal of Real Estate*, 10th ed. (Chicago: Appraisal Institute, 1992), p. 586.

The discounted economic income valuation method can easily be oriented toward developing an investment value. Whether or not the value thus developed also represents fair market value depends on whether the valuation projections used would be accepted by a consensus of market participants.

If sound analysis leads to a valid conclusion that the investment value to a particular owner exceeded market value at a given time, the rational economic decision for that owner would be not to sell at that time unless a particular buyer could be found to whom investment value would be higher than the consensus of value among a broader group of typical buyers.

Of course, the concept of investment value as described above is not completely divorced from the concept of fair market value, since it is the actions of many specific investors, acting in the manner just described, that eventually lead to a balancing of supply and demand through the establishment of an equilibrium market price that represents the consensus value of the collective investors.

Finally, the term *investment value* often has a different meaning when used in the context of dissenting stockholder suits. In this context, it often means a value based on earning power, as described above, except that the appropriate discount or capitalization rate is usually considered to be a consensus rate rather than a rate peculiar to any specific investor.

Intrinsic or Fundamental Value

Intrinsic value (sometimes called *fundamental value*) differs from *investment value* in that it represents an analytical judgment of value based on the perceived characteristics inherent in the investment, not tempered by characteristics peculiar to any one investor, but rather tempered by how these perceived characteristics are interpreted by one analyst versus another.

In the analysis of stocks, *intrinsic value* is generally considered the appropriate price for a stock according to a security analyst who has completed a *fundamental analysis* of the company's assets, earning power, and other factors.

> *Intrinsic value.* The amount that an investor considers, on the basis of an evaluation of available facts, to be the "true" or "real" worth of an item, usually an *equity security.* The value that will become the market value when other investors reach the same conclusions. The various approaches to determining intrinsic value of the *finance* literature are based on expectations and discounted cash flows. See *expected value; fundamental analysis; discounted cash flow method.*[8]

> *Fundamental analysis.* An approach in security analysis which assumes that a security has an "intrinsic value" that can be determined through a rigorous evaluation of relevant variables. Expected earnings is usually the most important variable in this analysis, but many other variables, such as dividends, capital structure, management quality, and so on, may also be studied. An analyst estimates the "intrinsic value" of a security on the basis of those fundamental variables and compares this value with the current market price of this security to arrive at an investment decision.[9]

---

[8]*W.W.* Cooper and Yuri Ijiri, eds., *Kohler's Dictionary for Accountants,* 6th ed. (Englewood Cliffs, NJ: Prentice Hall, 1983), p. 285.

[9]Ibid., p. 228.

> The purpose of security analysis is to detect differences between the value of a security as determined by the market and a security's "intrinsic value"—that is, the value that the security *ought* to have and will have when other investors have the same insight and knowledge as the analyst.[10]

If the market value is below what the analyst concludes is the intrinsic value, then the analyst considers the stock a "buy." If the market value is above the assumed intrinsic value, then the analyst suggests selling the stock. (Some analysts also factor market expectations into their fundamental analysis.)

It is important to note that the concept of intrinsic value cannot be entirely divorced from the concept of fair market value, since the actions of buyers and sellers based on their *specific* perceptions of intrinsic value eventually lead to the *general* consensus market value and the constant and dynamic changes in market value over time.

Case law often refers to the term *intrinsic value*. However, almost universally such references do not define the term other than by reference to the language in the context in which it appears. Such references to *intrinsic value* can be found both in cases where there is no statutory standard of value and in cases where the statutory standard of value is specified as *fair value* or even *fair market value*. When references to *intrinsic value* appear in the relevant case law, the analyst should heed the notions ascribed to that term as discussed in this section.

Fair Value

To understand what the expression *fair value* means, you have to know the context of its use. In business appraisal, the term *fair value* is a legally created standard of value that applies to certain specific transactions.

In most states, fair value is the statutory standard of value applicable in cases of dissenting stockholders' appraisal rights. In these states, if a corporation merges, sells out, or takes certain other major actions, and the owner of a minority interest believes that he is being forced to receive less than adequate consideration for his stock, he has the right to have his shares appraised and to receive fair value in cash. In states that have adopted the Uniform Business Corporation Act, the definition of fair value is as follows:

> "Fair value," with respect to a dissenter's shares, means the value of the shares immediately before the effectuation of the corporate action to which the dissenter objects, excluding any appreciation or depreciation in anticipation of the corporate action unless exclusion would be inequitable.[11]

Even in states that have adopted this definition, there is no clearly recognized consensus about the interpretation of fair value in this context, but published precedents established in various state courts certainly have not equated it to fair market value. When a situation arises of actual or potential stockholder dissent, it is necessary to research carefully the legal precedents applicable

---

[10]James H. Lorie and Mary T. Hamilton, *The Stock Market: Theories and Evidence* (Burr Ridge, IL: Richard D. Irwin, 1973), p. 114.

[11]Oregon Revised Statutes, Section 60.551(4).

to each case. The appraiser should solicit the view of counsel as to the interpretation of fair value and, in most cases, cannot assume that there is a definition that is clear and concise.

The term *fair value* is also found in the dissolution statutes of those few states in which minority stockholders can trigger a corporate dissolution under certain circumstances (e.g., California Code Section 2000). Even within the same state, however, a study of case law precedents does not necessarily lead one to the same definition of fair value under a dissolution statute as under that state's dissenting stockholder statute.

Several countries undergoing privatization have adopted the term *fair value* to apply to certain transactions, often involving specific classes of buyers, such as employees. Such statutes vary widely in their definitions of fair value.

Exhibit 2–2 gives some examples of matching certain valuation purposes with the applicable standards of value.

Exhibit 2–2

Examples of Matching the Valuation Purpose with the Standard of Value

Valuation Purpose	Applicable Standard of Value
Gift and estate taxes and charitable contributions	Fair market value (governed by federal statute and case law; very large and reasonably consistent body of case law precedent)
Inheritance taxes	Fair market value (governed by state law, but usually follows federal)
Ad valorem taxes	Fair market value or market value (governed by state law, and some important statutory and/or regulatory differences are found from state to state; it is important to note whether the appraisal subject is a bundle of assets or a bundle of securities)
Employee Stock Ownership Plans (ESOPs)	Fair market value (governed by both federal tax law and ERISA)
Buy–sell agreements	Anything the parties choose to agree on
Financial acquisition*	Fair market value
Strategic acquisition*	Investment value (buyers, of course, do the best they can to avoid paying for the synergistic value)
Going private	Fair value in most states (governed by state statutes; even where statutory language is consistent among several states, case law interpretation often varies considerably)
Dissenting stockholder actions	Fair value in most states (governed by state statutes; even where statutory language is consistent among several states, case law interpretation often varies considerably)
Corporate or partnership dissolutions under minority oppression statutes	Fair value (only California, New York, and Rhode Island have such statutes at press time; case law interpretations in those states tend to be different from case law interpretations of fair value in dissenting stockholder actions in the same states)
Marital dissolution	No standard of value specified in most state statutes. Case law inconsistent, often within the same state. Case law also tends to be confusing, e.g., even if "fair market value" specified in decision, actual valuation practice used frequently differs markedly from strict interpretation of fair market value as found in tax case law.
Antitrust cases	Damages based on federal case law precedent, with variations from circuit to circuit
Other damage cases (e.g., breach of contract, lost profits, lost business opportunity, condemnation, insurance claims, wrongful franchise termination)	Mostly governed by state statute and case law precedent; vary by type of case and from state to state

*Note that most acquisitions can trigger minority stockholder dissenters' rights, entitling dissenters to be paid the value of their shares according to state statutes, which is "fair value" in most states.

Going-Concern versus Liquidation Premise of Value

Virtually all businesses or interests in businesses may be appraised under each of these following four alternative premises of value:

1. *Value as a going concern*—Value in continued use, as a mass assemblage of income producing assets, and as a going-concern business enterprise.
2. *Value as an assemblage of assets*—Value in place, as part of a mass assemblage of assets, but not in current use in the production of income, and not as a going-concern business enterprise.
3. *Value as an orderly disposition*—Value in exchange, on a piecemeal basis (not part of a mass assemblage of assets), as part of an orderly disposition; this premise contemplates that all of the assets of the business enterprise will be sold individually, and that they will enjoy normal exposure to their appropriate secondary market.
4. *Value as a forced liquidation*—Value in exchange, on a piecemeal basis (not part of a mass assemblage of assets), as part of a forced liquidation; this premise contemplates that the assets of the business enterprise will be sold individually and that they will experience less than normal exposure to their appropriate secondary market.

While virtually any business enterprise may be appraised under each of these four alternative fundamental premises, the value conclusions reached under each premise, for the same business, may be dramatically different.

Each of these alternative premises of value may apply under the same standard, or definition, of value. For example, the fair market value standard calls for a "willing buyer" and a "willing seller." Yet, these willing buyers and sellers have to make an informed economic decision as to how they will transact with each other with regard to the subject business. In other words, is the subject business worth more to the buyer and the seller as a going concern that will continue to operate as such, or as a collection of individual assets to be put to separate uses? In either case, the buyer and seller are still "willing." And, in both cases, they have concluded a set of transactional circumstances that will maximize the value of the collective assets of the subject business enterprise.

The selection of the appropriate premise of value is an important step in defining the appraisal assignment. Typically, in a controlling interest valuation, the selection of the appropriate premise of value is a function of the highest and best use of the collective assets of the subject business enterprise. The decision regarding the appropriate premise of value is usually made by the appraiser, based upon experience, judgment, and analysis.

Sometimes, however, the decision regarding the appropriate premise of value is made "for" the appraiser. This occurs when the appraiser knows—or is told—that the subject business enterprise will, in fact, be continued as a going concern or will be sold in a certain set of transactional circumstances. For example, if the business assets are, in fact, going to be sold on a value in exchange basis, it is not relevant for the appraiser to consider the value in continued use—or going-concern—premise of value. Of course, if appraising a minority interest, one would normally adopt the premise of business as usual unless given reason to do otherwise.

In some circumstances, it may be relevant—and, in fact, critical—to appraise the subject business enterprise under several alternative premises of value. For example, it may be extremely important to conclude the value of the same business enterprise under several alternative premises of value in appraisals performed for bankruptcy and reorganization or for financing securitization and collateralization purposes.

Sources of Guidance as to Applicable Standards and Premises of Value

The experience and expertise of the professional appraiser include the skill to seek out and interpret guidance as to the standard and premises of value that are relevant to the assignment at hand. Some of the most important sources of guidance as to the applicable standard and premise of value for the given situation are the following:

- Statutory law (state and federal).
- Case law (cases decided under the controlling statutory or common law).
- Administrative regulations (e.g., IRS Revenue Rulings).[14]
- Company documents (e.g., articles of incorporation or partnership, bylaws, meeting minutes, agreements).
- Contracts between the parties (e.g., buy–sell agreements, arbitration agreements).
- Precedent established by prior transactions.
- Directives issued by the court (in some litigated cases where the standards or premises are not clear, the appraiser may take the initiative to seek direction from the court regarding the relevant definition of value).
- Discussions with an attorney involved in the valuation matter or experience in similar matters.
- Legal case documents (e.g., complaint, response, and so forth).
- The appraiser's experience and judgment.

Form of the Work Product

In many cases, the purpose of the report will largely determine the form of the report. The appraiser's report to the client can be oral, written, or a combination.

An oral report can be anything from a quick phone call to lengthy meetings with the principals, attorneys, brokers, and/or other parties involved. The form and extent of a written report can range from a single-page letter report to a detailed, hundred-page-plus volume.

---

[14]Note that administrative rulings do not have the force of law, but represent the position of the agency administering the law as to their interpretation of the law and rules for applying it.

An oral report is common in estate planning engagements, especially when the purpose of the exercise is to help the client get an approximate idea of the business's value in order to decide what action to take. A preliminary oral report is often the first deliverable product when the business valuation is being conducted for litigation because the client attorney is concerned with the expert's opinion before a firm stance is taken, which, if taken in writing, could be discovered and used by the opponents. Even oral reports, however, are covered by USPAP. Although some departures from full reports are permitted, there must be a supportable basis for the opinions expressed.

When the purpose of the assignment is to prepare a feasibility analysis for a potential employee stock ownership plan (ESOP), the client, or client's attorney, will usually require a brief opinion letter that can be used for further planning. Once the business's value is approximated, the rest of the ESOP team is engaged, the size of the ESOP can be determined, and the amount and cost of bank financing can be identified.

In most cases, especially those involving taxes or tax implications, such as gift or estate tax valuations, the appraiser will be required to prepare a formal written opinion report.

The valuation opinion report will typically include the following sections:

1. A valuation opinion letter summarizing the appraisal procedures and the valuation conclusions.
2. Several sections summarizing the relevant valuation theory, methodology, procedures, analyses, and conclusions.
3. A valuation synthesis and conclusion.
4. An exhibit section presenting a summary of the quantitative and qualitative appraisal analyses.
5. A listing of the data and documents relied upon by the appraiser.
6. A statement of appraisal contingent and limiting conditions.
7. An appraisal certification.
8. The professional qualifications of the principal appraisers.

Effective July 1, 1994, USPAP provided for more limited reporting procedures. However, a supportable basis for the conclusions expressed is still required.

Scheduling

One of the most important tools for conducting a business valuation thoroughly and on a timely basis is a proper schedule. Most first-time, or infrequent, business appraisal clients tend to underestimate the amount of lead time necessary for the appraiser to prepare a thorough and professional opinion. Scheduling problems often arise because the client delays in committing to the project, hoping that the valuation problem will go away. When it doesn't, there is little time left for anything but a crash assignment. Another common source of scheduling conflicts is a major change in some aspect of the assignment midway through the project—another good reason for the client and the appraiser to carefully think through and agree on the details of the appraisal assignment as thoroughly as possible at the outset.

The appraisal assignment should describe when the work is expected to be completed. But it should also make clear that the appraiser's ability to meet the proposed schedule depends on receipt of the necessary material on a timely basis, and that changes midway through the assignment will likely cause changes in the schedule. To expedite getting necessary data to the appraiser on a timely basis, we recommend that anyone contemplating an appraisal refer to Exhibit 4–1, "Preliminary Documents and Information Checklist for Business Valuation of a Typical Corporation" (the exhibit can be readily modified for noncorporate forms of organization), and make sure the information is readily available.

One tactic often used, especially during December when clients make gifts of property or are conducting other estate planning activities, is to ask the appraiser to arrive at an oral opinion of value and later provide a formal, written, documented report.

Fee Arrangements

The appraisal budget may be a fixed price or a range of estimated fees, or it may be based on an hourly or daily rate. The more clearly and thoroughly defined is the scope of the assignment, the more likely it is that the appraiser will be able to quote a total fixed fee or a narrow range.

If third-party independence of judgment is required of the appraiser—as in cases involving expert testimony in pending or potential litigation—the appraiser's fees must be fixed, hourly, or set in some manner totally independent of the outcome of any litigation, or the appraiser's independent third-party status will be jeopardized. For those appraisal assignments requiring independence, the independent professional appraiser is legally and ethically prohibited from entering into an arrangement making the appraiser's fee contingent on a certain settlement amount or the outcome of a court decision.

The fee arrangements should include the terms of payment as well as the basis for establishing the fee.

Summary

This chapter has provided guidance to both the appraiser and the client (or the client's attorney) as to matters that should be considered when entering into the appraisal engagement. Most of these matters should be incorporated into the engagement letter; some will be resolved after execution of the engagement letter or left to the appraiser's judgment. Even for those matters discussed in this chapter that ultimately are left to the appraiser's judgment, it often is helpful for the appraiser and the client (or the client's attorney) to discuss them at the onset of the engagement.

The basic elements of the appraisal assignment are:

1. Name of the client and of the appraiser.
2. Definition of the legal interest and business interests to be appraised.
3. Date or dates of the valuation (the date as of which the appraiser's opinion of value applies).
4. Purpose or purposes of the appraisal (the use to which the valuation exercise is expected to be put).
5. Applicable standard and premises of value.
6. Form and extent of written and/or verbal report.
7. Schedule and fee arrangements.

At some point, whether in the engagement letter or in some other transmittal, additional topics typically are addressed, such as: contingent and limiting conditions, limited use of the appraisal (only for the purpose intended and the effective date of valuation), confidentiality, and compliance with USPAP and/or ASA Business Valuation Standards.

Exhibit 2–3 is a sample engagement letter that covers the elements discussed in this chapter, as well as a few other important points such as indemnification of the appraiser.

Exhibit 2–3
Sample Professional Services Agreement

John Doe Associates, hereafter called "Doe," and __Estate of Alan B. Client__, hereafter called "Client," agree as follows:

1. Description of services. Doe agrees to perform certain professional services for Client, described briefly as follows as to purpose and assignment, with the understanding that any modification to the assignment as stated below will be by a letter agreement signed by both parties.

Appraisal of the fair market value of a 100% nonmarketable, controlling interest in the outstanding common stock of ABC, Inc., an Illinois corporation, held by the estate of Alan B. Client, as of August 30, 1994, for estate tax purposes.

2. Use of appraisal. Client warrants that this appraisal will be relied on only for the use indicated above and only as of the date indicated above. Client understands that this appraisal is not valid for any other use or for any other appraisal date.

3. Date(s) services due. Doe will begin performance upon receipt of all information requested of Client, and will complete assignment(s), unless delayed or prevented by matters beyond Doe's control, according to the following schedule:

Full, formal report within 90 days of receipt of signed agreement and all requested documents.

4. Fees. Doe's fees for such professional services will be calculated on standard hourly rates in effect at the time services are rendered for staff members assigned to Client's project, plus out-of-pocket expenses. The fee is estimated at a range of $_____ to $_____ , exclusive of expenses such as travel, long distance telephone, purchases of data, copying and printing costs.

5. Retainer. $_____ is due as a retainer upon execution of this Agreement. Retainer paid by Client will be applied to the **final** billings.

6. Payment terms. Client will receive regular twice-monthly invoices, including fees and expenses incurred, for which payments will be due at Doe offices within 15 days of dates of invoices. Balances which remain unpaid 30 days from dates of invoices will be assessed a finance charge of 1.5% monthly (18% annual percentage rate).

If Doe is to provide expert witness testimony as part of its assignment, Client agrees that payment of all fees and expenses invoiced and/or incurred to date will be received at Doe offices before Doe provides expert witness testimony, or if travel for testimony is necessary, payment will be received before travel is incurred.

Client agrees that the fees and expenses invoiced by Doe must be paid current per the terms of this Agreement before Doe provides any report or analysis conclusions.

7. Client understands that Doe will need prompt access to documents, materials, facilities, and/or Client's personnel in order to perform its services in a timely and professional manner, and Client agrees to fulfill all such requests in a timely manner and to cooperate fully with Doe. Client further understands and agrees that delays in providing data or information may result in a delay of the completion date of the project.

Exhibit 2-3 (continued)

8. Doe agrees to perform its services in a professional and objective manner. Client understands that Doe does not guarantee the results of any analysis which it may undertake, but only agrees that any report or analysis shall represent Doe's professional opinion based on the data given to or compiled by it. Doe attempts to obtain and compile its data from reliable sources, but it cannot guarantee its accuracy or completeness.

9. Client warrants that the information and data it supplies to Doe will be complete and accurate in every respect to the best of Client's knowledge; that any reports, analysis, or other documents prepared by Doe will be used only in compliance with all applicable laws and regulations; and that Client will hold Doe harmless for any breach of this warranty.

10. Client agrees to indemnify and hold Doe harmless against any and all liability, claim, loss, cost, and expense, whatever kind or nature, which Doe may incur, or be subject to, as a party, expert witness, witness or participant in connection with any dispute or litigation involving Client. This indemnity includes all out-of-pocket expenses (including travel costs and attorney fees) and payment for all Doe staff members' time at standard hourly rates in effect at the time rendered to the extent Doe attends, prepares for, or participates in meetings, hearings, depositions, trials, and all other proceedings, including travel time. If Doe must bring legal action to enforce this indemnity, Client agrees to pay all costs of such action, including any sum as the Court may fix as reasonable attorney fees.

11. If this Agreement, or any monies due under the terms hereof, is placed in the hands of an attorney for collection of the account, Client promises and agrees to pay Doe's attorney fees and collection costs, plus interest at the then legal rate, whether or not any legal action is filed. If any suit or action is brought to enforce, interpret, or collect damages for the breach of this agreement, Client agrees to pay Doe's reasonable attorney fees and costs of such suit or action, including any appeal as fixed by the applicable Court or Courts.

Dated this 30th day of September 1994, at Portland, Oregon.

By:_____   By:_____
Name: Martha Client, Executor   Name: John Doe, President
Estate of Alan B. Client   **John Doe Associates**

Address: 100 North 4th Street, Decatur, Illinois 64156
Telephone: (708) 555-4455
FAX: (708) 555-4457

SOURCE: Willamette Management Associates.

Chapter 3

Business Valuation Theory and Principles

One of the frequent sources of legal confusion between cost and value is the tendency of courts, in common with other persons, to think of value as something inherent in the thing valued, rather than as an attitude of persons toward that thing in view of its estimated capacity to perform a service . . . Certainly, for the purpose of a monetary valuation, property has no value unless there is a prospect that it can be exploited by human beings.[1]

There continues to be much controversy about the appropriate criteria by which to measure the value of a business or business interest. The previous chapter discussed the issues surrounding the choices that determine the standard of value and the premise of value. Now that those critical decisions have been made, the basic principles of business valuation are considered.

Generally Accepted Theory

In the simplest sense, the theory surrounding the value of an interest in a business depends on the future benefits that will accrue to the owner of it. The value of the business interest, then, depends upon an estimate of the future benefits and the required rate of return at which those future benefits are discounted back to the valuation date.

Thus, the theoretically correct approach is to project some category or categories of the future benefits of ownership (usually some measure of economic income, such as cash flow, earnings, or dividends) and to estimate the present value of those future benefits by discounting them based upon the time value of money and the risks associated with ownership. Direct implementation of this theoretically correct approach is discussed in Chapter 9, "Income Approach: Discounted Economic Income Methods." That chapter concentrates on net cash flow as a measure of economic income, both for conceptual reasons and also because it is the focus of most merger and acquisition income value analysis in the mid-1990s.

While there is general acceptance of a theoretical framework for business valuation, translating it into practice in an uncertain world poses one of the most complex challenges of economic and financial theory and practice. The reasonableness of the business valuation conclusions will usually depend upon whether the projections and variables used to estimate future economic income benefits are acceptable to the decision maker for whom the business valuation is being prepared (e.g., the buyer, the seller, the opponent, the IRS, the judge).

Getting two or more parties with different economic and business expectations to agree on projected future benefits and the risks associated with achieving those projections is, perhaps, the most difficult task for the business appraiser. Therefore, business valuation practitioners have developed various approaches that use historical as well as projected data to arrive at a valuation.

In general, approaches using current or historical data, if properly carried out, should yield a result that is reasonably reconcilable with what a well-implemented discounted economic income approach would derive. It is essential, however, that any historical data used in the valuation bear relevance to future expectations.

---

[1]James C. Bonbright, *The Valuation of Property*, Vol. I (Charlottesville, VA: The Michie Company, 1965 [reprint of 1937 ed.]), p. 21.

Reliance on Projected versus Historical Benefits

In virtually any business valuation, there is more than one point of view. Business appraisers are rarely engaged to conduct an assignment unless the client anticipates that the conclusions of the assignment will be scrutinized and challenged by someone with an adverse interest. Very often, the challenges surround the predictability of future benefits as they compare to the historical record.

In court, the parties to an action and the judge rely on *evidence* to support a particular position. Historical facts are often considered more credible evidence in the eyes of the court than projections of what somebody thinks will happen. Therefore, when legal evidence is required, the focus tends to be on the historical record of financial performance; future benefits and their predictability as of the valuation date are more difficult to establish. The courts generally prefer provable historical results to unprovable expectations of future results. The extent to which a court will accept projections as evidence in a valuation case is probably a function of the degree of confidence the court has in the validity of those projections based upon information available as of the valuation date, as well as the credibility of the witness.

In the real world of business valuation, the situations that most closely approach using a theoretical discounted economic income model to arrive at a value are in the merger market and, to a lesser extent, in the markets for publicly traded securities. In valuing businesses for investment purposes, one must make estimates of the future economic benefits that are sufficiently credible to persuade an investor to act on them. Businesspeople are trained to make and evaluate business and economic projections and use them as a basis for daily decision making. Businesspeople can (and should) use their knowledge and experience in allocating resources entrusted to them for the purpose of taking business risks and should accept calculated risks inherent in decision making based on forecasts of an uncertain future.

When preparing a business valuation for reorganization proceedings under bankruptcy statutes, the parties will frequently rely on the capitalization of anticipated future cash flow. This makes sense because, unless there is a reasonable expectation that the future will be more rewarding than the recent past, the reorganization would appear to be fruitless.

Other categories in which projections are usually necessary are antitrust; lost business opportunity; breach of contract; infringement of patents, copyrights, or trademarks; and certain other types of damage calculations that need to address the amount of value lost as a result of a wrongful act. Eminent domain, a legal taking of property often subject to compensation for lost value, may also give rise to projections of lost future economic income.

As a practical matter, because of the lack of a set of projections and variables acceptable to all parties, many business valuations tend to rely on historical data, which are evaluated and often adjusted to reflect reasonable expectations about foreseeable results.

In summary, this difference in focus between the future projections and the historical record is dictated by what the respective decision makers are willing to rely on. There may be a big difference in this respect between an investment decision in the market, where future performance of the business interest is critical, and a judicial decision in a court, where evidence rules the day, and the court may not believe it can assess the reliability of projections. To be practically useful, the business valuation procedure selected must conform to the criteria acceptable to those who ultimately decide what action to take as a result of the valuation process. There is some trend toward more court recognition of modern investment theory, which is based on discounting expected economic income at a discount rate that reflects the risk of achieving the expectations.

In the 1930s, Bonbright recognized the valuation controversy surrounding the reliance on historical earnings and projected earnings:

> *Realized Earnings versus Prophesied Earnings.* In the valuation of entire business enterprises or of shareholdings in these enterprises, one of the most sharply contested questions has concerned the relative weight to be given to the earnings actually realized, as shown by the companies' financial statements after proper auditing, and the future earnings as estimated by the witnesses for the two parties to the controversy. Sometimes, indeed, the controversy arises from a denial by one of the parties that prophesied earnings should even be admitted as competent evidence. It is alleged that these prophecies are necessarily too highly speculative to merit consideration; that they are based on guesses as to future business conditions and as to managerial efficiency, the validity of which cannot adequately be checked by cross-examination or by the countervailing testimony of opposing experts. Hence, it is argued, only the realized earnings, whose amount can be approximately established by a careful audit, should be brought to the attention of the tribunal for such weight as it sees fit to give this type of data. Lawyers who take this position generally concede that facts having a general bearing on the immediate prospects of the business may be brought to the attention of the court. They object, however, to the false appearance of precision which is given by any estimate, in monetary amounts, of future net earnings. Their objection is likely to be even more strenuous if the case is being tried by a jury or by any other unsophisticated tribunal. Such bodies are in danger of taking the prophecies at their face value, without applying those drastic discounts for risk of nonoccurrence which cautious appraisal experts would apply.
>
> These practical objections to the admission of prophesied gross and net earnings are well taken. Indeed, the courts have shown a wholesome tendency to belittle the significance of the prophecies, and even on occasion to refuse to let them get into the record. But the language by which they have justified their treatment of this type of evidence has not always been acceptable to appraisal theory and has sometimes been very confusing. At times the courts have come close to stating that, as a matter of principle, the *present* value of a business property depends on *present* earnings, and that future earnings are irrelevant because they will determine merely future value. More frequently they have stated that present value depends on both present *and* future earnings, but with the implication that the present earnings have the more direct bearing on the worth of the property as it exists today.
>
> In fact, neither of these two statements correctly expresses the relevance of realized earnings and of prospective earnings. *The truth is that, when earnings have once been "realized," so that they can be expressed with some approach to accuracy in the company's accounts, they are already water under the mill and have no direct bearing on what the property in question is now worth. Value, under any plausible theory of capitalized earning power, is necessarily forward looking. It is an expression of the advantage that an owner of the property may expect to secure from the ownership in the future. The past earnings are therefore beside the point, save as a possible index of future earnings.*[2]

---

[2]James C. Bonbright, *The Valuation of Property, Vol. I.* (Charlottesville, VA: The Michie Company, 1965 [reprint of 1937 ed.]), pp. 249–50. (Emphasis supplied.)

In a litigated appraisal, a more convincing argument for the capitalization of realized earnings, rather than of prophesied earnings, can be found in the possibility . . . of capitalizing the realized earnings at a rate objectively determined by rates established on the marketplace. Assume, for example, that the case at bar requires the valuation of a railroad enterprise, the net earnings of which have averaged $10 million per year. Assume also that the securities issued by this particular railroad have no established market value, since they are closely held. If the various securities of other, comparable railroad companies are quoted at prices which average 20 times current annual net earnings, a rate of 5 percent suggests itself as the appropriate rate at which the current earnings of the instant railroad company may fairly be capitalized. Of course, any such conclusion involves a number of highly shaky assumptions assumptions, not only as to the comparability of the various railroad enterprises, but also as to the relevance of quoted security prices as bearing on the value of an entire enterprise. But the errors implicit in this method of arriving at a proper rate of capitalization are probably far less serious than are the errors implicit in any other method available to an inexpert tribunal.[3]

The above quotation, written over a half century ago, continues to offer wisdom regarding the same issues today. Financial theory and accounting theory have advanced dramatically since this time making the prospective valuation approaches more common, acceptable, reasonable, reliable, and verifiable.

Basic Variables Affecting Value

Whether one actually attempts to make future projections or relies on historical data to derive some proxy for reasonable future expectations, the business valuation will focus on certain key variables. The relative importance of the relevant variables will vary in different situations. For generations, theorists will continue to argue about which variables deserve the most attention and should be given the most weight in various valuation situations.

There are internal valuation factors that are a function of the performance of the business and there are external valuation factors that are a function of the environment in which the business operates.

One way or another, the financial benefits of ownership of an interest in a business enterprise must come from the following sources:

1. Earnings or cash flow:
   a. from operations, or
   b. from investments (e.g., interest and/or dividends).
2. Liquidation or hypothecation of assets.
3. Sale of the interest.

Therefore, any valuation approach—at least from a financial point of view—must focus on quantifying the ability of the business interest to provide benefits to its owner from one or some combination of the above sources.

---

[3]Ibid., p. 263.

In many instances, a conclusion as to value is tempered by other internal variables, often variables relative to the specific shareholding as opposed to the company as a whole, such as:

1. Size of the subject interest (reflecting not only magnitude but also control issues).
2. The right to vote and to impact the direction of the business.
3. Restrictive provisions affecting ownership rights.
4. The marketability of the ownership position.
5. Special ownership or management perquisites.

There is no universal answer concerning which variable among the future benefit statistics deserves the greatest attention. Generally, earning power is the important internal variable affecting the going-concern value of the business. Earning power may be expressed in terms of the ability to realize cash flows, dividends, net income, or any of several other measures.

The external variables that affect a business's value are collectively referred to as "the market." It is the amount of expected return that is required to attract investment—the *cost of capital*. The cost of capital depends on the general level of interest rates and the amount of premium for risk (above the return available on a safe, fixed-income investment) that the market demands, as well as the risks attributable to the subject business.

Impact of Risk on Value

The appraiser must be sure to consider the expected returns in two dimensions: the magnitude of the expected returns and the risk that these returns will or will not be realized. In this book, we will define *risk* as *the degree of certainty or uncertainty as to the realization of expected future returns*. For a given level of expected future returns, the market will pay more for a company's stock to the extent that a realization of those returns is more certain or less to the extent that their realization is less certain. In other words, for a given level of expected future earnings (or cash flow, dividends, and the like), the lower the risk, the higher the present value or, conversely, the higher the risk, the lower the present value.

Risk generally is reflected in the valuation through the discount rate or the capitalization rate applied to the financial variables. The market determines a basic risk-free required rate of return and the amount of premium required for assuming various levels of risk. Of course, one thing the owners can do to lower their cost of capital, and thus increase the value of their enterprise, is lower the degree of risk associated with it. All else being equal, the lower the appraisers perceive the risk to be, the lower will be the cost of capital considered applicable in the valuation and, thus, the higher will be the resulting value.

Specific assessment and treatment of the all-important factor of risk is discussed in detail in the chapters on implementing the various valuation approaches.

Accepted Business Valuation Approaches and Methods

Background and Structure

Business valuation as it is practiced today reflects a blending of two streams of academic and professional background:

1. The securities profession, which deals with financial analysis of stocks, bonds, and other financial instruments and with business acquisitions, divestitures, and mergers.
2. The real estate profession, which deals with land and the improvements affixed thereto.

The body of knowledge required to estimate the value of a business or business interest is far more akin to that required by the securities profession than by the real estate profession. That fact is reflected by the material in this book and the academic and professional backgrounds of many of those in the business appraisal field.

However, the generalized field of "appraisal" (defined by The Appraisal Foundation as "the act or process of estimating value"[4]) is dominated by real estate appraisers. Among individual members of professional member organizations comprising The Appraisal Foundation, real estate appraisers outnumber business appraisers more than 20 to 1. The field of real estate appraisal is far more familiar to both the public and the courts than is the field of business appraisal.

Consequently, the American Society of Appraisers Business Valuation Standards recognizes an "income approach," a "market approach" (or sales comparison approach), and an "asset-based approach" (somewhat analogous to real estate's "cost" approach), thus following the three-pronged structure familiar to real estate appraisers. The term *method* is often used to refer to more specific ways to implement a business valuation within one of the three broad "approaches." For example, discounted cash flow is a method within the broader category of the income approach, the guideline company method would fall within the market approach, and the "capitalization of excess earnings" could be one method within the "asset-based approach."

We have reorganized the presentation of business valuation methodology in this third edition to more closely parallel the real estate appraisers' traditional three-pronged structure, as well as the structure of the American Society of Appraisers Business Valuation Standards. Thus, the reader will find:

Chapter 9:   Income Approach: Discounted Economic Income Methods
Chapter 10:   Market Approach: Guideline Company Method
Chapter 11:   Market Approach: The Merger and Acquisition Method
Chapter 12:   Asset-Based Approach
Chapter 13:   Excess Earnings Method

---

[4]*Uniform Standards of Professional Appraisal Practice* (Washington, DC: The Appraisal Foundation, 1995), p. 7.

Comparison with Real Estate Appraisal Approaches

Interrelationship of the Three Broad Approaches. In both business and real estate appraisal, the three broad approaches are interrelated.[5] The income approach requires some kind of a rate of return at which to discount or capitalize the income. These rates are driven by the forces of the market. All comparative appraisal approaches relate some market value observation to some unit of measure that is: (1) indicative of a property's ability to produce income and (2) a measure of the condition of its assets. The cost approach considers the investment required to replace the utility of the appraised subject, and it uses depreciation and obsolescence factors that are based, to a certain extent, on a measure of market values of assets. Thus, whether in business appraisal or real estate appraisal, the three broad approaches discussed so often are not discrete from each other, but are interrelated.

Income Approach. Within the income approach, the real estate appraisal profession recognizes certain methods similar to earning power discounting and capitalization methods used in business appraisal. For example, what real estate appraisers call *yield capitalization* uses procedures similar to what we refer to in Chapter 9 as the discounted economic income method. What real estate appraisers call *direct capitalization* uses procedures similar to what we refer to in Chapter 10 as capitalizing cash flow or earnings based upon market-derived capitalization rates or valuation multiples. In business appraisal, as in real estate appraisal, the two primary methods within the income approach require different rates at which to discount or capitalize the income stream. (See Chapter 9 for an explanation of the relationship between discount and capitalization rates in the context of business appraisal.)

While the appraisal procedures are similar, in many cases, estimating the future benefits for an operating business is somewhat more difficult than estimating the future benefits for an apartment building, an office building, or a similar income-producing real estate property. Furthermore, the risks of an operating business are somewhat more complex to assess and quantify than are the risks of operating real estate, and the resulting cash flows tend to be more volatile. Hence, the selection of appropriate discount and capitalization rates is somewhat more difficult in the context of the business appraisal. The business appraiser needs a broad understanding of relevant economic and industry factors, capital market conditions, business management, and accounting.

Pretax income streams from direct investments in real estate tend to be capitalized at lower rates of return than comparably defined pretax income streams from investments in business securities. One reason for this may be the lower perceived risk in the typical real estate investment. Another reason for this may be that real estate investments often enjoy tax benefits not available to the pretax income stream achieved by a business.

Real estate investors may accept a lower rate of return from their cash flow stream than they would accept from other assets because they expect extra return in the form of capital appreciation on the property. This is in sharp contrast to a business investment that includes machinery and equipment that will eventually lose value through wear and tear and/or obsolescence, or an investment that includes intangible assets that will become obsolete.

---

[5]For a discussion of this interrelationship with respect to real estate appraisal, see *The Appraisal of Real Estate,* 10th ed. (Chicago: Appraisal Institute, 1992), p. 409.

Market Approach. As for the market or sales comparison approach (covered in more detail in Chapters 10 and 11), the real estate appraiser will seek data on sales of comparable properties, and the business appraiser will seek data on transactions of guideline businesses. The business appraiser will interpret the transaction data for guidance in estimating applicable valuation parameters—such as capitalization rates for earnings or cash flow—and ratios of the entity's market value to asset value measures, such as book value or adjusted book value.

There is a tendency for the market for businesses to change more rapidly than the market for real estate. After all, a business can be thought of as a collection of tangible and intangible assets, each with its own price volatility and risks of ownership. Effects of these risks can be observed in volatility of stock prices every day.

Asset-Based Approach. The business appraiser's asset-based or adjusted net worth method (see Chapter 12) has some similarities to the real estate appraiser's cost approach. The asset-based approach provides an indication of the value of the business enterprise by developing a valuation-based balance sheet. All the assets of the business are identified and listed on the balance sheet (note: this balance sheet is not the cost-based balance sheet that is prepared in accordance with generally accepted accounting principles), and all the business's liabilities are brought to current value as of the valuation date.[6] The difference between the value of the assets and the current value of the liabilities is an indication of the business enterprise equity value under the asset accumulation approach.

Businesses Typically Owned through Securities. As discussed more fully elsewhere in the book, the fact that businesses typically are owned through either corporate stock or partnership interests introduces an element of complexity not present in direct ownership of assets. These securities represent bundles of rights determined by articles of incorporation or partnership, bylaws, and many contractual and legal rights and restrictions not relevant to direct ownership of physical assets. The valuation of stock or a partnership interest requires an understanding of the bundle of rights and restrictions encompassed therein.

Also, the income tax consequences of ownership and/or transfer of stock or partnership interests usually are quite different from those of ownership and/or transfer of direct investment in underlying assets. These income tax implications often have a significant bearing on value.

The U.S. Supreme Court in 1925 firmly established the principle that ownership of stock was not tantamount to ownership of a company's assets:

> The capital stock of a corporation, its net assets, and its shares of stock are entirely different things . . . The value of one bears no fixed or necessary relation to the value of the other.[7]

As George Lasry explains it:

> A share of common stock does not represent a share in the ownership of the assets of a business.[8]

---

[6]For example, if the company has a 6 percent bond outstanding due in 10 years, and the current market rate for a comparable bond was 8 percent, the bond would be revalued downward on the liability side of the balance sheet to a value equivalent of an 8 percent yield-to-maturity bond, unless it was contemplated that the bond would be paid before maturity.

[7]*Ray Consol. Copper Co. v. United States*, 45 S. Ct. 526 (1925).

[8]George Lasry, *Valuing Common Stock* (New York: AMACOM, 1979), p. 1.

Only the corporation itself holds title to all its assets and liabilities . . . A thirsty shareholder of a brewery cannot walk into "his" company and demand that a case of beer be charged to his equity account.[9]

Dozens of court cases have elaborated on the distinction between ownership of stock or partnership interests and direct ownership of assets.[10]

Fractional Interests. Stocks and partnership units are designed to be readily divisible into fractional interests in an enterprise, while fractional interests in direct investment in real estate or other assets are far less common and generally more cumbersome to transfer. To implement the market approach when valuing minority interests, market data on fractional interest transactions in direct investment in real estate are meager, at best, while minority interest public stock transactions abound.

Generally, minority holders of stocks and partnership units enjoy fewer rights if they are dissatisfied with management than do direct fractional interest holders in real estate. As a consequence, discounts from a pro rata portion of the value of 100 percent of the business or property taken as a whole generally are greater for stocks and partnership interests than for direct fractional interests in real estate.

Impact of Controlling versus Minority Interest

The owner of a controlling interest in an enterprise enjoys some very valuable rights that an owner not in such a position does not. Consequently, if control is an issue in the valuation, the analyst should assess the extent to which the various elements of control do or do not exist in the particular situation and consider the impact of each element on the value of control. (The most important elements of control are discussed in Chapter 14, "Minority Discounts, Control Premiums, and Other Discounts and Premiums.") A minority holder may not be totally stripped of control factors. For instance, a minority holder may be in a position to cast a crucial swing vote and, to some degree, influence important business policies.

The distribution of ownership can affect the value of a particular business interest. If each of three stockholders or partners owns a one-third interest, no one has complete control. However, no one is in a relatively inferior position unless only two of the three have close ties with each other. In this situation, the analyst could recognize that the size of the discount from pro rata value for each equal interest normally will be less than that for a minority interest that has no control whatsoever.

Many typical control rights may be denied to a company through relations with other stakeholders in the company, such as its banker. Indenture provisions in conjunction with debt obligations or senior classes of stock frequently prevent the company from taking such actions as dividend payments, increases in management compensation, liquidation of assets, acquisitions, or changes in the direction of the business, for example. Shareholder agreements also may contain several restrictions.

---

[9]Ibid., p. 15.

[10]See, for example, *Charles S. Foltz, et al.* v. *U.S. News & World Report, et al.*, 865 F.2d 364 (D.C. Cir. 1989); *Sommers Drug Stores* v. *Corrigan Enterprises, Inc.*, 793 F.2d 1456 (5th Cir. 1986); and *Estate of Edwin A. Gallun*, 33 T.C.M. 1316 (1974).

Government regulations may preempt the usual prerogatives of control. Liquidating such highly regulated businesses as insurance companies, railroads, or utilities can be a lengthy and sometimes impossible process, for example. Government regulations may prevent certain acquisitions and, similarly, prevent a company from selling to certain other companies or investors.

State statutes can affect the respective rights of controlling and minority stockholders. In about half the states, a simple majority can approve major actions such as a merger, sale, liquidation, or recapitalization of the company. Other states require a two-thirds or greater majority to approve such actions, which means that a minority of just over one-third (or even less in some states) has the power to block such actions. Under California and some other states' statutes, minority stockholders enjoy certain rights under specific circumstances. The variations in state law concerning which rights are given to what proportion of ownership can have an important bearing on the valuation of certain percentage interests in some cases.

Voting rights constitute one of the most difficult variables to quantify in terms of impact on value. For extremely small minority interests, the market accords very little value to voting rights. However, where swing votes or majority interests are involved, the impact on value can be significant. In fact, a majority block of nonvoting stock may actually be worth less per share than a smaller block of voting stock, since there are fewer potential buyers for the large block without the right to vote on corporate matters.

In most cases, a minority interest is worth less than a pro rata proportion of the value of the enterprise as a whole. The quantification of the difference between minority and control values is addressed in considerable detail in Chapter 14, "Minority Discounts, Control Premiums, and Other Discounts and Premiums."

Impact of Marketability

Ready marketability definitely adds value to a security. Conversely, lack of marketability detracts from the security's value as compared to a security that is identical but marketable. In other words, the market pays a premium for liquidity or exacts a discount for the lack of it.

Since ownership interests in closely held businesses do not, by definition, enjoy the ready market of a publicly traded stock, a share in a privately held company usually is worth less than an otherwise comparable share in a publicly held company. Many factors affect the relative marketability of different business interests. Sometimes size of the interest is a factor; a smaller block may be easier to market than a larger block, and in other cases the reverse is true. In most cases, the lack of marketability factor impacts minority interests most severely. However, even controlling interests in closely held businesses obviously are not as readily marketable as shares of publicly traded stock.

The existence of shareholder agreements can severely affect the transferability of shares. Some buy–sell agreements require that the shareholders be employed by the company and be a resident of a certain state. Others determine the price at which, and the circumstances under which, the shares are to be voluntarily or involuntarily transferred, put and call provisions, and who may be entitled to a right of first refusal on transactions. The presence of practically any type of restrictive agreement tends to reduce the appraised market value established for a closely held company's stock.[11]

Chapter 15, "Discounts for Lack of Marketability," presents extensive empirical evidence on the quantification of discounts for lack of marketability.

Distinction between Discount for Minority Interest and Discount for Lack of Marketability

Confusion can result when clients, appraisers, and the audience for the analysis (e.g., the court) fail to distinguish between a discount for minority interest and a discount for lack of marketability. These are two separate concepts, although they are somewhat interrelated. Sometimes people overlook the fact that discounts are meaningless until the bases from which they are to be taken have been clearly defined.

Since a minority interest discount reflects a value decrement due to lack of control, the value base from which the minority interest discount is subtracted is its proportionate share of the value of the total equity (or at least the common equity), taken as a whole, including all rights of control. Since a discount for lack of marketability reflects a value decrement due to lack of liquidity, the value base from which the discount is subtracted is the value of an entity or interest that is otherwise comparable but enjoys higher liquidity (that is, can more readily be sold and converted to cash).

If a minority interest in a closely held business is valued by reference to day-to-day trading prices of publicly held stocks, minority interests are being compared with other minority interests. The closely held stock should be discounted for its lack of marketability with respect to the public stock, but not for minority interest. If a minority interest in a closely held business is being valued by capitalization of earnings, book value, adjusted book value, or some other statistic, but with such multiples based on controlling interest transactions, discounts may be appropriate to reflect *both* the minority interest and the lack of marketability. Conversely, if a controlling interest in a closely held business is being valued with reference to day-to-day trading prices of public stocks, which are minority interests, it may be appropriate to add a premium for control to the price that otherwise would appear to be indicated.

When using a discounted economic income method, such as discounted cash flow, it is common to develop the present value discount rate based on data from the publicly traded stock market—that is, transactions in publicly traded minority shares. This would imply that, when valuing a minority interest, it would be appropriate to adjust the results from the method for a discount for lack of marketability, but not for minority interest. This is a correct implication, providing that the cash flows being discounted are not adjusted for changes or factors that would benefit a control owner but would not inure to the benefit of a minority owner. This is discussed in some detail in Chapter 9, "Income Approach: Discounted Economic Income Methods," and in the subsequent chapters on discounts and premiums.

---

[11]See, for example, W. Terrance Schreier and O. Maurice Joy, "Judicial Valuation of 'Close' Corporation Stock: *Alice in Wonderland* Revisited," *Oklahoma Law Review* 31 (1978), p. 865.

Even controlling interests can suffer to some extent from a lack of marketability. A majority but less than 100 percent control position may take longer to sell, thereby reducing its present value by the time value of money, for example. The relationship between the discount for lack of marketability and that for minority interest lies in the fact that even after reducing the pro rata value of an ownership interest in a business in order to reflect its lack of complete control, it is usually much more difficult, more time consuming, and more expensive to sell an ownership interest in a closely held company than a publicly traded one.

In some cases, the premium value of control may just offset the disadvantage of lack of marketability. However, this should be the result only after careful consideration of the specific circumstances surrounding those factors and not the result of only an uninformed assumption.

Many court decisions, especially older ones involving valuations for gift and estate tax purposes, have taken a single lump-sum discount to reflect minority, marketability, and sometimes still other factors. However, conceptual thinking in the valuation exercise, supported by the use of empirical data, usually can isolate and separately quantify the various valuation factors, especially the more important ones. Fortunately, in recent years, both valuation practitioners and courts increasingly have been giving separate recognition to the impact of minority interest and marketability factors. A 1982 estate tax decision articulated the distinction between the minority and marketability discounts very clearly:

> In their arguments, neither petitioner nor respondent clearly focuses on the fact that two conceptually distinct discounts are involved here, one for lack of marketability and the other for lack of control. The minority shareholder discount is designed to reflect the decreased value of shares that do not convey control of a closely held corporation. The lack of marketability discount, on the other hand, is designed to reflect the fact that there is no ready market for shares in a closely held corporation. Although there may be some overlap between these two discounts in that lack of control may reduce marketability, it should be borne in mind that even controlling shares in a nonpublic corporation suffer from lack of marketability because of the absence of a ready private placement market and the fact that flotation costs would have to be incurred if the corporation were to publicly offer its stock.[12]

Many court decisions since the above case have distinguished between the concepts of minority and marketability and have separately quantified their decisions regarding the impact of the respective factors. Several of these decisions are cited in later chapters.

Other Qualitative Factors Affecting Value

Qualitative factors bear on value yet defy quantification on the basis of empirical data within the valuation factors discussed up to this point. In some cases, such factors may influence the analyst's judgment and be reflected in a specific adjustment in arriving at the value conclusion. The analyst may incorporate these factors into the analysis when choosing valuation multiples or capitalization rates. In some cases, the qualitative factors may be important enough to warrant a separate, specific (and therefore quantified) adjustment to value.

---

[12]*Estate of Woodbury G. Andrews,* 79 T.C. 938 (1982).

Perhaps the most important qualitative factor in many closely held companies is reliance on one key individual or a few key management personnel. Limited product diversity can restrict the categories of potential customers, curtail the number of potential customers within a category, and increase the risks arising from shortages of critical supplies or competitive product information. Lack of vertical integration can leave a closely held business vulnerable to vagaries in sources of supply or to a particular customer relationship—an example being the original equipment component manufacturer who is vulnerable should the customer decide to manufacture in-house.

Other factors to consider in various cases include the company's research and development efforts, industry position, quantity and quality of asset base relative to competitors, and the quality and relationship with its workforce.

Matching the Valuation Methodology with the Standard of Value and Ownership Characteristics

Perhaps the single most prevalent broad reason many valuation work products miss the mark is failure to use valuation approaches and methods that are consistent with the definition of value being sought.

In the previous chapter, we discussed standards and premises of value and ownership characteristics and presented an exhibit giving examples of how the purpose of the valuation can affect the appropriate definition of value. In this chapter we have, at least broadly, introduced the topic of approaches to value and elaborated a bit further on two of the most important ownership characteristics, control versus minority interests and degree of marketability. *All these matters must be considered together in deciding exactly which valuation methods to use and what assumptions and data will go into the implementation of those methods.*

This art of matching the methodology to the valuation context will become clearer as the reader moves through Part III, "Reaching the Valuation Conclusion," and Part VII, "Business Valuations for Specific Purposes." When either preparing or reviewing a business valuation work product, always be alert to consider whether each step of the procedure is consistent with the standard and premises of value and the ownership characteristics applicable to the specific valuation context.

Sum of Parts Not Necessarily Equal to Whole

Since partial interests in a business enterprise are impacted by discounts and premiums differently than are controlling interests, the sum of the individual ownership positions may not add up to the overall business enterprise value. In most cases, the sum of the values of the partial ownership interests taken individually is less than what might be received if a single buyer purchased the entire entity. The company in its entirety has a different value because it conveys different rights and interests than the sum of all the interests taken on a minority basis. This economic fact, of course, is a catalyst for both merger and acquisition activity and dissenting shareholder lawsuits.

It is also important for attorneys and other advisors to alert clients entering into buy–sell agreements at "fair market value" that that usually means something less than a pro rata proportion of the total enterprise value, unless other provisions are specified.

Since estate tax planning is seriously impacted by the fact that the sum of the parts do not always equal the whole, Chapter 14, the special valuation provision of the Internal Revenue Code, was added by the Revenue Reconciliation Act of 1990. These provisions mandate certain departures from strict fair market value in valuations for certain family company recapitalizations. However, there still are many opportunities in estate planning to benefit from the fact that the sum of the values of parts often is considerably less than the value of the whole. These issues and opportunities are discussed further in Chapter 27, "Taxation Planning and Compliance—Gift and Estate."

Summary of Business Valuation Principles

The specific methods and procedures for valuing a business or a fractional business interest vary from one situation to another. However, several basic principles are fundamental to the business valuation discipline:

1. From a financial point of view, the value of a business or business interest is the sum of the expected future economic benefits to its owner, each discounted back to a present value at an appropriate discount rate.

2. The appropriate discount rate is usually dependent upon the market for capital. The discount rate is the expected rate of return that would be required to attract capital to the investment, which takes into account the rate of return available from other investments of comparable risk.

3. Projecting future economic benefits and determining an appropriate discount rate is difficult, especially when trying to bring two sides to a transaction or dispute to an agreement. There are accepted methods of estimating value by using current or historical rather than projected financial data. These often require adjustments to the historical data to reflect the impact of future expectations. Values estimated from such procedures should be reconcilable with estimates of value from a discounted economic income approach.

4. When relying on specific comparative market transactions for guidance in estimating the value of a subject business or interest, investors' specific expectations regarding future returns and risk that are incorporated into capitalization rates, multipliers, and other valuation parameters are not known. This makes it imperative that financial variables used in the valuation be defined on a consistent basis between the guideline and subject companies and that measurements for estimating variables be taken as of the same point in time or over the same time period relative to the valuation date for the guideline companies and the subject company.

5. Shareholders have no direct claim on a corporation's assets because a corporate entity intervenes between the assets and the shareholder. Therefore, the value of a share of stock can be more than or less than a proportionate share of the underlying net asset value and sometimes bears little relationship to the underlying net asset value.

6. Lack of control and lack of marketability are distinct concepts, although they are related. Both controlling and minority interests may suffer somewhat from lack of marketability, defined as the ability to convert the asset to cash very quickly, at minimal costs, with a high degree of certainty of realizing the anticipated amount of proceeds. The impact of both minority and marketability factors is influenced by both internal and external facts and circumstances as of the valuation date.

7. Minority shareholders lack control over various decisions affecting the business enterprise. Therefore, minority interests may be worth considerably less than a pro rata portion of the business value if it were valued as a single 100 percent ownership interest.

8. The market pays a premium for liquidity or, conversely, demands a discount for lack of liquidity. Business interests that lack ready marketability generally are worth less than otherwise comparable business interests that are readily marketable.

9. The sum of the values of individual fractional interests in a business is not necessarily (or even usually) equal to the value of a 100 percent ownership interest in the business.

Within the scope of these business valuation principles, different standards, characteristics, and premises of value apply for different valuation purposes and within different legal contexts. These can affect both the valuation procedures to be utilized and the final estimation of value. The appraiser should understand the applicable purpose and objective for the assignment and the implications of each.

These principles, though broad, provide a framework for consistency in the practice of the business valuation discipline. Many errors and unreasonable valuation conclusions can be avoided if these principles are understood and implemented. These principles provide the business appraisal user with a basic perspective from which to review and evaluate a business appraisal work product.

Part II

Preparing for the Business Valuation

Chapter 4

Gathering Company Data

Behind every stock is a company. Find out what it's doing.[1]

The next step in the valuation process, after carefully defining the assignment, is to gather the data necessary to conduct the assignment. These data can be categorized into three groups:

1. Company-specific data.
2. Data about the company's industry and economic environment.
3. Data about the subject property's market (market for ownership interests in the subject company).

The company-specific data are gathered from the subject company in written form and during site visits and interviews with people knowledgeable about the company. The gathering of this information is the subject of this and the next chapter.

The industry and economy data often can be provided by the subject company and can be gathered from publicly available sources. This is the subject of Chapter 6. Data about the market for ownership interests in the subject company include information about changes of ownership of competitors, about guideline company transactions, and about premiums and discounts that might apply to the subject property. These two categories of information gathering are covered in subsequent chapters in Part III.

The manner and sequence in which the data are gathered are important only to the extent that the process be complete and efficient. For example, supporting analysts may be collecting industry, economic, rate of return, and guideline transaction information at the same time that the principal analyst is working directly with the management of the subject company. In any case, it is important to convey a sufficient overview of the company and the assignment to all valuation team members at an early meeting so that all the analysts will be in a position to recognize important data as they proceed on the project.

If time allows, information gathered should be reviewed before the visit to the company so as to focus the interviewing process on the most essential factors that affect the value of the company, thereby minimizing the inconvenience of management interviews and also maximizing the productivity of the site visit.

Some of the information necessary to conduct the business valuation will need to be obtained through interviews with company management. Sometimes, however, the analyst merely inspects voluminous or highly sensitive documents and gets copies only of the information necessary to perform the assignment.

Generalized Company Information Checklist

Written company-specific information that is generally used in business valuations is presented in Exhibit 4–1. This list is generic. Not every item on the list will be required for every appraisal, and in many circumstances, documents not listed must be reviewed. Working with this list, nevertheless, will assist the ana-

---

[1]Peter Lynch, with John Rothchild, *Beating the Street* (New York: Simon & Schuster, 1994), p. 305.

lyst in developing a subject-company-specific information request list. It will also be helpful to company officials and attorneys in the planning stages of a potential valuation engagement.

Financial Statements

According to the American Institute of Certified Public Accountants (AICPA), the term *financial statements* refers to a presentation of financial data, including accompanying notes, derived from accounting records and intended to communicate an entity's economic resources or obligations at a point in time, or the changes therein for a period of time, in accordance with a comprehensive basis of accounting.[2]

Four traditional statements, along with the footnotes, together comprise the financial statements of a business entity. These are:

- Balance sheet (statement of financial position).
- Income statement (statement of income, statement of operations, or statement of earnings).
- Statement of cash flows (formerly, statement of changes in financial position).
- Statement of stockholders' equity (or statement of partners' capital).

The amounts of a company's assets, liabilities, and equity, as determined under generally accepted accounting principles (which is not necessarily the fair market value of these accounts) as of a given point in time, is the statement of financial position, more commonly referred to as the company's balance sheet. In contrast, the statement of results of operations, or the income statement, presents a financial summary of a company's operating results for a certain time period. The third statement, the statement of cash flows, is designed to provide information about the important changes in financial position that occurred during the accounting period. This statement is critical if net cash flow is an important measure of economic income in the valuation (as it is in many, if not most, cases), because it is a source of information on capital expenditures and changes in working capital.

It is important to recognize that, even within the scope of generally accepted accounting principles (GAAP), there are many decisions that management makes with respect to the accounting treatment of various company transactions. These include, for example, such things as choices of capitalizing or not capitalizing certain items, inventory accounting methods, and depreciation methods. The footnotes to financial statements and supporting schedules usually are helpful in understanding the company's treatment of such items.

The appraiser's function is not to audit, but to express an opinion of value on the basis of available financial information. In some situations, nevertheless, the accountants' work papers and/or company books may provide additional insight that is relevant to the appraisal, and the appraiser may request to see such information.

---

[2]American Institute of Certified Public Accountants, *AICPA Professional Standards,* vol. A (Chicago: Commerce Clearing House, 1989), p. 3312.

Exhibit 4–1

Preliminary Documents and Information Checklist for the Business Valuation of a Typical Corporation

Financial Statements for Typical Corporation

Balance sheets, income statements, statements of changes in financial position, and statements of stockholders' equity for the last five fiscal years

Income tax returns for the same years

Latest interim statements and interim statements for comparable period(s) of previous year

Other Financial Data

Summary property, plant, and equipment list and depreciation schedule

Aged accounts receivable summary

Aged accounts payable summary

List of marketable securities and prepaid expenses

Inventory summary, with any necessary information on inventory accounting policies

Synopsis of leases for facilities or equipment

Any other existing contracts (employment agreements, covenants not to compete, supplier agreements, customer agreements, royalty agreements, equipment lease or rental contracts, loan agreements, labor contracts, employee benefit plans, and so on)

List of stockholders, with number of shares owned by each

Schedule of insurance in force (key-person life, property and casualty, liability)

Budgets or projections, for a minimum of five years

List of subsidiaries and/or financial interests in other companies

Key personnel compensation schedule, including benefits and personal expenses

Company Documents

Articles of incorporation, bylaws, and any amendments to either

Any existing buy–sell agreements, options to purchase stock, or rights of first refusal

Franchise or operating agreements, if any

Other Information

Brief history, including how long in business and details of any changes in ownership and/or bona fide offers recently received

Brief description of the business, including position relative to competition and any factors that make the business unique

Marketing literature (catalogs, brochures, advertisements, and so on)

List of locations where company operates, with size and recent appraisals

List of competitors, with location, relative size, and any relevant factors

Organization chart

Résumés of key personnel, with age, position, compensation, length of service, education, and prior experience

Personnel profile: number of employees by functional groupings, such as production, sales, engineering/R&D, personnel and accounting, customer service/field support, and so forth

Trade associations to which the company belongs or would be eligible for membership

Relevant trade or government publications (specially market forecasts)

Any existing indicators of asset values, including latest property tax assessments and any appraisals that have been performed

List of customer relationships, supplier relationships, contracts, patents, copyrights, trademarks, and other intangible assets

Any contingent or off-balance-sheet liabilities (pending lawsuits, compliance requirements, warranty or other product liabilities, estimate of medical benefits for retirees, and so on)

Any filings or correspondence with regulatory agencies

Information on prior transactions in the stock or any related party transactions

Relevant Time Period

When asking for historical financial statements on the subject property, one should endeavor to study statements during a *relevant period*. The most common period of such study is five years. However, conceptually, the relevant period covers the most recent time period immediately before the valuation date during which the statements represent the company's general operations.

If the company significantly changed its operations a few years before the valuation date, the relevant period may include only the previous three or four years. On the other hand, if the business has a long history and some or all recent years were abnormal in some way (such as during a cyclical peak or trough in the company's industry), statements for the past 7, 10, or more years may constitute a relevant period for valuation purposes.

Levels of Financial Statement Preparation

In the United States, we sometimes take for granted the standardization of the financial statement presentation. One only needs to work with financial statements from other countries to truly appreciate our financial reporting standards, as complicated and as curious as they are.

Valuation analysts prefer to work with audited financial statements because of the statements' completeness and reliability, but the large majority of closely held businesses do not go to the trouble and expense of having their financial statements examined by an independent auditor. There are various levels of scrutiny represented by audited, reviewed, and compiled financial statements. The same company might have different levels of scrutiny performed for different years.

Audited Statements. In *audited statements,* the independent auditor expresses an opinion, or if circumstances require, disclaims an opinion, regarding the fairness with which the financial statements present the financial position, the results of operations, and the changes in financial position, in accordance with generally accepted accounting principles.

Reviewed Statements. The accountant expresses limited assurance in *reviewed statements* that no material modifications should be made to the statements for them to be in conformity with generally accepted accounting principles. A review does not provide assurance that the accountant will become aware of all significant matters that would be disclosed in an audit.

Compiled Statements. Finally, the *compiled statements* are management's representations presented in the form of financial statements, but the accountant has not undertaken any efforts to express assurance on the statements.

Sometimes, statements are prepared internally by management without the services of an outside accountant.

As the level of outside examination of the financial statements declines, the analysts should make more extensive inquiries and use judgment as to the quality of the information available.

Impact of Enterprise Legal Structure

When the legal structure of the company is different from the traditional corporation, the analyst should be cognizant of the potential impact on the analysis. Several of these legal organizations, and the valuation implications of the choice of legal structure, are discussed in later chapters.

It is important to point out that a different legal status of the business can have a dramatic impact on the valuation conclusions. Especially when it comes to partnerships, where partners do not share the earnings (or losses) in the same proportion (as their partnership share is entitled to upon liquidation, for instance), the legal rights and privileges of one equity owner could be substantially different from that of another owner, resulting in a substantially different value conclusion. The analyst valuing a partnership interest subject to any such complications probably will need to read the partnership agreement to be sure that the partners' rights are understood.

Federal Income Tax Returns

There are common reasons for discrepancies between the amounts and items reported on financial statements and those reported on federal income tax returns. Many of the differences are simply resulting from timing differences, such as different methods of revenue recognition and cost recovery of capital expenditures.

For corporations filing Form 1120, "U.S. Corporate Income Tax Return," a summary of differences between tax return reporting and financial statement reporting is found in Schedule M-1, "Reconciliation of Income per Books with Income per Return."

If such differences exist, the analyst must use his or her professional judgment to determine which figures will provide the most appropriate basis for appraisal purposes. A general rule is that the analyst should select the statements that most closely conform to industry practices and would most fairly represent the company's financial position and earning power. Normally, the financial data and ratios derived from income tax return data would not be relied upon when comparing the subject company to the financial data and ratios derived from the audited financial statements of publicly traded guideline companies.

It is not unusual to find small companies without any formally prepared financial statements. In this case, the analyst has only the income tax returns as a basis for financial statements. In this situation, financial statements can be formatted in the conventional manner by the analyst by recasting information from the tax returns.

Many federal income tax forms may contain relevant data for a particular valuation assignment. A discussion of the various forms and their use would be too detailed to fit within the scope of this book. Internal Revenue Service "Package X" is a two-volume set of informational copies of federal tax forms, along with their instructions, which is available on a complimentary basis from the IRS.

Interim Statements

Interim statements are those prepared as of a date other than the last day of the fiscal year. Analysis of interim statements can give a more timely indication of the financial performance of the subject company and can provide a better understanding of businesses with highly seasonal operations whose trends the analyst may want to track on a monthly or quarterly basis.

Some privately held companies prepare interim statements monthly. It is important, however, that the analyst have an idea of these statements' usefulness before demanding the effort required to develop this information.

Several factors influence the usefulness of interim statements, particularly:

1. The proximity of the valuation date to the fiscal year-end.
2. The quality of the interim statements.
3. The importance of seasonality to the subject company.
4. The extent to which interim statements are likely to affect the conclusion.

Often, information regarding the latest 12 months (LTM) of operations can provide a worthwhile perspective about the company's condition. When LTM analysis is conducted, the interim statements for the subject time period plus the interim statements for the corresponding period during the prior fiscal year are needed.

Interim statements usually do not contain certain adjustments typically made when closing the books at year-end for a variety of accrual items, such as a physical inventory inspection, prepaid expenses, and bad debt accounts.

Therefore, to interpret interim statements and use them as if they were comparable to fiscal year-end statements, the analyst probably will need to obtain additional information with which to approximate such adjustments.

Other Financial Schedules

The purpose of requesting financial information regarding equipment lists, aged receivables, aged payables, and prepaid expenses is to give the analyst familiarity with the accounting policies of the company and to alert the analyst to special situations that could affect the valuation. Also, when applying the asset accumulation approach to business valuation (see Chapter 12), normal operating assets should be distinguished from excess assets and should be separately identified and valued. Chapter 7 on analyzing financial statements discusses when and how some of this information may be used.

Current Assets and Liabilities

Depending on the situation, any or all of the following schedules may be relevant:

*   Aged receivables list.
*   Aged payables list.
*   Marketable securities list.
*   Prepaid expense list.
*   Inventory list.

Among other things, an understanding of a company's current assets and liabilities gives insight into the company's working capital needs.

Aged Receivables and Payables Lists. The *aged receivables list* can yield insight into the company's profitability, and even viability. However, many relatively small companies do not prepare them. Because the aged list gives the appraiser a useful means for recognizing situations that could affect the company's value, the analyst should have either the client's accounting department or a member of his or her own staff prepare one, if appropriate.

The *aged payables list* may be particularly relevant if it appears that a company's working capital may be deficient.

Marketable Securities List. For companies that maintain an investment portfolio of marketable securities, knowing what they are helps to understand how they should best be treated in the valuation process.

Prepaid Expense List. Adjustments to prepaid expenses may be appropriate in some cases, and a listing will help to make this determination as well as provide insight into working capital needs.

Inventory List. The amount of detail desired in the inventory list will vary from one appraisal to another. Depending upon the inventory's importance to the valuation conclusion and to the extent to which inventory accounting methods vary within the particular industry, the amount of inventory data to be gathered will vary. In any case, the total should be reconcilable with the inventory as presented on the financial statements, using whatever adjustments conform to the company's method of inventory valuation. The company's inventory write-down policy may also call for a market value adjustment.

Plant and Equipment

Property Lists. Lists of property owned should include the acquisition date, a description adequate for identifying each piece or group, the original cost, the depreciation method and life used, and the net depreciated value. The totals of such schedules should reconcile with line items in the financial statements. For real estate, the schedule should show the size (acres of land and dimensions and square feet of floor space of buildings), with a brief description of the construction and any special features. It should also indicate the dates and costs of additions and remodeling.

Evidence of Real and Personal Property Values. Indicators of current real estate and equipment asset values can be helpful. An independent appraisal by a qualified practitioner, if available, usually is a more reliable guide to asset value than either a property tax assessment or an insurance appraisal. Property tax assessments are usually readily available but may represent a standard of value that is different from the one required for the business valuation. Insurance appraisals have a tendency to use the replacement value standard instead of the market value standard and thereby overvalue used property. This is because insurance appraisals attempt to ensure that the insurance will be adequate to cover potential losses.

Officers' and Directors' Compensation Schedule

An officers' and directors' compensation and benefits schedule usually should be prepared for the same number of years as the financial statements. The income statement could conceivably be adjusted in order to identify the company's earning capacity (see Chapter 7). The benefits of ownership should be identified.

Employees related to the owners should be included on the list. The analyst should be mindful that the IRS sometimes attempts to depict compensation paid to owners as excessive, so as to get dividend tax treatment for a portion of it. The analyst should be careful to describe any adjustments made to compensation in order to avoid triggering unfavorable tax consequences for the client. These benefits might include:

- Base salary.
- Bonuses or commissions.
- Pension contributions.
- Profit sharing plans.
- Other employee benefit funds.
- Life insurance policies.
- Noncash contributions:
  — Stock options.
  — Company cars.
  — Country club memberships.
  — Other company property used (plane, boat, condominium, etc.).
  — Expenses paid or reimbursed to the employee.

Distribution of Ownership

The list of equity owners should include each owner's name and the number of shares or partnership units held by each as of the valuation date. The ownership list should describe and quantify individual and other entity ownership, especially if there is more than one class of equity. Family members and other relationships among the equity owners should be identified.

Dividend or Partnership Withdrawal Schedule

The *dividend schedule* normally should cover the same time period as the financial statements. It should show the date of each dividend payment and the per share amount for each class of stock or per unit amount for each class of partnership unit.

Schedule of Key-Person Life Insurance

In many companies, the loss of a single key employee can have a significant impact on the company's operations. It is always desirable to know how much of this risk is covered by life insurance. A schedule of key-person life insurance will help identify how much key employee risk affects the value of the business.

Off-Balance-Sheet Assets or Liabilities

Many financial items that can significantly affect the business's value do not appear as line items on the balance sheet, usually because they are of a contingent nature. Such items may or may not be referenced in footnotes.

One of the most common "off-balance-sheet" assets or liabilities is a prospective award or payment arising from a lawsuit. The appraiser should inquire about any pending or potential suits and note the details.

This category could also include the potential cost of compliance with environmental, OSHA, or other government requirements. The adequacy of reserves for claims or other product-related liabilities should also be explored. Overfunded pension plans are another potential hidden asset, or, conversely, underfunded plans a hidden liability.

Information regarding intangible assets, both those recorded on the balance sheet and those off-balance-sheet intangibles, such as patents, copyrights, and trademarks, should include a description of the property protected by this legal right and the expiration date of the right. The list of intangibles should include a brief description and enough information to understand these items. The importance to the business's value of these legal rights and degree of detail required varies by situation. The importance of intangible assets is covered in Part VI of this book along with some of the documentation necessary to reflect their impact on the business's value.

Related Party Transaction Information

When it comes to related party transactions, it is important that the analyst gather as much information as is available to determine the nature of the transactions and their propriety.

As the Financial Accounting Standards Board (FASB) states in its *Statement No. 57* regarding *related party transactions:*

> Related party[3] transactions may be controlled by one of the parties so that those transactions may be affected significantly by considerations other than those in arm's-length transactions with unrelated parties.[4]
>
> Without disclosure to the contrary, there is a general presumption that the transactions reflected in the financial statements have been consummated on an arm's-length basis between independent parties... Because it is possible for related party transactions to be arranged to obtain certain results desired by the related parties, the resulting accounting measures may not represent what they usually would be expected to represent.[5]

Related party transactions may be controlled entirely by one of the parties so that those transactions may be affected significantly by considerations other than those in arm's-length transactions with unrelated parties.

In the absence of audited financial statements, which will include related party information in their accompanying notes, the analyst should have a list prepared that describes the terms of the transactions. These types of related party transactions could include loans to and from related parties, leases, or purchases from or sales to related parties, guarantees to or for related parties, and so on.

---

[3]Defined in *Statement of the Financial Accounting Standards Board No. 57,* Appendix B(f).

[4]*SFAS No. 57,* Appendix A, para. 13 (1982).

[5]Ibid., para. 15.

Operating Information

Company History

The history of the company should put the business in the proper context for the user of the valuation analysis. A relatively brief history will suffice in most cases. The history should indicate how long the company has been in business and some chronology of major changes, such as form of organization, controlling ownership, location of operations, and lines of business. Sometimes predecessor companies are a relevant part of the background. A detailed explanation of the history may be required in some instances, and sometimes certain transactions that fundamentally contributed to the company's composition, as of the valuation date, should be included.

Brochures, Catalogs, and Price Lists

The company should furnish the analyst with a set of its sales materials, such as brochures, catalogs, and price lists. These items will enable the analyst to become familiar with the company's products, services, and pricing and to evaluate the written sales materials. As with many of the written items furnished, these will help the analyst get an overview of the company and prepare relevant questions for the visit to the company's facilities and inquiries of company personnel.

Key Personnel

Hiring, stimulating, and retaining human resources is often the closely held business owner's biggest challenge. Key personnel include directors and officers, heads of departments or divisions, and anyone else who plays an important part in the company's operation. Data on key personnel should include the person's age, position, tenure with the company and in the industry, educational and professional credentials, and compensation. An organization chart may help the analyst identify key personnel.

Customer and Supplier Base

Customer Base. A customer base is especially important for businesses that rely on only a few customers for a significant portion of their revenue and/or profit. Many businesses fall under the "80/20 rule" where 80 percent of their revenue is attributable to 20 percent of their customers. The information to analyze the impact on value attributable to a customer base includes a list, in order of size of revenue (or profit), of the largest customers. The list should include revenue by customer for the most recent fiscal period and the dollar amounts of revenue for several prior periods. The columns for the prior periods should also show customers that accounted for a significant proportion of the revenue in the prior period, even if they are not on the current period's largest customer list. Sometimes a budgeted figure for each customer for the forthcoming period is available.

Order Backlog. If the company's order backlog (customer orders yet to be filled) is a significant factor in the business, the analyst should compare the backlog on the valuation date with that on previous dates. Such comparison, especially with the backlog one year before the valuation date, is one indication of the company's prospects.

Supplier Base. Like the customer base, the supplier base can be an important factor affecting the value of a business, especially if the future availability of supplies is uncertain enough to increase the company's risk. The supplier list could take the same format as the customer base.

Contractual Agreements and Obligations

Also, a variety of other contractual commitments (e.g., leases, loans, franchise agreements, distributor agreements, customer contracts, etc.) can have a significant impact on the value of a particular business interest. The list of potential contractual commitments is nearly infinite. The analyst should draw on personal experience to inquire about contracts that typically occur in certain lines of business and ask management whether any significant contracts exist. Some factors that should be analyzed are the rights of ownership for the specific term, restrictive covenants, transferability, favorable or unfavorable rates relative to rates available as of the valuation date, renewal options, personal guarantees, and the penalties that the company could suffer for lack of performance under these commitments.

Industry and Trade Association Information

Industry information can be provided by the subject company, in many cases, more readily than relying on independent research. A description of the industry, its trends, and competitive environment is usually accessible from the company. It is also helpful if the company can furnish a list of trade associations to which it belongs, or is eligible to belong, along with the name and address of the executive director of each. Copies of relevant publications from trade associations, governmental agencies, and other industry sources can often be readily supplied by the company.

List of Past Transactions in the Stock or Offers to Buy

To the extent that past transactions in the stock were at arm's length, they provide objective evidence of value. Even if not accepted, a bona fide offer, particularly if submitted in writing, can at least corroborate the value. In preparing the record of past transactions or offers, it is important to list any relationships among the parties to determine whether each transaction was at arm's length. The transaction record usually should go as far back as the number of years of financial statements used. On this basis, past transaction prices can be compared with then current book values, earnings, or other relevant variables.

If the company has made an acquisition, details of the acquisition may be an extremely relevant past transaction. This is an important category of past transactions that often is overlooked.

Budgets and Forecasts

Budgets or forecasts prepared by closely held companies vary widely from no written budget ("It's all in my head. It doesn't need to be written down.") to fairly detailed and accurate ones. Since the value of a business interest ultimately depends on what the business will accomplish in the future, reasonable estimates of future expectations should help in arriving at a value. A good way to test the quality of a company's budgeting process is to compare past budgets to actual results.

Budgets and forecasts are an important component in valuations for mergers and acquisitions. On the other hand, some courts, such as divorce courts in California, are reluctant to accept budgets because the future is inherently unprovable and because they may incorporate fruits of a spouse's future efforts. In most cases, however, a company that produces convincing budgets will command a higher value than one that does not.

Capital Requirements

The needs of the business for capital play a part in the valuation because they are an integral part of estimating net cash flow and dividend-paying capacity. Capital requirements include items such as:

- Making capital expenditures.
- Remedying deferred maintenance.
- Increasing working capital.

The proper amount paid to the seller would be the total value of a properly financed business, less the amount of the required cash infusion. When cash infusions are known or reasonably expected to be required in the foreseeable future to support the expected earnings, they must be reflected as a cash outflow, the present value of which should represent a decrease in the value of the business as otherwise determined.

Capital Expenditures

Capital expenditures include replacements of worn out or obsolescent existing plant and equipment plus any additions to plant and equipment necessary to produce any revenues contemplated in the valuation. The latter category would include items needed to remain competitive and maintain the company's position, plus anything needed to support whatever level of growth is contemplated in the valuation methodology and parameters used.

Capital expenditures are a specific component in the discounted or capitalized economic income methods. When using a market comparison approach to valuation, capital expenditure requirements may influence valuation multiples chosen if the subject company's capital expenditure requirements are significantly different relative to guideline companies. Alternatively, abnormal capital expenditure requirements may be treated as a direct decrement or increment to value determined through income or market valuation methods.

Deferred Maintenance

Some businesses have not maintained their plant and equipment to a competitive level of efficiency and productivity. While expenditures to remedy this condition may be expensed for accounting and tax purposes, they nevertheless require an outlay of funds that detracts from value. The treatment as to how they impact value can be handled essentially the same as capital expenditures.

Working Capital Requirements

A company's working capital requirements can be estimated based on analysis of its past operations, industry data, guideline company data, and discussions with management. It is common to find companies with either excessive or inadequate working capital. Excesses or inadequacies in the valuation data can be treated in the valuation much as other capital requirements may be treated.

If revenue growth is anticipated, growth in working capital generally must also be anticipated. Changes in net working capital are a specific component in the discounted or capitalized economic income methods. When using a market approach to valuation, working capital requirements that differ significantly from guideline companies may be reflected in valuation multiples.

Company Documents Relating to the Rights of Owners

Corporate or Partnership Records

The official documents of a corporation or partnership often hold facts that significantly affect the valuation of the entity or of certain specific interests in the entity. The articles of incorporation or the partnership agreement, along with any amendments, and documents specifying rights attaching to each class of outstanding equity provide information that is particularly important for businesses with more than one class of equity. Other information in the articles or bylaws may be relevant to the value. Partnership agreements should describe the rights and privileges of each partner.

Board of directors' meeting and shareholders' meeting minutes may be important, especially regarding transactions with related parties.

Buy–Sell and ESOP Agreements

Buy–sell or repurchase agreements among stockholders—or between stockholders and the company—may contain provisions that can severely impact the value of the shares to which they apply. These agreements often restrict the marketability of the subject shares, and they can, correspondingly, affect the value of other classes of equity as well. Provisions in such agreements may address the question of value directly or may restrict transferability, which may bear on the value of the affected shares. On the other hand, in certain litigation scenarios, the restrictive provisions of a buy–sell agreement may not be applicable to the standard of value being sought and, at the instruction of counsel, are to be ignored.

If the company has an employee stock ownership plan (ESOP), then the terms of the buy-back provisions can have a major bearing on the marketability of the shares involved and, thus, must be considered when valuing ESOP shares. In some cases, the existence of an ESOP may provide a limited market for non-ESOP shares.

Employment and Noncompete Agreements

Employment agreements with key personnel may affect the company's value, as may agreements not to compete. These agreements could have either a positive or negative effect on value depending on the relationship between the cost of the contract and the person's value to the company.

Summary

Gathering and analyzing the foregoing information will give the analyst the groundwork on which to base the company interview and pinpoint still-needed details that are relevant to the valuation assignment. The specific material needed will vary with the valuation assignment and is a matter of the analyst's judgment. Following the suggestions in this chapter will help the analyst to avoid the common pitfall of overlooking certain company data that may have a significant bearing on the value of the business or interest being appraised. The chapter should also help company officials and/or attorneys to be well prepared for an efficient and productive data gathering process.

Chapter 5

Site Visits and Interviews

This chapter provides a guide for the valuation analyst to conduct an efficient site visit that will contribute in a meaningful way to the valuation process. It also should help company officials and any attorney involved to know what to expect and how to prepare for the visit to make it as productive as possible.

In most cases, the analyst's understanding and impressions of the business can be dramatically improved by seeing the operations firsthand and by participating in face-to-face interviews. The historical financial statements and other written material—and their implications—can become more meaningful to the analyst as a result of the site visit. Current and potential changes that might cause the company's future to differ from that indicated by a mere extrapolation of the historical data can be identified. The field trip and interviews should focus on establishing the relationship between the data gathered and the existing and prospective company situation and economic environment.

The need for the valuation analyst to visit the company facilities and have personal contact with the company personnel and other related people varies greatly from one valuation to another. The extent of the necessary fieldwork depends on many things, including the purpose of the valuation, the nature of the operation, and the size and complexity of the case. Another determining factor is the degree to which the analyst was able to gather and interpret the written material described in the previous chapter.

The title of the person to be interviewed is not as important as the categories of topics to be probed. To cover the topics described in this chapter, the analyst may be interviewing the company's president, chief operating officer, marketing or sales manager, and chief financial officer. In some companies, these job titles are all the responsibility of one person. In some companies, these responsibilities are carried out by people who are not even employees of the subject company. The analyst can work with the client to determine exactly who should be interviewed in order to gain an understanding of the important information that affects the value of the business.

This chapter presents a generalized discussion of interview topics. The actual topics and sequence of coverage will vary considerably from one situation to the next. The top-to-bottom comprehension of the business that the analyst is pursuing may not be provided in top-to-bottom order.

The limitless number of inquiries obviously has such broad potential implications for the valuation, and will vary so much from one company to another, that only the most general discussion of these topics is possible within the scope of this chapter. The analyst will attempt to understand what moves the company and what might accelerate it, slow it, or bring it to a halt.

A broader perspective of the business and its operations is the primary objective of the site visit. In addition, details missing from an analysis of the written material can be filled in. Developing some level of comfort with people at the company is also an important objective of the fieldwork, so that if additional information is required after the fieldwork is complete, it can be more readily obtained.

Generally, it is advisable to prepare a thorough list of questions in advance of the site visit. By studying the financial statements and other basic information, the analyst can gain an overview of the company and prepare a list of specific questions that will make the fieldwork more meaningful and productive. Also, after seeing the operation and talking with management, the analyst will be able to read and analyze the written material with greater insight.

It is usually best to visit company facilities and interview management fairly early in the valuation process—after obtaining and reviewing enough preliminary information to get a general overview of the company. This way, other necessary steps can be planned or some previously planned steps can be dismissed as irrelevant. Other sources of information (e.g., trade associations, periodicals, government agencies, customers, suppliers, and competitors) can be identified.

History

An appropriate beginning is often the company's history. This will give the analyst a perspective on how the business got where it is and can often put the valuation assignment in focus.

The history of the company should cover when the business, or any of its predecessors, was founded, any acquisitions or divestitures along the way, any changes in the basic form of organization, any major changes in lines of business, and any changes in the geographical areas served. It should cover major changes in ownership and how they came about.

Although the business's total history should be sketched briefly, the parts most relevant to the valuation analysis usually will be the most recent past. A chronology of major events will help the analyst decide how many years of the company's financial data are relevant to the current valuation assignment and identify any major changes in the business or special circumstances to consider in analyzing the financial statements.

Description of the Business

The analyst should try to gain an understanding of how the company perceives itself:

- What does the company do?
- Why does it need to be done?
- What makes this company particularly well qualified to do it?
- What is the company's perception of the economic niche into which it fits?
- How does it try to do the best job of fitting in its niche?
- What are the company's major strengths and weaknesses?
- What are the key factors that enable it to operate profitably?
- What is the company doing that will cause the future to differ from recent history?

The analyst should try to gain an understanding of how the company perceives the industry and the particular segment of the industry within which it operates:

- What are the nature and rate of technological changes affecting the industry?
- What developments or trends are expected in the industry in the foreseeable future?

- What special industry factors have a bearing on this particular company?
- To what extent are its fortunes subject to outside forces over which it has no control?
- What is the progress and prognosis for new products or services, locations, channels of distribution, etc.?
- What other aspects of the operation and of the industry are in a developmental or transitional stage?
- How will all these forces impact the future compared with the recent history?

The analyst will want to know about the company's program for corporate development, including further development of existing and/or new products and markets. The company's program for capital expenditures, acquisitions, divestitures, and research and development should also be discussed. These inquiries should cover capacity constraints, how much is being spent for what, and how much of it is being financed.

If future growth is to be financed by issuing additional stock, then the analyst must assess the effect of the potential dilution. If the future growth is to be financed using debt, then the analyst should consider both the direct expense and the risk of the additional financial leverage.

Present management's policies toward the future direction of the company are much more crucial for the analyst to understand if a minority equity interest is the subject of the valuation assignment than if a controlling equity interest in the company is being valued. Nevertheless, even in the case of a controlling ownership interest valuation, the perspective of the existing management team on the major opportunities and problems facing the company and how it plans to deal with them is an important area of inquiry.

The strength of the company's intangible assets, whether or not they are carried on the company's books, seems to be more important today than ever before. Often, sometimes without necessarily realizing it, management lists intangible assets when responding to questions about what makes this company unique. The analyst should be curious about the proprietary products and services, especially about the unique characteristics that generate a comparative advantage over their competition. Can management help quantify the benefit attributable to brand names, trademarks, copyrights, or patents? Does the company enjoy economic benefits from a favorable location, favorable supplier contracts, sustainable customer relationships?

Management and Management Compensation

Another critical factor is the assessment of management's competency, breadth, and depth.

Many closely held companies are somewhat lacking when it comes to providing for management succession.

The analyst should inquire about age, health, education and professional credentials, experience, background, and history with the company. Generally, each key person's compensation package and level of compensation should be considered. This includes participation in all employee benefit plans, fringe benefits, expense allowances, and other perquisites. Part of the purpose of this inquiry is to help the analyst judge whether key people are being compensated well enough to discourage them from leaving the company and part of the purpose is to judge whether there may be excess compensation that the company could reduce if it fell on hard times, whether by direct reductions or by replacement of certain personnel with others who could do a comparable job at a lower cost.

The time and effort devoted to the business by each key person usually should be discussed. Many closely held companies carry people—usually family members—at full salary even though they have only a figurehead role and work only occasionally. On the other hand, some senior people who devote only limited hours may make a significant contribution because of experience and acumen.

The matter of excess compensation should be considered after considering the manager's hours devoted to the company and the job responsibilities of the manager. Some managers in closely held companies are paid at what some consider to be excessive compensation levels.

In many cases, the managers of the closely held business are also the owners. By taking income in the form of compensation for services rendered instead of in the form of dividends, owner-managers avoid a layer of income tax at the corporate level. A hypothetical buyer of the subject business would want to be able to separate the existing owner's take-home pay from the amount the buyer would have to spend to pay a substitute employee to perform the same duties and the amount that is attributable to a return on the buyer's investment.

When the business valuation is of a controlling ownership interest in the subject company, the existing total compensation less normal compensation is often considered excess compensation and is adjusted out of the expense category and into income. This adjustment is often made in order to better reflect the expected economic performance of the company on a go-forward basis. New controlling owners are in a position to eliminate the excess compensation.

If the business valuation is of a minority ownership interest where no control over compensation levels is part of the equity position being valued (such as in the case of a gift of a 10 percent interest in the equity of a business, for example), then the excess compensation of the owner is generally not added back to the income statement. This is because the ownership of the minority position doesn't possess the rights necessary to correct the imbalance.

To make the appropriate adjustments regarding executive compensation of the closely held business, the appraiser typically identifies the total compensation from all sources being paid to the existing executive and compares that to the total compensation required to attract an executive of similar skills. If public company executives are the appropriate basis for comparison, then total compensation from all sources paid to the public company executive (including stock options, bonus plans, pension plans, perquisites, etc.) must be evaluated along with the contribution to the company provided by the executive.

Operations

The objective when discussing operations of the company is to learn what operations the company carries out, how efficiently and effectively it does so, and the prospects for either improvement or deterioration.

Supplies

Supplies are vital to the operations of any business enterprise. To what extent does the company fabricate versus assemble, and how much flexibility does it have in this respect? How much is the make-or-buy decision within the company's control?

Access and pricing are the two key factors that the analyst should typically pursue in questioning the company's supply situation. The extreme—which is less rare than one might think—is the existence of a single source for a critical supply that, if cut off, could shut down the company's operations. Most distributorships, for example, can be terminated on 30 days' notice. For many manufacturing companies, one or more raw materials with limited sources of supply are essential to the operation. For some companies, a reliable source for energy is a critical component of the subject company's prospects.

The analyst will often identify key suppliers and alternates, including names of individuals with whom the company deals. It may be appropriate for the analyst to contact suppliers directly, whether for additional information about the present or potential supply situation or for references concerning the company's credit, reputation, or other attributes.

Labor and Government Relations

The availability and cost of labor can be another critical factor in the successful operation of the business. When on the facilities tour, the analyst should be alert to clues about labor morale and efficiency. What labor contracts exist? When do they expire, and what are the prospects for satisfactory renewal in terms of both acceptable costs and risk of work stoppage? How do company compensation policies compare with other companies in the industry and in this locale? What is the company's experience with personnel turnover, and how does this compare with industry norms?

Government relations may impinge on the company's operations. To what extent is the company subject to industry regulations, such as food quality standards or the rate-of-return limitations imposed on some utilities? Does the company face costs associated with environmental protection or with OSHA? Does the company have problems meeting these requirements? What is the impact of these regulations on the company's earning capacity, flexibility, and future prospects?

Plant and Equipment

When touring the company's facilities, the analyst should gain an understanding of the adequacy of the plant and equipment. The business enterprise appraiser may make a general assessment of the adequacy and condition of plant assets, and he may obtain the assistance of appraisers specializing in real estate, machinery, or personal property when needed. It may be desirable to take pictures, especially if the analyst will need to communicate some description of the facilities to someone not able to visit the site, such as a judge in a court case. It may be useful to note the size and the type of construction, too. Is the equipment well maintained, new, highly utilized? Is there unused capacity and room for expansion? In general, will the plant be a source of future cost savings or a source of increasing costs?

Inventory

Inventory consists of raw material, work in progress, and finished goods. The analyst is interested in assistance in interpreting how much inventory is obsolete, damaged, excessive, or inadequate. The facilities tour is a good time to inquire about inventory turnover and quality. Since it can have a significant effect on reported earnings and net worth in some types of companies, the analyst should consider near-worthless inventory that is carried on the books at original cost or valuable inventory that has been written off.

Markets and Marketing

The objective of the marketing interview is for the analyst to identify and describe the company's markets and its program for reaching them. Who are its customers? Why do customers buy from this company instead of from the competition? Is its target market growing or shrinking? Overall, what are the company's prospects?

What forces determine the demand and changes in demand for the company's products or services? To what extent can the company rely on repeat business and customer continuity? Does the market have identifiable seasonal, cyclical, or secular characteristics?

Are there technological changes in progress or in prospect that will alter its share of the market? What is this business planning to do to remain competitive? What does the company do to anticipate and cope with market changes, and how effective are its efforts?

It is common for the marketing manager to understate the company's competition and overstate the defined market's potential. Asking questions on a similar topic from a slightly different perspective or at a different point in the interview will help the analyst verify the responses without challenging the respondent.

One of the most important aspects of the marketing interview is determining how the company competes. The analyst will often list the identified competitors for each product or service and in each target market segment. This leads to market share estimates and market share trends. What is the economic outlook for these markets and what are the competitors' likely actions? Many companies, especially smaller ones, are blindsided by competition that has not yet been identified.

The company's policies about pricing, warranty, providing quality services, on-time or in-stock delivery, and terms and conditions of sale are typical areas of inquiry.

The interview should also cover personnel. Does the company have its own direct sales force or does it rely on distributors? What is the degree of turnover? Where do the sales and marketing people come from and where do they go? What are the structure and level of compensation for marketing people, and how do they compare with the competition?

With respect to the order backlog, how does this year's compare to last year's and to next year's expectations? What is the customer turnover rate? To what extent is the company dependent on one or a few key customers? What are the customers' motivations in choosing to do business with this company or its competitors, and how is the company addressing those motivations?

What changes are anticipated for the marketing program? How does the company plan to capitalize on future opportunities? If competitive forces or other problems are building, what is the company doing to protect itself?

At the conclusion of the marketing discussion, the analyst should have a good grasp of the future prospects of the company and potential constraints.

Finance

As an aid in financial analysis, the analyst may conduct interviews with the chief financial officer, controller, outside accountant, or attorney. Adjusting financial statements is covered in Chapter 7, and many of the most important lines of interrogation are discussed there.

Interviews can contribute a great deal toward genuine understanding of a company's financial position beyond simply what the financial statements show.

Current Assets

It may be important, given the scope of the assignment, to verify the cash and cash equivalents account and to assess the company's cash management techniques. The accounts receivable account may be analyzed to understand the extent to which the figure represents an amount that is genuinely collectible and how long it will take to collect it. What is the prognosis for collection of any notes or other receivables? The company's policy for accounting for the inventory is an important factor affecting value. The physical flow and the accounting flow are likely to be different in a manufacturing operation, and they may be treated differently between the subject company and its competitors. What is the write-off policy? To what extent does the inventory figure represent the value of the inventory in a going-concern context?

Fixed Assets

The subject company's real estate and equipment are presented on the balance sheet according to a historical cost less accumulated depreciation, and these asset account balances may not represent the fair market value of those assets. The method for capitalizing assets and the depreciation method adopted by the subject company also may differ from the methods chosen by others in the industry and could affect the valuation conclusion. If a liquidation—or other value in exchange—premise is to be considered, then the analyst should discuss the probable time and cost of liquidating all or any part of the assets, as well as their potential net realizable value.

Intangible Assets

Management's perception of the factors that make the subject company different from its competitors usually introduces a discussion of the intangible assets of the company such as a trademark, patent, or copyright. It may be unpatented technology, a trained and assembled workforce, special know-how, customer relationships, supplier relationships, or other intangible assets that make the company a viable competitor and give it earning power. Some closely held business owners call these intangibles "blue sky" or "goodwill." The accounting practices for these assets and the legal protection of these assets should be explored. These types of assets are covered in more detail later in the book.

Current Liabilities

The company's banking relationship may be an important factor to consider when studying the company's current liabilities. If the company has a line of credit, what are the costs and terms? Is it under pressure to pay down the line or is there unused credit? How is the line used during the operating cycle? What are the relationships with suppliers, and what are the terms of payment? What are the terms, conditions, and expectations regarding other current liabilities items?

Capital Structure

If there is long-term debt maturing in the foreseeable future, what are the company's options and intentions about rolling it over? What is the company's debt capacity and is it assumable by a hypothetical buyer? Are personal guarantees on the company loans necessary? Convertible notes, puts, calls, warrants, or options could mean the current shareholders will be facing dilution. What changes to the capital structure might be anticipated? In virtually every valuation, the analyst will want to discuss who owns the shares currently outstanding and what are the shareholders' relationships with each other.

Off-Balance-Sheet Items

Potential asset items and potential liability claims against the company should be investigated. If the company is involved in pending litigation, what is its substance, and are there any pending judgments that might be favorable or unfavorable? Are leases of real or personal property favorable or unfavorable? The pension liability may be underfunded or overfunded. Is there any potential tax liability or refund? Lack of compliance with environmental protection, OSHA, or other governmental regulations may mean an unstated liability would be imposed on a hypothetical buyer of the company. Product liability claims or a generous warranty policy could represent a significant unstated liability.

Profitability

A review of past and current budgets can be a good starting point from which to gain greater insight into the company's profit history and potential. Budgeting is an important area of inquiry. How far into the future does the company budget its operations, and how often is the budget reviewed? In some industries, an evaluation of the company's sales outlook should include an analysis that distinguishes between changes in unit sales and price changes. The most profitable products or product lines, including the outlook for maintaining profitability, should also be considered. An analysis of fixed and variable expenses may help the analyst understand the extent to which increased or decreased volume will affect operating margins. What can be done to make the company more profitable and what are the associated costs?

Insurance

An uninsured catastrophe could wipe out a business. The questions about insurance should investigate the adequacy of the company's coverage for key-person life insurance, product and other liability insurance, and casualty insurance, including fire, theft, and business interruption. If no insurance is carried, the analyst should assess the adequacy of reserves.

Dividends

The analyst should try to obtain a complete record of past dividend payments. Beyond that, the analyst should assess both the company's dividend-paying capacity and management's intentions with regard to dividends if dividend-paying capacity exists.

Prior Transactions or Offers

Verification of the completeness of the list of prior transactions or offers and the circumstances surrounding them is a good idea. Overlooking or overemphasizing prior transactions is a common area of controversy in business valuations. What price was paid for the stock? Was it an arm's-length transaction? Was it a distinct transaction for stock or were there strings attached?

If there were one or more offers to buy stock but a transaction was not consummated, then the offer may provide some evidence of value. If it was a bona fide, arm's-length offer, it may provide particularly good evidence of value. The analyst should seek anything in writing about such an offer.

Prior transactions of significance may include acquisitions by the company as well as transactions in its own stock, so the analyst should inquire about acquisitions. If the company made a meaningful acquisition, then it may be a useful guideline transaction to use in the valuation.

Catchall Question

If the person performing the business valuation fieldwork follows this chapter as an outline, the result should be a reasonably comprehensive facility visit and set of interviews. This will be especially true if the person is an experienced interviewer, because many interview subjects will call for more in-depth interrogation than shown here, and personal style and technique alone can uncover critical information. Depending on the analyst's assignment, the ramifications of certain topics may call for a different depth of questioning, beyond the scope of reasonable explanation in a single book, much less in one chapter.

Nevertheless, even the most experienced interviewer may fail to ask just the right questions in order to elicit responses on every aspect bearing on the valuation. Therefore, somewhere near the end of each interview, the analyst might ask each interviewee a catchall question. This can be something like: "Is there any information you know that hasn't been covered and that could have a bearing on the valuation of the company?" This helps protect the analyst against material omissions in the questioning process and places the burden on company management if it is deliberately withholding material information.

Interviews of Outsiders

It is usually a good idea to get the names of outsiders who are involved with the company because an interview may be desirable. Sometimes interviews with the company's outsiders are helpful not only for specific technical information but also for independent viewpoints on certain aspects of the company. However, for many valuation assignments, where the purpose is confidential and sensitive, it is inappropriate to contact outsiders, especially without the client's permission and introduction.

Professionals Related to the Company

Attorney. There are times when the analyst may work very closely with the company's attorney. The wording of the legal documents when structuring a recapitalization, a buy–sell agreement, or an ESOP, for example, may have a considerable bearing on the valuation. In these circumstances, the attorney may solicit the analyst's opinion about the impact on the valuation due to certain prospective provisions. On the other hand, the analyst may need a legal interpretation of a company document or contract or need an assessment of a pending lawsuit or potential litigation.

Independent Accountant. To get an explanation or interpretation of something on the financial statements, or to consult working papers for details that augment the financial statements, it may be necessary to interview the company's outside independent accountant. This is most often the case when the financial statements are not audited, not completely footnoted, or contain some kind of qualified opinion by the independent accountant.

Banker. If the company's banking relationship is important or in jeopardy, it is a good idea to hear firsthand how the banker perceives it. The banker also may be a good source of general information about the company and the industry.

Other Possible Outside Interviews

Customers. The company's customers can be a good source of information about the subject company's products, strengths, and weaknesses. Customers can often provide an indication of the longer-term outlook of the subject company, and they can help the analyst evaluate the continuing demand for products and services. Customers may also provide a viewpoint about the competition and the customer's perceptions of the differences in product design, quality, service, pricing, and the various intangible assets (e.g., trade name) among competitors. Under some circumstances, former customers could be contacted to find out why they no longer patronize the company.

Suppliers. Particularly if the subject company deals in a technological area, the suppliers may be able to explain technology changes in the industry and, in some cases, evaluate the subject company's expertise.

Competitors. When it is appropriate to contact competitors, it is usually necessary to avoid violating confidentiality. The analyst may ask the competitor many of the same questions asked of the subject company regarding demand, supply, and pricing factors, technological changes in the industry, and relative merits of the products and services of the various companies in the industry, including the subject company.

Former Employees. Sometimes former employees may be useful as information sources—about why they left and other aspects of the company as seen in hindsight and from an objective viewpoint.

Summary

An experienced valuation analyst can gain a great deal of insight into a company through the field trip and management interview process. The preceding queries should provide the analyst with a perspective on the company being valued and yield a multitude of details relevant to the valuation assignment. What the analyst gets from the process will depend partly on the thoroughness of preparation and partly on the degree of cooperation provided by the subject company and those being interviewed.

It may be helpful for relevant company officials to review this chapter before the valuation analyst's site visit in order to be better prepared to make the visit as efficient and meaningful as possible. Also, it often is helpful for the attorney involved in the matter for which the valuation is being done to review the chapter before the valuation analyst's visit.

Chapter 6

Researching Economic and Industry Information

It is difficult to overemphasize the importance of thorough and relevant economic and industry research for a well-prepared business valuation. First, Revenue Ruling 59-60 requires consideration of "the economic outlook in general and the condition and outlook of the specific industry in particular." Second, an understanding of the economic and industry outlook is fundamental to developing reasonable expectations about the subject company's prospects. This chapter introduces some of the most useful sources of economic and industry information that can bear on a company valuation.

This chapter is organized in a top-down fashion. Because the general economic outlook influences all industries and all companies, this chapter starts with a discussion of general economic research, highlighting useful sources for researching both the national and regional economies. The chapter then turns to the topic of industry research for both general industry information and composite company statistics. Since the potential sources are so numerous, the chapter concludes with references to several indexes of economic and industry data sources.

The economic and industry outlooks included in appraisal reports should be clearly related to the company being valued. It is particularly important to point out how the outlooks will affect the subject company and to focus on those issues most relevant to a thorough understanding of the company's competitive position in its market. As a corollary to this issue, it is important to understand the subject company's relationship to the structure of the industry. Each segment of an industry or an economy may be affected differently by a particular trend or development. Therefore, it is important to focus on the logical impact of each relevant factor on the subject company, whether positive or negative. Applying economic and industry research to the valuation of the subject company is too often neglected.

National Economic Information

Generally, economic outlooks should include a discussion of each of the most important leading economic indicators. For example, it typically is appropriate for appraisal reports to discuss such variables as economic growth—usually measured by gross domestic product (GDP) on a national level or real gross state product (GSP) on a state level—inflation, employment, consumer spending, business investment, construction, interest rates, and population trends. The following sections outline some of the most useful sources of economic information for both national and regional economic research.

In addition to the economic indicators discussed above, the economic outlook should include the most relevant national economic issues at the time of the valuation. In the economic environment of the mid-1990s, for example, such issues would include the U.S. budget deficit, the U.S. foreign trade deficit, and national health care. Because of the huge variety of national economic data available, only a few of the most generally useful sources are mentioned. Beyond that, the reader is referred to the section at the end of this chapter on indexing services that can lead to the specific types of economic data sought.

The Federal Statistical System

The United States collects, analyzes, and disseminates more economic data than any other country. While most countries have central statistical offices, this has never been the case in the United States. The remarkable range and extent of the government's statistical efforts developed piecemeal, according to the dictates of legislation and in response to emerging needs. Thus evolved the far-flung, highly decentralized federal statistical system. Only about a half dozen federal agencies exist solely to create statistics, but over 100 other governmental units also participate in the statistical process.[1] Four of the most widely used publications are the *Federal Reserve Bulletin, Survey of Current Business, Statistical Abstract of the United States,* and the *Economic Report of the President.*

- *Federal Reserve Bulletin* (Board of Governors of the Federal Reserve System, Washington, D.C.): Published monthly, the *Federal Reserve Bulletin* includes such data as employment, industrial production, housing and construction, consumer and producer prices, GDP, personal income and savings, and key interest rates. Three years of annual historical data are usually presented for each set of statistics, and data for the current year are provided in monthly or quarterly units. It is usually available at public and university libraries. This is the best single service for finding current U.S. banking and monetary statistics. The board also publishes a quarterly *Federal Reserve Chart Book* with an annual *Historical Chart Book,* providing graphic trends for many of the statistics in the *Bulletin.*
- *Survey of Current Business* (U.S. Department of Commerce): This monthly publication has two sections. The first deals with basic business trends and starts with an article, "The Business Situation," that reviews business developments, pointing out relative strengths and weaknesses. The second section contains an extensive compilation of basic statistics on all phases of the economy. This is the most important single source for current U.S. business statistics. It can be found in most major libraries.
- *Statistical Abstract of the United States* (U.S. Department of Commerce): This annual publication contains statistics on all phases of U.S. life— economic, social, political, industrial—and some comparative international statistics. It is well indexed and easy to use and is available at most public libraries.
- *Economic Report of the President,* prepared annually by the U.S. Council of Economic Advisers, is another valuable source of summary data on the U.S. economy. Released each year in January or February, the document is essentially a report from the executive branch to Congress on the state of the economy. About two-thirds of the report consists of narrative analysis of the economy, with the remainder devoted to statistical tables. An important feature of the narrative section is a five-year outlook for the U.S. economy, including projections for GDP and other key indicators.

---

[1]Michael R. Lavin, *Business Information: How to Find It, How to Use It,* 2nd ed. (Phoenix, AZ: Oryx Press, 1992), pp. 326–27.

Banks

Bank letters are excellent sources for statistics, analysis, and projections of regional, national, and international economic and financial conditions. Several private and many government-owned banks, both in the United States and abroad, publish these periodicals and often distribute them free. Many foreign banks publish their bank letters in English-language editions.

Although bank letters may vary in size from four pages to journal-length issues of over 100 pages, many of them follow a similar format, beginning with a narrative summary of state, regional, or national economic and financial conditions. Such areas as government policies, inflation rates, trade balances, employment, manufacturing, and investment are discussed for the reporting period (e.g., monthly or quarterly). Some bank letters end such summaries with predictions of trends in the economy, including changes in interest rates, wages and prices, and government monetary policies. A second part of these bank letters consists of a statistical summary of major economic indicators for the reporting period. Several banks will include a section of international economic statistics to compare their economic situations with other countries.

Most bank letters concentrate on their state, region, or country of origin. For example, several of the banks in the Federal Reserve System publish data only on the states within their districts (e.g., New England or the Southeast). Three excellent bank letters are *Economic and Business Outlook* (Bank of America), *Economic Trends* (Federal Reserve Bank of Cleveland), and *U.S. Financial Data* (Federal Reserve Bank of St. Louis). A comprehensive listing of bank letters is included at the end of this chapter.

- *Economic and Business Outlook* (Bank of America): Issues are published six times a year and feature a particular aspect of the economy such as the U.S. economy and long-term outlook; short-term outlook; the California economy; and the global economy. This publication, previously known as *Economic Report,* was published by Security Pacific National Bank before its merger with the Bank of America.
- *Economic Trends* (Federal Reserve Bank of Cleveland): This monthly publication is an excellent source of economic variables, ranging from GDP and its components to money supply aggregates. The figures for such indicators as consumer income, business fixed investment, housing starts, producer and consumer prices, and so on, are usually given quarterly and monthly. Most major libraries have *Economic Trends* on hand, along with publications of the other 11 Federal Reserve Bank Districts, which also contain economic information.
- *U.S. Financial Data* (Federal Reserve Bank of St. Louis): This letter is published weekly and is an especially good compilation of statistics on the money supply, commercial paper and business loans, interest rates, and securities yields.

Business Periodicals and Statistical Services

Business periodicals, such as *Barron's, Business Week, Forbes, Fortune,* the *New York Times,* and the *Wall Street Journal,* are good sources of timely information on the national economy, as well as other types of information. In every issue, both *Business Week* and *Fortune* include forecasts for certain segments of the economy and articles on recent economic developments. They and other magazines also publish extensive economic forecasts in their January issues. The *New York Times* and the *Wall Street Journal* are particularly valuable sources for the most current national economic information, since they are published daily. In addition to frequent articles on the most recent economic developments, the *Wall Street Journal,* in particular, includes a great deal of information on the financial markets. By using the *Wall Street Journal/Barron's Index,* which lists articles by subject and by company, the analyst can also find historical economic information in both the *Wall Street Journal* and *Barron's.*

Standard & Poor's Statistical Service, which is updated monthly, is one of the best sources of summary economic data. Appearing in loose-leaf format, it contains economic statistics with special emphasis on banking and finance, production and labor, commodities prices, and the levels of activity in such industries as building and building materials, metals, and chemicals. It is a good source of historical economic and industrial data.

The *American Statistics Index* is a comprehensive tool to locate statistical information in the United States. This annual publication is in two volumes with monthly updates. The first volume is an index that refers to one or more abstracts in the second volume, which also contains full citations to the source publication. It is published by the Congressional Information Service, Inc.

Regional Economic Information

In addition to data on the national economic outlook, it is sometimes appropriate to gather data on the outlook for the region or regions in which the subject company operates. The regional economic outlook is more relevant in some valuation analyses than in others. More often than not, however, the outlook for a specific city, county, or group of counties, cities, or states is relevant to the valuation of a particular company. It is crucial to recognize the importance of properly defining the region to be researched for a particular valuation. Even within the same state, the economic outlook can differ dramatically in different locales.

The primary sources for regional economic data are bank economics departments, public utilities, chambers of commerce, and various state agencies, such as departments of economic development and bureaus of labor statistics. Most major local banks publish statistical tabulations of economic indicators, although their availability is limited. Although major libraries usually subscribe to one or more bank economic publications, the selections at libraries are usually limited to those published nearest to the particular library. The best way to obtain regional bank publications is to write or call the particular bank's economic department.

Some universities publish regional and local economic data, sometimes focused on one or a few industries important to the region. Most states and multistate regions now have regular monthly business magazines that give economic statistics, and most metropolitan areas now have weekly newspapers that focus on business developments. The business sections of some metropolitan daily newspapers offer economic analysis and statistics, sometimes regularly in Sunday editions and sometimes irregularly in special features that focus on some specific part of the local economic scene.

Additional sources of information on regional and local economies are listed below.

- *Regional Economies and Markets:* Published quarterly by the Economic and Business Environment Program of the Conference Board, this analysis looks at groups of states in terms of manufacturing production, employment, and income.
- *The Complete Economic and Demographic Data Source:* Published by Wilson & Poole Economics, this is an excellent source for statistical profiles of metropolitan areas, counties, and states. Historical as well as projected data are included in this source. Other publications from Wilson & Poole include *State Profiles* and *MSA Profiles,* which currently include statistical economic data and forecasts through the year 2010.
- *Metro Insights:* For larger metropolitan areas, this publication of Data Resources Inc./McGraw Hill provides 10 to 15 pages of narrative economic discussion well supported with statistics. This source contains information on the 100 largest metropolitan areas in the United States. Each area profile includes an economic profile, forecasts for growth, infrastructure evaluation, and construction and demographic data.
- *Survey of Buying Power:* Published annually in two monthly editions of *Sales & Marketing Management* magazine, this publication breaks down demographic and income data by state, metropolitan area, and county. Retail sales data are presented for store groups and merchandise lines. Also included are population and retail sales forecasts for local areas.

Industry Information

This section is divided into three parts. The first focuses on researching the industry outlook and briefly discusses some of the most useful sources for industry research. The second covers the various sources of composite financial statistics that can be used for comparison with the subject company. The third overviews sources of information on management compensation.

After reviewing the standard industry sources and while gathering more detailed information on the industry, the researcher should begin developing an outline of the relevant factors and events influencing the industry outlook. It is also advisable to keep a thorough bibliography of all information gathered, including the full name of the source and the date of the publication or meeting. The researcher should also comb through sources for additional references. Many articles cite individuals or other sources that will provide more informative and authoritative data.

In addition, the researcher must analyze the information in order to evaluate how the subject company is—and will be—affected by the various industry trends. For example, how will it be affected by price increases for key commodities? How will it be affected by shifts in demand, changes in technology, or shifts in the competitiveness of the industry? The researcher must consider the possible answers to these questions in the analysis and valuation of the subject company. The industry section of the report should include the researcher's conclusion as to the impact of the industry outlook on the valuation of the subject company, particularly as to how the subject company may respond differently or to a different degree than the guideline companies, and should provide an overview of the industry outlook at the time of the valuation.

General Industry Information

The first step in conducting industry research is to develop a general overview of the industry. This will allow the researcher to get a firm grasp on where the subject company fits into the industry and which industry factors or events are most relevant to the subject company. This general overview will also provide enough information about the overall industry to assist the researcher in finding additional information and analyzing the relevance of new information as it is gathered. Several standard industry sources provide this general overview for most industries.

Standard Industry Sources. Three standard sources that provide a very good overview of most industries are the *U.S. Industrial Outlook, Standard & Poor's Industry Surveys,* and *Moody's Investor's Industry Review.*

The *U.S. Industrial Outlook* was produced annually by the U.S. Department of Commerce through 1994. Accordingly, the *U.S. Industrial Outlook* provides an excellent data source for appraisals performed as of historical valuation dates. It provides information on the prospects for over 350 industries, focusing on the structure of the industry and the most significant factors influencing it. The *Outlook* includes forecasts for industries' revenue growth for the coming year as well as over the long term. In addition, this publication provides a very useful list of additional references for each industry covered.

Standard & Poor's Industry Surveys is also a useful starting point in researching an industry. It is organized into 36 broad industry groups and indexed for reference into 500 subgroups. It gives each industry group a reasonably comprehensive background analysis about once a year, with occasional updates in the form of a shorter current analysis. *Industry Surveys* generally includes discussion of the industry's structure, trends and outlook, and a section with financial statistics on publicly traded companies in the industry.

Moody's Investor's Industry Review complements the Standard & Poor's service with a more micro analysis, focusing on the major players in an industry.

Trade Associations and Trade Magazines. Perhaps the most valuable source of authoritative information on a particular industry is that industry's trade association(s). Trade associations often collect financial statements from their members and compile composite financial data. More often, though, trade associations publish general industry information and may include annual industry reports or articles in their trade magazines. Generally, the executives of the subject company have information on the industry's trade associations and whether or not such data are available.

The *Encyclopedia of Associations,* published annually by Gale Research, and *National Trade and Professional Associations of the United States,* published annually by Columbia Books, are two good sources to identify the association or associations that represent a particular industry or business sector. Many of these associations have regular publications that provide a wealth of data on their respective industries. They often provide periodic reviews and forecasts as well as statistical data.

While trade associations often have their own publications, most industries have at least one or two trade magazines as well. If the subject company's management cannot furnish information on relevant trade magazines, the researcher can turn to one of several directories of trade publications. One directory that is useful is the *Guide to Special Issues and Indexes of Periodicals,* published by the Special Libraries Association in Washington, D.C. This directory classifies periodicals into general industry categories and provides information on each periodical, including the publisher's phone number. An even more comprehensive source is the *Standard Rate & Data Service Directory,* published by Standard Rate & Data Service. While this publication is designed for the magazine advertising industry, it is useful as a directory of industry information sources because it lists periodicals by industry.

After identifying the appropriate periodicals, the researcher can usually obtain them directly from the publishers or a local business library. Often it is worthwhile to call the publisher and ask if any articles on the industry were published over a time period relevant to the valuation date to avoid ordering a year's worth of back issues with no relevant information. While not always successful, it is generally worth trying.

Government Agencies and Government Publications. Federal and state agencies compile astronomical amounts of data, most of which are indexed in some form or another. However, one disadvantage of government publications is that they often are somewhat outdated by the time they are published. The *Statistical Abstract of the United States* can help direct the researcher to various federal agencies, state agencies, and other sources of industry information. Regulatory agencies are often good sources of data on industries that are—or used to be—regulated, such as communications, trucking, airlines, food, and drugs.

Business Press. A wide variety of business publications cover companies and industries on an intermittent basis. The *Wall Street Journal, Fortune, Barron's,* and *Forbes* are but a few of the publications that frequently include industry articles. The two best ways to find these articles are to use a standard reference source such as the *Business Periodicals Index* or the *Wall Street Journal/Barron's Index,* or to perform an on-line search through an electronic database vendor (e.g., Predicast's database PROMT, file 16 in DIALOG). Often, articles in the business press will provide valuable leads to authoritative sources or important industry observers.

Brokerage Houses. Brokerage houses can provide current information in published report form on publicly traded companies. Such reports are an important source of information in order to gain insight into the functioning of an industry. In addition to providing information on publicly traded companies, brokerage houses can often provide stock prices, financial data on companies, estimated earnings on those companies, information on interest rates, and historical graphs. Many brokerage houses publish weekly and monthly reports. Contacting the particular analyst who reports on a specific industry is one way of obtaining reports. A directory such as *Nelson's Directory of Investment Research,* published annually by W.R. Nelson & Company, is an excellent tool for identifying analysts and their areas of specialization. Another resource is through Investext (accessible on-line through DIALOG file 545), a full-text database of brokerage house reports analyzing industries and companies.

Composite Company Data

Business Source Books. The Business Source Books, prepared annually by the Statistics of Income Division, Internal Revenue Service, are by far the most comprehensive set of composite company statistics. However, they generally are about three to four years out of date. They include the *Corporation Source Book, Partnership Source Book,* and *Sole Proprietorship Source Book.* A sample page from the *Corporation Source Book of Statistics of Income* is presented in Exhibit 6–1.

Almanac of Business and Industrial Financial Ratios. The data used in the *Almanac* are compiled from corporate tax returns by the U.S. Treasury, Internal Revenue Service. They are disaggregated into 181 fields of business and industry.

Exhibit 6–2 is a typical data presentation from the *Almanac,* in this case for grocery stores. Each industry group is presented in two tables. One table includes corporations that reported a profit as well as those that did not; the second table includes only those that reported a profit.

Each group for which there are sufficient data is presented in 13 asset size categories, compared with six in the *RMA Annual Statement Studies* data. The *Almanac* gives more income statement line items than does *RMA,* while *RMA* gives more balance sheet line items and more ratios.

The various ratios used are defined in the front part of the *Almanac.* Computations of some of the ratios differ from computations used by *RMA.*

The biggest drawback to the *Almanac* is the degree to which the information is outdated. The 1994 edition covers tax returns for fiscal years ended July 1990 through June 1991, the most recent year for which authoritative figures derived from tax return data of the Internal Revenue Service are available. Nevertheless, operating figures for most industries have at least some degree of stability over time, and the *Almanac* offers some income statement items not found elsewhere.

RMA Annual Statement Studies. Probably the most popular source of composite company data, including privately owned company data, is the *RMA Annual Statement Studies,* which is a product of a national association of bank loan and credit officers. The 1994 edition was based on more than 107,000 financial statements submitted by representatives of their member banks. One reason for the broad appeal of the *Annual Statement Studies* is the over 400 industries it covers. *Annual Statement Studies* is also available in computerized form from several sources.

Exhibit 6–3 is a typical page from *RMA Annual Statement Studies,* in this case "Retailers—Groceries & Meats." Note that each industry group is presented in six size categories, based on total assets. (No figures are presented for the two largest size categories in this particular industry group because *RMA* defines fewer than 10 financial statements in a particular size category to be too small a sample to be considered representative and could be misleading.) Also, data are presented in the aggregate for five years, so that year-to-year comparisons can be made.

Exhibit 6–1
Sample Page from *Corporation Source Book*

1991 corporation source book of statistics of income, income
tax returns of active corporations with accounting periods ended July 1991 through June 1992—
Balance sheet, income statement, and selected items, by minor industry, by size of total assets
(all figures are estimates based on samples—money amounts and size of total assets are in thousands of dollars)

Wholesale and retail trade:
Retail Trade: Food Stores

	Major Group 38 Returns with and without net income	Total	Zero Assets	Size of Total Assets: 1 under 100	100 under 250	250 under 500	500 under 1,000	1,000 under 5,000	5,000 under 10,000	10,000 under 25,000	25,000 under 50,000	50,000 under 100,000	100,000 under 250,000	250,000 or More
1	Number of returns	65463	2763	31314	17175	6578	3498	3368	342	179	111	39	48	46
2	Total assets	99198829	-	1413093	2656136	2363126	2383282	6456185	2343484	2755507	3897620	2672010	8481007	63777379
3	Cash	6296801	-	185495	338400	246665	297184	721205	218781	255389	330934	215054	426527	3061167
4	Notes and accounts receivable	6520626	-	42715	148307	162153	139432	432196	225357	212435	256956	197964	554905	4148206
5	Less: Allowance for bad debts	88890	-	*60	*276	*494	-	*2139	*822	3558	16897	4861	14591	45191
6	Inventories	22591517	-	465367	808322	714669	753768	1881247	632327	654289	826545	531703	1909104	13414175
7	Investment in govt. obligations: Total	400373	-	[illegible]	6744	-	*784	*2154	-	*25798	*16385	94	25197	383417
8	Tax-exempt securities	395940	-	*24	-	-	*10325	-	-	*394	*4769	1574	18141	360713
9	Other current assets	3017334	-	15447	86211	87703	72636	226539	12917	74451	152081	99914	279884	1793253
10	Loans to stockholders	497269	-	*53757	81833	88766	32771	98440	10199	27512	13229	3070	68470	19222
11	Mortgage and real estate loans	294651	-	*14	*71429	*11289	*29685	33596	*1309	*15395	*47810	64865	2800	16459
12	Other investments	8062101	-	*40970	51806	79689	137205	419202	79795	241359	199517	146039	420596	6245923
13	Depreciable assets	62748587	-	1381409	2009476	1794537	1782122	4735242	1700584	2093016	3239158	1899228	5562860	36550954
14	Less: Accumulated depreciation	28450713	-	951237	1278518	1099002	1078643	2564957	835260	1050632	1572493	830359	2276251	14913361
15	Depletable assets	*99736	-	-	-	-	*123	*3585	-	*3709	-	-	81	92240
16	Less: Accumulated depletion	*25579	-	-	-	-	*123	*2689	-	*1699	-	-	-	21069
17	Land	5086237	-	*9706	78776	73777	88229	234078	101682	115972	190532	150786	436652	3606047
18	Intangible assets (amortizable)	3507545	-	127202	160358	177210	69900	145955	37456	65035	108194	118976	504344	1992915
19	Less: Accumulated amortization	726429	-	78738	78899	69142	31385	48451	15585	20603	39615	38114	108115	197783
20	Other assets	8911524	-	121023	172167	95306	79269	140982	58443	47245	140516	116077	670405	7270092
21	Total liabilities	99198829	-	1413093	2656136	2363126	2383282	6456185	2343484	2755507	3897620	2672010	8481007	63777379
22	Accounts payable	17337266	-	342539	4613561	431703	496036	1367737	627309	571903	760666	423692	1340094	10512026
23	Mort, notes, and bonds under 1 yr	5820928	-	246841	215082	154766	180884	470849	242913	199633	185646	260547	996716	2667050
24	Other current liabilities	11228552	-	90644	138543	168284	155047	364943	185880	213495	330847	289560	944808	8346500
25	Loans from stockholders	2524356	-	471580	495579	323794	274825	342814	*84825	30530	*22697	11177	186621	279913
26	Mort, notes, bonds, 1 yr or more	36849446	-	360109	652057	742305	546011	1852810	667949	595993	1162812	788678	2618729	26861993
27	Other liabilities	6805630	-	13433	8900	21517	8976	42998	38764	110549	155862	82766	501983	5819862
28	Net worth	18632651	-	-112055	682414	520756	721502	2014035	495843	1033403	1279091	815571	1892056	9290036
29	Capital stock	3672402	-	324676	319287	231994	153810	331429	49769	81504	104812	89272	402155	1583693
30	Paid-in or capital surplus	8886901	-	119543	156336	125767	174323	181995	95805	285636	152592	229205	1122958	6242741
31	Retained earnings, appropriated	70309	-	*9	-	*5496	*15000	*24288	*1016	-	*3901	3232	17366	-
32	Retained earnings, unapropriate	5214569	-	-298874	427089	193081	487089	891104	285541	290760	636142	252123	333873	1716640
33	Retained earnings (S corp)	2404326	-	-193681	-19494	59378	-30786	738423	113802	423763	469146	254834	109704	479237
34	Less: Cost of treasury stock	1615856	-	*63728	*200805	*94961	77934	153205	50090	48261	87503	13096	93999	732275
35	Total receipts	360310604	3537891	9338510	15160496	13590350	13050465	35748312	13522570	13678766	18355085	10216702	30088375	184023081
36	Business Receipts	354253319	3419879	9293431	15049623	13435711	12908355	35317637	13331835	13465212	18096926	10018527	29526559	180389624
37	Interest	828027	*13351	4225	11011	10348	14729	38170	11743	15994	25072	22594	69339	591451
38	Interest on govt. obligations, state and local	41750	8	-	*716	*690	*1134	*337	*320	*1168	*1124	817	625	34812
39	Rents	885236	*8029	-	*7063	*4715	7476	38796	18478	18261	36654	11118	63485	671161
40	Royalties	47136	-	-	-	-	-	*4741	*12232	*5925	*15	12384	7744	4095
41	Net S-T gain less net LT loss	8224	-	*103	*819	-	*50	*450	*5128	-	*184	209	2	1278
42	Net L-T cap gain less net ST loss	286655	*62	-	*2125	*9634	*5654	26808	*7178	*4289	7065	7567	23907	192369
43	Net gain, noncapital assets	139615	*22972	*2826	*15790	*3261	*825	11846	17482	15508	5847	6625	8461	28174
44	Dividends, Domestic Corporations	9944	7	*3	*63	*60	*1470	1388	*81	*274	*509	1301	611	4178
45	Dividends, foreign corporations	*7769	-	-	-	-	-	*12	-	-	*504	-	108	7146
46	Other receipts	3802928	73583	37923	73287	125932	110773	308127	118095	152136	181185	135559	387535	2098794
47	Total deductions	356638921	3567882	9397003	15116788	13520144	13062996	25473977	13468680	13563813	18196449	10070492	29914152	181286544
48	Cost of sales and operations	270092152	2655970	6452987	11570997	10555112	10080418	28069930	10692883	10583361	14003794	7825214	22321202	135280283
49	Compensation of officers	2081110	29384	343746	354815	317685	174244	312851	114067	67323	68455	35890	84208	178441
50	Repairs	2085619	25358	75641	109723	70567	87311	199432	76349	77983	103240	54232	208176	997607
51	Bad debts	317887	8574	6538	11921	8714	9760	27367	9991	15999	12036	6512	32392	168081
52	Rent paid on business property	6607068	86099	461954	333818	255171	228728	533852	234023	250855	283773	180331	564720	3193745
53	Taxes paid	5142626	49926	208193	273595	200614	192208	445803	163687	176678	281613	135100	392126	2623083
54	Interest paid	4425033	61257	53913	99688	86597	84145	223161	83607	73342	114926	105120	381247	3058029
55	Contributions or gifts	76572	*1385	610	1906	1828	1648	3376	2009	2386	2595	3132	7275	48422
56	Amortization	376787	*8627	17394	31111	27914	7520	24863	11808	10349	11862	27783	55371	142182
57	Depreciation	4862187	40397	110248	160491	139788	138937	353115	140906	148584	245649	158076	413124	2812868
58	Depletion	*87	-	-	-	-	-	-	*86	-	-	-	1	**
59	Advertising	3303255	31635	65434	99632	128906	160108	361168	126551	117146	199343	73223	276783	1663326
60	Pension, prof sh, stock, annuity	973279	11548	*3731	*3527	*5204	5902	50294	37308	27742	73602	27643	55524	671253
61	Employee benefit programs	3859166	31547	17382	38484	51919	49645	186400	87069	153691	153232	81018	434901	2573878
62	Net loss, noncapital assets	245505	*18908	*5360	*3132	*220	*7418	3702	*428	1847	2181	1910	52807	147592
63	Other deductions	52190590	507266	1573871	2023949	1669903	1835002	4678662	1687907	1856527	2640148	1355306	4634296	27727753
64	Total receipts less total deducts	3671683	-29991	-58493	43708	70206	-12531	274335	53891	114953	158636	146209	174223	2736537
65	Const taxable inc frm rel frn corps	1452	-	-	-	-	-	-	-	-	-	-	47	1406
66	Net income (less deficit), total	3631385	-29998	-58493	42992	69516	-13665	273997	53571	113786	157511	145392	173646	2703130
67	Net income, total	5310549	73453	133224	198361	200868	124039	462471	125875	167303	201113	196226	380696	3046919
68	Deficit, total	1679164	103452	191718	155369	131352	137704	188473	72304	53517	43602	50834	207051	343789
69	Net income (less def), form 1120-A	*-2696	-	*-2041	*-656	-	-	-	-	-	-	-	-	-
70	Net income (less def), form 1120F	-	-	-	-	-	-	-	-	-	-	-	-	-
71	Net income (less def), form 1120S	547271	-24811	-26633	27532	49913	-37128	191052	30193	67358	56139	68761	58328	86565
72	Statutory special deductions, total	195500	*9549	14145	32836	*14603	19251	39292	*1722	9222	13428	4149	10103	27200
73	Net operating loss deduction	187769	*9545	14143	32793	*14561	18234	38283	*1665	*9030	*12587	3139	9649	24140
74	Dividends received deduction	7731	5	*2	*44	*42	*1016	1009	*56	*192	841	1009	454	3060
75	Public utility div paid deduction	-	-	-	-	-	-	-	-	-	-	-	-	-
76	Income subject to tax	4034926	*34737	22365	68935	63016	54332	159129	63113	80750	125751	123330	310096	292374
77	Income tax before credits, total	1373868	*11485	3354	11646	11140	10935	47008	22126	28904	47559	43798	110938	1024975
78	Regular tax	1329006	*11811	3354	11085	11140	10043	46244	21135	27395	42676	41932	106215	995975
79	Personal holding company tax	*190	-	-	-	-	*190	-	-	-	-	-	-	-
80	Recapture of investment credit	549	-	-	-	-	-	-	-	*1	*516	1	5	25
81	Alternative minimum tax	39154	445	-	*8	-	*170	1518	*995	*1362	4377	1394	4545	24339
82	Environmental tax	5383	24	-	-	-	-	-	-	*52	87	149	436	4635
83	Foreign tax credit	*2174	-	-	-	-	-	-	-	-	*96	-	2062	17
84	U.S. Possessions tax credit	3121	-	-	-	-	-	-	-	-	+-	-	3121	-
85	Orphan drug credit	-	-	-	-	-	-	-	-	-	-	-	-	-
86	Nonconventional source fuel credit	-	-	-	-	+-	-	-	-	-	-	-	-	-
87	General business credit	33456	142	-	-	*301	*277	*320	*414	*202	1900	812	2028	27060
88	Prior year minimum tax credit	9033	*93	-	-	-	*73	*345	*503	*477	*121	322	630	6470
89	Income tax after credits, total	1326084	*11250	3354	11646	10840	10585	46343	21210	28225	45442	42664	103099	991427

SOURCE: *Corporation Source Book of Statistics of Income, 1991–92* (Washington, DC: Internal Revenue Service, 1994), p. 166.

Exhibit 6–2

Sample Page from *Almanac of Business and Industrial Financial Ratios*

Table II

Corporations with Net Income

**Retail Trade
5410**

Grocery Stores

MONEY AMOUNTS AND SIZE OF ASSETS IN THOUSANDS OF DOLLARS

Item Description for Accounting Period 7/90 Through 6/91		Total	Zero Assets	Under 100	100 to 250	251 to 500	501 to 1,000	1,001 to 5,000	5,001 to 10,000	10,001 to 25,000	25,001 to 50,000	50,001 to 100,000	100,001 to 250,000	250,001 and over
Number of Enterprises	1	19368	13	7341	5527	2215	1864	2005	127	122	66	-	-	35

Revenues ($ in Thousands)

Net Sales	2	248916	1154	2682	5652	5521	8522	23575	4655	11438	10464	-	-	143250
Portfolio Income	3	2030	10	38	4.	26	15	40	8	25	31	-	-	1709
Other Revenues	4	3641	15	32	41	68	67	258	73	118	132	-	-	2436
Total Revenues	5	254587	1180	2751	5697	5615	8604	23873	4736	11582	10627	-	-	147396
Average Total Revenues	6	13145	90733	375	1031	2535	4641	11907	37291	94934	161019	-	-	4211304

Operating Costs/Operating Income (%)

Cost of Operations	7	76.7	73.8	75.9	78.5	78.7	77.8	80.2	81.0	80.7	79.2	-	-	74.7
Rent	8	1.6	1.1	2.9	1.7	1.3	1.3	1.4	1.4	1.5	1.4	-	-	1.6
Taxes Paid	9	1.4	1.6	1.3	2.2	1.6	1.5	1.2	1.3	1.3	1.4	-	-	1.5
Interest Paid	10	1.4	2.1	0.7	0.4	0.5	0.4	0.5	0.6	0.4	0.6	-	-	2.0
Depreciation, Depletion, Amortization	11	1.4	1.3	0.8	0.7	0.7	0.9	0.9	1.2	1.0	1.3	-	-	1.7
Pensions and Other Benefits	12	1.3	2.5	0.3	0.1	0.4	0.6	0.7	0.7	0.9	0.8	-	-	1.6
Other	13	16.0	17.3	14.4	12.9	14.3	15.6	13.7	13.6	13.6	14.9	-	-	17.3
Officers Compensation	14	0.4	0.4	3.0	2.5	2.3	1.3	1.0	0.8	0.5	0.4	-	-	.01
Operating Margin	15	-	-	0.8	1.2	0.4	0.7	0.4	-	0.1	-	-	-	-
Oper. Margin Before Officers Compensation	16	0.3	0.3	3.8	3.6	2.6	2.0	1.4	0.4	0.6	0.5	-	-	-

Selected Average Balance Sheet ($ in Thousands)

Net Receivables	17	247	-	6	5	34	48	127	483	1658	2791	-	-	95610
Inventories	18	815	-	19	60	140	223	577	1795	3831	7804	-	-	300611
Net Property, Plant and Equipment	19	1424	-	9	33	61	177	626	2402	6086	15570	-	-	579262
Total Assets	20	3698	-	47	156	348	665	1917	6683	15778	35059	-	-	1495564
Notes and Loans Payable	21	1765	-	36	49	111	182	619	2212	3936	12851	-	-	799443
All Other Liabilities	22	1205	-	17	29	76	168	481	2161	5636	10213	-	-	503485
Net Worth	23	727	-	-6	79	161	314	818	2310	6207	11994	-	-	192636

Selected Financial Ratios (Times to 1)

Current Ratio	24	1.0	-	1.3	2.9	2.4	2.0	1.8	1.4	1.2	1.4	-	-	0.8
Quick Ratio	25	0.3	-	0.5	1.0	0.9	0.9	0.7	0.6	0.6	0.6	-	-	0.2
Net Sales to Working Capital	26	-	-	48.3	15.9	17.4	21.9	25.5	38.5	-	36.3	-	-	-
Coverage Ratio	27	2.6	2.1	5.7	5.6	5.3	5.3	4.2	3.5	4.5	3.8	-	-	2.3
Total Asset Turnover	28	3.5	-	7.7	6.5	7.2	6.9	6.1	5.5	6.0	4.5	-	-	2.7
Inventory Turnover	29	-	-	-	-	-	-	-	-	-	-	-	-	-
Receivables Turnover	30	-	-	-	-	-	-	-	-	-	-	-	-	-
Total Liabilities to Net Worth	31	4.1	-	-	1.0	1.2	1.1	1.4	1.9	1.6	1.9	-	-	6.8

Selected Financial Factors (in Percentages)

Debt Ratio	32	80.3	-	-	49.5	53.8	52.7	57.4	65.5	60.7	65.8	-	-	87.1
Return on Assets	33	12.7	-	31.9	15.6	18.1	13.6	13.1	10.5	10.6	9.9	-	-	12.7
Return on Equity	34	29.0	-	-	24.0	30.4	21.9	20.0	16.5	16.9	17.5	-	-	37.3
Return Before Interest on Equity	35	-	-	-	30.9	-	28.8	30.7	30.3	27.0	29.0	-	-	-
Profit Margin, Before Income Tax	36	2.3	2.2	3.4	2.0	2.1	1.6	1.6	1.4	1.4	1.6	-	-	2.6
Profit Margin, After Income Tax	37	1.6	1.8	3.3	1.9	2.0	1.5	1.4	1.1	1.1	1.3	-	-	1.8

Trends in Selected Ratios and Factors, 1986–1994

		1986	1987	1988	1989	1990	1191	1992	1993	1994
Cost of Operations (%)	38	77.9	77.5	77.7	77.5	77.1	77.6	78.4	77.6	76.7
Operating Margin (%)	39	0.3	-	0.2	0.1	-	0.1	0.3	-	-
Oper. Margin Before Officers Comp. (%)	40	0.8	0.6	0.7	0.6	0.3	0.6	1.0	0.4	0.3
Average Net Receivables ($)	41	152	203	191	205	218	195	104	437	247
Average Inventories ($)	42	565	643	685	788	668	678	478	698	815
Average Net Worth ($)	43	762	875	963	1090	984	862	693	1268	727
Current Ratio (x1)	44	1.4	1.4	1.4	1.3	1.3	1.3	1.4	1.5	1.0
Quick Ratio (x1)	45	0.5	0.5	0.5	0.4	0.5	0.5	0.5	0.7	0.3
Coverage Ratio (x1)	46	4.5	4.1	4.4	4.2	4.3	3.3	4.6	2.6	2.6
Asset Turnover (x1)	47	5.1	4.6	4.5	4.3	4.3	4.3	4.3	3.3	3.5
Operating Leverage	48	-	0.3	2.3	0.6	-	-	2.9	-	1.9
Financial Leverage	49	-	1.0	1.1	0.9	1.1	1.0	1.2	0.8	1.0
Total Leverage	50	-	0.3	2.5	0.6	-	-	3.5	-	1.8

SOURCE: Leo Troy, *Almanac of Business and Industrial Financial Ratios* (Englewood Cliffs, NJ: Prentice Hall, 1994), pp. 245–46. Reprinted with permission from Prentice Hall Career and Personal Development.

Exhibit 6–3

Sample Page from *RMA Annual Statement Studies*

RETAILERS - GROCERIES & MEATS. SIC# 5411

Current Data Sorted By Assets							Comparative Historical Data	
7	6	8	8	3	4	# Postretirement Benefits		
						Type of Statement		
1	12	21	35	11	25	Unqualified	95	71
10	34	53	10	2		Reviewed	87	78
49	91	47	8			Compiled	190	178
22	15	4				Tax Returns		4
36	66	39	24	5	3	Other	177	144
	225(4/1-9/30/93)		398(10/1/93-3/31/94)				6/30/89-3/31.90	4/1/90-3/31.91
0-500 M	500 M-2MM	2-10MM	10-50MM	50-100MM	100-250MM		All	All
118	218	164	77	18	28	NUMBER OF STATEMENTS	549	475
%	%	%	%	%	%	**ASSETS**	%	%
9.8	10.8	12.0	9.2	7.7	9.0	Cash & Equivalents	10.7	9.5
5.8	5.7	4.4	5.4	4.8	6.7	Trade Receivables (net)	4.8	5.5
42.5	32.6	29.4	25.6	24.2	24.0	Inventory	34.8	33.5
1.7	2.7	1.6	1.6	1.5	1.9	All Other Current	2.2	1.9
59.8	51.8	47.4	41.8	38.1	41.6	Total Current	52.5	50.5
29.5	34.1	39.0	46.4	46.1	46.2	Fixed Assets (net)	34.8	37.9
4.0	1.7	1.8	1.8	8.4	5.7	Intangibles (net)	2.0	2.5
6.7	12.3	11.8	10.1	7.4	6.5	All Other Non-Current	10.7	9.2
100.0	100.0	100.0	100.0	100.0	100.0	Total	100.0	100.0
						LIABILITIES		
7.1	5.8	4.1	3.3	6	1.6	Notes Payable-Short Term	5.7	5.3
5.7	5.0	5.0	4.3	3.9	2.8	Curr. Mat.-L/T/D	5.3	4.7
17.9	20.3	20.3	19.7	17.9	17.3	Trade Payables	20.5	20.7
8	1.3	7	6	1.3	3	Income Taxes Payable	.8	.6
12.0	9.3	9.8	9.2	12.7	10.0	All Other Current	8.4	8.9
43.5	41.8	39.8	37.1	36.4	32.0	Total Current	40.7	40.2
27.2	22.2	24.5	24.5	30.6	25.6	Long Term Debt	25.6	27.3
.0	.2	.5	.9	1.8	1.2	Deferred Taxes	.4	.4
3.8	3.8	2.5	2.8	1.7	4.7	All Other Non-Current	2.3	2.0
25.6	32.0	32.7	34.7	29.5	36.5	Net Worth	31.0	30.2
100.0	100.0	100.0	100.0	100.0	100.0	Total Liabilities & Net Worth	100.0	100.0
						INCOME DATA		
100.0	100.0	100.0	100.0	100.0	100.0	Net Sales	100.0	100.0
24.8	23.6	22.2	22.8	21.9	25.5	Gross Profit	22.6	22.3
22.7	22.9	21.4	21.6	20.3	23.6	Operating Expenses	21.5	21.2
2.2	.8	.8	1.2	1.6	1.9	Operating Profit	1.0	1.1
.2	-.2	-.2	-.2	.5	.8	All Other Expenses (net)	.0	.2
2.0	1.0	1.0	1.4	1.0	1.1	Profit Before Taxes	1.1	1.0
						RATIOS		
2.7	1.9	1.6	1.5	1.3	1.5		1.9	1.9
1.5	1.4	1.3	1.2	1.1	1.2	Current	1.4	1.3
1.1	.9	.9	.8	1.0	1.0		1.0	.9
.8	.8	.7	.5	.6	.6		.7	.7
(117) .4	(215) .4	(163) .4	.3	.3	.3	Quick	(540) .3	(467) .3
.1	.2	.2	.2	.2	.2		.2	.2
0 Und	1 645.4	1 609.2	1 351.6	2 200.8	2 150.7		0 799.3	1 718.7
1 620.9	1 254.6	1 245.1	2 149.8	4 97.5	5 78.9	Sales/Receivables	1 260.5	1 264.7
3 115.8	3 109.3	3 113.4	4 100.5	5 67.6	11 34.6		3 113.6	3 107.2
19 19.0	16 22.9	16 22.6	16 22.9	18 20.2	25 14.4		17 22.0	17 20.9
27 13.6	22 16.6	22 16.4	19 18.8	24 14.9	30 12.0	Cost of Sales/Inventory	23 16.0	23 15.6
38 9.5	29 12.6	28 12.9	27 13.4	31 11.9	44 8.3		31 11.8	30 12.3
3 109.4	7 53.5	10 36.6	10 35.9	14 27.0	20 18.6		8 46.4	8 43.4
8 43.3	12 29.6	14 25.6	15 24.2	17 21.1	24 15.2	Cost of Sales/Payables	13 28.9	14 26.0
17 21.8	19 19.1	21 17.6	21 17.4	24 15.1	30 12.2		20 18.6	21 17.7
18.0	27.0	28.9	32.5	50.0	23.7		24.2	23.7
38.3	52.3	56.9	102.4	122.4	44.1	Sales/Working Capital	55.4	61.9
502.3	-209.4	-130.6	-120.5	NM	310.4		-440.7	-112.9
6.6	7.8	6.3	6.9	6.5	5.1		5.4	5.4
(98) 3.1	(197) 3.1	(151) 3.0	(75) 2.7	3.2	(24) 1.6	EBIT/Interest	(494) 2.5	(428) 2.2
.9	1.1	1.1	1.7	1.3	.9		1.2	1.0
1.8	3.2	4.0	3.9	6.1	3.7	Net Profit + Depr. Dep.	3.9	4.1
(20) .7	(71) 2.1	(72) 1.7	(48) 2.1	(10) 3.1	(13) 1.2	Amort/Cur. Mat L/T/D	(267) 2.1	(234) 2.2
.2	.8	1.0	1.2	.7	.6		.9	1.1
.4	.4	.7	1.0	1.3	1.1		.5	.6
1.4	1.1	1.2	1.6	1.6	1.6	Fixed/Worth	1.1	1.4
45.3	3.4	3.0	2.2	6.4	2.0		3.8	3.5
.9	.8	1.0	1.2	1.4	1.3		1.0	1.1
2.4	2.4	2.0	2.2	2.4	2.2	Debt/Worth	2.1	2.3
129.3	7.6	5.8	3.7	12.0	3.1		7.4	7.5
67.9	35.8	38.2	25.4	41.2	18.7	% Profit Before Taxes/Tangible	40.4	34.0
(91) 25.5	(189) 18.1	(147) 18.0	(73) 17.1	(15) 21.6	(26) 9.0	Net Worth	(464) 18.8	(409) 17.0
5.5	4.3	5.2	8.3	12.1	1.8		5.7	3.4
18.6	12.3	12.3	9.9	9.3	6.7	% Profit Before Taxes/Total	12.8	11.5
7.3	5.5	5.4	4.4	6.1	3.4	Assets	5.7	4.9
.4	.4	.6	2.5	1.9	.2		.9	.2
70.1	48.1	28.8	18.5	14.3	10.7		45.5	36.5
36.8	23.8	15.9	11.7	9.9	7.0	Sales/Net Fixed Assets	20.6	18.3
12.5	11.0	9.8	7.5	8.0	4.4		11.0	9.3
10.6	9.2	8.0	6.6	5.4	4.6		8.7	8.7
7.3	6.4	5.8	5.2	4.6	3.6	Sales/Total Assets	6.6	6.1
4.9	4.5	4.5	4.0	3.9	2.4		4.5	4.4
.5	.6	.8	1.0	1.2	1.3		.7	.7
(102) .9	(210) 1.0	(155) 1.1	1.3	1.4	(17) 1.6	%Depr., Dep. Amort./Sales	(497) 1.0	(437) 1.1
1.8	1.4	1.5	1.6	1.6	1.8		1.5	1.5
1.2	1.0	.6	.3				.8	.8
(61) 2.5	(110) 1.6	(71) 1.1	(14) .9			% Officers, Directors Owners' Comp./Sales	(209) 1.4	(192) 1.4
5.0	2.8	1.8	1.3				2.7	2.6
255555M	1768160M	4699859M	9879497M	5583255M	16290645M	Net Sales ($)	28109225M	23736953M
34401M	243368M	749430M	1806980M	1169042M	4643768M	Total Assets ($)	5883944M	4860586M

©Robert Morris Associates 1994

M = $thousand   MM = $million
See Pages 1 through 15 for Explanation of Ratios and Data

Interpretation of Statement Studies Figures. RMA cautions that the Studies be regarded only as a general guideline and not as an absolute industry norm. This is due to limited samples within categories, the categorization of companies by their primary Standard Industrial Classification (SIC) number only, and different methods of operations by companies within the same industry. For these reasons, RMA recommends that the figures be used only as general guidelines in addition to other methods of financial analysis.

Each of the ratios presented is defined in a section several pages long at the beginning of each annual volume. Note that "all ratios computed by *RMA* are based on year-end statement data only." For example, the cost of sales/inventory (inventory turnover ratio) is computed by dividing the cost of goods sold for the year by the ending inventory. A truer picture of inventory would be derived by dividing cost of goods sold by average inventory, but the data on which the *RMA* ratios are based are not sufficient to make that computation.

Standard & Poor's Analyst's Handbook. One of the primary sources of composite financial information on the larger publicly traded companies is the *Standard & Poor's Analyst's Handbook.* The handbook is published annually, with income statement and balance sheet items and related ratios grouped by industry. Approximately 90 industry groups are included, with data going back 30 years. A sample page from the *Analyst's Handbook* is shown in Exhibit 6–4.

Information on Management Compensation

As discussed later in this book, management compensation often must be adjusted when valuing a company on a control basis. Following is a brief overview of some of the sources of comparative information on management compensation.

RMA Annual Statement Studies, the *Corporation Source Book of Statistics of Income,* and the *Almanac of Business and Industrial Financial Ratios,* described earlier, provide information on management compensation as a percentage of revenues.

The *Officer Compensation Report* is a valuable source of information on officer or management compensation. It is a comprehensive study of officer compensation at over 1,400 companies with annual revenues of under $60 million. Compensation data are presented by such categories as officer position, company size, profit performance, and general industry group (manufacturing, technology, general products manufacturing, or service). The survey reports the compensation in effect early in the year in which the report is published; therefore, the results are very timely.

The proxy statements of guideline publicly traded companies are another useful source, since they generally present detailed information on the compensation of companies' top executives. Trade associations are another frequent source of information on management compensation, depending on the industry. For particularly small businesses, *Financial Statement Studies of the Small Business,* published annually, is a useful source. Additional sources are listed in the bibliography at the end of this chapter.

On-Line Information

Sometimes information needs can best be met by a database search. On-line information retrieval is computer-assisted access to several hundred databases covering information that includes multifaceted aspects of business. Some databases provide references to magazines and newspaper articles; others cover conference papers, statistical data, and technical reports. The capability to access remote databases of business information provides the smallest information center with the same resources as a very large library. The number of databases available on-line is expanding rapidly.

Exhibit 6–4

Sample Page from the *Standard and Poor's Analyst's Handbook*

RETAIL (FOOD CHAINS)

Per Share Data—Adjusted to stock price index level. Average of stock price indexes, 1941-1943=10

	Sales	Oper. Profit	Profit Margin %	Depr.	Income Taxes	Cash Flow	Earnings Per Share	Earnings % of Sales	Dividends Per Share	Dividends % of Earn.	Prices 1941-1943=10 High	Prices Low	Price/Earn. Ratio High	Price/Earn. Ratio Low	Div. Yields % High	Div. Yields % Low	Book Value Per Share	Book Value % Return	Work-ing Capital	Capital Expend-itures
1963	318.81	10.87	3.41	3.23	3.85		3.79	1.19	2.25	59.37	71.05	58.35	18.75	15.40	3.86	3.17	34.27	11.06	18.13	3.93
1964	331.89	11.45	3.45	3.41	3.79		4.13	1.24	2.36	57.14	76.60	61.00	18.55	14.77	3.87	3.08	36.27	11.39	19.11	4.62
1965	339.20	11.29	3.33	3.50	356		4.16	1.23	2.45	58.89	81.32	65.67	19.55	15.79	3.73	3.01	37.45	11.11	18.72	5.23
1966	367.21	12.03	3.28	3.77	3.76		439	1.20	2.53	57.63	69.11	49.54	15.74	11.28	5.11	3.66	39.55	11.10	18.22	6.16
1967	377.07	11.61	3.08	3.98	3.46		4.13	1.10	2.61	63.20	57.90	49.00	14.02	11.86	5.33	4.51	41.08	10.05	19.25	5.48
1968	399.19	12.72	3.19	4.96	4.15		4.29	1.07	2.49	58.04	70.40	52.59	16.41	12.26	4.71	0.51	40.07	9.96	13.33	3.77
1969	439.97	13.97	3.18	4.37	4.68		4.70	1.07	2.54	54.04	67.01	56.28	14.26	11.97	4.51	3.79	46.14	10.19	18.29	7.94
1970	464.40	14.82	3.19	4.48	4.87		5.09	1.10	2.56	50.29	67.38	51.59	13.24	10.14	4.96	3.80	48.04	10.60	21.45	10.81
1971	482.38	13.35	2.77	4.77	3.76		4.44	0.92	2.66	59.91	79.36	58.99	17.87	13.29	4.51	3.35	50.10	8.86	22.37	10.12
1972	526.29	10.01	1.90	5.12	1.71		2.80	0.53	2.11	75.36	68.92	54.34	24.61	19.41	3.88	3.06	50.43	5.55	23.31	10.84
1973	563.16	13.94	2.48	5.46	3.26		4.37	0.78	1.83	41.88	63.35	43.59	14.50	9.97	4.20	2.89	52.38	8.34	25.65	11.12
1974	588.26	15.19	2.58	5.62	3.38		1.61	0.27	2.15	...	60.35	40.01	37.48	24.85	5.37	3.56	47.95	3.36	20.92	12.74
1975	637.67	16.16	2.53	6.05	4.46		5.71	0.90	2.08	36.43	60.39	43.90	10.58	7.69	4.74	3.44	50.61	11.28	23.25	10.67
1976	619.07	15.68	2.53	5.68	4.31		5.41	0.87	2.23	41.22	62.87	51.93	11.62	9.60	4.29	3.55	48.11	11.25	24.10	9.77
1977	667.55	18.40	2.76	6.95	4.31	12.43	5.49	0.82	2.49	45.36	62.31	51.93	11.35	9.46	4.79	4.00	50.19	10.94	23.44	14.18
1978	690.69	23.19	3.36	7.88	5.93	14.33	6.45	0.93	2.68	41.55	62.27	49.32	9.65	7.65	5.43	4.30	50.72	12.72	21.68	15.04
1979	R714.74	23.01	3.22	8.00	5.24	15.48	7.47	1.05	3.03	40.56	63.45	54.31	8.49	7.27	5.58	4.78	51.94	14.38	20.47	18.58
1980	808.53	23.47	2.90	9.27	4.95	15.98	6.71	0.83	3.24	48.29	58.50	46.13	8.72	6.87	7.02	5.54	54.61	12.29	20.73	22.08
1981	871.91	25.85	2.96	10.30	5.30	15.37	5.08	0.58	3.55	69.88	63.36	49.70	12.47	9.78	7.14	5.60	56.65	8.97	21.08	20.26
1982	904.98	30.11	3.33	10.95	6.50	20.87	9.98	1.10	3.94	39.48	89.54	52.01	8.97	5.21	7.58	4.40	60.85	16.40	23.73	22.13
1983	872.31	30.40	3.49	11.08	7.03	20.53	9.47	1.09	4.20	44.35	104.58	81.43	11.04	8.60	5.16	4.02	63.60	14.89	21.75	21.05
1984	937.78	33.08	3.53	12.20	8.08	22.90	10.70	1.14	4.32	40.37	107.28	83.48	10.03	7.80	5.17	4.03	69.56	15.38	21.15	37.46
1985	982.07	36.66	3.73	14.03	7.87	25.61	11.58	1.18	4.41	38.08	141.30	105.07	12.20	9.07	4.20	3.12	79.24	14.61	19.55	28.36
1986	951.16	37.21	3.91	14.23	7.60	24.48	9.79	1.03	4.50	45.97	188.25	133.60	19.23	13.65	3.37	2.39	79.73	12.28	10.07	37.68
1987	1187.98	48.05	4.04	17.06	11.94	32.24	15.17	1.28	4.95	32.63	238.45	170.08	15.72	11.21	2.91	2.08	87.11	17.41	20.59	29.29
1988	2031.82	80.63	3.97	29.42	13.24	47.91	18.49	0.91	7.73	41.81	311.49	178.94	16.85	9.68	4.32	2.48	d30.84	def	29.64	50.52
1989	2157.74	94.57	4.38	30.62	14.83	51.09	20.47	0.95	6.61	32.29	425.85	303.91	20.80	14.85	2.17	1.55	d15.41	def	22.22	45.21
1990	2268.30	106.65	4.70	33.73	18.76	61.58	27.85	1.23	7.45	26.75	470.11	352.03	16.88	12.64	2.12	1.58	3.70	...	24.57	41.99
1991	2167.99	98.11	4.53	32.58	18.26	60.02	27.44	1.27	7.92	28.86	559.12	390.56	20.38	14.23	2.03	1.42	29.23	93.88	27.79	40.73
1992	2140.22	99.81	4.66	33.79	14.84	56.77	22.98	1.07	8.66	37.68	568.69	427.60	24.75	18.61	2.03	1.52	41.84	54.92	32.08	51.36
1993	2213.40	I07.60	4.86	36.87	21.04	68.69	31.83	1.44	9.36	29.41	582.08	503.72	18.29	15.83	1.86	1.61	104.40	30.49	26.45	60.43

SOURCE: *Standard & Poor's Analyst's Handbook*, 1994 Annual Edition (New York: Standard & Poor's Corporation, 1994), one of the McGraw-Hill companies, p. 140.

The computer provides powerful flexibility and control for the researcher. A quick search can retrieve a specific bit of data, or a carefully composed strategy can be used to probe a complex problem or to assemble more comprehensive information. In addition to actual on-line searching, CD-ROM (compact disk-read only memory) has made a major impact on the variety of on-line resources that are available. By attaching a CD-ROM player to a computer, one can search databases that have been purchased on compact disks.

The advantages of searching on-line for information include:

- Faster and more efficient information retrieval than is usually possible in printed sources.
- The timeliness of business news.
- The ability to combine different facets of a subject in a single search statement.
- The interactive search process that provides a means of adjusting search strategy until the desired information is found.
- The ease of searching several databases in sequence to produce a comprehensive survey of the available literature.
- The increased number of access points for standard reference sources.

- The growing amount of information accumulating in databases (which can be quickly scanned by the computer).
- The ability to retrieve data and store them on a disk for later editing and manipulation of figures.

Several thousand on-line services are presently marketed by dozens of database vendors. One can choose from an extraordinary number of business-related databases. DIALOG Information Service (Dialog Information Services Inc., now a subsidiary of Knight-Ridder) is one of the largest, most diversified vendors of on-line services. DIALOG offers more than 450 databases, approximately two-thirds of which have direct business applications. Business information on DIALOG runs the gamut from company directories, financial services, and statistical files, to news wires, periodical indexes, and full-text files of newspapers, journals, and newsletters.

Several major vendors have concentrated on supplying full-text services for searchers who do not have large libraries at their disposal. Mead Data Central (a subsidiary of the Mead Corporation) LEXIS/NEXIS databases offer electronic editions of a growing number of publications. LEXIS/NEXIS business offerings include corporate annual reports, state corporation filings, Wall Street brokerage reports, and the complete text of newsletters, trade journals, and local business newspapers.

On-line systems remain the most heavily used electronic sources for business searching, but they are by no means the only medium at the researcher's disposal. Important business databases can be found with increasing frequency on CD-ROMs. Database searching on CD-ROM has become an extremely popular alternative to on-line information retrieval in recent years. Using laser technology, information producers are able to store an incredible amount of data on a single compact disk. Because a single CD can hold up to 1,500 times the data on a floppy diskette, large databases can be installed on a microcomputer for local use. Many libraries subscribe to CD-ROM services and allow their patrons to search for themselves.

Information on how to contact database vendors is included in the bibliography at the end of this chapter.

Indexes to Economic and Industry Information

Several books and indexes are available to assist in finding additional sources of economic and industry data. Some indexes were already mentioned, such as the *American Statistics Index* and the *Wall Street Journal/Barron's Index*. Other indexes, such as the *Business Periodical Index*, the *Public Affairs Information Service* (PAIS), which tends to have more economic information, and *Predicasts*, generally are available in public libraries.

Predicasts provides several business reference publications. Two of this company's publications, *Predicasts Basebook* and *Predicasts Forecasts*, provide summary information on economic indicators and refer the reader to the original source. The *Basebook* provides historical data on U.S. business and economic activities, while *Forecasts* cumulates both short- and long-range projections for products, markets, industries, and the economy. *Predicasts Forecasts* is published quarterly, with an annual cumulative volume. *Forecasts* is particularly valuable as a source of long-term inflation forecasts.

In addition to these indexes, several directories can provide additional sources of economic and industry information. Two particularly valuable resources are *Encyclopedia of Business Information Sources,* 10th edition, edited by James Woy, and Michael R. Lavin's book *Business Information: How to Find It, How to Use It.*

Summary

This chapter has briefly described some of the sources of economic and industry data that appraisers and economists find particularly useful. Since the variety of potential sources is virtually boundless, the final section lists several of the most useful indexing services for locating sources relevant to a particular topic or industry. Locations of the sources' publishers and other information appear in the following bibliography.

To get maximum benefit from economic and industry research, the analyst must focus on the implications of the data for the value of the subject company. This focus must be maintained while conducting the research, using it in arriving at an opinion as to value, and including the research as an integral part of the ultimate appraisal report.

Bibliography

National Economic Information

Business Conditions Digest. U.S. Bureau of Economic Analysis, Department of Commerce. Washington, DC: Government Printing Office, monthly.
Includes charts and statistical tables for leading economic time series. Sections include cyclical indicators; composite indicators and their components; cyclical indicators by economic process; diffusion indexes and rates of change; national income and product; prices, wages, and productivity; labor force, employment, and unemployment; government activities; U.S. international transactions and international comparisons. The U.S. Department of Commerce provides the Economic Bulletin Board on-line for current information, and current and historical data from *Business Conditions Digest* are available on diskette.

Business Statistics. U.S. Bureau of Economic Analysis, Department of Commerce. Washington, DC: Government Printing Office, biennial.
This publication constitutes an amazing collection of economic and industrial statistics. It covers 1,900 separate data series used by the BEA in calculating the gross domestic product. It is intended for publication on a biennial basis as a supplement to the monthly *Survey of Current Business.*

EconBase: Time Series and Forecasts. Bala Cynwyd, PA: WEFA Group, monthly.
This on-line database is compiled by the WEFA Group, a respected econometric forecasting firm formed in 1987 through the merger of Wharton Econometric Forecasting

Associates and Chase Econometrics. Although *EconBase* covers a wide variety of economic time series, almost all historical data come from government sources. Data are not limited to broad economic indicators; many industry-specific series are also included. Among the latter are detailed price indexes from the CPI and PPI, industrial production indexes, employment by industry, and manufacturers' shipments and inventories.

Economic Report of the President. Transmitted to the Congress in February of each year together with the *Annual Report of the Council of Economic Advisers.* U.S. Council of Economic Advisers. Washington, DC: Government Printing Office, 1947–, annual.
This annual review of the nation's economic conditions presents projections of the current economic policy, a review of the existing economic conditions, and prospective changes in economic policies.

Federal Reserve Bulletin. Washington, DC: Board of Governors of the Federal Reserve System, monthly.
Current U.S. banking and monetary statistics. Includes such basic business statistics as employment, prices, national income, and construction. Includes the FRB index of industrial production.

Monthly Labor Review. U.S. Bureau of Labor Statistics, Department of Labor. Washington, DC: Government Printing Office, monthly.
A compilation of economic and social statistics. Most are given as monthly figures for the current year and one prior year. Features articles on the labor force, wages, prices, productivity, economic growth, and occupational injuries and illnesses. Regular features include a review of developments in industrial relations, book reviews, and current labor statistics.

Standard & Poor's Statistical Service. New York: Standard & Poor's Corporation, monthly, with cumulations.
Standard & Poor's Statistical Service is a collection of important business statistics, including the *Security Price Index Record, Business and Financial Statistics,* and cumulative monthly *Current Statistics* providing new information. The *Security Price Index Record,* published every two years, provides information to help in determining the performance history of particular stock groups during recessions, recovery periods, or periods of increasing or declining interest rates. The *Security Price Index Record* provides performance/activity indicators, such as price/earnings ratios, earnings, and dividends on a quarterly and, in some cases, weekly basis.

Standard & Poor's Trends and Projections. New York: Standard & Poor's Corporation, monthly.
This popular and affordable newsletter from Standard & Poor's is available as part of the loose-leaf version of its *Industry Surveys* or as a separate subscription. The newsletter provides a two- to four-page narrative economic outlook, plus a table of key forecasts from S&P economists. The list of variables is extensive, including GDP and its major components, various measures of personal and corporate income, the personal savings rate, the CPI, several key interest rates, the Index of Industrial Production, housing starts, auto sales, and the unemployment rate. Projections are given for the coming two years (both quarterly and annually). Actual data for the latest current year are provided for comparative purposes.

Statistical Abstract of the United States. U.S. Bureau of the Census, Department of Commerce. Washington, DC: Government Printing Office, annual.
The *Statistical Abstract* is as well known and frequently consulted as the *World Almanac and Book of Facts.* In it the user can find data on population, vital statistics, health, law enforcement, education, politics, and other areas of general interest. Although it contains much more than economic statistics, fully two-thirds of the material can be characterized as economic or industrial data. Most of the information is provided by government agencies, but nongovernment sources are also utilized. In addi-

tion, the book contains an excellent bibliography of statistical publications arranged by subject, a list of state statistical abstracts, and a fairly detailed subject index to tables. While not always the best choice for obtaining general economic statistics, with 1,600 tables, it is a viable and convenient source.

Survey of Current Business. U.S. Bureau of Economic Analysis, Department of Commerce. Washington, DC: Government Printing Office, monthly.

This periodical gives information on trends in industry, the business situation, outlook, and other points pertinent to the business world. It is the primary source of information on the national income and product accounts (NIPA). Although the accounts are tabulated quarterly, they are revised each month and presented here. The *Survey of Current Business* contains the most extensive breakdown of current NIPA values found in any ongoing publication. Each segment of the model is shown in considerable detail, because many components are themselves critical economic indicators. Another regular feature is the monthly "Business Situation," which offers an overview of economic conditions. The balance of each issue consists of narrative and statistical articles on special topics. Many are quite technical, explaining the methodology of NIPA revisions or similar topics, but most are understandable and worthwhile for the serious reader.

U.S. Industrial Outlook. U.S. Bureau of Industrial Economics, Department of Commerce. Washington, DC: Government Printing Office, annual.

Information on recent trends and outlook for about five years on over 350 industries. Narrative with statistics contains discussions of changes in supply and demand, developments in domestic and overseas markets, price changes, employment trends, and capital investment. Published in January of each year, the *U.S. Industrial Outlook* is helpful not only for its succinct narratives and summary statistics, but also for its highly regarded forecasts. Together with the *Economic Report of the President,* it has served as one of the government's key sources of economic projections.

Bank Letters[2]

Bank of Hawaii. *Business Trends.*

Federal Reserve Bank of Atlanta. *Economic Review.*

Federal Reserve Bank of Atlanta. *Southeastern Economic Insight.*

Federal Reserve Bank of Boston. *Conference Series.*

Federal Reserve Bank of Boston. *New England Economic Indicators.*

Federal Reserve Bank of Boston. *New England Economic Review.*

Federal Reserve Bank of Chicago. *Agricultural Letter.*

Federal Reserve Bank of Chicago. *Economic Perspectives.*

Federal Reserve Bank of Cleveland. *Economic Commentary.*

Federal Reserve Bank of Cleveland. *Economic Review.*

Federal Reserve Bank of Cleveland. *Economic Trends.*

Federal Reserve Bank of Dallas. *Economic Review.*

Federal Reserve Bank of Kansas City. *Economic Review.*

Federal Reserve Bank of Kansas City. *Financial Letter.*

Federal Reserve Bank of Minneapolis. *Quarterly Review.*

Federal Reserve Bank of New York. *Quarterly Review.*

[2]List compiled by Jeanie M. Welch, Reference Unit Head, J. Murrey Atkins Library, University of North Carolina at Charlotte in Jeanie M. Welch, "Free Bank Letters as Sources of Economic and Financial Information," *Journal of Business & Finance Librarianship* 1, no. 2 (1990), pp. 5–17.

Federal Reserve Bank of Philadelphia. *Business Review.*

Federal Reserve Bank of Philadelphia. *Fed in Print (index).*

Federal Reserve Bank of Richmond. *Economic Review.*

Federal Reserve Bank of St. Louis. *International Economic Conditions.*

Federal Reserve Bank of St. Louis. *Monetary Trends.*

Federal Reserve Bank of St. Louis. *National Economic Trends.*

Federal Reserve Bank of St. Louis. *Review.*

Federal Reserve Bank of St. Louis. *U.S. Financial Data.*

Federal Reserve Bank of San Francisco. *Economic Review.*

Federal Reserve Bank of San Francisco. *Weekly Letter.*

International Monetary Fund. *Finance and Development.*

Manufacturers Hanover Trust. *Economic Report.*

Manufacturers Hanover Trust. *Financial Digest.*

Morgan Guaranty Trust of New York. *Morgan Guaranty Survey.*

Morgan Guaranty Trust of New York. *World Financial Markets.*

Wells Fargo Bank. *Business Review.*

World Bank. *World Bank Research News.*

Regional Economic Information

American Business Climate & Economic Profiles. Priscilla Cheng Geahigan, ed.
Washington, DC: Gale Research, 1994.
This is a concise compilation of facts, rankings, incentives, and resource listings for all
319 metropolitan statistical areas (MSAs) and the 50 states.

*Census of Manufactures, Census of Retail Trade, Census of Wholesale Trade, Census of
Service Industries, Census of Mineral Industries, Census of Construction Industries,*
and *Census of Transportation.* U.S. Bureau of the Census, Department of Commerce.
Washington, DC: Government Printing Office.
The economic census is produced as seven separate titles grouped according to type of
business. Each title consists of three subseries: geographic data for each state, detailed
industry data by SIC numbers, and a subject series for special topics, though for some
titles the industry and subject series are combined.

City and County Databook and the State Metropolitan Area Databook. U.S. Bureau of
the Census, Department of Commerce. Washington, DC: Government Printing Office.
Contains statistics on housing, population, construction activity, and many other economic indicators.

The Complete Economic and Demographic Data Source. Washington, DC: Wilson and
Poole Economics, Inc., annual.
An excellent source for statistical profiles of metropolitan areas, counties and parishes,
and states. Historical as well as projected data are included in this source. Other publications from Wilson & Poole include annual *State Profiles* and *MSA Profiles,* which
currently include statistical economic data and forecasts through the year 2010.

Economic Bulletin Board. U.S. Bureau of Economic Analysis, Department of Commerce.
Washington, DC, (202) 377-1986.
This organization has a regional economics program that provides estimates, analyses,
and projections by region, state, metropolitan statistical area, and county or parish.
Regional reports are released approximately six times a year with summary estimates
of state personal income. This information is available on-line on the *Economic
Bulletin Board.*

Metro Insights. Lexington, MA: DRI/McGraw-Hill, annual.

For larger metropolitan areas, Metro Insights provides 10 to 15 pages of narrative economic discussion well supported with statistics. This source contains information on the 100 largest U.S. metropolitan areas. Each area profile includes an economic profile, forecasts for growth, and construction and demographic data.

Sales & Marketing Management Annual Survey of Buying Power. New York: Bill Communications, Inc., annual.

This publication breaks down demographic and income data by state, metropolitan area, and county or parish. Retail sales data are presented for store groups and merchandise lines. Also included are population and retail sales forecasts for local areas.

Industry Information

Almanac of Business and Industrial Financial Ratios. Englewood Cliffs, NJ: Prentice Hall, annual.

This reference profiles financial and operating ratios for approximately 181 fields of business including manufacturing, wholesaling, retailing, banks, and financial industries and services. It profiles corporate performance in two analytical tables. There is a time lag, since the statistics are based on corporate activity reported in the latest published IRS tax returns.

Census of Manufactures, Census of Retail Trade, Census of Wholesale Trade, Census of Service Industries, Census of Mineral Industries, Census of Construction Industries, and *Census of Transportation.* U.S. Bureau of the Census, Department of Commerce. Washington, DC: Government Printing Office.

The economic census is produced as seven separate titles grouped according to type of business. Each title consists of three subseries: geographic data for each state, detailed industry data by SIC numbers, and a subject series for special topics, though for some titles the industry and subject series are combined.

Corporation Source Book: Statistics of Income; Partnership Source Book: Statistics of Income; and *Sole Proprietorship Source Book: Statistics of Income.* Internal Revenue Service. Washington, DC: Government Printing Office, annual.

Balance sheet, income statement, tax and investment credit items by major and minor industries, broken down by size of total assets. Tables provide detailed industry data. Published three to five years after subject period (i.e., the 1994 edition might be based on 1990 data).

Industry Norms and Key Business Ratios. New York: Dun & Bradstreet, Inc., annual.

Balance sheet and profit and loss ratios based on a computerized financial statements file. The 14 key ratios are broken down into median figures, with upper and lower quartiles. Covers over 800 lines of business, broken down into three size ranges by net worth for each SIC.

Manufacturing USA, 4th ed. Detroit: Gale Research, 1994.

Profiles and top company rankings for about 460 manufacturing industries, organized by four-digit SIC code. Synthesizes relevant data from the *Census of Manufactures,* the *Annual Survey of Manufactures, County Business Patterns,* the *U.S. Industrial Outlook,* and the *Industry-Occupation Matrix* produced by the U.S. Department of Labor. Profiles provide general industry statistics, indexes of change, selected ratios, product share, statistical analyses of states and regions, and more.

Market Share Reporter. Detroit: Gale Research, 1994.

Presents comparative business statistics in a clear, straightforward manner. Arranged by four-digit SIC code, contains data from more than 2,000 entries. Each entry includes a descriptive title, data and market description, a list of producers/products along with their assigned market share, and more.

Moody's Industry Review. New York: Moody's Investors Service, biweekly.

Covers approximately 4,000 companies in nearly 150 industry groups. Every company is ranked within its industry by five financial characteristics (revenues, net income, total assets, cash and marketable securities, and long-term debt) and five ratios (profit margin, return on capital, return on assets, P/E, and dividend yield). Every industry report also provides additional data in an unranked display, including earnings per share, book value, and 12-year stock price summaries.

Predicasts Basebook. Foster City, CA: Information Access Company, annual.

This loose-leaf reference provides historical data on U.S. business and economic activities. Arranged by a modified, seven-digit SIC number, the industry statistics include production, consumption, plant and equipment expenditures, payroll, and exports/imports. The figures cover approximately 15 years. The sources of statistic and annual growth are also provided.

Predicasts PROMT. Foster City, CA: Information Access Company, updated daily.

This multi-industry resource provides broad, international coverage of companies, products, markets, and applied technologies for all industries. Available on-line through Dialog file 16, *PTS PROMT* is comprised of abstracts and full-text records from more than 1,000 of the world's important business publications, including trade journals, local newspapers and regional business publications, national and international business newspapers, trade and business newsletters, research studies, S1 SEC registration statements, investment analysts' reports, corporate news releases, and corporate annual reports.

RMA Annual Statement Studies. Philadelphia: Robert Morris Associates, annual.

Robert Morris Associates' member banks submit the raw data; thus, the contents are not strictly consistent from year to year. Although the financial data submitted reflect companies' overall operations, the data are categorized only by the companies' primary SICs. Comparative historical data are also included.

Service Industries USA: Industry Analyses, Statistics, and Leading Organizations. Arsen J. Darnay, ed. Detroit: Gale Research, biennial.

Organizes widely scattered and sometimes difficult-to-use federal economic information, as well as data from other sources, into a workable and easy-to-read format. Four indexes provide easy access to the material: SIC index; services index containing keyword listings of services with references to SIC codes and page numbers; company institution; and occupation indexes.

Standard & Poor's Analyst's Handbook. New York: Standard & Poor's Corporation, Inc., annual.

A statistical workbook that enables anyone concerned with company or industry performance to conveniently compare the most vital per share data and financial statistics for the S&P 400 industrial stocks and the 90 industries comprising the index. Also includes 15 transportation, financial, and utility groups. Contains industry charts. Available with monthly updating.

Standard & Poor's Industry Surveys. New York: Standard & Poor's Corporation, Inc., quarterly and annual.

Provides continuous economic and business information on all major U.S. industries and numerous related industries. Financial data on more than 1,000 companies are included in the 22 surveys now published. Publishes annual *Basic Survey* and periodic *Current Surveys* for each industry grouping. Also includes a monthly *Trends and Projections* Economics Letter and a monthly *Earnings Supplement.* Over 1,500 pages annually of accurate, timely information on important industry trends and developments. *Trends and Projections* reviews the state of the economy by highlighting major topics and evaluating leading indicators. Makes specific projections for gross domestic product and several of its components. A variety of charts show trends in interest rates, employment, housing starts, industrial production, and retail sales.

U.S. Industrial Outlook. U.S. Bureau of Industrial Economics, Department of Commerce. Washington, DC: Government Printing Office.

Information on recent trends and outlook for about five years on over 350 individual industries. Narrative with statistics contains discussions of changes in supply and demand, developments in domestic and overseas markets, price changes, employment trends, and capital investment. Published in January of each year through 1994. The *U.S. Industrial Outlook* is helpful not only for its succinct narratives and summary statistics but also for its highly regarded forecasts.

Industry Information Directories

Encyclopedia of Associations. Detroit: Gale Research, annual.

Available in print and electronic formats. This is the largest compilation of nonprofit associations and organizations available anywhere. Contains descriptions of professional associations, trade and business associations, labor unions, chambers of commerce, and groups of all types in virtually every field.

National Trade and Professional Associations of the United States. Washington, DC: Columbia Books, annual.

Excellent sourcebook for trade and industry sources of industry information. Restricted to trade and professional associations and labor unions with national memberships.

Nelson's Directory of Wall Street Research. Rye, NY: W.R. Nelson & Company, annual.

The "Research Sources" section gives names, addresses, telephone numbers, and specialties of research personnel at over 600 firms.

Management Compensation Sources

Almanac of Business and Industrial Financial Ratios. Leo Troy, Ph.D. Englewood Cliffs, NJ: Prentice Hall, annual.

Presents financial ratios of companies by SIC code, asset size, and profitability. Compensation of officers includes salary and wages, bonuses or bonds, and other identified benefits paid to officers for personal services rendered. Pensions, profit sharing, stock bonuses, annuity, and other deferred compensation is specifically excluded from officer compensation and is reported elsewhere.

Executive Compensation: Survey Results. New York: National Association of Business Management, Inc., annual.

Presents the results of surveys conducted by BDO/Seidman and the Research Institute of America, Inc. The results are separated into officer position.

Officer Compensation Report. Frederick, MD: Panel Publishers, Inc., annual.

A comprehensive study of officer compensation for more than 1,000 companies with annual revenues of less than $60 million, based on a survey of 50,000 companies. The study examines the ownership structure, profitability, and economic profile and is further broken down by officer position and industry. Compensation is defined as salary plus all other direct remuneration received.

RMA Annual Statement Studies. Philadelphia: Robert Morris Associates, annual.

Contains composite financial data on companies in manufacturing, wholesaling, retailing, service, and contracting. The information is collected by member banking institutions from their borrowing customers and is presented by SIC code. The officer compensation to sales ratio measures the total amount of monetary remuneration paid to the company officers (exclusive of pension contributions).

Source Book Statistics of Income. Washington, DC: Internal Revenue Service, annual.

A collection of balance sheet, income statement, tax, and selected other financial information by industry type and asset size. The information is collected by the Internal Revenue Service from a sampling of corporate tax returns filed.

On-Line Information

You may contact these vendors directly for more information about their services:

CompuServe
5000 Arlington Center Boulevard
Columbus, OH 43220
800-524-3388

DIALOG
Dialog Information Services Inc.
3460 Hillview Avenue
Palo Alto, CA 94304
800-334-2564

Dow Jones News/Retrieval
Post Office Box 300
Princeton, NJ 08543-0300
609-452-1511

LEXIS/NEXIS
Mead Data Central Inc.
9393 Springboro Pike
Post Office Box 933
Dayton, OH 45401
800-227-4908

Wilsonline
The H.W. Wilson Company
950 University Avenue
Bronx, NY 10452
800-367-6770
212-588-8400

Indexes and Guides to Business Information

American Statistics Index: A Comprehensive Guide and Index to the Statistical Publications of the U.S. Government. Washington, DC: Congressional Information Service, 1973–, monthly, with annual cumulations.
    Published by a reputable firm specializing in providing access to government publications, the ASI provides access to federal statistics. Each edition is two volumes, *Index* and *Abstracts*. Also included in the index volume are a title index, a guide to the Standard Industrial Classification code, the Standard Occupation Classification, and a list of standard metropolitan statistical areas (SMSAs).

The Basic Business Library: Core Resources, 3rd ed. Bernard S. Schlessinger. Phoenix, AZ: Oryx Press, 1994.
    New electronic formats and new publications are covered in the annotated core list of nearly 200 prime information sources, including on-line and CD-ROM databases, periodicals, newsletters, and books. The bibliography, including over 300 abstracts covering the business reference literature, has been updated to 1994.

Business Information: How to Find It, How to Use It, 2nd ed. Michael R. Lavin. Phoenix, AZ: Oryx Press, 1992.
    Combines in-depth descriptions of major business publications and databases with explanations of concepts essential for using them effectively. Readers will gain a greater appreciation of the enormous diversity of published information and the wide range of specific questions that can be answered.

Business Information Sources, rev. ed. Lorna M. Daniells. Berkeley, CA: University of California Press, 1985.

Annotates sources arranged by subject, such as industry statistics. Indexed by title, author, and subject. An updated edition is forthcoming.

Business Periodicals Index (BPI). New York: H.W. Wilson, 1958–, monthly, with quarterly and annual cumulations.

Subject index to approximately 350 periodicals in the business field. The periodicals indexed are English-based and come from trade and professional associations and government agencies. Articles indexed under specific business subject headings, including names of executives and corporations. Available in print, on CD-ROM disk, and on-line. *Wilson Business Abstracts* is a powerful resource that provides not only high-quality indexing, but also comprehensive abstracts written by subject experts, ranging from 50 to 150 words each. Over 57,000 subject terms for immediate access—search by subjects, keywords, company names, and SIC codes. Available on CD-ROM disk or on-line.

Directory of Business and Financial Services, 8th ed. Mary McNierney Grant and Riva Berleant-Schiller. Washington, DC: Special Libraries Association, 1984.

A fine companion to the Daniells book, this source deals with services that provide regularly or irregularly updated information on some category of business activity.

Encyclopedia of Business Information, 9th ed. James Woy, ed. Detroit: Gale Research, 1994.

A bibliographic guide to more than 24,000 citations covering over 1,100 subjects of interest to business personnel. Includes abstracting and indexing services, almanacs and yearbooks, bibliographies, biographical sources, directories, encyclopedias and dictionaries, financial ratios, handbooks and manuals, on-line databases, periodicals and newsletters, price sources, research centers and institutes, statistics sources, trade associations and professional societies, and other sources of information on each topic.

Guide to Special Issues and Indexes of Periodicals, 4th ed. Miriam Uhlan and Doris B. Katz, eds. Washington, DC: Special Libraries Association, 1994.

This handy resource details, in alphabetical order, 1,748 U.S. and Canadian periodicals that publish special issues, such as factbooks/yearbooks, buyers guides/directories, reviews/forecasts, statistical reports, rankings, marketing studies, and more. An annotation for each *Special Issue* is given when the title is not sufficiently descriptive. The heart of the *Guide* is its comprehensive subject index, which provides quick reference to the contents of each publication's recurring specials.

International Business Information: How to Find It, How to Use It. Ruth A. Pagell and Michael Halperin. Phoenix, AZ: Oryx Press, 1994.

Covering both print and electronic sources, this reference includes all major business environments outside the United States, with special up-to-date examinations of the most recent sources on Eastern Europe, the former Soviet Union, and Asia.

Predicasts F&S Index United States. Foster City, CA: Information Access Company, weekly, with cumulations.

Provides comprehensive reference indexes of business and economic information. *PTS F&S Index* covers worldwide company, product, and industry information. One- and two-line article summaries offer access to information on international companies, business and financial activities, demographics, government regulations, and economics. Detailed coverage of more than 750 trade journals, newspapers (including the *Wall Street Journal*), government documents, and special studies.

Predicasts Forecasts. Foster City, CA: Information Access Company, quarterly with annual cumulations.

Nearly 50,000 short- and long-range projections for products and industries, along with leading economic indicators for U.S. business are available in this reference. Arranged by modified seven-digit SIC code, each forecast gives the subject, quantities for a base year, short- and long-term projections, unit of measure, source of data, and projected annual rate.

Public Affairs Information Service Bulletin (PAIS). New York: Public Affairs Information Service, biweekly with quarterly and annual cumulations.

A selected subject list of the latest books, pamphlets, government publications, reports of public and private agencies, and periodical articles relating to economic and social conditions, public administration, and international relations.

Statistical Reference Index. Washington, DC: Congressional Information Service, monthly with annual cumulation.

Since 1980, *Statistical Reference Index* has indexed and abstracted statistical reports from agencies other than the federal government. Nonprofit organizations, trade and professional associations, state government agencies, university research centers, and commercial publishers are just some of the sources of statistical information included. Since 1983, CIS has also published the *Index to International Statistics,* which includes statistical publications of over 50 international, intergovernmental agencies such as the United Nations and OECD.

Tapping the Government Grapevine: The User-Friendly Guide to U.S. Government Information Sources, 2nd ed. Judith Schiek Robinson. Phoenix, AZ: Oryx Press, 1993.
The new edition incorporates material about recent developments, notably the advent of CD-ROM as a major medium of dissemination. It is a concise, well-designed guide to many mystifying realms of government information that has now been brought up-to-date.

Trade & Industry Index. Foster City, CA: Information Access Company, weekly.
Business journals relating to trade, industry, and commerce are indexed and selectively abstracted in *Trade & Industry Index.* This on-line database provides, in a single source, current and comprehensive coverage of major trade journals and industry-related periodicals representing all Standard Industrial Classifications. *Trade & Industry Index* (Dialog file 148) provides indexing and selective abstracting of over 300 trade and industry journals, as well as comprehensive but selective coverage of business and trade information from nearly 1,200 additional publications. *Trade & Industry ASAP* (Dialog file 648) contains the complete text of records from more than 200 of the covered journals.

Using Government Information Sources: Print and Electronic, 2nd ed. Jean L. Sears and Marily K. Moody. Phoenix, AZ: Oryx Press, 1994.
This resource covers all the changes in formats and accessibility of the new generation of government information sources, including CD-ROM products, on-line databases, diskettes, electronic bulletin boards, and telephone hot-line numbers, as well as print sources.

Chapter 7

Analyzing and Adjusting Financial Statements

One of the most significant changes in financial reporting is the erosion of the relative importance of financial statements.[1]

The experienced analyst knows some latitude is permitted in the preparation of financial statements. Rarely do any two companies follow exactly the same set of accounting practices in keeping their books and preparing their financial statements, even within the broad confines of generally accepted accounting principles (GAAP). When it comes to closely held companies, most financial statements are not audited and many provide financial statements that deviate from GAAP, to put it kindly. Therefore, the analyst must evaluate each item and adjust for differences in accounting practices, where appropriate, in order to compare two or more companies or to measure a company against an industry or other standard.

When there is a choice among accounting practices, private companies tend toward a more conservative selection to minimize taxes, while public companies may account more aggressively in order to please shareholders with higher reported income. Also, some public companies try to "manage" their earnings to minimize earnings peaks and valleys by making more conservative accounting decisions in good years and more aggressive accounting decisions in bad ones. Typically, the smaller the private company, the more pronounced the difference between public companies and private companies tends to be.

It is important to remember, then, that shareholders who have control over the company may have the right to change business policies, including the accounting policies followed by the company. This fact should be recognized when the appraisal subject is a controlling ownership interest—versus a minority ownership interest.

All discussion of financial statement analysis in this book is subject to the caveat that generally accepted accounting principles are constantly being reviewed and updated. Also, publicly traded companies are subject to certain disclosure requirements of the Securities and Exchange Commission (SEC), which continue to be challenged and interpreted by the courts.

Complete books are dedicated to the subject of financial statement analysis (see the bibliography at the end of this chapter). The material presented in this chapter is only a refresher to those who are presented with the task of appraising a business or of reviewing an appraisal prepared by others.

The purpose of analyzing income statements is to better understand and interpret the economic earning capacity of the company, since earning capacity is a very important element of the value of a business. Therefore, adjustments to the income statements, in order to better present the earning capacity of the business, generally fall into any or all of three categories:

1. Methods the company has elected to account for its activities, as discussed earlier.
2. Nonrecurring events, discontinued operations, or other aspects of past operations that may not represent future economic earning capacity.
3. Certain discretionary items, such as generous management bonuses.

---

[1] Kay, Robert S., and D. Gerald Searfoss, eds., *Handbook of Accounting and Auditing*, 2nd ed. (Boston: Warren, Gorham & Lamont, 1989), pp. 1–24.

In many valuations, asset values also play an important role and, therefore, adjustments to the balance sheet may or may not be necessary for analytical purposes. Some variables adjusted for income statement analysis will imply adjustments to the balance sheet because of their interdependence. In other situations, it may be appropriate to make adjustments to balance sheet items that will not affect the company's earning capacity or to make adjustments to the income statement that will not affect the balance sheet.

This chapter discusses the most common categories of adjustments to the income statement and balance sheet in the valuation. It begins with adjustments for different means of measuring asset and liability items. Then it examines a number of items arising from the treatment of revenue and expense items. Finally, it looks at a number of miscellaneous items. More complete discussions of financial statements and the appropriate adjustments of various financial statement accounts can be explored by the reader by referring to other sources, including those in the bibliography at the end of this chapter.

Adequacy of Allowance and Reserve Accounts

It is common to find that a company is either under- or over-reserved for certain items. Some "reserve accounts" should not be considered reserve accounts at all but merely portions of equity that management has chosen to earmark for some future expenditure or contingency. If under-reserved, the effect is an overstatement of earnings due to inadequate reserve charges to expenses, with an accompanying overstatement of net asset value. If over-reserved, the opposite occurs. The analyst may encounter an endless variety of reserve or allowance accounts from time to time and should question and analyze each on its own merits.

Allowance for Doubtful Accounts

Accounts Receivable. Most companies carry accounts receivable and deduct some allowance for potentially uncollectible accounts. The typical policy is to charge some percentage of credit sales to bad debt expense at the time the sales are made. Often a charge (or debit) is made at the end of each month, reflecting that month's credit sales, with a credit to the allowance for doubtful accounts (which is recorded as a deduction from accounts receivable on the balance sheet). Then, as individual accounts are written off, they are credited against accounts receivable and debited against the allowance for doubtful accounts, with no direct effect on either earnings or net asset value at the time of the write-off.

Since the expense charge (or debit) actually represents an estimate of future write-offs, the analyst may wish to make some judgment as to that estimate's accuracy, at least if the effect is material. One way is to compare the historical percentage of bad debt losses with the percentage of current credit sales being charged to bad debt expense to see if too little or too much is being charged. Another procedure is to compare the aged accounts receivable schedule allowance relative to the amount of overdue accounts. Some companies tend to carry receivables on their books indefinitely, with little or no doubtful account allowance; this results in an overstatement of earnings and net asset value. Other companies follow a very aggressive write-off policy, removing from their books many accounts that eventually are collected; this tends to understate earnings and net asset value.

Notes Receivable.   While examining accounts receivable, the analyst should check to see whether any notes or other receivables are questionable and make any appropriate adjustments. Notes receivable may be taken to improve the company's chance of collecting a delinquent trade receivable, but their collectability may be in question. Notes receivable from stockholders may really be more in the nature of long-term loans, or even undeclared dividends, even though they may be carried on the balance sheet in the current asset section. A review of prior period balance sheets—to see how long some "current" items have been carried—often can provide some insight into the probability of collection during the company's normal operating cycle.

Pension Liabilities

The procedures for accounting for pension liabilities were substantially revised by SFAS No. 87.[2] Although explanation of the revision is beyond the scope of this book, the analyst should become familiar with the revised accounting standards and be aware that they must be in place for all companies with audited financial statements no later than fiscal years on or after December 16, 1988. For companies still not using GAAP accounting after that time, this could be a major item of financial statement adjustment.

Inventory Accounting Methods

FIFO, LIFO, and Other Methods

The *FIFO,* or *first-in, first-out,* inventory accounting method, assumes that the first unit of an inventory item purchased is the first unit sold. The *LIFO,* or *last-in, first-out,* method assumes that the last unit of an inventory item purchased is the first unit sold. The difference between FIFO and LIFO accounting shows up in the ending inventory on the balance sheet, affecting both the cost of goods sold and earnings. To the extent that inventory prices go up, the LIFO inventory accounting method produces lower reported earnings and inventory than does FIFO. Since LIFO accounting is acceptable for federal income tax purposes, many companies have adopted LIFO over FIFO inventory accounting in response to inflation.

However, it should be noted that if inventory has been accounted for using LIFO, and if that inventory *declines* over the course of the year—that is, with-

---

[2]FAS-87, "Employers' Accounting for Pensions," *GAAP Guide 1995* (New York: Harcourt Brace Professional Publishing, 1995), pp. 35.08—.12.

drawals from inventory exceed purchases—a phenomenon known as a *LIFO liquidation occurs*. This event reduces inventories to a point at which LIFO cost layers from prior years are matched to current inflated prices. If prices from the "old" inventory layer are much lower than current prices, a distortion of income occurs. Audited and reviewed financial statements should disclose whether LIFO liquidation has occurred and the extent of its effects. If a decline in inventory that is being accounted for using LIFO occurs, and the financial statements lack proper disclosures, the analyst should conduct further examination and inquiry to eliminate the distorting effects of the LIFO liquidation.

When comparing two or more companies for valuation purposes, all the companies' earnings and asset values should have been derived based on the same inventory accounting method if the difference is substantial enough to affect the valuation. If they do not all use the same accounting method, the analyst can adjust the earnings and asset values to the same basis using information in the financial statements.

As a simple example, let's assume that a company started its accounting period with 30 widgets, purchased for $10 each. Later in the period, it purchased 60 more widgets at $15 each, and before its next fiscal year-end it sold 50 widgets, ending the period with 40 widgets in inventory. The cost of goods sold would be computed under the FIFO and LIFO methods as presented in Table 7–1. In other words, LIFO accounting perpetrates the fiction that the original units in the inventory are the ones that are still there. In the above case, if sales were $1,000, the gross margin would be $400 under FIFO inventory accounting and $250 under LIFO inventory accounting.

For most companies that report on FIFO, the data needed to adjust earnings and inventory to the LIFO basis are not readily available. If a company reporting on LIFO has audited statements, however, the footnotes will provide a figure for the LIFO in inventory reserve that can be used to adjust earnings and inventory values from LIFO to FIFO. If the statements are not audited, the company's accountant should be able to provide the necessary information for adjusting to a FIFO basis. Therefore, because of the availability of this information, if one or more companies' inventory accounting needs to be adjusted for comparative purposes, the analyst will typically adjust the LIFO-reporting companies to a FIFO basis rather than vice versa.

The analyst should keep in mind that if earnings are adjusted from LIFO to FIFO, the adjustment should be net of the associated income tax effect (either additional taxes or benefit). Selecting the correct income tax rate to use in making the adjustment may be more complicated than just using the effective or marginal tax rate. The analyst should scrutinize the income tax characteristics of the company in order to estimate the most likely consequences of the additional income or losses, as adjusted, on income taxes.

Besides adjusting the income statement from a LIFO to a FIFO basis, it may be necessary to adjust the balance sheet, generally in three areas. First, the inventory level should be adjusted to the FIFO basis. Second, an income tax liability account should be adjusted to account for the additional income taxes that would have resulted from the adjustment to inventory. Third, retained earnings should be adjusted by the net difference between the inventory and income tax liability adjustments.

Table 7–1

	FIFO	LIFO
Beginning inventory	30 Units @ $10 = $ 300	30 Units @ $10 = $ 300
Plus: Purchases	60 Units @ $15 = $ 900	60 Units @ $15 = $ 900
Equals: Goods available for sale	$1,200	$1,200
Less: Ending inventory	40 Units @ $15 = $ 600	30 Units @ $10 = $ 300
		10 Units @ $15 = $ 150
		$ 450
Equals: Cost of goods sold	$ 600	$ 750

Table 7–2

Continuing with the example above:

Assume:	
Effective income tax rate	30%
LIFO reserve	$150
Adjust ending inventory to FIFO:	
LIFO inventory	$450
Add LIFO reserve	150
Equals: Adjusted ending inventory	$600
Compute accrued income tax liability, and add to an income tax liability account:	
LIFO reserve	$150
Multiply by tax rate	0.30
Equals: Addition to accrued income tax liability	$ 45
Add net effect to retained earnings:	
LIFO reserve	$150
Less related accrued income tax	45
Equals: Addition to retained earnings	$105

Continuing with the our widget company example, let's assume the company is using LIFO accounting and the appropriate income tax rate for the adjustment is 30 percent. The company has a LIFO reserve of $150. Therefore, to adjust the inventory to FIFO, the analyst adds $150 to the ending inventory level of $450 to reach an adjusted inventory level of $600. Then the analyst adds $45 ($150 × 30 percent tax rate) to an income tax liability account and $105 ($150 − $45) to retained earnings. Table 7–2 illustrates these calculations.

In some lines of business, specific inventory items are clearly identifiable from the time of purchase through the time of sale and are accounted for and costed on this basis. Some companies also account for inventory on an *average cost basis.*[3] In particular, in some industries it is possible to adjust inventory from LIFO only to average cost, not to FIFO. The adjustment is calculated in the same way as the adjustment to FIFO.

Write-Down and Write-Off Policies

Regardless of whether the company uses FIFO, LIFO, specific identification, or average cost inventory accounting, most companies adhere to the *lower-of-cost-or-market* accounting principle, which says the carrying value should be reduced

---

[3]For a discussion of the average cost method, see Leopold A. Bernstein, *Financial Statement Analysis: Theory, Application, and Interpretation,* 5th ed. (Burr Ridge, IL: Richard D. Irwin, 1993), p. 148.

if the market value is less than cost. *Market value* for this purpose is defined as "current replacement cost except that market shall not be higher than net realizable value nor should it be less than net realizable value reduced by the normal profit margin."[4] Implementation of the lower-of-cost-or-market principle varies tremendously—one company may have stockrooms full of obsolete inventory and another company may have an aggressive program of automatic write-downs and write-offs of inventory based on the number of months it has been in stock. If the company goes to one extreme or to the other in its implementation of this principle, the analyst may need to adjust earnings and asset values.

Depreciation Methods and Schedules

The five most common methods of computing depreciation charges are the straight-line, declining-balance, sum-of-the-years'-digits, accelerated cost recovery systems (ACRS), and modified accelerated cost recovery system (MACRS) introduced by the Tax Reform Act of 1986. The method that produces the largest annual depreciation deduction is the one most often selected by closely held businesses, since they are most eager to minimize reported taxable income.

Code Section 197 was enacted by the Revenue Reconciliation Act of 1993, providing a uniform 15-year amortization period for most intangible assets.

The *straight-line method* simply charges depreciation on the asset in even increments over the asset's useful life. The declining-balance, sum-of-the-years'-digits, ACRS, and MACRS methods are called *accelerated methods* because, unlike the straight-line method, they charge a higher proportion of the total depreciation in the early years of the asset's useful life than in later years.

Declining-Balance Method

The *declining-balance method* uses some multiple, such as two times or one and one-half times the straight-line annual depreciation rate. For example, if an asset had a useful life of 10 years, straight-line depreciation would be at the rate of 10 percent per year. Double-declining-balance depreciation would be at twice that rate, or 20 percent per year, but with the percentage always applied to the remaining book value. In other words, in the first year a $100,000 piece of equipment with a 10-year life would be depreciated at 20 percent of $100,000 or $20,000, leaving a depreciated original cost balance of $80,000. In the second year, the asset would be depreciated at 20 percent of $80,000, or $16,000, leaving a depreciated original cost balance of $64,000.

Sum-of-the-Years'-Digits Method

In the *sum-of-the-years'-digits method,* the depreciation charge is a fraction whose denominator is the sum of the years' digits of the asset's useful life and the numerator is the number of years of remaining useful life. Thus, for a 10-year

---

[4]Ibid., p. 152.

useful life, the denominator is 55 (1 + 2 + 3 + 4 + 5 + 6 + 7 + 8 + 9 + 10 = 55), and the numerator the first year is 10. Therefore, the first year's depreciation charge is 10/55 of the asset's value, in the second year 9/55, and so on.

For some assets, the company estimates a residual or salvage value at the end of the depreciable life. In these cases, the difference between the cost and salvage value is the depreciable amount. Salvage value may not be deducted from cost in the declining-balance method, however, because that method never results in the asset being depreciated to zero.

ACRS and MACRS[5]

The fourth widely used depreciation method is *ACRS* (accelerated cost recovery system), which was enacted as part of the Economic Recovery Tax Act of 1981. It is used principally for federal income tax purposes as compared to financial accounting purposes. The Tax Reform Act of 1986 revised the use of ACRS for property placed in service after 1986, thus creating the MACRS (modified accelerated cost recovery system). One can consult a periodic tax guide for a presentation of the original and the modified provisions of ACRS.

Still another depreciation method sometimes used is *units of production* (also referred to as *units of utilization*). For example, if a $100,000 asset is expected to provide 10,000 hours of useful service, it might be depreciated on the basis of $10 for each hour it is used.

Exhibit 7–1 illustrates the depreciation computations under the straight-line, declining-balance, sum-of-the-years'-digits, and MACRS methods for an asset with an original cost of $50,000, no salvage value, and an estimated useful life of five years.

Analytical Implications

The analyst should make some judgment of the appropriateness of the depreciation schedule, both as it stands alone and in relation to other companies, if such comparisons are to be made. For example, a company may use an eight-year useful life for equipment that it manufactures and leases to customers, but most other companies in the industry may use a six-year useful life for the same type of equipment, assuming the machinery will be technologically obsolete in six years. In valuing the company using an eight-year depreciation schedule, the analyst may apply a downward adjustment to both the earnings base and the equipment's net remaining book value in order to reflect the relatively inadequate depreciation charges, if such an adjustment would be material. There can be a fairly wide range of normal practices within any industry, and the analyst must be prepared to perform considerable research in order to reach an informed judgment as to the reasonable depreciation life for some types of assets.

Let's say we are valuing a closely held company using an earnings capitalization method and that a 10 times earnings multiple is appropriate based on current capital market multiples of publicly traded guideline companies. Suppose,

---

[5]The MACRS example is quite complex and beyond the scope of this book. The reader may wish is refer to the *U.S. Master Tax Guide*, 79th ed. (Chicago: Commerce Clearing House, 1995), for a comprehensive discussion of MACRS.

Exhibit 7–1

Alternative Depreciation Methods

Data used for the following examples:
Piece of equipment, purchased at beginning of Year 1
Original cost of equipment $50,000
Salvage value   zero
Estimated useful life   5 years

Year	Computation			Annual Depreciation Charge	Balance Accumulated Depreciation	Book Value at Year-End
			Straight-Line Method			
1	1/5 (20%)	x	$50,000	$10,000	$10,000	$40,000
2	20%	x	50,000	10,000	20,000	30,000
3	20%	x	50,000	10,000	30,000	20,000
4	20%	x	50,000	10,000	40,000	10,000
5	20%	x	50,000	10,000	50,000	0
			200% Declining-Balance Method			
1	40%	x	$50,000[a]	$20,000	$20,000	$30,000
2	40%	x	30,000	12,000	32,000	18,000
3	40%	x	18,000	7,200	39,200	10,800
4	40%	x	10,800	4,320	43,520	6,480
5	40%	x	6,480	2,592	46,112	3,888
			Sum-of-the-Years'-Digits Method			
1	5/15	x	$50,000[b]	$16,667	$16,667	$33,333
2	4/15	x	50,000	13,333	30,000	20,000
3	3/15	x	50,000	10,000	40,000	10,000
4	2/15	x	50,000	6,667	46,667	3,333
5	1/15	x	50,000	3,333	50,000	0
			Modified Accelerated Cost Recovery System			
1	20.00%	x	$50,000[c]	$10,000	$10,000	$40,000
2	32.00%	x	50,000	16,000	26,000	24,000
3	19.20%	x	50,000	9,600	35,600	14,400
4	11.52%	x	50,000	5,760	41,360	8,640
5	11.52%	x	50,000	5,760	47,120	2,880
6	5.76%	x	50,000	2,880	50,000	0

[a]Based on double the straight-line rate of 20%, multiplied by the undepreciated book value.
[b]Numerator is the remaining estimated useful life. Denominator is the sum of the years (5 + 4 + 3 + 2 + 1 = 15).
[c]Statutory percentages for MACRS five-year property used for federal income tax purposes.

Note: The above are examples of the more popular depreciation methods now in use. An introductory accounting text can be consulted for a thorough presentation of potential depreciation methods. The modified accelerated cost recovery system (MACRS) was enacted as part of the Economic Recovery Tax Act of 1986 and is used for federal tax purposes. One of the periodic tax guides can be consulted for a thorough presentation of the provisions of the MACRS.

however, the publicly traded guideline companies are reporting straight-line depreciation for financial statement purposes while the subject company is reporting on an accelerated depreciation basis. If the difference is material, then the analyst may want to restate the closely held company's earnings to a straight-line depreciation basis (remembering to also adjust the related income taxes) before applying the publicly traded company multiple so that the earnings to be capitalized will be stated on a comparable basis. Usually a reasonable approximation suffices for this kind of adjustment.

Depletion

Depletion is the process of charging the cost of a natural resource to expense over the time during which it is extracted. It applies to such natural resources as metals and hydrocarbons in the ground and to timber stands. The basic concept of depletion accounting is simple: If a natural resource costs $1 million and 5 percent of it is removed in a year, the depletion expense charge is 5 percent $\times$ $1,000,000 = $50,000. A like amount is credited to the allowance for depletion account on the balance sheet, reducing the net carrying value of the natural resource asset. The IRS also accepts this method of calculating depletion and refers to it as *cost depletion.*

An unrelated method, *percentage depletion,* also appears in the Internal Revenue Code and is defined so as to allow an excess tax deduction in prescribed circumstances. Percentage depletion, as defined by the IRS, has no conceptual basis and is allowed only for calculating a depletion deduction for income tax purposes. The problems of applying depletion are basically ones of measurement. How much of the natural resource is there? What is included in "cost" of a natural resource undergoing continuous development? If depletion is involved, the analyst should ask how it is measured and how thoroughly the company's depletion accounting practices conform to (or depart from) industry norms. Although depletion is relatively easy to define, it is very difficult to measure. Reasonable estimates can be subject to wide variations.

Treatment of Intangibles

It may be necessary to adjust the balance sheet and income statement for the diverse accounting treatments (or lack thereof) for intangible assets.

Leasehold Interests

If a company owns a leasehold at something other than fair market rent, the balance sheet may be adjusted by the analyst to show an asset or liability representing the present value of the difference between the leasehold (contract) rent and the current market rent. One formula for estimating the value of a leasehold interest is as follows:

Formula 7–1

$$PV = \sum_{i=1}^{n} \frac{E}{(1 + k)^i}$$

where:

PV = Present value
E = Expected amount of difference per period between leasehold rent and market rent
n = Number of periods remaining on the lease
k = Discount rate per period at which to capitalize the leasehold interest
i = ith period

For example, suppose a company has 25 months remaining on its lease at $5,000 per month and a new lease on comparable space today would cost $6,500 per month. (Alternatively, the company could sublet the space at $6,500 per month for the 25 months remaining on the lease.) The appropriate yield capitalization rate for a real property interest is 12 percent per annum. The present value of the company's leasehold interest is computed as follows:

Formula 7–2

$$PV = \sum_{i=1}^{25} \frac{\$6{,}500 - \$5{,}000}{\left(1 + \dfrac{.12}{12}\right)^i}$$

$$= \sum_{i=1}^{25} \frac{\$1{,}500}{(1 + .01)^i}$$

An upward adjustment of $33,035 may be made by the analyst to the asset side of the balance sheet in order to recognize the value of the leasehold interest.

Other Intangible Assets

For federal income tax purposes:

> Effective for acquisitions after August 10, 1993, all "Section 197 intangibles" must be amortized over 15 years…Much like MACRS, § 197 forces the taxpayer to use the 15-year period even if the useful life is actually more or less than 15 years. Section 197 intangibles include a number of items such as goodwill, going-concern value, covenants not to compete, information bases such as customer or subscription lists, know-how, customer-based intangibles, governmental licenses and permits (e.g., liquor licenses, taxicab medallions, landing or takeoff rights, regulated airline routes, television or radio licenses), franchises, trademarks, and trade names.[6]

Following are some other examples of intangible assets:

1. Patents.
2. Copyrights.
3. Employment contracts.
4. "Intangible drilling costs" or similar natural resource development costs.
5. Natural resource exploration rights.

Financial accounting principles state that purchased intangibles are to be carried on the books at cost and amortized over their expected remaining useful lives. However, for federal income tax purposes:

> The costs of developing, maintaining, or restoring intangibles which are unidentifiable, have indeterminate lives, or are inherent in a continuing enterprise should be expensed as incurred. By contrast, such intangible assets which are purchased must be carried at cost and amortized over their useful lives and cannot be written down or written off at date of acquisition.[7]

---

[6]James W. Pratt and William N. Kulsrud, eds., *Federal Taxation 1995* (Burr Ridge, IL: Richard D. Irwin, 1995), pp. 9–35.
[7]Ibid., p. 176.

Thus, a company may have spent a great amount of money internally developing valuable intangible assets without showing their value on the balance sheet, while another company may show comparable intangible assets on the balance sheet and be charging amortization expenses as deductions from earnings because the latter company purchased the intangibles instead of developing them internally. If a company's intangible assets have true economic value, that value is likely to be reflected in earnings. In comparing companies with very different accounting practices, one simple way for an analyst to adjust for intangible items on the financial statements is to eliminate intangible assets from the balance sheets and amortization charges from the income statements.

Capitalization versus Expensing of Various Costs

Many cost items fall into a gray area, in which the decision to expense or to capitalize the expenditure is subjective. One such decision is the dividing line between maintenance expenditures, which are expensed, and capital improvements, which are capitalized. For example, many seasonal operations, such as resorts and food processing plants, employ skeletal crews year-round. Their compensation generally is expensed, even though they make improvements during the slow period. Such improvements would probably be capitalized if outside contractors were hired for the same job. Companies that want to report a good bottom line will capitalize items that fall into this gray area, and companies that want to minimize income taxes will elect to expense rather than capitalize whenever possible. In analyzing the quality of the company's earnings and balance sheets, the appraiser should watch for opportunities to select between capitalization and expensing and should ask management about the company's practice of accounting for these items.

Timing of Recognition of Revenues and Expenses

Certain types of companies have considerable latitude in their choice of accounting practices in the timing of recognition of some of their revenues and expenses.

Contract Work

Contract work can be accounted for either on a completed-contract or on a percentage-of-completion basis. The latter is conceptually preferable. However, for financial accounting purposes, it can be implemented only under strict guidelines established by the AICPA.[8] Furthermore, the method is only as good as the estimates of the percentage completed. If the company being valued is in the contracting business, its accounting practices deserve scrutiny. This can be one of the most difficult areas for the outside analyst to evaluate critically. If it is a major issue in the valuation, it may necessitate considerable inquiry into the company's records as well as investigation of industry experience in comparable situations.

---

[8]AICPA *Statement of Position, 81-1.*

Installment Sales

When is a sale a sale? For years many companies recognized considerable profits by selling land on high-face-value contracts with 5 or 10 percent down and the balance over extended periods at low interest. The down payments were not high enough to deter many buyers from defaulting, and even good contracts were worth nowhere near their face value because of the low interest rate. In 1982, the FASB released *Statement of Financial Accounting Standards No. 66*[9] to help prevent such abuses, but there is still some latitude for differences in treatment from one company to another. If installment sales are a significant part of the company's business, the analyst should look into their accounting treatment.

Sales Involving Actual or Contingent Liabilities

Generally, sales involving actual future liabilities are those in which certain services are due to the customer in conjunction with the transaction. Such sales would include service contracts and subscriptions or products with future servicing warranted for some period. The unearned portion of the revenues is usually carried on the balance sheet as a liability account, commonly called deferred income, and then transferred to income as it is earned. Knowing when to recognize such deferred income as current revenue may require considerable judgment. Thus, the analyst should scrutinize the accounting treatment in companies that make sales involving future liabilities.

Sales involving contingent liabilities most commonly are those in which the customer has certain rights to return the product for a refund. If contingent liabilities exist, the analyst should assess the adequacy of their accounting treatment because they will affect the reported earnings and assets.

Prior-Period Adjustments

For a variety of reasons a company may find that its revenues or expenses, or both, were under- or overstated in certain prior accounting periods. The most common reasons are errors in accounting and under- or overpayment of income taxes. The company usually records such an adjustment in the accounting year in which it is discovered by charging or crediting the adjustment to the opening balance of retained earnings. Thus, the adjustment does not affect net income during the current period. In assessing the company's earnings history, the analyst should spread the effect of the adjustment back over the prior periods to which it applies. Sometimes the information needed for accurately allocating the adjustment to the appropriate prior periods is available; in other cases, it is not. Even if a rough estimate of the appropriate prior-period allocation is the best one can make, usually it is better, for analytical purposes, to spread the adjustment on the basis of such an estimate rather than leave it in the period in which it was reported.

---

[9]*FASB Statement of Financial Accounting Standards No. 66*, "Accounting for Sales of Real Estate."

Accounting for Leases

According to the *Statement of Financial Accounting Standards No. 13* as amended and interpreted, leases that are of a financial nature (those that transfer essentially all the benefits and risks incident to ownership of the property) must be capitalized as assets on the lessee's balance sheet. All other leases are accounted for as operating leases; that is, the lease payments are simply expensed as they are incurred. Since there is sometimes room for argument about which method of accounting is appropriate (and because unaudited closely held companies are less prone to strictly adhere to GAAP than are audited public companies), the analyst may want to examine leases. This examination may allow the analyst to judge whether to make any adjustments to the company's accounting treatment for analytical purposes.

Net Operating Loss Carryforwards

An item that may cause controversy in a business valuation is the value of a net operating loss carryforward. The amounts are presented in the footnotes to the balance sheet rather than in the body, because their value is contingent upon generating future profits against which to use them. The ability to generate such profits usually is questionable, since if the company had an unbroken profit history there would be no net operating loss carryforwards.

As far as the income statement is concerned, net operating loss carryforwards properly are classed as extraordinary credits in the periods in which they are used. They should be adjusted out of the earnings base in those periods for analytical purposes. It may be reasonable to spread back the net operating loss carryforward credits that actually were used to offset the losses in the periods in which the net operating loss carryforwards were generated in order to normalize the taxes in the historical loss periods.

Treatment of Interests in Affiliates

For financial accounting purposes, if a company owns 50 to 100 percent of another company's stock, it generally prepares consolidated financial statements. However, in some situations, the parent company properly accounts for the subsidiary by the equity method, defined below. If a company owns 20 to 50 percent of another company's stock, it may account for it by either the equity method or the cost method, depending on whether the parent exerts "significant influence"[10] over the company in which it holds the ownership interest. If a company owns less than 20 percent of another company's stock, it almost always accounts for it by the cost method, although accounting principles leave the door open for using the equity method if a significant degree of control can be demonstrated.

---

[10]*APB Opinion No. 18*, 1971.

Consolidated statements treat the parent and subsidiaries as if they were all one company, with minority interests in subsidiaries, if any, shown as deductions on the financial statements. When subsidiaries are accounted for by the equity method, the parent's share of the subsidiary's earnings or losses (net of intercorporate eliminations, if any) is shown on its income statement, and the carrying value of the interest in the subsidiary is adjusted accordingly on its balance sheet. When subsidiaries are accounted for by the cost method, the parent shows only dividends received on its income statement and continues to carry the investment on its balance sheets at cost. This is true except if it has a permanent impairment in its value, in which case accounting principles state that the investment should be written down. Frequently an analyst would consider an adjustment appropriate on the basis of the valuation, even though the account would not necessarily recognize permanent impairment.

The greatest distortions in the reporting of a parent company's overall results, of course, arise under the cost method, which does not reflect earnings or losses of the subsidiary interest in the parent's financial statement. If a subsidiary's earnings and losses are significant, the analyst may wish to make appropriate adjustments. On the other hand, presenting consolidated statements or accounting using the equity method implies that a dollar of the subsidiary's earnings is worth a dollar to the parent, which is not necessarily true. There may be restrictions on distributions of the subsidiary's earnings due to loan agreements, regulatory authorities, or other reasons. Also, the analyst should ensure that the parent has allowed for any income taxes incident to potential transfer of funds from subsidiary to parent.

Extraordinary or Nonrecurring Items

In analyzing a company's historical earnings as a guide to estimating the company's earnings base, the analyst should make every reasonable effort to distinguish between past earnings that represent ongoing earning power and those that do not. The analyst should adjust the income statements to eliminate the effects of past items that would tend to distort the company's current and future earning power. The implementation of this analysis and adjustments requires some judgment.

Ordinary versus Extraordinary Items

Accounting Principles Board Opinion No. 30, issued in 1973, is very restrictive as to what may be reported as an "extraordinary" gain or loss. *APB Opinion No. 30* states that an item must be *both* unusual in nature and infrequent in occurrence to be categorized as extraordinary. It defines these two requirements as follows:

> *Unusual nature*—the underlying event or transaction should possess a high degree of abnormality and be of a type clearly unrelated to, or only incidentally related to, the ordinary and typical activities of the entity, taking into account the environment in which the entity operates.

> *Infrequency of occurrence*—the underlying event or transaction should be of a type that would not reasonably be expected to recur in the foreseeable future, taking into account the environment in which the entity operates.[11]

---

[11]*APB Opinion No. 30,* 1973.

If an item meets these definitions, it almost certainly cannot be considered representative of ongoing earning power. That does not necessarily mean it should be ignored, however, since an extraordinary item could indicate a risk that the company may face again in the future.

Other Nonrecurring Items

Since the use of the extraordinary designation is so restrictive, many items do not meet the strict definition for accounting purposes but, nevertheless, should be regarded as nonrecurring for analytical purposes. Some examples of such items would be:

1. Gains or losses on the sale of assets, especially when the company clearly lacks a continuing supply of assets available for sale.
2. Gains or losses on disposition of a segment of the business.
3. Insurance proceeds from life insurance on a key person or from some type of property and casualty claim.
4. Proceeds from the settlement of lawsuits.
5. Effects of a strike or of an extended period in which critical raw materials are unavailable.
6. Effects of abnormal price fluctuations, especially those of a very short-term nature that are due to regulatory, industry, or other aberrations that are not likely to be repeated.

It is possible for most of these unusual events to recur, resulting in a greater or smaller effect on the company's financial results. The analyst must carefully consider the likelihood of their recurrence and decide whether and how to adjust the financial statements in order to produce a best estimate of the company's continuing earning power.

Discontinued Operations

Apart from any onetime gain or loss associated with the disposal or discontinuation of an operating segment, the analyst must also consider how to treat the operating earnings or losses generated by that segment before its discontinuation. If the amounts can be distinguished from the results of the ongoing operations, the analyst may decide to adjust the earnings of the ongoing operations by removing the effect of the discontinued operations. The analyst must also consider the effect on the company's overall resources, however, because lost earnings from one source may be replaced by redeploying the resources in other efforts.

Operating versus Nonoperating Items

Depending on the method of valuation, it may be useful to distinguish between operating and nonoperating earnings even if the latter are recurring. The nonoperating item most commonly found on financial statements is income from investments. We suggest elsewhere in this book that it may be appropriate to value certain portions of a company, such as an investment portfolio, with a current value approach and the operating portions of a company primarily on a capitalization of economic income approach. If the analyst values nonoperating assets separately, he must be sure to exclude any income generated or expenses incurred by the nonoperating assets from the earnings base capitalized in the appraisal of the company's operations.

Management Compensation and Perquisites

In closely held companies, compensation and perquisites to owners and managers may be based on the owners' personal desires and the company's ability to pay—rather than on the value of the services these individuals perform. How much to adjust the earnings base to reflect discrepancies between compensation paid and value of service performed depends, in part, upon the purpose and objective of the appraisal.

Owners of successful closely held businesses may distribute what normally would be considered profits in the form of compensation and discretionary expenses. This practice may be an effort to avoid the double taxation that arises from paying a corporate income tax and then paying a personal income tax on what the closely held business pays to the owner in the form of dividends. It is not uncommon to find an owner/manager of a successful closely held company earning a greater amount in annual compensation than the amount an equivalent nonowner employee would earn as compensation.

If the above owner/manager wants to sell the business and retire, the difference between the compensation and the cost to replace the owner's services will become available as a part of pretax profits, and the company's economic earning capacity should be adjusted accordingly in estimating the business's selling price. On the other hand, if the principal owner wants to establish an ESOP but plans to continue working and maintain a similar compensation program for the next 10 years, the analyst probably should not adjust the earnings base for an ESOP valuation, since the level of compensation can be expected to continue.

It is also common for management to be undercompensated because the company lacks the ability to pay. The analyst may assume the underpayment will be corrected when adequate resources are available and should make an appropriate upward adjustment to the management compensation expense in estimating the company's economic earnings capacity.

In general, adjustments for compensation, if appropriate, will be made when valuing controlling interests, because it will be within the power of the controlling interest's owner to change such compensation. Adjustments for compensation may *not* be appropriate when valuing minority interests, because the minority stockholder may receive no benefit from such compensation and lacks the power to change it.

Transactions Involving Company Insiders

The analyst should carefully scrutinize and evaluate any transaction involving owners or management. One of the most common situations is one in which the business leases premises from a person associated with the company. In such cases, the analyst usually should evaluate whether the lease amounts are equivalent to what the company would pay on an arm's-length basis. If not, the appropriate adjustment will depend on the situation, especially the length of time over which the present lease arrangement can be expected to continue and the ability of the stockholder whose stock is being valued to change the arrangement.

Another common occurrence in closely held businesses is loans to or from stockholders or officers. Here the analyst should examine the borrower's ability and intent to repay. If there is little or no likelihood of collecting a receivable from an insider, it should be removed from the balance sheet for analytical purposes. If interest is being accrued and is unlikely to be collected, it should be adjusted out of the earnings used to evaluate the economic earning capacity. It is also common to find a demand note payable in the current liability section of the balance sheet, even though there is no intent to pay the note any time soon or even ever. Interest may or may not be paid on it. For analytical purposes, it may be more appropriate to treat such an item as if it were long-term debt or even subordinated capital of a nature more like equity than debt.

Contingent Assets and Liabilities

One of the most difficult categories of items to treat analytically for valuation purposes is contingencies. The very fact that an item is a contingency defies precise quantification. Nevertheless, the valuation analyst must try to discover contingent assets and liabilities, whether or not they are on the financial statements in some form, and deal with them within the scope of the available information.

The most common categories of contingent assets and liabilities are those that arise from existing or potential litigation. If the outcomes were known, there would be no need for litigation. These situations are so varied that it is virtually impossible to generalize about how to treat them for valuation purposes. The analyst should at least be alert to opportunities to investigate and evaluate contingencies.

Adjustments to Asset Valuations

Marketable Securities

It is generally agreed that marketable securities should be adjusted to fair market value for most asset valuation purposes. However, there is not necessarily total agreement that such an adjustment should be accompanied by a partially offsetting adjustment for the related income tax effects, implied by the unrealized gain or loss to which the adjustment gives rise. The U.S. Tax Court's treatment of this matter has been inconsistent. Adjustments may also affect liability accounts that are carried on the books. There has not been any clarification of this issue since the Tax Reform Act of 1986. That act amended Sections 336 and 337 of the Internal Revenue Code. As a result, the sale of a C corporation's assets followed by a liquidation of the corporation can no longer be accomplished without incurring a corporate-level capital gains tax on the sale of the assets.

Other Assets

The appropriateness of adjusting various other categories of balance sheet assets for business valuation purposes is not unambiguous and depends partly on the situation. Revenue Ruling 59-60 states that for gift and estate tax purposes, values of assets of an investment nature (as opposed to operating assets) should be adjusted. The economic theory apparently is that such assets could be liquidated without impairing the company's operations. Sometimes, however, that will not be true, such as if the assets must be maintained as loan collateral or are necessary for maintaining certain financial ratios that lenders or regulatory agencies require. Other portions of this book, especially on the asset-based valuation approach, discuss the appropriateness of adjusting different categories of asset values under various circumstances.

Computation of Earnings per Share

Weighted-Average Basis

Earnings per share should be computed on a weighted-average basis, that is, the number of shares weighted by the length of time they have been outstanding. Let's say a company had 100,000 shares outstanding at the beginning of the year and issued 30,000 more shares on May 1. The 100,000 shares would be outstanding for four months and the 130,000 shares for eight months, or two-thirds of the year. The weighted-average number of shares outstanding for the year would be computed as follows:

Formula 7–3

$$1/3 \times 100,000 = 33,333$$
$$2/3 \times 130,000 = \underline{86,667}$$

Weighted average
shares outstanding $= 120,000$

If the earnings were $300,000, the proper computation of earnings per share would be $300,000/120,000 = $2.50 per share.

Primary versus Fully Diluted Earnings

In general, primary earnings per share are computed by dividing the earnings available to common equity by the weighted average number of common shares outstanding, plus "dilutive common stock equivalents." The definition and computations can be very technical, and the reader who needs this detail should turn to a technical, accounting-oriented manual, such as Bernstein's.[12]

For analytical purposes, it seems that the earnings per share are best stated on a fully diluted basis, that is, showing the maximum potential dilution that could have resulted had all possible conversions and exercises of options and warrants

---

[12]Bernstein, *Financial Statement Analysis*, pp. 412–19.

been exercised. Naturally, the effect of any interest or dividends paid on the convertible issues would have to be added back to the earnings base. Any conversions that would be antidilutive in their effect should not be included.

Computation of Book Value per Share

Book value per share is based on the number of shares outstanding at the end of the accounting period rather than the weighted average used in computing earnings per share. Also, book value normally is computed without considering possible dilutive effects of conversions, although the analyst may wish to make such a computation for analytical purposes. Thus, the computation of book value per share usually is a simple matter of dividing the total common equity by the number of shares outstanding. (Treasury stock—that is, stock once issued and subsequently reacquired—is *not* included in the number of shares outstanding.)

On most balance sheets, the common equity consists of the common stock account, any paid-in capital in excess of par or stated value, any unrealized currency translation gains or losses, and the accumulated retained earnings or deficit. Of course, if there were any contingent payments on senior securities not presented on the balance sheet, such as preferred dividends in arrears, such amounts would have to be deducted from common equity in computing book value per share. Several investment services, including *S&P Corporation Records* (referenced elsewhere in this book), exclude intangibles in their computed book values per share.

Exhibit 7–2 illustrates the impact on reported earnings of using different methods of accounting for a particular set of operations.

Adjusting the Balance Sheet to Current Values

If it is appropriate to rely heavily on an asset approach in the valuation, the analyst may prepare a pro forma balance sheet with some or all of the line items adjusted to current values. Depending on the valuation criteria to be used, the adjustments may affect only nonoperating assets or may affect all assets (see Chapter 12, "Asset-Based Approach"). The treatment of the income tax effect on the built-in capital gains on the unrealized appreciation remains a matter of some controversy, as noted earlier. Consensus is building among appraisers that the built-in capital gains tax should be recognized one way or another, either in the form of a balance sheet adjustment or some type of a discount.[13]

Summary

Adjustments to the financial statements require both analytical judgment and an understanding of accounting principles. This chapter has presented the categories of financial statement adjustments that are most frequently appropriate for the business valuation. The chapter has presented both the accounting mechanics and

---

[13]For a well-reasoned discussion on this, see John R. Gasiorowski, "Is a Discount for Built-In Capital Gain Tax Justified?" *Business Valuation Review*, June 1993, pp. 76–79.

Exhibit 7–2

Example of the Effect of the Variety of Accounting Principles on Reported Income

Rival Manufacturing Company
Consolidated Statement of Income
for Year Ended 19xx

	Method A	Adjustments Debit		Adjustments Credit	Method B
Net sales	$365,800,000				$365,800,000
Cost of goods sold	(276,976,200)		[1]	1,730,000	
			[2]	88,000	
			[3]	384,200	
			[4]	346,000	
			[5]	78,000	(274,350,000)
Gross profit	88,823,800				91,450,000
Selling, general, & administrative expenses	(51,926,000)		[6]	9,226,000	(42,700,000)
Operating profit	36,897,800				48,750,000
Other income (expense):					
Interest expenses	(3,085,000)	10,000			(3,095,000)
Net income—subsidiaries	1,538,000	78,000			1,460,000
Amortization of goodwill	(390,000)		[7]	220,000	(170,000)
Miscellaneous expenses	(269,000)			40,000	(229,000)
Total other income (expense)	(2,206,000)				(2,034,000)
Income before taxes	34,691,800				46,716,000
Taxes:					
Income taxes—deferred	(556,000)	294,000			(850,000)
Income taxes—current	(13,906,500)	4,733,000			(18,639,500)
Net income	$ 20,229,300				$ 27,226,500
Earnings per share	$6.98				$9.39

Explanations:

[1]	Inventories	Difference: $1,780,000
	A uses last-in, first-out	
	B uses first-in, first-out	
[2]	Administrative costs	Difference: $88,000
	A includes some administrative costs as period costs	
	B includes some administrative costs as inventory costs	
[3]	Depreciation	Difference: $384,200
	A uses sum-of-the-years'-digits method	
	B uses straight-line method	
[4]	Useful lives of assets	Difference: $346,000
	A uses conservative assumption—8 years (average)	
	B uses liberal assumption—14 years (average)	
[5]	Pension costs	Difference: $78,000
	A uses realistic assumptions regarding rates of return on assets and future inflation	
	B uses less realistic assumptions regarding rates of return on assets and future inflation	
[6]	Executive compensation	Difference: $840,000
	A compensates executives with cash bonuses	
	B compensates executives with stock options	
[7]	Goodwill from acquisition	Difference: $220,000
	A amortizes over 10 years	
	B amortizes over 40 years	

SOURCE: Leopold A. Bernstein, *Financial Statement Analysis: Theory, Application, and Interpretation,* 5th ed. (Burr Ridge, IL: Richard D. Irwin, 1993), p. 402.

also some discussion of the judgmental factors that the analyst should consider in analyzing the financial statements for appropriate adjustments. The analyst should be guided by common sense, experience, and an understanding of the company in determining what adjustments should be made to present the statements in the manner most appropriate for valuation purposes. In some cases, there may not be enough information to make certain adjustments or the process may be too time consuming relative to the results achieved. Which adjustments to make should be a matter of professional judgment as to their materiality in the context of the specific valuation objective.

Select Bibliography

Articles

Bergevin, Peter M., and Lisa K. Miller. "Financial Statement Analysis: The Research Process in a Business Library." *Journal of Business & Finance Librarianship* 1, no. 4 (1993), pp. 49–59.

Bernstein, Leopold A. "Accounting for Goodwill: Some Analytical Implications." *Business Credit,* October 1994, pp. 14–15.

Clark, Lynne. "Demystifying Dilution." *CA Magazine,* May 1993, pp. 62–64.

Craig, Thomas, and Timothy Hoerr. "Recasting Income Statements in Valuations of Closely Held Businesses." *Business Valuation Review,* September 1993, pp. 134–39.

Davis, Harry Zvi, and Yoram C. Peles. "Measuring Equilibrating Forces of Financial Ratios." *Accounting Review,* October 1993, pp. 725–47.

Dennis, Michael C. "Understanding Cash Flow Statements." *Business Credit,* January 1994, pp. 40–42.

Evans, Frank C. "Analyzing a Financial Statement." *Management Review,* November 1993, pp. 52–53.

Fridson, Martin S. "Financial Statement Analysis for Perilous Times." *Corporate Cashflow,* October 1992, pp. 46–50.

King, Alfred M. "GAAP Financial Statements: Turning Myth into Reality." *Business Credit,* November/December 1992, pp. 333–35.

Lee, Cheng F., and Chunchi Wu. "Rational Expectations and Financial Ratio Smoothing." *Journal of Accounting, Auditing & Finance,* Spring 1994, pp. 283–306.

Miller, Barry E. "Mastering Cause-and-Effect Ratio Analysis." *Business Credit,* February 1993, pp. 24–27.

Posner, Bruce G. "Minding Your Ratios—Annual Statement Studies/Industry Norms & Key Business Ratios." *Inc.,* November 1993, p. 136.

Schuppe, Walter. "Cash Flow, Liquidity and Solvency—Getting behind the Numbers." *Secured Lender,* July/August 1993, pp. 42–45.

Taub, Maxwell J. "The Treatment of Taxes on the Corporate Adjusted Income Statement." *Business Valuation Review,* December 1994, pp. 163–64.

Turner, Mark A. "Accounting for Inventory in a Reorganization or Liquidation." *Management Accounting,* February 1993, pp. 29–32.

Reference Books

Bailey, Larry P. *Miller GAAS Guide,* 1995. New York: Harcourt Brace Professional Publishing, 1995.

Bandler, James. *How to Use Financial Statements: A Guide to Understanding the Numbers.* Burr Ridge, IL: Irwin Professional Publishing, 1994.

Bernstein, Leopold A. *Analysis of Financial Statements,* 4th ed. Burr Ridge, IL: Irwin Professional Publishing, 1993.

_____. *Financial Statement Analysis: Theory, Application, and Interpretation,* 5th ed. Burr Ridge, IL: Irwin Professional Publishing, 1993.

Costales, S.B. *Guide to Understanding Financial Statements,* 2nd ed. New York: McGraw-Hill, 1993.

Fraser, Lyn M., and Aileen Ormiston. *Understanding Financial Statements,* 4th ed. Englewood Cliffs, NJ: Prentice Hall, 1994.

Fridson, Martin S. *Financial Statement Analysis: A Practitioner's Guide,* 2nd ed. New York: John Wiley & Sons, 1995 (forthcoming).

Stickney, Clyde P. *Financial Statement Analysis: A Strategic Perspective,* 2nd ed. New York: Dryden Press, 1993.

White, Gerald I.; Sondi C. Ashwinpaul; and Dov Fried. *The Analysis and Use of Financial Statements.* New York: John Wiley & Sons, 1993.

Williams, Jan R. *Miller GAAP Guide,* 1995. New York: Harcourt Brace Professional Publishing, 1995.

Chapter 8

Comparative Ratio Analysis

Use and Interpretation of Ratio Analysis
Common-Size Statements
Short-Term Liquidity Measures
    Current Ratio
    Quick (Acid-Test) Ratio
Activity Ratios
    Accounts Receivable Turnover
    Inventory Turnover
    Sales to Net Working Capital
    Sales to Fixed Assets and Total Assets
Risk Analysis
    Business Risk
    Financial Risk
Balance-Sheet Leverage Ratios
    Total Debt to Total Assets
    Equity to Total Assets
    Long-Term Debt to Total Capital
    Equity to Total Capital
    Fixed Assets to Equity
    Debt to Equity
Income Statement Coverage Ratios
    Times Interest Earned
    Coverage of Fixed Charges
Income Statement Profitability Ratios
Return on Investment Ratios
    Return on Equity
    Return on Investment
    Return on Total Assets
Asset Utilization Ratios
Summary

Basic to the analyst's work is the ability to reconstruct the business transactions that are summarized in the financial statements. One can visualize this important skill as the ability to replicate the accountant's work but in reverse order.[1]

Use and Interpretation of Ratio Analysis

When properly employed, analysis of financial statement ratios can be a useful tool in a business valuation. In particular, it can help identify and quantify some of the company's strengths and weaknesses, both on an absolute basis and relative to other companies or industry norms.

The implications gleaned from financial statement analysis may be considered in arriving at the value of the business or business interest in several ways. The most common method of incorporating the results of ratio analysis of financial statements in the final valuation is to make appropriate adjustments to the selection of various fundamental financial multiples (e.g., P/E multiple). To the extent that the ratios indicate sustainable growth, the business should be worth a higher multiple than it would if they did not indicate growth. The higher the degree of risk factors the ratios reveal, the lower should be the business's worth relative to earnings, book value, and other fundamental financial variables.

One use of ratio analysis is to compare a company's figures over time, a method sometimes called *trend analysis*. In this way, one can identify aspects of the business that demonstrate any trends of improvement or deterioration. It can also indicate levels of the different variables that have been normal within the period studied, as well as ranges that reveal high and low points for each variable.

Another way to use ratio analysis is to compare the subject company with other companies, either specific companies or industry averages. Patterns of strength in the subject company relative to guideline companies would tend to support a multiple in the high end of the industry range. Conversely, poor performance ratios relative to similar companies would suggest lower multiples for the subject company.

In comparing ratios from one period to another or from company to company, one should inquire into the extent to which comparative ratios are based on comparable accounting policies. The previous chapter noted that different choices among accounting methods can result in wide variations in reported figures. If one is making a comparative analysis of a company's financial statements over time, one should make an appropriate allowance for any changes in accounting policies. When comparing a company with others in its industry, one should allow for any material differences in accounting policies between the subject company and industry norms.

Another consideration is whether to calculate the ratios before or after any adjustments in the balance sheet or income statement for things such as nonrecurring items, inventory adjustments, or pro forma adjustments. In many cases, these adjustments can significantly affect the magnitude of the company's ratios.

---

[1]Leopold A. Bernstein, *Financial Statement Analysis: Theory, Application, and Interpretation*, 5th ed. (Burr Ridge, IL: Richard D. Irwin, 1993), p. 71.

Two factors should guide the analyst in making this decision. First, if the ratios are to be compared to those of similar publicly traded companies, the analyst should make the same adjustments to the statements of both the subject company and the guideline companies. Second, if the computed ratios are to be compared to industry norms, the analyst should make only those adjustments that are likely to put the subject company on a basis comparable to other companies in the industry. In most cases, however, ratios calculated on adjusted statements will reveal a more accurate picture of the company's financial health.

The relative significance of the various ratios will differ in each valuation. Certain ratios have greater significance for value in particular industries. A ratio may be especially significant in some situations because it departs markedly from industry norms. The analyst must judge each individual case when selecting and evaluating the significance of figures as they apply to the particular situation.

If the analyst performs the ratio computations before making the field trip to interview company personnel, the ratio analysis usually will generate some questions about any departures from industry norms. Of course, if the ratio work follows the field trip, the analyst can cover such questions in later telephone interviews.

This chapter discusses ratios that help evaluate the company's financial position. First, it looks at those that measure short-term liquidity, followed by the commonly used longer-term balance-sheet leverage ratios. Then, the chapter discusses a variety of operating ratios. Each ratio is illustrated with an example from our hypothetical company, ABC Grocery Company. A summary of ABC Grocery Company ratios appears in Exhibit 18–3 in Chapter 18, "A Sample Report." All exhibits referred to in this chapter may be found in Chapter 18.

Common-Size Statements

Usually, the first step in ratio analysis of financial statements is to prepare what are sometimes called *common-size statements*. On these statements, each line item is expressed as a percentage of the total. On the balance sheet, each line item is shown as a percentage of total assets. On the income statement, each item is expressed as a percentage of sales.

Exhibit 18–1 presents five years of balance sheets and Exhibit 18–2 presents five years of income statements for ABC Grocery Company presented on a common-size basis.

Short-Term Liquidity Measures

Generally, *liquidity ratios* demonstrate the company's ability to meet its current obligations. Liquidity ratios can help resolve one of the common controversies in business valuations: whether the company has any assets in excess of those required for its operating needs or, conversely, whether its assets fall short of its needs.

Current Ratio

The most commonly used short-term liquidity ratio is the *current ratio*, which is defined as current assets divided by current liabilities. Its greatest significance is as an indicator of the company's ability to pay its short-term liabilities on time.

The old rule of thumb—that a satisfactory current ratio is 2.0:1—is not widely followed because of vastly different conditions typical in various industries, such as accounts receivable collection periods and inventory turnover periods. As with most ratios, the adequacy of the current ratio for a given company can be better gauged by comparison with industry norms than by comparison with any absolute standard.

Using figures from Exhibit 18–1, the current ratio for ABC Grocery Company for 1993 is calculated as follows:

Formula 8–1

$$\frac{Current\ assets}{Current\ liabilities} = \frac{\$181,174}{\$118,842} - 1.52$$

Quick (Acid-Test) Ratio

The next most commonly used liquidity ratio is the *quick ratio,* which some analysts refer to as the *acid-test ratio.* It is defined as the sum of cash and cash equivalents plus receivables (usually all current assets listed above inventory) divided by current liabilities. For most companies, the only other significant current asset is inventory—usually the slowest of the current assets to be converted to cash. The old rule of thumb is that a satisfactory quick ratio is 1.0:1; but, as with the current ratio, comparison with industry norms is more meaningful in most cases than comparison with an absolute standard.

Using figures from Exhibit 18–1, the quick or acid-test ratio for 1993 is calculated as follows:

Formula 8–2

$$\frac{\begin{array}{l} Cash \\ + \ Cash\ equivalents \\ + \ Investments\ (generally\ marketable\ securities) \\ + \ Receivables \end{array}}{Current\ liabilities} = \frac{\$44,806 + \$1,850 + \$12,679}{\$118,842} = .50$$

It is important to realize that both the current ratio and the quick ratio measure liquidity at a point in time and may not reflect a company's use of short-term credit to finance its short-term liquidity needs. To be most meaningful, the investments that qualify as current assets should be computed at market value.

Activity Ratios

Activity ratios generally measure how efficiently a company uses its assets.

Accounts Receivable Turnover

The *accounts receivable turnover* can be expressed either as the number of times per year the accounts turn over on average or as the average number of days required for collecting accounts. A slow accounts receivable turnover (i.e., long average collection period) not only puts a strain on a company's short-term liquidity, but it also can indicate excessive bad debt losses. On the other hand, a fast accounts receivable turnover (short average collection period) can indicate an overly stringent credit policy that may be limiting sales.

The accounts receivable turnover typically is computed by dividing net credit sales by average accounts receivable. If cash sales (as opposed to credit sales) are insignificant, or if the available figures do not distinguish between cash and credit sales, total sales may be used in the computation. Because of limitations on available data, average accounts receivable may have to be computed by averaging the receivables at the beginning and at the end of the period. The procedure of averaging receivables figures at the end of each quarter or each month gives a more accurate picture, especially if the business is subject to seasonal variations. In any case, if the ratio is for comparative purposes, the amount of data available for the guideline companies may limit the extent of fine-tuning that is possible in computing this ratio.

Using data from Exhibits 18–1 and 18–2, the accounts receivable turnover for ABC Grocery Company for 1993 is computed as follows:

Formula 8–3

$$\frac{1993\ Sales}{(Accounts\ receivable\ end\ 1993 + Account\ receivable\ end\ 1992)/2} = \frac{\$1,628,251}{(\$12,679 + \$10,383)/2} = 141.2$$

The accounts receivable turnover is divided into 365 days to express this variable in terms of average collection period. For ABC Grocery Company, we divide 365 days by the turnover of 141.2 times a year for an average collection period of 2.6 days. Incidentally, some analysts use 360 days instead of 365 days—one of many inconsistencies in valuation practice.

The sales-to-receivables ratio reported in Robert Morris Associates' (RMA) *Annual Statement Studies*[2] is net sales for the year divided by accounts and trade notes receivable *as of the end of the year.* Therefore, if the analyst wishes to compare the subject company with RMA statistics, the ratio for the subject company should be computed in the same manner as the RMA ratio. For ABC Grocery Company, this simplifies the computation to the following:

Formula 8–4

$$\frac{1993\ Sales}{Accounts\ receivable\ end\ 1993} = \frac{\$1,628,251}{\$12,679} = 128.4$$

This level of accounts receivable turnover is equivalent to (365/128.4) = 2.8 average days' collection period. (Of course, this ratio is generally meaningful only for companies with a significant amount of sales on account, not generally for a grocery store.)

Inventory Turnover

The *inventory turnover ratio* typically is computed by dividing the cost of goods sold by the average inventory. As is true of accounts receivable turnover, a slow inventory turnover (long average holding period) not only puts a strain on the

---

[2]*RMA Annual Statement Studies*, 1994 (Philadelphia: Robert Morris Associates, Inc.), published annually. See Exhibit 18–4A for Interpretation of Statement Studies Figures.

company's liquidity but also can indicate obsolete or otherwise undesirable inventory. On the other hand, a fast inventory turnover may indicate that sales are being lost due to insufficient inventory on hand.

Also, as with accounts receivable turnover, the ratio is more meaningful if it can be computed using quarterly or monthly inventory data, especially for companies with seasonal aspects in their operation; however, data limitations more often than not make these computations impractical.

Using data from Exhibits 18–1 and 18–2, the inventory turnover for ABC Grocery Company for 1993 is computed as follows:

Formula 8–5

$$\frac{1993\ Cost\ of\ goods\ sold}{(Inventory\ end\ 1993\ +\ Inventory\ end\ 1992)/2} = \frac{\$1,209,590}{(\$121,259 + \$116,634)/2} = 10.2$$

Like accounts receivable turnover, inventory turnover can be expressed as the average number of days in inventory. For ABC Grocery Company, average days in inventory is calculated by dividing 365 days by an inventory turnover of 10.2 times per year for an average of 35.8 days needed for selling inventory.

RMA Annual Statement Studies[3] reports inventory turnover in the same manner as accounts receivable turnover—dividing cost of sales *by ending inventory*. For making comparisons with RMA data, this ratio should be computed by RMA's formula. For ABC Grocery Company, this ratio is computed as follows:

Formula 8–6

$$\frac{1993\ Cost\ of\ goods\ sold}{Inventory\ end\ 1993} = \frac{\$1,209,590}{\$121,259} = 10.0$$

From an inventory turnover of 10.0 times per year, we calculate an average of 36.5 days in inventory (365/10.0 = 36.5).

Sales to Net Working Capital

Net working capital may be defined as current assets minus current liabilities. If a company's current ratio, accounts receivable collection period, and inventory turnover remain constant as its sales go up, the working capital must rise, because the company will have to carry more receivables and inventory to support the increased sales level. A simple way to compute the sales-to-net-working-capital ratio is to divide sales for the fiscal year just ended by net working capital at the fiscal year-end. This ratio can be useful in comparing the company's own history with those of other companies in the industry.

Using the figures from Exhibits 18–1 and 18–2, the sales-to-net-working-capital ratio for ABC Grocery Company is calculated as follows:

Formula 8–7

$$\frac{Sales}{Current\ assets\ -\ Current\ liabilities} = \frac{\$1,628,251}{\$181,174\ -\ \$118,842} = 26.1$$

---

[3]Ibid. See Exhibit 18–4A for Interpretation of Statement Studies Figures.

A more sophisticated way to compute the ratio would be to use average net working capital rather than ending net working capital as the denominator. Again, using the figures from Exhibits 18–1 and 18–2, sales to average net working capital is calculated as follows:

Formula 8–8

$$\frac{1993\ Sales}{(Working\ capital\ end\ 1993 + Working\ capital\ end\ 1992)/2} = \frac{\$1,628,251}{[(\$181,174 - \$118,842) + (\$187,710 - \$131,325)]/2} = 27.4$$

A high ratio of sales to net working capital results from a favorable turnover of accounts receivable and inventory and indicates efficient use of current assets. However, a high sales-to-net-working-capital ratio also can indicate risk arising from possibly inadequate short-term liquidity. The economy and most industries are subject to some degree of cyclicality in economic activity and liquidity that do not necessarily run exactly in tandem. To assess the company's ability to meet peak needs, the analyst should consider the highest reasonable level of sales that might be anticipated, couple it with the largest accounts receivable and longest inventory turnover periods that might occur, and assess the adequacy of the working capital under that scenario.

Sales to Fixed Assets and Total Assets

Sales-to-fixed-assets and *sales-to-total-assets ratios,* sometimes called a*sset utilization ratios*, measure how efficiently a company's assets are generating sales. They are calculated by dividing sales by either ending assets levels or by an average of the asset levels over the last two years. The results indicate the number of dollars of sales being generated by a dollar of assets. When observed over time, these ratios can indicate changing levels of asset productivity and reveal possible nonoperating assets relative to guideline companies.

Using the figures in Exhibits 18–1 and 18–2, the simplest way to calculate these ratios is as follows:

Formula 8–9

$$\frac{Sales}{Fixed\ assets} = \frac{\$1,628,251}{\$188,778} = 8.6$$

$$\frac{Sales}{Total\ assets} = \frac{\$1,628,251}{\$456,024} = 3.6$$

A more sophisticated approach would be to use the average asset levels over the last two years. In this instance, monthly or quarterly figures are less important, since one would not expect to see seasonality in total or fixed assets levels in the same manner as current assets. Using the figures in Exhibits 18–1 and 18–2, the calculation of these ratios using this method is as follows:

Formula 8–10

$$\frac{1993\ Sales}{(Fixed\ assets\ end\ 1993 + Fixed\ assets\ end\ 1992)/2} = \frac{\$1,628,251}{(\$188,788 + \$147,906)/2} = 9.7$$

$$\frac{1993\ Sales}{(Total\ assets\ end\ 1993 + Total\ assets\ end\ 1992)/2} = \frac{\$1,628,251}{(\$456,024 + \$424,755)/2} = 3.7$$

These ratios are subject to misinterpretation. The age and, thus, depreciated book value of the assets used in these calculations should be considered, particularly when comparing them to those of other, similar companies.

Risk Analysis

At this point it is appropriate to briefly investigate risk analysis, since it is closely related to the leverage ratios and coverage ratios discussed in the following sections. The purpose of risk analysis is to ascertain the uncertainty of the income flows to the company's various capital suppliers. Generally, there are two classes of capital suppliers: (1) those that provide debt capital and receive a fixed return and (2) those that provide equity capital and receive a variable return but can participate in the company's growth through increased future returns. The higher the risk to any category of capital suppliers to the company, the higher the cost of that class of capital.

The capital asset pricing model (CAPM) suggests using the factor called *beta* to measure risk. However, because of a lack of regularly quoted market prices for their stocks, betas for closely held companies cannot be measured directly. One can make a good case for the fact that the nonsystematic portions of risk (those not reflected in beta) are more important for closely held companies than for publicly traded companies. Therefore, the risk analysis portion of financial statement analysis is a very important part of the valuation process.

It is possible to examine the uncertainty of income to the various suppliers of capital by investigating the uncertainty of income to the company. The greater the uncertainty of income to the company, the greater the uncertainty of income to the investor in the company. There are two general classes of risk: business risk and financial risk.

Business Risk

Business risk is the uncertainty of income due largely to two factors: (1) fluctuation in sales and (2) the level of the company's fixed operating costs, which is a function of how the company operates. There are basically two ways to measure a company's business risk.

The first—and simpler—way is to measure the coefficient of variation of earnings, which is equal to the standard deviation of net income divided by the mean of net income:

Formula 8–11

$$Business\ risk = \frac{Standard\ deviation\ of\ net\ income}{Mean\ of\ net\ income}$$

For example, using the figures from Exhibit 18–2, the standard deviation of net income is $5,847 and the mean of net income is $29,664. Substituting into the above equation produces a measure of business risk:

Formula 8–12

$$Business\ risk = \frac{\$5,847}{\$29,664} = .20$$

For many companies, sales volatility is the most important determinant of the fluctuation of net income measured by the standard deviation. Although companies have some control over this variable, sales volatility is, to a considerable extent, a function of the economy's overall health and consumers' willingness to spend their disposable income.

The second method used to measure business risk is the calculation of the degree of operating leverage. *Operating leverage* reflects both the variability of sales and the level of the company's fixed operating costs. These fixed operating costs are a function of the manner in which the company produces its product. The operating earnings of companies with high variable operating costs fluctuate at about the same rate as sales do, whereas those of companies whose production processes entail high fixed operating costs fluctuate more widely than sales.

Operating leverage is measured by the percentage change in operating earnings relative to the percentage change in sales during any given period:

Formula 8–13

$$Degree\ of\ operating\ leverage = \frac{Percentage\ change\ in\ operating\ earnings}{Percentage\ change\ in\ sales}$$

Financial Risk

The second type of risk to investigate is financial risk. Whereas business risk, as measured by operating leverage, reflects the incidence of fixed operating costs and their effect on the income flows to capital suppliers, *financial risk* reflects the incidence of fixed financial costs, or interest, and their effect on the fluctuation of income flows to investors. A company's financial risk occurs in addition to business risk. If there were only business risk, the fluctuation of earnings available to stockholders would be the same as that of operating earnings. However, when fixed financial costs—that is, the interest associated with the use of financial leverage—are introduced, the fluctuation of earnings available to shareholders is greater than that of operating earnings. When the company uses debt to finance some of its activities, the payments to the holders of this debt come before any payments to shareholders. During good times, there is plenty left over for shareholders. In bad times, however, the company's operating earnings are used to pay the interest on the debt and little may be left over for shareholders, increasing the fluctuation in their earnings.

Financial risk is measured in two ways: (1) through calculating the degree of financial leverage and (2) through calculating various leverage ratios. The degree of financial leverage is similar to the degree of operating leverage in that both measure relative volatility. Financial leverage measures the fluctuation of earnings available to the common shareholders relative to the fluctuation of operating earnings (measured as earnings before interest and taxes (EBIT)):

Formula 8–14

$$Degree\ of\ financial\ leverage = \frac{Percentage\ change\ in\ income\ to\ common\ stockholders}{Percentage\ change\ in\ EBIT}$$

For example, using the figures from Exhibit 18–2, the degree of financial leverage for ABC Grocery Company for 1993 is:

Formula 8–15

$$Degree\ of\ financial\ leverage = \frac{(\$34,456 - \$35,728)/\$35,728}{(\$63,442 - \$65,088)/\$65,088} = 1.5$$

This result indicates a 1.0 percent change in operating income is accompanied by approximately a 1.5 percent change in income available to common shareholders.

The higher the degree of financial leverage, the more risk exists for the company's equity investors, because there is a greater possibility that they will receive lower cash flows both today and in the future.

The balance-sheet leverage ratios discussed in the next section are also used to measure financial leverage. They are used in conjunction with the degree of financial leverage to indicate the company's overall financial riskiness.

Balance-Sheet Leverage Ratios

The general purpose of capital structure or *balance-sheet leverage ratios* is to aid in making some quantifiable assessments of the long-term solvency of the business and its ability to deal with financial problems and opportunities as they arise. As with most ratios, such analysis generally is most meaningful when compared with other companies in the same industry. Comparisons within the same company over time also can be useful.

There are numerous variations of balance-sheet leverage ratios, but the following are the ones most frequently used.

Total Debt to Total Assets

Of the various balance-sheet ratios designed to measure the long-term adequacy of the company's capital structure, the *total-debt-to-total-assets* ratio probably is the most popular. It is defined as total debt divided by total assets and measures the total amount of the company's funding provided by all categories of creditors as a percentage of the company's total assets.

Using the figures from Exhibit 18–1, the total-debt-to-total-assets ratio for ABC Grocery Company at the end of 1993 is calculated as follows:

Formula 8–16

$$\frac{Total\ liabilities}{Total\ assets} = \frac{\$214,543}{\$456,024} = .47$$

Equity to Total Assets

The *equity-to-total-assets ratio,* or simply *equity ratio,* is computed by dividing the company's total equity by its total assets. It is equal to 1 minus the total-debt-to-total-assets ratio. Since these two ratios are merely alternative ways of stating the same thing, most analysts would include one or the other, but not both, in the presentation.

Using figures from Exhibit 18–1, the equity-to-total-assets ratio for ABC Grocery Company at the end of 1993 is calculated as follows:

Formula 8–17

$$\frac{Total\ equity}{Total\ assets} = \frac{\$241,480}{\$456,024} = .53$$

Long-Term Debt to Total Capital

Unfortunately, there is considerable ambiguity in the terminology of financial statement analysis, especially in ratio definitions. By *debt ratio,* some analysts mean debt divided by total assets, the ratio discussed above, but others mean long-term debt divided by total capital. Therefore, to avoid misinterpretation, it seems best to avoid the term *debt ratio* and use the more specific term *long-term-debt-to-total-capital ratio.* There is some consensus that *total capital* should be defined as total assets minus current liabilities. However, many analysts include all interest-bearing debt as part of total capital.

Using figures from Exhibit 18–1, and using the first definition above, the long-term-debt-to-total-capital ratio for ABC Grocery Company is computed as follows:

Formula 8–18

$$\frac{Long\text{-}term\ debt}{Total\ assets - Current\ liabilities} = \frac{\$90,993}{\$456,024 - \$118,842} = .27$$

The analyst should check to ensure that any ratios used for comparisons actually are computed by the same definitions, or the comparisons may be misleading. For example, some analysts include deferred taxes in the denominator as part of long-term capital, and others do not.

Equity to Total Capital

The *equity-to-total-capital ratio* is simply 1 minus the long-term-debt-to-total-capital ratio, so there usually is no need to compute both.

Using the figures from Exhibit 18–1, the equity-to-total-capital ratio for ABC Grocery Company at the end of 1993 is calculated as follows:

Formula 8–19

$$\frac{Total\ equity}{Long\text{-}term\ debt + Equity} = \frac{\$241,480}{\$90,993 + \$241,480} = .73$$

Fixed Assets to Equity

One can develop another view of the company's leverage by looking at the proportion of the fixed assets that are financed by equity as opposed to long-term debt. A larger value for the *fixed-assets-to-equity ratio* indicates that much of the company's productive capacity is being financed by borrowed funds rather than owners' funds.

Using the figures from Exhibit 18–1, the fixed-assets-to-equity ratio for ABC Grocery Company in 1993 is calculated as follows:

Formula 8–20

$$\frac{Net\ fixed\ assets}{Total\ equity} = \frac{\$188,778}{\$241,480} = .78$$

Debt to Equity

Sometimes the company's debt is expressed as a ratio to equity rather than to total assets. Again, some analysts prefer to focus on total debt and others just on long-term debt. The *RMA Annual Statement Studies* use *total debt* and only *tangible equity*.[4] In other words, the RMA *debt-to-equity ratio* is computed as follows:

Formula 8–21

$$\frac{Total\ liabilities}{Total\ equity - Intangible\ assets}$$

This ratio is also sometimes expressed in reverse, that is, equity to total debt or equity to long-term debt.

Income Statement Coverage Ratios

In general, *income statement coverage ratios* are designed to measure the margin by which certain of the company's obligations are being met.

Times Interest Earned

The most popular income statement coverage ratio is times interest earned (referred to as the *interest coverage ratio*). It is designed to measure the company's ability to meet interest payments. The *times-interest-earned ratio* is defined as earnings before interest and taxes (EBIT) divided by interest expense.

Using figures from Exhibit 18–2, the times-interest-earned ratio for ABC Grocery Company for 1993 is:

Formula 8–22

$$\frac{Earnings\ before\ interest\ and\ taxes}{Interest\ expense} = \frac{\$52,855 + \$8,774 + \$1,813}{\$8,774 + \$1,813} = 6.0$$

Note that the ABC Grocery Company statements are presented in the conventional manner, showing interest expense as a separate deduction after operating income. Since some closely held companies do not present the statements in this way, the EBIT figure may have to be computed rather than taken directly from a line item on the income statement.

---

[4]Ibid. See Exhibit 18–4A for Interpretation of Statement Studies Figures.

Another way to look at interest coverage is to calculate the ratio based on earnings before depreciation, interest, and taxes (EBDIT) rather than EBIT. EBDIT is basically pretax, pre-interest cash flow that is available to pay the interest expense.

Using figures from Exhibit 18–2, the EBDIT interest coverage ratio for ABC Grocery Company for 1993 is computed as follows:

Formula 8–23

$$\frac{\text{Earnings before depreciation, interest, and taxes}}{\text{Interest expense}} = \frac{\$52,855 + \$8,774 + \$1,813 + \$25,345}{\$8,774 + \$1,813} = 8.4$$

Coverage of Fixed Charges

The *coverage of fixed charges* is a more inclusive ratio than the times-interest-earned ratio in that it includes coverage of items in addition to interest. It is defined as the sum of earnings before interest and taxes and fixed charges divided by fixed charges. This definition leaves open an almost unlimited spectrum of possibilities for determining which fixed charges to include. The most common items are lease payments and required installments of principal payments toward debt retirement.

In the ABC Grocery Company example, the information presented in Exhibits 18–1 and 18–2 is inadequate for computing this ratio. Typically, the analyst must request some schedules or ask questions beyond the normal statement presentations to acquire the information necessary for computing this ratio. Audited financial statements normally contain such information in the footnotes.

Let's assume that the current portion of long-term debt (in this example, notes and mortgage payable, as presented in the current liability section of the balance sheet in Exhibit 18–1) is an annual required reduction of debt principal and that the operating expenses shown in Exhibit 18–1 include \$4,000,000 per year lease payments on the premises the company occupies. The coverage of fixed charges for ABC Grocery Company, then, can be computed as:

Formula 8–24

$$\frac{\text{Earnings before interest and taxes} + \text{Lease payments}}{\text{Interest} + \text{Current portion of long-term debt} + \text{Lease payments}}$$

or

$$\frac{\$52,855 + \$8,774 + \$1,813 + \$4,000}{\$8,774 + \$1,813 + \$1,298 + \$4,000} = 4.2$$

Income Statement Profitability Ratios

The four most commonly used measures of operating performance are *gross profit to sales, operating profit to sales, pretax income to sales,* and *net profit to sales.* Since all are percentages of sales, they may be read directly from the common-size income statements presented in Exhibit 18–2.

Return on Investment Ratios

Analysts will debate whether return on equity, return on investment, or return on assets is the most meaningful measure of investment return. Proponents of return on equity say the return on stockholder investment is what counts, and most adhere to this argument. Return on investment recognizes both the shareholders and the debtholders and can be quite important if the company is contemplating a change in the capital structure. However, proponents of return on assets say management should be measured by the return on total assets utilized, without regard for the company's capital structure, which can have a considerable bearing on return on equity if return on assets is held constant. Each measure is useful for its own purpose.

Return on Equity

Return on equity usually means return on common equity capital. If a company has preferred stock outstanding, the analyst might consider computing return on total equity and return on common equity, since both can be useful measures. If comparing one or more ratios of return on equity for other companies with preferred stock outstanding, the analyst should ensure that the ratios are being computed on the same basis for the subject company as for the comparative companies.

Unless otherwise specified, return on equity means *after* taxes. Once in a while, someone—perhaps a broker trying to sell a business—quotes return on equity computed on a pretax basis. This definition can be very misleading, since *income taxes are a very real cost,* and the investor's return is what remains after corporate taxes. In fact, if the computation is being made for a subchapter S corporation, a partnership, or a sole proprietorship, many analysts recommend that the taxes the company would pay if it were a regular corporation be deducted from the net income before making the calculations. Sometimes there are legitimate reasons for comparing companies' returns on equity on a pretax basis, but when doing so it should be clearly specified—and recognized by the parties using the data—that it is a departure from the conventional meaning and computation of return on equity. Perhaps the best way to specify this is to use the expression *pretax return on equity* when that is what is being presented.

One other issue to be resolved in the return-on-equity analysis is whether the selected equity base is the one at the beginning of the period, the end of the period, or the average for the period. There is consensus among analysts that the average equity provides the basis for the most meaningful analysis. However, an emerging group believes that beginning equity is the most important measure, since that is the equity *base* on which the earnings are generated. Still, the most commonly used method is to divide the earnings for the year by the average of the beginning and ending equity. If adequate information is available, return on equity can be further fine-tuned by averaging quarterly or monthly equity figures.

Since return on equity is a percentage, the result should be the same whether the computations are made on a total-company basis or on a per share basis, at least if there is no dilution. If a weighted average number of shares has been used in the per share earnings computation, the calculation will work out if the average equity base is weighted in the same manner.

Using the data from Exhibits 18–1 and 18–2, the return on equity for ABC Grocery Company for 1993 is calculated as follows:

Formula 8–25

$$\frac{Net\ income}{Average\ common\ stockholders'\ equity} = \frac{\$34,356}{(\$241,480 + \$207,124)/2} = 15.3\%$$

Using beginning equity yields the following:

Formula 8–26

$$\frac{Net\ income\ for\ 1993}{Stockholders'\ equity\ for\ 1992} = \frac{\$34,356}{\$207,124} = 16.6\%$$

On a per share basis, with 1,431,770 shares outstanding for ABC Grocery Company, the computation is as follows:

Formula 8–27

$$\frac{Earnings\ per\ share}{Average\ book\ value\ per\ share} = \frac{\$22.24}{(\$156.33 + \$134.09)/2} = 15.3\%$$

Another way to look at the above ratio (that is, net income divided by equity), and perhaps to understand and appreciate it more fully, is in terms of the components that make up return on equity. These components of return on equity are:

$$ROE = Profitability \times Turnover \times Leverage$$

Stated more completely:

Formula 8–28

$$\frac{Net\ income}{Equity} = \frac{Net\ income}{Sales} \times \frac{Sales}{Assets} \times \frac{Assets}{Equity}$$

Formula 8–28 above is commonly referred to as the Du Pont formula, since the Du Pont Company was widely known to use that formula as an integral part of its financial planning and control.

Return on Investment

The computations for *return on investment,* sometimes called *return on total capital,* are similar to those for return on equity. One key difference is that interest should be added back to net income to reflect the return to *both* equity *and* debt. Whether interest should be adjusted for taxes depends on the information to be conveyed in the ratio presentation. One may adjust interest for taxes by multiplying interest by 1 minus the tax rate, yielding a product that is the equivalent of computing the ratio on a debt-free basis, as if all of the investment were in the form of equity. If, on the other hand, there is no adjustment for taxes, the ratio will reflect the return under the company's existing capital structure. Again, the issue of average investment versus beginning investment must be recognized. In addition, the debt portion of the investment figure in the denominator could be long-term debt plus interest-bearing short-term debt, since the interest expense in the numerator is *total* interest expense.

Looking at it all four ways and using figures from Exhibits 18–1 and 18–2, the computation of return on investment for ABC Grocery Company for 1993 is as follows:

Formula 8–29

$$\frac{Net\ income + Interest\ (1 - Tax\ rate)}{\left[\left(\begin{array}{c}Beginning\ stockholders'\ equity \\ + Long\text{-}term\ debt\end{array}\right) + \left(\begin{array}{c}Ending\ stockholders'\ equity \\ + Long\text{-}term\ debt\end{array}\right)\right]/2}$$

$$\frac{\$34,356 + (\$1,813 + \$8,774)\,(1 - .35)}{[(\$207,124 + \$82,280) + (\$241,480 + \$90,993)]/2} = 13.3\%$$

or

$$\frac{Net\ income + Interest}{\left[\left(\begin{array}{c}Beginning\ stockholders'\ equity \\ + Long\text{-}term\ debt\end{array}\right) + \left(\begin{array}{c}Ending\ stockholders'\ equity \\ + Long\text{-}term\ debt\end{array}\right)\right]/2}$$

$$\frac{\$34,356 + \$1,813 + \$8,774}{[(\$207,124 + \$82,280) + (\$241,480 + \$90,993)]/2} = 14.5\%$$

Based on beginning investment, return on investment becomes:

Formula 8–30

$$\frac{Net\ income + Interest\ (1 - Tax\ rate)}{\begin{array}{c}Beginning\ stockholders'\ equity \\ + Long\text{-}term\ debt\end{array}} = \frac{\$34,356 + (\$1,813 + \$8,774)(1 - .35)}{\$207,124 + \$82,280} = 14.2\%$$

or

$$\frac{Net\ income + Interest}{Beginning\ stockholders'\ equity + Long\text{-}term\ debt} = \frac{\$34,356 + \$1,813 + \$8,774}{\$207,124 + \$82,280} = 15.5\%$$

It is important to note that conceptually the amount of interest expense that should be added back is only the interest expense that relates to the company's long-term debt, since that is the figure in the denominator. However, in practice, while one may be able to get this information for the subject company, the data for the guideline companies will rarely be available. Another alternative is to use total interest expense in the numerator and total interest-bearing debt in the denominator. The problem with this, however, is that often the fiscal year-end amount of short-term interest-bearing debt does not relate to the amount of interest expense that was paid over the year on the average amount of short-term interest-bearing debt utilized. One would have to find out what the average amount of short-term interest-bearing debt was over the course of the year.

Due to these complexities, for practical purposes it is acceptable to use the ratio as we have defined it. However, the analyst is advised to research both the subject and guideline companies' use of short-term debt to determine whether to adjust this ratio to include all interest-bearing debt.

The analyst should be aware of two other potential problems with Formula 8–30. First, the comparisons among rates of return may not be meaningful when comparing companies with dissimilar capital structures. Second, the rates of return can be misleading in the cases of many (especially smaller) companies that show on their balance sheet short-term liabilities that actually are being used as long-term financing.

Return on Total Assets

The computations for *return on total assets* are similar to those for return on investment, with the same issues of tax adjustments and beginning or average assets. A realistic analysis of return on total assets should not be influenced by how the company chooses to use debt in its capital structure.

Again, using figures from Exhibits 18–1 and 18–2, the computation of return on assets for ABC Grocery Company for 1993 is as follows:

Formula 8–31

$$\frac{Net\ income\ +\ Interest\ (1\ -\ Tax\ rate)}{(Beginning\ total\ assets\ +\ Ending\ total\ assets)/2} = \frac{\$34,356 + (\$1,813 + \$8,774)(1 - .35)}{(\$424,755 + \$456,024)/2} = 9.4\%$$

or

$$\frac{Net\ income\ +\ Interest}{(Beginning\ total\ assets\ +\ Ending\ total\ assets)/2} = \frac{\$34,356 + \$1,813 + \$8,774}{(\$424,755 + \$456,024)/2} = 10.2\%$$

Based on beginning assets, the ratio becomes:

Formula 8–32

$$\frac{Net\ income\ +\ Interest\ (1 - Tax\ rate)}{Beginning\ total\ assets} = \frac{\$34,356 + (\$1,813 + \$8,774)(1 - .35)}{\$424,755} = 9.7\%$$

or

$$\frac{Net\ income\ +\ Interest}{Beginning\ total\ assets} = \frac{\$34,356 + \$1,813 + \$8,774}{\$424,755} = 10.6\%$$

One must be careful when comparing these ratios to published ratios to determine whether the base is an average or whether beginning or ending figures are being used. The return on investment ratios shown in Exhibit 18–3 are calculated using average equity and total assets.

Asset Utilization Ratios

Asset utilization ratios indicate how efficiently the company is employing its assets in its operations. These are almost always based on average asset levels, unless a study used for industry comparative ratio analysis calculates them using year-ending asset figures. This series of ratios relates sales to each of several assets or asset groups. Ratios sometimes computed include sales to cash, to accounts receivable, to inventories, to working capital, to fixed assets, to other assets, and to total assets (discussed under "Activity Ratios").

Summary

Comparative ratio analysis helps identify and quantify some of the company's strengths and weaknesses, both on an absolute basis and relative to guideline companies or industry norms.

The analyst should allow for changes in the subject company's accounting policies during the period under analysis and differences in accounting policies between the subject company and the guideline companies or industry norms. The analyst should also be aware of off-balance-sheet financing that may not be reflected in the ratio analysis.

Analysis of the various ratios will help the analyst to evaluate the subject company's financial position and to understand the risks it may be facing. The relative significance of the various ratios will differ in each valuation.

A further discussion of the valuation implications of these comparative ratios is included in Chapter 18, "A Sample Report."

Part III

Reaching the Value Conclusion

Chapter 9

Income Approach: Discounted Economic Income Methods

THEORY OF VALUATION
...the value of an asset is the present value of the expected returns. Specifically, you expect an asset to provide a stream of returns during the period of time that you own it. To convert this stream of returns to a value for the security you must discount this stream at your required rate of return. This process of valuation requires estimates of (1) the stream of expected returns, and (2) the required rate of return on the investment.[1]

Value today always equals future cash flow discounted at the opportunity cost of capital.[2]

This chapter presents the most commonly accepted methods of discounting or capitalizing expected economic income. It is the very heart of valuation.

This chapter necessarily has many algebraic formulas and quantitative examples. We have tried to present each formula clearly and precisely, with each variable defined in understandable terms, and with examples. In doing so, we hope to make a somewhat technical topic clear and understandable not only to appraisers, but also to accountants, attorneys, business owners, and other appraisal users who do not necessarily have a finance background.

We will touch briefly on some slightly complex economic concepts, in particular the capital asset pricing model and, to a lesser extent, arbitrage pricing theory. These economic concepts are crucial to modern financial theory, and one needs at least a rudimentary understanding of them in order to fully understand what makes business enterprise values and business interest values what they are. Again, we present these concepts in basic terms that do not require an extensive economics background to understand.

Introduction: Theoretical and Practical Soundness of Approach

What is someone who buys a company or an interest in a company really buying? Management? Markets? Technological skills? Products? Although each of these factors may be involved in the investment decision, what is actually being bought is a stream of prospective economic income.

It may be worthwhile to define the term economic income, as we will use it in this discussion of the income approach to valuation. As the term implies, we define income according to the economists' definition and not the accountants' definition. In the landmark text *Economics,* Paul D. Samuelson and William D. Nordhaus define income as: "The flow of wages, interest, payments, dividends, and other receipts accruing to an individual or nation during a period of time (usually a year)."[3]

For purposes of this discussion of the income approach, we will use a similarly broad definition of economic income. We define economic income as any inflow into an economic unit in exchange for goods, services, or capital.

[1]Frank K. Reilly, *Investment Analysis and Portfolio Management,* 4th ed. (Fort Worth, TX: The Dryden Press, 1994), pp. 380–81.

[2]Richard A. Brealey and Stewart C. Myers, *Principles of Corporate Finance,* 4th ed. (New York: McGraw-Hill, Inc., 1991), p. 63.

[3]Paul A. Samuelson and William D. Nordhaus, *Economics,* 14th ed. (New York: McGraw-Hill, Inc., 1992), p. 738.

In this definition, the economic unit can be either a business entity (e.g., corporation, partnership, professional practice) or an individual (e.g., an individual investor). And, the inflow can be gross (before recognition of any outflows) or net (after recognition of certain outflows). So, from the perspective of a business entity, economic income could mean gross revenues, gross profits, net operating profits, net income before tax, net income after tax, operating cash flow, net cash flow before tax, net cash flow after tax, or net cash flow available for distribution to owners (e.g., dividends). Any of these measures of economic income could be converted into a value indication, based upon a capitalization (or discount) rate appropriate to that measure of economic income. Of course, different capitalization (or discount) rates would be appropriate to each different measure of economic income.

In theory, the value of a business or an interest in a business depends on the future benefits that will accrue to it, with the value of the future economic benefits discounted back to a present value at some appropriate discount rate. In other words, the basic concept of the income approach is to project the future economic income associated with the investment and to discount the projected income stream to a present value at a discount rate appropriate for the expected risk of the prospective economic income stream.

The income approach is based upon the economic principle of anticipation (sometimes also called the principle of expectation). In this approach, the value of the subject investment (i.e., the subject business interest) is the present value of the economic income expected to be generated by the investment. As the name of this economic principle implies, the investor "anticipates" the "expected" economic income to be earned from the investment. This expectation of prospective economic income is converted to a present worth—that is, the indicated value of the subject business interest.

For valuation purposes the measurement of economic income to be analyzed can be defined in several different ways, as discussed in various sections of the chapter. Some of the different measurements of economic income that are commonly analyzed in this approach include:

1. Payouts (e.g., dividends, interest, security sale proceeds, partnership withdrawals).
2. Cash flow (often measured as net cash flow).
3. Some measure of accounting earnings (often net income or net operating income).

In any event, it is essential that the economic income stream that is projected be clearly defined and that a discount rate appropriate for that definition of economic income be used in the analysis.

The discounted economic income method of the income approach to valuation is often used in the context of merger and acquisition analysis. In these instances, this method is not always used to estimate a fair market value conclusion. This is because the projections and the discount rate used in a merger and acquisition analysis may be specific to the individual acquirer, as suggested by the first quote above. Accordingly, such an analysis would estimate investment value, use value, acquisition value, or some other buyer-specific standard of value.

However, the same discounted economic income analysis could be performed—but with market-derived projections of economic income and with a market-derived discount rate, as suggested by the second quote above—in order to estimate the fair market value of the subject business interest.

The discounted economic income method may also be used to appraise a wide range of appraisal subjects. For example, this method may be used in the valuation of both controlling and minority interests, provided that: (1) the prospective economic income stream is consistent with the business interest subject to appraisal, and (2) the discount rate is appropriate for that measure of economic income and for that particular appraisal subject.

Since the value of a business interest depends on its prospective economic income, the correct application of this approach requires a projection of the economic income that is relevant to the appraisal subject, be that dividends, cash flow, accounting earnings, or some other measure of economic income. The discounted economic income method is practical only to the extent that the projections used are reasonable to the decision maker for whom the valuation is being prepared. Without supportable projections, the discounted economic income method can convey an aura of precision that is not justified.

Such economic income projections may be difficult to make—and even more difficult to get two or more parties with different investment perspectives and transaction expectations to agree on. Therefore, appraisers have developed various other approaches to valuation, based on both historical and prospective economic data. These approaches are discussed in subsequent chapters.

However, the preparer or user of a business valuation should keep in mind that the value of an investment is a function of what it will do for an owner in the future, not what it has done for an owner in the past. Therefore, *regardless of what valuation approach is used, in order for it to make rational economic sense from a financial view, the results should be compatible with what would result if a well-supported discounted economic income analysis were carried out.*

The Basic Discounted Economic Income Framework

The basic arithmetic of the present value calculation is presented as Exhibit 9–1.

The basic formula for valuation using the discounted economic income approach is as follows:

Formula 9–1

$$PV = \sum_{i=1}^{n} \frac{E_i}{(1+k)^i}$$

where:

PV = Present value

Σ = Sum of

n = The last period for which economic income is expected; n may equal infinity (i.e., ∞) if the economic income is expected to continue in perpetuity

E_i = Expected economic income in the ith period in the future

k = Discount rate (the cost of capital, e.g., the expected rate of return available in the market for other investments of comparable risk and other investment characteristics)

i = The period (usually stated as a number of years) in the future in which the prospective economic income is expected to be received

Exhibit 9–1

Arithmetic of Present Value: Discounting versus Compounding

Discounting is the mathematical opposite of compounding. In compounding, we ask the question: "If I invest a dollar today at x percent interest for a period of x years, how much will it be worth at the end of x years?" In discounting, we ask the opposite question: "In order to receive a dollar x years in the future, based on x percent assumed compound rate of return, how much do I have to invest today?"

Compounding*

The formula to estimate the future value of an amount invested at annually compounded interest for a certain number of years is as follows:

$$FV = PV(1 + k)^i$$

where:

$$
\begin{aligned}
FV &= \text{Future value} \\
PV &= \text{Present value} \\
k &= \text{Interest rate} \\
i &= i\text{th year (the number of years into the future that the principal plus the compound rate of return will be received)}
\end{aligned}
$$

Example

Assume that we invest $1,000 for 3 years at a 10% interest rate. Substituting in the above formula gives us the following:

$$
\begin{aligned}
FV &= \$1,000(1 + .10)^3 \\
&= \$1,000(1.10 \times 1.10 \times 1.10) \\
&= \$1,000(1.331) \\
&= \$1,331
\end{aligned}
$$

Discounting

Start with the formula for compounding:

$$FV = PV(1 + k)^i$$

As we learned in basic algebra, we can divide both sides of an equation by the same factor:

$$\frac{FV}{(1 + k)^i} = \frac{PV(1 + k)^i}{(1 + k)^i}$$

Also, if the same factor appears in both the numerator and the denominator of an expression, we can cancel it out:

$$\frac{FV}{(1 + k)^i} = \frac{PV\cancel{(1 + k)^i}}{\cancel{(1 + k)^i}}$$

And, then, we have the formula for discounting from a future value to a present value! Since it is customary to put the dependent variable (i.e., the value we are solving for) on the left side of the equation, the basic formula for discounting is written as follows:

$$PV = \frac{FV}{(1 + k)^i}$$

Example

If we can earn 10% annually compounded interest, how much do we have to invest today to receive a lump-sum payment of $1,331 exactly 3 years from now? Substituting in the above formula gives us the following:

$$
\begin{aligned}
PV &= \frac{\$1,331}{(1 + .10)^3} \\[6pt]
&= \frac{\$1,331}{1.331} \\[6pt]
&= \$1,000
\end{aligned}
$$

Discounting a Stream of Prospective Economic Income

Discounting a stream of prospective economic income simply involves discounting each individual future economic income receipt and adding up the present values of each receipt to calculate a total present value for the stream of economic income. The formula for discounting a stream of economic income may be written as follows:

Exhibit 9–1 (concluded)

$$PV = \sum \frac{E_i}{(1 + k)^i}$$

where:

E_i = Expected economic income in the ith year

All other variables as defined on previous page

The capital Greek letter sigma (Σ) stands for "sum of." It means to add up each of the components that follow, in this case the present values of each of the prospective economic income amounts.

Example

Assume that a bond pays $100 interest at the end of each year for 3 years, and pays $1,000 principal at the bond's maturity date at the end of 3 years. If the market requires a 10% total yield rate of return on bonds of this quality and maturity at this time, what is the present value of the bond? Substituting in the above formula gives us the following:

$$PV = \frac{\$100}{(1 + .10)} + \frac{\$100}{(1 + .10)^2} + \frac{\$100}{(1 + .10)^3} + \frac{\$1,000}{(1 + .10)^3}$$

$$PV = \frac{\$100}{1.10} + \frac{\$100}{(1.10 \times 1.10)} + \frac{\$100}{(1.10 \times 1.10 \times 1.10)} + \frac{\$1,000}{(1.10 \times 1.10 \times 1.10)}$$

$$PV = \frac{\$100}{1.10} + \frac{\$100}{1.21} + \frac{\$100}{1.331} + \frac{\$1,000}{1.331}$$

$$= \$90.91 + \$82.64 + \$75.13 + \$751.32$$

$$= \$1,000$$

It readily can be seen from the above that if the discount rate (the yield or rate of return required to attract capital to the investment) increases, the present value decreases, and vice versa.

*In all the examples in this book, for simplicity, it is assumed that compounding is on an annual basis and that all returns are received at the end of each year. With minor adjustments in the arithmetic, assumptions of semiannual, quarterly, monthly, daily, or even continuous compounding can be accommodated. It can also be assumed that proceeds are received at some time other than the end of the year. For example, proceeds received at the middle of the year are accommodated by the "mid-year discounting convention," which also often is used when proceeds are expected to be received more or less continuously throughout the year.

This basic formula can be expanded very simply as follows:

Formula 9–2

$$PV = \frac{E_1}{(1+k)} + \frac{E_2}{(1+k)^2} + \frac{E_3}{(1+k)^3} + \dots + \frac{E_n}{(1+k)^n}$$

where:

$E_{1,2,3,etc.}$ = Expected economic income in the 1st, 2nd, 3rd periods, and so on

E_n = Expected economic income in the nth or last period in which an element of income is expected. (An investment with an expected perpetual life can be assumed to terminate at some point, since income in the remotely distant future will have only negligible impact when discounted to present value.)

k = Discount rate

This basic valuation model, which is central to the income approach to valuation, has only two variables:

1. The amount of the expected prospective economic income in each period.
2. The required rate of return (or yield rate) by which each of the expected prospective economic income receipts should be discounted.

Before attempting to quantify the numbers to go into the above model, it is first necessary to more specifically define each of the variables.

The Numerator: Expected Prospective Economic Income

Income Associated with What? The answer to this question depends on the answer to one of the questions in Chapter 2, "What exactly are we valuing?" Usually the focus is on the amount of economic income available to one of the following categories of investments:

1. One class of common equity.
2. All classes of common equity.
3. All classes of equity.
4. All equity and all long-term debt.
5. All equity and all interest-bearing debt.
6. All equity and all debt (i.e., total business assets).

When debt is included in what is being valued, the result is often referred to either as "the value of the business entity," "the business enterprise value," "the total capital value," or "market value of invested capital" (MVIC). For more discussion of defining the capital structure when debt is included, see the subsequent section on defining the capital structure under the discussion of discounting returns to overall capital.

Of course, we are sometimes interested in projecting economic income associated with other types of investments, such as: asset/property investments (e.g., income-producing real estate), security investments (e.g., minority interests in shares of stocks or in bonds), or intangible asset investments (e.g., patents, trademarks, or copyrights).

Obviously, the economic income to be measured should be that level of income that is associated with—and available to—whatever business or investment interest is being valued.

Definition of Economic Income Measured. Depending partly on the answer to the question, "Income associated with what?" there can be many definitions of economic income to be estimated. Some of the most common measurements of economic income include the following:

1. Dividends (or other payouts to security holders, such as partnership withdrawals).
2. Net cash flow to equity (NCF_e in the notation used in this book):

Formula 9–3

    Net income (after taxes)
 + Noncash charges (e.g., depreciation, amortization, deferred taxes)
 − Capital expenditures (the net changes in fixed and other noncurrent assets)*

    − Changes in net working capital*
    + Net changes in long-term debt*
    = Net cash flow to equity

> *Assumes that the amounts are the levels necessary to support projected business operations. If there are preferred dividends, they would have to be subtracted if the objective is to estimate net cash flow available to common equity holders. If one wants to project net cash flow available to all equity and interest-bearing debt holders, then interest needs to be added to the income measurement, but changes in long-term debt need not be considered (see following point 3).

3. Net cash flow to overall invested capital (NCF_f in the notation used in this book):[4]

Formula 9–4

    Net income (after taxes) available to common shareholders
    + Noncash charges
    − Capital expenditures*
    − Changes in working capital*
    + Interest expense, net of the tax effect (interest expense $\times$ [1 − tax rate])
    + Preferred dividends, if any
    = Net cash flow to overall invested capital

> *Assumes that the amounts are the levels necessary to support projected business operations.

4. Net income (after taxes).

It is noteworthy that the capital expenditures, net changes in working capital, and net changes in long-term debt components to net cash flow may be negative. In other words, if there are not reductions (sales) of capital assets, decreases in net working capital, or decreases in long-term debt, these components would represent negative numbers. And, the subtraction of a negative number (e.g., a decrease in net working capital) would represent an increment—instead of a decrement—to net cash flow.

It is also noteworthy that the measures of cash flow defined above (i.e., to equity and to overall capital) are a different measure of cash flow than that reported in a Statement of Cash Flow prepared in accordance with generally accepted accounting principles.

Of course, many other variables representing some relevant measurement of economic income may be estimated. These might include, for example, pretax income, net operating income, or some other measure of accounting income. However, for many of these other economic income measures, it may be difficult, if not impossible, to develop an empirically supportable discount rate.

The Denominator: The Discount Rate

Definition of a Discount Rate. In economic terms, a present value discount rate is an "opportunity cost," that is, the expected rate of return (or yield) that an investor would have to give up by investing in the subject investment—instead of in available alternative investments that are comparable in terms of risk and other investment characteristics.

---

[4]An alternative formula for net cash flow to overall invested capital is the following:

    Earnings before interest and taxes
    − Taxes on EBIT at effective tax rate
    + Noncash charges
    − Capital expenditures
    − Changes in working capital
    = Net cash flow to overall invested capital

The discount rate is the cost of capital for that particular category of investment. The discount rate is determined by market conditions as of the valuation date as they apply to the specific characteristics of the subject contemplated investment.[5]

Matching the Discount Rate with the Definition of the Prospective Economic Income. The choice of the discount rate is driven by the definition of economic income used in the numerator. The discount rate used in the analysis must be appropriate for the definition of the economic income in the numerator and for the class of capital (or other type of investment) to which it applies.

As a practical matter, the choice of economic income used in the numerator may be constrained by the ability, or lack of it, to develop an empirically supportable discount rate. For this reason, we sometimes find definitions of economic income used in market approach methods, where a market-derived capitalization rate is available, that are not used in discounting methods. (Later in this chapter, we explain the relationship between discount rates and capitalization rates.)

In any case, we cannot overemphasize how important it is that *the discount rate developed must be matched conceptually and empirically to the definition of economic income being discounted.* Also, the discount rate must reflect the degree of risk, discussed in some detail later.

Constant or Variable Discount Rate? A question that sometimes arises is whether the discount rate should remain constant over the projection period or whether it should vary with time. The argument for varying it is that the investment risk may be greater—or less—later in the projection period than it is at the beginning of the projection period. This is a highly judgmental (and usually quite subjective) matter. Most commonly, analysts use a constant discount rate—reflecting the average amount of investment risk—throughout the projection period.

Relationship between Discount Rates and Capitalization Rates

A *discount rate* converts *all* of the expected future return on investment (however defined) to an indicated present value.

In contrast to the more comprehensive method of discounting *all* of the expected returns, a *capitalization rate* converts *only a single return flow number* to an indicated present value.

Discount rate	A rate of return used to convert a monetary sum, payable or receivable in the future, into a present value.
Capitalization rate	Any divisor (usually expressed as a percentage) that is used to convert income into value.[6]

---

[5]To the extent that a particular buyer or seller chooses to use a discounted economic income analysis using a discount rate that would deviate from the market consensus rate as of the valuation date, the resulting indicated value would depart from the strict standard of *fair market value* and, likely, approximate *investment value,* as defined in Chapter 2.

[6]American Society of Appraisers, *Business Valuation Standards, Definitions* (Herndon, VA: American Society of Appraisers, 1994).

Discounting, for which a *discount rate* is used, is a process applied to one or a series of specific expected income amounts as of a specified time or times in the future to convert those expected amounts to an estimate of present value. The discount rate is applied to all the expected future economic income. Therefore, any expected future growth in returns is captured in the numerator of the discounted economic income formula.

Capitalizing, for which a *capitalization rate* is used, is a process applied to an amount representing some measure of economic income for some single period to convert that economic income amount to an estimate of present value. Capitalization procedures can be used with expected, current, historical, or "normalized" (or "stabilized") measures of economic income. If growth is expected from the base level of economic income being capitalized, then that expected growth is reflected in the capitalization rate.

This leads to the logical answer to the difference between the discount rate and the cap rate: *For an investment with perpetual life, the difference between the discount rate and the cap rate is the annually compounded percentage rate of growth or decline in perpetuity in the economic income variable being discounted or capitalized.*

The above relationship can be expressed as a formula very simply:

Formula 9–5

$$c = k - g$$

where:

c = Capitalization rate (a rate to be used as a divisor to convert a return flow variable, such as net cash flow, to an indication of value)

k = Discount rate

g = Annually compounded rate of growth in the economic income variable being capitalized over the life of the investment (if there is an expected rate of decline, the g is negative, so the effect is that the rate of decline is *added* to the discount rate to get the capitalization rate)

The Perpetual Economic Income Stream Model

Consider the case of a preferred stock that has no maturity and no call provision (i.e., no expected redemption), paying a fixed dividend in perpetuity. The basic discounted economic income formula would value this preferred stock as follows:

Formula 9–6

$$PV = \sum_{i=1}^{n} \frac{E_i}{(1 + k_p)^i}$$

where:

k_p = Cost of capital of the subject preferred stock

All other variables are the same as in Formula 9–1

It can be shown mathematically that where the expected economic income is a constant amount in perpetuity, the above formula can be simplified to:

Formula 9–7

$$PV = \frac{E}{k}$$

In this unique case, the result is that the expected level amount of economic income can be capitalized by dividing it by the discount rate, and the capitalization rate equals the discount rate. Thus, in this case:

$$c = k$$

In other words, *in the unique case where the expected economic income is a net level amount in perpetuity (i.e., there is no growth in the expected economic income), the discount rate is equal to the capitalization rate.*

In any other case, where expected future amounts of economic income differ from the amount used in the capitalization formula, the difference between expected prospective amounts and the amount being capitalized is reflected in the difference between the appropriate discount rate (i.e., total yield or total required rate of return) and the capitalization rate (the divisor by which a single period return is converted to an estimate of value).

Converting a Discount Rate to a Capitalization Rate— The Constant Growth Model

If the level of economic income expected in the 12 months immediately following the valuation date is expected to grow after that time at a constant average annually compounded rate in perpetuity, then it can be demonstrated mathematically that the basic discounted economic income formula of:

$$PV = \sum_{i=1}^{n} \frac{E_i}{(1+k)^i}$$

can be simplified to:

Formula 9–8

$$PV = \frac{E_1}{k - g}$$

or:

$$PV = \frac{E_1}{c}$$

where:

PV = Present value
E_1 = Expected amount of economic income in the period immediately ahead
k = Discount rate (required yield rate or total rate of return)
g = Growth rate of E, annually compounded in perpetuity
c = Capitalization rate

In this formula, it is noteworthy that the capitalization rate is the reciprocal of a multiplier. For example, if next year's earnings are projected to be $1.00, and the stock is priced at $12.50, it is selling at 12.5 times next year's earnings. This equates to a capitalization rate of 8 percent—that is, $1 \div 12.5 = 0.08$.

A commonly encountered slight variation of this formula starts with the last 12 months' economic income figure as the base and assumes the constant perpetual growth rate proceeds from there:

Formula 9–9

$$PV = \frac{E_0 (1 + g)}{k - g}$$

where:

PV = Present value
E_0 = Amount of economic income in the period immediately past
k = Discount rate (required yield rate or total rate of return)
g = Growth rate of E, annually compounded in perpetuity

Formulas 9–8 and 9–9 above are often referred to as the Gordon growth model or the dividend growth model.[7] They represent a technically correct simplification of the basic discounted economic income model, *provided that the critical assumption underlying this simplification is met, that is, the economic income variable is expected to have a constant average annually compounded rate of growth in perpetuity.*

Since this assumption rarely comports to reality, this growth model is often used only as one stage of a multistage discounted economic income model. For example, it is common to make specific income forecasts for some period (often, five years or until the company is expected to reach a reasonably stable state), and then use the constant growth model to reflect income expectations from that point forward. An example of this will be shown later in the chapter.

Estimating the Discount Rate

As noted in Chapter 3 on business valuation theory and principles and earlier in this chapter, in an appraisal estimating fair market value *the discount rate is a market-driven rate. It represents the expected yield rate—or rate of return—necessary to induce investors to commit available funds to the subject investment, given its level of risk.*

Return and Rate of Return Defined

When we speak of *return* and *rate of return*, we are referring to the *total yield to the investor*, reflecting all dividends, interest, or other cash or cash equivalent received, plus or minus any realized or unrealized appreciation or depreciation in the investment's value. The yield, or rate of return, on an investment for a given time period is as follows:

Formula 9–10

$$R = \frac{Ending\ price - Beginning\ price + Cash\ distributions}{Beginning\ price}$$

---

[7]For a mathematical proof of this formula, see Brealey and Myers, *Principles of Corporate Finance*, pp. 33–34.

where:

R = Rate of return (for the period)

This formula simply says that the investment yield—or rate of return—is equal to the ending price of an investment, minus the beginning price, plus any cash flows received from holding that investment, divided by the initial price. For example, if Paola Pizza Parlours stock started the year at $10 per share, paid $.50 in cash dividends during the year, and ended the year at $11.50 per share, then the total investment yield or rate of return for the year would be computed as follows:

$$R = \frac{\$11.50 - \$10.00 + \$.50}{\$10.00} = .20$$

Given a series of prices for a particular investment and the economic income received by the owner of that investment, it is possible to calculate the rate of return over any time period—or over any number of subperiods.

The *discount rate* is the expected total yield rate—or rate of return—that investors require for the particular class of investment.

Components of the Discount Rate

Broken into its simplest components, the discount rate, or the rate of return that investors require, incorporates the following elements:

1. A "risk-free rate" (the amount that an investor feels certain of realizing over the holding period). This includes:
    a. A "rental rate" for forgoing the use of funds over the holding period.
    b. The expected rate of inflation over the holding period.[8]

2. A premium for risk. This includes:
    a. Systematic risk (that risk that relates to movements in returns on the investment market in general).
    b. Unsystematic risk (that risk that is specific to the subject investment).

Other important characteristics of an investment that are sometimes incorporated into the discount rate are: (1) the degree of minority ownership versus control position represented by the investment and (2) the degree of ready marketability or lack of marketability.

It is noteworthy that *discount rates developed through traditional capital asset pricing model (CAPM) analysis are based on minority transactions in highly marketable publicly traded securities. Therefore, discount rates based on CAPM relate to marketable, minority ownership positions in the subject investment.* Any considerations of investment control and/or lack of marketability require separate consideration and are addressed elsewhere in the book. Although

---

[8]This assumes the projected returns are in nominal terms, that is, including expected inflation over the projection period. In economies characterized by hyperinflation, the practical procedure is to perform a discounted income analysis in "real" terms; that is, to remove inflation from both the income projection and the discount rate. In any case, the projected income and the discount rate must match in this respect; that is, either both the projection and the discount rate include inflation or neither of them do.

there are exceptions, appraisers often explicitly treat the important valuation issues of control and lack of marketability separately rather than implicitly incorporating those issues in the estimation of the appropriate discount rate.[9]

The "Risk-Free" Rate

The "risk-free" rate generally used is that rate available on instruments considered to have virtually no possibility of default, such as U.S. Treasury obligations. As noted above, such instruments compensate the holders for renting out their money and for the expected loss of purchasing power (inflation) during the holding period.

The ultimate riskless security is considered to be the short-term U.S. Treasury bill. However, in estimating cost of capital for equity investments, the short-term Treasury bill has an important shortcoming: its maturity does not match the anticipated investment horizon (or holding period) of most equity investors. The Treasury bill rate is much more volatile than longer-term Treasury rates, and the yield may not reflect longer-term inflation expectations. Therefore, most analysts prefer to use a long-term Treasury bond yield—such as the 20-year Treasury bond—as the "risk-free" component for estimating the cost of equity capital.[10]

The "Equity Risk Premium"

Over and above a risk-free return, investors must expect some additional rate of return to induce them to invest in non-Treasury bonds, in equities, or in similar securities—to compensate them for the additional risk incurred in such an investment. In the context of cost of capital, we define *risk* as *the degree of uncertainty as to the realization of the expected future returns.*

For a given level of expected future returns, the market will pay more to the extent that realization of those returns is more certain and less to the extent that their realization is less certain. In other words, for a given level of expected prospective economic income (e.g., cash flow, dividends, accounting earnings, and the like), the lower the risk, the higher the present value, or conversely, the higher the risk, the lower the present value.

The mechanism by which the assessment of risk is translated into its effect on value normally is the discount rate.[11]

Since the cost of capital is one of the most important variables in the valuation of a business or a business interest, both academicians and practitioners have expended an enormous amount of theoretical and empirical research effort in an attempt to quantify the effect of risk on the cost of capital for equity investments. The state of the art in the mid-1990s involves incorporating one or all of the following elements into the discount rate to reflect risk:

---

[9]One notable exception is in the field of venture capital, where buyers of interests often incorporate the lack of marketability characteristic into their required rate of return in their discounted economic income analysis.

[10]The reason for using 20-year rather than 30-year Treasury bonds is that Ibbotson Associates publishes equity risk premium data related to 20-year Treasury coupon bond maturities, but no such equity risk premium data are available for 30-year maturities.

[11]Bierman and Smidt, two Cornell professors, make a convincing argument that the theoretically most correct way to handle the element of risk is to adjust the future expectations stream to what they call a *certainty adjusted equivalent.* They adjust the expectations downward by some factor that reflects the probability that the expectations will be achieved. They then apply the same cost of capital to the valuation of all alternative investment choices. They do quite a good job, in our opinion, of explaining the rationale for this approach [Harold Bierman Jr., and Seymour Smidt, *The Capital Budgeting Decision,* 4th ed. (New York: Macmillan, 1975)]. Notwithstanding Bierman and Smidt's fine presentation, the more commonly used approach to incorporating risk in the valuation of a business is to reflect it in the cost of capital.

1. A basic "equity risk premium" over the risk-free rate selected as the base.
2. One or more coefficients modifying the basic equity risk premium based on industry or other characteristics expected to affect the degree of risk for the subject investment.
3. An element reflecting the "size effect."
4. A final adjustment reflecting judgments about investment-specific risk for the subject investment not captured in the first three elements.

Extensive empirical research is available that attempts to quantify the effect on the discount rate of the first three of the elements above. Nonetheless there are choices to be made based on informed analysis of the evidence at each step. The fourth element, the unsystematic risk specific to the subject business or business interest, still remains largely a matter of the analyst's judgment, without a commonly accepted set of empirical support evidence. The analyst will base this judgment on factors discussed in Part II of this book, such as financial statement and comparative ratio analysis and the qualitative matters to be considered during the site visit and management interviews. However, after carefully analyzing these elements of investment-specific risk, there is no specific model for quantifying the exact effect of these factors on the discount rate. The analyst must depend on experience and judgment in this final element of the discount rate, but should explicitly describe the factors that impact this final element.

Exhibit 9–2 gives a schematic summary of the elements of a discount rate applicable when net cash flow is the measure of economic income being discounted. The basic equity risk premium, modifications to it, and the effect of company size on the equity risk premium are discussed in some detail in subsequent sections.

Later in the chapter, a procedure is presented to convert a discount rate applicable to net cash flow to a discount rate applicable to net income, providing that certain fairly stringent assumptions are met.

The Capital Asset Pricing Model

The capital asset pricing model (CAPM) is part of a larger body of economic theory known as *capital market theory* (CMT). CMT also includes *security analysis* and *portfolio management theory,* a *normative* theory that describes how investors *should* behave in selecting common stocks for their portfolios, under a given set of assumptions. In contrast, the CAPM is a *positive* theory, meaning it describes the market relationships that *will* result *if* investors behave in the manner prescribed by portfolio theory.

The capital asset pricing model is a conceptual cornerstone of modern capital market theory. Its relevance to business valuations is that businesses and business interests are a subset of the investment opportunities available in the total capital market; thus, the determination of the prices of businesses theoretically should be subject to the same economic forces and relationships that determine the prices of other investment assets.

Exhibit 9–2

Schematic Diagram and Example of Elements of a Discount Rate Applicable to Expected Net Cash Flow Available to Common Equity

	Explanation of Component	Component Value	Source
"Risk-free" rate	In the United States, usually 20-year, 5-year, or 30-day U.S. Treasury obligation yield available as of the valuation date. (Empirical equity risk premium data are available to match each of these 3 Treasury instrument maturities.)	7.26	20-year U.S. Treasury bond yield as of April 6, 1995. Source: *New York Times*, April 7, 1995, p. C20
Equity risk premium (reflecting systematic risk)	Data available from Ibbotson Associates based on S&P 500 stock returns over income yields on 20-year, 5-year, or 30-day U.S. Treasury instrument rates. May be modified by one or more coefficients, such as beta, based on the capital asset pricing model, and/or other coefficients based on the arbitrage pricing model theory.	7.0 x 1.20 = 8.40	Long horizon expected equity risk premium times beta. Source for long-horizon equity risk premium: *SBBI 1995 Yearbook*, p. 157. Source for beta: average of beta from *Value Line*, February 3, 1995, for guideline companies used in the market approach.
Impact of "size effect" on risk	Incremental addition to the discount rate to reflect research showing additional returns to stocks of companies smaller than S&P 500. Ibbotson data suggest that this is appropriate for stocks with a market value of equity of less than $150 million as of 1995. The data also include equity size premiums for low-capitalization stocks (about $150–$600 million in 1995) and mid-capitalization stocks (up to about $2.5 billion in 1995).	4.0	Expected size premium. Source: *SBBI 1995 Yearbook*, p. 157.
Specific risk	Matter of analyst's judgment. May be based on ratio analysis of subject compared to industry averages or specific guideline companies and/or on qualitative factors such as depth and quality of management, competitive position, and so on. This element of the discount rate will be supported conceptually by the analysis done pursuant to Part II of this book, "Preparing for the Business Valuation." However, there is no widely accepted model or set of formulas to convert the results of these analyses into an exact quantified effect on the discount rate.	(1.00)	Based on superior ratio analysis results for subject company compared with guideline companies used.
		18.66	
Total discount rate (rounded)		18.7	It is common to round to one decimal place. However, it is not uncommon to see discount rates either rounded to a full percentage point or carried to two decimal points.

Systematic and Unsystematic Risk

In the previous section, we defined risk conceptually as *the degree of uncertainty as to the realization of expected future returns.* Capital market theory divides risk into two components: systematic risk and unsystematic risk. Stated in nontechnical terms, *systematic risk* is the uncertainty of future returns due to the sensitivity of the return on the subject investment to movements in the return for the investment market as a whole. *Unsystematic risk* is a function of characteristics of the industry, the individual company, and the type of investment interest. Company characteristics could include, for example, management's ability to weather economic conditions, relations between labor and management, the possibility of strikes, the success or failure of a particular marketing program, or any other factor specific to the company. Total risk, therefore, depends on both these systematic and unsystematic factors.

A fundamental assumption of the capital asset pricing model is that the risk premium portion of the expected return of a security is a function of that security's systematic risk. This is because capital market theory assumes that investors hold or have the ability to hold common stocks in large, well-diversified portfolios. Under that assumption, the unsystematic risk attaching to a particular company's stock is eliminated because of the portfolio's diversification. Therefore, the only risk pertinent to a study of capital asset pricing theory is systematic risk.

Beta: The Measure of Systematic Risk

Systematic risk is measured in the capital asset pricing model by a factor called *beta.* Beta is a function of the relationship between the return on an individual security and the return on the market as measured by a broad market index such as the Standard & Poor's 500 Stock Composite Index. It is sometimes measured as a function of the excess return on an individual security relative to the *excess* return on the market index. By the "excess return," we mean the return over and above the return available on a risk-free investment (e.g., U.S. Treasuries).

For the market index as a whole, the average beta, by definition, is 1.0. If a stock tends to have a positive excess return greater than the market when the market return is greater than the risk-free return, and a negative excess return greater than the market when the market return is less than the risk-free return, then the stock's beta is greater than 1.0. If the difference between the stock's return and the risk-free return tends to be less than the difference between the market return and the risk-free return, then the stock's beta is less than 1.0.

In other words, beta measures the volatility of the excess return on an individual security relative to that of the market. Securities that have betas greater than 1.0 are characterized as aggressive securities and are more risky than the market. Securities that have betas of less than 1.0 are characterized as defensive securities and have systematic risks lower than the market.

It is possible (although not very common) for securities to have a negative beta (i.e., a beta less than zero). Such a beta would indicate that the returns of these securities are counter-cyclical to the returns of the broad investment market index.

One common method for calculating beta is illustrated in Exhibit 9–3. (The computation may be performed by regressing the excess stock return compared to the excess market return.)

(Is there a variability measurement that can identify stocks that go up more than the market when the market goes up, and down less than the market when the market goes down? Unfortunately, the answer is no. This is because research shows that stocks that have demonstrated such a pattern in the past do not tend to continue to demonstrate the same pattern in the future.)

Using Beta to Estimate Expected Rate of Return

The capital asset pricing model leads to the conclusion that the equity risk premium (the required excess rate of return for a security over and above the risk-free rate) is a linear function of the security's beta. This linear function is described in the following univariate linear regression formula:

Formula 9–11

$$E(R_i) = R_f + B(RP_m)$$

where:

$E(R_i)$ = Expected return on an individual security

R_f = Rate of return available on a risk-free security (as of the valuation date)

B = Beta

RP_m = Equity risk premium for the market as a whole (or, by definition, the equity risk premium for a security with a beta of 1.0)

Exhibit 9–3

Illustrative Example of One Common Method for the Calculation of Beta

Month End, t[a]	Return on Security A[b]	Return on S&P Index[c]	Calculated Covariance[d]	Calculated Variance[e]
1/78	(0.038)	(0.080)	0.0046	0.00757
2/78	0.076	0.048	0.0025	0.00168
3/78	0.062	0.008	0.0005	0.00001
.				
.				
.				
9/78	(0.004)	0.040	(0.0063)	0.01090
10/87	0.091	0.016	0.0068	0.00080
11/87	0.174	0.109	0.1622	0.10400
12/87	0.083	(0.030)	0.0363	0.01370
Sum	1.800	0.840	0.20952	0.23374
Average	0.015	0.007	0.00175[f]	0.00194[g]

$$\text{beta} = \frac{\text{Covariance (Security A, S\&P Index)}}{\text{Variance of S\&P Index}} = \frac{0.00175}{.00194} = .90$$

[a] 10 years or 120 months.
[b] Returns based on end-of-month prices and dividend payments.
[c] Returns based on end-of-month S&P Index.
[d] Values in this column are calculated as:
(Observed return on Security A − Avg. return on Security A) x (Observed return on S&P Index − Avg. return on S&P Index)
0.00046 = [(0.038) - 0.015] x (0.080) − 0.007]
[e] Values in this column are calculated as:
(Observed return on S&P Index − Avg. return on S&P Index)^2
0.00757 = [(0.080) - 0.007]^2
[f] The average of this column is the covariance between Security A and the S&P Index.
[g] The average of this column is the variance of return on the S&P Index.

To illustrate using the above formula as part of the process of estimating a company's cost of equity capital, consider stocks of average size, publicly traded companies i, j, and k, with betas of 0.8, 1.0, and 1.2, respectively, a risk-free rate in the market at the valuation date of 7 percent (.07), and the market equity risk premium of 8 percent (.08). The expected investment rate of return on common equity for stocks of these companies would be computed as follows:

Formula 9–12

$$
\begin{aligned}
E(R_i) &= .07 + .8(.08) \\
       &= .07 + .064 \\
       &= .134 \\
E(R_j) &= .07 + 1.0(.08) \\
       &= .07 + .08 \\
       &= .15 \\
E(R_k) &= .07 + 1.2(.08) \\
       &= .07 + .096 \\
       &= .166
\end{aligned}
$$

Exhibit 9–2 and later sections of this chapter discuss sources for the market risk-free rate, the equity risk premium, and betas.

The above linear relationship is presented schematically in Exhibit 9–4, which presents the security market line (SML). According to capital asset pricing theory, if the combination of the expected rate of return on a given security and its risk, as measured by beta, places it below the security market line, such as security X in Exhibit 9–4, that security (e.g., common stock) is mispriced. It is mispriced in the sense that the return on that security is less than what it would be if the security were correctly priced, assuming fully efficient capital markets.

For the return on a security to be appropriate for that security's risk, the price of the security must decline, allowing the rate of return to increase until it is just sufficient to compensate the investor for bearing the security's risk. All common stocks in the market, in equilibrium, adjust in price until the rate of return on each is sufficient to compensate investors for holding them. In that situation, the systematic risk/expected rate of return characteristics of all those securities will place them on the security market line.

Levered and Unlevered Betas

Published betas for publicly traded stocks reflect the actual capital structure of each respective company. As such, they can be referred to as *levered betas,* betas reflecting the actual financial leverage in the company's capital structure. If the leverage of the company subject to appraisal differs significantly from the leverage of the guideline companies selected for analysis, it may be desirable to adjust the guideline betas for use in estimating the required rate of return on equity in the context of the CAPM.

This adjustment is performed by first computing the *unlevered betas* for the guideline companies. An *unlevered beta* is the beta the company would have if it had no debt. The second step is to decide where the subject company's risk would fall on an unlevered basis relative to the guideline companies. The third

Exhibit 9–4

Security Market Line

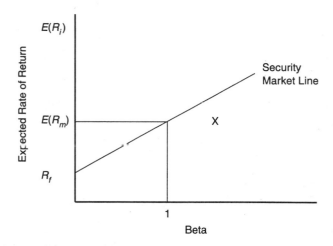

In the above diagram

$E(R_i)$ = Expected return for the individual security.
$E(R_m)$ = Expected return on the market.
R_f = Risk-free rate available as of the valuation date.

In a market in perfect equilibrium, all securities would fall on the security market line. The security X is mispriced, with a return less than it would be on the security market line.

and final step is to relever the beta for the subject company on the basis of one or more assumed capital structures. The result will be a market-derived beta that has been specifically adjusted for the degree of financial leverage of the subject company.[12]

To summarize, the steps are as follows:

1. Compute an unlevered beta for each of the guideline companies.
2. Decide where the risk would fall for the subject company relative to the guideline companies, assuming all of the guideline companies had 100 percent equity capital structures.
3. Re-lever the beta for the subject company based on one or more assumed capital structures.

The formulas and an example for carrying out this process are presented in Exhibit 9–5. Of course, this financial leverage adjustment procedure takes as given all the assumptions of the capital asset pricing model.

Keep in mind that capital structures both for the guideline and for the subject companies are assumed to be at *market value* in this process. If the relevered beta is used to estimate the market value of the company on a controlling basis, and if it is anticipated that the actual capital structure will be adjusted to the proportions of debt and equity in the assumed capital structure, then only one assumed capital

---

[12]Robert S. Hamada, "Portfolio Analysis, Market Equilibrium and Corporation Finance," *Journal of Finance* 24 (March 1969), pp. 19–30.

Exhibit 9–5

Computing Unlevered and Relevered Betas

The following is the formula for computing an unlevered beta (a beta assuming 100% equity in the capital structure).

$$B_u = \frac{B_L}{1 + (1 - t)W_d/W_e}$$

where:

B_u = Beta unlevered
B_L = Beta levered
t = Tax rate for the company
W_d = Percent debt in the capital structure
W_e = Percent equity in the capital structure

Example

Assume that for guideline company A:
  Levered (published) beta: 1.2
  Tax rate: .40
  Capital structure: 30% debt, 70% equity

$$B_u = \frac{1.2}{1 + (1 - .40).30/.70}$$

$$= \frac{1.2}{1 + .60(.429)}$$

$$= \frac{1.2}{1.257}$$

$$= .95$$

Assume you made the above calculation for all the guideline companies, the average unlevered beta was .90, and you believe the riskiness of your subject company, on an unlevered basis, is about equal to the average for the guideline companies. The next step is to relever the beta for your subject company based on its tax rate and one or more assumed capital structures. The formula to adjust an unlevered beta to a levered beta is as follows:

$$B_L = B_u(1 + (1 - t)W_d/W_e)$$

where the definitions of the variables are the same as in the formula for computing unlevered betas.

Example

Assume for the subject company:
  Unlevered beta: .90
  Tax rate: .30
  Capital structure: 60% debt, 40% equity

$$B_L = .90(1 + (1 - .30).60/.40)$$
$$= .90(1 + .70(1.5))$$
$$= .90(2.05)$$
$$= 1.85$$

structure is necessary. However, if the amount of debt in the subject capital structure will *not* be adjusted, an iterative process may be required. The initial *assumed* capital structure for the subject will influence the cost of equity, which will, in turn, influence the relative proportions of debt and equity at market value. It may be necessary to try several assumed capital structures until one of them produces an estimate of equity value that actually results in the assumed capital structure.

This process of unlevering and relevering betas to an assumed capital structure is based upon the assumption that the business interest subject to appraisal has the ability to change the capital structure of the subject company. In the case of the valuation of a minority ownership interest, for example, the appraisal subject may not have that ability.

Assumptions Underlying the Capital Asset Pricing Model

The assumptions underlying the capital asset pricing model are as follows:

1. Investors are risk averse.
2. Rational investors seek to hold efficient portfolios; that is, portfolios that are fully diversified.
3. All investors have identical investment time horizons (i.e., expected holding periods).
4. All investors have identical expectations about such variables as expected rates of return and how capitalization rates are generated.
5. There are no transaction costs.
6. There are no investment-related taxes (i.e., there may be corporate income taxes).
7. The rate received from lending money is the same as the cost of borrowing money.
8. The market has perfect divisibility and liquidity (i.e., investors can readily buy or sell any desired fractional interest).

Obviously, the extent to which the above assumptions are or are not met in the real world will have a bearing on the application of the CAPM for the valuation of closely held businesses.

The Size Premium

Several research studies demonstrate convincing evidence that, on average, smaller companies have higher rates of return than larger companies.[13] The *total* risk, or standard deviation of annual returns, also increases with decreasing company size.[14]

The *SBBI 1995 Yearbook* states:

> The greater risk of small stocks does not, in the context of the Capital Asset Pricing Model, fully account for their higher returns over the long term. In the CAPM, only systematic or beta risk is rewarded. Small company stocks have had returns in excess of those implied by the betas of small stocks.[15]

The implication would seem to be that the investment market does *not* ignore unsystematic risk and, indeed, demands and achieves extra return for accepting it. The 1995 Ibbotson data showing higher returns to higher standard deviation stocks are consistent with Pratt's research as far back as 1966, which showed increasing returns to risk as measured by the standard deviation.[16]

---

[13]See, for example, Eugene Fama and Kenneth French, "The Cross Section of Expected Stock Returns," *Journal of Finance* 47 (1992), pp. 427–65; Eugene Fama and Kenneth French, "Common Risk Factors in the Returns on Stocks and Bonds," University of Chicago working paper no. 360, November 1992; Eugene Fama and Kenneth French, "The Economic Fundamentals of Size and Book-to-Market Equity," University of Chicago working paper no. 361, September 1992; Christopher B. Barry and Stephen J. Brown, "Differential Information and the Small Firm Effect," *Journal of Financial Economics* 13 (1984), pp. 283–94; and Rolf W. Banz, "The Relationship between Return and Market Value of Common Stocks," *Journal of Financial Economics* 9 (1981), pp. 3–18. Also, see Chapter 7 of *Stocks, Bonds, Bills & Inflation 1995 Yearbook (SBBI 1995 Yearbook)* (Chicago: Ibbotson Associates, 1995).

[14]*Stocks, Bonds, Bills & Inflation 1995 Yearbook* (Chicago: Ibbotson Associates, 1995), p. 124.

[15]Ibid.

[16]Shannon P. Pratt, "Relationship between Variability of Past Returns and Levels of Future Returns for Common Stocks, 1926–1960" (abridged version, previously unpublished), in *Frontiers of Investment Analysis,* rev. ed., ed. E. Bruce Fredrikson, (Scranton, NY: Intext Educational Publishers, 1971), pp. 338–53.

We believe that the reflection of this unsystematic risk in the discount rate is especially important for the valuation of closely held stocks. Most owners of closely held businesses or interests in closely held businesses do not diversify their investment portfolios nearly to the extent to which investors diversify their holdings of publicly traded securities. Thus, since the unsystematic portion of total risk is unlikely to be diversified away to the same extent as for a portfolio of publicly traded securities, it is worth considering reflecting at least some part of unsystematic risk—as well as systematic risk—in estimating an appropriate expected rate of return.

An explanation of the data quantifying the size premium is contained in the following section on sources of data.

Arbitrage Pricing Theory

The concept of the *arbitrage pricing theory* (APT) was introduced by academicians in 1976,[17] but it was not until 1988 that data in a commercially usable form became generally available to permit the application of the theory to the estimation of required rates of return in day-to-day practice.

As noted in the previous section, the CAPM is a univariate model, that is, it only recognizes one risk factor—systematic risk relative to a market index. In a sense, APT is a multivariate extension of the CAPM, in that it recognizes a variety of risk factors that may bear on an investment's required rate of return, one of these being systematic or "market timing" risk. However, in another sense, it may be argued that the CAPM and APT are not mutually exclusive, nor are they of greater or lesser scope than one another. It can be argued that the CAPM beta implicitly reflects the information included separately in each of the APT "factors." Under APT, the required rate of return for an investment varies according to that investment's sensitivity to each risk factor. The APT model takes the following form:

Formula 9–13

$$E(R_i) = R_f + (B_{i1}K_1) + (B_{i2}K_2) + \ldots + (B_{in}K_n)$$

where:

$E(R_i)$ = Expected rate of return on the subject security

R_f = Rate of return on a risk-free security

$K_1 \ldots K_n$ = Risk premium associated with factor K for the average asset in the market

$B_{i1} \ldots B_{in}$ = Sensitivity of security i to each risk factor relative to the market average sensitivity to that factor

The risk factors considered in current APT applications, in addition to market timing risk, include:

---

[17]Stephen A. Ross, "The Arbitrage Theory of Capital Asset Pricing," *Journal of Economic Theory,* December 1976, pp. 241–60, and Stephen A. Ross, "Return, Risk, and Arbitrage," in *Risk and Return in Finance,* ed. Irwin I. Friend and J. Bisksler (Cambridge, MA: Ballinger, 1977), pp. 189–218. See also, Stephen A. Ross, Randolph W. Westerfield, and Jeffrey F. Jaffe, *Corporate Finance,* 3rd ed. (Burr Ridge, IL: Irwin Professional Publishing, 1993), chap. 11, pp. 315–37.

Exhibit 9–6

Explanation of APT Risk Factors

Confidence Risk

Confidence Risk is the unanticipated changes in investors' willingness to undertake relatively risky investments. It is measured as the difference between the rate of return on relatively risky corporate bonds and the rate of return on government bonds, both with 20-year maturities, adjusted so that the mean of the difference is zero over a long historical sample period. In any month when the return on corporate bonds exceeds the return on government bonds by more than the long-run average, this measure of Confidence Risk is positive. The intuition is that a positive return difference reflects increased investor confidence because *the required yield on risky corporate bonds has fallen relative to safe government bonds.* Stocks that are positively exposed to this risk then will rise in price. (Most equities *do* have a positive exposure to Confidence Risk, and small stocks generally have greater exposure than large stocks.)

Time Horizon Risk

Time Horizon Risk is the unanticipated changes in investors' desired time to payouts. It is measured as the difference between the return on 20-year government bonds and 30-day Treasury bills, again adjusted to be mean zero over a long historical sample period. A positive realization of Time Horizon Risk means that the price of long-term bonds has risen relative to the 30-day Treasury bill price. This is a signal that investors require a lower compensation for holding investments with relatively longer times to payouts. The price of stocks that are positively exposed to Time Horizon Risk will rise to appropriately decrease their yields. (Growth stocks benefit more than income stocks when this occurs.)

Inflation Risk

Inflation Risk is a combination of the unexpected components of short- and long-run inflation rates. Expected future inflation rates are computed at the beginning of each period from available information: historical inflation rates, interest rates, and other economic variables that influence inflation. For any month, Inflation Risk is the unexpected surprise that is computed at the end of the month, i.e., it is the difference between the actual inflation for that month and what had been expected at the beginning of the month. Since most stocks have negative exposures to Inflation Risk, a positive inflation surprise causes a negative contribution to return, whereas a negative inflation surprise (a deflation shock) contributes positively toward return.

Industries whose products tend to be "luxuries" are most sensitive to Inflation Risk. Consumer demand for "luxuries" plummets when real income is eroded through inflation, thus depressing profits for industries such as retailers, services, eating places, hotels and motels, and toys. In contrast, industries least sensitive to Inflation Risk tend to sell "necessities," the demands for which are relatively insensitive to declines in real income. Examples include foods, cosmetics, tire and rubber goods, and shoes. Also companies that have large asset holdings such as real estate or oil reserves may benefit from increased inflation.

Business Cycle Risk

Business Cycle Risk represents unanticipated changes in the level of real business activity. The expected values of a business activity index are computed both at the beginning and end of the month, using only information available at those times. Then, Business Cycle Risk is calculated as the difference between the end-of-month value and the beginning-of-month value. A positive realization of Business Cycle Risk indicates that the expected growth rate of the economy, measured in constant dollars, has increased. Under such circumstances firms that are more positively exposed to business cycle risk—for example, firms such as retail stores that do well when business activity increases as the economy recovers from a recession—will outperform those such as utility companies that do not respond much to increased levels in business activity.

Market Timing Risk

Market Timing Risk is computed as that part of the S&P 500 total return that is not explained by the first four macroeconomic risks and an intercept term. Many people find it useful to think of the APT as a generalization of the CAPM, and by including this Market Timing factor, the CAPM becomes a special case: If the risk exposures to all of the first four macroeconomic factors were exactly zero, then Market Timing Risk would be proportional to the S&P 500 total return. Under these extremely unlikely conditions, a stock's exposure to Market Timing Risk would be equal to its CAPM beta. Almost all stocks have a positive exposure to Market Timing Risk, and hence positive Market Timing surprises increase returns, and vice versa.

A natural question, then, is: "Do Confidence Risk, Time Horizon Risk, Inflation Risk, and Business Cycle Risk help to explain stock returns better than I could do with just the S&P 500?" This question has been answered using rigorous statistical tests, and the answer is very clearly that they do.

SOURCE: Presented in a talk based on a paper, "A Practitioner's Guide to Arbitrage Pricing Theory," by Edwin Burmeister, Richard Roll, and Stephen A. Ross, written for the Research Foundation of the Institute of Chartered Financial Analysts. The exhibit is drawn from Notes for "Controlling Risks Using Arbitrage Pricing Techniques," by Edwin Burmeister.

- Confidence risk.
- Time horizon risk.
- Inflation risk.
- Business cycle risk.

Each of these risk factors is discussed in Exhibit 9–6. Like the CAPM, APT ignores risk factors that are unique to a particular company, since investors theoretically could avoid such risks through diversification.

Ibbotson and Brinson make the following observations regarding APT:

> In theory, a specific asset has some number of units of each risk; those units are each multiplied by the appropriate risk premium. Thus, APT shows that the equilibrium expected return is the risk-free rate plus the sum of a series of risk premiums.
>
> APT is more realistic than CAPM because investors can consider other characteristics besides the beta of assets as they select their investment portfolios.[18]

Research suggests that, on average, the cost of equity as estimated using APT tends to be slightly higher than the cost of equity as estimated using CAPM. Early research also suggests the multivariate APT model explains expected rates of return better than the univariate CAPM.[19]

A source of data for required rates of return using APT is included later in this chapter.

Sources of Data to Estimate the Cost of Equity Capital

Risk-Free Rate

The risk-free rate should be the yield available to investors as of the valuation date. In the United States, the yield most often used is for 20-year, 5-year, or 30-day U.S. Treasury obligations, because those are the maturities for which matching equity risk premium data are available.

The Ibbotson risk premium data are based on yields on U.S. Government coupon bonds. Therefore, the coupon bond yield as of the valuation date is appropriate to use with the Ibbotson equity risk premium data.

Equity Risk Premium

Ibbotson Associates publishes its three equity risk premium series annually, as presented in Exhibit 9–7. These are based on arithmetic (as opposed to geometric) means of differences between stock market returns and riskless security returns, for reasons explained in Exhibit 9–8. This is a widely (but not universally) accepted procedure for estimating the equity risk premium.[20]

---

[18]Roger G. Ibbotson and Gary P. Brinson, *Investment Markets* (New York: McGraw-Hill, Inc., 1987), p. 52. For a more extensive discussion of APT, see Frank K. Reilly, *Investment Analysis and Portfolio Management,* 4th ed. (Fort Worth, TX: The Dryden Press, 1994), pp. 288–91.

[19]Tom Copeland, Tim Koller, and Jack Murrin, *Valuation: Measuring and Managing the Value of Companies,* 2nd ed. (New York: John Wiley & Sons, 1994), p. 267.

[20]For example, the Ibbotson view that the arithmetic mean is appropriate for estimating discount rates is supported by Brealey and Myers in one of the leading corporate finance texts: Brealy and Myers, *Principles of Corporate Finance,* p. 130. However, for a contrary view (i.e., that the geometric mean differences more closely approximate the market's required return), see Tom Copeland, et al., *Valuation: Measuring and Managing the Value of Companies,* 2nd ed., pp. 261–63.

Exhibit 9–7

Key Variables in Estimating the Cost of Equity Capital

Variable Description	Value
Yields (Riskless Rates)[a]	
Long-term (20-year) U.S. Treasury Coupon Bond Yield	8.0%
Intermediate-term (5-year) U.S. Treasury Coupon Note Yield	7.8
Short-term (30-day) U.S. Treasury Bill Yield	4.7
Risk Premia[b]	
Long-horizon expected equity risk premium: large company stock total returns minus long-term government bond income returns	7.0
Intermediate-horizon expected equity risk premium: large company stock total returns minus intermediate-term government bond income returns	7.4
Short-horizon expected equity risk premium: large company stock total returns minus U.S. Treasury bill total returns[c]	8.4
Size Premia	
Expected mid-capitalization equity size premium: capitalization between $617 and $2,570 million	1.3
Expected low-capitalization equity size premium: capitalization between $149 and $617 million	2.1
Expected micro-capitalization equity size premium: capitalization below $149 million	4.0

[a] As of December 31, 1994. Maturities are approximate.
[b] Expected risk premia are based on the simple differences of historical arithmetic mean returns from 1926 to 1994.
[c] For U.S. Treasury bills, the income return and total return are the same.

SOURCE: *Stocks, Bonds, Bills, & Inflation 1995 Yearbook™* (Chicago: Ibbotson Associates, 1995), p. 157. Annual updates work by Roger G. Ibbotson and Rex. A. Sinquefield. Used with permission. All rights reserved.

Beta

Since privately held companies by definition have no market quotes and thus no market fluctuations, they have no observable betas. The most common procedure in using CAPM to develop a discount rate for a privately held company is to derive an estimate of betas from publicly traded guideline companies, most often guideline companies in the same industry as the subject company.

Many different financial reporting services publish betas for publicly traded securities. These include *Value Line Investment Survey, Wilshire Associates,* and *Tradeline.* Betas are also available from various on-line data sources, such as Compustat and Compuserve. See the bibliography at the end of the chapter for details on locating these sources.

One will find significant differences among betas for the same stock published by different financial reporting services. This is because of differences in computation methods. See Exhibit 9–9 for a discussion of the controversy over different details of computing betas, which can sometimes lead to widely divergent results. One of the implications is that betas for guideline companies used in a valuation should all come from the same source. If all betas for guideline companies are not available from a single source, the best solution probably is to use the source providing betas for the most guideline companies, and not use betas for the others. Otherwise an "apples and oranges" mixture will result.

Exhibit 9–8

Ibbotson Associates' Discussion of Arithmetic versus Geometric Mean for Calculating the Expected Equity Risk Premium for Estimating Cost of Capital (Discount Rate)

Arithmetic versus Geometric Differences

For use as the expected equity risk premium in the CAPM, the *arithmetic* or *simple difference* of the *arithmetic means* of the stock market returns and riskless rates is the relevant number. This is because the CAPM is an additive model where the cost of capital is the sum of its parts. Therefore, the CAPM expected equity risk premium must be derived by arithmetic, *not geometric,* subtraction.

Arithmetic versus Geometric Means

The expected equity risk premium should always be calculated using the arithmetic mean. The arithmetic mean is the rate of return which, when compounded over multiple periods, gives the mean of the probability distribution of ending wealth values. (A simple example given below shows that this is true.) This makes the arithmetic mean return appropriate for computing the cost of capital. The discount rate that equates expected (mean) future values with the present value of an investment is that investment's cost of capital. The logic of using the discount rate as the cost of capital is reinforced by noting that investors will discount their expected (mean) ending wealth values from an investment back to the present using the arithmetic mean, for the reason given above. They will therefore require such an expected

(mean) return prospectively (that is, in the present looking toward the future) in order to commit their capital to the investment.

For example, assume a stock has an expected return of +10% in each year and a standard deviation of 20%. Assume further that only two outcomes are possible each year— +30 percent and −10% (that is, the mean plus or minus one standard deviation) and that these outcomes are equally likely. (The arithmetic mean of these returns is 10%, and the geometric mean is 8.2%.) The growth of wealth over a two-year period is shown in the previous column.

Note that the median (middle outcome) and mode (most common outcome) are given by the geometric mean, 8.2%, which compounds up to 17% over a 2-year period (hence a terminal wealth of $1.17). However, the *expected value,* or probability-weighted average of all possible outcomes, is equal to:

(.25	x	1.69)	=	0.4225
+ (.50	x	1.17)	=	0.5850
+ (.25	x	0.81)	=	0.2025
Total				1.2100

Now, the rate that must be compounded up to achieve a terminal wealth of $1.21 after 2 years is 10%; that is, the expected value of the terminal wealth is given by compounding up the arithmetic mean, not the geometric. Since the *arithmetic mean* equates the expected future value with the present value, it is the discount rate.

Stated another way, the arithmetic mean is correct because an investment with uncertain returns will have a higher expected ending wealth value than an investment which earns, with certainty, its compound or geometric rate of return every year. In the above example, compounding at the rate of 8.2% for two years yields a terminal wealth of $1.17, based on a dollar invested. But holding the uncertain investment, with a possibility of high returns (two +30% years in a row) as well as low returns (two −10% years in a row), yields a higher expected terminal wealth, $1.21. In other words, more money is gained by higher-than-expected returns than is lost by lower-than-expected returns. Therefore, in the investment markets, where returns are described by a probability distribution, the arithmetic mean is the measure that accounts for uncertainty, and is the appropriate one for estimating discount rates and the cost of capital.

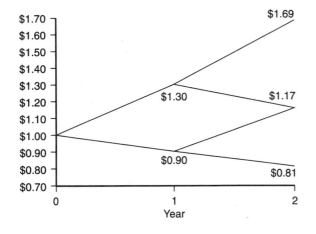

Size Premium

As noted earlier, a substantial body of published research indicates that the size of the company is important in that stocks of smaller companies are riskier than larger ones and that small-company stocks command a higher expected rate of return in the market. Ibbotson Associates quantifies this in the *SBBI Yearbook* in the section titled "Size Premia," as presented in Exhibit 9–7.

Exhibit 9–9

Beta Measurement Problems

A major weakness of using CAPM for its original purpose of understanding the value of securities in a portfolio is the measurement of the various components of the CAPM equation. In particular, there is no single accepted source of data or method for measuring the beta coefficient component of the model.

First, different financial reporting services provide different estimates of beta—for the same industry, and even for the same individual security. And, there are at least a dozen reputable financial reporting services that analysts may refer to in order to obtain a beta for a particular security.

Second, different market indexes provide different estimates of the "market risk premium" component of CAPM. Some financial reporting services use the Standard & Poor's 500 as their benchmark market index; some use the Value Line index; some use the Russell 1000, 2000, or 0000, etc.

Third, different time frames for beta estimates obviously can provide different estimates of the subject beta. In order to compare the subject security prices to the guideline market index, some financial reporting services use weekly observations; some use monthly observations; some make their observations on the last trading day of each; some make their observations on the last Friday of each month (or of each week); etc. These differences in data collection—particularly the differences between weekly observation and monthly observation—can have a material impact on the estimation of beta—for the same security.

These first three beta measurement problems are illustrated by the data in the table below; this table presents the beta measurement characteristics of several commonly used financial reporting services.

Fourth, betas are typically measured infrequently; therefore, they can be "out of date" as of the particular valuation date. It is common that the most recent betas reported in reputable financial reporting services may have been estimated several months before the publication date of the financial service. And, most financial reporting services do not estimate individual betas on a real time basis. Rather, they will estimate the beta for an individual security periodically—typically only a few times each year.

Fifth, betas are not available for many securities. For example, betas are not generally available for infrequently traded securities. And, there are literally thousands of publicly listed securities that are not followed by the financial reporting services. So, published betas are not readily available for those securities.

Therefore, with all of these beta measurement problems, the analyst is often uncertain as to:

1. What is the correct beta for the selected guideline companies used in the subject valuation analysis, and
2. What is the correct beta for the subject company (whether or not a "published" beta is estimated directly or a beta based upon guideline companies is estimated indirectly)?

Beta Measurement Characteristics of Common Financial Reporting Services

Financial Reporting Service	Market Index	Measurement Interval	Measurement Time Period
CompuServe	S&P 500	Weekly (Friday close)	5 years
Media General Financial Services	Media General Composite Index (6400+ common stocks)	Per market movement of 5% (up or down)	No set time span
Merrill Lynch	S&P 500	Monthly	5 years
S&P Compustat	S&P 500	Monthly (end of month)	5 years
Tradeline	S&P 500	Weekly (Friday close)	3 years
Value Line	NYSE Composite	Weekly	5 years
Wilshire Associates	S&P 500	Monthly	5 years

Starting with *1995 Yearbook*, SBBI has expanded the size premium data to include three tiers based on data from the University of Chicago Center for Research on Security Prices. What used to be called the "Small Stock Premium" size tier is now called the "micro-capitalization equity size premium." It still includes the smallest 20 percent of stocks on the New York Stock Exchange as measured by market value of common equity—in 1994 up to approximately $150 million.

The two size premium categories added in the *1995 Yearbook* are the "low-capitalization equity risk premium," which includes the sixth through eighth NYSE size deciles, encompassing market values of common equity from about $150 to $617 million, and the "mid-capitalization equity risk premium," covering market value of common equity from $617 million to about $2.5 billion.[21]

It is noteworthy that the size premium is *in addition* to the basic equity risk premium already modified by the effect of the beta, and betas for smaller stocks tend to be greater than for larger stocks. The correct formula, reflecting *both* beta and the size premium, is the following:[22]

Formula 9–14

$$E(R_i) = R_f + B(RP_m) + RP_s$$

where:

$$
\begin{aligned}
E(R_i) &= \text{Expected return on an individual security} \\
R_f &= \text{Rate of return available on a risk-free security (as of the valuation} \\
&\quad\ \text{date); when using the Ibbotson size premium data, the risk-free rate} \\
&\quad\ \text{should be 30-day, 5-year, or 20-year government bond yields, used} \\
&\quad\ \text{in conjunction with the corresponding equity risk premium} \\
B &= \text{Beta} \\
RP_m &= \text{Equity risk premium for a security with a beta of 1.0} \\
RP_s &= \text{Risk premium for size (size premium)}
\end{aligned}
$$

Investment-Specific Risk

The estimation of the effect of investment-specific (unsystematic) risk is often a matter for the analyst's professional judgment. The risk factors will be developed as part of the quantitative and qualitative analyses discussed in Part II of this book, and the significant positive and negative factors related to these analyses should be noted in the valuation report. These analyses will reveal many things that will affect the economic income projections, as well as the risk of achieving those projections. The analyst should be careful to distinguish between those factors that influence the *magnitude* of the projection (the numerator in the model) and those factors that affect the *degree of uncertainty* of achieving the mathematical expectation projection (that is, the *risk,* which determines the discount rate, the denominator in the model). The analyst must be especially careful to avoid undue double counting, such as reflecting a negative factor fully by a reduction in the same economic income projection and then magnifying the effect by an increase in the discount rate—for the negative factor.

Having carefully analyzed all the investment-specific risk factors, there is no specific model or formula for quantifying their exact effect on the discount rate. This ultimately is based on the analyst's experience and judgment. It is noteworthy that the analysis may lead to the conclusion that the subject company is *less risky* than industry or guideline company averages, in which case the investment-specific risk adjustment may *reduce* the discount rate.

---

[21]*SBBI 1995 Yearbook,* p. 135.
[22]Ibid., p. 155.

Arbitrage Pricing Theory Factors

Two major sources exist for arbitrage pricing theory data. The Alcar Group, Inc., markets a software package and database service called *APT!* that estimates bond ratings using standard financial ratios. Alcar's address is 5215 Old Orchard Road, Skokie, Illinois 60077 (708-967-4200). Birr Portfolio Analysis, Inc., publishes *BIRR Risks and Returns Analyzer*, a PC-based software text. Birr's address is 2200 West Main Street, Suite 210, Durham, North Carolina 27705 (919-687-7053).

Estimating a Discount Rate Directly from Market Data

Sometimes a discount rate can be estimated from market data by converting observed market capitalization rates into discount rates. The most likely economic income measure to lend itself to this exercise is net income. Recall that the primary difference between a discount rate and a capitalization rate is growth. For some companies, earnings growth estimates can be obtained for as much as five years in the future.[23] Adding the growth rate to the capitalization rate (the reciprocal of the P/E multiple in the case of net income) provides a rough estimate of the implied discount rate. There are at least two problems with this method. First, to be valid, the growth rate used in the conversion should be an expected growth rate in perpetuity. The five-year growth rate could differ considerably from the longer-term growth rate. Second, the five-year projected growth rates found in such publications leave much to be desired in terms of accuracy. Nevertheless, in some cases, the method provides at least a useful tool for approximating a discount rate.

Rate of Return Allowed to Regulated Companies

Additional cost of capital data are available when estimating the appropriate discount rate for a regulated company.

Public utility commissioners in all 50 states allow regulated utilities to charge rates to their customers that provide what supposedly is a fair rate of return on investment (often called the rate base). These allowed rates of return generally are based on the respective commissions' perceptions of the cost of debt capital and the cost of equity capital based on studies by their staffs. Utility commissions' allowed rate-of-return orders usually also specify an allowed overall rate of return on invested capital, based on their conclusions as to the appropriate capital structure. Megamillions of dollars are involved in these rate-setting decisions, based on hard-fought negotiations and hearings that sometimes culminate in lawsuits and rate case decisions rendered in court.

Regulated companies usually are regulated because they have a captive market and are in a monopoly position to supply a needed service; thus, their cost of capital should be considerably lower than that for an average company. Therefore, allowed rates of return for regulated companies can be viewed as a reasonable benchmark for a minimum boundary of the overall cost of capital.

---

[23]*Value Line Investment Survey* is one source of such estimates.

Each year, *Public Utilities Fortnightly* publishes the results of research compiled on natural gas utility and electric utility rate orders issued during the previous year by state public utility commissions throughout the United States. The published research results include the rate of return on common equity authorized by each public utility commission order, along with various other information related to the order. The published research is organized by state and by individual utility within each state. The most current research published on the natural gas utility rate orders covers the 12-month period ending August 31, 1994, while the electric utility rate order published research covers the 12-month period ending March 31, 1994.

Research based on *Public Utilities Fortnightly* data indicates that during the 12 months ended August 31, 1994, the authorized rates of return on common equity for natural gas utilities, as ordered by the state public utilities commissions, ranged from 10.13 to 13.4 percent after excluding outlying authorized rates of return that were affected by special circumstances. The authorized rate of return on common equity for electric utilities during the 12 months ended March 31, 1994, ranged from 9.89 percent to 14.25 percent.

Ibbotson *Cost of Capital Quarterly*

A new source, available starting in 1995, combines several of the above data items plus other information relevant to estimating the cost of equity, and also other information useful for valuation work. Exhibit 9–10 is an example of the double-page spread offered in the *Cost of Capital Quarterly* for each of over 300 SIC code groups (see the bibliography at the end of this chapter).

This is a convenient and potentially powerful new compilation of data for use in valuation work. We caution readers who use it, however, to study carefully the definitions of all data items before using them in a valuation analysis. Some definitions are not completely implied by the short titles describing the data points in the tables. Other definitions are not what we may ideally desire, usually because of limitations on the availability of data. The definitions *are* explained in detail. Used carefully, this can be a very useful new reference source for the valuation analysis.

Discounting Economic Income Available to Overall Capital

Until now in this chapter, we have focused on discounting economic income available to the common equity holders. In some situations (which will be described elsewhere in this book), it is desirable to value more than just the common equity—often all the equity and all the interest-bearing debt, sometimes referred to as the entire capital structure or the value of the company or market value of invested capital (MVIC).

In these instances, the projected cash flow (or other economic income) must include that which is available to *all* the components of the capital structure being valued. The discount rate must be the weighted average of the cost of each of the components in the capital structure, *each weighted average based on the market value of that capital component.* This is called the "weighted-average cost of capital" (WACC). In other words, the cost of a company's overall capital is the weighted average of the costs of all its financing sources in its capital structure.

Defining the Capital Structure

When people refer to "the value of the company" (as opposed to just the value of equity), they usually mean the value of the capital structure. However, this still may leave ambiguity as to exactly what is included in the capital structure.

Treatment of Interest-Bearing Debt. The most commonly used conceptual definition of *capital structure* is all equity and all long-term debt (including current maturities of long-term debt). However, to value the capital structure by this definition using the discounted economic income method, it is necessary to include the interest on the long-term debt in the income being discounted and treat other interest (such as on a bank operating line of credit) as an expense. If it is not practical to get the necessary information to separate the two elements of interest, then a commonly used solution to the problem is to define the capital structure to include all interest-bearing debt.

Treatment of Noninterest-Bearing Items. Another issue in some cases is whether or not to include certain noninterest-bearing long-term liabilities in the capital structure. This may include, for example, such items as deferred taxes and pension liabilities. If any such items were to be included, some portion of the capital structure would have zero cost of capital.

Conceptually, the most commonly accepted answer is that they should be included if it is expected they will be paid and excluded if not. This, then, requires a judgment call. Keep in mind also that weightings of the components of the capital structure for the purpose of estimating a WACC are at *market value*. Therefore, if noninterest-bearing liabilities are to be included, an estimate of when they will be paid is required so the face value can be discounted to a present market value to determine their weight. As a practical matter, noninterest-bearing liabilities usually are not included in calculations of a WACC, but there are times that they are important enough to consider.

In any case, when discounting economic income available to the company, it is important to specify what is assumed to be included in the capital structure.

Weighted Average Cost of Capital (WACC) Formula

The basic formula for computing the after-tax WACC is as follows:

Formula 9–15

$$WACC = (k_e \times W_e) + (k_d[1 - t] \times W_d)$$

where:

$WACC$ = Weighted average cost of capital
k_e = Company's cost of common equity capital
k_d = Company's cost of debt capital
W_e = Percentage of equity capital in the capital structure
W_d = Percentage of debt capital in the capital structure
t = Company's effective income tax rate

Assume:

Cost of equity capital:	.25
Cost of debt capital:	.10
Proportion of equity in capital structure:	.70
Proportion of debt in capital structure:	.30
Income tax rate:	.40

Exhibit 9–10

Sample Pages from Ibbotson *Cost of Capital Quarterly*

STATISTICS FOR SIC CODE 2834

Pharmaceutical Preparations

(This Industry Comprises 59 Companies)

Industry Description:

Establishments primarily engaged in manufacturing, fabricating, or processing drugs in pharmaceutical preparations for human or veterinary use. The greater part of the products of these establishments are finished in the form intended for final consumption, such as tablets, capsules, vials, and ointments.

Sales–Current Year (in $Millions)			Total Capital–Current Year (in $Millions)		
Industry					
Total	$68,902.8		Total	$212,833.1	
Average	$1,167.8		Average	$3,607.3	
Largest Companies					
MERCK & CO.	$10,498.2		MERCK & CO.	$47,723.2	
ABBOTT LABORATORIES	$8,407.8		ABBOTT LABORATORIES	$26,327.7	
AMERICAN HOME PRODUCTS CORP	$8,304.8		PFIZER INC	$25,042.7	
PFIZER INC	$7,477.7		AMERICAN HOME PRODUCTS CORP	$20,364.6	
LILLY (ELI) & CO	$6,452.4		LILLY (ELI) & CO	$19,470.3	

Distribution	*Latest*	*5 Yr. Avg.*		*Latest*	*5 Yr. Avg.*
90th Percentile	$4,631.8	$3,972.3	90th Percentile	$12,094.7	$10,282.0
75th Percentile	$377.8	$294.8	75th Percentile	$1,794.8	$1,453.7
Median	**$33.1**	**$24.2**	**Median**	**$147.6**	**$126.0**
25th Percentile	$4.5	$3.8	25th Percentile	$37.5	$67.9
10th Percentile	$1.4	$1.9	10th Percentile	$18.6	$36.0

For Total Industry Over Last Five Years ($Billions)

Sales, Operating Income, and Net Income	Market Capitalization–Equity and Debt
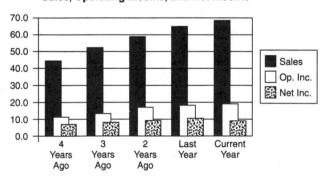	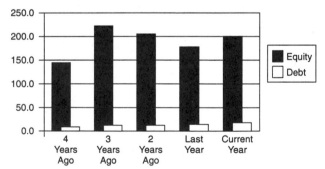

Compound Annual Equity Returns			Growth Over Last Five Years		
	5 Years	*10 Years*	*Net Sales*	*Operating income*	*Net Income*
90th Percentile	29.49%	24.97%	46.26%	54.89%	62.26%
75th Percentile	19.94%	20.09%	26.53%	30.16%	26.42%
Median	**7.16%**	**14.51%**	**14.65%**	**11.99%**	**9.72%**
25th Percentile	−2.27%	−2.73%	6.96%	−10.73%	−11.05%
10th Percentile	−19.79%	−11.82%	−18.07%	−37.08∞	−38.47%
Ind. Composite	**14.09%**	**23.93%**	**10.45%**	**12.19%**	**7.16%**
Lg. Composite	12.40%	21.81%	8.93%	11.26%	4.56%
Sm. Composite	−7.86%	17.71%	−24.50%	−21.37%	−23.97%

Exhibit 9-10 (concluded)

	Ending Value of $1 Invested Over		Annualized Stats. for Last 10 Years	
	5 Years	**10 Years**	**Avg. Return**	**Std. Deviation**
S&P	$1.62	$3.99	16.19%	17.59%
Ind. Composite	**$1.93**	**$8.54**	**26.33%**	**25.01%**
Lg. Composite	$1.79	$7.19	24.17%	24.53%
Sm. Composite	$.66	$5.10	34.91%	76.30%

Margins

	Operating Margin		Net Margin		Return on Assets		Return on Equity	
	Latest	*5-Yr. Avg.*	*Latest*	*5-Yr. Avg.*	*Latest*	*5-Yr. Avg.*	*Latest*	*5-Yr. Avg.*
90th Percentile	29.15%	29.06%	19.04%	17.28%	15.49%	17.64%	6.83%	5.65%
75th Percentile	23.60%	20.06%	10.77%	8.61%	10.19%	10.54%	4.02%	4.27%
Median	**10.56%**	**8.99%**	**2.55%**	**-0.91%**	**3.18%**	**-1.86%**	**1.03%**	**-0.32%**
25th Percentile	-87.19%	-64.51%	-86.22%	-78.78	-33.71	-21.75%	-7.94%	-5.41%
10th Percentile	-601.00%	-445.00%	-593.00%	-477.00%	-44.64%	-52.80%	-21.97%	-9.53%
Ind. Composite	**27.44%**	**26.74%**	**13.04%**	**14.98%**	**11.22%**	**13.91%**	**4.96%**	**4.73%**
Lg. Composite	29.78%	28.48%	13.78%	16.16%	12.14%	15.57%	5.04%	4.97%
Sm. Composite	-2048.00	-356.00%	-2142.00%	-388.00%	-45.21%	--39.79%	-21.28%	-10.69%

Capital Structure Ratios | | | | **Yields (% of Price)**

	Debt/Total Capital		Debt/M.V. Equity		Dividends		Cash Flow	
	Latest	*5-Yr. Avg.*	*Latest*	*5-Yr. Avg.*	*Latest*	*5-Yr. Avg.*	*Latest*	*5-Yr. Avg.*
90th Percentile	15.43%	13.41%	18.25%	15.49%	3.10%	2.96%	4.47%	4.28%
75th Percentile	8.64%	8.72%	9.46%	9.56%	0.86%	1.25%	2.97%	2.47%
Median	**4.06%**	**3.58%**	**4.24%**	**3.72%**	**0.00%**	**0.00%**	**-0.29%**	**-1.41%**
25th Percentile	0.00%	0.83%	0.00%	0.84%	0.00%	0.00%	-14.74%	-6.88%
10th Percentile	0.00%	0.00%	0.00%	0.00%	0.00%	0.00%	-50.55%	-9.72%
Ind. Composite	**6.94%**	**5.97%**	**7.42%**	**6.35%**	**2.93%**	**2.60%**	**2.40%**	**2.95%**
Lg. Composite	6.11%	4.79%	6.49%	5.03%	3.31%	2.81%	2.44%	3.13%
Sm. Composite	2.09%	4.51%	1.67%	4.72%	0.00%	0.00%	-34.79%	-11.41%

Equity Valuation Ratios | | | | | | **Betas**

	Price/Earnings		Market/Book		Price/Sales		Unlev.	Levered
	Latest	*5-Yr. Avg.*	*Latest*	*5-Yr. Avg.*	*Latest*	*5-Yr. Avg.*	*Asset Beta*	*Equity Beta*
90th Percentile	NMF	NMF	7.54	12.89	44.05	66.78	2.28	2.35
75th Percentile	NMF	NMF	5.43	7.50	11.77	14.63	1.79	1.85
Median	**79.37**	**NMF**	**3.41**	**4.90**	**3.64**	**5.13**	**1.34**	**1.48**
25th Percentile	21.62	23.42	2.42	3.29	1.89	2.38	0.94	1.03
10th Percentile	16.35	17.69	0.96	2.84	1.22	1.43	0.50	0.69
Ind. Composite	**22.12**	**21.14**	**4.72**	**5.33**	**2.89**	**3.17**	**1.05**	**1.09**
Lg. Composite	21.88	20.12	4.99	5.61	3.01	3.25	1.06	1.10
Sm. Composite	NMF	NMF	1.39	4.78	58.67	36.28	2.02	2.13

Costs of Equity Capital | | | | | **DCF Growth Rates**

	CAPM		Discounted Cash Flow			Sustainable	
	S-L Form	**Empirical**	**Analysts**	**Sustainable**	**3-Stage**	**Analysts**	**Growth**
90th Percentile	25.01%	21.32%	30.08%	25.66%	18,26%	23.62%	21.40%
75th Percentile	21.41%	19.08%	24.49%	22.92%	16.10%	11.46%	14.65%
Median	18.75%	17.43%	15.75%	15.64%	14.88%	10.38%	0.00%
25th Percentile	15.51%	15.42%	13.59%	NMF	13.66%	10.38%	-44.35%
10th Percentile	13.04%	13.90%	11.64%	NMF	12.53%	8.90%	-146.00%
Ind. Composite	15.94%	15.69%	15.11%	14.50%	15.00%	10.38%	9.77%
Lg. Composite	16.01%	15.74%	15.10%	20.54%	15.18%	10.13%	15.57%
Sm. Composite	23.43%	20.33%	NMF	NMF	NMF	10.38%	-65.84%

SOURCE: *Cost of Capital Quarterly, 1994 Yearbook* (Chicago: Ibbotson Associates, 1994), pp. 2-87–2-88.

The above would be substituted in Formula 9–15 as follows:

$$(.25 \times .70) + (.10[1 - .40] \times .30)$$
$$= .175 + (.06 \times .30)$$
$$= .175 + .018$$
$$= .193$$

So, the overall cost of capital in the above example is 19.3 percent.

In many cases, there is a more complex capital structure, perhaps with a preferred stock and more than one class of debt. Formula 9–14 simply would be expanded to include a term for each class of capital.

Should an Actual or Hypothetical Capital Structure Be Used?

If the company is to be valued *as it is* (for example, under the strict fair market value standard, assuming the capital structure will remain intact), then the amount of debt in the company's actual capital structure should be used. Certainly, if a minority interest is to be valued by a procedure involving (first) valuing overall capital and (then) subtracting debt, the company's actual amount of debt in its capital structure would seem appropriate. This is because it would be beyond the power of a minority stockholder to change the capital structure.

Keep in mind that the weightings in the capital structure are at *market value*. Therefore, if there is a fixed amount of debt and the WACC is used to estimate market value of equity, computations may need to be iterated with different assumed capital structures until the estimated market value of equity results in the assumed market value capital structure weights.

If a controlling interest is to be valued and the standard of value is fair market value, an argument can be made that an industry-average capital structure should be used, since a control buyer would have the power to change the capital structure and the industry average could represent the most likely result. However, it would be important to understand how the industry-average capital structure is derived and whether or not it is reasonable to expect the subject company to achieve it, given current conditions of the company itself as well as financial market conditions. If a controlling interest is to be valued under the standard of investment value, then the buyer's or owner's capital structure could be used.

Specific Projection Period Plus a Terminal Value

Earlier in the chapter we presented the basic discounted economic income model, where specific projections of economic income are made over the life of the investment. We also presented two simplifications of that model, one assuming a constant perpetual economic income and one assuming constant growth in the economic income in perpetuity.

The most common multistage variation of the discounted economic income model is a two-stage model that projects economic income for a finite number of periods, usually somewhere between 3 and 10 years, and then assumes a terminal value at the end of the discrete projection period.

This terminal value is sometimes also called the residual value, the reversionary value, or the future value. The formula for this model can be generalized as follows:

Formula 9–16

$$PV = \frac{E_1}{(1+k)} + \frac{E_2}{(1+k)^2} + \ldots + \frac{E_n}{(1+k)^n} + \frac{FV}{(1+k)^n}$$

where:

$E_1 \ldots E_n$ = Expected amounts of the economic income (often net cash flow) in each of periods E_1 through E_n

k = Discount rate

n = Number of periods in the discrete projection period

FV = Future value or terminal value (the prospective value as of the end of the discrete projection period)

The immediately obvious characteristic of the above formula is that it depends partly on a projection of the value of the subject several periods in the future to estimate the value of the subject today! It is not uncommon for the present value of the terminal value in this formulation to account for over half of the total present value. Therefore, the matter of how the terminal value is estimated is an important part of the estimate of present value.

One of the most common ways to estimate the terminal value is to use the constant growth model presented earlier. This assumes that, after the discrete projection period, the economic income will grow at some constant compound rate in perpetuity. This version of the terminal value estimate merely continues the projection of prospective economic income with a simplifying assumption of a constant growth rate past the discrete projection period.

Using the constant growth model to estimate the terminal value results in Formula 9–16, modified as follows:

Formula 9–17

$$PV = \frac{E_1}{(1+k)} + \frac{E_2}{(1+k)^2} + \ldots + \frac{E_n}{(1+k)^n} + \frac{\dfrac{E_n(1+g)}{k-g}}{(1+k)^n}$$

where:

$E_1 \ldots E_n$ = Expected amounts of the economic income (often net cash flow) in each of periods E_1 through E_n

k = Discount rate

n = Number of periods in the discrete projection period

g = Annually compounded growth rate projected in perpetuity for the prospective economic income, beyond the discrete projection period

Another common way to estimate the terminal value is to capitalize some measure of economic income (which may or may not be the same measure as the one used in the discrete projection period) at a projected market rate of capitalization. For example, one may base the terminal value on a multiple of prospective net income for the final year of the discrete projection period (in other words, projecting the terminal value by using a P/E multiple). One could say that this mixes what we more commonly classify as a "market approach" (P/E multiples) with the income approach. This also introduces the added dimension of projecting a multiple or capitalization rate as of the date of the terminal value estimate. A commonly encountered solution to this is to use the current market multiple or capitalization rate as the best estimate of the rate expected to prevail at some time in the future. For cyclical companies, a normalized multiple may be more appropriate.

Under certain circumstances, the terminal value may be based on the premise that the company will be liquidated at the end of the discrete projection period. This terminal value requires an estimate of liquidation value of the subject company assets as of that future date.

The "Midyear Discounting Convention"

In the formulas presented up to this point, we have implied (by using whole integer exponents) that the cash flows (or other economic income) are expected to be received at the *end* of each period. This is reasonable, since many closely held companies wait until the end of their fiscal year to see how things are and assess capital requirements and decide on shareholder distributions.

On the other hand, sometimes it seems more reasonable to project that cash flows are received (or at least available) more or less evenly throughout the year. This projection can be reflected in the discounted economic income model by using the "midyear discounting convention." This convention projects cash flows being received at the middle rather than the end of each year, thus more or less approximating the valuation effect of even cash flows throughout the year.

The modification to Formula 9–17 to accommodate the midyear discounting convention results in the following:

Formula 9–18

$$PV = \frac{E_1}{(1+k)^{.5}} + \frac{E_2}{(1+k)^{1.5}} + \ldots + \frac{E_n}{(1+k)^{n-.5}} + \frac{\dfrac{E_n(1+g)}{k-g}}{(1+k)^n}$$

where the variables are defined the same as in Formula 9–17. (To be technically correct, note that use of the perpetual growth model in the final term of the above formula ignores the midyear convention with respect to the terminal value.)

Of course, the midyear discounting convention increases the indicated present value, since it projects that the cash flows will be received earlier on the average than the more common year-end discounting model assumes.

The model can be varied to accommodate any projections about the timing of cash flows, such as monthly, quarterly, or irregularly. The calculations for any such variations can be done on any modern, inexpensive pocket financial calculator.

Exhibit 9–11A

Stealth Electronic Investigations, Inc.

Balance Sheets

End of Year	Actual 19X0	Projected 19X1	Projected 19X2	Projected 19X3
Current assets	$300,000	$ 315,000	$ 330,750	$ 347,288
Plant & equipment	900,000	1,010,000	1,125,500	1,246,775
Less: Accumulated depreciation	600,000	690,000	784,500	883,725
Net plant & equipment	300,000	320,000	341,000	363,050
Total assets	$600,000	$ 635,000	$ 671,750	$ 710,338
Current liabilities	$100,000	$ 105,000	$ 110,250	$ 115,763
Long-term debt	400,000	420,000	441,000	463,050
Equity	100,000	110,000	120,500	131,525
Total liabilities & equity	$600,000	$ 635,000	$ 671,750	$ 710,338

Income Statements

	19X1	19X2	19X3
Sales	$2,000,000	$2,100,000	$2,205,000
Cost of sales	1,200,000	1,260,000	1,323,000
Gross margin	800,000	840,000	882,000
General operating expenses	520,000	546,000	573,300
Depreciation	90,000	94,500	99,225
Earnings before interest & taxes (EBIT)	190,000	199,500	209,475
Interest (10% of beginning LTD)	40,000	42,000	44,100
Taxable income (EBT)	150,000	157,500	165,375
Income taxes (40%)	60,000	63,000	66,150
Net income	$ 90,000	$ 94,500	$ 99,225

Other Information

Expected growth rate in perpetuity: 5%
  (applies to all income statement items, net working capital, capital expenditures, and long-term debt)
Capital expenditures year 19X1: $110,000
Market value of long-term debt = Book value of long-term debt
All net cash flow to equity will be paid out in dividends

Calculation of Net Cash Flow to Equity

(Formula 9–3)

	19X1	19X2	19X3
Net income	$ 90,000	$ 94,500	$ 99,225
+ Depreciation	90,000	94,500	99,225
− Capital expenditures	110,000	115,500	121,275
− Increase in net working capital	10,000	10,500	11,025
+ Increase in long-term debt	20,000	21,000	22,050
= Net cash flow to equity	$ 80,000	$ 84,000	$ 88,200

Statements of Stockholders' Equity

	19X1	19X2	19X3
Balance at beginning of year	$100,000	$110,000	$120,500
+ Net income	90,000	94,500	99,225
− Dividends paid	80,000	84,000	88,200
= Balance at end of year	$110,000	$120,500	$131,525

Calculation of Net Cash Flow to Invested Capital

(Formula 9–4)

	19X1	19X2	19X3
Net income	$ 90,000	$ 94,500	$ 99,225
+ Depreciation	90,000	94,500	99,225
− Capital expenditures	110,000	115,500	121,275
− Increase in net working capital	10,000	10,500	11,025
+ Interest expense (net of 40% income taxes)	24,000	25,200	26,460
= Net cash flow to invested capital	$ 84,000	$ 88,200	$ 92,610

Exhibit 9–11B

Illustrative Example Discount Rate Applicable to Equity

Risk-free rate (20-Year U.S. Government Bonds)[a]		10.50
+ Systematic risk:		
Long-horizon expected equity risk premium[b]	7.0	
× Beta[c]	1.2	
		8.40
+ Expected size premium[b]		4.00
+ Specific (unsystematic) risk[d]		2.00
		24.90
Rounded		25.00

[a]Rate available as of valuation date per, *The Wall Street Journal.*
[b]*Stocks, Bonds, Bills & Inflation 1995 Yearbook*, p. 157.
[c]Median of guideline companies used in valuation report, from *Value Line*, xx/xx/xx.
[d]Analyst's estimate, as discussed in valuation report.

Example of Application of Discounted Economic Income Methods

In a series of exhibits, we present several of the basic discounted economic income methods applied to value of 100 percent of the equity of Stealth Electronic Investigations, Inc., as of December 30, 19X0. The basic information, including the December 30, 19X0, balance sheet, three years of projected balance sheets, income statements, cash flows to equity, cash flows to invested capital, and other information are presented as Exhibit 9–11A on page 187.

The example projects stable growth for the entire projection period. This projection allows us to show how any of four methods can be used, all resulting in a similar value:

1. Discounted net cash flow available to equity.
2. Perpetual growth model using net cash flow available to equity.
3. Discounted net cash flow available to all invested capital (market value of invested capital) less value of debt.
4. Perpetual growth model using net cash flow available to all invested capital (market value of invested capital) less value of debt.

Estimating an Equity Discount Rate

Exhibit 9–11B illustrates the estimation of the cost of equity capital for the subject company using the capital asset pricing model. The sources of all components are footnoted in the exhibit, so one can seek out the sources and replicate the work.

Discounting Net Cash Flow to Equity

Exhibit 9–11C illustrates discounting the cash flow to equity using the projected net cash flows to equity from Exhibit 9–11A and the discount rate developed in Exhibit 9–11B. This example uses the perpetual growth model to estimate the terminal value.

Note that, with a very short specific projection period, the terminal value constitutes over half the total value. The shorter the specific projection period and the lower the discount rate, the higher the proportion of the total value will be accounted for by the terminal value. When using the perpetual growth model to estimate the terminal value, it often is useful to check its reasonableness by computing implied market multiples, such as price/earnings multiples and so on (see Chapters 10 and 11 on the market approach).

Estimating Equity Value by the Perpetual Growth Model

Exhibit 9–11D illustrates capitalizing the cash flow to equity using the cash flows and growth projection from Exhibit 9–11A with the discount rate developed in Exhibit 9–11B. This example also calculates the estimated value of the equity one year and two years past the valuation date, using the same information.

Exhibit 9–11E illustrates how the total rate of return achieved comports to the cost of equity capital. It is assumed that all net cash flows to equity are paid out in dividends. The *total return* equals the cash distributions during the period plus the appreciation in value during the period (ending value less beginning value). Thus, the total *rate of return* equals the total return during the period divided by the beginning value. If this example were carried out for additional years, it would show that the investor achieves a rate of return on equity equal to the market's cost of equity capital (at the valuation date) in each year.

Estimating a Weighted Average Cost of Capital

Exhibit 9–11F illustrates the estimation of the weighted average cost of capital (WACC) using the information provided in Exhibit 9–11A and the equity discount rate developed in Exhibit 9–11B.

Exhibit 9–11C

Estimation of Value of Equity (Discounted Cash Flow Model—Formula 9–2)

	19X1		19X2		19X3		Terminal Value
	$\dfrac{\$80,000}{(1+.25)}$	+	$\dfrac{\$84,000}{(1+.25)^2}$	+	$\dfrac{\$88,200}{(1+.25)^3}$	+	$\dfrac{\frac{\$88,200(1.05)}{.25-.05}}{(1+.25)^3}$
=	$\dfrac{\$80,000}{(1.25)}$	+	$\dfrac{\$84,000}{(1.25)^2}$	+	$\dfrac{\$88,200}{(1.25)^3}$	+	$\dfrac{\frac{\$92,610}{.20}}{(1.25)^3}$
=	$\$64,000$	+	$\$53,760$	+	$\$45,158$	+	$\dfrac{\$463,050}{(1.25)^3}$
=	$\$64,000$	+	$\$53,760$	+	$\$45,158$	+	$\$237,082$
=	$\$400,000$						

Exhibit 9–11D

Estimation of Value of Equity (Perpetual Growth Model—Formula 9–6)

End of Year		19X0	19X1	19X2
Net cash flow to equity		$80,000	$84,000	$88,200
Equity discount rate – growth		.25 − .05	.25 − .05	.25 − .05
Indicated value of equity*	=	$400,000	$420,000	$441,000

*Indicated values as of end of each year based on projection for following year.

Discounting Net Cash Flow to Invested Capital

Exhibit 9–11G illustrates discounting the cash flow available to all invested capital using the projected cash flow to invested capital from Exhibit 9–11A and the WACC from Exhibit 9–11F. This example also uses the perpetual growth model to estimate the terminal value.

Note that, with the short projection period and the WACC, which is much lower than the equity discount rate, the terminal value accounts for over three-quarters of the total market value of invested capital! Some market multiples that might be used as a check on the reasonableness of the terminal value are discussed in Chapter 11 on mergers and acquisitions.

The market value of debt, as of the valuation date, is subtracted from the MVIC to arrive at the market value of equity.

Exhibit 9–11E

Calculation of Rate of Return on Equity (Formula 9–9)

$$\frac{\text{Dividends paid} + (\text{Ending value} - \text{Beginning value})}{\text{Beginning value}}$$

Year 1

$$\frac{\$80,000 + (\$420,000 - \$400,000)}{\$400,000}$$

$$= \frac{\$100,000}{\$400,000} = .25$$

Year 2

$$\frac{\$84,000 + (\$441,000 - \$420,000)}{\$420,000}$$

$$= \frac{\$105,000}{\$420,000} = .25$$

Exhibit 9–11F

Estimation of Weighted Average Cost of Capital

Capital Component	Amount	Percent of Capital		Cost of Capital		Weighted Average Cost
Market value of debt	$400,000	.50	x	.06*	=	.030
Market value of equity	$400,000	.50	x	.25	=	.125
Weighted average cost of capital						.155

*Cost of debt x (1 − Tax rate) = .10(1 − .40) = .06.

Exhibit 9–11G
Estimation of Market Value of Invested Capital
(Discounted Cash Flow Model—Formula 9–2)

Less Market Value of Debt

	19X1		19X2		19X3		Terminal Value
	$\dfrac{\$84,000}{(1+.155)}$	+	$\dfrac{\$88,200}{(1+.155)^2}$	+	$\dfrac{\$92,610}{(1+.155)^3}$	+	$\dfrac{\frac{\$92,610(1.05)}{.155-.05}}{(1+.155)^3}$
=	$\dfrac{\$84,000}{(1.155)}$	+	$\dfrac{\$88,200}{(1.155)^2}$	+	$\dfrac{\$92,610}{(1.155)^3}$	+	$\dfrac{\frac{\$97,240.50}{.105}}{(1.155)^3}$
=	\$72,727	+	\$66,116	+	\$60,105	+	$\dfrac{\$926,100}{(1.155)^3}$
=	\$72,727	+	\$66,116	+	\$60,105	+	\$601,052
=	\$800,000						
Less:	\$400,000	Value of debt					
Equals:	\$400,000	Indicated value of equity					

Estimating the Market Value of Invested Capital by the Perpetual Growth Model

Exhibit 9–11H illustrates capitalizing the cash flow to invested capital using the cash flows and growth projection from Exhibit 9–11A with the WACC developed in Exhibit 9–11F. This example also calculates the estimated market value of invested capital one year and two years past the valuation date, using the same information.

The market value of debt as of the valuation date and as of each of the following two years is subtracted from the MVIC to arrive at the value of equity in each of those years.

Caveats in Using Discounted Economic Income Methods

The discounted economic income methods are extremely sensitive to changes in the input variables—that is, the projected cash flows and the discount rate. This is especially true of the market value of invested capital (MVIC) version, where one values the entire invested capital using a WACC discount rate and then subtracts the value of existing debt to get an estimate of the value of the equity.

Exhibit 9–11H
Estimation of Market Value of Invested Capital (Perpetual Growth Model—Formula 9–6)

End of Year	19X0	19X1	19X2
Net cash flow to invested capital*	\$84,000	\$88,200	\$92,610
WACC – Growth	.155 – .05	.155 – .05	.155 – .05
Indicated value of invested capital	= \$800,000	\$840,000	\$882,000
– Market value of debt	400,000	420,000	441,000
= Indicated market value of equity	\$400,000	\$420,000	\$441,000

*Projections under 19X0 column are for 19X1, etc.; indicated market value of equity is for end of 19X0, etc.

In the previous example, four versions of the discounted economic income method produced identical values for the equity. However, that example only illustrates the mechanics of the methods. Changes in the projections, sometimes seemingly small, can result in different methods yielding strikingly different results.

For example, let us assume a 6 percent growth rate instead of 5 percent. In the direct estimation of the value of equity in the perpetual growth model (Exhibit 9–11D), this change would result in the following:

$$\frac{NCF_e}{k_e - g} = \frac{\$80,000}{.25 - .06} = \frac{\$80,000}{.19} = \$421,053$$

This is an increase of $21,053 or 5.3 percent from the value of $400,000 using a 5 percent growth rate.

However, capitalizing the market value of invested capital at the WACC minus the 6 percent growth rate (using the same model as presented in Exhibit 9–11H), the one percentage point change in the estimated growth rate would result in the following:

$$\frac{NCF_f}{WACC - g} = \frac{\$84,000}{.155 - .06} = \frac{\$84,000}{.095} = \$884,211$$

This is an increase of $84,211 or 10.5 percent in the market value of all invested capital from the value of $800,000, using a 5 percent growth rate. If one subtracts the actual debt of $400,000, the result is an indicated value of equity of $484,211 ($884,211 - $400,000 = $484,211). This increase of $84,211 is a material 21.1 percent increase over the previously indicated value of $400,000, all because of a single percentage point increase in the projected rate of growth in cash flow available to invested capital!

When the projected growth rate reaches or exceeds the discount rate in the perpetual growth model, mathematically, the capitalization rate is zero or negative. This relationship leads to the generally unreasonable conclusion that the company is infinitely valuable.

Because of such potentially large impacts of relatively small changes in input variables, it is often enlightening to perform some sensitivity analysis in conjunction with a discounted economic income method. This could take the form of a sensitivity table showing the impact of a range of discount rates, terminal value multiples, growth rates, and cash flow projections.

Converting a Discount Rate Applicable to Net Cash Flow to a Discount Rate Applicable to Net Income

If it can be assumed that the relationship (ratio) of net income to net cash flow is constant over time, then the formula to convert a discount rate applicable to net cash flow to a discount rate applicable to net income for use in the multiperiod discounted economic income model is as follows:[24]

---

[24]For a proof of the derivation of this formula, see Christopher Z. Mercer, *Valuing Financial Institutions* (Burr Ridge, IL: Irwin Professional Publishing, 1992), pp. 262–64.

Formula 9–19

$$k_{ni} = [\frac{NI}{NCF_e} (k_e - g)] + g$$

where:

k_{ni} = Discount rate applicable to net income

$\frac{NI}{NCF_e}$ = Assumed constant ratio of net income to net cash flow to equity

k_e = Discount rate applicable to net cash flow

g = Annually compounded growth rate in perpetuity for both net income and net cash flow

Note carefully the *critical assumptions* inherent in the above formula:

1. Net income and net cash flow bear a constant relationship to each other over time.
2. Both grow at the same constant annually compounded rate in perpetuity.

One way to assess whether these assumptions are realistic is to compute the ratio of net income to net cash flow for the subject company for several years in the past to see whether the ratio has been steady historically. One would still need to judge whether this stability would be expected to continue to hold true.

Another avenue is to research publicly traded companies in the industry to see the extent to which the ratio is reasonably consistent from company to company and over time. One would then have to analyze the extent to which the subject company could be expected to parallel the public companies in this respect.

If the subject company comes close enough to the above assumptions to realistically use this formula, then it is useful to know the following characteristics about how it works out:

1. The higher the cash flow discount rate, the higher the difference between the cash flow discount rate and the net income discount rate.
2. The higher the ratio between net income and net cash flow, the higher the difference between the net cash flow discount rate and the net income discount rate. For any given combination of discount rate and growth rate, this relationship moves proportionately with changes in the percentages by which net income exceeds net cash flow.
3. The higher the growth rate, the less the difference between the net cash flow discount rate and the net income discount rate.

Examples of the application of this formula are presented in Exhibit 9–12. As can be seen, the greatest differences between net cash flow discount rates and net income discount rates are found in situations of high net cash flow discount rates, high ratios of net income to net cash flow, and low growth rates.

Net cash flow is generally lower than net income or any other economic income measures that the appraiser is likely to discount or capitalize. Therefore, the discount rate applicable to other measures is generally higher than the discount rate applicable to net cash flow.

Exhibit 9–12

Differences between Net Cash Flow Discount Rate and Net Income Discount Rate

Formula:

$$k_{ni} = [\ \frac{NI}{NCF_e}\ (k_e - g)] + g$$

k_e = 30% Growth Rate	Constant Ratio of Net Income to Net Cash Flow					
	150%	140%	130%	120%	110%	100%
2%	14.0%	11.2%	8.4%	5.6%	2.8%	0.0%
4%	13.0%	10.4%	7.8%	5.2%	2.6%	0.0%
6%	12.0%	9.6%	7.2%	4.8%	2.4%	0.0%
8%	11.0%	8.8%	6.6%	4.4%	2.2%	0.0%
k_e = 25% Growth Rate						
2%	11.5%	9.2%	6.9%	4.6%	2.3%	0.0%
4%	10.5%	8.4%	6.3%	4.2%	2.1%	0.0%
6%	9.5%	7.6%	5.7%	3.8%	1.9%	0.0%
8%	8.5%	6.8%	5.1%	3.4%	1.7%	0.0%
k_e = 20% Growth Rate						
2%	9.0%	7.2%	5.4%	3.6%	1.8%	0.0%
4%	8.0%	6.4%	4.8%	3.2%	1.6%	0.0%
6%	7.0%	5.6%	4.2%	2.8%	1.4%	0.0%
8%	6.0%	4.8%	3.6%	2.4%	1.2%	0.0%

where:

k_{ni} = Discount rate applicable to net income

$\frac{NI}{NCF_e}$ = Constant assumed ratio of net income to net cash flow to equity

k_e = Discount rate applicable to net cash flow to equity

g = Annually compounded growth rate in perpetuity for both net income and net cash flow

CAUTION: The above critical assumptions for the conversion of a discount rate applicable to net cash flows to equity to a discount rate applicable to net income are rarely met in real world situations. Therefore, we strongly recommend the use of net cash flow as the measure of economic income to use in the discounted economic income method.

It is also noteworthy that the discount rate conversion procedures described above are appropriate for the multiperiod (or yield capitalization) discounted economic income model. They are not necessarily appropriate for the single-period (or direct capitalization) discounted economic income model.

Does the Discounted Economic Income Model Produce a Control or a Minority Value?

As noted earlier in the chapter, the discounted economic income model can produce either a control value or a minority value, depending on the model inputs regarding the valuation variables. Generally, if the inputs in the valuation model reflect changes that only a control owner would (or could) make (e.g., changed capital structure, reduced owner's compensation, and so on), then the model would be expected to produce a control value.

If the economic income projections merely reflect the continuation of present policies, then the model would be expected to produce a minority value. If every facet of the company is being so well optimized that a control owner could not improve on it, then there may be little or no difference between a control value and a minority value. Further discussion of this notion will be found in Chapter 14 on control premiums and minority discounts.

The argument often is made that, because discount rates typically are developed from minority trades in publicly traded stocks, the discount rate is a minority interest discount rate and the value indicated by a discounted economic income model must, therefore, be a minority value. There are at least two problems with this argument. First, *most, if not all, of the difference between a control value and a minority value in a discounted economic income model results from differences in the projected economic income (the numerator) and not from differences in the discount rate.* Second, while the costs of equity capital are estimated from trades of minority ownership interests, the capital structure (i.e., the percent of debt versus percent of equity) of the subject company is clearly influenced by the controlling stockholder. And, the capital structure mix is at least as important as the cost of equity capital in the estimation of a company's overall WACC—that is, the discount rate associated with net cash flow. In other words, the cost of equity capital may be the same, or nearly the same, whether a control or a minority interest is being transacted. However, the controlling owner (and, generally, not the minority owner) influences the projection of economic income (the numerator in the model) and the capital structure component of the WACC (the denominator in the model).

What Standard of Value Does a Discounted Economic Income Model Produce?

As with the control/minority ownership issue, the answer to this question depends to some extent on the individual valuation variable inputs that go into the model.

If valuing a company on a stand-alone basis, use of that company's own economic income projections and a market-derived cost of capital as the discount rate would be expected to estimate *fair market value.* If, on the other hand, a particular acquirer with a lower cost of capital would discount an economic income projection at that acquirer's lower cost of capital, then the result would be *investment value,* the value of the subject—but only to that individual acquirer. Similarly, if the particular acquirer were to include synergistic benefits or other enhancements in the economic income projections, then the result would be *investment value* rather than *fair market value.*

Common Errors

While simple in basic concept, the application of the discounted economic income method provides virtually limitless opportunities for errors. The following are a few of the common errors that are made:

Mismatching the Discount Rate with the Economic Income Measure

The most common error in application of the income approach is using a discount or capitalization rate that is not appropriate for the definition of economic income being discounted or capitalized. This general category of error has almost infinite variations. The following are only a few.

Using a "Safe" Rate to Discount or Capitalize a Risky Return. While not the most common error, this certainly is one of the most egregious. Some analysts have even erroneously discounted a highly risky series of projected economic income by the Treasury bill rate!

Applying a Discount Rate to an Income Variable Defined Differently Than That to Which the Discount Rate Is Applicable. This general error in itself has many variations. As discussed earlier, most of the methods and sources for developing discount rates used in the practical application of contemporary financial theory and discussed in this book produce a rate at which to discount net cash flow, as defined in an earlier section. The *SBBI 1995 Yearbook* makes the following point:

> It should be noted that from a valuation specialist's point of view, the stock market returns presented in this book are after corporate taxes but before personal taxes and should be applied to cash flows calculated on the same basis.[25]

Applying a Discount Rate in Real Terms to an Economic Income Projection in Nominal (Current) Terms. Some analysts erroneously subtract the anticipated inflation rate from the discount rate and then apply the adjusted discount rate to an economic income projection that includes inflation (and vice versa). It is noteworthy that all the Ibbotson data are in nominal terms—that is, including inflation.

Confusing Discount Rates with Capitalization Rates

The *discount rate* is the cost of capital and applies to all prospective economic income. The *capitalization rate* is a divisor applied to some particular economic income (e.g., latest 12 months' earnings, cash flow, and so on). Only when the expected level of economic income is constant in perpetuity are these two rates equal, other than by sheer coincidence.

Nevertheless, some appraisers fall into the trap of using the discount rate (i.e., cost of capital) as a capitalization rate. We also see the opposite from time to time: using a capitalization rate to discount prospective cash flow or other expected economic income to a present value.

Projecting Growth Beyond What the Capital Being Valued Will Support

As businesses grow, they typically need additional working capital and capital expenditures to support the increased level of operations. One of the many advantages of using net cash flow as the prospective economic income measure is that it forces the analyst to explicitly consider these needs. Nevertheless, they often are underestimated.

---

[25]*SBBI 1995 Yearbook*, p. 147.

Projecting Near-Term Growth Will Continue in Perpetuity

One error commonly encountered is the use of high short-term (one- to five-year) growth expectations as the rate of growth (the "g" factor) in the perpetual growth model (Gordon growth model). Very high rates of growth generally are not sustainable for very long periods. If high growth is expected in the early years, a multistage projection model may make the most economic sense.

Projecting That Extrapolation of the Recent Past Represents the Best Estimate of Future Results

All economic, financial, and regulatory literature makes it clear that valuation is a function of expected prospective economic income. The past history is relevant only to the extent that it may, in some cases, provide useful guidance in projecting future economic income. Nevertheless, it is not as uncommon as one might think to see "projections" that are nothing more than a statistical extrapolation of past results, with no analysis as to the extent to which the future generating forces will or will not duplicate the recent past. Usually, they will not.

Discounting a Terminal Value for an Incorrect Number of Periods

Referring back to Formula 9–15, it can be seen that the terminal value usually is projected to be the value at the *beginning* of the period immediately following the discrete projection period. Therefore, it usually should be discounted back to present value by the same number of years as the last term in the discrete projection period (n in the formula). A common error is to discount the terminal value for $n + 1$ periods, which would be appropriate only if the terminal value represented the estimated value one year following the end of the discrete projection period.

Internally Inconsistent Capital Structure Projection

"Debt-free" methods and methods using betas adjusted for leverage require projections about the subject company's capital structure. These projected capital structures are on the basis of *market value*. Often appraisers assume a capital structure in the process of estimating a market value of equity, and the resulting estimated market value of equity makes the capital structure, at the estimated market value, different from that which was assumed.

In such cases, the projected capital structure needs to be adjusted and the process iterated until the estimated market value of equity results in a capital structure consistent with that which is projected in estimating the cost of capital.

Assumptions That Produce a Standard or Premise of Value Other Than That Called for in the Valuation Engagement

A common example of this type of error is making unsupported adjustments to projected economic income that only a control owner could cause to happen (e.g., lowering the control owner's salary) when valuing a minority interest.

Another common error is projecting a capital structure other than the company's actual capital structure (thereby getting a weighted average cost of capital different from the company's actual WACC) when the standard of value is fair market value on a minority basis. If an acquirer were to use its own WACC, the implied result would be *investment value* to that acquirer instead of fair market value. Moreover, if the interest is a minority interest, the holder could not force a change in capital structure.

Summary

This chapter has presented the rationale of the discounted economic income method and step-by-step explanations of each important aspect of its implementation. It has also presented a simplified version, the constant growth or Gordon growth model, and an explanation of the difference and relationship between discount rates and capitalization rates as those two terms are commonly used today. The chapter has explained the conceptual elements of discount and capitalization rates and sources of information to develop estimates of appropriate betas.

Discounted economic income methods can be used in conjunction with almost any combination of standards of value and ownership characteristics, as long as the projections underlying the valuation variables used in the calculation are consistent with the definition of value being sought.

Bibliography

Articles

Abrams, Jay B. "Cash Flow: A Mathematical Derivation." *ASA Valuation*, March 1994, pp. 64–71.

Bendixen, Christian L. "Improved Estimation of Equity Risk Premiums." *Business Valuation Review*, March 1994, pp. 22–32.

Bielinski, Daniel W. "Putting a Realistic Dollar Value on Acquisition Synergies." *Mergers & Acquisitions*, November/December 1992, pp. 9–12.

————. "The Debt-Free DCF Model: A Fix on Intrinsic Values." *Mergers & Acquisitions*, September/October 1989, pp. 43–47.

Black, Fischer. "A Simple Discounting Rule." *Financial Management*, Summer 1988, pp. 7–11.

————. "Estimating Expected Return." *Financial Analysts Journal*, September–October 1993, pp. 36–38.

Carlton, Willard T., and Josef Lakonishok. "Risk and Return on Equity: The Use and Misuse of Historical Estimates." *Financial Analysts Journal*, January–February 1985, pp. 38–47.

Chen, Nai-fi; Richard Roll; and Stephen A. Ross. "Economic Forces and the Stock Market: Testing the APT and Alternative Asset Pricing Theories." UCLA Graduate School of Management working paper no. 20-83 (December 1983).

Dilbeck, Harold R. "A Constant-Dollar Discount Rate for Closely Held Businesses Based on Risk Premiums from Five-Year Holding Periods." *Business Valuation Review*, March 1994, pp. 11–18.

Dukes, William P., and Oswald D. Bowlin. "A Comparison of Valuation Techniques for Closely Held Firms." *Business Valuation Review,* June 1993, pp. 80–91.

Fama, Eugene, and Kenneth French. "Common Risk Factors in the Returns on Stocks and Bonds." University of Chicago working paper no. 360 (November 1992).

_____. "The Cross Section of Expected Stock Returns." *Journal of Finance,* 47 (1992), pp. 427–65.

Fishman, Jay E., and Francis W. Donahue. "Applying Common Sense to Capitalization of Earnings." *FAIR$HARE: The Matrimonial Law Monthly,* September 1991, pp. 3–5.

Harper, Charles P., and Lawrence C. Rose. "Accuracy of Appraisers and Appraisal Methods of Closely Held Companies." *Entrepreneurship Theory & Practice,* Spring 1993, pp. 21 33.

Hempstead, John E. "Delaware Court Embraces Cash Flow Valuation Method with Both Arms." *Business Valuation Review,* December 1991, pp. 182–83.

Hickman, Kent, and Glenn H. Petry. "A Comparison of Stock Price Predictions Using Court Accepted Formulas, Dividend Discount, and P/E Models." *Financial Management,* Summer 1990, pp. 76–87.

Howitt, Idelle A. "Valuing Closely Held Stock." *CPA Journal,* September 1993, pp. 44–45 ff.

Jackson, Marcus. "The Gordon Growth Model and the Income Approach to Value." *Appraisal Journal,* January 1994, pp. 124–28.

Kenny, Thomas J. "Closely-Held Corporation Valuation: Determining a Proper Discount Rate." *Business Valuation Review,* March 1992, pp. 22–30.

King, David W. "The Equity Risk Premium for Cost of Capital Studies: Alternatives to Ibbotson." *Business Valuation Review,* September 1994, pp. 123–29.

Knight, Ray A., and Lee G. Knight. "Three Key Methods for Valuing Profitable Closely Held Companies." *Journal of Corporate Accounting & Finance,* Autumn 1993, pp. 79–94.

LeClair, Mark S. "Valuing the Closely-Held Corporation: The Validity and Performance of Established Valuation Procedures." *Accounting Horizons,* September 1990, pp. 31–42.

Lippitt, Jeffrey W., and Nicholas J. Mastracchio, Jr. "Valuing Small Businesses: Discounted Cash Flow, Earnings Capitalization, and the Cost of Replacing Capital Assets." *Journal of Small Business Management,* July 1993, pp. 52–61.

Maxson, Mark J. "Will You Get Your Money's Worth?" *Financial Executive,* May/June 1993, pp. 54–58.

McGillivray, Duncan, and Stephanie McGillivray. "Scenario Planning To Help Buyers In Dynamic Industries." *Mergers & Acquisitions,* January/February 1995, pp. 37–40.

McMullin, Scott G. "Discount Rate Selection." *Business Valuation News,* September 1986, pp. 16–19.

Melcher, Albert G. "A Comparison of Built-Up Capitalization and Discount Rate Development Procedures." *Business Valuation Review,* December 1994, pp. 168–71.

Mercer, Z. Christopher. "Adjusting Capitalization Rates for the Differences between Net Income and Net Free Cash Flow." *Business Valuation Review,* December 1992, pp. 201–207.

Nevers, Thomas J. "Capitalization Rates." *Business Valuation News,* June 1985, pp. 3–6.

Pratt, Shannon P. "Understanding Capitalization Rates." *ASA Valuation,* June 1986, pp. 12–29.

Pratt, Shannon P., and Ralph Arnold. "Misuse of the Discounted Future Returns Valuation Method." *FAIR$HARE,* March 1990, pp. 3–5.

Proctor, Richard J. "Business Valuation Litigation: Concepts & Issues." *Connecticut CPA Quarterly,* March 1992, pp. 8–10.

Reilly, Robert F. "Business Valuation Methodology." *Ohio CPA Journal,* Winter 1986, pp. 42–44.

Schilt, James H. "Selection of Capitalization Rates—Revisited." *Business Valuation Review,* June 1991, pp. 51–52.

Sharpe, William F. "Capital Asset Prices with and without Negative Holdings." Nobel Lecture, December 1990, The Nobel Foundation, Royal Swedish Academy of Sciences, Sweden.

————. "Factor Models, CAPMs, and the ABT." *Journal of Portfolio Management,* Fall 1984, pp. 21–25.

Skolnik, Martin A. "Taking the Mystery Out of Discounted Cash Flow Analysis." *Assessment Journal,* January/February 1995, pp. 36–41.

Sliwoski, Leonard. "Capitalization Rates Developed Using the Ibbotson Associates Data: Should They Be Applied to Pretax or After Tax Earnings?" *Business Valuation Review,* March 1994, pp. 8–10.

————. "Capitalization Rates, Discount Rates, and P/E Ratios: One More Time." *Business Valuation Review,* September 1992, pp. 122–34.

Swad, Randy. "Discount and Capitalization Rates in Business Valuations." *CPA Journal,* October 1994, pp. 40–46.

Taggart, Robert A., Jr. "Consistent Valuation and Cost of Capital Expressions with Corporate and Personal Taxes." *Financial Management,* Autumn 1991, pp. 8–20.

Reference Texts

Bierman, Harold, Jr., and Seymour Smidt. *The Capital Budgeting Decision: Economic Analysis of Investment Projects,* 8th ed. New York: Macmillan, 1992.

Brealey, Richard A., and Stewart C. Myers. *Principles of Corporate Finance,* 4th ed. New York: McGraw-Hill, Inc. 1991.

Cornell, Bradford. *Corporate Valuation: Tools for Effective Appraisal and Decision Making.* Burr Ridge, IL: Irwin Professional Publishing, 1993.

Copeland, Tom; Tim Koller; and Jack Murrin. *Valuation: Measuring and Managing the Value of Companies,* 2nd ed. New York: John Wiley & Sons, 1994.

Damodaran, Aswath. *Damodaran on Valuation: Security Analysis for Investment and Corporate Finance.* New York: John Wiley & Sons, 1994.

Dewing, Arthur Stone. *The Financial Policy of Corporations,* 5th ed. New York: Ronald Press, 1953.

Ehrhardt, Michael C. *The Search for Value: Measuring the Company's Cost of Capital.* Boston: Harvard Business School Press, 1994.

Hackel, Kenneth S., and Joshua Livnat. *Cash Flow and Security Analysis.* Burr Ridge, IL: Irwin Professional Publishing, 1992.

Ibbotson, Roger G., and Gary P. Brinson. *Global Investing: The Professional's Guide to the World Capital Markets.* New York: McGraw-Hill, Inc. 1993.

————. *Investment Markets.* New York: McGraw-Hill, Inc. 1987.

Reilly, Frank K. *Investment Analysis and Portfolio Management,* 4th ed. Fort Worth, TX: The Dryden Press, 1994.

Ross, Stephen A.; Randolph W. Westerfield,; and Jeffrey F. Jaffe. *Corporate Finance,* 3rd ed. Burr Ridge, IL: Irwin Professional Publishing, 1993.

Sharpe, John. *Texas Property Tax Manual for Discounting Oil and Gas Income.* Austin, TX: Texas Comptroller of Public Accounts, 1994.

Sharpe, William F., and G. J. Alexander. *Investments,* 4th ed. Englewood Cliffs, NJ: Prentice Hall, 1989.

Stocks, Bonds, Bills & Inflation 1995 Yearbook. Chicago: Ibbotson Associates, 1995.

Williams, John Burr. *The Theory of Investment Value.* Cambridge, MA: Harvard University Press, 1938.

Arbitrage Pricing Theory Data Sources

Birr Portfolio Analysis, Inc.
BIRR Risks and Returns Analyzer
220 West Main Street, Suite 210
Durham, NC 27705
(919) 687-7053

The Alcar Group
APT!
5215 Old Orchard Road
Skokie, IL 60077-1035
(708) 967-4200

Sources of Beta

CompuServe
5000 Arlington Centre Boulevard
P.O. Box 20212
Columbus, OH 43220
(800) 848-8990

Merrill Lynch
Merrill Lynch Capital Markets
Global Securities Research & Economics Group
World Financial Center
North Tower, 19th Floor
New York, NY 10281-1320
(212) 449-1069

Standard & Poor's Compustat and
Standard & Poor's Stock Reports
Standard & Poor's Corporation
25 Broadway
New York, NY 10004
(212) 208-8000

Tradeline
IDD Information Services
100 Fifth Avenue
Waltham, MA 02154
(617) 890-7227

Value Line Investment Survey
220 East 42nd Street, 6th Floor
New York, NY 10017
(212) 907-1500

Wilshire Associates Inc.
1299 Ocean Avenue, 7th Floor
Santa Monica, CA 90401-1085
(310) 451-3051

Other Cost of Capital Data

Ibbotson Associates, Inc.
Cost of Capital Yearbook
Cost of Capital Quarterly
225 North Michigan Avenue
Suite 700
Chicago, IL 60601-7676
(312) 616-1620

Chapter 10

Market Approach: The Guideline Company Method

The use of comparable publicly held corporations as a guide to valuation, as a practical matter, may be the most important and appropriate technique for valuing a privately held operating business. Obviously finding a business exactly the same as the enterprise to be valued is an impossibility. The standard sought is usually one of reasonable and justifiable similarity. This degree of likeness is attainable in most cases.[1]

In the market determined price of a stock, thousands of investors act through Adam Smith's "invisible hand" to arrive at an equilibrium value.[2]

While the income approach discussed in the previous chapter is the core of valuation theory, actual market transaction data can provide compelling empirical evidence of value.

There is an enormous storehouse of reliable guideline transaction data from the day-to-day transactions in publicly traded companies, of which over 12,000 are reasonably actively traded in the United States alone. We agree with the above quote that publicly traded corporation capital market data may provide relevant valuation guidance in many cases.

The scope of this vast U.S. public stock market is summarized in Exhibit 10–1, which indicates the number of issues trading and the criteria for eligibility to trade in each of several major segments of the public market. Exhibit 10–2 summarizes the mechanisms available to effect a public offering.

The size requirements for a public offering and public trading are far less than many people think. Many closely held companies that might be thought of as small actually are large enough to go public if they so desired. However, it is not necessary for a company to be eligible to go public in order to use valuation guidance from the public market. The capital markets provide general guidelines as to how securities in many industries are being priced.

The public capital markets in the United States (as well as in other countries) reprice thousands of securities every day, mostly through transactions among financial buyers and sellers who are well informed (because of stringent disclosure laws at least in the United States) and have no special motivations or compulsions to buy or to sell. This constant repricing gives up-to-the-minute evidence of prices that buyers and sellers agree on for securities in all kinds of industries relative to the fundamental variables perceived to drive their values, such as dividends, cash flows, and earnings. Multiples of these and other relevant financial variables are important investor valuation yardsticks.

Furthermore, companies already public are high on the list of potential acquirers for many private companies, and valuation parameters of the potential acquirers' stock certainly will influence the pricing of a potential acquiree. If the subject company *could* be a candidate to go public, this makes the comparison even more directly relevant.[3]

---

[1] Frank M. Burke Jr., *Valuation and Valuation Planning for Closely Held Businesses* (Englewood Cliffs, NJ: Prentice Hall, Inc., 1981), p. 49.

[2] Kent Hickman and Glen H. Petry, "A Comparison of Stock Price Predictions Using Court Accepted Formulas, Dividend Discount, and P/E Models," *Financial Management*, Summer 1990, p. 84.

[3] It should be noted that minority stockholders cannot force a public offering. This fact typically is recognized by a discount for lack of marketability for the private shares when valued by reference to public market shares. This adjustment to value is discussed in detail in Chapter 15 on discounts for lack of marketability.

Exhibit 10–1

Stock Issues Traded and Criteria for Trading in Major U.S. Public Markets

National Exchange	No. of Issues	Initial Listing	Maintenance
		Requirements	
New York Stock Exchange (NYSE)	3,064	2,000 holders of at least 100 shares or 2,200 holders and at least 100,000 shares average monthly volume for the last six months 1,100,000 public shares outstanding with a market value of $18,000,000 $18,000,000 in net tangible assets $2,500,000 pretax income in the most recent year and $2,000,000 for each of the two preceding years, or pretax income of $6,500,000 in aggregate for the last three years and $4,500,000 for the most recent year, and all three years must be profitable Must have two outside directors Voting rights policies prohibit disenfranchisement of existing stockholders	Not measured mathematically, but consideration given to: Must have at least 1,200 round-lot holders 600,000 or more shares in public hands Aggregate market value of publicly held shares must be $500,000,000
American Stock Exchange (AMEX)	980	Alternate 1: 800 shareholders and 500,000 public shares outstanding Alternate 2: 400 shareholders, 1,000,000 public shares outstanding Alternate 3: 400 shareholders, 500,000 public shares outstanding, and average daily volume of 2,000 Regular: $750,000 pretax income in latest fiscal year or two of the three most recent years, $3,000,000 market value of shares, minimum bid price $3 and $4,000,000 in shareholders' equity, and two outside directors Alternate: $15,000,000 market value of public shares, with shareholders' equity $4,000,000, an operating history of three years, and two outside directors	Not measured mathematically, but consideration given to: The financial condition and/or operating results of the company Adequate public distribution and market value of security Compliance with listing agreements
AMEX Emerging Company Marketplace **Note:** This market was discontinued in May 1995.	37	Companies traded in Nasdaq: Regular: 300 shareholders and 250,000 public shares outstanding with a market value of $2,500,000; capital and surplus $1,000,000; total assets of $2,000,000; two outside directors; and a minimum bid price of $1 Alternate: Same requirements as regular except capital and surplus of $2,000,000 with a minimum bid price below $1 Companies not traded in Nasdaq: Regular: 300 shareholders and 250,000 public shares outstanding, with a $2,500,000 market value; total assets of $4,000,000; capital and surplus of $2,000,000; two outside directors; and a minimum bid price of $3 Alternate: 300 shareholders and 400,000 public shares outstanding, with a market value above $10,000,000; total assets of $3,000,000; capital and surplus of $2,000,000; two outside directors; and a minimum bid price of $2	For all companies: Regular: 300 shareholders and 250,000 shares outstanding, with a total market value of $500,000; total assets of $2,000,000; capital and surplus of $1,000,000; and minimum bid price of $1 Alternate: 300 shareholders and 250,000 shares with market value of $1,000,000; total assets of $2,000,000; capital and surplus of $2,000,000; and minimum price below $1
Nasdaq National Market	3,757	Registration under Sec. 12(g) of Securities Exchange Act of 1934 or equivalent Alternate 1: Shareholders—if between 0.5 and 1 million shares publicly held, 800; if more than 1 million public shares, 400; if more than 0.5 million shares held and average daily volume in excess of 2,000 shares, 400. Net tangible assets must equal $4 million or more, net income (in latest fiscal year or two of last three fiscal years) of $400,000; pretax income (in latest fiscal year or 2 of last 3 fiscal years) of $750,000; 500,000 public shares outstanding with a market value of $3,000,000; and a minimum bid price of $5. Must have two market makers. Alternate 2: Net tangible assets of $12 million; 1 million public shares outstanding with a market value of $15 million; an operating history of three years; and a minimum bid price of $3. Must have two market makers.	Registration under Sec. 12(g) of Securities Exchange Act of 1934 or equivalent Net tangible assets of $1.2 million or $4 million; 200,000 public shares outstanding with a market value of $1 million; minimum bid price $1 and 400 shareholders. Must have two market makers. Voting rights policies prohibit disenfranchisement of existing shareholders
Nasdaq SmallCap Market	1,974	Registration under Sec. 12(g) of Securities Exchange Act of 1934 or equivalent 300 shareholders with 100,000 shares outstanding with a market value of $1 million; $2 million total stockholders' equity; and total assets of $4 million. Must have two market makers.	Registration under Sec. 12(g) of Securities Exchange Act of 1934 or equivalent Must have 300 shareholders with 100,000 shares outstanding with a market value of $200,000; total stockholders' equity of $1 million; and total assets of $2 million. Minimum bid price must be $1; if less than $1, company must maintain $1 million market value of public float and $2 million in capital and surplus. Must have two market makers.

SOURCE: Telephone conversations on December 12, 1994, with representatives from the NYSE, AMEX, and Nasdaq; and Carl W. Schneider, Joseph M. Manko, and Robert S. Kant, *Going Public: Practice, Procedure and Consequences* (New York: Bowne & Co., 1992).

The authors have observed that those quickest to downplay the usefulness of this vast database for guidance in the valuation of closely held companies may be those least schooled in its use. This chapter is designed to help both the veteran and the neophyte make the best possible use of guideline market transaction data. It should also be helpful to those reviewing business appraisals to evaluate the thoroughness and appropriateness of the valuation work product.

Exhibit 10–2
Mechanisms for Going Public in the United States

Registration statements are of two principal types: (1) "offering" registrations filed under the Securities Act of 1933, and (2) "trading" registrations filed under the Securities Exchange Act of 1934.

"Offering" registrations are used to register securities before they are offered to investors. Part I of the registration, a preliminary prospectus or "red herring," contains preliminary information that will be in the final prospectus. Included in Part I (or incorporated by reference) in many registration statements are:

- Description of securities to be registered.
- Use of proceeds.
- Risk factors.
- Determination of offering price.
- Potential dilution.
- Selling security holders.
- Plan of distribution.
- Interests of named experts and counsel.
- Information with respect to the registrant (description of business; legal proceedings; market price and dividends on common equity; financial statements; management discussion and analysis; changes in and disagreements with accountants, directors, and executive officers; security ownership of certain beneficial owners and management; and certain relationships and related transactions).

Part II of the registration contains information not required in the prospectus. This includes:

- Expenses of issuance and distribution.
- Indemnification of directors and officers.
- Recent sales of unregistered securities, undertakings, exhibits, and financial statement schedules.

"Offering" registration statements vary in purpose and content according to the type of organization issuing stock:

S-1   Companies reporting under the 1934 Act for less than 3 years. Permits no incorporation by reference and requires complete disclosure in the prospectus.

SB-2 A simpler form of S-1, adopted by the SEC in August 1992, to be used for cash offerings by small business issuers (revenues under $25 million, and $25 million in public float, which is the estimated price of the initial public offering as well as the value of securities held by nonaffiliates prior to the offering). May be used by issuer for newly issued securities, as well as secondary offerings. Does not require financial statements be prepared in accordance with Regulation S-X (the SEC accounting rules), but in accordance with generally accepted accounting standards and is somewhat less demanding in terms of details required to be disclosed.

S-2   Companies reporting under the 1934 Act for 3 or more years but not meeting the minimum voting stock requirements. Reference to 1934 Act reports permits incorporation and presentation of financial information in the prospectus or in an Annual Report to Shareholders delivered with the prospectus.

S-3   Companies reporting under the 1934 Act for 3 or more years and having at least $150 million of voting stock held by nonaffiliates, or

as an alternative test, $100 million of voting stock coupled with an annual trading volume of 3 million shares. Allows minimal disclosure in the prospectus and maximum incorporation by reference of 1934 Act reports.

S-4   Registration used in certain business combinations or reorganizations.

S-6   Filed by unit investment trusts registered under the Investment Act of 1940 on Form N-8B-2.

S-8   Registration used to register securities to be offered to employees under stock option and various other employee benefit plans.

S-11 Filed by real estate companies, primarily limited partnerships and investment trusts.

S-18 Short-form initial registration of up to $7.5 million in securities.

SE   Nonelectronically filed exhibits made by registrants filing with the EDGAR Project.

N-1A Filed by open-end management investment companies.

N-2   Filed by closed-end management investment companies.

N-5   Registration of small business investment companies.

N-14 Registration of the securities of management investment and business development companies to be issued in business combinations under the Investment Act of 1940.

F-1   Registration of securities by foreign private issuers eligible to use Form 20-F, for which no other form is prescribed.

F-2   Registration of securities by foreign private issuers meeting certain 1934 Act filing requirements.

F-3   Registration of securities by foreign private issuers offered pursuant to certain types of transactions, subject to the 1934 Act filing requirements for the preceding 3 years.

F-4   Registration of securities issued in business combinations involving foreign private registrants.

F-6   Registration of depository shares evidenced by the American Depository Receipts (ADRs).

Regulation A Offerings   Exempts from registration public offerings not exceeding $5 million in the aggregate in any one year. Documentation required to establish exemption. Sometimes referred to as "short form" of registration. Unavailable to reporting companies under the 1934 Securities Act.

Regulation D Offerings   Private and limited offerings. Exempt from registration requirements but not antifraud prohibitions. Offerees must receive or have access to important information about issuer; offer must be made without general advertising or mass media circulation; number of offerees and purchasers must be limited; and securities are not to be redistributed by initial purchasers.

Intrastate Offering   Offerings within a single state are exempt from registration requirements, without any fixed limit on size of the offering or number of offerees. Company must be incorporated in the state in which it makes the offering, must do a significant portion of its business in the state, and all offerees must be residents of the state.

Pending Proposal   Would allow certain small offerings to use a new Form SB-1 that makes alternative presentation formats available.

SOURCE: Adapted from *A Guide to SEC Corporate Filings* (Bethesda, MD: Disclosure, Inc., 1990).

Overview of the Guideline Public Company Method

The purpose of compiling guideline company tables is to develop value measures based on prices at which stocks of similar companies are trading in a public market. The value measures thus developed will be applied to the subject company's fundamental data and correlated to reach an estimate of value for the subject company or its shares or other interests.

A "value measure" is usually a multiple computed by dividing the price of the guideline company's stock as of the valuation date by some relevant economic variable observed or calculated from the guideline company's financial statements. Some variables, such as projections of next year's earnings, may be estimated by security analysts. The reciprocal of the multiple is the capitalization rate for that variable.

The income statement variables most often used to develop business value measures from guideline companies are the following:

- Net sales.
- Net income.
- Gross cash flow (net income plus noncash charges).
- Net free cash flow (gross cash flow adjusted for capital expenditures, changes in working capital, and sometimes changes in debt).
- Net income before taxes.
- Gross cash flow before taxes (earnings before depreciation, other noncash charges, and taxes, sometimes called EBDT).
- Dividends or dividend-paying capacity.

In addition to business value measures using only the value of the common stock to develop the multiple, some measures address the value of *all* the invested capital. In this case, the numerator for the value measure multiple is often called market value of invested capital (MVIC). This is also sometimes called "adjusted market value of capital structure," "aggregate market value of capital structure," and even by that overly ambiguous term, "enterprise value." This includes the market value of all classes of stock and all interest-bearing debt. Many analysts *deduct* cash and marketable securities. The denominator used to compute the value measure must include the returns available to all classes of capital reflected in the numerator, for example, preferred dividends and interest.

The income statement variables most often used to develop business value measures for MVIC are:

- Net sales.
- Earnings before interest and taxes (EBIT).
- Earnings before depreciation, amortization, interest, and taxes (EBDIT or EBDITA).
- Net free cash flow available to invested capital.

The above variables usually are computed on an operating basis, with nonoperating items treated separately. Any of the above income variables may be measured for any or all of a variety of time periods to create the denominator for a value measure. The typical time periods used are:

- Latest 12 months.
- Latest fiscal year.
- Straight average of some number of past years.
- Weighted average of some number of past years.
- Estimates for the forthcoming year.

All of the above performance variables and time periods may have various other permutations, depending on availability and relevance of data.

Business value measures also may be developed based on balance sheet data. Such measures normally are developed by dividing the price as of the valuation date by the balance sheet variables as of a date as close as possible preceding the valuation date for which both guideline company and subject company data are available. Balance sheet variables typically used are:

- Book value.
- Tangible book value.
- Adjusted book value.
- Adjusted tangible book value.

As with business value measures based on operating data, business value measures based on asset values may also be performed on a value of total capital basis. In such cases the market value of the senior equity and interest-bearing liabilities generally is added into both the numerator and the denominator in developing the business value measure.

Note that *unlike* operating variables, which are measured over one or more *periods* of time, asset value variables normally are measured only at the latest practical *point* in time.

The actual value measure applied to the subject company may be anywhere within (or sometimes even outside) the range of value measures developed from the market data. Where each value measure should fall will depend on the quantitative and qualitative analysis of the subject company relative to analysis of the companies that comprise the market transaction data.

When Is the Guideline Public Company Method Most Useful?

The initial value derived from the guideline public company method, before adjustment for shareholder-level factors such as size of the block and degree of marketability or lack of it, is often called a publicly traded equivalent value or "as if freely traded" value—that is, the price at which the stock would be expected to trade if it were traded publicly. In other words, the valuation indication is appropriate for a marketable, minority ownership interest, typically appraised using the valuation premise of value in continued use, as a going-concern business.

The method can be used in conjunction with an appraisal for any standard of value, certainly most importantly for fair market value. Use of the method in conjunction with each of the standards of value is discussed in the first part of this section.

Adjustments when the method is used to value a nonmarketable minority stock and to value controlling interests are discussed in the second part of this section.

Finally, we discuss the impact of the quantity and quality of available data on the use of the method.

Standard of Value

Fair Market Value. While the guideline company method can be used in conjunction with any standard of value, it generally is most useful when the standard of value is fair market value. By definition, the method is based on making comparisons between the subject stock and active market transactions in guideline stocks.

Fair market value is the standard of value in most income tax-related transactions. (Revenue Ruling 59-60 references the public markets no less than seven times.) It is also the standard of value for all ESOP valuations.

Fair Value. As noted in Chapter 2, fair value is a statutorily mandated standard of value. In the United States, it is applicable in almost all states to dissenting stockholder actions and, in the few states that have corporate and partnership dissolution statutes, to such dissolutions. It is interpreted differently by judicial precedent in each state. As a generality, in most states it is a broader standard that incorporates market value along with values indicated by income and asset approaches. Therefore, we would say a guideline company approach usually would be a part of the analysis when fair value is the standard.

Investment Value. This is the standard of value that could depart the most from the value developed by a strict application of the guideline company method. The guideline company method would be expected to develop a value based on a *consensus* of market participants, as evidenced by their transactions. Investment value, by definition, is the value to a *particular* buyer or seller. Therefore, the income approach gives more opportunity for a specific party to project income flows and use discount and capitalization rates that are appropriate to their individual investment criteria.

Even a party primarily interested in investment value, however, generally would want to have some notion of what a consensus value would be. Furthermore, the valuer interested in investment value can always adjust the financial variables on a pro forma basis reflecting anticipated changes in the subject company and use the guideline company method to see the sensitivity of market value to various possible changes in the financial variables.

Ownership Characteristics

Marketable versus Nonmarketable. The guideline company method would be most ideal, of course, when valuing marketable shares by direct comparison with marketable shares. The most obvious application of this would be when pricing an IPO.

Marketability, or lack of it, like most shareholder-level attributes of securities, is often an issue that is not totally black or white. For example, private placements of stocks that already have a public market generally will be restricted for a time and then will enjoy full marketability. Most ESOP stock by law enjoys the right of a "put," which guarantees a market at the appraised price at the occurrence of specified triggering events. There are much data and precedent for adjusting for the limited marketability in such situations.

The use of the guideline public company method to value stocks of closely held companies that have no market has been significantly enhanced in the late 1980s and early 1990s by two important developments.

1. A vastly increased number of available actively traded public companies to choose from, especially smaller companies that may be more comparable in many respects to many closely held companies than those traded in public markets a decade ago.

2. Development of extensive new databases that provide empirical guidance not previously available to assist in quantifying the discount for lack of marketability between a publicly traded security equivalent value and an otherwise similar closely held security value. These data are described in detail in Chapter 15, "Discounts for Lack of Marketability."

Control versus Minority. Since guideline public company transactions are, by definition, minority interests, they are most directly relevant for valuation of other minority interests.

In applying the guideline company method, qualitative and quantitative differences between the guideline and subject companies are reflected in arriving at the publicly traded equivalent value of the subject stock, usually in the choice of multiples applied to the subject's fundamental data relative to the guideline companies' multiples. Adjustments may also be made for other factors such as relative excess assets or deficiencies in arriving at a publicly traded equivalent value. Thus, having arrived at a publicly traded equivalent value, the only remaining adjustment necessary for a minority interest value is the shareholder-level attribute of lack of marketability. As already noted, there are a plethora of empirical data on which to base this adjustment.

When valuing controlling interests, it might be ideal to apply the market approach by using only guideline controlling-interest transactions, which is the subject of Chapter 11. However, the practical reality is that there are far more reliable guideline public company minority transaction data available than data on control transactions. Therefore, it often is useful to use the guideline public company method even when valuing controlling interests. This usually requires some adjustment from the publicly traded minority stock value equivalent to account for control. (In the case of a controlling interest, some prefer to call this a discount for lack of liquidity.) This may be offset in part or even fully by a discount for lack of marketability. This is a complicated issue, which is addressed briefly toward the end of this chapter in the section on typical adjustments to reach the value conclusion and in considerable detail in Chapter 14, "Minority Interest Discounts, Control Premiums, and Other Discounts and Premiums," and Chapter 15, "Discounts for Lack of Marketability."

Going-Concern Value versus Liquidation Value

In almost all cases, the public market is pricing stocks on the assumption that they will continue as a going concern. Unless there is evidence to the contrary, the guideline public company method would be expected to produce a value on the premise that the subject is expected to continue as a going concern. The various forms of liquidation value are addressed in the subsequent chapter on the asset-based approach.

Quantity and Quality of Available Data

As with any valuation method, the quantity and quality of relevant data available to implement it will have an important bearing on the usefulness of the method. As noted earlier, there are more publicly traded companies, especially small ones, than most people realize, and it is important to search them out.

After discussing criteria for selection of companies, we address the question of how many guideline companies would ideally be used in this method. We usually would not reject the method just because we were not satisfied with either the number or the degree of comparability of available guideline companies. In the final analysis, the quantity and quality of the guideline company data compared to the quantity and quality of data available for other methods will influence the weight accorded the method in correlating the results of various methods and reaching a value conclusion.

Criteria for Guideline Company Selection

One succinct quote summarizes the essence of the key characteristic that should be present in a guideline company:

> Do the underlying economics driving this comparable company match those that drive our company?[4]

In Revenue Ruling 59-60, the IRS, one of the strongest proponents of the guideline public company method, makes the following observation:

> Although the only restrictive requirement as to comparable corporations specified in the statute is that their lines of business be the same or similar, yet it is obvious that consideration must be given to other relevant factors in order that the most valid comparison possible will be obtained.[5]

In analyzing whether or not a particular public company should be considered an appropriate guideline or which of the guideline public companies are most comparative to the subject and therefore deserve more weight in the valuation, the analyst must consider several important factors.

The comparability of guideline publicly traded companies used in a valuation frequently has become a central issue in litigated valuations, partly because of the difficulty of choosing truly comparative companies. In *Tallichet* v. *Commissioner,* the Tax Court emphasized that there are "guideposts in determining comparability."[6] According to the court, the following factors are among those to consider in determining comparability:

1. Capital structure.
2. Credit status.
3. Depth of management.
4. Personnel experience.
5. Nature of competition.
6. Maturity of the business.

In *Estate of Victor P. Clarke,* the Tax Court reemphasized that it is "imperative that the characteristics of the subject company and the purportedly comparable company relevant to the question of value be isolated and examined so that a significant comparison can be made."[7] In that case, the court cited the following as relevant factors:

---

[4]Daniel W. Bielinski, "The Comparable-Company Approach: Measuring the True Value of Privately Held Firms," *Corporate Cashflow Magazine,* October 1990, pp. 64–66.
[5]Revenue Ruling 59-60 (1959-1 C.B. 237), Section 4(h).
[6]*Tallichet* v. *Commissioner,* 33 T.C.M. 1133 (1974).
[7]*Estate of Victor P. Clarke,* 35 T.C.M. 1482 (1976).

1. Products.
2. Markets.
3. Management.
4. Earnings.
5. Dividend-paying capacity.
6. Book value.
7. Position of company in industry.

Although these lists are fairly comprehensive, depending on the nature of the industry, the analyst may need to consider additional factors, such as number and size of retail outlets, sales volume, product mix, territory of operations, and customer mix. Clearly, even this additional list is not exhaustive, and we cannot overemphasize the necessity of tailoring the list of factors to be considered to fit each valuation. Much of this information can be gathered in a thorough review of each public company's Form 10-K, but it may also be necessary to consult additional sources such as industry and trade publications (discussed in Chapter 6, "Researching Economic and Industry Information") or to call the company for additional information.

It is also useful to analyze the financial statements for both the subject company and the guideline companies to uncover similarities and differences to consider in the valuation. Bearing in mind the company being valued and the nature of the industry, we generally compare the performance of the subject company to the guideline companies by analyzing financial ratios that measure liquidity, leverage, activity, and profitability, as well as historical trends in revenues, expenses, and profitability. This type of analysis is illustrated in Chapter 8, "Comparative Ratios." In particular, if this analysis indicates the guideline companies' capital structures differ significantly from that of the subject (one of the examples cited by the IRS in Revenue Ruling 59-60 regarding factors relevant to comparability), this difference can be factored out by using market value of invested capital procedures referred to earlier.

In many valuation situations, the subject company is so unique that it is difficult to find a set of good guideline companies. In these cases, the analyst may find a group of guideline companies that can shed some light on the valuation question but may consider only one or a few guideline companies more comparative to the subject company than the rest. In such cases, the analyst may tabulate data for the whole group but elect to accord more weight to the data for those guideline companies considered most comparative.

Sometimes, though, the subject company seems so unique that even an exhaustive search produces no companies for use as guideline companies. The appraiser should keep in mind that there are over 30,000 small public companies that have sold stock through public offerings at one time or another and are still operating. Their data may not be as extensive or reliable as larger companies, but in most cases it is better than no guideline company at all. Also, if the valuation is for federal gift and estate taxes, Revenue Ruling 59-60 states the companies may be in the same "or similar" industries. This phrase gives the analyst latitude to exercise reasonable judgment in selecting companies from related industries if unable to find guideline companies in the subject company's industry group.

In considering "the same or similar lines of business," keep in mind the comparability of the driving underlying economics. Important economic factors include the market(s) into which the company sells, its brand acceptance, or lack of it, and, sometimes, the raw material supply conditions. Three quick examples will help to illustrate the point.

Example 1: Industrial Equipment Manufacturer

We were retained to value a company whose line of business was the manufacture of electronic control equipment for the forest products industry. We found plenty of manufacturers of electronic control equipment, but none for whom the forest products industry was a significant part of their market. Therefore, for guideline companies, we selected manufacturers of other types of industrial equipment and supplies that sold to the forest products and related cyclical industries. We decided the markets served were more of an economic driving force than the physical nature of the products produced.

Example 2: The Gallo Wine Company

At the valuation date in the *Estate of Mark Gallo*,[8] there was only one publicly traded wine company stock, a tiny company compared to the huge Gallo and, for other reasons as well, not a good guideline company. Experts for both the taxpayer and the IRS recognized this and used as guideline companies distillers, brewers, soft drink bottlers, and food companies that enjoyed strong brand recognition and were subject to seasonal crop conditions and grower contracts.

Example 3: The Hallmark Greeting Card Co.

At the valuation date in the *Estate of Joyce Hall*,[9] there was only one good publicly traded greeting card guideline company. The expert for the IRS used that company and also other companies that manufactured consumer consumable products and whose consumer brand names commanded the dominant market share for their respective products. The court commented very positively on this procedure.

However, the analyst who has difficulty finding suitable guideline companies should also remember that in several cases courts have decided the comparability between the subject company and the guideline publicly traded company was insufficient. In *Righter* v. *U.S.,* for example, the court decided companies that manufactured toys or toys and games were not sufficiently comparable to a company that produced two types of games, partly because their products appealed to and were used by different age groups.[10] In *Estate of Joseph E. Salsbury*, the Tax Court rejected several companies one expert had chosen as comparable because they "did not even have divisions engaged in the animal and poultry health industry" (which was the subject company's business). As a result, the court concluded the selection of these companies "fails to satisfy the 'same or similar line of business' requirement of the regulations." Additional cases that address comparables are listed in Exhibit 10–3.

A problem also arises if an appraiser establishes criteria that are too restrictive. By unnecessarily limiting the number of guideline companies considered, an appraiser may miss relevant market evidence that would have led to a different valuation. Several court cases have noted that experts were too selective, excluding companies that would have provided useful valuation guidance. A few of these court cases are also listed in Exhibit 10–3. In *Estate of Victor P. Clarke*, the

---

[8]*Estate of Mark S. Gallo*, 50 T.C.M. 470 (1985).
[9]*Estate of Joyce C. Hall*, 92 T.C. No. 19 (1989).
[10]*Righter* v. *U.S.*, 439 F.2d 1244 (1971).

Exhibit 10–3

A Partial List of Court Cases Pertinent to the Issue of Comparability

Court Rejected Comparables*

Bader v. *U.S.,* 172 F. Supp. 833 (D.C. Ill., 1959)
Blass v. *U.S.,* 344 F. Supp. 669 (1972)
Central Trust Company v. *U.S.,* 305 F.2d 393 (Ct. Cl., 1962)
Righter v. *U.S.,* 439 F.2d 1244 (1971)
Estate of Joseph E. Salsbury, 34 T.C.M. 1441 (1975)
Tallichet v. *Commissioner,* 33 T.C.M. 1133 (1974)
Estate of Lida R. Tompkins, 20 T.C.M. 1763 (1961)
Worthen v. *U.S.,* 192 F. Supp. 727 (D.C. Mass., 1961)

Court Accepted Comparables

Estate of Mark S. Gallo, 50 T.C.M. 470 (1985)
Estate of Joyce C. Hall, 92 T.C. No. 19 (1989)

Court Found Criteria for Comparables Chosen too Restrictive

Drayton Cochran, et al. v. *Commissioner,* 7 T.C.M. 325 (1948)
Estate of Victor P. Clarke, 35 T.C.M. 1482 (1976)
Estate of Ethyl L. Goodrich, 37 T.C.M. 1062 (1978)

* Did not reject the concept, but rejected certain companies for lack of comparability.

Tax Court addressed this problem forcefully by stating that the definition of a guideline corporation cannot be "unduly restrictive, as it strips the inquiry into the valuation of closely held stock of the flexibility needed to make an informed judgment."[11] The U.S. Court of Claims stated its opinion on this issue quite succinctly in *Central Trust Company* v. *U.S.* In employing the guideline public company method, "every effort should be made to select as broad a base of comparative companies as is reasonably possible, as well as to give full consideration to every possible factor in order to make the comparison more meaningful."[12] In *Estate of Mark S. Gallo,* this point was again emphasized when the Tax Court commended one of the experts for making "careful and reasoned comparisons with each comparable instead of arbitrarily relying upon the outer limit of a range."[13] Clearly, the message of these cases is that the appraiser must choose guideline companies logically and be able to justify their selection.

How Many Guideline Companies?

The answer to this question depends on a number of factors:

1. Similarity to the subject—the more similar, the fewer needed.
2. Trading activity—again, the more actively traded, the fewer needed.
3. Dispersion of value measure data points—the wider the range of relevant value measure data points, the more companies it takes to identify a pattern relevant to the subject company.

---

[11]*Estate of Victor P. Clarke,* p. 1501.
[12]*Central Trust Company* v. *U.S.,* 305 F.2d 393 (Ct. Cl., 1962).
[13]*Estate of Mark S. Gallo.*

In the *Gallo* and *Hall* cases cited earlier, where companies in other industries but with related characteristics were used, the guideline company lists encompassed 10 to 16 companies. In *Hall,* the court rejected the reliance by one appraiser on the only other company in the greeting card industry, even though it was an excellent comparable, stating "one company does not a market make."

On occasion, we have used as few as two or three guideline companies. However, in those cases we have not relied on the guideline company method exclusively. Our confidence rises sharply when we can find four to seven good guideline public companies. In those rare cases where it seems that there are a dozen or more good guideline companies in terms of line of business, we often narrow down the criteria in terms of size, earning pattern, and other factors to utilize what our analysis indicates to be the best ones.

Time Period to Consider

In the absence of a compelling reason to do otherwise, the time period most commonly used for analysis of operating data is five years. This conventional time period should not, however, be blindly and mechanistically adopted. The operative phrase is "relevant time period."

For a cyclical industry, a complete economic cycle for that industry is widely considered to be a good choice of time period from which to develop average operating results to be used as the basis for value measures. This has led us on occasion to use averages of operating data for as long as 10 years.

Sometimes the relevant time period is constrained by major changes that affected either the subject company or the industry as a whole. Such events may render comparative financial data before such changes irrelevant for valuation purposes. In these cases it may only be relevant to use one or a few years' comparative data.

Once in a while, the historical data include an aberration that is so clearly nonrecurring for either the subject company or the industry that the best thing to do is to omit that year when computing the value measures, unless one can clearly isolate and adjust for the nonrecurring event. In such cases, however, the data normally are tabulated and presented and the reason for omitting that year from the value measure calculations is explained.

Typically, whatever time period is used for gathering and presenting data is used for both income statement and balance sheet data. Value measures based on income statement data typically are computed by dividing the valuation date price by the income variables or averages of variables for one or a number of prior periods, usually (but not necessarily) years. Value measures based on balance sheet variables (e.g., price/book value) typically are computed by dividing the valuation date price by the most recent balance sheet variable. The reason for collecting and presenting several years of balance sheet information is to identify and interpret comparative trends among the guideline and subject companies, although the earlier years' balance sheet data usually are not used directly in the computation of value measures.

Deciding Which Value Measures to Use

As was noted earlier in the chapter, there is a wide variety of financial variables for which capitalization rates for the guideline companies can be computed. For the income variables, there is also a wide choice of time periods and possible weighting schemes for each variable. The analyst's skill, experience, and judgment play an important role in making these choices and, ultimately, in deciding the appropriate weight to accord to each. This section discusses criteria to consider to make relevant choices in each case.

Influence of the Ownership Characteristics

Control versus Minority Value. When valuing a controlling interest, emphasis often is heavily on measures of the market value of invested capital (MVIC) rather than the equity only, because the controlling interest holder would be able to make the financial decision to change the capital structure if so desired. Conversely, when valuing a minority interest, focus logically is on measures that directly value the subject equity interest. Sometimes, however, measures of the MVIC are used to value minority interests, subtracting the debt to reach an indication of the value of equity. This is most often done when the subject and guideline companies have wide variations in capital structure, to even out the effects of the differences in leverage.

Marketable versus Nonmarketable. Public companies tend to focus more on net income than do private companies, while private companies tend to focus more on cash flows than do public companies. Therefore, when valuing a private company, one may choose to focus a bit more on cash flow variables than net income variables. However, even though public company reports and press releases tend to focus on income variables, the market pricing for many public companies will be found to be more oriented to cash flows than to net income.

Going-Concern Value versus Liquidation Value

Going-concern value tends to be based largely, and sometimes entirely, on income and cash flow analyses. Liquidation value often involves an analysis of individual asset values, so the emphasis is on balance sheet items. As noted earlier, however, the guideline company valuation method is generally used for a going-concern premise of value.

Type of Company

Operating versus Holding Companies. In the broadest general sense, valuation of operating companies tends to focus on earning power variables, while valuation of holding companies tends to focus on asset value variables. Therefore, for operating companies, focus tends to be on ratios of price to cash flows, earnings, and dividends. For holding companies, focus tends to be on ratios of price to book value or price to adjusted book value.

Stage of Company in Life Cycle. The more mature or stable the company is, the more the focus may be on cash flow variables, whereas companies in a growth phase may focus more on net income. In fact, young companies in a very high growth phase may be expected to have negative net free cash flow for years, so that net free cash flow would be meaningful in a long-term discounted cash flow valuation method but meaningless for the same company in a capital market approach using current guideline company data. This is not to imply diminished importance of ultimate ability to produce meaningful net cash flows, but only because multiples of negative current numbers are meaningless.

Line of Business. The more meaningful the tangible assets are to the type of business, the more they should be considered in the value measures computed. In particular, assets are more important the more liquid they are. Furthermore, they are easier to deal with in valuation if their GAAP values are close to their market values. For example, for financial institutions, the financial assets and liabilities are extremely important, and price-to-book-value ratios are much more important than for most other types of operating companies. For distribution companies (especially wholesalers, but also retailers), inventories (and in some cases receivables) are a major part of their asset mix, usually making price to book value a relevant measure to consider. For manufacturing companies, plant and equipment vary tremendously from one to another, both in age and condition and also in importance to their operations, so that price-to-asset-value measures are difficult to implement on a comparative basis and frequently are not very meaningful. For service companies, tangible assets play a very minor role, if any, in value measures.

Availability of Data

We often face the frustrating obstacle of lack or limited availability of data for the value measures we would conceptually most prefer to use in the guideline company method. Our advice is to do the most thorough possible search for the data you would *like* to use, and then make the best possible use of whatever is available.

Gross Cash Flow versus Net Cash Flow. A good example of this problem is the choice between gross cash flow and net cash flow as an economic income variable in a guideline company value measure. In the discounted economic income method, we generally prefer and generally use net cash flow, and most experienced appraisers tend to prefer it in the guideline company method also. If one is willing to do the work, using the statement of cash flows along with the income statements and balance sheets, one can compute net cash flow for most public companies for each year. However, if data such as capital expenditures have been subject to wide variations, as they frequently are, these data generally are harder to adjust objectively for abnormal or nonrecurring items than most other data. Thus, gross cash flow is more commonly used because it is straightforward, easier to compute, and simple to explain.

Ratios of Market Prices to Asset Values. When using ratios of market prices of stock or invested capital to underlying tangible asset values, it is more meaningful if the tangible asset values are adjusted to their respective fair market values. For example, publicly traded, closed-end investment companies are required to reprice their tangible assets at market value regularly, so price to adjusted net tangible asset value is available for such companies.

Real estate investment trusts (REITs) and other real estate holding companies are not required to disclose market prices of their assets, but many choose to do so. Thus, if one is valuing a real estate holding company and has market values for the subject company tangible assets, one may limit guideline company selection to those that report market values of their holdings. Alternatively, one may use those that report market values for a price-to-adjusted-net-asset-value measure and a broader list for income-related value measures. (The availability of market prices of assets does not necessarily mean that assets are the primary value drivers. For example, at this writing, REIT prices are heavily driven by yields.)

Data on values of timber holdings for many forest products companies are available from Wall Street analysts. Therefore, when valuing a company with timber holdings, a value measure of price to net asset value adjusted for timber holdings can be developed.

For most other types of public companies, market values of asset holdings are not available. This leaves the analyst with no choice, if desiring to use a measure based on asset value in the guideline company method, but to use a simple price-to-book-value ratio. As noted earlier in the "Type of Company" section, the price-to-book-value ratio tends to have more relevance if assets are of such a nature that book values tend to be fairly close to market values.

Use of Only a Portion of the Guideline Companies for Some Value Measures. It is not necessary to use every guideline company selected for every value measure utilized. For example, one of the guideline companies may have had deficit net income so it can't be used for the price-to-earnings (P/E) value measure, but it may still have had meaningful gross cash flow so it could be considered in developing a price-to-gross-cash-flow measure. Sometimes an industry group includes a good guideline company that went public recently, say only three years ago, so it would not be available for the price-to-five-year-average-income multiples, but would be available for the price-to-latest-12-months'-income multiples. The analyst must use caution and careful judgment, however, to be sure that the use of certain guideline companies for some value measures and not others does not introduce bias or distortion to the value implications.

This section has touched on some of the more common general problems of availability of data to implement the guideline company method. Sometimes, we find that the guideline company data we have been able to develop are not as strongly and compellingly convincing of value as we would like. Generally, to the extent that they provide some general guidance with respect to value, we still would tend to present them rather than ignore them. And, the strength of the data leads to the judgment as to the weight ultimately accorded to them among the various value measures within the guideline company method, and accorded to the guideline company method among other valuation methods.

Compiling Guideline Company Tables

The purpose of gathering data on guideline publicly traded companies is to derive some benchmarks by which to value the subject privately held company. For example, public companies in the industry selling at price-to-earnings multiples higher than the overall market average indicate that the public market is optimistic about the industry's future relative to its recent earnings, and this optimism should also be reflected in the private companies' P/E multiples. Similarly, the public market can provide benchmarks concerning the relation of stock prices to such variables as book values, adjusted underlying net asset values, dividends, and gross revenues. Any or all of these parameters can be relevant to a specific valuation situation, as discussed throughout this book.

Compiling a comprehensive list of guideline publicly traded companies is not simple. No single source provides an exhaustive list. It is much easier to find good guideline companies in some industries than in others. A complete search requires creativity, ingenuity, and experience. This chapter presents the most comprehensive general sources available. If not satisfied with the list developed through these sources, the analyst can consult trade association membership lists and regional investment publications or ask the management of the subject company and of the companies discovered through the conventional search for additional prospects.

Of all the criteria by which different companies may be judged as comparative for valuation purposes, the one that typically receives the most attention is the industry in which the subject company operates. In fact, Revenue Ruling 59-60 specifically states that of the factors that "are fundamental and require careful analysis in each case" for gift and estate tax valuations, one is "the market price of stocks of corporations engaged in the same or a similar line of business having their stocks actively traded on a free and open market, either on an exchange or over-the-counter."[14]

Therefore, the starting point in compiling a list of guideline companies is to form a list of the companies that operate in the subject company's industry group. The most widely accepted categorization of industry groups is the U.S. government's *Standard Industrial Classification Manual,* which publishes and defines Standard Industry Classification (SIC) codes. (The SIC code is the statistical classification standard underlying all establishment-based federal economic statistics classified by industry.) The latest edition of the manual was published in 1987 and revised to take into account technological changes; institutional changes such as deregulation in the banking, communications, and transportation industries; and the tremendous expansion in the service sector.

The search for guideline publicly traded companies should be as exhaustive as the scope of the particular valuation case permits. Frequently, the most obvious public companies in an industry are the largest ones and, for this and related reasons, may be less comparative to most closely held companies than some of the smaller, more obscure public companies. A comprehensive search for guideline companies also demonstrates that the appraiser took into account all companies that might be considered reasonably comparable and selected for analysis the most comparative companies available. The analyst must establish and adhere to an objective set of selection criteria so that the final list will not tend to bias the valuation result either upward or downward.

Developing a List of Guideline Companies

The use of the SIC code as a means of identifying potential guideline publicly traded companies has already been discussed. The starting point in a search for developing similar guideline publicly traded enterprises is a search for the appropriate SIC code that applies to the subject company. Data concerning publicly traded companies by SIC group are found in a number of sources, including printed material, CD-ROM technology, and on-line databases.

---

[14]Revenue Ruling 59-60 (1959-1 C.B. 327), Section 4.

Print sources:

Moody's Manuals. This service consists of annual hard-back volumes updated by loose-leaf reports with detailed financial information and bond ratings in separate sets according to type of business or government entity. There is a master index to identify the industry volume in which each of the over 15,000 public companies is included.

SEC Directory. The *Directory of Companies Required to File Annual Reports with the Securities and Exchange Commission under the Securities Exchange Act of 1934* is published annually. It lists companies alphabetically and classified by industry group according to the *Standard Industrial Classification Manual.* The latest Directory (1993) lists 12,764 companies required to file annual reports with the SEC.

Standard & Poor's Corporation Records. In cases in which budget or time constraints do not permit an exhaustive search for guideline companies, a shortcut is to use the "Classified Index of Industrial Companies" published annually as part of the *Standard & Poor's Corporation Records* instead of the S&P Register. The index, classified by SIC code, includes every public company that appears in the *S&P Corporation Records.* The two limitations are that the *Corporation Records* excludes some smaller public companies included in the *S&P Register,* and there is no distinction for primary SIC code.

Standard & Poor's Register. The *S&P Register* is perhaps the most comprehensive directory of companies by SIC group, but it does not distinguish which companies are public and which are private. However, if a company is public and has been quoted in the *National Daily Quotation Service,* it will be listed in the *National Monthly Stock Summary.* Therefore, the *S&P Register* and the *National Monthly Stock Summary* can be used together to develop a list of publicly quoted companies in a particular SIC group.

CD-ROM technology:

Compact D/SEC contains lengthy extracts from major SEC documents for over 12,000 public companies. Its powerful capabilities and user-friendly approach have made it one of the best-selling CD-ROMs for business libraries. Produced by Disclosure, Incorporated, Compact D/SEC provides extensive reports—a typical report is about 12 pages with over 200 variables, including a narrative description of the company, primary and secondary SIC codes, annual sales, and earnings information. The information is updated monthly.

Standard & Poor's Corporation produces a CD-ROM product known as *Dialog on Disc.* Detailed descriptions of general operations, financial structure, sales, earnings, and corporate news are covered for over 9,000 public companies. This information is also updated monthly.

On-Line databases:

Company Intelligence is a combined directory and company news file published by Information Access Company. It contains current addresses, financial, and marketing information on approximately 150,000 private and public U.S. companies. Approximately 90,000 of these companies are listed in the three-volume set of *Ward's Business Directory.* A search for primary SIC code on public companies can be accomplished in powerful command-based language.

Media General Plus provides timely and detailed financial and stock price information on approximately 5,100 public companies. It covers all New York Stock Exchange and American Stock Exchange companies, plus all Nasdaq National Market System companies and selected over-the-counter companies.

Moody's Corporate Profiles provides descriptive and financial information on important publicly held U.S. companies. The file covers all companies on the New York and American Stock Exchanges, and approximately 1,300 of the most active, emerging companies traded over the counter. The data include concise narrative descriptions of the most essential company information and, for most companies, five-year financial histories and key statistics.

None of the databases can guarantee complete accuracy, and variables may be defined differently from one source to another. Therefore, if complete accuracy and consistency are essential, it often is necessary to go to the original source documents.

Financial Statement Adjustments to Guideline Companies

Generally, the same types of adjustments should be made to the financial statements of the guideline companies as are made to the financial statements of the subject company. Some main categories of adjustments are the following:

- Remove nonrecurring items from income statements.
- Put guideline and subject companies on a comparable accounting basis (e.g., adjust any companies accounting for inventory on LIFO basis to FIFO basis, use consistent depreciation methods and lives)
- Adjust for nonoperating items.
- Adjust for discontinued operations.

Comparative Ratio Analysis

For purposes of comparative performance and other ratios between the subject company and the guideline companies, the comparisons will be more meaningful if the ratios are computed *after* the adjustments to the financial statements of the guideline companies as well as the subject company.

On the other hand, it is much faster and cheaper to use ratios for publicly traded companies from one of the many handy on-line services, such as Standard & Poor's, Compustat, Disclosure's Compact D/SEC, or Media General Plus. Whether to use ratios computed by a service or compute them oneself depends on the analyst's judgment as to the extent to which the difference in results is likely to justify the cost, which is a case-by-case decision.

An example of comparative ratio analysis based on guideline companies is included in Exhibit 18–5B in Chapter 18, "A Sample Report." This is a part of the analysis that helps guide the valuer's judgment as to where the various value measures for the subject company should fall relative to the range of the respective value measures for the guideline companies.

Typically, the comparative ratio analysis exercise is done only for the latest available comparative year, or latest 12 months, even if value measures are based on several years' average results. If the comparative ratio analysis is used to help decide where the subject's value measures should be relative to the guideline companies' value measures, the analyst should be careful to recognize any distortions or abnormalities in the year for which the ratios were calculated that would cause the ratios to be misleading for use in pinpointing a relevant value measure. It may be helpful to calculate the ratios for past years, as well, to identify any possible distortions.

Obtaining the Guideline Companies' Market Value Data

If the value measures to be used are only those that relate to common equity, then all that is needed is the price for each guideline company's stock as of the valuation date.

If value measures based on the market value of invested capital (MVIC) are to be used, then the market value of all the components of the invested capital needs to be estimated. Some of the guideline companies' senior securities (e.g., debt and/or preferred stock) may not be publicly traded. In that case, book value often is used as a proxy for market value. If, however, the analyst suspects the book value may be far enough apart from market value to create a significant distortion in the value measure computed, the senior securities should be revalued to market value. (Chapters 20 and 21 on debt securities and preferred stock, respectively, discuss how to do this.)

Market value per share of stock normally would reflect all shares outstanding plus all options and convertibles that would be dilutive if exercised. However, in a few cases, these could be "out of the money" options that should be considered if they are both long-term and significant in amount.

Presenting Guideline Company Tables

Guideline company tables typically are presented on a per share basis. They usually show the name of the guideline company, the market in which it is traded (e.g., New York Stock Exchange, American Stock Exchange, Nasdaq, and so on), the per share market price as of the valuation date, the fundamental variable of interest (e.g., earnings per share, gross cash flow per share, and so on), and the resulting valuation multiple (the price divided by the fundamental variable of interest). If space permits, there may be columns for more than one fundamental variable and valuation ratio on the same table. The table typically has a line at the bottom presenting the corresponding fundamental data for the subject company.

For each valuation multiple presented, the table typically shows a mean average, median, standard deviation, coefficient of variation, and sometimes a range. Harmonic means may be computed for ratios where the price or MVIC is the numerator, as well. The sample case in Chapter 18 presents guideline company tables for a variety of fundamental value measures.

A question often arises as to what extent value measures that were not ultimately used in reaching the value conclusion should be presented in the tables in the report. There is no clear-cut, right or wrong answer to this. We might suggest that there is not much point in presenting value measures that were never seriously considered to be used. If, however, a value measure was considered but discarded because of the nature of the data (perhaps a very wide dispersion of value ratios) it might be worthwhile to present it, so the reader can see the data that led to its being discarded in the final analysis.

Selecting and Weighting Multiples for the Subject Company Based on Guideline Companies

The result of the guideline company analysis is an array of multiples for each of several value measures. At this point, it is necessary to again visit the question of which measures to use in reaching an indication of value and the relative weight to be accorded to each of those used.

For each value measure used, it is also necessary to decide what the multiple for the subject company should be relative to the observed multiples for the guideline companies.

Impact of Guideline Company Data Evaluation

The same general thought processes and decision criteria apply to both deciding on whether or not to rely on any particular value measure at all and also to deciding on the relative weight to be accorded each value measure ultimately used in reaching the opinion of value.

The earlier discussion of the relative conceptual significance of different value measures as more or less applicable to different types of companies with different ownership characteristics applies here, of course. However, a study of the data developed may lead to greater or lesser reliance on certain value measures than one might have expected before compiling the data.

Number of Data Points Available. If it turns out that very few data points are available for a particular value measure, that problem may lead one to abandon that measure or to put relatively little weight on it, even though it might be conceptually significant if there were more data. A common example is price to latest 12 months' earnings. If only two of seven guideline companies had meaningful positive earnings (and thus meaningful P/Es), the analyst has to decide whether the two convey enough information to be accorded weight in the final analysis. The analyst might, for example, decide instead to use a price-to-gross-cash-flow multiple or a price to some number of years average earnings. One must be careful, however, that this procedure does not give undue weight to companies with losses if the subject is a profitable company.

Comparability of Data Measurement. Another issue to consider is the extent to which the analyst is satisfied that the adjustments, if any, to the subject and guideline companies' fundamental financial data have resulted in stating the data on a comparable basis. The analyst's confidence regarding the comparability of fundamental data may influence the analyst's judgment regarding the use of or weight accorded to value measures based on that particular fundamental variable.

Comparability of Data Patterns. Another factor in assessing comparability is the extent to which the data for the subject company "tracks" with the data for the guideline companies. For example, if the subject and six of the seven guideline companies had a generally upward earnings trend, but one guideline company had a downward trend, the analyst might omit the maverick company when deciding on appropriate value measures relative to earnings.

In the case of one of our annual valuations, the subject company's earnings always followed a pattern somewhat similar to a good group of guideline companies, and each year we put considerable weight on the multiple of price to latest 12 months' earnings. Then, one year, our company had a banner year while the guideline group struggled. Having satisfied ourselves that this sudden divergence was an aberration, in that year we placed most of the weight on the price to five years' average earnings instead of the latest 12 months, which would have resulted in an inflated valuation.

Apparent Market Reliance. The extent to which the value measures are tightly clustered or widely dispersed tends to indicate the extent to which the market is inclined to focus on that particular measure in pricing stocks in the particular industry. For this reason, it is helpful if the guideline company tables present not only measures of central tendency (such as mean and median), but also measures of dispersion (such as standard deviation and coefficient of variation).

Generally, the lower the dispersion of the value measure, the greater the weight the analyst might consider according to that measure. In some cases, the guideline company table may lead the analyst to conclude that the value measures based on some particular fundamental financial variable are so widely dispersed that those measures have no usefulness as guidance to value.

Measures of Central Tendency and Dispersion

Measures of Central Tendency. The *median* (the number in the middle of the array) usually, but not always, provides a better measure of central tendency for multiples than the *mean* (the arithmetic average).[15] This is because one or a few outliers (extreme observations) may have more of a distorting effect on the mean than on the median.

Another problem with the arithmetic average is that when it is used to summarize ratios that have stock price or MVIC in the numerator (such as the P/E multiple) it weights each guideline company in proportion to that company's ratio. It does not give equal weight to each guideline company. For example, the arithmetic mean P/E multiple of two guideline companies' P/E multiples of 15 and 5 is 10. While it might appear that this mean is giving equal weight to each company, it actually gives three times as much weight to the first company because its P/E multiple is triple that second's. Assuming that we invest a total of $200 in both companies, the only way the resulting portfolio's P/E multiple is 10 is by investing $150 (for $10 of earnings) in the first company and $50 (for $10 of earnings) in the second.

---

[15]A little knowledge of statistics is helpful here, but beyond the scope of this book. Relevant basic references would be, for example, Gerald I. White, Ashwinpaul C. Sondi, and Dov Fried, *The Analysis & Use of Financial Statements* (New York: John Wiley and Sons, 1993), which is listed as recommended reading by the Association for Investment Management & Research (AIMR) for all levels of the chartered financial analyst program. See also Owen P. Hall Jr., and Harvey E. Adelman, *Business Statistics: Text, Cases, and Software* (Burr Ridge, IL: Irwin Professional Publishing, 1991).

The harmonic mean is used to give equal weight to each guideline company in summarizing ratios that have stock price or MVIC in the numerator. It is the reciprocal of the average of the reciprocals of the guideline company multiples. In the example above, the reciprocal of the P/E multiple of 15 is .0667, the reciprocal of the P/E multiple of 5 is .200, the average of the two reciprocals is .1334, and the reciprocal of the average is 7.5. This P/E multiple of 7.5 is the same as the P/E of a $200 portfolio with $100 invested (for $6.67 of earnings at a P/E multiple of 15) in the first company, and $100 invested (for $20 of earnings at a P/E multiple of 5) in the second company. With the $200 invested equally in each guideline company, the total earnings are $26.67, and the P/E multiple is 7.5.

Measures of Dispersion. A simple but important measure of dispersion is the *range*—that is, the spread between the highest and lowest observation. Generally, the tighter the range of the data points, the less room for judgmental error in deciding on the appropriate multiple for the subject company relative to the guideline companies.

Occasionally, differences between the subject and guideline companies lead the analyst to conclude that a multiple for the subject should be outside the range for the guideline companies. When this occurs, it is important that the analyst explain carefully the reason for choosing a multiple outside the guideline company range.

The most familiar measure of dispersion is the *standard deviation*.[16] When using the standard deviation, it is generally helpful to focus primarily on the *coefficient of variation,* which is the standard deviation divided by the mean. By using the coefficient of variation, the relative dispersion of data for different value measures with different mean or median values can be compared directly with each other.

Multiples of Earnings or Cash Flow

Multiples of economic income variables (price/earnings multiples, price/cash flow multiples, and so on) are the reciprocals of the capitalization rates applicable to those variables. For example, a multiple of 8 is the same as a capitalization rate of .125 $(1 \div 8 = .125)$. Therefore, valuation multiples are influenced by the same forces that influence capitalization rates, the two most important of which are:

1. Risk.
2. Expected growth in the operating variable being capitalized.

Therefore, to make an intelligent estimate of what multiple is appropriate for the subject company relative to the multiples observed for the guideline companies, the analyst must make some judgments as to the relative risk and growth prospects of the subject compared with the guideline companies.

Relative Risk. Since a closely held stock does not have a regular price trading history from which to compute a *beta* (as described in Chapter 9), other means must be used to assess relative risk. One such means is a study of comparative

---

[16]For the mathematical formula for the standard deviation, see one of the statistics books referenced in the prior footnote. In any case, many pocket calculators are programmed to compute standard deviations.

financial ratios between the subject and guideline companies, as discussed in Chapter 8. Operating and financial leverage ratios are of the greatest importance in assessing relative risk. The analyst can then use judgment to adjust multiples up or down from those of the guideline companies to reflect relative risk as revealed by the comparative financial ratios.

Another way to assess relative risk is to compare historical earnings or cash flow volatility between the subject and the guideline companies. Any of several measures of dispersion, such as a standard deviation, may be used for this purpose. It then becomes a matter of analysts' judgment as to how much to adjust multiples from those observed for the guideline companies to reflect differences in risk evidenced by differences in earnings or cash flow volatility.

The size factor is also an important indicator of risk. We presented data in Chapter 9 that showed companies of the size of the smallest quintile of the New York Stock Exchange required a discount rate several points above the average for the New York Stock Exchange. This differential in the discount rate can translate directly into a difference in the capitalization rate.

Relative Growth. As discussed in Chapter 9, the expected growth rate in perpetuity for cash flow translates point for point into the capitalization rate for that variable. Therefore, if the subject company has very long-term growth prospects above or below those of the subject company, those growth rate differentials should be reflected in the capitalization rate chosen. Be careful, however, not to understate the proper capitalization rate by making a large adjustment for growth prospects that are only short or intermediate term.

An Example. We will continue with the example where the guideline company indicated price/cash flow multiple is 8, resulting in a capitalization rate for cash flow of 12.5 percent. Let's assume the comparative risk analysis leads us to conclude the discount rate for the subject company would be five percentage points higher than for the guideline companies, which would bring the capitalization rate to 17.5 percent (12.5 + 5.0 = 17.5). On the other hand, let's assume our smaller, riskier company had two percentage points higher infinitely sustainable long-term growth prospects than the guideline companies. This offsetting factor would bring the capitalization rate back down to 15.5 percent (17.5 − 2.0 = 15.5). This, then, equates to a valuation multiple of 6.5 (1 ÷ 15.5 = 6.5).

Capitalization of Dividends or Dividend-Paying Capacity

Dividends from operations ultimately are possible only as a result of earnings and adequate available cash flow. Therefore, capitalization of dividends or dividend-paying capacity may or may not be analyzed as a valuation method separate from capitalization of earnings and/or cash flow, depending on the circumstances and the valuation's purpose. Revenue Ruling 59-60 states that dividends or dividend-paying capacity should be one factor in the valuation of a business interest for federal estate or gift tax purposes. In court cases involving valuations of shares under dissenting stockholder appraisal rights, capitalization of dividends has been a factor specifically recognized in the courts' determinations of value in only a minority of cases. Most potential acquirers are not specifically interested in the acquiree's dividend-paying capacity, since the acquiree will not continue to operate as an independent entity.

If the valuation is of a controlling interest, dividend-paying capacity is more important than actual dividends paid, since the controlling stockholder has the discretion to pay or not pay dividends as long as the company has the capacity to do so. In valuing a minority interest, however, the actual dividends the company pays usually are more important than the dividend-paying capacity, since the minority stockholder generally cannot force the company to pay dividends even if it unquestionably has the capacity to do so.

When the capitalization of dividends method is used as an element in valuation, it usually is by reference to dividend yields on guideline publicly traded companies. For example, if guideline publicly traded companies were found to have an average dividend yield (market price per share divided by annual dividends per share) of 5 percent and the subject company paid dividends or was estimated to have a dividend-paying capacity of $1 per share, the capitalization of dividends method would be to simply divide the dividend-paying capacity per share by the appropriate capitalization rate or dividend yield—in this case, .05, which implies a $20 per share value by the capitalization of dividends method.

An estimate of dividend-paying capacity may be based in part on typical payout ratios of publicly traded companies in the subject company's industry. For example, if public companies in that industry typically pay out 30 percent of their earnings in dividends, 30 percent of earnings might be a good starting point from which to estimate the subject company's dividend-paying capacity. However, the typical closely held company generally is less well capitalized than its publicly traded counterpart and may have less dividend-paying capacity per dollar of earnings capacity than most of the publicly traded companies with which it might be compared. This factor must be considered in estimating the subject company's dividend-paying capacity.

Multiples of Revenue

Multiples of revenue tend to be most highly correlated with return on sales, but the strength of the correlation varies greatly from one industry to another. Therefore, when considering using a multiple of sales, it is useful to first see whether the guideline company multiples of revenue are well correlated with return on sales. This value measure tends to be more useful for industries where such a correlation is high than for those where it is not. In a way, capitalization of revenues can be considered a shortcut to capitalization of earnings, since generally there is an implicit assumption that a certain level of revenues should be able to generate a specific earnings level in a given type of business.

Capitalization of revenues is applied most frequently to service businesses, such as advertising agencies, insurance agencies, mortuaries, professional practices, and some types of publishing operations. It generally tends not to work very well for manufacturing companies.

One can find guidance in arriving at an appropriate multiple of revenues for a particular business in both public stock market data and merger and acquisition data. There are quite a few publicly traded companies in most service business categories, such as insurance agencies and advertising and public relations firms. If the subject company's true return on sales is known, an estimate of a reasonable price/sales multiple can be derived by simple regression analysis using guideline companies' price/sales ratios and returns on sales.

Exhibit 10–4A

Correlation between Price/Revenues and Return on Revenues

	September 30, 1993	
Company	Return on Revenues	Price/Revenues
Marsh & McLennan Companies, Inc.	19.1%	1.96
Arthur J. Gallagher & Co.	17.1%	1.90
Poe & Brown, Inc.	12.4%	1.73
Hilb, Rogal & Hamilton Company	11.3%	1.38
Alexander & Alexander Services, Inc.	5.2%	0.60

$r^2 = 0.9055$

The regression formula to be solved is:
$$y = a + bx$$
Price/revenues ratio = $a + b$ (return on revenues)
where:
  a = Price/revenues ratio (y) intercept
  b = Slope of the line
Using a calculator capable of linear regression analysis, the analyst can calculate the y intercept a and slope of the line b using return on revenues and price/revenues ratios data from the guideline companies.

Using the returns on revenues and price/revenues ratio data for 9/30/93, we calculate:
  $a = 0.2398$
  $b = 9.7796$
  $y = 0.2398 + 9.7796(x)$
Substituting in the subject company's return on revenues, .10, we compute an indicated price/revenues ratio:
  $y = 0.2398 + 9.7796(.10)$
  $y = 0.2398 + 0.97796$
  $y = 1.22$

Exhibit 10–4A illustrates the relationship between return on sales and price to revenue multiples for publicly traded insurance agency companies as of September 30, 1993. The exhibit also presents the computation of a suggested price-to-revenue multiple for a subject insurance agency company realizing a 6 percent return on revenue at that time.

Valuations by multiples of revenue are particularly susceptible to distortion because of differences in capital structure between subject and guideline companies. Therefore, this value multiple is often done on a market value of invested capital basis, as discussed in a later section.

One step removed from a multiple of revenues is a multiple of some measure of unit volume or capacity. Examples would include nursing homes at so much per bed, forest products plants at so much per thousand board feet of production, service stations and fuel distributors at so much per gallon sold per month, and so on. The implication of this method is that so much volume can be expected to translate into some anticipated amount of sales and economic income.

Multiple of Stock Value to Asset Value

When the analyst has determined that book value or some adjusted book value figure provides a useful representation of the company's underlying net asset values, the next step is to translate that figure into its implication for the value of the shares of stock or partnership interest being valued. This usually is performed by referring to the relationship of the prices of guideline companies' stocks to their respective underlying net asset values. The data for the guideline companies may be based on prices of stocks traded on the open market, prices paid in acquisitions, or both, depending on several factors, including the percentage ownership interest being valued.

As in any aspect of valuation based on comparisons with other companies, the analyst must use experience and expertise to ensure that the comparisons are as valid as possible within the limitations of data availability.

Exhibit 10–4B
Price/Revenues Compared to Return on Revenues

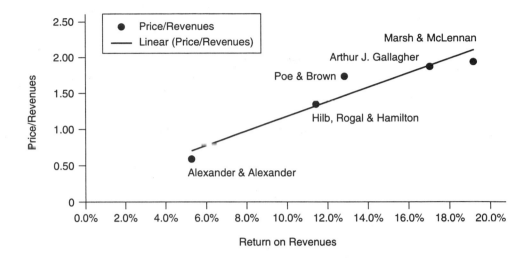

Price/Book Value Multiple. It may be possible to compute the multiple of market price to book value for a group of guideline companies that have stock trading in the public market and apply a multiple somewhere within the range of such multiples to the subject company's book value. If the book values of the subject and guideline companies were computed on comparable bases, and if the assets' composition is comparative, this procedure may provide a reasonably realistic figure for the value of the business interest.

If accounting methods for the subject and guideline companies significantly differ, the analyst should make appropriate adjustments before computing the market price/book value multiples and applying them to the valuation. There can be additional significant differences, such as in asset mix, that challenge the validity of using one company's price-to-book-value multiple in valuing another's stock.

Often the value measure multiples are computed on only *tangible* book value. This may help to avoid distortions, since some companies may have created their own intangibles, and thus expensed them for accounting purpose, while others may have acquired their intangibles, and thus carry them on the balance sheet.

If the subject company's return on equity is high relative to the guideline companies', the appropriate price-to-asset-value multiple probably should be in the upper end of the relevant range, and vice versa. As common sense would suggest, empirical tests indicate a significant degree of correlation between price/book value multiples and return on equity for both publicly traded stocks and acquisition prices in most industries. As a consequence, an analysis of the relationship between price/book value multiples and return on equity for the guideline companies often can provide objective guidance in deciding on an appropriate price/book value multiple for the subject company. If the correlation between the price/book value multiples and return on equity for the guideline companies is reasonably good, the analyst might use a simple linear regression to compute an indicated price/book value multiple for the subject company based on market data. The mechanics of this analysis are the same as for the price/sales analysis presented in Exhibit 10–4B.

Price/Adjusted Net Asset Value. For a limited number of industries, data on market values of underlying assets are available. Where this is the case, it is possible to compute multiples of the public stock's price to its adjusted net asset value.

In particular, market values for some real estate companies are provided in *Realty Stock Review*. Also, estimates of timber values for many forest products companies are available from brokerage house analysts. When using multiples of price to adjusted net asset value, it is important to make the same kinds of adjustments to the subject company as have been made to the asset values for the guideline companies. For example, some real estate company adjusted net asset values are reported net of impounded capital gains taxes and some are not.

Treating Nonoperating Assets, Excess Assets, and Asset Deficiencies

If the subject company has significant nonoperating assets, excess assets, or asset deficiencies that distinguish it from the guideline companies, adjustments for those items may be appropriate. If some of the guideline companies also have such asset anomalies, it is important, of course, to make similar adjustments to them for consistency.

Nonoperating Assets

Many privately held companies own assets that are not part of their operations. Such assets may add some value to the closely held stock over and above the values indicated by the ratios of guideline company stock prices to their underlying financial fundamentals.

If nonoperating assets are to be given separate consideration, they should be separated from the operating company data. Any income they generate (or expenses incurred on behalf of their maintenance) should be removed from earnings or cash flows capitalized. If a price/asset value multiple is used based on guideline companies, they should be removed from the asset value. These financial statement adjustments should be made before the ratio analysis of the financial statements if such analysis is to be used to help decide on multiples relative to guideline company multiples.

The question then becomes, "How much extra value do they contribute to the stock?"

The theory of valuing nonoperating assets separately from operating assets rests on the assumption that the nonoperating assets could be liquidated without impairing operations. Thus, if the market value of nonoperating assets is higher than their book value and the analyst is going to mark the nonoperating assets up to their market value to perform the valuation, the analyst should also consider offsetting factors. These factors might include the capital gains or ordinary income tax, as the case might be, that the company would have to pay if it liquidated the assets, any costs of liquidation, and any discounts that might be appropriate in reflecting the estimated time required to liquidate and the risk that the actual amounts realized might be less than the estimated market values as of the valuation date.

From there, it often makes a significant difference whether one is valuing a minority interest or a controlling interest. It also is important to know, if possible, the likelihood of sale of the assets. The market attributes very little weight to non-income-producing, nonoperating assets, unless they are likely to be sold, because their existence provides little, if any, benefit to the minority stockholder. Even when valuing a controlling interest, they normally would be discounted from their net realizable value, because most control buyers would rather buy a pure operating company and not have to deal with disposing of nonoperating assets.

Marginal Operating Real Estate

An issue that often is a gray area in stock valuations is whether certain real estate should be valued separately when using the guideline company valuation method.

One factor is the degree of comparability. If the subject company owns its real estate and the guideline companies do not, then it often is appropriate to value the real estate separately. This is more true for controlling than for minority interests for the same reasons discussed in connection with nonoperating assets. Of course, if this is done, fair market rent must be reflected as an example.

Real estate used in operations but used far below its highest and best use often is controversial. This becomes a matter of the analyst's judgment. Certainly, the imminence—or lack of it—of prospective development or sale of the real estate will play a role in the judgment.

Excess Assets or Asset Deficiencies

An often controversial area for possible adjustment may arise when the subject company has significantly greater amounts of some assets relative to its operations than do the guideline companies. The most common assets giving rise to such a potential adjustment are cash and marketable securities.

If it appears that some assets may be held in excessive amounts, the analyst should ask the company officials if there is a rationale for why such apparent excesses may be necessary for operations. If they are not necessary, then some adjustment may be appropriate. The same reasoning regarding minority and control valuation characteristics discussed earlier also applies here.

It is also common to find the reverse situation—that is, one in which it might be appropriate to value the company by a capitalization of earnings method but then to subtract an amount reflecting the inadequacy of operating assets. This can easily be the case if net working capital is inadequate to support the level of business or if certain plant and equipment are in imminent need of replacement or major repair. Evaluating such inadequacies may require more subjective judgment than would assessing excess or nonoperating assets, but the potential problem of measurement does not render recognition of the concept of asset inadequacy any less important.

Multiline Companies

There are a variety of ways to handle multiline companies within the application of the guideline company method.

Procedures for Valuation

Separate Valuations.   When a company has two or more separate and different operations, and if the financial information can be adequately segregated between them, the valuation of the combined operations might be handled as if it were two or more separate and independent valuations, using the valuation multiples most applicable for each.

Blended Valuation Multiples.   More often, it is not possible to separate revenues and expenses so that values of different operating groups can be estimated separately. In this case, valuation multiples from the respective guideline company industry groups may be weighted in accordance with the subject company's fundamental weights, such as sales or gross margin dollars.

Use of Conglomerates.   One alternative for multiline companies is to use value measures from publicly traded conglomerates. We would recommend this procedure only if the industry lines of the subject company bear some reasonable resemblance to the industry lines of the guideline company conglomerates used.

"Portfolio Effect"

Multiline companies sometimes are valued at some discount from the sum of the indicated values of their various operations. This is because most buyers tend to seek a participation in a particular industry and are less enthusiastic about a participation in somebody else's predetermined combination of some group of industries. This discount tends to apply whether valuing a minority or a controlling interest. Guidance to quantify this discount can sometimes be observed in the marketplace by comparing prices of conglomerate companies with the aggregate values of their parts, sometimes referred to as their breakup value.

Typical Adjustments to Reach a Value Conclusion

As discussed earlier, the guideline company method is based on minority interest day-to-day transactions in publicly traded stocks. Therefore, if valuing a closely held minority interest, it would not be appropriate to take a minority interest discount, but it would be appropriate to take a discount for lack of marketability (discussed in Chapter 15, "Discounts for Lack of Marketability").

If a controlling interest is being valued, it may or may not be appropriate to apply a premium for control. This is discussed in Chapter 14, "Minority Interest Discounts, Control Premiums, and Other Discounts and Premiums." Also, as discussed in Chapter 15, a control premium may be fully or partially offset by a discount for lack of marketability.

Value Measures Using Market Value of Invested Capital

Sometimes it is desirable to address the value of the entire invested capital. As noted in the section on defining the capital structure in Chapter 9, "Income Approach," the most commonly used conceptual definition of *invested capital* is all equity and long-term debt (including current maturities of long-term debt).

Valuing the entire capital structure often is useful when valuing a controlling interest, since a control buyer usually is interested in the value of the entire company irrespective of its current capital structure, which a control buyer might change.

Valuing all the invested capital based on guideline company values and then subtracting the value of the senior securities may also be useful for valuing minority interests where the capital structures differ significantly between the subject and guideline companies. This procedure can even out distorting effects of widely differing capital structures.

As a practical matter, when using the guideline company method, it generally is necessary to include *all* interest-bearing debt. Unless repayment at face is imminent, it usually should be valued at market. It often is difficult or even impossible to separate out how much of each of the guideline companies' interest expenses is attributable to long-term versus short-term debt.

Therefore, the numerator for market value of invested capital (MVIC) ratios in the guideline company method usually is the aggregate market value of all equity and all interest-bearing debt. Some practitioners subtract cash, which then would be added on at the end of the valuation procedures.

As noted earlier in the chapter, the denominators for MVIC measures typically are the following:

- Gross or net sales.
- Earnings before interest and taxes (EBIT).
- Earnings before depreciation, amortization, interest, and taxes (EBDIT or EBDITA).
- Net free cash flow available to invested capital.

Exhibit 10–5 presents a simple illustration of a valuation exercise using MVIC for three guideline companies where the capital structures for the guideline companies differed significantly from the subject company. As can be seen in Exhibit 10–5, the range of indicated values for the subject company using MVIC for the guideline companies is much tighter than the wide scatter using typical straight equity value measures. In particular, the straight equity measures distort the price/book value multiple on the high side and the price/sales multiple on the low side.

The analysis suggests that a control buyer might be willing to pay $27 to $32 a share for the equity on the assumption that the buyer could leverage the purchase with debt similar to the industry average. On the other hand, a minority buyer could not take advantage of the leverage opportunity and probably would not be willing to pay nearly as much.

Exhibit 10–5

Market Value of Invested Capital Valuation Using Guideline Companies with Different Capital Structures Than Subject

Figures in $000s	Company A	Company B	Company C	Subject
Comparative Balance Sheets				
Current assets	$25,000	$15,000	$12,000	$10,000
Net plant and equipment	45,000	35,000	18,000	15,000
Total assets	$70,000	$50,000	$30,000	$25,000
Current liabilities	$15,000	$10,000	$10,000	$ 5,000
Long-term debt	30,000	20,000	10,000	0
Stockholders' equity	25,000	20,000	10,000	20,000
Total liabilities and equity	$70,000	$50,000	$30,000	$25,000
Book value of invested capital (equity + interest-bearing debt)	$55,000	$40,000	$20,000	$20,000
Comparative Income Statements				
Sales	$90,000	$60,000	$40,000	$30,000
Cost of sales	55,000	35,000	25,000	18,000
Gross margin	35,000	25,000	15,000	12,000
General and administrative	16,000	12,000	7,000	5,500
Earnings before depreciation, interest, and taxes (EBDIT)	19,000	13,000	8,000	6,500
Depreciation	7,000	5,000	3,000	2,500
Earnings before interest and taxes (EBIT)	12,000	8,000	5,000	4,000
Interest	3,000	2,000	1,000	0
Net income before taxes	9,000	6,000	4,000	4,000
Taxes	4,000	2,500	1,500	1,500
Net income	$ 5,000	$ 3,500	$ 2,500	$ 2,500
Market value per share	$6.00	$5.00	$ 25.00	
Shares outstanding	10,000	6,000	1,000	1,000
Aggregate market value of equity	$60,000	$30,000	$25,000	
Add: Market value of debt[a]	30,000	20,000	10,000	0
Market value of invested capital	$90,000	$50,000	$35,000	
Debt/Equity ratio (at market)	0.33	0.40	0.29	0.00

	Company A	Company B	Company C	Average	Implied Value of Subject[b] ($000)	Implied Value per Share
Valuation Multiples						
Price/Book	2.4	1.5	2.5	2.1	$42,000	$42.00
Price/Sales	0.7	0.5	0.6	0.6	18,000	18.00
Price/Earnings	12.0	8.6	10.0	10.2	25,500	25.50
Price/Gross cash flow (Net income + Depreciation)	5.0	3.5	4.5	4.3	21,500	21.50
MVIC/BVIC	1.6	1.3	1.8	1.6	32,400	32.40
MVIC/Sales	1.0	0.8	0.9	0.9	27,000	27.00
MVIC/EBIT	7.5	6.3	7.0	6.9	27,600	27.60
MVIC/EBDIT	4.7	3.8	4.4	4.3	27,950	27.95

[a]Assumes market value of debt = Book value of debt.
[b]Using averages of guideline company multiples in all cases, since fundamentals are similar except for capital structure.

Common Errors

The guideline company method can be a powerful and useful tool in the valuation of closely held business interests. Proper application of it, however, requires some expertise in the analysis of publicly traded securities. This section discusses a few of the most common categories of errors frequently encountered in the use of the guideline company method.

Failure to Conduct an Adequate Search for Guideline Transaction Data

As noted early in the chapter, there are thousands of publicly traded stocks. Some services report only on a fraction of them, usually the largest ones. It is common to see reports that say something to the effect that, "We searched for publicly traded companies in the industry, but there were none," when, in fact, a more thorough search might unearth several. A related error is to use only companies listed in some service such as *Value Line Investment Survey,* which generally covers larger companies, when smaller companies not included in *Value Line* may be more comparative to the subject company.

Failure to Make Appropriate Financial Statement Adjustments to Guideline Companies

We frequently see a good job done on adjustments to the subject company statements, but little or no consideration given to possible appropriate adjustments to the guideline companies' financials. It is important that the analyst peruse the financial statements of the guideline companies to determine whether adjustments may be appropriate for one or more of the companies to put them on a basis as comparative as possible to the subject.

Along the same line, we generally like to use the guideline companies' original financial statements and SEC filings rather than secondary sources, especially if the guideline company method is to be the primary method relied on. Secondary sources often do not provide the detail of data needed for certain adjustments. Also, analysts sometimes are not careful to understand the definition a secondary source may use for certain data and thus may get caught in a mismatch when using it to value the subject company.

Multiples that Mismatch Numerator and Denominator

There are many ways to mismatch the numerator in a value multiple (the multiple selected on the basis of guideline company market evidence) with the denominator (the fundamental data for the subject company to which the numerator is applied to get an indication of value). Two of the most common are mismatched time periods and mismatched definitions.

Mismatched Time Periods. It is not uncommon to find value multiples computed from guideline company data for some time period applied to subject company data for a different time period. This inconsistency can result in serious distortions, especially if industry conditions differed significantly between the time periods. At a market turning point for a cyclical industry, a single quarter's difference in the fundamental data used between the guideline companies and the subject company can result in seriously misleading value multiples.

To avoid such distortion, it is often necessary to work with interim (versus fiscal year-end) data for the guideline companies in order to match time periods as closely as possible with available subject company data closest to the effective date of the valuation. This usually requires more work on the part of the analyst but often is worth it to produce a more highly reliable result.

Mismatched Definitions of Variables. If a value multiple is computed based on guideline company data defined in a certain way, that multiple should be applied to fundamental data defined the same way for the subject company. Looking at the same point another way, if subject company data are defined in a certain way, the same definition should be used for guideline company data from which a value multiple is computed.

Elementary as this sounds, we have seen hundreds of instances of data mismatches. A few of the most often encountered are:

- Fully diluted data used for the guideline companies or subject company, but not for both.
- Subject but not guideline company data adjusted for nonrecurring items.
- After-tax multiples for guideline companies applied to pretax data for subject.
- Income data after officers' compensation for guideline companies applied to subject company income data before owner/officer compensation.

The above just gives a flavor of typical mismatches. Be on the lookout to avoid them.

Simple Reliance on Average of Guideline Company Multiples without Comparative Analysis

Unless the guideline and subject companies are extremely homogenous in their financial characteristics, the mean or median of the guideline company value ratios may not be the most appropriate multiples for the subject company. Yet, we frequently see the mean or median multiple used with no explanation to justify the implied notion that the subject company's characteristics indicate it should be valued right at the average of the guideline companies.

A section of this chapter was devoted to choosing the multiple for the subject company relative to guideline company multiples. Such analysis is little more than common sense; yet it is amazing how often it is ignored!

Summary

This chapter has presented the procedures and sources for implementing the guideline company method of valuing the equity ownership of a business. It is widely used and accepted, but it must be implemented vary carefully.

Exhibit 10–6 summarizes the steps in carrying out the guideline company method.

The guideline company method usually uses measures that indicate the value of the equity directly, such as price/earnings multiples. However, sometimes the market value of the total invested capital is estimated and the value of debt subtracted to reach an indicated value for the equity.

Because the guideline company method usually uses publicly traded minority interest stock transactions, the value reached usually is minority interest value on a fully marketable basis. If valuing a minority interest in a private company, it normally requires adjusting for a discount for lack of marketability. If valuing a

Exhibit 10–6

Steps in the Guideline Public Company Method

1. Set criteria for selection of guideline companies.
2. Search for and identify the companies that meet the criteria.
3. Decide on the relevant time period for comparative analysis of the subject and guideline companies.
4. Obtain the guideline companies' financial statements for the time period decided in Step 3. Broaden or narrow the criteria, if necessary, to provide the best group of guideline companies, adding or deleting companies according to the revised criteria.
6. Analyze and adjust the subject and/or guideline company financial statements as appropriate (Chapter 7).
7. Compile comparative financial ratios for the subject and guideline companies (Chapter 8).
8. Decide which guideline company value measures to use.
9. Obtain the market price of each guideline company's stock as of the valuation date. (If market value of invested capital is used in any of the value measures, it is necessary to obtain the market value of all the guideline companies' securities that are included in their invested capital.)
10. Compile guideline company value measure tables for the value measures decided in Step 8.
11. Based on analysis of the value measure tables in conjunction with the comparative financial analysis of the subject and guideline companies, decide on the appropriate multiple for the subject company for each value measure to be used.
12. Multiply each value measure to be used by the relevant financial variable for the subject company to get indications of value according to each value measure.
13. Weight or otherwise correlate the indications of value from Step 11 to reach an estimate of "value as if publicly traded" (a marketable, minority ownership value).
14. Make adjustments to this value, if appropriate, for factors in the definition of value not reflected in the value as if publicly traded, such as discount for lack of marketability and/or premium for control. Also, adjust any other elements of value, if appropriate, that were adjusted out of the guideline company analysis, such as nonoperating assets.

controlling interest, a premium for control might or might not be appropriate, and such a premium may be fully or partially offset by a discount for the lack of liquidity of the privately held company controlling interest.

The chapter should be helpful both for those preparing a valuation utilizing the guideline company method and also for those reviewing and evaluating a valuation report that uses the method.

Bibliography

Alford, Andrew W. "The Effect of the Set of Comparable Firms on the Accuracy of the Price-Earnings Valuation Method." *Journal of Accounting Research*, Spring 1992, pp. 94–108.

Bielinski, Daniel W. "The Comparable-Company Approach: Measuring the True Value of Privately Held Firms." *Corporate Cashflow Magazine,* October 1990, pp. 64–68.

Bjorklund, Victoria B., and Susan A. Meisel. "Valuation: When Are Comparables Comparable Enough?" *Practical Tax Lawyer,* Spring 1991, pp. 45–47.

Englebrecht, Ted D., and Cathy H. Leeson. "Valuation of Closely Held Stock *Tax Executive,* October 1978, pp. 57–64.

Fishman, Jay E. "The Alternate Market Comparison Approach in Valuing Closely Held Enterprises." *FAIR$HARE: The Matrimonial Law Monthly*, October 1988, pp. 7–8.

_____. "The Problem with Rules of Thumb in the Valuation of Closely Held Entities." *FAIR$HARE: The Matrimonial Law Monthly*, December 1984, pp. 13–15.

Graham, Michael D. "Selection of Market Multiples in Business Valuation." *Business Valuation Review,* March 1990, pp. 8–12.

Hickman, Kent, and Glenn H. Petry. "A Comparison of Stock Price Predictions Using Court Accepted Formulas, Dividend Discount, and P/E Models." *Financial Management,* Summer 1990, pp. 76–87.

Randisi, Martin P. "Comparable Company Method of Valuing a Closely-Held Business." *FAIR$HARE: The Matrimonial Law Monthly,* January 1991, pp. 3–5.

Schreier, W. Terrance, and O. Maurice Joy. "Judicial Valuation of 'Close' Corporation Stock: *Alice in Wonderland* Revisited." *Oklahoma Law Review* 31 (1978), pp. 853–85.

Summers, S. Chris. "The Myth of Public Company Comparisons." *Business Valuation Review,* June 1992, pp. 59–62.

Taub, Maxwell J. "Can Market Comparables Be Used in Valuing Small Businesses?" *IBBA Journal,* October 1991, pp. 10–14.

_____. "Mid-Size Companies—How Do They Differ from Small Businesses and Publicly Held Firms?" *IBBA Journal,* Fall 1993, pp. 25–32.

West, Thomas L. "Pricing Businesses: The Use of Comparables." *The Business Broker,* June 1992, pp. 1–4.

Chapter 11

Market Approach: The Merger and Acquisition Method

The most difficult decision an executive faces in negotiating an acquisition is the price to be paid. The decision is difficult because there are so many factors to consider—the process by which the target company is being sold, the expected competition, the future profitability of the target, expected synergies, complex tax rules, alternate legal forms of effecting a transaction and accounting considerations.[1]

The essential difference between this chapter and the previous chapter on the guideline public company method is the nature of the market data used as a starting point. In the previous chapter, we started with minority interest transactions, mostly in the public stock market and thus fully marketable. In this chapter, we start with data on transfers of controlling interests, usually (but not entirely) 100 percent ownership interests.

The business interest transferred often includes the entire capital structure, not necessarily just equity. The company being sold may have been either public or private before the transaction. The nature of the transaction and the nature and availability of data about it varies much more than public market guideline company transaction data.

The quote introducing this chapter helps explain why there may be different values under different valuation criteria and different circumstances. It also explains why we should examine merger and acquisition transactions as carefully as possible when using them as guidance in the market approach to valuing a company, and why we need to be very careful in interpreting and applying the results of our analysis.

Overview of the Merger and Acquisition Method

The previous chapter dealt with data on day-to-day trading prices of securities. However, one can also derive indications of value from prices at which entire companies or operating units of companies have been sold or the prices at which significant interests in companies changed hands. Such data are harder to find than daily stock trading data, since there are far fewer such transactions and there is no centrally organized mechanism for collecting and making such price information available.

The general notion of merger and acquisition analysis is the same as guideline public company analysis—one relates the price at which the transaction took place to fundamental financial variables that affect the value. As noted earlier, the financial variables used in the valuation of the entire company usually focus on the market value of the entire invested capital rather than on the equity alone. This is because the transaction often involves the entire capital structure, or if it does not, at least the acquiring control owner usually has the power to change the capital structure.

Also, it is common to consider transactions over a fairly long time. This might involve analyzing transactions over several years in the subject company's industry or similar industries. This is partly because there are fewer transactions, but also because acquisition value multiples seem to fluctuate somewhat less over time than public stock market valuation multiples.

---

[1]Joseph H. Marren, *Mergers & Acquisitions: A Valuation Handbook* (Burr Ridge, IL: Irwin Professional Publishing, 1993), p. v.

Generally, the criteria for selection of merger and acquisition guideline transactions are similar to those for selecting publicly traded stock guideline companies. However, because of the fewer companies available, the criteria may have to be broadened.

When Is the Merger and Acquisition Method Most Useful?

The initial value derived from the merger and acquisition method, before adjustment for factors such as size of block and degree of marketability, is an indication of transaction prices of major ownership interests, usually controlling interests. The characteristics of each transaction need to be analyzed carefully to make judgments as to what adjustments may be necessary in order to use the transaction value multiples as guidance in a specific valuation assignment.

Standard of Value

Merger and acquisition transaction prices may be representative of *fair market value, investment value,* or somewhere in between. At one end of the spectrum, a sale to a pure financial buyer (one who is buying strictly for a return on investment from the company as a stand-alone entity) usually would be representative of fair market value, although even financial buyers may have some special motivations and advantages. At the other end of the spectrum, the more unique the synergies between the acquirer and the acquiree, the more the transaction is representative of investment value rather than fair market value, because the pricing may reflect the synergistic benefits to a *particular* buyer rather than the price a typical *hypothetical* buyer would pay (as required in the definition of fair market value).

William D. Rifkin, managing director and co-head of the Merger and Acquisition Group, Solomon Brothers, Inc., explained how investment value characteristics often influence merger and acquisition prices:

> The same acquisition target will have different values to different buyers, due both to perception and reality. Potential buyers will have different views on: (1) the expected financial performance of the target; (2) what can be done to enhance performance; and (3) the risk of deviation from expected results. Certain potential buyers, regardless of their perception of the future, may have a true economic advantage over others. This could be due to tax factors (such as ability to utilize net operating loss carry forwards), potential economies of scale, or opportunities to achieve synergies. Economic benefits which may result from the combination of two going concerns would not, for instance, be available to a so-called financial buyer, such as a leveraged buyout firm. Unless a company is purchased for immediate resale, as in a "bust-up" acquisition, the potential acquiror's first step must be a determination of what the target is worth specifically to it, not others—and this requires a careful and honest assessment of what the acquiror can do with the combined company.[2]

---

[2]William D. Rifkin, "Valuing and Pricing Mergers and Acquisitions I: Concepts and Mechanisms," Chap. 3 in *Mergers, Acquisitions, and Leveraged Buyouts,* Robert Lawrence Kuhn, ed. (Burr Ridge, IL: Irwin Professional Publishing, 1990), p. 39.

The same distinction arises when using merger and acquisition data in the context of *fair value*. Most state statutes defining fair value specifically exclude the value of any benefits arising from the merger itself.

There is no formula to sort out the amount by which a price that was paid in a transaction reflected synergistic value over and above a strict, stand-alone fair market value price. This is a continuing source of contention in using such data to resolve disputed valuations and a challenge to the analyst's judgment.

Ownership Characteristics

Marketable versus Nonmarketable. As we go to press, the issue of adjustments for marketability or lack of it relative to control transactions is a subject of controversy among business valuation professionals.

In many respects, this controversy is more semantic than real. Everyone recognizes that the sale of a controlling or major interest in a company obviously is not marketable in the sense of a publicly traded stock, which can be sold in seconds at or very near a recently established and known price, with cash delivered to the seller within five business days. Thus, if merger and acquisition data are used as guidance to estimate fair market value—a cash equivalent value as of a certain date—certain adjustments may be appropriate. This issue is discussed more fully in Chapter 15.

Control versus Minority. Since mergers and acquisitions usually represent control transactions, they are most directly relevant for valuation of other control interests.

If valuing a minority interest, it usually would be necessary to apply a minority interest discount to a value indicated by merger and acquisition data. It may also be appropriate to apply a further discount for lack of marketability.

Going-Concern Value versus Liquidation Value.

Sometimes, but not often, it is possible to analyze a transaction to estimate the extent to which a price represents a going-concern value or a liquidation value. Often, a transaction price reflects some combination of the two, where some assets acquired will be liquidated while others will be operated as part of a going-concern business. This is a matter that varies on a case-by-case basis.

Quantity and Quality of Data Available

Some industries are characterized by lots of acquisition activity while others are not. Even one good transaction generally is better than nothing, if it is a reasonably good guideline transaction and the data are complete and reliable. We generally would want to see at least a few transactions, however, if we were to weight the merger and acquisition method heavily in the final analysis.

If the acquiree(s) were public, generally adequate data are available. On the other hand, if the acquirees were private, rarely are there good, verifiable data available. Reported purchase prices may or may not reflect considerations such as covenants not to compete or employment contracts. It often is difficult to determine exactly what assets were included in the purchase price or what liabilities were or were not assumed. It often is difficult to get any reliable data on profitability. All these problems must be factored into a decision to use or not use private company acquisition data and, if so, the weight to be accorded to such data in the final analysis.

Control Transaction (Acquisition) Value Measures

When valuing a controlling interest, one often focuses on guidance from other controlling interest transactions (mergers and acquisitions). Control transaction valuation analysis typically focuses on market value of invested capital (MVIC, as defined in Chapter 10) or on *aggregate consideration,* defined as *"purchase price of equity plus total debt less cash."*[3] This comports to common sense, since the control owner has the power to change the capital structure, and control buyers very frequently do.

This, of course, means that all the return available to both equity and debt must be included in the denominator when computing the value measure multiple. Control transaction value measures (often called *deal multiples* or *acquisition multiples*) often use the following measures of returns in the denominator:

- Sales.
- Operating income available to invested capital (EBIT).
- Operating cash flow available to invested capital (EBIT plus depreciation and amortization).
- Tangible book value.

The above assumes that nonoperating income, expenses, and the assets and/or liabilities that produce them are treated separately if they are significant. (As a practical matter, we believe that practitioners tend to separate out nonoperating items more carefully when calculating operating cash flow than when calculating operating income.)

Exhibit 11–1 presents a very typical example of the use of the merger and acquisition method to develop an indicated value range for an acquisition candidate. Note that five value measures are computed but only three of them are used in the valuation analysis applied to the subject company. The reason seems obvious: three value measures fall into a fairly tight range while the other two are widely dispersed. Note that the three used involve aggregate consideration as the numerator (defined similarly to our definition of market value of invested capital, but not exactly the same). Had the tangible book value ratio also been computed on the basis of aggregate consideration instead of only price paid for equity securities, the range for that value measure may have been more usable.

Robert Kuhn recognizes that comparative transaction data are widely used in the merger market, but also cautions to carefully analyze differences between companies, time period differences, and market aberrations:

> In merger market valuation models, we compare prices among similar companies, much like comparison shopping for a consumer item among similar retail stores. Merger market value arrays reasonably similar transactions (i.e., similar industry, company size, financial structure, time frame, etc.) and uses these prices to judge the relative worth of the target company. Investment bankers favor this technique, generating long lists of comparable transactions to advise clients on both buy and sell sides.
>
> In theory, the M&A market is the true reflection of current interaction between willing sellers and willing buyers. In the real world, however, this is rarely the case. Corporations are not yellow pencils, quickly stacked and easily matched; it is difficult to make true comparisons of complex situations—in one way or another virtually every

---

[3]Marren, *Mergers & Acquisitions: A Valuation Handbook,* p. 188.

Exhibit 11–1

Example Application of Merger and Acquisition Method Analysis of Selected Transactions Involving Building Material Retailers (Figures in millions except ratios)

Date Final	Target/Acquirer	AC PP	Sales AC/Sales	OCF AC/OCF	EBIT AC/EBIT	Net Income PP/Net Income	TBV PP/TBV
7/89	Scotty's/	$303.8	$574.4	$32.4	$19.4	$11.9	$174.6
	GB Inno BM SA	$243.9	0.53 x	9.40 x	15.70 x	20.50 x	1.40 x
10/88	Payless Cashways/	$1,189.3	$1,844.9	$131.0	$93.0	$52.4	$397.5
	PCI Acquisition Corp.	$911.9	0.64 x	9.10 x	12.80 x	17.40 x	2.29 x
3/88	Pay 'N Pak Stores/	$292.3	$398.1	$29.6	$19.3	$5.7	$100.1
	PNP Prime Corp.	$212.6	0.73 x	9.90 x	15.10 x	37.30 x	2.12 x

Statistical Summary

Low:	0.53	9.08	12.79	17.40	1.40
High:	0.73	9.87	15.66	37.30	2.29
Mean:	0.64	9.44	14.53	25.07	1.94
Median:	0.64	9.38	15.15	20.50	2.12
Sample:	3	3	3	3	3

PP = Purchase price for all equity securities including options and convertible debt.
AC = Aggregate consideration (PP plus total debt less cash).
EBIT = Earnings before interest and taxes.
OCF = Operating cash flow (EBIT plus depreciation and amortization).
TBV = Tangible book value (total book value less intangibles).

Comparable Transactions Valuation Analysis
(Figures in millions except ratios)

	Comparable Transaction Multiples		Target Company LTM[a] Results	Valuation Range	
	Mean	Median		Mean	Median
Aggregate consideration[b] sales	0.64	0.64	$1,050	$668	$677
Aggregate consideration[b] operating cash flow[c]	9.44	9.38	55	519	516
Aggregate consideration[b] EBIT	14.53	15.15	35	509	530
			Range	$509	$677

[a]LTM means last 12 months.
[b]Aggregate consideration equals purchase price of equity plus total debt less cash.
[c]Operating cash flow equals EBIT plus depreciation and amortization.

SOURCE: Joseph H. Marren, *Mergers & Acquisitions: A Valuation Handbook* (Burr Ridge, IL: Irwin Professional Publishing, 1993), pp. 188–89.

M&A sale can be considered special or extraordinary. Furthermore, the M&A market often evinces aberrations—companies selling too low when suffering distressed conditions and companies selling too high when faddish or foolish buyers are over-eager to acquire. The feeding frenzy of M&A in recent years—the search for synergy and hostile takeover battles—have bid up many M&A prices to unrealistic levels.[4]

---

[4]*Mergers, Acquisitions, and Leveraged Buyouts*, p. 61.

Caveat: Check the Deal Structure

Deal Terms

For guideline valuation purposes, and certainly if the standard of value is fair market value, it is necessary that the deal price used to develop a value measure be a cash or cash equivalent price. In many acquisitions, the consideration paid is all or partly something other than cash, such as common or preferred stock (sometimes convertible), notes (also sometimes convertible), and so on. The cash value of such consideration often is less than its face value (rarely more). If using a guideline transaction in which the consideration paid was not all cash, the analyst should make the best possible effort to convert the consideration paid to a cash equivalent value.

If the standard of value is *fair value,* then the deal structure may be extremely important in some states. Fair value may be interpreted stringently in a dissenting stockholder action in a cash buyout, where the seller's interest in a going concern may be forced to be terminated. The fair value standard may be interpreted differently in a stock-for-stock merger where participants retain an interest in a somewhat similar going concern.

Exactly What Was Transacted?

When using publicly traded guideline company stock transactions, we know that what was sold was stock. When entire companies are sold, however, the deal often is structured as an asset sale. In such instances, it is important to know exactly what assets were sold and what liabilities assumed. In addition to the fact that not everything on the seller's balance sheet (or off-balance-sheet assets or liabilities) may have been included in the transaction, the income tax ramifications of an asset sale usually are considerably different than for a stock sale.

Differences in the structure between the guideline transaction and the contemplated subject transaction should be noted and adjusted or accounted for appropriately in developing value measures. This is of particular importance when the guideline transaction was an asset sale instead of a stock sale.

Sources of Merger and Acquisition Data

Generally, sources of price and underlying financial data on control transactions are more expensive and less consistent in content and reliability than public market stock transaction data. Public stock financial data are subject to very consistent reporting requirements by the SEC and the accounting profession. Data on acquisitions of private companies are not subject to any such regulation, and data on mergers and acquisitions of public companies vary tremendously in scope and format.

The bibliography at the end of the chapter gives specific information for several merger and acquisition sources as we go to press.

Information about mergers is obtained from disclosure filings, the news media, and business intermediaries (business brokers and investment bankers). When publicly held companies are involved, the participants must submit disclosure documents known collectively as Williams Act reports. The two major filings are forms 14D-1 and 13D. The first is submitted by companies attempting to purchase another company in the open market (called a tender offer). The second is filed by individuals purchasing 5 percent or more of a company's stock with the intent to obtain substantial voting control or otherwise influence the management of the company. There are also many other relevant required reports, depending on the transaction, such as 14D-9's, proxy statements, and prospectuses. News stories, including press releases from the participants, are the primary source of information on private transactions. The business media can also provide additional details on mergers involving public companies.

An amazing variety of reporting services, newsletters, and on-line databases utilize information from disclosure filings, company announcements, the media, and business intermediaries to provide extensive, organized analysis of merger transactions as they unfold. General business indexes and news databases can be useful in conducting merger research, but the following sources provide specific coverage of merger and acquisition activities. As with any secondary sources, errors and inconsistencies occur, so the original source documents are the only guarantees of absolute accuracy.

The *Mergerstat Review* is published annually in book form. In addition to a transaction roster covering transactions announced during the year and either completed or still pending at year's end, *Mergerstat Review* includes extensive analysis of the transaction data. In particular, it contains useful analyses of control premiums.

The Merger & Acquisition Sourcebook is published annually by Quality Services Company. This reference tool contains detailed analysis of transactions in every industry. Of special interest is the section that presents the average purchase price ratios to seller's sales, earnings, and net worth for acquisitions in every industry. Typically, more than 3,000 transactions are included, organized by SIC code. Also published by Quality Services is a weekly newsletter, *Corporate Growth Report,* covering transactions announced or completed after the last *Sourcebook* was published.

The Merger Yearbook is published annually by Securities Data Company. All the data contained in the *Yearbook* are collected, analyzed, verified, and compiled by the staff of Securities Data Company, a leading provider of merger and acquisition and financial information worldwide. Drawing upon an extensive proprietary database of merger and acquisition information, and backed by the worldwide resources of Thomson Financial Networks, *The Merger Yearbook* is very comprehensive. It is organized by SIC code and industry sector.

Mergers & Acquisitions magazine is published bimonthly by Investment Dealers' Digest. Most issues contain articles about mergers and acquisitions and also a "Mergers & Acquisitions Roster." The rosters list every corporate acquisition over $1 million that the publisher can identify, including private transactions. Selected information in the publication is provided by Securities Data Company. Investment Dealers' Digest also publishes biweekly *Mergers+Acquisitions International.* This magazine covers the world marketplace.

Several newsletters cover the merger and acquisition scene. Among them are *Mergers & Acquisitions Report,* published weekly by Investment Dealers' Digest;

Mergers & Corporate Policy, published weekly by Securities Data Publishing; and *Buyouts,* published every other week by Venture Economics Publishing Company. The newsletters vary in price, but most tend to be expensive.

BIZCOMPS is produced by Jack R. Sanders, an active business broker in San Diego. He collects data on several hundred transactions per year from a group of about 40 business brokers. His 1995 *Study of Larger Business Sales* covers 230 sales of manufacturing, wholesale/distribution, and larger service businesses. The average price of these 230 transactions was $605,000. Data include the asking price and actual deal terms, as well as the face value deal price.

In addition to traditional print sources, on-line databases provide a powerful and wide variety of information sources for tracking merger and acquisition–related information. DIALOG has a varied group of news and financial databases. These include the following:

- *BUSINESS DATELINE* (File 635) is an important source of company and industry news written from a local perspective. It provides the complete text of stories appearing in more than 130 regional business publications. This database often covers smaller companies not referenced in national publications.

- *BUSINESSWIRE* (File 610) and *PR NEWSWIRE* (File 613), which contain the full text of news releases issued by companies, trade associations, government agencies, and other organizations, provide details of the latest company announcements within minutes of their release on the wire.

- *MOODY'S CORPORATE NEWS—U.S. & International* (Files 556, 557) supply both textual and tabular information on the merger and acquisition activities of over 13,000 U.S. and 5,000 international companies. Special event names or codes help extract merger and acquisition–related information.

- *PTS PROMT* (File 16) provides key information on public and private companies from thousands of international trade and business publications. PTS PROMT abstracts and full-text records cover national and international events and activities of public and private companies throughout the world.

- *SDC WORLDWIDE MERGERS & ACQUISITIONS* (File 551) is produced by Securities Data Company and includes information on all partial, completed, or rumored transactions that involve a change in ownership of at least 5 percent of the target's equity ownership. U.S. and international targets are covered in depth, with 60 data items available for each transaction. Sources for information provided in this database include: the *Wall Street Journal,* the *New York Times,* Dow Jones Newswire, Corporate News Releases, Proxy Statements, Williams Act Filings (14-d-1, 13E-3, E-4), 8-Ks and other periodic SEC reports, and S-4s and S-3s.

- *STANDARD & POOR'S NEWS* (Files 132, 134) provides daily news and financial reports on over 12,000 publicly held corporations. Transactions such as leveraged buyouts, spin-offs, and tenders are indexed by event name for easy retrieval.

- *TRADE & INDUSTRY ASAP* (File 648) indexes and delivers the full text of articles from popular journals and magazines and trade-specific publications, plus stories and releases from three newswires. Information on both public and private mergers and acquisitions is covered.

Adjusting for Time Period Differences

A major difference between merger and acquisition guideline transaction analysis and publicly traded guideline company analysis is the proximity of the guideline transaction date to the subject company's effective valuation date. In the public guideline company method, guideline transaction prices usually are as of the same date as the subject company effective valuation date. In the merger and acquisition method, guideline transaction dates are whenever they occurred.

This creates the additional problem of adjusting for differences in conditions between the guideline transaction dates and the subject company effective valuation date. If enough transactions are available, the analyst may wish to omit those that occurred when economic conditions were significantly different rather than try to make drastic adjustments to account for the differences.

A common way to adjust for time differences is through either industry average stock price differences or industry average differences in valuation multiples, such as price/earnings multiples. Generally, we have found adjusting for industry valuation multiples more effective than adjusting for industry price indexes if the subject and guideline companies are similar in terms of profitability and other operating characteristics. However, it should also be recognized (as discussed more fully in Chapter 14 on minority discounts and control premiums) that the relation between market multiples and acquisition multiples varies over time.

Past Subject Company Transactions

Past transactions involving the subject company may be fruitful subjects to analyze for guidance as to value.

Past Subject Company Changes of Control

If the subject company itself has changed control in the last few years, the transaction may be an excellent source of value measures. The value measures used would generally be the same as those discussed earlier. The value measures indicated by the prior transaction may need some adjustment to reflect internal changes in the company or changes in merger and acquisition market conditions for companies in the industry.

Bona Fide Offers

Documentable, arm's-length, bona fide offers to buy or sell may also be useful evidence of value. It is usually difficult, however, to obtain adequate documentation or to verify the arm's-length relationship of the potential buyer/seller.

Past Acquisitions by the Subject Company

If the company has made one or more acquisitions in the last several years, such transactions may prove to be excellent sources of value measures. Again, adjustments may be necessary for changes between the dates of the acquisitions and the relevant valuation date.

It may be easy to overlook such acquisitions, because they may not come to light in any of the search procedures normally used to identify merger and acquisition transactions. The subject company may be the *only* source for such data, but typically is a very comprehensive and reliable source. Therefore, if considering using a merger and acquisition method, it often is a good idea to ask the company whether it has made any acquisitions.

Formulas or Rules of Thumb

Some industries have rules of thumb (sometimes given an aura of credibility by being referred to as industry valuation formulas) about how companies in their industry are valued for transfer of controlling interests. On the one hand, if such rules of thumb are widely disseminated and referenced in the industry, they probably should not be ignored. On the other hand, there usually is no credible evidence of how such rules were developed nor how well they actually comport to actual transaction data.

Rules of thumb usually are quite simplistic. As such, they obscure much important detail. They fail to differentiate how differences in either operating characteristics or assets from one company to another affect the valuation. They also fail to differentiate changes in conditions for companies in various industries from one time period to another.

Furthermore, it is common for companies in many industries to sell on terms rather than for cash, so the "prices" generated by the rules of thumb often are not cash equivalent values. The terms may vary considerably from one transaction to another, but usually are worth less than cash equivalent value. Rules of thumb, therefore, may tend to overstate a cash equivalent value. Consequently, rules of thumb rarely, if ever, should be used without other, more reliable valuation methods.

In an article targeted primarily to valuations for divorce, and still widely quoted after 10 years, Jay Fishman offers the following summary:

> There are no "quick fixes" to the valuation of closely held entities. It is essential to remember that industry formulas or rules of thumb are commonly not market derived representations of actual transactions. Since most industry formulas or rules of thumb are derived from textbooks, trade publications, verbal representations, or other similar sources of information, they are poor substitutes for the Direct Market Comparison Approach.[5]

Under a heading "Cautions about Using Formulas" in his book *Handbook of Small Business Valuation Formulas and Rules of Thumb,* Glenn Desmond makes the following observations:

Formulas Are General in Nature

Formulas are general in nature. Adjustments must be made to account for variations in revenue and cash flow trends; location; lease; condition of the plant, fixtures, and equipment; reputation with customers, suppliers, bankers, and others; special skills required; difficulty in starting the business; and so forth.

---

[5]Jay E. Fishman, "The Problem with Rules of Thumb in the Valuation of Closely-Held Entities," *FAIR$HARE: The Matrimonial Law Monthly,* December 1984, p. 13.

There Is No Single, All-Purpose Formula

There is no single formula that will work for every business. Formula multipliers offer ease of calculation, but they also obscure details. This can be misleading. Net revenue multipliers are particularly troublesome because they are blind to the business's expense and profit history. It is easy to see how two businesses in any given industry group might have the same annual net revenue (ANR), yet show very different cash flows. A proper valuation will go beyond formulas and include a full financial analysis whenever possible.[6]

Reaching the Value Conclusion

Relative weighting of valuation multiples is similar to that used in the public guideline company method, except that assets may get a little more weight in a control valuation, since the control owner has discretion over their use or disposal. The same observations apply to nonoperating assets, excess assets, and asset deficiencies. (See Chapter 10, "Market Approach: The Guideline Public Company Method," for a detailed discussion of these topics.)

One should recognize, of course, that an actual accomplished merger or acquisition observed in the market usually has been consummated at the highest possible value to the seller, not at some average of possible values. For every such transaction observed, there have been many attempts at transactions in which compensation acceptable to the potential seller was unable to be attained. Furthermore, many transactions reflect some synergistic value, which would contain elements of investment value over and above pure fair market value. All these factors must be considered when deciding on what multiples to apply to the subject transaction, and the relative weight to be accorded to each.

Since merger and acquisition value analysis usually focuses on market value of invested capital, the value of the debt must be subtracted to reach the market value of equity. This debt would be valued at market if it is expected to remain outstanding, but usually at face if it is expected to be retired in conjunction with the transaction.

If a minority interest is being valued, both minority interest and lack of marketability discounts should be considered. Even in the case of a controlling interest, it may be appropriate to make some adjustment for lack of marketability (or "lack of liquidity") relative to the values indicated from actual consummated transactions. This is discussed in Chapter 15.

Summary

The merger and acquisition method is similar in concept to the guideline public company method, seeking valuation guidance from actual sale transactions in the market. Since the transaction data used usually are controlling interests, it is most directly applicable for valuing other controlling ownership interests, although it can be used for minority ownership interest valuations with proper adjustments.

---

[6]Glenn M. Desmond, *Handbook of Small Business Valuation Formulas and Rules of Thumb*, 3rd ed. (Camden, ME: Valuation Press, 1993), p. 12.

Merger and acquisition data come from diverse sources and are less consistent (and sometimes less reliable) than data on day-to-day public stock market transactions. Sometimes, past transactions involving the subject company are a good source of value measures.

Since merger and acquisition transaction dates almost always differ from the subject company effective valuation date, adjustments often are needed to reflect differences in economic and industry conditions between the dates.

Merger and acquisition prices often, to some extent, reflect synergies between acquirer and acquiree. To the extent that this is true, a transaction may be more reflective of *investment value* (value to that particular buyer) than *fair market value* (the value to a hypothetical, typically motivated buyer). For this reason, the circumstances of the merger and acquisition transactions must be carefully analyzed.

Select Bibliography

Albo, Wayne P., and A. Randal Henderson. *Mergers & Acquisitions of Privately-Held Businesses,* 2nd ed. Toronto: Canadian Institute of Chartered Accountants, 1989.

Kuhn, Robert Lawrence, ed. *Mergers, Acquisitions, and Leveraged Buyouts.* Burr Ridge, IL: Irwin Professional Publishing, 1990.

Marren, Joseph H. *Mergers & Acquisitions: A Valuation Handbook.* Burr Ridge, IL: Irwin Professional Publishing, 1993.

Reed, Stanley Foster, and Lane and Edson, P.C. *The Art of M&A: A Merger Acquisition Buyout Guide.* Burr Ridge, IL: Irwin Professional Publishing, 1989.

Rock, Milton L., ed. *The Mergers and Acquisitions Handbook.* New York: McGraw-Hill Book Company, 1987.

West, Thomas L. *Business Reference Guide,* 1995. Concord, MA: Business Brokerage Press, *1995.*

Additional Resources

BIZCOMPS
Jack R. Sanders, CBC, CBI
Asset Business Appraisal
P.O. Box 711777
San Diego, California 92171
(619) 457-0366
> *BIZCOMPS National Industrial Edition* (annual)
> *BIZCOMPS Western, Central, and Eastern States Regional Studies* (annual)

Dialog Information Services, Inc.
A Knight-Ridder Company
Worldwide Headquarters
3460 Hillview Avenue
P.O. Box 10010
Palo Alto, California 94303-9993
(800) 334-2564
> Dialog Databases and File Number:
> *BUSINESS DATELINE* (File 635)
> *BUSINESSWIRE* (File 610)

MOODY'S CORPORATE NEWS—U.S. & INTERNATIONAL
  (Files 556, 557)
PR NEWSWIRE (File 613)
PTS PROMT (File 16)
SDC WORLDWIDE MERGERS & ACQUISITIONS (File 551)
STANDARD & POOR'S NEWS (Files 132, 134)
TRADE & INDUSTRY ASAP (File 648)

Investment Dealers' Digest
2 Worth Trade Center
18th Floor
New York, New York 10048
(212) 227-1200
  Mergers & Acquisitions (bimonthly)
  Mergers & Acquisitions Report newsletter (weekly)
  Mergers+Acquisitions International (biweekly)

Houlihan Lokey Howard & Zukin
1930 Century Park West
Los Angeles, California 90067
(310) 553-8871
  Mergerstat Review (annual)

Quality Services Company
5290 Overpass Road, Suite 126
Santa Barbara, California 93111
(805) 964-7841
  Corporate Growth Report (weekly)
  The Merger & Acquisition Sourcebook (annual)

Securities Data Company
Securities Data Publishing, Inc.
A Division of Thomson Financial Services
40 West 57th Street, 11th Floor
New York, New York 10019
(212) 765-6123
  Mergers & Corporate Policy newsletter (weekly)
  The Merger Yearbook (annual)

Venture Economics Publishing Co.
A Division of SDC Publishing
40 West 57th Street, Suite 802
New York, New York 10019
(212) 765-5311
  BUYOUTS newsletter (biweekly)

Chapter 12

Asset-Based Approach

Generally, business financial statements prepared in accordance with generally accepted accounting principles (GAAP) are prepared based on the historical cost principle. That is, all assets and liabilities recognized on a statement of financial position (i.e., a business balance sheet) are recorded at their historical acquisition price to the business entity (i.e., at historical cost). This historical cost principle is true even for a corporate acquisition of the assets of a going-concern business. While the purchased assets are recorded at their market value at the time of the acquisition, that value represents the "cost" of those purchased assets to the corporate acquirer.

This GAAP-based historical cost valuation principle allows for conservatism, consistency, and efficiency in the preparation of the periodic financial statements of the business entity.

Because of this historical cost *accounting principle,* and because of the fundamental principle of accounting identity, the book value of assets minus the book value of liabilities equals the book value of equity.

However, the basic principles of economics allow us to create this valuation identity: the defined value of assets minus the defined value of liabilities equals the defined value of equity of a business entity.

From a valuation perspective, the relevant standard (or definition) of value is the one that is appropriate given the purpose and objective of the appraisal. Chapter 2 presented several alternative standards of value, including fair market value, investment value, intrinsic or fundamental value, and fair value. These—and other similar—standards of value are the appropriate value definitions to use in the analysis and appraisal of a business entity—and particularly a going-concern business entity—using the asset-based valuation approach.

Accordingly, based on the purpose and objective of the appraisal, the appraiser will first select the appropriate standard of value to apply to the business interest subject to appraisal. In the asset-based valuation approach, the appraiser will apply that appropriate standard of value to all assets and all liabilities of the business entity.

In other words, the appraiser will restate the value of all assets and liabilities of the business from historical cost to, for example, fair market value. After the restatement of all asset and liability accounts from historical cost to fair market value, the appraiser can then apply the axiomatic "assets minus liabilities" formula to conclude the fair market value of the company's equity interests.

Also, it is possible to conclude a standard of value other than fair market value for the subject equity interest from an asset-based analysis that uses the fair market value standard. In that case, the appraiser will first estimate the fair market value of the subject equity interest from an asset-based valuation method. Then, the appraiser will apply appropriate discounts and premiums—to adjust the fair market value estimate to the definition of value that is appropriate for that appraisal.

At this point, the appraiser has typically concluded the value of 100 percent of the equity of the company, on a marketable, controlling interest basis. If the appraisal subject is other than 100 percent of the equity of the company (e.g., the value of a nonmarketable, minority ownership equity interest), then several security valuation discounts and/or premiums will need to be considered.

In some cases, a discount for lack of marketability and/or other premiums or discounts will be appropriate even when valuing 100 percent of the equity. Such premiums or discounts often are affected by the standard of value applicable to the subject equity interest.

Fundamentals of the Asset-Based Approach

If properly applied, asset-based valuation approach methods are, arguably, the most complex and challenging business valuation and security analysis techniques from an analytical perspective. The costs and benefits of asset-based business valuation methods will be described below. Before we consider these costs and benefits, or the various asset-based valuation methods, several important fundamentals should be reiterated.

First, in properly applying asset-based valuation methods, historical cost-based financial statements are only a starting point in the analysis. They are never the ending point in a valuation analysis.

Appraisers use the company's statement of financial position (i.e., balance sheet) prepared in accordance with GAAP only as a point of departure from which to begin the appraisal analysis. While the final format of the valuation-based balance sheet is cosmetically similar to the historical-cost-based balance sheet (e.g., the assets may be on the left-hand side and the liabilities may be on the right-hand side), it substantially differs in both content and intent.

First, the valuation-based balance sheet is materially different from the historical cost-based balance sheet in at least two ways:

1. The balances in the asset and the liability accounts have been revalued to the appropriate standard of value, as of the valuation date.
2. Several additional asset and liability accounts are likely to be added to the balance sheet and several original asset and liability accounts are likely to be deleted from (or consolidated on) the balance sheet.

Second, in properly applying asset-based valuation methods, all assets and liabilities should be restated to a standard of value consistent with the standard of value selected for the business valuation. As will be described below, if the asset and liability account balances are immaterial, or if the revaluation changes are immaterial, then the appraiser may elect to leave those account balances at their historical cost value. Otherwise, the appraiser will separately consider and analyze each asset and liability account—either individually (item by item) or collectively (grouped by major account categories).

The appraiser will then conclude the defined value (e.g., fair market value) of each asset and liability account, in the process of ultimately concluding the defined value (e.g., fair market value) of the company's equity structure. As will be explained below, it is inappropriate and incorrect (except by sheer coincidence) to estimate the value of the company's assets and liabilities—and the value of the company's equity—at net book value.

Third, in properly applying asset-based methods, *all* the company's assets and *all* the company's liabilities should be considered for revaluation to the selected appropriate standard of value. Where the appraiser is unskilled in individual asset appraisal methods, he or she may need to rely on experts in real estate, tangible personal property, intangible personal property, or other appraisal disciplines.

Typically, many of a company's most valuable assets are not recorded on a historical-cost-based balance sheet. This omission may include the entire spectrum of the company's intangible assets and intellectual properties. These intangible assets are typically not included on a historical-cost-based balance sheet prepared in accordance with GAAP (unless the intangible assets were acquired as part of a business acquisition and accounted for as an asset purchase transaction).

Also, many of the company's most significant liabilities are often not recorded on the company's historical-cost-based balance sheet. This may include the entire spectrum of the company's contingent liabilities. Accordingly, as part of the asset-based valuation, new asset and, possibly, new liability accounts may be recorded on the company's revaluation-based balance sheet.

Asset-Based Methods versus Book Value

It is important to distinguish between asset-based business valuation methods and the naive reliance on book value as a valuation conclusion. As mentioned above, the true defined value of a business enterprise, under any standard of value, may equal the company's book value (or net book value) only by sheer coincidence. More likely, the defined value (e.g., fair market value) of the business will be either higher or lower than its book value.

There is no theoretical underpinning, conceptual justification, empirical data, or economic reasoning to suggest that the value of a business enterprise (under any selected standard of value) would equal the company's historical cost-based book value.

The terms *book value* or *net book value* are unfortunate colloquialisms from an appraisal perspective, because book value is not related to any concept of economic "value" or to the valuation process. Book value is an accounting convention.

From an accounting perspective, the book value of a company is the historical cost of all the company's assets less total accumulated contra-asset reserves (e.g., reserves for depreciation of tangible assets, amortization of intangible assets, bad debt allowances for receivables, and shrinkage and obsolescence for inventory).

The net book value of a company is the company's book value of recorded assets less the recorded liabilities.

As another accounting identity, net book value (often called book value in the vernacular) is also synonymous with the company's owners' equity. Therefore, net book value can also be calculated as the sum of the owners' direct equity investments in the company (i.e., total capital contributions less capital withdrawals) plus the cumulative amount of the company's retained earnings.

In any event, book value is not a rigorous business valuation method. And book value is not a conceptually sound asset-based valuation method. It is naive and generally inappropriate to conclude a business valuation based on book value. Not only are the values presented on a GAAP—or historical-cost-based—balance sheet often not representative of the appropriate standard of value for business valuation purposes, but there also may be one or several important asset and/or liability accounts not presented on the GAAP balance sheet.

Various Asset-Based Valuation Methods

In the appraisal literature, there are several names for very similar asset-based methods. These methods are sometimes referred to as the net asset value method, the adjusted net worth method, the adjusted book value method, the asset buildup method, or the asset accumulation method. In fact, these are all very similar methods within the same broad valuation approach. These methods will be referred to collectively as asset-based methods for the remainder of this chapter.

Asset-based methods are balance-sheet-oriented valuation methods. Essentially, the company's balance sheet is restated to the defined value. This typically involves the identification and valuation of otherwise unrecorded tangible and intangible assets, as well as the revaluation of the asset and liability accounts already recorded on the GAAP balance sheet.

Two general methodological alternatives in the application of the asset-based valuation approach are:

1. The discrete (or individual) identification and revaluation of all the company's asset and liability accounts; this method is typically called the asset accumulation method.
2. The collective identification and revaluation of all (or major categories of) the company's asset and liability accounts; as will be discussed shortly, the capitalized excess earnings method is the most common of these collective revaluation asset-based methods.

Each of these two alternative methods will be described briefly below. In some cases, practicality will dictate analytical procedures somewhere in between these two methodological alternatives.

Discrete (Separate) Revaluation of Assets and Liabilities

In the discrete revaluation method, all the company's assets and liabilities are analyzed and appraised individually.

This involves a separate identification and revaluation of the company's:

1. Financial assets (e.g., cash, receivables, prepaids, inventory, etc.).
2. Tangible personal property (e.g., machinery and equipment, furniture and fixtures, trucks and automobiles, etc.).
3. Tangible real estate (e.g., land, land improvements, buildings, etc.).
4. Intangible real property (e.g., leasehold interests, easements, mineral development rights, air and water rights, etc.).
5. Intangible personal property (e.g., patents, trademarks and trade names, computer software, customer relationships, going-concern value, goodwill, etc.).
6. Current liabilities (e.g., accounts payable, taxes payable, salaries payable, etc.).
7. Long-term liabilities (e.g., bonds, notes, mortgages, and debentures payable, etc.).
8. Contingent liabilities (e.g., pending tax disputes, pending environmental matters, pending bankruptcy or other commercial litigation, etc.).
9. Special obligations (e.g., unfunded pensions, earned and otherwise unrecorded vacations, ESOP repurchase liabilities, etc.).

Under this method, the value of the discretely appraised assets (both tangible and intangible) less the value of the discretely appraised liabilities (both recorded and contingent) represents the business value of the company.

Collective Revaluation of Assets and Liabilities

In the collective revaluation method, all of the revaluation of the company's assets and liabilities (and, hence, owners' equity) is made in one analysis and calculation. Typically, this collective revaluation is concluded in the identification and quantification of the company's incremental value over and above (or decremental value below) the book value of its recorded assets.

Using this method, the company's intangible value in the nature of goodwill is defined globally as the total of all the appreciation (or depreciation) in the value of the company, as compared to the book value of the company.

Under the capitalized excess earnings method, the value of the company's equity is the value of the company's net tangible assets plus the value of the company's collective intangible assets, much or all of which may be in the nature of goodwill. This collective intangible value may be quantified using the capitalized excess earnings method.

So, when viewed from the perspective of the asset-based business valuation approach, the capitalized excess earnings method is considered an asset-based valuation method, where the total amount of the company's asset revaluation is concluded on a collective basis. This single collective adjustment in the revaluation of all the company's assets and liabilities is often labeled as "intangible value in the nature of goodwill."

As will be noted in Chapter 13, "The Excess Earnings Method," in the variation of the excess earnings method that is presented in Revenue Ruling 68-609, all tangible assets are revalued to fair market value, and the excess earnings method is used only to quantify the total intangible value of the company in excess of tangible asset value.

Partial Revaluation of Individual Assets and Liabilities

Very often, it is practical to revalue some—but not all—the company's specific assets and liabilities. The analysts often use the capitalized excess earnings method to quantify the balance of the remaining increment or decrement to the company's total equity value. When choosing a capitalization rate to apply to the excess earnings associated with a partial revaluation, the appraiser should consider the extent to which the excess earnings arise totally from intangibles (which indicates a higher capitalization rate) and the extent to which the excess earnings partially reflect the unrecognized tangible asset values. (For ease of exposition, we present the excess earnings method separately in the following chapter.)

Which Asset-Based Valuation Method to Use

Theoretically and practically, the business value concluded under the collective revaluation method should equal the business value concluded under the discrete revaluation method.

In fact, if the revaluation analyses are all performed consistently, and if an appropriate excess earnings income capitalization rate is estimated, then even the partial revaluation method will result in a consistent business valuation conclusion.

The determination of which valuation method to use in a given appraisal should be a function of:

1. The experience and judgment of the professional appraiser.
2. The quantity and quality of available data.
3. The purpose and objective of the appraisal.
4. The scope and timing of the appraisal assignment.

As will be discussed below, both costs and benefits are associated with the discrete valuation method—or the asset accumulation method—to business valuation. In the remainder of this chapter, we will describe the steps in the application of the asset accumulation method—or the individual asset valuation method—in the asset-based business valuation approach. In the next chapter, we will describe the steps in the application of the capitalized excess earnings method—or the collective asset valuation method—in the asset-based business valuation approach.

Steps in the Application of the Asset Accumulation Method

This section lists and briefly discusses the asset accumulation method, as summarized in the following six steps:

1. Obtain or develop a GAAP-or historical-cost-based balance sheet for the subject business entity.
2. Determine which categories of assets and liabilities currently recorded on the GAAP-basis balance sheet that require a revaluation adjustment and then revalue these assets and liabilities to the appropriate standard of value.
3. Identify all off-balance-sheet assets—typically intangible assets—that should be recognized and valued.
4. Identify all off-balance-sheet—typically contingent—liabilities that should be recognized and valued.
5. Value the previously unrecognized (under GAAP) assets and liabilities identified in steps 2 through 4 to the appropriate standard of value.
6. Construct a valuation-based balance sheet (reflecting the appropriate standard of value) using the results of steps 1 through 5.

Obtain or Develop a GAAP-Basis Balance Sheet

As mentioned above, first, the appraiser starts with a GAAP or historical-cost-based balance sheet for the subject business entity, prepared as of the valuation date. If a historical-cost-based balance sheet is not available because the valuation is being conducted as of an interim (i.e., nonfiscal period end) date, then the appraiser has three options:

1. The client (or an accountant retained by the client) may prepare a historical-cost-based balance sheet as of the valuation date and give it to the appraiser as a basic tool to start the appraisal.
2. The appraiser may prepare a historical-cost-based balance sheet as of the valuation date, assuming the appraiser has the requisite basic accounting expertise to prepare such a financial statement.

3. The appraiser may rely on the most recent historical-cost-based balance sheet prepared at a fiscal period end just before the valuation date. A recent fiscal period end balance sheet will require more revaluation adjustments than a valuation date balance sheet, but it is usually better than not having a starting point. (Of course, the appraiser should consider any changes in the financial position of the company that occurred between the balance sheet date and the valuation date.)

Identify Assets and Liabilities to Be Revalued

Second, the appraiser will carefully analyze and understand each material recorded asset category and liability category of the subject company. The objective of this analysis is to determine which material recorded asset and liability categories will need to be revalued according to the selected standard of value appropriate for the subject business valuation.

As a convention throughout the remainder of this discussion, let's assume that fair market value is the appropriate standard of value for the subject business valuation. Accordingly, in this step, the appraiser will analyze which material recorded assets and liabilities of the subject company should be revalued to conclude fair market value.

Identify Off-Balance-Sheet Assets that Should be Recognized

Third, the appraiser will identify which unrecorded (sometime called off-balance-sheet) assets need to be recognized on the valuation-based balance sheet of the company. For example, while intangible assets are not normally recorded on the company's financial statements under GAAP, they often represent the largest component of economic value for many business entities.

The value of the company's tangible and intangible assets represents the allocation of the elements of the overall business value into specific assets. It represents the identification of the specific factors (i.e., the specific assets or asset groups) responsible for the company's earning capacity, cash flow generation capacity, and dividend-paying capacity. In the case of intangible assets, they normally would not appear on the balance sheet if developed internally. As mentioned above, typically, intangible assets are recognized under GAAP accounting only if they were acquired in a purchase. Some tangible assets may have been expensed rather than capitalized when acquired, and others may be fully depreciated—even though they may still have significant remaining economic life.

Identify Off-Balance-Sheet and Contingent Liabilities that Should Be Recognized

Fourth, the appraiser will identify what unrecorded material contingent liabilities, if any, need to be recognized on the valuation-based balance sheet of the subject company. If there are potential environmental liabilities, specialized expert opinion may be needed.

Under GAAP accounting, contingent liabilities are not recorded on a historical-cost-based balance sheet. However, in audited and reviewed financial statements, material contingent liabilities are subject to footnote disclosure.

The identification and valuation of contingent liabilities is a less common step in an asset accumulation method of business valuation. This does not mean, however, that many business entities do not have material contingent liabilities. Therefore, the appraiser should carefully consider this procedure in every asset accumulation method business valuation. Certainly, for those companies that have material pending commercial or other litigation against them, tax claims against them, environmental claims against them, product liability claims against them, bankruptcy claims against them, and so forth, these contingent liabilities have a significant (and often quantifiable) effect on the risk of the business. Therefore, these material contingent liabilities have a significant effect on the business enterprise value of the subject company

Value the Items Identified Above

Fifth, after the analysis of recorded assets and liabilities and after the identification of unrecorded assets and liabilities, the appraiser will begin the quantitative process of revaluing each of the subject company's assets and, if necessary, each of the subject company's liabilities.

Typically, the appraiser will perform these valuation analyses by category of assets. The standard categorization of assets, for purposes of applying the asset accumulation method, was described above. These standard categories of assets are:

1. Financial assets.
2. Tangible personal property.
3. Tangible real estate.
4. Intangible real property.
5. Intangible personal property.

For some of these categories, the business appraiser may need to rely on specialized experts.

The general valuation approaches, methods, and procedures for appraising these asset categories (and the component tangible and intangible assets) will be summarized in a later section of this chapter.

Construct a Valuation-Based Balance Sheet

Sixth, after concluding the defined value for all the company's financial, tangible, and intangible assets—and for all the company's recorded and contingent liabilities—the appraiser will construct a valuation-basis balance sheet for the company, as of the valuation date.

From this valuation-based (as opposed to the historical-cost-based) balance sheet, it is mathematically simple for the appraiser to subtract the value of the company's liabilities (recorded and contingent) from the value of the company's assets (tangible and intangible). The remainder of this subtraction is the value of a 100 percent interest in the company's equity structure (on a marketable, controlling business enterprise basis).

At this point, the asset accumulation method has produced the value of the total owners' equity of the company. Of course, if the company has several classes of equity securities outstanding, then additional security analysis and valuation allocation procedures are required.

In addition, if the appraisal assignment relates to something less than the overall business equity value (e.g., to a nonmarketable, minority ownership interest in the class B nonvoting common stock of the company), then additional business valuation discount and/or premium analyses and procedures are required.

Premises of Value for Individual Assets

Before considering the various valuation methods with respect to the individual assets of the company, the appraiser should first consider both the appropriate standard (or definition) of value and the appropriate premise of value for each asset category. Usually (but not always), the appropriate standard of value selected for each asset category should be the same standard of value as selected for the overall business valuation.

With regard to individual asset appraisal, appraisers may elect from among four alternative premises of value. Each of these four alternative premises of value may apply under each of the alternative standards of value.

While the standard (or definition) of value answers the general question "value to whom?" the premise of value answers the general question "value under what type of hypothetical market transaction?" For example, under the fair market value standard of value, the same asset category may be appraised under four different premises of value.

So, while fair market value answers the question of "value to whom?" (i.e., to a hypothetical willing buyer and to a hypothetical willing seller), the selected premise of value answers the question "in what type of market transaction—or under what set of transactional circumstances—will these parties interact?"

The four alternative premises of value for individual asset appraisal are:

1. Value in continued use, as part of a going concern.
2. Value in place, as part of a mass assemblage of assets.
3. Value in exchange, as part of an orderly disposition.
4. Value in exchange, as part of a forced liquidation.

Value in Continued Use, as Part of a Going Concern

Under this premise, it is assumed the subject assets are sold as a mass assemblage of assets and as part of an income-producing, going-concern business enterprise.

This premise of value contemplates the mutually synergistic relationships of the company's tangible assets to the company's intangible assets—and the relationship of the intangible assets to the tangible assets.

Value in Place, as Part of a Mass Assemblage of Assets

Under this premise, it is assumed the subject assets are sold as a mass assemblage, but that the mass assemblage is capable of being, but not currently operating as, an income-producing business enterprise.

This premise of value contemplates some of the mutual contributory value of the tangible assets vis-à-vis the intangible assets and of the intangible assets vis-à-vis the tangible assets. However, while there is a value in place component to the subject assets (including such intangible assets as patents, trademarks, copyrights, and computer software), this premise would exclude the contributory value of such common intangible assets as a trained and assembled workforce, going-concern value, and goodwill.

Value in Exchange, as Part of an Orderly Disposition

Under this premise, it is assumed the subject assets are sold piecemeal and not as part of a mass assemblage. It is assumed the assets are given an adequate exposure to their normal secondary market.

However, due to the orderly disposition market transaction assumption, this premise does not contemplate any contributory value effect of the tangible assets on the intangible assets, or of the intangible assets on the tangible assets.

Value in Exchange, as Part of a Forced Liquidation

Under this premise, it is assumed the subject assets are sold piecemeal and not as part of a mass assemblage. It is also assumed the assets are not allowed a normal exposure to their usual secondary market. Rather, the assets are permitted an abbreviated exposure to a market of the highest bidders present (who may or may not represent the collective demand-side marketplace for that asset). As an aside, this valuation premise may conclude a fair market value standard of value if the seller voluntarily decides to auction his assets (for example, as his plan of selling his business) and if the auction bidders are willing (but not compelled) to bid. Under this valuation premise, the seller and the potential buyers are both willing and not under compulsion.

Due to the forced liquidation market transaction assumption, this premise assumes no contributory value (or other interrelationships) from tangible assets to intangible assets, or vice versa.

Selecting the Appropriate Premise of Value

Any of the four above described premises of value may be applied to the same asset (or category of assets) being appraised under the same standard of value. For example, an appraiser may select the fair market value standard and assume that a willing buyer and a willing seller transact to exchange an asset.

The selected premise of value describes the assumed market conditions under which this willing buyer and willing seller meet (i.e., during the sale of an up-and-running business, during the sale of a temporarily closed business, during the brokered sale of individual assets, or during the auction sale of individual assets).

The appraiser will select the appropriate premise or premises of value based on the purpose and objective of the appraisal and based on the most likely form of the ultimate sale of the subject business (and, accordingly, of the assets of the subject business). The selection of the appropriate premise or premises of value is a critical decision in the application of the asset accumulation method of business valuation.

Even under the same standard of value, the subject business can have materially different business enterprise valuation conclusions—given the premise or premises of value selected for valuing various assets.

Individual Asset Valuation Approaches and Methods

After the appropriate premise of value is selected, the next step in the asset accumulation method is to apply one or more widely recognized appraisal methods to each individual asset category.

The conceptual cornerstone of the asset accumulation method is the identification and valuation of all the company's assets. This includes the financial assets, the tangible assets (real and personal), and the intangible assets (real and personal).

In Chapter 7, the procedures related to adjusting the balance sheet were discussed. Those adjustment procedures should be considered when analyzing the company's balance sheet in preparation for *any* business valuation approach or method. The procedures discussed below are common asset appraisal procedures, as compared to common balance-sheet adjustment procedures. These asset appraisal procedures should be considered when using the asset accumulation method of business valuation.

Since this is not a text devoted to individual asset appraisal, this discussion will be introductory. In the bibliography to this chapter, appropriate references to specialized textbooks will be presented with regard to the appraisal of individual tangible assets for those business appraisers who wish to study these subjects in detail. References to articles on appraising intangible assets are included in the bibliographies at the end of Chapters 23, 24, and 25.

Financial Assets

The most common assets included in this category are: cash, accounts and notes receivable, prepaid expenses, and inventory.

With regard to cash, no revaluation procedures need to be performed, of course. However, the appraiser should verify the amount of cash on hand as of the valuation date.

With regard to accounts and notes receivable, the appraiser may estimate the net realizable value of these receivables. The net realizable value is, essentially, the present value of the expected realization of (i.e., collection of) the receivables.

For businesses with audited or reviewed financial statements (or more sophisticated accounting systems), a reserve for uncollectible accounts is typically established as a contra-asset valuation account. Particularly if the valuation date is other than a fiscal period end, the appraiser should assess the adequacy of this reserve for uncollectible accounts.

For businesses that have not established reserves for uncollectible accounts, the appraiser should assess the ultimate collectibility of the gross receivables. Based on this assessment of historical collection patterns, the appraiser will, typically, discount the gross accounts receivable to conclude an estimate of net cash collections.

Lastly, if the expected realization of the receivables is anticipated to occur over an extended time period (i.e., longer than the normal collection cycle), then the appraiser may also apply a present value analysis to the longer-term receivables.

The net balance of the accounts and notes receivable, after the analysis for uncollectible accounts and the present value of extended period receivables (if applicable), represents the net realizable value of this asset category.

With regard to prepaid expenses, the appraiser may estimate the net realizable value of this asset category. Prepaid expenses typically include deposits and prepaid rent, insurance, utilities expenses, and so forth.

Normally, the business expects to realize the economic benefit of these assets within the usual course of the business cycle. Therefore, commonly, no revaluation adjustment is required with respect to recorded prepaid expenses. However, if the appraiser determines the company will not enjoy an economic benefit from a prepaid expense during the business cycle, then a revaluation adjustment is appropriate. For example, if the company has recorded prepaid rent expense on a facility that it is no longer using, then that asset will likely have little economic value.

The expected realization of the prepaid expenses represents the net realizable value of this asset category. It is noteworthy that under the valuation premise of value in-exchange-forced liquidation, prepaid expenses may have no net realizable value.

With regard to inventory, the appraiser should distinguish between the work-in-process inventory of a professional service firm (e.g., accounting firms, law firms, etc.) and the merchandise inventory of a manufacturer or wholesale/retail company.

The work-in-process inventory of a professional service firm is, essentially, the unbilled receivables of the firm. Therefore, with regard to this asset category, the same net realizable value rules discussed with respect to accounts and notes receivable would apply to this asset as well.

With regard to tangible merchandise inventory, there are at least three common valuation methods. These alternative valuation methods apply equally to raw material, work-in-process, and finished goods inventory. These three common merchandise inventory valuation methods are: (1) the cost of reproduction method, (2) the comparative sales method, and (3) the income method.

While these three inventory valuation methods are discussed elsewhere in the appraisal literature, they are concisely summarized in Internal Revenue Service Revenue Procedure 77-12. Revenue Procedure 77-12 (Exhibit 12–1) was originally issued with respect to the valuation of merchandise inventory for purchase price allocation purposes. Nonetheless, these valuation methods provide reasonable guidelines for the appraisal of merchandise inventory for business valuation purposes, as well.

The cost of reproduction valuation method generally provides a good indication of fair market value if the inventory is readily replaceable in the volume and in the mix equal to the subject quantity on hand. In valuing inventory under this method, however, other factors may be relevant. For example, a well-balanced inventory available to fill customers' orders in the ordinary course of business may have a fair market value in excess of its cost of reproduction, because it provides a continuity of business. Whereas, an inventory containing obsolete merchandise unsuitable for customers might have a fair market value of less than the cost of reproduction.

The comparative sales valuation method uses the actual or expected selling prices of finished goods to customers as a basis of determining the fair market value of that inventory. When the expected selling price is used as a basis for valuing inventory, consideration should be given to the time that would be required to dispose of this inventory, the expenses that would be expected to be incurred in such disposition, applicable discount (including those for quantity),

Exhibit 12–1
Revenue Procedure 77-12

26 CFR 601.105: Examination of returns and claims for refund, credit or abatement; determination of correct tax liability. (Also Part I, Section 334; 1.334-1.)

Rev. Proc. 77-12

SECTION 1. PURPOSE.

The purpose of this Revenue Procedure is to set forth guidelines for use by taxpayers and Service personnel in making fair market value determinations in situations where a corporation purchases the assets of a business containing inventory items for a lump sum or where a corporation acquires assets including inventory items by the liquidation of a subsidiary pursuant to the provisions of section 332 of the Internal Revenue Code of 1954 and the basis of the inventory received in liquidation is determined under section 334(b) (2). These guidelines are designed to assist taxpayers and Service personnel in assigning a fair market value to such assets.

SEC. 2. BACKGROUND.

If the assets of a business are purchased for a lump sum, or if the stock of a corporation is purchased and that corporation is liquidated under section 332 of the Code and the basis is determined under section 334(b) (2), the purchase price must be allocated among the assets acquired to determine the basis of each of such assets. In making such determinations, it is necessary to determine the fair market value of any inventory items involved. This Revenue Procedure describes methods that may be used to determine the fair market value of inventory items.

In determining the fair market value of inventory under the situations set forth in this Revenue Procedure, the amount of inventory generally would be different from the amounts usually purchased. In addition, the goods in process and finished goods on hand must be considered in light of what a willing purchaser would pay and a willing seller would accept for the inventory at the various stages of completion, when the former is not under any com-

pulsion to buy and the latter is not under any compulsion to sell, both parties having reasonable knowledge of relevant facts.

SEC. 3. PROCEDURES FOR DETERMINATION OF FAIR MARKET VALUE.

Three basic methods an appraiser may use to determine the fair market value of inventory are the cost of reproduction method, the comparative sales method, and the income method. All methods of valuation are based on one or a combination of these three methods.

.01 The cost of reproduction method generally provides a good indication of fair market value if inventory is readily replaceable in a wholesale or retail business, but generally should not be used in establishing the fair market value of the finished goods of a manufacturing concern. In valuing a particular inventory under this method, however, other factors may be relevant. For example, a well balanced inventory available to fill customers' orders in the ordinary course of business may have a fair market value in excess of its cost of reproduction because it provides a continuity of business, whereas an inventory containing obsolete merchandise unsuitable for customers might have a fair market value of less than the cost of reproduction.

.02 The comparative sales method utilizes the actual or expected selling prices of finished goods to customers as a basis of determining fair market values of those finished goods. When the expected selling price is used as a basis for valuing finished goods inventory, consideration should be given to the time that would be required to dispose of this inventory, the expenses that would be expected to be incurred in such disposition, for example, all costs of disposition, applicable discounts (including those for quantity), sales commissions, and freight and shipping charges, and a profit commensurate with the amount of investment and degree of risk. It should also be recognized that the inventory to be valued may represent a larger quantity than the

normal trading volume and the expected selling price can be a valid starting point only if customers' orders are filled in the ordinary course of business.

.03 The income method, when applied to fair market value determinations for finished goods, recognizes that finished goods must generally be valued in a profit motivated business. Since the amount of inventory may be large in relation to normal trading volume the highest and best use of the inventory will be to provide for a continuity of the marketing operation of the going business. Additionally, the finished goods inventory will usually provide the only source of revenue of an acquired business during the period it is being used to fill customers' orders. The historical financial data of an acquired company can be used to determine the amount that could be attributed to finished goods in order to pay all costs of disposition and provide a return on the investment during the period of disposition.

.04 The fair market value of work in process should be based on the same factors used to determine the fair market value of finished goods reduced by the expected costs of completion, including a reasonable profit allowance for the completion and selling effort of the acquiring corporation. In determining the fair market value of raw materials, the current costs of replacing the inventory in the quantities to be valued generally provides the most reliable standard.

SEC. 4. CONCLUSION.

Because valuing inventory is an inherently factual determination, no rigid formulas can be applied. Consequently, the methods outlined above can only serve as guidelines for determining the fair market value of inventories.

SOURCE: Rev. Proc. 77-12, 1977-1 C.B. 569.

sales commissions, freight and shipping charges, and a profit commensurate with the amount of investment and degree of risk.

It should also be recognized that the inventory to be valued may represent a larger quantity than the normal trading volume and the expected selling price can be a valid starting point only if customers' orders are filled in the ordinary course of business.

The income valuation method when applied to the fair market value determination of inventory recognizes that the subject inventory must generally be valued in a profit-motivated business. Since the amount of inventory may be large in relation to the normal trading volume, the highest and best use of the inventory will be to provide for a continuity of the marketing operation of the going business.

Additionally, the subject inventory will usually provide the only source of revenue of the subject business during the period it is being used to fill customers' orders. The historical financial data of the subject company can be used to determine the amount that could be attributed to inventory in order to pay all costs of disposition and provide a return on the investment during the period of disposition.

The appraiser will apply one or more of these inventory valuation methods based on the quantity and quality of available data and the most likely ultimate disposition of the subject inventory. The appraiser will estimate the value of the subject inventory based on the results concluded from one or more of these inventory valuation methods.

Tangible Real Estate

Tangible real estate includes such assets as owned land, land improvements, buildings, and building improvements.

Technically, in the appraisal literature, real estate is called tangible real property. Real estate is distinguished from intangible real property, which represents a limited legal interest (i.e., less than a fee simple interest) in real estate.

There is a prodigious body of literature with respect to the appraisal of real estate, and both the appraisal regulatory agencies and the various professional appraisal membership organizations have promulgated professional standards with respect to the valuation of tangible real estate. For example, the Uniform Standards of Professional Appraisal Practice (USPAP)—which are principally real estate related—were discussed earlier in this text.

Nonetheless, all real estate is valued by reference to these three traditional valuation approaches: (1) the cost approach, (2) the income approach, and (3) the sales comparison approach. However, each of these three approaches represents a general category of several discrete appraisal methods. Each of these three approaches will be described briefly below.

Cost Approach. The cost approach is based on the economic principle of substitution. That is, no one would pay more for an asset than the price required to obtain (by purchase or by construction) a substitute asset of comparable utility.

This assumes, of course, that the subject asset is fungible. In other words, the cost approach assumes substitute properties of comparable utility may be obtained. If the subject asset is unique in one or more respects, then the cost approach may not be a reliable valuation approach.

Using the cost approach, the value of land is appraised separately from the value of all appurtenance to land. The subject land is valued as if vacant and unimproved. Although other appraisal methods are available, the subject land is typically valued using the sales comparison approach. That is, the value of vacant land is determined by reference to the sale of comparable land parcels in the reasonably proximate marketplace.

The appraiser collects and analyzes data with respect to recent sales of comparable vacant land parcels. If necessary, quantitative adjustments are made for size, access, services, frontage, topography, distance, time of sale (i.e., market condition), special financing, and special terms of sale. Based on an analysis of these adjusted comparable property sales data, the appraiser concludes the value of the subject land.

The subject site improvements (i.e., buildings and improvements) are valued by reference to the current cost to re-create their functional utility. There are several commonly used cost approach methods, including both reproduction cost and replacement cost methods. One of the most common methods for appraisal of buildings and improvements is the depreciated reproduction cost method.

This method is algebraically described as follows:

	Reproduction cost new of buildings and improvements
less:	Allowances for curable functional and technological obsolescence
equals:	Replacement cost new
less:	Allowance for physical deterioration
equals:	Depreciated replacement cost
less:	Allowance for external (either economic or locational) obsolescence
less:	Allowances for incurable functional and technological obsolescence
equals:	Market value of buildings and improvements

To complete the cost approach, the value of the land (as if vacant) is added to the value of the buildings and improvements. The sum of these two values represents the value of the subject tangible real estate, per the cost approach.

Income Approach. The income approach is based on the economic principles of anticipation and expectation. Using this approach, the value of the real estate is the present value of the expected economic income that could be earned through the ownership of the subject asset.

There are two categories of valuation methods under the income approach: (1) the direct capitalization method and (2) the yield capitalization method. From an investment analysis perspective, both of these methods are conceptually identical; and, therefore, from a theoretical perspective, both methods should conclude identical values for the same parcel of real estate.

Using the direct capitalization method, the appraiser first estimates the stabilized (or normalized) economic income that would be earned from the rental (whether hypothetical or actual) of the subject real estate. Economic income may be defined in many ways (i.e., before-tax income, after-tax income, potential gross income, effective gross income, etc.).

The most common definition of economic income used in the direct capitalization method is (before-tax) net operating income. This estimate of economic income is stabilized (or normalized) to represent an average or typical period's effective gross rental income (including normal rental rates and occupancy levels) and operating expenses (including normal repairs and maintenance, real estate taxes, insurance, management fees, and an allowance for replacement reserves).

The stabilized economic income is capitalized, typically as an annuity in perpetuity, by a capitalization rate commensurate with the risk of investment and consistent with the measurement of economic income. For example, if projected economic income is measured on an after-tax basis, then the capitalization rate should be derived on an after-tax basis. If economic income is measured before tax, then the capitalization rate should be derived before tax, and so forth.

Consistent with the definition of economic income as (before-tax) net operating income, the most common derivation of the direct capitalization rate is a (before-tax) blended rate of return to both the debt holder and the equity holder— in other words, a weighted average cost of capital.

The equity component of this blended rate represents the typical real estate investor's current income yield expectation for similar rental properties; it excludes the investor's derived long-term capital appreciation expectation for the subject property. The return represents the return to the equity holder in the subject real estate.

The debt component of this blended rate represents the current typical mortgage debt rate for similar properties; it includes a yield component for the amortization of mortgage principal as well as the payment of mortgage interest. The return (typically expressed as a mortgage constant) represents the return to the mortgage holder in the subject real estate.

The debt component and the equity component are blended, or weighted together, based on the typical loan-to-value ratio for new mortgages offered on comparable properties. The result of this analysis is the direct capitalization rate.

Using the direct capitalization method, the value of the subject real estate is presented algebraically, as follows:

Formula 12–1

$$Value = \frac{Expected\ economic\ income}{Direct\ capitalization\ rate}$$

Using the yield capitalization method, the value of the subject real estate is the present value of the projected economic income to be derived from the property over a discrete period. While there is no theoretically correct projection period, discrete projection periods of from 5 to 10 years are common. The projection period typically represents the average investment holding period for real estate such as the subject.

The appraiser projects the economic income to be derived from the rental of the subject property for each individual year in the discrete projection period. Again, (before-tax) net operating income is the most common measurement of economic income.

The appraiser next derives a present value discount rate to calculate the present value of the discrete projection of economic income. This present value discount rate is often called the *going-in capitalization rate*. A blended cost of debt and cost of equity is the most common derivation of the going-in capitalization rate.

The appraiser then estimates the normalized economic income to be generated by the property after the conclusion of the discrete projection period. This is sometimes called an estimate of the residual value (or reversionary period) income. This is the average or typical level of economic income to be generated by the property after the end of the projection period.

The appraiser next derives a capitalization rate consistent with this estimate of residual value (or reversionary period) income. This rate is often called the *residual (or reversionary) capitalization rate;* it is sometimes called the *coming-out capitalization rate.*

The coming-out capitalization rate is often different from the going-in capitalization rate due to the changing relative remaining life of the property and the different risk positions of the two investment periods.

The estimate of residual normalized economic income is capitalized by the residual capitalization rate. The result is the estimated value of the property at the end of the discrete projection period. This residual value is brought back to its present value, using the discrete projection period present value discount rate.

Finally, under the income approach, the value of the subject real estate is the sum of discrete projection period present value plus the residual value present value.

Sales Comparison Approach (Market Approach). The sales comparison approach is based on the economic principles of efficient markets and of supply and demand. That is, when there is a relatively efficient and unrestricted secondary market for comparable properties, and when that market accurately represents the activities of a representative number of willing buyers and willing sellers, then the market is most determinative of the market value of the subject property.

Using the sales comparison approach, the appraiser first collects data with regard to relatively recent sales of comparable real estate properties. Next, the appraiser analyzes each of these sale transactions to determine if any quantitative adjustments are necessary due to the lack of comparability of the subject property when compared to the comparable properties.

The appraiser would consider these factors, among others, when determining if quantitative adjustments to the sales comparison data are necessary:

1. Age of each transaction (i.e., elapsed time from the valuation date).
2. Land-to-building ratio of each property.
3. Absolute location and relative location of each property compared to population centers, highways, and so forth.
4. Age of each property.
5. Physical condition of each property.
6. Municipal and other services available to each property.
7. Frontage and access of each property.
8. Topography of land and soil type of each comparable property.
9. Environmental aspects of each property.
10. Special financing or other terms regarding each sale transaction.

Accordingly, if necessary, the appraiser adjusts the sales comparison data to make each transaction as comparable to the subject property as possible. Based on these adjusted sales comparison data, the appraiser will conclude a market-derived valuation multiple.

This multiple is typically expressed in terms of value per square foot of improved building space, as a common unit of value measure.

Next, the appraiser applies the market-derived valuation multiple to the size characteristics of the subject property. The resulting product is the estimate of value of the subject real estate, per the sales comparison approach.

To reach a final valuation synthesis and conclusion regarding the subject real estate, the appraiser will carefully consider the quantitative results of each of the valuation approaches used. In reaching the valuation conclusion, the appraiser will consider the quantity and quality of available data used in each valuation approach.

The appraiser will also assess the appropriate degree of confidence in the applicability and validity of each approach, with respect to unique characteristics of the subject real property. Based on these factors, the appraiser will synthesize the results of each approach and conclude a final value estimate for the subject real estate.

Tangible Personal Property

Tangible personal property assets include such items as: office furniture and fixtures, computer and office automation equipment, store racks and fixtures, manufacturing machinery and equipment, processing equipment, tools and dies, trucks and automobiles, and material handling and transportation equipment.

There is a considerable body of literature with regard to the appraisal of industrial and commercial tangible personal property. There is also authoritative literature regarding the appraisal of special purpose and technical tangible personal property, such as scientific and laboratory equipment, medical and health care equipment, mining and extraction equipment, and so forth. Many of these references are presented in the bibliography related to this chapter.

Nonetheless, all the various tangible personal property appraisal methods and procedures can be grouped into the three traditional asset appraisal approaches: (1) the cost approach, (2) the income approach, and (3) the sales comparison (or market) approach.

Cost Approach. The conceptual underpinnings of the cost approach for tangible personal property are essentially identical to that for tangible real estate. Again, the cost approach is based on the economic principle of substitution.

Particularly with respect to tangible personal property, a willing buyer will pay no more to a willing seller than the cost associated with replacing the subject asset with an asset of comparable functional utility.

As with real estate, there are several common cost approach methods that appraisers use as a starting point related to tangible personal property. These methods include depreciated reproduction cost method, depreciated replacement cost method, creation cost method, re-creation cost method, and others.

For special purpose tangible personal property (which may experience considerable obsolescence), the depreciated reproduction cost method is a common valuation method. However, for most general purpose tangible personal property, the depreciated replacement cost method is the most common valuation method.

The depreciated replacement cost method for tangible personal property is presented algebraically on the next page.

	Replacement cost new of the subject asset
less:	Allowance for physical deterioration
equals:	Depreciated replacement cost
less:	Allowance for external (either economic or locational) obsolescence
less:	Allowance for incurable functional and technological obsolescence
equals:	Fair market value, of the subject asset

If the subject asset is no longer produced, the replacement cost of the most comparable available substitute asset is used as the starting point in the cost approach (and, specifically, in the depreciated replacement cost method).

Income Approach. The income approach is based on the economic principles of anticipation and risk/expected return investment relationships. Using the income approach, the value of the tangible personal property is often quantified as the present value of the estimated rental income from the hypothetical rental of the subject property over its remaining useful life.

First, the appraiser estimates the remaining useful life of the subject asset. This is typically the shortest of the asset's remaining physical, functional, techno-logical, or economic lives. Second, the appraiser estimates a fair rental rate for the subject asset. This gross rental income is reduced by insurance, maintenance, and other expenses that are the responsibility of the lessor. The result is a projection of the net rental income (real or hypothetical) to be derived from the subject asset over the asset's expected remaining life.

Next, the appraiser derives an appropriate present value discount rate. This discount rate is intended to provide for a fair, risk-adjusted rate of return to the property lessor over the term of the lease.

The present value of the projected rental income over the expected remaining life of the property represents the value of the subject asset, per the income approach. (Since tangible personal property has a finite life, appraisers typically do not have to consider a residual value to tangible personal property—as would be appropriate with tangible real property.)

Sales Comparison Approach. Using the sales comparison (or market) approach, the value of the subject asset is the price it would command in its appropriate secondary market. This valuation approach is based on the economic principles of efficient markets and of supply and demand.

The use of this approach assumes that an efficient secondary market exists with regard to the exchange of the subject asset. The use of this approach also assumes that reliable information is available regarding this tangible personal property exchange market.

Using this approach, appraisers first obtain data regarding secondary transactions with respect to comparable assets. Next, appraisers analyze these data with regard to a set of reasonable comparability criteria. The market transactional data are adjusted, if necessary, to enhance their comparability and applicability to the subject asset.

Based on the adjusted transactional data, the appraiser selects the comparable sales most indicative of a hypothetical transaction involving the subject asset. These adjusted sales data are used to estimate the value of the subject asset, per the market approach.

Lastly, the appraiser concludes a final value estimate of the subject asset based on a synthesis of the results of the various valuation approaches used. Based on the appraiser's perceived reliability of, and confidence in, the various approaches, the appraiser will reach a final valuation estimate for the subject tangible personal property.

Intangible Real Property

Intangible real property assets represent intangible legal claims on tangible real estate. The types of assets encompassed by this category include: leasehold interests (and various other leasehold estates), possessory interests (associated with franchise ordinances or other permits), exploration rights, exploitation rights, air rights, water rights, land rights, mineral rights, use rights, development rights, easements (including scenic easements), and associated intangible rights and privileges related to the use or exploitation of real estate.

As intangible claims on tangible real estate, the value of these assets is generally a subset of, or a derivative of, the value of the associated tangible real estate.

As with tangible real estate, there are many individual methods and techniques to appraise intangible real property. However, as with real estate, all these methods can be conveniently grouped into the three traditional appraisal approaches: the cost approach, the income approach, and the sales comparison approach.

Each of these three approaches (and some associated methods) were discussed above, with respect to the value of tangible real estate. Accordingly, we will not reiterate those general discussions here.

It is noteworthy, however, that the cost approach is rarely used to value intangible real property. Intangible real property typically represents a legal claim on the use of, exploitation of, development of, or forbearance of real estate.

Accordingly, the cost of the underlying real estate is generally irrelevant to the intangible property right holder. Rather, the income approach is typically the most widely used approach with respect to the valuation of intangible real estate interests.

The sales comparison approach is also used to value certain intangible real estate interests. For example, there is a reasonable sales transaction secondary market for certain intangible real estate interests—such as the unexpired portion of assignable below-market industrial and commercial leases (i.e., leasehold interests).

As with the appraisal of real estate, the appraisal of intangible real property interests is based on a synthesis of all available valuation data and the conclusions of whatever valuation approaches were used. The appraiser considers and synthesizes the results of the various valuation approaches and concludes a final value estimate for the subject intangible real property interests.

Intangible Personal Property

Intangible personal property assets include most of the assets generally called intangible assets and intellectual properties. There are, arguably, over 100 individual types of intangible assets and intellectual properties. However, many of these individual intangible assets are industry-specific.

Generally, all intangible assets can be conveniently grouped into the following eight categories:

1. Customer related (e.g., customer lists).
2. Contract related (e.g., favorable supplier contracts).
3. Location related (e.g., certificates of need).
4. Market related (e.g., trademarks and trade names).
5. Data processing related (e.g., computer software).
6. Technology related (e.g., engineering drawings and technical documentation).
7. Employee related (e.g., employment agreements).
8. Goodwill related (e.g., going-concern value).

In addition, all intellectual properties can be conveniently grouped into the following two categories of intellectual properties:

1. Creative (e.g., copyrights).
2. Innovative (e.g., patents).

Chapters 23, 24, and 25 will discuss in detail the identification, valuation, and remaining useful life analysis of intangible assets and intellectual properties. Therefore, we will not expand on these issues here.

As with all other assets, intangible personal property assets are valued by application of one or more of the three basic asset valuation approaches: the cost approach, the income approach, and the sales comparison (or market) approach. The appraiser will apply one or more of these three approaches to the valuation of each intangible personal property asset. Then, the appraiser will derive a final value estimate based on a synthesis of the results of the various intangible personal property valuation approaches used.

Although the discussion of intangible asset valuation is deferred to Chapter 24, the identification, valuation, and remaining useful life analysis of intangible personal property assets is the conceptual cornerstone of the asset accumulation method.

It is possible for a thorough analysis of intangible personal property assets to indicate a nominal—or even a zero—economic value for the subject intangible assets. It is also possible for a thorough analysis to even indicate a negative economic value for the subject intangible assets. In such a case, the overall business valuation of the company cannot generate adequate economic support for the values assigned to the discrete tangible real estate and personal property assets.

When that situation occurs, the valuation phenomenon of economic obsolescence exists. For intangible asset valuation purposes, economic obsolescence is defined as the amount, if any, of negative intangible asset value calculated in an asset accumulation method business valuation (given the indicated values for the tangible real and personal property assets).

When economic obsolescence exists in a business valuation using the asset accumulation method, the indicated values of the tangible real estate and personal property assets are overstated—from an economic perspective—and must be reduced. In fact, the indicated values of the tangible real estate and personal property assets must be reduced (i.e., allocated down, typically in direct proportion to their indicated values) until the final estimates of value for these assets indicates no economic obsolescence.

At that final valuation estimate, there may be no positive intangible personal property value indicated by the intangible asset valuation. But there will also be no negative intangible personal property value indicated by the intangible asset valuation.

In other words, after any calculated economic obsolescence is allocated to the subject company's tangible real estate and personal property assets, then the remaining amount of intangible asset value in the subject company will be zero.

Of course, based on the standards and premises of value applied, the industry in which the company operates, and the microeconomic dynamics of the company, the analysis and appraisal of the subject assets of any subject company may indicate little or no (or even negative) intangible asset value. Nonetheless, such an analysis and appraisal should be performed as an integral part of any asset-based method business valuation.

As mentioned above, when using the asset accumulation method of business valuation, the company's intangible assets may be valued collectively (e.g., using the capitalized excess earnings method) or the company's intangible assets may be valued individually and discretely. But the company's intangible assets must be appraised as part of the valuation process.

As will be discussed in Chapter 24, several important concepts with regard to the valuation of intangible assets are part of an asset accumulation method business valuation. Several of these concepts will be introduced briefly below.

First, there is an important sequencing to the identification and valuation of these intangible assets. For example, it is important to understand and follow the flow (or funnel) of income from customers/clients/patients into the company and appraise the intangible assets in the order of how they are affected by this flow.

Second, there is an important prioritization to the identification and valuation of intangible assets. Typically, intangible assets to be appraised using a sales comparison (or market) approach will be valued first; intangible assets to be appraised using a cost approach will be valued second; and intangible assets to be appraised using an income approach will be valued last.

Third, it is important to avoid double counting (or over counting) of economic business value when appraising intangible assets. For example, the appraiser must procedurally avoid identifying one component of economic business value and then, inadvertently through various valuation techniques, assigning some or all of the same economic value to the company's trademarks and trade names, patents, customer relationships, goodwill, and so forth. As will be further described in Chapter 24, the use of "capital changes" in the intangible asset valuation will help to avoid this double counting of intangible asset values.

Fourth, like tangible assets, intangible assets may be valued using either a cost approach, an income approach, or a sales comparison (or market) approach. If several different intangible assets are identified as part of an asset accumulation method business valuation, it is likely that some intangible assets will be valued using a cost approach, while others will be valued using an income approach, and still others may be valued using a market approach. Clearly, given the economic function and the business purpose of each individual intangible asset, the appraiser should use the valuation approach (or approaches) that is (are) most determinative of the true economic value of the subject intangible asset.

Nonetheless, as a general rule, at least one intangible asset should be valued using an income approach as part of each asset accumulation method business valuation. In this way, the appraisal will verify and validate the income-earning economic capacity of the subject company's assets. The intangible assets valued using the income approach confirm the economic support for the tangible real estate and personal property assets (and other intangible assets) of the company. And the intangible assets valued using the income approach confirm that there is no (or that there is) economic obsolescence associated with the tangible real estate and personal property assets of the company. And, the intangible asset(s) valued using the income approach will help to confirm that there was no inadvertent previous double counting or omission of intangible asset values.

Illustrative Example

To illustrate the general application of the asset accumulation method, let's create a hypothetical business entity and call it Typical Corporation.

Typical Corporation is a substantial family-owned widget manufacturing company. To make this example relatively simple, let's assume the current generation of the owners of Typical Corporation are contemplating the sale of this going-concern business enterprise.

Therefore, the objective of this appraisal is to estimate the fair market value of the overall business enterprise. In other words, we can eliminate from consideration the identification and quantification of various business valuation discounts and premiums.

The purpose of this appraisal is to provide an independent valuation opinion to the current owners to allow them to assess the most likely transaction price regarding the sale of the company.

To more finitely identify the components of the Typical Corporation business value by the selling family members and to potential buyers, we have elected to use the asset accumulation method. We will apply this business valuation method on a discrete asset valuation basis (as opposed to a collective asset valuation basis).

Given the purpose and objective of the appraisal, we will conclude the fair market value (as the standard of value) of all the tangible and intangible assets of Typical Corporation, as of the valuation date.

Given the successful historical operations of the company and management's plans to sell the business as an ongoing business, we have selected the individual asset valuation premise of value in continued use, as a going-concern business enterprise.

Exhibit 12–2 presents the statement of financial position (i.e., balance sheet) of Typical Corporation as of June 30, 1995, the valuation date. Let's assume this statement of financial position is prepared in accordance with generally accepted accounting principles. In other words, the Exhibit 12–2 statement of financial position is prepared on a historical-cost basis.

Exhibit 12–2, then, is the basic working document that is the starting point for our asset accumulation method business valuation.

Exhibit 12–3 presents the final summary of the asset accumulation method business valuation for Typical Corporation. It presents both the historical-cost-basis values for all the recorded assets and liabilities of Typical Corporation (just slightly rearranged from the GAAP-basis balance sheet). And Exhibit 12–3 shows the fair market values for all the assets and liabilities—both tangible and intangible—of Typical Corporation.

Exhibit 12–2

Typical Corporation Statement of Financial Position as of June 30, 1995 (in 000s)

Assets

Current assets:

Cash	$ 200,000
Accounts and notes receivable	500,000
Prepaid expenses	200,000
Inventory	600,000
Total current assets	1,500,000

Noncurrent assets:

Plant, property, and equipment, at cost:

Land	200,000
Buildings and improvements	1,200,000
Office furniture and fixtures	300,000
Machinery and equipment	500,000
Tools and dies	300,000
Total plant, property, and equipment	2,500,000
Less: Accumulated depreciation	1,000,000
Net plant, property and equipment	1,500,000

Other noncurrent assets:

Long-term notes receivable	250,000
Note receivable from supplier	250,000
Total other noncurrent assets	500,000
Total Assets	**$3,500,000**

Liabilities and Owners' Equity

Current liabilities:

Accounts payable	$ 400,000
Wages payable	200,000
Taxes payable	100,000
Accrued liabilties	300,000
Total current liabilities	1,000,000

Noncurrent liabilities:

Bonds payable	200,000
Notes payable	200,000
Mortgages payable	700,000
Debentures payable	200,000
Total noncurrent liabilities	1,300,000

Owners' equity:

Capital stock	200,000
Additional paid-in capital	500,000
Retained earnings	500,000
Total owners' equity	1,200,000
Total Liabilities and Owners' Equity	**$3,500,000**

Let's review each of the individual asset and liability fair market value estimates in Exhibit 12–3. The following paragraphs describe an illustrative valuation conclusion for each asset and liability and a typical valuation approach that may be used in a business valuation such as Typical Corporation.

The cash balance remains at its historical-cost value. The appraiser would confirm whether or not the cash balances would be transferred to the new owner when the business was sold.

The accounts and notes receivable assets remain at their historical-cost value. This conclusion was reached after an assessment of the timing and collectibility of the receivables.

Exhibit 12–3

Typical Corporation Business Enterprise Valuation Asset Accumulation Method as of June 30, 1995 (in 000s)

	At Historical Cost	At Fair Market Value
Assets		
Financial assets:		
Cash	$ 200,000	$ 200,000
Accounts and notes receivable	500,000	500,000
Prepaid expenses	200,000	200,000
Inventory	600,000	700,000
Long-term notes receivable	250,000	250,000
Note receivable from supplier	250,000	150,000
Total financial assets	2,000,000	2,000,000
Tangible real estate:		
Land	200,000	300,000
Buildings and improvements	1,200,000	1,000,000
Less: Accumulated depreciation	400,000	
Net tangible real estate	1,000,000	1,300,000
Tangible personal property:		
Office furniture and fixtures	300,000	200,000
Machinery and equipment	500,000	300,000
Tools and dies	300,000	200,000
Less: Accumulated depreciation	600,000	
Net tangible personal property	500,000	700,000
Intangible real property:		
Leasehold interests	0	100,000
Net intangible real property	0	100,000
Intangible personal property:		
Trademarks and trade names	0	200,000
Computer software	0	150,000
Patents	0	150,000
Favorable supplier contracts	0	100,000
Intangible value in the nature of goodwill	0	100,000
Net intangible personal property	0	700,000
Total Assets	$3,500,000	$4,800,000
Liabilities and Owners' Equity		
Current liabilities:		
Accounts payable	$ 400,000	$ 400,000
Wages payable	200,000	200,000
Taxes payable	100,000	100,000
Accrued liabilties	300,000	300,000
Total current liabilities	1,000,000	1,000,000
Noncurrent liabilities:		
Bonds payable	200,000	200,000
Notes payable	200,000	200,000
Mortgages payable	700,000	650,000
Debentures payable	200,000	200,000
Total noncurrent liabilities	1,300,000	1,250,000
Contingent liabilities:		
Contingent claims	0	150,000
Total contingent liabilities	0	150,000
Total Liabilities	2,300,000	2,400,000
Total Liabilities and Owners' Equity	$3,500,000	$4,800,000
Total Owners' Equity	$1,200,000	$2,400,000

Prepaid expenses remain at their historical cost value. This estimate was reached after an assessment of the net realizable value of the prepaid expenses to the going-concern business.

Inventory is revalued upward. This revaluation is based upon the sales comparison method described in IRS Revenue Procedure 77-12.

Long-term notes receivable are valued at their historical cost. This estimate is based upon an analysis of the stated interest rate versus current interest rates for similar risk notes—and based upon the historical and likely prospective payment pattern regarding the notes.

The note receivable from the supplier is revalued downward. Let's assume that some years ago, this business extended a loan to one of its key suppliers. This decremental revaluation was based on an analysis of the below-market interest rate on the note—and of the erratic historical payment history from the supplier on the note.

Land is revalued upward. This incremental revaluation is based on a market value appraisal of the land, as if vacant and improved, using the sales comparison approach.

Buildings and improvements are revalued incrementally, as market value exceeds the (depreciated) historical cost of these properties. This appraisal is based on depreciated reproduction cost analysis of the subject properties.

Office furniture and fixtures, machinery and equipment, and tools and dies are revalued incrementally—that is, the fair market value estimates for each asset category exceed their (depreciated) historical cost. The depreciated replacement cost method would be a typical valuation method for the appraisal of these assets.

A leasehold interest is identified and capitalized on the valuation basis balance sheet. In this illustrative example, Typical Corporation enjoys a favorable rental advantage (i.e., below-market rental rates) on some warehouse space that it leases. The appraiser used the income approach to project and capitalize this favorable (below-market) lease rate advantage and to conclude the fair market value of the leasehold interest. This leasehold interest intangible asset was not previously recorded on the historical-cost basis balance sheet.

The entire category of intangible personal property would not be recorded on a GAAP-basis, or historical-cost-based, balance sheet. However, these intangible assets are identified and appraised for business valuation purposes.

Trademarks and trade name are an important intangible asset for Typical Corporation. Typical Corporation management spends much time and money promoting the company's name: they advertise, send promotional announcements, sponsor booths at trade shows, and so forth.

The appraiser used the re-creation cost method to estimate the value of this intangible asset. The appraiser estimated the current cost required for the company to re-create its current level of customer awareness, brand recognition, and consumer loyalty. This estimated cost to re-create this level of name awareness is capitalized as the value of this intangible asset.

Computer software is an important intangible asset for Typical Corporation. This computer software was internally developed, instead of externally purchased. Accordingly, the value of this computer software may not be recorded on a GAAP-basis balance sheet.

The systems analysts at Typical Corporation have developed and implemented an automated materials requirement planning (MRP) system. This system is extremely useful to the company with regard to material purchasing, labor scheduling, and production planning.

The appraiser used the sales comparison (or market) approach to estimate the value of this intangible asset, as there is a relatively similar (in terms of functionality) MRP system available on the market from a commercial software vendor. After consideration of the market value of a comparable commercial system, and after including the costs of customization, installation, testing, and training, the appraiser concluded the market value of the Typical Corporation computer software.

The product patent that Typical Corporation holds is a valuable intangible asset. The widgets that Typical Corporation manufactures have certain unique and proprietary technological advancements compared to the widgets manufactured by competitors. And other manufacturers cannot reverse-engineer and copy the Typical Corporation advanced features, because the subject product is protected by a U.S. product patent.

Because of the advanced features (protected by the product patent), Typical Corporation estimates that it sells more widgets than it would otherwise and its average selling price per widget is higher than its competitors' prices. Accordingly, the appraiser used the income approach to estimate the intangible value of the Typical Corporation patent.

Typical Corporation has a favorable supply contract with a key supplier. The materials buyer for Typical Corporation is a particularly skilled negotiator. Using these superior negotiating skills, the materials buyer convinced the key supplier to agree to supply an essential raw material to Typical Corporation at 20 percent below the prices the supplier charges to its other, similarly sized customers. This agreement is documented in a three-year-term supply contract.

The appraiser used the income approach to estimate the economic value of the Typical Corporation favorable supply contract.

Goodwill is typically considered the accumulation of all the other economic value of the company not specifically identified with (or allocated to) individual tangible and intangible assets. The analysis and quantification of goodwill (or the lack of goodwill) is an important component in the asset accumulation method business valuation of a company like Typical Corporation.

With respect to the subject company, the appraiser used a capitalized excess earnings method to identify and value goodwill. First, the appraiser identified and valued all the other individual assets of Typical Corporation—both tangible and intangible. Second, the appraiser applied a market-derived fair rate of return against each category of identified assets of the company—both tangible and intangible. Third, the appraiser compared the total calculated fair return on the total identified tangible and intangible assets to the total economic income actually expected to be earned by the company. Fourth, any excess economic income (above a fair return on all identified tangible and intangible assets) was capitalized as an annuity in perpetuity.

This capitalization conclusion, then, is the indicated fair market value of the Typical Corporation intangible value in the nature of goodwill.

The current liabilities of Typical Corporation were also analyzed by the appraiser. Given the short-term nature of these monetary liabilities, the appraiser estimated their fair market value at their historical-cost carrying amounts.

The noncurrent liabilities were also analyzed. Given the term of these liabilities and their stated (or implied) interest rates, the appraiser estimated the fair market value of the bonds, notes, and debentures at their historical cost carrying amounts.

The mortgage payable, however, has a substantial remaining term and has an interest rate that is considerably below current market rates. The appraiser confirmed with the mortgage bank that it would allow Typical Corporation to pay off the mortgage at a discount compared to the remaining outstanding principal balance. The appraiser estimated the amount of this discount and estimated the fair market value of the mortgage payable.

There is an outstanding product liability lawsuit against Typical Corporation. The plaintiff, a customer that used a Typical Corporation widget, alleges the Typical Corporation product exploded during normal use and caused him substantial physical impairment. Although there were extenuating circumstances, Typical Corporation management realized it did produce one batch of defective products and it owes damages to the customer.

While the trial is not yet scheduled, and no one can predict the court's final decision regarding either liability or damages, Typical Corporation management believes that an offer of $150 million will be adequate to settle the case and satisfy all future product liability to the current and potential plaintiffs.

The appraiser analyzed this estimate and then used it to capitalize a contingent liability on the Typical Corporation valuation-based balance sheet.

Finally, the appraiser summed the estimated fair market values for all the tangible and intangible assets of Typical Corporation. Next, the appraiser summed the estimated fair market values for all the recorded and contingent liabilities of Typical Corporation. Last, the appraiser subtracted the total liability value from the total asset value. The remainder is the fair market value of the total owners' equity of Typical Corporation, per the asset accumulation method.

Advantages of the Asset Accumulation Method

As should be apparent from the above discussion of the theoretical concepts and the practical applications of this valuation method, there are a number of advantages of the asset accumulation method of business valuation.

First, the results of the asset accumulation approach are presented in a traditional balance sheet financial statement format. This format should be comfortable and familiar to anyone who has ever worked with basic financial statements.

Second, this method categorizes all the business value of the company. In the example above, the valuation conclusion was exactly two times book value for Typical Corporation. Other valuation methods would, presumably, reach the same valuation conclusion. But those other valuation methods would not explicitly explain why the company is worth two times book value. This method identifies exactly which assets (tangible and intangible) are contributing value to the company and how much value each asset is contributing.

Third, this method is useful when structuring the sale of a business. This method can immediately quantify the effects on business value of many common seller structural considerations, such as:

1. What if the seller retains the company's cash on hand?
2. What if the seller retains (or leases back to the company) the operating real estate facilities?
3. What if the seller personally retains title to the patent or some other valuable assets of the company?
4. What if the seller personally retains any or all of the debt instruments of the company?

Fourth, this method is useful to the seller when negotiating the sale of the company. If the buyer offers a lower price than the asset accumulation method concludes, then the seller can ask: "Since you're not willing to pay for all of the identified assets of the business, which of these assets don't you want me to sell to you as part of the transaction?"

Fifth, this method is useful to the buyer when negotiating the purchase of the company. If the seller wants a higher price than the conclusions of the asset accumulation method, the buyer can ask: "What other identified assets are you willing to sell to me—in addition to what has already been appraised on this balance sheet—in order to justify the price that you are asking?"

Sixth, after the sale transaction is consummated, this business valuation method allows for a fast and reasonable allocation of the lump-sum purchase price among the individual assets acquired. This purchase price allocation is often required for both financial accounting purposes and tax accounting purposes. Depending on the structure of the sale, many of the identified intangible assets may be subject to amortization cost recovery for federal income tax purposes.

Seventh, this method is useful with regard to financing the subject transaction. Typically, all categories of lenders (secured, unsecured, mezzanine, etc.) will want to know the value of the company's individual assets—both tangible and intangible—before they will commit to financing the proposed deal. This business valuation method generally provides lenders with the information they need.

Eighth, this method is particularly useful in litigation support and dispute resolution controversy matters. Since this method identifies the individual value components of the assets of the company, it allows for the easy measurement of the impact of certain alleged actions (or lack of actions) on the value of the company.

Also, this method can be used to allocate assets (as well as—or instead of—stock) in a stockholder/partner dissolution dispute or in a marital dissolution dispute.

Ninth, this method can be used with virtually any standard of value or any premise of value. In other words, using the same comparative balance-sheet format, appraisers can value the same business under several alternative standards (i.e., definitions) of value. Likewise, using the same comparative balance-sheet format, appraisers can value the same business under several alternative premises of value. Therefore, the impact of changing standards of value or premises of value can be immediately identified and quickly quantified.

Tenth, this method requires the most rigorous analysis and thorough understanding of company operations on the part of the appraiser. Such required rigorous analyses can only help to enhance the quality of the valuation. Also, this method generally requires much more active participation of company management in the valuation process. This active interest and participation can only help to enhance the quality of the valuation.

Disadvantages of the Asset Accumulation Method

The primary disadvantage of the asset accumulation method is that, if taken to its ultimate extreme, it could be quite expensive and time consuming. It also may necessitate involvement of appraisal specialists in several fields, such as inventory appraisers, personal property appraisers, real estate appraisers, and intangible asset appraisers. Certainly, business appraisers who perform the asset accumulation method should have experience and expertise in each of these specialty fields; otherwise they should consult with appraisal specialists in these fields.

Also, as described in this chapter, capturing all the assets means the intangibles as well as the tangibles. Most intangible asset values depend especially heavily on income approaches. Therefore, taken to its extreme, the asset accumulation method may ultimately depend as much, or more, on income variables as on values of tangible assets. In this sense, the appellation *asset accumulation method* may seem to some like a misnomer. However, this latter is a semantic problem, not a conceptual problem.

Summary

The asset-based business valuation approach can be performed either on a discrete asset valuation basis or on a collective asset valuation basis.

This chapter discussed the asset accumulation method—an individual asset valuation method within the asset-based approach. Chapter 13 will discuss the excess earnings method—a collective asset valuation method within the asset-based approach.

The asset accumulation method is a common asset-based business valuation method. The theoretical underpinning of this method is simple: the value of the business is the value of the business assets (tangible and intangible) less the value of the business liabilities (recorded and contingent).

Basically, this method recognizes that all the economic value of a business has to come from—and be identified back with—the productive assets of the business.

The asset-based approach can be applied on a collective basis, where all of the economic value of the company greater than the tangible value is aggregated and called goodwill. A common implementation of this method is the capitalized excess earnings method.

Also, the asset-based approach can be applied on a discrete basis, where all the company's tangible and intangible assets are individually identified and appraised. The discrete application of the asset accumulation method was illustrated in this chapter.

It is naive and conceptually incorrect to automatically conclude that the value of a business is based on the value of the tangible assets of the business only. Likewise, it is naive and conceptually incorrect to conclude that the value of a business is equal to its accounting book value—without substantial valuation procedures and rigorous fundamental analysis to support that conclusion.

The intangible assets of the company may contribute substantial economic value. They may contribute little or no economic value. Or they may contribute negative economic value, which is recognized as economic obsolescence—or a decrease in the value of the tangible assets of the company. Again, the ultimate application of an asset-based valuation approach requires a structured, rigorous, and comprehensive valuation analysis of all the assets of the company.

There are numerous advantages to the asset accumulation method of business valuation. These advantages include application to transaction pricing and structuring, deal negotiation, acquisition financing, purchase accounting, and dispute resolution.

However, there are costs associated with the asset accumulation method of business valuation. This method requires more time and effort on the part of the appraiser than many other business valuation methods. This method requires more access to company facilities and management than many other business valuation methods. And this method requires more access to company data, particularly operational data, than many other business valuation methods. This method also requires more time and effort on the part of company management and more involvement of company management in the valuation process.

Lastly, the asset accumulation method requires that the appraiser has experience and expertise in the identification and valuation of both the tangible and intangible assets of the company. Certainly, this method is recommended only for appraisers who have adequate experience and expertise in the appraisal of the individual component assets of a business enterprise. The use of supporting appraisers, with the requisite experience and qualifications, may fill the void for a particular asset type for which the business appraiser lacks the technical expertise.

Bibliography

American Society of Appraisers. *Appraising Machinery and Equipment.* New York: McGraw-Hill, Inc., 1989.

Appraisal of Real Estate, 10th ed. Chicago: Appraisal Institute, 1992.

Dictionary of Real Estate Appraisal, 3rd ed. Chicago: Appraisal Institute, 1993.

Dratler, Jay Jr. *Licensing of Intellectual Property.* New York: Law Journal Seminars-Press, 1994.

Fisher, Jeffrey D., and Robert S. Martin. *Income Property Valuation.* Chicago: Dearborn Financial Publishing, Inc., 1994.

Lee, Lewis C., and J. Scott Davidson. *Managing Intellectual Property Rights.* New York: John Wiley & Sons, 1993.

Marston, Anson; Robley Winfrey; and Jean C. Hempstead. *Engineering Valuation and Depreciation,* 8th ed. Ames: Iowa State University Press, 1979.

Parr, Russell L. *Intellectual Property Infringement Damages.* New York: John Wiley & Sons, 1993.

_____. *Investing in Tangible Assets: Finding and Profitting from Hidden Corporate Value.* New York: John Wiley & Sons, 1991.

Rushmore, Stephen. *Hotels, Motels, and Restaurants: Valuations and Market Studies.* Chicago: Appraisal Institute, 1983.

Simensky, Melvin, and Lanning G. Bryer. *The New Role of Intellectual Property in Commercial Transactions,* 2nd ed. New York: John Wiley & Sons, 1994.

Smith, Gordon V., and Russell L. Parr. *Intellectual Property Licensing and Joint Venture Profit Strategies.* New York: John Wiley & Sons, 1993.

_____. *Valuation of Intellectual Property and Intangible Assets,* 2nd. ed. New York: John Wiley & Sons, 1993, supplemented in 1995.

Chapter 13

The Excess Earnings Method

In applying the "formula" approach, the average earnings period and the capitalization rates are dependent on the facts pertinent thereto in each case.

The past earnings to which the formula is applied should fairly reflect the probable future earnings.[1]

The above quotations from Revenue Ruling 68-609 are frequently overlooked, resulting in serious misapplications of the excess earnings method.

The excess earnings method of business valuation can be classified as an asset-based valuation approach, in that, as with the asset accumulation method, the excess earnings method starts with—and ends with—the balance sheet for the subject business entity. Of course, the accounts on the subject balance sheet have been revalued to the appropriate standard of value.

The excess earnings method does involve an earnings capitalization—to estimate the intangible value in the nature of goodwill of the subject business entity. Certainly an earnings capitalization method is a form of the income approach to value. And, as was explained in the last chapter, the income approach is one of three traditional approaches (i.e., the cost approach, the income approach, and the sales comparison approach) in the valuation of virtually all assets, which is the fundamental basis of the asset-based valuation approach.

The excess earnings method has been written about widely. It is often used by courts in divorce proceedings for estimating the value of goodwill in business valuations. Yet the Internal Revenue Service, which first articulated the method in 1920, now often denounces it.

History of the Excess Earnings Method

The excess earnings method is sometimes called the *Treasury Method* because the method originally appeared in a 1920 publication by the U.S. Treasury Department, ARM 34, which stands for Appeals and Review Memorandum Number 34. It was adopted to estimate the value of the goodwill that breweries and distilleries lost because of Prohibition.

Since then, both taxpayers and IRS agents have widely used (and misused) it in connection with valuations of businesses for gift and estate taxes and for other taxation-related purposes. Also, partly because of its wide publicity and partly because of its apparently simplistic nature, it has been adopted in one form or another for various business valuation purposes.

In 1968, the Internal Revenue Service updated and restated the ARM 34 method, with the publication of Revenue Ruling 68-609, which is reproduced as Exhibit 13–1. Revenue Ruling 68-609 is still in effect.

How It Works

A Step-by-Step Explanation

While there are several variations to this method, the typical steps in the excess earnings method can be summarized as follows:

---

[1]Revenue Ruling 68-609, 1968-2, C.B. 327.

Exhibit 13–1
Revenue Ruling 68-609

The "formula" approach may be used in determining the fair market value of intangible assets of a business only if there is no better basis available for making the determination; A.R.M. 34, A.R.M. 68, O.D. 937, and Revenue Ruling 65-192 superseded.

SECTION 1001.—DETERMINATION OF AMOUNT OF AND RECOGNITION OF GAIN OR LOSS

26 CFR 1.1001-1: Computation of gain or loss. (Also Section 167; 1.167(a)-3.)

Rev. Rul. 68-609[1]

The purpose of this Revenue Ruling is to update and restate, under the current statute and regulations, the currently outstanding portions of A.R.M. 34, C.B. 2, 31 (1920), A.R.M. 68, C.B. 3, 43 (1920), and O.D. 937, C.B. 4, 43 (1921).

The question presented is whether the "formula" approach, the capitalization of earnings in excess of a fair rate of return on net tangible assets, may be used to determine the fair market value of the intangible assets of a business.

The "formula" approach may be stated as follows:

A percentage return on the average annual value of the tangible assets used in a business is determined, using a period of years (preferably not less than five) immediately prior to the valuation date. The amount of the percentage return on tangible assets, thus determined, is deducted from the average earnings of the business for such period and the remainder, if any, is considered to be the amount of the average annual earnings from the intangible assets of the business for the period. This amount (considered as the average annual earnings from intangibles), capitalized at a percentage of, say, 15 to 20 percent, is the value of the intangible assets of the business determined under the "formula" approach.

The percentage of return on the average annual value of the tangible assets used should be the percentage prevailing in the industry involved at the date of valuation, or (when the industry percentage is not available) a percentage of 8 to 10 percent may be used.

The 8 percent rate of return and the 15 percent rate of capitalization are applied to tangibles and intangibles, respectively, of businesses with a small risk factor and stable and regular earnings; the 10 percent rate of return and 20 percent rate of capitalization are applied to businesses in which the hazards of business are relatively high.

The above rates are used as examples and are not appropriate in all cases. In applying the "formula" approach, the average earnings period and the capitalization rates are dependent upon the facts pertinent thereto in each case.

SOURCE: Rev. Rul. 68-609, 1968-2, C.B. 327.

The past earnings to which the formula is applied should fairly reflect the probable future earnings. Ordinarily, the period should not be less than five years, and abnormal years, whether above or below the average, should be eliminated. If the business is a sole proprietorship or partnership, there should be deducted from the earnings of the business a reasonable amount for services performed by the owner or partners engaged in the business. See *Lloyd B. Sanderson Estate* v. *Commissioner,* 42 F. 2d 160 (1930). Further, only the tangible assets entering into net worth, including accounts and bills receivable in excess of accounts and bills payable, are used for determining earnings on the tangible assets. Factors that influence the capitalization rate include (1) the nature of the business, (2) the risk involved, and (3) the stability or irregularity of earnings.

The "formula" approach should not be used if there is better evidence available from which the value of intangibles can be determined. If the assets of a going business are sold upon the basis of a rate of capitalization that can be substantiated as being realistic, though it is not within the range of figures indicated here as the ones ordinarily to be adopted, the same rate of capitalization should be used in determining the value of intangibles.

Accordingly, the "formula" approach may be used for determining the fair market value of intangible assets of a business only if there is no better basis therefor available.

See also Revenue Ruling 59-60, C.B. 1959-1, 237, as modified by Revenue Ruling 65-193, C.B. 1965-2, 370, which sets forth the proper approach to use in the valuation of closely-held corporate stocks for estate and gift tax purposes. The general approach, methods, and factors, outlined in Revenue Ruling 59-60, as modified, are equally applicable to valuations of corporate stocks for income and other tax purposes as well as for estate and gift tax purposes. They apply also to problems involving the determination of the fair market value of business interests of any type, including partnerships and proprietorships, and of intangible assets for all tax purposes.

A.R.M. 34, A.R.M. 68, and O.D. 937 are superseded, since the positions set forth therein are restated to the extent applicable under current law in this Revenue Ruling. Revenue Ruling 65-192, C.B. 1965-2, 259, which contained restatements of A.R.M. 34 and A.R.M. 68, is also superseded.

_____

[1]Prepared pursuant to Rev. Proc. 67-6, C.B. 1967-1, 576.

1. Estimate the net tangible asset value for the subject business entity. Note that this value is for net tangible assets only. However, as was explained above, the definition of *net tangible assets* may be expanded to include all identified tangible and intangible assets of the subject business; such identified assets would include leaseholds, patents, copyrights, and so on. However, for simplicity, and for strict conformity with the exact language of Revenue Ruling 68-609, we will consider only identified tangible assets as part of net tangible assets used in this method for the remaining sections of this chapter.

2. Estimate a normalized level of economic income for the subject business entity.

3. Estimate an appropriate or "fair" percentage rate of return or, in the parlance of this book, a capitalization rate on the net tangible asset value. Multiply the net tangible asset value from Step 1 by that fair rate of return to estimate the amount of economic income attributable to the net tangible assets. Subtract that amount of fair return on assets from the normalized economic income estimate developed in Step 2. The result of this step is called the *excess earnings:* that is, the amount of economic income above a fair return on the net tangible asset value of the subject business entity.

4. Estimate an appropriate capitalization rate to apply to the excess earnings, which are presumably the level of earnings attributable to the intangible value in the nature of goodwill or other intangible assets, instead of to the net tangible assets. The next step is to capitalize the excess earnings at that rate.

5. Add the values from steps 1 and 4.[2]

Ah...Sweet Simplicity!

The apparent simplicity of this method is deceptive. In fact, it is quite a complicated valuation method.

In a subsequent section, we will examine the many decisions and pitfalls encountered in each of the above steps. But first, let's look at a simple example and a few choice words from the IRS.

An Example

Let's assume Client Corporation has a net tangible asset value of $20 million. Let's also assume that, on a net income basis, Client Corporation earns $8 million per year.

For this example, we will use a rate of return of 15 percent on the net tangible assets. We will assume this capitalization rate was derived in a manner consistent with our estimate of economic income. And we will capitalize the indicated excess earnings at a 20 percent rate. (The issue of estimating the applicable rates is discussed later in the chapter.) In this example, the indicated value of Client Corporation would be computed as follows:

Net tangible asset value		$20,000,000
Normalized economic income	$8,000,000	
Earnings attributable to net tangible assets ($20,000,000 × .15) =	3,000,000	
Excess economic earnings	$5,000,000	
Indicated value of excess earnings ($5,000,000 ÷ .20) =		25,000,000
(i.e., indicated value of the company's intangible value in the nature of goodwill)		
Indicated total value of the subject business enterprise		$45,000,000

Denunciation by the IRS

The IRS Appellate Conferee Valuation Training Program has denounced the naive application of ARM 34 or the excess earnings method of business valuation. The following are some pertinent excerpts:

---

[2]As an alternative to using the present net tangible asset value and normalized earnings, some appraisers base the computations of the value of excess earnings on average net tangible assets and average earnings for some time period, usually five years. This procedure is satisfactory if the period used is representative of reasonable future expectations. If this procedure is used, the value of excess earnings is still added to the present net tangible asset value to arrive at the value for the total entity. Also, if there is interest-bearing debt, some analysts use returns available to overall capital (debt and equity), and then subtract the value of the interest-bearing debt as a final step to arrive at an equity value.

One of the most frequently encountered errors in appraisal is the use of a formula to determine a question of fact, which on a reasonable basis must be resolved in view of all pertinent circumstances...ARM 34 has been applied indiscriminately by tax practitioners and by members of the Internal Revenue Service since it was published. On occasion the Tax Court has recognized ARM 34 as a means of arriving at a fair market value. The latest and most controlling decisions on valuation, however, relegate the use of a formula to a position of being a last resort. ARM 34 was published in 1920, but since that time it has continually appeared in the annals of tax valuation and resulted in many improper appraisals.

By such a formula the same value would be found in 1960 as in 1933, although values per dollar of earnings were very different in those two years. The basic defect is apparent; the rates of return which are applied to tangibles and to intangibles are completely arbitrary and have no foundation in fact...

The 8 percent rule, or any other arbitrary rate of earnings as a normal return on tangible assets, cannot be demonstrated to have a reasonable basis. Similarly, the 15 percent rate or any specific rate on intangible assets is not in itself a supportable figure. If there were a somewhat comparable business which had earned $50,000 per year as an average for five years and which had been sold for $400,000 cash it could be said that there was a 12 percent indicated rate of return on total investment but no one could ascertain what has been the rates of return on the tangible and intangible assets. All that can be said for ARM 34, or a similar formula method of capitalization using two rates of interest, is that you hope to get a good answer based upon two bad guesses. It is difficult enough to get one reasonably accurate rate of capitalization using normal appraisal methods...To get two fairly accurate rates, one for tangibles and the other for intangibles, other than by the use of pure guesswork, is impossible...

Any capitalization of earnings must take into consideration the economic conditions prevailing at the specific date of appraisal, including those conditions controlling in the industry in this particular company's area, and even in the national economy.

If we assume that a fair rate of return for this type of business is 8 percent, the better procedure is to capitalize a representative earnings figure (in this instance 1953 income) at that rate. To attempt to segregate value based on earnings as between normal income and that induced by whatever goodwill or other intangible assets the business may possess, is to aspire to a higher degree of clairvoyance than has yet been demonstrated as obtainable by mere man.[3]

Analysis of the Method

A method that apparently has been denounced by its own promulgators and yet is one of the most widely used business valuation methods in practice deserves some analysis.

The Treasury Department did not initiate this method to estimate the value of the total business entity; rather this method was developed to estimate the value of the goodwill or other intangible value, if any (above the tangible asset value of a business entity). However, since it is economically logical that any intangible value identified by the excess earnings method must be added to the tangible value in order to estimate a total business value, the method has attained popularity for estimating the value of a total entity.

---

[3]U.S. Internal Revenue Service, *IRS Appellate Conferee Valuation Training Program* (Chicago: Commerce Clearing House, 1978), pp. 82–86. The section was repeated with no substantive changes in the 1980 revision, but not carried forward in the 1994 version.

Revenue Ruling 68-609 contains many ambiguities and leaves many unanswered questions. Various practitioners have adopted a wide variety of interpretations to the ambiguities and a wide variety of answers to the questions. We will discuss these ambiguities and open questions in the same order as the step-by-step explanation in an earlier section.

Estimating Net Tangible Asset Value

Step 1 in the excess earnings method is to estimate a net tangible asset value. Revenue Ruling 68-609 does not define net tangible asset value, nor is it very specific with respect to the important question "net of what?"

Defining Tangible Asset Value. Revenue Ruling 68-609 offers no guidance as to either the appropriate standard or the appropriate premise of value that is intended in conjunction with the phrase *net tangible asset value*. Does it mean replacement cost? Liquidation value? Book value?

In the valuation of a business entity (on a going-concern basis), there is some consensus among valuation practitioners that the best conceptual interpretation of the phrase *tangible asset value* in this context is fair market value, on a going-concern basis. Typically, this would be measured by replacement cost new less allowances for physical deterioration and for any functional or economic obsolescence.

Furthermore, IRS Private Letter Ruling 79-05013 (also promulgated as an IRS National Office Technical Advice Memorandum) takes a firm position that the standard of value of the net tangible assets should be fair market value:

> Rev. Rul. 68-609 addresses the determination of fair market value of intangible assets by the formula approach, and for this reason it is proper that all terms used in the formula be consistent. The formula uses value in terms of fair market value, so the term "...value of the tangible assets used in a business," in the formula, should be in terms of fair market values, as defined in Rev. Rul. 59-60.

Should Asset Value Adjustments Be Tax-Affected? Because the purpose of the analysis is to estimate the value of the net tangible assets on a going-concern basis (on which a reasonable rate of return should be earned), the appraiser normally does not make any adjustment to recognize the tax effect of unrealized gains or losses. However, there could be cases (e.g., a large inventory write-up where a tax payment on the sale of the inventory is imminent) where a tax adjustment may be appropriate.

Treatment of Nonoperating Assets. There is general consensus that it is preferable to remove nonoperating and/or excess assets from the balance sheet (and the related revenue from the income statement) and to treat such items separately in the excess earnings method.

Treatment of Real Estate Owned. Many practitioners prefer to remove the owned real estate of the subject business from the balance sheet and to impute fair market rental expense on the income statement.

What Is "Netted Out" in Estimating Tangible Asset Value? Depreciation? All liabilities? All current liabilities? All noninterest-bearing liabilities?

There is a general consensus among practitioners that net tangible asset value should be net of all depreciation, amortization, and obsolescence. However, it often is not practical to measure all these items in terms of current economic values.

In the simplest straight equity application of the excess earnings method, all liabilities would be deducted to arrive at a net tangible asset value.

However, the only reference to the netting of liabilities in Revenue Ruling 68-609 is taking out noninterest-bearing current liabilities.[4] Furthermore, experienced valuation practitioners recognize that differences in leverage from one company to another can lead to distortions in valuation results derived from the excess earnings method. Therefore, in many cases, a more reliable result will be achieved by using a "debt-free" version of the excess earnings method. This involves removing all interest-bearing debt from the balance sheet and all interest (adjusted for taxes) from the income statement. The excess earnings exercise is then carried out to produce an indicated value for all invested capital (defined here to include all equity and interest-bearing debt). Finally, the value of interest-bearing debt would be subtracted to determine the value of the owners' equity.

Do You Value Debt at Face Value or Fair Market Value?   The conceptual answer to this question is that it depends on when the debt is likely to be paid. If payment at face value is imminent (e.g., payment triggered by the very transaction for which the valuation is being performed), then it is appropriate to value the debt at face value. If it is contemplated that the debt will remain outstanding, then most practitioners would prefer to value the debt at fair market value.

Estimating a Normalized Level of Earnings

Step 2 in the excess earnings method is to estimate a normalized level of earnings. Revenue Ruling 68-609 does not try to define *earnings*. It does, however, make the key statement that the earnings "*should fairly reflect the probable future earnings*" (emphasis supplied). In suggesting the use of past years' earnings as a basis, it notes that abnormal years should be eliminated. Practitioners also agree that nonrecurring items should be eliminated from any year used for earnings base calculations.

Treatment of Nonoperating Income.   Consistent with removing nonoperating assets from the net tangible asset base, related nonoperating income should be removed from the earnings base.

Treatment of Owners' Compensation.   Revenue Ruling 68-609 states, "If the business is a sole proprietorship or partnership, there should be deducted from the earnings of the business a reasonable amount for services performed by the owner or partners engaged in the business." Valuation practitioners also concur that abnormal compensation should be adjusted to a normal level. The normal level is generally considered to be the cost of employing someone else to perform like services.

---

[4]The actual phrase used in Revenue Ruling 68-609 is "accounts and bills receivable in excess of accounts and bills payable."

Treatment of Income Taxes.   Earnings to be capitalized should normally be net of federal and state income taxes paid by the entity being valued.

However, a case can be made for tax affecting the income even where the subject entity does not pay income taxes (e.g., as in the case of an S corporation or a partnership). For example, if the entity were to be sold to a corporation that would have to pay taxes on the entity's income, the buyer almost surely would tax-affect the income in doing a valuation calculation. If that buyer were the typical buyer, the tax-affected earnings probably would also lead to the fair market value. Also, a significant (and not uncommon) problem arises when tax liability is flowed through to an owner but the earnings giving rise to the tax liability are not paid out. Tax affecting the entity's earnings is one of several possible ways to treat this problem for purposes of valuation.

Definition of "Earnings."   Revenue Ruling 68-609 is silent with respect to any definition of *earnings*. Is it net income? Net cash flow? Or some other measure of economic income?

There is some consensus among valuation practitioners that the variable best suited to represent *earnings* in the context of the excess earnings method is net cash flow (as defined in Chapter 9). If net cash flow is used as the appropriate measure of earnings, then it is important to use an equity rate of return applicable to the variable being capitalized, as discussed in Chapter 9 on the income approach.

Appropriate Rate of Return on Net Tangible Assets

No one has convincingly refuted the position stated by the IRS that any arbitrary rate of earnings as a normal return on net tangible assets cannot be demonstrated to have a reasonable basis. Nevertheless, there are some ways to look at the problem of estimating a fair rate of return on net tangible assets that could be helpful.

There is a consensus among valuation practitioners that the appropriate percentage rate of return on net tangible assets in the excess earnings method depends on the asset mix.[5] Assets that are highly liquid, low in risk, and/or readily acceptable as loan collateral require lower rates of return than assets that are less liquid, more risky, and/or less acceptable as loan collateral. A reasonable procedure would be to develop a weighted average cost of capital based on the percentage of debt financing that the asset mix would support.

Appropriate Capitalization Rate for Excess Earnings

Net tangible assets provide a measure of safety in that, if earnings fail to materialize as expected, then the assets usually can be liquidated for something. Goodwill, on the other hand (as well as most other intangible assets), has no liquidation value in the absence of earnings, since its economic value depends on its ability to generate economic income. Therefore, the risk attached to the intangible portion of the assets would seem to be greater and demand a higher rate of return.

---

[5]See, for example, Jay E. Fishman, and Shannon P. Pratt, et al., *Guide to Business Valuations,* 5th ed. (Fort Worth, TX: Practitioners Publishing Co., 1995), chap. 7; and Thomas L. West and Jeffrey D. Jones, eds., *Handbook of Business Valuation* (New York: John Wiley & Sons, 1992), chap. 15.

Furthermore, a case can be made that the tangible assets have a more persistent and predictable life than goodwill or other intangible assets in many cases.

In general, investors are not willing to pay cash up front for more than one to five years' worth of earnings from commercial goodwill, sometimes even less. The length of expected future earnings from goodwill for which investors are willing to pay depends primarily on the perceived persistence of those earnings in the future, independent of further investment of time and effort to perpetuate them.

One way to estimate a capitalization rate to apply to excess earnings is to think in terms of converting the number of years' worth of expected future excess earnings the investor would be willing to pay for in terms of cash up front into an implied capitalization rate. The implied capitalization rate in this scenario is simply the reciprocal of the number of years' expected excess earnings for which the investor would be willing to pay cash up front. For example, if the typical investor would pay cash equivalent to four years' excess earnings, the calculation would be:

$$1 \div 4 = .25$$

The following table presents implied capitalization rates that may be appropriate for excess earnings based on assumed investors' tolerances for a range of investment payback periods (the length of time the investor is willing to accept to recover the initial outlay):

Investment Payback Period	Implied Capitalization Rate
6 months	200%
1 year	100
2 years	50
3 years	33⅓
4 years	25
5 years	20

Summary: Conceptual Basis for the Two Capitalization Rates

In light of the foregoing discussion, it is reasonable, conceptually, to determine appropriate capitalization rates to apply to earnings generated both from a base of net tangible assets and from intangible factors over and above an acceptable return on the investment in tangible assets. The conceptual basis is that the difference in the cost of capital depends on the presence or lack of tangible assets. Generally, the greater the value of the tangible assets the buyer receives for his investment, the less risky the buyer perceives the investment to be, thus the lower his required rate of return.

Some practitioners suggest that the rate to be applied as a return on tangibles be a weighted average of the cost of borrowing and the cost of equity. The weighting would logically depend on what percentage of the assets could be financed by borrowing.

Some practitioners also suggest that the capitalization rate for the excess earnings be at or above the high end of a range of reasonable required rates of return on equity, because the risk would be perceived to be greater with no tangible asset backing. The determination of the rate in each case should depend on the expected duration and the perceived risk of the excess earnings.

Exhibit 13–2

Illustrative Business Valuation Using the Excess Earnings Method

Assumptions:

Net current assets	$100,000,000
Fixed assets, net	25,000,000
(Above assets valued at fair market value)	
Borrowing base	80% of net current assets
Borrowing rate	10%
Cost of equity capital	25%
Capitalization rate for excess earnings	20%
Pretax net cash flow	25,000,000
(After reasonable compensation to business owners)	

Scenario A: Company Pays No Income Taxes

Borrowing base:

Net current assets	$100,000,000	
	x .80	
Tangible assets financed by debt	$ 80,000,000	64%
Tangible assets financed by equity	45,000,000	36%
Total net tangible assets	$125,000,000	100%
(Before interest-bearing debt)		

	Proportion in the Capital Structure	Cost of Capital	Weighted Cost of Capital
Debt	.64	.10	.064
Equity	.36	.25	.09
Required return on net tangible assets			.154

Pretax net cash flow		$ 25,000,000
Net tangible assets	$125,000,000	
Required return on net tangible assets	.154	
		19,250,000
"Excess" earnings		$ 5,750,000
Capitalized at		20%
Value of excess earnings		$ 28,750,000
Add: Value of net tangible assets		125,000,000
Total business equity value		$153,750,000

In the above scenario, a willing buyer could pay $153,750,000 for the fixed assets, net current assets, and intangible value. If the buyer used the full borrowing power, the purchase price could be financed with $80,000,000 debt and $73,750,000 equity.

Scenario B: Company Pays 20% Income Taxes

Borrowing base is same as in Scenario A, but cost of debt reduced 20% of debt cost because of deductibility of taxes.

	Proportion in the Capital Structure	Cost of Capital	Weighted Cost of Capital
Debt	.64	(.10 x .80) = .08	.0512
Equity	.36	.25	.0900
Required return on net tangible assets (rounded)			.141

Pretax net cash flow		$ 25,000,000
Less: Income taxes at 20%		5,000,000
After-tax net free cash flow		$ 20,000,000
Net tangible assets	$125,000,000	
Required return on net tangible assets	.141	
		17,625,000
"Excess" earnings		$ 2,375,000
Capitalized at		20%
Value of excess earnings		11,875,000
Add: Value of net tangible assets		125,000,000
Total value		$136,875,000

In the above scenario, the buyer could pay $136,875,000 for the fixed assets, net current assets, and intangible value. If the buyer used the full borrowing power, the purchase price could be financed with $80,000,000 debt and $56,875,000 equity.

An example of the application of the excess earnings method is presented as Exhibit 13–2. While the excess earnings method is most often used for small businesses and professional practices, it may also be used for large companies, as shown in Exhibit 13–2, if it is performed extremely rigorously.

Negative Goodwill

The excess earnings method deals with how to value the earnings, if any, over and above a reasonable rate of return on the net tangible assets. What if the earning power is less than a reasonable rate of return on the net tangible assets? Such a circumstance could indicate the phenomenon that some call negative goodwill; it could mean the value of the total entity would be less than the value of its net tangible assets.

Common Errors in Applying the Excess Earnings Method

The excess earnings method is widely misused in business valuation practice. Some of the errors most commonly encountered are discussed in the following sections.

Failure to Allow for Owners' Salaries

As noted in Revenue Ruling 68-609 (Exhibit 13–1), "If the business is a sole proprietorship or partnership, there should be deducted from the earnings of the business a reasonable amount for services performed by the owner or partners engaged in the business."

Unfortunately, valuations are often performed by the excess earnings method that do not include a reasonable allowance for compensation to the owner or owners for services performed. This error results in an overstatement of the true economic earnings, which in turn leads to an overstatement of the value of the business entity.

Failure to Use Realistic Normalized Earnings

To the extent that the method is valid, it depends on a reasonable estimate of normalized earnings. As noted in Revenue Ruling 68-609, "The past earnings to which the formula is applied should fairly reflect the probable future earnings."

We have frequently seen the method naively applied to the latest year's earnings, or to some simple or weighted average of recent years' earnings, without regard to whether or not the earnings base used reflects fairly the probable future earnings. Such a naive use of some historical earnings base usually results in an undervaluation or overvaluation.

Using Book Values of Assets without Adjustment

As noted in the previous chapter, book value is something of a misnomer, since it is not an indication of economic value at all, but rather an accounting term meaning the dollar amount at which the item is carried on the company's financial records. The book value of assets usually represents the acquisition cost of assets less any depreciation recorded for financial accounting and/or income tax purposes. The longer the company has held the assets, the less likely it is that their book value will be a reasonable approximation of any kind of economic value.

Net tangible asset value used in the excess earnings method should reflect an informed judgment about the value of the tangible assets. Understatement of the value of the net tangible assets results in a high capitalization rate being applied to too large a portion of the total earnings, which leads to an undervaluation of the total entity, or vice versa if the net tangible asset value is overstated.

Errors in Estimating Appropriate Rates

The estimation of the two capitalization rates is critical to the validity of the result of the excess earnings method. A conceptual approach to determine the rates to use was suggested earlier. However, one clearly erroneous practice that recurs in the selection of the rates is using the rates suggested in the ruling itself.

The ruling, written in 1968, suggests rates of 8 to 10 percent on tangible assets, with 15 to 20 percent applied to the excess earnings. However, the ruling states, "The percentage of return...should be the percentage prevailing in the industry involved at the date of the valuation...The above rates are used as examples and are not appropriate in all cases...The capitalization rates are dependent upon the facts pertinent thereto in each case."[6]

Both the wording of the ruling and common sense indicate that the specific rates mentioned in the ruling are examples, and the actual rates to use depend on the facts at the time. Despite that, even in the 1990s, we find people using the rates for the excess earnings method used in the ARM 34 example back in 1920, and again in Revenue Ruling 68-609 in 1968, when prevailing rates were much lower. The average yield on long-term government bonds in 1968 was about 5 percent. They have not been that low in recent history. Using capitalization rates that are too low inevitably results in overstating the value of the entity.

Summary

The excess earnings method (also called the formula method) dates back to Prohibition. It was the U.S. Treasury Department method of determining the amount to compensate distilleries for their loss of intangible value in the nature of goodwill. The IRS's current position on the method is embodied in Revenue Ruling 68-609 and in Private Letter Ruling 79-05013, both referenced in this chapter. The IRS says the method "may be used in determining the value of intangible assets of a business only if there is not a better basis for making the determination."

Despite this lack of enthusiasm on the part of the IRS, the excess earnings method is one of the most widely used and misused methods of business valuation. Moreover, the guidance in the proper implementation of the method contained in the above three references is widely ignored, resulting in a plethora of misapplications.

---

[6]Revenue Ruling 68-609, 1968-2 C.B. 327.

This chapter developed the proper use of the excess earnings method. It quoted the relevant guidance provided in each of the IRS references cited above. Of most critical importance, the chapter (along with the previous chapter) provided guidance on how to develop the four key variables in the excess earnings method:

1. Net tangible asset value.
2. Earnings base to be capitalized.
3. Reasonable rate of return on tangible assets.
4. Capitalization rate to be applied to "excess earnings."

Finally, the chapter concluded with a discussion of each of the most commonly encountered errors found in attempted implementations of the excess earnings method. By following the guidance in this chapter, the reader should be able to implement the excess earnings method properly and identify any of the most common errors in other implementations of the excess earnings method.

Bibliography

Fox, Jeffery D. "Closely Held Business Valuations: The Uninformed Use of the Excess Earnings/Formula Method." *Taxes,* November 1982, pp. 832–36.

Gallinger, George W., and Glenn A. Wilt Jr. "The Excess Earnings Model's Necessary Assumptions." *ASA Valuation,* February 1988, pp. 74–78.

Gomes, Glenn M. "Excess Earnings, Competitive Advantage, and Goodwill Value." *Journal of Small Business Management,* July 1988, pp. 22–31.

Schilt, James H. "An Objection to the Excess Earnings Method of Business Appraisal." *Taxes,* February 1980, pp. 123–26.

_____. "Challenging Standard Business Appraisal Methods." *ASA Valuation,* June 1985, pp. 2–10.

_____. "Goodwill and Excess Earnings." *Business Law News,* Winter 1982, pp. 18–20.

Shayne, Mark. "A Reexamination of Revenue Ruling 68-609." *FAIR$HARE: The Matrimonial Law Monthly,* July 1992, pp. 5–8.

Vinso, Joseph D. "Excess Earnings Estimation of Intangibles (A Note)." *Business Valuation News,* December 1984, pp. 15–17.

Chapter 14

Minority Interest Discounts, Control Premiums, and Other Discounts and Premiums

Minority stock interests in a "closed" corporation are usually worth much less than the proportionate share of the assets to which they attach.[1]

The above statement, from a 1935 stock valuation case that is still widely quoted 60 years later, captures the essence of the minority stockholder's situation. Yet·this revelation comes as a shock to many people, who may have always assumed that a partial interest is worth a pro rata portion of the value of the total enterprise.

The major areas of premiums or discounts are the degree of control, or conversely, lack of it (minority status), and the degree of marketability (or lack of it). The issue of control versus minority is a major subject of this chapter. Other possible discounts, discussed at the end of the chapter, include voting versus nonvoting shares (akin to the control/minority issue), blockage, a key person discount, and a "portfolio" discount. The matter of discounts for lack of marketability is the subject of the next chapter.

Critical to the discussion of discounts or premiums is the notion that they have no meaning until the base to which they are applied is clearly defined. We have seen an incredible number of buy–sell agreements and appraisals written that refer to discounts or premiums with no reference to the base from which those discounts or premiums are to be taken. This is a typical error in business appraisal. Throughout our discussions of premiums and discounts, we will attempt to be very specific as to what premiums and/or discounts are properly applied to what base definition of value.

In Chapter 3, we discussed the fact that minority (the degree of control or lack of it) and marketability (the ability to liquidate the ownership interest) are separate and distinct concepts, although to some extent they are interrelated. The difficulty in liquidating a minority interest in a closely held company generally is much greater than the difficulty in liquidating a controlling interest. One form of schematic presentation is presented as Exhibit 14–1.

The traditional schematic diagram shown in Exhibit 14–1 reflects the value of the elements of control versus the minority stockholder's situation as discussed in the section immediately following. This schematic usually would represent *fair market value* on a *going-concern basis.* In some cases, there may be yet another layer of value, which may reflect synergies with certain third-party buyers (for example, reducing combined overhead by consolidation of operations or raising prices by reducing competition). There is not a widely used term for this additional layer of possible premium over fair market, going-concern value, but this premium combined with the control premium on a stand-alone basis is sometimes called an "acquisition premium." The value reflecting these synergies usually would be considered *investment value,* because it reflects *value to a particular buyer,* generally referred to as a *synergistic buyer,* rather than value to a hypothetical buyer buying the company strictly on its own merits, generally referred to as a *financial buyer.*

It is noteworthy that the issue of minority versus control covers a broad spectrum of factors that influence the impact of this issue on value. One category of factors is the degree of control elements that may or may not be present in any specific ownership interest. Another factor is the potential ability of a controlling

---

[1]*Cravens* v. *Welch,* 10 Fed. Supp. 94 (1935).

Exhibit 14–1

Example of Relationships between Control Premiums, Minority Interest Discounts, and Discounts for Lack of Marketability

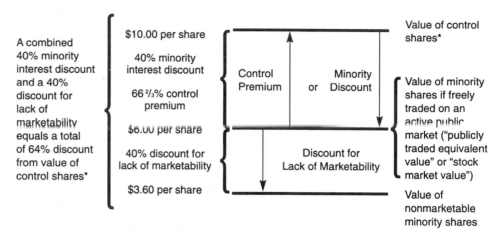

*Control shares in a privately held company may also be subject to some discount for lack of marketability, but usually not nearly as much as minority shares.

Note: Empirical data to assist in the quantification of discounts for lack of marketability for both minority and controlling interests are presented in the following chapter.

SOURCE: Jay E. Fishman and Shannon Pratt, et al., *Guide to Business Valuations*, 5th ed. (Fort Worth, TX: Practitioners Pubishing Co., 1995). Reprinted with permission.

shareholder to implement policies that will enhance the value of control versus minority shares. This chapter provides detail on how various facts and circumstances may impact the difference in value between control and minority ownership positions.

The Concept and Importance of Control

Elements of Control

The following is a list of some of the more common prerogatives of control:

1. Appoint management.
2. Determine management compensation and perquisites.
3. Set policy and change the course of business.
4. Acquire or liquidate assets.
5. Select people with whom to do business and award contracts.
6. Make acquisitions.
7. Liquidate, dissolve, sell out, or recapitalize the company.
8. Sell or acquire Treasury shares.
9. Register the company's stock for a public offering.
10. Declare and pay dividends.
11. Change the articles of incorporation or bylaws.
12. Block any of the above actions.

From the above list, it is apparent that the owner of a controlling interest in an enterprise enjoys some very valuable rights that an owner not in a controlling position does not.

In their *Control Premium Study,* Houlihan Lokey Howard & Zukin define a control premium as "the additional consideration that an investor would pay over a marketable minority equity value (i.e. The Wall Street Journal price) in order to own a controlling interest in the common stock of a company."[2] They list major factors that impact the potential magnitude of a control premium.

> A controlling interest is considered to have greater value than a minority interest because of the purchaser's ability to effect changes in the overall business structure and to influence business policies. Control premiums can vary greatly. Factors affecting the magnitude of a given control premium include:
>
> - The nature and magnitude of nonoperating assets.
> - The nature and magnitude of discretionary expenses.
> - The perceived quality of existing management.
> - The nature and magnitude of business opportunities which are not currently being exploited.
> - The ability to integrate the acquiree into the acquiror's business or distribution channels.[3]

The Minority Stockholder's Situation

The above are important and valuable elements of control, rights that do *not* attach to minority stock. H. Calvin Coolidge, a former bank trust officer with extensive experience in dealing with and selling (or attempting to sell) minority interests in closely held companies, presents a cogent précis of the minority stockholder's position:

> The holder of a minority interest can at best elect only a minority of the directors and for corporations chartered in states which do not permit cumulative voting, he may not be able to elect even one director. Lacking control of the board of directors, he cannot compel payment of dividends which must be declared equally and which would give him his pro rata share of earnings. Lacking control of the board of directors, he cannot compel his election as an officer or his employment by the corporation, which the holders of the controlling interest can do, often with resultant no voice in corporate affairs and is at the mercy of the holders of the controlling interest who have no reason to pay anything but a token dividend, if any, and no reason to buy out the minority holder except at a nominal price.
>
> A willing buyer contemplating purchase from a willing seller of a minority interest, being under no compulsion to buy (which would exclude a buyer already owning some shares whose new purchase would cover control), would suffer the same disadvantages of lack of control. The buyer is asked to make an investment with no assurance as to certainty of current yield or as to when, or the amount at which, he may be able to liquidate his investment. Regardless, therefore, of the value of 100% of the corporation, the buyer will not purchase a minority interest except at a discount from its proportionate share of the value of 100% of the corporation.[4]

---

[2]*Control Premium Study* (Los Angeles: Houlihan Lokey Howard & Zukin, 1995), p. 1

[3]Ibid.

[4]H. Calvin Coolidge, "Discount for Minority Interest: Rev. Rul. 79-7's Denial of Discount Is Erroneous," *Illinois Bar Journal* 68 (July 1980), p. 744.

The lack of concurrence between the value of stock and the corporation's underlying assets was clearly established by the U.S. Supreme Court in 1925:

> The capital stock of a corporation, its net assets, and its shares of stock are entirely different things...The value of one bears no fixed or necessary relation to the value of the other.[5]

An oft-cited U.S. Tax Court case quoted the above, adding: "This is particularly true as to minority interests in a closed corporation..."[6]

That minority shareholders often find themselves disadvantaged compared to controlling shareholders is attested to by the fact that the often quoted, scholarly, two-volume treatise *O'Neal's Oppression of Minority Shareholders* is doing well in its second edition, published in 1985. In the preface to that edition, the authors comment on the growing amount of minority shareholder litigation:

> Most American lawyers do not realize the tremendous amount of litigation in this country arising out of shareholder disputes. Since the publication of the first edition of this treatise, the volume of litigation grounded on minority shareholder oppression—actual, fancied, or fabricated—has grown enormously, and the flood of litigation shows no sign of abating. The increase in litigation has been pronounced in both federal and state courts, with an especially large number of suits challenging the validity of "cash-out" mergers. Also worthy of note is that in the last four or five years there has been a substantial increase in the number of suits minority shareholders have brought for involuntary dissolution of their corporation or to force majority shareholders to purchase their shares.[7]

The above discussion makes it obvious why there may be considerable difference in the value of shares that have some or all of the elements of control compared with minority shares lacking elements of control.

How the Valuation Approach Used Affects the Minority Discount/Control Premium Issue

The approach or approaches used in the valuation each lead to a value with certain characteristics (control/minority, marketable/nonmarketable, and so on). The type of value each approach may produce was discussed in the chapters on the respective approaches. The characteristics of the value produced by the approach dictate, to a large degree, the premiums and/or discount(s) appropriate for the standard and premises of value being sought. This section discusses how the valuation approach(es) used may impact the control premium/minority discount issue.

The Income Approach

Recall that the various methods within the income approach all have two basic elements in common:

---

[5]*Ray Consol. Copper Co.* v *United States*, 45 S. Ct. 526 (1925).

[6]*Drayton Cochran, et al.,* 7 T.C.M. 325 (1948).

[7]F. Hodge O'Neal and Robert B. Thompson, *O'Neal's Oppression of Minority Shareholders*, 2nd ed., vol. 1 (Wilmette, IL: Callaghan & Company, 1985), p. iii. The term *cash-out merger* is sometimes used to mean a *squeeze-out* or *freeze-out merger*, in which minority shareholders receive cash for their shares. They cannot block the merger or demand consideration other than cash. If they are not satisfied with the amount of cash offered, their remedy is to demand an appraisal of the stock under dissenters' appraisal rights statutes. See, for example, *Roland International Corp.* v. *Najjar*, 407 A.2d 1032, 1033 (Del. S. Ca. 1979).

1. A numerator consisting of an amount or amounts of expected economic income.
2. A denominator consisting of a rate of return at which the economic income is discounted or capitalized.

Almost all the difference in control versus minority value in the income approach is found in the numerator—the expected economic income—rather than in the denominator—the discount or capitalization rate.

Consider, for example, a public company acquiring a controlling interest in another company, whether public or private. The acquirer generally will not be willing to accept a lower rate of return than the cost of capital for its own publicly traded minority stock just because it is acquiring control, because that would be dilutive and detrimental to the acquirer's existing stockholders. An argument can be made that acquiring control reduces risk compared to acquiring a minority interest, and the reduced risk should be reflected in a lower discount rate. While this may well be a major factor in certain instances, surveys show that in the typical instance the control versus minority issue has little or no impact on the discount rate.

More importantly, many argue that the discount rate should be the target's, not the acquirer's. That certainly is true if the standard of value is fair market value. Even if the standard of value is investment value, the higher risk of the target may raise the acquirer's overall cost of capital.

The big difference between control and minority ownership in the income approach generally is found in the economic income projections. To the extent that the economic income projections reflect the ability of a controlling shareholder to realize more for the controlling interest than a minority holder could realize under the status quo, the income approach reflects the impact of control, and the resulting value would represent the value of those elements of control. If a controlling stockholder could enhance value to controlling shares, but the impact of such potential actions is not reflected in the economic income projections, then the indication of value tends to be on a minority basis, and a premium for control over the indicated value could be warranted.

The most common example of economic income projections that would lead to a minority or control value is whether or not owners' compensation is adjusted to reflect value of services rendered. Such an adjustment would move an income approach value toward a control value rather than a minority value.

The implication of this discussion is that the justification for and amount of any control premium over the value indicated in an income approach largely depends on the ability of a control owner to enhance the income to control shares over and above the amounts of income already accounted for in the income approach. This matter needs to be assessed in consideration of the facts and circumstances in each case.

The Capital Market (Guideline Company) Method

By definition, since the capital market method derives a value based on publicly traded minority shares, the method provides a marketable, minority ownership indication of value. If conditions in the market for companies in the industry at the valuation date are such that controlling interests can be sold for more than the aggregate value of the publicly traded minority shares, then a control premium probably is warranted if valuing a controlling interest. (Such a control premium may be partially or fully offset by a discount for lack of marketability, as discussed in the next chapter.)

Sources of empirical data to assist in quantifying a control premium over a stock market value (value as if publicly traded) are presented in a subsequent section. As further discussed in conjunction with the presentation of such data, they might more properly be called acquisition premiums, since in many cases they include the impact of synergies and other factors beyond pure elements of control. In any case, such premiums vary considerably from one time to another, from one industry to another at any given time, and from company to company within an industry. The market conditions at or near the valuation date and the circumstances of the company relative to others must be analyzed in each case if it appears that a control premium should be applied to an indication of value from the capital market method.

Merger and Acquisition Method

Most (but not all) merger and acquisition transactions are controlling interests. Therefore, if an indication of value is developed based on merger and acquisition data, a control premium generally would not be appropriate. If valuing a minority ownership interest, then a minority interest discount usually would be appropriate.

Asset Accumulation Method (Adjusted Net Asset Value)

Adjusted net asset value generally represents a controlling ownership interest value, since only a controlling stockholder could decide to replace or liquidate assets or put them to their highest and best use in a going-concern context. If the full value of all intangible assets is fully reflected in the asset-based valuation approach, then minority shares typically sell at a minority discount from such value.

On the other hand, we would like to think that if the income approach, the market approach, and the asset-based approach were all perfectly implemented for a controlling interest value, we would reach the same value by all three approaches, and the discount to move from a control to a minority value would be the same. However, rarely do the data allow us to do it so neatly. As suggested in Exhibit 14–1, in the typical situation (and especially when using a market approach) the available market data provide guidance for a minority interest discount to move from a control to a minority marketable value and then another set of data on discounts for lack of marketability to move from a marketable, minority value to a nonmarketable minority value.

When using the asset-based approach, we may use this two-step discounting process to reach a nonmarketable, minority interest value. The data for the minority interest discount portion of this process are better for some industries than others. When using adjusted net asset value as a base, however, some empirical data lump the minority and marketability aspects so they cannot be separately quantified. This is especially true for limited partnership interests, as will be seen in a later section. When starting from adjusted net asset value as an indicator of controlling interest, and the objective is to value a minority, nonmarketable interest, one can either discount first for minority interest and then take a separate discount for lack of marketability or lump the two factors into a single discount. Which is preferable depends on the type of company and the quality of the empirical data available for quantification of the discounts for the particular type of interest.

The Excess Earnings Method

Generally, the excess earnings method can be viewed as a variant of the asset accumulation method, adjusting tangible assets to fair market value and simply aggregating all the intangible asset value into a single calculation based on excess earnings. The earnings typically are adjusted to reflect the prerogatives of control. Thus, the excess earnings method would produce a control value.

If the earnings do not, however, reflect the prerogatives of control, and the assets are not adjusted to market value, then the excess earnings method could produce a minority value. Therefore, when considering whether a control premium or minority discount should be applied to a value using the excess earnings method as the base, the analyst must consider whether or not prerogatives of control have been reflected in the economic income used in the calculation.

How the Applicable Standard of Value Affects Minority Discounts or Control Premiums

As discussed in Chapter 2, the applicable standard of value for the majority of valuation situations falls into one of four categories: (1) fair market value, (2) investment value, (3) intrinsic value, or (4) fair value. The applicable standard of value is determined primarily by the purpose and objective of the valuation. In some situations, the applicable standard of value is mandated by law. In others, the selection of the appropriate standard of value lies within the discretion of the parties involved.

Fair Market Value

Recall from Chapter 2 that the *fair market value* standard implies a price at which an arm's-length transaction would be expected to occur between normally motivated investors under open market conditions, without considering any special benefits for any particular buyer or seller. Considering the unattractiveness of minority interests in closely held companies to investors at large, the discount from a proportionate share of enterprise value under the fair market value standard normally is large. There are substantial amounts of transaction data (presented later in the chapter) to assist in quantifying minority interest discounts or control premiums when the standard of value is fair market value.

Investment Value

In Chapter 2, we defined the *investment value* standard as the value to a particular investor considering that investor's cost of capital, perception of risk, and other unique characteristics. Because of the particular attributes of ownership that may have unique appeal to any specific investor, the investment value of a minority interest in a certain enterprise may be equal to, greater than, or less than fair market value and also equal to, greater than, or less than a pro rata portion of the total enterprise value.

Because investment value, by definition, depends on the attributes of a particular buyer or seller, there obviously aren't market data to assist in quantifying premiums or discounts directly relative to that standard of value, since the premiums or discounts would vary with the individual buyer or seller rather than necessarily representing a market consensus as in the case of fair market value. Thus, although market evidence usually would have a bearing on appropriate premiums or discounts under the investment value standard, they would be more judgmental based on analysis of the individual facts and circumstances than under the fair market value standard.

This suggests that under the investment value standard, one might be more inclined to select a valuation method that directly produces the desired level of value (control or minority) than to reach some other level and then have to adjust for a minority discount or control premium.

A study published in 1995 by *Buyouts* distinguishes between multiples of EBIT paid by strategic buyers versus those paid by financial buyers. This study shows the following results:

Table 14–1
Average Acquisition to EBIT Multiples

	1989	1993	1995
Financial buyers	7.41	5.40	6.50
Strategic buyers	7.76	6.11	7.24

SOURCE: Jennifer Lea Reed, "Purchase Multiples Press to Rarefied Heights," *Buyouts,* February 20, 1995, p. 1.

Certainly, the excess multiples paid by strategic buyers over financial buyers represents elements of investment value over fair market value. However, it should also be recognized that elements of investment value often are also present in financial buyer transactions.

Intrinsic Value

Intrinsic value (sometimes called *fundamental value*), as defined in Chapter 2, is the value inherent in the characteristics of the investment itself. It is rarely used as a standard of value in and of itself. More commonly, the term is referred to, and some of the notions it implies used, in the context of one of the other three standards of value.

As it is used by public market security analysts, intrinsic value usually is a publicly traded, minority value. If this is the case, then a control premium could be applicable if exercise of elements of control could enhance the value elements reflected in the intrinsic value analysis.

Fair Value

As noted in Chapter 2, the *fair value* standard suffers from lack of consistent definition from one context to another. It most often arises as the statutory standard of value applicable to appraisals under dissenting stockholders' rights or rights to dissolution. Such valuations by their nature are valuations of minority interests. The need to interpret the meaning of this standard of value from a study of the legal precedents in minority stockholder actions in each of the 50 states and Canada poses a continuing challenge to the appraisal profession.

Certain precedents—including those pursuant to California Corporations Code Section 2000—have suggested that fair value may be interpreted to mean fair market value without a minority interest discount (a proportionate share of enterprise value).

Even when a proportionate share of enterprise value is an indicated interpretation of "fair value," precedent as to which factors to consider and the relative weights to accord each varies considerably. Generally, but not always, unless liquidation is prospect, emphasis will be on factors that bear on the enterprise's going-concern value rather than on its liquidation value. Therefore, case precedent may dictate not only what premiums and/or discounts may or may not be applicable, but also how such premiums or discounts are defined and the base to which they may be applied. We cannot emphasize enough that research of the specifically applicable legal precedent is very important in each context to which the fair value standard is determined to apply.

Impact of State Statutes on Minority versus Control Value

Statutes affecting minority stockholders' rights vary greatly from state to state. These statutes, and the case law developed pursuant to each, can have an extremely important bearing on the values of certain minority or majority interests in many situations.

Requirements for Supermajority Votes

In some states, a simple majority can approve major actions such as a merger or sale of the company. Other states require a two-thirds or even greater majority to approve such actions, which means a minority of just over one-third has the power to block them, thus giving large minority interests a form of blocking power.

Both the types of actions that require a supermajority vote and the size of the supermajority required for each action vary considerably from state to state, and many states are undergoing review and change.

Dissenting Stockholder Appraisal Rights

Most states have statutes allowing minority stockholders to dissent if a company merges, sells nearly all its assets, or undergoes other fundamental change. In most cases, the dissenters' remedy is to have their shares appraised and be paid that value in cash. In most states, the standard of value for dissenting stockholder actions is "fair value," as discussed in Chapter 2 and later in this chapter. A few state statutes still specify "fair market value," but recently several have changed their dissenting stockholder statutory standard of value to "fair value." In any case, standards for appraisal under dissenting stockholder rights vary considerably and it is necessary to study the relevant case law.

Most states require that if a minority stockholder wishes to dissent to a corporate action, the decision must be registered in writing at or within a few days following the stockholder meeting at which the action is approved by the majority of stockholders. This registration of the dissent often is referred to as *perfecting dissenters' appraisal rights*. The courts are virtually unanimous in prohibiting dissenters' appraisal rights unless they have been perfected within the time specified in the statute. The impact on minority versus control value aspects was discussed briefly in the earlier section on fair value.

Rights to Dissolution or Sale of Stock

A few states have statutes enabling minority shares aggregating some specified percentage of the total outstanding to petition the courts to force dissolution of the corporation under certain circumstances. Such statutes generally provide that controlling stockholders can prevent dissolution in such cases by paying the petitioners for dissolution the "fair value" of their shares. By far, the largest amount of litigation regarding the value of shares under such statutes has been pursuant to California Corporation Code Section 2000.

In states that have such dissolution statutes, case law does not necessarily interpret *fair value* the same for dissolution statutes as for dissenting shareholder statutes in the same state. This was discussed in the earlier section on fair value. In any case, states that have such statutes provide minority stockholders with one facet of control that is lacking in other states.

Other Factors Impacting Degree of Control

Effect of Distribution of Ownership

If one shareholder owns 49 percent of a company's stock and another shareholder owns 51 percent, the 49 percent shareholder has little or no control. However, if two shareholders own 49 percent each and a third owns 2 percent, the 49 percent shareholders may be on a par with each other depending on who owns the other 2 percent. The 2 percent shareholder may be able to command a premium over the normal minority interest value for that particular block of stock because of its swing vote power.

If each of three shareholders or partners owns a one-third interest, no one has complete control. However, no one is in a relatively inferior position, unless two of the three have close ties with each other that the third does not share. Each of equal individual interests normally are worth less than a pro rata portion of the total enterprise's worth; thus, the sum of the values of the individual interests usually is less than what the total enterprise could be sold for to a single buyer. However, the percentage discount from pro rata value for each such equal interest normally would be smaller than that for a minority interest with no control.

Each situation must be analyzed individually with respect to the degree of control, or lack of it, and the implications for the minority interest's value, keeping in mind the simple—or super—majority voting requirements as mandated by the company's own governing documents or by state law.

Articles of Incorporation, Bylaws, and Shareholder Agreements

A myriad of possible provisions in companies' articles of incorporation, bylaws, and shareholder agreements can impact the relative degree of control or lack of it for any particular block of stock or partnership interest. For example, even in states that require only a simple majority for any corporate action, many companies write requirements for supermajorities for certain actions into their articles of incorporation.

Buy–sell agreements frequently contain provisions specifying certain valuation premiums or discounts. Often these provisions differ depending on the triggering event that activates the buy–sell agreement provisions.

The analyst should understand any provisions in company documents or shareholder agreements that may impact the degree of control when quantifying a minority discount or control premium for a specific ownership interest.

Potential Dilution

Another factor that can affect the degree of control or lack of it is changes in the relative distribution of ownership as a result of either issuance of shares or redemption of outstanding shares. Many companies have stock options outstanding, the exercise of which could affect the balance of control. An ESOP could have control at a point in time, but lose that control position as a result of retiring participants exercising options to "put" their stock to the company. Even if an ESOP has a right of first refusal, it may not always have the resources available to exercise the right.

Preemptive Rights

Some companies give their stockholders *preemptive rights*. The *Encyclopedia of Banking & Finance* defines this right as follows:

> **PREEMPTIVE RIGHT** Stockholders' privilege to subscribe to new issues of voting stock, usually the common stock or securities convertible into voting stock, before such offerings are made to nonstockholders. A preemptive right is often referred to as a privileged subscription right. The preemptive right has been eroded in recent years.[8]

Such rights are designed to protect stockholders from dilution. However, they can make it awkward for a company to issue new shares, having first to offer stock to existing stockholders in accordance with the preemptive right provisions. Consequently, the trend in recent years has been toward elimination of preemptive rights.

Even if preemptive rights exist on paper, they may not be of equal efficacy to each respective holder of such rights because one owner may have adequate resources to exercise such rights while another owner may not.

---

[8]Charles J. Woelfel, *Encyclopedia of Banking & Finance,* 10th ed. (Chicago: Probus Publishing Company, 1994), p. 912.

Cumulative versus Noncumulative Voting

Either state statutes or a company's articles of incorporation may allow for cumulative voting. Under noncumulative voting, a simple majority of the stock can elect *all* the directors. Under cumulative voting, votes may be "cumulated" for a single director. For example, if five directors are to be elected, the owner of a share of stock could cast five votes for a single director, thus enabling minority shareholders with a sufficient number of shares to elect one or more directors.

The *Encyclopedia of Banking & Finance* offers the following formula for determining how many shares are required to elect one or more directors with cumulative voting:

Formula 14–1

$$\frac{\text{Total number of shares voting} \times \text{Number of directors desired}}{\text{Total number of directors} + 1} + 1$$

To illustrate: If there are five directors to be elected and 500 shares are outstanding and voting for the election of directors, the minimum number of shares necessary to elect one director would be 84 shares. Proof: 84 shares times five directors to be elected equals 420 votes, all cast for one director. Assuming the rest of the stock (416 shares) votes en bloc as the majority, such total of 2,080 votes distributed among five directors would be 416 votes each. Therefore, the individual representing the minority and receiving its 420 votes is sure to get one of the places on the board, the majority getting the other four places. The minority in this example must be sure to vote all of its 420 votes for one director; if it distributed the 420 votes among two, it obviously would not win any places on the board.

Cumulative voting, therefore, does *not* automatically assure the minority of representation on the board; the minority must have the minimum shares necessary for election of the directors desired and, second, must concentrate its cumulative votes properly. A good general rule to remember is Dr. Harry G. Guthmann's generalization: the minority for election of at least one director fraction of the total board must own the next lower fraction plus one share; e.g., on a board of five directors, the minority must have one-sixth of the stock plus one share; six directors, one-seventh of the stock plus one share, etc. Cumulative voting, moreover, requires a majority of the stock to be able to elect a majority of the board; in the above example, to elect three of the five directors, 251 shares are necessary, or a majority of the 500 shares total.[9]

Contractual Restrictions

Many typical control rights may be denied to a company through contractual restrictions. For example, indenture provisions in conjunction with debt obligations frequently prevent dividend payments, increased management compensation, liquidation of assets, acquisitions, or changes in the direction of the business.

---

[9]Woelfel, *Encyclopedia of Banking & Finance*, p. 276.

Effect of Regulation

Government regulation of operations may preempt the usual prerogatives of control. For example, it is a lengthy and sometimes even impossible process to liquidate companies in such regulated industries as insurance and utilities. Government regulation may prevent certain acquisitions and similarly prevent a company from selling to certain other companies or investors.

Financial Condition of Business

Many of the rights associated with control are rendered economically empty or of little value simply because of the company's financial condition. These could include the right to decide on management compensation, dividends, stock or asset purchases, or acquisition of other companies.

Three General Methods for Valuing Minority Interests

This section suggests three broad methods for valuing minority interests:

1. *Top down*—control value less discount(s).
2. *Horizontal*—comparison with other minority interest transactions.
3. *Bottom up*—start with nothing and find sources of value.

Method #1: Proportion of the Enterprise Value Less Discount(s), if Applicable

The first broad method for the valuation of a minority interest involves a three-step process:

1. Estimate the value of the equity of the total enterprise (control basis).
2. Compute the minority owner's pro rata interest in the total.
3. Estimate the amount of discounts, if any, applicable to the pro rata value of the total enterprise to properly reflect the value of the minority interest. This step must also include estimating whether a further discount for lack of marketability is applicable, and if so, how much.

Estimating the Enterprise Value. The Business Valuation Committee of the American Society of Appraisers has defined a *business enterprise* as "a commercial, industrial, or service organization pursuing an economic activity." This definition suggests that an enterprise be viewed as any integral, operating unit rather than as a collection of individual assets and liabilities. This is consistent with quotes presented earlier in the chapter from the U.S. Supreme Court and other sources, indicating there is little, if any, direct relationship between the value of stock in the enterprise and the value of assets the enterprise owns. One of the quotes cited earlier notes that this is particularly true for minority interests in close corporations. In this section, we will define "enterprise value" as the value of all of the classes of equity taken as a whole, assuming no long-term debt. (Unfortunately, the term "enterprise value" means many things to many people, often including the value of long-term debt.)

All the basic valuation methods discussed in earlier chapters could bear on the value of the entire enterprise or on the value of minority interests. However, our own experience, as well as our study of the literature and of court decisions on valuation issues, reveals a thread of distinction, in terms of the relative weight accorded to various factors, between estimating the enterprise value for a controlling interest and estimating the enterprise value as a starting point for valuing a minority interest. In estimating an enterprise value as a starting point for valuing minority shares, greater emphasis usually is on operating factors, such as earnings and dividends or dividend-paying capacity, than on values of assets.

An example of this focus is illustrated in the following quote from an oft-cited estate tax case:

> A prospective buyer would give some consideration to the book value of $145 a share. He would realize, however, that the company was a going concern, and that, even if it be assumed that the book value could be realized upon the liquidation of the corporation, there was no indication that it was to be liquidated. Moreover, he would also realize that "minority stock interests in a 'closed' corporation are usually worth much less than the proportionate share of the assets to which they attach." *Cravens* v. *Welch,* 10 Fed. Supp. 94. In our opinion, the factor which he would consider as the most important would be what the stock would earn.[10]

In the above case, the court determined a value of $45 per share, a little less than one-third of the $145 per share book value.

The following excerpt is typical of statements of the same position from the literature:

> Control evaluations differ markedly from noncontrol evaluations, because the way in which control buyers analyze businesses is different from the way in which passive investors analyze stocks. Control buyers generally concentrate on only a few situations and tend to analyze asset values. Situations are evaluated from a long-term perspective, because the control buyer is contemplating a large economic reevaluation in a single move. Alternatively, passive or noncontrol investors generally emphasize earnings.[11]

Another distinction between estimating the enterprise value for a controlling interest and estimating the enterprise value as a starting point for valuing a minority interest is in the adjustments to financial statements or in the projections. The control buyer normally will assume changes that the buyer would make, while the minority interest valuation will not project any changes that the existing control owners do not contemplate.

Computing the Minority Pro Rata Interest. In cases in which there is only a single class of stock and no warrants or contingent interests are outstanding, the proportionate value per share is given by the straightforward exercise of dividing the enterprise value by the number of shares outstanding. If there are different classes of interests, the total enterprise value must be allocated among the classes and the dilution resulting from any contingent interests must be reflected.

---

[10]*Hooper* v. *C.I.R.,* 41 U.S.B.T.A. 114 (1949).

[11]Arthur N. Haut and William P. Lyons, "Issues in the Valuation of Control and Noncontrol Shares in Connection with the Acquisition of Stock by Employee Stock Ownership Plans," *Journal of Pension Planning & Compliance,* Winter 1986, p. 319.

Estimating Applicable Discount(s) from Enterprise Value. As suggested in the schematic diagram in Exhibit 14–1, this discounting from control value usually is done as a two-step process, first for minority interest, then for marketability, each step drawing as much as possible on empirical data available to assist in quantifying the respective discounts. Done this way, the discounts for minority interest and marketability are *multiplicative,* as presented in Exhibit 14–1, *not additive.* That is, the discounts are taken in chain. The discount for minority interest is taken first; then the discount for lack of marketability is taken from the *net* amount after the minority interest discount. Thus, the total of the two 40 percent discounts presented on the diagram is *not* 80 percent, but 64 percent:

Control value	$10.00	
Discount for minority interest	x .60	(1 − .40)
Value as if publicly traded	$ 6.00	
Discount for lack of marketability	x .60	(1 − .40)
	$ 3.60	(represents a total of 64% discount from the control value of $10.00)

One reason for the above procedure is the conceptual preference for distinguishing between the discount for minority interest and the discount for lack of marketability. However, perhaps more importantly, for most types of companies and ownership interests, far more empirical evidence is available for quantifying each of the two discounts taken one at a time than for quantifying them together. Sources of empirical data for guidance in quantifying discounts for minority interest are presented in subsequent sections of this chapter. Sources of data for quantification of discounts for lack of marketability are presented in the next chapter.

There are exceptions to this general procedure. For example, in the case of minority interests in limited partnerships, several studies have been done relating transaction prices to adjusted net asset values. These studies generally have not attempted to distinguish how much of the total discount is due to minority interest and how much to lack of marketability.

Also, courts have not always followed the multiplicative procedure. For example, in the *Estate of Roy Martin,*[12] the expert for the IRS testified the discount for minority interest should be 35 percent and the discount for lack of marketability should be 35 percent. The court accepted these figures and determined a total discount of 70 percent from the aggregate underlying component values. It is not clear from reading the case whether the expert for the IRS testified that the two discounts should be added together rather than taken in chain, or whether the court decided on that procedure on its own.

Method #2: Direct Comparison with Sales of Other Minority Interests

We have often heard the question, "How can you possibly value a minority interest without knowing what the whole company is worth?" The answer is that you may value a minority interest by reference to other minority interest transactions. Then it is not necessary to wrestle with the difficult and often controversial issue

---

[12]*Roy O. Martin Jr.,* 50 T.C.M. 768 (1985).

of minority interest discounts and control premiums. If the indication of value produced by the valuation approach is a "publicly traded equivalent value" as presented in the schematic in Exhibit 14–1, then the only discount usually necessary is the discount for lack of marketability. Occasionally, one or more of the other discounts discussed at the end of this chapter is appropriate. If a direct comparison can be made with other closely held minority interests, no discounts or premiums may be necessary. However, except for past transactions in the subject company's own stock, it usually is very difficult (generally impossible) to find reliable data on minority transactions in guideline closely held company stocks.

If using past transactions in the company's own stock, one should update to reflect any changes in fundamental factors. One should also consider the extent to which the transactions could be considered arm's length, and whether they represent the standard of value applicable to the current valuation, such as fair market value.

As discussed in the previous section, it should be remembered that when valuing minority interests, more weight usually should be put on earnings-related approaches and less on asset-related approaches than when valuing a controlling interest. Also, when valuing minority interests, actual dividends rather than dividend-paying capacity are relevant, since the minority stockholder can't force the payment of dividends, regardless of how much dividend-paying capacity the company has.

As noted elsewhere in the book (e.g., the chapter on the guideline company method and various chapters relating to litigation), this "horizontal" method is widely accepted by courts.

Method #3: The "Bottom-Up" Method

In contrast to the two broad methods just discussed, the "bottom-up" method starts with nothing and builds up whatever elements of value to ownership of the minority interests exist.

This approach is the preference of Joel Adelstein, partner in charge of closely held company valuations for the Toronto office of Coopers & Lybrand. In a presentation at the 1985 ASA Advanced Business Valuation Seminar, Adelstein explained:

> Starting with zero and trying to find some value is my preference—why try to value the total enterprise at all? For many minority interests, ownership is just a long-shot speculation on something happening to get something out of the stock. The interest may have value someday, but it's sometime between now and never.[13]

In most cases, the values the minority interest holder may realize fall into two categories: (1) distributions, usually in the form of dividends, and (2) proceeds to be realized on the sale of the interest. The mechanics of this approach are the same as those discussed in Chapter 9, with expected cash contributions as the economic income returns to be discounted. The steps in this approach are as follows:

---

[13]Joel Adelstein, "Real World Challenges in Valuing Minority Shareholdings in Private Corporations" (Fourth Annual ASA Advanced Business Valuation Seminar, New Orleans, November 7–8, 1985).

1. Project the flow of expected distributions (timing and amounts).
2. Project an amount realizable on sale of the interest (timing and amount).
3. Discount the results of steps 1 and 2 to present value at an appropriate discount rate, reflecting the degree of uncertainty of realizing the expected returns at the times and in the amounts projected.

As an alternative to projecting an amount realizable on sale, the analyst could project the flow of expected distributions into perpetuity and not assume any residual sale value.

In doing this exercise, the analyst may want to project a best-case and worst-case scenario and perhaps one or more scenarios in between. The analyst might base the value on the most-likely scenario or assign probabilities to each scenario and compute the expected value (weighted average) of the possible values indicated by the various scenarios.

The lack of marketability of the closely held minority interest can be reflected in either of two ways. First, the discount rate can be increased to reflect the disadvantages of illiquidity as well as the other risks inherent in the investment. Second, the discount for lack of marketability can be handled as a separate step.

Market Evidence Regarding Control Premiums and Minority Interest Discounts

The market evidence available to assist in quantifying control premiums and/or minority interest discounts generally compares control acquisition prices with pre-acquisition minority interest transaction prices.

The general idea of control premium studies is to measure the premium over minority interest transaction prices at which a controlling interest in the same company was transacted. Such studies compare public market trading prices before the announcement of a merger or acquisition to the merger or acquisition price. The percentage of the acquisition price over the prior minority trading price is commonly called the control premium. Conversely, the percentage below the acquisition price at which the minority stock had been trading is commonly called the minority discount.

In reality, it might be better to call this premium an acquisition premium rather than a control premium. The data do measure the difference between prices at which control transactions took place in the stock of a company compared with previous minority interest transaction prices. It is important to keep in mind, however, that these price differences often reflect additional factors over and above the elements of control discussed in this chapter, such as the value of synergistic benefits.

Mergerstat Review Studies

Mergerstat Review describes its database as follows:

> The Mergerstat Review Research Department tracks publicly announced formal transfers of ownership of at least 10% of a company's equity where the purchase price is at least $1,000,000, and where at least one of the parties is a U.S. entity. These transactions are recorded as they are announced, not as they are completed.

Exhibit 14–2

Premium Offered over Market Price*

Year	DJIA High	DJIA Low	Premium Offered Average	Premium Offered Median	Base
1985	1,553.10	1,184.96	37.1%	27.7%	331
1986	1,955.60	1,502.30	38.2	29.9	333
1987	2,722.42	1,738.74	38.3	30.8	237
1988	2,183.50	1,879.14	41.9	30.9	410
1989	2,791.41	2,144.64	41.0	29.0	303
1990	2,999.75	2,365.10	42.0	32.0	175
1991	3,168.83	2,470.30	35.1	29.4	137
1992	3,413.21	3,136.58	41.0	34.7	142
1993	3,794.33	3,241.95	38.7	33.0	173
1994	3,978.36	3,593.35	41.9	35.0	260

* Premium calculations for the years 1985–94 are based on the seller's closing market price five business days before the initial announcement.

SOURCE: *Mergerstat Review 1994* (Los Angeles: Houlihan Lokey Howard & Zukin, 1995), p. 98.

Open market stock purchases are not recorded. For sellers in our database with competing bids, only the highest offer is included in our calculations. Cancelled transactions are deducted from total announcements for that period. Unless otherwise noted, all merger and acquisition statistics contained in this publication reflect completed or pending transactions as of the end of the applicable period.[14]

Exhibit 14–2 presents average and medium premiums offered over market price for transactions collected according to the above criteria. To convert the premiums to discounts from the acquisition price, the formula is:

Formula 14–2

$$1 - \frac{1}{(1 + \text{Premium})}$$

For example, using 1994's median premium, the discount would be:

$$1 - \frac{1}{(1 + .35)} \approx .26$$

Note that Exhibit 14–2 states that the minority trading price from which the premium is computed is five business days before the initial announcement. Studies show that stocks have some tendency to rise somewhat earlier on speculation of a possible takeover. Thus, the *Mergerstat* data may understate the premium from a strictly unaffected price (also understating the implied minority interest discount).

The *Mergerstat* data show a strong relationship between the level of the market (as measured by P/E multiples) and the premiums paid over the market average P/E multiple in acquisition transactions. When the market is low, P/E multiples offered relative to the general market P/E multiple are high, and vice versa. Exhibit 14–3 shows this relationship quite emphatically. Many times individual stocks, and even entire industries, may be priced so high that it would not be prudent to make takeover bids high enough to be successful. In such instances, a public market minority price may be equal to or even greater than a control price.

---

[14]*Mergerstat Review 1994* (Los Angeles: Houlihan Lokey Howard & Zukin, 1995), p. i.

Exhibit 14–3
Price to Earnings Ratios
Percent Offered over S&P 500
1980–1994

Year	S&P 500 P/E Ratio*	Average P/E Offered	Percent Offered over S&P 500 P/E Ratio
1980	9.1	15.2	67.0%
1981	8.1	15.6	92.6
1982	10.2	13.9	36.3
1983	12.4	16.7	34.7
1984	10.8	17.2	59.3
1985	11.5	18.0	56.5
1986	16.0	22.2	39.0
1987	19.3	23.3	20.7
1988	12.4	21.6	74.1
1989	13.3	20.9	57.1
1990	15.2	20.1	32.2
1991	18.6	20.0	7.5
1992	24.2	22.7	−6.2
1993	23.4	24.4	4.3
1994	19.9	24.5	23.1

*Based on an average of weekly prices and quarterly earnings.

SOURCE: *Mergerstat Review 1994* (Los Angeles: Houlihan Lokey Howard & Zukin, 1995), p. 108.

HLHZ Control Premium Studies

Houlihan Lokey Howard & Zukin also publishes a somewhat similar set of control premium data quarterly, with an annual compilation. In an attempt to overcome the potential distortion from stock price run-ups in speculative anticipation of a possible deal, they show minority stock prices one day, one week, one month, and two months before the acquisition announcement date, as well as a "Houlihan Lokey Unaffected Price." The latter involves analysis of price and volume data and selection of a price just before observed changes in normal pricing activity. The average and median Houlihan Lokey control premiums thus calculated tend to run somewhat higher than those calculated by *Mergerstat,* as shown in Exhibit 14–4. Note, however, as the following table shows, at least for the fourth quarter of 1994, that the premiums over prices one month and two months before the announcement date were even higher than the "Houlihan Lokey Unaffected Price."

Table 14–2

		Houlihan Lokey Control Premium	Premium 1 Day	Premium 1 Week	Premium 1 Month	Premium 2 Months
Range:	High	105.3%	105.3%	105.3%	81.7%	105.3%
	Low	17.6	8.8	19.0	19.0	23.4
Median:		31.9	31.9	32.5	36.8	45.2
Mean:		41.8	36.3	37.6	42.8	46.8

SOURCE: *Control Premium Study,* 1st Quarter 1995, (Los Angeles: Houlihan Lokey Howard & Zukin, 1995) p. 33.

Exhibit 14–4

Houlihan Lokey Howard & Zukin Industrywide *Control Premium Study*
Comparative Results

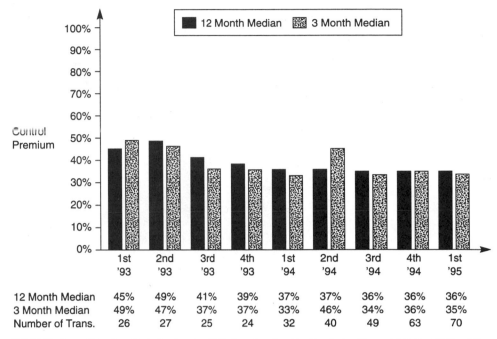

	1st '93	2nd '93	3rd '93	4th '93	1st '94	2nd '94	3rd '94	4th '94	1st '95
12 Month Median	45%	49%	41%	39%	37%	37%	36%	36%	36%
3 Month Median	49%	47%	37%	37%	33%	46%	34%	36%	35%
Number of Trans.	26	27	25	24	32	40	49	63	70

SOURCE: *Control Premium Study,* 1st Quarter 1995, (Los Angeles: Houlihan Lokey Howard & Zukin, 1995) p. 54.

Discounts from Net Asset Value

As noted several times in this book, net asset value or adjusted net asset value is not equal to the value of a company's stock unless a complete asset accumulation valuation exercise recognizing all intangible assets and all forms of obsolescence has been carried out, as per Chapter 12. Thus, the discount from some measure of the underlying net asset value at which a transaction occurs does not necessarily represent a pure minority interest discount. Nevertheless, there are many instances in which valuation guidance can be found in the relationship between transaction prices and some measure of net asset value. This section notes some of those categories of data.

Holding Companies

Adjusted net asset values are available for most publicly traded closed-end investment companies (including both REITs and operating real estate companies with significant holdings), for some real estate holding companies, and for some companies with significant timber holdings. If one were to assume the company could be liquidated for its adjusted net asset value and, therefore, that value represented a control value, then the price at which minority shares trade might be an indication of minority interest discount. There could also be other factors at play, however, especially taxes on built-in gains on unrealized appreciation of asset values.

One study showed significantly greater discounts from net asset value for real estate operating companies than for REITs. The author opined that:

The primary reason for the different median discounts is that, by law, shareholders in REITs receive almost all of the cash flow generated. Because the cash flow is paid directly to shareholders, they control how that cash is used.[15]

The same study identified four factors that affect the size of the discount:

1. Revenues.
2. Earnings.
3. Dividend payout ratio.
4. Unrealized capital gains.

Exhibit 14–5 shows the effects of these factors graphically.

Exhibit 14–5

Minority Interest Discounts for Publicly Traded Real Estate Companies

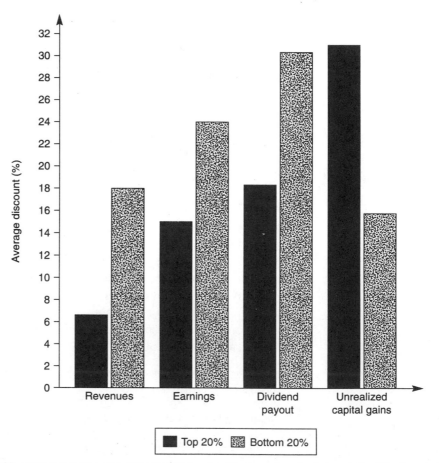

SOURCE: Lance S. Hall, "Valuation of Fractional Interests: A Business Appraiser's Perspective," *The Appraisal Journal*, April 1989, p. 176.

---

[15]Lance S. Hall, "Valuation of Fractional Interests: A Business Appraiser's Perspective," *The Appraisal Journal*, April 1989, p. 175.

Limited Partnerships

Most market transactions in limited partnership interests in recent years have been at substantial discounts from underlying net asset value. Unlike stocks, most limited partnerships sold in public offerings never developed a secondary public trading market. Therefore, without liquid public markets, most of the transactions are individually negotiated. Therefore, unlike most stocks, where one body of empirical data helps to quantify minority interest discounts and another discounts for lack of marketability, the discounts from net asset value for limited partnership transactions reflect aspects of both minority interest and lack of marketability.

One study tabulated discounts from net asset value for 146 syndicated limited partnerships that traded in the secondary market in April and May 1993. The study found an average discount of 38 percent.[16] They also found that those with no cash distributions sold at significantly greater discounts than those with cash distributions.

An article in *Trusts & Estates* cites such empirical evidence of minority interest discounts for real estate limited partnerships, apparently influenced to some extent by less than optimum marketability:

> A comparison of net asset values and secondary market prices for 85 real estate-based partnerships reported that actual transactions occurred at an average discount of 44 percent from liquidation values. For 21 of the 85 partnerships, the trading discount was 60 percent or more. Partnerships not currently distributing cash to investors tended to have larger discounts. This survey focused on partnerships whose units were traded relatively more frequently and in better organized markets. For other partnerships and related entities, the market imperfections would be larger and the discounts greater.[17]

Trust and Estate Sales Study

H. Calvin Coolidge, a bank trust officer responsible for administering trusts and estates that owned all or portions of closely held businesses, did two studies in which he compiled data on actual sales prices of closely held businesses. As an introduction, he offers the following generalities:

> A number of years of experience has demonstrated that it is extremely difficult to find any market for minority interests…, despite efforts to do so… On the relatively rare occasions when an offer is made to buy a minority interest, it is almost always for an amount far less than the fiduciary and the beneficiary expect to get.[18]

In his first study, Coolidge compiled data on 30 actual sales of minority interests. He found that the average transaction price was 36 percent below book value and concluded with the following observations:

> Only 20 percent of the sales were made at discounts less than 20 percent. A little more than half the sales (53 ⅓ percent) were made at discounts that ranged from 22 percent to 48 percent, and 23 ⅓ percent of the sales were made at discounts of from 54.4 percent to 78 percent.

---

[16]Steven Kam, Hans Schroeder, and Curt Smith, "Pricing Non-Publicly Traded Limited Partnerships," *Houlihan Valuation Advisors Valuation Report,* Spring 1994, p. 5.

[17]Mark S. Thompson and Eric S. Spunt, "The Widespread Overvaluation of Fractional Ownership Positions," *Trusts & Estates,* June 1993, p. 63, citing Partnership Profiles, Inc., "LP Secondary Market Discounts How Much?" *The Perspective,* May/June 1992, pp. 1–2.

[18]H. Calvin Coolidge, "Fixing Value of Minority Interest in Business,: Actual Sales Suggest Discount as High as 70%," Reprinted with permission from *Estate Planning,*© Spring 1975, p. 141, Warren, Gorham & Lamont, 31 St. James Avenue, Boston, MA 02116. All rights reserved.

It would be dangerous to draw too many generalizations from the survey, but those sales where the discounts were below 20 percent involved, with one exception, purchases from close relatives where friendly relations existed. The exception was the sale by a holder of swing shares who used his leverage well, but still took a 4.3 percent discount. At the other end of the spectrum was the settlement of a three year bitter dispute between two families; the majority family raised its token offer only after threat of a lawsuit, but the price the minority interest took nonetheless represented a 78 percent discount.[19]

It is noteworthy that the discounts in the foregoing surveys were from book value, not from the value of the enterprise as a whole. Book value, of course, recognizes no appreciation in assets above depreciated net asset value, although, in a very few cases in the above survey, the discounts were computed from an adjusted book value, reflecting appreciation in real estate values. I would expect that the total enterprise value would be above the book value in most cases. If that was true in the survey, then the discounts from the owners' proportionate shares of the total enterprise values were even greater than the discounts as shown in the survey, which were from book value.

An update published in 1983 indicated a trend toward even higher discounts when disposing of minority interests in closely held corporations. That study found a much higher concentration of discounts from book value at the high end of the range, and the average discount for the two studies combined was approximately 40 percent. The updated study concludes as follows:

> Each of the sales used in the survey involved a combination of factors that made it somewhat unique. To use any of the data, or any classification of the data, as definitive proof of the discount to be applied in a prospective valuation would be dangerous. This should not, however, obscure the true significance of the data, which is that in the actual marketplace, the typical discount is not of token size, but of substantial magnitude.[20]

Discounts for Direct Undivided Minority Interests in Real Estate

Market data on sales of fractional interests in real estate are scarce, but the data available do support the concept that fractional direct interests in real estate, when they are sold, generally are transacted at less than a pro rata portion of the value of the total parcel.

One study covered 54 undivided interests, with the undivided interest discounts ranging from zero to 82 percent, with a median discount of 35 percent.[21] Another study covered 21 undivided interests, with the undivided interest discounts ranging from 5 percent to 94 percent, with a median discount of 30 percent.[22]

[19]Ibid., p. 141.

[20]H. Calvin Coolidge, "Survey Shows Trend Toward Larger Minority Discounts," *Estate Planning,* September 1983, p. 282.

[21]Peter J. Patchin, "Market Discounts for Undivided Minority Interests in Real Estate," *Real Estate Issues* (Fall/Winter 1988), pp. 14–16.

[22]Don L. Harris, Philip A. McCormick, and W.D. Davis Sr., "The Valuation of Partial Interests in Real Estate," *ASA Valuation* (December 1983), pp. 62–73.

Discounts tend to be considerably less than for stocks or partnership interests. This probably is accounted for in large part by differences in the respective rights of the ownership interests. An owner of a direct minority interest in real estate may sue for partition—that is, to have the property divided and give each owner his or her pro rata share. If the court finds the property not divisible, it orders the property sold. Owners of minority stock and partnership interests have no such rights.

It is interesting to note that a recent case for the first time distinguished between minority interest and marketability discounts for an undivided interest in real estate. The court stated:

> "A minority interest discount for an interest in real property may be allowed on account of the lack of control which accompanies co-ownership." The minority interest discount should consider "the cost, uncertainty, and delays attendant upon partition proceedings…The marketability discount, by contrast, measures the diminution in value attributable to the lack of a ready market for the property." This two-step process is similar to prior Tax Court decisions regarding corporate and partnership interests.[23]

Other Discounts

In considering the following possible discounts, which may be taken independently of more common (and usually larger) discounts, the reader is cautioned to avoid double-counting. These discounts in some cases may already be reflected in market multiples, discount or capitalization rates, or in other discounts.

Voting versus Nonvoting Shares

The difference in value, if any, between voting and nonvoting minority shares depends largely on the size of the block and the distribution of ownership. In general, the greater the extent to which control is involved, the greater the impact of voting rights on the stock's value. As noted earlier, when swing votes are involved, the value impact can be considerable.

There have been several empirical studies on the price differentials between voting and nonvoting publicly traded stocks. The market data indicate that for small minority interests, the market generally accords very little or no value to voting rights. Where differentials in favor of voting stock exist, they generally have been under 5 percent, and no study has indicated a differential of over 10 percent. Again, the distribution of the stock can have a bearing. If one stockholder has total control anyway and there is no cumulative voting, the question of whether the minority shares are voting or nonvoting is academic unless a split of the control block is foreseeable.

Restrictive agreements also can have a bearing. Some voting stocks are subject to an agreement that causes them to be converted to nonvoting stock in the event of transfer. Such a provision can render voting rights virtually impotent for valuation purposes.

---

[23] *Samuel J. LeFrak* v. *Commissioner*, 66 T.C.M. 1297 (1993).

Blockage

The notion of a discount for blockage is applicable where the subject block of stock is of a size that would be difficult to sell without a discount in the normal course of trading. It is normally applied to blocks of public stock where the size of the block might represent several weeks or more of normal trading. The concept is well recognized by the courts,[24] but careful empirical evidence of trading must be presented to support it in each case.

The concept of blockage is not usually applied directly in the case of closely held stocks, since there is no record of average trading volume with which to compare the size of the block. The data shown in the chapter on discounts for lack of marketability do, however, suggest that larger blocks tend to sell at a greater discount than smaller blocks, so the large size of a block could be a factor that influences the magnitude of the discount for lack of marketability.

Key Person Discount

Some businesses are so dependent on a few key people or a single key person that a discount is warranted to reflect the impact of the actual or potential lack of availability of the key person's services. This may be the case in an estate where the key person has died, or when there is cause for concern about the key person's health or continued availability for whatever reasons. Following are the elements to be investigated in establishing any discount or diminution from the loss of a key person.

First, the appraiser determines the deceased executive's actual duties and areas of active involvement. A key person may contribute value to a company in both day-to-day management duties and from strategic judgment responsibilities based on long-standing contacts and reputation within an industry.

Second, the appraiser assesses the ability of existing successor management to move up the organizational ladder and take over the duties of the vacated position. Ideally, a strong and stable corporate organization will provide this capability. This assumes a succession plan exists. All too often, however, private business owners create "spider web" organization structures with themselves at the center—that is, all management decisions are made by the key executive-owner. The extent of organizational damage may also be related to the suddenness of the key manager's death.

Third, the appraiser calculates the amount of compensation necessary for replacing the key executive or filling the positions vacated or created when successors move up.

Fourth, to this quantitative calculation the appraiser adds the damages arising from risks to the business in bringing in replacement executives who may be unfamiliar with the company's operations. These risks can be compounded by the appraiser's assessment of the complexity or precariousness of the company's competitive or financial position. This is especially true if the deceased was personal guarantor of the company's debts, as often is the case with closely held business loans. Sometimes these risks can be quantified as estimates of sales losses or profit margin declines over estimated future periods.

---

[24]See, for example, *Edwin A. Gallun,* 33 T.C.M. 1316 (1974), in which the experts agreed that blockage reduced the value of an investment portfolio from $18,087,263 to $16,204,439, a difference of over 10 percent.

There are at least two offsets to these potential losses. One is the compensation, net of any continuing obligations, that the company ceases to pay to the deceased executive. The other is any insurance on the key person's life that is payable to the company and not earmarked for other purposes, such as repurchase of the deceased's stock in the company.

The estimates of key person losses can be directly incorporated into the valuation methods appropriate for the particular case. This may be accomplished by adjusting normalized earnings or price-to-earnings multiples, or as reductions in estimated future cash flows to be discounted. Otherwise, the loss can be subtracted from the company's indicated value as a separate item, much like the discount for lack of marketability.

Evidence for the amount of the loss in securities' values in the public market caused by the key person's death shows that the magnitude of the decline varies with the circumstances. Generally, public companies have larger and more flexible professional management teams and thus can better absorb the shock of the loss of any one key person. An instructive example of a catastrophic loss of key executives, however, was the tragic death of most of the top management of Arrow Electronics in a hotel fire in December 1980. Arrow's New York Stock Exchange listed common stock fell approximately 20 percent after the announcement of the news.

Courts often have recognized a key person discount. One of the highest such discounts was in the *Estate of Milton Feldmar,* where the court recognized a 25 percent key person discount.[25]

"Portfolio" Discount

The concept of a "portfolio" discount is a discount for a company that owns anywhere from two to several dissimilar operations and/or assets that do not necessarily fit well together. Many private companies have accumulated such a package of disparate operations and/or assets over the years, the combination of which probably would not be particularly attractive to a buyer seeking a position in any one of the industries, necessitating a discount to sell the entire company as a package. Research indicates that conglomerate public companies tend to sell at a discount of about 10 to 15 percent from their breakup value, although the relationship is not consistent from company to company nor necessarily over time.

Summary

The types and amounts of appropriate discounts and/or premiums often are the major matters of dispute in the resolution of business valuation differences between parties. The primary discounts are for minority interest and lack of marketability. Market evidence indicates that these discounts are quite substantial, generally greater than most people realize until they have become acquainted with the actual market data.

---

[25]*Estate of Milton Feldmar,* T.C. Memo 1988-429.

When dealing with discounts and/or premiums, it is essential to be very precise as to the level of value to which the discount or premium applies. (This also means the basic valuation work product must be precise in indicating the level of value it has developed.) It is essential that the level of discounts and/or premiums be appropriately matched to the level of value developed.

Many of the same indicators of market value (price/earnings multiples, capitalization of dividends, discounted economic income, price/book value multiples, and so on) used in valuing controlling interests can also be used to value minority interests. However, in valuing minority interests, the focus of value normally is on the business as a going concern rather than in either total or partial liquidation, and relatively more emphasis goes to operating variables, such as earnings and dividends, and less to asset values than when valuing a controlling interest. Also, the assumptions underlying the minority interest valuation usually reflect business as usual rather than any changes that an outside buyer might introduce.

If existing or potential litigation is involved, it is important to understand relevant statutory standards of value and their interpretation by the courts. The range of court case outcomes in disputes regarding valuations of minority interests is extremely wide, even under comparable statutory law. Therefore, in litigated situations, a thorough analysis of the facts and circumstances of the particular interest is essential, along with strong supporting data and careful reasoning that lead to an objective conclusion that is consistent with applicable statutes and legal precedent.

This chapter discussed the concepts, factors influencing, and empirical data sources to help quantify minority interest discounts and control premiums, and it discussed a number of other discounts sometimes applicable. The next chapter analyzes and presents empirical data regarding discounts for lack of marketability.

Bibliography

Abrams, Jay B. "A Breakthrough in Calculating Reliable Discount Rates." *ASA Valuation,* August 1994, pp. 8–24.

Arneson, George S. "Minority Discounts beyond Fifty Percent Can Be Supported." *Taxes,* February 1981, pp. 97–107.

_____. "The Case for No Majority-Control Premium." *Taxes,* March 1981, pp. 190–93.

Asbell, William R. Jr. "An Analysis of When Minority Discounts Will Be Available to Family-Controlled Corporations." *Journal of Taxation,* June 1982, pp. 336–40.

Barron, Michael S. "Is a Discount for Locked-In Capital Gains Tax Justified after General Utilities Repeal?" *Journal of Taxation,* April 1992, pp. 218–23.

Berkery, Peter M. Jr. "IRS Approves Minority Discounts." *Accounting Today*, March 1, 1993, p. 6.

Bolotsky, Michael J. "Adjustments for Differences in Ownership Rights, Liquidity, Information Access, and Information Reliability: An Assessment of 'Prevailing Wisdom' versus the 'Nath Hypotheses.'" *Business Valuation Review,* September 1991, pp. 94–110.

Bolten, Steven E. "Discounts for Stocks of Closely Held Corporations." *Trusts & Estates*, December 1990, pp. 47–48.

Braswell, John M. "Valuing Fractional Interests in Real Estate for Federal Estate and Gift Tax Purposes: A Current Assessment of the Law." *Tax Management Memorandum* 19 (1993), pp. 275 ff.

Bringardner, Bruce W. "Discounting the Value of Undivided Interests in Realty." *Journal of Taxation,* January 1990, pp. 12–16.

Coolidge, H. Calvin. "Fixing Value of Minority Interest in Business: Actual Sales Suggest Discounts as High as 70%." *Estate Planning*, Spring 1975, pp. 138–41.

Curtis, Andrew M. "Discounting Minority Stock Interests in Closely Held Corporations: When and How Much?" *Journal of Taxation of Estates and Trusts,* Spring 1991, pp. 26–30.

Dant, Thomas W., Jr. "Courts Increasing Amount of Discount for a Minority Interest in a Business." *Journal of Taxation,* August 1975, pp. 104–9.

Davidson, Brad. "Valuation of Fractional Interests in Real Estate Limited Partnerships—Another Approach." *Appraisal Journal,* April 1992, pp. 184–94.

DenHollander, Darlene. "Minority Interest Discounts and the Effect of the Section 2704 Regulations." *Tax Lawyer,* Spring 1992, pp. 877–87.

"Discounts Involved in Purchases of Common Stock." *Institutional Investor Study Report of the Securities and Exchange Commission.* Document No. 92-64, Part 5 (March 10, 1971), pp. 2444–56. In U.S. 92d Congress, 1st Session. Washington, DC: U.S. Government Printing Office.

Fiore, Nicholas J. "All in the Family: Determining the Value of a Minority Interest in Stock in a Closely Held Corporation." *Journal of Accountancy,* September 1991, p. 14.

Fishman, Jay E.; Shannon P. Pratt; J. Clifford Griffith; et al. "Premiums and Discounts in Business Valuations." Parts I and II. *FAIR$HARE: The Matrimonial Law Monthly,* May and June 1992, pp. 11–17; 14–16.

Fowler, Anna C. "Valuation of Undivided Interests in Realty: When Do the Parts Sum to Less than the Whole?" *Journal of Real Estate Taxation,* Winter 1986, pp. 123–67.

Gasiorowski, John R. "Is a Discount for Built-In Capital Gain Tax Justified?" *Business Valuation Review,* June 1993, pp. 76–79.

Greenside, Myron. "Discounts in the Valuation of Stock of Closely-Held Investment Corporations." *Massachusetts CPA Review*, July/August 1976, pp. 33–34.

Hall, Lance S. "Minority Interests in Closely Held Real Estate: Lessons from Estate of Berg." *Journal of Real Estate Taxation,* Winter 1993, pp. 170–77.

————. "The Service Limits Discounts for Undivided Interests in Real Estate: Why the Service Is Wrong." *Journal of Real Estate Taxation*, Winter 1994, pp. 344 ff.

————. "Valuation of Fractional Interests: A Business Appraiser's Perspective." *Appraisal Journal,* April 1989, pp. 173–79.

Hall, Lance S., and Timothy G. Polacek. "Higher Discounts in Offing for Real Estate Interests." *Journal of Financial Planning,* April 1994, pp. 76–80.

————. "Strategies for Obtaining the Largest Valuation Discounts." *Estate Planning,* January–February 1994, pp. 38–44.

Harper, John S. Jr. "Minority Shareholders: It's the Cash You Get that Counts: Discounting Expected Future Cash Distributions to Determine the Fair Market Value of a Minority Ownership Interest in a Partnership or Corporation." *Tax Management Estates, Gifts, and Trusts Journal,* November–December 1990, pp. 215–21.

Harper, John S. Jr., and Peter J. Lindquist. "Quantitative Support for Large Minority Discounts in Closely Held Corporations." *Appraisal Journal,* April 1983, pp. 270–77.

Harris, James Edward. "Minority and Marketability Discounts: Are You Taking Enough?" *Probate and Property,* January/February 1990, pp. 6–11.

_____. "Valuation of Closely Held Partnerships and Corporations: Recent Developments Concerning Minority Interest and Lack of Marketability Discounts." *Arkansas Law Review 42* (1989), pp. 649–70.

Herber, William C.; Patrick K. Schmidt; and Robert J. Strachota. "Fairness in Minority Interest Valuation." *Business Valuation Review*, September 1992, pp. 140–46.

Herpe, David A., and Carter Howard. "Minority Discounts Revisited: The Estate of Murphy." *Trusts & Estates,* December 1990, pp. 35–38.

Hitchner, James R., and Gary Roland. "Marketability and Control Govern Value of Family Businesses." *Taxation for Accountants,* January 1994, pp. 24–28.

Hitchner, James R., and Kevin J. Rudd. "The Use of Discounts in Estate and Gift Tax Valuations." *Trusts & Estates,* August 1992, pp. 49–52.; 60.

Hopson, James F., and William J. Sheehy. "Valuation of Minority Discounts in Closely-Held Companies." *National Public Accountant,* December 1993, pp. 30–33.

Horsman, Steven E. "Minority Interest Discounts on Gifts among Family Members." *Trusts & Estates*, July 1987, pp. 54–55.

Ives, H. Bryan III. "Valuation Discounts for Partnership and LLC Member Interests." *Journal of Limited Liability Companies,* Winter 1994, pp. 110–17.

Jankowske, Wayne C. "Valuing Minority Interests in Relation to Guideline Firms." *Business Valuation Review*, December 1991, pp. 139–43.

Jones, Patrick G. "Rev. Rul. 81-253: Will the Service Ever Allow a Minority Discount?" *Estates, Gifts, and Trusts Journal,* March–April 1982, pp. 17–27.

Lansche, James. J. "A Lawyer's Guide to Finding Goodwill Minority Discounts and Going-Concern Value." *Washington State Bar News,* April 1991, pp. 37–39.

Lauer, Eliot, and Bernard V. Preziosi Jr. "A Fair Share for Minority Shareholders." *New York Law Journal,* June 1, 1992, p. 7.

Lease, Ronald C.; John J. McConnell; and Wayne H. Mikkelson. "The Market Value of Control in Publicly-Traded Corporations, *Journal of Financial Economics* 11, 1983, pp. 439–71.

Lerch, Mary Ann. "Discount for Key Man Loss: A Quantitative Analysis." *Business Valuation Review,* December 1992, pp. 183–94.

_____. "Quantitative Measures of Minority Interest Discounts." *Business Valuation Review,* March 1991, pp. 14–20.

Lyons, Robert P., and Michael J. Wilczynski. "Discounting Intrinsic Value." *Trusts & Estates,* February 1989, pp. 22–27.

Lyons, William P., and Martin J. Whitman. "Valuing Closely Held Corporations and Publicly Traded Securities with Limited Marketability: Approaches to Allowable Discounts from Gross Values." *Business Lawyer,* 33 July 1978, pp. 2213–29.

Maher, J. Michael. "An Objective Measure for a Discount for a Minority Interest and Premium for a Controlling Interest." *Taxes,* July 1979, pp. 449–54

_____. "Application of Key Man Discount in the Valuation of Closely-Held Businesses." *Taxes,* June 1977, pp. 377–80.

Moreland, E. R. "The Control Value of Noncontrolling Shares." *Review of Taxation of Individuals*, Fall 1984, pp. 291–348.

Moroney, Robert E. "No Minority Discount for Interest in Trust." *Estate Planning,* May/June 1986, p. 167.

Mulligan, Michael D., and Angela Fick Braly. "Family Limited Partnerships Can Create Discounts." *Estate Planning,* July/August 1994, pp. 195–204.

Murdock, Charles W. "The Evolution of Effective Remedies for Minority Shareholders and its Impact upon Valuation of Minority Shares." *Notre Dame Law Review* 65 (1990), pp. 425–89.

Nath, Eric W. "Control Premiums and Minority Interest Discounts in Private Companies." *Business Valuation Review,* June 1990, pp. 39–46.

_____. "Tale of Two Markets." *Business Valuation Review,* September 1994, pp. 107–12.

Obstler, David M. "The Investment Company Discount: Estate of Folks and Beyond." *Taxes,* January 1983, pp. 47–50.

Oliver, Robert P. "Valuing Fractional Interests in Closely Held Real Estate Companies." *Real Estate Review,* Spring 1986, pp. 44–46.

O'Shea, Keven C., and Robert M. Siwicki. "Stock Price Premiums for Voting Rights Attributable to Minority Interests." *Business Valuation Review,* December 1991, pp. 165–71.

Osteryoung, Jerome S., and Derek Newman. "Key Person Valuation Issues for Private Businesses." *Business Valuation Review,* September 1994, pp. 115–19.

Patchin, Peter J. "Market Discounts for Undivided Minority Interests in Real Estate." *Real Estate Issues,* Fall/Winter 1988, pp. 14–16.

Penn, Thomas A. "Premiums: What Do They Really Measure?" *Mergers & Acquisitions,* Fall 1981, pp. 30–34.

Polacek, Timothy C., and Richard A. Lehn. "Tax Court Allows Sizable Fractional Interest Discounts." *Trusts & Estates,* September 1994, pp. 29–40.

Pratt, Shannon P. "Valuing a Minority Interest in a Closely Held Company." *Practical Accountant,* June 1986, pp. 60–64 ff.

Reynolds, Bruce M. "IRS Modifies Position and Allows Discounts on Intra-Family Stock Transfers." *Taxes,* June 1993, pp. 381–87.

Rothschild, Gideon. "IRS Turns around on Discounts for Intra-Family Gifts of Businesses." *Practical Accountant,* April 1993, pp. 59–60.

Schubert, Walt, and Les Barenbaum. "Control Premiums and the Value of the Closely-Held Firm." *Journal of Small Business Finance* 1, no. 2 (1991), pp. 155–59.

Shenkman, Martin M., and Cal R. Feingold. "Minority, Marketability Discounts Affect Valuation of Partnership Interest." *Real Estate Finance Journal,* Summer 1993, pp. 18–25.

Shishido, Zenichi. "The Fair Value of Minority Stock in Closely Held Corporations." *Fordham Law Review,* October 1993, pp. 65–110.

Simpson, David W. "Minority Interest and Marketability Discounts: A Perspective, Part I." *Business Valuation Review,* March 1991, pp. 7–13.

Sirmans, C. F.; John C. Doiron; and Krisandra A. Guidry. "A Survey of Appraisers Regarding Factors in Discounting Partial Interests." *Appraisal Journal,* October 1993, pp. 600–67.

Solberg, Thomas A. "Valuing Restricted Securities: What Factors Do the Courts and the Service Look For?" *Journal of Taxation,* September 1979, pp. 150–54.

Spradley, Ronald C. "Litigating Rights of Dissenting Shareholders—'Fair Value.'" *Journal of the Missouri Bar,* June 1990, pp. 273–80.

Thompson, Mark S., and Eggert Dagbjartsson. "Market Discounting of Partial Ownership Interests." *Appraisal Journal,* October 1994, pp. 535–41.

Thompson, Mark S., and Eric S. Spunt. "The Widespread Overvaluation of Fractional Ownership Positions." *Trusts & Estates,* June 1993, pp. 62–66.

Timble, Suzanne M. "Built-In Capital Gains: The Argument for Discounting Value." *Illinois Bar Journal,* July 1989, pp. 602–6.

Treynor, Jack L. "The Value of Control." *Financial Analysts Journal,* July–August 1993, pp. 6–9.

Trieschmann, James S.; E. J. Leverett; and Peter J. Shedd. "Valuating Common Stock for Minority Stock and ESOPs in Closely Held Corporations." *Business Horizons,* March–April 1988, pp. 63–69.

Trout, Robert R. "Estimation of the Discount Associated with the Transfer of Restricted Securities." *Taxes,* June 1977, pp. 381–85.

Vaughan, Jack M.; Chris B. Parsons; and Thomas J. Featherston Jr. "Valuation of Community Property Interests in Closely Held Stock: The Minority Interest Discount Controversy Continues." *Community Property Journal,* Winter 1982, pp. 3–14.

Warnken, Wayne L., and Pamela R. Champine. "Securing the Minority Discount for Family Business Transfers." *Trusts & Estates,* April 1993, pp. 49–50 ff.

Chapter 15

Discounts for Lack of Marketability

Perhaps the most difficult aspect in the valuation of closely held stocks is the quantification of the size of the discount to apply to the gross value ascertained for the stock due to the absence of a public market for the stock.[1]

In the absence of an effective exit vehicle, private placements normally sell at a significant discount—often 30%–60% or even more—from freely traded securities.[2]

All other things being equal, an interest in a business is worth more if it is readily marketable or, conversely, worth less if it is not. Investors prefer liquidity to lack of liquidity. Interests in closely held businesses are illiquid relative to most other investments. This problem may be further compounded by restrictions on transfer of interests found in buy–sell agreements or other governing documents in many companies. The appraiser of closely held businesses must quantify the effect of marketability, or lack of it, on the value of the business interest being considered. In many valuations of closely held businesses or business interests, the discount for lack of marketability is the largest single issue to resolve—and an important issue in almost all such valuations.

The first quotation above was written over 20 years ago, just before the mountains of empirical data summarized in this chapter to help quantify the discount for lack of public market started to become available. The data cited in this chapter, along with analysis of the relevant facts and circumstances in each case, will help enormously in the difficult task of quantifying the size of the discount for lack of marketability.

The second (much more contemporaneous) quote above suggests a range of 30 percent to 60 percent discount for lack of marketability, which is a little higher than many people's "conventional wisdom" of a norm of about 35 percent, and is based largely on the data on restricted public company stock transactions that were available in the 1970s and early 1980s. However, this higher range is consistent with the more recent series of data on closely held stock transactions before initial public offerings (IPOs) cited herein, which began to become available in the late 1980s. Actual discounts for lack of marketability are higher than most people realize, and this chapter presents evidence of the market realities of this issue.

Concept and Importance of Marketability

The concept of *marketability* deals with the liquidity of the interest—that is, how quickly and certainly it can be converted to cash at the owner's discretion.

For this text, we will define *marketability* as *the ability to convert the property to cash quickly, with minimum transaction and administrative costs in so doing, and with a high degree of certainty of realizing the expected amount of net proceeds.*

Our definition is consistent with the definition offered by the *Encyclopedia of Banking & Finance,* which focuses on securities for which *some* public market already exists:

---

[1] Milton Gelman, "An Economist-Financial Analyst's Approach to Valuing Stock of a Closely Held Company," *Journal of Taxation,* June 1972, p. 354.

[2] Daniel W. Bielinski, "The Comparable-Company Approach: Measuring the True Value of Privately Held Firms," *Corporate Cashflow Magazine,* October 1990, p. 68.

MARKETABILITY The relative ease and promptness with which a security or commodity may be sold when desired, at a representative current price, without material concession in price merely because of the necessity of sale. Marketability connotes the existence of current buying interest as well as selling interest and is usually indicated by the volume of current transactions and the spread between the bid and asked price for a security—the closer the spread, the closer are the buying and selling interests to agreement on price resulting in actual transactions. To look at it from the standpoint of a dealer maintaining the MARKET, the closer his bid to current transactions and the smaller his markup as to asking prices, the larger the volume will be. By contrast, inactive securities that rarely trade or for which buyers have to be located or sales negotiated are characterized by large spreads between the bid and asked prices.[3]

With respect to the investment characteristics of assets, the terms *marketability* and *liquidity* are sometimes used interchangeably. *The Encyclopedia of Banking & Finance* offers the following:

LIQUIDITY The amount of time required to convert an asset into cash or pay a liability. For noncurrent assets, liquidity generally refers to marketability...

In economics, liquidity is the desire to hold assets in the form of cash. Common elements often included in the concept of liquidity include marketability, realizability, reversibility (as to the difference between buying and selling prices), divisibility of the asset, predictability or capital certainty, and plasticity (ease of maneuvering into and out of various yields after the asset has been acquired). Firms and individuals often prefer to hold money for the sake of holding money. Liquidity may be desired for the following reasons: (1) the transactions motive, (2) the precautionary motive, and (3) the speculative motive. Money is desired to carry out future monetary transactions, to save for a rainy day, or to take advantage of movements in the price level.[4]

The market for securities in the United States is the most liquid market for any kind of property anywhere in the world. This is one of the major reasons companies are able to raise investment capital from both institutional and individual investors: the ability to liquidate the investment immediately, at little cost, and with virtual certainty as to realization of the widely publicized market price. Empirical evidence demonstrates that investors are willing to pay a high premium for this level of liquidity, or, conversely, extract a high discount relative to actively traded securities for stocks or other investment interests that lack this high degree of liquidity.

Benchmark for Discount for Lack of Marketability for Minority Interests

For a "discount" to have a precise meaning, there must be a precise definition of the level of value from which the discount is taken. Since minority ownership interests in stocks and partnership interests are typically valued by reference to prices of relevant actively traded securities, the benchmark for marketability for minority interest securities normally is the active public securities markets. This publicly traded counterpart value is often called the publicly traded equivalent value or value as if publicly traded.

---

[3]Charles J. Woelfel, *Encyclopedia of Banking & Finance*, 10th ed. (Chicago: Probus Publishing Company, 1994), p. 729.
[4]Ibid., p. 703.

In the U.S. public markets, a security holder is able to sell a security over the telephone in seconds, usually at or within a small fraction of a percent of the last price at which the security traded, with a very small commission cost, and receive the cash proceeds within three working days.

By contrast, the universe of realistically potential buyers for most closely held minority ownership securities is an infinitesimally small fraction of the universe of potential buyers for publicly traded securities. In any case, it is *illegal* for a person or company to sell privately held securities to the general public without a registration with either the SEC or the state corporation commission, an expensive and time-consuming process. Furthermore, *a minority stockholder cannot register stock for public trading;* only the company can register its stock for public trading.

Besides the problems of actually trying to sell the stock (and because of them), the liquidity of closely held stock is further impaired by banks and other lending institutions' unwillingness to accept it as loan collateral—as they would accept public stock.

Because of these extreme contrasts between the ability to sell or hypothecate closely held minority stock as compared with publicly traded stock, empirical evidence (as we will see shortly in this chapter) suggests that discounts for lack of marketability for minority interest closely held stocks tend to cluster in the range of 35 to 50 percent from their publicly traded counterparts. Naturally, each situation must be analyzed on the basis of its individual facts and circumstances, which may in some cases justify a discount for lack of marketability above or below this typical range.

Evidence for Quantification of Discount for Lack of Marketability

Two general types of empirical studies have been designed to quantify the discounts for lack of marketability for minority interests in closely held companies:

1. Discounts on sales of restricted shares of publicly traded companies.
2. Discounts on sales of closely held company shares compared to prices of subsequent initial public offerings of the same company's shares.

As noted earlier, the above sources of empirical data indicate that the base from which to take the discount in each case is the actual or estimated price at which the shares could be sold if registered and freely tradable in a public trading market.

The immediately following sections of this chapter summarize the findings of these two (each very extensive) lines of empirical evidence. The second line of studies is more recent and brings us closer to the true discount for lack of marketability for most closely held stocks.

As discussed conceptually in Chapter 3, the data presented in this chapter relate to the quantification of the discount for lack of marketability only, separately and distinctly from any discount for minority interest, which is discussed in the previous chapter.

The body of evidence to quantify discounts for lack of marketability for controlling interests is much less extensive and of a somewhat different nature. This subject will be covered later in the chapter.

Marketability Discounts Evidenced by Prices of Restricted Stocks

One body of empirical evidence specifically isolates the value of the factor of marketability from all other factors: the body of data on transactions in letter stocks. A *letter stock* is identical in all respects to the freely traded stock of a public company except it is restricted from trading on the open market for a certain period. The duration of the restrictions varies from one situation to another. Since marketability is the only difference between the letter stock and its freely tradable counterpart, the appraiser should try to find differences in the price at which letter stock transactions take place compared with open market transactions in the same stock on the same date. This difference will provide some evidence of the price spread between a readily marketable security and one that is identical but subject to certain restrictions on its marketability.

Publicly traded corporations frequently issue letter stock in making acquisitions or raising capital, because the time and cost of registering the new stock with the SEC would make registration at the time of the transaction impractical. Also, founders or other insiders may own portions of a publicly traded company's stock that have never been registered for public trading. Even though such stock cannot be sold to the public on the open market, it may be sold in private transactions under certain circumstances. Such transactions usually must be reported to the SEC and thus become a matter of public record. Therefore, data on the prices of private transactions in restricted securities or letter stocks can be used for comparison with prices of the same but unrestricted securities eligible for trading on the open market.

Since the data represent hundreds of actual arm's-length transactions, anyone who might consider negotiating a deal involving these securities (such as receiving letter stock in connection with selling out to a public company) would be well advised to become familiar with the information. Furthermore, courts frequently reference the data on letter stock discounts in determining the amount of discount for lack of marketability appropriate in valuing interests in closely held companies.

SEC Accounting Release No. 113 specifically points out that the discount for lack of marketability is frequently substantial:

> Restricted securities are often purchased at a discount, frequently substantial, from the market price of outstanding unrestricted securities of the same class. This reflects the fact that securities which cannot be readily sold in the public market place are less valuable than securities which can be sold, and also the fact that by the direct sale of restricted securities, sellers avoid the expense, time and public disclosure which registration entails.[5]

It is exceedingly important to keep in mind that restrictions on the transfer of letter stock eventually lapse, usually within 24 months. At that point, the holder can sell the shares into the existing market, subject to whatever volume and other restrictions may be imposed by SEC Rule 144. Consequently, all other things being equal, shares of closely held stock, which may never have the benefit of a

---

[5]Securities and Exchange Commission, *Accounting Series Release No. 113: Statement Regarding Restricted Securities* (Chicago: Commerce Clearing House, Federal Securities Law Reports, 1977), pp. 62, 285.

public market, would be expected to require a higher discount for lack of marketability than that applicable to restricted stock of a public company. The market does impose a higher discount on closely held stock than on restricted stock of a public company, as we shall see in a later section.

SEC Institutional Investor Study

In a major SEC study of institutional investor actions, one topic was the amount of discount at which transactions in restricted stock (letter stock) occurred compared to the prices of identical but unrestricted stock on the open market.[6] The most pertinent summary tables from that study are reproduced in Exhibits 15–1 and 15–2.

Exhibit 15–1 presents the amounts of discount from open market price on letter stock transactions broken down by the market in which the unrestricted stock trades. The four categories are the New York Stock Exchange, American Stock Exchange, over-the-counter (OTC) reporting companies, and over-the-counter nonreporting companies. A *reporting company* is a publicly traded company that must file forms 10-K, 10-Q, and other information with the SEC. A *nonreporting* company is a company whose stock is publicly traded OTC but is not subject to the same reporting requirements. A company whose stock is traded OTC can avoid becoming an SEC reporting company either by maintaining its total assets under $1 million or by keeping its number of stockholders under 500.

Because many closely held companies are small compared to typical well-known public companies, the smaller nonreporting public companies often may have more characteristics comparable to those of the closely held subject company. However, since they need not report to the SEC, the analyst may have trouble obtaining annual and interim reports for them.

Exhibit 15–1 indicates that, compared to their free-trading counterparts, the discounts on the letter stocks were the least for NYSE-listed stocks and increased, in order, for AMEX-listed stocks, OTC reporting companies, and OTC nonreporting companies. For OTC nonreporting companies, the largest number of observations fell in the 30 to 40 percent discount range. Slightly over 56 percent of the OTC nonreporting companies had discounts greater than 30 percent on the sale of their restricted stock compared with the market price of their free-trading stock. A little over 30 percent of the OTC reporting companies were discounted over 30 percent, and over 52 percent had discounts over 20 percent.

Using midpoints of the discount range groups from Exhibit 15–1—and even including those that sold at premiums for one reason or another—the overall mean average discount was 25.8 percent and the median was about the same. The study also noted, "Average discounts rose over the period January 1, 1966, through June 30, 1969," and average discounts were "27.9 percent in the first half of 1969."[7] For nonreporting OTC companies, which are more likely to resemble most closely held companies, the average discount was 32.6 percent and the median discount again was about the same.

[6]"Discounts Involved in Purchases of Common Stock," in U.S. 92nd Congress, 1st Session, House, *Institutional Investor Study Report of the Securities and Exchange Commission* (Washington, DC: Government Printing Office, March 10, 1971, 5:2444–2456, Document No. 92-64, Part 5).

[7]Ibid., p. 2452.

Exhibit 15–1

Table XIV–45 of SEC *Institutional Investor Study*: Discount by Trading Market

| | Discount | | | | | | | | | | | | | | |
| Trading Market | −15.0% to 0.0% | | 0.1% to 10.0% | | 10.1% to 20.0% | | 20.1% to 30.0% | | 30.1% to 40.0% | | 40.1% to 50.0% | | 50.1% to 80.0% | | Total | |
	No. of Trans-actions	Value of Purchases	No. of Trans-actions	Value of Purchases	No. of Trans-actions	Value of Purchases	No. of Trans-actions	Value of Purchases	No. of Trans-actions	Value of Purchases	No. of Trans-actions	Value of Purchases	No. of Trans-actions	Value of Purchases	No. of Trans-actions	Value of Purchases
Unknown	1	$ 1,500,000	2	$ 2,496,583	1	$ 205,000	0	$0	2	$ 3,332,000	0	$0	1	$ 1,259,995	7	$ 8,793,578
New York Stock Exchange	7	3,760,663	13	15,111,798	13	24,503,988	10	17,954,085	3	11,102,501	1	1,400,000	4	5,005,068	51	78,838,103
American Stock Exchange	2	7,263,060	4	15,850,000	11	14,548,750	20	46,200,677	7	21,074,298	1	44,250	4	4,802,404	49	109,763,439
Over-the-Counter (reporting companies)	11	13,828,757	39	13,613,676	35	38,585,259	30	35,479,946	30	58,689,328	13	9,284,047	21	8,996,406	179	178,477,419
Over-the-Counter (nonreporting companies)	5	8,329,369	9	5,265,925	18	25,122,024	17	11,229,155	25	29,423,584	20	11,377,431	18	13,505,545	112	104,253,033
Total	26	$34,681,849	67	$52,337,982	78	$102,965,021	77	$110,863,863	67	$123,621,711	35	$22,105,728	48	$33,569,418	398	$480,145,572

Exhibit 15–2

Table XIV–47 of SEC *Institutional Investor Study*: Discount by Size of Transaction and Sales of Issuer

| | Discount | | | | | | | | | | | | | | |
| Sales of Issuer (Thousands of Dollars) | 0.1% to 10.0% | | 10.1% to 20.0% | | 20.1% to 30.0% | | 30.1% to 40.0% | | 40.1% to 50.0% | | 50.1% or More | | Total | |
	No. of Trans-actions	Size of Trans-actions	No. of Trans-actions	Size of Trans-actions	No. of Trans-actions	Size of Trans-actions	No. of Trans-actions	Size of Trans-actions	No. of Trans-actions	Size of Trans-actions	No. of Trans-actions	Size of Trans-actions	No. of Trans-actions	Size of Trans-actions
Less than 100	9	$12,566,000	6	$12,267,292	16	$12,197,394	17	$19,642,364	7	$ 2,554,000	11	$ 2,894,999	66	$ 62,122,049
100–999	2	3,877,500	1	1,018,500	1	500,000	0	0	2	1,221,000	7	474,040	13	7,091,040
1,000–4,999	3	2,295,200	10	9,351,738	15	9,865,951	12	10,675,150	13	8,170,747	8	4,605,505	61	44,964,291
5,000–19,999	47	12,750,481	24	21,441,347	25	27,238,210	13	25,986,008	4	1,147,305	6	1,620,015	19	90,183,366
20,000–99,999	17	36,481,954	18	22,231,737	8	11,817,954	6	11,499,250	3	4,372,676	3	605,689	55	87,009,260
100,000 or More	7	10,832,925	10	24,959,483	3	7,903,586	2	2,049,998	0	0	2	1,805,068	24	47,551,060
Total	85	$78,804,060	69	$91,270,097	68	$69,523,095	50	$69,852,770	29	$17,465,728	37	$12,005,316	238	$338,921,066

SOURCE: *Institutional Investor Study Report of the Securities and Exchange Commission*, Chapter XIV, Section F.8., "Discounts Involved in Purchases of Common Stock," H.R. Doc. No. 64, Part 5, 92d Cong., 1st Sess. (1971), pp. 2444–56.

Since the time of the SEC study, the efficiency of the OTC market has improved considerably, aided by the development of inexpensive and virtually instantaneous electronic communications and the advent of the Nasdaq system. Since the market in which restricted OTC shares will eventually trade once the restrictions expire or are removed is now somewhat more efficient, one would expect the differential in discount for restricted listed versus OTC stocks to be less pronounced, and this generally has been the case.

Exhibit 15–2 presents the discounts from open market prices on letter stock transactions broken into six groups by the subject companies' annual sales volume. Companies with the largest sales volumes tended to receive the smallest discounts and companies with the smallest sales volumes the largest discounts. Well over half the companies with sales under $5 million (the three smallest of the six size categories used) had discounts of over 30 percent. However, this may not be a size effect but just further evidence of the influence of the trading market, since most of the largest companies were listed on the NYSE, by far the most liquid market at that time.

One of the outgrowths of the SEC *Institutional Investor Study* was *SEC Accounting Series Releases, No. 113,* dated October 13, 1969, and *No. 118,* dated December 23, 1970, which require investment companies registered under the Investment Company Act of 1940 to disclose their policies for the cost and valuation of their restricted securities. The result was that an ongoing body of data became available on the relationship between restricted stock prices and their freely tradable counterparts, which can provide empirical benchmarks for quantifying marketability discounts.

Gelman Study

In 1972, Milton Gelman published the results of his study of prices paid for restricted securities by four closed-end investment companies specializing in restricted securities investments.[8] From 89 transactions between 1968 and 1970, Gelman found that both the arithmetic average and median discounts were 33 percent and that almost 60 percent of the purchases were at discounts of 30 percent and higher. The distribution of discounts found in the Gelman study is presented in Table 15–1.

Table 15–1

Size of Discount	Number of Common Stocks	% of Total
Less than 15.0%	5	6
15.0–19.9	9	10
20.0–24.9	13	15
25.0–29.9	9	10
30.0–34.9	12	13
35.0–39.9	9	10
40.0 and Over	32	36
Total	89	100

SOURCE: Milton Gelman, An Economist-Financial Analyst's Approach to Valuing Stock of a Closely Held Company," *Journal of Taxation*, June 1972, p. 354.

---

[8]Milton Gelman, "An Economist-Financial Analyst's Approach to Valuing Stock of a Closely Held Company," *Journal of Taxation*, June 1972, pp. 353–54.

Trout Study

In a study of letter stocks purchased by mutual funds from 1968 to 1972, Robert Trout attempted to construct a financial model that would provide an estimate of the discount appropriate for a private company's stock.[9] His multiple regression model involved 60 purchases and found an average discount of 33.45 percent for restricted stock from freely traded stock. As the SEC study showed, he also found that companies with stock listed on national exchanges had lower discounts on their restricted stock transactions than did companies with stock traded over-the-counter.

Moroney Study

In an article published in the March 1973 issue of *Taxes,* Robert E. Moroney presented the results of a study of the prices paid for restricted securities by 10 registered investment companies.[10] The study reflected 146 purchases. The average discount for the 146 transactions was 35.6 percent, and the median discount was 33.0 percent. Exhibit 15–3 shows the results of the study.

Moroney points out:

> It goes without saying that each cash purchase of a block of restricted equity securities fully satisfied the requirement that the purchase price be one, "at which the property would change hands between a willing buyer and a willing seller, neither being under any compulsion to buy or to sell and both having reasonable knowledge of relevant facts." Reg. Sec. 20.2031-1(b)[11]

Moroney contrasts the evidence of the actual cash deals with the lower average discounts for lack of marketability adjudicated in most prior court decisions on gift and estate tax cases. He points out, however, that the empirical evidence on the prices of restricted stocks was not available as a benchmark for quantifying marketability discounts at the time of the prior cases and suggests that higher discounts for lack of marketability be allowed in the future now that the relevant data are available. As Moroney puts it:

> Obviously the courts in the past have overvalued minority interests in closely held companies for federal tax purposes. But most (probably all) of those decisions were handed down without benefit of the facts of life recently made available for all to see.
>
> Some appraisers have for years had a strong gut feeling that they should use far greater discounts for nonmarketability than the courts had allowed. From now on those appraisers need not stop at 35 percent merely because it's perhaps the largest discount clearly approved in a court decision. Appraisers can now cite a number of known arm's-length transactions in which the discount ranged up to 90 percent.[12]

Maher Study

Another well-documented study on marketability discounts for closely held business interests was performed by J. Michael Maher and published in the September 1976 issue of *Taxes.*[13] Maher's approach was similar to Moroney's in that it compared prices paid for restricted stocks with the market prices of their

---

[9]Robert R. Trout, "Estimation of the Discount Associated with the Transfer of Restricted Securities," *Taxes,* June 1977, pp. 381–85.

[10]Robert E. Moroney, "Most Courts Overvalue Closely Held Stocks," *Taxes,* March 1973, pp. 144–54.

[11]Ibid., p. 151.

[12]Ibid., p. 154.

[13]J. Michael Maher, "Discounts for Lack of Marketability for Closely-Held Business Interests," *Taxes,* September 1976, pp. 562–71.

Exhibit 15–3

Original Purchase Discounts for Restricted Stocks
(Discounts from the Quoted Market Value of the Same Corporation's "Free" Stock of the Same Class)

Investment Company	Original Purchase Discount	Number of Blocks
Bayrock Growth Fund, Inc., New York City (formerly Florida Growth Fund)	4 blocks bought at discounts of 12%, 23%, 26%, 66%, respectively	4
Diebold Venture Capital Corp., New York City	6 blocks bought at discounts of 16%, 20%, 20%, 23%, 23%, 50%, respectively	6
Enterprise Fund, Inc., Los Angeles	10 blocks bought at discounts of 31%, 36%, 38%, 40%, 49%, 51%, 55%, 63%, 74%, 87%, respectively	10
Harbor Fund, Inc., Los Angeles	1 block bought at a discount of 14%	1
Inventure Capital Corp., Boston	At acquisition dates all blocks were valued at cost	—
Mates Investment Fund, Inc., New York City	1 block bought at a discount of 62%	1
New America Fund, Inc., Los Angeles (formerly Fund of Letters, Inc.)	32 blocks bought at discounts of 3%, 3%, 14%, 14%, 16%, 21%, 25%, 26%, 27%, 33%, 33%, 33%, 35%, 36%, 36%, 37%, 37%, 39%, 40%, 40%, 43%, 44%, 46%, 47%, 49%, 51%, 53%, 53%, 56%, 57%, 57%, 58%, respectively	32
Price Capital Corp., New York City	7 blocks bought at discounts of 15%, 29%, 29%, 32%, 40%, 44%, 52%, respectively	7
SMC Investment Corp., Los Angeles	11 blocks bought at 30% premium, discounts of 4%, 25%, 26%, 32%, 33%, 34%, 38%, 46%, 48%, 50%, 78%, respectively	12
Value Line Development Capital Corp., New York City	35 blocks bought at discounts of 10%, 15%, 15%, 15%, 15%, 15%, 20%, 23%, 28%, 28%, 28%, 30%, 30%, 30%, 30%, 30%, 32.5%, 35%, 40%, 40%, 40%, 40%, 40%, 40%, 45%, 50%, 50%, 50%, 50%, 53%, 55%, 55%, 65%, 70%, 90%, respectively	35
Value Line Special Situations Fund, Inc., New York City	37 blocks bought at discounts of 10%, 13%, 15%, 15%, 17%, 17%, 20%, 20%, 20%, 23%, 25%, 25%, 25%, 25%, 26.5%, 27%, 27%, 30%, 30%, 30%, 30%, 30%, 30%, 30%, 30%, 33%, 37.5%, 40%, 40%, 40%, 40%, 45%, 55%, 56%, 56%, 60%, 81%, respectively	38

SOURCE: Robert E. Moroney, "Most Courts Overvalue Closely Held Stocks," *Taxes* (March 1973), pp. 154-55. Published and copyrighted 1973 by Commerce Clearing House, Inc., in Chicago.

unrestricted counterparts. He found that mutual funds were not purchasing restricted securities during 1974 and 1975, which were very depressed years for the stock market. Therefore, the data actually used covered the five-year period from 1969 through 1973. The study showed, "The mean discount for lack of marketability for the years 1969–73 amounted to 35.43 percent."[14] He further eliminated the top and bottom 10 percent of purchases in an effort to remove especially high- and low-risk situations. The result was almost identical with the outliers removed, with a mean discount of 34.73 percent.

Maher concludes:

The result I have reached is that most appraisers underestimate the proper discount for lack of marketability. The results seem to indicate that this discount should be about 35 percent. Perhaps this makes sense because by committing funds to restricted common stock, the willing buyer (a) would be denied the opportunity to take advantage of other investments, and (b) would continue to have his investment at the risk of the business until the shares could be offered to the public or another buyer is found.

---

[14]Ibid., p. 571.

The 35 percent discount would not contain elements of a discount for a minority interest because it is measured against the current fair market value of securities actively traded (other minority interests). Consequently, appraisers should also consider a discount for a minority interest in those closely held corporations where a discount is applicable.[15]

Standard Research Consultants Study

In 1983, Standard Research Consultants (SRC) analyzed recent private placements of common stock to test the current applicability of the SEC study.[16] SRC studied 28 private placements of restricted common stock from October 1978 through June 1982. Discounts ranged from 7 percent to 91 percent, with a median of 45 percent.

Willamette Management Associates Study

Willamette Management Associates (Willamette) analyzed private placements of restricted stocks for the period of January 1, 1981, through May 31, 1984. The early part of this unpublished study overlapped the last part of the SRC study, but few transactions took place during the period of overlap. Most of the transactions in the Willamette study occurred in 1983.

Willamette identified 33 transactions during that period that could reasonably be classified as arm's length and for which the price of the restricted shares could be compared directly with the price of trades in identical but unrestricted shares of the same company at the same time. The median discount for the 33 restricted stock transactions compared to the prices of their freely tradable counterparts was 31.2 percent.

The slightly lower average percentage discounts for private placements during this time may be attributable to the somewhat depressed pricing in the public stock market, which in turn reflected the recessionary economic conditions prevalent during most of the period of the study. This study basically supports the long-term average discount of 35 percent for transactions in restricted stock compared with the prices of their freely tradable counterparts.

Silber Study

In a 1991 article in the *Financial Analysts Journal,* William L. Silber presented the results of analysis of 69 private placements of common stock of publicly traded companies between 1981 and 1988.[17] He found that the average discount was 33.75 percent, very consistent with earlier studies.

He also found that the size of the discount tended to be higher for private placements that were larger as a percentage of the shares outstanding. He found a small effect on the discount on the basis of the size of the company as measured by revenues. "Tripling the revenues from $40 million (the mean of his sample) to $120 million increases the relative price of the restricted shares by only 2.9 points."[18]

---

[15]Ibid.

[16]Charles H. Stryker and William Pittock, "Revenue Ruling 77-287 Revisited," *SRC Quarterly Reports,* Spring 1983, pp. 1–3.

[17]William L. Silber, "Discounts on Restricted Stock: The Impact of Illiquidity on Stock Prices," *Financial Analysts Journal,* July–August 1991, pp. 60–64.

[18]Ibid., p. 64.

FMV Opinions, Inc., Study

An article in the January/February 1994 issue of *Estate Planning* referenced a study by FMV Opinions, Inc., that "examined over 100 restricted stock transactions from 1979 through April 1992."[19] The FMV study found a mean discount of only 23 percent.

Summary of Studies on Restricted Stock Transactions

The nine independent studies of restricted stock transactions reported above cover several hundred transactions spanning the late 1960s through 1992. Considering the number of independent researchers and the very long time span encompassing a wide variety of market conditions, the results are remarkably consistent, as summarized in Table 15–2.

In many of the cases of restricted stock transactions tabulated in Table 15–2, the purchaser of the stock had the right to register the stock for sale in the existing public market. Sometimes investors get a commitment from the issuer to register the securities at a certain future date; sometimes investors have "demand" rights, where they can force the issuer to register the securities at a time of their choosing. Sometimes they get "piggyback" rights where there is no obligation other than to include the securities on any future registration that the issuer undertakes. And sometimes the purchasers have to rely on Rule 144, where they can sell after two years if other parts of the rule are followed. In recent years, more transactions have occurred under Rule 144(a), which relaxes some of the restrictions on such transactions, thus making the restricted securities more marketable. In any case, they generally expect to be able to resell the stock in the public market in the foreseeable future.

The IRS specifically recognized the relevance of restricted stock transaction data as evidence for quantifying the discount for lack of marketability in Revenue Ruling 77-287, presented in full as Exhibit 28–3 in Chapter 28, "Taxation Planning and Compliance—Gifts and Estates."

Studies of Private Transactions before Public Offerings

Before the 1980s, virtually all the empirical research directed at quantifying the value of ready marketability, or the discount for lack of it, focused on comparisons between the prices of freely tradable shares of stock and restricted but otherwise identical shares of stock. Observers agreed that discounts for lack of marketability for shares of closely held companies were greater than those for restricted shares of publicly held companies, since the closely held shares had no established market in which they could eventually sell following the removal of certain trading restrictions. However, data for quantifying how much greater this discount should be had not yet been developed and analyzed.

---

[19]Lance S. Hall and Timothy C. Polacek, "Strategies for Obtaining the Largest Valuation Discounts," *Estate Planning*, January/February 1994, pp. 38–44.

Table 15–2

Summary of Restricted Stock Studies

Study	Years Covered in Study	Average Discount (%)
SEC Overall Average[a]	1966–69	25.8%
SEC Nonreporting OTC Companies[a]	1966–69	32.6
Gelman[b]	1968–70	33.0
Trout[c]	1968–72	33.5[k]
Moroney[d]	[j]	35.6
Maher[e]	1969–73	35.4
Standard Research Consultants[f]	1978–82	45.0[k]
Willamette Management Associates[g]	1981–84	31.2[k]
Silber[h]	1981–88	33.8
FMV Opinions, Inc.[i]	1979–April 1992	23.0

[a] From "Discounts Involved in Purchases of Common Stock (1966–1969)," *Institutional Investor Study Report of the Securities and Exchange Commission*, H.R. Doc. No. 64, Part 5, 92nd Congress, 1st Session, 1971, pp. 2444–2456.

[b] From Milton Gelman, "An Economist-Financial Analyst's Approach to Valuing Stock of a Closely Held Company," *Journal of Taxation*, June 1972, pp. 353–54.

[c] From Robert R. Trout, "Estimation of the Discount Associated with the Transfer of Restricted Securities," *Taxes*, June 1977, pp. 381–85.

[d] From Robert E. Moroney, "Most Courts Overvalue Closely Held Stocks," *Taxes*, March 1973, pp. 144–54.

[e] From J. Michael Maher, "Discounts for Lack of Marketability for Closely-Held Business Interests," *Taxes*, September 1976, pp. 562–71.

[f] From "Revenue Ruling 77-287 Revisited," *SRC Quarterly Reports*, Spring 1983, pp. 1–3.

[g] From Willamette Management Associates study (unpublished).

[h] From William L. Silber, "Discounts on Restricted Stock: The Impact of Illiquidity on Stock Prices," *Financial Analysts Journal*, July–August 1991, pp. 60–64.

[i] From Lance S. Hall and Timothy C. Polacek, "Strategies for Obtaining the Largest Valuation Discounts," *Estate Planning*, January/February 1994, pp. 38–44.

[j] Although the years covered in this study are likely to be 1969–72, no specific years were given in the published account.

[k] Median discounts.

During the 1980s, an investment banking firm and a valuation consulting firm independently undertook the development of data with which to address this question. The research proceeded along basically parallel lines, although each firm was unaware of the other's efforts until their respective research was far along and each had enough data to reach some conclusions.

Both firms utilized data from *registration statements*, forms that companies must file with the SEC when they sell securities to the public. Each of the series of studies reported in the following sections used data from these forms to analyze prices of the private transactions relative to the public offering prices and market prices following initial public offerings.

Robert W. Baird & Company Studies

Six studies were conducted under the direction of John D. Emory, first vice president of appraisal services at Robert W. Baird & Company, a regional investment banking firm headquartered in Milwaukee, Wisconsin.[20] The studies covered various time periods from 1981 through 1993.

---

[20]John D. Emory, "The Value of Marketability as Illustrated in Initial Public Offerings of Common Stock—January 1980 through June 1981," *Business Valuation News*, September 1985, pp. 21–24, also in *ASA Valuation*, June 1986, pp. 62–66; "The Value of Marketability as Illustrated in Initial Public Offerings of Common Stock, January 1985 through June 1986," *Business Valuation Review*, December 1986, pp. 12–15; "The Value of Marketability as Illustrated in Initial Public Offerings of Common Stock (August 1987–January 1989)," *Business Valuation Review*, June 1989, pp. 55–57; "The Value of Marketability as Illustrated in Initial Public Offerings of Common Stock, February 1989–July 1990," *Business Valuation Review*, December 1990, pp. 114–16; "The Value of Marketability as Illustrated in Initial Public Offerings of Common Stock, August 1990 through January 1992," *Business Valuation Review*, December 1992, pp. 208–12; "The Value of Marketability as Illustrated in Initial Public Offerings of Common Stock, February 1992 through July 1993," *Business Valuation Review*, March 1994, pp. 3–5.

The basic methodology for the six studies was identical. The population of companies in each study consisted of initial public offerings during the respective period in which Baird & Company either participated in or received prospectuses. The prospectuses of these 1,191 offerings were analyzed to determine the relationship between the price at which the stock was initially offered to the public and the price at which the latest private transaction occurred up to five months before the initial public offering. Emory gives the following explanatory statements regarding the studies:

> In most cases, the transactions were stated to have been at fair market value. All ultimately would have had to be able to withstand Securities and Exchange Commission (SEC), IRS, or judicial review, particularly in light of the subsequent public offering. The transactions primarily took one of two forms: (1) the granting of stock options at the stock's then fair market value; or (2) the direct sale of stock.
>
> In order to provide a reasonable comparison of prices before and at the IPO, I felt it necessary both for the company to have been financially sound, and for the private transaction to have occurred within a period of five months prior to the offering date.[21]

Following the above guidelines, and after eliminating development-stage companies (companies with a history of operating losses) and companies with no transactions within the five months before the initial public offering, 173 qualifying transactions remained in the six studies.

The mean discount for the 173 transactions was 47 percent and the median 46 percent. The fact that these averages are a little more than 10 percentage points greater than those shown in restricted stock studies is about what one might reasonably expect, since the transactions occurred when there was not yet any established market for the stocks at all. A summary of the results of each of the six Baird studies is presented as Exhibit 15–4.

Emory concludes with the following observations:

> Since an initial public offering often takes four or five months from conception to completion, the transactions mentioned in the prospectuses in the study would almost certainly have reflected the likelihood of marketability within the next half year.

The final question to be answered is that if these kinds of discounts are appropriate for promising situations where marketability is probable, but not a certainty, how much greater should discounts be for the typical company's stock that has no marketability, little if any chance of ever becoming marketable, and is in a neutral to unpromising situation?

It is apparent that the lack of marketability is one of the most important components of value, and the public marketplace emphasizes this point.[22]

Willamette Management Associates Studies

Over the last several years, Willamette Management Associates has conducted 12 studies on the prices of private stock transactions relative to those of subsequent public offerings of stock of the same companies. The 12 studies covered the years 1975 through 1992.

---

[21]Emory, "The Value of Marketability, February 1992 through July 1993," p. 14.

[22]Ibid., pp. 3–4. Further elaboration is to be found in "Letters to the Editor," *Business Valuation Review,* June 1987, pp. 93–94, and September 1987, pp. 143–45.

Exhibit 15–4

The Value of Marketability as Illustrated in Initial Public Offerings of Common Stock

Study	Number of IPO Prospectuses Reviewed	Number of Qualifying Transactions	Discount Mean	Median
1991–93	443	54	45%	44%
1990–92	266	35	42	40
1989–90	157	23	45	40
1987–89	98	27	45	45
1985–86	130	21	43	43
1980–81	97	13	60	66
		173 (Total)	47% (Mean)	46% (Mean)

SOURCE: John D. Emory, "The Value of Marketability as Illustrated in Initial Public Offerings of Common Stock," February 1992 through July 1993, *Business Valuation Review* (March 1994), p. 3.

The Willamette studies differed from the Baird studies in several respects. One important difference was that the source documents for the Willamette studies were complete SEC registration statements primarily on Form S-1 and Form S-18, whereas the source documents for the Baird studies were prospectuses. Although the prospectus constitutes a portion of the registration statement, it is required to disclose only transactions with affiliated parties. Form S-1 and Form S-18 registration statements require disclosure of *all* private transactions in the stock within the three years before the public offering, in a section of the registration statement separate from the prospectus portion. The Willamette studies attempted to include only transactions that were on an arm's-length basis. The data analyzed included sales of stock in private placements and repurchases of treasury stock by the companies. All stock option transactions and sales of stock to corporate insiders were eliminated unless there was reason to believe they were bona fide transactions for full value. In some cases, the companies were contacted by telephone to either validate the arm's-length nature of the transaction or eliminate the transaction from the study. Therefore, although there was considerable overlap in the 13 years of public offerings studied by Baird and the 19 years of offerings studied by Willamette, the actual transactions included in the two sets of studies differed almost totally.

The Willamette studies considered all initial public offerings in the files of the *IPO Reporter*. According to the *IPO Reporter*, they included all public offerings during the respective period. Eliminated from each of the studies were financial institutions, natural resource companies, offerings priced at $1 or less per share, and offerings that included units or warrants, since such offerings might be thought to have unique characteristics. The private transactions analyzed took place from 1 to 36 months before the initial public offering. If a company had more than one transaction that met the study's criteria, all such transactions were included.

Each private transaction price was compared with the subsequent public offering price. In addition, for each transaction for which meaningful earnings data were available in the registration statement as of both the private transaction and public offering dates, the price-earnings multiple of each private transaction was compared with the subsequent public offering price-earnings multiple.

Because some of the companies had no meaningful earnings as of the private transaction date and/or the public offering date, the population of transactions compared on a P/E multiple basis was a subset of the population of transactions compared on a price basis.

Also, because the private transactions occurred over a period of up to three years before the public offering, Willamette made adjustments to reflect differences in market conditions for stocks of the respective industries between the time of each private transaction and the time of each subsequent public offering. Prices were adjusted by an industry stock price index. P/E multiples were adjusted for differences in the industry average P/E multiple between the time of the private transaction and that of the public offering.

For the price comparison, the formula used to derive the discount for the private transaction price from the public offering price was as follows:

Formula 15–1

$$\frac{P_o - P_p \left(\dfrac{I_o}{I_p} \right)}{P_o}$$

where:

P_o = Price per share of the public offering
P_p = Price per share of the private transaction
I_o = Industry price index at time of offering
I_p = Industry price index at time of private transaction

As an example, consider the public offering at $10 per share of Riley's Restaurant, an upscale gourmet restaurant, whose largest stockholder and chairman of the board was Rusty Riley, a prominent entrepreneur who knew a good thing when he saw it. About a year before the $10 per share offering, Riley had arranged for the company to buy back the stock held by a major outside investor for $4 per share. The restaurant industry stock price index stood at 77 at the time of the public offering and at 70 at the time of the private transaction. Substituting in the above formula, the percentage discount of the private transaction price from the public offering price, adjusted for the change in the industry price index, was as follows:

Formula 15–2

$$\frac{\$10 - \$4 \left(\dfrac{77}{70} \right)}{\$10} = \frac{\$19 - \$4.40}{\$10} = 56\%$$

where:

$10 = Price per share of the public offering
 $4 = Price per share of the private transaction
 77 = Industry price index at time of offering
 70 = Industry price index at time of private transaction

For the price-earnings multiple comparison, the formula used to derive the discount for the private transaction price from the public offering price was as follows:

Formula 15–3

$$\frac{P/E_0 - P/E_p \left(\dfrac{IP/E_o}{IP/E_p} \right)}{P/E_o}$$

where:

P/E_o = Price/earnings multiple of the public offering

P/E_p = Price/earnings multiple of the private transaction

IP/E_o = Industry average price/earnings multiple at the time of the public offering

IP/E_p = Industry average price/earnings multiple at the time of the private transaction

Continuing with the same example, assume that Riley's earnings for the year before the offering were $1 per share. Thus, the offering was at a P/E multiple of 10 ($10/$1 = 10) and Riley's earnings for the year prior to the private transaction were $.80 per share and the private transaction was at a P/E multiple of 5 ($4/$.80 = 5). At the time of the public offering, the restaurant industry average P/E multiple was 12, and at the time of the private transaction it was 10. Substituting the information in the above formula, the percentage discount of the private transaction P/E multiple from the public offering P/E multiple, adjusted for the change in the industry average P/E multiple, was as follows:

Formula 15–4

$$\frac{10 - 5 \left(\dfrac{12}{10} \right)}{10} = \frac{10 - 6}{10} = 40\%$$

where:

10 = Price/earnings multiple of the public offering

 5 = Price/earnings multiple of the private transaction

12 = Industry average price/earnings multiple at the time of the public offering

10 = Industry average price/earnings multiple at the time of the private transaction

The results of the 14 Willamette studies described above are summarized in Exhibit 15–5. As the table indicates, the average discounts varied from period to period, but in all cases, were higher than the average discounts shown in the studies for restricted stocks of companies that already had an established public trading market—which is the result one would expect.

While both sets of discount data deserve attention, we believe the data based on P/E multiples present a more accurate estimate of the amount of discount attributable to lack of marketability, since it eliminates the effects of both changes in the subject company's earnings and changes in market P/E multiples.

In one of the studies, Willamette checked trading prices six months after the initial public offering to see whether the IPO prices were upwardly or downwardly biased compared to a more seasoned market price. While after six months some prices increased and some decreased, the *average* change from the IPO price was insignificant.

Exhibit 15–5

Average Discounts for Private Transaction Prices Compared with Public Offering Prices

**Summary of Discounts for Private Transaction Prices
Compared to Public Offering Prices
Adjusted for Changes in Industry Stock Price Indexes**

Time Period	Number of Companies Analyzed	Number of Transactions Analyzed	Median Discount
1975–78	28	59	64.3%
1979	11	30	68.2
1980–82	98	185	68.2
1984	53	94	80.5
1985	39	75	61.3
1986	NA	NA	NA
1987	NA	NA	NA
1988	NA	NA	NA
1989	NA	NA	NA
1990	38	68	50.4
1991	75	152	39.1
1992	86	216	64.9

**Summary of Discounts for Private Transaction P/E Multiples
Compared to Public Offering P/E Multiples
Adjusted for Changes in Industry P/E Multiples**

Time Period	Number of Companies Analyzed	Number of Transactions Analyzed	Median Discount
1975–78	17	31	54.7%
1979	9	17	62.9
1980–82	58	113	55.5
1984	20	33	74.4
1985	18	25	43.2
1986	47	74	47.5
1987	25	40	43.8
1988	13	19	51.8
1989	9	19	50.4
1990	17	23	48.5
1991	27	34	31.8
1992	36	75	52.4

SOURCE: Willamette Management Associates.

For certain time periods, Willamette examined the effect of the size of the block transacted relative to the total shares outstanding. For one period, no discernible difference was evident. For another time period, more significant size blocks (10 to 30 percent of the outstanding shares) had greater average discounts than the overall average for the same time period, supporting the findings of the Silber and FMV restricted stock studies.

Summary of Conclusions from Private Transaction Studies

The evidence from the Baird and Willamette studies taken together seems compelling. The studies covered hundreds of transactions over 19 years. Average differentials between private transaction prices and public market prices varied under different market conditions, ranging from about 40 to 63 percent, after eliminating the outliers. This is very strong support for the hypothesis that the fair market values of minority ownership interests in privately held companies are greatly discounted from their publicly traded counterparts.

Option Pricing as a Proxy for Discount for Lack of Marketability

A recent article in the *Business Valuation Review* suggests estimating the cost of a put option as a proxy for measuring discounts for marketability. Chaffe gives the following explanation for this approach:

> When provided with an option to sell, otherwise nonmarketable shares are given marketability. (For instance, we see this type of provision in Employee Share Ownership Plans where, in such cases, marketable level values are found.)
>
> Following this logic, the cost or price of the option to sell (a put option) represents all (or a major portion) of the discount to be taken from the marketable price to price the nonmarketable shares.
>
> To summarize, if one holds restricted or nonmarketable stock and purchases an option to sell those shares at the free market price, the holder has, in effect, purchased marketability for the shares. The price of the put is the discount for lack of marketability.[23]

The article goes on to present empirical results of a study of the cost of such options. He concludes, "A range of put prices of approximately 28% to 41% of the marketable price is shown at the two-year intercept."[24] This is supportive of the discounts concluded in restricted stock studies, where restrictions usually lapse in two years or less.

Chaffe goes on to disclose, "At the four-year intercept, these ranges are 32% to 49%, after which time increases do not substantially change the put price."[25] This range is supportive of the higher discounts concluded in the Baird and Willamette studies, where there was no guaranteed market within two years.

Regulation S Transactions

Regulation S, enacted in 1990, allows public companies to sell stock to offshore investors without registering the shares with the SEC. After a holding period of *only 40 days* the shares may be resold in the United States, still without having to be registered. *The Wall Street Journal* reports:

> Onyx, of Miami, tells public companies they can raise millions of dollars in less than a month by selling stock at discounts of 20% to 30% below market prices to offshore buyers who won't sell the shares for at least 40 days.[26]

The *Journal* reports, "Nearly all of the large U.S. investment banks have marketed Regulation S transactions." Despite the required holding period being only 40 days, the *Journal* cites several specific transactions at discounts in excess of 30 percent. The short required holding period enables buyers to sell short the equivalent freely tradable shares in the U.S. market and then cover their short sales with shares bought in the Regulation S transaction.

With discounts of this magnitude for stocks with such limited resale restrictions, is it any wonder investors demand much larger discounts for stocks for which no market exists?

---

[23]David B. H. Chaffe III, "Option Pricing as a Proxy for Discount for Lack of Marketability in Private Company Valuations," *Business Valuation Review,* December 1993, p. 182.

[24]Ibid., p. 184.

[25]Ibid.

[26]Laurie P. Cohen, "Rule Permitting Offshore Stock Sales Yields Deals that Spark SEC Concerns," the *Wall Street Journal,* April 26, 1994, p. C1.

Discounts for Lack of Marketability for Controlling Interests

It often is necessary to agree on the cash equivalent value today (or as of some date certain) for a controlling interest in a closely held business, whether or not the business will actually be sold. Examples of this cash equivalency analysis include *federal estate taxes* (in the case of a death of the controlling equity holder) or the value of a closely held business as *marital property* (in the case of a divorce).

Federal estate taxes, by law, require a cash equivalency value as of a date certain. The taxes themselves are paid in cash—not in kind by tendering shares of stock. Therefore, it seems reasonable to make an adjustment from the estimated (but uncertain) sale value of the subject controlling business interest at some undetermined time in the future to a cash equivalency value as of the valuation date, reflecting the time, costs, and risks attendant to achieving such a sale. This valuation adjustment—or discount—is often referred to as a discount for lack of marketability, or as a discount for illiquidity.

In many reported decisions, the U.S. Tax Court has recognized that discounts for lack of marketability for controlling interests in closely held companies are appropriate. The courts have used language such as the following:

> Even controlling shares in a nonpublic corporation suffer from lack of marketability because of the absence of a ready private placement market and the fact that flotation costs would have to be incurred if the corporation were to publicly offer its stock.[27]

Similarly, in the marital dissolution situation, the spouse most actively involved in the business usually gets the controlling stock in the closely held corporation; and the nonoperating spouse usually gets much more liquid assets, such as cash, marketable securities, and real estate.

A rational argument can be made that the same factors discussed above should be reflected in the value of the illiquid controlling block of stock of the closely held business for marital dissolution valuation purposes.

Marketability Factors Affecting Controlling Interests

Unlike the owner of publicly traded securities, the owner of a controlling block of stock in a closely held corporation cannot call up a securities broker, sell that controlling interest in seconds at a predetermined price and with a nominal transaction commission, and realize the cash proceeds of the sale in three business days. Rather, selling a controlling interest in a closely held company is a lengthy, expensive, and uncertain undertaking.

The typical means of liquidating a controlling ownership interest in a closely held business include:

1. Consummate a public offering of the controlling block of stock.
2. Sell the company in a private transaction:
    a. Sell the overall business enterprise (and equitably allocate the sale proceeds to the minority stockholders).
    b. Sell the controlling block of stock only (either to the other, minority ownership stockholders or to an independent third-party buyer).

---

[27]*Estate of Woodbury G. Andrews*, 79 T.C. 938 (1982).

Under various conditions in the public capital markets for stocks and the merger/acquisition markets for companies, one or more of the above transactional alternatives may be clearly more or less attractive—at any point. The values realizable from these transactional alternatives usually have some relationship to each other. This is because potential business acquirers may themselves be public companies, and there is a tendency for public company acquirers to avoid stock price dilution by paying a higher P/E multiple for an acquisition target than the multiple at which their own stock is selling. In the highly valued public markets of 1993 and 1994, public market minority interest valuation multiples were as high or higher than those attainable by selling a controlling interest in many industries.

The controlling owner of a closely held company who wishes to liquidate a controlling equity interest generally faces the following transactional considerations:

1. Uncertain time horizon to complete offering or sale.
2. Cost to prepare for and execute offering or sale.
3. Risk as to eventual price.
4. Form of transaction proceeds.
5. Inability to hypothecate.

Time Horizon. It takes many months, and in some cases years, to complete either an offering or a sale. To some extent, the time factor may be offset by cash flows available to the owner awaiting sale, if they are equal to or greater than the company's cost of capital on a stand-alone basis.

Costs. There will be many costs attendant to the sale:

1. Auditing and accounting fees, to provide potential buyers or underwriters the financial information and assurances they demand.
2. Legal costs, at a minimum to draft all the necessary documents and often to clear away potential perceived contingent liabilities and/or to negotiate warranties.
3. Administrative costs on the part of management to deal with the accountants, lawyers, potential buyers, and/or their representatives.
4. Transaction and brokerage costs, if a business broker, investment banker, or other transactional intermediary is involved.

The most comprehensive, and still most often quoted, study on the cost of flotation is one published by the SEC in December 1974, which covered 1,599 initial public offerings. The average direct expenses of the offering, broken down by size of offering, are presented in Exhibit 15–6.

The typical costs of a public flotation today are considerably greater than they were in 1972. For example, for an equity value offering under $7.5 million (the maximum allowed at the time of this writing under a form S-18 registration), you rarely see direct compensation to the underwriters of less than 12 to 13 percent—compared to the 6.7 percent presented in Exhibit 15–6 for issues of $5.00 million to $9.99 million. (The SEC and many state regulators tend to frown on underwriting commissions over 15 percent, but smaller offerings often approach this figure.) Furthermore, other direct transactional expenses currently tend to run higher than those presented in Exhibit 15–6. A summary of another empirical study of the direct expenses of going public is presented in Exhibit 15–7.

Exhibit 15–6

Cost of Flotation

Size of Issue (Millions)	Number	Compensation (Percent of Gross Proceeds)	Other Expense (Percent of Gross Proceeds)
Under .5	43	13.24%	10.35%
.5 – .99	227	12.48	8.26
1.0 – 1.99	271	10.60	5.87
2.0 – 4.99	450	8.19	3.71
5.0 – 9.99	287	6.70	2.03
10.0 – 19.99	170	5.52	1.11
20.0 – 49.99	109	4.41	0.62
50.0 – 99.99	30	3.94	0.31
100.0 – 499.99	12	3.03	0.16
Over 500.00	0	—	—
Total/Averages	1,599	8.41%	4.02%

SOURCE: *Cost of Flotation of Registered Issues 1971–72.* (Washington, DC: Securities and Exchange Commission, 1974), p. 9.

Risk. There is a high degree of risk as to the amount of the actual sale price that will be realized relative to the estimated sale price, partly because of a reasonable margin of error in business valuation estimates and partly because internal and/or external factors may influence the business value during the sale negotiation period.

Furthermore, in many cases, there is substantial risk as to whether the business can be sold at all. As Jay Abrams notes in the September 1994 *Business Valuation Review,* "The market for privately held businesses is very thin and fairly volatile. Far more than half of the businesses offered for sale never sell."[28]

There is always considerable risk as to whether an initial public offering can actually be completed at any given stock price. The capital markets are more or less receptive to stocks of companies in different industries at different points, and some companies will not be accepted by the public markets at all.

Form of Proceeds. Even when a sale is completed, the proceeds may not be all in cash. Often, the seller may receive part of the proceeds in a note or contingent compensation—or in stock of the acquiring company (and usually restricted stock, if the acquiring company is a publicly traded company).

As presented in Exhibit 15–8 the trend over the last 20 years has been away from straight cash for assets or cash for stock acquisition structures. Whereas from 1975 to 1979, almost half the reported business acquisitions were for all cash, this figure was halved by 1993–94, with only about 25 percent of the acquisitions all cash, 40 percent all stock, and 35 percent a combination of cash and stock. In most of these cases, the stock (in the stock for assets or stock transfer) is restricted stock. Accordingly, the cash equivalency value of the business sale transaction may be substantially lower than the announced deal price.

---

[28]Jay B. Abrams, "Discount for Lack of Marketability: A Theoretical Model," *Business Valuation Review,* September 1994, p. 133.

Exhibit 15–7

Direct Expenses of Going Public as a Percentage of Gross Proceeds (1977–1982)

Gross Proceeds[a] ($)	Number of Offers	Underwriting Discount[b] (%)	Other Expenses[c] (%)	Total Cash Expenses (%)
Firm Commitment Offers				
100,000–1,999,999	68	9.84%	9.64%	19.48%
2,000,000–3,999,999	165	9.83	7.60	17.43
4,000,000–5,999,999	133	9.10	5.67	14.77
6,000,000–9,999,999	122	8.03	4.31	12.34
10,000,000–120,174,195	176	7.24	2.10	9.34
All offers	664	8.67	5.36	14.03
Best-Efforts Offers				
100,000–1,999,999	175	10.63%	9.52%	20.15%
2,000,000–3,999,999	146	10.00	6.21	16.21
4,000,000–5,999,999	23	9.86	3.71	13.57
6,000,000–9,999,999	15	9.80	3.42	13.22
10,000,000–120,174,195	5	8.03	2.40	10.43
All offers	364	10.26	7.48	17.74

[a]Gross proceeds categories are nominal; no price level adjustments have been made.
[b]The underwriting discount is the commission paid by the issuing firm; this is listed on the front page of the firm's prospectus.
[c]The other expenses figure comprises accountable and nonaccountable fees of the underwriters, cash expenses of the issuing firm for legal, printing, and auditing fees, and other out-of-pocket costs. These other expenses are described in footnotes on the front page of the issuing firm's prospectus. None of the expense categories includes the value of warrants granted to the underwriter, a practice that is common with best-efforts offers.

SOURCE: Jay R. Ritter, "The Costs of Going Public," *Journal of Financial Economics,* January 1987, p. 272.

Exhibit 15–8

Payment Trends (1975–1994)

Year	Total Number Disclosing Form of Payment	Cash		Stock		Combination		Debt	
1975	1,225	585	48%	325	27%	285	23%	30	2%
1976	1,255	656	52	327	26	250	20	22	2
1977	1,238	663	54	322	26	224	18	29	2
1978	1,182	539	46	353	30	273	23	17	1
1979	1,233	654	53	323	26	247	20	9	1
1980	1,121	522	47	345	31	237	21	17	1
1981	1,309	542	42	448	34	301	23	18	1
1982	1,083	405	38	317	29	338	31	23	2
1983	1,108	350	32	387	35	362	33	9	0
1984	1,079	465	43	281	26	320	30	13	1
1985	1,468	742	51	344	23	377	26	5	0
1986	1,303	545	42	411	32	345	26	2	0
1987	724	298	41	248	34	176	24	2	1
1988	777	437	56	166	21	170	22	4	1
1989	664	307	46	199	30	153	23	5	1
1990	657	260	40	207	31	186	28	4	1
1991	645	221	34	221	34	197	31	6	1
1992	818	178	22	328	40	303	37	9	1
1993	929	236	25	369	40	321	35	3	0
1994	1,202	317	26	466	39	412	34	7	1

SOURCE: *Mergerstat Review 1994* (Los Angeles: Houlihan Lokey Howard & Zukin, 1995), p. 55.

For smaller company sales through business brokers, seller financing through a note is involved in the vast majority of transactional cases. Usually, these seller paper notes are at interest rates well below market rates for notes of comparable risk. Furthermore, many smaller "deal prices" have a portion of the payments contingent on given levels of revenues or earnings, thus further reducing the cash equivalent value.

In the initial public offering transaction scenario, normally, it is not possible to sell 100 percent of the company's stock at one time. Underwriters generally are not willing to sell an offering in which insiders are bailing out of all their stock. Thus, the business seller usually is left with some unregistered (restricted) stock, which then still would be subject to the discount for lack of marketability for restricted stocks as discussed in an earlier section.

Inability to Hypothecate. Stock of closely held corporations, even controlling interest stock, generally does not make satisfactory bank collateral. If an owner of a controlling interest wants cash while awaiting a sale, for an emergency or an opportunity or whatever, it will be somewhere between time consuming and impossible to borrow against the estimated value of the stock.

Benchmark for the Discount for Lack of Marketability for Controlling Interests

If the appropriate standard of value is fair market value, then the price ultimately expected to be achievable between "a willing buyer and a willing seller"—before the above listed costs and risks are considered—would be a benchmark from which the discount for lack of marketability would be taken. This generalized statement leaves the following possibilities as to the appropriate base from which a discount for lack of marketability, on a controlling ownership interest, should be taken:

1. The price one might get in an initial or secondary public stock offering (i.e., the publicly traded equivalent value).
2. The price achievable in the private sale of the entire closely held company, which itself may be estimated in a variety of ways.

In addition to the underwriting commissions and the direct expenses presented in Exhibits 15–6 and 15–7, underwriters frequently receive stock warrants, especially in connection with smaller initial public offerings. Although this is not an immediate cash expense, it is a very real cost of the transaction if the company is successful, possibly amounting to several percentage points of dilution. There are also other indirect transaction costs, such as a large commitment of top management's time to negotiate and carry out a successful stock offering. If the lack of marketability discount is a critical issue in the subject valuation, then it might be appropriate to obtain more current data with regard to the cost of a public flotation.

There are also many of the same or similar costs involved in preparing a company for a private sale, not to mention the cost of an intermediary to effect the sale. Also, if the benchmark for the estimated sale price is valuation multiples observed in acquisitions of public companies, data indicate that valuation multiples for acquisitions of private companies tend to be less. This phenomenon is discussed in the following section.

Differences between Private and Public Company Acquisition P/E Multiples

Every year, *Mergerstat Review* publishes a table presenting the average P/E multiples for the acquisitions of private companies for which they have data—compared with the average P/E multiples for the acquisitions of companies that had been publicly traded. Every year the average P/E multiple for the acquisitions of private companies is significantly lower than the average P/E multiple for the acquisitions of public companies. The public versus private acquisition P/E multiple table from the 1994 *Mergerstat Review* is presented in Exhibit 15–9.

Only in 1993 and 1994 were private company acquisition P/E multiples higher than public company acquisition P/E multiples; and these results could well be an anomaly, because only 14 such private company acquisitive transactions were analyzed by *Mergerstat Review* in 1993 and only 18 in 1994.

Observers have hypothesized a number of reasons for this consistent and significant acquisition pricing differential; the most common reasons for this phenomenon are the following:

1. Exposure to the market.
2. The quality of financial accounting and other information.
3. The size effect.

Exposure to the Market. The names and stock prices of publicly traded companies are published in hundreds of newspapers throughout the world every day. Publicly traded companies also issue many press releases every year with quarterly earnings and other information; these press releases are also published in hundreds of newspapers. Many computer databases have financial information on thousands of publicly traded companies, including SIC codes, which anyone can access on-line. Publicly traded companies are required to file Forms 10-K, 10-Q, and 8-K, as well as other detailed financial information, with the SEC, which anyone can obtain copies of. Any company—or financial intermediary—interested in an acquisition in any industry has this list of publicly traded companies and the detailed financial information on them at its fingertips.

Exhibit 15–9
Median P/E Offered
Public versus Private (1985–1994)

Year	Acquisitions of Public Companies (Base)		Acquisitions of Private Companies (Base)	
1985	16.4	(240)	12.3	(187)
1986	24.3	(259)	16.5	(105)
1987	21.7	(191)	15.2	(25)
1988	18.3	(309)	12.8	(50)
1989	18.4	(222)	12.7	(42)
1990	17.1	(117)	13.2	(36)
1991	15.9	(93)	8.5	(23)
1992	18.1	(89)	17.6	(15)
1993	19.7	(113)	22.0	(14)
1994	19.8	(184)	22.0	(18)

SOURCE: *Mergerstat Review 1994* (Los Angeles: Houlihan Lokey Howard & Zukin, 1995), p. 107.

By contrast, there is no such comprehensive and reliable listing of privately owned companies, and privately owned companies normally do not disclose financial data. Many privately owned companies do not even disclose gross revenues. Therefore, acquisition seekers do not have privately owned companies constantly exposed to them. Acquirers have difficulty making a comprehensive list of available closely held businesses if they decide to work at it. Generally, acquirers cannot get financial information regarding closely held corporations—short of a direct approach to the company, which they are often reluctant to do.

Quality of Financial Accounting and Other Information. The SEC requirements for accounting information and other disclosures are far more stringent and extensive than what is required for an unqualified audit opinion under normal GAAP rules. Many analysts believe this difference in the quantity and reliability of financial data has an impact on the differential in average P/E multiples paid for the acquisition of public companies versus the acquisition of private companies.

Size Effect. Empirical studies have proven that larger companies tend to be less risky than smaller companies. This phenomenon would generally result in a lower present value discount rate and a higher price for larger companies. On average, the privately owned companies reported in the *Mergerstat Review* acquisitions are smaller than the publicly traded companies reported in *Mergerstat Review* data. As a footnote to his article, "Should Marketability Discounts Be Applied to Controlling Interests in Private Companies?" Chris Mercer makes the following point:

> According to data in *Mergerstat Review 1992,* about one half of all recorded public company acquisitions have purchase prices of $50 million or more. About 70% of all the private company deals for which transaction pricing is available have deal prices of $25 million or less. These relationships have been fairly consistent for several years. See *Mergerstat Review 1992,* pp. 80–81, p. 91, and p. 6.[29]

This appears to be a contributing factor to the P/E multiple differential between privately owned and publicly traded company acquisitions reported in the *Mergerstat Review* data. However, it is highly questionable whether this much difference in average acquisition size is significant enough to account for the large magnitude of difference between privately owned and publicly traded company acquisition P/E multiples.

It is not possible, with the data currently available, to completely explain the relative impact of the various influences that cause privately owned company acquisitions to be consistently based on much lower P/E multiples than publicly traded company acquisitions. In any case, the data are clear that privately owned companies realize lower acquisition P/E multiples, on the average, when compared to publicly traded companies. Additional research on this point is clearly warranted. Nonetheless, the three factors listed above (i.e., exposure to market, quality of financial accounting, and size effect) generally explain this phenomenon.

[29]Z. Christopher Mercer, "Should Marketability Discounts Be Applied to Controlling Interests in Private Companies?" *Business Valuation Review,* June 1994, p. 64.

If the analysis of the value of a controlling ownership interest in a privately owned company is based on market prices for the acquisitions of publicly traded companies, then these data suggest some amount of valuation discount is applicable. For convenience, we may refer to this valuation phenomenon as a part of the discount for the lack of marketability of a controlling block of stock in a closely held business—or (to distinguish it from the lack of marketability of minority ownership interests) we may refer to it as the discount for the illiquidity in the overall closely held business enterprise. Nonetheless, regardless of what we call this phenomenon, empirical data clearly suggest that a valuation discount is appropriate for controlling interests (and, for that matter, 100 percent ownership interests) in closely held businesses. And this lack of marketability discount (or illiquidity discount) applies—although to varying degrees—regardless of whether the subject company is valued by reference to publicly traded guideline companies, consummated guideline acquisitions, or discounted economic income analyses.

A Question of Semantics?

In his regular column, "How Do You Handle It?" in *Business Valuation Review,* Brad Fowler, an experienced business appraiser as well as a business brokerage intermediary, discusses many of the problems involved in liquidating a controlling interest in a closely held business. He offers the following observations regarding both this transactional phenomenon and what label to put on this valuation adjustment:

> The inability to exit an investment holding can be a substantial negative, whether or not one is in control...[30]
>
> Is this a question of semantics? When control is involved, should we call the penalty for the prospect of being locked in a discount for lack of marketability?... Or should we recognize the penalty but call it something else...?
>
> In lieu of calling this liquidity problem "lack of marketability" and taking it as a discount late in the valuation equation, it is always possible to incorporate it as a risk factor assuming a higher investor's required rate of return or capitalization rate. The venture capital industry does essentially this, when declining to consider an early stage investment unless at least a 40 to 50% per annum rate of return is deemed likely. These high required rates of return are usually considered to incorporate all risk factors, including lack of marketability.
>
> As valuation consultants we constantly strive to write better, more understandable, reports. We might be shooting ourselves in the foot to take a stand that the illiquidity penalty when controlling interests are involved is not "lack of marketability." The inability to cash out of an investment is what is involved. When we call this lack of marketability it tends to be understood and accepted by those who read the report. Although it is probably inappropriate to simply round up Moroney, Maher, Emory and the other usual suspects and "go for 35%," it is also inappropriate to say that lack of marketability is not a factor when control positions are being valued.[31]

If the objective of the appraisal is to estimate a cash equivalency value today based on the estimated proceeds of an initial public offering or from the private sale of the company (or the controlling block of stock) at some time in the future, some adjustment from the estimated final transaction proceeds to arrive at

---

[30]Bradley A. Fowler, "How Do You Handle It?" *Business Valuation Review,* December 1993, p. 189.
[31]Ibid., p. 191.

a current cash equivalency price may be appropriate to reflect these factors. For simplicity and for lack of a better term, we may call this adjustment a discount for lack of marketability. However, as an alternative term, this valuation adjustment may also be called a discount for illiquidity (either of the overall closely held company or of the controlling ownership interest).

Alternatively, instead of a separate, quantified adjustment, the cost and risk factors may be handled through analytical judgments of appropriate valuation multiples and discount or capitalization rates. In this case, it would be desirable to make it clear how much adjustment is related to the marketability factor.

Factors That Affect the Discount for Lack of Marketability

It is important to recognize that the discount for lack of marketability is not a black and white issue; that is, a stock is not necessarily simply "marketable," freely tradable in a public market, or "nonmarketable," not freely tradable. There are *degrees* of marketability or lack of it, which depend on the circumstances in each case. Following are some factors that affect the degree of marketability or lack of it. Although there is no quantitative formula to assess the impact of each, consideration of these factors should guide the analyst's judgment as to where the subject interest should fall within the reasonable range of discounts for lack of marketability.

"Put" Rights

Generally, the most powerful factor that could reduce or eliminate a discount for lack of marketability would be the existence of a "put" right. A put is a contractual right that entitles the holder, at his option, to sell the stock to a specified party at some time or under some specified circumstances, at the price or mechanism for determining the price specified in the contract. In other words, a put *guarantees* a market under specified circumstances. Puts are found most commonly in connection with ESOP-owned stock.

Dividend Payments

Stocks with no or low dividends typically suffer more from lack of marketability than stocks with high dividends. Besides being empirically demonstrable, this makes common sense. If the stock pays no dividend, the holder is dependent *entirely* on some future ability to sell the stock to realize any return. The higher the dividend, the greater the return the holder realizes without regard for sale of the stock. For this reason (because of the high dividends), preferred stocks typically have far less discount for lack of marketability than common stocks.

Potential Buyers

The existence of a reasonable number of potential buyers or even one strong potential buyer (often as demonstrated by past activity in the stock) could dampen the discount for lack of marketability. For example, if an ESOP regularly purchases shares, the possibility of sometime selling shares to the ESOP may cause the discount for lack of marketability to be less than if the ESOP did not exist.

Size of Block

Strictly from a marketability perspective, the empirical evidence cited in earlier sections suggests that larger blocks may tend to have larger discounts for lack of marketability than smaller blocks. There may be fewer potential buyers for a large block, and a large block transaction may be more difficult to finance.

One might logically note that a larger block may have higher value because of possible elements of control, such as a swing vote position or a seat on the board. However, this is another matter and was discussed in the previous chapter under minority discounts and control premiums.

Prospect of Public Offering or Sale of Company

An imminent public offering or sale of the company could decrease the discount for lack of marketability. However, such prospects are almost never certain, and the degree of offset to the discount for lack of marketability is problematical. In some cases, even if such an event were to occur, all minority shareholders might not necessarily have the right to participate.

Conversely, if a company is committed to remaining private and in the hands of current control owners for the foreseeable future, this would tend to exacerbate the discount for lack of marketability.

Information Access and Reliability

The degree to which information is or is not made available to minority owners and the reliability of that information affects the discount for lack of marketability. For example, a recent article on partnership interest valuations states, "An important basis for illiquidity discounts is the difficulty faced by prospective purchasers in obtaining information."[32]

Restrictive Transfer Provisions

Many closely held stocks are subject to provisions that severely restrict the right of the holder to transfer stock. Any provision that limits the right of the holder to transfer the stock would tend to increase the amount of the discount for lack of marketability. In some cases, the restrictive provision may fix the value or put a ceiling on value. The impact of such restrictions is a matter of judgment that must be analyzed in light of the provisions in each case, in some cases with the aid of consultation with counsel regarding enforceability.

Court Decisions on Discounts for Lack of Marketability

Four years after Moroney's 1973 article, referenced earlier, Moroney wrote that courts have started to recognize higher discounts for lack of marketability:

---

[32]Mark S. Thompson and Eric S. Spunt, "The Widespread Overvaluation of Fractional Ownership Positions," *Trusts & Estates,* June 1993, pp. 62–66. See also Michael J. Bolotsky, "Adjustments for Differences in Ownership Rights, Liquidity, Information Access, and Information Reliability: An Assessment of 'Prevailing Wisdom' versus the 'Nath Hypotheses,'" *Business Valuation Review,* September 1991, pp. 94–110. Bolotsky's position is that, conceptually, this is a factor separate from marketability, but he recognizes the reality that we have no good way to measure this factor separately.

The thousands and thousands of minority holders in closely held corporations throughout the United States have good reason to rejoice because the courts in recent years have upheld illiquidity discounts in the 50 percent area. (*Edwin A. Gallun,* CCH Dec. 32,830(M), 33 T.C.M. 1316 (1974) allowed 55 percent. *Est. of Maurice Gustave Heckscher,* CCH Dec. 33,023, 63 T.C. 485 (1975) allowed 48 percent. Although *Est. of Ernest E. Kirkpatrick,* CCH Dec. 33,524(M), 34 T.C.M. 1490 (1975) found per share values without mentioning discount, expert witnesses for both sides used 50 percent—the first time a government witness recommended 50 percent. A historic event, indeed!)

Nevertheless, perhaps we appraisers ought to think of 75 percent or thereabouts as the norm, subject to adjustment up or down according to the facts of each case. We shall certainly gain strong support from many minority stockholders who have tried to sell at that level without getting so much as a nibble.[33]

Solberg Study of Court Decisions on Restricted Shares

Thomas A. Solberg studied 15 cases in which the courts valued restricted securities.[34] He discussed Revenue Ruling 77-287 and federal securities law, especially Rules 144 and 237. Of the 15 cases, the range of discounts from market value was 10 to 90 percent, with a median of 38.9 and a mean of 37.4 percent. He concluded:

> The valuation of restricted securities is not a numbers game, and each case must stand on its own facts as presented to the court. Legal precedent, in terms of discounts granted in cases previously decided, is not as important as the nature, quality, and quantity of the evidence and the skill with which that evidence is marshaled and presented. The cases indicate that the courts, if provided with the factual basis to do so, are willing to grant significant discounts for restricted securities to properly reflect the economic realities of the marketplace.[35]

The results of the Solberg study are presented in Exhibit 15–10.

Court Decision on Restricted Shares

At his death, Saul Gilford was the largest stockholder in a company that traded OTC; he owned 23 percent of the stock, all restricted shares. The IRS contended the stock should be valued at a substantial premium over the market price at the time of death, based on the price of a merger six months later. The expert for the taxpayer testified the stock should be discounted 35 percent from the public trading price, 33 percent to reflect the lack of marketability of the restricted shares, and an additional 2 percent to reflect blockage. The IRS presented no expert testimony. The court rejected the position of reflecting the subsequent merger, ruled the stock should be discounted 33 percent to reflect lack of marketability, and rejected the additional 2 percent for blockage.[36]

There have been a substantial number of other court cases on restricted stock in recent years, but we think the Gilford case is the most on target.

---

[33]Robert E. Moroney, "Why 25 Percent Discount for Nonmarketability in One Valuation, 100 Percent in Another?" *Taxes,* May 1977, p. 320.

[34]Thomas A. Solberg, "Valuing Restricted Securities: What Factors Do the Courts and the Service Look For," Reprinted with permission from *Journal of Taxation,*© September 1979, pp. 150–54, Warren, Gorham & Lamont, 31 St. James Avenue, Boston, MA 02116. All rights reserved.

[35]Ibid., p. 153.

[36]*Estate of Saul R. Gilford,* 88 T.C. 38 (1987).

Exhibit 15–10

Cases in Which the Court Valued Restricted Securities

Case Name and Citation	Discounts Considered	Market Price	IRS Value	Taxpayer's Value	Court's Value	Discount from Market
1. *Goldwasser*, 47 BTA 445 (1942) aff'd 142 F.2d 556 (CA-2, 1944) cert. den.	Restricted securities	$82.25	$75.88	$54.87	$68.00	17.3%
2. *Conroy*, TCM 1958-6	Restricted securities	5.00	NA	1.00–2.00	3.50	30.0
3. *Victorson*, TCM 1962-231	Restricted securities	0.85	0.85	NA[1]	0.50	40.0
4. *Simmons*, TCM 1964-237 (involved two securities)	Restricted securities and blockage	3.50 / 1.00	2.75 / 1.00	NA[1] / NA[1]	2.75 / 0.75	21.4 / 25.0
5. *Specialty Paper and Board Co., Inc.*, TCM 1965-208	Restricted securities and blockage	5.12	4.50	NA[1]	2.85	44.4
6. *LeVant*, 45 TC 185 (1965) *rev'd* 376 F.2d 434 (CA-7, 1967)	Restricted securities	39.06	39.06	31.50	31.50	19.4
7. *Husted*, 47 TC 644 (1967)	Restricted securities and blockage	11.25	11.25	4.20–5.25	7.00	37.7
8. *Jacobowitz*, TCM 1968-261	Restricted securities	10.00[2]	10.00	1.00[3]	4.50	55.0
9. *Alves*, DC Mo., 4/11/69	Restricted securities and voting trust certificates	103.00[4]	103.00	77.25	77.25	25.0
10. *Bolles*, 69 TC 342 (1977) (involved three securities)	Restricted securities and blockage	22.62 / 14.30 / 12.60	15.00 / 6.50 / 12.00 / 12.00[6]	NA[5] / NA[5] / NA[5] / 0.00	12.44 / 1.43 / 9.83 / 0.00	45.0 / 90.0 / 22.0
11. *Roth*, TCM 1977-426	Restricted securities and blockage	2.68	2.00	0.75[7]	1.07	60.0
12. *Stroupe*, TCM 1978-55 (involved two dates)	Restricted securities	36.00 / 34.00	34.00 / 32.00	6.00 / 6.00	21.00 / 19.20	40.0 / 43.5
13. *Estate of Doelle*, DC Mich., 5/19/78	Restricted securities and voting trust	NA[8]	3.12	0.083	0.085[1] / 0.09[9]	NA[10]
14. *Wheeler*, TCM 1978-208	Restricted securities blockage denied	5.87	NA	2.15	5.29	10.0
15. *Kessler*, TCM 1978-491	Restricted securities	7.09	4.96	0.50	3.67	48.2

[1] Taxpayer argued that the stock had no ascertainable value due to Securities Act restrictions.
[2] Public offering took place 2½ months after the valuation date. Offering price to public was $10.
[3] Taxpayer reported value initially at $5.50, but later changed his value to $1.00. Taxpayer's expert testified stock was worth $1.10.
[4] Market price for shares was $101 bid, $105 asked. Plaintiff made gift of voting trust certificates representing shares and valued them at 75% of mean share value.

[5] Taxpayer sought greater discounts than court allowed on debentures. The court probably adopted the taxpayer's value on the warrants and common stock, but this is not clear from opinion.
[6] Taxpayer had a guaranty of questionable enforceability that the three securities would have a total value of $45.50. IRS valued the guaranty agreement at $12.00. The court disregarded the guaranty.
[7] Reduced from $1.00 claimed on original tax return.
[8] No evidence introduced as to market value.
[9] Stock in voting trust was valued at $.085 and stock not in voting trust at $.09.
[10] Cannot be computed without a market value figure.

SOURCE: Thomas A. Solberg, "Valuing Restricted Securities: What Factors Do the Courts Look For?" Reprinted with permission from *Journal of Taxation*,© September 1979, pp. 150–54, Warren, Gorham & Lamont, 31 St. James Avenue, Boston, MA 02116, All rights reserved.

Moore Study of Court Decisions on Closely Held Interests

Philip W. Moore, president of J. & W. Seligman Valuations Corporation, published a study analyzing 14 decisions of the U.S. Tax Court involving discounts for lack of marketability for interests in closely held businesses from 1969 through 1982.[37] Such an analysis is quite difficult, because the wording of some opinions leaves the reader uncertain as to exactly what weight was accorded to lack of marketability in the discounts finally arrived at. As Moore explains,

> The discounts vary quite considerably, depending on many factors. However, it is oftentimes not easy to isolate the weight of the so-called "lack-of-marketability" factor, and difficult to compare even equal discounts when taken from the varied basis, i.e., net asset value, book value, or appraised value.[38]

Moore concludes, however, "The tendency seems to have been for discounts for lack of marketability to have risen slowly in size over the years."[39] He groups the 14 cases into three time periods, as presented in Table 15–3.

Table 15–3
Discounts for Lack of Marketability

Years	Number of Cases	Range (%)	Average (%)
1969–76	4	15 to 25%	18.75%
1978–79	5	10 to 35	24.00
1980–82	5	10 to 50	28.60

SOURCE: Philip W. Moore, "Valuation Revisited," *Trusts & Estates,* February 1987, p. 48.

Recent Court Decisions on Closely Held Interests

Several U.S. Tax Court cases since the Moore study have addressed the issue of discount for lack of marketability. We selected the following cases for inclusion here because they are particularly relevant among the many recent cases in which discount for lack of marketability has been an issue.

Virginia Z. Harwood v. *Commissioner.*[40] In this case, the court ruled for a combined discount from net asset value of 50 percent to reflect combined minority interest and lack of marketability, the latter influenced by a restrictive agreement. The court recognized that lack of marketability was the basis for a further discount beyond the discount for minority interest, even though in the final decision the discount was given as a lump amount.

One witness said the marketability discount could be between 20 and 50 percent and chose 35 percent. The court said, "He failed to adequately substantiate the discount he chose to apply." This leads us to believe the combined discount would have been higher had the 35 percent marketability discount been adequately substantiated.

---

[37]Philip W. Moore, "Valuation Revisited," *Trusts & Estates,* February 1987, pp. 40–52.
[38]Ibid.
[39]Ibid.
[40]*Virginia Z. Harwood* v. *Commissioner,* 82 T.C. 239 (1984).

Estate of Mark Gallo* v. *Commissioner.[41] At trial, the estate presented three expert witnesses. The primary valuation expert for the estate testified the per share value was $237. This value was derived by using a price/earnings multiple based on guideline publicly traded companies' price/earnings ratios and then discounting by 36 percent to reflect the stock's lack of marketability.

The Tax Court held for a value of $237 per share, holding, among other findings, that a company's size and market dominance do not necessarily mean that a lack of marketability discount should be lower than normal.

Roy O. Martin, Jr. and Barbara M. Martin* v. *Commissioner.[42] This complicated case involved a series of gifts of minority interests of common stock in a closely held personal holding company. The holding company owned minority interests in each of seven closely held companies. The court determined the one company that clearly was an operating company should be valued on a capitalization of earnings basis, two companies that clearly were nonoperating companies should be valued on an asset value basis, and four companies should be valued with one-third of the weight given to capitalized earnings and two-thirds to asset values. To the values thus derived, the court applied a 70 percent discount, "to reflect the marketability/minority considerations." Finally, the court allowed a 5 percent second-stage discount at the holding company level.

Estate of Market B. Watts.[43] In this case, the court allowed a discount for lack of marketability of 35 percent from the estimated price at which minority interests would have traded in a public market had such a market existed for them.

Estate of Joyce C. Hall.[44] The *Estate of Joyce C. Hall* involved a fairly large minority interest in Hallmark Cards, Inc. As in the Gallo case, experts for both the IRS and the taxpayer relied primarily on a publicly traded guideline company method, less a discount for lack of marketability. The court determined the discount for lack of marketability should be 36 percent, the amount testified to by the taxpayer's expert.

Summary

This chapter presented a substantial amount of evidence to assist in estimating appropriate discounts for lack of marketability for both minority and controlling interests in closely held businesses. In the final analysis, however, as with many other valuation issues, the estimation must be made in light of a careful examination of the facts of each case. The specific data the analyst collects and relies on for each situation must relate as closely as possible in time and other characteristics to the particular valuation for which they are being used.

Shares of closely held companies, most of which will never be freely tradable, suffer much more from lack of marketability than do restricted shares of publicly traded companies. In general, they also have less prospect of being marketable than do shares of companies that are considering or already in the process of attempting to go public.

[41]*Estate of Mark Gallo* v. *Commissioner,* 50 T.C.M. 470 (1985).

[42]*Roy O. Martin Jr. and Barbara M. Martin* v. *Commissioner,* 50 T.C.M. 68 (1985).

[43]*Estate of Martha B. Watts,* 87-2 U.S.T.C., paragraph 13726 (11th Cir. 1987); 51 T.C.M. 60 (1985).

[44]*Estate of Joyce C. Hall,* 92 T.C. No. 19 (1989).

Courts have tended to recognize higher discounts for lack of marketability in recent years than earlier, and the trend toward higher discounts for lack of marketability has continued since the second edition of this book. However, the levels of discounts for lack of marketability allowed in most court decisions still seem to be below those at which the empirical evidence indicates that arm's-length transactions tend to occur in the real-world market between willing buyers and willing sellers.

Court decisions necessarily rely on the evidence that experts and others submit to the court for its consideration. Reading the cases reveals that in many instances where low discounts for lack of marketability were concluded, it was because the types of market evidence summarized in this chapter were not adequately presented. *It is imperative that market evidence such as that presented in this chapter be marshaled and presented, including analysis that applies it as specifically as possible to the individual set of facts and circumstances of each case.*

We hope that appraisers, attorneys, and owners of business interests will use the types of data presented in this chapter, along with continuing related research, to continue to reduce the disparity between inadequate marketability discounts often found in prior court decisions and marketability discounts typically evidenced in actual market transactions.

Bibliography

Abrams, Jay B. "Discount for Lack of Marketability: A Theoretical Model." *Business Valuation Review,* September 1994, pp. 132–39.

Arneson, George S. "Nonmarketability Discounts Should Exceed Fifty Percent." *Taxes,* January 1981, pp. 25–31.

Bolten, Steven E. "Discounts for Stocks of Closely Held Corporations." *Trusts & Estates,* December 1990, pp. 47–48.

Chaffe, David B. H. III. "Option Pricing as a Proxy for Discount for Lack of Marketability in Private Company Valuations." *Business Valuation Review,* December 1993, pp. 182–88.

Emory, John D. "The Value of Marketability as Illustrated in Initial Public Offerings of Common Stock—February 1992 through July 1993." *Business Valuation Review,* March 1994, pp. 3–7.

Garber, Steven. "A Proposed Methodology for Estimating the Lack of Marketability Discount Related to ESOP Repurchase Liability." *Business Valuation Review,* December 1993, pp. 172–81.

Hall, Lance S., and Timothy C. Polacek. "Strategies for Obtaining the Largest Valuation Discounts." *Estate Planning,* January/February 1994, pp. 38–44.

Harris, James Edward. "Minority and Marketability Discounts: Are You Taking Enough?" *Probate and Property,* January/February 1990, pp. 6–11.

_____. "Valuation of Closely Held Partnerships and Corporations: Recent Developments Concerning Minority Interest and Lack of Marketability Discounts." *Arkansas Law Review,* 42, no. 3 (1989), pp. 649–70.

Hertzel, Michael, and Richard L. Smith. "Market Discounts and Shareholder Gains for Placing Equity Privately." *Journal of Finance,* June 1993, pp. 459–85.

Hitchner, James R., and Gary Roland. "Marketability and Control Govern Value of Family Businesses." *Taxation for Accountants,* January 1994, pp. 24–28.

Hitchner, James R., and Kevin J. Rudd. "The Use of Discounts in Estate and Gift Tax Valuations." *Trusts & Estates,* August 1992, pp. 49–56, 60.

Holthausen, Robert W., Richard W. Leftwich, and David Mayers. "The Effect of Large Block Transactions on Security Prices: A Cross-Sectional Analysis." *Journal of Financial Economics* 19 (1987), pp. 237–67.

Johnson, Richard D., and George A. Racette. "Discounts on Letter Stock Do Not Appear to Be a Good Base on Which to Estimate Discounts for Lack of Marketability on Closely Held Stocks." *Taxes,* August 1981, pp. 574–81.

Lyons, Robert P., and Michael J. Wilczynski. "Discounting Intrinsic Value." *Trusts & Estates,* February 1989, pp. 22–27.

Lyons, William P., and Martin J. Whitman. "Valuing Closely Held Corporations and Publicly Traded Securities with Limited Marketability: Approaches to Allowable Discounts from Gross Values." *Business Lawyer,* July 1978, pp. 2213–29.

Maher, J. Michael. "Discounts for Lack of Marketability for Closely Held Business Interests." *Taxes,* September 1976, pp. 562–71.

Mercer, Z. Christopher. "Should 'Marketability Discounts' Be Applied to Controlling Interests of Private Companies?" *Business Valuation Review,* June 1994, pp. 55–65.

Moore, Philip W. " 'Blockage' Redux: The Challenge Posed by Blockage." *Trusts & Estates,* February 1992, pp. 35–36 ff.

Moroney, Robert E. "Why 25 Percent Discount for Nonmarketability in One Valuation, 100 Percent in Another?" *Taxes,* May 1977, pp. 316–20.

Shenkman, Martin M., and Cal R. Feingold. "Minority, Marketability Discounts Affect Valuation of Partnership Interest." *Real Estate Finance Journal,* Summer 1993, pp. 18–25.

Silber, William L. "Discounts on Restricted Stock: The Impact of Illiquidity on Stock Prices." *Financial Analysts Journal,* July–August 1991, pp. 60–64.

Smith, Ronald C. "Leveraged Buildups, Mergers and Acquisitions." *Secured Lender,* March/April 1994, pp. 72–74.

Chapter 16

Valuation Synthesis and Conclusion

When all the relevant factors have been individually analyzed and assessed, they must be brought together to arrive at a final number that represents the valuation conclusion. Sometimes it will be obvious that the analyst should rely on a single approach, because of the nature of the company or the interest being appraised. In other cases, two or more valuation approaches may yield such similar results that it matters little how much weight one approach receives. However, in the real world, business valuation approaches and methods sometimes lead to apparently inconsistent value indications. When the different valuation approaches result in materially different value indications, they must be reconciled into a single number to be used for the valuation at hand.

The Reconciliation Process

During the reconciliation process, it is important for the analyst to review all the steps of the business valuation. The first step in this reconciliation process is for the appraiser to review the appraisal assignment. At this point, the appraiser must answer the question: "Did I accomplish what I set out to accomplish?"

A review of the appraisal assignment should consider:

1. The purpose and objective of the appraisal.
2. The business enterprise ownership interest to be appraised.
3. The bundle of legal rights to be appraised.
4. The ownership characteristics of the business interest to be appraised.
5. The date of the appraisal.
6. The standard (or definition) of value to be estimated.
7. The premise of value to be used (based upon the highest and best use of the subject business interest).

The appraisal is performed to answer a client's question about the value of a business enterprise or business interest. Even within the same valuation approach, different methods will typically result in different indications of value. For example, it is likely that different indicated values will result from two different income approach methods (e.g., from a direct capitalization method versus a yield capitalization method).

The process of reconciliation is the analysis of the alternative valuation conclusions to arrive at a final estimate for the subject business enterprise. Before reaching a final value estimate, the appraiser should review the entire business valuation for appropriateness and accuracy. Reviewing the business appraisal work product is the subject of Chapter 19. Suffice it here, however, to emphasize that the definition of value sought and its relationship to each step in the valuation process should be borne in mind throughout the reconciliation process.

Criteria for the Selection of Valuation Approaches and Methods

Of the recommended business valuation approaches discussed in this text, there are no clearly right or wrong approaches. This assertion deliberately excludes valuation approaches that are not recommended, of course, such as the naive book value approach. There is also no precise guideline or quantitative formula for selecting which approach or approaches are most applicable in a given business valuation situation. However, the following list presents the most common and most important factors to be considered by the appraiser when selecting among alternative valuation approaches.

1. The quantity and quality of available data.
2. The degree of access to available data.
3. The supply of industry transactional data.
4. The type of business, nature of business assets, and type of industry subject to appraisal.
5. The nature of the business interest subject to appraisal.
6. Statutory, judicial, and administrative considerations.
7. The informational needs of the appraisal audience.
8. The purpose and objective of the appraisal.
9. The professional judgment and expertise of the appraiser.

Quantity and Quality of Available Data

Practically, this may be the most important of the valuation approach selection criteria. An appraiser simply cannot perform a valuation approach (no matter how conceptually robust it is) if the requisite financial, operational, or market data are not available.

Degree of Access to Available Data. In business valuations performed for litigation support, dispute resolution, or other controversy purposes, the appraiser may not have unrestricted access to company data, company management, company facilities, and so forth. In these cases, all the desired historical and prospective data may exist. However, the appraiser may not be granted reasonable access to the existing data. Accordingly, in selecting among valuation approaches, the appraiser may have to consider not only what data exist, but also what data are available to the appraiser.

Supply of Industry Transactional Data. Some industries have a large quantity of publicly available data regarding business purchase and sale transactions. When the supply of such reliable industry transactional data is substantial, then the appraiser will more likely select and rely on transaction-based business valuation approaches.

Type of Business, Nature of Business Assets, and Type of Industry Subject to Appraisal

Certain industries have rules of thumb that are used as quick estimates regarding the valuation of businesses. While these industry rules of thumb, guidelines, or conventions should not be relied on in a rigorous business valuation, they should not be ignored either. Depending on the nature of the subject business (e.g., whether it is capital-asset intensive or intangible-asset intensive), different valuation approaches may be more or less applicable.

Nature of the Business Interest Subject to Appraisal

Obviously the valuation of a marketable, controlling ownership interest in a business enterprise is a different assignment than the valuation of a nonmarketable, minority ownership interest in the restricted, nonvoting stock of the same business enterprise. In selecting the most appropriate valuation approach, the appraiser should consider that some valuation approaches are more appropriate for overall business enterprise valuations while other approaches are more appropriate for the analysis of fractional ownership interests.

Statutory, Judicial, and Administrative Considerations

For those business valuations performed for certain taxation, ESOP, and litigation purposes, the appraiser should be cognizant of whether certain valuation approaches are required—and whether certain valuation approaches are prohibited—by the appropriate regulatory authority. For example, the IRS has published valuation procedures and guidelines for appraisals performed for gift and estate tax purposes, such as the specific Chapter 14 guidelines that apply to business valuations performed for estate freeze purposes. And certain states (often as a result of judicial precedent) require some valuation approaches—and prohibit other valuation approaches—for business valuations performed for appraisal rights pursuant to minority squeeze-out mergers, other shareholder appraisal rights cases, marital dissolution cases, and so forth. The appraiser should be aware of whatever specific statutory requirements, administrative guidance, or judicial precedent affects the subject business valuation.

Informational Needs of the Appraisal Audience

The ultimate audience for the appraisal may affect the selection of business valuation approaches. These considerations include the level of sophistication of the appraisal audience and the degree of familiarity of the audience with the subject company. The ultimate purpose of the appraisal—as either notational or transactional—may also affect which valuation approach (and how many valuation approaches) will be selected.

Purpose and Objective of the Appraisal

Overall, the purpose and objective of the business valuation may influence the selection of the valuation approaches. The factors encompassed in the appraisal objective include the description of the business interest subject to appraisal, the description of the ownership characteristics of the subject business interest, the definition (or standard) of value applied, the premise of value applied (including consideration of the highest and best use of the subject business interests), and the valuation date. The factors encompassed in the appraisal purpose include the audience for the appraisal and the decision (or decisions) to be influenced by the appraisal.

Professional Judgment and Expertise of the Appraiser

Ultimately, the most fundamental factors affecting the selection of the appropriate business valuation approach or approaches are the professional judgment, technical expertise, and experienced common sense of the appraiser.

Reconciling Divergent Results among Business Valuation Methods

Ideally, the appraiser will use two or more approaches in the subject business valuation and these approaches will all yield virtually identical value conclusions. Practically, this rarely happens.

Appraisers expect to estimate a range of valuation conclusions when several alternative valuation approaches are used. The normal situation occurs when the several valuation approaches all conclude a reasonably narrow dispersion of valuation conclusions. These alternative conclusions, then, indicate the reasonable range of values for the subject business. They also provide mutually supportive evidence as to the final valuation synthesis and conclusion.

Occasionally, two or three valuation methods produce value estimates within a reasonable range—and then one valuation method produces a clear and obvious value estimate outlier.

An illustrative example of this valuation conclusion outlier phenomenon is shown in Table 16–1:

Table 16–1

Illustrative Business Enterprise, Inc.
Business Valuation Methods and Value Estimates
Valuation Synthesis and Conclusion

Valuation Method	Value Estimate
Capital market method	$18,000,000
Discounted economic income method	$20,000,000
Asset-based approach, capitalized excess earnings method	$22,000,000
Asset-based approach (discrete), asset accumulation method	$10,000,000
Valuation synthesis and conclusion	$22,000,000

In this example, the value estimate of the asset accumulation method is a clear and obvious outlier compared to the three other value estimates. Accordingly, this appraisal requires further analysis and consideration before a valuation conclusion may be reached.

The question is: What is the appraiser to do regarding such an outlier value estimate? There are three alternatives.

First, the appraiser could discard the valuation method that yields the outlier value estimate. This action is based on the rationale that the outlier valuation method simply does not work given the subject set of facts and circumstances.

Second, the appraiser could keep the outlier valuation method but assign a very low weight to the outlier value estimate. This action is based on the rationale that if the method is fundamentally sound, even an unreasonable value estimate should be given some weight in the final valuation conclusion.

Third, the appraiser could thoroughly investigate why the outlier valuation method is producing outlier value estimates. The appraiser could attempt to reconcile all the value estimates. The appraiser could search for an answer, or at least an explanation, to this apparent anomaly. As part of this investigation and reconcilement, the appraiser should recheck all the quantitative analyses and rethink all the qualitative conclusions. The appraiser is most likely to find that an error was made in the analysis and application of the outlier method. (An example may be that one significant unrecorded intangible asset was inadvertently missed in the asset accumulation method.)

After the analytical or data error is discovered, it can be corrected. Then, the outlier method may produce a more reasonable, and more consistent, value estimate.

Of course, this third alternative—which involves additional analyses and reconciliation procedures—to handling the phenomenon of an outlier business value estimate is the preferred procedure. Only with such analysis can a discrepancy be adequately explained and reconciled with the other indications of value.

If, after careful review, one of the appraisal methods that appears to have merit still produces an outlier, then it becomes a matter of appraisal judgment as to the extent to which the factors reflected in the valuation method actually contribute to the value of the business or interest being appraised, with weight accorded commensurately to the method in the final value estimate.

Weighting of Valuation Method Results

As with the selection of which valuation methods to use, there are no scientific formulas or specific rules to use with regard to the weighting of the results of two or more business valuation methods. In fact, the same factors or guidelines that affect the selection of the valuation methods will influence the appraiser with regard to weighting the conclusions of these valuation methods.

This section is really only a brief summary of relative applicability of different methods in different circumstances. The chapters on the various approaches and methods contain more extensive discussion of the circumstances under which each is most useful, and the reader is encouraged to visit those sections for guidance in weighting of approaches and methods.

Keep in mind that different approaches to value are not discrete but have considerable overlap. For example, within the market approach, heavy emphasis may appropriately be placed on a multiple of an economic income figure, such as a price/earnings multiple. It could be argued that this is an alternate form of an income approach, thus lessening the need for separate weight on an income approach per se. Similarly, income approaches are dependent on information about market conditions to estimate appropriate discount and capitalization rates. Thus, the better the job an income approach does on capturing and documenting market-required discount and/or capitalization rates, the less the need for separate weight on a market approach per se.

The appraiser must ask, "What attributes of ownership of this business or business interest give rise to the value of owning it?" If the income available for distribution to the owner is the primary value driver, then it may be appropriate that one or more methods within the income approach dominate the value conclusion. Of course, a capitalization of dividends (for a minority interest) or dividend-paying capacity (for a controlling interest) within the market approach could very well also capture the income-related value.

If the ability to sell the business or interest in the business is the primary value driver, then it may be appropriate that one or more methods within the market approach dominate the value conclusion.

If the value derives primarily from ownership of assets, then an asset approach may dominate. However, a market approach using a multiple of the market price of stock to underlying net asset value may also be a satisfactory way to capture asset-driven value. As a generality, an asset approach tends to be more appropriate in valuing a controlling interest than a minority interest, since one of the important things that a control owner controls—and a minority owner does not—is the utilization of the assets.

Through all of this, the analyst must keep in mind the operative standard of value and court interpretations of the standard of value, if applicable. For example, family law courts in some states adhere to a strict definition of *fair market value* as value in exchange. In such cases, personal goodwill that could not be transferred would not be considered a marital asset, even though it may give rise to considerable value to the owner and would be considered if *investment value* was the applicable standard of value.

The final estimate should typically be a number within the final range of values indicated by the various business valuation methods used in the analysis. The final value estimate may be a number indicated by one of the valuation methods, or it may be heavily weighted to the result of the valuation method relied on most heavily, or it may be another number within the indicated range.

It is generally inappropriate to simply calculate an arithmetic average to arrive at a final value estimate. A simple arithmetic mean implies that all the valuation methods have equal validity and equal weight. While this may occur in certain instances, this is usually not the case.

The final value opinion regarding the subject business enterprise or business interest should be derived from the appraiser's reasoning and judgment of all the factors considered and from the impartial weighting of the market evidence.

At What Point Are Discounts and Premiums Applied?

The appropriate point at which to apply discounts or premiums depends on the types of value premise (type of value) implied by each method used. As discussed in earlier chapters, the most important discounts or premiums usually are for the degree of minority or control status of the appraised interest and for the degree of marketability or lack of it. Therefore, it is necessary to examine, for each valuation method to be reflected in the final analysis, the extent to which that valuation method implies a control or minority ownership interest and a fully marketable or less than fully marketable characteristic of ownership.

If all the methods used imply a conclusion reflecting the same ownership characteristics (e.g., a marketable, minority ownership value), then any applicable premiums and/or discounts may be taken at the end of the exercise, after whatever relative weightings are applied to the various methods used. If, on the other hand, different valuation methods imply different ownership characteristics, then premiums and/or discounts normally would be applied separately for the different methods before the relative weighting of the methods.

For example, let's say a guideline public company method and a discounted cash flow method were used. Let's also say there were no adjustments to earnings to reflect control factors, and that valuation multiples and discount rates were based on public market minority share transaction data. In this case, both the methods used would produce an indication of minority, fully marketable value. If the interest being appraised is a minority interest in a closely held company, the results of the two methods could be combined and a discount for lack of marketability applied to the combined estimate of minority but fully marketable value.

Let's say, however, in addition to the foregoing two methods, a market approach using merger and acquisition transaction data was also used. The valuation multiples found in merger and acquisition data frequently reflect control or acquisition premiums. If that were the case, it would be appropriate to apply a minority interest discount to the results of the merger and acquisition method before weighting it in with the results of the other two methods.

A common error that we see is the application of a single premium or discount to an indication of value developed from two or more valuation methods that imply dissimilar ownership characteristics. This can produce a conclusion that is not clearly either fish or fowl—that is, not clearly a minority or control value nor clearly a fully marketable or nonmarketable value. Be sure in each situation that any discount or premium applied is appropriate to adjust from the definition of value implied in the valuation method to the definition of value being sought in the appraisal.

Presenting the Value Conclusion

Explicit Weighting

An intuitively appealing method of presenting the value conclusion is for the analyst: (1) to use subjective but informed judgment and decide on a percentage weight to assign the results of each relevant valuation approach or method used and (2) to base the final valuation on a weighted average of the results of the various methods. Suppose, for example, the analyst is valuing a minority ownership interest in a closely held manufacturing company and ultimately relies on three value measures developed through the guideline public company (capital market) method. Since it is an operating company but has a substantial asset base, the analyst thinks the appropriate price-to-earnings multiple should be accorded 60 percent of the total weight, the capitalization of dividends 10 percent, and the price-to-asset-value multiple 30 percent. We will assume in this case that the company has been unable to generate a good rate of return on its asset base—thus, the result would be that presented in Table 16–2.

Table 16–2

	Value per Share	Weight	Total
Capitalization of earnings:			
$2.00 per share x 5.0	$10.00	.6	$ 6.00
Capitalization of dividends:			
$0.60 per share ÷ .05	12.00	.1	1.20
Capitalization of net asset value:			
$20.00 book value x .8	16.00	.3	4.80
			$12.00
Less discount for lack of marketability:			
.35 x 12.00			4.20
Indicated value per share			$ 7.80

In the case presented in Table 16–2, although companies in the same industry generally are selling below book value, the subject company is valued at a larger discount from book value than the average in its industry because of poorer earnings. However, the asset base is accorded some weight, and the company is valued at a lower discount from book value than it would be if it were valued strictly on a multiple of earnings basis. As it turns out, in this case, the effect of the capitalization of dividends is neutral.

The main weakness of the above valuation synthesis procedure is that no acceptable mathematical model is available for use in deriving the weights to assign to the results of each valuation method. The relative weights to assign each method depend on the analyst's judgment; however, it forces the analyst to present his or her thinking in clearly quantified terms. The above narrative, coupled with the explicit weighting, provides important information as to the appraiser's thought process. The procedure also has the appeal of being clear and simple to understand. If someone evaluating the results disagrees with some aspect of the analyst's judgment, the point of departure is readily identifiable and it is easy to apply an alternate set of numbers and quickly recompute the result.

Court cases in which values of stocks must be estimated under dissenting stockholders' appraisal rights have tended to rely on this weighting procedure. However, the wording of Revenue Ruling 59-60 does not embrace the method. The ruling states:

> Because the valuations cannot be made on the basis of a prescribed formula, there is no means whereby the various applicable factors in a particular case can be assigned mathematical weights in deriving the fair market value. For this reason, no useful purpose is served by taking an average of several factors (for example, book value, capitalized earnings, and capitalized dividends) and basing the valuation on the result. Such a process excludes active consideration of other pertinent factors, and the end result cannot be supported by a realistic application of the significant facts in the case except by mere chance.[1]

Despite this wording, the method has been used successfully in many gift and estate tax cases both in dealing with the IRS and in cases decided in court. The wording of Revenue Ruling 59-60 indicates concern that the averaging or weighted average method leaves room for omission of pertinent factors. However, it is possible to use the basic weighted average of factors procedure and still, at one stage or another, incorporate consideration of all the pertinent factors mentioned in Revenue Ruling 59-60. Of course, it is important to be careful to demonstrate in each case that all other pertinent factors were actively considered and reflected in the result to the appropriate extent.

---

[1]Revenue Ruling 59-60 (1959-1 C.B. 237).

Implicit Weighting

Some appraisers use an implicit weighting scheme in their final valuation synthesis and conclusion. That is, they present the valuation indications for each method performed and then simply present a final value estimate. They do not document or justify the valuation synthesis process.

An example of this implicit weighting scheme is provided in Table 16–3.

Table 16–3

Illustrative Business Enterprise, Inc.
Business Valuation Methods and Value Estimates
Valuation Synthesis and Conclusion

Valuation Method	Value Estimate
Capital market method	$18,000,000
Discounted economic income method	$20,000,000
Asset accumulation method	$24,000,000
Valuation synthesis and conclusion	$22,000,000

This analysis presents the final valuation conclusion. However, it is incomplete unless the appraiser explains and justifies the final value estimate concluded from this synthesis. The explanation can cover both the conceptual preferability among the methods used and also the degree of confidence in each based on the relative quantity and quality of data available.

Final Value Estimate

Any of the following types of final value estimates may be appropriate, given the purpose and objective of the business valuation:

1. A point estimate—usually the business valuation final value estimate is stated as a single figure or point estimate.
2. A range of value—in this conclusion, the business valuation indicated value is said to fall somewhere within a range of values. This may be reported solely, as the conclusion of value, or in conjunction with a point estimate.
3. A relationship value—in this conclusion, the business valuation estimate is expressed as a relationship to a given value. For example, the value estimate is indicated to be "no less than $X million" or "no more than $Y million."

Summary

The final value estimate is ultimately based on the accumulated evidence as analyzed and assessed by the reasoned professional judgment of the appraiser. The valuation process should be presented in such a way as to lead the reader to the same final value estimate conclusion reached by the appraiser. Accordingly, all qualitative and quantitative data and analyses should be presented in the appraisal. And all the appraiser's judgments and thought processes should be documented in the appraisal. In this way, the reader of the business valuation should understand—and be able to re-create—exactly how the appraiser reached the final valuation conclusion.

Part IV

Presenting the Valuation Report

Chapter 17

Writing an Appraisal Report

This chapter will present the following professional standards topics related to the preparation and issuance of business valuation reports:

1. An overview of the appraisal reporting process.
2. USPAP appraisal reporting standards.
3. The form, format, and content of various common types of appraisal reports, as categorized by USPAP.
4. The documentation and retention requirements of USPAP.
5. The confidentiality requirements of USPAP.

In addition, this chapter will present some general principles with regard to effective business valuation report writing.

An Overview of the Appraisal Report

According to the Uniform Standards of Professional Appraisal Practice (USPAP), the definition of an appraisal report is any communication, written or oral, of an appraisal. This definition encompasses any written document that is transmitted to the client upon completion of an appraisal assignment. An appraisal report leads the reader from the definition of the appraisal problem through the analysis and the relevant descriptive data to a specific value conclusion.

The length, type, and content of business valuation reports may be dictated by:

1. The client.
2. The applicable regulatory requirements.
3. The courts.
4. The type of business ownership interest being appraised.
5. The nature of the appraisal problem.

Appraisal Reporting Standards

The Uniform Standards of Professional Appraisal Practice dictate minimum standards to be applied in all types of appraisal reports. USPAP states that each written or oral appraisal report must:

1. Clearly and accurately set forth the appraisal in a manner that will not be misleading.
2. Contain sufficient information to enable those who receive or rely on the report to understand it properly.
3. Clearly and accurately disclose any extraordinary assumption or limiting condition that directly affects the appraisal, and indicate its impact on the concluded value.

The professional standards related to reporting the results of the business appraisal are presented in USPAP Standard 10. Since this standard is so vitally important to the production of a professional business valuation report, it is presented here, in its entirety, in Exhibit 17–1.

Exhibit 17–1

USPAP Standard 10

STANDARD 10

In reporting the results of a business or intangible asset appraisal an appraiser must communicate each analysis, opinion, and conclusion in a manner that is not misleading.

<u>Standards Rule 10-1</u>

Each written or oral business or intangible asset appraisal report must:

(a) **clearly and accurately set forth the appraisal in an manner that will not be misleading.**

<u>Comment</u>: <u>Departure from this binding requirement is not permitted.</u>

(b) **contain sufficient information to enable the intended user(s) to understand it. Any specific limiting conditions concerning information should be noted.**

<u>Comment</u>: <u>Departure from this binding requirement is not permitted</u>. Any specific limiting conditions should be noted in the engagement letter as well as in the report itself. A failure to observe this rule could cause the intended users of the report to make a serious error even though each analysis, opinion, and conclusion in the report is clearly and accurately stated.

(c) **clearly and accurately disclose any extraordinary assumption that directly affects the appraisal and indicate its impact on value.**

<u>Comment</u>: <u>Departure from this binding requirement is not permitted</u>. This rule requires a clear and accurate disclosure of any extraordinary assumptions or conditions that directly affect an analysis, opinion, or conclusion. Examples of such extraordinary assumptions or conditions might include items such as the execution of a pending lease agreement, atypical financing, infusion of additional working capital or making other capital additions, or compliance with regulatory authority rules. The report should indicate whether the extraordinary assumption or condition has a positive, negative or neutral impact on value.

<u>Standards Rule 10-2</u>

Each written business or intangible asset appraisal report must comply with the following specific reporting guidelines:

(a) **identify and describe the business enterprise, assets or equity being appraised.**

(b) **state the purpose and intended use of the appraisal.**

(c) **define the value to be estimated.**

(d) **set forth the effective date of the appraisal and the date of the report.**

<u>Comment</u>: If the appraisal concerns equity, it is not enough to identify the entity in which the equity is being appraised without also identifying the nature of the equity, for example: the number of shares of common or preferred stock. The purpose may be to express an opinion of value but the intended use of the appraisal must also be stated.

The report date is when the report is submitted; the appraisal date or date of value is the effective date of the value conclusion.

(e) **describe the extent of the appraisal process employed**

(f) **set forth all assumptions and limiting conditions that affect the analyses, opinions, and conclusions.**

(g) **set forth the information considered, the appraisal procedures followed, and the reasoning that supports the analyses, opinions, and conclusions.**

(h) **set forth any additional information that may be appropriate to show compliance with, or clearly identify and explain permitted departures from, the requirements of Standard 9.**

(i) **set forth the rationale for the valuation methods and procedures considered and employed.**

(j) **include a certification in accordance with Standards Rule 10-3.**

<u>Standards Rule 10-3</u>

Each written business or intangible asset appraisal report must contain a certification that is similar in content to the following:

> **I certify that, to the best of my knowledge and belief:**
>
> — **the statements of fact contained in this report are true and correct.**
> — **the reported analyses, opinions, and conclusions are limited only by the reported assumptions and limiting conditions, and are my personal, unbiased professional analyses, opinions, and conclusions.**

Exhibit 17–1 (concluded)

— **I have no (or the specified) present or prospective interest in the property that is the subject of this report, and I have no (or the specified) personal interest or bias with respect to the parties involved.**
— **my compensation is not contingent on an action or event resulting from the analyses, opinions, or conclusions in, or the use of, this report.**
— **my analyses, opinions, and conclusions were developed, and this report has been prepared, in conformity with the Uniform Standards of Professional Appraisal Practice.**
— **no one provided significant professional assistance to the person signing this report. (If there are exceptions, the name of each individual providing significant professional assistance must be stated.)**

Comment: Departure from this binding requirement is not permitted.

Standards Rule 10-4

To the extent that it is both possible and appropriate, each oral business or intangible asset appraisal report (including expert testimony) must address the substantive matters set forth in Standards Rule 10-2 and state conformity with Standards Rule 10-3.

Standards Rule 10-5

An appraiser who signs a business or intangible asset appraisal report prepared by another, even under the label "review appraiser," must accept full responsibility for the contents of this report.

Comment: Departure from this binding requirement is not permitted. This requirement is directed to the employer or supervisor signing the report of an employee or subcontractor. The employer or supervisor signing the report is as responsible as the individual preparing the appraisal for the content and conclusions of the appraisal and the report. Using a conditional label next to the signature of the employer or supervisor or signing a form report on the line over the words "review appraiser" does not exempt that individual from adherence to these Standards.

This requirement does not address the responsibilities of a review appraiser, the subject of Standard 3.

SOURCE: *Uniform Standards of Professional Appraisal Practice* (Washington, DC: The Appraisal Foundation, 1995), pp. 55–56. The complete annual edition of USPAP is available for purchase from The Appraisal Foundation, 1029 Vermont Avenue, N.W., Suite 900, Washington, DC 20005.

Written Appraisal Report Standards

As it relates to business valuations, USPAP also requires that each written appraisal report must:

1. Identify and describe the business and the business ownership interest being appraised.
2. Identify the bundle of legal rights being appraised.
3. State the purpose of the appraisal.
4. Define the value to be estimated (described in this book as the standard of value and applicable ownership characteristics, e.g., control/minority and marketable/nonmarketable).
5. Set forth the effective date of the appraisal and the date of the report.
6. Describe the extent of the process of collecting, confirming, and reporting data.
7. Set forth all assumptions and limiting conditions that affect the analyses, opinions, and conclusions.
8. Set forth the information considered, the appraisal procedures followed, and the reasoning that supports the analyses, opinions, and conclusions.

9. Set forth the appraiser's opinion of the highest and best use of the business enterprise being appraised, when such an opinion is necessary and appropriate.
10. Explain and support the exclusion of any of the usual valuation approaches.
11. Set forth any additional information that may be appropriate to show compliance with, or clearly identify and explain permitted departure from, the requirements of all USPAP standards.
12. Include a signed certification in accordance with USPAP Standard Rule (SR) 2-3.

Oral Reports

USPAP provides the following guidance with regard to the preparation and issuance of an oral report:

1. An appraiser may make an oral report when the circumstances or the needs of the client do not permit or warrant a written report.
2. Expert testimony, in depositions or in court, is considered to be an oral report.
3. To the extent that it is possible and appropriate, oral reports *must* address the substantive matters set forth in SR 2-2.
4. Each oral report should include a description of the subject business and business ownership interest and the facts, assumptions, conditions, and reasoning on which the conclusions are based.
5. After communicating an oral report, the appraiser should keep on file all notes and data relating to the assignment and a complete memorandum on the analysis, conclusion, and opinion.

Limited Reports

USPAP provides the following guidance with regard to the preparation and the issuance of a limited report:

1. Sometimes, by prior agreement with the client, an appraiser submits the results of the business valuation in a limited report.
2. Although these reports are abbreviated, they still must conform in all respects to the Uniform Standards of Professional Appraisal Practice.
3. The departure provision of USPAP specifies which elements of the appraisal report may be omitted under certain circumstances.
4. Other elements of the appraisal report are binding requirements and they may not be omitted.
5. The most common types of limited reports are:
   • Letter reports.
   • Form reports.

Letter Reports. USPAP considers a letter report to be a type of limited report and provides the following guidance:

1. Under the Uniform Standards of Professional Appraisal Practice, a letter report must comply with all the reporting requirements.
2. A letter report should indicate that all significant data and other information that support the analyses, opinions, and conclusions in the report have been retained in the appraiser's files.
3. A statement regarding the limited nature of the report must also be included.
4. The client should be informed that many regulatory agencies and third-party users of appraisal reports do not accept letter reports.

Form Reports. USPAP considers a form report to be a type of limited report and provides the following guidance:

1. Form reports meet the needs of many financial institutions, insurance companies, and government agencies.
2. Form reports must qualify as limited reports under the conditions set forth in USPAP.
3. Some forms may not conform to the USPAP reporting standards and additional material must be included.
4. Certain forms do not contain a certification statement that complies with these standards and, therefore, supplementary material must be added.
5. A form appraisal report is unacceptable if the appraiser fails to:
    *   Consider the purpose of the report, the value definition, and the assumptions and conditions inherent in the report.
    *   Question the client about any engagement criteria that may conflict with proper appraisal practice.
    *   Review the report before signing it.

Narrative Reports

Narrative valuation reports are the most complete type of report. They reflect the appraiser's ability to interpret relevant data and select appropriate valuation methods and procedures to estimate a specifically defined value.

It is important to consider that the report is the appraiser's "representative" before the audience that will rely on the appraiser's analysis. The report will reflect the appraiser's competence and reputation. Some suggestions for the presentation of narrative valuation reports including the following:

1. The paper, cover, and binding should be good quality.
2. The report should be professionally typed and printed.
3. Graphics and charts should be carefully prepared.
4. Illustrations should ideally be on pages facing the material being discussed.
5. The contents should be designed for maximum communication.
6. The sections should be clearly labeled and identified in the table of contents.
7. All superfluous material should be eliminated.
8. There should be good writing style and clear expression.
9. Technical jargon and slang should be avoided.

USPAP Standards Regarding Levels of Appraisal and Types of Appraisal Reports

Early in 1994, the Appraisal Standards Board of The Appraisal Foundation adopted modifications to certain standards and adopted Statement of Appraisal Standards No. 7. These new USPAP provisions provide important professional guidance with regard to alternative levels of appraisal analysis and alternative levels of appraisal reporting. These types of appraisals and appraisal reports are discussed in Exhibit 17–2, which is a reprint of an article from the Willamette Management Associates' quarterly client newsletter, *Insights*.

Premises of the Appraisal

The following premises with regard to business valuation should be affirmatively stated in the content of each narrative valuation report:

1. The contingent and limiting conditions.
2. The purpose and use of the appraisal.
3. The standard or definition of value estimated.
4. The date of the value estimate and the date of the valuation report.
5. The business ownership bundle of rights being appraised.
6. The scope of the appraisal—that is, the extent of the process of collecting, confirming, and reporting data. The scope of the appraisal will vary according to the nature of the business ownership interest being appraised.

Retention of Appraisal Reports and Files

The record keeping section of the ethics provision of USPAP states:

> An appraiser must prepare written records of appraisal, review, and consulting assignments—including oral testimony and reports—and retain such records for a period of at least five years after preparation or at least two years after final disposition of any judicial proceeding in which testimony was given, whichever period expires last.
>
> 1. Written records include true copies of written reports, written summaries of oral testimony, and reports and all data required by the USPAP Standards.
> 2. Written records also include information stored on electronic or magnetic files.
> 3. All supporting notes, documentation, and file memoranda should likewise be retained.

USPAP Confidentiality Provisions

The confidentiality section of the ethics provision of USPAP addresses the confidential nature of the appraiser–client relationship. It states:

> An appraiser must not disclose confidential factual data obtained from a client or the results of an assignment prepared for a client or anyone other than:

Exhibit 17–2
Uniform Standards of Professional Appraisal Practice Update

Introduction

The Appraisal Standards Board (ASB) of The Appraisal Foundation recently adopted new Statements of Appraisal Standards pertaining to any permitted departure from the Uniform Standards of Professional Appraisal Practice (USPAP) specific guidelines. These statements are effective for all appraisals prepared after July 1, 1994.

While these specific statements apply directly to real estate appraisals, the professional guidance they provide has conceptual application to the appraisal of other (non-real estate) types of property interests. Accordingly, appraisers of all types of property interests should be generally aware of these new USPAP guidelines.

In the summer 1994 issue of *Insights,* we reported on the USPAP revisions and modifications that focused on the development of Complete and Limited Appraisals and use of three approved reporting options.

Levels of Appraisal

The USPAP definition of an appraisal is "an estimate of value." When the purpose of an assignment is a value estimate, USPAP considers the assignment to be an appraisal and requires the development of the value estimate to be in compliance with USPAP Standard 1 and requires the reporting of the value estimate to be in compliance with USPAP Standard 2.

The revised standards allow for two different levels of appraisal development:

1. Complete Appraisal: A complete appraisal is the result of an appraisal assignment performed without invoking the "departure provision."

2. Limited Appraisal: A limited appraisal is the result of an appraisal assignment when the "departure provision" is invoked. An appraiser can accept and perform a limited appraisal in which the "departure provision" is invoked as long as the request for something less than or different from a complete appraisal would not result in a misleading analysis and report.

The revised standards allow for three different types of appraisal reports:

1. Self-Contained Appraisal Report: The self-contained appraisal report is the most all-encompassing of the reporting options.

2. Summary Appraisal Report: The Summary appraisal report is less detailed in its presentation.

3. Restricted Appraisal Report: The restricted appraisal report is intended for use only by the client and is the least detailed reporting option.

Appraisers may report the results of either complete appraisals or limited appraisals by using any of the three allowable types of appraisal reports.

Statement on Appraisal Standards No. 7 (SMT-7)

Statements on Appraisal Standards are authorized by the bylaws of The Appraisal Foundation and are issued specifically for the purpose of clarification, interpretation, explanation, or elaboration of the Uniform Standards of Professional Practice. Statements have the full weight of a standards rule.

The subject of SMT-7 is the permitted departure from USPAP specific guidelines. The issue addressed by SMT-7 is when is it appropriate to invoke the departure provision in performing real estate appraisals, and what are the reporting requirements when the departure provision is utilized?

In the definitions section of USPAP, the comment to the definition of *appraisal practice* states: "The use of other nomenclature by the appraiser (e.g., analysis, counseling, evaluation, study, submission, valuation) does not exempt an appraiser from adherence to these standards."

The departure provision of USPAP states: "An appraiser may enter into an agreement to perform an assignment that calls for something less than, or different from, the work that would otherwise be required by the specific guidelines."

This provision goes on to permit limited departures from specific guidelines provided the *appraiser* determines the appraisal process is not *so limited as to mislead the client* and intended users of the report, the appraiser advises the client of the limitations and discloses the limitations in the report, and the client agrees that the limited service would be appropriate.

Definitions

The following definitions from USPAP are also relevant to the understanding of the SMT-7 response to this issue:

Appraisal
   The act or process of estimating value; an estimate of value.

Complete Appraisal
   The act or process of estimating value or an estimate of value performed without invoking the departure provision.

Limited Appraisal
   The act or process of estimating value or an estimate of value performed without invoking the departure provision.

Binding Requirement
   All or part of a standards rule of USPAP from which departure is not permitted.

Specific Guideline
   All or part of a standards rule of USPAP from which departure is permitted under certain limited conditions.

Exhibit 17–2 (concluded)

Report

Any communication, written or oral, of an appraisal, review, or consulting service that is transmitted to the client upon completion of an assignment.

Self-Contained Appraisal Report

A written report prepared under Standards Rule 2-2(a) of a complete or limited appraisal performed under Standard 1.

Summary Appraisal Report

A written report prepared under Standards Rule 2-2(b) of a complete or limited appraisal performed under Standard 1.

Restricted Appraisal Report

A written report prepared under Standards Rule 2-2(c) of a complete or limited appraisal performed under Standard 1.

SMT-7 Response to the Issue

The departure provision and Standard 1 permit the development of two types of appraisals (complete appraisal and limited appraisal). Appraisers are trained and qualified to identify when a limited appraisal is appropriate. At the same time, appraisers must adhere to USPAP in the performance of all types of assignments.

As long as the appraiser determines that the request for something less than, or different from, a complete appraisal would not result in a misleading analysis, then the departure provision can be invoked and the assignment can be accepted and performed.

SMT-7 Clarification of Nomenclature

Various nomenclature has been developed by clients for certain appraisal assignments. The development of the Statement on Appraisal Standards is a response to inquiries about several types of appraisal assignments, and it is appropriate to clarify the meaning of these terms for future reference.

The term "letter opinion of value" has been used to describe a one-page letter that stated a value estimate and referenced the file information and experience of the appraiser as the basis for the estimate. This service does not comply with USPAP and should be eliminated from appraisal practice.

USPAP recognizes that the results of any appraisal assignment may be presented in a letter format provided that the content items in one of the three report options under Standards Rule 2-2 are addressed. The "restricted report" is the minimum report format and replaces the concept of the "letter opinion of value."

Summary and Conclusion

USPAP now allows appraisers to provide a level of analysis that is less than a full appraisal. These revisions to USPAP also allow appraisers, and consumers of appraisal services, to select from three levels of appraisal work product reports. The revisions to USPAP Standards 1 and 2 acknowledge that not all appraisal clients require—and not all appraisal assignments deserve—a complete appraisal and a self-contained, narrative appraisal report.

The issuance of SMT-7 provides important guidance to appraisers as to when limited appraisals are appropriate, as to what the content and intent of such limited appraisals should be, and as to the appropriate terminology to use in such limited appraisals.

SOURCE: Robert P. Schweihs, "Uniform Standards of Professional Appraisal Practice Update," *Insights,* Winter 1995, pp. 18–19.

1. The client and persons specifically authorized by the client.
2. Such third parties as may be authorized by due process of law.
3. A duly authorized professional peer review committee.

Summary

The report is the final product of the valuation process. It must convince the reader of the quality, completeness, and accuracy of the valuation analyses, and of the reasonableness of the valuation conclusions.

The Uniform Standards of Professional Appraisal Practice provide significant guidance with regard to business valuation reporting standards. Appraisers should be familiar with these standards—both with regard to the form and content of appraisal reports and with regard to workpaper files and confidentiality requirements.

Principles of Effective Report Writing[1]

As mentioned above, the purpose of the appraisal report is to convey to the client the logic, data, underlying premises, and analyses that support the final estimate of value. The real task involves doing this clearly, accurately, and convincingly. Even a simple business valuation employs procedures and terminology that are unfamiliar to many clients. Consequently, the reporting process is not a simple one, but recognizing various elements in that process will help to produce better reports and more satisfied clients.

The Reader

Probably the greatest pitfall in appraisal report writing is to ignore the reader. It is easy for writers to be so involved in their ideas that they forget the reader. Everyone has read material that is almost incomprehensible. Usually, this results from the writer's failure to consider the reader's needs.

The first step in effective report writing requires that the appraiser consider the actual reader. Think about the average reader's knowledge of the subject being written about. Appraisers should be mindful that appraisal reports may be read by anyone, not just the client, so taking only the client into consideration may not be enough.

While a business valuation assignment may serve a unique reader or audience, all readers benefit when the report author adheres to the principles of good writing. The following sections address some of the basic principles of effective appraisal report writing.

Clarity.   Phrase ideas so that they are understandable. This principle may sound simplistic, but it has many implications for appraisal writing. One sign of a good writer is his or her ability to explain complex ideas in a simple and straightforward manner. Remember that the two greatest impediments to clear writing are unclear ideas and inappropriate words. Irrelevant material is also a hindrance.

Begin with an Outline.   When ideas are put down on paper it is easier to spot a lack of clarity in the thinking processes. The writing process itself can force people to organize and clarify their thoughts. Others need some kind of outline or planning stage to organize the writing process. In any case, the ideas must be clear before they can be clearly expressed.

Avoid Inappropriate Language.   The appraisal field is full of jargon, acronyms, and expressions not normally used by the general population. If appraisal report writers use pompous and bloated phrases and try to impress the reader with their expertise, the result is often unreadable prose and dissatisfied clients.

Use Precise Definitions.   Recognize that all jargon, acronyms, and terminology need explanation and, in some cases, precise definition. Clients usually do not need an exact definition of a term like *weighted average cost of capital*. Rather, they need an explanation of the procedure. On the other hand, net income can mean different things to various readers, so a precise definition is necessary for

---

[1]This entire section is adapted from "Report Writing and Valuation Analysis," Course 540 (Chicago: The Appraisal Institute, 1994), pp. 97–102.

clarity. The use of acronyms when writing is convenient, but they must first be defined. Writing out a well-known symbol such as *net operating income* (NOI) the first time it appears in a report is not insulting and provides the reader with precise information.

Keep the Language Simple and Familiar.   If a simple word will suffice, don't use a complex one. *About* works just as well as *approximately*; *enough* usually says as much as *a sufficient quantity of.* Moreover, the shorter word allows the client to read faster and concentrate on the important ideas, not on the verbiage.

Readers Expect and Deserve Accuracy.   To convince anyone of the validity of the final value estimate, the language and presentation of the research, analysis, and data must be correct. The valuation report must be an image of the appraiser's professionalism. Consequently, inaccuracies in language, sentence structure, grammar, and even spelling detract from the report's persuasiveness.

The time devoted to the careful editing of a report is not a luxury but a necessity in the appraisal profession. Appraisers should ensure accuracy in the data and the analysis throughout the writing process.

Business Readers Like Reports to Be Short and to the Point.   Time is precious, and few clients can afford the burden of reading needlessly long reports. Keeping a report brief involves thinking while one writes.

Decide what is truly important to the appraisal and eliminate what is irrelevant. Constantly ask yourself, "Does this fact or idea directly affect the value of the business interest?" If not, consider eliminating it. If it is important, ask whether its significance is revealed in the writing.

Conciseness in language comes from simplification. Focus on what is essential and significant, and say it simply. Professionals are able to separate the important from the irrelevant. Appraisal writing should reflect this ability.

Readers Don't Like to Get Lost in the Woods.   Business valuation reports are usually long, complex documents that contain many complicated procedures and much data. The report writer is always more familiar with the analysis presented in the report than the reader is. Solving this problem involves breaking down large, complicated concepts or processes into manageable chunks.

One function of the introduction to each section is to introduce readers to the information and show how that section relates to the whole report—in other words, what to look for and why it is important.

Another organizational technique involves using section headings and subheadings as signals along the way. These headings tell readers where they are in the report and facilitate comprehension, which keeps readers happy.

It is important to look at the report from the reader's perspective. What is clear to the informed writer is not always meaningful to the reader. Reveal logic, show the relationship between ideas, and never assume that the basis for a conclusion is obvious.

Readers Like Breathing Room.   Long-winded paragraphs may have achieved a high grade in college, but they do not always work in the business world. Shorter paragraphs are more effective because they put ideas into digestible bits.

Effectiveness is further increased in business valuation reports when the paragraphs are separated by white space. Headings and subheadings also create white space that helps make the report visually pleasing.

A good way to organize and present random items is to create a bulleted list. Other listed information, such as steps in an analytical process, may need numbers to suggest a required sequence. Either format creates both white space and a sense of order.

Raw data and numbers are easier to grasp in tables than in text. Showing calculations in a one- or two-line table works much better than does a prose description. Similarly, a tabular presentation of raw data provides organization and breathing room.

The Writing Process

While everyone wishes to dash off a valuation report quickly and be done with it, the process is seldom so simple. Few people are able to plan a report while they are writing it, and then leave it unedited after the first draft. Good report writing involves the following process:

- Brainstorming
- Organizing
- Drafting
- Editing
- Proofreading

Each of these steps involves a different kind of thought process. Most people cannot perform all of them at once.

Brainstorming.   This stage is the creative and uninhibited step in the writing process. One needs to be free and noncritical. Jot down ideas, good or bad, in a random list to bring out thoughts that may otherwise be squelched by self-criticism.

Organizing.   This is the time to be critical. Look at the random list of ideas that came from the brainstorming session and edit them. Try to find patterns and develop organization from the brainstorming. Exactly how detailed this organizational step becomes is a personal choice. Some people like very detailed outlines; others feel constrained by them. Everyone, however, needs some general plan that will lead to a specific conclusion.

Drafting.   When writing the first draft of the report, let the ideas flow freely and don't be concerned about editing or proofreading for mistakes. The benefit of this is being able to quickly produce a draft report that can be worked with. Don't be caught staring for hours at a blank page. As with organizing, the drafting mode is a personal preference. Do whatever produces results, but get something on paper.

Editing.   Now the real work beings. First, concentrate on the ideas and the organization. Once the content is satisfactory, work on the language and wording. Spelling and punctuation are not the concern here, but expression and clarity of ideas are. Play the role of the opposing attorney with your writing. Does it say exactly what you mean?

Proofreading. At this stage you must concentrate on the details. Most people cannot work on the organization of ideas and content while checking for spelling errors. The proofreading step works on correctness in all forms: mathematics, data, grammar, spelling, punctuation, and format.

Approach the report writing process with a clear sense of what each step involves and the task will be less painful and more efficient.

Summary

First, this chapter presented the professional standards related to reporting the results of the business valuation. In particular, the USPAP guidelines were discussed.

Second, this chapter discussed both the content and organization of an effective business valuation report. Several principles related to effective report writing were presented.

Well-researched and documented written appraisal reports, presented in a complete, logical, and readable manner, can be instrumental in expediting sound transactions and in reducing the risks of subsequent litigation pursuant to the subject transactions. Conversely, poorly written appraisal reports may delay or prevent transactions and invite litigation, even if the transaction itself was basically sound.

It is hoped this chapter will help report writers to prepare sound reports that will be readable by—and acceptable to—the parties who must be satisfied, whether buyers, sellers, beneficiaries, fiduciaries, regulators, or others related to the subject appraisal.

Bibliography

While this chapter does not contain a complete end-of-chapter bibliography, such as the more technical chapters do, several books on technical report writing and on English style and usage are highly recommended. A brief review of these recommended books is presented below.

Technical Report Writing

Himstreet, William C. *Communicating the Appraisal: The Narrative Report.* Chicago: The Appraisal Institute, 1988.
   This reference specializes in real estate appraisal report writing and is the latest revision of the report writing guides. Because of its focus on the appraisal profession, it is highly recommended.

Houp, Kenneth W., and Thomas E. Pearsall. *Reporting Technical Information,* 4th ed. Beverly Hills, CA: Glencoe, 1980.
   This book is well-respected in the technical writing field. It is both comprehensive and literate. The authors discuss almost every type of report that one might encounter in technical writing. A comprehensive handbook follows the text.

MacGregor, A. J. *Graphics Simplified: How to Plan and Prepare Effective Charts, Graphs, Illustrations, and Other Visual Aids.* Toronto: University of Toronto Press, 1979.

> This excellent standard text provides detailed information on the various types of graphics, their functions, their most effective use, and how to prepare them well.

Miles, James; Donald Bush; and Allin A. Kaplan. *Technical Writing: Principles and Practice.* Chicago: Science Research Associates, 1982.

> The technical report writer will find this text useful because it stresses on-the-job applications rather than library research. And it provides several excellent examples gleaned from business. Its step-by-step analysis shows how to design everything from clear business correspondence to technical reports, including progress reports and technical proposals.

English Style and Usage

The Chicago Manual of Style, 14th ed. Chicago: University of Chicago Press, 1993.

> *The Chicago Manual of Style* has long been the standard reference text for writers in many fields. Its precise rules leave little room for doubt about style matters.

Hodges, John C., and Mary E. Whitten. *Harbrace College Handbook,* 11th ed. San Diego: Harcourt Brace Jovanovich, 1990.

> The staying power of the *Harbrace College Handbook* can be attributed to its straightforward instruction in grammar, mechanics, and punctuation. It provides a wide variety of excellent examples and leads the reader through the information in a logical and concise manner. It includes the Modern Language Association documentation guide.

Strunk, William, Jr., and E. B. White. *Elements of Style,* 3rd ed. New York: Macmillan, 1979.

> This is one of the standards in the composition field, and for a very good reason: in fewer than 100 pages, Strunk and White effectively communicate the most important aspects of good writing.

Chapter 18

A Sample Report

ABC Grocery Company Fair Market Value Nonmarketable, Minority Ownership Interest in Voting Common Stock as of November 10, 1993

The Grocery Industry Outlook
    Overview
    Increased Competition
    Response to Increased Competition
    Unemployment and Demographics
    Outlook
Fundamental Position of the Company
    Introduction
    History
    Retail Operations
    Expansion
    Distribution
    Real Estate
    Competition
    Dividend Policy
    Employees
    Litigation
    Restrictions on Share Transfer
    Prior Transactions in the Company's Stock
    Summary of Positive and Negative Factors
The Selection of Guideline Companies
Financial Statement Analysis
    Overview
    Balance Sheets
    Income Statements
    Ratios
    Comparison to Industry Average
Appraisal of Fair Market Value
    Valuation Methods Used
    Guideline Company Method
    Discounted Economic Income Method
    Summary before Discount for Lack of Marketability
    Discount for Lack of Marketability
    Selection of Applicable Discount for ABC Grocery Minority Interests
    Concluded Fair Market Value
Appendixes
    Exhibits
    Definition of Financial and Operating Ratios
    Appraisal Certification
    Statement of Contingent and Limiting Conditions
    Professional Qualifications of the Principal Appraiser

ABC Grocery Company is a sample case contrived to illustrate the application of many of the principles and procedures presented in several chapters of this book.

This is a hypothetical company and is not intended to be patterned after any real-world company. The reader should not be concerned whether the hypothetical fact pattern resembles the reader's perception of reality in the retail grocery industry. The point of the case is to demonstrate an example of a full, narrative appraisal report (as discussed in Chapter 17) and to illustrate by example the application of some procedures commonly used in valuation reports.

August 24, 1994

Mr. Robert Kline, Executor
Estate of John Smith
ABC Grocery Company
123 Uphill Road
Portland, Oregon 97999

Dear Mr. Kline:

At your request, we have appraised a nonmarketable, minority ownership interest in the voting common stock of ABC Grocery Company, as of November 10, 1993. We are pleased to submit the results of our findings in the following report.

PURPOSE AND OBJECTIVE OF THE APPRAISAL

The objective of this appraisal is to estimate the fair market value of the nonmarketable, minority ownership interest in the voting common stock of ABC Grocery Company owned by the Estate of John Smith, as of November 10, 1993.

The purpose of this appraisal is to provide an independent valuation opinion to assist you in filing the estate tax return for the Estate of John Smith.

DEFINITION AND PREMISE OF VALUE

For purposes of this appraisal, we define fair market value as the price at which the property would change hands between a willing buyer and a willing seller when the former is not under any compulsion to buy and the latter is not under any compulsion to sell, both having reasonable knowledge of relevant facts, and with both seeking their maximum economic self-interests.

We have appraised the voting common stock of ABC Grocery Company under the appraisal premise of value in continued use, as part of a going-concern business entity. We concluded that this appraisal premise was appropriate based upon our analysis of the highest and best use of the subject operating business.

SUMMARY DESCRIPTION OF ABC GROCERY COMPANY

ABC Grocery Company ("ABC Grocery" or "the Company") is a privately owned retail grocery chain incorporated in Portland, Oregon, in 1930. As of the Company's fiscal year ended September 30, 1993, ABC Grocery Company operated 139 food stores in Oregon, Washington, and California. Of this total, 119 stores were food supermarkets operating under the name of *ABC Grocery Store,* and 20 stores were super food warehouse stores operating under the name of *Giant ABC Grocery Store.* Approximately 85.0 percent of the sales of products sold in ABC Grocery stores are supplied by distribution centers owned by the Company. Net sales for the Company were $1.62 billion for the Company's 1993 fiscal year.

VALUATION PROCEDURES

This appraisal was performed in accordance with the Uniform Standards of Professional Appraisal Practice (USPAP), as promulgated by The Appraisal Foundation.

We relied on two valuation methods to estimate the fair market value of the nonmarketable, minority interest in the common stock of ABC Grocery. These methods were the guideline publicly traded company method and the discounted economic income method.

In the guideline publicly traded company method, we estimated the value of ABC Grocery Company's equity by analyzing the prices of publicly traded companies in the retail grocery store industry.

We performed the discounted economic income method based on financial projections provided to us by the Company's management. We estimated the value of the Company's equity by discounting the projected economic income of the Company by the appropriate present value discount rate.

We then performed a valuation synthesis and reached an overall valuation conclusion based upon the result of the analyses summarized above.

The indicated value from these methods represents the publicly traded equivalent value, or a fully marketable price, for ABC Grocery Company's common stock. Since there is no active market for the block of stock owned by the Estate, we then discounted the estimated publicly traded equivalent value for lack of marketability.

A more detailed description of our quantitative and qualitative analyses and valuation conclusions is presented in the attached narrative valuation opinion report.

VALUATION SYNTHESIS AND CONCLUSION

Based on our analysis and considering all relevant factors that affect the valuation, it is our opinion that the fair market value of the nonmarketable, minority ownership interest in ABC Grocery Company voting common stock held by the Estate of John Smith, as of November 10, 1993, is:

$152 per share

VALUATION TERMS AND CONDITIONS

During this appraisal, we were provided with audited and unaudited financial and operational data with respect to ABC Grocery Company. We have accepted these data without independent verification or confirmation.

We are independent of ABC Grocery Company, and we have no financial interests in the securities subject to appraisal. Our fee for this appraisal is in no way influenced by the result of our valuation conclusion.

This valuation opinion report is prepared solely for the purpose stated herein. No other purpose is intended or should be inferred.

The attached valuation opinion report and exhibits further describe the analyses performed and conclusions reached during this appraisal.

The attached appraisal certification, statement of contingent and limiting conditions and qualifications of the principal appraiser are integral parts of this valuation opinion.

Sincerely,
WILLAMETTE MANAGEMENT ASSOCIATES

James G. Rabe, CFA, ASA

Introduction

Description of the Assignment

We were retained by the Estate of John Smith to appraise the fair market value of an approximate 5.45 percent ownership interest in the common stock of ABC Grocery Company ("ABC Grocery" or "the Company") for federal estate tax purposes. The valuation date is the date of death of John Smith, November 10, 1993.

Standard and Definition of Value

The standard of value for gift and estate taxes is fair market value. Fair market value is defined as:

> The price at which the property would change hands between a willing buyer and a willing seller when the former is not under any compulsion to buy and the latter is not under any compulsion to sell, both parties having reasonable knowledge of relevant facts. Court decisions frequently state in addition that the hypothetical buyer and seller are assumed to be able, as well as willing, to trade and to be well informed about the property and concerning the market for such property.[1]

Among other factors, this appraisal takes into consideration all elements of appraisal listed in Internal Revenue Service Ruling 59-60, which generally outlines the valuation of closely held stocks and includes the following:

1. The nature of the business and the history of the company.
2. The economic outlook in general and the outlook of the retail grocery industry in particular.
3. The book value and the financial condition of the company.
4. The earning capacity of the company.
5. The dividend-paying capacity of the company.
6. Whether or not the company has goodwill or other intangible value.
7. Sales of stock and the size of the block to be valued.
8. The market prices of stocks of corporations engaged in the same or similar lines of business as the company and whose stocks are actively traded in a free and open market, either on an exchange or over-the-counter.

---

[1] Revenue Ruling 59-60, 1959-1, C.B. 237.

Implied within this standard of value is that the consideration for the fair market value is expressed in cash, or the customary economic equivalent, paid at closing.

In addition, we have appraised the subject company's stock under the premise of value in continued use, as a going-concern business entity. This premise assumes the business will continue to operate as an income-producing entity.

Summary Description of the Company

ABC Grocery is a privately owned retail grocery chain incorporated in Portland, Oregon, in 1930. As of the Company's fiscal year ended September 30, 1993, ABC Grocery Company operated 139 food stores in Oregon, Washington, and California. Of this total, 119 stores were food supermarkets operating under the name of *ABC Grocery Store,* and 20 stores were super food warehouse stores operating under the name of *Giant ABC Grocery Store.* Approximately 85.0 percent of the sales of products sold in ABC Grocery stores are supplied by distribution centers owned by the Company. Net sales for the Company were $1.62 billion for the Company's 1993 fiscal year.

Capitalization and Ownership

The Company is capitalized with one class of voting common shares. As of the valuation date, the Company had authorized 10,000,000 shares of $1.00 par value, voting common stock. The Company issued 1,544,678 shares, with 112,908 shares in treasury stock. As of November 10, 1993, there were 1,431,770 shares of voting common stock outstanding. Of these, 78,031, or approximately 5.45 percent of the outstanding shares, were held by the Estate of John Smith.

The ownership distribution of the shares of the Company's stock, as of the valuation date, was as follows:

Table 18–1

Shareholder	Number of Shares Owned	Percentage of Total Outstanding Shares
Frank Adams	609,223	42.55%
Robert Beck	136,251	9.52
James Crowley	201,158	14.05
Susan Miller	407,107	28.43
Estate of John Smith	78,031	5.45
Total	1,431,770	100.00%

Sources of Information

We used the following information and documents in our appraisal:

- Company audited financial statements for the fiscal years ended September 30, 1989–1993.
- ABC Grocery corporate income tax returns for 1989 through 1993.
- ABC Grocery's five-year strategic plan, dated September 30, 1993, for fiscal years 1994 through 1998.

- Internally prepared budget for fiscal 1994.
- Equipment list and depreciation schedule as of September 30, 1993.
- List of stockholders for fiscal 1989 through 1993.
- Copies of store leases.
- Excerpts from minutes of recent board of directors' meetings.
- Articles of incorporation and bylaws.
- Historical stock sales and purchases of ABC Grocery Company common stock.
- Information on the outlook for the U.S. economy was derived from the following sources: *Forecast 1993–1994,* First Interstate Bancorp; *Barron's; Business Week; The Wall Street Journal; The Outlook* and *Trends & Projections,* Standard & Poor's Corporation; *Value Line Investment Survey; Value Line Convertibles; U.S. Financial Data,* Federal Reserve Bank of St. Louis; *The Chicago Fed Letter,* Federal Reserve Bank of Chicago; *Monthly Business Notes,* The Conference Board; *Economic & Financial Market Outlook,* American National Bank; *U.S. Economic Outlook,* The Northern Trust Company; *The Oregonian;* and *Fortune.*
- Information on the Oregon, Washington, and California economies was derived from the following sources: *Western Blue Chip Economic Forecast;* First Interstate's *Forecast 1993–1994; Northwest Portrait 1993,* U.S. Bank; *Washington State Labor Area Summary,* August 1993; and *Oregon Economic and Revenue Forecast,* September 1993.
- For information on the grocery store industry, the following sources were relied upon: *Transportation & Distribution; New York Times; Distribution; Progressive Grocer; Marketing News; Advertising Age; Value Line Investment Survey;* Standard & Poor's *Industry Surveys; U.S. Industrial Outlook 1994; Brandweek;* and Association for Investment Management Research, *Industry Analysis—The Retail Industry.*

In addition, James Rabe of our firm visited ABC Grocery's offices in Portland, Oregon, on June 25, 1994, interviewed key management personnel, and toured various stores and distribution centers owned by the Company.

Summary of Valuation Conclusions

We considered all relevant factors in arriving at our appraisal conclusions for the shares owned by the Estate of John Smith.

We relied on two valuation methods to estimate the fair market value of the minority interest in the common stock of ABC Grocery. These methods were the guideline publicly traded company method and the discounted economic income method.

In the guideline publicly traded company method, we estimated the value of ABC Grocery's common stock by analyzing the prices of publicly traded companies in the grocery store industry. Due to the differences in leverage between the guideline publicly traded companies and ABC Grocery, we used a debt-free method to estimate the market value of the Company's invested capital and then subtracted the market value of the Company's interest-bearing debt to estimate the market value of the Company's equity.

We relied on multiples of earnings before interest and taxes (EBIT); earnings before depreciation, interest, and taxes (EBDIT); debt-free net income (DFNI); debt-free cash flow (DFCF); revenues; and tangible book value of invested capital (TBVIC) of the guideline companies to estimate the market value of ABC Grocery's invested capital.

We then subtracted the market value of the Company's interest-bearing debt to result in an estimated value for the equity of the Company.

We performed the discounted economic income method based on financial projections provided to us by the Company's management. We used net cash flow as the measure of economic income in our discounted economic income analysis.

We developed net cash flow estimates for ABC Grocery based on management's income statement projections and then discounted these projections to a present value based on the appropriate weighted average cost of capital for ABC Grocery.

We then subtracted the market value of the Company's interest-bearing debt to result in an estimated value for the equity of the Company.

The indicated values from each of these methods represent the publicly traded equivalent value, or a fully marketable price, for ABC Grocery's common stock. Since there is no active market for the block of stock owned by the Estate, we then discounted the estimated publicly traded equivalent value for lack of marketability.

Based on our analysis and considering all relevant factors that affect the valuation, it is our opinion that the fair market value of ABC Grocery common stock for estate tax purposes, as of November 10, 1993, is:

$152 per share

U.S. Economic Outlook

In the valuation of any company, the general economic outlook as of the appraisal date should be considered, since the national economic outlook influences how investors perceive alternative investment opportunities at any given time.

In our appraisal of ABC Grocery, we considered the consensus forecast for the U.S. economy that prevailed as of November 10, 1993. In particular, we focused on the outlook for aspects of the economy that are most directly related to the retail grocery industry and ABC Grocery.

Overview

The recession officially ended in March 1991; however, news of below-average employment growth, continued layoffs, and financially strapped state and local governments has obscured other signs of economic progress. The U.S. economy now boasts slower inflation, smaller private and public debt burdens, and lower interest rates than in recent years.

According to the U.S. Department of Commerce, gross domestic product (GDP) increased at an annual rate of 2.8 percent in the third quarter of 1993, above the rate of increase for the first and second quarters of 1993 of 0.8 percent and 1.9 percent, respectively. Most of the increase in the third quarter was due to increased consumer purchases of durable goods and new homes and increased business investment in capital equipment. Economic activity is expected to continue to be modestly positive in the remaining months of 1993 and during 1994, hindered by the combination of higher tax rates and a continued high rate of unemployment.

Inflation

The Consumer Price Index for all urban consumers (CPI-U) was 145.7 in October 1993, up from 145.1 in September 1993 and 144.8 in August 1993. Economists expect inflation to remain within a 2.5 percent to 3.5 percent range over the next two years. Long-term projections are for moderate price increases through 1996–1998. Low inflation continues to be one of the few bright spots in the economy.

Employment

The unemployment rate for October 1993 was 6.8 percent. Although employment increased in the third quarter of 1993, the new jobs are lacking in quantity and quality. The new jobs created during this recovery are in the services industries, mainly in the temporary help, health, restaurant, and social services areas. The average hourly salary in these sectors is $8.74, compared with the average hourly wage of $10.86 for the entire nonfarm sector. During the past year, these four sectors have created over 54 percent of all new jobs.

By this point in time in the three recoveries previous to this one, payrolls increased 7.4 percent, while they have increased only 1.7 percent in this recovery. Three reasons given for this lack of job creation are: (1) sluggish economic growth, (2) the growth in labor productivity, and (3) significant structural labor market changes. Of the jobs lost during the most recent recession, 76 percent (the highest percentage on record) have not been recovered and are considered permanent losses.

A very difficult environment for wage increases accompanies the current sluggish job growth. The Bureau of Labor Statistics (BLS) employment cost index for private industry indicates a declining pattern of wage gains. The increase of 3.5 percent in 1993 just keeps pace with inflation. The annual increase in hourly pay has been in the 2.3 percent to 2.5 percent range for the past year.

About 22.0 percent of 870 companies surveyed by the American Management Association plan to reduce staff during the year ending in June 1994. The projected layoffs are expected to affect very large corporations more than small businesses. Corporate cutback decisions are no longer based on a business downturn but on improved staff productivity and new technology.

Interest Rates

Interest rates are as low as they have been in 20 years and are expected to remain low for the rest of the year. Long-term rates have decreased since late May. The difference between three-month Treasury bills, yielding 3.2 percent as of November 10, 1993, and 30-year Treasury bonds, which are yielding 6.2 percent, is now three percentage points. *Value Line* estimates that three-month Treasury bill rates will remain at 3.2 percent through year end and estimates a 3.4 percent to 4.0 percent range in 1994. The Federal Reserve discount rate has been at 3.0 percent since July 2, 1992. This is the longest period without a change since 1989–1990. The yield on three-month Treasury bills has ranged between 2.69 percent to 3.48 percent since July 1992. Long-term Treasury bond rates are expected to stay at current levels for the remaining months of the year.

While borrowers have profited from falling interest rates, savers have experienced sharp income decline. In the household sector, for example, total interest payments fell by $5.8 billion between the end of 1991 and the end of 1992, while total interest income received by households plunged $73.1 billion. Net interest income decreased another $45.0 billion in the second quarter of 1993, down 14.0 percent from its peak in late 1990.

Below is a summary of some key interest rate projections for 1994 and 1995:

Table 18–2

Forecast of Interest Rates
(Quarterly Averages)

	1994				1995			
	Q1	Q2	Q3	Q4	Q1	Q2	Q3	Q4
Short-term								
Fed funds (overnight)	3.17	3.33	3.50	3.75	3.75	3.92	4.00	4.25
Treasury bills (3-month)	3.18	3.32	3.45	3.65	3.65	3.82	3.90	4.15
CDs (3-month, secondary)	3.28	3.44	3.61	3.86	3.86	4.03	4.11	4.36
LIBOR (3-month)	3.40	3.56	3.73	3.98	3.98	4.15	4.23	4.48
Prime rate	6.00	6.00	6.00	6.00	6.17	6.33	6.50	6.50
Long-term								
U.S. government bonds (30-yr.)	6.10	6.18	6.25	6.30	6.30	6.37	6.40	6.50
Corporate Aaa (Moody's)	6.71	6.76	6.83	6.91	6.91	7.00	7.04	7.18
Mortgage rate (fixed)	6.95	7.03	7.10	7.18	7.18	7.27	7.31	7.45

SOURCE: *Forecast 1994–1995*, First Interstate Bancorp, October 1993.

Consumer Spending

Retail sales increased at an annual rate of 6.5 percent during the third quarter of 1993 and have increased 6.1 percent since September 1992. First Interstate Bancorp predicts in *Forecast 1994–1995* that retail sales will advance 5.5 percent in 1994 and 1995. Auto sales are included in those predictions, increasing to 14.2 million auto sales in 1994 and 14.3 million in 1995, due to the fact that the average automobile is now seven years old.

Accounting for approximately two-thirds of the nation's total economic activity, consumer spending is crucial to an economic recovery. Consumer spending rose 0.3 percent in September after rising 0.2 percent in August and 0.3 percent in July. Since spring of this year, consumers have been increasing personal consumption at a faster rate than the growth rate in personal income, resulting in a decrease in the savings rate from 4.7 percent in April to 3.7 percent at the end of September 1993.

The Conference Board's Index of Consumer Confidence rose to 63.8 in September from 59.3 in August. This is its highest level since April 1993. The Consumer Confidence Index had fluctuated downward since January 1993, when it was 76.7, reaching a low in August 1993.

The Stock Markets

The Dow Jones Industrial Average (DJIA) stood at 3,685.34 at November 10, 1993, up 12.9 percent from the previous 12 months. The Standard & Poor's 500 Index was 463.62 at the close of business on November 10, 1993, up 7.7 percent from the previous 12 months. The continuing positive increase in the stock market averages has been fueled by a combination of rising corporate profits, low inflation, and declining interest rates.

The following table presents various stock market averages at the end of each quarter of 1992 and 1993 and the related price/earnings multiples and dividend yields for the Standard & Poor's 400 Industrials and 500 Composite.

Table 18–3

Historical Stock Market Data

	1992				1993		
	3/31	6/30	9/30	12/31	3/31	6/30	9/30
Dow Jones Industrial Average	3249.10	3318.50	3200.61	3301.11	3435.11	3516.08	3555.12
S&P 400 Industrials	479.14	483.64	480.84	507.46	504.36	514.26	516.16
P/E multiple	28.44	28.60	26.86	26.95	25.86	25.11	27.66
Dividend yield	2.65	2.67	2.75	2.60	2.54	2.54	2.49
S&P 500 Composite	401.55	411.77	410.47	435.71	441.67	450.53	458.93
P/E multiple	25.14	25.43	24.07	24.14	23.10	22.47	23.67
Dividend yield	3.05	3.02	3.08	2.89	2.83	2.82	2.75
Nasdaq (OTC) Industrials	647.72	598.85	604.61	676.95	669.85	703.95	762.78

SOURCE: *Barron's* and *The Wall Street Journal.*

An increasing number of companies are using the equity markets to raise funds. Corporations raised $8 billion with new stock offerings in the second quarter of 1993, up from $6.7 billion in the first quarter of the year.

Summary

It appears that the economic expansion is continuing to slowly broaden its base,; although weakness still persists in some sectors, such as some manufacturing areas and employment. At the end of the third quarter consumers are spending at an increasing rate, businesses continue to invest in new equipment, and home building and housing demand are beginning to respond to lower interest rates. Industrial production is showing signs of an upturn. New jobless claims are at a four-year low. Lower interest rates are providing stimulus to rate-sensitive sectors of the economy.

Economic activity should increase modestly through the end of 1993 and during 1994, but will be hindered by higher tax rates, the decreasing rate of family formations, and a continued high rate of joblessness. Inflation should remain in a 2.5 percent to 3.5 percent range possibly through the latter part of the decade.

The U.S. economic outlook as summarized above would have a moderately positive impact on the value of the shares of ABC Grocery. However, since the Company's stores are located in Oregon, Washington, and California, we also reviewed the economic outlook for these states, as presented in the next section of this report.

The Oregon, Washington, and California Economies

The economic outlook for Oregon, Washington, and California is also relevant to the analysis of ABC Grocery, since the Company's stores are located throughout those three states. Due to the nature of the Company's business, ABC Grocery will be more directly influenced by changes in the economic outlook for these specific areas than the U.S. economy as a whole. Therefore, we considered the economic outlook for these three states as of November 10, 1993.

Overview

The 1980s were a turbulent decade for the Pacific Northwest's economy. The back-to-back recessions of 1980 and 1982 were more intense and longer in the region than for the nation. The recessions were followed by a period of stagnant growth in the mid-1980s, but the economy has recovered strongly during the last two years of the decade. Since 1989, job and income growth have outpaced the nation. During the 1991–92 period, the Northwest continued the pattern of performing better than the national averages in terms of income and employment.

However, the Northwest economy has not been immune to the forces affecting the rest of the nation. Washington has been hit by the decline in the aerospace and defense sector and the end of the construction boom. These forces have significantly changed the growth pattern in the Seattle area while other portions of the state continue to grow. With the depressed economy in southern California, some of that state's small manufacturing companies have come to the Northwest seeking lower costs, a better quality of life, and a more robust economy. The construction real estate sector in the region continues to fare better than that of the nation. A synopsis of the economic outlook for Oregon, Washington, and California is presented below.

Oregon

Oregon's economy has continued to increase at a moderate pace since the U.S. recession ended in the spring of 1991. Wage and salary jobs have increased by 2.2 percent following the end of the recession. Since March of 1991, Oregon's personal income has increased at a 5.5 percent annual rate versus a 4.4 percent rate for the nation. Personal income is expected to increase 6.2 percent in 1993, with net job growth increasing by 1.9 percent. The state's economic outlook is looking brighter, and growth should continue into early 1994. Income growth and job growth during 1994 should reach 7.1 percent and 3.0 percent, respectively.

Nonresidential building permits increased 8.6 percent from October 1992 to October 1993, to total $371.9 million. Residential permits increased 18.6 percent from October 1992 to October 1993.

The unemployment rate decreased to 7.0 percent in October 1993, down from 7.5 percent in September 1993. This unemployment rate is slightly below the unemployment figure for the past 12 months. The primary contributor to job growth in 1993 is the services sector. The services sector increased 4.3 percent from October 1992 to October 1993, which is at a rate twice that of the rest of the economy.

Key forces to improved conditions in Oregon are an expanding high-technology sector, increased construction activity, continued in-migration, and improving agricultural conditions. Major limiting factors in the state's economy expected over the next two years are weakness in the timber industry, layoffs in the utilities sector, cutbacks in the aerospace industry, and downsizing of state government.

In contrast to the 1980s, Oregon's economy is expected to increase faster than the U.S. economy during the remainder of the 1990s. Oregon employment is expected to increase 20.3 percent over the next 10 years, while U.S. employment is expected to increase 13.8 percent. The state's population is expected to increase at nearly twice the national average.

Washington

The Washington economy slowed dramatically in 1991, 1992, and so far in 1993. Over this time period the manufacturing sector lost jobs, led by Boeing, but with losses in lumber and wood products, primary metals, and some nondurable sectors as well.

The location of job growth in Washington has shifted in the 1990s. During the 1980s, growth pressures in the Seattle metropolitan area led to the passage of the Growth Management Act by the state legislature. Since the passage of this legislation, growth has shifted to outside the Seattle area. Every other metropolitan area in the state experienced increases in wage and salary employment.

Several factors have played a role in the slow economic advancement of the Puget Sound region during 1993. These major factors are weak foreign economies, the fragile recovery of the U.S. economy, and soft local demand for goods and services. Washington is affected by foreign economies since most of its major industries (transportation equipment, forest products, agriculture, fishing, and aluminum) are export dependent. The sluggish recovery of the U.S. economy is affecting Washington through decreases in airline travel, housing starts, tourism travel, and goods consumption. The local weak economic areas are currently aerospace, agriculture, forest products, and construction, while the relatively strong areas are high technology and government. Stable economic areas are trade and services, tourism, and food processing.

Nonresidential building permits for the state totaled $902.9 million for the year-to-date October 1993. Nonresidential building permits increased 22.5 percent over the same period in 1992. Residential units increased only 0.8 percent for the period October 1992 to October 1993.

The July 1993 unemployment rate in the Seattle area was 7.1 percent, up 20 percent from July 1992. Job growth in the Seattle area is expected to be approximately zero from 1992 to 1993. The outlook for job growth in 1994 for the Seattle area is also essentially flat. The continued layoffs at Boeing between January 1993 and mid-1994 will have a negative effect on the state and local economy.

The seasonally adjusted unemployment rate for Washington in October 1993 was 7.5 percent versus 7.9 percent during October 1992. Looking to the future, Washington should expect an upturn conditional on a continued national recovery, but a modest rate of expansion in comparison with the rest of the nation.

California

After a prosperous mid-to-late 1980s, California's economy slumped into a recession in late 1990, and the state is experiencing its worst recession since the 1930s. Factors negatively affecting growth in California include lower consumer and business confidence due to the following: decreased defense expenditures, overvalued real estate, high business taxes, and cumbersome business regulations. Most analysts anticipate that the economy will begin to recover by the end of 1993 or the first half of 1994.

Trends in nonfarm employment reflect the overall health of the state's economy. The unemployment rate for California increased to 7.4 percent in late 1991; 1992 unemployment increased another 1.8 percent, and there are no signs of improvement in the near future. The unemployment rate was 9.0 percent as of August 1993, and California was one of three states in the nation to have an unemployment rate of 8.5 percent or above in September 1993. The national average unemployment rate during September 1993 was 6.7 percent. California's unemployment rate is expected to fluctuate between 9 percent and 10 percent during 1994.

Personal income increased a modest 2.4 percent in 1992, and an increase of 3.7 percent is projected for 1993. Personal income for the state was estimated at $647 billion for 1992 and 1993's estimate is $671 billion.

The residential real estate market in California struggled in 1991 and 1992. For the three years before 1990, the California real estate market had been explosive, with home prices rising over 20 percent per year. Recently, however, the California housing market has shown signs of recovery. Sales of existing homes in September 1993 increased 11.5 percent over September 1992. The housing market is expected to recover as the job market stabilizes. The percent of households that can afford a median priced home (32 percent) has increased to its highest level since 1987, the year that a rapid escalation in home prices and sales began.

Private nonresidential construction virtually collapsed during the recent recession and is expected to remain at low levels during 1993, with an oversupply of existing space of about 20 percent. In California, this is expected to impact future construction for up to five years.

Employment is showing a slight improvement in 1993 and should strengthen further in 1994. Personal income should increase modestly (4.5 percent) during 1993 and increase further in 1994. Inflation should remain at low to moderate levels. Current low interest rates should be beneficial to California's housing industry. As the national economy improves, demand for California goods and services should increase. California currently represents 13 percent of the national economy.

Summary

The outlook for the economies of Oregon, Washington, and California is important to the overall appraisal of ABC Grocery, since (everything else being equal) the equity of a business that serves a growing regional economic area is more valuable than the equity of a business serving an area with little or no economic growth. Overall, the outlook for the economies of the states served by ABC Grocery Company is mixed. Although the outlook for Oregon is above the national average, the outlook for Washington and California is somewhat below the national average.

The Grocery Industry Outlook

Since the outlook for the grocery industry has an impact on the value of ABC Grocery Company, we considered the consensus outlook for the industry as of November 10, 1993, as an important part of our appraisal.

Overview

Due primarily to increased competition, supermarkets have experienced decreased growth in sales and profits over the past two years. With price becoming the primary concern of consumers due to the recent U.S. recession, warehouse clubs and discount chains have put intensive competitive pressure on supermarkets. Mass merchandisers and club stores now account for an estimated 8 percent of food industry sales, with prices that average 25 percent less than those of traditional supermarkets.

In 1992, grocery sales increased just 1.7 percent over 1991 sales, to $382.6 billion. After considering food price inflation of 0.7 percent in 1992, the real growth for grocery industry sales was only 1.0 percent. Supermarkets with $2 million or more in sales reported the best performance in 1992, with sales growth of 2.5 percent, according to *Progressive Grocer.* This sales increase was the smallest gain in over 40 years for stores with sales over $2 million. Furthermore, sales for independent grocery stores increased only 1.1 percent in 1992.

The table below presents grocery store sales by size and ownership for 1992 (the latest data available as of the valuation date).

Table 18–4
Grocery Store Sales—1992
(By Size and Ownership)

	Number of Stores	% of Total	$ Sales (millions)	% of Total
All stores	138,000	100.0	382,600	100.0
Supermarkets (over $2.0 million)	30,400	22.0	286,300	74.8
Independent supermarkets	17,690	12.8	204,300	53.4
Chain supermarkets	12,710	9.2	82,000	21.4
Convenience stores*	58,200	42.2	27,000	7.1
Wholesale club stores†	500	0.4	16,500	4.3
Other stores	48,900	35.4	52,800	13.8

*Supermarket items only.
†Excludes sales of gasoline.

SOURCE: *Progressive Grocer*'s Annual Report of the grocery industry.

Increased Competition

In the mature supermarket business, price-based competition has intensified recently, especially due to the added competition from discount stores and warehouse clubs. Discount stores, such as Kmart Corp. and Wal-Mart Stores, Inc., generally offer a specialized merchandise line at discount prices in large superstores or smaller regional discount stores. Warehouse clubs, such as Costco, are large retail establishments that usually offer at discount prices a limited product line with an extensive array of complementary merchandise.

Warehouse clubs are currently supermarkets' biggest rival. According to a July 1993 article in *The Economist,* the number of warehouse retailers has doubled to more than 600 in three years. The clubs experienced double-digit growth in sales and earnings until the early 1990s, but since then sales and earnings growth has slowed somewhat. According to a September 1993 article in *Marketing News,* approximately 8 percent of clubs' $33–40 billion volume was stolen from grocers.

Grocers have begun stocking bulk items at matching prices while offering a wider grocery selection and better service than the clubs. Warehouse clubs are responding to the competition by downsizing and restructuring, changing their merchandise mix, adding more services, and opening new warehouse club stores.

An even larger threat for traditional supermarkets may come from the supercenters developed by discount stores such as Kmart and Wal-Mart, according to *Progressive Grocer.* Supercenters sell general merchandise and a broad array of foods and average 110,000 square feet. These outlets offer one-stop shopping that supermarkets can't duplicate. Weaknesses inherent within the concept include the quality of perishables and the very large size of the stores. The size of the stores may limit their expansion possibilities. Kmart and Wal-Mart plan to become two of the largest supermarket operators in the United States by the year 2000. Kmart currently operates four supercenters and plans to add 15 more during 1993, while Wal-Mart plans to double the number of supercenters with groceries to 80 by the end of 1993.

ABC Grocery faces competition from both Kmart and Wal-Mart supercenters. As mentioned above, both Kmart and Wal-Mart plan an aggressive expansion of supercenters in the future. James M. Degan & Co. predicted in *Progressive Grocer*'s June 1993 issue that supercenters will total 458 by the end of 1994 with sales of $16.4 billion. A total of 305 supercenters were in operation at the end of 1992.

Response to Increased Competition

Supermarkets have lost sales to drugstores and warehouse clubs in the last several years. Grocers are fighting back with better inventory management, expanding offerings of private-label products, and stocking bulk items at matching prices while offering a wider grocery selection and better service.

Aided by falling costs of new technology, retailers are making a considerable effort to reduce the resources devoted to holding and handling inventory. Advances in computer-assisted bar code scanning, on-line receiving, merchandise tracking, and labor management are enabling companies to reduce inventory, speed inventory turnover, and shorten lead times. These techniques lower working capital requirements and provide a higher return on investment.

Slowly, the burden of inventory management is being shifted to the manufacturers. Vendors are being given access to the retailer's point of sale terminals so the vendors can track the retail movement of their own products instantaneously. The manufacturer, the retailer, and the customer all benefit from this partnership.

Expanded offerings of private-label products have become a competitive weapon for large supermarket chains. For some stores, private-label products account for as much as 20.0 percent of sales. Nationally, private-label products now account for $25.5 billion in supermarket sales, over 18.0 percent of supermarket unit volume. Although private-label goods usually sell for 20 percent to 30 percent less than national name brands, they carry higher margins. Premium private-label goods are rapidly taking market share from national brands. In addition, the quality and packaging of private labels have begun to match those of national brands.

Supermarkets are also competing with supercenters and warehouse clubs by stocking bulk items and offering a wider variety of groceries and better service.

Unemployment and Demographics

Retail demand had been negatively impacted by the recent U.S. recession and demographic changes. Although unemployment peaked at 7.7 percent in June 1992 and decreased to 6.8 percent in October 1993, widespread layoffs for both white- and blue-collar workers decreased consumer optimism.

Demographic changes also have contributed to slower retail demand. These changes include a growing proportion of elderly, retired, and semi-retired Americans. Also, the baby-boom generation has discovered frugality, and grocers have faced lower average customer transaction size. Price sensitivity is higher now than it was in the 1980s, and grocers are trying new merchandising concepts to counteract this trend.

The single largest group of retail customers is persons in their 40s. This group is shifting consumption away from status and conspicuous consumption and toward caution about debt levels. A study developed by Mimi Lieber of LAR Management Consultants revealed consumers are spending 32 percent less time shopping than they did in 1990. One cause of decreased shopping could be that people are spending more time at work. Of those surveyed, 39 percent said they are working longer hours than they did in 1990.

Outlook

Retailers of nondurable merchandise face a slow-growing market and changes in demographics and consumer buying habits. Retailers who adjust their strategies and take advantage of new marketing techniques should improve their market position. Retail food store sales tend to mirror changes in general business conditions as reflected in the gross domestic product (GDP), which is forecast to increase by about 3.0 percent in 1994. Most of the competition in the industry is based on price, and a number of efficiency measures to achieve an optimum cost structure must be initiated by the retailer in order to continue to gain market share.

Over the long term, the retail sector is not expected to grow as fast as it has in the past due to the changes in demographics and consumer buying patterns. During the years 1990–2005, an average annual growth rate of 2.5 percent is expected, compared to 3.5 percent annually during the previous 15 years, according to *U.S. Industrial Outlook.*

An estimate from Willard Bishop Consulting in *Advertising Age* predicts warehouse club sales should increase 30 percent to nearly $36 billion in 1993. According to a July 1993 article in *Brandweek,* warehouse club sales are projected to reach $70 billion by 1998. A 1992 study by Cornell University estimated that warehouse clubs hold approximately 4.5 percent of U.S. grocery sales and will likely hold 9.5 percent by 2000. A report published by the Food Marketing Institute in 1992 warned that the discounters could more than double their share of the market within 10 years.

The outlook for the retail grocery industry negatively impacts the value of ABC Grocery's stock, due to the expected slower growth rate for grocers and increased competition.

Fundamental Position of the Company

Introduction

Founded in 1930, ABC Grocery Company is a privately owned retail food chain headquartered in Portland, Oregon. As of the Company's fiscal year ended September 30, 1993, ABC Grocery Company operated 139 food stores in Oregon, Washington, and California. Of this total, 119 stores were food supermarkets operating under the name of *ABC Grocery Store*, and 20 stores were super food warehouse stores operating under the name of *Giant ABC Grocery Store.* Approximately 85.0 percent of the sales of products sold in ABC Grocery stores are supplied by distribution centers owned by the Company. Net sales for the Company were $1.62 billion for the 1993 fiscal year.

History

ABC Grocery's history dates back to June 1, 1930, when Ben Adams, late founder of ABC Grocery, opened an ABC Grocery Store in Portland, Oregon.

1930s and 1940s.   During the 1930s and 1940s, the ABC Grocery organization grew to 12 stores located throughout Oregon.

1950s.   Foremost in ABC Grocery's accomplishments during the 1950s was constructing produce and grocery warehouses. By the close of the 1950s, ABC Grocery had grown to 18 stores and 400 employees.

1960s.   By 1961, ABC Grocery opened its first store across the Oregon state line, in Seattle, Washington. ABC Grocery incurred heavy initial losses upon entering the Seattle market until it was able to achieve a reputation with its customers comparable to the reputation it enjoyed in Oregon.

By the early 1960s, the warehouse facilities constructed in 1953 had become too small to meet ABC Grocery's needs. ABC Grocery opened a new 175,000-square-foot distribution center in 1962.

1970s.   The 1970s was a period of rapid growth for ABC Grocery. It opened 38 stores, including ABC Grocery's first store in California, bringing the total number of stores to 65 by the close of the decade. New store construction and remodeling steadily increased the average size of ABC Grocery's stores. By the close of the 1970s, stores averaged more than 17,500 square feet with two stores exceeding 30,000 square feet. ABC Grocery also added 71,000 square feet to its distribution center in 1974.

1980s.   To provide a broader range of stores to its customers, ABC Grocery decided to diversify its store operations by opening its first super food warehouse store in 1982.

1990s.   Changes in the 1990s included the following:

- In 1990, the Company subleased an existing warehouse in Eugene, Oregon, to better serve ABC Grocery's stores in Oregon and northern California.
- ABC Grocery began construction of a 115,000-square-foot cold storage distribution facility at its Portland, Oregon, complex. The facility, with storage capacity of nearly 3 million cubic feet, will improve distribution efficiency for frozen foods, ice cream, and novelties.

Retail Operations

Introduction.   At the end of fiscal 1993, ABC Grocery operated 139 food stores using two formats, that is, 119 traditional food supermarkets operating under the name of *ABC Grocery Store* and 20 super food warehouse stores operating under the name of *Giant ABC Grocery Store.*

ABC Grocery offers a broad selection of national, regional, and private-label merchandise in its stores, the majority of which are open seven days a week. Sales in stores open at least one year averaged approximately $12 million in 1993.

ABC Grocery Stores.   At the end of 1993, ABC Grocery operated 119 food stores under the name of ABC Grocery Store. Approximately 40 percent of the ABC Grocery Stores are supplied out of ABC Grocery's distribution center located at its Portland, Oregon, headquarters. Remaining stores are supplied from the distribution centers located in Eugene, Oregon, and Tacoma, Washington. ABC Grocery distributes merchandise to all its stores on a wholesale basis at a price to each store that includes a markup that ABC Grocery believes is similar to the markup that would take place in arm's-length transactions.

ABC Grocery stores range in gross size from approximately 15,000 to 62,000 square feet. The cost of land, construction, and equipment for a new ABC Grocery Store ranges from $2.0 million to $3.0 million, depending on the size and location of the store. ABC Grocery has never purchased existing stores; it has always constructed its own stores.

A typical ABC Grocery Store carries over 15,000 items of general merchandise in addition to over 15,000 different food items. General merchandise includes limited men's, women's, and children's apparel, auto accessories, health and beauty aids, cosmetics, toys, hardware, housewares, shoes, small appliances, plants, fresh flowers, and gardening supplies. Prescription drugs are available through store pharmacies.

Giant ABC Grocery Stores.   ABC Grocery opened its first Giant ABC Grocery Store in Bellevue, Washington, in 1982. At the end of fiscal 1993, ABC Grocery operated 20 Giant ABC Grocery Stores.

The Giant ABC Grocery Stores offer almost all of the departments and features offered in the ABC Grocery stores. The primary difference is lower prices that are made available because of scaled-down decor and lower labor costs. The warehouse structure allows goods to be stocked to the ceiling, thus eliminating some backroom storage, while reinforcing the price image of the store. Management estimates that prices are 15 percent to 20 percent lower at a Giant ABC Grocery Store than at a conventional supermarket.

ABC Grocery supplies a majority of its Giant ABC Grocery Stores from its own distribution centers. The merchandise is distributed at a cost representing what ABC Grocery believes to be a competitive wholesale markup established by ABC Grocery.

Expansion

ABC Grocery's unit expansion for the past five fiscal years is presented in the table below.

Table 18–5
Store Unit Expansion

	Fiscal Years Ended Approximately September 30:				
	1993	1992	1991	1990	1989
ABC Grocery Stores					
Units beginning of year	118	118	119	119	118
Openings	3	4	5	1	2
Closings	2	4	6	1	1
Units end of year	119	118	118	119	119
Average sq. ft. per store at year-end	33,900	32,850	31,500	30,100	29,000
Giant ABC Grocery Stores					
Units beginning of year	17	15	14	11	9
Openings	5	3	2	3	2
Closings	2	1	1	0	0
Units end of year	20	17	15	14	11
Average sq. ft. per store at year-end	59,000	55,000	53,000	52,000	52,000

ABC Grocery normally devotes a significant portion of its capital budget to the remodeling and expansion of existing stores. The cost of substantial remodeling and expansion ranges from $1 to $2 million per store including fixtures. ABC Grocery completed major expansions of three and five stores in 1992 and 1993, respectively. Many less substantial store remodels are undertaken and completed each year.

Distribution

The grocery and produce items supplied by ABC Grocery's distribution centers constitute approximately 85 percent of sales of the products sold in ABC Grocery stores. The balance of the merchandise is provided by direct store deliveries of various suppliers (principally beverages such as soft drinks, beer, various snack and bakery goods, and other items typically distributed directly to stores on a local basis).

ABC Grocery uses 103 trucks, 271 trailers, and 290 automobiles in its business. All the trucks are serviced out of either ABC Grocery's main distribution center complex in Portland or at its Tacoma facility. ABC Grocery leases approximately 40 percent of its trucks, tractors, and autos;, and the remaining vehicles are owned by ABC Grocery.

Real Estate

Of the 139 stores that ABC Grocery operated at the end of fiscal 1993, ABC Grocery owned 27 buildings and related land parcels. The remaining 112 stores consist of buildings and land that ABC Grocery has leased on a long-term basis.

Competition

ABC Grocery has faced severe competitive pressures in the majority of the cities in which its stores are located, and management anticipates even more intense competition in 1994. ABC Grocery competes with large regional and national chains, as well as local chains and independent, single-store operators.

Dividend Policy

Historically, the Company has paid no cash dividends to shareholders. In addition, management does not anticipate paying dividends over the next five years.

Employees

ABC Grocery has 11,890 regular employees, of whom approximately 60 percent are part-time employees.

ABC Grocery's employees have never been covered by a collective bargaining agreement, and historically there have been good relations between management and employees.

Key management personnel are presented below:

Frank Adams (50), is president of ABC Grocery and is responsible for overall corporate strategy and expansion. Mr. Adams is the son of the founder of the Company and has been employed by ABC Grocery since his graduation from college.

Robert Beck (49), executive vice president, is responsible for the Company's marketing strategy and also assists with overall corporate planning activities.

James Crowley (45), vice president–finance, joined the Company in 1980 after working for several years for a national accounting firm. Mr. Crowley is a CPA and is responsible for all of the Company's accounting and financial functions.

Susan Miller (57), vice president–operations, is responsible for analyzing and improving store operating performance. Ms. Miller has been with ABC Grocery for 20 years.

Litigation

ABC Grocery is not subject to material legal proceedings, other than ordinary routine litigation incidental to its business. ABC Grocery believes it has adequate insurance to cover ordinary claims that may be made in the normal course of business.

Restrictions on Share Transfer

According to the bylaws of the Company, ABC Grocery has a right of first refusal on the sale of shares in the stock. If the Company fails to exercise its option to purchase the stock at the proposed price within 90 days, the shareholder may sell the shares. Otherwise, there are no restrictions on the sale or transfer of the Company's stock.

Prior Transactions in the Company's Stock

During the five years before the November 10, 1993, appraisal date, there were no sales of the Company's stock.

Summary of Positive and Negative Factors

Valuation methodology encompasses the analysis of quantitative fundamental data and empirical capital market evidence, and also of qualitative factors relevant to a subject industry and company. The quantitative fundamental data and empirical capital market evidence will be discussed in later sections of this report. Qualitative factors generally refer to certain aspects specific to an industry or business that are critical in assessing the risk and expected return for such an investment. Perceptions of differences between ABC Grocery Company and comparable alternative investment opportunities provide a basis for identifying risk as well as return potential.

The following is a summary of positive and negative qualitative factors pertaining to ABC Grocery:

Positive Factors.

1. The Company has a leading market position in many of the markets served in Oregon, Washington, and California.
2. The Company has a strong management team with considerable experience in the grocery industry.
3. The Company has a strong reputation for excellent service and competitive prices.

Negative Factors.

1. The industry is becoming increasingly competitive, due to the recent entry into the grocery market by warehouse clubs and supercenters.

2. Grocers have recently faced lower average transaction sizes due in part to a lack of strength in the national economy.

3. Annual sales growth for the grocery industry is expected to decrease from 3.5 percent for the past 15 years to 2.5 percent over the next decade due partly to demographic changes, including a growing population of elderly Americans.

4. Many of the Company's older stores need to be remodeled and enlarged to remain competitive, which will require a significant amount of capital over the next decade.

5. Many of the competitors of ABC Grocery are much larger than the Company and have access to greater financial resources.

The Selection of Guideline Companies

Since no marketplace exists for the common stock of ABC Grocery, an alternative to estimate the value of the Company is to analyze the prices investors are willing to pay for the publicly traded common stock of companies that are similar to ABC Grocery Company.

The following section of this report describes the process of selecting companies that were considered to be similar to ABC Grocery Company.

The first step in selecting guideline publicly traded companies is to identify the most appropriate Standard Industrial Classification (SIC) code. ABC Grocery most closely resembles companies with the SIC code 5411-Grocery Stores.

Using CD-ROM technology, we performed a search for companies with SIC code 5411. Standard & Poor's Corporation's CD-ROM product covers 9,000 public companies. In addition, we searched Disclosure's Compact D/SEC, which has information filed by more than 12,000 public companies. All information in the Disclosure database is extracted from various documents that have been filed with the U.S. Securities and Exchange Commission.

These databases were searched by primary SIC code. That is, every publicly traded company with SIC code 5411 listed as its primary SIC in the databases was reviewed for comparability. The primary SIC code is determined by identifying the predominant product or group of products produced or handled or services rendered.

From these various databases, we obtained information on companies in the selected SIC code using Standard & Poor's *Corporations* and *Disclosure*. We examined a description of each of these companies. And, after reviewing the companies' financial data and pricing information, we determined if they were, in fact, reasonable valuation guidelines for ABC Grocery. Through this process, we concluded that 10 companies in SIC 5411 were reasonable valuation guidelines. The companies were selected based on similarity in retailing operations to ABC Grocery. The final selection of the guideline publicly traded companies was based on the following selection criteria:

- Revenues between $700 million and $3 billion for the last fiscal year.
- An active public market for the common stock.
- No companies in financial distress.
- No companies generating negative cash flow (defined as net income plus depreciation).
- No foreign stocks.

The 10 guideline companies that we selected are described below:

Brunos, Inc., (Brunos) operates 257 supermarkets and combination food and drug stores, of which 124 are located in Alabama, 91 in Georgia, 17 in Florida, 7 in Mississippi, and 9 each in Tennessee and South Carolina. Brunos operates 81 stores under the Food World format that range in size from 40,000 to 48,000 square feet. Brunos operates 51 stores under the Food Max format that range from 48,000 to 65,000 square feet. Brunos operates 30 stores under the Food Fair format that range in size from 17,000 to 32,000 square feet. Revenues were $2.872 billion for the fiscal year ended June 30, 1993.

Delchamps, Inc., (Delchamps) has operated for over 70 years and has 118 supermarkets in Alabama, Florida, Louisiana, and Mississippi. The average square footage of selling area per supermarket in 1993 was 28,314. Revenues were $1.035 billion in the fiscal year ended June 30, 1993.

Eagle Food Centers, Inc., (Eagle) operates 109 supermarkets in Illinois and Iowa. Eagle supermarkets offer a full line of groceries, meats, fresh produce, dairy products, delicatessen and bakery products, health and beauty aids, and other general merchandise, as well as video rental and floral service. Stores under the name of Eagle Country Market range from 38,000 to 56,000 square feet. The pricing strategy is the same as the Eagle Food Centers, which is to offer overall lower prices than comparable supermarket competition. Eagle Food Centers range from 25,000 to 42,000 square feet. Revenues were $1.082 billion for fiscal year ended January 20, 1993.

Hannaford Brothers Company (Hannaford) operates 93 supermarkets under the names Martin's, Sun Foods, Alexander's, and Shop 'n Save. The supermarkets are in Maine, New Hampshire, New York, Massachusetts, and Vermont. Hannaford's wholesale distribution is made to 112 supermarkets, six retail drugstores, and 38 pharmacies in five states. Revenues for Hannaford were $2.066 billion for the fiscal year ended December 31, 1992.

Ingles Markets, Inc., (Ingles) operates 170 supermarkets in North Carolina, South Carolina, Georgia, Tennessee, and Virginia. The average size of the existing stores is approximately 31,000 square feet. A 450,000-square-foot distribution center supplies approximately 65 percent of the inventory requirements of its supermarkets. During the past five years, the number of supermarkets operated by Ingles has grown from 122 to 170. Revenues were $1.142 billion for the fiscal year ended September 25, 1993.

Penn Traffic Company (Penn Traffic) operates 217 supermarkets in western Pennsylvania, upstate New York, Ohio, and northern Virginia. The stores are operated under the names Riverside Markets, Bi-Lo Foods, Quality Markets, P&C Foods, and Big Bear and Big Bear Plus. Penn also operates a wholesale food distribution business that serves 133 licensed franchisees and 127 independent operators and a discount general merchandise business with 17 stores. Revenues were $2.788 billion in the fiscal year ended January 30, 1993.

Riser Foods, Inc., (Riser) operates 45 supermarket stores in the greater Cleveland area. Riser operates 43 of the stores under the "Rini-Rego Stop-N-Shop" format. The company is involved in the distribution of groceries and related items through its retail supermarket and wholesale subsidiaries. Many of the stores have specialty departments, such as delicatessens, video rental, photo processing, pharmacies, and banking. Riser operates, through a subsidiary the largest wholesale grocery operation in the Midwest—doing business as Seaway. Revenues for Riser were $1.108 billion for the fiscal year ended June 20, 1993.

Smith's Food & Drug Centers, Inc., (Smith's) operates 125 stores in Arizona, California, Idaho, New Mexico, Nevada, Texas, Utah, and Wyoming. The breakdown of stores is as follows: 109 large combination food and drug centers averaging 68,400 square feet; 14 superstores averaging 40,900 square feet; and two conventional stores averaging 26,000 square feet. The combination stores range in size from 45,000 to 84,000 square feet and offer a full line of supermarket, nonfood, and drug products. Revenues were $2.649 billion for calendar 1992.

Village Super Market, Inc., (Village) operates a chain of 22 ShopRite supermarkets in New Jersey and Pennsylvania. Village also belongs to the Wakefern Food Corporation, the nation's largest retailer-owned food cooperative and owner of the ShopRite name, which provides Village with many of the economies of scale in purchasing, distribution, and advertising associated with chains of greater size and geographic reach. Village is concentrating on the development of superstores, which in addition to being larger in size offer higher margins from specialty service departments. Revenues were $714 million for the fiscal year ended July 31, 1993.

Weis Markets, Inc., (Weis) operates 103 retail food markets in Pennsylvania, Maryland, Virginia, New York, and West Virginia. All but two stores operate under the name Weis Markets. The other two stores operate under the name Erb's. Weis supplies its stores from distribution centers in Sunbury, Northumberland, and Milton, Pennsylvania. Revenues were $1.289 billion for the fiscal year ended December 26, 1992.

Financial Statement Analysis

Overview

An essential step in the valuation of any company is an analysis of its financial performance over time. Analyzing a company's financial statements provides an indication of historical growth, liquidity, leverage, and profitability, all of which influence the value of a company's equity. The following sections of this report examine the trend of ABC Grocery's balance sheets, income statements, and financial ratios over the past five fiscal years. In addition, the Company's financial performance is compared to its peers in the grocery industry as a means of measuring the Company's relative historical performance.

Frequently, the appraisal of closely held companies requires adjusting the historical balance sheets and income statements to eliminate items such as nonoperating assets and nonrecurring or unusual income or expenses. Our analysis of ABC Grocery indicates that no adjustments to the Company's historical financial statements were necessary.

Balance Sheets

Exhibit 18–1 presents ABC Grocery's balance sheets as of the fiscal years ended September 30, 1989, through 1993. All exhibits are located at the end of this chapter in Appendix 18A.

As of September 30, 1993, the Company's assets totaled $456.0 million, up 7.4 percent from the end of fiscal 1992. Current assets totaled $181.2 million, or 39.7 percent of total assets, and consisted primarily of inventory (26.6 percent of total assets) and cash (9.8 percent of total assets). Over the past five years, inventory decreased as a percent of total assets, from 30.4 percent at the end of fiscal 1989 to 26.6 percent at the end of fiscal 1993. The cash balance of the Company increased by approximately 76 percent over the last year, to $44.8 million as of September 30, 1993.

A majority of the Company's assets over the past five years were fixed assets including equipment, buildings and parking lots, land, and transportation equipment. As of September 30, 1993, ABC Grocery's fixed assets were depreciated to 53 percent of their original cost. Due to continued investments in new stores and improvements to existing stores, net fixed assets increased from 36.2 percent of total assets at the end of fiscal 1989 to 41.4 percent of total assets at the end of fiscal 1993.

Current liabilities were $118.8 million as of September 30, 1993, or 26.1 percent of total assets. Trade accounts payable and accrued expenses were the largest current liabilities of the Company at the end of fiscal 1993, accounting for 13.8 percent and 9.8 percent of total liabilities, respectively.

ABC Grocery is modestly leveraged, with $91 million of long-term debt at the end of fiscal 1993, or approximately 20.0 percent of total liabilities and equity. The Company's long-term debt increased in each of the past five years, from $56.6 million in 1989 to $91.0 million in 1993, or a compound annual growth rate of 12.6 percent. However, as a percentage of total liabilities and equity, long-term debt has decreased, from 22.6 percent in 1989 to 20.0 percent in 1993.

Due to consistent profitability of the Company over the past five years, shareholders' equity increased from $115.1 million (or 46.0% of total liabilities and equity) at the end of fiscal 1989 to $241.5 million (or 53.0% of total liabilities and equity) at the end of fiscal 1993. This increase in equity indicates the Company's financial risk decreased somewhat over the past five years.

Income Statements

Exhibit 18–2 presents ABC Grocery's income statements for the fiscal years ended September 30, 1989, through 1993.

The table below presents the Company's annual revenues over the past five fiscal years:

Table 18–6

Fiscal Year Ended September 30	Revenues ($000)	% Change
1989	1,183,979	14.1
1990	1,348,304	13.9
1991	1,440,023	6.8
1992	1,526,509	6.0
1993	1,628,251	6.7

As presented, the Company reported increases in revenues in each of the past five years, from $1.2 billion in 1989 to $1.6 billion in 1993, for a compound annual growth rate of 8.3 percent. ABC Grocery's revenue increase over the past five years was well above the 3.5 percent revenue growth reported by the overall grocery industry. However, the annual revenue increases reported by the Company have dropped from 14.1 percent in 1989 to 6.7 percent in 1993. Since 1990, the Company's revenue growth slipped to a 6.5 percent annual rate.

Cost of goods sold as a percentage of revenues has fluctuated within a narrow range, from 74.1 percent to 75.1 percent, over the past five years. Operating expenses ranged from 22.4 percent to 23.0 percent from fiscal 1989 to fiscal 1993. For fiscal 1993, the Company's cost of goods sold was 74.3 percent of revenues, and operating expenses were 22.9 percent of revenues.

The Company reported consistent profitability over the past five years. In fiscal 1993, net income was $34.3 million, or 2.1 percent of revenues. In addition, ABC Grocery's net profit margin in 1993 was improved over the net profit margin of 1.9 percent in fiscal 1989.

Ratios

Exhibit 18–3 presents various financial and operating ratios for ABC Grocery for the last five fiscal years. Appendix 18B presents the definitions of the financial and operating ratios summarized in Exhibit 18–3.

Liquidity ratios indicate the ability of the company to meet current obligations as they come due. The liquidity ratios presented in Exhibit 18–3 indicate the Company's liquidity has improved over the past five years. The current ratio increased from 1.42 at the end of 1989 to 1.52 at the end of 1993. Similarly, the quick ratio increased from 0.41 to 0.50, and the Company's working capital increased to 62.3 million, from 31.5 million over the same time frame.

Activity ratios indicate how effectively a company is utilizing its assets. The average number of days the Company's accounts receivables were outstanding (as measured by days in receivables) steadily decreased over the past five years, from 3.7 to 2.6. However, the average number of days inventory remained on the shelves before being sold (as measured by days in inventory) increased from 28.9 in 1989 to 35.9 in 1993. Three other activity ratios, including working capital turnover, fixed asset turnover, and asset turnover, all reflected decreased efficiency in the Company's ability to manage its assets over the past five years.

Coverage ratios indicate the ability of the company to meet interest payments, and leverage ratios indicate how much debt the company has outstanding. Highly leveraged companies and companies with low coverage ratios are more vulnerable to business downturns. ABC Grocery's coverage ratios based on earnings before interest and taxes (EBIT) and earnings before depreciation, interest, and taxes (EBDIT) indicate the Company has sufficient cash flow to meet interest charges. Leverage ratios reflect the Company's modest amount of debt outstanding. Equity as a percent of total capital was 72.6 percent at the end of fiscal 1993, up from 67.0 percent in 1989.

Profitability ratios reflect the returns earned by the Company and assist in evaluating management performance. ABC Grocery has been consistently profitable in each of the past five years. The Company's return on sales improved from 1.9 percent in 1989 to 2.1 percent in 1993, while return on average assets decreased from 9.5 percent in 1990 to 7.8 percent in 1993. In addition, return on average equity decreased from 19.9 percent in 1989 to 15.3 percent in 1993.

Comparison to Industry Average

In addition to analyzing the trends in the Company's historical financial statements, we also compared the financial statements of the company to the industry average, as measured by both Robert Morris Associates and the 10 guideline publicly traded companies.

Robert Morris Associates (RMA).   ABC Grocery's common-size balance sheets and income statements and financial and operating ratios are presented in comparison to Robert Morris Associates (RMA) data for retailers of groceries in Exhibits 18–4A and 18–4B. The main differences between ABC Grocery and the average company of a similar size are as follows:

- ABC Grocery's net fixed assets as a percent of total assets in 1993 were lower than the average company, at 41.4 percent compared to 53.5 percent.
- ABC Grocery is less leveraged than the average company in the industry, with total liabilities equal to 47.0 percent of total liabilities and equity for 1993, versus 65.9 percent for the industry average.
- ABC Grocery is more profitable than the average company of similar size, with a pretax profit margin of 3.2 percent for 1993, compared to 1.4 percent for the industry average.
- The assets of ABC Grocery are somewhat more liquid than the average company, with a current ratio of 1.5 for 1993, compared to 1.3 for the average.
- Interest expense coverage for ABC Grocery is much greater than the industry average, at 6.0 compared to 2.1.

Guideline Publicly Traded Companies.   Exhibits 18–5A and 18–5B present the Company's common-size balance sheets and income statements and various financial and operating ratios in comparison to the 10 selected guideline publicly traded companies. The highlights from Exhibits 18–5A and 18–5B are as follows:

- ABC Grocery is somewhat larger than the median of the guideline companies based on revenues, with $1.6 billion in revenues for fiscal 1993, compared to $1.2 billion for the guideline companies.
- ABC Grocery's net fixed assets as a percent of total assets in 1993 were lower than the median for the guideline companies, at 41.4 percent compared to 52.4 percent.
- ABC Grocery is less leveraged than the median of the guideline companies, with total liabilities equal to 47.0 percent of total liabilities and equity for 1993 versus 63.8 percent.
- ABC Grocery is more profitable than the median of the guideline companies, with a net profit margin of 2.1 percent for 1993, compared to 1.2 percent.
- The assets of ABC Grocery are somewhat more liquid than the median for the guideline companies. ABC Grocery's current ratio of 1.52 is above the median of the guideline companies of 1.33. In addition, ABC Grocery's quick ratio of 0.50 is well above the 0.28 median of the guideline companies.
- ABC Grocery's days in receivables and days in inventory are lower than the guideline companies, at 3 and 36, compared to 4 and 41, respectively.
- Interest expense coverage for ABC Grocery is much greater than the median of the guideline companies, at 6.0 compared to 2.3.
- By nearly all profitability measures presented on Exhibit 18–5B, ABC Grocery is more profitable than the median of the guideline companies.

Appraisal of Fair Market Value

Several approaches are available for the appraisal of private business interests. In our analysis and appraisal presented in this section of the report, we will discuss:

- Our consideration and selection of the appropriate approaches and methods for valuation for the 5.45 percent block of common stock of ABC Grocery.
- Application of the methods to estimate the fair market value of the minority ownership interest in ABC Grocery as of November 10, 1993.
- Analysis and selection of the appropriate discount for the relative lack of marketability of the subject minority block of common stock.

Valuation Methods Used

All relevant valuation approaches and methods were considered during the course of our work. The subject business interest to be appraised is a 5.45 percent interest owned by the Estate of John Smith. Based on the size of the block being appraised, the subject interest is a minority ownership interest.

Minority interests typically lack the unilateral capacity to initiate and control the liquidation of the company or the direct control of the use of the underlying assets of the company. For this reason, we considered, but did not use, an asset-based valuation approach in arriving at our value for the subject minority interest.

We relied on two valuation approaches to estimate the value of the subject minority interest: a market approach and an income approach.

The market approach is appropriate in this case, given the minority interest represented by the subject block of ABC Grocery common stock. In addition, the Company, with revenues in 1993 of over $1.6 billion, is similar in size to many of the guideline publicly traded companies that we selected. Within the market approach, we relied on a guideline publicly traded company method to estimate the value of the subject minority interest in ABC Grocery.

In addition, within the income approach, we relied on the discounted economic income method. This discounted economic income analysis was based on financial projections prepared by management dated September 30, 1993, as part of the Company's five-year strategic plan.

In each of the two methods discussed above, an adjustment was necessary to reflect the relative lack of marketability of the privately held subject shares.

Debt-Free Analysis. As part of our analysis of the Company, we noted that ABC Grocery has historically been somewhat less leveraged than the average of the guideline publicly traded companies. To minimize the impact of the difference in leverage between ABC Grocery and the guideline companies, we used a debt-free analysis to estimate the value of the subject security.

Under a debt-free valuation analysis, the market multiples are based on the market value of invested capital (MVIC). MVIC for the guideline publicly traded companies is calculated as follows:

$$\begin{array}{rl} & \text{Market value of common stock} \\ + & \text{Market value of preferred stock} \\ + & \text{Market value of interest-bearing debt} \\ \hline = & \text{Market value of invested capital} \end{array}$$

Debt-free analysis results in an indication of value of a company's aggregate MVIC. Therefore, to arrive at the market value of common stock for ABC Grocery, the market value of interest-bearing debt must be subtracted from the MVIC.

We also conducted our discounted economic income method on a debt-free basis, using projected debt-free net cash flow as the economic income measure to discount. The present value discount rate was based on the Company's weighted average cost of capital. We subtracted the value of the Company's interest-bearing debt from the total value of invested capital to arrive at the indicated value of ABC Grocery's common stock on an aggregate minority interest basis.

Treatment for Relative Lack of Marketability. The indicated values derived from the two methods we estimated to be most appropriate—the guideline company method and the discounted economic income method—were derived from data relating to prices and returns on minority blocks of *publicly* traded common stock securities. The subject ABC Grocery shares are *privately* held minority interests.

We will discuss the appropriate magnitude of the adjustment for the relative lack of marketability in the "Discount for Lack of Marketability" section of this report.

Guideline Company Method

Overview. The first method we relied on was the guideline company method. As discussed previously, we analyzed the valuation multiples from the selected guideline companies on a debt-free basis. In adjusting earnings measures to a debt-free basis, we analyzed pretax earnings. To adjust pretax earnings to a debt-free basis, total interest expense is added to pretax income, since if a company had no debt, it would have no interest expense. The resulting figure is earnings before interest and taxes (EBIT). Because the companies in the grocery store industry use somewhat different methods of recognizing depreciation and amortization, we also analyzed earnings before depreciation and amortization. Adding depreciation and amortization back to EBIT results in earnings before depreciation/amortization, interest, and taxes (EBDIT).

In addition, we analyzed after-tax earnings measures, including debt-free net income (DFNI) and debt-free cash flow (DFCF). DFNI is calculated as net income plus tax affected interest expense. DFCF equals DFNI plus depreciation and amortization.

Book value adjusted to a debt-free basis, referred to in this report as tangible book value of invested capital (TBVIC), is equal to the sum of the tangible book value of a company's equity and the book value of interest-bearing debt.

Data used for the guideline company method are presented in Exhibits 18–6A through 18–6I. Exhibit 18–6A presents the determination of the MVIC for the guideline companies. Exhibits 18–6B through 18–6H present the calculation of EBIT, EBDIT, DFNI, DFCF, revenues, and TBVIC for ABC Grocery and the guideline companies. To maintain comparability, we relied on data from the latest available financial statements for each company before the November 10, 1993, valuation date.

MVIC/EBIT. Exhibit 18–6B presents the 10 guideline companies' EBIT performance in comparison to each other and ABC Grocery for the past five years. The median growth rate in EBIT for the guideline companies was 1.0 percent.

ABC Grocery's EBIT increased at an annual rate of 11.2 percent over the past five years, well above the mean of the guideline companies. The trend in EBIT for the last 12 months has been mixed among the guideline companies, with 4 of the 10 companies reporting decreased EBIT in the last 12 months.

The table below presents the expected earnings growth for the 10 guideline companies and ABC Grocery, based on Value Line and Zack's earnings estimates. Note that ABC Grocery's earnings are expected to increase at an annual rate of 5.6 percent over the next five years, versus a 12.5 percent expected growth rate for the guideline companies.

Table 18–7

| | Expected Annual Earnings Growth Rate over Next Five Years | |
Company	Value Line*	Zack's†
Brunos, Inc.	13.0%	12.6%
Delchamps, Inc.	15.0%	12.5%
Eagle Food Centers, Inc.	NA	NA
Hannaford	11.5%	14.2%
Ingles Markets, Inc.	NA	8.0%
Penn Traffic Company	NA	NA
Riser Foods, Inc.	NA	12.0%
Smith's Food & Drug	12.5%	15.6%
Village Super Market, Inc.	NA	NA
Weis Markets, Inc.	1.0%	5.8%
Mean	10.6%	11.5%
Median	12.5%	12.5%
ABC Grocery	5.6%††	

*As of November 19, 1993.
†As of October 31, 1993.
††Management estimate, as presented in Exhibit 18–7A.
NA = Not available.

Last 12 Months.   The MVIC/EBIT multiples for the last 12 months (LTM) for the guideline companies ranged from 7.5 to 14.4, with a mean of 10.5 and a median of 10.9.

In our opinion, ABC Grocery would command an MVIC/EBIT multiple less than the median of the guideline companies. Although over the past five years ABC Grocery's EBIT growth has been greater than that reported by the guideline companies, ABC Grocery is expected to report annual earnings growth over the next five years of 5.6 percent, well below the expected growth of 12.5 percent for the median of the guideline companies. We estimated that a 20 percent discount from the median multiple is appropriate to reflect the differential in expected growth rates. Applying a 20 percent discount to the median multiple of 10.9 results in a multiple of 8.7.

Applying the selected multiple of 8.7 to the LTM EBIT of $64,226,000 for ABC Grocery results in a market value of invested capital of $558,766,000 (rounded).

Five-Year Average.   Five-year average EBIT multiples were also examined. These multiples ranged from a low of 6.4 to a high of 13.4, with a median of 10.5. We selected an EBIT multiple 20 percent less than the median multiple for reasons mentioned above. Discounting the median multiple of 10.5 by 20 percent results in a multiple of 8.4.

Applying the selected multiple of 8.4 to ABC Grocery's five-year average EBIT of $55,594,000 results in an MVIC of $466,990,000 (rounded).

Indicated MVIC. In our opinion, both the last 12 months and five-year average EBIT multiples provide relevant valuation indications. In the grocery industry, which is not especially sensitive to business cycle fluctuations, investors would be equally concerned with the Company's earnings in the most recent period and over the past five years. Therefore, we placed equal weight on the LTM and five-year average indications of value ($558,766,000 and $466,990,000, respectively). This results in an indicated MVIC from the EBIT method of $512,878,000.

MVIC/EBDIT. Exhibit 18–6C presents the 10 guideline companies' EBDIT performance in comparison to each other and ABC Grocery for the past five years. The median EBDIT growth rate for the guideline companies over the past five years was 4.3 percent. ABC Grocery's EBDIT increased at an annual rate of 9.1 percent over the past five years, above the mean of the guideline companies. However, in the most recent fiscal year, ABC Grocery's EBDIT decreased by 1.3 percent. Only 2 of the 10 guideline companies reported decreased EBDIT over the last year. In addition, as discussed above, expected earnings growth for ABC Grocery is well below the median for the guideline companies.

Last 12 Months. The MVIC/EBDIT multiples for the LTM for the guideline companies ranged from 4.0 to 8.7, with a mean of 6.3 and a median of 6.5.

In our opinion, ABC Grocery would command an MVIC/EBDIT multiple equal to the median of the guideline companies discounted by 20 percent. Although over the last five years the Company's EBDIT growth has been superior to its peers, over the next five years the Company's earnings growth is expected to be well below the guideline companies. Discounting the median multiple of 6.5 by 20 percent results in a multiple of 5.2.

Applying the selected multiple of 5.2 to ABC Grocery's LTM EBDIT of $89,571,000 results in a market value of invested capital of $465,769,000 (rounded).

Five-Year Average. Five-year average EBDIT multiples were also examined. These multiples ranged from a low of 3.8 to a high of 8.7, with a median of 7.7. We again selected an EBDIT multiple equal to the median multiple discounted by 20 percent for reasons mentioned above. Discounting the median multiple of 7.7 by 20 percent results in a multiple of 6.2.

Applying the selected multiple of 6.2 to ABC Grocery's five-year average EBDIT of $79,568,000 results in an MVIC of $493,322,000 (rounded).

Indicated MVIC. In our opinion, both the last 12 months and five-year average EBDIT multiples provide relevant valuation indications. In an industry that is not as sensitive to business cycle fluctuations such as the grocery industry, investors would be equally concerned with the Company's earnings in the most recent period and over the past five years. Therefore, we placed equal weight on the LTM and five-year average indications of value ($465,769,000 and $493,322,000, respectively). This results in an indicated MVIC from the EBDIT method of $479,546,000.

MVIC/DFNI. Exhibit 18–6D presents the historical DFNI for the 10 guideline companies and ABC Grocery. The median growth rate for the 10 guideline companies over the past five years was 0.5 percent, compared to a growth rate of 11.2 percent for ABC Grocery's DFNI. However (similar to the trend for EBIT and EBDIT presented above), ABC Grocery's DFNI decreased in the last year, while only 3 of the 10 guideline companies reported a decrease in DFNI in the last year. In addition, ABC Grocery's earnings over the next five years are expected to increase significantly less than the median of the guideline companies.

Last 12 Months. The LTM MVIC/DFNI multiples for the guideline companies ranged from 11.8 to 23.7, with a mean of 17.0 and a median of 17.6.

For reasons mentioned earlier in this report, we selected the median multiple of the guideline companies, discounted by 20 percent. Discounting the median multiple of 17.6 by 20 percent results in a multiple of 14.1. Applying the selected multiple of 14.1 to the LTM DFNI of $41,747,000 for ABC Grocery results in a market value of invested capital of $588,633,000 (rounded).

Five-Year Average. Five-year average DFNI multiples were also examined. These multiples ranged from a low of 10.5 to a high of 22.1, with a median of 15.7. We selected a DFNI multiple equal to the median multiple, discounted by 20 percent, for reasons mentioned above. Discounting the median multiple of 15.7 by 20 percent results in a multiple of 12.6.

Applying the selected multiple of 12.6 to ABC Grocery's five-year average DFNI of $36,136,000 results in an MVIC of $455,314,000 (rounded).

Indicated MVIC. We placed equal weight on the LTM and five-year average indications of value for reasons mentioned earlier in this report. Weighting these indications of value equally results in an indicated MVIC from the DFNI method of $521,974,000.

MVIC/DFCF. Exhibit 18–6E presents the historical DFCF for the 10 guideline companies and ABC Grocery. ABC Grocery's DFCF increased at an annual rate of 8.5 percent over the past five years, above the 5.1 percent growth reported by the guideline companies. However, in fiscal 1993, ABC Grocery's DFCF decreased by 1.4 percent, while only 3 of the 10 guideline companies reported a decrease in DFCF in the last year. Over the next five years, ABC Grocery's earnings are expected to increase at 5.6 percent per year, versus 12.5 percent for the median of the guideline companies.

Last 12 Months. The LTM MVIC/DFCF multiples for the guideline companies ranged from 5.0 to 12.2, with a mean of 8.3 and a median of 8.6.

Since ABC Grocery's earnings growth is expected to be less than the guideline companies, we selected the median multiple of the guideline companies, discounted by 20 percent. Discounting the median multiple of 8.6 by 20 percent results in a multiple of 6.9.

Applying the selected multiple of 6.9 to the LTM DFCF of $67,092,000 for ABC Grocery results in a market value of invested capital of $462,935,000 (rounded).

Five-Year Average.   Five-year average DFCF multiples were also examined. These multiples ranged from a low of 5.0 to a high of 11.8, with a median of 10.0. We selected a DFCF multiple equal to the median multiple, discounted by 20 percent, for reasons mentioned earlier in this report. Discounting the median multiple of 10.0 by 20 percent results in a multiple of 8.0.

Applying the selected multiple of 8.0 to ABC Grocery's five-year average DFCF of $60,110,000 results in an MVIC of $480,880,000 (rounded).

Indicated MVIC.   We placed equal weight on the LTM and five-year average indications of value for reasons mentioned earlier in this report. Weighting these indications of value equally results in an indicated MVIC from the DFCF method of $471,908,000.

MVIC/Revenues.   Exhibit 18–6F presents the historical revenues reported by the guideline companies and ABC Grocery, and Exhibit 18–6G presents various debt-free returns on revenues for both the LTM and five-year average.

A revenue method can be considered a derivative of an earnings method, since generally there is an implicit assumption that a certain level of revenues should be able to generate a certain level of earnings in a given type of business.

In choosing a multiple of revenues to apply to the revenues of ABC Grocery, we reviewed debt-free returns on revenues. Generally, the higher a company's return on revenues, the higher a multiple of revenues investors are willing to pay. The following table presents the EBDIT returns and the MVIC/Revenues for the guideline companies.

Table 18–8

Company	LTM EBDIT Return on Revenues	MVIC/LTM Revenues
Village Super Market, Inc.	1.9%	0.10
Riser Foods, Inc.	3.3	0.15
Eagle Food Centers, Inc.	4.5	0.18
Delchamps, Inc.	4.5	0.20
Brunos, Inc.	4.7	0.40
Ingles Markets, Inc.	4.9	0.32
Penn Traffic Company	7.0	0.52
Smith's Food & Drug	7.4	0.49
Hannaford	7.9	0.57
Weis Markets, Inc.	10.0	0.88
ABC Grocery	5.5	0.37
R-squared	92%	

As presented in this table, there is a strong positive relationship between the returns generated by the guideline companies and the price investors are willing to pay for the revenues of the companies. As presented in the table, the r-squared for this relationship is 92 percent, which implies a very strong correlation between the two variables. Based on this information, the estimated MVIC/LTM revenues for ABC Grocery is 0.37, as presented in the table above. In our opinion, this is an appropriate multiple to use for the revenue method to estimate ABC Grocery's market value of invested capital.

Applying the multiple of 0.37 to ABC Grocery's revenues of $1,628,251,000 results in an indicated market value of invested capital of $602,453,000 (rounded).

MVIC/TBVIC. Exhibit 18–6H presents the ratios of MVIC to TBVIC for the guideline companies and the debt-free returns on TBVIC for the latest 12 months and the five-year average. The table below presents the EBDIT returns on TBVIC for the latest 12 months and the MVIC/TBVIC for the guideline companies.

Table 18–9

Company	LTM EBDIT Return on TBVIC	MVIC/TBVIC
Village Super Market, Inc.	15.9%	0.83
Smith's Food & Drug	15.9	1.05
Ingles Markets, Inc.	15.9	1.03
Weis Markets, Inc.	19.4	1.69
Brunos, Inc.	19.6	1.65
Riser Foods, Inc.	22.4	1.02
Eagle Food Centers, Inc.	24.4	0.98
Delchamps, Inc.	25.6	1.16
Hannaford	26.6	1.92
Penn Traffic Company	26.6	1.97
ABC Grocery	25.7	1.55

Note that there is not a strong correlation between the MVIC/TBVIC and the debt-free returns on TBVIC.

As presented in this table, ABC Grocery has reported debt-free returns most similar to Penn Traffic, Hannaford, and Delchamps. Note, however, the wide range of multiples of TBVIC for these three companies—between 1.16 and 1.97. Based on a regression of the variables presented in Table 18–9, the indicated multiple for ABC Grocery is 1.55. Although the r-squared for this regression is relatively low at 0.27, this multiple appears reasonable based on the multiple for Penn Traffic, Hannaford, and Delchamps.

Applying the multiple of 1.55 to ABC Grocery's TBVIC of $347,908,000 results in an indicated market value of invested capital of $539,257,000 (rounded).

Summary of Indicated Value—Guideline Company Method. The following table presents the indicated values for the guideline company method.

Table 18–10

Method	Indicated MVIC ($000)	Method Weighting
MVIC/EBIT	512,878	10.0%
MVIC/EBDIT	479,546	25.0
MVIC/DFNI	521,974	10.0
MVIC/DFCF	471,908	25.0
MVIC/Revenues	602,453	15.0
MVIC/TBVIC	539,257	15.0

As presented, the indicated values ranged from $471,908,000 to $602,453,000. The weightings selected for each method to estimate the MVIC for the Company are summarized in the table above. Since we are appraising the Company as a going concern, we placed primary emphasis (a total of 70 percent) on the earnings methods. Also, in our opinion, the earnings methods that eliminate depreciation should be accorded greater weight than the other methods, due to the relatively high amount of depreciation expense for the guideline companies relative to earnings.

Weighting the methods as presented above results in an indicated market value of invested capital from the guideline company method of $512,605,000. Subtracting the value of the Company's interest-bearing debt as of the valuation date of $96,584,000 results in an estimated value for the equity of the Company of $416,021,000 (rounded).

This indicated value is based on data from publicly traded securities—hence, a further adjustment is necessary to reflect the relative lack of marketability of the subject privately held stock. This adjustment is presented in the "Discount for Lack of Marketability" section of this report.

Discounted Economic Income Method

Overview.   The second method that we relied on was the discounted economic income method. This method is intuitively appealing, since it reflects the trade-off between risk and expected return that is critical to the investment process. Generally, common stocks are purchased in light of anticipated stock price appreciation, which, in turn, is strongly influenced by expectations about a company's cash flow capacity.

Discounted economic income analyses estimate value on the basis of future return flows over an investment horizon. Using empirical market data, macroeconomic and industry evidence, and the underlying fundamental trends for the subject company, discounted economic income methods apply a present value discount rate, known as the required rate of return on investment, to expected future cash flows, which results in a determination of the net present value of a series of cash flows.

We selected net cash flow as the appropriate measure of economic income to analyze. Accordingly, the particular discounted economic income method that we used was a discounted cash flow (DCF) analysis.

We conducted this DCF analysis on an after-tax, debt-free basis and used net cash flow on a debt-free basis (referred to as net cash flow) as our economic income measure. A debt-free method was used to eliminate the impact of the company's leverage (albeit modest) on the value of the equity. ABC Grocery's weighted average cost of capital (WACC) is the appropriate discount rate to apply to net cash flow. The value calculated from this analysis is the market value of ABC Grocery's invested capital. We then subtracted the value of the interest-bearing debt as of the valuation date to result in the aggregate publicly traded equivalent value of ABC Grocery's common stock.

Derivation of Cash Flows.

Interim Cash Flows.   Since we used the capital asset pricing model (CAPM) to estimate the present value discount rate, the returns from which this discount rate was drawn represent potential cash flows available to the investor in the form of dividends plus capital appreciation. As stated above, a debt-free method is appropriate to appraise ABC Grocery's common stock due to the differences in leverage between ABC Grocery and the guideline companies. We define debt-free net cash flow (referred to as net cash flow) as:

> After-tax earnings
> +   Interest $\times$ (1 − Tax rate)
> +   Depreciation and amortization
> −   Capital expenditures
> −   Increases (or + decreases) in working capital requirements
> ---
> =   Net cash flow (NCF)

    Exhibit 18–7A presents a summary of the projections for fiscal years ended September 1994 through 1998 prepared by ABC Grocery management. This exhibit also presents the estimated future net cash flow for the Company for 1994 through 1998. Exhibit 18–7C presents the implied additional working capital needs of the Company based on working capital requirements of the Company as a percent of revenues for fiscal 1989 through 1993.

Terminal Cash Flows.   Although the projections run through 1998, ABC Grocery has value beyond 1998, since it is expected to continue to generate cash flow. The value of the Company in the last year of the projections is defined as the terminal value. The terminal cash flows are based on the 1998 projected results, utilizing the value measures EBDIT, and NCF, as presented in Exhibit 18–7B.

    The multiple applied to the Company's projected EBDIT is based on the last 12 months' EBDIT multiple selected from the guideline companies, as presented in the "Guideline Company Method" section of this report. The multiple assigned to ABC Grocery's projected 1999 NCF is based on the inverse of the WACC (described below), less an estimated 4.0 percent projected long-term growth rate. The 4.0 percent long-term growth rate is conservative, considering projected growth of net income for the Company of 5.6 percent from 1994 through 1998.

    We estimated 1999 NCF by projecting a modest increase of approximately 4.0 percent from the Company's projected 1998 NCF.

Required Discount Rate.   The required rate of return on ABC Grocery invested capital was estimated by analyzing the weighted average cost of capital on all forms of capital for the Company, both debt and equity. The box in Exhibit 18–7B presents the calculation of the WACC for the Company at 10.0 percent. The WACC incorporates the market evidence of the cost of debt and equity as of the valuation date. These expected rates of return were then weighted based on the Company's current capital structure.

Required Rate of Return on Equity.   In a rational investment environment, an investor has various alternative investments for funds. The investor will require a rate of return on these investments that is a function of: (1) the expected rate of inflation, (2) the rate of return currently offered above inflation on a riskless investment, and (3) a return to compensate for the relative uncertainty (additional risk) of the projected future cash flows. The required return on an investment is therefore a function of the investment risk inherent in the return flows.

The required rate of return for ABC Grocery common shares must incorporate the perceived risks, as they were known on the valuation date, relative to the empirical evidence of guideline investments of comparable risk. In developing this rate of return, we used the capital asset pricing model, defined as follows:

Risk-free rate + (Equity risk premium × Beta)

We began the process of estimating the required rate of return on ABC Grocery's equity with the appropriate risk-free rate of return, which incorporates investors' expectations for the real rate of return on a riskless investment and the impact of expected inflation on the investors' purchasing power. The risk-free rate proxy we selected is based on long-term U.S. Treasury securities. The 20-year U.S. Treasury bond yield, as of November 10, 1993, was 6.2 percent.

To estimate the premium for the required rate of return for equity investments in relation to the risk-free rate of return, we researched historical equity returns net of the risk-free rate over a long-term investment horizon. According to the *Stocks, Bonds, Bills and Inflation:, 1993 Yearbook*[2] (SBBI '93), the arithmetic equity risk premium on the Standard & Poor's 500 Composite Common Stock Index above the risk-free rate was 7.3 percent over the 65-year period of the study. This historical risk premium was used as the estimate for the equity risk premium.

Exhibit 18–7B presents the calculation of the required equity rate of return for ABC Grocery's common shares. As presented, ABC Grocery's equity risk premium was calculated by multiplying the estimated beta for the Company's shares by the historical equity risk premium for large stocks. The beta for the Company was estimated by analyzing the betas for the guideline companies. The betas for these 10 companies, as of October 1993, according to *Compustat*, were as follows:

Table 18–11

Company	Beta
Brunos, Inc.	0.68
Delchamps, Inc.	0.58
Eagle Food Centers, Inc.	1.68
Hannaford	0.72
Ingles Markets, Inc.	0.38
Penn Traffic Company	1.08
Riser Foods, Inc.	0.96
Smith's Food & Drug	1.52
Village Super Market, Inc.	0.30
Weis Markets, Inc.	0.70
Median	0.71
Rounded	0.70

Based on this information, we selected a beta of 0.70 for ABC Grocery, equal to the median of the betas from the 10 selected guideline companies.

---

[2]*Stocks, Bonds, Bills and Inflation:, 1993 Yearbook* (Chicago: Ibbotson Associates, 1993).

Therefore, the equity risk premium for ABC Grocery is 5.1 percent (or the equity risk premium of 7.3 percent, multiplied by the selected beta of 0.70). Adding the equity risk premium to the risk-free rate of 6.2 percent results in a required equity rate of return for ABC Grocery of 11.3 percent.

In our opinion, no further specific company risk adjustment is necessary, since ABC Grocery is very similar to the guideline companies in terms of size, management depth, and geographic diversification.

Cost of Debt. We derived the cost of debt capital for ABC Grocery by reviewing the current interest rate costs of the Company's long-term debt as of the latest reporting period before the valuation date. The estimated pretax cost of debt for the Company is 8.5 percent.

Because debt is tax deductible, we also adjusted the rate for ABC Grocery's projected tax rate for 1994 through 1998 of 35 percent. This after-tax adjustment is appropriate, since the interim cash flows and terminal values were determined on an after-tax basis. The after-tax cost of ABC Grocery's debt is therefore 5.5 percent, which we utilized as our proxy for the Company's cost of debt.

Weighted Average of Debt and Equity Costs. As presented in Exhibit 18–7B, we estimated the market value of ABC Grocery's interest-bearing debt as a percentage of the market value of total capital at 20.0 percent in estimating the weighted average cost of capital for the company. This is somewhat less than the book value of ABC Grocery's interest-bearing debt as a percent of total capital. However, it is appropriate to base these weightings on market value, not book value.

Based on this weighting, the calculated WACC is therefore the weighted average of 5.5 percent for debt and 11.3 percent for equity, or 10.0 percent overall.

Total Discounted Cash Flow Value. The resulting value of the discounted interim cash flows and the terminal value cash flow is $472,825,000, as presented in Exhibit 18–7B. This represents the total indicated MVIC of the Company under this method of analysis. Subtracting total interest-bearing debt of $96,584,000, as of the latest financial statement dated September 28, 1993, results in a value attributable to the common equity of ABC Grocery of $376,200,000 (rounded).

This indicated value is based on data from publicly traded securities—hence, a further adjustment is necessary to reflect the relative lack of marketability of the subject privately held stock. This adjustment is presented in the "Discount for Lack of Marketability" section of this report.

Summary before Discount for Lack of Marketability

The two methods yield indicated publicly traded equivalent values as follows:

Table 18–12

Valuation Method	Indicated Value ($)	Weighting (%)
Guideline company	416,021,000	50
Discounted economic income	376,200,000	50

In our opinion, both of the valuation methods provide meaningful indications of value for the minority interest in ABC Company. In addition, the guideline company method, as presented, relies primarily on historical data, and the discounted economic income method relies on projected data. In our opinion, a purchase of the minority interest in ABC Grocery would be concerned with both the actual performance of the company and the expected performance. Therefore, we weighted each of the methods equally, resulting in a publicly traded equivalent value for ABC Grocery, before consideration for any discounts for lack of marketability, of $396,111,000.

Discount for Lack of Marketability

A major difference between ABC Grocery's shares and those of its publicly traded counterparts is their lack of marketability. All other things being equal, an investment is worth more if it is marketable than if it is not, since investors prefer liquidity over lack of liquidity. Interests in closely held businesses are illiquid relative to most other investments.

The market places a far greater value differential on the liquidity factor alone in its pricing of common stocks than in its pricing of any other class of investment assets, for sound reasons. For common stocks as a group, investors expect to realize the majority of their return in the form of capital gains at the time of the stock's sale and only a small part of their total return in the form of dividends while they hold the stock. This situation is taken to the extreme, of course, in the case of common stock that has not paid dividends in the past, such as ABC Grocery's. Thus, the ability to sell the stock is crucial to the realization of the investor's expected return for buying and holding it.

A stock that pays no dividends, has no market, and cannot be legally offered to the general public but might possibly be salable under certain limited circumstances and at a totally undeterminable price must be discounted heavily from an otherwise comparable stock that is both legally salable to the general public and has an established market.

Another reason that liquidity takes on a high degree of importance for common stocks is that prices of common stocks tend to be much more volatile than prices of real estate or other securities such as preferred stocks or bonds. Consequently, the investor's choice as to the timing of the sale of the stock is much more important in determining the amount of return to be earned on the investment than is the case with other security investments. Numerous studies concerning the size of marketability discounts have been published.[3]

Summary and Conclusion of Empirical Research.   The restricted stock studies are quite consistent in indicating an average discount for lack of marketability of at least 35 percent. In addition, the IPO studies provide convincing support for a somewhat higher discount for lack of marketability of approximately 45 percent.

---

[3]These studies normally would be presented in an appraisal report. However, due to the limited amount of space available in presenting this sample case, we have not presented them here. See Chapter 15, "Discounts for Lack of Marketability," for a detailed discusssion.

Such a result is rational since the restricted securities will have access to an established public market upon the expiration of the restrictions. Also, the discounts based on private transactions before access to a public capital market (i.e., the IPO studies) would be expected to more closely represent the actual discount for lack of marketability required by an actual investor in connection with the investment in the shares of a closely held security.

Selection of Applicable Discount for ABC Grocery Minority Interests

For the Estate of John Smith's minority interest, we considered the following factors that might have an impact on the selection of the appropriate discount for lack of marketability:

- *Size of the block.* The subject block is a minority interest with very little ability to influence corporate policies. This represents a factor that would increase the appropriate marketability discount.
- *Transaction activity.* There have been no transactions in the common stock of ABC Grocery over the last five years. This factor would indicate a higher discount for lack of marketability.
- *Dividends.* The Company has historically paid no cash dividends to shareholders and has indicated its intention not to pay any in the foreseeable future. This factor would also increase the indicated marketability discount.

Based on the analysis set forth above regarding the factors that influence the lack of marketability of ABC Grocery shares, it is our opinion that the appropriate discount for lack of marketability falls within the range of 45 percent to 50 percent from the indicated publicly traded minority interest value based on the publicly traded guideline company method and the discounted economic income method. We selected a lack of marketability discount of 45 percent to apply to the subject securities, based on all relevant information.

Applying a 45 percent lack of marketability discount to the previously derived publicly traded equivalent value of $396,111,000 results in a nonmarketable value of $217,861,000. Dividing by the number of outstanding shares of 1,431,770 results in a per share nonmarketable value of $152.00 (rounded).[4]

Concluded Fair Market Value

After consideration of all relevant issues, it is our opinion that the fair market value of the 5.45 percent nonmarketable, minority ownership interest in the voting common stock of ABC Grocery Company held by the Estate of John Smith as of the date of death, November 10, 1993, is:

$152.00 per share

---

[4]Again, this discussion in an actual report normally would be more detailed, presenting information such as that in Chapter 15.

Appendix 18A

Exhibits

Exhibit 18–1
ABC Grocery Company
Balance Sheets

	September 30:					September 30:				
	1993 ($000)	1992 ($000)	1991 ($000)	1990 ($000)	1989 ($000)	1993 (%)	1992 (%)	1991 (%)	1990 (%)	1989 (%)
ASSETS										
Current Assets:										
Cash & Equivalents	44,806	25,352	15,351	21,824	19,226	9.8	6.0	4.5	7.6	7.7
Investments	1,850	34,165	15,369	493	1	0.4	8.0	4.5	0.2	0.0
Accounts Receivable	12,679	10,383	12,519	16,276	11,232	2.8	2.4	3.7	5.7	4.5
Prepaid Expenses	580	1,176	1,190	2,105	258	0.1	0.3	0.4	0.7	0.1
Inventory	121,259	116,634	90,921	84,052	76,187	26.6	27.5	26.8	29.3	30.4
Total Current Assets	181,174	187,710	135,350	124,751	106,904	39.7	44.2	39.9	43.5	42.7
Fixed Assets:										
Land	17,114	15,785	12,876	9,509	7,566	3.8	3.7	3.8	3.3	3.0
Buildings & Parking Lots	130,628	101,626	77,779	65,524	47,412	28.6	23.9	22.9	22.8	18.9
Equipment & Fixtures	196,485	170,163	170,217	164,094	155,843	43.1	40.1	50.2	57.2	62.2
Transportation Equipment	11,401	8,188	5,642	2,868	954	2.5	1.9	1.7	1.0	0.4
Total Fixed Assets, Cost	355,628	295,762	266,514	241,995	211,775	78.0	69.6	78.5	84.3	84.6
Accumulated Depreciation	(166,850)	(147,857)	(146,559)	(141,372)	(121,062)	(36.6)	(34.8)	(43.2)	(49.3)	(48.3)
Total Fixed Assets, Net	188,778	147,906	119,956	100,623	90,713	41.4	34.8	35.3	35.1	36.2
Other Assets:										
Capitalized Leases, Net	47,838	53,308	52,623	44,023	46,026	10.5	12.6	15.5	15.3	18.4
Deferred Taxes	8,833	12,074	10,201	5,890	2,582	1.9	2.8	3.0	2.1	1.0
Prepaids, Noncurrent	3,661	2,981	2,551	1,726	1,695	0.8	0.7	0.8	0.6	0.7
Miscellaneous Assets	25,738	20,776	18,728	10,022	2,538	5.6	4.9	5.5	3.5	1.0
Total Other Assets	86,071	89,139	84,103	61,661	52,841	18.9	21.0	24.8	21.5	21.1
TOTAL ASSETS	456,024	424,755	339,409	287,035	250,459	100.0	100.0	100.0	100.0	100.0
LIABILITIES & EQUITY										
Liabilities:										
Current Liabilities:										
Demand Overdrafts	0	14,561	0	0	8,474	0.0	3.4	0.0	0.0	3.4
Capital Lease Obligations	4,293	3,814	2,846	1,317	1,027	0.9	0.9	0.8	0.5	0.4
Trade Accounts Payable	62,953	66,999	49,620	60,451	52,612	13.8	15.8	14.6	21.1	21.0
Accounts Payable—Affiliates	2,946	2,598	5,701	4,997	1,982	0.6	0.6	1.7	1.7	0.8
Notes & Mortgages Payable	1,298	1,211	879	551	570	0.3	0.3	0.3	0.2	0.2
Income Taxes Payable	2,780	1,772	3,786	1,801	0	0.6	0.4	1.1	0.6	0.0
Accrued Expenses & Taxes Payable	44,572	40,371	28,959	10,823	10,714	9.8	9.5	8.5	3.8	4.3
Total Current Liabilities	118,842	131,325	91,792	79,939	75,378	26.1	30.9	27.0	27.8	30.1
Long-Term Debt:										
Notes & Mortgages Payable	32,423	18,395	9,251	8,153	1,022	7.1	4.3	2.7	2.8	0.4
Capital Lease Obligations	58,570	63,886	63,201	54,862	55,594	12.8	15.0	18.6	19.1	22.2
Total Long-Term Debt	90,993	82,280	72,452	63,016	56,617	20.0	19.4	21.3	22.0	22.6
Other Debt:										
Deferred Compensation	4,708	4,025	3,769	3,474	3,326	1.0	0.9	1.1	1.2	1.3
Total Other Debt	4,708	4,025	3,769	3,474	3,326	1.0	0.9	1.1	1.2	1.3
Total Liabilities	214,543	217,631	168,013	146,428	135,321	47.0	51.2	49.5	51.0	54.0
Equity:										
Common Stock	2,457	2,457	2,457	2,457	2,457	0.5	0.6	0.7	0.9	1.0
Paid-In Capital	263	263	263	263	263	0.1	0.1	0.1	0.1	0.1
Retained Earnings	244,273	209,917	174,189	143,399	117,930	53.6	49.4	51.3	50.0	47.1
Treasury Stock	(5,513)	(5,513)	(5,513)	(5,513)	(5,513)	(1.2)	(1.3)	(1.6)	(1.9)	(2.2)
Total Shareholders' Equity	241,480	207,124	171,396	140,606	115,137	53.0	48.8	50.5	49.0	46.0
TOTAL LIABILITIES & EQUITY	456,024	424,755	339,409	287,035	250,459	100.0	100.0	100.0	100.0	100.0
Common shares outstanding (000)	1,432	1,432	1,432	1,432	1,432					
Per-share book value	$168.66	$144.66	$119.71	$98.20	$80.42					

SOURCE: Audited financial statements.

Exhibit 18–2
ABC Grocery Company
Income Statements

	Fiscal Years Ended September 30:					Fiscal Years Ended September 30:				
	1993 ($000)	1992 ($000)	1991 ($000)	1990 ($000)	1989 ($000)	1993 (%)	1992 (%)	1991 (%)	1990 (%)	1989 (%)
Revenues	1,628,251	1,526,509	1,440,023	1,348,304	1,183,979	100.0	100.0	100.0	100.0	100.0
Cost of Goods Sold	1,209,590	1,130,856	1,066,439	1,012,982	885,340	74.3	74.1	74.1	75.1	74.8
Gross Margin	418,661	395,653	373,584	335,323	298,639	25.7	25.9	25.9	24.9	25.2
Operating Expenses:										
Selling, General & Administrative	348,313	323,556	306,721	278,591	246,426	21.4	21.2	21.3	20.7	20.8
Depreciation	25,345	25,771	24,562	23,006	21,185	1.6	1.7	1.7	1.7	1.8
Total Operating Expenses	373,658	349,327	331,283	301,597	267,611	22.9	22.9	23.0	22.4	22.6
Operating Income	45,004	46,326	42,301	33,726	31,029	2.8	3.0	2.9	2.5	2.6
Other Recurring Income (Expense):										
Interest on Capitalized Leases	(8,774)	(8,778)	(8,140)	(7,784)	(7,879)	(0.5)	(0.6)	(0.6)	(0.6)	(0.7)
Advertising Allowances & Other Income	20,831	21,121	15,940	16,170	12,508	1.3	1.4	1.1	1.2	1.1
Interest Expense	(1,813)	(1,343)	(702)	(979)	(307)	(0.1)	(0.1)	(0.0)	(0.1)	(0.0)
Profit-Sharing Expense	(2,393)	(2,359)	(2,030)	(1,950)	(1,537)	(0.1)	(0.2)	(0.1)	(0.1)	(0.1)
Total Other Recurring Income	7,852	8,641	5,068	5,458	2,784	0.5	0.6	0.4	0.4	0.2
Pretax Income, Continuing Operations	52,855	54,967	47,369	39,183	33,813	3.2	3.6	3.3	2.9	2.9
Provision for Income Taxes	18,499	19,238	16,579	13,714	11,834	1.1	1.3	1.2	1.0	1.0
Net Income	34,356	35,728	30,790	25,469	21,978	2.1	2.3	2.1	1.9	1.9
Average shares outstanding (000)	1,432	1,432	1,432	1,432	1,432					
Per-share net income from continuing operations	$24.00	$24.95	$21.50	$17.79	$15.35					

SOURCE: Audited financial statements.

Exhibit 18–3

ABC Grocery Company

Financial and Operating Ratios

	Fiscal Years Ended September 30:				
	1993	1992	1991	1990	1989
LIQUIDITY RATIOS					
Current Ratio	1.52	1.43	1.47	1.56	1.42
Quick Ratio	0.50	0.54	0.48	0.51	0.41
Working Capital ($MM)	62.3	56.4	43.6	44.8	31.5
ACTIVITY RATIOS					
Sales/Receivables	141.2	133.3	100.0	98.0	NA
Days in Receivables	2.6	2.7	3.6	3.7	NA
Cost of Sales/Inventory	10.2	10.9	12.2	12.6	NA
Days in Inventory	35.9	33.5	29.9	28.9	NA
Working Capital Turnover	27.4	30.5	32.6	35.3	NA
Fixed Asset Turnover	9.7	11.4	13.1	14.1	NA
Asset Turnover	3.7	4.0	4.6	5.0	NA
COVERAGE/LEVERAGE RATIOS					
Interest Expense Coverage:					
EBIT	6.0	6.4	6.4	5.5	5.13
EBDIT	8.4	9.0	9.1	8.1	7.72
Cash Flow/Cur. Mat. LTD	10.7	12.2	14.9	26.0	27.04
Fixed Assets/Equity	0.8	0.7	0.7	0.7	0.79
Equity/Total Capital (%)	72.6	71.6	70.3	69.1	67.0
PROFITABILITY RATIOS (%)					
Net Income/Equity	15.3	18.9	19.7	19.9	NA
Net Income/Assets	7.8	9.4	9.8	9.5	NA
Net Income/Sales	2.1	2.3	2.1	1.9	1.9
Cash Flow/Equity	26.6	32.5	35.5	37.9	NA
Cash Flow/Assets	13.6	16.1	17.7	18.0	NA
Cash Flow/Sales	3.7	4.0	3.8	3.6	3.6

EBIT = Earnings before interest and taxes.

EBDIT = Earnings before depreciation, interest, and taxes.

LTD = Long-term debt.

Cash Flow = Net Income plus depreciation expense.

NA = Not available.

SOURCE: Exhibits 18–1 and 18–2 and WMA calculations.

Exhibit 18–4A

ABC Grocery Company
and Robert Morris Associates (RMA)
SIC No. 5411 - Retailers - Groceries & Meats
Common-Size FInancial Statements

	1993		1992		1991		1990		1989	
	ABC Grocery	RMA	ABC Grocery	RMA	ABC Grocery	RMA	ABC Grocery	RMA	ABC Grocery	RMA
Number of Observations	1	20	1	15	1	10	1	18	1	18
Average Asset Size ($MM)	456	171	425	169	339	157	287	167	250	155
Average Sales Volume ($MM)	1,628	615	1,527	673	1,440	639	1,348	699	1,184	655
	%	%	%	%	%	%	%	%	%	%

Common-Size Balance Sheets

ASSETS

Current Assets:

Cash & Equivalents	9.8	7.7	6.0	4.2	4.5	6.6	7.6	5.8	7.7	10.4
Accts. & Notes Receivable (Trade)	2.8	5.1	2.4	4.2	3.7	6.5	5.7	5.0	4.5	4.9
Inventory	26.6	23.1	27.5	24.0	26.8	25.3	29.3	25.2	30.4	35.8
All Other Current Assets	0.5	0.9	8.3	2.0	4.9	1.1	0.9	0.8	0.1	2.1
Total Current Assets	39.7	36.8	44.2	34.4	39.9	39.6	43.5	36.8	42.7	53.2
Net Fixed Assets	41.4	53.5	34.8	54.2	35.3	46.7	35.1	48.3	36.2	35.7
Net Intangible Assets	0.0	3.7	0.0	2.4	0.0	3.5	0.0	7.5	0.0	1.3
Net Other Assets	18.9	6.0	21.0	8.9	24.8	10.2	21.5	7.3	21.1	9.7
TOTAL ASSETS	100.0	100.0	100.0	100.0	100.0	100.0	100.0	100.0	100.0	100.0

LIABILITIES & EQUITY

Liabilities:

Current Liabilities:

Notes Payable	0.3	1.7	0.3	1.2	0.3	3.5	0.2	1.9	0.2	6.0
Current Mat. LTD	0.9	2.0	0.9	3.0	0.8	3.0	0.5	3.9	0.4	4.6
Accounts & Notes Payable (Trade)	13.8	16.9	15.8	16.9	14.6	17.2	21.1	17.4	21.0	20.0
Income Taxes Payable	0.6	0.4	0.4	0.3	1.1	0.2	0.6	0.0	0.0	0.8
All Other Current Liabilities	10.5	8.6	13.5	10.4	10.2	9.1	5.4	7.2	8.5	8.3
Total Current Liabilities	26.1	29.5	30.9	31.8	27.0	32.9	27.8	30.5	30.1	39.8
Total Long-Term Debt	20.0	26.5	19.4	32.2	21.3	36.0	22.0	38.5	22.6	27.1
Total Other Noncurrent Debt	1.0	9.9	0.9	6.5	1.1	4.6	1.2	6.1	1.3	2.5
Total Liabilities	47.0	65.9	51.2	70.5	49.5	73.5	51.0	75.1	54.0	69.4
Total Equity	53.0	34.2	48.8	29.5	50.5	26.4	49.0	24.9	46.0	30.6
TOTAL LIABILITIES & EQUITY	100.0	100.0	100.0	100.0	100.0	100.0	100.0	100.0	100.0	100.0

Common-Size Income Statements

Net Sales	100.0	100.0	100.0	100.0	100.0	100.0	100.0	100.0	100.0	100.0
Cost of Goods Sold	74.3	75.1	74.1	75.0	74.1	77.1	75.1	76.1	74.8	77.5
Gross Profit	25.7	24.9	25.9	25.0	25.9	22.9	24.9	23.9	25.2	22.5
Operating Expenses	22.9	22.9	22.9	23.3	23.0	20.6	22.4	21.8	22.6	20.9
Operating Income	2.8	2.0	3.0	1.7	2.9	2.4	2.5	2.1	2.6	1.6
Other Income (Expense), Net	0.5	(0.6)	0.6	(0.8)	0.4	(1.2)	0.4	(1.6)	0.2	(0.1)
PRETAX PROFIT	3.2	1.4	3.6	0.9	3.3	1.1	2.9	0.5	2.9	1.5

Interpretation of Statement Studies Figures: RMA cautions that the studies be regarded only as a general guideline and not as an absolute industry norm. This is due to limited samples within categories, the categorization of companies by their primary Standard Industrial Classification (SIC) number only, and different methods of operations by companies within the same industry. For these reasons, RMA recommends that the figures be used only as general guidelines in addition to other methods of financial analysis.

SOURCE: Audited financial statements and Robert Morris Associates, *Annual Statement Studies*, 1989–1993.

Exhibit 18–4B
ABC Grocery Company and Robert Morris Associates (RMA)
SIC No. 5411 - Retailers - Groceries & Meats
Financial and Operating Ratios

		1993 ABC Grocery	1993 RMA	1992 ABC Grocery	1992 RMA	1991 ABC Grocery	1991 RMA	1990 ABC Grocery	1990 RMA	1989 ABC Grocery	1989 RMA
Number of Observations		1	20	1	15	1	10	1	18	1	18
Average Asset Size ($MM)		456	171	425	169	339	157	287	167	250	155
Average Sales Volume ($MM)		1,628	615	1,527	673	1,440	639	1,348	699	1,184	655
Liquidity Ratios											
Current Ratio	High		1.5		1.4		1.6		1.3		1.9
	Median	1.5	1.3	1.4	1.0	1.5	1.1	1.6	1.1	1.4	1.4
	Low		1.0		0.9		0.9		1.0		1.0
Quick Ratio	High		0.5		0.3		0.5		0.6		0.7
	Median	0.5	0.3	0.5	0.3	0.5	0.3	0.5	0.2	0.4	0.3
	Low		0.2		0.2		0.2		0.2		0.2
Working Capital ($MM)	Median	62.3	12.5	56.4	14.4	43.6	10.5	44.8	10.5	31.5	0.8
Activity Ratios											
Sales/Receivables	High		183.1		174.1		164.7		141.9		790.5
	Median	128.4	128.4	147.0	97.8	115.0	111.7	82.8	91.7	105.4	256.2
	Low		66.8		74.5		54.7		76.0		116.0
Cost of Sales/Inventory	High		19.3		20.0		18.3		17.4		20.5
	Median	10.0	12.8	9.7	14.0	11.7	13.5	12.1	12.0	11.6	15.5
	Low		8.6		9.7		9.0		9.0		11.7
Cost of Sales/Payables	High		22.1		20.7		22.4		17.8		44.4
	Median	19.2	16.7	16.9	17.7	21.5	18.5	16.8	14.7	16.8	27.7
	Low		14.2		13.3		16.5		11.6		18.2
Sales/Working Capital	High		25.2		40.8		24.2		39.0		23.6
	Median	26.1	50.9	27.1	50.5	33.1	101.9	30.1	101.3	37.6	52.8
	Low		NA		(194.2)		(229.4)		(698.5)		(360.8)
Sales/Net Fixed Assets	High		9.6		10.3		13.1		9.0		38.0
	Median	8.6	6.2	10.3	7.2	12.0	8.7	13.4	7.4	13.1	19.0
	Low		4.8		5.5		5.8		5.5		11.0
Sales/Total Assets	High		4.8		4.8		5.2		4.2		8.4
	Median	3.6	3.5	3.6	3.8	4.2	4.1	4.7	3.6	4.7	6.4
	Low		2.8		3.0		3.1		2.9		4.7
Coverage/Leverage Ratios											
Earnings before Interest	High		3.0		5.0		3.3		3.7		5.5
and Taxes/Int. Expense	Median	6.0	2.1	6.4	1.8	6.4	2.1	5.5	1.4	5.1	2.6
	Low		1.4		1.2		1.4		0.7		1.2
Fixed Assets/Net Worth	High		1.3		1.4		1.2		1.8		0.5
	Median	0.8	1.8	0.7	2.1	0.7	2.0	0.7	2.1	0.8	1.2
	Low		2.8		3.1		32.2		NA		3.2
Debt/Net Worth	High		1.3		1.3		1.5		2.0		1.1
	Median	0.9	2.0	1.1	2.8	1.0	3.2	1.0	3.6	1.2	2.3
	Low		3.1		4.1		67.2		NA		7.3
Equity/Total Capital (%)	Median	72.6	56.3	71.6	47.8	70.3	42.3	69.1	39.3	67.0	53.0
Profitability Ratios											
Pretax Profit/	High		22.7		24.6		25.2		28.2		39.9
Tangible Net Worth (%)	Median	24.9	15.6	29.7	14.7	30.1	15.5	29.2	18.5	29.4	20.9
	Low		7.5		7.2		7.0		-1.6		5.2
Pretax Profit/	High		6.7		8.1		9.0		9.1		13.0
Total Assets (%)	Median	11.6	3.4	12.9	3.3	14.0	4.5	13.7	3.0	13.5	6.2
	Low		1.8		1		2.0		-2.9		0.9
Pretax Profit/Sales (%)	Median	3.2	1.4	3.6	0.9	3.3	1.1	2.9	0.5	2.9	1.5

Note: Ratio calculations on this exhibit may differ from the calculation in Exhibit 18–3 due to different definitions for the ratios used for Exhibit 18–3 and Robert Morris Associates. For example, Robert Morris Associates calculates inventory turnover as the cost of sales divided by ending inventory, while the calculation on Exhibit 18–3 is based on average inventory.

SOURCE: Audited financial statements, Robert Morris Associates, *Annual Statement Studies*, 1989–1993, and WMA calculations.

Exhibit 18–5A
ABC Grocery Company
Guideline Publicly Traded Companies
Common-Size Financial Statements

	Brunos 6/30/93 (%)	Delchamps 6/30/93 (%)	Eagle Food Centers 1/31/93 (%)	Hannaford Brothers 12/31/92 (%)	Ingles Markets 9/30/93 (%)	Penn Traffic 1/31/93 (%)	Riser Foods 6/30/93 (%)	Smith's Food & Drug Ctrs. 12/31/92 (%)	Village Super Market 7/31/93 (%)	Weis Markets 12/31/92 (%)	Median (%)	ABC Grocery 9/28/93 (%)
Size												
Assets ($MM)	917	252	332	769	457	1,375	233	1,479	141	762	609	456
Revenues ($MM)	2,872	1,035	1,082	2,066	1,142	2,788	1,108	2,650	714	1,289	1,215	1,628
Balance Sheet												
ASSETS												
Cash & Equivalents	2.2	4.8	3.5	13.0	3.9	4.0	1.9	1.0	4.7	55.2	3.9	9.8
Accounts Receivable	2.8	3.2	4.6	1.6	3.1	3.8	15.5	1.1	3.0	2.9	3.0	2.8
Inventory	28.3	38.5	32.3	16.2	22.3	19.9	31.1	23.1	18.6	12.8	22.7	26.6
Other Current Assets	1.0	1.3	0.3	1.7	0.6	1.6	2.0	0.9	2.9	1.6	1.4	0.5
Total Current Assets	34.2	47.8	40.7	32.5	29.9	29.3	50.5	26.2	29.2	72.5	33.4	39.7
Fixed Assets (at Cost)	73.6	97.0	84.6	77.5	96.8	56.0	67.5	87.5	88.1	59.1	81.1	78.0
Accumulated Depreciation	(21.2)	(47.7)	(27.8)	(23.1)	(28.3)	(13.8)	(24.0)	(14.7)	(35.6)	(32.3)	(25.9)	(36.6)
Net Fixed Assets	52.4	49.3	56.8	60.6	68.5	42.2	43.4	72.8	52.4	26.9	52.4	41.4
Intangible Assets	4.7	2.1	0.8	1.1	0.0	24.5	0.0	0.0	10.4	0.6	1.0	0.0
Other Assets	8.7	0.8	1.7	5.7	1.7	4.1	6.1	1.0	8.0	0.0	2.9	18.9
TOTAL ASSETS	100.0	100.0	100.0	100.0	100.0	100.0	100.0	100.0	100.0	100.0	100.0	100.0
LIABILITIES & EQUITY												
Accounts Payable	12.7	15.8	18.8	10.3	17.5	14.0	20.3	12.4	16.6	6.5	14.9	13.8
Accrued Expenses	4.5	7.3	5.3	6.6	0.0	6.6	13.1	6.6	10.3	1.8	6.6	9.8
Current Portion LTD	0.3	2.3	0.8	0.9	9.6	0.2	3.7	1.4	3.3	0.0	1.1	0.9
Other Interest-Bearing Debt	3.8	2.2	0.0	0.2	0.0	0.6	0.7	0.0	0.3	0.0	0.3	0.3
Other Current Liabilities	0.1	0.6	5.0	0.9	0.0	1.3	2.3	0.1	0.3	0.7	0.7	1.3
Total Current Liabilities	21.4	28.2	29.9	18.8	27.1	22.7	40.0	20.5	30.8	9.0	24.9	26.1
Long-Term Debt	29.3	15.7	34.5	29.5	35.7	72.2	28.7	40.0	27.9	0.0	29.4	20.0
Deferred Income Tax	5.1	5.9	0.4	3.3	4.8	0.7	0.4	4.2	3.6	1.6	3.5	0.0
Other Liabilities	0.2	0.2	13.7	3.0	0.0	3.0	6.6	0.4	0.0	0.0	0.3	1.0
Total Liabilities	56.1	49.9	78.5	54.6	67.7	98.6	75.8	65.2	62.4	10.7	63.8	47.0
Stockholders' Equity	43.9	50.1	21.5	45.4	32.3	1.4	24.2	34.8	37.6	89.3	36.2	53.0
TOTAL LIABILITIES & EQUITY	100.0	100.0	100.0	100.0	100.0	100.0	100.0	100.0	100.0	100.0	100.0	100.0
Income Statements												
Net Sales	100.0	100.0	100.0	100.0	100.0	100.0	100.0	100.0	100.0	100.0	100.0	100.0
Cost of Sales	78.1	74.5	75.0	75.1	78.1	80.0	80.5	77.1	75.8	74.6	76.4	74.3
Gross Profit	21.9	25.5	25.0	24.9	21.9	20.0	19.5	22.9	24.2	25.4	23.6	25.7
Operating Expenses	17.1	21.1	20.2	17.3	17.5	14.5	16.4	15.7	22.3	17.5	17.4	21.4
Depreciation Expense	1.7	1.7	2.0	2.7	1.8	2.5	1.2	2.6	1.2	2.0	1.9	1.6
Operating Profit	3.2	2.7	2.7	5.0	2.6	3.1	1.9	4.7	0.7	5.9	2.9	2.8
Interest Expense	0.6	0.5	1.5	1.0	1.5	4.2	0.6	1.4	4.5	0.0	1.2	0.6
Other Income (Expenses), Net	0.0	0.0	0.0	0.0	0.5	1.6	(0.4)	0.0	4.1	2.7	0.0	1.1
Pretax Income	2.6	2.2	1.2	4.0	1.6	0.5	0.9	3.3	0.3	8.6	1.9	3.2
Income Taxes	0.9	0.8	0.5	1.6	0.6	0.4	0.3	1.3	0.1	3.0	0.7	1.1
NET INCOME	1.6	1.4	0.8	2.4	1.0	0.2	0.6	2.0	0.2	5.6	1.2	2.1

SOURCE: Individual companies' annual reports and Forms 10-K, and WMA calculations.

Exhibit 18–5B

ABC Grocery Company
Guideline Publicly Traded Companies
Financial and Operating Ratios

	Brunos 6/30/93	Delchamps 6/30/93	Eagle Food Centers 1/31/93	Hannaford Brothers 12/31/92	Ingles Markets 9/30/93	Penn Traffic 1/31/93	Riser Foods 6/30/93	Smith's Food & Drug Ctrs. 12/31/92	Village Super Market 7/31/93	Weis Markets 12/31/92	Median	ABC Grocery 9/28/93
LIQUIDITY												
Current Ratio	1.60	1.70	1.36	1.73	1.10	1.29	1.26	1.28	0.95	8.03	1.33	1.52
Quick Ratio	0.23	0.28	0.27	0.77	0.26	0.34	0.43	0.11	0.25	6.44	0.28	0.50
Working Capital ($Mill)	117.5	49.5	35.8	105.2	12.4	90.7	24.4	84.6	(2.3)	483.6	67.1	62.3
ACTIVITY												
Sales/Receivables (Avg.)	106.5	140.6	86.2	165.0	88.8	59.0	35.3	166.3	181.1	65.0	97.6	141.2
Days in Receivables	3	3	4	2	4	6	10	2	2	6	4	3
COGS/Inventory (Avg.)	9.0	8.0	8.1	11.3	8.7	8.6	12.8	6.5	20.4	10.1	8.9	10.2
Days In Inventory	40	46	45	32	42	42	28	56	18	36	41	36
Sales/Working Capital (Avg.)	25.1	23.5	8.9	23.8	28.0	32.2	46.2	46.0	(241.2)	2.7	24.5	18.0
Sales/Net Fixed Assets (Avg.)	6.1	8.4	5.9	4.5	4.0	5.2	11.5	2.7	9.2	6.4	6.0	9.7
Sales/Total Assets (Avg.)	3.3	4.1	3.4	2.8	2.7	2.1	5.1	2.0	5.0	1.7	3.0	3.7
COVERAGE/LEVERAGE												
Interest Expense Coverage	5.0	5.2	1.8	4.9	2.1	1.1	2.5	3.4	1.1	NA	2.3	6.0
Cash Flow/Curr. Mat. LTD	41.2	6.3	14.1	22.7	3.5	10.2	6.3	7.9	2.8	NA	7.1	10.7
Fixed Assets/Equity	1.2	1.0	2.6	1.3	2.1	30.3	1.8	2.1	1.4	0.3	1.6	0.8
LTD/LTD + Equity	0.40	0.24	0.62	0.39	0.52	0.98	0.54	0.53	0.43	0.00	0.48	0.27
Total Debt/Equity	1.3	1.0	3.6	1.2	2.1	70.9	3.1	1.9	1.7	0.1	1.8	0.9
PROFITABILITY (%)												
Net Income/Sales	1.6	1.4	0.8	2.4	1.0	0.2	0.6	2.0	0.2	5.6	1.2	2.1
Net Income/Equity (Avg.)	11.3	12.0	12.1	15.2	8.1	4.5	11.7	2.7	0.7	2.7	9.7	15.3
Net Income/Assets (Avg.)	5.3	5.8	2.6	6.7	2.7	0.1	2.8	1.0	0.3	2.4	2.6	7.8
EBIT/Sales	3.2	2.7	2.7	5.0	3.1	4.7	1.5	4.7	4.8	8.6	3.9	3.9
DFNI/Sales	3.3	3.1	2.7	5.0	2.8	0.2	1.8	2.0	0.2	5.6	2.8	2.6

COGS = Cost of goods sold.
LTD = Long-term debt.
EBIT = Earnings before interest and taxes.
DFNI = Debt-free net income.
NA = Not available.

SOURCE: Individual companies' annual reports and Forms 10-K, and WMA calculations.

Exhibit 18–6A

ABC Grocery Company
Guideline Publicly Traded Companies
Market Value of Invested Capital

Company	Mkt./Sym.	FYE	Lat. Qtr. TBV ($000)	Lat. Qtr. BV IBD ($000)	Lat. Qtr. TBVIC ($000)	Lat. Qtr. MV IBD [a] ($000)	As of or for Period Ending	Bid/Close Price per Common Share 11/10/93 ($)	Common Shares Outstg. [b] (000s)	MV Common Equity ($000)	MV Preferred Equity ($000)	MVIC ($000)
Brunos, Inc. [f]	OTC/BRNO	6/30/93	365,617	328,709	694,326	328,709	9/93	10.500	78,065	819,685	0	1,148,394
Delchamps, Inc. [g,f]	OTC/DLCH	7/03/93	132,750	50,352	183,102	50,352	10/93	22,750	7,114	161,834	0	212,186
Eagle Food Centers, Inc. [h,f]	OTC/EGLE	1/31/93	72,833	123,797	196,630	123,797	10/93	6,250	10,994	68,709	0	192,506
Hannaford Brothers Company [f]	NYSE/HRD	12/31/92	386,053	228,493	614,546	228,493	9/93	23,125	41,147	951,514	0	1,180,007
Ingles Markets, Inc.	OTC/IMKTA	9/30/93	147,689	206,846	354,535	206,846	9/93	8.875	17,904	158,895	0	365,741
Penn Traffic Company [i,f]	AMER/PNF	1/31/93	(348,858)	1,142,769	793,911	1,142,769	10/93	38.750	10,833	419,796	0	1,562,565
Riser Foods, Inc. [j,f]	AMER/RSR	6/30/93	69,829	93,695	163,524	93,695	9/93	8.875	8,081	71,718	1,804	167,217
Smith's Food & Drug Centers, Inc.	NYSE/SFD	12/31/92	536,291	752,212	1,288,503	752,212	9/93	20.000	29,866	597,312	0	1,349,524
Village Super Markets, Inc. [f]	OTC/VLGEA	7/31/93	42,900	43,331	86,231	43,331	10/93	9.750	2,910	28,371	0	71,702
Weis Markets, Inc. [f]	NTSE/WMK	12/31/92	724,664	0	724,664	0	9/93	28.000	43,804	1,226,524	0	1,226,524
ABC Grocery Company [f]	NA	9/28/93	251,324	96,584	347,908	NM	9/93	NA	2,244	NM	0	NM

Definitions, sources, and footnotes are presented on Exhibit 18–6I.

Exhibit 18–6B

ABC Grocery Company
Guideline Publicly Traded Companies
Earnings before Interest and Taxes

Company	LTM EBIT ($000)	Ending	Earnings before Interest & Taxes (EBIT)					5-Yr. Avg. [c] EBIT ($000)	5-Yr. Avg. Annual Compound Growth [d] (%)	Coeff. of Var. [e] (%)	MVIC/EBIT		
			1993 ($000)	1992 ($000)	1991 ($000)	1990 ($000)	1989 ($000)				MVIC ($000)	LTM	5-Yr. Avg.
Brunos, Inc. [f]	86,360	9/93	86,849	97,012	125,374	112,914	96,359	103,702	(2.5)	13.2	1,148,394	13.3	11.1
Delchamps, Inc. [g,f]	28,457	10/93	28,349	12,372	29,934	28,990	27,041	25,337	1.2	25.9	212,186	7.5	8.4
Eagle Food Centers, Inc. [h,f]	25,574	10/93	29,412	29,596	31,491	33,853	28,207	29,985	(2.0)	9.1	192,506	7.5	6.4
Hannaford Brothers Company [f]	106,923	9/93	98,693	95,061	84,855	73,616	56,350	91,830	14.4	12.6	1,180,007	11.0	12.8
Ingles Markets, Inc.	35,586	9/93	35,586	24,621	33,522	31,374	34,567	31,934	0.7	12.3	365,741	10.3	11.5
Penn Traffic Company [i,f]	134,453	10/93	122,544	122,291	108,991	96,035	43,464	116,863	26.8	11.3	1,562,565	11.6	13.4
Riser Foods, Inc. [j,f]	22,277	9/93	22,155	22,727	26,489	21,191	3,685	19,249	52.7	41.5	167,217	7.5	8.7
Smith's Food & Drug Centers, Inc.	126,297	9/93	124,180	103,716	80,309	67,821	53,508	100,465	19.8	23.2	1,349,524	10.7	13.4
Village Super Markets, Inc. [f]	4,989	10/93	5,314	5,493	8,823	13,229	14,584	9,489	(22.3)	40.5	71,702	14.4	7.6
Weis Markets, Inc. [f]	111,177	9/93	112,778	125,014	136,711	136,503	129,701	124,437	(3.2)	8.9	1,226,524	11.0	9.9
Mean									8.6	19.8		10.5	10.3
Median									1.0	12.9		10.9	10.5
Standard deviation									20.8	12.5		2.4	2.5
Coefficient of variation (%)									242.6	63.1		22.9	24.4
ABC Grocery Company [f]	64,226	9/93	64,226	65,013	56,579	50,154	41,999	55,594	11.2	15.7	NM	NM	NM

Definitions, sources, and footnotes are presented on Exhibit 18–6I.

Exhibit 18–6C

ABC Grocery Company
Guideline Publicly Traded Companies
Earnings before Depreciation, Interest, and Taxes

Company	LTM EBDIT ($000)	Ending	Earnings before Depreciation, Interest & Taxes (EBDIT)					5-Yr. Avg. [c] EBDIT ($000)	5-Yr. Avg. Annual Compound Growth [d] (%)	Coeff. of Var. [e] (%)	MVIC/EBDIT		
			1993 ($000)	1992 ($000)	1991 ($000)	1990 ($000)	1989 ($000)				MVIC ($000)	LTM	5-Yr. Avg.
Brunos, Inc. [f]	136,061	9/93	135,567	141,273	166,132	149,280	129,007	144,252	1.3	8.9	1,148,394	8.4	8.0
Delchamps, Inc. [g,f]	46,905	10/93	46,448	27,971	44,804	43,012	39,691	40,385	4.0	16.3	212,186	4.5	5.3
Eagle Food Centers, Inc. [h,f]	48,032	10/93	50,765	48,046	49,873	55,546	51,851	50,452	(1.6)	5.0	192,506	4.0	3.8
Hannaford Brothers Company [f]	163,557	9/93	153,607	145,715	120,378	101,747	80,175	137,001	16.2	19.9	1,180,007	7.2	8.6
Ingles Markets, Inc.	56,425	9/93	56,425	44,198	51,515	46,692	47,321	49,230	4.5	8.7	365,741	6.5	7.4
Penn Traffic Company [i,f]	210,988	10/93	191,291	185,845	170,298	149,466	64,206	181,578	28.5	25.5	1,562,565	7.4	8.6
Riser Foods, Inc. [j,f]	36,664	9/93	35,740	34,925	38,373	33,146	14,325	31,302	24.7	27.6	167,217	4.6	5.3
Smith's Food & Drug Centers, Inc.	205,193	9/93	191,961	154,211	120,886	100,606	79,836	154,571	22.0	25.7	1,349,524	6.6	8.7
Village Super Markets, Inc. [f]	13,681	10/93	14,032	14,215	16,694	20,698	21,730	17,474	(10.3)	18.4	71,702	5.2	4.1
Weis Markets, Inc. [f]	140,383	9/93	139,136	150,145	159,907	158,551	149,253	149,624	(1.3)	5.0	1,226,524	8.7	8.2
Mean									8.8	16.1		6.3	6.8
Median									4.3	17.4		6.5	7.7
Standard deviation									13.1	8.7		1.7	2.0
Coefficient of variation (%)									148.9	54.3		26.5	28.8
ABC Grocery Company [f]	89,571	9/93	89,571	90,784	81,141	73,160	63,184	79,568	9.1	13.0	NM	NM	NM

Definitions, sources, and footnotes are presented on Exhibit 18–6I.

Exhibit 18–6D
ABC Grocery Company
Guideline Publicly Traded Companies
Debt-Free Net Income

Company	LTM DFNI ($000)	Ending	Debt-Free Net Income (DFNI) 1993 ($000)	1992 ($000)	1991 ($000)	1990 ($000)	1989 ($000)	5-Yr. Avg. [c] DFNI ($000)	5-Yr. Avg. Annual Compound Growth [d] (%)	Coeff. of Var. [e] (%)	MVIC/DFNI MVIC ($000)	LTM	5-Yr. Avg.
Brunos, Inc. [f]	51,995	9/93	55,496	62,750	79,504	70,788	61,292	65,966	(3.8)	12.7	1,148,394	22.1	17.4
Delchamps, Inc. [g,f]	17,960	10/93	17,920	8,963	19,589	18,851	18,420	16,748	(0.6)	23.5	212,186	11.8	12.7
Eagle Food Centers, Inc. [h,f]	15,857	10/93	18,236	17,787	18,913	20,582	17,348	18,275	(1.9)	6.2	192,506	12.1	10.5
Hannaford Brothers Company [f]	63,285	9/93	59,448	56,733	51,367	44,122	34,579	54,991	13.6	16.49	1,180,007	18.6	21.5
Ingles Markets, Inc.	22,753	9/93	22,753	16,072	21,705	19,220	21,294	20,209	1.7	11.7	365,741	16.1	18.1
Penn Traffic Company [i,f]	85,919	10/93	79,587	114,127	132,158	69,969	33,578	96,352	21.5	26.9	1,562,565	18.2	16.2
Riser Foods, Inc. [j,f]	13,822	9/93	13,669	13,431	15,226	12,076	2,211	11,323	53.9	41.2	167,217	12.1	14.8
Smith's Food & Drug Centers, Inc.	72,942	9/93	75,664	63,726	50,366	42,672	33,704	61,074	17.6	24.4	1,349,524	18.5	22.1
Village Super Markets, Inc. [f]	3,022	10/93	3,227	3,352	4,931	7,662	8,646	5,564	(21.9)	39.9	71,702	23.7	12.9
Weis Markets, Inc. [f]	71,738	9/93	73,314	81,114	89,672	88,037	82,492	80,775	(2.9)	7.2	1,226,524	17.1	15.2
Mean									7.7	21.0		17.0	16.1
Median									0.5	19.9		17.6	15.7
Standard deviation									20.5	12.5		4.1	3.7
Coefficient of variation (%)									265.3	59.5		24.2	23.2
ABC Grocery Company [f]	41,747	9/93	41,747	42,258	36,777	32,600	27,299	36,136	11.2	15.7	NM	NM	NM

Definitions, sources, and footnotes are presented on Exhibit 18–6I.

Exhibit 18–6E
ABC Grocery Company
Guideline Publicly Traded Companies
Debt-Free Cash Flow

Company	LTM DFCF ($000)	Ending	Debt-Free Cash Flow (DFCF) 1993 ($000)	1992 ($000)	1991 ($000)	1990 ($000)	1989 ($000)	5-Yr. Avg. [c] DFCF ($000)	5-Yr. Avg. Annual Compound Growth [d] (%)	Coeff. of Var. [e] (%)	MVIC/DFCF MVIC ($000)	LTM	5-Yr. Avg.
Brunos, Inc. [f]	101,696	9/93	104,214	107,011	120,262	107,154	93,940	106,516	1.9	7.9	1,148,394	11.3	10.8
Delchamps, Inc. [g,f]	36,408	10/93	36,019	24,562	34,459	32,873	31,070	31,796	3.8	12.5	212,186	5.8	6.7
Eagle Food Centers, Inc. [h,f]	38,315	10/93	39,589	36,237	37,295	42,275	40,992	38,742	(1.4)	5.8	192,506	5.0	5.0
Hannaford Brothers Company [f]	119,919	9/93	114,362	107,387	86,890	72,252	58,403	100,162	16.4	20.9	1,180,007	9.8	11.8
Ingles Markets, Inc.	43,591	9/93	43,591	35,649	39,698	34,538	34,048	37,505	6.4	9.7	365,741	8.4	9.8
Penn Traffic Company [i,f]	162,454	10/93	148,334	142,161	193,465	123,400	54,320	153,963	25.4	17.0	1,562,565	9.6	10.1
Riser Foods, Inc. [j,f]	28,209	9/93	27,254	25,629	27,110	24,031	12,851	23,375	20.3	23.1	167,217	5.9	7.2
Smith's Food & Drug Centers, Inc.	151,838	9/93	143,445	114,221	90,943	75,457	60,032	115,181	21.6	25.5	1,349,524	8.9	11.7
Village Super Markets, Inc. [f]	11,714	10/93	11,945	12,075	12,803	15,131	15,792	13,549	(6.8)	11.8	71,702	6.1	5.3
Weis Markets, Inc. [f]	100,944	9/93	99,672	106,245	112,868	110,085	102,044	105,963	(0.2)	4.6	1,226,524	12.2	11.6
Mean									8.7	13.9		8.3	9.0
Median									5.1	12.2		8.6	10.0
Standard deviation									11.2	7.4		2.5	2.7
Coefficient of variation (%)									128.7	53.2		29.9	30.1
ABC Grocery Company [f]	67,092	9/93	67,092	68,029	61,339	55,606	48,484	60,110	8.5	12.2	NM	NM	NM

Definitions, sources, and footnotes are presented on Exhibit 18–6I.

Exhibit 18–6F
ABC Grocery Company
Guideline Publicly Traded Companies
Revenues

Company	LTM Revenues ($000)	Ending	Revenues 1993 ($000)	1992 ($000)	1991 ($000)	1990 ($000)	1989 ($000)	5-Yr. Revenues DFCF ($000)	5-Yr. Avg. Annual Compound Growth [d] (%)	Coeff. of Var. [e] (%)	MVIC/Revenues MVIC ($000)	LTM	56-Yr. Avg.
Brunos, Inc. [f]	2,871,514	9/93	2,872,327	2,657,846	2,585,934	2,394,788	2,134,093	2,528,998	7.2	9.9	1,148,394	0.40	0.45
Delchamps, Inc. [g,f]	1,045,727	10/93	1,034,531	949,849	949,169	948,257	899,532	958,268	3.6	4.5	212,186	0.20	0.22
Eagle Food Centers, Inc. [h,f]	1,068,537	10/93	1,081,538	1,113,303	1,124,030	1,120,355	1,066,010	1,100,510	0.0	0.0	188,588	0.18	0.17
Hannaford Brothers Company [f]	2,078,944	9/93	2,066,023	2,007,960	1,687,649	1,520,600	1,261,668	1,872,235	11.1	16.1	1,180,007	0.57	0.63
Ingles Markets, Inc.	1,141,800	9/93	1,141,800	1,066,332	1,044,452	1,006,790	903,831	1,032,641	6.0	7.6	365,741	0.32	0.35
Penn Traffic Company [i,f]	3,025,413	10/93	2,787,566	2,729,537	2,770,875	2,699,847	1,179,924	2,802,648	21.9	22.4	1,562,565	0.52	0.56
Riser Foods, Inc. [j,f]	1,105,371	9/93	1,108,178	979,277	1,022,024	1,054,496	1,083,130	1,049,421	0.5	4.3	167,217	0.15	0.16
Smith's Food & Drug Centers, Inc.	2,767,374	9/93	2,649,860	2,217,437	2,031,373	1,731,559	1,393,391	2,279,521	15.5	18.7	1,349,524	0.49	0.59
Village Super Markets, Inc. [f]	707,029	10/93	713,856	715,059	686,002	681,174	658,143	690,847	1.7	3.1	71,702	0.10	0.10
Weis Markets, Inc. [f]	1,397,545	9/93	1,289,195	1,294,332	1,271,806	1,239,272	1,189,236	1,298,430	3.5	3.0	1,226,524	0.88	0.94
Mean									7.1	9.2		0.38	0.42
Median									4.8	6.0		0.36	0.40
Standard deviation									7.1	7.3		0.24	0.27
Coefficient of variation (%)									100.2	79.9		63.1	63.7
ABC Grocery Company [f]	1,628,251	9/93	1,628,251	1,526,509	1,440,023	1,348,304	1,183,979	1,425,413	8.3	10.7	NM	NM	NM

Definitions, sources, and footnotes are presented on Exhibit 18–6I.

Exhibit 18–6G
ABC Grocery Company
Guideline Publicly Traded Companies
Revenue Performance Ratios

Company	LTM Return on Revenues EBIT (%)	EBDIT (%)	DFNI (%)	DFCF (%)	5-Yr. Avg. Return on Revenues EBIT (%)	EBDIT (%)	DFNI (%)	DFCF (%)
Brunos, Inc. [f]	3.0	4.7	1.8	3.5	4.1	5.7	2.6	4.2
Delchamps, Inc. [g,f]	2.7	4.5	1.7	3.5	2.6	4.2	1.7	3.3
Eagle Food Centers, Inc. [h,f]	2.4	4.5	1.5	3.6	2.7	4.6	1.7	3.5
Hannaford Brothers Company [f]	5.1	7.9	3.0	5.8	4.9	7.3	2.9	5.3
Ingles Markets, Inc.	3.1	4.9	2.0	3.8	3.1	4.8	2.0	3.6
Penn Traffic Company [i,f]	4.4	7.0	2.8	5.4	4.2	6.5	3.4	5.5
Riser Foods, Inc. [j,f]	2.0	3.3	1.3	2.6	1.8	3.0	1.1	2.2
Smith's Food & Drug Centers, Inc.	4.6	7.4	2.6	5.5	4.4	6.8	2.7	5.1
Village Super Markets, Inc. [f]	0.7	1.9	0.4	1.7	1.4	2.5	0.8	2.0
Weis Markets, Inc. [f]	8.0	10.0	5.1	7.2	9.6	11.5	6.2	8.2
Mean	3.6	5.6	2.2	4.2	3.9	5.7	2.5	4.3
Median	3.1	4.8	1.9	3.7	3.6	5.2	2.3	3.9
Standard deviation	2.0	2.4	1.3	1.7	2.3	2.6	1.5	1.8
Coefficient of variation (%)	56.0	42.9	57.6	39.4	59.5	45.4	61.4	42.4
ABC Grocery Company [f]	3.9	5.5	2.6	4.1	3.9	5.6	2.5	4.2

Definitions, sources, and footnotes are presented on Exhibit 18–6I.

Exhibit 18–6H

ABC Grocery Company
Guideline Publicly Traded Companies
Book Value of Invested Capital and Performance Ratios

Company	MVIC ($000s)	MVIC/ Lat. Qtr. TVBIC	IBD/ TBVIC (%)	MV of IBD/ MVIC (%)	EBIT Return On TBVIC LTM (%)	EBIT Return On TBVIC 5-Yr. Avg. (%)	EBDIT Return On TBVIC LTM (%)	EBDIT Return On TBVIC 5-Yr. Avg. (%)	DFNI Return On TBVIC LTM (%)	DFNI Return On TBVIC 5-Yr. Avg. (%)	DFCF Return On TBVIC LTM (%)	DFCF Return On TBVIC 5-Yr. Avg. (%)
Brunos, Inc. [f]	1,148394	1.65	47.3	28.6	12.4	14.9	19.6	20.8	7.5	9.5	14.6	15.3
Delchamps, Inc. [g,f]	212,186	1.16	27.5	23.7	15.5	13.8	25.6	22.1	9.8	9.1	19.9	17.4
Eagle Food Centers, Inc. [h,f]	192,506	0.98	63.0	64.3	13.0	15.2	24.4	25.7	8.1	9.3	19.5	19.7
Hannaford Brothers Company [f]	1,180,007	1.92	37.2	19.4	17.4	14.9	26.6	22.3	10.3	8.9	19.5	16.3
Ingles Markets, Inc.	365,741	1.03	58.3	56.6	10.0	9.0	15.9	13.9	6.4	5.7	12.3	10.6
Penn Traffic Company [i,f]	1,562,565	1.97	143.9	73.1	16.9	14.7	26.6	22.9	10.8	12.1	20.5	19.4
Riser Foods, Inc. [j,f]	167,217	1.02	57.3	56.0	13.6	11.8	22.4	19.1	8.5	6.9	17.3	14.3
Smith's Food & Drug Centers, Inc.	1,349,524	1.05	58.4	55.7	9.8	7.8	15.9	12.0	5.7	4.7	11.8	8.9
Village Super Markets, Inc. [f]	71,702	0.83	50.2	60.4	5.8	11.0	15.9	20.3	3.5	6.5	13.6	15.7
Weis Markets, Inc. [f]	1,226,524	1.69	0.0	0.0	15.3	17.2	19.4	20.6	9.9	11.1	13.9	14.6
Mean		1.33	54.3	43.8	13.0	13.0	21.2	20.0	8.0	8.4	16.3	15.2
Median		1.10	53.8	55.9	13.3	14.3	21.0	20.7	8.3	9.0	15.9	15.5
Standard deviation		0.4	36.8	23.9	3.6	3.0	4.5	4.1	2.3	2.4	3.4	3.4
Coefficient of variation (%)		32.2	67.7	54.7	27.9	23.2	21.0	20.7	28.9	28.4	20.8	22.5
ABC Grocery Company [f]	NM	NM	27.8	NM	18.5	16.0	25.7	22.9	12.0	10.4	19.3	17.3

Definitions, sources, and footnotes are presented on Exhibit 18–6I.

Exhibit 18–6I

ABC Grocery Company
Guideline Publicly Traded Companies
Definitions, Footnotes, and Sources to Exhibits

BV	=	Book value
DF	=	Deficit
FIFO	=	First-in, first out
FYE	=	Fiscal year-end
IBD	=	Interest-bearing debt
IC	=	Invested capital
LIFO	=	Last-in, first-out
LTM	=	Latest 12 months
MV	=	Market value
MVIC	=	LTD + ST interest-bearing debt + MV of preferred + MV of common equity
NA	=	Not available
NM	=	Not meaningful
T	=	Tangible
TBVIC	=	Stockholders' equity - goodwill + LTD + ST interest-bearing debt

Footnotes:
a. Book value if not publicly traded.
b. Per most recently available data prior to the valuation date.
c. Includes latest 12 months if at least 6 months beyond latest fiscal year-end.
d. From earliest year on the table to the latest 12-month period.
e. (Standard deviation/Mean) × 100.
f. Company reports earnings based on LIFO inventory accounting. Earnings adjusted to reflect inventory accounting on a FIFO basis.
g. Excludes losses on sale of property and equipment in 1991–93.
h. Excludes effect of 1991 store closings and asset revaluations.
i. Excludes acquisition and financing costs and expenses in 1989 and 1990.
j. Excludes restructuring charges in 1992 and 1993.

SOURCE: Individual companies' Forms 10-K, Forms 10-Q, and annual reports; *The Wall Street Journal*; WMA calculations; CompuServe; and *Moody's Bond Guide.*

Exhibit 18–7A
ABC Grocery Company
Discounted Economic Income Method
Projected Income Statements

	Actual	Projected				
	1993	**1994**	**1995**	**1996**	**1997**	**1998**
	($000)	($000)	($000)	($000)	($000)	($000)
Revenues	1,628,251	1,725,854	1,856,235	1,925,640	2,051,457	2,147,896
Percent Increase		*6.0%*	*7.6%*	*3.7%*	*6.5%*	*4 7%*
Gross Margin	418,661	448,722	482,621	491,038	523,122	547,713
Percent of Revenues	*25.7%*	*26.0%*	*26.0%*	*25.5%*	*25.5%*	*25.5%*
Operating Expenses	373,658	396,946	426,934	433,269	461,578	483,277
Percent of Revenues	*22.9%*	*23.0%*	*23.0%*	*22.5%*	*22.5%*	*22.5%*
Pretax Income	52,855	51,776	55,687	57,769	61,544	64,437
Taxes	18,499	18,121	19,490	20,219	21,540	22,553
Tax Rate	*35.0%*	*35.0%*	*35.0%*	*35.0%*	*35.0%*	*35.0%*
Net Income	34,356	33,654	36,197	37,550	40,003	41,884
Determination of Net Cash Flow:						
Net Income		33,654	36,197	37,550	40,003	41,884
Tax-Affected Interest Expense [a]		7,292	7,843	8,136	8,667	9,075
Depreciation and Amortization [b]		34,517	37,125	38,513	41,029	42,958
Capital Expenditures [c]		(47,720)	(51,325)	(53,244)	(56,723)	(59,389)
Working Capital Requirements [d]		(3,319)	(4,433)	(2,360)	(4,278)	(3,279)
Net Cash Flow		24,425	25,406	28,595	28,699	31,249

[a] Interest expense estimated at 0.65% of sales, based on management projections.
[b] Estimated at 2.0% of sales, based on management projections.
[c] Estimated at 70% of net income plus depreciation, based on historical results.
[d] 3.4% of sales increase, as derived in Exhibit 18–7C.

SOURCE: ABC Grocery management projections, WMA calculations.

Exhibit 18–7B
ABC Grocery Company
Discounted Economic Income Method
Indicated Value

	Fiscal Years Ended September:				
	Projected				
	1994	1995	1996	1997	1998
	($000)	($000)	($000)	($000)	($000)
Net Income [a]	33,654	36,197	37,550	40,003	41,884
Earnings before Interest and Taxes (EBIT) [a]	62,994	67,753	70,286	74,878	78,398
Depreciation and Amortization [a]	34,517	37,125	38,513	41,029	42,958
Earnings before Depreciation, Interest, and Taxes [a]	97,511	104,877	108,799	115,907	121,356
Net Cash Flow (NCF) [a]	24,425	25,406	28,595	28,699	31,249
Discount Factor [b]	0.953	0.867	0.788	0.716	0.651
Present Value Interim NCF	23,288	22,022	22,532	20,559	20,350

Present Value Sum Interim NCF $108,751

Weighted Average Cost of Capital (WACC):

Risk-Free Rate [c]		6.2%
Plus:		
Equity Risk Premium [d]	7.3%	
Multiplied by: Beta [e]	0.70	
ABC Grocery Equity Risk Premium		5.1%
Equity Rate of Return		11.3%
Cost of Debt (Pretax) [f]	8.5%	
Multiplied by: (1 − Tax Rate)	0.65	
Cost of Debt (Tax-Affected)		5.5%
Debt/Total Capital [g]		20.0%

Computation of WACC:

	Cost		Proportion		
Equity	0.113	×	0.80	=	.090
Debt	0.055	×	0.20	=	.011
					0.101
WACC (Rounded)					10.0%

Terminal Value:

Fundamentals	($000)	Multiple	Terminal Value ($000)
Projected EBDIT	121,356	5.2	631,052
Projected NCF	32,498	16.7 [j]	541,641
Terminal Value [i]			586,346
Present Value Factor		×	0.621
Present Value of Terminal Value			364,075

Residual Equity Value Calculation:

	($000)
Present Value of Interim NCF	108,751
Present Value of Terminal Value	364,075
Total Market Value of Invested Capital	472,825
Less: Total Interest-Bearing Debt [h]	96,584
Indicated Equity Value	376,241
Rounded	376,200

[a] As derived in Exhibit 18–7A.
[b] Based on mid–year convention.
[c] 20-year U.S. government bond yield as of November 10, 1993, per *Standard & Poor's The Outlook* dated November 17, 1993.
[d] *SBBI 1993 Yearbook,* Ibbotson Associates.
[e] Based on Compustat data for October 1993, median of betas for the 10 guideline companies.
[f] Estimated embedded cost of debt of ABC Grocery.
[g] Based on estimated market value of debt to total capital for ABC Grocery as of the valuation date.
[h] As of September 28, 1993.
[i] Based on weightings of 50% for EBDIT and 50% for NCF.
[j] Based on expected long-term growth of 4.00%.

SOURCE: Exhibit 18–7A, WMA calculations.

Exhibit 18–7C
ABC Grocery Company
Discounted Economic Income Method
Working Capital Requirements

	Fiscal Years Ended September:				
	1993 ($000)	1992 ($000)	1991 ($000)	1990 ($000)	1989 ($000)
Sales	1,628,251	1,526,509	1,440,023	1,348,304	1,183,979
Total Current Assets	181,174	187,710	135,350	124,751	106,904
Total Current Liabilities	118,842	131,325	91,792	70,030	75,070
Less: Current Interest-Bearing Debt (IBD)	5,591	5,024	3,725	1,868	1,596
Total Non-IBD Current Liabilities	113,251	126,301	88,067	78,071	73,782
Net Working Capital	67,923	61,409	47,283	46,680	33,122
Increase	*6,514*	*14,126*	*603*	*13,558*	
Average Working Capital Turnover [a]	25.2	28.1	30.7	33.8	
Implied Working Capital Requirement					
as % of Sales [b]	3.97%	3.56%	3.26%	2.96%	
Median, 1990–93	3.41%				
Rounded	3.40%				

[a] Calculated based on average working capital.
[b] Calculated as the inverse of the working capital turnover.

SOURCE: Exhibits 18–1 and 18–2, WMA calculations.

Appendix 18B

Definition of Financial and Operating Ratios

Current ratio	Year-end current assets divided by year-end current liabilities.
Quick ratio	(Year-end cash, accounts receivable, and all assets shown between cash and accounts receivable) divided by year-end total current liabilities.
Working capital ($000s)	(Year-end current assets less year-end current liabilities) divided by 1,000.
Sales/Receivables	Year's sales divided by the average of year-beginning and year-end accounts receivable.
Days in Receivables	365 divided by the sales/receivables ratio (above).
Cost of sales/Inventory	Year's cost of sales divided by the average of the year-beginning inventory and year-end inventory.
Days in inventory	365 divided by the cost of sales/inventory ratio (above).
Working capital turnover	Year's sales divided by the year's average working capital (year-beginning total current assets plus year-end total current assets less year-beginning total current liabilities less year-end total current liabilities divided by 2).
Fixed asset turnover	Year's sales divided by the average of year-beginning and year-end net fixed assets.
Asset turnover	Year's sales divided by average of year-beginning and year-end total assets.
Interest expense coverage, EBIT	(Year's pretax income from continuing operations plus year's interest expense) divided by year's interest expense.
Interest expense coverage, EBDIT	(Year's pretax income from continuing operations plus year's interest expense plus year's depreciation/amortization expense) divided by year's interest expense.
Cash flow/Current maturity of long-term debt	(Year's net income from continuing operations plus year's depreciation/amortization expense) divided by year-ending current maturities of long-term debt.
Fixed assets/Equity	Year-end net fixed assets divided by year-end net worth.
Equity as a % of total capital	Year-end equity divided by (year-end equity plus year-end long-term debt).
Net income/Equity	Year's net income divided by the average of year-beginning and year-ending net worth.
Net income/Assets	Year's net income divided by the average of year-beginning and year-ending total assets.
Net income/Sales	Year's net income divided by year's sales.
Cash flow/Equity	(Year's net income plus depreciation expense) divided by the average of year-beginning and year-ending net worth.
Cash flow/Assets	(Year's net income plus depreciation expense) divided by the average of year-beginning and year-ending total assets.
Cash flow/Sales	(Year's net income plus depreciation expense) divided by year's sales.

Appendix 18C

Appraisal Certification

We hereby certify the following statements regarding this appraisal:

1. We have personally inspected the assets, properties, or business interests encompassed by this appraisal.
2. We have no present or prospective future interest in the assets, properties, or business interests that are the subject of this appraisal report.
3. We have no personal interest or bias with respect to the subject matter of this report or the parties involved.
4. Our compensation for making the appraisal is in no way contingent upon the value reported or upon any predetermined value.
5. To the best of our knowledge and belief, the statements of facts contained in this report, upon which the analyses, conclusions, and opinions expressed herein are based, are true and correct.
6. Our analyses, opinions, and conclusions were developed, and this report has been prepared, in conformity with the Uniform Standards of Professional Appraisal Practice, as promulgated by The Appraisal Foundation.
7. No persons other than the individuals whose qualifications are included herein have provided significant professional assistance regarding the analyses, opinions, and conclusions set forth in this report.
8. The reported analyses, opinions, and conclusions are limited only by the reported contingent and limiting conditions, and they represent our unbiased professional analyses, opinions, and conclusions.
9. The reported analyses, opinions, and conclusions were developed, and this report has been prepared, in conformity with the requirements of the Code of Professional Ethics and the Standards of Professional Appraisal Practice of The Appraisal Institute, of the American Society of Appraisers, and of the other professional organizations of which we are members.
10. Disclosure of the contents of this report is subject to the requirements of The Appraisal Institute, the American Society of Appraisers, and the other professional organizations of which we are members related to review by their duly authorized representatives.

Appendix 18D

Statement of Contingent and Limiting Conditions

This appraisal is made subject to the following general contingent and limiting conditions:

1. We assume no responsibility for the legal description or matters including legal or title considerations. Title to the subject assets, properties, or business interests is assumed to be good and marketable unless otherwise stated.
2. The subject assets, properties, or business interests are appraised free and clear of any or all liens or encumbrances unless otherwise stated.
3. We assume responsible ownership and competent management with respect to the subject assets, properties, or business interests.
4. The information furnished by others is believed to be reliable. However, we issue no warranty or other form of assurance regarding its accuracy.
5. We assume no hidden or unapparent conditions regarding the subject assets, properties, or business interests.
6. We assume that there is full compliance with all applicable federal, state, and local regulations and laws unless the lack of compliance is stated, defined, and considered in the appraisal report.
7. We assume that all required licenses, certificates of occupancy, consents, or legislative or administrative authority from any local, state, or national government, or private entity or organization have been or can be obtained or reviewed for any use on which the opinion contained in this report is based.
8. Unless otherwise stated in this report, we did not observe, and we have no knowledge of, the existence of hazardous materials with regard to the subject assets, properties, or business interests. However, we are not qualified to detect such substances. We assume no responsibility for such conditions or for any expertise required to discover them.
9. Possession of this report does not carry with it the right of publication. It may not be used for any purpose by any person other than the client to whom it is addressed without our written consent and, in any event, only with proper written qualifications and only in its entirety.
10. We, by reason of this opinion, are not required to furnish a complete valuation report, or to give testimony, or to be in attendance in court with reference to the assets, properties, or business interests in question unless arrangements have been previously made.
11. Neither all nor any part of the contents of this report shall be disseminated to the public through advertising, public relations, news, sales, or other media without our prior written consent and approval.
12. The analyses, opinions, and conclusions presented in this report apply to this engagement only and may not be used out of the context presented herein. This report is valid only for the effective date(s) specified herein and only for the purpose(s) specified herein.

Appendix 18E

Professional Qualifications of the Principal Appraiser

James G. Rabe, CFA, ASA

Mr. Rabe is co-director of the Portland office of Willamette Management Associates.

Mr. Rabe has performed the following types of valuation assignments: gift tax appraisals, estate tax appraisals, ESOP appraisals, business and stock valuations, litigation support appraisals, merger and acquisition appraisals, fairness opinions, post-acquisition purchase price allocation appraisals, ad valorem assessment appeal appraisals, intangible asset appraisals, marital dissolution appraisals, and appraisal review.

Mr. Rabe has performed business and stock appraisals in the following industries: accounting, advertising, apparel, automobile dealerships, aviation, broadcasting, brokerage, cable television, chemical, construction and contracting, distribution, entertainment, fast food, food service, forest products, retail grocery stores, health care, insurance, leasing, manufacturing, medical and dental practice, newspaper, pharmaceuticals, printing, publishing, railroads, real estate holding companies, recreational services, restaurant, retailing, shipping, telecommunications, transportation and trucking, and wholesaling.

Previous Experience

Before joining Willamette Management Associates, Mr. Rabe was a senior consultant in the financial consulting group with Ernst & Young, the Big Six international accounting firm. During his employment with Ernst & Young, Mr. Rabe completed several business and stock valuations and litigation support appraisals.

Prior to that, Mr. Rabe was a securities analyst with Edward D. Jones & Co., a national brokerage firm. During his employment with Edward D. Jones & co., Mr. Rabe appraised publicly traded securities and made purchase and sale recommendations to stockbrokers.

Education

Master of Business Administration, Finance, Washington University, Graduate School of Business

Bachelor of Science, Business Administration, Finance, University of Missouri at Columbia
Chartered Financial Analyst

American Society of Appraisers, Accredited Senior Appraiser, Business Valuations

Professional Affiliations

Portland Society of Financial Analysts

2nd Vice President, American Society of Appraisers, Portland Chapter

Institute of Chartered Financial Analysts

Member, International Board of Examiners, American Society of Appraisers

Publications

Contributing author, *Valuing a Business: The Analysis and Appraisal of Closely Held Companies,* 3rd ed., Burr Ridge, IL: Irwin Professional Publishing, 1995.

"The Use and Misuse of Limited Liability Companies as an Estate Planning Device," *Insights,* Autumn 1994.

"The Valuation of Intangible Assets as Part of a Unitary Assessment for Ad Valorem Property Tax Purposes," *Journal of Property Tax Management,* Winter 1994.

"The Impact of Safe Harbor Regulations on Medical Practice Transactions," *Insights,* Spring 1993.

Chapter 19

Reviewing a Business Valuation Report

Many parties from time to time need to review a business appraisal, for a wide variety of purposes, such as:

- A fiduciary for an ESOP, estate, charitable trust, or other entity for adequate due diligence relative to a transaction.
- A judge deciding a business valuation issue on the basis of appraisal reports and expert testimony submitted.
- An attorney involved in litigation or potential litigation relating to a business valuation.
- An owner, personal representative, or taxing entity estimating value for various tax purposes, such as estate and gift taxes, inheritance taxes, and state and local ad valorem taxes.
- A professional advisor, such as an attorney or CPA, who may be asked to review a client's business valuation report for any of a variety of reasons.
- An owner considering a sale or a buyer considering a purchase of all or some part of a business.
- A spouse for marital property settlement.
- A commercial loan officer evaluating a credit.
- A professional appraiser asked to review someone else's appraisal report.

In many cases, such persons will not have theoretical or technical training in the complex discipline of business valuation. Nevertheless, significant decisions, often involving substantial sums of money, must be made based on the acceptability of business appraisal reports.

This chapter provides a working tool for use by those who review business valuation reports or related work products. We have attempted to present the chapter in a way that will be useful to any reviewer, from the experienced business valuation professional to the attorney or business owner who is faced with reviewing a valuation report for the first time. It is designed to assist anyone who must rely on a business appraisal report in their efforts to critically assess the validity of the report and the reliability of its conclusion.

It has been our experience that clients (and often their attorneys), especially those serving in a fiduciary capacity such as a trustee, accept an appraisal conclusion without having the understanding that they should as to the methods and analysis used in reaching the conclusion. It frequently is very constructive to have a client/appraiser meeting to review the work product. Often such a meeting is advisable before the appraisal is finalized, so that any questionable analyses can be examined and corrected if appropriate. One of the uses of this checklist would be in preparing for such a meeting to make it as productive as possible.

An example of the importance of understanding the appraisal is reflected in a quote from Judge Barrington Parker's often-cited decision upholding disputed appraisals of the stock of U.S. News & World Report:

> Mr. Padrutt was a methodical, thorough, and knowledgeable executive who knew what was required as chief financial officer under the circumstances. He understood the methodology employed by the appraisers and believed that their approach was appropriate.[1]

Judge Parker also noted that the independent CPA firm's audit of the plan's financial statements included a review of the appraisal methodology and that they found the methodology appropriate and reasonable.

---

[1]*Charles S. Foltz, et al.* v *U.S. News & World Report, Inc., et al.,* U.S. District Court, District of Columbia, Civil Action No. 85-2195, June 22, 1987.

In the case of litigation, obvious uses of the checklist are: preparation of interrogatories, preparation for deposition, and preparation of examination or cross-examination in court. It also should be very helpful in the preparation of rebuttal testimony.

Organization of the Checklist

This chapter is presented in a checklist format. It frequently provides references to chapters in this book where the subject is discussed in detail. In some cases, there are also references to the Uniform Standards of Professional Appraisal Practice (USPAP). Notes to reviewers are included at some points where they might be helpful in clarifying or focusing on the implication of the checklist question.

We have tried to organize the checklist in the logical sequence in which the reviewer would seek or expect to find the material. Certain items such as the appraisers' certification, statement of contingent and limiting conditions, and appraisers' professional qualifications are at the beginning of the checklist, even though they probably will be found in an appendix. This is because the reviewer usually would want to know these things at the outset of the review process. Obviously, different appraisers will present their reports in different sequences. In some cases, it may be more convenient for the reviewer to go over the report in the sequence presented, finding the appropriate sections of this checklist as necessary.

In some cases, the desired information will be found only in the appraiser's work papers. The necessity of going to the work papers will depend on the scope and purpose of the review. Many times desired information not contained in the appraisal report itself can be obtained through a telephone or personal interview with the appraiser. This checklist should help facilitate that process.

Boxes are provided to the left of many questions. Where there are two boxes, the reader can check the left-hand box if the answer to the question is satisfactory, or the right-hand box if the item is omitted or not handled satisfactorily. Of course, some items will simply be "not applicable" (N/A). Lines have been left below some questions to fill in answers or notations about problems with the report or questions to raise.

The user should recognize that the chapter is a very broad checklist. Not every item on the checklist will be applicable for every appraisal. Although professional standards have evolved significantly in the early 1990s, good business appraisal will always depend on the appraiser's professional judgment based on technical expertise and experience.

Appraisers' Certification

Is there an appraisers' certification that is similar in content to the following:

We certify that ...

- ☐ ☐ The statements of fact contained in this report are true and correct.
- ☐ ☐ The reported analyses, opinions, and conclusions are limited only by the reported assumptions and limiting conditions and are my (our) personal, unbiased professional analyses, opinions, and conclusions.

☐ ☐   I (we) have no (or the specified) present or prospective interest in the property that is the subject of this report, and I (we) have no (or the specified) personal interest or bias with respect to the parties involved.

☐ ☐   My (our) compensation is not contingent on an action or event resulting from the analyses, opinions, or conclusions in, or the use of, this report.

☐ ☐   My (our) analyses, opinions, and conclusions were developed, and this report has been prepared, in conformity with the Uniform Standards of Professional Appraisal Practice.

☐ ☐   No one provided significant professional assistance to the person(s) signing this report. (If there are exceptions, the name of each individual providing significant professional assistance must be stated.)

USPAP Standards Rule 10-3
Chapter 17, Writing an Appraisal Report

Contingent and/or Limiting Conditions or Assumptions

☐ ☐   Is there a statement of contingent and/or limiting conditions?

☐ ☐   If there are any extraordinary limiting conditions, are they stated, along with some statement regarding their impact on value?

USPAP Standards Rule 10-1(b) and (c)

Professional Qualifications of Appraisers

It is often helpful to have a general understanding of the background of the appraiser(s) before actually getting into the content of the report. Other than basic certifications and academic credentials, each category of qualifications is really a matter of degree, which could be rated from strong to very weak.

Professional Certifications

Examples are AM, ASA, FASA, CFA, CBA, CPA, and so on.

Chapter 1, Business Valuation Professional Standards

Other Qualifications

- Academic degrees. _____
- Relevant experience. _____
  _____
  _____

- Professional involvement (membership and activities in professional organizations, committee service, offices held, speeches, courses taught, publications, etc.). _____

_____

_____

- Expert testimony on business valuation and related matters. _____

_____

_____

Definition of Appraisal Assignment

Definition of Property Appraised

Definition of Entity.

☐ ☐   Name of entity. _____

☐ ☐   State or country of incorporation or registration. _____

☐ ☐   Legal form of organization:

        ☐ C corp.   ☐ S corp.   ☐ Limited liability company.

        ☐ General partnership.   ☐ Limited partnership.

        ☐ Sole proprietorship.   ☐ Other. _____

Definition of Interest Being Appraised. Type of ownership interest:

☐ ☐   Common stock.

☐ ☐   Partnership interest.

☐ ☐   Assets.

☐ ☐   Other (e.g., debt, preferred stock, special class of stock).

_____

_____

Relationship of interest to total entity:

☐ ☐   100% interest.

☐ ☐   Partial interest.

If partial interest, relationship of interest to total entity (e.g., 375 shares out of 1,000 outstanding, 20 percent interest in general partnership):

_____

_____

Any special rights or restrictions (e.g., restricted stock in public company, stock or interest subject to restrictive agreement):

_____

_____

Chapter 2, Defining the Assignment

Purpose of Appraisal

☐ ☐ Is the purpose and intended use of the appraisal clearly spelled out (e.g., sale or purchase, estate or gift taxes, ESOP, marital dissolution)?

_____

_____

USPAP Standards Rule 10-2
Chapter 2

Standard of Value

☐ ☐ Is the standard of value clearly defined?
  ☐ Fair market value   ☐ Fair value _____

  ☐ Investment value   ☐ Other _____

☐ ☐ If the appraisal is made according to binding legal authority (e.g., statute, buy–sell agreement, arbitration agreement), is that controlling authority specified?

_____

_____

☐ ☐ Is the authority not only cited, but also quoted? For example:

The standard of value was fair value, as set forth by Section 30-1-91 of the Idaho Code. According to the statute, "fair value" of shares means their value immediately before the effectuation of the corporate action to which the dissenter objects, excluding any appreciation or depreciation in anticipation of such corporate action unless such exclusion would be inequitable.

Reviewer's note: *Definitions of standards of value, such as "fair market value," and "fair value," vary somewhat from one legal context to another. Thus, it is extremely important that the standard of value that the appraisal represents be clearly specified.*
Chapter 2

Characteristics of Ownership

Control versus Minority.

☐ Control   ☐ Minority   ☐ 50 percent
☐ Control, but less than absolute   ☐ Minority, but with some elements of control

_____

_____

Note that control or minority are not necessarily absolutes—a majority may not have absolute control, and a minority may have some elements of control.

Marketability.

☐ ☐ Is the marketability status clear? Marketability status:
  ☐ Fully marketable public stock.
  ☐ Restricted stock or partnership interest in public company.
  ☐ Closely held interest, but no restrictions.

☐ Closely held interest subject to buy–sell agreement or other restrictions.
☐ ESOP:
　☐ Put option.　☐ No put option.

Chapter 2

Premise of Value

☐ Value in continued use.
☐ Value in place.
☐ Value in exchange:
　☐ Orderly disposition.　☐ Forced liquidation.

Chapter 2

Effective Date and Date of Report

☐ ☐ Effective date (appraisal date, the date as of which the appraisal applies). _____

☐ ☐ Date of report (date the report is completed or submitted).

Note: The report must be in compliance with the latest version of USPAP available as of the date of the report, regardless of USPAP Standards Rule 10-2. USPAP currently requires that the date of the report as well as the effective appraisal date be disclosed.

Chapter 2

Sources of Information

In general, the sources of information should be complete and should be identified well enough that the reader of the report can locate the source and verify the information if so desired.

Site Inspection and Interviews

☐ ☐ Did the appraiser visit the operation(s)? If so, when? _____
☐ ☐ Did the appraiser interview appropriate management personnel?

Chapter 5, Site Visits and Interviews

Company Financial Statements

☐ ☐ Is there a complete list of the statements (and tax returns, if any) consulted by year, including the designation of the fiscal year-end?
☐ ☐ Does the report indicate for each year whether the statements are internally compiled, compiled by a CPA firm, reviewed by a CPA firm, or audited by a CPA firm?

☐ ☐ Did the appraiser use an adequate set of financial statements and schedules, including footnotes, if available, for an adequate number of years for the purpose of the appraisal?

Chapter 7, Analyzing and Adjusting Financial Statements

Publications

☐ ☐ Are publications used cited adequately, including issue date for periodicals, so the reader can locate the publication and verify the information?

Note: There are additional checkpoints on sources of information under headings on specific valuation approaches and methods.

Chapter 6, Researching Economic and Industry Information

Data Known or Knowable as of Valuation Date

☐ ☐ Were all data used known or susceptible of being known as of the effective date of the valuation (except to the limited extent, if any, of permissible ex post data)?

Past Transactions

☐ ☐ Is there either a list of past transactions in the company's stock or partnership interests or a statement that there have not been any for a relevant period (along with the source of such information)?

☐ ☐ If there were past transactions, is there information to evaluate their relevance to value (i.e., date(s), number of shares, price, identity and relationship of parties, whether pursuant to any contractual agreement).

Chapter 4, Gathering Company Data

Description of Company

The main consideration is: Does the report provide adequate information for the reviewer to evaluate the appraisal in the context of what the company is and does, and whether the subject interest is being appraised appropriately relative to the total capitalization?

Capitalization and Ownership

☐ ☐ Is the amount outstanding and description of each class of stock or partnership interest clearly described?

Reviewer's note: *In a multi-class capitalization structure, the rights of one class of ownership may have an important bearing not only on the value of the ownership interest in that class but on the value of other classes of ownership interests as well.*

☐ ☐ Is the distribution of ownership clearly described (list of major owners, usually those over 10 percent, number of other owners, broken down by class of ownership interest if more than one class of stock or other interest)?

Reviewer's note: *If less than 100 percent ownership position is being appraised, the distribution of the remaining ownership may have a bearing on the value of the interest. For example, a 49 percent owner normally would have much more control over a company if there were many other small owners than if there were one 51 percent controlling owner.*

Company Background and Operations

Following are some major points about the company that the reviewer typically would want to know:

- ☐ ☐   Brief history of company leading to where it stands today.
- ☐ ☐   Location(s) of operations.
- ☐ ☐   Product/service lines.
- ☐ ☐   Markets served.
- ☐ ☐   Customer base (type, degree of concentration/dispersion).
- ☐ ☐   Competition.
- ☐ ☐   Position of subject company relative to its industry.
- ☐ ☐   Competitive strengths and weaknesses (uniqueness of product, quality, service, price, location, etc.).
- ☐ ☐   Description of facilities (site, plants, equipment, etc.).
- ☐ ☐   Management and workforce (size of workforce, description and degree of dependence on key personnel, the latter especially if highly dependent on one or a few key people).
- ☐ ☐   Status of labor/union relations/contract(s).
- ☐ ☐   If the company has subsidiaries, affiliates, or significant interests in other entities, are the relationships (percentage ownership, methods of accounting, basis for transfer pricing, etc.) clearly spelled out?
- ☐ ☐   Overall, have the positive and negative aspects of the company's operations and resources been pointed out and/or summarized?

Economic and Industry Data and Analysis

- ☐ ☐   Are the economic data and analysis adequate and relevant to the appraisal date and the subject of the appraisal?
- ☐ ☐   Are the industry data and analysis adequate and relevant to the appraisal?

Chapter 6

Analysis and Adjustment of Subject Company Financial Statements

- ☐ ☐   Have the financial statements been analyzed by the appraiser and either:
  - ☐   A statement made to the effect that the statements were analyzed and no adjustments were deemed necessary OR
  - ☐   Adjustments were made.

☐ ☐   If adjustments were made, are they adequately described and justified?

_____

Were there any adjustments omitted that you believe possibly should have been made or adjustments made that you believe may be questionable either in concept or in magnitude?

Reviewer's note: *When considering the appropriateness or lack of it of financial statement adjustments, the reviewer should be particularly mindful of the extent to which they are or are not consistent with the standard of value, ownership characteristics (e.g., minority, nonmarketable), and premise of value. For example, if the standard of value is fair market value or fair value, the appraiser normally would not make any adjustments to reflect synergies with an acquirer, although such adjustments may be appropriate if the standard of value is investment value. Similarly, if the appraisal subject is a minority interest, it normally would not be appropriate to make adjustments to reflect changes that only a control owner could make, unless such changes were known or thought to be imminent.*

☐ ☐   Adequacy of allowance and reserve accounts (e.g., allowance for doubtful receivables).

_____

☐ ☐   Adjustments for inventory accounting methods.

_____

☐ ☐   Depreciation methods and schedules.

_____

☐ ☐   Treatment of intangible assets.

_____

☐ ☐   Capitalization versus expensing of costs.

_____

☐ ☐   Timing of recognition of revenues and expenses.

_____

☐ ☐   Accounting for leases.

_____

☐ ☐   Treatment of tax loss carryforwards.

_____

☐ ☐   Treatment of interests in affiliates.

_____

☐ ☐   Extraordinary or nonrecurring items.

_____

☐ ☐   Recognition and treatment of operating versus nonoperating items.

_____

☐ ☐   Management compensation and perquisites.

_____

☐ ☐   Transactions involving company insiders.

_____

☐ ☐ Contingent assets and liabilities.

☐ ☐ Adjustments to values of marketable securities.

☐ ☐ Adjustments to values of other assets.

Computation of earnings and book value (or adjusted asset value) per share:

☐ ☐ Was it done on a weighted average basis? (as required by GAAP)?

☐ ☐ If there were options or other potential dilution outstanding, was the potential dilution properly accounted for?

☐ ☐ If book value per share was utilized, was it computed correctly?

☐ ☐ If book value or adjusted asset value was used, was it made clear whether it was total book or asset value versus tangible book or asset value, and was it used appropriately (e.g., if tangible book value used in guideline companies, was it the same for the subject)?

☐ ☐ If there were liability accounts on the balance sheet that should have been adjusted, were they properly adjusted?

☐ ☐ If it was appropriate to tax-effect any of the financial statement adjustments, was this done?

Chapter 7

Comparative Ratio Analysis

☐ ☐ Is some type of comparative financial ratio analysis used to evaluate the company's financial strengths and weaknesses? If yes, to what industry data population was the subject company compared (e.g., industry code, size category, etc.) and what was the source?

☐ ☐ Are you satisfied that it is a relevant comparison, in terms of such comparative characteristics as industry group and relative company size?

☐ ☐ Are the ratios computed clearly defined, so that the reviewer could go to the subject company financial documents and make the same computations?

☐ ☐ Were the ratios calculated for the subject company data defined and measured in the same way as the industry ratios with which they are being compared?

☐ ☐ Were the ratios calculated for the subject company as close in time as reasonably possible to the time period for which the industry ratios were calculated?

☐ ☐ Are the significant relative strengths and weaknesses noted?

☐ ☐ Are you satisfied that relative strengths and weaknesses ultimately are reflected in the valuation?

Note: Ratio analysis compared to specific guideline companies (as opposed to composite industry data) is discussed in a subsequent section under the market approach.

Chapter 8, Comparative Ratios

Income Approach

☐ ☐ If an income approach (e.g., discounted or capitalized net cash flow or some other measure of economic income) was NOT used, is there a satisfactory explanation as to why not?

☐ ☐ If an income approach WAS used, was there a:
    ☐ Discounted economic income method?
    ☐ Capitalization of economic income method?
(Check both above if both were used)

What level of economic income was discounted or capitalized?

    ☐ Economic income available to equity.
    ☐ Economic income available to total invested capital.
       (Check both boxes above if both methods were used.)

☐ ☐ If there was a method used that discounts income to total invested capital, was the definition of total invested capital made clear?

☐ ☐ If the income to total invested capital was used, is the rationale for using it—as opposed to income available to equity—explained?

What definition of economic income is discounted or capitalized?

    ☐ Net cash flow.
    ☐ Net income.
    ☐ Other. _____

☐ ☐ Are the analyses underlying the projected cash flow or other economic income made clear?

☐ ☐ Are the analyses consistent with the standard of value, ownership characteristics, and premise of value?
(See reviewer's note under financial statement adjustments.)

☐ ☐ Is there support that the economic income discounted or capitalized is representative of reasonable future expectations?

Reviewer's note: *A common error is to mechanistically extrapolate future results based on a trend or average of historical results. The future rarely conforms to a pure extrapolation or average of past results. It is important to have analysis and support for estimations as to how the generating forces will cause future results to conform to or depart from a continuation of past trends.*

If a present value discount rate is used, how is it supported?

☐ ☐ Built up (risk-free rate plus equity risk premium plus other applicable adjustments such as size premium and/or specific company adjustment).

☐ ☐ Capital asset pricing model (same as above, but equity risk premium adjusted for beta).

☐ ☐ Arbitrage pricing model.

☐ ☐ Other. _____

☐ ☐ Does the support offered appear to be appropriate?

If a capitalization rate is used, how is it supported?

☐ ☐ Discount rate minus expected growth.
☐ If above, then is growth used a reasonable expectation in perpetuity?

Reviewer's note: *If too high a growth rate is subtracted from a discount rate to get a capitalization rate, the capitalization rate will be too low, resulting in overvaluation when applied to the immediately foreseeable cash flow or other income stream being capitalized.*

☐ Other support for capitalization rate:

If a weighted average cost of capital (WACC) is used, what is the weighting based on?
☐ Subject company's capital structure at market value.
☐ Industry average capital structure at market value.
☐ Other: _____

Reviewer's note: *A common error is to approximate weightings in the capital structure by using book value for the weighting, even though there may be significant differences between market value and book value. For example, if market value of debt approximates book value of debt but market value of equity substantially exceeds book value of equity, a weighting of the capital structure components based on book value would overstate the debt component weighting and understate the equity component weighting, thus understating the WACC, since the cost of equity capital almost always is greater than the cost of debt capital. This, of course, would result in an overvaluation when applied to the cash flow or other measure of income being discounted or capitalized.*

☐ ☐ Is the discount rate or capitalization rate appropriate to the definition of economic income being discounted or capitalized?

Reviewer's note: *Much empirical data is available to develop a discount rate or a capitalization rate applicable to net cash flow, as defined in Chapter 9. While it is also possible to develop discount or capitalization rates applicable to other definitions of economic income, a common error is to develop a rate applicable to net cash flow and apply it to something else, such as net income. Since net income usually is higher than net cash flow (at least for a growth company), applying a net cash flow discount or capitalization rate to net income generally will result in an overvaluation.*

Chapter 9, Income Approach: Discounted Economic Income Methods

---

Market Approach

☐ ☐ Was some type of market approach valuation method used?
☐ ☐ If no, is there an explanation that you find satisfactory as to why not?

If yes, what form of market approach method?
☐ Guideline public company.
☐ Merger/acquisition.
☐ Other. _____

☐ ☐ Is the population of possible companies from which the guideline companies were chosen clearly defined?

☐ ☐ Are you satisfied that the population from which the guideline companies were drawn is adequate?

☐ ☐ Are the selection criteria clearly spelled out?

☐ ☐ Are you satisfied that the selection criteria are appropriate?

☐ ☐ If there were companies that appeared to meet the selection criteria, but were omitted, is there a satisfactory explanation as to why?

☐ ☐ Are the prices used for the guideline company stocks prices as of the valuation date?

☐ If not, is there a satisfactory explanation as to why not?

☐ ☐ Is the source of the price data clearly disclosed so that you can check the prices for accuracy?

What is the source of the guideline company data?
☐ SEC filings
☐ Other _____

☐ ☐ Are you satisfied that the source(s) used contained adequate data for the guideline company valuation measures and procedures utilized?

☐ ☐ Were adjustments made to any of the guideline company financial data before computing value ratios?

☐ ☐ If no, is there a satisfactory statement that the guideline company data were examined and no adjustments were necessary?

☐ If yes, are you satisfied that the adjustments made were appropriate?

☐ ☐ Do you believe that adjustments should have been made that were not?

What value measures were computed for the guideline companies and for what date or time period were the data used?

Value Measure	**Time Period or Date**

☐ ☐ Is each value measure clearly defined so that you or your expert can replicate the computation of the value measure from the source data?

☐ ☐ Are you satisfied that the value measures used are appropriate for the situation at hand?

☐ ☐ Were there value measures not used that you believe should have been considered?

☐ ☐ Is there a satisfactory explanation of why the measures used were chosen and (if applicable) why others were not?

☐ ☐ Is there a satisfactory explanation of why the time periods used were chosen and (if applicable) why others were not?

☐ ☐ Does it seem to be clear that the fundamental financial data for the guideline companies was calculated the same way as the fundamental financial data for the subject company to which the multiple from the guideline companies was applied?

☐ ☐ Are the time periods over which the fundamental financial data for the guideline company value measures were calculated the same as the time periods for the subject company financial data to which the guideline company multiples were applied? (Or, if not, appropriately adjusted?)

☐ ☐ Are relevant comparative financial ratios computed and presented for the guideline companies and subject company?

☐ If yes, are ratios computed clearly defined so that the reviewer could go to the same source documents and make the same computations?

☐ ☐ Is there appropriate notation of relative strengths and weaknesses between the guideline companies and the subject company?

☐ ☐ Are you satisfied that the relative strengths and weaknesses are reflected in the value measures used for the subject company?

☐ ☐ Was the mathematical calculation of the ratios consistent between the subject company and guideline companies?

☐ ☐ For each value measure used, is there a satisfactory explanation of how the multiple for the subject company was chosen relative to the various multiples for the guideline companies? (The selection of the multiple to apply to the subject company could be based, for example, on the comparative financial ratios.)

☐ ☐ Is there a satisfactory explanation of the weighting of the various value measures considered in arriving at an indication of value? (**Note:** The "weighting" may be percentage weights assigned to each value measure or may be a more subjective discussion of the relative weights attributable to different value measures.)

The guideline public company method normally produces a minority as-if-publicly traded value.

☐ ☐ If a minority closely held interest is the subject, is there an adjustment for lack of marketability? (More on this in a later section of this review checklist, but there should be NO discount for minority interest, since guideline publicly traded stock transactions are minority interests.)

☐ ☐ If a controlling interest is the subject, is there a discussion of possible premium for control (which may be fully or partially offset by a discount for lack of marketability or lack of liquidity)?

Chapter 10, Market Approach: The Guideline Company Method
Chapter 11, Market Approach: The Merger and Acquisition Method

Asset-Based Approach

☐ ☐ Was an asset-based approach valuation method used?
☐ If no, is there an explanation that you find satisfactory as to why not?

☐ If yes: Were all assets and liabilities on the balance sheet revalued that should have been?

☐ ☐ Were all off-balance-sheet assets and liabilities recognized and valued if appropriate?

☐ ☐ Were there any adjustments made that should *not* have been made in accordance with the standard, characteristics, and premises of value or for other reasons?

☐ ☐ Are all the revaluations adequately supported?

☐ ☐ Are the adjustments and conclusions presented with adequate clarity so that the reviewer could reconstruct them if desired?

Chapter 12, Asset Based Approach

Excess Earnings Method

The following checklist points relate to the various steps in the excess earnings method as presented on the following page:

Step 1:	Net tangible asset value		$2,000,000
Step 2:	Normalized economic income	$800,000	
Step 3:	Earnings attributable to net tangible assets		
	($2,000,000 × 0.15) =	300,000	
	Excess economic income	$500,000	
Step 4:	Indicated value of excess earnings		
	($500,000 ÷ 0.20) =		2,500,000
Indicated total value of the subject business enterprise			$4,500,000

☐ ☐   In general, is the procedure used consistent with the steps and example presented above?

☐ ☐   Does the amount used for the asset base represent the value of net tangible assets (exclusive of intangibles)?

Reviewer's note: *As an alternative to using the current net tangible asset value and normalized earnings, some appraisers base the computations of the value of excess earnings on average net tangible assets and average earnings for some period of time, usually five years. This procedure is satisfactory if the period used is representative of reasonable future expectations. If this procedure is used, the value of excess earnings still is added to the present net tangible asset value to arrive at the value for the total entity.*

☐ ☐   Is the earnings base used representative of ongoing economic income generating capacity of the entity?

☐ ☐   Is the earnings base net of reasonable compensation to any owner(s) involved in managing the business?

☐ ☐   If a C corporation, is the earnings base used net after taxes?

☐ ☐   Is the required rate of return applicable to net tangible assets adequately justified?

Reviewer's note: *This normally should be at least the company's cost of borrowing, which generally is dependent on its asset mix. A common error is to use some "safe" rate, such as the current rate on risk-free U.S. Treasury bills, or a rate of 8 to 10 percent as used in an illustrative example in Revenue Ruling 68-609, reflecting economic and market conditions prevalent in 1968.*

☐ ☐   Is the rate at which the "excess earnings" (earnings over and above the amount required to support the tangible asset base) adequately justified?

Reviewer's note: *This normally should be a higher rate than the rate of return applicable to tangible assets because of the considerably higher risk. As with the rate applicable to tangible assets, a common error is to use a rate of 15 to 20 percent because that was the range of rates used in the illustrative example in Revenue Ruling 68-609, reflecting economic and market conditions in 1968.*

Reviewer's note: *In many businesses, there are no "excess earnings," because the total earnings are not even enough to justify the investment in the net tangible assets. In some such cases, the business may even be worth less than the net tangible asset value (unless the asset values could actually be realized by net proceeds from liquidation).*

Chapter 13, The Excess Earnings Method

Discounts and Premiums

Each method of valuation produces an indication of value that has inherent in it certain characteristics and premises. The most important of these premises usually are:

1. Is the value indicated by the method a control basis value or a minority interest value? (Control premiums and minority interest discounts are discussed in Chapter 14.)
2. Does the value indicated imply full, immediate ready marketability (publicly traded equivalent value) or not? (Discounts for lack of marketability are discussed in Chapter 15.)

☐ ☐ For each method used, is it made clear what characteristics and premises of value are implied?

Reviewer's note: *An income approach valuation method could produce either a minority value or a control value, generally depending on whether the projected cash flow or other definition of economic income reflected what a minority owner would expect or what a control owner could expect, given the power of control. Discount and capitalization rates used in the income approach usually are derived from the publicly traded securities markets and therefore could be interpreted to imply full marketability. The guideline public company method generally implies a minority, fully marketable value; the merger and acquisition and asset-based methods normally would imply a control value.*

☐ ☐ From the value indicated by each of the valuation methods, are appropriate premiums and/or discounts applied, if applicable, to adjust from the type of value implied by the method to the type of value being sought, as indicated in the definition of the appraisal assignment?

☐ ☐ Are there any premiums or discounts applied that are *not* appropriate adjustments from the type of value indicated by the method to the type of value being sought as indicated in the definition of the appraisal assignment?

☐ ☐ Has appropriate recognition been accorded to the size of the block and its voting rights with respect to the degree of control or lack of it?

Reviewer's note: *Minority or control is not necessarily a black or white issue. Minority ownership interests may have some elements of control, while majority interests may not have complete control. See Chapter 14 for more discussion of this issue.*

If a minority interest discount or control premium is applied, what data are referenced in support of the amount of the discount or premium?

_____

_____

☐ ☐ Do these data support the amount of the discount or premium applied?

_____

☐ ☐ Has appropriate recognition been accorded the degree of marketability (liquidity) or lack of it, including any special rights or restrictions?

_____

☐ ☐ If a discount for lack of marketability is applied, what data are referenced in support of the amount of the discount?
   ☐ Restricted stock data.

_____

_____

   ☐ Studies of transactions before IPOs:
      ☐ Baird & Co. studies.
      ☐ Willamette Management Associates studies.
      ☐ Other. _____
   ☐ Other data. _____

_____

_____

☐ ☐ Do the data, along with analysis of the characteristics and special rights and/or restrictions applicable to the subject interest, support the amount of the discount applied?

_____

Chapter 14, Minority Interest Discounts, Control Premiums, and Other Discounts and Premiums
Chapter 15, Discounts for Lack of Marketability

Synthesis and Conclusion

Ultimately, what approaches and methods were relied on in reaching the final value conclusion?

_____

_____

_____

Was the weighting of methods presented:
☐ ☐ Mathematically, in terms of percentages to each.

☐ ☐   Subjectively.

☐ ☐   Was the rationale for the relative weightings among methods
          made clear?

☐ ☐   Is there adequate support that the approaches and methods chosen were
          appropriate in light of the standard, characteristics, and premise of value
          as defined in the valuation assignment and the quantity and quality of
          available data?

Chapter 16, Valuation Synthesis and Conclusion

Overall Assessment

Comprehensiveness

☐ ☐   Does the report do everything it promises to do? (E.g., if it says it
          considered each of the eight factors listed in Revenue Ruling 59-60, are
          they all addressed in the report?)

☐ ☐   Are there topics or information omitted from the report that seem
          necessary to support the conclusion or that seem to beg to be addressed?
          (In other words, are all relevant factors addressed?)

Accuracy

☐ ☐   Are the mathematical calculations correct?

Reviewer's note: *It is suggested that the reviewer at least spot check a few
critical calculations—a thorough review might check a broader sampling of calculations. Most mathematical errors fall into one of three broad categories: (1)
simple mathematical calculation error, (2) plugging an incorrect number into a
formula, and (3) using a formula that is different from the one specified in the
report. The latter often occurs when calculations are done by computer and the
formula programmed into the computer is different from the formula specified in
the report.*

☐ ☐   Are there any errors in the data presented in the report?

Reviewer's note: *The degree of checking for data accuracy depends on the
scope of the review. Sometimes there are simply errors in extracting numbers
from their source. Sometimes numbers (e.g., interest rates) are taken from a
source that does not represent the time period most applicable to the appraisal.
Sometimes numbers are defined differently in their source than what they are purported to represent in the appraisal report, often resulting in "apples to oranges"*

comparisons. One common source of error is the use of secondary rather than original sources for guideline company data. The secondary sources may define or adjust numbers differently than the definitions purported in the report, sometimes causing material distortions in results.

Coherence and Cohesion

☐ ☐   Replicability: Are the steps taken clearly spelled out so the reviewer could independently replicate the steps and reach the same conclusion?

☐ ☐   Definitions: Where esoteric or potentially ambiguous terms are used, and are they defined so the reader always knows exactly what is meant?

☐ ☐   Formulas: Where formulas are used, and is each term clearly defined?

☐ ☐   Relevance: Is all the material presented relevant to the valuation report?

☐ ☐   Are questions raised in the mind of the reader that are not addressed?

☐ ☐   Do the data and analysis presented clearly support the conclusion reached?

☐ ☐   Is the degree of attention accorded to various factors in the report adequate relative to the degree of impact that each of such factors has on the ultimate conclusion of the report?

☐ ☐   Are there any leaps of faith (i.e., presentation of a fact or conclusion with no accompanying documentation of source or supporting analysis or data) that might be open to question by the reader?

☐ ☐   Is there any overemphasis of past data without analysis suggesting it is reasonably representative of future expectations?

Internal Consistency

☐ ☐   Are the data and analysis used consistently appropriate to the standard of value, ownership characteristics, and premise of value stated in the definition of the appraisal assignment?

Reviewer's note: *If legal standards or definitions of value are applicable, the requirement for consistency with legal standards may go beyond standards, ownership characteristics, and premise actually stated in the report. If the reviewer believes this may be an issue, then the reviewer should raise the question. Resolution of the issue may require research and analysis of the relevant statutory and/or case law.*

☐ ☐ If information is presented that has positive or negative implications for value, are those factors ultimately recognized and reflected in the valuation?

☐ ☐ Are all statements made in any part of the report consistent with statements made in any other part of the report?

☐ ☐ Is the conclusion consistent with all statements made and procedures used to lead up to that conclusion?

Incisiveness

Finally, is the report incisive? Webster defines *incisive* as follows:

1. Having a cutting edge or piercing point—facilitating cutting or piercing, as sharp …
2. Marked by sharpness and penetration—especially in keen, clear, unmistakable resolution of matter at issue or in pointed decision effectiveness of presentation …
3. Clear genius which states in a flash the exact point at issue …
4. Keen penetration and sharp presentation that is decisive or effective—rapier quality of highly tempered steel …
5. Unmistakably clear outlining, analysis, and presentation that defies disbelief or question.[2]

Wouldst that all valuation reports be so characterized!

---

[2]*Webster's Third New International Dictionary*, p. 1142.

Part V

Valuing Specific Business Interests

Chapter 20

Debt
Securities

Although debt securities play an important role in the analysis and appraisal of closely held companies, their valuation cannot be thoroughly discussed in a single chapter. Therefore, this chapter confines discussion to general areas of reference that the analyst may want to consider when valuing debt securities.[1]

This chapter first discusses common situations that require the valuation of debt securities; it then moves to the general method of valuing them. The chapter discusses the discount for lack of marketability, if any, and then examines the impact on value of special characteristics that many debt securities have.

Common Situations Requiring the Valuation of Debt Securities

The most frequently encountered reasons for needing to value debt securities are the following:

1. Purchase or sale for cash.
2. Exchange of equity for debt, or vice versa.
3. Gift and estate taxes.
4. Allocating total enterprise value among classes of securities in a leveraged buyout, recapitalization, or bankruptcy reorganization.
5. Adjusting a balance sheet for debt securities owned or owed.

Purchase or Sale for Cash

From time to time, a company may purchase or sell debt securities for cash. If they are existing securities, it is necessary to estimate their cash equivalent value. If they are to be newly issued securities, it is necessary to structure the provisions so the value will be equal to the price paid or received.

Exchange of Equity for Debt

If debt securities are to be exchanged for some consideration other than cash, such as stock or other property, it usually is most expedient to estimate the cash equivalent values of both the debt securities and the stock or other consideration to be exchanged.

Most typically, a company or some or all of its stock is to be sold and a debt security received as all or part of the consideration. The seller needs to know the cash equivalent value of the consideration being received for the company or stock being given up. It is not uncommon for notes or other debt securities issued in connection with the acquisition of a company to have a cash equivalent value of 20 percent or more below the securities' face value.[2]

---

[1]For a more extensive discussion of this topic, see, for example, Frank J. Fabozzi, *Handbook of Fixed-Income Securities,* 3rd ed. (Burr Ridge, IL: Irwin Professional Publishing, 1990).

[2]While this may be true in a business of any size, it is particularly prevalent in the sale of small businesses. For an extended discussion of this, see Shannon P. Pratt, Robert F. Reilly, and Robert P. Schweihs, *Valuing Small Businesses and Professional Practices,* 2nd ed. (Burr Ridge, IL: Irwin Professional Publishing, 1993), chap. 19.

Gift and Estate Taxes

Debt securities may be gifted, or they may be an asset in an estate. As in all gift and estate tax situations, the appropriate standard of value is fair market value. Quite often, debt securities presented as a gift or included in an estate have a fair market value considerably below the face value.

Allocation of Total Enterprise Value among Classes of Securities

A leveraged buyout, by its nature, results in the creation of new classes of securities, almost always including at least one class of debt. Therefore, in dealing with the valuation for a leveraged buyout, it usually is necessary not only to value the entire enterprise but also to allocate the total value among the various classes of participants.

Recapitalizations involving debt securities may be undertaken for a variety of reasons. A popular purpose in the late 1980s was leveraged recapitalizations—issuing debt to redeem a substantial portion of outstanding equity to create a more optimal capital structure. During the first couple of years of the 1990s, this trend was reversed as economic conditions forced companies to lower their debt levels.

Bankruptcy recapitalizations, by their nature, involve debt securities, sometimes both before and after the recapitalization. Creative structuring of debt and other securities to meet the varying objectives of the parties at interest can be an essential tool in achieving a successful bankruptcy reorganization.

Adjusting a Balance Sheet for Debt Securities Owned or Owed

For various reasons, the balance sheet may be analyzed to adjust each line item to its fair market value. In many cases, debt instruments may need to be adjusted to fair market value on both the asset (e.g., investment securities) and liability (e.g., notes payable) sides of the balance sheet. An example of the latter would be the use of "debt-free" methods to value the common stock, as discussed in Chapters 9, 10, and 11.

The amount of analysis undertaken for the valuation of debt securities will vary with the assignment and with the level of accuracy required. For example, generally more analysis will be undertaken in the valuation of a debt security when that security is to be gifted (and thus subject to gift tax consequences) than when the assignment is to value the common stock of a closely held company by a debt-free valuation method. Even if the analyst does not contemplate going through all the steps in the analysis of debt securities, it is important to understand them in order to have a general idea of the potential impact of an adjustment in the value of a debt security to market value.

Method of Valuation

Valuation theory states that the fair market value of a future stream of payments on debt is equal to the present value of the future payments, discounted back to the current time at an appropriate present value discount rate. The higher the risk or uncertainty associated with the payments, the higher the appropriate discount rate will be. This is precisely how the value of a debt security is estimated. The value of this type of security can be estimated by the following present value formula:

Formula 20–1

$$Present\ value = \sum_{i-1}^{n} \frac{PMT_i}{(1 + r)^i}$$

where:

PMT_i = Payment in the ith period in the future
i = Period when payments are generated
r = Interest rate at which payments are to be discounted back to the present
n = Maturity of the debt, in periods

There are extensive public trading markets both for capital market debt securities, including corporate bonds and notes, U.S. government and agency bonds and notes, some municipal government bonds and notes, and for short-term money market instruments. If the debt security being valued can be bought and sold in one of the public trading markets, its observed market price at any given time will reflect the present value of the future payments as determined by the market. The rate of interest that, when applied to the expected future payments on a debt security, produces a present value of the payments equal to the debt security's observed market price is called the *yield to maturity* of that security.

If the debt security cannot be purchased or sold in a public market (i.e., it is a closely held debt security), then its value must be estimated by using the above formula. The information needed for estimating the value of a closely held debt security from the above formula is the following: (1) the amount of future payments generated by the debt security; (2) the timing of the future payments generated by the security; and (3) the appropriate rate of interest—or yield to maturity—to apply to the future payments to estimate the present value. The timing and amounts of the contractually obligated payments can be estimated from the debt instruments themselves. The third item, an appropriate interest rate or yield to maturity to apply to the future payments, requires both quantitative analysis and the appraiser's judgment.

Amount and Timing of Future Payments

The amount of future payments generally is set by the contract establishing the debt security. Interest payments are specified at a certain amount, and, as determined by the contract, the principal will be repaid at some specific future time. Certain characteristics of some debt securities may alter the amount and timing of the future payments. Some of these characteristics include call provisions and sinking fund provisions, the debt's income taxation status, and whether the debt is a zero coupon debt issue or has conversion privileges. The nature of each of these characteristics is discussed later in the chapter.

Estimation of Yield to Maturity

The critical step in the final estimation of the value of a debt security is to choose an appropriate interest rate or yield to maturity to apply to the future payments. Many quantitative and qualitative factors help to estimate this figure at any point in time.

The yield to maturity for a debt security may differ from the security's coupon rate of interest (i.e., the rate expressed as a percentage of face value) at any point. If the market-determined yield to maturity for a debt security is equal to the security's coupon interest rate, then the security's fair market value is equal to its face or par value. If the coupon interest rate is greater than the yield to maturity, as indicated by the market yields of comparable bonds, then the debt security's market value is greater than its face or par value. Conversely, if the coupon interest rate for a debt security is less than the yield to maturity as indicated by the market, then the security's market value is less than its face or par value.

The coupon rate of interest determines the amount of the payments that can be expected from holding a debt security, but the yield to maturity required by the market establishes the market value of the payments generated by the debt security at any particular time.

Guideline Analysis. To estimate the yield to maturity to apply to a closely held debt security, it is necessary to examine several characteristics related to the security's issuer. By comparing the various characteristics of the closely held debt issuer with comparable characteristics of issuers of publicly traded debt securities that already have a market-determined yield to maturity, the analyst can gain insight into the proper yield to maturity to apply to the closely held debt security.

The first step in the guideline analysis is the quantitative analysis of the debt security issuer's operating performance and financial position. This analysis is very similar to that described in Chapter 8 and generally includes analysis of the debt issuer's balance-sheet leverage ratios, income statement coverage ratios, short-term liquidity ratios, profitability ratios, and return on investment. The relative importance of the various ratios may vary with the type of debt security being valued. For example, the short-term liquidity ratios are far more important in the valuation of short-term debt securities than in the valuation of long-term debt securities, since short-term liquidity ratios demonstrate the debt issuer's ability to meet its current obligations, one of which is the short-term debt.

The closely held debt issuer's operating performance and financial condition can be compared to those of a broad population of issuers of publicly traded debt securities. For example, Exhibit 20–1 presents key financial ratios calculated by Standard & Poor's Corporation for industrial long-term debt issuers for which it provides debt ratings. The exhibit also presents median three-year financial ratios for the debt issuers, by rating classification, for both 1988 to 1990 and 1991 to 1993. Exhibit 20–2 presents the definition of credit ratings issued by Standard & Poor's Corporation. By calculating these same ratios for the issuer of the closely held debt security over the same time period, the analyst can estimate into which rating classification the closely held debt might fall if it were rated by Standard & Poor's.

After having gained an idea of the general rating classification into which the closely held debt security might fall, the analyst can select specific publicly traded debt securities similar in debt rating and nature to the subject security. Several rating agencies, including Moody's Investors Service[3] and Standard & Poor's Corporation[4] provide listings of publicly traded debt securities, along with credit ratings for nearly all the securities. Exhibit 20–3 presents the yields to maturity for various bond indexes, segregated by rating, compiled by Standard & Poor's Corporation for 1984 through 1994. As would be expected, the lower-rated indexes have higher yields to maturity than the higher-rated indexes at any point in time.

---

[3]*Moody's Bond Record* (New York: Moody's Investors Service, 1995).
[4]*Standard & Poor's Bond Guide* (New York: Standard & Poor's Corporation, 1995).

Exhibit 20–1

Standard & Poor's Corporation
Key Industrial Financial Ratios and Definitions
By Rating Classification for Long-Term Debt Issuers

Three-Year Medians: 1991–1993	AAA	AA	A	BBB	BB	B
Pretax interest coverage (x)	16.66	8.81	4.63	2.51	1.59	0.69
Pretax fixed charge coverage including rents (x)	6.34	4.48	2.93	1.82	1.33	0.78
Pretax funds flow interest coverage (x)	22.99	13.31	7.21	4.29	2.75	1.31
Funds from operations/total debt (%)	134.70	74.60	44.40	28.80	17.90	8.50
Free operating cash flow/total debt (%)	49.20	32.30	17.00	4.00	0.90	(2.40)
Pretax return on permanent capital (%)	24.20	18.40	13.50	9.70	9.10	6.30
Operating income/sales (%)	22.50	15.90	13.80	11.80	10.60	10.10
Long-term debt/capitalization (%)	11.70	19.10	29.40	39.60	51.10	61.80
Total debt/capitalization (%)	23.20	26.20	36.70	48.10	56.30	71.00
Total debt + 8 times rent/capitalization (%)	35.70	37.90	48.10	57.60	65.90	75.80

Three-Year Medians: 1988–1990	AAA	AA	A	BBB	BB	B
Pretax interest coverage (x)	11.08	9.43	4.65	3.16	1.91	0.88
Pretax fixed charge coverage including rents (x)	5.46	5.10	3.00	2.18	1.54	0.94
Pretax funds flow interest coverage (x)	13.65	11.65	6.65	4.97	3.00	1.59
Funds from operations/total debt (%)	82.90	74.20	45.60	31.70	18.70	8.40
Free operating cash flow/total debt (%)	24.80	23.40	8.70	3.40	(0.50)	(3.40)
Pretax return on permanent capital (%)	26.20	21.10	16.70	13.00	11.10	7.40
Operating income/sales (%)	21.60	15.90	14.90	12.00	12.50	9.30
Long-term debt/capitalization (%)	12.90	16.60	29.50	39.40	45.70	63.50
Total debt/capitalization (%)	25.10	27.60	37.30	48.00	54.80	73.70
Total debt + 8 times rent/capitalization (%)	38.20	38.70	50.90	58.60	65.50	78.50

Formulas for Key Ratios

$$\text{Pretax interest coverage} = \frac{\text{Pretax income continuing operations} + \text{Interest expense}}{\text{Gross interest}}$$

$$\text{Pretax fixed charge coverage including rents} = \frac{\text{Pretax income continuing operations} + \text{Interest expense} + \text{Gross rents}}{\text{Gross interest} + \text{Gross rents}}$$

$$\text{Pretax funds flow interest coverage} = \frac{\text{Pretax funds flow} + \text{Interest expense}}{\text{Gross interest}}$$

$$\text{Funds operations as a \% of total debt} = \frac{\text{Funds operations}}{\text{Total debt}} \times 100$$

$$\text{Free operating cash flow as a \% of total debt} = \frac{\text{Free operating cash flow}}{\text{Total debt}} \times 100$$

$$\text{Pretax return on permanent capital} = \frac{\text{Pretax income continuing operations} + \text{Interest expense}}{\substack{\text{Sum of (1) average of beginning of year and end of year current} \\ \text{maturities, long-term debt, noncurrent deferred taxes, and equity and} \\ \text{(2) average short-term borrowings during year as disclosed in footnotes}}} \times 100$$

$$\text{Operating income as a \% of sales} = \frac{\text{Operating income}}{\text{Sales}} \times 100$$

$$\text{Long-term debt as a \% of capitalization} = \frac{\text{Long-term debt}}{\text{Long-term debt} + \text{Equity}} \times 100$$

$$\text{Total debt as a \% of capitalization} = \frac{\text{Total debt}}{\text{Total debt} + \text{Equity}} \times 100$$

$$\text{Total debt + 8 times rents as a \% of adjusted capitalization} = \frac{\text{Total debt} + 8 \text{ times gross rents paid}}{\text{Total debt} + 8 \text{ times gross rents paid} + \text{Equity}} \times 100$$

Glossary

Equity — Shareholders' equity (including preferred stock) plus minority interest.

Free operating cash flow — Funds from operations minus capital expenditures, minus (plus) the increase (decrease) in working capital (excluding changes in cash, marketable securities, and short-term debt).

Exhibit 20–1 (concluded)

Funds from operations	Net income from continuing operations plus depreciation, amortization, deferred income taxes and other noncash items.
Gross interest	Gross interest incurred before subtracting (1) capitalized interest, (2) interest income.
Gross rents	Gross operating rents paid before sublease income.
Interest expense	Interest incurred minus capitalized interest, plus amortization of capitalized interest.
Long-term debt	As reported on the balance sheet, including capitalized lease obligations.
Net cash flow	Funds from operations less preferred and common dividends.
Operating income	Sales minus cost of goods manufactured (before depreciation and amortization), selling, general and administrative, and research and development costs.
Pretax funds flow	Pretax income from continuing operations plus depreciation, amortization, and other noncash items.
Total debt	Long-term debt plus current maturities, commercial paper, and other short-term borrowings.

SOURCE: *Standard & Poor's Corporate Finance Criteria* (New York: Standard & Poor's Corporation, one of the McGraw-Hill Companies, 1994), pp. 74–75.

Exhibit 20–2

Standard & Poor's Corporate and Municipal Rating Definitions

DEBT

A Standard & Poor's corporate or municipal debt rating is a current assessment of the creditworthiness of an obligor with respect to a specific obligation. This assessment may take into consideration obligors such as guarantors, insurers, or lessees.

The debt rating is not a recommendation to purchase, sell or hold a security, inasmuch as it does not comment as to market price or suitability for a particular investor.

The ratings are based on current information furnished by the issuer or obtained by Standard & Poor's from other sources it considers reliable. Standard & Poor's does not perform any audit in connection with any rating and may, on occasion, rely on unaudited financial information. The ratings may be changed, suspended or withdrawn as a result of changes in, or unavailability of, such information, or based on other circumstances.

The ratings are based, in varying degrees, on the following considerations:

I.   Likelihood of default—capacity and willingness of the obligor as to the timely payment of interest and repayment of principal in accordance with the terms of the obligation;

II.   Nature of and provisions of the obligation;

III.   Protection afforded by, and relative position of, the obligation in the event of bankruptcy and other laws affecting creditor's rights.

AAA   Debt rated "AAA" has the highest rating assigned by Standard & Poor's. Capacity to pay interest and repay principal is extremely strong.

AA   Debt rated "AA" has a very strong capacity to pay interest and repay principal and differs from the higher rated issues only in small degree.

A   Debt rated "A" has a strong capacity to pay interest and repay principal although it is somewhat more susceptible to the adverse effects of changes in circumstances and economic conditions than debt in higher rated categories.

BBB   Debt rated "BBB" is regarded as having an adequate capacity to pay interest and repay principal. Whereas it normally exhibits adequate protection parameters, adverse economic conditions or changing circumstances are more likely to lead to a weakened capacity to pay interest and repay principal for debt in this category than in higher rated categories.

BB, B, CCC, CC, C   Debt rated "BB", "B", "CCC", "CC" and "C" is regarded, on balance, as predominantly speculative with respect to capacity to pay interest and repay principal in accordance with the terms of the obligation. "BB" indicates the lowest degree of speculation and "C" the highest degree of speculation. While such debt will likely have some quality and protective characteristics, these are outweighed by large uncertainties or major risk exposures to adverse conditions.

CI   The rating "CI" is reserved for income bonds on which no interest is being paid.

D   Debt rated "D" is in payment default. The "D" rating category is used when interest payments or principal payments are not made on the date due even if the applicable grace period has not expired, unless S&P believes that such payments will be made during such grace period. The "D" rating also will be used upon the filing of a bankruptcy petition if debt service payments are jeopardized.

Plus (+) or Minus (–)   The ratings from "AA" to "CCC" may be modified by the addition of a plus or minus sign to show relative standing within the major categories.

r   The "r" is attached to highlight derivative, hybrid, and certain other obligations that S&P believes may experience high volatility or high variability in expected returns due to non-credit risks. Examples of such obligations are: securities whose principal or interest return is indexed to equities, commodities, or currencies; certain swaps and options; and interest only and principal only mortgage securities.

The absence of an "r" symbol should not be taken as an indication that an obligation will exhibit no volatility or variability in total return.

NR   indicates that no public rating has been requested, that there is insufficient information on which to base a rating, or that S&P does not rate a particular type of obligation as a matter of policy.

Debt Obligations of issuers outside the United States and its territories are rated on the same basis as domestic corporate and municipal issues. The ratings measure the creditworthiness of the obligor but do not take into account currency exchange and related uncertainties.

Bond Investment Quality Standards   Under present commercial bank regulations issued by the Comptroller of the Currency, bonds rated in the top four categories ("AAA", "AA", "A", "BBB", commonly known as "Investment Grade" ratings) are generally regarded as eligible for bank investment. In addition, the Legal Investment Laws of various states may impose certain rating or other standards for obligations eligible for investment by savings banks, trust companies, insurance companies and fiduciaries generally.

SOURCE: *Standard & Poor's Bond Guide*, (New York: Standard & Poor's Corporation, one of the McGraw-Hill Companies, January 1995), pp. 10–11.

The list of prospective guideline publicly traded debt securities compiled from one of these two debt listings should then be narrowed to those with characteristics or provisions similar to the privately held debt security. Thus winnowing the selection will help eliminate securities whose yields to maturity differ because of varying contract provisions. If unable to eliminate any publicly traded debt securities whose provisions differ from those of the closely held debt security from the guideline list, the analyst should carefully consider the differences in the securities' provisions and the associated risk characteristics when estimating the appropriate yield to maturity to apply to the closely held debt security.

Exhibit 20–3
Standard & Poor's Corporation
Yield to Maturity for Bond Indexes
1984–1994

		Public Utility			Industrial						Composite			U.S. Government			
		AA	A	BBB	AAA	AA	A	BBB	BB	B	AA	A	BBB	Long-Term	Inter-mediate	Short-Term	Muni-cipals
Weekly Averages 1994																	
December 28		8.53	8.68	9.29	8.28	8.50	8.89	9.44	10.40	11.68	8.52	8.79	9.36	7.94	7.80	7.64	6.70
December 21		8.54	8.70	9.30	8.29	8.51	8.89	9.45	10.41	11.78	8.52	8.80	9.38	7.95	7.74	7.53	6.73
December 24		8.56	8.71	9.30	8.31	8.55	8.91	9.46	10.28	11.76	8.55	8.81	9.38	7.98	7.75	7.57	6.73
December 7		8.58	8.72	9.35	8.33	8.53	8.92	9.51	10.26	11.74	8.56	8.82	9.43	8.01	7.74	7.46	6.86
Monthly Averages 1994–1993																	
December		8.55	8.70	9.31	8.30	8.52	8.90	9.47	10.34	11.74	8.54	8.81	9.39	7.97	7.76	7.55	6.76
November		8.71	8.84	9.50	8.43	8.60	8.98	9.67	10.07	11.70	8.65	8.90	9.57	8.18	7.59	7.14	6.96
October		8.53	8.66	9.43	8.35	8.54	8.92	9.55	9.84	11.70	8.53	8.79	9.49	8.07	6.90	6.76	6.50
September		8.22	8.39	9.26	8.07	8.35	8.76	9.27	9.89	11.49	8.29	8.57	9.27	7.83	6.69	6.42	6.33
August		8.00	8.26	9.02	7.80	8.07	8.47	8.92	9.84	11.10	8.04	8.36	8.97	7.54	6.55	6.21	6.19
July		8.13	8.33	9.14	7.97	8.19	8.59	9.03	9.89	10.93	8.16	8.46	9.09	7.68	6.69	6.29	6.19
June		7.97	8.21	8.95	7.81	8.05	8.52	8.83	9.76	10.53	8.01	8.37	8.89	7.47	6.48	6.11	6.41
May		8.13	8.27	8.85	7.96	8.10	8.64	8.79	9.76	10.64	8.11	8.45	8.82	7.50	6.62	6.20	6.26
April		8.00	8.28	8.72	7.79	7.92	8.50	8.57	9.54	10.62	7.96	8.39	8.65	7.32	6.29	5.85	6.28
March		7.73	8.08	8.49	7.39	7.59	8.21	8.35	9.12	10.31	7.66	8.15	8.42	6.89	5.78	5.30	5.93
February		7.44	7.96	8.31	6.94	7.33	7.97	8.19	8.91	10.50	7.38	7.97	8.25	6.44	5.23	4.74	5.44
January		7.36	8.12	8.31	6.80	7.26	7.91	8.28	9.01	10.29	7.31	8.01	8.29	6.28	5.02	4.01	5.30
December		7.34	8.69	8.36	6.79	7.28	7.83	8.28	9.06	10.45	7.31	8.26	8.30	6.23	5.08	3.87	5.35
Annual Ranges																	
1994	High	8.75	8.87	9.53	8.46	8.64	9.01	9.69	10.41	11.82	8.69	8.94	9.60	8.22	7.83	7.64	7.03
	Low	7.26	7.82	8.21	6.66	7.19	7.82	8.06	8.89	10.06	7.23	7.89	8.14	6.15	4.90	3.90	5.27
1993	High	8.34	9.03	8.77	8.12	8.21	8.60	9.03	9.88	11.19	8.23	8.63	8.82	7.35	6.14	4.57	6.22
	Low	7.28	7.99	7.65	6.16	7.06	7.48	7.35	8.96	10.37	7.26	7.73	7.50	5.75	4.63	3.63	5.23
1992	High	9.02	9.24	9.32	8.69	8.86	9.38	9.50	11.52	12.53	8.94	9.31	9.39	8.07	7.45	6.03	6.71
	Low	8.40	8.63	8.70	7.89	8.08	8.49	8.82	9.84	10.94	8.28	8.56	8.82	7.07	5.53	3.65	5.88
1991	High	9.54	9.75	9.99	9.14	9.55	9.89	11.83	12.58	20.53	9.54	9.80	10.86	8.70	8.13	7.20	7.15
	Low	8.77	8.93	8.93	8.05	8.25	8.87	9.13	10.80	12.87	8.51	8.90	9.03	7.36	6.32	5.03	6.50
1990	High	10.17	10.36	10.60	9.76	10.13	10.50	11.48	14.12	19.85	10.15	10.43	10.98	9.32	9.13	8.99	7.56
	Low	9.09	9.39	9.68	8.78	9.06	9.55	10.06	11.94	13.80	9.07	9.47	9.87	8.22	7.75	7.22	6.99
1989	High	10.14	10.47	10.56	9.92	10.29	10.70	11.06	12.30	13.95	10.21	10.59	10.81	9.50	9.68	9.97	7.68
	Low	8.98	9.28	9.55	8.62	8.91	9.45	9.90	11.20	11.93	8.95	9.36	9.69	7.97	7.71	7.61	6.87
1988	High	10.38	10.65	10.97	9.95	10.33	10.85	11.22	11.35	12.51	10.35	10.66	10.98	9.60	9.24	9.18	8.10
	Low	9.27	9.52	9.93	9.05	9.41	9.89	10.44	10.96	11.89	9.34	9.71	10.24	8.44	7.99	7.15	7.41
1987	High	10.96	11.27	11.78	10.74	11.09	11.48	12.06	0.00	0.00	11.03	11.37	11.92	10.30	9.89	8.90	9.31
	Low	8.59	8.89	9.13	8.37	8.89	8.83	9.52	0.00	0.00	8.76	8.88	9.36	7.57	6.90	6.26	6.53
1986	High	10.24	10.69	11.06	9.80	10.41	10.58	11.26	0.00	0.00	10.32	10.58	11.15	9.51	9.15	8.44	8.21
	Low	8.76	9.05	9.36	8.50	9.18	8.99	9.81	0.00	0.00	8.98	9.19	9.61	7.23	6.98	6.27	6.73
1985	High	12.54	12.87	13.24	12.00	12.43	12.50	13.19	0.00	0.00	12.48	12.62	13.14	11.84	11.89	10.82	9.93
	Low	10.01	10.49	10.93	9.50	10.13	10.20	11.13	0.00	0.00	10.07	10.34	11.03	9.24	8.86	8.11	8.41
1984	High	14.45	14.78	15.60	13.66	14.13	14.42	15.12	0.00	0.00	14.23	14.54	15.32	13.89	13.79	13.22	11.14
	Low	11.94	12.31	12.80	11.40	11.73	12.06	12.78	0.00	0.00	11.84	12.18	12.79	11.25	11.30	10.19	9.48

SOURCE: *Standard & Poor's Bond Guide,* January 1995, p. 3.

Standard & Poor's attaches one of approximately 200 industry codes or sub-codes to nearly all the corporate bonds included in its listing. The analyst may want to consider including only publicly traded debt securities within the same general industry as that of the closely held debt security issuer, if enough publicly traded debt securities within that industry are available to provide meaningful insight into yields to maturity. Standard & Poor's description of the impact of industry analysis on its debt rating methodology is presented in Exhibit 20–4.

After selecting an appropriate set of publicly traded equivalent securities, the analyst should examine several quantitative and qualitative factors of the privately held debt security issuer and compare them to those of the publicly traded debt security issuers. This analysis is similar to that for valuing common stock in a closely held business.

The analyst should quantitatively analyze and compare the operating performance and financial position of the debt security issuer to those of the guideline publicly traded debt security issuers. This analysis is similar to that described above in comparing the operating performance and financial condition of the closely held debt security issuer to the broad population of its publicly traded counterparts. This comparison will offer the analyst insight into the appropriate yield to maturity for the closely held debt security relative to those of the guideline publicly traded debt securities.

If the valuation is to be performed in considerable depth, the appraiser may wish to analyze relevant economic and industry data, as well as the company's fundamental position, in some detail, as discussed elsewhere in the book.

After completing the quantitative and qualitative analysis discussed above, the analyst must develop an opinion of the risk associated with the payments from the closely held debt security in relation to the risk associated with the payments of the publicly traded debt securities. Based on the closely held security's risk and the publicly traded debt securities' yields to maturity, the analyst estimates the appropriate yield to maturity to apply to the closely held debt security payments.

Valuation Conclusion.   Having estimated the appropriate yield to maturity to apply to the future payments associated with a closely held debt security, the analyst may value the debt security simply by computing the present value of its payments, using Formula 20–1.

Marketability Aspects of Closely Held Debt Securities

Chapter 15, "Discounts for Lack of Marketability," presents much evidence in support of a discount for lack of marketability for the common stock of closely held businesses. On the surface, it appears that such a discount might also be appropriate for closely held debt securities. However, such a discount often is not required or, if required, would be much less than such a discount for a common stock.

Unlike investment returns on common stock, which are generated primarily by appreciation in the price of the common stock and contingent on the ability to sell the stock to realize the price appreciation, investment returns on most debt securities are generated predominantly by cash flows in the form of interest payments over the securities' lives. These payments are anticipated to be received by the debt security holder regardless of the security's marketability, and the repayment of principal is a contractual obligation for a given amount at a fixed point in time. Therefore, if the marketability of a debt security is to be considered at all, the discount associated with the security's lack of marketability should be much less than that associated with closely held common stock. If the analyst thinks that marketability is a valid consideration in the valuation of a particular closely held debt security, the adjustment can be handled by either increasing the appropriate yield to maturity to apply to the debt security payments to compensate for the additional risk associated with lack of marketability or taking a discount from the value estimated by applying a yield to maturity unadjusted for marketability considerations.

Special Characteristics of Various Debt Securities

In estimating the value of a debt security, it is extremely important to analyze the security's various characteristics or provisions that will impact on its value. In addition, if guideline publicly traded debt securities are used in the valuation, any differences between the provisions of the security being valued and those of the guideline securities should be considered. The following discussion focuses on some common provisions of various debt securities that should be analyzed in the valuation process.

Call Provisions

A feature associated with some debt securities is a *call* provision. This allows the debtor to repay the debt before its maturity. Usually, the debt may not be called for some period early in its life, often the first five years. Furthermore, the debtor usually must pay a premium in addition to the amount of debt outstanding to the

Exhibit 20–4

Standard & Poor's Rating Methodology

Each rating analysis begins with an assessment of the company's environment. To determine the degree of operating risk facing a participant in a given business, S&P analyzes the dynamics of that business. This analysis focuses on the strength of industry prospects, as well as the competitive factors affecting that industry.

The many factors assessed include industry prospects for growth, stability, or decline and the pattern of business cycles. It is critical to determine vulnerability to technological change, labor unrest, or regulatory interference. Industries that have long lead times or that require fixed plant of a specialized nature face heightened risk. The implications of increasing competition are obviously crucial. S&P's knowledge of investment plans of the major players in any industry offers a unique vantage point from which to assess competitive prospects.

While any particular profile category can be the overriding rating consideration, the industry risk assessment goes a long way toward setting the upper limit on the rating to which any participant in the industry can aspire. Specifically, it would be hard to imagine S&P assigning "AA" and "AAA" debt ratings or "A-1+" commercial paper ratings to companies with extensive participation in industries of above-average risk, regardless of how conservative their financial posture. Examples of these industries are integrated steel makers, tire and rubber companies, homebuilders, and most of the mining sector.

Conversely, some industries are regarded favorably. They are distinguished by such traits as steady demand growth, ability to maintain margins without impairing future prospects, flexibility in the timing of capital outlays, and moderate capital intensity. Industries possessing one or more of these attributes include manufacturers of branded consumer products, drug firms, and publishing and broadcasting. Again, high marks in this category do not translate into high ratings for all industry participants, but the cushion of strong industry fundamentals provides helpful support. The industry risk assessment also sets the stage for analyzing more specific company risk factors and establishing the priority of these factors in the overall evaluation. For example, if an industry is determined to be highly competitive, careful assessment of a firm's market position is stressed. If the industry has large capital requirements, examination of cash flow adequacy assumes major importance.

SOURCE: *Standard & Poor's Corporate Finance Criteria*, p. 17.

debtholder when the debt is called. A call provision generally benefits the debtor, since it allows the debtor to repay the debt early in a period of declining interest rates. A debt security with a call provision usually will require a higher yield to maturity than an identical security without such a provision. This is because if the debt security is called, the investor usually will be unable to find a comparable alternative investment vehicle with a yield to maturity as high as that of the original debt issue that was called. If the stated interest rate on the debt is above market rates, making exercise of the call provision likely, the analyst usually will focus on the yield-to-call date rather than on the yield to maturity.

Sinking Fund Provisions

A debt security may also have a *sinking fund* provision. This provision requires the debt issuer to call or retire a contractually determined portion of the entire debt issue periodically over time before the issue's maturity date. When a portion of a debt issue is retired under sinking fund provisions, the actual debt security to be retired is usually determined by lottery and the holder of the security typically is paid the security's face or par value. Although sinking fund provisions increase the uncertainty of the timing of future payments associated with a particular debt security, they are also thought to reduce the risk associated with the security. The sinking fund provisions ensure that a portion of the debt is retired periodically, thus reducing the amount of debt that will have to be paid off at maturity and lowering the risk of default on the debt.

Collateral Provisions

A debt security that has no pledge of specific property or assets as collateral for the debt is called a *debenture*. Although a debenture clearly will require a higher yield to maturity than an identical security secured by a specific asset, the relative risk associated with it will be reduced by indenture provisions designed to protect the debtholder. Such indenture provisions might include restrictions on the amount of additional debentures the debtor can issue before paying off the original debentures; restrictions on the payment of cash dividends to equity owners of the debt issuer while the debentures are outstanding; and provisions that require the issuer to meet minimum liquidity (such as working capital) requirements while the debentures are outstanding. Despite the protection such provisions provide, however, debentures generally are considered more risky than similar secured debt.

Income Tax Status

Interest earned on debt is subject to federal and state income taxation, with several exceptions. Interest earned on U.S. Treasury obligations and on many U.S. government agency obligations generally is exempt from income tax at the state level. Interest earned on most municipal obligations is exempt from federal income taxation and may also be exempt from state income taxation if the obligation originated in the state assessing the income tax. In addition, the purchaser must reside in the same state. As a result of this preferential tax status, debt securities not subject to some form of income taxation will require a lower yield to maturity than an identical security subject to income taxation. Conversely, a debt security subject to income taxation will require a higher yield to maturity than an identical security exempt from income taxation to compensate for the income tax liability associated with the interest on the debt security.

Zero Coupon Debt

An interesting form of debt security, known as a *zero coupon* debt security, allows the issuer to avoid paying cash to the debtholder for interest before the debt's maturity. The only cash payment from the debt issuer comes at maturity, when the debt's face value is repaid to the security holder. However, when the debt is originally issued, the debtor will receive proceeds substantially discounted from the debt's face amount. The difference between the amount of the proceeds the debtor receives at issue and the amount of debt the debtor repays at the maturity date is the investor's compensation in lieu of interest. The yield to maturity is simply the compound rate of return that equates the present value with the face value.

Convertible Debt

Corporations periodically issue bonds with conversion privileges, known as convertible bonds. These conversion privileges give the holder the right to convert the bond into a given number of shares of the issuing corporation's common stock at some future point. The bondholder has no obligation to convert the bond to stock if the conversion is not to the holder's advantage. The terms of the conversion privilege are usually set such that at the time the convertible debt is issued, there is no economic benefit in immediately converting the debt to stock. For example, if a $1,000-par-value convertible bond is issued for $1,000 and is convertible into 20 shares of the issuer's common stock that pays no dividend, there will be no economic benefit in converting the debt to stock as long as the common stock is selling for less than $50 per share.

A convertible bond is unique in that its value depends, to a certain extent, on the value of the common stock into which it can be converted. The convertible bond has a minimum value equal to its value as straight debt with no conversion privilege. However, as the value of the common stock into which the bond is convertible rises, the bond's value also will begin to depend on the common stock's value. Finally, as the common stock price continues to rise, there will be a point at which the incremental increase in the bond's value is nearly equal to the increase in the aggregate value of the number of common shares into which the bond can be converted. Once this relationship begins, the bond value has entered what is known as the *equity-equivalent region.* Continuing with the above example, if the bond value is indeed in the equity-equivalent region, as the value of a single share of common stock increases $1, the bond's value will increase $20 ($1 increase × 20 common shares per bond).

The valuation of closely held convertible debt securities presents a problem not associated with publicly traded convertible debt securities. Closely held debt securities are usually convertible into closely held stock with no readily determinable market price. Although it is theoretically correct to value closely held convertible debt by direct comparison with publicly traded convertible debt with comparable conversion privileges and other provisions, it is extremely difficult to find publicly traded convertible debt that meets these criteria. As a consequence, it is difficult to estimate the value of the closely held convertible debt by comparison with publicly traded convertible debt other than when determining the minimum value of the convertible debt as a straight, nonconvertible issue.

One reasonable alternative approach to this dilemma is to segregate the convertible debt security into two parts: a straight, nonconvertible debt security and a derivative security in the form of an option or warrant to purchase the common stock at a given price. The nonconvertible debt portion of the security would then be valued in the manner for valuing nonconvertible debt securities described above. Then these two values would be added to estimate the value of the convertible debt security.

Summary

Debt security valuations are required for a wide range of purposes. Some of the most frequent reasons include the possible purchase or sale of a debt security, an exchange of equity securities for debt securities, gift and estate taxes on debt securities, allocation of the enterprise value of a business entity among debt and other classes of securities, and the adjustment of the balance sheet for debt securities owned or owed.

The debt security valuation process includes an analysis of the debt security contract provisions to determine the amount and timing of payments associated with the security's ownership. Various contract provisions or characteristics that affect the amount, timing, and riskiness of payments include call provisions, sinking fund provisions, collateral provisions, income tax status, and whether the debt is a zero coupon issue or has conversion privileges.

The risk or uncertainty associated with the payments is further assessed through the use of guideline quantitative and qualitative analysis. This involves comparing the closely held debt security with a broad population of debt securities to estimate the general ratings classification into which the security would fall if it were publicly traded. Then, the closely held debt security is compared with specific guideline publicly traded debt securities similar in debt rating and nature in order to estimate an appropriate yield to maturity to apply to the subject security. The present value of the debt security payments is estimated by discounting the future payments at the appropriate yield to maturity. The analyst should consider the marketability of the debt security and determine whether a discount for lack of marketability or an increase in the debt security's yield to maturity is appropriate. However, such discounts, if any, are minor compared to discounts for lack of marketability for common stocks.

Finally, if a convertible debt security is being valued, the valuation process is further complicated by the security's "optionlike" features.

Chapter 21

Preferred Stock

Preferred stock is commonly found in closely held companies. The main characteristic of preferred stock is that the holder is promised a fixed dividend every period until its expiration. This dividend must be paid before any dividend can be paid to the common stockholders, hence the term *preferred*. The preferred distribution to a particular class of ownership can also exist in partnerships and limited liability companies.

In addition to the stated dividend, preferred stock can have many other characteristics that make it unique from the common stock. For example, preferred stock often has a preference over the common stock in the event that the corporation liquidates. And preferred stock need not have voting rights.

A good case can be made that preferred stock is really debt in disguise, a kind of equity bond. Unlike debt, however, preferred stock dividends cannot be deducted as interest expense when determining the taxable income of the issuing corporation. To the individual holder of preferred stock, the dividends received are taxable income. To the corporate owner of preferred stock, 70 percent of the dividends received are excluded from taxation.[1]

In this chapter, we consider the common situations that require the valuation of preferred stock, the special characteristics of closely held preferred stock, and the methods of valuing preferred stock.

Common Situations Requiring the Valuation of Preferred Stock

There are many reasons for valuing preferred stock; these reasons are very similar to those for valuing debt securities discussed in Chapter 20. The most frequently encountered reasons are:

1. Purchase or sale for cash.
2. Exchange of common equity or debt for preferred stock, or vice versa.
3. Gift and estate taxes.
4. Allocating total enterprise value among classes of securities in a leveraged buyout, recapitalization, or bankruptcy reorganization.
5. Adjusting a balance sheet for preferred securities owned or outstanding.

Purchase or Sale for Cash

As is the case with debt securities, a company may have occasion to purchase or sell preferred stock for cash. If the preferred stock is existing stock, it is necessary to estimate the cash equivalent value. If it is to be newly issued, it will be necessary to structure the provisions so the value will be equal to the price paid or received.

---

[1]According to Internal Revenue Code Section 243(a)(1). This 70 percent "dividends received deduction" applies as long as the corporation owns less than 20 percent of the distributing corporation. According to Section 243(c), the "dividends received deduction" is increased to 80 percent where the receiving corporation owns 20 percent or more of the distributing corporation.

Exchange of Common Equity or Debt for Preferred Stock

If preferred stock is to be exchanged for some consideration other than cash, such as common stock, debt securities, or other property, it usually is most expedient to estimate the cash equivalent values of both the preferred stock and the other consideration.

The most typical situation encountered is one in which a company, or some or all of its stock, is to be sold and a preferred stock received as all or part of the consideration. In this case, it is important that the seller know the cash equivalent value of the consideration being received for the company or stock being sold.

Gift and Estate Taxes

Preferred stock may be gifted or may be an asset in an estate. In either situation, an estimation of the preferred stock's fair market value is needed for gift and estate tax purposes. It is not uncommon to find that the fair market value of a preferred stock is considerably less than its par value.

Allocating Total Enterprise Value among Classes of Securities

In many acquisitions, attracting capital requires creativity. For example, a leveraged buyout, by its very nature, results in the creation of new classes of securities, almost always including at least one class of debt. In addition, preferred stock may be issued in a transaction. Therefore, it is usually necessary not only to value the total enterprise but also to allocate the total value among the various classes of securities.

The issuance of preferred stocks in acquisitions is becoming increasingly popular, especially in situations involving ESOPs. Typically, the preferred stock is issued to the ESOP with other shareholders taking common stock. Issuing the preferred stock to the ESOP gives the ESOP a claim that is senior to the common shareholders' and at the same time allows a form of equity participation, thereby reducing the risk to the employees in a leveraged buyout situation. One of the attractions of preferred stocks for ESOPs is that, under the current tax law, dividends paid on preferred ESOP stock can be a tax-deductible expense to the employer corporation in most circumstances. (See Chapter 30 on employee stock ownership plans.)

Recapitalizations very often involve preferred stock, thereby requiring a valuation of the security. In recapitalizations involving preferred stock, a new class of preferred stock is issued, which the current owners of the business typically retain, while the common stock is passed along to other shareholders.

Bankruptcy reorganizations or restructurings, by their nature, involve debt securities. Preferred stock often is issued along with the debt securities. The creative structuring of debt and preferred stock can be an essential tool in achieving a successful reorganization or restructuring.

Adjusting a Balance Sheet for Preferred Stock Owned or Outstanding

The most common situation requiring a balance-sheet adjustment for the preferred stock outstanding occurs when the appraiser is using debt-free methods to valuing common stock. In this situation, the market value of any preferred stock must be estimated as well as the market value of any debt outstanding. As discussed in Chapters 9, 10, and 11, when the market value of debt and preferred stock is deducted from the value of the company's total capital, what remains is the value of the company's equity.

Also, the subject company may own some preferred stock as an investment. This preferred stock investment may need valuing if the analyst is adjusting the various line items on the balance sheet to fair market value.

Special Characteristics of Closely Held Preferred Stocks

Preferred stock is often used to recognize that certain potential investors will have unique characteristics that call for special allocations of the proceeds of ownership. While the investor in preferred stock may be surrendering some of the upside potential that common shareholders have, the preferred stockholder will expect to be protected from some of the downside potential by demanding special characteristics and contingencies.

The special characteristics of the preferred stock we encounter include:

- Dividend rate.
- Liquidation preference.
- Cumulative versus noncumulative dividends.
- Redeemable (e.g., call options) versus nonredeemable rights (i.e., expected life).
- Put options.
- Voting versus nonvoting rights.
- Participating versus nonparticipating rights in any future earnings.
- Convertible versus nonconvertible rights into common equity.
- Foreign tax attributes.

The difficulties encountered in valuing closely held preferred stock result primarily from estimating the required yield rate given the stock's myriad characteristics. Because of the flexibility in characteristics, the ability to estimate the value of preferred stock of a closely held business depends on the analyst's experience and subjective judgment. The following discussion focuses on some common special characteristics found in closely held preferred stock.

Dividend Rate

The dividend rate in and of itself is not special, but the type of dividend can be unique.

Fixed Dividend Rate. The most common form of dividend is one that is fixed at an amount usually stated as a percentage of the preferred stock's par value. For example, a $100-par-value, 10 percent preferred stock would pay an annual dividend of $10 per share. The value attributable to the stated dividend rate of the preferred stock depends on the issuing company's current and expected ability to pay the stated dividend rate and the current market yields of preferred stocks with similar dividend payment risk.

Adjustable Dividend Rate. A somewhat less common form of dividend is an adjustable-rate dividend. This form of dividend typically is adjustable within a stated range and is pegged to the general level of interest rates. However, the adjustable rate can be pegged to just about anything. The dividend rate could be adjustable based on a given time period—for example, 10 percent from 1997 to 2000, 11 percent from 2000 to 2003, and so forth. There are situations in which the dividend rate is adjusted based on the corporation's profits (in effect, a specialized form of participating preferred stock). In this case, the dividend might have equaled some percentage of the average of the corporation's last three fiscal years' earnings or some other measure of profits.

To estimate the appropriate yield, or discount rate, to apply to the subject company's adjustable-rate preferred stock, publicly traded adjustable-rate preferred stocks can be used as a benchmark. However, the analyst must be careful to note the differences between the basis for the adjustability of the subject company's preferred stock dividend and that of the publicly traded guideline company's preferred stock dividends. The adjustability differences in the subject preferred stock compared to its publicly traded adjustable counterparts will require either an increase or a decrease in the adjustable dividend yield evidenced in the market. Just as the case with a "straight" or fixed-dividend preferred stock, the subject company's ability to pay the adjustable dividend and its liquidation preference must also be analyzed, making appropriate adjustments to the publicly traded adjustable dividend yields as necessary.

In general, all other things being equal, adjustable-rate preferred stocks require a lower dividend yield, thereby increasing the preferred stock's value. For example, as presented in Exhibit 21–1, market evidence for a small sample of preferred stock issues in December 1994 indicated that adjustable-rate preferred stocks may require yields in the range of 0 to 200 basis points[2] below the yields required on similar fixed-rate preferred stocks. However, at any given time, the reduction in required yield will depend on the level of interest rates prevailing in the market at the valuation date and the stated range of the adjustable dividend rate of the subject company's closely held preferred stock. For example, if market interest rates are at historically high levels at the valuation date, the likelihood of their going much higher is smaller. In this situation, the potential for a higher dividend rate in the future is diminished, thereby reducing the necessary adjustment to the yield. If the adjustable-rate range (or *collar)* on the closely held preferred stock is very small, there is less potential for an increase in the dividend, thereby reducing the required yield adjustment relative to an issue with a wider adjustable-dividend-rate range.

Liquidation Preference

Another important characteristic of a preferred stock is its liquidation preference and the subject company's ability to pay it in full at liquidation. In almost all cases, preferred stock carries a contractual right to preference (advantage) in the distribution of the issuing corporation's assets upon liquidation. The preferred stock's liquidation preference usually is stated as a certain dollar amount per share, such as $100 per share.

---

[2]100 basis points = 1 percentage point.

Exhibit 21–1

Adjustable- and Fixed-Rate Preferred Stock Yields

S&P Rating	Average Yield as of December 31, 1994				
	Adjustable %	Number of Observations	Fixed Rate %	Number of Observations	Yield Differential in Basis Points
AA	7.8	1	7.8	4	0
BBB	6.8	1	8.8	9	200
BB	8.2	1	8.8	2	60

SOURCE: *Standard & Poor's Corporation Records* (via *Dialog OnDisc*), *Standard & Poor's Stock Guide*, Disclosure's *Compact D/SEC*, and WMA calculations.

Revenue Ruling 83-120 requires that the issuing corporation's ability to pay the full liquidation preference at liquidation be considered in estimating the preferred stock's fair market value. According to the ruling, this risk can be measured by the protection afforded by the corporation's net assets. The ruling sets out the method of measuring this protection as follows:

Formula 21–1

$$Liquidation\ coverage\ = \frac{Market\ value\ of\ assets\ -\ Market\ value\ of\ liabilities}{Aggregate\ liquidation\ preference\ of\ preferred\ stock}$$

This ratio should be high enough that any unforeseen business downturns would not jeopardize the issuing corporation's ability to pay the liquidation preference. This ratio should be compared with ratios of publicly traded preferred stocks. All other things being equal, if the subject company's preferred stock liquidation coverage ratio is higher than the publicly traded preferred stock ratios, a lower yield (or, conversely, a higher value) will be required on the subject company preferred stock due to the lower risk of nonpayment of the liquidation preference upon liquidation. However, it should be noted that since most investors look at investments in preferred stock on a going-concern basis, the liquidation coverage ratio generally is a less important factor in the valuation than the dividend coverage ratio.

It should be noted that it is extremely difficult, if not impossible, to obtain adequate data about the guideline publicly traded preferred stocks to compute the market value of assets called for in the above liquidation coverage ratio. Therefore, as a practical matter, analysts will often use the book value of the issuing corporation's assets and liabilities in calculating the liquidation coverage ratios.

Cumulative versus Noncumulative Dividends

The term *cumulative,* when applied to preferred stock dividends, means that if the dividends are not paid for one or more periods, the corporation has a contractual obligation to make up the lapsed payments before declaring and paying any dividends on the common stock or on other junior issues. Furthermore, many cumulative issues also give preferred stockholders voting rights and/or the right to elect one or more members to the board of directors following the nonpayment of one or more dividends.

Cumulative dividends imply that the risk of nonpayment of dividends becomes secondary, because the cumulative feature requires that the shareholder not suffer a loss in income in the long run unless the company is never able to pay. In addition, when dividends are cumulative, liquidation coverage tends to become more important than dividend coverage, because in the event of liquidation, cumulative dividends in arrears must be paid in addition to the stated liquidation preference before making any assets available for distribution to common shareholders.

Noncumulative preferred stocks are rare in the public market, and those few that do exist typically have special characteristics, making them unlikely to be useful as comparative securities. In general, all other things being equal, the value of a noncumulative preferred stock would be significantly less than an otherwise comparable cumulative preferred stock, because dividends not paid on a noncumulative issue are lost permanently. Revenue Ruling 83-120 addresses the cumulative versus noncumulative feature as follows:

> The absence of a provision that preferred dividends are cumulative raises substantial questions concerning whether the stated dividend rate will, in fact, be paid. Accordingly, preferred stock with noncumulative dividend features will normally have a value substantially lower than a cumulative preferred stock with the same yield, liquidation preference, and dividend coverage.

According to Graham, Dodd, and Cottle:

> One of the chief objections to the noncumulative provision is that it permits the directors to withhold dividends even in good years, when they are amply earned, the money thus saved inuring to the benefit of the common stockholders. Experience shows that noncumulative dividends are seldom paid unless they are necessitated by the desire to declare dividends on the common and if the common dividend is later discontinued, the preferred dividend is almost invariably suspended soon afterward.[3]

However, the analyst must also look at the subject company's history of dividend payments on noncumulative preferred stock and evidence of the company's intention to pay or not to pay preferred stock dividends. If the company has a solid history of paying dividends on its noncumulative preferred stock and a stated intention to do so in the future, and the company has the financial capability to pay dividends in the future, the diminution in value resulting from the noncumulative feature will be minimal. In addition, if the holder of a noncumulative preferred stock has full voting control of the corporation, the noncumulative feature becomes moot, since the shareholder controls the votes to pay or withhold dividends. With all these factors to consider, the impact of the noncumulative feature on value requires a considerable amount of experienced subjective judgment.

Redeemable versus Nonredeemable

Most privately held preferred stock is nonredeemable—that is, the issue has an infinite life. However, in many instances, a preferred stock has a contractual redemption provision. The type of redemption provision can vary significantly. The most common forms of redemption provisions found in privately held companies are as follows:

---

[3]Benjamin Graham, David L. Dodd, and Sidney Cottle, *Security Analysis—Principles and Technique* (New York: McGraw-Hill, 1962), p. 391.

1. The entire issue is redeemable at the option of the issuing corporation at a specified price (typically par value) over a designated time period. These types of issues are commonly referred to as *callable.*
2. The entire issue is redeemable at the option of the issuing corporation at a specified price contingent upon a certain event, such as the death of a major shareholder, a change in ownership control, or issuance of other securities.
3. Future redemption by the issuing company is mandatory and based on a specific redemption schedule. These types of issues have sinking fund provisions similar to the vehicle by which bonds are retired at intervals up to their maturity dates and are referred to as *sinking fund preferreds.*

The impact on value of the redemption privilege varies depending on the specific redemption provisions. Therefore, it is extremely important that the analyst be aware of all the contractual provisions and contingencies of the redemption.

In general, the most important factors of the redemption provisions that affect value are:

1. Call (or redemption) price.
2. Length of time the issuing company is *not* permitted to call the preferred.
3. Likelihood that the contingent event triggering redemption will occur.
4. Redemption schedule.
5. Whether or not a sinking fund or some other means of financing the redemption is established.
6. Issuing company's financial ability to cash out the preferred shares without some sort of redemption financing fund.

For a preferred issue that is redeemable at the issuing corporation's option at a specified price, the most important provisions affecting value are the call price and the length of time the issuing company is not permitted to call the preferred stock (the call protection period). All other things being equal, the shorter the call protection period, the lower the preferred stock's value. This is because redemption of the entire issue of preferred stock eliminates the shareholder's right to a future stream of income and forces the shareholder to accept a price (equal to the call price) for the stock that may be substantially lower than the fair market value the preferred stock might have in the absence of the redemption feature. A lower redemption, or call, price also reduces value to the shareholder, both by increasing probability that the preferred will be called (assuming that redemption is not contingent on some future event) and by reducing the proceeds to shareholders on redemption.

Fortunately, the public market for preferred stocks makes the task of estimating the appropriate yield rate to apply to a callable preferred stock, such as that described above, relatively straightforward. To value this type of issue, the analyst uses the same procedure discussed in the section "Method of Valuation" with one important distinction: The guideline publicly traded preferred stocks will be callable preferred stocks with similar call protection periods. As discussed in that section, the analyst selects the appropriate yield based on a comparison of the dividend and liquidation payment risk of the subject preferred and the publicly traded callable preferred stock. An additional risk factor to consider in valuing callable preferred stock is the subject company's ability to fund redemptions.

When the preferred stock is redeemable contingent on a future event, it is extremely difficult to ascertain the impact on value. This stems from the fact that the analyst is forced to make an educated guess as to the likelihood that the event triggering redemption will or will not occur. In addition, "contingent" redemption privileges are extremely rare, if not nonexistent, in the public market. Because the redemption of this type of issue is contingent on some certain event, the importance of the likelihood of its occurring may outweigh the importance of the issuing corporation's financial ability to redeem the preferred shares should the contingent event occur when estimating the appropriate yield to apply to the stock's future income stream.

One way to approach the valuation of a contingently redeemable preferred stock is to estimate the appropriate yield to apply to the future income stream absent the contingent redemption privilege and then adjust the yield based on an analysis of the likelihood of the contingent event occurring. Alternatively, the matter of the contingency can be handled as a separate adjustment. It should be noted that if the redemption is contingent on the death of a major stockholder, the ability to use life insurance proceeds to redeem the preferred stock and the adequacy of those proceeds, or other evidence of the company's ability to pay, are important factors to consider in estimating the appropriate yield adjustment.

Sinking fund preferred stocks differ from the types of redeemable preferred stocks discussed above in that it is known with certainty that the preferred stock will be redeemed at a specified price over a given time period. Both the redemption price and the redemption schedule are specified in the preferred stock contract. Sinking fund preferred stocks provide two advantages to their holders that are worth noting. First, the continuous reduction in the issue's size allows greater certainty that dividends will be paid. Second, the specified redemption guarantees a market, albeit limited, for the preferred stock.

The primary impact on the value of a sinking fund preferred stock results from the fact that redemption creates a finite stream of income to the investor plus a terminal value versus an infinite stream of income available to the nonsinking fund preferred stockholder. This can be illustrated with a simplified example. Let's assume that issue A is $100-par-value, nonredeemable, fixed-rate, voting, cumulative preferred stock that requires a market-derived yield of 10 percent. Issue A's fixed dividend rate is 7 percent, or $7 per share. The value of issue A before consideration of lack of marketability is calculated as follows:

Formula 21–2

$$Value = \frac{Dividend}{Required\ yield} = \frac{\$7.00}{.10} = \$70\ per\ share$$

Now let's assume that issue B is identical to issue A in all respects except it is a sinking fund preferred stock that is redeemable at par value beginning in year 5, with 10 percent of the entire issue redeemable each year. There are 100 shares of issue B outstanding. To estimate the appropriate required yield for issue B, the procedure outlined in the "Method of Valuation" section is followed using guideline publicly traded, redeemable, fixed-rate, voting, cumulative, sinking fund preferred stock *with similar redemption schedules*. It is important to note that the appropriate yield measure for sinking fund preferred stock is yield to maturity (YTM) as opposed to the stated yield implied by the dividend rate alone.

Exhibit 21–2

Value of Sinking Fund Preferred

Year End	Income Stream			Present Value Factor @10.0% YTM	Value
	Dividends	Redemption	Total		
1	$700	$0	$700	0.909	$636.30
2	700	0	700	0.826	578.20
3	700	0	700	0.751	525.70
4	700	0	700	0.683	478.10
5	700	1,000	1,700	0.621	1,055.70
6	630	1,000	1,630	0.564	919.32
7	560	1,000	1,560	0.510	800.28
8	490	1,000	1,490	0.467	695.83
9	420	1,000	1,420	0.424	602.08
10	350	1,000	1,350	0.386	521.10
11	280	1,000	1,280	0.350	448.00
12	210	1,000	1,210	0.319	385.99
13	140	1,000	1,140	0.290	330.60
14	70	1,000	1,070	0.263	281.41
					8,258.61
				Shares outstanding	÷ 100
				Value per share	$82.59

YTM = Yield to maturity.

For simplicity, we will assume the appropriate yield to maturity given an analysis of issue B's dividend and liquidation payment risk is 10 percent. The value of issue B before consideration of lack of marketability, if applicable, is calculated as presented in Exhibit 21–2. In these illustrative examples, the value of issue B (the sinking fund preferred) is greater than the value of issue A (non-sinking fund preferred) because issue B is redeemed at par value, which, because the required yield is higher than the stated yield, is higher than its value absent the sinking fund provision. Therefore, a portion of issue B's return is derived from capital gains from the time of purchase to the time of redemption. If the stated yield and required yield in both issue A and issue B were equal, their values would be equal to par in both instances.

Put Option

A common characteristic of closely held preferred stock is a *put* option on the preferred shareholder's behalf. This option allows the shareholder to require the issuing corporation to buy back the stock at some fixed price, usually par value. When a preferred stock can be put back to the company at par value, its value usually is, at a minimum, its par value assuming the company has the financial ability to honor the put. This is true because if the preferred stock's value is estimated to be less than par value based on the stock's other characteristics, the holder always has the right to put the stock back to the company at par value.

Voting versus Nonvoting

In general, voting rights increase the value of preferred stock, for obvious reasons. Numerous studies of publicly traded preferred stocks have been conducted in an attempt to isolate the reduction in yield (and thus increase in value) investors accord to voting preferred stock. Unfortunately, these studies have yet to produce any meaningful results. Significant patterns of yield differentials due to voting versus nonvoting preferred stocks in the public market have not been developed on any consistent basis. Generally, this is because voting rights in publicly traded preferred stocks are incidental relative to the total outstanding voting power. Therefore, they have no significant impact on yield.

Lacking any concrete public market evidence, it is thus necessary for the analyst to judgmentally adjust the required yield downward in valuing voting preferred stock. Industry practice dictates a discount in yield for voting stock ranging from 5 to 10 percent of the yield otherwise indicated.

In closely held companies, it is common for the preferred stock as a class to have voting control of the corporation. If the voting preferred stock being valued represents a controlling interest, the value increases considerably more (or the yield decreases even more). Perhaps the easiest way to approach the valuation of preferred stock in this situation is to value the stock absent the control feature and then add a premium for control.

Participating versus Nonparticipating

A participating preferred stock gives the preferred stockholder the right to share in additional earnings beyond the amount described in the preferred stock contract (beyond the stated dividend rate). On the other hand, a nonparticipating preferred stockholder can receive dividends only in the amount specified in the contract. A fully participating preferred stock allows the stockholder to share with the common stockholder in any earnings disbursements after the common stockholders have received a certain specified annual payment. The incremental amount to the preferred shareholders in such a case normally is equal to that paid to common stockholders.

Another form of participating preferred stock, which is something less than fully participating, allows the preferred stockholder to share earnings disbursements with the common stockholder up to a certain dividend rate, and after this dividend has been paid in any one year, the right of the preferred stock to participate in the earnings ceases. The degree of participation allowed in any preferred stock can vary significantly from one issue to another, limited only by the creativity of financial advisors, legal counsel, and controlling stockholders' imaginations in designing the features of the issue. This is especially true of privately held participating preferred stock. Therefore, it is critical that the analyst review the preferred stock provisions in order to determine the level of participation.

The value of the participating feature in a preferred stock is derived from the stockholder's right to *potentially* higher dividends and depends on the likelihood that these potentially higher dividends will in fact be paid. Thus, the increment to value attributable to the participating feature is higher the greater the likelihood that dividends exceeding the stated dividend rate will be paid and the greater the participation (the higher the potential dividend).

When valuing a participating preferred stock, the analyst will need to analyze projected income statements, if available, and look at the common stock dividend payment history to estimate a level of future dividends to capitalize that can reasonably be expected given the preferred stock's contractual participation features.

A variation of a participating stock is a hybrid cumulative preferred stock. For example, a company might issue a preferred stock that has a stated cumulative dividend and also participates in common stock dividends. Theoretically, one might logically approach a valuation of this type of preferred stock by valuing the fixed dividend and participating dividends separately and then adding these values to get the preferred's total value. This approach demands that the required yield to be applied to the participating dividends be higher than the yield applied to the cumulative fixed dividends, because the risk of nonpayment of the participating dividends is much higher. Whether or not the preferred shareholder will receive additional dividends as a result of the participating feature depends on whether or not dividends are declared on the common. The analyst must look at the subject company's history of paying dividends on common stock and assess the likelihood that its payment history will continue in order to assess the additional risk inherent in the preferred shareholder's receipt of participating dividends.

In addition, the analyst should not view the appropriate required yield on the participating dividend portion of the preferred stock in isolation from the fact that the preferred stock does, in fact, carry a stated cumulative dividend right. This fact, combined with the participation, reduces the overall risk of the participating portion of the issue compared to an issue that has only participating dividend rights. Thus, estimating the appropriate required yield for the participating dividend requires a great deal of experienced subjective judgment.

Given these factors, perhaps a more appropriate approach to the valuation of such a hybrid preferred stock is to value both the cumulative stated dividends and the participating dividends together, adjusting the required yield to compensate for the added risk of nonpayment of the participating dividends. This process somewhat lessens the subjectivity required in estimating the appropriate required yield. Using this approach, the analyst can estimate the appropriate required yield to apply to the issue assuming that it lacked the participation feature by using public market evidence. Then the required yield is adjusted to reflect the added dividend payment risk attributable to the participating feature. If the valuation is approached by separating the cumulative stated dividend and the participating dividend, the analyst will be forced to estimate the required yield on the participating dividend portion with no empirical market evidence base from which to start.

Convertible versus Nonconvertible

Convertible preferred stock is similar to a convertible bond in that it is a combination of a preferred stock issue and an option on a common equity issue. The conversion feature gives the preferred stock a speculative quality in addition to its investment value as a fixed-income security, which is derived through future dividend payments. Because of the speculative quality that the equity conversion feature imparts to the preferred stock, the stock's value depends not only on its conversion rights and expected future income stream, but on the value of the common stock as well.

Method of Valuation

Simply stated, the value of a preferred stock lacking any common equity kicker, such as convertibility or other special features, is equal to the present value of its future income stream discounted at its market-derived required rate of return, or yield. The higher the risk inherent in the investment, the higher the required yield.

Assessing Dividend and Liquidation Payment Risk

The single most important factor in the value of most preferred stock is the stock's dividend rate. Another factor would be redemption in the case of a preferred stock that has a prospect of being redeemed. In most instances, the primary source of value to the preferred stockholder is the right to future levels of income through the receipt of dividends. Therefore, in estimating the appropriate required yield for the subject company preferred, the risk that the dividends on the preferred stock will not be paid is critical.

The most prevalent measure for assessing the likelihood of receiving future preferred dividends is the company's fixed-charge coverage ratio, defined as the sum of pretax income plus interest expense divided by the sum of interest expense plus preferred dividends adjusted for taxes.[4] The higher this ratio, the greater the subject company's capacity to pay its preferred dividends (or, conversely, the lower the risk that the company will miss dividend payments) and, therefore, the lower the required yield. Rating agencies use the fixed-charge coverage ratio as part of the analysis conducted to determine the appropriate rating to assign a particular preferred stock issue. Moreover, the Internal Revenue Service Revenue Ruling 83-120 (to be discussed later) specifically requires analysis of the fixed-charge coverage ratio for preferred stock valuations involving federal gift, estate, or income taxes.

Other ratios than the fixed-charge coverage ratio are used to assess the subject company's dividend payment risk. One example is the return on total capital, defined as the sum of pretax income plus interest expense divided by the sum of long-term debt and shareholders' preferred and common equity. Several variations of this ratio also can be used, such as pretax cash flow return on total capital or pretax earnings before interest and depreciation charges return on total capital. A higher ratio indicates superior profitability and, thus, a greater ability to meet preferred dividend obligations.

Another often-calculated ratio is the liquidation coverage ratio, defined as the sum of the market value of total assets less the market value of total liabilities divided by the aggregate liquidation value of the preferred stock. This ratio helps the analyst identify the risk that the preferred shareholder will not receive the full liquidation payment in the event of the corporation's liquidation. Analysis of this ratio is also specifically required in Revenue Ruling 83-120. A higher ratio implies greater protection of the shareholder's investment in the event of liquidation of company assets.

The problem with the above ratios is that they address the subject company's dividend payment risk only as of a certain point. Because many companies exhibit cyclical earnings fluctuations, recent operating results may not accurately reflect a company's long-term dividend payment risk. A company subject to large swings in profits is more likely to suspend preferred dividends in down years, even though its average earnings may far exceed the annual preferred stock dividend requirements. Depending on the situation, the analyst may want to compute the above ratios using historical average financial statement figures.

---

[4]The fixed-charge coverage ratio has many definitions. However, Standard & Poor's uses this definition of fixed-charge coverage in its preferred stock rating process. See *Standard & Poor's Debt Ratings Criteria: Industrial Overview* (New York: Standard & Poor's Corporation, one of the McGraw-Hill Companies, 1986).

Exhibit 21–3

Preferred Stock Dividend and Liquidation Payment Risk Ratios

$$\text{Fixed charge coverage} = \frac{EBIT}{1 + (\text{Preferred dividends}) + (1 - t)}$$

$$\text{Liquidation coverage} = \frac{(\text{Market value of assets} - \text{Market value of liabilities})^a}{\text{Aggregate liquidation value of preferred stock}}$$

$$\text{Capitalization ratio} = \frac{\text{Total debt} + \text{Liquidation value of all preferred stock}}{\text{Total debt} + \text{Total equity}}$$

$$\text{Pretax return on total capital} = \frac{\text{Pretax income} + \text{Interest expense}}{\text{Long-term debt} + \text{Total equity}}$$

[a]From a practical standpoint, total book value of equity is often used.

NOTE: All net income and cash flow figures are before preferred stock dividends, discontinued operations, nonrecurring items, and extraordinary items.

EBIT = Earnings before interest expense and taxes.
t = Effective tax rate.

The subject company's capitalization ratio is another measure of long-term dividend payment risk. The capitalization ratio is defined as the sum of long-term debt and the aggregate liquidation value of preferred stock divided by the sum of the long-term debt and total equity. This ratio measures the company's leverage and indicates how vulnerable the company will be in cyclical downturns. The higher the capitalization ratio, the greater the company's vulnerability to cyclical downturns; therefore, the risk of losing out on preferred dividend payments over the long term is higher.

The methods of calculating these ratios are shown in Exhibit 21–3. If the analyst is valuing a preferred stock that has not yet been issued, a situation that often occurs in recapitalizations, the subject company ratios must be calculated on a pro forma basis, assuming the subject preferred issue is outstanding.

Comparison with Publicly Traded Preferred Stocks

None of the ratios discussed above imply, in and of themselves, the appropriate required yield to apply to the subject preferred stock's income stream. To estimate the appropriate required yield, and thus the value of the preferred stock, the ratios determined for the subject company must be compared to similarly calculated ratios for a group of publicly traded preferred stocks having the *same rights and privileges as the subject company.* Once these ratios are calculated, the comparable publicly traded preferred stocks must be grouped by rating category.

Quantitative Comparison. Both Moody's and Standard & Poor's rate publicly traded preferred stock issues. Exhibit 21–4 presents Standard & Poor's ratings and its explanation of the nature of the risk of the preferred stocks contained in each category. Exhibit 21–5 presents the yields of nonconvertible publicly traded preferred stocks as they existed at the end of 1994. As can be seen from Exhibit 21–5, there were 364 nonconvertible, fixed-dividend-rate preferred stocks issued by 203 companies listed in *Standard & Poor's Corporation Records* (via Dialog OnDisc) as of December 1994.

It is extremely important that the guideline publicly traded preferred stocks used to determine appropriate yields for the subject stock be as similar as possible to the subject stock in rights, privileges, and all relevant characteristics. Differences in these factors can have a dramatic impact on the required yield. In addition, the analyst will probably want to exclude preferred stocks issued by utilities, banks, insurance companies, and other financial institutions when selecting guideline publicly traded preferred stocks (unless the preferred stock to be valued is issued by a utility, bank, or insurance company). The criteria the rating agencies use differ somewhat for these types of issues due to their unique financial statement presentation and the fact that they are regulated. Because preferred stock ratings affect the investor's perception of risk, they also impact the required yield.

Once the ratios are calculated for both the subject company and the publicly traded guideline companies and the publicly traded issues categorized by rating, then the yields of each issue must be calculated and averaged for each rating category. The ratios for each issue also need to be averaged in each rating category. Exhibit 21–6 presents an example of the end result of this process. Generally, the more favorable the ratios, the higher the rating and the lower the yield. In addition, once financial institutions and utilities are excluded, the number of guideline preferred stocks drops significantly. In most circumstances, it is not necessary to compute dividend yields and ratios for each rating category. This is because once the dividend and liquidation payment risk ratios for the subject company have been calculated, it often becomes clear to the analyst into which rating category the subject preferred generally would fit.

Exhibit 21–4
Standard & Poor's Preferred Stock Ratings

"AAA"   This is the highest rating that may be assigned by Standard & Poor's to a preferred stock issue and indicates an extremely strong capacity to pay the preferred stock obligations.

"AA"   A preferred stock issue rated AA also qualifies as a high-quality, fixed income security. The capacity to pay preferred stock obligations is very strong, although not as overwhelming as for issues rated AAA.

"A"   An issue rated A is backed by a sound capacity to pay the preferred stock obligations, although it is somewhat more susceptible to the adverse effects of changes in circumstances and economic conditions.

"BBB"   An issue rated BBB is regarded as backed by an adequate capacity to pay the preferred stock obligations. Whereas it normally exhibits adequate protection parameters, adverse economic conditions or changing circumstances are more likely to lead to a weakened capacity to make payments for a preferred stock in this category than for issues in the A category.

"BB," "B," "CCC"   Preferred stock rated BB, B, and CCC are regarded, on balance, as predominantly speculative with respect to the issuer's capacity to pay preferred stock obligations. BB

indicates the lowest degree of speculation and CCC the highest degree of speculation. While such issues will likely have some quality and protective characteristics, these are outweighed by large uncertainties or major risk exposures to adverse conditions.

"CC"   The rating CC is reserved for a preferred stock issue in arrears on dividends or sinking fund payments but that is currently paying.

"C"   A preferred stock rated C is a non-paying issue.

"D"   A preferred stock rated D is a non-paying issue with the issuer in default on debt instruments.

"NR"   This indicates that no rating has been requested, that there is insufficient information on which to base a rating, or that S&P does not rate a particular type of obligation as a matter of policy.

Plus (+) or Minus (−)   To provide more detailed indications of preferred stock quality, the ratings from AA to BB may be modified by the addition of a plus or minus sign to show relative standing within the major rating categories.

SOURCE: *Standard & Poor's Stock Guide* (New York: Standard & Poor's Corporation, one of the McGraw-Hill Companies, 1994).

Exhibit 21–5

Preferred Stock Dividend Yield Summary

	Companies %	Issues %	Range Low %	High %	Mean*	Median
AA	4	4	7.4	9.5	8.2	7.9
AA−	6	77	6.5	9.1	8.0	8.3
A+	13	15	5.8	9.4	8.1	8.3
A	15	23	7.7	9.6	8.9	8.8
A−	28	50	7.3	10.9	8.9	8.7
BBB+	25	48	5.7	9.9	8.9	8.9
BBB	21	39	6.8	9.9	9.0	9.1
BBB−	25	34	2.9	12.1	9.2	9.3
BB+	13	15	7.4	10.8	9.2	9.3
BB	3	4	7.4	11.6	9.6	9.8
BB−	4	6	0.0	10.4	8.4	7.9
B+	4	4	9.4	12.9	10.9	10.7
B	5	5	9.9	11.7	11.0	11.0
CCC	2	2	8.1	10.5	9.3	9.3
NR	35	38	0.0	18.2	8.6	9.2

*Excludes nondividend-paying issues.

SOURCE: *Standard & Poor's Corporation Records* (via *Dialog OnDisc*), *Standard & Poor's Stock Guide*, Disclosure's *Compact D/SEC*, and WMA calculations.

Once all the necessary guideline data are available, the next step is to determine the rating category into which the subject preferred stock would fall given the subject company's dividend and liquidation payment risk. The appropriate yield is selected for the subject company based on the yields in the appropriate rating category.

Qualitative Factors. At this point, the analyst must consider any unique qualitative factors that might cause the required yield to be higher or lower than that determined based on the quantitative ratio analysis. These include many of the nonquantitative factors generally considered in valuing common stock that would increase or decrease the issuing company's risk. However, when assessing risk,

Exhibit 21–6

Nonconvertible, Nonsinking Fund, Fixed Rate, Cumulative
Preferred Stocks Excluding Financial Institutions and Utilities

S&P Rating	Number Issues	Yield Range Low %	High %	Average Mean Yield %	Fixed Charge Coverage %	Liquidation Coverage	Total Debt/ Total Equity	EBIT Return on Total Capital %
AA	4	7.4	8.6	7.8	5.92	43.99	0.36	14.47
A	7	5.8	8.8	7.5	9.10	63.89	1.25	14.94
BBB	9	6.8	9.3	8.8	3.51	37.72	0.88	14.01
BB	2	8.2	9.3	8.8	0.62	20.21	1.20	3.41
B	2	11.6	12.9	12.3	0.00	5.58	2.26	1.39
CCC	1	11.7	11.7	11.7	1.59	3.60	1.64	10.56

SOURCE: *Standard & Poor's Corporation Records* (via *Dialog OnDisc*), *Standard & Poor's Stock Guide*, Disclosure's *Compact D/SEC*, and WMA calculations.

the preferred shareholder will be most concerned with qualitative factors that may change the company's ability to meet its preferred stock obligations. As suggested in an article in *Business Valuation Review*, these qualitative factors might include the following:

1. The competitive environment in the industry.
2. Depth and competence of management.
3. Proposed federal regulation of the business.
4. Rights of lenders and other stockholders to influence dividend policy.
5. Trends in and diversification of supply sources.
6. Trends in and diversification of revenue sources.[5]

Standard & Poor's extensively analyzes a company's qualitative factors in determining a security's appropriate rating. In addition, the outlook for the industry and economy also play an important role in assessing the subject company's preferred stock income stream risk.

Capitalizing the Income Stream

Once the appropriate required yield is estimated, the next step is to capitalize the preferred stock's future income stream by its required yield. Mechanically, this is a simple present value calculation. For a noncallable, nonsinking-fund preferred stock with no maturity and lacking a conversion feature, the formula for estimating the value is as follows:

Formula 21–3

$$Present\ value\ =\ \frac{Dividend}{Required\ yield}$$

If the issue is nonconvertible and callable or subject to a sinking fund, its value is calculated as follows:

Formula 21–4

$$Present\ value\ =\ \sum_{i=1}^{n} \frac{C_i}{(1+r)^i}$$

where:

C_i = Cash flow (including redemption price and dividends) in the ith period in the future
i = Period when cash flows are generated
r = Required yield at which cash flows are to be discounted back to the present
n = Number of periods until redemption

It is important to note that even if a preferred stock is callable at the company's option, it usually is appropriate to value the issue as if it were noncallable if the stated dividend rate is below the rate currently required by the market for comparable issues. For example, if a $100-par-value preferred stock, callable at

---

[5]Gerald R. Martin and E. Halsey Sandford, "Valuation of Preferred Stock," *Business Valuation Review*, March 1991, p. 35.

$100 per share and with a stated dividend of 6 percent, requires a yield of 10 percent under current market conditions, the call feature has little or no effect as a practical matter. If the required yield is above the stated yield, the company will not exercise its option to call the issue, which renders the call feature irrelevant for the preferred stockholder.

Marketability Aspects of Closely Held Preferred Stock

Chapter 15, "Discounts for Lack of Marketability," presented much evidence in support of a discount for lack of marketability on common stock of closely held businesses. On the surface, it appears that such a discount might also be appropriate for closely held preferred stocks. However, such a discount for preferred stocks, if required, would be different from such a discount for common stocks. Unlike investment returns on closely held common stock, which are predominantly generated by appreciation in the common stock's price and contingent on the ability to sell the stock to realize the price appreciation, investment returns on most preferred stocks, as on debt securities, are predominantly generated by cash flows in the form of dividend payments over the life of the security. These cash flows are anticipated to be received by the holder of the preferred stock regardless of how marketable the preferred stock happens to be. Therefore, the discount associated with the lack of marketability of a preferred stock is different from that associated with closely held common stock.

If the analyst thinks marketability is a valid consideration in the valuation of a particular closely held preferred stock, the adjustment can be handled by either increasing the appropriate yield to apply to the preferred stock's dividends or by taking a discount from the value estimated by applying a yield unadjusted for marketability considerations.

Revenue Ruling 83-120

At this writing, the only regulatory guidelines established for the valuation of closely held preferred stock are those issued by the Internal Revenue Service in Revenue Ruling 83-120 (see Exhibit 21–7). Although applicable to any valuation of preferred stock in a closely held corporation, the ruling was designed to prevent the relative overvaluation of preferred stock and concurrent undervaluation of common stock in "estate freezing recapitalizations" in closely held corporations.

In the section titled "Approach to Valuation—Preferred Stock," Revenue Ruling 83-120 invokes the standard tools of security analysis for the valuation of the closely held preferred stock based on the issuing company's ability to pay its dividend yield and its liquidation preference. Revenue Ruling 83-120 addresses the following factors affecting the value of preferred stock:

1. Stated dividend rate and the risk associated with payment of it.
2. Cumulative versus noncumulative dividends.
3. Ability to pay the preferred stock's liquidation preference at liquidation.
4. Voting rights.
5. Redemption privileges.

Exhibit 21–7
Revenue Ruling 83-120

Rev. Rul. 83-120

SECTION 1. PURPOSE

The purpose of this Revenue Ruling is to amplify Rev. Rul. 59-60, 1959-1 C.B. 237, by specifying additional factors to be considered in valuing common and preferred stock of a closely held corporation for gift tax and other purposes in a recapitalization of closely held businesses. This type of valuation problem frequently arises with respect to estate planning transactions wherein an individual receives preferred stock with a stated par value equal to all or a large portion of the fair market value of the individual's former stock interest in a corporation. The individual also receives common stock which is then transferred, usually as a gift, to a relative.

SEC. 2. BACKGROUND

.01 One of the frequent objectives of the type of transaction mentioned above is the transfer of the potential appreciation of an individual's stock interest in a corporation to relatives at a nominal or small gift tax cost. Achievement of this objective requires preferred stock having a fair market value equal to a large part of the fair market value of the individual's former stock interest and common stock having a nominal or small fair market value. The approach and factors described in this Revenue Ruling are directed toward ascertaining the true fair market value of the common and preferred stock and will usually result in the determination of a substantial fair market value for the common stock and a fair market value for the preferred stock which is substantially less than its par value.

.02 The type of transaction referred to above can arise in many different contexts. Some examples are:

(a) *A* owns 100% of the common stock (the only outstanding stock) of *Z* Corporation which has a fair market value of 10,500x. In a recapitalization described in section 368(a)(1)(E), *A* receives preferred stock with a par value of 10,000x and new common stock, which *A* then transfers to *A*'s son *B*.

(b) *A* owns some of the common stock of *Z* Corporation (or the stock of several corporations) the fair market value of which stock is 10,500x. *A* transfers this stock to a new corporation *X* in exchange for preferred stock of *X* corporation with a par value of 10,000x and common stock of corporation, which *A* then transfers to *A*'s son *B*.

(c) *A* owns 80 shares and his son *B* owns 20 shares of the common stock (the only stock outstanding) of *Z* Corporation. In a recapitalization described in section 368(a)(1)(E), *A* exchanges his 80 shares of common stock for 80 shares of new preferred stock of *Z* Corporation with a par value of 10,000x. *A*'s common stock had a fair market value of 10,000x.

SEC. 3. GENERAL APPROACH TO VALUATION

Under section 25.2512-2(f)(2) of the Gift Tax Regulations, the fair market value of stock in a closely held corporation depends upon numerous factors, including the corporation's net worth, its prospective earning power, and its capacity to pay dividends. In addition, other relevant factors must be taken into account. *See* Rev. Rul. 59-60. The weight to be accorded any evidentiary factor depends on the circumstances of each case. *See* section 25.2512-2(f) of the Gift Tax Regulations.

SEC. 4. APPROACH TO VALUATION— PREFERRED STOCK

.01 In general the most important factors to be considered in determining the value of preferred stock are its yield, dividend coverage and protection of its liquidation preference.

.02 Whether the yield of the preferred stock supports a valuation of the stock at par value depends in part on the adequacy of the dividend rate. The adequacy of the dividend rate should be determined by comparing its dividend rate with the dividend rate of high-grade publicly traded preferred stock. A lower yield than that of high-grade preferred stock indicates a preferred stock value of less than par. It the rate of interest charged by independent creditors to the corporation on loans is higher than the rate such independent creditors charge their most credit worthy borrowers, then the yield on the preferred stock should be correspondingly higher than the yield on high quality preferred stock. A yield which is not correspondingly higher reduces the value of the preferred stock. In addition, whether the preferred stock has a fixed dividend rate and is nonparticipating influences the value of the preferred stock. A publicly traded preferred stock for a company having a similar business and similar assets with similar liquidation preferences, voting rights and other similar terms would be the ideal comparable for determining yield required In arms length transactions for closely held stock. Such ideal comparables will frequently not exist. In such circumstances, the most comparable publicly-traded issues should be selected for comparison and appropriate adjustments made for differing factors.

.03 The actual dividend rate on a preferred stock can be assumed to be its stated rate if the issuing corporation will be able to pay its stated dividends in a timely manner and will, in fact, pay such dividends. The risk that the corporation may be unable to timely pay the stated dividends on the preferred stock can be measured by the coverage of such stated dividends by the corporation's earnings. Coverage of the dividend is measured by the ratio of the sum of pre-tax and pre-interest earnings to the sum of the total interest to be paid and the pre-tax earnings needed to pay the after-tax dividends. *Standard & Poor's Ratings Guide, 58* (1979). Inadequate coverage exists where a decline in corporate profits would be likely to jeopardize the corporation's ability to pay dividends on the preferred stock. The ratio for the preferred stock in question should be compared with the ratios for high quality preferred stock to determine whether the preferred stock has adequate coverage. Prior earnings history is important in this determination. Inadequate coverage indicates that the value of preferred stock is lower than its par value. Moreover, the absence of a provision that preferred dividends are cumulative raises substantial questions concerning whether the stated dividend rate will, in fact, be paid. Accordingly, preferred stock with noncumulative dividend features will normally have a value substantially lower than a cumulative preferred stock with the same yield, liquidation preference and dividend coverage.

.04 Whether the issuing corporation will be able to pay the full liquidation preference at liquidation must be taken into account in determining fair market value. This risk can be measured by the protection afforded by the corporation's net assets. Such protection can be measured by the ratio of the excess of the current market value of the corporation's assets over its liabilities to the aggregate liquidation preference. The protection ratio should be compared with the ratios for high quality preferred stock to determine adequacy of coverage. Inadequate asset protection exists where any unforeseen business reverses would be likely to jeopardize the corporation's ability to pay the full liquidation preference to the holders of the preferred stock.

.05 Another factor to be considered in valuing the preferred stock is whether it

Exhibit 21-7 (concluded)

has voting rights and, if so, whether the preferred stock has voting control. See, however, Section 5.02 below.

.06 Peculiar covenants or provisions of the preferred stock of a type not ordinarily found in publicly traded preferred stock should be carefully evaluated to determine the effects of such covenants on the value of the preferred stock. In general, if covenants would inhibit the marketability of the stock or the power of the holder to enforce dividend or liquidation rights, such provisions will reduce the value of the preferred stock by comparison to the value of preferred stock not containing such covenants or provisions.

.07 Whether the preferred stock contains a redemption privilege is another factor to be considered in determining the value of the preferred stock. The value of a redemption privilege triggered by death of the preferred shareholder will not exceed the present value of the redemption premium payable at the preferred shareholder's death (i.e., the present value of the excess of the redemption price over the fair market value of the preferred stock upon its issuance). The value of the redemption privilege should be reduced to reflect any risk that the corporation may not possess sufficient assets to redeem its preferred stock at

SOURCE: Rev. Rul. 83-120, 1983-2 C.B. 170.

the stated redemption price. *See* Section .03 above.

SEC. 5. APPROACH TO VALUATION— COMMON STOCK

.01 If the preferred stock has a fixed rate of dividend and is nonparticipating, the common stock has the exclusive right to the benefits of future appreciation of the value of the corporation. This right is valuable and usually warrants a determination that the common stock has substantial value. The actual value of this right depends upon the corporation's past growth experience, the economic condition of the industry in which the corporation operates, and general economic conditions. The factor to be used in capitalizing the corporation's prospective earnings must be determined after an analysis of numerous factors concerning the corporation and the economy as a whole. *See* Rev. Rul. 59-60, at page 243. In addition, after-tax earnings of the corporation at the time the preferred stock is issued in excess of the stated dividends on the preferred stock will increase the value of the common stock. Furthermore, a corporate policy of reinvesting earnings will also increase the value of the common stock.

.02 A factor to be considered in determining the value of the common stock is whether the preferred stock also has voting rights. Voting rights of the preferred stock, especially it the preferred stock has voting control, could under certain circumstances increase the value of the preferred stock and reduce the value of common stock. This factor may be reduced in significance where the rights of common stockholders as a class are protected under state law from actions by another class of shareholders, *see Singer v. Magnavox Co.,* 380 A.2d 969 (Del. 1977), particularly where the common shareholders, as a class, are given the power to disapprove a proposal to allow preferred stock to be converted into common stock. See ABA-ALI Model Bus. Corp. Act, Section 60 (1969).

SEC. 6. EFFECT ON OTHER REVENUE RULINGS

Rev. Rul. 59-60, as modified by Rev. Rul. 65-193, 1965-2 C.B. 370 and as amplified by Rev. Rul. 77-287, 1977-2 C.B. 319, and Rev. Rul. 80-213, 1980-2 C.B. 101, is further amplified.

Specifically, the revenue ruling calls on the valuation analyst to compute coverage ratios for the subject company's preferred stock dividend and liquidation value and to compare these ratios to those found for guideline publicly traded preferred stocks. The revenue ruling indicates that if the ratios for the subject stock are substandard, the value of the subject preferred should be discounted from its par value on the basis of these criteria. Although the revenue ruling is very specific with respect to these two factors, it leaves a wide area of uncertainty as to the value of features such as voting control and redemption rights, two extremely valuable features often found in closely held preferred stocks.

Summary

The combination of rights and privileges found in closely held preferred stock are limited only by the imaginations of the issuer, the financial advisor, and the legal counsel. The flexibility of the myriad characteristics of closely held preferred stock makes the determination of value so difficult. Some guidance is found in

Revenue Ruling 83-120, but the ruling fails to address the value implications of several of the most important features often found in closely held preferred stocks but not in publicly traded preferreds.

A judge's opinion in a 1981 estate tax case, in which the fair market value of closely held preferred stock was at issue, sums up the difficulties in valuing closely held preferred stock with many features not found in publicly traded preferred stocks:

> Since these consummate negotiators, who invariably achieve an agreeable bargain, are mythical persons endowed with characteristics prescribed in authoritative writings, the undertaking of determining what they would decide on given evidence not exactly like any recounted in precedents, might better be discharged with the benefit of interpretive insights and skills associated more often with the theater than with the court. Like the actor or actress who re-creates the character from the guidelines the playwright has given, I must try first to understand the characters created in the authoritative statute regulations and precedents, and then, departing from the custom of the stage, occupy not one but two roles simultaneously—those of the willing buyer and the willing seller—coming finally to an agreement with myself—or more precisely between the two whom I am simultaneously impersonating—on the value of the stock at issue. A judge might be daunted by such an undertaking were it not for the reassuring thought that as surely as one who...
>
> ... never saw a moor,
> [And] never saw the sea;
> Yet [may] know... how the heather looks,
> And what a wave must be.[6]

Bibliography

Ferreira, Eurico J.; Michael F. Spivey; and Charles E. Edwards. "Pricing New-Issue and Seasoned Preferred Stocks: A Comparison of Valuation Models." *Financial Management,* Summer 1992, pp. 52–62.

Friedrich, Craig W. "More Refined View of Preferred Stock Valuation by IRS May Jeopardize Common to Preferred Recapitalizations." *Journal of Corporate Taxation,* Spring 1984, pp. 81–87.

Houston, Arthur L., Jr., and Carol Olson Houston. "Financing with Preferred Stock." *Financial Management,* Autumn 1990, pp. 42–54.

_____. "The Changing Use of Preferred Stock." *Management Accounting,* December 1991, pp. 47–49.

Huffaker, John B. "Subtraction Method of Valuing Gift Illustrated by IRS." *Journal of Taxation,* June 1992, pp. 340–41.

Linn, S. C., and J. M. Pinegar. "The Effect of Issuing Preferred Stock on Common and Preferred Stockholder Wealth." *Journal of Financial Economics* 22 (1988), pp. 155–84.

Martin, Gerald R., and E. Halsey Sandford. "Valuation of Preferred Stock." *Business Valuation Review,* March 1991, pp. 33–36.

McDaniel, William R. "Sinking Fund Preferred Stock." *Financial Management,* Spring 1984, pp. 45–52.

---

[6]*Wallace* v. *United States,* 82-1 U.S.T.C. paragraph 13,442 (D. Mass. 1981). Verse from "Time and Eternity," in *Poems by Emily Dickinson,* Vol. IV, ed. George Monteiro (Delmar, NY: Scholars' Facsimiles & Reprints, 1967), p. XVII.

Osborne, Philip H. "Recent Valuation Developments: Tax Court Rules on Indirect Gift Issues in Preferred Stock Recapitalizations." *Business Valuation Review,* March 1990, pp. 28–31.

Shayne, Mark. "Valuation Issues under Chapter 14." *Tax Management: Estates Gifts & Trusts Journal,* September 9, 1993, pp. 146–52.

Sherman, Lawrence F. "Valuation of Preferred Capital Stock for Business Enterprises." *ASA Valuation,* March 1994, pp. 72–83.

Switzer, Ralph V., Jr., and Douglas E. Chestnut. "Evolution of the Estate Freeze." *National Public Accountant,* January 1994, pp. 20–25 ff.

Thompson, James. "Letter Ruling 9420001: A Taxable Gift on Conversion of Preferred Stock to Common Stock." *Tax Adviser,* October 1994, p. 611.

Chapter 22

Pass-Through Entities

Introduction

Businesses are usually structured as corporations or as partnerships. Among other legal forms, we also see businesses that are formed as sole proprietorships, S corporations, and limited liability companies.

This chapter discusses these various legal forms of business and the impact the form of the business may have on its value. In most cases, the form of the business has an impact on its value, especially when the appraiser is analyzing the value of a minority ownership interest in the business. Depending on the purpose of the appraisal assignment, the impact on the value of the business due to its form of ownership could be significant.

Characteristics of the Organizations

The analyst should understand the characteristics of the business's legal form. The legal form of the business defines its business-related characteristics and its tax-related characteristics.

Sole Proprietorships

The simplest form of a business is the sole proprietorship. Its simplicity is both its strength and its weakness. It is started without a lot of paperwork. Inexpensive, over-the-counter computer software allows for easy business record-keeping. All earnings and losses of the business are taxed to the sole proprietor personally. All risks of the business are the sole proprietor's, and all the sole proprietor's personal assets will be subject to those risks.

Corporations

Insulating personal assets from the liabilities of a business is frequently the reason the corporate form is selected. A corporation is a separate entity for income tax purposes, too. Shareholders own the corporation, and they elect a board of directors to govern the company. C corporations pay income taxes on taxable income, so the shareholder-owners might be subject to double taxation: once at the corporation level and again when corporate earnings are distributed as dividends. Instead of paying the extra level of taxes, closely held corporation shareholder-owners often pay themselves additional, but reasonable, compensation, which reduces the level of taxable income of the corporation.

Partnerships

Two entities are required to form a partnership, which can be either general or limited. In a general partnership, all partners are jointly and severally liable for the obligations of the partnership and are permitted to participate in the management of the partnership. General partners act primarily in their own interest subject only to their fiduciary duty owed to the other partners. In a limited partnership, the liability of the limited partners is limited to their agreed-upon capital contributions, but they are typically not permitted to participate in management (which right is reserved for the general partners). The net earnings of partnerships are taxed only at the partner level, thus avoiding double income taxation.

S Corporations

Generally, double taxation may also be avoided by electing S corporation status. Limited legal liability is also maintained. Generally, an S corporation's earnings are taxed only at the shareholder level. There are restrictions, however, on S corporation equity ownership: an S corporation may have only one class of stock, no more than 35 shareholders (all of which must be U.S. citizens), and only individual shareholders (with certain limited exceptions).

Limited Liability Companies

Some observers say the newest form of business entity, the limited liability company (LLC), is the entity of the future. At least two "members" are required to form an LLC. Members have limited legal liability and may participate in the management of the organization, but they are taxed on earnings only once at the member level—like a partnership. The LLC may have multiple classes of members that exceed 35 in number, members other than individuals, and foreign members. One drawback to this form of business is that not all states currently authorize LLCs, and there is no uniform legislation among states that do. This means multistate businesses may face different rules regarding business operations than they had expected. Some observers believe LLCs are so legally undeveloped that LLC ownership interests may not be considered securities. This may affect the marketability of the interest because of potential limitations on transferability and on the communications regarding the value of the interest.

Pass-Through Entities

The businesses that pass through earnings to their owners, subject only to federal taxation at the owner's personal income tax rate, are referred to as pass-through entities. Of the previously discussed legal organizations, the traditional corporation, sometimes called a type C corporation, is the only one that is not a pass-through entity. While the tax-related advantages are real, the business-related implications of a particular business form are complex, and there are many disadvantages to be considered. For example, no business structure protects a professional from his or her own negligence, malpractice, or misdeeds, of course.

Six factors, or characteristics, are considered when determining if an organization will be taxed as a corporation or as a pass-through entity. These characteristics also affect the rights and privileges of ownership and, hence, its value. The characteristics are:

1.   Associates.
2.   An objective to carry on a business and divide the gains therefrom.
3.   Continuity of life.
4.   Centralization of management.

5. Liability for corporate debts limited to corporate property.
6. Free transferability of interests.

Since the first two characteristics are common to most businesses, the focus of consideration shifts to the remaining four characteristics to determine the tax treatment of a business entity. An unincorporated organization will not be classified as a taxable corporation unless it has more corporate characteristics than noncorporate characteristics. Taxpayers, then, generally endeavor to prove that at least two of the remaining four characteristics do not apply to their organization, so the taxpayers can enjoy the advantages of being a pass-through entity.

Continuity of Life

An organization has a continuity of life if the death, insanity, bankruptcy, retirement, resignation, or expulsion of any owner will not cause dissolution. A limited partnership does not have continuity of life if the retirement, death, or insanity of the general partner will cause a dissolution—unless the remaining general partners or a majority of remaining partners agree to continue the partnership. As long as any owner has the power under local law to dissolve the organization, the organization does not possess continuity.

Centralized Management

An organization has centralized management if a group of persons (not necessarily all the owners) makes management decisions. Some authorities use as a test of centralized management the ability of persons to act as a representative on behalf of others (such as the board of directors in a corporation), while other tests focus on the centralization of authority to bind the entity (such as the general partner). Centralized management typically does not exist if all or substantially all the owners must agree on major management decisions or if managers own a substantial interest.

Limited Liability

An organization has limited liability if no owner is personally liable for its debts or for claims against the organization. Personal liability does not exist with respect to a general partner of a limited partnership if the general partner has no substantial assets other than the interest in the partnership and is merely a "dummy" acting on behalf of the limited partners.

Free Transferability

An organization has free transferability of interests if each of its owners or those owning "substantially all of the interests in the organization" may substitute, without the consent of other owners, another person who is not an owner of the organization. Owners may freely assign a right to share in the profits or distributions of the organization without resulting in free transferability—as long as there is no right to assign, without consent, rights to participate in management. Involuntary transfers required by law (e.g., death, dissolution, liquidation, bankruptcy, or insolvency of a owner) cannot result in free transferability because parties have no control over such transfers.

The contents of the entity's articles of organization and its operating agreements should be analyzed in order to understand the rights, privileges, and risks of ownership, because they can materially affect the value of the ownership interest subject to valuation.

Partnerships

The partnership agreement will describe the specific characteristics of the partnership and the rights, privileges, and risks of each partner's ownership position. Usually, general partners are jointly and severally responsible for the partnership's obligations, but general partners also have management responsibility.

The theory underlying the rule that there will be centralized management even though the limited partners own more than 80 percent of the partnership interests is that a general partner owning a relatively small interest is managing the business primarily for the other passive owners—which is the essence of centralized management—but a general partner that owns a significant interest is managing the business to a substantial degree for itself.

S Corporations

S corporations were created in 1958 as part of a tax program to aid small businesses, although they are not limited to small businesses. The congressional intent was to lessen income tax considerations in the choice of business form by giving certain corporate entities and shareholders the option of being taxed as if they were partnerships. Hence, S corporations achieved the coveted corporate characteristics of limited liability combined with the income flow-through attributes of a partnership. Currently, to qualify for S corporation status, certain requirements must be met:

1. The corporation must have no more than 35 shareholders (however, Revenue Ruling 94-43 provides for some relaxation of this limitation) and all shareholders must be U.S. citizens. (Spouses who hold stock are considered as one shareholder.)
2. Shareholders must be individuals (except for estates and certain trusts).
3. All shareholders must participate equally in the allocation of profits, losses, and distributions.
4. Only common stock can be issued by an S corporation. The corporation may not have more than one class of stock, except there can be voting and nonvoting shares as long as there are no unequal distribution rights.

These limitations present qualification barriers and necessitate continued monitoring to prevent a subsequent inadvertent termination of S status.

The shareholders of the S corporation increase or decrease the basis of their ownership interest in the S corporation to the extent of the income or loss of the corporation recognized by each shareholder. The consequences of such basis adjustment is that income or loss is not taxable to the shareholder again on distribution or, in the absence of distribution, on the sale or exchange of the shareholder's interest in the corporation. This allows earnings to be distributed to shareholders free of federal income tax, avoiding the double taxation inherent in C corporations—where federal income taxes are levied on earnings at the corporate level and on dividends or distributions at the shareholder level.

The companies gaining this income tax benefit are unlikely to be high-growth companies, because high-growth companies typically plow profits back into the company to fund growth, leaving little or no earnings to pay out to shareholders.

Therefore, S corporations that have a handful of shareholders, where employee-shareholders of the corporation are in the minority, and/or where the corporation has significant cash flow to distribute achieve the greatest advantage as measured by the income tax savings from their S election.

It is helpful for the appraiser to be aware of the advantages and disadvantages of S corporation status, so these attributes are reflected in the process of estimating the value of the subject company.

The major advantage of the S corporation status is avoiding the double income taxation on shareholder distributions. Income and loss items pass directly through to shareholders, where income is taxed at the personal tax rate of the shareholder—rather than at the corporate tax rate. This means the S corporation can sell assets (at a purchase price that is often greater than a similar sale of stock) and distribute the proceeds without the corporate-level tax (which would apply before a C corporation's dividend distribution).

S corporations are not subject to the accumulated earnings tax, and there are no personal holding company taxes applicable to S corporations. Non–tax–shelter S corporations are allowed to use the cash method of accounting. At the point of conversions to an S corporation, the C corporation's deferred income tax charges are adjusted to retained earnings, often improving the appearance of the balance sheet.

Other distinctions between S corporations and C corporations include:

1. S corporations are liable for taxes on income whether the income is distributed or not. Tax-free distributions are allowed only to the extent of the shareholder's basis in the stock. Shareholders typically demand enough cash distributions to pay their taxes, which may limit the amount of earnings available for reinvestment (see Exhibit 22–1).
2. S corporations must generally conform their tax years to their owner's tax years (usually calendar years).
3. Each shareholder's deductible share of the S corporation's loss in any year is limited to his adjusted basis in stock and direct shareholder loans, in general. Losses can be carried forward indefinitely at the shareholder level to future S corporation years in which the shareholder creates basis.
4. State and local tax compliance can be complicated with multistate S corporations.
5. Many fringe benefits for shareholders who own more than 2 percent of the S corporation's stock cannot be deducted by the S corporation.
6. The deductibility of pass-through losses for inactive owners is limited.
7. S corporations cannot own more than 79 percent of another corporation.

Exhibit 22–1

Depending upon Distributions, the S Corporation Election May Be Unfavorable

100% Earnings Distributed

	C Corporation	S Corporation
Profit before tax	$100.00	$100.00
Corporate tax at 34%	34.00	0.00
Net profit	66.00	100.00
Retain 0%	0.00	0.00
Dividends	66.00	100.00
Personal tax at 39.6%	26.14	39.60
Net after tax	$39.86	$60.40[a]

0% Earnings Distributed

	C Corporation	S Corporation
Profit before tax	$100.00	$100.00
Corporate tax at 34%	34.00	0.00
Net profit	66.00	100.00
Retain 100%	66.00	66.00[b]
Dividends	0.00	34.00
Personal tax at 39.6%	0.00	39.60[c]
Net after tax	$0.00	($5.60)[d]

[a]When 100% of earnings are distributed, the advantage is greater than 51%.

[b]Assumes same dollar amount is retained; this implies same growth requirement.

[c]Personal tax is due on the reported net profit.

[d]When earnings are retained, the shareholder in the 39.6% bracket has negative cash flow.

Limited Liability Companies (LLCs)

To be an LLC, the business must have at least two owners or "members." Thus, an S corporation is the only entity through which a sole proprietor can enjoy both a single level of tax and limited liability.

Pass-through tax treatment for many LLCs will depend on the absence of continuity of life and the absence of free transferability of interests because, for a variety of nontax reasons, an LLC may desire centralized management and, of course, limited liability. On the other hand, some organizations may specifically desire to lack centralized management—either because of business reasons or because they are unable to comply strictly with the ruling guidelines to lack continuity of life or free transferability of interests.

LLCs are not subject to the ownership restrictions applicable to S corporations and, thus, offer increased flexibility. An unlimited number of persons or entities (including partnerships, corporations, and nonresident aliens) may own interests in an LLC, and an LLC may be used in multitiered structures. LLCs may issue more than one class of equity, giving them the flexibility to use special allocations and to offer equity interests designed to meet the needs of different investors.

A large number of owners, however, may not be feasible from a practical standpoint, because the unanimous consent of all the remaining "members" may be required to prevent dissolution on the withdrawal of a single member. Obtaining unanimous consent to continue an LLC's business on the event of dissolution (e.g., death or bankruptcy of a member) may be extremely burdensome, especially for large organizations and fragile family arrangements.

A possible approach that could be considered for a large group of investors would be to have several limited partnerships (which do not dissolve on the withdrawal of an owner) form an LLC, provided that both the limited partnerships and the LLC can be classified as partnerships for income tax purposes.

The estate planning applications and implications of LLCs are discussed below and in Chapter 27. Obviously, the structure and flow of the rights and privileges of the subject ownership position need to be understood by the analyst before its value can be determined.

LLCs as an Estate Planning Device

It may be easier to transfer gifts of interests in property, such as real estate or stocks and bonds, with an LLC. For example, if an individual owns real estate, a gift of a fractional interest in a deed is cumbersome and potentially expensive with respect to filing fees and legal costs. On the other hand, the transfer of real estate to an LLC will allow the owners to then make annual gifts of "membership units" without needing to file fractional deeds. The transfer of real estate or other property either to an LLC or to a partnership will generally be income tax free, but this is not necessarily true for the transfer of property to a C corporation or to an S corporation.

Another advantage of an LLC (or of a partnership) over a corporation is that the liquidation or distribution of assets to members or partners can be tax free (per Section 731). However, the liquidation of a C corporation or an S corporation—or the distribution of an appreciated asset in an S corporation—will result in taxable income (per Section 336).

If business or nonbusiness assets are held in an LLC, the owners can make annual gifts of LLC units up to $10,000 in value ($20,000 if the taxpayer is married) to children and grandchildren, free of gift tax. Although the same annual gifting mechanism can be implemented with a corporation or a partnership, an S corporation has several limitations that complicate estate planning. Unlike an LLC, only certain types of trusts can hold S corporation stock—that is, a Section 1361(d) QSST Trust. These trusts must be carefully drafted or the S corporation can lose its S taxpayer status. Since trusts are often used in many estate plans, this limitation is significant.

Also, a QSST must always have only one income beneficiary, and income must be distributed annually. There is no similar problem with an LLC (or a partnership), since there are no restrictions as to who can own an LLC membership.

If the transferor dies during the process of transferring his or her interests to children or grandchildren, the use of an LLC is preferable to a corporation. This is because of the ability to elect to step up the basis of assets inside the LLC (per Section 754). This step-up in basis will allow greater depreciation deductions for inherited assets and a deferral of any gain on the sale of assets by the LLC.

An LLC can be used just like a limited partnership to hold a variety of assets (e.g., real estate, cash, securities, etc.). Such flexibility in asset ownership allows a business owner to transfer ownership to second- and third-generation family members while still keeping control of the assets in the parent generation.

Membership interests, just like limited partnership interests or shares in a corporation, can be limited as to voting power and transferability rights. Consequently, if assets are transferred into an LLC, the estate or gift valuation of the individual membership units transferred may be substantially discounted—perhaps by 30 to 40 percent for each lack of marketability and lack of control discount. (The same argument can be used for a corporation or a limited partnership.)

Caveats Regarding the Valuation of Transferred LLC Interests

It is unclear whether an LLC is preferable to a limited partnership for holding business or other assets for purposes of the marketability and minority discounts in a family transfer situation. Section 2704(b) provides that restrictions by agreement on liquidation rights should be ignored for gift and estate tax valuation purposes if: (1) family members control the entity before the transfer and (2) after the transfer, the family members could remove the restriction on liquidation.

For gift and estate tax purposes, Section 2704(b) may require that—for purposes of valuing membership units—any language in the LLC operating agreement limiting liquidation rights be ignored. Therefore, the value of a member's interest would be closer to the pro rata portion of what the entire asset could be sold for, without consideration of any lack of control or lack of marketability discounts. Until further guidance is issued by the IRS, it is unclear how Section 2704(b) impacts the valuation of an LLC. For this reason, a term of years structure is often utilized for LLCs in the same manner as it is for limited partnerships.

Some observers believe the above valuation problem will not apply to limited partnership interests because of the difference in the rights of limited partners on a dissolution of a limited partnership. Nevertheless, caution may require consideration of the use of a limited partnership rather than an LLC—for family transfer purposes—when lack of control and lack of marketability valuation discounts are desired.

Another way to address this Section 2704(b) concern, if the use of an LLC is desired, is to give someone other than a family member the right to limit the dissolution of the LLC. Because a nonfamily member is involved in determining dissolution, the LLC membership units should qualify for the lack of control and lack of marketability discounts.

Recapitalization of the Family-Owned Business

A C corporation recapitalization is still possible under Sections 2701-2704, but it is expensive due to the double taxation of dividends. An LLC can be drafted in such a way as to create an interest similar to preferred stock. However, since an LLC is not a taxable entity, there would be no double taxation of the dividends.

Use of an LLC Instead of a Trust

An LLC can function in many ways just like a trust, but without the adverse estate and income tax consequences. If a trust accumulates income, it will be subject to the 39.6 percent marginal tax bracket once it has $7,500 of taxable income. An LLC will pass through all of its income to the members, who may be in a lower income tax bracket. Also, the donor can retain interests in the LLC without causing all the assets in the LLC to be included in his or her estate, per the Section 2036 retained interest rules. Finally, an LLC may be changed to real-locate interests, while a trust would be irrevocable.

The use of an LLC may be a valuable new tool for estate planners and other advisors to closely held business owners. However, as with any new estate tax planning device, it must be used carefully. Both the potential tax benefits—and the potential tax costs—should be evaluated when considering the use of an LLC in an estate plan.

Comparing the LLC to the S Corporation

An S corporation may continue in perpetuity and is not subject to the fixed termination date imposed on LLCs in many states. The possibility of an inopportune termination may be of significance to a family-owned entity that may plan to continue through multiple generations.

From a nontaxation standpoint, S corporation shareholders unquestionably enjoy limited liability in all states; however, there are serious concerns about the limited liability protection that will be afforded LLCs doing business in states without LLC statutes (rapidly approaching approval in all 50 states, as of this writing).

An S corporation clearly may use the cash method of accounting, while an LLC with nonmanager members may be required to use the accrual method of accounting.

S corporations have flexibility concerning restrictions on the transferability of their stock, and there is no risk of dissolution on the occurrence of the death, disability, bankruptcy, retirement, or resignation of a shareholder. Many LLCs must restrict the transferability of their interests and provide for dissolution upon the occurrence of certain events. The consent requirements to transfer interests and to continue the business upon the occurrence of an event of dissolution may not be feasible.

The taxation of S corporations may be simpler in many situations than the taxation of LLCs. Because an S corporation may have only one class of stock, its items of income, loss and gain, and deductions are shared pro rata. Thus, the complexities associated with special allocations, available to an LLC, are avoided with an S corporation.

Changing the Form of the Business from Taxable to Pass-Through

An existing C corporation that meets the requirements of an S corporation can make an S election tax-free (although undistributed earnings and profits may eliminate the benefit). Because an LLC is taxed as a partnership, the tax-free-reorganization provisions will not apply to the conversion of a C corporation to a partnership or to an LLC. The conversion involves a liquidation of the C corporation, followed by the formation of a partnership or an LLC. The C corporation will be subject to tax on any appreciation in its assets, and each shareholder will be taxed on the excess of the fair market value of his or her share of the distributed assets over the stock basis. This double taxation means an S election is the only viable option for pass-through taxation to most C corporations.

The major disadvantage of the S corporation when converted from C corporation status is that any gain the corporation recognizes within the 10 postconversion years (i.e., the built-in gain) is taxed to the extent the asset giving rise to the gain or income was owned at the conversion date. Not only is the corporation subject to the built-in gains tax on these items, but also the gain or income flows through to the shareholders net of corporate-level tax paid. This creates near double-level tax to the corporation and to its shareholders. Generally, C corporations converting to S status will want to know the fair market value of each of their assets and their stock as of the date of the conversion. That becomes the property's basis for calculating taxable gains after the 10-year wait.

Other tax disadvantages of the conversion to S corporation status are that carry over tax attributes are generally lost (but may be available for built-in gains purposes). And, there may be a LIFO inventory method recapture tax.

The LLC is a unique entity that presents opportunities for innovative and flexible tax planning. Under present entity classification rules, LLCs can be structured to receive partnership tax treatment and may avoid many of the disadvantages associated with using other types of entities. There are, however, tax and state law uncertainties involving the use of this relatively new entity. Some states, for example, tax LLCs at corporate rates and others subject LLCs to franchise taxes. It is uncertain how much flexibility can be built into the structure while still maintaining pass-through status. Until all states have enacted statutes recognizing LLCs, limited liability is not assured for multistate operations. S corporations may continue to be the preferred form of doing business for many taxpayers because limited liability is certain and the applicable tax rules are familiar, predictable, and, in many cases, simpler.

LLCs are gaining more flexibility as state laws change to accommodate them—in order to aid in the formation of more small businesses. It is not yet clear whether LLCs are subject to the laws of the state in which they are organized or to the laws of the state in which their real estate is located, for example. Under many of the new laws, LLCs would be able to have only one member, there would be a choice between elected management or management by members, voting interests could be transferred with less than unanimous consent if the operating agreement so stipulated, and continuity of life of the LLC in the event of death could occur with less than unanimous consent if the operating agreement so stipulated.

Valuation Issues

In the valuation of the ownership interest of the pass-through entity, the central valuation issues are two-fold: First, is there an incremental value attributable to the income tax advantages of the pass-through status? If so, how can this incremental value be accounted for in the valuation process? Second, if the value of the pass-through entity is arrived at by comparison to the valuation characteristics of nonpass-through entities, what adjustments are necessary?

Business Enterprise Value

If the purpose of the valuation is to estimate the fair market value of a controlling interest in the pass-through entity for buying, selling, or merging the company, the company's tax attributes may have little or no impact on value. If the most likely buyer is a C corporation, then the C corporation will be unwilling to pay for the pass-through entity's income tax benefits, which are not available to it by definition of its being a C corporation. Generally, especially in appraisals for transaction purposes, valuation methods using pretax earnings fundamentals are used, because it is the buyer's tax status that is relevant—not the historical tax status of the selling company.

Valuation of Minority Interests

If the business interest being appraised is a minority ownership interest—that is, the appraisal of an ownership interest not having the prerogatives of control—then a direct comparison with values of other minority interests is the most appropriate method of valuation. As discussed earlier in this book, the prices at which the daily transactions in minority ownership interests of publicly traded companies occur offer guidance for the valuation of minority interests.

When the direct comparison method is applicable, the capitalization of owner's distribution method is usually used. However, direct comparison with other minority interests is not always an appropriate method (for any of a variety of reasons, such as a lack of publicly traded guideline companies), so a discounted economic income method should be considered.

Capitalization of Owner's Distribution Method

Of course, most publicly traded companies are not pass-through entities, making a direct comparison difficult. For pass-through entities, there exists in the public market a comparative subset that can be very useful for the valuation of minority interests. This group is made up of publicly traded limited partnerships (PLPs). PLPs are listed on stock exchanges and the Nasdaq over-the-counter quotation service. Traditionally, PLPs were used to finance oil and gas projects, real estate ventures, and natural resource exploration and development. However, the Tax Reform Act of 1986 and the repeal of the General Utilities doctrine triggered a rash of PLPs between 1985 and 1987—in a wide variety of industries.

Because Congress feared a wholesale conversion of corporations into partnerships, the Revenue Act of 1987 decreed that new publicly traded partnerships would be taxed as corporations. Existing PLPs were given a 10-year tax holiday. This stopped virtually all new PLP issuances beginning in 1988. However, a limited number of PLPs still exist. As partnerships, they have similar flow-through tax treatment of income as do pass-through entities, thus making them useful for comparative valuation purposes in the appraisal of pass-through entity interests. Unfortunately, the limited number of PLPs results in no PLPs or only one or two in many industry categories. As stated earlier, the majority of PLPs are still in such industries as natural resources and real estate. For those industries, such as forest products, where PLPs exist, they provide good comparative valuation guidance for pass-through entities.

Two sources of data on PLPs are the *Stanger Report* and the *Realty Stock Review.* Each publication publishes performance summaries for publicly traded limited partnerships, including listings by industry categories.

When using PLPs as valuation guidelines, the appraiser should be aware of several caveats. First, many publicly traded partnerships have multitier distribution policies calling for a large percentage of income (often 95 percent) to be paid to the limited partners for a specific length of time, followed by a change in the distribution policy in favor of the general partners. It is important to carefully read the partnership agreement and to be aware of the distribution policy, especially when applying the PLPs' dividend yields to shareholder distributions in the valuation of a pass-through entity.

If the only appropriate guideline companies are C corporations, then the appraiser is faced with deciding how to apply empirical market data derived from C corporations to the pass-through entity's fundamentals. The analyst should keep in mind the specific tax-related and business-related characteristics of the pass-through entity that is the subject of the valuation assignment. Often, the business-related characteristics (such as limited life and limited transferability) are considered as a separate step in the valuation process. There are three alternatives to quantifying the tax-related characteristics of the pass-through entity when using C corporation market data:

1. Apply the statutory C corporation income tax rate to the pass-through entity's earnings and apply price/earnings (P/E) multiples derived from the C corporation guideline analysis.

    This procedure does not recognize the income tax advantages accruing to the owner of the pass-through entity interest—from the positive differential between the highest corporate marginal income tax rate and the maximum marginal income tax rate for individuals. Some appraisers take this approach and add a premium to the indicated values to capture the economic advantage of pass-through entity status.

2. Capitalize the pass-through entity income (before taxes to owners) by applying guideline company P/E multiples.

    This procedure does not recognize the pass-through entity owners' exposure to taxes on the income that they don't receive in distributions from the company. It further suffers from a classic apples-to-oranges comparative flaw in its application of an after-tax-derived multiple being applied to a pre-tax earnings stream.

3. The third procedure is to apply the pass-through entity owner's highest personal income tax rate to the earnings and apply after-tax multiples derived from the guideline (C corporation) companies.

    This approach captures the economic benefit that accrues to the pass-through entities from the lower personal income tax rates. However, such a capitalization of earnings fails to capture the pass-through entity's ability to distribute earnings on a tax-free basis.

To capture the incremental value attributable to the tax advantages of the pass-through entity, one must capitalize owners' distributions. The capitalization of dividends or owners' distributions is given relatively minor weight in most minority interest valuations of C corporations. Ultimately, whether a C corporation or a pass-through entity, dividends are possible only as a result of earnings. In the valuation of a minority ownership interest, actual dividends—rather than dividend-paying capacity—are relevant, since the minority interest owner cannot force the payment of dividends, regardless of how much dividend-paying capacity the company has. Since many closely held C corporations either don't pay dividends or pay only minimal dividends because of double taxation on dividends, the capitalization of dividends generally receives relatively less weight than other earnings-based valuation methods. It should be noted, however, that for investors owning a nonmarketable minority interest position in a closely held C corporation, dividends *do* represent the only return the investor is able to realize.

However, the typical pass-through entity distributes a portion of earnings to its owners. In addition, it is the pass-through entity's ability to distribute proceeds on a tax-free basis (i.e., only taxed at one level—at the personal tax rate) that is at the crux of the entity's incremental value relative to the C corporation, as shown in Exhibit 22–1. Capitalizing the owners' distributions captures the incremental value reflected by both the difference in corporate and individual income tax rates and the elimination of double taxation. If a pass-through entity distributes all its earnings, this advantage can result in a 51 percent higher after-tax cash flow at the owner's level (see Exhibit 22–1). Thus, when valuing a pass-through entity or an interest in it, the capitalization of owners' distributions method should receive a relatively greater proportion of the total weight given to earnings-based methods than is appropriate when valuing a C corporation or an interest in it.

Estimation of Appropriate Distribution Rate

If guideline companies are C corporations, dividend yields are inappropriate to apply to the pass-through entity's distributions. Once again, PLPs provide useful guideline data. Ideally, specific PLPs or LPs in the specific industry should be used, if available. If the subject company operates in an industry in which there are no PLPs, a more diverse industry group may have to be used or the universe of available PLPs and LPs examined and used as an index.

The appraiser may want to compare the payout ratios of the PLPs with the subject company's payout ratio in selecting an appropriate rate at which to capitalize the owners' distributions from the subject company. Current, as well as average, distributions, or both, may be capitalized depending on which best represents the expected future distributions of the subject company.

If the subject pass-through entity is only distributing earnings sufficient to cover income taxes, then the capitalization of owners' distributions may not be a meaningful approach to value. Arguably, if a pass-through entity distributes earnings in addition to those necessary to pay taxes, those earnings only (total distribution less that portion of distributions necessary to pay taxes) should be capitalized. However, PLPs usually report only total distributions without reporting those distributions made to meet owners' taxes, making comparative analyses difficult except on a total distribution basis.

Discounted Economic Income Method

Often, a discounted economic income method is used in the appraisal of controlling interests. In such appraisals, the potential or hypothetical buyer will not pay for the pass-through entity's income tax advantages if they are not expected to continue in the future. However, if a discounted economic income method is being used in the appraisal of a minority interest, or the pass-through entity's status of the company is expected to continue in the future, then one approach is to apply the highest applicable personal tax rate to the taxable income and calculate net free cash flow. It is appropriate to select a discount rate as discussed in Chapter 9.

To capture the avoidance of double income taxation on net cash flow within this valuation framework, one must calculate the future income tax savings that would accrue to the pass-through entity because of its status. These income tax savings should then be present valued at a discount rate sufficient to reflect the risks that:

1. Future distributions may be insufficient to cover taxes.
2. The pass-through entity may lose its status.
3. The impact of tax legislation relative to personal tax rates may change.

These risks would seem to imply an equity rate of return as the appropriate present value discount rate.

In estimating the appropriate present value discount rate applicable to the net cash flow of a pass-through entity, the appraiser needs to consider whether the pass-through entity status of the subject company increases its cost of capital. The company's cost of debt capital may be adversely impacted because some banks are reluctant to lend to pass-through entities because of their distribution policies. A pass-through entity's cost of equity capital may be affected by its more circumscribed sources of capital—restricted by both number of investors (owners) and type. This increased cost of capital may offset any value increment from the present value of future income tax benefits.

Other Valuation Issues

The above methods of estimating value have attempted to explicitly deal with the incremental economic value of pass-through entities, which stems from the different income tax rates paid by a pass-through entity compared to a C corporation. But the appraiser must take into consideration some other characteristics of pass-through entities and their implications on value. Earlier in this chapter, we listed a number of tax-related advantages and disadvantages of pass-through entities as well as business concerns for pass-through entities. These characteristics need to be examined in the valuation of each pass-through entity to determine whether there are risks specific to the subject company that are not reflected in the comparative valuation methods discussed above. Specific factors to analyze are the outlook for continuation of the pass-through entity status; the proportion of earnings paid out both currently and prospectively (examine the historical record, capital needs, and management intentions); owner agreements; and the categories of potential buyers (of the entire company or the interest). These specific risks need to be considered in appraising a pass-through entity. These additional risks can be taken into account either in specific discounts or in the valuation multiples or capitalization rates used.

As an example, what would be the impact (presumably negative) of a pass-through entity paying out distributions insufficient to meet the owners' income tax obligations? Typically, distributions are set to meet the income tax obligations of the owner with the highest tax rate. Pass-through entities typically have strong cash flows, making this scenario unlikely. If it was anything but a short-term aberration, there would be little advantage to pass-through entity status, and owners would presumably act to disqualify the election. A more likely scenario that the appraiser may encounter is that distributions are made and then loaned back to the corporation by the owners in order to meet, for example, a large, one-time capital expenditure requirement. This avoids income tax shortfalls for shareholders and also increases their basis in the stock.

Lack of Marketability

A lack of marketability discount is still applicable to a pass-through entity having no ready market for its securities. However, several additional factors need to be considered in estimating the appropriate level of such a discount. The valuation discount may be lower because dividends or distributions are more likely to be paid by a pass-through entity. In fact, the typical pass-through entity may be distributing a large portion of its earnings. On the other hand, the marketability discount for stock of a pass-through entity that is not paying out sufficient distributions to cover the income tax obligations of its shareholders may be significantly increased. Furthermore, pass-through entities may be subject to greater limitations than C corporations with respect to their ability to continue to operate as a going concern (continuity of life) and to the transferability of the ownership interest (which may require approval of other owners).

Summary

The advantages and disadvantages of the pass-through form of business lead to the following important business concerns:

1. The articles of organization of the pass-through entity may significantly affect the rights, privileges, and risks of ownership and, hence, the value of ownership.
2. The pool of hypothetical willing buyers (i.e., the marketability of the subject business) may be limited because of the restrictions on ownership of partnership interests and S corporations and the lack of legislative history regarding LLC owners' rights.
3. The value of ownership of a pass-through entity is not only affected by its tax attributes. Other attributes such as its ability to continue in operation and the restrictions on the transferability of ownership can impact its value.

Bibliography

Banoff, Sheldon I. "New Ruling Adds Further Encouragement for Large Firms to Form LLCs." *Journal of Taxation,* July 1994, pp. 12–17.

_____; Richard M. Lipton, and Burton W. Kanter. "LLC Members: More Like General or Limited Partners?;" *Journal of Taxation,* June 1994, p. 380.

Barragato, Charles A. "The Final S Corporation Single-Class-of-Stock Regulations." *CPA Journal,* May 1993, pp. 46–49.

Berg, Mark E. "Pass-Through Entities." *Journal of S Corporation Taxation,* Summer 1993, pp. 84–91.

Brenman, Lawrence H. "Service Businesses Switch to LLC." *Journal of Partnership Taxation,* Summer 1994, pp. 167–74.

Burkhard, James R. "Final Regulations Simplify S Corporation One-Class-Of-Stock Rule." *Journal of Taxation of Investments,* Spring 1993, pp. 220–30.

Buss, David B. "LLCs Still Beat S Corps Despite IRS's Reversal." *Practical Accountant,* January 1995, pp. 52–53.

Cassiere, George G. "The Value of S-Corp Election—The C-Corp Equivalency Model." *Business Valuation Review,* June 1994, pp. 84–91.

Clariday, Mary J. "The Limited Liability Company: An S Corporation Alternative or Replacement?" *Journal of S Corporation Taxation,* Winter 1993, pp. 202–25.

Clolery, Paul. "LLPs/LLCs: Bulletproofing Your Firm." *Practical Accountant,* September 1994, pp. 24–32.

Condren, Gary. "S Corporations and Corporate Taxes." *Business Valuation Review,* December 1993, pp. 168–71.

Duffy, Robert E., and George L. Johnson. "Valuation of 'S' Corporations Revisited: The Impact of the Life of an 'S' Election under Varying Growth and Discount Rates." *Business Valuation Review,* December 1993, pp. 155–67.

Dunn, William J., and Samuel P. Starr. "Prop. Regs. on Built-In Gains Tax Provide Long-Awaited Guidance for S Corporations." *Journal of Taxation,* April 1993, pp. 202–8.

Eastland, S. Stacy. "Family Limited Partnerships: Non-Transfer Tax Benefits." *Probate & Property,* March/April 1993, pp. 11–13.

Engel, Barry S., and Ronald L. Rudman. "Family Limited Partnerships: New Meaning for 'Limited.'" *Trusts & Estates,* July 1993, pp. 46–48.

Englebrecht, Ted D.; Dana M. LeFever; and Steven C. Colburn. "Shareholder Guarantees of an S Corporation: Review and Analysis of the Basis Dilemma." *Taxes,* February 1993, pp. 114–25.

Hodgman, David R. "Grantor Retained Annuity Trusts and S Corporation Stock." *Trusts & Estates,* December 1993, pp. 38–58.

Horwood, Richard M. "Limited Liability Companies Provide New Planning Options." *Estate Planning,* September/October 1994, pp. 266–74.

_____, and Jeffrey A. Zaluda. "Asset Protection by Design." Tax Management Estates, *Gifts and Trusts Journal,* July 14, 1994, pp. 119–29.

Ives, H. Bryan, III. "Valuation Discounts for Partnership and LLC Member Interests." *Journal of Limited Liability Companies,* Winter 1994, pp. 110–17.

Johnson, Linda M., and Rodger A. Bolling. "Bringing an S Corporation Back to Life." *Practical Accountant,* June 1993, pp. 20–31.

Karlinsky, Stewart S., and Hughlene Burton. "S Corporation Current Developments: S Corporation Eligibility and Elections, Operations, Reorganizations and Proposed Legislation." *Tax Adviser,* October 1994, pp. 629–36.

Kato, Kelly. "Valuation of 'S' Corporations—Discounted Cash Flow Method." *Business Valuation Review,* December 1990, pp. 117–22.

Lemons, Bruce N., and Richard D. Blau. "Significant Issues May Remain for S Corporation Partners Despite IRS's Newest Ruling." *Journal of Taxation,* September 1994, pp. 132–36.

_____; Richard D. Blau; and Thomas P. Rohman. "Final Basis and Distribution Regs. Provide Additional Guidance for S Corporations." *Journal of Taxation,* April 1994, pp. 226–30.

Looney, Stephen R. "Important Developments Affecting S Corporations Since the Tax Reform Act of 1986." *Journal of S Corporation Taxation,* Spring 1993, pp. 312–44.

Pluth, Robert R., Jr. "The Limited Liability Company: A New Alternative." *Trusts & Estates,* September 1994, pp. 14–17.

Price, Charles E. "Tax Aspects of Limited Liability Companies." *Journal of Accountancy,* September 1992, pp. 48–52.

Shackelford, Aaron L. "Valuation of 'S' Corporations." *Business Valuation Review,* December 1988, pp. 159–62.

Starr, Sam. "A Better-Looking S Corp." *Inc.,* August 1994, pp. 29–30.

Steele, H. John; Allan J. Weiner; and Todd D. Snyder. "LLCs: The Death Knell for the Limited Partnership?" *Stanger Report,* February 1995, pp. 2–4.

Ware, Robert C. "The Limited Liability Company." *Life & Health Insurance Sales,* January 1994, pp. 85 92.

Part VI

Valuing Intangible Assets and Intellectual Property

Chapter 23

Identification of Intangible Assets

The analysis and appraisal of intangible assets and intellectual properties is a complex topic. This topic will be discussed in the next three chapters. This chapter will present the issues related to the identification of intangible assets. Chapter 24 will discuss the approaches and methods related to the valuation of intangible assets. And Chapter 25 will review the issues related to the remaining useful life analysis of intangible assets.

The following introductory topics will be presented in this chapter:

1.   The definition of an intangible asset.
2.   The distinctions between tangible assets and intangible assets, real estate and personal property, and intangible assets and intellectual properties.
3.   The common categories of intangible assets and intellectual properties.
4.   The professional standards that relate to intangible asset appraisals.
5.   The purpose and objectives of an intangible asset appraisal.
6.   The appropriate content of an intangible asset valuation report.

This chapter will also present a brief introduction to the basic intangible asset valuation approaches. Each valuation approach will be described in greater detail in Chapter 24.

Definition of an Intangible Asset

There are numerous legal, accounting, or taxation related definitions of the term *intangible asset*. Before conducting an intangible asset appraisal, the analyst should perform adequate research to ascertain if a particular definition is appropriate to the subject intangible asset analysis, given:

1.   The particular purpose and objective of the appraisal.
2.   The particular jurisdiction or venue in which the assets exist.

Appropriate professional advisors (e.g., lawyers, accountants, etc.) may have to be consulted in this research. For purposes of this discussion, we will focus on the definitional questions that are relevant to the economic analysis and valuation of intangible assets. Accordingly, from this economic valuation perspective, there are two definitional questions the analyst should consider:

1.   What economic phenomena are necessary for an intangible asset?
2.   What economic phenomena manifest—or are indicative of—value in an intangible asset?

Economic Phenomena That Result in an Intangible Asset

For an intangible asset to exist from a valuation or economic perspective, it must possess certain attributes. Some of these requisite attributes include the following:

1.   It must be subject to specific identification and recognizable description.
2.   It must be subject to legal existence and protection.
3.   It must be subject to the right of private ownership, and this private ownership must be legally transferable.

4. There must be some tangible evidence or manifestation of the existence of the intangible asset (e.g., a contract or a license or a registration document).

5. It must have been created or have come into existence at an identifiable time or as the result of an identifiable event.

6. It must be subject to being destroyed or to a termination of existence at an identifiable time or as the result of an identifiable event.

In other words, a specific bundle of legal rights (and other natural properties) must be associated with the existence of any intangible asset.

Economic Phenomena That Do Not Result in an Intangible Asset

Economic phenomena that do not meet the specific attribute tests described previously do not result in identifiable intangible assets. Some economic phenomena are descriptive or expository in nature. They describe conditions that contribute to the existence of—and value of—identified intangible assets. But these phenomena do not possess the requisite elements to distinguish themselves as intangible assets. Such "descriptive" economic phenomena—that do not qualify as identifiable intangible assets—may include:

1. Market share.
2. High profitability.
3. Lack of regulation (or a regulated environment).
4. Monopoly position.
5. Market potential.

However, these descriptive conditions may indicate the subject identifiable intangible assets do, indeed, have substantial economic value.

Economic Phenomena That Indicate Value in an Intangible Asset

For an intangible asset to have a quantifiable value from an economic analysis or appraisal perspective, it must possess certain additional attributes. Some of these additional requisite attributes include the following:

1. It must generate some measurable amount of economic benefit to its owner; this economic benefit could be in the form of an income increment or of a cost decrement.

2. This economic benefit may be measured in any of several ways, including net income or net operating income or net cash flow, etc.

3. It must enhance the value of other assets with which it is associated; the other assets may include tangible personal property and tangible real estate.

Clearly there may be a substantial distinction between the legal existence of an intangible asset and the economic value of an intangible asset. An example of this situation would be the new registration of a legally binding and enforceable patent that, upon creation, is immediately and permanently locked in the corporate vault. If the patent is never used in the production of, or in the protection of, income, then it has no economic value—even though it has legal existence.

Distinction between Tangible and Intangible Assets

A tangible asset generally possesses all the attributes previously discussed with regard to an intangible asset, in addition to the following attributes:

1. It must have physical existence and substantial form.
2. It must be capable of being touched and seen.

A tangible asset may be either immobile (affixed to the land) or mobile (not affixed to the land). Tangible assets are often necessary to realize the value (or the income-producing capacity) of intangible assets. For example, computer hardware (a tangible asset) is typically necessary to effectively exploit the positive attributes of computer software (an intangible asset). Intangible assets, in addition to possessing discrete economic value of and by themselves, often enhance the value of the tangible assets with which they are associated. As will be discussed later, this incremental value contributed by intangible assets to tangible assets is sometimes called the in-use value or the going-concern value elements of tangible asset value.

Four Categories of Property

For economic analysis and valuation purposes, it is often necessary to distinguish between tangible and intangible assets, as well as between realty and personalty assets. These distinctions are important for a variety of accounting, taxation, legal, and financial reasons. In fact, for valuation purposes, all assets or property types may be categorized into the following four groups:

1. Tangible real estate.
2. Intangible real property.
3. Tangible personal property.
4. Intangible personal property.

Each of these four categories of assets will be described and illustrated next.

Tangible Real Estate.   Real estate is the physical land and appurtenances affixed to the land, such as structures. Real estate is immobile and tangible. The legal definition of real estate includes land and all things that are a natural part of the land (e.g., tree, minerals), as well as all things that are attached to it by people (e.g., buildings, site improvements). All permanent building attachments (e.g., plumbing, electrical wiring, heating systems), as well as built-in items (e.g., cabinets, elevators), are usually considered part of the real estate. Real estate includes all attachments to the land, both below and above the ground.

Intangible Real Property.   Intangible real property includes all interest, benefits, and rights inherent in the ownership of physical real estate. A right or interest in real estate is also referred to as an estate. Specifically, an estate in land is the degree, nature, or extent of interest that a person has in it. Interests vary, so real property is said to include a "bundle of rights" that are inherent in the ownership of real estate. Real property ownership rights include, among others:

1. The right to use real estate.
2. The right to sell it.
3. The right to lease it.
4. The right to enter it.
5. The right to give it away.
6. The ability to choose to exercise all or none of these rights.

The bundle of rights is often compared to a bundle of sticks, with each stick representing a distinct and separate right or interest.

Tangible Personal Property.   Tangible personal property includes movable items of property that are not permanently affixed to, or part of, the real estate. Tangible personal property is not endowed with the rights of real property ownership. Examples of tangible personal property include furniture and fixtures, tools and dies, machinery and equipment, office and data processing equipment, trucks and automobiles, and so forth.

It is sometimes difficult to determine whether a particular asset should be considered tangible personal property or real estate. A fixture is an article that was once personal property but has since been installed or attached to the land or building in a rather permanent manner; it is regarded as part of the real estate. Although fixtures are real estate, trade fixtures are not. A trade fixture, also called a chattel fixture, is an article that is owned and attached to a rented space or building by a tenant and used in conducting business.

Intangible Personal Property.   Intangible personal property includes the two attributes of:

1. Not having substantial physical form or substance (at least to the extent that the value of the property is not dependent on the physical form or substance).
2. Not being physically attached to the land or other real estate.

Accordingly, intangible personal property is mobile. As with intangible real property, intangible personal property typically encompasses a specific bundle of legal rights, benefits, and interest. Other than real estate-related intangibles (e.g., leases, easements, etc.) most intangible assets generally fall into the category of intangible personal property.

Common Categories of Intangible Assets

Generally, appraisers and economists will categorize individual intangible assets into several distinct categories. This categorization of intangible assets is used for general asset identification and classification purposes. Intangible assets in each category are generally similar in nature and in function. Also, intangible assets are grouped in the same category when similar valuation methods apply to that group of assets.

A common categorization of intangible assets is presented as follows:

1. Technology-related (e.g., engineering drawings).
2. Customer-related (e.g., customer lists).
3. Contract-related (e.g., favorable supplier contracts).

4. Data processing-related (e.g., computer software).
5. Human capital-related (e.g., a trained and assembled workforce).
6. Marketing-related (e.g., trademarks and trade names).
7. Location-related (e.g., leasehold interests).
8. Goodwill-related (e.g., going-concern value).

Common Categories of Intellectual Properties

There is a specialized classification of intangible assets called intellectual properties. Intellectual properties manifest all the legal existence and economic value attributes of other intangible assets. However, because of their special status, intellectual properties enjoy special legal recognition and protection.

Unlike other intangible assets, which may be created in the normal course of business operations, intellectual properties are created by human intellectual and/or inspirational activity. Such activity (although not always planned) is specific and conscious. And such creativity can be attributed to the activity of identified, specific individuals. Because of this unique creation process, intellectual properties are generally registered under, and protected by, specific federal and state statutes.

Like other intangible assets, intellectual properties are generally grouped into like categories. The intellectual properties in each category are generally similar in nature, feature, method or creation, and legal protection. Likewise, similar valuation methods and economic analysis procedures would apply to the intellectual properties in each category.

A common categorization of intellectual properties is presented as follows:

1. Creative (e.g., copyrights).
2. Innovative (e.g., patents).

Motivations to Conduct an Intangible Asset Appraisal

While there are numerous individual reasons for conducting an intangible asset appraisal, typically all of these individual reasons can be grouped into a few categories of motivations:

1. Transaction pricing and structuring, for either the sale or license (i.e., transfer pricing) of intangible assets.
2. Financing securitization and collateralization, for both cash flow-based financing and asset-based financing.
3. Taxation planning and compliance, with regard to amortization, abandonment, charitable contribution, gifting, intercompany transfer pricing, and other federal taxation matters and with regard to state and local ad valorem taxation matters.
4. Management information and planning, including business value enhancement purposes, estate planning, and other long-range strategic issues.

5. Bankruptcy and reorganization analysis, including the value of the estate in bankruptcy, debtor in possession financing, traditional refinancing, restructuring, and assessment of the impact of proposed reorganization plans.

6. Litigation support and dispute resolution, including infringement, fraud, lender liability, and a wide range of deprivation-related reasons (e.g., eminent domain, property damages, infringement, etc.).

There are many requirements for, and opportunities related to, intangible asset appraisals. The following list briefly describes some reasons for conducting such an appraisal:

1. *Purchase price allocation for financial accounting purposes.* The promulgated accounting authority for the recording of purchased intangible assets as part of the purchase of a going-concern business is Accounting Principles Board Opinion Numbers 16 and 17.

2. *Purchase price allocation for tax accounting purposes.* Internal Revenue Code Section 1060 dictates the tax accounting for intangible assets, acquired as part of the purchase of the assets of a going-concern business. Internal Revenue Code Section 197 allows for the amortization of most acquired intangible assets.

3. *Preacquisition assessment of value.* After the question, "Should we buy this company?" the questions of "How much should we pay?" and "How should we structure the deal?" are the key issues in acquisition planning and execution. If intangible assets are an important component of the acquisition target, then a valuation will help answer many or all of these questions.

4. *The purchase of selected assets.* The acquisition strategy may involve only the purchase of particular intangible assets such as product designs, patents, special processes, proprietary technology, and so forth.

5. *Obtaining financing.* Many financial institutions are willing to consider the value of cash flow-generating intangible assets in their lending decisions. If so, they typically require an independent appraisal for asset-based financing and for cash flow-based financing, or for intangible assets that are pledged as collateral against loan commitments or lines of credit.

6. *Bankruptcy and reorganization analysis.* An appraisal of the intangible assets of a debtor may be necessary in the assessment of a proposed reorganization plan, the quantification of a secured creditor collateral position, the identification of any cancellation of debt income, or for other bankruptcy-related accounting and taxation considerations.

7. *Establishment of appropriate royalties for licensee or licensor.* An intangible asset appraisal is essential when determining appropriate royalty rates associated with the use, license, or franchise of patents, technology, trademarks or trade names, musical or literary creations, and so forth.

8. *Establishment of fair intercompany transfer pricing.* Internal Revenue Code Section 482, related to the allocation of income and deductions among taxpayers, states, "In the case of any transfer of intangible property, the income with respect to such transfer or license shall be commensurate with the income attributable to the intangible." An appraisal or economic analysis is often necessary to establish the appropriate transfer price—or royalty rate—for intangible assets transferred within a multinational taxpayer.

9. *Income taxation planning and compliance.* The appraisal of intangible assets may be necessary for substantiating a charitable contribution deduction or an abandonment loss deduction, for establishing the basis for amortization, for estimating built-in gain (BIG) tax on the conversion from C corporation to S corporation status, and for proving the reasonableness of royalty/dividend payments.
10. *Ad valorem property taxes.* The appraisal of intangible assets is an important part of valuing a taxable entity under the unitary method or under the summation method of property tax valuation.
11. *Litigation support and dispute resolutions.* Intangible asset appraisals are often required in infringement matters, breach of contract matters, tortious damages, and other types of commercial litigation.
12. *Business formation and dissolution.* When businesses or professional practices merge, the owners' equity allocation is often a function of relative contribution of intangible assets (e.g., clients, patients). When businesses or professional practices dissolve, the settlement payments often relate to the value of intangible assets (e.g., clients, patients) transferred from the business.

Professional Standards Related to Intangible Asset Appraisals

As is the case with respect to the valuation of business entities and business interests, there are several sets of professional standards that intangible asset appraisers should be familiar with, including:

1. The Uniform Standards of Professional Appraisal Practice (USPAP).
2. The American Society of Appraisers (ASA) Business Valuation Standards.

A brief overview of these two important sets of professional standards follows.

Uniform Standards of Professional Appraisal Practice

As has already been discussed, in 1987, The Appraisal Foundation promulgated, and its nine founding appraisal organization members adopted, USPAP. An outline of the principal content of USPAP follows:

1. The prefatory material contains, among other things, an ethics provision, a competency provision, and a departure provision, which apply to all appraisers.
2. Standards 1 through 6 deal with real estate appraisal.
3. Standard 3 deals with reviewing an appraisal. While Standard 3 is oriented to real estate, it is applicable to a business valuation or intangible asset appraisal with only minor modification.
4. Standards 7 and 8 deal with personal property appraisal.
5. Standards 9 and 10 deal with business appraisal and intangible asset appraisal.

ASA Business Valuation Standards

As has already been discussed, in 1992, the ASA, through its Business Valuation Committee, completed a series of Standards for Business Valuation. An outline of the principal content of these standards follows:

1. Business Valuation Standard I: Terminology.
2. Business Valuation Standard II: Full Written Business Valuation Report.
3. Business Valuation Standard III: General Performance Requirements for Business Valuation.
4. Business Valuation Standard IV: Asset-Based Approach to Business Valuation.
5. Business Valuation Standard V: The Guideline Company Valuation Method.
6. Business Valuation Standard VI: Market Approach to Business Valuation.
7. Business Valuation Standard VII: Income Approach to Business Valuation.
8. Business Valuation Standard VIII: Reaching a Conclusion of Value.
9. Business Valuation Standard IX: Financial Statement Adjustments.

Many of these ASA business valuation standards are directly applicable to an intangible asset appraisal. The ASA Business Valuation Standards are included in Appendix C of this book.

Purpose and Objective of the Appraisal

The objective of an intangible asset appraisal describes the appraisal assignment. The objective of an intangible asset appraisal should clearly articulate at least the following issues:

1. What specific asset is being appraised.
2. What ownership interest (or what bundle of legal rights) related to that asset is being appraised.
3. What standard or definition of value is being estimated.
4. What is the "as of" date of the appraisal.

The purpose of the appraisal describes who the audience (i.e., the expected reader) of the appraisal is and what decision (if any) will be influenced by the appraisal. The purpose of the appraisal should clearly indicate, at least, the following.

1. Why the appraisal is being performed.
2. What is the intended use of the appraisal.
3. Who is expected to rely on the appraisal.

It is highly recommended that both the purpose and objective of the appraisal should be agreed on, in writing, between the appraiser and the client before the start of the intangible asset appraisal.

Alternative Standards of Value

The term *standard of value* may be considered to be synonymous with the term *definition of value*. The standard of—or definition of—value means: what type of value is being estimated? The alternative standards of value generally answer the question: value to whom? That question is important because the same asset has different values to different parties.

With regard to intangible assets specifically, some of the more common alternative standards of value include:

1. Fair market value—what a typical (hypothetical) willing buyer will pay to a typical (hypothetical) willing seller, with neither being under undue influence to transact.
2. Fair value—the amount that will fairly compensate an owner who was involuntarily deprived of the benefit of an asset where there is neither a willing buyer nor a willing seller; this is primarily a legal concept.
3. Market value—the most probable price an asset should bring in a competitive and open market under all conditions requisite to a fair sale, the buyer and seller each acting prudently and knowledgeably, and assuming the price is not affected by undue stimulus.
4. Acquisition value—the price a particular identified buyer would be expected to pay for an asset with consideration given to any unique benefits of the asset to the identified buyer.
5. Use value—the value of an asset in a particular specified use (which may be different from the asset's current use or from the asset's highest and best use).
6. Investment value (or investor value)—the value of an asset given a particular defined set of individual investment criteria (e.g., given a definite set of internal rate of return or payback period investment criteria); this standard of value does not necessarily contemplate a sale transaction.
7. Owner value—the value of an asset to its current owner, given the owner's current use of the asset and current resources and capabilities for economically exploiting the asset; this standard of value does not necessarily contemplate a sale transaction.
8. Insurable value—the amount of insurance proceeds necessary to replace the subject asset with an asset of comparable utility, functionality, and income-producing capacity.
9. Collateral value—the amount a creditor would be willing to lend with the subject asset serving as security for the loan.
10. Ad valorem value—the value of an asset for property taxation purposes, given the statutory standards of the particular taxing jurisdiction.

The selection of the appropriate standard of value will be greatly influenced by the purpose (or intended use) of the appraisal. The selection of the appropriate standard of value, obviously, will directly impact the value estimate. It is important to emphasize that an appraiser "estimates" value—the market "determines" value.

Alternative Premises of Value

The *valuation premise* is the hypothetical set of asset transaction assumptions under which the subject intangible asset will be analyzed. The selection of the appropriate valuation premise is typically dictated by the highest and best use of the subject intangible assets.

The highest and best use of an intangible asset is the reasonably probable and legal use of the asset that is physically possible, appropriately supported, financially feasible, and that results in the highest value. The highest and best use must meet the following four criteria:

1. Legal permissibility.
2. Physical possibility.
3. Financial feasibility.
4. Maximum profitability.

Among all reasonable, alternative uses, the use of the intangible asset that yields the highest present value—after payments are made for labor, capital, and coordination—typically represents the highest and best use of the subject intangible asset. The assessment of the highest and best use of the subject intangible asset will determine which of the four alternative fundamental premises of value should be applied in the appraisal.

Virtually any type of intangible asset may be appraised under each of these following four alternative premises of value:

1. Value in continued use, as part of a mass assemblage of assets, and as part of a going-concern business enterprise; this premise contemplates the contributing value of the subject intangible asset to and from the other assets of an enterprise.
2. Value in place, as part of a mass assemblage of assets, but not in current use in the production of income, as part of a going-concern business enterprise.
3. Value in exchange, on a piecemeal basis (not part of a mass assemblage of assets), as part of an orderly disposition; this premise contemplates that the asset will enjoy normal exposure to its appropriate secondary market.
4. Value in exchange, on a piecemeal basis (not part of a mass assemblage of assets), as part of a forced liquidation; this premise contemplates that the asset will experience less than normal exposure to its appropriate secondary market.

While virtually any intangible asset may be appraised under each of these four alternative fundamental premises, the value conclusions reached under each premise, for the same asset, may be dramatically different. The appraiser will select the appropriate premise of value based on:

1. The purpose and objective of the appraisal.
2. The actual functional and economic status of the subject intangible asset.

Describing the Asset Subject to Appraisal

The description of the subject intangible asset should be complete enough to clearly identify the intangible asset to the reader of the appraisal. The description may include reference to the common categories of intangible assets and intellectual properties discussed previously. The description may identify the physical, functional, technical, or economic parameters of the subject intangible asset. The description of an intangible asset in an intangible asset appraisal serves the same informational purposes as the legal description does in a real estate appraisal.

Exhibit 23–1 lists many intangible assets that are commonly subject to economic analysis and appraisal.

Exhibit 23–1

Listing of Intangible Assets Commonly Subject to Appraisal and Economic Analysis

Advertising campaigns and programs	Goodwill	Possessory interest
Agreements	Government contracts	Prescription drug files
Airport gates and slots	Government programs	Prizes and awards
Appraisal plants	Governmental registrations	Procedural manuals
Awards and judgments	Historical documents	Production backlogs
Bank customers—deposit, loan, trust, and credit card	HMO enrollment lists	Product designs
Blueprints	Insurance expirations	Property use rights
Book libraries	Insurance in force	Proposals outstanding
Brand names	Joint ventures	Proprietary computer software
Broadcast licenses	Know-how	Proprietary processes
Buy–sell agreements	Laboratory notebooks	Proprietary products
Certificates of need	Landing rights	Proprietary technology
Chemical formulations	Leasehold estates	Publications
Claims	Leasehold interests	Purchase orders
Computer software	Literary works	Regulatory approvals
Computerized databases	Litigation awards and damages	Reputation
Contracts	Loan portfolios	Retail shelf space
Cooperative agreements	Location value	Royalty agreements
Copyrights	Management contracts	Schematics and diagrams
Credit information files	Manual databases	Securities portfolios
Customer contracts	Manuscripts	Security interests
Customer lists	Marketing and promotional materials	Shareholder agreements
Customer relationships	Masks and masters	Solicitation rights
Designs	Medical charts and records	Stock and bond instruments
Development rights	Mineral rights	Subscription lists
Distribution networks	Musical compositions	Supplier contracts
Distribution rights	Natural resources	Technical and specialty libraries
Drilling rights	Newspaper morgue files	Technical documentation
Easements	Noncompete covenants	Technology
Employment contracts	Nondiversion agreements	Technology sharing agreements
Engineering drawings	Open orders	Title plants
Environmental rights	Options, warrants, grants, rights	Trade secrets
FCC licenses	Ore deposits	Trained and assembled workforce
Favorable financing	Patent applications	Trademarks and trade names
Favorable leases	Patents—both product and process	Training manuals
Film libraries	Patterns	Unpatented technology
Food flavorings and recipes	Permits	Use rights—air, water, land
Franchise agreements	Personality contracts	Work in process
Franchise ordinances		
Going concern		

Bundle of Legal Rights Subject to Appraisal

An important step in the intangible asset valuation process is the identification of the specific bundle of legal rights subject to appraisal. According to the bundle of rights theory of valuation, complete intangible asset ownership, or title in fee, consists of a group of distinct rights. Each of these rights can be separated from the bundle and conveyed by the fee owner to other parties in perpetuity or for a limited time period.

When a right is separated from the bundle and transferred, a partial, or fractional, property interest is created. Property interests may be examined from many perspectives because the ownership, legal, economic, and financial aspects of intangible assets overlap. The ownership of intangible property interests can be divided in various ways.

Separate economic and legal interests derived from the bundle of rights are involved in many kinds of income-producing intangible assets and each of these interests is distinct in its form and content. Licensee, licensor, and sublicensee estates are created when licenses or franchises to intangible assets are conveyed in accordance with established legal procedures.

Some of the more common bundles of legal rights related to intangible assets include the following:

1. Fee simple interest.
2. Life or term estates.
3. Licensor/franchisor interests.
4. Licensee/franchisee interests.
5. Sublicensee/subfranchisee interests.
6. Reversionary interests.
7. Development rights.
8. Exploitation rights.
9. Use rights.
10. Other fractional ownership interests.

Obviously, the selection of the bundle of legal rights to be appraised will have a direct impact on the intangible asset value estimate.

Stating the Appropriate Valuation Date

The intangible asset value estimate must be "as of" a specified valuation date. The value of an intangible asset changes over time, due to both endogenous and exogenous factors. Valuation dates may be:

1. Historical—as of a previous date.
2. Contemporaneous—as of a current date.
3. Prospective—as of a future date.

Prospective valuation dates always result in hypothetical appraisals. According to the professional standards of the American Society of Appraisers, hypothetical appraisals should be clearly identified as such.

The selection of the appropriate valuation date will be a function of the purpose of the appraisal assignment and should be agreed to between the appraiser and the client.

The Form of the Valuation Report

The form of the intangible asset valuation report will be greatly influenced by the purpose of the valuation assignment. And the form should be agreed to between the appraiser and the client.

The Uniform Standards of Professional Appraisal Practice defines *report* as: "any communication, written or oral, of an appraisal, review, or consulting service ... that is transmitted to the client upon completion of assignment."[1] USPAP allows for two types of an appraisal:

---

[1] *Uniform Standards of Professional Appraisal Practice* (Washington, DC: The Appraisal Foundation, 1995), p. 8.

1. A complete appraisal, which is performed without invoking the departure provision.
2. A limited appraisal, which does invoke the departure provision.

USPAP also allows for three forms of an appraisal report:

1. A self-contained appraisal report (see USPAP Standards Rule 2-2(a)).
2. A summary appraisal report (see USPAP Standards Rule 2-2(b)).
3. A restricted appraisal report (see USPAP Standards Rule 2-2(c)).

A general discussion of business valuation reporting standards is presented in Chapter 17.

Three Approaches to Intangible Asset Valuation

Numerous methods, techniques, and analyses may be appropriate to the economic analysis and appraisal of intangible assets and intellectual properties. When appraisers consider the fundamental similarities and differences of these numerous methods, they all logically group into the three general categories of valuation analyses. These three general categories of methods—or fundamental ways of analyzing the economics of intangible assets—are often called the cost approach, the market approach (or the sales comparison approach), and the income approach.

Each of the numerous methods has the same objective: to arrive at a reasonable indication of a defined value for the subject intangible asset. Accordingly, methods that are premised on the same fundamental economic principles should be grouped together into overall valuation approaches. The three approaches to intangible asset value, collectively, encompass a broad spectrum of economic theory and of property investment concepts.

The cost approach is based on the economic principle of substitution. This basic economic principle asserts that an investor will pay no more for an investment than the cost to obtain (i.e., either purchase or construct) an investment of equal utility. For purposes of this economic principle, utility can be measured in many ways, including functionality, desirability, and so on. The availability (and the cost) of substitute investments is directly affected by shifts in the supply and demand functions with regard to the universe of substitute investments.

The market (or sales comparison) approach is based on the related economic principles of competition and equilibrium. These economic principles conclude that, in a free and unrestricted market, supply and demand factors will drive the price of an investment to a point of equilibrium. The principle of substitution also directly influences the market approach. This is because the identification and analysis of equilibrium prices for substitute investments will provide important evidence to the appraiser with regard to the indicated value for the subject investment (i.e., the subject intangible asset).

The income approach is based on the economic principle of anticipation (sometimes also called the principle of expectation). In this approach, the value of the subject investment (i.e., intangible asset) is the present value of the expected economic income to be earned from the ownership of the subject intangible asset.

As the name of this economic principle implies, the investor "anticipates" the "expected" economic income to be earned from the investment. This expectation of prospective economic income is converted to a present worth—that is, the indicated value of the subject intangible asset.

There are numerous alternative definitions of economic income. If properly analyzed, many different definitions of economic income can be analyzed to provide a reasonable indication of value for the subject intangible assets. This approach requires the appraiser to estimate the investor's required rate of return on the investment generating the prospective economic income. This required rate of return will be a function of many economic variables, including the risk—or the uncertainty—of the expected economic income.

Appraisers attempt to analyze intangible assets using all three of the basic valuation approaches in order to obtain a multidimensional perspective on the subject intangible asset. The final value estimate conclusion is typically based on a synthesis of the value indications derived from various alternative intangible asset valuation approaches and methods.

Introduction to Cost Approach Methods

Within the cost approach category, there are several groups of related methods. Each of these groups of methods uses a similar definition of the "type" of cost that is relevant to the analysis. Some of the most common types of—or definitions of—cost include the following:

1. Reproduction cost.
2. Replacement cost.
3. Creation cost.
4. Re-creation cost.

Definitions of Cost.   There are subtle but important differences in the definitions of each of these types of cost. Reproduction cost contemplates the construction of an exact replica of the subject intangible asset. Replacement cost contemplates the cost to re-create the functionality or utility of the subject intangible asset, but in a form or appearance that may be different from the actual intangible asset subject to appraisal. Creation cost considers the cost to originally create the subject intangible asset from its conceptual inception—with no guideline as a point of reference. Re-creation cost considers the cost to duplicate the subject intangible asset, assuming the owner possesses the knowledge, experience, and expertise already developed during the (actual) original creation process.

Several other definitions of cost are encompassed by the cost approach. Some analysts consider a measure of cost avoidance as a cost approach method. This method quantifies either historical or prospective costs that are avoided (i.e., not incurred) by the asset owner due to the ownership of the subject intangible asset. Some analysts consider trended historical costs as an identification of value. In this method, actual historical asset development costs are identified and quantified and then "trended" to the valuation date by an appropriate inflation-based index factor.

All cost approach methods typically include a comprehensive and all-inclusive definition of *cost*. These costs (reproduction, replacement, etc.) typically include all direct materials, labor, and overhead costs; the intangible asset developer's profit; and an entrepreneurial incentive (e.g., return on the capital employed during the intangible asset development period).

The Concept of Obsolescence within the Cost Approach.   Basic economic theory indicates that cost alone (regardless of the type of cost quantified) typically does not provide a reasonable indication of value. That is, various forms of obsolescence have to be identified, quantified, and subtracted from the cost of the intangible asset in order to estimate the value of the intangible asset. The most common forms of obsolescence include:

1. Physical deterioration.
2. Functional obsolescence.
3. Technological obsolescence.
4. Economic obsolescence.

Each of these forms of obsolescence indicates a decrease in value of the subject intangible asset due to a very specific reason. Clearly, not every intangible asset will suffer from each form of obsolescence. However, the consideration, identification, and quantification of the various forms of obsolescence (to the extent that they exist) is an important step in the cost approach valuation process.

The measure of cost (as defined by the individual method) less the measure of obsolescence (which will be greatly influenced by the type of cost methodology selected) will provide an indication of the defined value of the subject intangible asset.

Introduction to Market Approach Methods

There are somewhat fewer methods to select from within the market (sometimes called sales comparison) approach—as compared to the cost or income approaches. Nonetheless, the practical application of a market approach method is a very complex and rigorous analytical process.

There is a general systematic process—or framework—to the application of market approach methods to the valuation of intangible assets. The basic steps of this systematic process are summarized as follows:

1. Research the appropriate exchange market to obtain information on sale transactions, listings, and offers to purchase or sell guideline or comparable intangible assets that are similar to the subject intangibles—in terms of characteristics such as intangible asset type, intangible asset use, industry in which the intangible asset functions, date of sale, and so on.
2. Verify the information by confirming that the data obtained are factually accurate and that the sale or exchange transactions reflect arm's-length market considerations. This verification procedure may also elicit additional information about the current market conditions for the sale of the subject intangible asset.

3. Select relevant units of comparison (e.g., income multipliers or dollars per unit—units such as "per drawing," "per customer," "per location," and "per line of code") and develop a comparative analysis for each unit of comparison.

4. Compare guideline intangible asset sale transactions with the subject using the elements of comparison and adjust the sale price of each guideline transaction appropriately to the subject asset—or eliminate the sale transaction as a guideline for future consideration.

5. Reconcile the various value indications produced from the analysis of the guideline transactions into a single value indication or a range of values. In an imprecise market—subject to varying economics—a range of values may sometimes be a better conclusion than a single value estimate.

Introduction to the 10 Basic Elements of Comparison. There are 10 basic elements of comparison that should be considered when selecting and analyzing guideline sales (or license) transactions in the market approach valuation of an intangible asset. These 10 basic elements are summarized below:

1. The legal rights of intangible property ownership that were conveyed in the guideline transaction.
2. The existence of any special financing terms or arrangements (e.g., between the buyer and the seller).
3. Whether the elements of arm's-length sale conditions existed.
4. The economic conditions that existed in the appropriate secondary market at the time of the sale transaction.
5. The industry in which the intangible asset was—or will be—used.
6. The physical characteristics of the guideline sale assets—compared to the subject intangible assets.
7. The functional characteristics of the guideline sale assets—compared to the subject intangible assets.
8. The technological characteristics of the guideline sale assets—compared to the subject intangible assets.
9. The economic characteristics of the guideline sale assets—compared to the subject intangible assets.
10. The inclusion of other assets in the guideline sale transaction; this may include the sale of a bundle—or a portfolio—of assets that could include tangible personal property and/or real estate, as well as intangible assets.

The Reconciliation Step in the Market Approach. The reconciliation step is the last phase of any market approach valuation analysis, in which two or more value indications have been derived from guideline market data. In the reconciliation step, the appraiser summarizes and reviews the data and analyses that resulted in each of the value indications. These value indications are then resolved into a range of value or into a single value indication or a point estimate.

It is important that the appraiser consider the strengths and weaknesses of each guideline value indication derived, examining the reliability and appropriateness of the market data compiled and the analytical techniques applied.

Introduction to Income Approach Methods

There are numerous measures of economic income that may be relevant to the various income approach methods. Some of these measures of economic income include:

1. Gross or net revenues.
2. Gross income.
3. Net operating income.
4. Net income before tax.
5. Net income after tax.
6. Operating cash flow.
7. Net cash flow.
8. Several others.

Given the different measures of economic income that may be used in the income approach, an essential element in the application of this approach is to ensure that the discount rate or capitalization rate used in the analysis is derived on a basis consistent with the measure of economic income used. There are at least as many income approach valuation methods as there are measures of economic income. However, most of these methods may be grouped into several categories of methods. These categories have similar conceptual underpinnings and similar practical applications.

Categories of Income Approach Methods.   Several categories of illustrative income approach methods are introduced below:

1. Methods that quantify incremental levels of economic income (i.e., the intangible asset owner will enjoy a greater level of economic income by owning the asset as compared to not owning the asset).
2. Methods that quantify decremental levels of economic costs (i.e., the intangible asset owner will suffer a lower level of economic costs—such as otherwise required investments or operating expenses—by owning the asset as compared to not owning the asset).
3. Methods that estimate a relief from a hypothetical royalty or rental payment (i.e., the amount of a royalty or rental payment that the intangible asset owner would be willing to pay to a third party to obtain the use of—and the rights to—the subject intangible asset).
4. Methods that quantify the difference in the value of overall business enterprise—or similar economic unit—as a result of owning the subject intangible asset (and using it in the business enterprise), as compared to not owning the subject intangible asset (and not using it in the business enterprise).
5. Methods that estimate the value of the subject intangible asset as a residual from the value of an overall business enterprise (or of a similar economic unit), or as a residual from the value of an overall estimation of the total intangible value of a business enterprise (or of a similar economic unit).

Introduction to Direct Capitalization and Yield Capitalization.   All the various income approach methods may be grouped into the following two other analytical categories:

1. Those that rely on direct capitalization.
2. Those that rely on yield capitalization.

In a direct capitalization analysis, the analyst estimates the appropriate measure of economic income for one period (i.e., one period future to the valuation date) and divides that measure by an appropriate investment rate of return. The appropriate investment rate of return is called the capitalization rate. The capitalization rate may be appropriate for a perpetuity time period or for a specified finite period of time depending on the analyst's expectation of the duration of the economic income stream.

In a yield capitalization analysis, the analyst projects the appropriate measure of economic income for several discrete time periods into the future. This projection of prospective economic income is converted into a present value by the use of a present value discount rate. The present value discount rate is the investor's required rate of return—or yield rate—over the expected term of the economic income projection. The duration of the discrete projection period—and whether or not a residual or terminal value should be considered at the conclusion of the discrete projection period—depends on the analyst's expectation of the duration of the economic income stream.

The result of either a direct capitalization analysis or a yield capitalization analysis will provide an indication of the value of the subject intangible asset, per the income approach.

Introduction to the Valuation Synthesis and Conclusion

The analyst must consider and synthesize the various indications of value revealed by the various valuation approach methods into a final valuation conclusion for the subject intangible asset. The valuation synthesis is the analysis of alternative valuation indications to arrive at a final value estimate. A valuation synthesis is required because different value indications result both from the use of multiple valuation approaches and from the application of various methods within a single approach.

To perform the valuation synthesis, the appraiser reviews the entire appraisal to ascertain that the data, techniques, and logic used are valid and consistent. Inconsistencies among the valuation approaches should be reconciled. The appraiser should make sure the approaches and methods used relate to the same bundle of intangible asset legal rights being appraised, the same standard of value under consideration, and the same purpose and objective of the appraisal. A final, independent check of all mathematical calculations is recommended. The final value estimate conclusion is not derived simply by applying the technical and quantitative procedures; rather, it involves the application of the appraiser's professional judgment and experience to the valuation process.

Introduction to Reporting Valuation Conclusions

Regardless of the form or format of the report, the basic intangible asset valuation report should:

1. Conform to the Uniform Standards of Professional Appraisal Practice (USPAP) adopted by the Appraisal Standards Board of The Appraisal Foundation.
2. Be presented in a format or form that is sufficiently descriptive to enable the reader to ascertain the estimated defined value and the rationale for the estimate, and provide detail and depth of analysis that reflect the complexity of the intangible asset appraised.

3. Analyze and report on current market conditions and trends that will affect the projected income or the marketability of the intangible asset.
4. Contain sufficient supporting documentation to adequately describe to the reader the appraiser's logic, reasoning judgment, and analysis in arriving at the defined value reported.
5. Follow a valuation methodology that includes the market (sales comparison), income, and cost approaches; reconcile the three approaches; and explain the elimination of any approach not used.

The following practices should be considered unacceptable in an intangible asset valuation report:

1. The inclusion of inaccurate or incomplete data about the subject intangible asset.
2. The failure to report and consider any apparent factor that has an adverse effect on the value and marketability of the subject intangible asset.
3. The reliance in the valuation analysis on comparable, or guideline, market transactions that were not confirmed by the appraiser.
4. The reliance on any valuation analyses of inappropriate comparable, or guideline, sale transactions or the failure to use comparable, or guideline, sale transactions that are more similar, without adequate explanation.
5. The development of value and marketability conclusions that are not supported by available market data.
6. The failure to provide in the appraisal report a signed appraisal certification, statement of appraisal contingent and limiting conditions, and the professional qualifications of the responsible appraiser.

Summary

This chapter introduced the basic concepts related to the identification of intangible assets and intellectual properties. In assessing the existence of intangible assets, the analyst should consider both economic factors and legal factors.

In this chapter, we also considered some of the important distinctions between tangible and intangible assets, between real and personal property, and between intangible assets and intellectual properties. These distinctions are important both for classification reasons and for analytical reasons.

The following basic intangible asset valuation concepts were also discussed in this chapter: defining the purpose and objective of the intangible asset appraisal, selecting the appropriate standard of value, selecting the appropriate premise of value, describing the intangible asset subject to appraisal, describing the bundle of legal rights subject to appraisal, stating the appropriate valuation date, and selecting the appropriate form of valuation report.

Lastly, this chapter generally introduced the three basic approaches to intangible asset appraisal and the fundamental principles related to preparing the valuation synthesis and conclusion.

Bibliography

Alexander, Donald C. *Valuation of Intangibles.* New York: Institute on Federal Taxation, New York University, 1962, pp. 567–85.

Antognini, Walter G., and Mitchell J. Kassoff. "Section 197: Congress and the IRS Attempt to Settle Disputes Involving Amortization of Intangibles." *Tax Executive,* July/August 1994, pp. 281–90.

Avi-Yonah, Reuven S. "Amortization of Intangibles under Section 197." *Tax Management Memorandum,* May 30, 1994, pp. 22–32.

Blain, Davis R. "Valuation of Goodwill and Going Concern Value." *Mergers & Acquisitions,* Spring 1979, pp. 4–11.

Burckel, Daryl; Zoel W. Daughtrey; and Fonda Carter. "The Controversy Surrounding Customer-Based Intangibles." *CPA Journal,* May 1992, pp. 44–46 ff.

Carter, Stephen L. "The Trouble with Trademark." *Yale Law Journal,* January 1990, pp. 759–800.

Christensen, Barbara. "Computer Software—Is It Tangible or Intangible?" *Small Business Taxation,* January/February 1990, pp. 174–76.

Dance, Glenn E., and Alan Fortini-Campbell. "How Will the Temporary Regulations under Section 197 Affect Partnership Transactions?" *Journal of Partnership Taxation,* Fall 1994, pp. 199–215.

Dennis-Escoffier, Shirley. "Is a Solution to the Intangibles Problem on the Horizon?" *Journal of Corporate Accounting & Finance,* Winter 1992/1993, pp. 247–50.

Doering, James A. "The Amortization of Intangibles: Before and After Section 197." *Taxes,* October 1993, pp. 621–35.

Douglass, Michael J. "Tangible Results for Intangible Assets: An Analysis of New Code Section 197." *Tax Lawyer,* Spring 1994, pp. 713–72.

Flashner, Martin J. "Acquired Customer List Is Classified as Goodwill." *CPA Journal,* February 1992, p. 56.

Fuller, James P. "The Treatment of Intangible Property Rights in International Tax Planning." *Taxes,* December 1992, pp. 982–97.

Gross, Paul H. "Establishing Fair Market Value of Intangible Assets." *Journal of Business Valuation,* July 1977, pp. 5–17.

Henszey, Benjamin N. "Going Concern Value after *Concord Control, Inc.*" *Taxes,* November 1983, pp. 699–705.

Hodgson, Allan; John Okunev; and Roger Willett. "Accounting for Intangibles: A Theoretical Perspective." *Accounting and Business Research,* Spring 1993, pp. 138–50.

Jones, Ken C., and Joan L. Rood. "Evaluating the Service's Settlement Initiative for Intangible Assets." *Journal of Taxation,* April 1994, pp. 196–200.

King, Alfred M., and James Cook. "Brand Names: The Invisible Assets." *Management Accounting,* November 1990, pp. 41–45.

King, Jerry G., and Paul D. Torres. "The Purchase of a Going Concern: Planning for Intangibles." *National Public Accountant,* March 1991, pp. 32–35.

Kozub, Robert M. "Amortization of Intangibles under Section 197." *Ohio CPA Journal,* August 1994, pp. 15–21.

Levy, Marc D.; C. Ellen MacNeil; and Barbara J. Young. "Supreme Court's Decision on Amortizing Intangibles Removes One Barrier." *Journal of Taxation,* July 1993, pp. 4–10.

Luchs, Lorin D. "Proposed Intangible Asset Legislation." *Tax Adviser,* May 1993, pp. 313–14.

McMahon, Robert V. "Intangible Assets: Economic, Tax and Accounting Questions for Acquirers." *Bank Accounting & Finance,* Winter 1990–91, pp. 10–20.

Monath, Donald. "Differentiating Commercial Professional Goodwill from Personal Professional Goodwill." Parts I and II. *FAIR$HARE: The Matrimonial Law Monthly,* October and November 1990, pp. 13–15; 6–8.

Morgan, Bruce W. "Intangible Assets: A Primer for Bankers." *Bank Accounting & Finance,* Summer 1993, pp. 14–23.

Osborne, Philip H. "Amortization of Intangibles." *Business Valuation Review,* September 1991, pp. 127–28.

Paul, Robert S., and Wendy Sharon. "What Lenders Should Know about Intangible Asset Deductions." *Secured Lender,* September/October 1993, pp. 38–40 ff.

Paulsen, Jon. "Goodwill and Going Concern Value Revisited." *Mergers & Acquisitions,* Winter 1980, pp. 10–13.

————. "Measuring Rods for Intangible Assets." *Mergers & Acquisitions,* Spring 1984, pp. 45–49.

Rearick, Linda. "The Tangible Debate over Bank Intangibles." *ABA Banking Journal,* June 1991, pp. 14–15.

Reilly, Robert F. "Allocation of Value between Intangible Assets and Real Estate in Location-Dependent Businesses." *ASA Valuation,* January 1993, pp. 52–66.

————. "Interstate Intangible Asset Transfer Programs." *CPA Journal,* August 1992, pp. 34–40.

————. "What Appraisers Need to Know about Interstate Intangible Asset Transfer Programs." *ASA Valuation,* June 1992, pp. 42–51.

Reilly, Robert F., and Robert P. Schweihs. "The Valuation of Intangible Assets." *ASA Valuation,* June 1988, pp. 16–25.

Schlessinger, Michael R. "*Indopco & Newark*: Defining the Intangible Asset in the Larger Cost Recovery Context." *Taxes,* December 1992, pp. 929–47.

Varnadoe, James T. "Recent TC Decisions on Core Deposit Amortization Contain Inconsistencies." *Journal of Bank Taxation,* Spring 1993, pp. 19–26.

Wertlieb, Mark; Judy Scarabello; and Tracy L. Curran. "The Amortization of Purchased Intangible Assets." *Tax Adviser,* September 1993, pp. 583–92.

Whitmore, Daniel P. "A New Standard for Intangibles." *Corporate Growth Report,* September 28, 1992, pp. 62–74.

Wood, Robert W. "Intangible Hassles Continue." *Taxation of Mergers & Acquisitions,* April 1992, p. 5.

Chapter 24

Valuation of Intangibles

The following topics regarding the three basic approaches for the valuation of intangible assets—the cost approach, the market approach, and the income approach—will be presented in this chapter:

1. The basic economic principles underpinning each approach.
2. The applications—and the limitations—of using various methods under each approach.
3. The importance of remaining useful life estimation with regard to any valuation analysis of an intangible asset.
4. Definitions of—and differences between—replacement cost and reproduction cost.
5. The various forms of obsolescence that should be recognized in a cost approach appraisal.
6. The fundamental categories of—and procedures for—alternative market approach methods.
7. The estimation of the appropriate amount of—and the expected remaining term of—economic income for each income approach method.
8. The estimation of the appropriate present value discount rate and/or capitalization rate to be used in the various income approach methods.
9. Illustrative practical examples related to each valuation approach.
10. The preparation of the intangible asset valuation synthesis and conclusion, based on the indicated results of the three valuation approaches.

Cost Approach Methods

The theoretical underpinnings of the various cost approach methods relate to the following basic economic principles:

1. Substitution—affirms that no prudent buyer would pay more for an intangible asset than the cost to construct one of equal desirability and utility.
2. Supply and demand—shifts in supply and demand cause costs to increase and decrease and cause changes in the need for supply of different types of intangible assets.
3. Externalities—gains or losses from external factors may accrue to intangible assets. External conditions may cause a newly constructed intangible asset to be worth more or less than its cost.

Cost approach methods are most applicable to the valuation of intangible assets in the following situations:

1. When the cost to construct the intangible asset is well supported and when the intangible asset is relatively new or suffers from little obsolescence.
2. When appraising special purpose, internally developed intangible assets. These intangibles are not frequently exchanged in the marketplace, so there may be little or no sale or license transaction information.

3. When comparable (or guideline) sales or licenses are not available. The intangible asset may be of an unusual type and, if the intangible is not normally income producing, the income approach may be unusable. Sometimes, the only valuation approach left is the cost approach.

Analysts should consider several limitations in applying the cost approach, including:

1. When the intangible asset is older or suffers from extreme obsolescence.
2. In valuing income-producing intangibles, the income approach methods may be the preferred methods.
3. When the value estimates developed by the cost approach are not supported by observed market data.

Replacement Cost New

"Replacement cost new" typically establishes the maximum amount a prudent investor would pay for a fungible, tangible asset. However, this is not always the case with intangible assets. This is because intangible assets are, typically, less fungible than tangible assets.

To the extent that an intangible asset is less useful than an ideal replacement asset, the value of the subject intangible asset must be adjusted accordingly. The subject intangible asset's replacement cost new is adjusted for losses in economic value due to:

- Physical deterioration.
- Functional obsolescence.
- Technological obsolescence (a specific form of functional obsolescence).
- Economic obsolescence (which is often called external obsolescence).

Forms of Obsolescence

Physical deterioration is the reduction in the value of an intangible asset due to physical wear and tear resulting from continued use. Functional obsolescence is the reduction in the value of an intangible asset due to its inability to perform the function (or yield the periodic utility) for which it was originally designed. Technological obsolescence is a decrease in the value of an intangible asset due to improvements in technology that make an asset less than the ideal replacement for itself. Technological obsolescence occurs when, due to improvements in design or engineering technology, a new replacement intangible asset produces a greater standardized measure of utility production than the intangible asset being appraised. Economic (or external) obsolescence is a reduction in the value of the subject intangible asset due to the effects, events, or conditions, that are external to—and not controlled by—the current use or condition of the intangible asset. The impact of economic obsolescence is typically beyond the control of the intangible asset's owner. For that reason, economic obsolescence is typically considered incurable.

Sequence of Obsolescence Analyses.   In estimating the amounts (if any) of physical deterioration, functional obsolescence, technological obsolescence, and economic obsolescence related to the subject intangible asset, consideration of the subject asset's actual age—and its expected remaining useful life—is essential to the proper application of the cost approach.

Under the cost approach, the typical formula for quantifying an intangible asset's replacement cost is:

$$\text{Reproduction cost new} - \text{Curable functional and technological obsolescence} = \text{Replacement cost new}$$

To estimate the intangible asset value, the following formula is used:

$$\text{Replacement cost new} - \text{Physical deterioration} - \text{Economic obsolescence} - \text{Incurable functional and technological obsolescence} = \text{Value}$$

Curable versus Incurable Obsolescence.   An intangible asset's deficiencies are considered curable when the prospective economic benefit of enhancing or modifying it exceeds the current cost (in terms of material, labor, and time) to change it. An intangible asset's deficiencies are considered incurable when the current cost of enhancing or modifying it (in terms of material, labor, and time) exceed the expected future economic benefits of improving it.

Reproduction Cost

Reproduction cost is the cost (at current price) to construct an exact duplicate of the subject intangible asset. This duplicate would be created using the same materials, standards, design, layout, and quality of workmanship used to create the original intangible asset. Therefore, an intangible asset's reproduction cost encompasses all the deficiencies, "superadequacies," and obsolescence that exist in the subject intangible asset. Many of these conditions or characteristics are inherent in the subject intangible asset and are thus incurable.

Replacement Cost

The replacement cost of an intangible asset is the cost to create, at current prices, an asset having equal utility to the intangible asset subject to appraisal. However, the replacement asset would be created with modern methods and developed according to current standards, state-of-the-art design and layout, and the highest available quality of workmanship. The difference between an intangible asset's reproduction cost and its replacement cost is typically the quantification of incurable functional and technological obsolescence. That is, in an ideal replacement intangible asset, all elements of incurable functional and technological obsolescence are removed or "re-engineered" from the subject asset. An intangible asset's replacement cost is sometimes quantified using a green-field approach. That is, the replacement cost of an intangible asset is the cost to redesign and re-engineer an ideal replacement intangible asset on the drawing board from scratch—that is, on a virgin "green field."

Depreciated Replacement Cost Formula

The depreciated replacement cost method for appraising intangible assets is presented algebraically below:

	Reproduction cost new of the subject intangible asset
Less:	Allowance for curable functional and technological obsolescence
Equals:	Replacement cost new of the subject intangible asset
Less:	Allowances for physical deterioration
Equals:	Depreciated replacement cost
Less:	Allowance for economic or external obsolescence
Less:	Allowance for incurable functional and technological obsolescence
Equals:	Indicated value of the subject intangible asset

Intangible Assets That Are Often Appraised Using a Cost Approach

Some intangible assets lend themselves very well to the application of the cost approach to valuation. These intangible assets are typically used—or used up—in the generation of income for the company. Examples of intangible assets that may be likely candidates for the cost approach to valuation include:

- Computer software and automated databases.
- Technical drawings and documentation.
- Blueprints and engineering drawings.
- Laboratory notebooks.
- Technical libraries.
- Chemical formulations.
- Food and other product recipes, and so on.

Obviously, for intangible assets that are used or used up in the production of income for the company—and for which accurate replacement cost estimates are available—the appraiser should seriously consider the application of the cost approach as one method in the appraisal of the subject intangible asset.

Remaining Useful Life Analysis of Intangible Assets

One factor that is particularly important in the cost approach—particularly with regard to the estimation of obsolescence—is the estimation of the remaining useful life of the subject intangible asset. There are several methods for analyzing and estimating the remaining useful life for intangible assets. The most common methods are listed below:

1. Remaining legal (or legal protection) life (e.g., remaining term of trademark protection).
2. Remaining contractual term of period (e.g., remaining term on a lease).
3. Statutory or judicial life (e.g., some courts have allowed a "standardized" life of five years for computer software).
4. Remaining physical life (e.g., some intangible assets wear out from continued use, like blueprints).

5. Remaining functional life (e.g., some intangible assets become dysfunctional with the passage of time, like chemical formulations that need to be continuously updated).
6. Remaining technological life (e.g., period until the current technology becomes obsolete, for patents, proprietary processes, etc.).
7. Remaining economic life (e.g., period after which the intangible asset will no longer generate income, such as a legally valid copyright on a book that's out of print).
8. Analytical or actuarial mortality life analysis (e.g., estimating the remaining life of group assets—such as customer accounts—by reference to the historical turnover, or mortality, of such accounts).

Assessment of Remaining Useful Life

Generally, an appraiser should consider all these measures of remaining useful life in the analysis of an intangible asset. Also, generally, the shortest resulting measurement of remaining useful life will be used in the appraisal of each intangible asset. For example, it is not as relevant that the remaining legal life on a particular patent is 15 years if the expected remaining technological life on the patented technology is only 5 years. In any event, regardless of the valuation approach used, an assessment of the remaining useful life of the subject intangible is an important step in any valuation of intangible assets. This topic is covered in Chapter 25.

Illustrative Cost Approach Example—An Assembled Workforce Valuation

Let us assume the following set of hypothetical facts:

- You have been retained to estimate the value of the trained and assembled workforce of the XYZ Company.
- You have selected the cost approach—and the replacement cost method— as the most appropriate valuation method.
- You have obtained the requisite information regarding the number of, tenure of, and compensation of the company employees, as presented in Table 24–1:

Table 24–1

Assembled Workforce Valuation Workforce —Related Historical Cost Data Expressed as a Percent of Total Annual Compensation

Employee Years of Tenure with XYZ Company	Historical Cost to Recruit	Historical Cost to Hire andTrain
Less than 2 years	10%	20%
2–4 years	20	20
5–7 years	30	30
8–9 years	40	30
10 years or more	40	40

You are going to estimate the cost to replace the XYZ Company assembled workforce—that is, the cost to recruit, hire, and train new employees of comparable experience and expertise to the company's current employee base. Based on your research, you have concluded the replacement costs presented in Table 24–2 are relevant to your valuation.

Table 24–2

Valuation Data Regarding Current Assembled Workforce

Categories by Employment Tenure with XYZ Company	Current Number of Employees	Total Base Compensation	Average Total Compensation
Less than 2 years	238	$ 4,808,475	$20,204
2–4 years	141	3,504,736	24,856
5–7 years	129	4,037,876	31,301
8–9 years	70	2,398,975	34,271
10 years or more	271	9,900,803	36,534
Total	849	$24,650,865	

Table 24–3 presents the calculation of the cost approach replacement cost method valuation of subject assembled workforce.

Table 24–3

Assembled Workforce Valuation
Estimated Replacement Cost of
XYZ Company Assembled Workforce

Categories by Employment Tenure with XYZ Company	Estimated Total Base Compensation	Expressed as a Percent of Annual Compensation			Assembled Workforce Value
		Estimated Cost to Recruit	Estimated Cost to Train	Indicated Total Cost	
Less than 2 years	$4,808,475	10%	20%	30%	$ 1,442,543
2–4 years	3,504,736	20	20	40	1,401,894
5–7 years	4,037,876	30	30	60	2,422,726
8–9 years	2,398,975	40	30	70	1,679,283
10 years or more	9,900,803	40	40	80	7,920,642
Indicated Value of Assembled Workforfce					$14,867,088

Market Approach Methods

There are two fundamental categories of market approach methods with regard to the appraisal of intangible assets:

1. The market transaction methods—which involve the collection of data with respect to guideline intangible assets that have been bought and sold.
2. The market license/royalty methods—which involve the collection of data with respect to guideline intangible assets that have been licensed or are subject to a royalty transfer agreement.

Market Transaction Method

The market transaction method requires a well-established market that generates observable market prices for the guideline intangible assets. The first step in the analysis is an assessment of the economic strengths and weaknesses of each individual market observation and of the subject intangible asset. The second step in the related analysis is the identification and quantification of adjustment factors related to the differences between the market observations (i.e., guideline transactions) and the subject intangible asset. In the third step in the analysis, valuation multiples are estimated and are applied to the appropriate subject intangible asset financial parameter (e.g., sales, operating profit, cost, etc.) in order to estimate the value indication via the market transaction method.

Market License/Royalty Method

The market license royalty method requires that the appraiser be able to collect, confirm, and analyze a sample of license agreements that stipulate terms governing the use of—and compensation for—the license of the guideline intangible assets. In addition, for this method to function efficiently, the subject intangible asset must generate some identifiable stream of economic income so the appraiser can apply the royalty compensation formula (e.g., a percent of revenues, a percent of gross profits, etc.) derived from the guideline license agreements.

In the valuation analysis related to the market license/royalty method, the following procedures are typically performed:

1. Assess the terms of each guideline license agreement with special consideration of the following terms:
    *   The description of the guideline intangible licensed property.
    *   The description of any maintenance required for the guideline intangible property (e.g., product advertising, product enhancements, quality control, etc.).
    *   The effective date of the guideline license agreement.
    *   The termination date of the guideline license agreement.
    *   The degree of exclusivity of the guideline license agreement.
2. Assess the current status of the industry and the associated relevant markets and prospective trends.
3. Estimate an appropriate market-derived capitalization rate.
4. Apply the market-derived capitalization rate to the appropriate economic earnings measure with respect to the subject intangible asset in order to arrive at an indication of value.

Selection of Intangible Asset Sale and/or License Guideline Transactions

The following factors (among others) should be carefully considered—with respect both to each guideline intangible asset and to the subject intangible asset—when selecting and/or adjusting guideline transactions:

1. Relative selling price—does the product using the intangible asset command a premium selling price in the marketplace when compared to other products in the same category?

2. Relative sales volume—is the product using the intangible asset demanded by consumers at a higher rate than other products in the same category?
3. Relative profit gross margin—is the product using the intangible asset produced more cost effectively than other products in the same category?

To comprehensively analyze the comparative economic differences discussed above, the appraiser needs adequate financial and operational data for both the guideline and the subject intangible assets and product categories. Also required are market, market share, and selling price data for both the guideline and the subject intangible assets and product categories.

The analyst should compare selling prices, cost structures, and sales volume levels of the subject intangible asset with the guideline intangible asset sales and/or license transactions in order to select and/or adjust the guideline transaction data.

In addition, in order to select the appropriate valuation multiples from the guideline sale and/or license transaction data, the analyst should consider the following factors:

1. The industry that the subject intangible operates in compared to the guideline intangibles.
2. The bundle of legal rights subject to appraisal compared to the legal rights conveyed in the guideline transactions.
3. The age (and relative age) of the subject intangible compared to the guideline intangibles.
4. The functional, technological, and economic characteristics of the subject intangible compared to the guideline intangibles.

Ability to Value Intangible Assets Using Market Approach Methods

The various market approach methods have broad applications with regard to the valuation of numerous categories of intangible assets. The following list presents several examples of the types of intangible assets that are often appraised using one or more variations of a market approach method:

1. *Customer-related intangible assets.* Analysts often use the market transaction method to appraise credit card portfolios, core deposit customer lists, and mortgage servicing portfolios.
2. *Marketing-related intangible assets.* Analysts often use the market license/royalty rate method or income differential method to appraise trademarks and trade names and advertising programs.
3. *Proprietary technology-related intangible assets.* Analysts often use the market transaction method, market license/royalty rate method, or the income differential method to appraise commercialized computer software and patented and unpatented propriety technology.

Limitations of Using the Market Approach

Analysts should carefully consider the following limitations to—and weaknesses of—the use of market approach methods with regard to the economic analysis and appraisal of intangible assets:

- The analyst must be able to associate a particular stream of economic income with the subject intangible asset.
- There are few well-established transaction markets generating observable (and confirmable) prices with regard to the outright sale of operating intangible assets.
- Therefore, it is typically difficult to obtain and to confirm guideline data with regard to the sale and/or license of intangible assets.
- It is often difficult to assess the degree of economic and/or functional comparability between the guideline intangible assets and the subject intangible asset.

Sources of Guideline Comparative Data

Analysts often refer to the following sources, among others, to obtain information with respect to either the sale of guideline intangible assets, the license of guideline intangible assets, or the level of economic income that is generated by guideline intangible assets:

1. Company data of industry participants using guideline intangible assets, including:
   - SEC reports (10K, 10Q, etc.).
   - Standard & Poor's Corporation publicly traded security database.
   - Disclosure Compact D/SEC publicly traded security database.
   - Dialog Information Services.
   - Moody's *Corporate Profiles.*
   - *Company Intelligence.*
2. Industry data regarding economic income data with respect to the industry in which the guideline and subject intangible assets operate:
   - *U.S. Industrial Outlook.*
   - Industry trade journals and publications (e.g., for the banking industry— *The American Banker,* or for the food industry—*The Food Institute Report*).
   - Financial periodicals.
3. The following other sources are often used to research both the economics and the functionality of the guideline intangible assets and the subject intangible assets:
   - Litigated court cases concerning similar intangibles (e.g., U.S. Tax Court cases, patent and trademark infringement cases, international and interstate transfer pricing cases).
   - Professional and trade journals and periodicals (e.g., food industry publications, licensing executives society publications, etc.).

Quantitative Analysis of Guideline Intangible Asset and Subject Data

Particularly with regard to intangible assets that are in use in a going-concern business, it is extremely useful for the analyst to compute the following financial ratios for both the businesses using the guideline intangibles and the business using the subject intangible. This financial ratio analysis should encompass several years. The analysis allows the appraiser to assess the comparative strengths and weaknesses of the guideline companies to the subject company and to assess the economic contribution of the subject intangible asset to the financial condition and results of operations of the subject company.

The analyst should compute the following financial ratios over a period of time such as, for example, five years. The analyst should also compute the historical rates of change in the following financial ratios over a period of time, such as five years, and compare the following financial ratios to published industry ratios, in order to assess and quantify the contributing economic effects of the subject intangible asset:

1. Liquidity ratios, including:
    -   Current ratio.
    -   Quick ratio.
2. Activity ratios, including:
    -   Annual sales to average receivables.
    -   Cost of goods sold to average inventory balance.
    -   Days in outstanding inventory.
    -   Annual sales to average working capital balance.
    -   Annual sales to average net fixed assets.
    -   Annual sales to average total assets.
3. Coverage/leverage ratios, including:
    -   EBIT to interest expense coverage.
    -   Net fixed assets to owners' equity.
    -   Long-term debt to total capital (Long-term debt + Owners' equity).
    -   Interest-bearing debt to equity.
    -   Interest-bearing debt to total capital.
4. Profitability ratios, including:
    -   EBIT to average total assets.
    -   Pretax income to average owners' equity.
    -   Net income to average owners' equity.
    -   Pretax income to average total assets.
    -   Net income to average total assets.
    -   EBIT to average total capital.
    -   DFNI to average total capital.

The following economic variables are often important in the application of market approach methods to intangible asset valuation:

-   Average selling price.
-   Average unit volume.
-   Net revenue.
-   Gross margin.
-   Net cash flow.
-   Operating income.
-   Investment requirements.

To identify and quantify the appropriate valuation multiples, it is important for the analyst to compute trends for the relevant intangible asset economic variables, for both the guideline companies and the subject company, with regard to the above-mentioned economic variables.

Selection and Application of Valuation Multiples

Obviously, the most important step in any market approach method is the selection and application of one or more valuation multiples. The following represent typical market transaction approach price multiples:

1. Earnings before interest and taxes.
2. Earnings before depreciation, interest, and taxes.
3. Debt-free net income.
4. Debt-free cash flow.
5. Revenues.

The following represent typical market license/royalty approach valuation procedures:

1. Estimate the appropriate market-derived royalty rate.
2. Convert the selected royalty rate to a "common-size" royalty rate that will be easily applicable to the subject intangible asset (e.g., percent of net sales).
3. Apply the common-size royalty rate to the appropriate projected economic income measure with regard to the subject intangible asset in order to estimate a measure of economic royalty income.
4. Apply the market-derived capitalization rate to the estimate of economic royalty income in order to conclude an indication of the value of the subject intangible asset.

The following represent typical comparative income differential approach procedures:

1. Determine the projected normalized economic income differential associated with the use of the subject intangible asset.
2. Apply the market-derived capitalization rate to this estimate of prospective economic income differential in order to conclude an indication of the value of the subject tangible asset.

Estimation of the Appropriate Income Capitalization Rate

It is necessary to estimate an empirical or market-derived capitalization rate in order to use either the market license/royalty method or the comparative income differential method. To estimate the appropriate income capitalization rate for the subject intangible asset, it is important for the analyst to consider the following risk and expected return investment variables:

1. The relationship between risk and expected return with regard to an investment in the subject intangible asset.
2. The cost of debt capital in the subject company.
3. The cost of equity capital in the subject company.
4. The weighted average cost of capital in the subject company.
5. Capitalization rates derived directly from the analysis of transactional data.

6. A built-up rate, starting with a risk-free rate and adding various risk-adjusted components.
7. The appropriate income tax adjustments.
8. The expected long-term growth rate.
9. The expected remaining useful life of the subject intangible asset.
10. The consistency of the selected capitalization rate with the selected economic income measure.

Estimation of the Appropriate Income Capitalization Rate—An Illustrative Example

Let us assume the following market-derived facts in our estimation of the appropriate income capitalization rate:

After-tax cost of equity	14.0%
Pretax cost of equity	22.9
Tax rate	39.0
Pretax cost of debt	8.2
After-tax cost of debt	5.0
Equity as a percent of capital	55.0
Debt as a percent of capital	45.0
Projected long-term growth rate	5.0

The estimation of the appropriate market-derived income capitalization rates is presented in Table 24–4.

Table 24–4

Estimation of Market-Derived Income Capitalization Rates

		Pretax Capitalization Rate (%)	After-Tax Capitalization Rate (%)
	Cost of equity capital	22.9	14.0
Times:	Equity capital as a percent of total capital	55.0	55.0
Equals:		12.6	7.7
	Cost of debt capital	8.2	5.0
Times:	Debt capital as a percent of total capital	45.0	45.0
Equals:		3.7	2.3
	WACC (weighted average cost of capital)	16.3	10.0
Minus:	Projected long-term growth rate in economic income	5.0	5.0
Equals:	Estimate of appropriate market-derived income capitalization rate	11.3	5.0

Income Approach Methods

The following list presents the most commonly used income approach methods with regard to the economic analysis and appraisal of intangible assets:

1. Yield capitalization method.
2. Direct capitalization method.

3. Relief from royalty method.
4. Profit split method.
5. Capitalized excess earnings method.
6. Residual from business enterprise method.
7. Residual from purchase price method.
8. Postulated loss of income method.

Each of these eight income approach methods will be described and illustrated in the following sections.

Yield Capitalization Method

The definition of the yield capitalization method of intangible asset valuation is the present value of projected economic income over a discrete time period.

The first step in the yield capitalization method is the estimation of an appropriate measurement of economic income to be used in the valuation analysis. The second step is the estimation of the appropriate capitalization rate or present value discount rate, used to convert the projection of economic income to a present value. The third step in the yield capitalization method is the estimation of the remaining expected term of the economic income projection or, in other words, the expected remaining life of the subject intangible assets. The fourth step is an indication of the value of the subject intangible value—by calculating the present value of the projected economic income stream over the expected term of the economic income—at the appropriate present value discount rate.

Identification of the appropriate economic income measurement is an important step in the valuation. The typical alternative measures of economic income related to intangible assets include the following:

1. Average selling price differential.
2. Net revenue.
3. Gross cash flow (net income with an add-back for depreciation).
4. Net cash flow (net income plus depreciation, minus capital expenditures, minus working capital addition).
5. Operating income.
6. Net income.

Some additional questions to consider in the identification and projection of economic income related to the valuation of intangible assets include the following:

1. Should the measure of economic income be before tax or after tax? (The measure of economic income should correspond with the derivation of the discount rate.)
2. Should the measure of economic income be before or after debt service? (Again, the assumption regarding debt service should correspond to the assumption regarding the derivation of the discount rate.)

The following economic income projection variables should be carefully considered by an analyst when the yield capitalization method is used:

1. Revenue projection.
2. Expense projection.

3.   Investment projection (i.e., capital expenditures and net working capital increments).
4.   Capital charge analysis (i.e., charges for the use of other assets in the production of the projected income stream).
5.   Capital structure (i.e., the debt-to-equity ratio and the cost of capital).
6.   Residual value projection (i.e., the value of the intangible asset—if any—beyond the discrete projection period).

An analyst should be prepared to justify each of the economic income projection variables, typically by reference to historical comparison, industry average comparison, or capital market guideline companies.

The following factors should be carefully considered in the estimation of the appropriate capitalization rate or present value discount rate:

- The relationship between risk and expected return for the subject intangible asset.
- The cost of debt capital for the company using the subject intangible asset.
- The cost of equity capital for the company using the subject intangible asset.
- The weighted average cost of capital for the company using the subject intangible asset.
- A market-derived capitalization rate, based on consummated intangible asset sale transactions.
- A built-up rate, based on a risk-free rate plus a risk premium appropriate to the subject intangible asset.
- A before-tax or after-tax discount rate.
- An estimation of the appropriate long-term growth rate in the projected economic income.

The assessment of the appropriate yield capitalization may be affected by the definition and premise of value selected for the subject appraisal. The estimation of the appropriate yield capitalization will be directly affected by the expected remaining life of the subject intangible asset. Most importantly, there must be a direct consistency between the selection of the yield capitalization rate and the measurement of the projected economic income stream.

The following determinants should be considered by the analyst with regard to the estimation of the expected remaining useful life for the subject intangible asset:

- Legal life.
- Contractual life.
- Statutory/judicial life.
- Physical life.
- Functional life.
- Technological life.
- Economic life.
- Actuarial mortality life.

Generally, of these various measurements of remaining useful life, the shortest life estimate typically applies in the yield capitalization method valuation. It is important to emphasize that this estimation of the remaining useful life is directly necessary to the estimation of the value of the subject intangible asset.

In addition, the estimation of the remaining useful life of an intangible asset may be used in tax and accounting amortization, transfer pricing, contract negotiation, financing, property tax, and other analyses. In the valuation of intangible assets using the yield capitalization method, it is important to distinguish between the various definitions of life, such as total *life* of the intangible asset, average life of the intangible asset, or average remaining life of the intangible asset. These different definitions will be discussed in the next chapter.

Yield Capitalization Method—An Illustrative Example

Table 24–5 presents an illustrative example with regard to the use of the yield capitalization method to value a customer list intangible asset.

Let us assume the following hypothetical set of facts in our illustrative example:

Economic Variable	Projection
Next year projected revenues directly related to the customer list	$3,000,000
Economic income growth rate	5%
Present value discount rate	18%
Income tax rate	36%
Average remaining life of the subject customer list	4 years
Gross margin, EBIT margin, depreciation expense, capital expenditures	Discretely projected below

To simplify, we assume there will be no annual changes in net working capital or any other economic variables that will affect net cash flow in this example.

Table 24–5
Yield Capitalization Method
A Customer List Valuation
(in $000s)

Projection Variable	Year 1	Year 2	Year 3	Year 4
Revenue	$3,000	$3,150	$3,308	$3,473
Gross profit margin	1,268	1,370	1,452	1,510
− Operating expenses	1,056	1,141	1,209	1,258
= EBIT	212	229	243	252
− Income tax expense	76	82	87	91
= Debt-free net income	136	147	156	161
+ Depreciation	40	42	44	46
− Capital expenditures	42	44	46	48
= Net cash flow	134	145	154	159
x Present value discount factor	.92	.78	.66	.56
= Discounted net cash flow	123	113	102	89
Indicated value of the customer list				$427

Direct Capitalization Method

The definition of the direct capitalization method of intangible asset valuation is: The capitalization, meaning the division by an appropriate rate of return, of a static measurement of normalized economic income.

The direct capitalization method starts with the estimation of an appropriate measurement of economic income to be used in the valuation analysis. The second step is the determination of the appropriate capitalization rate or present value discount rate, used to convert the projection of economic income to a present value. The third step in the direct capitalization method is the estimation of the remaining expected term of the economic income projection or, in other words, the expected remaining life of the subject intangible assets. The fourth step is an indication of the value of the subject intangible asset—by calculating the present value of the projected economic income stream over the expected term of the economic income—at the appropriate direct capitalization rate.

Identification of the appropriate economic income measurement is an important step in the valuation. The typical alternative measures of economic income related to intangible assets include the following:

1. Average selling price differential.
2. Net revenue.
3. Gross cash flow (net income with an add-back for depreciation).
4. Net cash flow (net income plus depreciation, minus capital expenditures, minus working capital addition).
5. Operating income.
6. Net income.

Additional questions for the analyst to consider in the identification and projection of economic income related to the valuation of intangible assets include the following:

1. Should the measure of economic income be before tax or after tax? (The measure of economic income should correspond with the derivation of the discount rate.)
2. Should the measure of economic income be before debt service or after debt service? (Again, the assumption regarding debt service should correspond to the assumption regarding the derivation of the discount rate.)

The following economic income projection variables should be carefully considered by an analyst when the direct capitalization method is used:

- Revenue projection.
- Expense projection.
- Investment projection (i.e., capital expenditures and net working capital increments).
- Capital charge analysis (i.e., charges for the use of other assets in the production of the projected income stream).
- Capital structure (i.e., the debt to equity ratio and the cost of capital).
- Residual value projection (i.e., the value of the intangible asset, if any, beyond the discrete projection period).

An analyst should be prepared to justify each of the economic income projection variables, typically by reference to historical comparison, industry average comparison, or capital market guideline companies.

The following factors should be carefully considered in estimating the appropriate capitalization rate:

1. The relationship between risk and expected return for the subject intangible asset.
2. The cost of debt capital for the company using the subject intangible asset.
3. The cost of equity capital for the company using the subject intangible asset.
4. The weighted average cost of capital for the company using the subject intangible asset.
5. A market-derived capitalization rate, based on consummated intangible asset sale transactions.
6. A built-up rate, based on a risk-free rate plus a risk premium appropriate to the subject intangible asset.
7. A before-tax or after-tax discount rate.
8. An estimation of the appropriate long-term growth rate in the projected economic income.

The assessment of the appropriate direct capitalization may be affected by the definition and premise of value selected for the subject appraisal. It will also be directly affected by the expected remaining life of the subject intangible asset. Most importantly, there must be a direct consistency between the selection of the direct capitalization rate and the measurement of projected economic income stream.

The following determinants should be considered by the analyst with regard to the estimation of the expected remaining useful life for the subject intangible asset:

- Legal life.
- Contractual life.
- Statutory/judicial life.
- Physical life.
- Technological life.
- Economic life.
- Actuarial mortality life.

Generally, of these various measurements of remaining useful life, the shortest life estimate typically applies in the application of a direct capitalization valuation. It is important to emphasize that this estimation of the remaining useful life is directly necessary to the estimation of the value of the subject intangible asset.

In addition, the estimation of the remaining useful life of an intangible asset may be used in tax and accounting amortization, transfer pricing, contract negotiation, financing, property tax, and other analyses. In the valuation of intangible assets using the direct capitalization method, it is important to distinguish between the various definitions of *life*, such as total life of the intangible asset, average life of the intangible asset, or average remaining life of the intangible asset. These different definitions will be discussed in the next chapter.

Direct Capitalization Method—An Illustrative Example

Let us consider the illustrative example of the direct capitalization method, with regard to the valuation of a customer list that is presented in Table 24–6.

Let us assume the following hypothetical set of facts with regard to our example:

Economic Variable	Projection
Projected revenue for next year	$3,000,000
Projected economic income growth rate	5%
Present value discount rate	18%
Income tax rate	36%
Average remaining life of the subject customer list	4 years
Gross margin, EBIT margin, depreciation expense, capital expenditures, net working capital increments	As indicated below

Table 24–6
Direct Capitalization Method
A Customer List Valuation
(in $000s)

Projection Variable	Next Year Projection
Revenue	$3,000
Gross margin	1,268
− Operating expenses	1,056
= EBIT	212
− Income tax	76
= Debt-free net income	136
+ Depreciation expense	40
− Capital expenditures	42
− Additional net working capital investments	32
= Debt-free cash flow	102
x Present value annuity factor for four years related to the direct capitalization rate (i.e., 18% − 5%)	2.92
= Indicated fair market value of customer list	$ 298

Relief from Royalty Method

In the relief from royalty method, the analyst estimates the amount of hypothetical royalty income that could be generated if the subject intangible asset were licensed from an independent, third-party owner to the business currently using the intangible, in an arm's-length transaction. The value of the subject intangible asset is the present value of the prospective stream of hypothetical royalty income that would be generated over the expected remaining useful life of the subject intangible asset.

Since the relief from royalty method often involves the analysis and selection of market-derived royalty rates, this valuation tends to merge aspects of both the income and market approaches. That is, the guideline royalty rates that are used in this analysis should be derived, either directly or indirectly, from empirical data with respect to actual arm's-length license agreements. As with other income approach methods, the analyst must consider the question of the correct economic income measurement.

The next step in the valuation process is the estimation of the appropriate capitalization rate or present value discount rate. The final step in the valuation process is the capitalization or discounting of the projected stream of the hypothetical royalty income associated with the hypothetical license of the subject tangible asset. The sum of the present values of the projected royalty income stream is one indication of the value of the subject intangible.

When selecting the sample of guideline license agreements from which to conclude a market-derived royalty rate, there are several important factors for the analyst to consider including the following:

1. An assessment of whether the agreements under consideration as guidelines are, in fact, independent party, arm's-length agreements.
2. An assessment of whether the agreements are directly comparable to the subject intangible asset or whether they are useful only as guideline transactions to give the analyst guidance with respect to the appropriate royalty rate.
3. The degree of comparability of the subject to the guideline intangible assets.

The following facts, among others, should be considered in the selection of guideline agreements and in the assessment of, and adjustment of, guideline or comparable agreements:

- The industry in which the subject intangible asset is used.
- The age of the intangible asset.
- The degree of consumer or other market recognition.
- The geographical coverage of the agreement.
- The remaining legal protection.
- The remaining term of the license agreement.
- The functionality and/or utility of the subject intangible asset—in comparison to the guideline intangibles.

After selecting comparable and/or guideline royalty rates, adjustments to the market-derived hypothetical royalty rate may be made for:

1. Differences between the subject intangible asset and the guideline intangible assets including:
   - Location of use of the various intangibles.
   - Term of the various agreements.
   - Functionality of the various intangibles.
   - Economics of the various intangibles.
2. Conversion to a common-size royalty rate basis, if the guideline license agreements encompass various royalty formulas.

After the adjustments are made, the next step in this method is to apply the selected comparable or guideline royalty rate to the applicable economic income measurement related to the subject intangible asset.

Identification of the appropriate economic income measurement is an important step in the valuation. The typical alternative measures of economic income related to intangible assets include the following:

- Average selling price differential.
- Net revenue.
- Gross cash flow (net income with an add-back for depreciation).
- Net cash flow (net income plus depreciation, minus capital expenditures, minus working capital addition).
- Operating income.
- Net income.

Additional questions to consider in the identification and projection of economic income related to the valuation of intangible assets include the following:

1. Should the measure of economic income be before tax or after tax? (The measure of economic income should correspond to the derivation of the discount rate.)
2. Should the measure of economic income be before debt service or after debt service? (Again, the assumption regarding debt service should correspond to the assumption regarding the derivation of the discount rate.)

The next step in this valuation method is to either capitalize or to discount the projected hypothetical royalty income stream either over the subject intangible asset's expected remaining useful life or over an infinite period, as an annuity in perpetuity.

Clearly, the selection of the capitalization period is influenced by the analyst's estimate of the expected remaining useful life of the subject intangible asset. The next step in the valuation method is the selection of the appropriate capitalization rate or present value discount rate.

The following factors should be carefully considered in estimating the appropriate capitalization rate or present value discount rate:

1. The relationship between risk and expected return for the subject intangible asset.
2. The cost of debt capital for the company using the subject intangible asset.
3. The cost of equity capital for the company using the subject intangible asset.
4. The weighted average cost of capital for the company using the subject intangible asset.
5. A market-derived capitalization rate, based on consummated intangible asset sale transactions.
6. A built-up rate, based on a risk-free rate plus a risk premium appropriate to the subject intangible asset.
7. A before-tax or after-tax discount rate.
8. An estimation of the appropriate long-term growth rate in the projected economic income.

The assessment of the appropriate capitalization rate may be affected by the definition and premise of value selected for the subject appraisal. The estimation of the appropriate capitalization rate will be directly affected by the expected remaining life of the subject intangible asset. Most importantly, there must be a direct consistency between the selection of the capitalization rate and the measurement of projected economic income stream.

Relief from Royalty Method—An Illustrative Example

Table 24–7 presents an example of the relief from royalty method used in the valuation of a trademark.

Let us assume the following hypothetical set of facts in our illustrative example:

Economic Variable	Propjection
Next year revenues associated with the use of the subject intangible asset	$600,000
Projected long-term growth rate	3%
Market-derived royalty rate	5%
Expected remaining useful life of the subject trademark	Perpetuity

Table 24–7

Relief from Royalty Method

A Trademark Valuation

	Revenues related to intangible subject	$600,000
Times:	Market-derived royalty rate	5%
Equals:	Projected royalty income	30,000
Divided by:	Capitalization rate (i.e., 13% rate − 3% rate)	10%
Equals:	Indicated value of the trademark	$300,000

Profit Split Method

Using this valuation method, the analyst has to estimate the amount of the economic income that is generated by the subject intangible asset that could be hypothetically split between a hypothetical licensee and a hypothetical licensor for the use of the subject intangible asset. As with the relief from royalty method, this method assumes an independent third party owns the subject intangible and licenses it—for a percent, or split, of the associated profit—to the business that uses the subject intangible.

The first step in the profit split method is estimation of the appropriate economic income measurement. The second step in the method is estimation of the hypothetical "split" of the economic income measure between a hypothetical licensor and a hypothetical licensee. The third step is application of the derived split to the estimated normalized economic income that will be generated by the use of the subject intangible. The fourth step is estimation of the appropriate capitalization rate or present value discount rate. The fifth step in the method is capitalizing or discounting of the estimated "profit split" economic income.

Identification of the appropriate economic income measurement is an important step in the valuation. The typical alternative measures of economic income related to intangible assets include the following:

- Average selling price differential.
- Net revenue.
- Gross cash flow (net income with an add-back for depreciation).
- Net cash flow (net income plus depreciation, minus capital expenditures, minus working capital addition).
- Operating income.
- Net income.

Additional questions to consider in the identification and projection of economic income related to the valuation of intangible assets include the following:

1. Should the measure of economic income be before tax or after tax? (The measure of economic income should correspond with the derivation of the discount rate.)
2. Should the measure of economic income be before debt service or after debt service? (Again, the assumption regarding debt service should correspond to the assumption regarding the derivation of the discount rate.)

The next step in the process is to estimate the normalized economic income associated with the use of the subject intangible asset. In this projection of economic income related to the subject intangible asset, it is important to consider all applicable capital charges—these are "charges," or decrements, against the projected income stream associated with assets other than the subject intangible that are used or used up in the production of income associated with the subject intangible.

The next step in the process is to estimate the hypothetical split between a licensor and a licensee related to the projected economic income. Analysts should carefully consider the following factors when estimating the appropriate profit split:

1. The qualities/attributes of assets used in the production of income.
2. The degree of market acceptance or consumer recognition.
3. The decisions in published court cases with regard to profit split percentages.
4. Licensing standards related to the industry in which the subject intangible is used.

The next step in the process is to apply the profit split percentage to the projected normalized economic associated with the subject intangible. The final step is to capitalize or discount the projected profit split income to arrive at an indication of value of the subject intangible asset.

The following factors should be carefully considered in the estimation of the appropriate capitalization rate or present value discount rate:

1. The relationship between risk and expected return for the subject intangible asset.
2. The cost of debt capital for the company using the subject intangible asset.
3. The cost of equity capital for the company using the subject intangible asset.
4. The weighted average cost of capital for the company using the subject intangible asset.
5. A market-derived capitalization rate, based on consummated intangible asset sale transactions.
6. A built-up rate, based on a risk-free rate plus a risk premium appropriate to the subject intangible asset.
7. A before-tax or after-tax discount rate.
8. An estimation of the appropriate long-term growth rate in the projected economic income.

The assessment of the appropriate capitalization or discount rate may be affected by the definition and premise of value selected for the subject appraisal. The estimation of the appropriate capitalization or discount rate will be directly affected by the expected remaining life of the subject intangible asset. Most importantly, there must be a direct consistency between the selection of the yield capitalization or discount rate and the measurement of projected economic income stream.

Profit Split Method—An Illustrative Example

Table 24–8 presents an example of the profit split method, with regard to a trademark valuation.

Let us assume the following hypothetical set of facts in our illustrative example:

Economic Variable	Projection
Next year revenues	$600,000
Operating profit margin	35%
Projected long-term growth	3%
Income tax rate	35%
Present value discount rate	13%
Estimated profit split	50%
Expected remaining life of the asset	Annuity

Table 24–8
Profit Split Method
A Trademark Valuation

	Revenues	$600,000
Times:	Operating profit percentage	35%
Equals:	Operating profit	210,000
Less:	Income taxes	73,500
Equals:	After-tax operating profit	136,500
Times:	Profit split percentage	35%
Equals:	Profit split	47,775
Divided by:	Capitalization rate (13% − 3%)	10%
Equals:	Indicated fair market value of trademark	$477,750

Capitalized Excess Earnings Method

The definition of the capitalized excess earnings method of intangible asset valuation is the capitalization, or division by an appropriate rate of return, of the excess economic earnings generated by a business enterprise using the subject intangible asset.

The first step in the capitalized excess earnings method is estimation of the fair rates of return and the values of the investment in the identified assets used in the production of economic income to be used in the valuation analysis. The second step is estimation of the actual economic income associated with the subject intangible asset for the "next" time period. The third step is estimation of the "excess earnings" associated with the subject intangible—that is, the amount of projected economic income in excess of the amount of required economic income. The fourth step in the capitalized excess earnings method is an indication of the value of the subject intangible value—by calculating the present value of the projected excess earnings over the expected term of the economic income—at the appropriate capitalization rate.

The first step in this method is the estimation of fair rates of return for all net tangible assets (i.e., net property, plant and equipment), identified intangible assets, and net working capital that are employed in the production of the income stream associated with the subject intangible asset.

In the selection of these fair rates of returns, analysts may consider published industry average rates of return and selected guideline company rates of return.

The next step in the method is to multiply the selected fair rates of return by the values of the net tangible assets, the identified intangible assets, and the net working capital balances that are employed in the business that uses the subject intangible asset.

The next step in this method is to project the actual economic earnings—for the next time period—associated with the business operations that use the subject intangible asset. As mentioned previously, the analyst may consider numerous different measures of economic income. However, two of the more common measures of economic income, for purposes of the capitalized excess earnings method, are net cash flow and operating cash flow.

The next step in the method is to subtract a fair return on the net tangible assets, identified intangible assets, and the net working capital that are used with the subject intangible from the projected actual economic earnings generated by the business operations that use the subject intangible. If, after this subtraction step, there is a positive amount difference remaining, then that positive amount represents the excess economic earnings associated with the subject intangible.

The next step in the method is to capitalize the excess economic earnings into a valuation indication.

The following factors should be carefully considered in the determination of the appropriate capitalization rate:

1. The relationship between risk and expected return for the subject intangible asset.
2. The cost of debt capital for the company using the subject intangible asset.
3. The cost of equity capital for the company using the subject intangible asset.
4. The weighted average cost of capital for the company using the subject intangible asset.
5. A market-derived capitalization rate, based on consummated intangible asset sale transactions.
6. A built-up rate, based on a risk-free rate plus a risk premium appropriate to the subject intangible asset.
7. A before-tax or after-tax discount rate.
8. An estimation of the appropriate long-term growth rate in the projected economic income.

The assessment of the appropriate capitalization rate may be affected by the definition and premise of value selected for the subject appraisal. The estimation of the appropriate capitalization rate will be directly affected by the expected remaining life of the subject intangible asset. Most importantly, there must be a direct consistency between the selection of the capitalization rate and the measurement of the projected economic income stream.

Capitalized Excess Earnings Method—An Illustrative Example

Table 24–9 presents an example of the application of the capitalized excess earnings method with regard to the valuation of intangible value in the nature of goodwill.

Let us consider the following set of hypothetical facts in our illustrative example:

Economic Variable	Projection
Economic income associated with the business operations using the subject intangible asset	$60,000
Required return on net tangible assets, identified intangible assets, and net working capital	15%
Estimated value of net tangible assets, identified intangible assets, and net working capital	$300,000
Expected long-term growth rate	3%
Present value discount rate	13%

Table 24–9

Capitalized Excess Earnings Method
Valuation of Intangible Value
in the Nature of Goodwill

	Projected economic income for the next time period		$60,000
	Value of net tangible assets, identified intangibles, and net working capital	300,000	
Times:	Required rate of return	15%	
Equals:	Required return on net tangible assets, identified intangible assets, and net working capital		45,000
Equals:	Excess economic income		15,000
Divided by:	Capitalization rate (i.e., 13% − 3%)		10%
Equals:	Indicated value of the intangible value in the nature of goodwill		$150,000

Residual from Business Enterprise Method

This valuation method estimates the value of the subject intangible as the arithmetic result of the subtraction of the net financial assets, the net tangible assets, and the identifiable intangible assets from the overall business enterprise value of the business that operates the subject intangible asset.

The first step in this method is estimation of the overall business enterprise value of the business that operates the subject intangible. The second step is the estimation of the value of all the other assets employed in the business other than the subject intangible asset. These other assets include:

1. All net working capital accounts.
2. All net tangible real and personal property.
3. All identified intangible assets—that is, all intangible assets other than the subject (unidentified—at least from a value perspective) intangible asset.

The final step in this method is the mathematical calculation of the residual, or subtraction, value. This is the overall business enterprise value less the value of all the identified tangible and intangible assets. This residual represents an indication of the value of the subject intangible asset.

Again, the first step in this method is to estimate the value of the overall business enterprise that uses the subject intangible asset. Some of the more common business valuation approaches that are often used in the residual from business enterprise method include the capital market approach, the market data transaction approach, and the income (or discounted cash flow) approach.

The next step in the method is estimation of the value of all the identifiable assets of the business, including the following categories of identifiable assets:

1. Financial assets (e.g., net current assets).
2. Tangible real property (e.g., real estate).
3. Tangible personal property (e.g., machinery and equipment).
4. Identifiable intangible assets.

Each of the individual identified assets of the subject business may be valued using one or more of the generally accepted asset valuation approaches, including the market (or sales comparison) approach, the income approach, or the cost approach.

The final step in this method is to subtract the value of all of the identifiable assets from the subject business enterprise value to estimate the value of the subject intangible asset.

Residual from Business Enterprise Method—An Illustrative Example

Table 24–10 presents an example of the application of the residual from business enterprise method. In this example, we will estimate the value of a franchise agreement.

Let us assume the following set of hypothetical facts:

Economic Variable	Projection
Subject business long-term debt value	$100,000
Subject business owners' equity value	400,000
Value of current assets	225,000
Value of current liabilities	200,000
Value of net fixed assets	60,000
Value of subject business identifiable intangible assets:	
Assembled workforce value	30,000
Computer software value	100,000
Going-concern value	35,000

Table 24–10
Residual from Business Enterprise Method
Valuation of a Franchise Agreement

	Value of current liabilities	$200,000
Plus:	Business enterprise value	
	(i.e., long-term debt + owners' equity)	500,000
Equals:	Total liabilities + owners' equity	700,000
Less:	Value of current assets	225,000
	Value of net fixed assets	60,000
	Value of identified intangible assets:	
	Assembled workforce	30,000
	Computer software	100,000
	Going-concern value	35,000
Equals:	Indicated value of the subject franchise agreement	$250,000

Residual from Purchase Price Method

This valuation method estimates the value of the subject intangible as the arithmetic result of the subtraction of the actual purchase price of the net financial assets, the net tangible assets, and the identifiable intangible assets from the actual purchase price (including assumed liabilities) of the business that operates the subject intangible asset.

The first step in this method is calculation of total purchase price of the business that operates the subject intangible. The second step is estimation of the value of all the other assets employed in the business other than the subject intangible asset. These other assets include:

1. All net working capital accounts.
2. All net tangible real estate and personal property.
3. All identified intangible assets—that is, all intangible assets other than the subject (unidentified—at least from a value perspective) intangible asset.

The final step in this method is the mathematical calculation of the residual, or subtraction, value. This is the overall business purchase price less the value of all the identified tangible and intangible assets. This residual represents an indication of the value of the subject intangible asset.

The first step in this method is to calculate the total purchase price and confirm that the actual purchase price is equivalent to the fair market value of the total business interest that was purchased. In the calculation of the total purchase price, it is important to include all assumed liabilities and all transaction-related purchase costs.

The next step in the method is the estimation of the value of all the identifiable assets of the business, including the following categories of identifiable assets:

1. Financial assets (e.g., net current assets).
2. Tangible real property (e.g., real estate).
3. Tangible personal property (e.g., machinery and equipment).
4. Identifiable intangible assets.

Each of the individual identified assets of the subject business may be valued using one or more of the generally accepted asset valuation approaches—the market (or sales comparison) approach, the income approach, or the cost approach.

The final step in this method is to subtract the value of all the identifiable tangible and intangible assets from total purchase price of the overall business in order to estimate the value of the subject intangible asset.

Residual from Purchase Price Method—An Illustrative Example

Table 24–11 presents an example of the application of the residual from purchase price method. In this example, we will estimate the amount of intangible value in the nature of goodwill.

For purposes of this example, let us assume the following set of hypothetical facts:

Economic Variable	Projection
Total business enterprise purchase price	$500,000
Value of current assets	225,000
Value of current liabilities	200,000
Value of net fixed assets	60,000
Value of identified intangible assets:	
Assembled workforce	30,000
Computer software	100,000
Customer list	35,000

Table 24–11

Residual from Purchase Price Method
Valuation of Intangible Value
in the Nature of Goodwill

	Total business enterprise purchase price (includes all assumed liabilities)	$500,000
Less:	Value of net working capital (i.e., current assets minus current liabilities)	25,000
	Value of net fixed assets	60,000
	Value of identified intangible assets:	
	Assembled workforce	30,000
	Computer software	100,000
	Computer list	35,000
Equals:	Indicated value of the intangible value in the nature of goodwill	$250,000

Postulated Loss of Income Method

This valuation method requires that the analyst quantify the loss of economic income that would occur to the business operation that uses the subject intangible if it did not have possession of the subject intangible asset. This method can be applied on a comparative overall business basis or on a product line basis.

The first step in this method is calculation of two discounted cash flow business—or business segment—valuations. The second step is to analyze and quantify the appropriate adjustments to the second discounted cash flow valuation analysis. The third step is quantification of the comparative cash flow analysis. The difference in the two discounted cash flow valuation analyses indicates the value of the subject intangible asset.

Step one involves calculating two discounted cash flow valuation analyses or scenarios. The first business valuation scenario assumes the possession of the subject intangible asset. The second business valuation scenario assumes the absence of the subject intangible asset. The second business valuation scenario (the "without" the subject intangible scenario) is typically a derivative of the first—or base case—business valuation scenario (the "with" the subject intangible scenario).

Adjustments to the base case discounted cash flow business valuation scenario, to create the second discounted cash flow business valuation, may include:

1. Decreased revenues due to the subject business not having the use of the subject intangible.
2. Increased operating expenses due to the subject business not having the use of the subject intangible.
3. Increased capital requirements due to the subject business not having the use of the subject intangible.

The next step in the method is quantification of the two comparative discounted cash flow valuation scenarios. The difference between the two indicated valuation conclusions represents the postulated loss of income and, thus, the indicated value of the subject intangible asset.

Postulated Loss of Income Method—An Illustrative Example

The following example illustrates the application of the postulated loss of income method. In this example, we will estimate the value of a noncompetition agreement.

Let us assume the following set of hypothetical facts with regard to our example for scenario I projections:

Economic Variable	Projection
Projected short-term growth rate	5%
Present value discount rate	18%
Projected long-term growth rate	4%
Projected loss in revenue	10%
Effective income tax rate	36%
Other economic variable projections	Presented below

The calculation of the "with noncompetition agreement" scenario illustrative example is presented in Table 24–12.

Table 24–12
Postulated Loss of Income Method
Scenario I Projections
With Noncompetition Agreement in Place
(in $000s)

Projection Variable	Year 1	Year 2	Year 3	Year 4	Residual Value
Revenue	$3,000	$3,150	$3,308	$3,473	
Gross margin	1,268	1,370	1,452	1,510	
− Operating expenses	1,056	1,141	1,209	1,258	
= EBIT	212	229	243	252	
− Income tax expense	76	82	87	91	
= Debt-free net income	136	146	156	161	
+ Depreciation expense	40	42	44	46	
− Capital expenditures	42	44	46	48	
− Additional net working capital investments	32	28	23	16	
= Net cash flow	102	116	131	143	1,062
x Present value discount factor	.92	.78	.66	.56	.47
= Discounted net cash flow	94	91	86	80	499
Sum of discounted net cash flow					$ 850

Let us also assume the following set of hypothetical facts with regard to our example for scenario II projections:

Economic Variable	Projection
Projected short-term growth rate	5%
Present value discount rate	18%
Projected long-term growth rate	4%
Projected loss in revenue	10%
Effective income tax rate	36%
Other economic variable projections	Presented below

The calculation of the "without noncompetition agreement" scenario illustrative example is presented in Table 24–13.

Table 24–13
Postulated Loss of Income Method
Scenario II Projections
Without Noncompetition Agreement in Place
(in $000s)

Projection Variable	Year 1	Year 2	Year 3	Year 4	Residual Value
Revenue with subject intangible	$3,000	$3,150	$3,308	$3,473	
– Revenue decrement	300	315	331	347	
= Revenue without subject intangibles	2,700	2,835	2,977	3,126	
Gross margin	968	1,055	1,121	1,163	
– Operating expenses	856	841	859	925	
= EBIT	112	214	262	238	
– Income tax expense	40	77	94	86	
= Debt-free net income	72	137	168	152	
+ Depreciation expense	40	42	44	46	
– Capital expenditures	42	44	46	48	
– Additional net working capital investments	32	28	23	16	
= Net cash flow	38	107	143	134	996
x Present value discount factor	.92	.78	.66	.56	.47
= Discounted net cash flow	35	83	94	75	468
Sum of discounted net cash flow					$ 755

Table 24–14 presents the final value estimate of the subject noncompetition agreement, based on this postulated loss of income method analysis.

Table 24–14
Postulated Loss of Income Method
Final Value Estimate
for Subject Noncompetition Agreement
(in $000s)

	Sum of discounted net cash flow business valuation—Scenario I	$ 850
Less:	Sum of discounted net cash flow business valuation—Scenario II	755
Equals:	Indicated value of the subject noncompetition agreement	$ 95

Applications and Limitations of Various Income Approach Methods

This section will outline the more significant applications and limitations with regard to the use of the various income approach methods to the valuation of intangible assets.

Yield Capitalization Method—Application and Limitations

Application: When an economic income stream can be specifically associated with the subject asset.

Limitations:
1. Ensuring consistency of measure of economic income and discount or capitalization rate.
2. Double counting of the economic income.
3. Not counting all the economic income.
4. Estimating the expected remaining useful life of economic income.
5. Estimating the risk of the projected economic income.
6. Ensuring consistency with the purpose and objective of the appraisal.

Direct Capitalization Method—Application and Limitations

Application: When an economic income stream can be specifically associated with the subject intangible asset.

Limitations:
1. Ensuring consistency of measure of economic income and discount or capitalization rate.
2. Double counting of the economic income.
3. Not counting all the economic income.
4. Estimating the expected remaining useful life of economic income.
5. Estimating the risk of the economic income.
6. Ensuring consistency with the purpose and objective of the appraisal.

Relief from Royalty Method—Applications and Limitation

Applications:
1. When an economic income stream can be specifically associated with the subject intangible asset.
2. When either guideline or comparable arm's-length license agreements and royalty rates can be found.

Limitation: The degree of comparability of license agreement and royalty rate may affect the degree of accuracy of the value conclusion.

Profit Split Method—Application and Limitation

Application: When an economic income stream can be specifically associated with the subject asset.

Limitation: The degree of accuracy of assessing the hypothetical profit split percentage between the willing licensor and the willing licensee may affect the degree of accuracy of the value conclusion.

Capitalized Excess Earnings Method—Application and Limitations

Application: When all intangible assets are valued in the aggregate or when there is only one intangible asset subject to appraisal.

Limitations: 1. The degree of accuracy in estimating the required rates of return on net tangible assets, identified intangible assets, and net working capital may affect the degree of accuracy of the value conclusion.

2. This method cannot easily estimate the value of a single individual intangible asset (because the value has to be allocated among all the unidentified intangible assets).

Residual from Business Enterprise Method—Applications and Limitations

Applications: 1. When intangible assets are valued in aggregate or when there is only one unidentifiable intangible asset.

2. When other identifiable tangible and intangible assets are easily valued.

Limitations: 1. The degree of accuracy in estimating the value of the subject enterprise and the other identifiable tangible and intangible assets may affect the degree of accuracy of the value conclusion.

2. This method cannot easily estimate the individual value of multiple unidentifiable intangible assets.

Residual from Purchase Price Method—Applications and Limitations

Applications: 1. When intangible assets are valued in aggregate or when there is only one unidentifiable intangible asset.

2. When other identifiable tangible and intangible assets are easily valued.

Limitations: 1. The degree of accuracy in estimating the value of other identifiable tangible and intangible assets may affect the degree of accuracy of the value of conclusion.

2. This method cannot easily estimate the individual value of multiple unidentifiable intangible assets.

Postulated Loss of Income Method—Application and Limitation

Application: When the contributory value of the subject intangible assets has a direct link to the economic income produced by the business enterprise that uses the subject intangibles.

Limitation: The degree of accuracy in estimating the value of the subject business enterprise—both with and without the subject intangible asset—may affect the degree of accuracy of the value conclusion.

Valuation Synthesis and Conclusion

In this section, we will discuss the final step in the intangible asset appraisal process: performing the valuation synthesis and reaching the valuation conclusion.

The Reconciliation Process

During the reconciliation process, it is important for the analyst to review all the steps of the intangible asset appraisal process. To begin with, a review of the intangible asset appraisal assignment should consider the following:

1. The purpose and objective of the appraisal.
2. The intangible asset business interest to be appraised.
3. The date of the appraisal.
4. The definition of value to be estimated.
5. The premise of value to be applied.

An appraisal is performed to answer a client's question about an intangible asset. To answer this question, the appraiser follows the valuation process. When more than one valuation approach is used, each usually results in a different value indication. Even within approaches, there are different indications of value. For example, there may be several indicated values resulting from different income approach methods. Reconciliation is the analysis of alternative valuation indications in order to arrive at a final value estimate.

The Review Process

The appraiser should review the entire intangible asset appraisal for appropriateness and accuracy. Some items to be considered during this process include the following:

1. Validity—Was it verified and transcribed correctly?
2. Pertinence—Is it pertinent to the appraisal problem? Does it help the reader arrive at the same conclusion? Is it just fluff? Have you overlooked any data that could be employed?
3. Consistency—Are the same numbers used throughout? Is the same description of the intangible asset in all sections of the report?

4. Quantity of data—Is there enough to be meaningful?
5. Quality of data—Are the comparable intangibles really comparable? Are the data believable?

The appraisal review process should also consider the appraisal procedures, mathematics of the analysis, and presentation of the analysis.

Appraisal Procedures.

1. Appropriateness—Are the methods and procedures used by the appraiser the best to measure the reaction of the marketplace? Are the methods and procedures appropriate in light of:
   - The definition of value sought?
   - The legal interests appraised?
   - The qualifying conditions imposed?
2. Logic—Are the procedures applied logically? Do they lead to meaningful conclusions related to the purpose and use of the appraisal?
3. Consistency—Are the procedures used consistently? Do they use reasonable consistent amounts of data? Is rounding employed consistently throughout the appraisal?

Mathematics of the Analysis.

1. Check for math errors.
2. Have someone else check your math.

Presentation of the Analysis.

1. Check spelling and grammar.
2. Neatness does count.
3. The overall completeness and legibility of your thinking and report presentation affects the client's impression of your ability and of the validity of your conclusions.

Relationship to the Valuation Process. Considerations and calculations in each valuation approach must be consistent with the purpose and use of the appraisal. Data and assumptions must be consistent in all parts of the valuation process. The definition of the appraised value and its relation to each step in the valuation process should be re-examined in the reconciliation. The relationship between non–arm's-length arrangements and atypical market conditions should be reconciled and explained in relation to the final value estimate.

Reconciliation Criteria

The analyst weighs the relative significance, applicability, and defensibility of each value indication and relies most heavily on the approach that is most appropriate to the nature of the particular intangible asset appraisal.

Appropriateness.

1. Weigh the strengths and weaknesses of each valuation approach as it applies to the particular type of intangible asset subject to appraisal:
    *   Market (sales comparison) approach—applicable to all types of intangible assets *providing* there are adequate data available.
    *   Cost approach—works well with internally developed intangible assets.
    *   Income approach—should typically be used with income-producing intangible assets.
2. Appropriateness is also used to judge the relevance of each guideline or comparable transaction and each significant adjustment made.

Accuracy.   Accuracy is measured by the appraiser's confidence in the reliability of the data, the calculations in each approach, and the adjustments made to the comparable transactions. The adjusted values are examined for the:

1. Number of adjustments.
2. Net adjustments.
3. Gross adjustments.

Quantity of Evidence.   Appropriateness and accuracy affect the *quality* of the evidence. Both factors must be studied in relation to the *quantity* of evidence.

Final Value Estimate

The following types of final value estimates may be appropriate:

1. Point estimate—usually, the final value estimate is stated as a single figure, or a point estimate.
2. Range of value—the indicated value is said to fall somewhere within a range of values. This may be reported solely, as the conclusion of value, or in conjunction with a point estimate.

A range of value estimates may be helpful additional information in helping a client reach a decision and is inevitably a part of the appraiser's reasoning process anyway.

Summary

The following concepts regarding the cost approach methods were discussed in this chapter:

1. The different definitions of *cost*—and when each definition may be appropriate.
2. The different types of obsolescence that intangible assets may suffer—and how they affect the cost approach analysis.
3. The importance of the remaining useful life estimate to the cost approach analysis.

The following concepts regarding the market approach methods were discussed in this chapter:

1. The fundamental categories of alternative market approach methods.
2. The ability to value intangible assets using market approach methods.
3. Sources of guideline comparative data.
4. Selection and application of various market approach valuation methods.

The following concepts related to the income approach methods were discussed in this chapter:

1. An assessment of the theoretical and the practical strengths and weaknesses of each method.
2. The estimation of the appropriate measure of economic income to be used in each method.
3. The estimation of the remaining expected term of the economic income for each method.
4. The estimation of an appropriate discount rate and/or capitalization rate to be used in various income approach methods.

In this chapter we also discussed the final step in the intangible asset appraisal process—concluding the final value estimate. Specifically, we considered:

1. How to conduct a thorough and effective review of the intangible asset appraisal work.
2. How to reconcile different value estimates developed from the different approaches into one estimate of the single, most probable, price the subject intangible asset will bring under the market conditions at the time of the appraisal and in conformance with a client's instructions, legal considerations, and the contingent and limiting conditions used by the appraiser.

The final value estimate should generally be a number within the final range of values indicated by the various valuation approaches. The final value estimate may be one of the numbers indicated by one of the approaches, or the approach relied on most heavily, *or* another number within the range. Do not average the numbers to arrive at a final value estimate. A simple arithmetic mean implies that all approaches have equal validity and equal weight—this is usually not the case. The final value opinion should be derived from the appraiser's reasoning and judgment of all factors and from the impartial weighing of the market evidence.

Bibliography

Berry, Jon. "Opinion: Brand Value Isn't about Stocks, It's Sales & Profits." *Brandweek,* June 28, 1993, p. 14.

Blackett, Tom. "Brand and Trademark Valuation—What's Happening Now?" *Marketing, Intelligence & Planning,* November 1993, pp. 28–30.

Boose, Mary Ann, and Virginia S. Ittenbach. "Depreciation of Customer-Based Intangibles: Good News for Taxpayers." *CPCU Journal,* December 1993, pp. 232–42.

Dal Santo, Jacquelyn. "Valuation Concerns in the Appraisal of Covenants Not to Compete." *Appraisal Journal,* January 1991, pp. 111–14.

Diana, James C. "Amortization of Customer-Based Intangibles—*Newark Morning Ledger v. U.S." Tax Management Memorandum,* July 26, 1993, pp. 223–28 ff.

Driscoll, Barrie K., and Stephen C. Gerard. "A Round for Buyers on Depreciation of Intangible Assets." *Mergers & Acquisitions*, July/August 1993, pp. 22–25.

Ellsworth, Richard K. "Minimizing Financial Institution Taxes." *Tax Adviser,* September 1992, pp. 604–7.

Farineau, Don F., and Royce E. Chaffin. "Amortizing Intangible Assets." *National Public Accountant,* August 1992, pp. 32–36.

Fenton, Edmund D.; Lucinda VanAlst; and Patricia Isaacs. "The Determination and Valuation of Goodwill: Using a Proven, Acceptable Method to Withstand IRS Challenge." *Tax Adviser,* September 1991, pp. 602–12.

Fuller, David N. "Amortizing Intangibles—A Break-Even Analysis." *Journal of Accountancy,* June 1994, pp. 31–34.

Grabowski, Roger J. "Supreme Court Rules Two-Pronged Test Applicable when Amortizing Intangible Assets." *Tax Adviser,* July 1993, pp. 438–42.

Hollingsworth, Danny P., and Walter T. Harrison, Jr. "Deducting the Cost of Intangibles." *Journal of Accountancy,* July 1992, pp. 85–90.

Horvath, James L., and Patrick J. Canham. *CA Magazine,* August 1988, pp. 65–68.

Jaeger, David G. "Supreme Court Decides *Newark Morning Ledger Co." Taxes,* July 1993, pp. 406–13.

Laverde, Lorin, and Eric Knapp. "Evaluating Intangible Assets in the Sale of Technology-Based Companies." *Corporate Growth Report,* October 1990, pp. 23–25.

Levy, Marc D.; C. Ellen MacNeil; and Barbara J. Young. "Supreme Court's Decision on Amortizing Intangibles Removes One Barrier." *Journal of Taxation,* July 1993, pp. 4–10.

Locke, Dennis H. "A Systematic Approach to Patent Valuation." *Business Valuation News,* September 1986, pp. 23–27.

Lubow, Nathan; Michael Nanus; Jack Panitch; and Stanley Weinstein. "Demystifying Intangible Asset Lending." *Secured Lender,* May/June 1991, pp. 52–53.

Martin, Michael J. "Valuing the Glamour in Brand Name Acquisitions." *Mergers & Acquisitions,* January–February 1991, pp. 31–37.

McMullin, Scott G. "The Valuation of Patents." *Business Valuation News*, September 1983, pp. 5–13.

Millon, Thomas J. "Computer Software Valuation: Don't Be Led Astray by a Quick Approach." *National Public Accountant*, September 1992, pp. 14–17.

———. "Software Development: Cost vs. Value (Determining Fair Market Value of Internally Developed Computer Software)." *Practical Accountant,* October 1992, p. 48.

———. "The Valuation and Amortization of Non-Compete Agreements." *CPA Litigation Service Counselor,* May 1991, pp. 1–3.

Morgan, Bruce W. "Amortizing Intangible Assets: Current Practices and Guidelines." *Bank Accounting & Finance,* Fall 1992, pp. 12–30.

———. "Valuing Deposit Intangibles." *Bank Accounting & Finance,* Summer 1990, pp. 15–21.

Mullen, Maggie. "How to Value Intangibles." *Accountancy,* November 1993, pp. 92–94.

———. "What Is a Brand Name or Trademark Really Worth—How Can That Value Be Measured?" *Journal of Business,* October 1990, pp. 203–12.

Murphy, John. "A Brand New Look to Valuations." *World Accounting Report*, August/September 1992, pp. ii–iii.

————. "Assessing the Value of Brands." *Long Range Planning*, June 1990, pp. 23–29.

Nellen, Annette, and Donald L. Massey. "Supreme Court Clarifies Depreciation of Acquired Intangibles." *Taxation for Accountants*, August 1993, pp. 68–75.

Oswald, Lynda J. "Goodwill and Going-Concern Value: Emerging Factors in the Just Compensation Equation." *Boston College Law Review*, March 1991, pp. 283–376.

Ourusoff, Alexandra; Michael Ozanian; Paul B. Brown; and Jason Starr. "'What's in a Name': What the World's Top Brands Are Worth." *Financial World*, September 1992, pp. 32–49.

Persellin, Mark B. "Depreciation of Customer-Based Intangibles Confirmed by Supreme Court in *Newark Morning Ledger*." *Tax Executive*, May/June 1993, pp. 211–16.

Rabe, James G., and Robert F. Reilly. "Valuation of Intangible Assets for Property Tax Purposes." *National Public Accountant*, April 1994, pp. 26–28 ff.

————. "Valuing Intangible Assets as Part of Unitary Assessment." *Journal of Property Tax Management*, Winter 1994, pp. 12–20.

Reilly, Robert F. "Appraising and Amortizing Noncompete Covenants." *CPA Journal*, July 1990, pp. 28–38.

————. "Maximizing Amortization Deductions for Noncompete Covenants." *The Practical Accountant*, December 1991, pp. 40–46 ff.

————. "The Valuation and Amortization of Noncompete Covenants." *Appraisal Journal*, April 1990, pp. 211–20.

————. "The Valuation of Computer Software." *ASA Valuation*, March 1991, pp. 34–54.

————. "The Valuation of Intangible Assets and Intellectual Properties." *Financial Managers' Statement*, March 1988, pp. 50–56.

————. "Valuation of Intangible Assets for Bankruptcy and Reorganization Purposes." *Ohio CPA Journal*, August 1994, pp. 25–30.

————. "Valuing Economic Loss." *Management Accounting*, July 1993, pp. 44–48.

Reilly, Robert F., and Daniel Lynn. "The Valuation of Leasehold Interests." *Real Estate Accounting & Taxation*, Winter 1991, pp. 24–33.

————., and Robert P. Schweihs. "The Valuation of Intangible Assets." *ASA Valuation*, June 1988, pp. 16–25.

Russell, Lee C. "How to Value Covenants Not to Compete." *Journal of Accountancy*, September 1990, pp. 85–92.

Schlesinger, Michael. "Covenants Not to Compete are Still Useful after RRA '93." *Taxation for Lawyers*, November/December 1993, pp. 165–70.

Schweihs, Robert P., and Robert F. Reilly. "The Valuation of Intellectual Properties." *Licensing Law and Business Report*, May–June 1988, pp. 1–12.

Seetharaman, Ananth; Stephen B. Shanklin; and Gregory A. Carnes. "Section 197: Methods for Treating Intangibles." *National Public Accountant*, October 1994, pp. 28–31 ff.

Shanda, Lawrence P. "Incorporating Intangible Assets into the Transfer Price Formula." *Taxes*, February 1991, pp. 100–105.

————. "Intangible Assets: To Amortize or Not?" *Management Accounting*, December 1992, pp. 39–42.

Shearlock, Peter. "Valuing Route Rights." *Airfinance Journal*, July 1993, pp. 4–8.

Sherwood, Stanley G.; Michael Godbee; and Siv D. Janger. "The Price of Flexibility: The New Section 482 Regulations." *Tax Planning International Review*, March 1993, pp. 3–15.

Stoller, Lee J. "Amortization of Intangible Assets and Goodwill after Section 197 and *Newark Morning Ledger*." *Tax Lawyer*, Winter 1994, pp. 467–77.

Tang, Roger Y. W. "Transfer Pricing in the 1990s." *Management Accounting*, February 1992, pp. 22–26.

Varnadoe, James T. "Recent TC Decisions on Core Deposit Amortization Contain Inconsistencies." *Journal of Bank Taxation*, Spring 1993, pp. 19–26.

Wacker, Raymond F. "Treasury's Proposed Regulations Allow Profit Split Method on Self-Developed Intangibles." *International Tax Journal*, Fall 1993, pp. 12–29.

Wertlieb, Mark; Judy Scarabello; and Tracy L. Curran. "The Amortization of Purchased Intangible Assets." *Tax Adviser*, September 1993, pp. 583–92.

Wilkins, Mira. "The Neglected Intangible Asset: The Influence of the Trade Mark on the Rise of the Modern Corporation." *Business History*, January 1992, pp. 66–95.

Wood, Robert W. "What Cheer: Core Deposits Amortizable." *Mergers & Acquisitions*, January 1992, pp. 6–7.

Chapter 25

Remaining Useful Life Analysis

This chapter will introduce the following topics with regard to estimation of the remaining useful life of intangible assets:

1. The importance of—and the application of—remaining useful life analysis to all three intangible asset valuation approaches.
2. The conceptual underpinnings of remaining useful life estimation.
3. The principal "determinants" of remaining useful life estimation.
4. The use of analytical methods of remaining useful life estimation.
5. The cause of—or reasons for—attrition or obsolescence with regard to intangible assets.

We will discuss survivor curve analysis at some length. We will review the construction of a survivor curve and the associated statistical curve fitting procedure. And we will present an illustrative example of the use of an Iowa-type curve in the estimation of the remaining useful life of an intangible asset. Lastly, we will review the final elements the analyst should consider in the conclusion of an intangible asset analysis and appraisal.

However, since this is not a textbook on statistical analysis techniques, our discussion of the analytical methods of remaining useful life analysis will be presented at a summary level.

Reasons to Estimate the Remaining Life (RL) of an Intangible Asset

The following represent common reasons to estimate the remaining useful life of an intangible asset:

1. Valuation of an asset—for transaction pricing and/or licensing purposes.
2. Amortization—for income tax accounting and/or financial accounting purposes.
3. Cost accounting—for capital recovery purposes.
4. Percent-good studies—for financing purposes and ad valorem property tax purposes.
5. Other—for miscellaneous purposes.

Priority of Estimating the RL for Each Valuation Approach

As described below, the estimation of the remaining useful life of an intangible asset is an integral part of each of the standard approaches to intangible asset valuation:

Valuation Approach	Remaining Useful Life Estimation Priority
1. Income approach	Lifing analysis should be performed in order to estimate the period for the economic income projection subject to capitalization.

Valuation Approach	Remaining Useful Life Estimation Priority
2. Cost approach	Lifing analysis should be performed to estimate the amount of obsolescence, if any, from the measure of reproduction, replacement, creation, or re-creation cost.
3. Market (or sales comparison) approach	Lifing analysis should be performed to select or reject and/or to adjust the comparable or guideline intangible asset sale and/or license transaction data.

Effect of RL Estimation on Each Approach

As described below, the analysis of the remaining useful life of an intangible asset will typically have a direct and predictable effect on the value of that intangible asset:

Valuation Approach	Expected Effect on the Intangible Asset Value
1. Income approach	1. Normally, a longer RL results in a higher indicated value. 2. The value estimate is particularly sensitive when the RL is less than 10 years. 3. The value estimate is not very sensitive when the RL is greater than 20 years.
2. Cost approach	1. Normally, a longer RL results in a higher indicated value. 2. Normally, a shorter RL results in a lower indicated value.
3. Market (or sales comparison) approach	1. The market must indicate an acceptance for the RL of the subject intangible asset. 2. If the subject's RL is different from the guideline transactions, then adjustments are typically appropriate. 3. If the subject's RL is substantially different from the guideline transactions, then this may indicate a lack of marketability of the subject intangible asset.

Various Means—or Determinants—to Estimate the RL of an Intangible Asset

The following list presents the most common determinants—or factors—that directly influence the remaining useful life of most intangible assets. This list also presents several examples of typical intangible assets that are most commonly influenced by the indicated remaining life determinant:

1. Legal determinants:
   a. Patents.
   b. Copyrights.
2. Contractual determinants:
   a. Loans.
   b. Leases.
3. Judicial determinants, such as computer software.

4. Physical determinants, such as engineering drawings.
5. Functional determinants, such as computer software.
6. Technological determinants:
    a. Proprietary technology.
    b. Technical documentation.
7. Economic determinants:
    a. Proprietary technology.
    b. Computer software.
8. Analytical determinants:
    a. Customer lists.
    b. Credit card portfolios.

Data Requirements Regarding Various Life Determinants

The following list indicates the type of remaining useful life estimate resulting from each life determinant—and the type of information or documentation required for the analyst to consider that type of life determinant:

Life Determinants	Type of Life Estimation	Information or Data Required
1. Legal	Definite	Document
2. Contractual	Definite	Document
3. Judicial	Definite	Document
4. Physical	Subjective	Engineering
5. Functional	Subjective	Engineering
6. Technological	Subjective	Technical
7. Economic	Quantitative	Engineering, economic
8. Analytical	Quantitative	Various age data

Causes of Attrition/Retirements/Obsolescence in Intangible Assets

The following list presents some of the more common causes of—or reasons for—the attrition, or retirement, of intangible assets. Each of these causes of attrition represent legitimate retirements with regard to the application of analytical methods of remaining useful life estimation:

1. Physical:
    a. Accident.
    b. Catastrophe.
    c. Deterioration/wear and tear.
2. Functional:
    a. Inadequacy.
    b. Obsolescence.
    c. Interrelated assets.
    d. Evolution—technology.
3. Operational:
    a. Accounting.
    b. Management policy.
    c. Regulatory.

4. Economic:
    a. Lack of demand.
    b. Interest rates.
    c. Inflation.
    d. Financing.

Analytical Methods to Remaining Life Estimation

There are two important categories of procedures related to the application of analytical methods to intangible asset remaining useful life estimation:

1. The estimation of a historical attrition rate.
2. The development of "survivor curves" based on the observed historical attrition rates.

Survivor Curve Analysis

Exhibit 25–1 is a graphical representation of the application of a survivor curve analysis as part of the analytical method to remaining useful life estimation.

Survivor Curve Terminology

The following definitions are important for the analyst to understand with regard to the use of survivor curve analysis:

1. Average service life (ASL)—the total number of years (i.e., time periods) of service provided by the group of like assets (e.g., credit card holders) divided by the number of units (e.g., number of credit card holders) in the group.

Formula 25–1

$$ASL = \frac{Area\ under\ the\ complete\ survivor\ curve}{Total\ number\ of\ units\ at\ age\ zero}$$

The area under the survivor curve can be approximately calculated by adding the height (i.e., percent surviving) of the survivor curve at each age (e.g., 0, 1, 2, . . . years).

2. Total life (TL)—the maximum life of the last surviving unit of the group. In the graphical representation of the survivor curve presented in Exhibit 25–1, the TL is approximately 30 years.
3. Average remaining life (ARL)—similar to ASL except it is defined as of an age other than age zero.

Formula 25–2

$$ARL = \frac{Area\ under\ the\ survivor\ curve\ to\ the\ right\ of\ an\ age}{Number\ of\ units\ surviving\ at\ that\ age}$$

Exhibit 25–1

Analytical Methods to Remaining Life Estimation
Survivor Curve Analysis

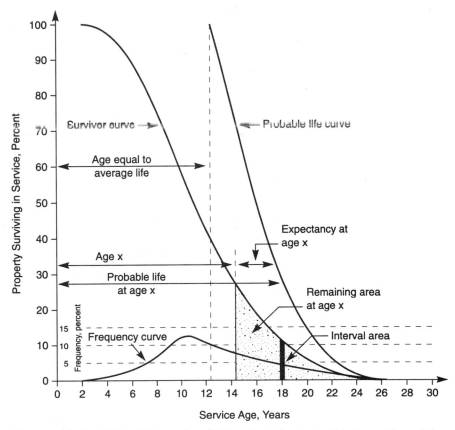

SOURCE: Anson Marston, Robley Winfrey, and Jean C. Hempstead, *Engineering Valuation and Depreciation*
(Ames, IA: Iowa State University Press, 1953), p. 147.

Either of the following types of data collection may be used in a survivor curve remaining useful life analysis:

1. Actuarial data (i.e., the age of the "retired" members of the group is known).
2. Semi-actuarial data (i.e., the age of the "retired" members of the group is unknown).

The following definitions are important to the understanding of the use of survivor curve analysis:

Formula 25–3

$$Retirement\ ratio = \frac{Number\ of\ units\ retired\ during\ a\ time\ period\ ``t"}{Number\ of\ units\ exposed\ to\ retirement\ (i.e.,\ active)\ at\ beginning\ of\ time\ period\ ``t"}$$

Formula 25–4

$$Survivor\ ratio = 1 - retirement\ ratio$$

Construction of Survivor Curve—An Illustrative Example (Actuarial Data)

Let's consider an example of the use of survivor curve analysis to estimate the remaining useful life of an intangible asset. Exhibit 25–2 presents a set of hypothetical placement and retirement data with regard to a customer list intangible asset account we will use in our example.

The box on the left of Exhibit 25–2 presents historical account placement ("opening") and retirement ("closing") data for the customer accounts subject to analysis. The box on the right side of Exhibit 25–2 presents the age intervals, the annual retirement ratios, and the corresponding survivor curve percentages with regard to the customer accounts subject to analysis.

From these annual retirement ratios—and the corresponding survivor curve percentages—we can begin to construct the survivor curve presented in Exhibit 25–3. The survivor curve percentages calculated in Exhibit 25–2 are plotted as the "actual stub curve" on Exhibit 25–3. This "actual stub curve" is smoothed and extrapolated by "fitting" the actual stub curve data to a standardized curve (i.e., the "fitted curve" in Exhibit 25–3).

This customer list example illustrates the construction of a typical survivor curve. The steps involved in the survivor curve construction process are summarized below.

Statistical Curve Fitting Process

The following procedures describe the statistical curve fitting process associated with the use of survivor curve analysis:

1. Curve fitting—the determination of the trend or pattern developed from known actual historical placement (e.g., account opening) and retirement (e.g., account closing) data (i.e., the actual stub survivor curve).
2. Extension of the stub curve—the actual stub curve must be extended down to the zero percent surviving line to enable:
   a. The calculation of an ASL.
   b. The calculation of an ARL.

The following are several of the more common types of survivor curves:

1. Iowa-type curves (the exponential function is a special case of this curve type).
2. Weibull distribution (the Iowa-type curves are a special case of this curve type).
3. Gompertz-Makeham curves.
4. Polynomial equations.

Iowa-Type Survivor Curves

The following describes the historical development of—and the conceptual support for—the use of Iowa-type curves to estimate the remaining useful life of intangible assets:

Exhibit 25–2
Construction of a Survivor Curve
Hypothetical Data Set Regarding Customer Account
Placements and Retirements

	Experience								(b.o.y.'89)
Placements	1981	1982	1983	1984	1985	1986	1987	1988	Active '88
1973 7	7 (0)	7 (0)	7 (0)	7 (0)	7 (1)	6 (1)	5 (0)	5 (0)	5
1974 3	3 (0)	3 (0)	3 (0)	3 (1)	2 (0)	2 (0)	2 (0)	2 (0)	2
1975 6	6 (0)	6 (0)	6 (0)	6 (1)	5 (0)	5 (1)	4 (0)	4 (1)	3
1976 7	7 (1)	6 (1)	5 (0)	5 (0)	5 (0)	5 (2)	3 (0)	3 (0)	3
1977 8	8 (2)	6 (0)	6 (0)	6 (0)	6 (1)	5 (1)	4 (0)	4 (0)	4
1978 2	2 (0)	2 (0)	2 (0)	2 (0)	2 (0)	2 (0)	2 (0)	2 (0)	2
1979 8	8 (0)	8 (0)	8 (1)	7 (1)	6 (1)	5 (1)	4 (0)	4 (0)	4
1980 4	4 (0)	4 (1)	3 (0)	3 (1)	2 (1)	1 (0)	1 (0)	1 (0)	1
1981 5	5 (0)	5 (0)	5 (1)	4 (1)	3 (1)	2 (0)	2 (0)	2 (0)	2
1982 13		13 (0)	13 (2)	11 (3)	8 (1)	7 (1)	6 (1)	5 (3)	2
1983 19			19 (0)	19 (4)	15 (2)	13 (8)	5 (3)	2 (0)	2
1984 16				16 (0)	16 (3)	13 (7)	6 (2)	4 (0)	4
1985 16					16 (0)	16 (5)	11 (5)	6 (0)	6
1986 23						23 (0)	23 (4)	19 (5)	14
1987 22							22 (0)	22 (5)	17
1988 26								26 (0)	26
Total 185									97
Balance Retired	50 (3)	60 (2)	77 (4)	89 (12)	93 (11)	105 (27)	100 (15)	111 (14)	

Curve Construction (Exp. Band 1981–88)

Age Interval	Exposures to Retirement	Retired	Retirement Ratio	Survivor Curve
9–10				24.14%
8–9	34	1	2.94%	24.67%
7–8	30	1	3.33%	25.73%
6–7	34	5	14.71%	30.16%
5–6	34	4	11.76%	34.19%
4–5	40	9	22.50%	44.11%
3–4	50	12	24.00%	58.04%
2–3	86	24	27.91%	80.51%
1–2	118	23	19.49%	100.00%
0–1	140	0	0.00%	100.00%

Note: 1. In each cell, top number represents "exposed to retirements" at beginning of year end. Bottom number represents "retirements" during the year.
     2. For each age interval, Retirement ratio = Retirements/Exposed to retirement.

1. History:
   a. Initial data for the development of Iowa-type curves: 1916.
   b. First Iowa-type curves published: 1931.
   c. The series of Iowa-type curves expanded to O-type curves: 1957.
   d. The data related to the development of the Iowa-type curves revalidated: 1978.
2. The actual asset placement and retirement data used in the original development of Iowa-type survivor curves included the following:
   a. Railroad ties, boxcars, flatcars.
   b. Telephone poles, central office equipment, cable.
   c. Waterworks pumps, steam engines, boilers.
   d. Electrical poles, transformers, conductors.
   e. Motor cars, trucks, mowers, plows.

Exhibit 25–3
Hypothetical Customer Account Data
Survivor Curve Fitting Process

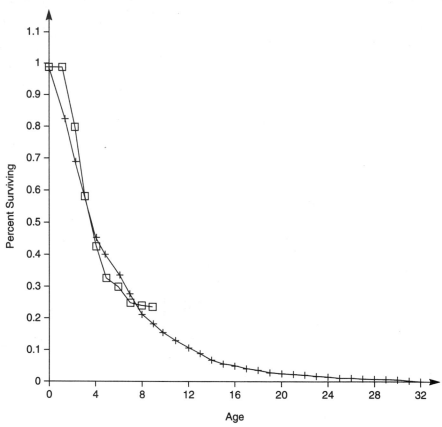

☐   Actual Stub Curve (from data in Exhibit 25–2)
+   Fitted Curve

3. Conceptual support for the use of Iowa-type curves:
    a. The empirical mathematical derivation is statistically sound and is
        derived from a variety of asset types subject to different combinations of
        the various forces that cause asset retirements.
    b. The different methods of the construction of the Iowa-type curves
        emphasized the forces of asset retirements in different ways.
    c. The Iowa-type curves have been generalized and the curves themselves
        are disassociated from the retirement forces that relate to specific assets.
    d. The idea for the derivation of the Iowa-type curve was originated from
        human mortality studies.
    e. The easy-to-communicate retirement/survivor characteristics of this
        curve type are based on the O,L,S, and R type curves.

Iowa-Type Survivor Curves—Characteristics

The following describes the asset retirement pattern characteristics of the four
"families" of Iowa-type curves:

1. Type O:
    a. Very high retirements far left of the average life, indicating a high degree
        of "infant mortality."

    b. "Relationship" oriented, if the subject asset does not fail during the break-in period, then the asset life may last longer.

2. Type L:

    a. More retirements occur before the average life of the asset.

    b. This implies older group members tend to be more "loyal" than younger group members.

3. Type S:

    a. The retirements before and after the average life are equal.

    b. This implies the customer base is exposed to a competitive environment.

4. Type R:

    a. Retirements are higher after the average life of the asset.

    b. Personalty and realty assets usually display the right mode tendency, where minimal breakdown occurs initially—but high asset maintenance occurs after a certain period (typically after the average life of the asset).

Iowa-Type Survivor Curves—Various Graphical Representations

Exhibits 25–4 through 25–7 present the typical "families" or types of Iowa-type survivor curves.

Calculation of the Average Service Life of an Intangible Asset

The following steps summarize the analysis necessary to estimate the average service life (ASL) of an intangible asset, using the analytical approach:

1. Calculate the amount of the area under the complete survivor curve (using integral calculus).

2. Calculate the ordinate approximation (as described previously in this chapter).

3. Calculate the expectancy of the average service life of the subject intangible asset as follows:

$$ASL = \frac{\textit{The area to the right of a particular age under the curve}}{\textit{The proportion surviving at that age of the curve}}$$

Survivor Curve Analysis for DCF Calculations

The following points are particularly noteworthy with regard to the use of survivor curve analysis in the various income approach methods (e.g., the yield capitalization method and the discounted cash flow procedure) to intangible asset valuation:

1. The survivor curve is required for estimating the future revenues (and, ultimately, economic income) to be generated from the wasting or "decaying" intangible asset (e.g., a credit card portfolio).

2. From the actuarial data with regard to the historical placements and retirements of that asset, a fitted standardized survivor curve (e.g., Iowa-type, Weibull, etc.) is only representative of a new intangible asset (i.e., at age zero), while the existing intangible asset is already several years old. Therefore, additional computations are required to estimate the remaining useful life of the existing "seasoned" intangible asset from the fitted survivor curve.

Exhibit 25–4

Illustrative Original Model Type Curves

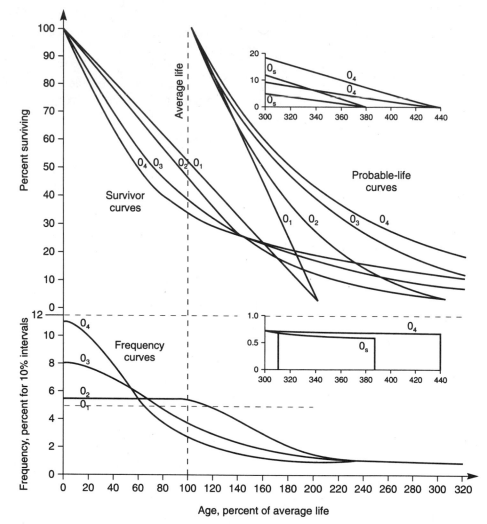

SOURCE: Robley Winfrey, *Statistical Analyses of Industrial Property Retirements* (Ames, IA: Engineering Research Institute, Iowa State University, 1935). Revised April 1967 by Harold A. Cowles, p. 179.

Exhibit 25–5

Illustrative Left Model Type Curves

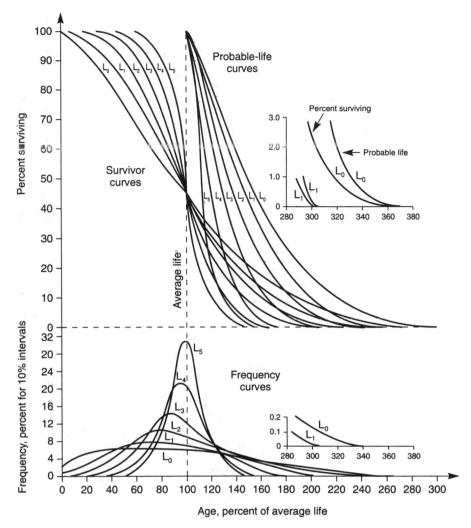

SOURCE: Robley Winfrey, *Statistical Analyses of Industrial Property Retirements* (Ames, IA: Engineering Research Institute, Iowa State University, 1935). Revised April 1967 by Harold A. Cowles, p. 70.

Exhibit 25–6
Illustrative Right Model Type Curves

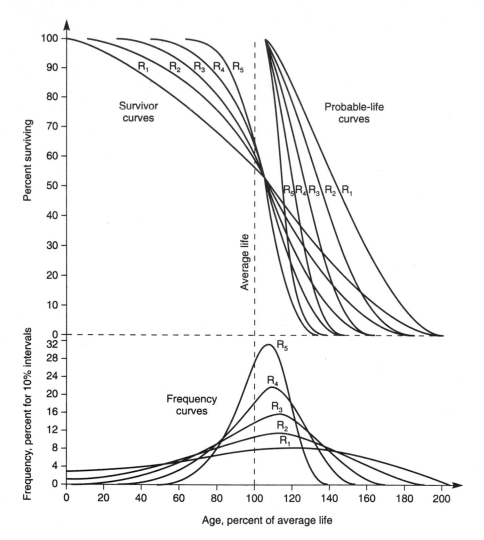

SOURCE: Robley Winfrey, *Statistical Analyses of Industrial Property Retirements* (Ames, IA: Engineering Research Institute, Iowa State University, 1935). Revised April 1967 by Harold A. Cowles, p. 71.

Exhibit 25–7
Illustrative Symmetrical Type Curves

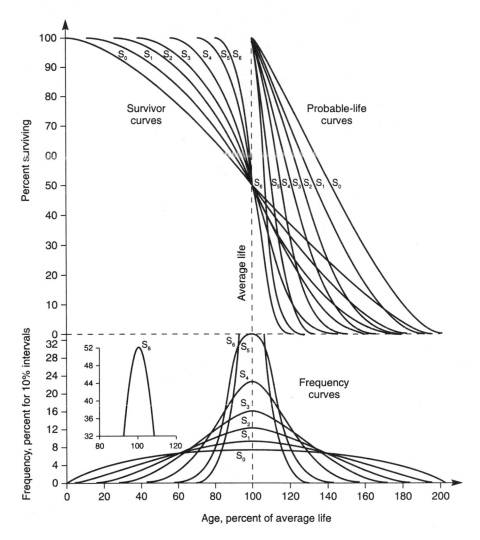

SOURCE: Robley Winfrey, *Statistical Analyses of Industrial Property Retirements* (Ames, IA: Engineering Research Institute, Iowa State University, 1935). Revised April 1967 by Harold A. Cowles, p. 72.

Valuation Summary and Conclusion—Remaining Useful Life Analyses

In summary, the following factors should be considered with respect to the estimation of the remaining useful life of the subject intangible asset:

1. Determinants of remaining useful life:
   a. Legal life.
   b. Contractual life.
   c. Statutory/judicial life.
   d. Physical life.
   e. Functional life.
   f. Technological life.
   g. Economic life.
   h. Actuarial mortality life.
2. Generally, for valuation purposes, the shortest remaining useful life estimate applies.
3. A useful life estimation is necessary to quantify the value of an intangible asset regardless of the valuation approach used.
4. The estimation of the remaining useful life of intangible assets is used in amortization, transfer pricing, contract, financing, property tax, and other intangible asset analyses.
5. The analyst should distinguish between the following definitions of *life* with regard to any intangible asset remaining useful life analysis:
   a. Total life.
   b. Average life.
   c. Average remaining life.

Valuation Summary and Conclusion—Other Valuation Issues

The following miscellaneous valuation issues should be considered by the analyst in the valuation synthesis and conclusion phase of any intangible asset appraisal:

1. What is the bundle of rights subject to appraisal?
2. Does the owner have the right to sell the bundle of rights?
3. Are there tangible manifestations of intangible asset existence?
4. Are there economic manifestations of intangible asset value?
5. What is the estimate of the remaining useful life?
6. Can you determine the existence of a secondary market for asset transfers?
7. What has been the legal protection and historical defense of the subject intangible asset?
8. Is there a proper identification and assignment of intangible asset values, related to:
   a. Avoiding double counting value?
   b. Avoiding not counting value?
9. Is there a proper sequencing of intangible asset values, related to the interdependence of intangibles?

10. Has there been a proper prioritization of intangible asset values and analyses?
11. Has there been a confirmation of the economic value of the total bundle of intangible assets (by the use of the income approach, for example)?

Summary

This chapter outlined the following topics and concepts related to intangible asset remaining useful life analysis:

1. The importance of remaining useful life estimation with regard to each approach to intangible asset valuation.
2. Alternative methods for the estimation of the remaining useful life of intangible assets.
3. Approaches, methods, and procedures with regard to the analytical remaining useful life estimation methods.
4. Final caveats and comments regarding the valuation of intangible assets.

Bibliography

Boehm, Ted. " 'Hoskold's Formula' for the Valuation of Intangibles." *Capital University Law Review,* Winter 1980, pp. 293–307.

Clark, Stanley J., and Charles E. Jordan. "Seeking Guidance: How and When to Group Old Assets for New Write-Downs." *National Public Accountant*, December 1994, pp. 17–19 ff.

Ellerman, David. "New Results of the Straight Line and Hoskold Methods of Capitalization." *Real Property Perspectives,* July 1994, pp. 29–36 ff.

Ellsworth, Richard K. "Amortization of Core Deposit Intangibles: A Matter of Proof." *Journal of Bank Taxation,* Spring 1992, pp. 11–13.

_____. "Supporting Cable Television Subscriber Amortization." *ASA Valuation*, January 1992, pp. 42–47.

Falk, Charles Edward. "Amortizing Insurance Expirations: The Meaning of *Decker.*" *Taxes,* June 1989, pp. 391 ff.

Fuller, David N. "Amortizing Intangibles—A Break-Even Analysis." *Journal of Accountancy,* June 1994, pp. 31–34.

Gehan, Raymond F. "How to Establish a Limited Useful Life in Order to Amortize Purchased Intangibles." *Taxation for Accountants*, June 1986, pp. 356–59.

Paschall, Robert H. "Measuring Functional Obsolescence at Manufacturing Plants." *ASA Valuation,* March 1994, pp. 56–62.

Reilly, Robert F. "How to Determine the Value and Useful Life of Core Deposit Intangibles." *Journal of Bank Taxation,* Winter 1991, pp. 10–18.

Part VII

Business Valuation for Specific Purposes

Chapter 26

Taxation Planning and Compliance—Income

Introduction

First, this chapter will discuss many of the reasons to appraise business entities and business interests for federal income tax purposes. These income taxation-related appraisal purposes may be grouped into two general categories: planning opportunities and compliance opportunities. Planning opportunities include valuations that may cause the deferral of an income tax liability or that may reduce a current or future income tax liability. Compliance opportunities typically involve transactions that cause an immediate taxable event that must be quantified or otherwise measured in terms of value.

We will list several income taxation transactions where a valuation is relevant. We will describe the taxation-related reason for the valuation requirement—often in terms of a reference to the appropriate statutory authority, administrative rulings, or judicial precedent. And we will discuss any unusual or particular valuation considerations that relate directly to that particular taxation-related valuation requirement.

Second, we will briefly discuss a state income taxation-related reason to conduct a valuation analysis. This reason relates to the state income tax consequences of an intercompany (and interstate) transfer of corporate intangible assets—and the resulting intercompany (and interstate) royalty payments related to the intangible asset transfer.

Third, we will briefly discuss several of the valuation-related federal income tax penalties. Valuation practitioners, tax practitioners, and taxpayers all should be mindful of these penalties when accounting for a taxable transaction where valuation is relevant.

This chapter will exclude consideration of federal gift and estate tax-related valuation issues, which will be addressed in Chapter 27. This chapter also will exclude a discussion of state and local ad valorem property tax valuation issues. These issues will be addressed in Chapter 29.

As with all chapters in this book, this chapter is written from an appraisal and economic perspective. It is not intended to offer legal, accounting, or taxation advice. Appropriate professional advisors should be consulted for such advice.

Federal Income Tax Reasons to Conduct an Appraisal

Table 26–1 lists several federal income tax transactions where valuation is relevant; however, this list is not intended to be exhaustive. This list is intended to illustrate many of the more common income taxation-related reasons to conduct a valuation. Several of the most common income taxation-related reasons to conduct a valuation will be described in greater detail in the following sections.

While Table 26–1 does indicate numerous taxable transactions that may require a valuation, most of these transactions may be grouped into a few common categories of taxable "events." For example, the first category of taxable events involves a valuation that is needed when a taxpayer (whether individual, partnership, or corporation) claims a deduction for property that the taxpayer abandons or donates; for example, this occurs in the case of abandonment losses, casualty losses, charitable contributions, and so forth.

Table 26–1

Taxable Transactions Requiring Valuations

Abandonment losses	Incorporation of a business
Bargain purchases	Insolvent corporation recapitalized
"Boot" in tax-free transfer	Intercompany transfer of goods or services
Casualty losses	Liquidation, when property is received by a
Charitable contributions of property	shareholder
Compensation received in the form of property	Lump sum acquisition of various assets or
Conversion of C corporation status to	properties (purchase price allocation)
S corporation status	"Reasonableness" of compensation
Dividends received in the form of property	(determination of)
Employee stock options	Rents received in the form of property
Excess accumulated earnings	Recapitalization
(the quantification of)	Residence converted to a rental property
Exchange of properties	Stock rights
Foreclosure of mortgaged property	Tax shelters

The second category involves a valuation that is needed when a business owner and/or employee receives noncash distributions from a business (whether the business is a proprietorship, corporation, or partnership); this occurs in the case of property distributed to employees as compensation, property distributed to shareholders as dividends, property distributed to shareholders as part of a partial or complete liquidation, employee stock options or other stock rights distributed to employees, and so on. In these instances, the valuation may affect the amount of the tax deduction available (if any) to the business; and it may affect the amount of income (as compensation or otherwise) recognized by the employee or shareholder.

A third category of events relates to the amount of recognition of income (if any) associated with economic benefits received by a business. Examples of this category of taxable events include the valuation of property received as rents and the valuation (or the solvency/insolvency test) related to the recognition (or nonrecognition) of cancellation of indebtedness income by a business involved in a debt restructuring.

A fourth category of taxable events involves the conversion of one property (or form of property) for another. Examples of this category of taxable events that may require valuations are the conversion of C corporations to S corporations (and the estimation of the associated built-in gains associated with the assets subject to the conversion of corporate form), the conversion of a personal residence to a business (such as a rental property or home office), and the general taxable or tax-free exchange of properties.

A fifth category of taxation-related events that may involve valuations are tests of reasonableness. These tests of reasonableness include, for example, the reasonableness of the amount of compensation paid to the owner of a business, the reasonableness of the amount of undistributed "excess" accumulated earnings retained in a corporation, or the reasonableness of the transfer price (or royalty payment) related to the intercompany transfer of goods, services, or properties between controlled or otherwise related taxpayers.

A sixth (and very common) category of taxable events that typically requires a valuation involves establishing the value-related tax basis for assets transferred into, purchased by, or transferred out of a business (whether a proprietorship, partnership, or corporation). Examples of this category of valuation opportunities include the incorporation of a business (i.e., when assets other than cash are transferred into the corporation in exchange for securities) and the allocation of a lump-sum purchase price paid for an assemblage of assets, properties, or business interests (i.e., for purposes of establishing a basis in each asset purchased).

The following sections will describe several of these income taxation–related valuation opportunities in greater detail.

Valuation of Property Received in a Transaction

When any type of property (other than money) is received on a sale, exchange, or other disposition, the amount realized on the receipt of that property is its fair market value. This basic rule of income taxation valuation in property transactions is presented in Internal Revenue Code Section 1001(b). The definition of fair market value used for property transaction and property basis purposes is the familiar: the most probable price that, at a particular time, will induce a willing buyer to buy and a willing seller to sell, neither being under undue pressure to buy or to sell.[1] This familiar definition of value has been slightly expanded with regard to the income taxation valuation of transactional property so as to include consideration of: (1) the availability of a buyer at the particular time and place and (2) the assumption that the buyer is not only willing but also able to pay for the particular quantity involved.[2]

Determining Basis in a Property

When there is a sale or exchange of property, taxpayers must determine the amount of the property transaction gain or loss, and they must determine whether the amount of the gain or loss is taxable or deductible. For income tax purposes, the following factors are considered in finding the amount of the property transaction gain or loss:

$$Basis + Additions - Reductions = Adjusted\ basis$$
$$Amount\ realized - Adjusted\ basis = Gain$$
$$Adjusted\ basis - Amount\ realized = Loss$$

Basis is the measurement of the taxpayer's investment in the property for income tax purposes. A taxpayer must know the property's basis to determine such taxation-related elements as depreciation, casualty losses, and gain or loss on the property's sale or exchange. Basis is ordinarily the property's cost or purchase price. Basis normally includes cash, debt assumed, and the fair market value of any other property given up. However, if a taxpayer receives property in some other way, such as by gift or inheritance, the taxpayer must normally use a basis other than cost.

Various transactional and taxation events may occur that change the taxpayer's original basis in the property. These events increase or decrease the original basis. The result is called the adjusted basis.

---

[1] See *H.H. Marshman*, CA-6, 60-2 USTC 9484, 279 F. 2d 27, cert. denied, 364 U.S. 918.

[2] See *A.E. Walbridge*, CA-2 4 USTC 1284, 70 F. 2d 683 (1934), cert. denied, 293 U.S. 594.

In certain situations, the fair market value of property on a particular date is the key factor in determining its basis. For determining basis based on value, actual sales of similar property on the open market are typically reliable evidence of value. For example, for this purpose, various courts have concluded that stock exchange quotations are usually good evidence of a stock's fair market value.

A taxable exchange is an exchange of property in which the gain is taxable or the loss is deductible. If a taxpayer acquires one property for another property in a taxable exchange, then the basis of the property received is generally its fair market value at the time of the exchange.

There are two allowable methods for determining the basis of property received in exchange for other property:

1. The basis is its fair market value when the property is received; or
2. The basis is the fair market value of the property exchanged for it, increased by any payments made or decreased by any payments received when the two properties are of unequal value.

Occasionally, it may be impracticable to estimate the fair market value of the property given up (in order to measure the cost of the property received). In these situations, taxpayers may presume the values of the exchanged properties are equal, if the exchange was made at arm's length.

If a taxpayer receives property for services, then the original basis of the property to that taxpayer is its fair market value. According to Treasury Regulation Section 1.61-2(d), the taxpayer will include this amount in his or her taxable income. The basis of any restricted property received as payment for services is the sum of any amount paid for the property, plus any amount the taxpayer includes in gross income when the property is no longer subject to a substantial risk of forfeiture. The rules related to restricted property received as payment for services are presented in Regulation Section 1.83-4.

Joint Ownership of Property

The death of a joint tenant or a tenant by the entirety may create a problem in determining a property's basis for the survivor. The part of the property included in the decedent's estate is considered to be acquired from the decedent by the survivor. The survivor's basis in this inherited part of the property is its fair market value on the date of death (or on the alternate valuation date). The basis of the part of the joint property not included in the decedent's estate is its cost or other basis, per Internal Revenue Code Section 2040. These rules apply to *all* joint interests in property *except* for those involving a husband and wife, as discussed below.

For qualified joint ownership interests created after December 31, 1976, only half of the joint ownership interest's fair market value is included in the gross estate regardless of who paid for the property. For married decedents dying after December 31, 1981, qualified joint interests include *any* interest in property held by the decedent and by the spouse as tenants by the entirety, or as joint tenants with right of survivorship (but only if decedent and spouse are the only joint tenants).

Property Acquired from a Decedent

Generally, if a taxpayer inherits property from a decedent, then the property's basis will be its fair market value when the decedent died. This property valuation rule is according to Internal Revenue Code Section 1015. However, if the executor of the estate elects the alternate valuation date for estate tax purposes, then the property's basis will be its fair market value on that alternate valuation date.

Valuation Requirements for Charitable Contribution Deductions

Individuals can deduct contributions they make to—or for the use of—qualified charitable organizations. A qualified charitable organization may be public or private, or a governmental unit.

According to Internal Revenue Code Section 170(c), a contribution to an organization may be deducted only if the organization meets the following qualifications and if, in some cases, the gift is used for a stated purpose:

1. *Community chest, corporation, trust, fund, or foundation.* These organizations must be created under federal or state laws or laws of U.S. possessions and operated exclusively for religious, charitable, scientific, literary, or educational purposes, or to prevent cruelty to children or animals.
2. *Veterans' organizations.* A post, group, trust, or foundation for war or non-war veterans' organizations must be organized in the United States or its possessions.
3. *Fraternal organizations.* Only contributions that are used for the same religious, charitable, and so forth purposes as community chests or funds qualify as deductible contributions. The society, order, or association must be a domestic organization operating under the lodge system.
4. *Cemetery organizations.* These must be company-owned and operated solely for the benefit of its members or a nonprofit corporation chartered solely for burial purposes and no other business.
5. *Governmental units.* Only contributions made exclusively for a public purpose may be deducted. They may be made to a state, U.S. possession, or any political subdivision, or the United States, or the District of Columbia.

A list of qualified charitable organizations, to which contributions are tax deductible, is contained in U.S. Treasury Department Publication 78.

Individual taxpayers have a percentage limitation as to the amount of charitable contributions allowed for any one tax year; this deduction limitation is based on their "contribution base." According to Internal Revenue Code Section 170(b)(1), this percentage limitation is based on two factors:

1. The type of the organization to which the charitable contribution is made.
2. The type of the property donated.

According to Internal Revenue Code Section 170(b)(1)(F), an individual taxpayer's "contribution base" is his or her adjusted gross income, computed without regard to any net operating loss carryback.

The 1993 Omnibus Budget Reconciliation Act added considerable documentation and substantiation requirements with regard to the charitable contribution of property. This section will summarize these appraisal-related documentation and substantiation requirements.

Documentation Requirements—Contributions of Property

A corporate or individual taxpayer making a charitable contribution of property—other than money—must have a receipt from the donee charitable organization and a reliable written record of specified information with respect to the donated property, per Regulation Section 1.170A-13(b)(2).

The receipt must include the name of the donee, the date and location of the contribution, and a description of the property in detail reasonable under the circumstances, including the value of the property.

In cases where it is impractical to obtain a receipt (such as leaving property at a charity's unattended drop site), the taxpayer is nevertheless required to maintain a reliable written record of specified information with respect to each item of donated property.

A reliable written record should include the following information:

1. Name and address of the donee organization.
2. Date and location of the contribution.
3. A description of the property in reasonable detail, including the value of the property (including, in the case of securities, the name of the issuer, the type of security, and whether such security is regularly traded on a stock exchange or on an over-the-counter market).
4. In the case of ordinary income property (including capital gain property held for less than 12 months), the cost or basis of the property.
5. If less than the entire interest in the property is contributed, the total amount claimed as a deduction for the tax year and for prior years and the name of any person other than the donee organization that has actual possession of the property.
6. The terms of any agreement entered into by the taxpayer relating to the use, sale, or other disposition of the contributed property.
7. If an election is made to treat contributions and carryovers of 30 percent capital gain property as ordinary income property, the years for which the election is made and the contributions to which the election is made.

Noncash Property Contributions—Post December 31, 1993

No deduction is allowed for any charitable contribution of $250 or more made on or after January 1, 1994, unless the taxpayer substantiates the contribution by a contemporaneous written acknowledgment from the donee organization of the contribution.

However, substantiation is not required if the donee organization files a return with the Internal Revenue Service reporting the information that is required to be included in the written acknowledgment to substantiate the amount of the deductible contribution.

Written Acknowledgment.   An acknowledgment is required to include the following information:

1. The amount of cash and a description, but not the value, of any property other than cash contributed.
2. Whether the donee organization provided any goods or services in consideration, in whole or in part for any property contributed.
3. A description and good-faith estimate of the value of any goods or services provided to the donor, or, if the goods and services consist solely of intangible religious benefits, a statement to that effect.

An intangible religious benefit is any benefit that is provided by an organization organized exclusively for religious purposes and that generally is not sold in a commercial transaction outside the donative context.

Contemporaneous Requirement.   Substantiation is considered contemporaneous for purposes of the charitable contribution deduction if the taxpayer obtains the acknowledgment on or before the earlier of:

1. The date the taxpayer files a tax return for the taxable year in which the contribution was made; or
2. The due date, including extensions, for filing the tax return.

Appraisals for Noncash Contributions

Most donors, including individuals, partnerships, S corporations, closely held corporations, and personal service corporations, must attach Form 8283, Noncash Charitable Contributions, to their federal income tax return when claiming charitable contributions deductions that include noncash gifts of more then $500.

However, C corporations, other than personal service corporations and closely held corporations, need to attach Form 8283 to their income tax returns only when the amount of the noncash contribution deduction is more than $5,000.

Form 8283 must be completed by all donors if the aggregate claimed or reported value of such property—and all similar items of property for which charitable deductions are claimed or reported by the same donor for the same tax year (whether or not donated to the same donee)—is more than $5,000. The phrase *similar types of property* means property of the same generic category or type, such as stamps, books, land, buildings, or nonpublicly traded stock.

In cases where the noncash charitable contributions deduction includes items with a value in excess of $5,000, then Form 8283 must include an acknowledgment of receipt signed by the donee charity and a signed appraiser's certification of appraisal, per Regulation Section 1.170A-13(c)(3).

Publicly Traded Stock.   Neither a qualified appraisal nor an appraisal summary is required for securities that are publicly listed and regularly traded on a national, regional, or over-the-counter established securities market or for mutual funds for which quotations are published daily in general-circulation newspapers.

Closely Held Stock.   Qualified appraisals are not required for deductions of $10,000 or less of nonpublicly traded stock. However, a partially completed appraisal summary signed by the donee must be attached to his or her tax return for charitable contributions of closely held stock valued between $5,000 and $10,000.

Qualified Appraisals. Pursuant to Regulation Section 1.170A-13(c)(3), a qualified appraisal is an appraisal document that:

1. Relates to an appraisal that is made not earlier than 60 days before the date of contribution of the appraised property and that must be updated if made earlier.
2. Is prepared, signed, and dated by a qualified appraiser.
3. Does not involve a prohibited type of appraisal fee, such as that in which a part or all of the fee arrangement is based on a percentage (or set of percentages) of the appraised value of the property.
4. Includes the following information:
   a. A description of the donated property.
   b. In the case of tangible property, the physical condition of the property.
   c. The date of contribution.
   d. The terms of any agreement entered into by the donor which relates to the use, sale, or other disposition of the contributed property.
   e. The name, address, and taxpayer identification number of the qualified appraiser and the appraiser's employer or partnership.
   f. The qualifications of the qualified appraiser.
   g. A statement that the appraisal was prepared for income tax purposes.
   h. The date on which the property was valued.
   i. The appraised fair market value of the property on the date of contribution.
   j. The method of valuation used.
   k. The specific basis for valuation, if any, such as any specific comparable sales transactions.
   l. A description of the fee arrangement between the donor and the appraiser.

The appraisal summary, which is made on Form 8283 (Noncash Charitable Contributions), must be signed and dated by both the donee and the qualified appraiser, and it must be attached to the donor's return on which a deduction for the appraised property is first claimed or reported.

The person who signs the appraisal summary for the donee must be an official authorized either to sign the tax or information returns of the donee or to sign appraisal summaries. The signature of the donee does not indicate concurrence with the appraised value of the contributed property.

No part of the fee paid for a charitable contribution appraisal can be based on a percentage of the appraised value of the property—that is, the appraiser's fee cannot be a contingent fee (or other similar arrangement).

Also, the appraisal fees may not be deducted as part of the charitable contribution.

Qualified Appraisers. According to Regulation Section 1.170A-13(c)(5), a qualified appraiser is an individual who:

1. Holds himself out to the public as an appraiser or who regularly performs appraisals.
2. Is qualified to appraise property because of his qualifications.
3. Is aware of the appraiser penalties associated with the overvaluation of charitable contributions.

Certain individuals, however, may not act as qualified appraisers, including:

1. The property's donor (or the taxpayer who claims the deduction).
2. The property's donee.
3. A party to the property transfer transaction (with certain very specific exceptions).
4. Any person employed by, married to, or related to any of the above persons.
5. An appraiser who regularly appraises for the donor, donee, or party to the transaction and does not perform a majority of his or her appraisals for other persons.

Summary of Charitable Contribution Valuation Requirements

Subsequent to the 1993 Omnibus Budget Reconciliation Act, the substantiation and documentation requirements have increased with regard to the appraisal of noncash property claimed for charitable contribution deductions.

Taxpayers, and their valuation advisors, should be familiar with these appraisal substantiation and documentation requirements when planning a noncash charitable contribution.

Valuation of Worthless and Abandoned Property

When misfortune strikes, leaving a taxpayer with worthless property, the taxpayer normally has a deductible loss equal to the adjusted basis of the worthless property. It is noteworthy, however, that the loss in these situations does not technically arise from a sale or exchange. The following discussion will summarize how the taxpayer is to justify and to quantify this deductible loss.

Worthless Securities

In the event that a qualifying security (e.g., stock or bond) becomes worthless at any time during the taxable year, then the resulting loss is treated as having arisen from the sale or exchange of a capital asset on the last day of the taxable year. This tax treatment is according to Internal Revenue Code Section 165(g). Losses from worthless securities are then treated as either short-term or long-term capital losses, depending on the taxpayer's holding period with regard to the subject securities.

This fictional sale or exchange treatment applies only to qualifying securities. To qualify, the security must be: (1) a capital asset and (2) a security as defined by the Internal Revenue Code. Under Internal Revenue Code Section 165, the term *security* means stock, stock rights, and bonds, notes, or other forms of indebtedness issued by a corporation or the government. When these rules do not apply (e.g., for property other than securities), the taxpayer suffers an ordinary loss. Whether a security actually becomes worthless during a given year is a question of fact, and the burden of proof is on the taxpayer to show that the security became worthless during the tax year in question.

Worthless Securities in Affiliated Corporations.   The basic rule for worthless securities is modified for a corporate taxpayer's investment in the securities of an affiliated corporation. If securities of an affiliated corporation become worthless, then the loss is treated as an ordinary loss and the limitations that normally apply if the loss were a capital loss are avoided. This rule is according to Internal Revenue Code Section 165(g)(3).

A corporation is considered affiliated to a parent corporation if the parent owns at least 80 percent of the voting power of all classes of stock and at least 80 percent of each class of nonvoting stock of the affiliated corporation. In addition, to be treated as an affiliated corporation for purposes of the worthless security provisions, the defunct corporation must have been truly an operating company. This test is met if the corporation has less than 10 percent of the aggregate of its gross receipts from passive sources such as rents, royalties, dividends, annuities, and gains from sales or exchanges of stock and securities. This condition prohibits ordinary loss treatment for what are really investments.

Abandoned Property.   While the tax law creates a fictional sale or exchange for worthless securities, it takes a different approach for abandoned property. When worthless property (other than stocks and securities) is abandoned, the abandonment is not considered a sale or exchange. Consequently, any loss arising from an abandonment is treated as an ordinary loss rather than a capital loss—a much more favorable taxation result. It is noteworthy, however, that the loss is deductible only if the taxpayer can demonstrate that the property has been truly abandoned and not simply taken out of service temporarily.

Valuation Aspects of Internal Revenue Code Section 165

Many businesses have experienced operating losses during the recent prolonged economic recession. In addition, the economic value of many businesses, business assets, or security interests become zero or negative.

Businesses that own worthless assets or worthless security interests should consider the possibility of taking an abandoned asset or worthless security loss deduction under Internal Revenue Code Section 165. Particularly as businesses generate taxable income as the economic recovery progresses, this deduction would give rise to either current or future income tax benefits.

The federal income tax rules for taking the loss deduction vary greatly, depending on the type of nondepreciable business asset or security interest involved and the taxpayer's actions.

Internal Revenue Code Section 165(a) provides that the taxpayer "shall be allowed as a deduction any loss sustained during the taxable year and not compensated for by insurance or otherwise." The amount of the loss equals the adjusted basis of the property calculated under Code Section 1011, as if the asset had been sold or exchanged at a loss.

However, the amount of the loss must be adjusted for any salvage value or for compensation received. If the loss arises from a capital asset, Code Sections 1211 and 1212 (relating to the capital loss limitation and carryover) restrict the deductibility of the loss.

A deduction is not permitted under Code Section 165 if the loss results from an actual sale or exchange of the worthless or abandoned property. In addition, if the abandonment or worthlessness loss was incurred by an individual, it must have been incurred in a trade or business, in a transaction entered into for profit, or from an event classified as a casualty or theft.

The worthlessness or abandonment loss is deductible in the year sustained. However, it cannot be deducted if there is a reasonable prospect of recovery. The possibility of recovery is a question of fact that must be determined by the particular circumstances involved.

Abandonment Loss for Nondepreciable Business Assets

The proper treatment of abandonment losses from nondepreciable business assets is found in the Regulations under Code Section 165 and in the related case law. Regulation Sections 1.165-1(b) and (d) state that the loss is deductible when "evidenced by closed and completed transactions and as fixed by identifiable events occurring in such taxable year."

Regulation Section 1.165-2(a) states that the deduction of a loss is permitted for "the sudden termination of the usefulness in such business or transaction of any nondepreciable property, in a case where such business or transaction is discontinued or when such property is permanently discarded from use therein . . ."

Accordingly, the Regulations indicate that an abandonment loss on nondepreciable business assets (other than securities) is deductible, even though the assets may not be totally worthless.

The criteria for establishing an abandonment loss for nondepreciable business assets—in cases other than worthlessness—are:

1. The occurrence of a closed and completed transaction coupled with the termination of the asset's usefulness.
2. The discontinuation of the use of the asset.
3. The discontinuation of the business.

An event that meets either of the latter two conditions qualifies as the abandonment of the asset. For a taxpayer to claim an abandonment loss for a business asset, there must be both the intent to abandon plus an actual act designed to accomplish that intent. The actual proof of an asset abandonment will be determined based on the facts and circumstances of the event.

The deductibility of an abandonment comes from the requirement in Regulation Section 1.165-2(a) that the taxpayer discontinue the use of the asset or the business in which the asset is used.

Technical Advice Memorandum 9220003

As the recent Letter Ruling 9220003 indicates, the Internal Revenue Service may allow a taxpayer to claim an abandonment loss before the actual abandonment is made by the taxpayer.

In this Letter Ruling, a public utility was permitted an abandonment loss deduction with regard to a nuclear power plant even though the taxpayer had not yet transferred ownership of the plant, still had employees on the premises, and had not yet been granted permission to transfer the plant.

The abandonment loss was allowed because of the difficulty in abandoning a nuclear power plant and because the taxpayer had taken all the steps necessary to abandon the plant and could not reverse course to recover the property.

Letter Ruling 9220003 stated, "The act necessary to evidence the intent to abandon property need only be appropriate to the particular circumstances. The actual transfer of title is not a requirement for abandonment." This conclusion should apply to any taxpayer who encounters legal or other restrictions on his or her ability to physically abandon property.

Worthless Stock Deduction

In addition to allowing a deduction for the abandonment of nondepreciable business assets, Internal Revenue Code Section 165(g) allows a deduction for the loss sustained by a taxpayer resulting from the worthlessness of a security.

For there to be a deduction without a sale, the security must be totally worthless and, therefore, unsalable. The loss deduction must be taken only for the year in which the security becomes completely worthless. A partial worthlessness of a security caused simply by a drop in value in the market price is not deductible until the taxpayer has sold the security. The loss is a capital loss if the security is a capital asset. To determine if the capital loss is treated as long-term or short-term, the taxpayer is considered to have held the worthless stock or security until the last day of the year in which it became worthless.

For purposes of the worthlessness deduction, a *security* is defined (in Internal Revenue Code Section 165(g)(2)) as follows:

1. Bonds, debentures, notes, or certificates, or other evidences of indebtedness issued by a corporation (including those issued by a government or its political subdivision), with interest coupons or in registered form.
2. A share of stock in a corporation.
3. A right to subscribe for, or to receive, a share of stock in a corporation.

The loss from a worthless security is treated as resulting from a sale or exchange on the last day of the tax year in which the security becomes worthless. In most cases, this worthlessness event will result in a long-term capital loss for the taxpayer.

As mentioned above, the worthless security loss will be treated as an ordinary deduction if it involves the security of an affiliated corporation (e.g., the stock of a subsidiary). To be an affiliated corporation, the taxpayer must own stock possessing at least 80 percent of the voting power and at least 80 percent of each class of nonvoting stock. In addition, the "worthless" subsidiary must obtain over 90 percent of its gross receipts from active sources.

The determination of worthlessness is a question of fact. In a case in which the Internal Revenue Service had urged a finding that stock did not become worthless in the year chosen by the taxpayer, for want of an "identifiable event," such as appointment of a receiver, cessation of normal business operation, bankruptcy, or liquidation, the Tax Court held that exceptional circumstances—that is, the lack of liquidating value and potential operating value—justified the taxpayer's choice.[3]

---

[3]See *C.W. Steadman*, CA-6, 70-1 USTC 9328, 424 F.2d 1, cert. denied, 400 U.S. 869.

A taxpayer's deduction for a loss sustained on a worthless security is based on his or her adjusted basis in the security. A cash-method taxpayer may deduct, for worthless stock purchased on the installment basis and not entirely paid for, only the amount paid up to the close of the tax year.

Summary of Worthless and Abandoned Property Valuation

Due to the recent prolonged recession, many business taxpayers have suffered economic losses over the past few years. In addition to operating losses, many businesses have abandoned nondepreciable business assets or have experienced the worthlessness of owned securities (in particular, the stock of corporate subsidiaries). This section has briefly summarized the rules related to substantiating a deduction for the abandonment of nondepreciable business assets or the worthlessness of owned securities.

Valuation Aspects of Cancellation of Indebtedness Income

When creditors cancel all or part of a business's debt, its tax consequences are determined by whether the business is in bankruptcy proceedings or is insolvent, according to Internal Revenue Code Section 108(a). When debt is canceled under bankruptcy proceedings, there is no taxable income currently. The taxpayer has a choice in how the reduction is recorded. First, the recognition of any income associated with the cancellation of debt may be offset by seven tax attributes:

1. Net operating losses (NOLs) and NOL carryovers.
2. The general business credit.
3. The minimum tax credit.
4. Capital loss carryovers.
5. The basis of the taxpayer's property.
6. Passive activity loss and credit carryovers.
7. Foreign tax credit carryovers.

Although not involved in a bankruptcy proceeding, a business may still be insolvent—that is, the value of its liabilities exceed the value of its assets. And the question of business insolvency (and the relative values of assets and liabilities) is answered by a business valuation.

If a business continues to be insolvent after debt cancellation, the decrease in debt is offset by the seven tax attributes listed above. If, however, the business is insolvent before but solvent after the debt cancellation, than the debt cancellation—to the extent of solvency—is subject to the rules governing solvent businesses. In contrast, when the debt of a solvent business not in bankruptcy is canceled, then the taxpayer must report the debt reduction as taxable income.

Unfavorable Tax Consequences of Debt Restructuring

In almost every debt restructuring, some amount of debt is forgiven by the lender to the borrower. As introduced above, there are usually unfavorable income tax consequences associated with such debt restructurings. Without adequate tax planning, and without a thorough and rigorous valuation analysis, these unfavorable tax consequences may surprise the unwary taxpayer.

These negative tax consequences typically occur when the taxpayer can least afford them. Generally, income recognition occurs without the taxpayer enjoying any cash receipts. Therefore, a tax liability is due even though the taxpayer may not have any cash to pay the tax liability. And this tax liability arises when the borrower is trying to restructure debt. Presumably, the debt restructuring is due to the severe economic condition of the borrower, the depressed value of property owned by the borrower, or by the borrower's attempt to avoid the stigma and costs associated with bankruptcy. In any event, the tax liability is created when the borrower is least able to pay it.

The two most common negative tax consequences of debt restructuring are (1) the recognition of gain or loss on the direct transfer of property to a creditor in exchange for debt discharge;, and (2) the recognition of discharge of indebtedness income when debt is partially or totally forgiven. Both of these common negative income tax consequences are directly affected by the valuation of the borrower's property.

Insolvency Provisions of Code Section 108

Internal Revenue Code Section 61(a)(12) includes as gross income the "discharge of indebtedness" associated with the reduction or forgiveness of debt. Code Section 108 provides for an exclusion of "discharge of indebtedness" income from gross income if the debt discharge occurs when the taxpayer is insolvent. The Code Section 108 income exclusion is limited to the amount by which the taxpayer is insolvent at the time of the discharge.

Pursuant to Code Section 108(a), a taxpayer will not recognize income from the discharge of indebtedness if the discharge occurs when the taxpayer is insolvent, even if the taxpayer is not in Title 11 bankruptcy proceedings. An insolvent taxpayer is permitted to exclude from gross income any amount of indebtedness forgiven by a creditor—subject only to the limitation that the amount excluded cannot exceed the amount of insolvency.

Code Section 108(d)(3) defines *insolvency* as the amount by which a taxpayer's liabilities exceed the fair market value of the taxpayer's assets immediately before the discharge of indebtedness. Accordingly, the determination of insolvency is entirely a valuation matter. This determination requires the fair market value appraisal of all the assets owned by the borrower just before the debt forgiveness.

The statutory authority and judicial precedent related to Code Section 108 make it clear that *all* of the taxpayer's assets are subject to appraisal in the determination of insolvency. These assets include: tangible personal property (e.g., machinery and equipment), tangible real estate (e.g., land and buildings), intangible real property (e.g., leasehold interests and easements), and intangible personal property (e.g., trademarks and goodwill). And the statutory and judicial guidance is clear that traditional valuation approaches (i.e., cost approach, market approach, and income approach) are appropriate for the appraisal of the fair market value of the taxpayer's assets.

Unquestionably, a rigorously prepared and thoroughly documented independent appraisal is required to support a claim of insolvency under Code Section 108.

The Internal Revenue Code does not provide a definition of *liabilities* in the determination of insolvency. Accordingly, the determination of what liabilities are included in the solvency test has become a matter of judicial and administrative interpretation. The rationale for Code Section 108 has been to provide the economically distressed taxpayer with a fresh start, not hampered by the imposition of an income tax liability that the taxpayer is not able to pay.

Insolvency Test Illustrative Example

The following simple example illustrates the application of the Code Section 108 insolvency test.

Real Estate Development Corporation is in financial distress. It has successfully negotiated with its bank for a partial reduction of the loan associated with its current office building construction project. The analysis of insolvency for Real Estate Development Corporation is presented in Table 26–2.

Table 26–2
Real Estate Development Corporation
Analysis of Assets and Liabilities
as of Date of Debt Discharge

	Tax Basis	Fair Market Value Basis
Assets		
Cash and other assets	$ 100,000	$ 100,000
Office building	10,000,000	7,000,000
Goodwill and other intangibles	0	400,000
Total assets	$10,100,000	$ 7,500,000
Liabilities		
Current liabilities	$ 100,000	$ 100,000
Construction project debt	9,000,000	9,000,000
Total liabilities	$ 9,100,000	$ 9,100,000

In this example, Real Estate Development Corporation is "insolvent" in the amount of $1,600,000 (i.e., the $9,100,000 of total liabilities less the fair market value of $7,500,000 in total assets).

Accordingly, in this example, Real Estate Development Corporation could exclude up to $1,600,000 of discharge of indebtedness income from its gross income. In other words, its bank could discharge, or forgive, up to $1,600,000 in debt without the recognition of discharge of indebtedness income to Real Estate Development Corporation.

The "Costs" of Code Section 108

Of course, this Code Section 108 exclusion from discharge of indebtedness income is not without any negative income tax consequences. Taxpayers will not recognize income from the discharge of indebtedness if they are in bankruptcy, to the extent they are insolvent (as illustrated above), if the debt is qualified farm indebtedness. However, in exchange for this income exclusion, taxpayers are required to reduce certain favorable tax attributes. These tax attributes, other than certain credits, are reduced by the amount of the discharge of indebtedness income that is excluded from gross income by the taxpayer. (General business credits and foreign tax credits are reduced at the rate of 33.3 cents for every dollar of excluded discharge of indebtedness income.)

Unless the taxpayer elects to reduce the basis in his or her depreciable assets (e.g., real estate) before reducing other tax attributes, the taxpayer must reduce tax attributes in the following sequence:

1. Net operating losses or carryovers.
2. Carryovers of the general business tax credit.
3. Capital losses and carryovers.
4. Basis in depreciable and nondepreciable assets.
5. Foreign tax credit carryovers

As an alternative to the above described reduction of tax benefits, the borrower may elect to apply the amount of excluded discharge of indebtedness income from the basis of any depreciable assets, but not below his or her basis in the assets.

In summary, the Code Section 108 insolvency discharge of indebtedness income exclusion is designed to provide a borrower with greater flexibility in arranging his or her financial affairs. It is not intended to allow taxpayers to avoid future taxes. Therefore, depending on the beneficial tax attributes otherwise available to the borrower, the Code Section 108 discharge of indebtedness income exclusion may provide some taxpayers with a permanent income exclusion and some taxpayers with only a temporary income exclusion.

Summary of Cancellation of Indebtedness Income Valuation

In the current economic climate, particularly as magnified in many real estate markets, debt restructurings are a normal part of the business environment. These debt restructurings take many forms and include direct forgiveness of debt (partial or total) and direct transfers of assets to creditors in exchange for (partial or total) debt cancellation. Without proper planning and structured valuation analysis, these debt restructuring techniques could have unexpected—and undesirable—income tax consequences.

In this section, we considered the unfavorable taxation consequences of debt restructuring and the discharge of indebtedness income exclusion provisions of Code Section 108. All these unfavorable taxation consequences of debt restructuring are affected by the valuation of the taxpayer's assets.

Valuation-Related Income Tax Penalties

Internal Revenue Code Sections 6662 and 6664 provide for a series of penalties with regard to the underpayment of income tax related to either the undervaluation or the overvaluation of assets, properties, or business interests for taxation-related purposes. First, we will introduce the general category of accuracy-related income tax penalties. Second, we will describe the specific accuracy-related penalties associated with either undervaluation or overvaluation.

General Accuracy-Related Penalties

An accuracy-related penalty is applied to the portion of any underpayment of federal income tax that is attributable to one or more of the following: (1) negligence or disregard of the rules and regulations, (2) any substantial understatement of income tax, (3) any substantial valuation misstatement, (4) any substantial overstatement of pension liabilities, and (5) any substantial estate or gift tax valuation understatement.

The penalty equals 20 percent of the income tax underpayment. An income tax underpayment, for purposes of the accuracy-related penalty and the fraud penalty is the excess of the correct tax over the tax shown by the taxpayer on the income tax return. In determining this excess, the tax shown on the income tax return is: (1) increased by any amounts previously assessed but not so shown (or collected without assessment) and (2) decreased by the amount of any rebates made. A rebate is that portion of an abatement, credit, refund, or other repayment made on the grounds that the tax imposed was less than the excess of the tax shown on the return (increased as in item (1)) over any rebates previously made.

The accuracy-related penalty does not apply to any portion of an income tax underpayment that is subject to a penalty for fraud.

Substantial Valuation Overstatement Penalty

There is a substantial valuation overstatement for purposes of the accuracy-related penalty if the claimed value (or the adjusted basis) of any property is 200 percent or more of the amount determined to be the correct value (or the basis) of that property. If the portion of the underpayment that is subject to the penalty is attributable to one or more gross valuation misstatements, then the penalty rate is 40 percent rather than 20 percent. A gross valuation misstatement occurs if the claimed value (or the adjusted basis) is 400 percent or more of the value amount determined to be correct.

No penalty is imposed on a taxpayer for a substantial valuation overstatement unless the portion of the underpayment for the tax year attributable to substantial valuation overstatements exceeds $5,000 ($10,000 in the case of a corporation other than an S corporation or a personal holding company). This penalty is provided for in Internal Revenue Code Section 6662(e).

Substantial valuation overstatements of charitable contribution property that result in underpayments of income tax are subject to the general accuracy-related penalty provisions. There is a charitable contribution deduction penalty waiver for qualified appraisers.

No penalty is imposed for an underpayment of income tax resulting from a substantial or gross overvaluation of charitable deduction property, if the taxpayer shows that there was reasonable cause for the underpayment and that the taxpayer acted in good faith. This exception does not apply unless the claimed value of the property was based on an appraisal made by a qualified appraiser. In addition to obtaining the appraisal, the taxpayer must make a good-faith investigation of the value of the contributed property. This penalty is provided for in Internal Revenue Code Section 6664(c).

The penalty for substantial valuation overstatement also applies to intercompany transfer price misstatements. This penalty is provided for under Internal

Revenue Code Section 482. Transfer prices are the intercompany amounts purportedly charged for the exchange of goods and services among commonly owned or commonly controlled businesses.

A transfer price adjustment is an allocation by the Internal Revenue Service of income, deductions, credits, and other items among such a group. A substantial valuation overstatement has occurred if a claimed intercompany transfer price is 200 percent or more (or 50 percent or less) of the amount determined to be correct or if the Internal Revenue Service transfer price adjustments increase taxable income by more than the lesser of $5,000,000 or 10 percent of the taxpayer's gross receipts for a tax year.

If the net adjustment exceeds the lesser of $20,000,000 or 20 percent or less, or if the claimed transfer price is 400 percent or more (or 25 percent or less) of the correct amount, a gross valuation misstatement has occurred, according to Internal Revenue Code Sections 6662(e) and (h).

Estate and Gift Tax Valuation Understatements

This topic will be presented in Chapter 27, which discusses gift and estate tax–related valuation matters.

Valuation of Intellectual Properties for State Income Taxation Purposes

In recent years, many corporations have formed intellectual property holding companies and then transferred legal title to various intangible assets and intellectual properties to them. In the most common structure for this program, the entity transfers intangible assets such as trademarks and trade names to the newly organized intellectual property holding company. As part of its normal business operations, the holding company licenses the use of the trademarks and trade names to the related business interests in other states. The business pays a license fee or royalty payment to the holding company for the use of the trademarks and trade names now owned by the holding company.

There is no tax liability in many states on the income derived from the licensing or leasing of intangible assets, such as royalties received for the use of trademarks. The intercompany payments from outside the holding company state—the same royalty payments for the use of the trademarks—represent deductible expenses for determining taxable income in other states in which the entity generates business income. The net result, therefore, can be a reduction in the total state income tax obligation of the consolidated entity. The taxpayer's consolidated federal income tax expense, however, is obviously not affected by this intercompany asset transfer program.

This section presents the valuation, economic, and corporate management aspects related to the design and implementation of an intellectual property transfer program. Some of the issues include identification of specific intellectual properties to transfer, creation of the holding company, methods of quantifying arm's-length transfer prices for the intangible assets, and the most significant economic pros and cons of implementing an intellectual property transfer program.

Trademarks and Trade Names

Corporate trademarks and trade names are the most common intangible assets found in intangible asset transfer programs. Because of the critical importance of corporate trademarks and trade names combined with the need to protect, manage, and control their use, corporations in the retail industry frequently avail themselves of this intangible asset transfer strategy. Corporations in wholesale distribution, manufacturing, service, and other industries may also have the same needs, making the use of an interstate intangible asset transfer program a viable strategic option for many industries.

Transfer of Intellectual Properties

In determining which intangible assets to include in an interstate transfer program, a taxpayer should consider which corporate intangible assets:

- Have legal existence.
- Have economic substance.
- Can be legally transferred to a holding company.
- Have a practical business reason for being transferred to the holding company.
- Are actually used, or used up, in normal business operations in other states.
- Can be associated with a determinable royalty rate or other transfer price, in order to effectively quantify the asset transfer program.
- Have a reasonably long-term and determinable, remaining useful life.
- Will not have to be sold, abandoned, or otherwise transferred back out of the holding company in the foreseeable future.

In the case of trademarks and trade names, a number of additional issues should be considered including:

- Should all trademarks and trade names be transferred?
- Should only the overall corporation trademark be transferred?
- Should all individual brand, product, and service marks be transferred?
- Should future trademarks and trade names be transferred as they are developed?
- Should the trademarks be transferred in perpetuity or for a specified limited term?

These questions cannot be answered in a vacuum. They can be answered only after careful consideration of the above selection criteria and after thorough consideration of the corporate purpose and objectives of the intangible asset transfer program.

Creation of the Intellectual Property Holding Company

Besides advising in the creation of an intellectual property holding company, qualified legal counsel is also necessary before the taxpayer implements any intangible asset transfer program. Title to the trademarks, trade names, and/or other intangibles should be effectively transferred to the newly created holding company, using legal counsel familiar with intellectual property law.

The newly created holding company should have both form and substance. There should be a legitimate business purpose, other than the exclusive goal of minimizing consolidated state tax liability. One traditional corporate purpose for the intangible asset transfer program is to allow the business entity to better control its intangibles. This means internal, as well as external, control, and this would include accounting, legal, administrative, and operational controls. Another common corporate purpose for the asset transfer program is to allow the corporation to explore the possibility of licensing its trademarks, trade names, technology, copyrights, and other intangible assets. The holding company would be the vehicle to license various intangible assets to independent, third-party licensees in arm's-length transactions. As with all stated corporate goals and objectives, these purposes do not ultimately have to be achieved.

To accomplish its business purpose, and to achieve substance as well as form, it is not unusual for the corporate parent to transfer assets, other than intangibles, to the newly created holding company. Often, the parent will transfer cash balances and certain banking relationships to the state of the holding company incorporation. Also, employees are frequently placed on the payroll of the holding company. These employees may be responsible for the management and control of the firm's intangible assets. They may also be accountable for developing and implementing the firm's intangible asset licensing program.

As with any functioning business enterprise, the newly created holding company should prepare financial statements on a periodic basis. These statements should report the results of operations and the financial position of the corporation. The results of operations will include any licensing and investment income less the payroll, rent, utilities, and administrative costs of the business operations. Administrative, accounting, or other services provided to the holding company business operations should be charged through intercompany accounts to the holding company. The holding company's balance sheet will include among its assets the transferred intangibles.

Valuation of the Transferred Intangible Assets

Intangible assets and intellectual properties included in an intercompany asset transfer program are valued using the traditional cost approach, market approach, and income approach valuation methods. These general approaches and specific methods are discussed in detail in Chapter 24, which deals with the valuation of intangible assets.

Other Considerations

As with any asset management or other corporate strategy program, there are costs as well as benefits. These costs should be understood and budgeted before management chooses to implement an intellectual property transfer program.

The asset program could include significant setup costs such as qualified legal and valuation advice, a new holding company entity, as well as the costs associated with transferring assets, personnel, and operations. Also, consideration should be given to the indirect costs associated with possible disruption to the business enterprise during the creation and implementation of the intellectual property program.

In addition to the startup costs, there will probably be continuing administrative costs associated with maintaining the intellectual property transfer program. These costs, as noted earlier, include ongoing periodic legal and valuation advice. In addition, various states may challenge the appropriateness of the intellectual property transfer price. These challenges may come as part of an audit of the impact of the intercompany transfer pricing on the parent corporation's total state income tax liability.

The greatest risk facing a prospective user in an intellectual property transfer program is an unexpected change in the value of the transferred asset—and the corresponding change in the transfer price. After the program is implemented and the assets are transferred, the fair arm's-length transfer price may change due to unanticipated asset obsolescence or economic changes in the industry or in the subject business entity. This is one reason many corporations re-evaluate the fair transfer price formula periodically. Such events could materially affect the cost/benefit considerations concerning an asset transfer program. There is no effective way to ensure against the occurrence of such events.

A valuation firm experienced with intercompany transfer pricing analysis should be able to reasonably estimate a fair transfer price formula and an expected remaining life of the transfer agreement on a preliminary basis. These preliminary estimates should be adequate for planning, evaluation, and decision-making purposes. A more rigorous and thorough valuation and analysis of the remaining economic life of the intangible asset would be required in the actual pricing and structuring phase of implementing the intellectual property transfer program.

Summary of Intellectual Property Valuation for State Income Taxation

As with any strategic planning technique, there are pros and cons to implementing an intellectual property transfer program.

In terms of the pros, the business entity may enjoy increased internal and external control over its intellectual properties. It may implement a legal and an organizational structure to investigate licensing, or otherwise maximize the value of its intellectual properties. And there may be substantial state income tax management opportunities associated with an intellectual property transfer program.

As to the cons, the business entity may experience significant transfer program implementation costs, including the expenses of a cost/benefit analysis study, legal fees, valuation consulting fees, and all the temporary organizational disturbances associated with implementing the program. There may be recurring legal and valuation consulting fees, particularly if certain states decide to challenge the transfer pricing formula. Last, there is the risk that the value—and the associated transfer price—of the transferred assets may change over time. And this risk is not always within the control of corporate management.

Summary

This chapter discussed some of the many reasons to appraise business entities and business interests for federal income tax purposes. In this chapter, we also explored several specific reasons to conduct federal income taxation-related valuations, including setting basis after a property transfer transaction, substantiating charitable contribution deductions, substantiating property abandonment and worthless security deductions, and assessing corporate insolvency with regard to the nonrecognition of cancellation of indebtedness income. In addition, we presented the accuracy-related federal income tax penalties associated with the undervaluation or overvaluation of assets, properties, or business interests. Lastly, we discussed the valuation aspects of the interstate transfer of intellectual properties for state income taxation-related purposes.

Each of these topics was presented from an appraisal and economic perspective. This chapter was not intended to provide legal, accounting, or taxation advice. Appropriate professional advisors should be consulted for such advice.

Chapter 27

Taxation Planning and Compliance—Gifts and Estates

Say not that you know another entirely until you have shared an inheritance with him.
Johann Kaspar Lavater
Swiss theologian, 1788

Introduction

The three most important objectives of estate planning for owners of closely held businesses are:

1.   Provision for liquidity for themselves or their heirs, or both.
2.   Minimization of federal gift and estate taxes and state inheritance taxes.
3.   Provision for continuity of the business.

Liquidity during the owner's lifetime can be achieved by going public, selling the company, selling shares to an employee stock ownership plan (ESOP), or selling shares by other means. Liquidity at the owner's death can be provided by any of the same means or through a buy–sell agreement funded by life insurance. The need for liquidity relates to the business owner's desires not only to cash in on the company's successful growth, but also to have funds available to pay the associated income or estate taxes that the above transactions typically trigger. This chapter discusses the valuation issues that arise in connection with estate and gift planning based on these three key objectives.

Other chapters in Part VII carry this topic further. Chapter 28 focuses on buy–sell agreements. Additional estate planning–related information is contained in Chapter 30 on ESOPs. Elsewhere in the book, Chapter 21 discusses the valuation of preferred stocks, which often have been used in estate freezing recapitalizations.

The first section of this chapter sets forth the nature of estate and gift taxes and the current rates, exemptions, special provisions, and penalties under the current Internal Revenue Code and Regulations. The next section discusses the guidelines for valuation for estate and gift tax purposes (which also can be applied to income tax matters) and includes the complete texts of the most relevant IRS Revenue Rulings. The last section deals with valuation issues arising from specific estate and gift tax planning techniques, including the special valuation rules under Chapter 14. No doubt, over time, new estate planning techniques will continue to be developed in response to the constantly changing economic and tax environment.

The material in this book generally is limited to a discussion of the valuation issues. Anyone involved in appraisal work with tax planning or tax litigation implications should consult a competent attorney and CPA for guidance with regard to legal and tax issues.

Current Tax Rates and Penalties

Estate and gift taxes are a unified system of excise taxes levied on the transfer of wealth during life and at death. In other words, in calculating an individual's final estate taxes, the amount of all taxable gifts that were made during life are added to the estate's gross value and all gift taxes that were paid during life are subtracted from the estate tax payable. The current rates on taxable amounts are presented in Exhibit 27–1.

The law provides for several basic exemptions and exclusions from the amount of net assets that otherwise would be taxable. These adjustments include:

- The first $600,000 of the fair market value of estate or previously gifted assets.[1]
- Any amounts given to one's spouse, either by gift or by will.[2]
- Up to $10,000 gifted annually from any one donor to each of any number of donees.

  Other special provisions affect:

- The value of farm or small-business, special-use real estate (Internal Revenue Code (Section 2032A).
- The time over which estate tax payments can be made and the interest rate charged on such payments on the portion of the estate consisting of interests in a privately owned company engaged in an active trade or business (Section 6166).
- The income tax treatment of redemptions of corporate stock owned by the estate whose proceeds are used to pay estate expenses and taxes (Section 303).
- The choice of the estate asset valuation date (either as of date of death or an alternative valuation date six months after death).

An additional tax can be levied on certain generation-skipping transfers of assets.

There are also penalties for undervaluation of estate and gift assets (Section 6660); these are presented in Table 27–1. The Section 6660 penalties presented in Table 27–1 are triggered by asset undervaluation and computed as a percentage of the tax underpayment. The IRS may decide not to apply these penalties if the returned value was made in good faith and had a reasonable basis. A qualified appraisal prepared by a competent appraiser may constitute part of the establishment of a "reasonable basis."

Table 27–1
Undervaluation Penalties

For Estate and Gift Taxes over $1,000:

Value Claimed on the Tax Return as a Percentage of the Value Finally Determined	Additional Penalty
50% or more	0%
25%–49%	20%
Below 25%	40%

---

[1]There is a unified credit of $192,800 applicable against either the gift or estate tax. This credit is equal to the tax on the first $600,000 of taxable value.

[2]The transfers to the spouse must be "qualified," that is, they must be in a form that would cause the property to be taxed in the spouse's estate if retained until death.

Exhibit 27–1

Current Unified Transfer Tax on Gifts and Estates

If the Amount Is:		Tentative Tax Is:*		
Over $	But Not Over $	Tax + $	%	Of Excess Over $
0	10,000	0	18	0
10,000	20,000	1,800	20	10,000
20,000	40,000	3,800	22	20,000
40,000	60,000	8,200	24	40,000
60,000	80,000	13,000	26	60,000
80,000	100,000	18,200	28	80,000
100,000	150,000	23,800	30	100,000
150,000	250,000	38,800	32	150,000
250,000	500,000	70,800	34	250,000
500,000	750,000	155,800	37	500,000
750,000	1,000,000	248,300	39	750,000
1,000,000	1,250,000	345,800	41	1,000,000
1,250,000	1,500,000	448,300	43	1,250,000
1,500,000	2,000,000	555,800	45	1,500,000
2,000,000	2,500,000	780,800	49	2,000,000
2,500,000	3,000,000	1,025,800	53	2,500,000
3,000,000	- - - - -	1,290,800	55	3,000,000

* Tentative tax is applied to the sum of the taxable estate and all taxable gifts made by the deceased after 1976. The tentative tax shown above is calculated before the application of the unified credit and other credits and certain adjustments. (After 1986 this is $192,800 in tax—equal to $600,000 in assets.)

NOTE: There is a 5% additional tax levied on amounts between $10,000,000 and $21,040,000. This additional tax essentially recaptures the benefits received from the lower brackets and the unified credit for large estates.

Appraisers are subject to a civil penalty of $1,000 for aiding and abetting an understatement of tax liability (Section 6701). Even more serious, the IRS may impose an administrative sanction barring the appraiser from submitting probative evidence in future IRS tax proceedings.

These penalties are similar to the overvaluation penalties imposed on taxpayers who overstate charitable gift values (Section 6659) or depreciable investment asset values for income tax deductions. The charitable contribution penalty is a flat 30 percent of the tax underpayment due to a valuation overstatement if the latter exceeds the finally determined value by 150 percent or more. Charitable gift valuation issues are discussed later in the chapter.

Guidelines for Federal Gift and Estate Tax Valuations

The basic guidelines for the appraisal of closely held business equity for federal gift and estate tax purposes are set forth in the Internal Revenue Code, the Treasury Regulations to the Code, and various revenue rulings, technical advice memorandums, and private letter rulings.

The Internal Revenue Code addresses the valuation of closely held securities in Section 2031(b). The standard of value applied to all gift, estate, and income tax matters concerning the IRS is fair market value. *Fair market value* is defined as the price at which the subject interest would change hands between a willing buyer and a willing seller, neither being under any compulsion to buy or sell and both having knowledge of all relevant facts.

The next most important source of guidance for valuation is the Treasury Regulations, which set forth the IRS's interpretation of the laws set forth in the Code. Each regulation is numbered in the same fashion as the Code section to which it relates. Regulation Section 20.2031-2(f) covers corporate stock and Section 20.2301-3 covers unincorporated interests in businesses. Parallel regulations cover gift taxes in Sections 25.2512-2(f) and 25.2512-3.

Revenue rulings are similar to regulations, except they are drafted to provide guidance for general types of situations not requiring a specific change in the regulations. The basic guidelines for the valuation of closely held common stocks for gift and estate tax purposes are contained in Revenue Ruling 59-60, which Exhibit 27–2 presents in its entirety.

Other forms of IRS opinions are issued in the form of technical advice memorandums (TAMs) and private letter rulings (PLRs), which refer to specific situations in which a taxpayer has sought advice on a specific matter from the IRS. Although these TAMs and PLRs cannot be cited as precedent for anyone but the individual taxpayer, they do provide good evidence of the direction of the IRS thinking on a topic.

Of course the courts have final jurisdiction over tax matters. IRS regulations and positions taken in revenue rulings can be overturned by a single or series of adverse rulings. The United States Tax Court, Federal District Court, and Court of Federal Claims systems all hear cases involving valuation issues for gift and estate taxes.

Revenue Ruling 59-60 has also been modified and amplified by other subsequent revenue rulings.

Exhibit 27–2
Revenue Ruling 59-60

SECTION 1. PURPOSE.

The purpose of this Revenue Ruling is to outline and review in general the approach, methods and factors to be considered in valuing shares of the capital stock of closely held corporations for estate tax and gift tax purposes. The methods discussed herein will apply likewise to the valuation of corporate stocks on which market quotations are either unavailable or are of such scarcity that they do not reflect the fair market value.

SEC. 2. BACKGROUND AND DEFINITIONS.

.01 All valuations must be made in accordance with the applicable provisions of the Internal Revenue Code of 1954 and the Federal Estate Tax and Gift Tax Regulations. Sections 2031(a), 2032 and 2512(a) of the 1954 Code (sections 811 and 1005 of the 1939 Code) require that the property to be included in the gross estate, or made the subject of a gift, shall be taxed on the basis of the value of the property at the time of death of the decedent, the alternate date if so elected, or the date of gift.

.02 Section 20.2031-1(b) of the Estate Tax Regulations (section 81.10 of the Estate Tax Regulations 105) and section 25.2512-1 of the Gift Tax Regulations (section 86.19 of Gift Tax Regulations 108) define fair market value, in effect, as the price at which the property would change hands between a willing buyer and a willing seller when the former is not under any compulsion to buy and the latter is not under any compulsion to sell, both parties having reasonable knowledge of relevant facts. Court decisions frequently state in addition that the hypothetical buyer and seller are assumed to be able, as well as willing, to trade and to be well informed about the property and concerning the market for such property.

.03 Closely held corporations are those corporations the shares of which are owned by a relatively limited number of stockholders. Often the entire stock issue is held by one family. The result of this situation is that little, if any, trading in the shares takes place. There is, therefore, no established market for the stock and such sales as occur at irregular inter-

vals seldom reflect all of the elements of a representative transaction as defined by the term "fair market value."

SEC. 3. APPROACH TO VALUATION.

.01 A determination of fair market value, being a question of fact, will depend upon the circumstances in each case. No formula can be devised that will be generally applicable to the multitude of different valuation issues arising in estate and gift tax cases. Often, an appraiser will find wide differences of opinion as to the fair market value of a particular stock. In resolving such differences, he should maintain a reasonable attitude in recognition of the fact that valuation is not an exact science. A sound valuation will be based upon all the relevant facts, but the elements of common sense, informed judgment and reasonableness must enter into the process of weighing those facts and determining their aggregate significance.

.02 The fair market value of specific shares of stock will vary as general economic conditions change from "normal" to "boom" or "depression," that is, according to the degree of optimism or pessimism with which the investing public regards the future at the required date of appraisal. Uncertainty as to the stability of continuity of the future income from a property decreases its value by increasing the risk of loss of earnings and value in the future. The value of shares of stock of a company with very uncertain future prospects is highly speculative. The appraiser must exercise his judgment as to the degree of risk attaching to the business of the corporation which issued the stock, but that judgment must be related to all of the other factors affecting value.

.03 Valuation of securities is, in essence, a prophesy as to the future and must be based on facts available at the required date of appraisal. As a generalization, the prices of stock which are traded in volume in a free and active market by informed persons best reflect the con-

Exhibit 27–2 (continued)

sensus of the investing public as to what the future holds for the corporations and industries represented. When a stock is closely held, is traded infrequently, or is traded in an erratic market, some other measure of value must be used. In many instances, the next best measure may be found in the prices at which the stocks of companies engaged in the same or a similar line of business are selling in a free and open market.

Sec. 4. Factors to Consider.

.01 It is advisable to emphasize that in the valuation of the stock of closely held corporations or the stock of corporations where market quotations are either lacking or too scarce to be recognized, all available financial data, as well as all relevant factors affecting the fair market value, should be considered. The following factors, although not all-inclusive are fundamental and require careful analysis in each case:

(a) The nature of the business and the history of the enterprise from its inception.

(b) The economic outlook in general and the condition and outlook of the specific industry in particular.

(c) The book value of the stock and the financial condition of the business.

(d) The earning capacity of the company.

(e) The dividend-paying capacity.

(f) Whether or not the enterprise has goodwill or other intangible value.

(g) Sales of the stock and the size of the block of stock to be valued.

(h) The market prices of stock of corporations engaged in the same or a similar line of business having their stocks actively traded in a free and open market, either on an exchange or over-the-counter.

.02 The following is a brief discussion of each of the foregoing factors:

(a) The history of a corporate enterprise will show its past stability or instability, its growth or lack of growth, the diversity or lack of diversity of its operations, and other facts needed to form an opinion of the degree of risk involved in the business. For an enterprise which changed its form of organization but carried on the same or closely similar operations of its predecessor, the history of the former enterprise should be considered. The detail to be considered should increase with approach to the required date of appraisal, since recent events are of greatest help in predicting the future; but a study of gross and net income and of dividends covering a long prior period, is highly desirable. The history to be studied should include, but need not be limited to, the nature of the business, its products or services, its operating and investment assets, capital structure, plant facilities, sales records and management, all of which should be considered as of the date of the appraisal, with due regard for recent significant changes. Events of the past that are unlikely to recur in the future should be discounted, since value has a close relation to future expectancy.

(b) A sound appraisal of a closely held stock must consider current and prospective economic conditions as of the date of appraisal, both in the national economy and in the industry or industries with which the corporation is allied. It is important to know that the company is more or less successful than its competitors in the same industry, or that it is maintaining a stable position with respect to competitors. Equal or even greater significance may attach to the ability of the industry with which the company is allied to compete with other industries. Prospective competition which has not been a factor in prior years should be given careful attention. For example, high profits due to the novelty of its product and the lack of competition often lead to increasing competition. The public's appraisal of the future prospects of competitive industries or of competitors within an industry may be indicated by price trends in the markets for commodities and for securities. The loss of the manager of a so-called "one-man" business may have a depressing effect upon the value of the stock of such business, particularly if there is a lack of trained personnel capable of succeeding to the management of the enterprise. In valuing the stock of this type of business, therefore, the effect of the loss of the manager on the future expectancy of the business, and the absence of management-succession potentialities are pertinent factors to be taken into consideration. On the other hand, there may be factors which offset, in whole or in part, the loss of the manager's services. For instance, the nature of the business and of its assets may be such that they will not be impaired by the loss of the manager. Furthermore, the loss may be ade-

quately covered by life insurance, or competent management might be employed on the basis of the consideration paid for the former manager's services. These, or other offsetting factors, if found to exist, should be carefully weighed against the loss of the manager's services in valuing the stock of the enterprise.

(c) Balance sheets should be obtained, preferably in the form of comparative annual statements for two or more years immediately preceding the date of appraisal, together with a balance sheet at the end of the month preceding that date, if corporate accounting will permit. Any balance sheet descriptions that are not self-explanatory, and balance sheet items comprehending diverse assets or liabilities, should be clarified in essential detail by supporting supplemental schedules. These statements usually will disclose to the appraiser (1) liquid position (ratio of current assets to current liabilities); (2) gross and net book value of principal classes of fixed assets; (3) working capital; (4) long-term indebtedness; (5) capital structure; and (6) net worth. Consideration also should be given to any assets not essential to the operation of the business, such as investments in securities, real estate, etc. In general, such nonoperating assets will command a lower rate of return than do the operating assets, although in exceptional cases the reverse may be true. In computing the book value per share of stock, assets of the investment type should be revalued on the basis of their market price and the book value adjusted accordingly. Comparison of the company's balance sheets over several years may reveal, among other facts, such developments as the acquisition of additional production facilities or subsidiary companies, improvement in financial position, and details as to recapitalizations and other changes in the capital structure of the corporation. If the corporation has more than one class of stock outstanding, the charter or certificate of incorporation should be examined to ascertain the explicit rights and privileges of the various stock issues including: (1) voting powers, (2) preference as to dividends, and (3) preference as to assets in the event of liquidation.

(d) Detailed profit-and-loss statements should be obtained and considered for a representative period immediately prior to the required date of appraisal, preferably five or more years. Such statements should show (1) gross income by principal items; (2) principal deductions from gross income including major prior items of operating expenses, interest and other expense on each item of long-term debt, depreciation and depletion if such deductions are made, officers' salaries, in total if they appear to be reasonable or in detail if they seem to be excessive, contributions (whether or not deductible for tax purposes) that the nature of its business and its community position require the corporation to make, and taxes by principal items, including income and excess profits taxes; (3) net income available for dividends; (4) rates and amounts of dividends paid on each class of stock; (5) remaining amount carried to surplus; and (6) adjustments to, and reconciliation with, surplus as stated on the balance sheet. With profit and loss statements of this character available, the appraiser should be able to separate recurrent from nonrecurrent items of income and expense, to distinguish between operating income and investment income, and to ascertain whether or not any line of business in which the company is engaged is operated consistently at a loss and might be abandoned with benefit to the company. The percentage of earnings retained for business expansion should be noted when dividend-paying capacity is considered. Potential future income is a major factor in many valuations of closely held stocks, and all information concerning past income which will be helpful in predicting the future should be secured. Prior earnings records usually are the most reliable guide as to the future expectancy, but resort to arbitrary five-or-ten-year averages without regard to current trends or future prospects will not produce a realistic valuation. If, for instance, a record of progressively increasing or decreasing income is found, then greater weight may be accorded the most recent years' profits in estimating earning power. It will be helpful, in judging risk and the extent to which a business is a marginal operator, to consider deductions from income and net income in terms of percentage of sales. Major categories of cost and expense to be so analyzed include the consumption of raw materials and supplies in the case of manufacturers, processors and fabricators; the cost of purchased merchandise in the case of merchants; utility services; insurance; taxes; depletion or depreciation; and interest.

(e) Primary consideration should be given to the dividend-paying

Exhibit 27–2 (continued)

capacity of the company rather than to dividends actually paid in the past. Recognition must be given to the necessity of retaining a reasonable portion of profits in a company to meet competition. Dividend-paying capacity is a factor that must be considered in an appraisal, but dividends actually paid in the past may not have any relation to dividend-paying capacity. Specifically, the dividends paid by a closely held family company may be measured by the income needs of the stockholders or by their desire to avoid taxes on dividend receipts, instead of by the ability of the company to pay dividends. Where an actual or effective controlling interest in a corporation is to be valued, the dividend factor is not a material element, since the payment of such dividends is discretionary with the controlling stockholders. The individual or group in control can substitute salaries and bonuses for dividends, thus reducing net income and understating the dividend-paying capacity of the company. If follows, therefore, that dividends are less reliable criteria of fair market value than other applicable factors.

(f)   In the final analysis, goodwill is based upon earning capacity. The presence of goodwill and its value, therefore, rests upon the excess of net earnings over and above a fair return on the net tangible assets. While the element of goodwill may be based primarily on earnings, such factors as the prestige and renown of the business, the ownership of a trade or brand name, and a record of successful operation over a prolonged period in a particular locality, also may furnish support for the inclusion of intangible value. In some instances it may not be possible to make a separate appraisal of the tangible and intangible assets of the business. The enterprise has a value as an entity. Whatever intangible value there is, which is supportable by the facts, may be measured by the amount by which the appraised value of the tangible assets exceeds the net book value of such assets.

(g)   Sales of stock of a closely held corporation should be carefully investigated to determine whether they represent transactions at arm's length. Forced or distress sales do not ordinarily reflect fair market value nor do isolated sales in small amounts necessarily control as the measure of value. This is especially true in the valuation of a controlling interest in a corporation. Since, in the case of closely held stocks, no prevailing market prices are available, there is no basis for making an adjustment for blockage. It follows, therefore, that such stocks should be valued upon a consideration of all the evidence affecting the fair market value. The size of the block of stock itself is a relevant factor to be considered. Although it is true that a minority interest in an unlisted corporation's stock is more difficult to sell than a similar block of listed stock, it is equally true that control of a corporation, either actual or in effect, representing as it does an added element of value, may justify a higher value for a specific block of stock.

(h)   Section 2031(b) of the Code states, in effect, that in valuing unlisted securities the value of stock or securities of corporations engaged in the same or a similar line of business which are listed on an exchange should be taken into consideration along with all other factors. An important consideration is that the corporations to be used for comparisons have capital stocks which are actively traded by the public. In accordance with section 2031(b) of the Code, stocks listed on an exchange are to be considered first. However, if sufficient comparable companies whose stocks are listed on an exchange cannot be found, other comparable companies which have stocks actively traded in on the over-the-counter market also may be used. The essential factor is that whether the stocks are sold on an exchange or over-the-counter there is evidence of an active, free public market for the stock as of the valuation date. In selecting corporations for comparative purposes, care should be taken to use only comparable companies. Although the only restrictive requirement as to comparable corporations specified in the statute is that their lines of business be the same or similar, yet it is obvious that consideration must be given to other relevant factors in order that the most valid comparison possible will be obtained. For illustration, a corporation having one or more issues of preferred stock, bonds or debentures in addition to its common stock should not be considered to be directly comparable to one having only common stock outstanding. In like manner, a company with a declining business and decreasing markets is not comparable to one with a record of current progress and market expansion.

SEC. 5.   WEIGHT TO BE ACCORDED VARIOUS FACTORS.

The valuation of closely held corporate stock entails the consideration of all relevant factors as stated in section 4. Depending upon the circumstances in each case, certain factors may carry more weight than others because of the nature of the company's business. To illustrate:

(a)   Earnings may be the most important criterion of value in some cases whereas asset value will receive primary consideration in others. In general, the appraiser will accord primary consideration to earnings when valuing stocks of companies which sell products or services to the public; conversely, in the investment or holding type of company, the appraiser may accord the greatest weight to the assets underlying the security to be valued.

(b)   The value of the stock of a closely held investment or real estate holding company, whether or not family owned, is closely related to the value of the assets underlying the stock. For companies of this type the appraiser should determine the fair market values of the assets of the company. Operating expenses of such a company and the cost of liquidating it, if any, merit consideration when appraising the relative values of the stock and the underlying assets. The market values of the underlying assets give due weight to potential earnings and dividends of the particular items of property underlying the stock, capitalized at rates deemed proper by the investing public at the date of appraisal. A current appraisal by the investing public should be superior to the retrospective opinion of an individual. For these reasons, adjusted net worth should be accorded greater weight in valuing the stock of a closely held investment or real estate holding company, whether or not family owned, than any of the other customary yardsticks of appraisal, such as earnings and dividend paying capacity.

SEC. 6.   CAPITALIZATION RATES.

In the application of certain fundamental valuation factors, such as earnings and dividends, it is necessary to capitalize the average of current results at some appropriate rate. A determination of the proper capitalization rate presents one of the most difficult problems in valuation. That there is no ready or simple solution will become apparent by a cursory check of the rates of return and dividend yields in terms of the selling prices of corporate shares listed on the major exchanges of the country. Wide variations will be found even for companies in the same industry. Moreover, the ratio will fluctuate from year to year depending upon economic conditions. Thus, no standard tables of capitalization rates applicable to closely held corporations can be formulated. Among the more important factors to be taken into consideration in deciding upon a capitalization rate in a particular case are: (1) the nature of the business; (2) the risk involved; and (3) the stability or irregularity of earnings.

SEC. 7.   AVERAGE OF FACTORS.

Because valuations cannot be made on the basis of a prescribed formula, there is no means whereby the various applicable factors in a particular case can be assigned mathematical weights in deriving the fair market value. For this reason, no useful purpose is served by taking an average of several factors (for example, book value, capitalized earnings and capitalized dividends) and basing the valuation on the result. Such a process excludes active consideration of other pertinent factors, and the end result cannot be supported by a realistic application of the significant facts in the case except by mere chance.

SEC. 8.   RESTRICTIVE AGREEMENTS.

Frequently, in the valuation of closely held stock for estate and gift tax purposes, it will be found that the stock is subject to an agreement restricting its sale or transfer. Where shares of stock were acquired by a decedent subject to an option reserved by the issuing corporation to repurchase at a certain price, the option price is usually accepted as the fair market value for estate tax purposes. See Rev. Rul. 54-76, C.B. 1954-1, 194. However, in such case the option price is not determinative of fair market value for gift tax purposes. Where the option, or buy and sell agreement, is the result of voluntary action by the stockholders and is binding during the life as well as at the death of the stockholders, such agreement may or may not, depending upon the circumstances of each case, fix the value for estate tax purposes. However, such agreement is a factor to be considered, with other relevant factors, in determining fair market value. Where the stockholder is free to dispose of his shares during life and the option is to become effective only upon his death, the fair

Exhibit 27–2 (concluded)

market value is not limited to the option price. It is always necessary to consider the relationship of the parties, the relative number of shares held by the decedent, and other material facts, to determine whether the agreement represents a bonafide business arrangement or is a device to pass the decedent's shares to the natural objects of his bounty for less than an adequate and full consideration in money or money's worth. In

this connection see Rev. Rul. 157 C.B. 1953-2, 255, and Rev. Rul. 189, C.B. 1953-2, 294.

SEC. 9. EFFECT ON OTHER DOCUMENTS.
Revenue Ruling 54-77, C.B. 1954-1, 187, is hereby superseded.

SOURCE: Rev. Rul. 59-60, 1959-1, C.B. 237.

Revenue Ruling 77-287, presented as Exhibit 27–3, amplifies Revenue Ruling 59-60 by specifically recognizing criteria for determining an appropriate discount for lack of marketability. It also provides guidance for discounts to be applied to publicly traded securities restricted under federal securities laws (see Chapter 15). Revenue Ruling 83-120, discussed in Chapter 21, contains guidelines for valuing preferred stock. Revenue Ruling 93-12, presented in Exhibit 27–4, acknowledged that stock interest transfers among family members, who in the aggregate own a controlling interest in the company, would not be valued as controlling interests solely due to the family relationship among the shareholders. This acknowledgment that minority interest transfers among relatives would normally be treated as minority interests for valuation purposes follows a long series of IRS losses in court on this issue.

If the analyst follows the valuation procedures presented in this book with reasonable thoroughness, the requirements of these rulings should be satisfied. Consequently, beyond including the relevant rulings as exhibits, this section will simply call attention to a few points in Revenue Ruling 59-60. The following chapters discuss a variety of key factors in the context of various positions taken and decisions reached in court cases.

Revenue Ruling 59-60, Section 3, "Approach to Valuation," makes the general point that the public marketplace best reflects the consensus of the investing public, and it concludes by suggesting as a measure of value "the prices at which the stocks of companies engaged in the same or similar line of business are selling in a free and open market." The section also recognizes that the value can change as a result of factors internal to the company and external economic factors. The section emphasizes the complexity of the factors affecting valuation and the degree of uncertainty involved.

Revenue Ruling 59-60, Section 4, "Factors to Consider," lists eight key factors to consider with regard to the valuation of closely held corporations and elaborates on each. In any appraisal involving gift and estate taxes, the appraiser should review Section 4 to ensure that each of the eight points has been addressed in the total valuation process.

Revenue Ruling 59-60, Section 4.02(c) notes, "In computing the book value per share of stock, assets *of the investment type* should be revalued on the basis of their market price and the book value adjusted accordingly [emphasis supplied]." It is important to recognize that this requirement to adjust asset values specifically applies to assets "of the investment type," not operating assets.

Section 4.02(d) notes that the profit and loss statements to be considered should be for a "representative period." The section states the appraiser should separate recurrent from nonrecurrent items and operating income from investment income. It suggests putting more weight on recent years if there appears to be a trend in the earnings pattern.

Exhibit 27–3
Revenue Ruling 77-287

SECTION 1. PURPOSE.

The purpose of this Revenue Ruling is to amplify Rev. Rul. 59-60, 1959-1 C.B. 237, as modified by Rev. Rul. 65-193, 1965-2 C.B. 370, and to provide information and guidance to taxpayers, Internal Revenue Service personnel, and others concerned with the valuation, for Federal tax purposes, of securities that cannot be immediately resold because they are restricted from resale pursuant to Federal securities laws. This guidance is applicable only in cases where it is not inconsistent with valuation requirements of the Internal Revenue Code of 1954 or the regulations thereunder. Further, this ruling does not establish the time at which property shall be valued.

SEC. 2. NATURE OF THE PROBLEM.

It frequently becomes necessary to establish the fair market value of stock that has not been registered for public trading when the issuing company has stock of the same class that is actively traded in one or more securities markets. The problem is to determine the difference in fair market value between the registered shares that are actively traded and the unregistered shares. This problem is often encountered in estate and gift tax cases. However, it is sometimes encountered when unregistered shares are issued in exchange for assets or the stock of an acquired company.

SEC. 3. BACKGROUND AND DEFINITIONS.

.01 The Service outlined and reviewed in general the approach, methods, and factors to be considered in valuing shares of closely held corporate stock for estate and gift tax purposes in Rev. Rul. 59-60, as modified by Rev. Rul. 65-193. The provisions of Rev. Rul. 59-60, as modified, were extended to the valuation of corporate securities for income and other tax purposes by Rev. Rul. 68-609, 1968-2 C.B. 327.

.02 There are several terms currently in use in the securities industry that denote restrictions imposed on the resale and transfer of certain securities. The term frequently used to describe these securities is "restricted securities," but they are sometimes referred to as "unregistered securities," "investment letter stock," "control stock," or "private placement stock." Frequently these terms are used interchangeably. They all indicate that these particular securities cannot lawfully be distributed to the general public until a registration statement relating to the corporation underlying the securities has been filed, and has also become effective under the rules promulgated and enforced by the United States Securities & Exchange Commission (SEC) pursuant to the Federal securities laws. The following represents a more refined definition of each of the following terms along with two other terms—"exempted securities" and "exempted transactions."

(a) The term "restricted securities" is defined in Rule 144 adopted by the SEC as "securities acquired directly or indirectly from the issuer thereof, or from an affiliate of such issuer, in a transaction or chain of transactions not involving any public offering."

(b) The term "unregistered securities" refers to those securities with respect to which a registration statement, providing full disclosure by the issuing corporation, has not been filed with the SEC pursuant to the Securities Act of 1933. The registration statement is a condition precedent to a public distribution of securities in interstate commerce and is aimed at providing the prospective investor with a factual basis for sound judgment in making investment decisions.

(c) The terms "investment letter stock" and "letter stock" denote shares of stock that have been issued by a corporation without the benefit of filing a registration statement with the SEC. Such stock is subject to resale and transfer restrictions set forth in a letter agreement requested by the issuer and signed by the buyer of the stock when the stock is delivered. Such stock may be found in the hands of either individual investors or institutional investors.

(d) The term "control stock" indicates that the shares of stock have been held or are being held by an officer, director, or other person close to the management of the corporation. These persons are subject to certain requirements pursuant to SEC rules upon resale of shares they own in such corporations.

(e) The term "private placement stock" indicates that the stock has been placed with an institution or other investor who will presumably hold it for a long period and ultimately arrange to have the stock registered if it is to be offered to the general public. Such stock may or may not be subject to a letter agreement. Private placements of stock are exempted from the registration and prospectus provisions of the Securities Act of 1933.

(f) The term "exempted securities" refers to those classes of securities that are expressly excluded from the registration provisions of the Securities Act of 1933 and the distribution provisions of the Securities Exchange Act of 1934.

(g) The term "exempted transactions" refers to certain sales or distributions of securities that do not involve a public offering and are excluded from the registration and prospectus provisions of the Securities Act of 1933 and distribution provisions of the Securities Exchange Act of 1934. The exempted status makes it unnecessary for issuers of securities to go through the registration process.

SEC. 4. SECURITIES INDUSTRY PRACTICE IN VALUING RESTRICTED SECURITIES.

.01 *Investment Company Valuation Practices.* The Investment Company Act of 1940 requires open-end investment companies to publish the valuation of their portfolio securities daily. Some of these companies have portfolios containing restricted securities, but also have unrestricted securities of the same class traded on a securities exchange. In recent years the number of restricted securities in such portfolios have increased. The following methods have been used by investment companies in the valuation of such restricted securities:

(a) Current market price of the unrestricted stock less a constant percentage discount based on purchase discount;

(b) Current market price of unrestricted stock less a constant percentage discount different from purchase discount;

(c) Current market price of the unrestricted stock less a discount amortized over a fixed period;

(d) Current market price of the unrestricted stock; and

(e) Cost of the restricted stock until it is registered.

The SEC ruled in its Investment Company Act Release No. 5847, dated October 21, 1969, that there can be no automatic formula by which an investment company can value the restricted securities in its portfolios. Rather, the SEC has determined that it is the responsibility of the board of directors of the particular investment company to determine the "fair value" of each issue of restricted securities in good faith.

.02 *Institutional Investors Study.* Pursuant to Congressional direction, the SEC undertook an analysis of the purchases, sales, and holding of securities by financial institutions, in order to determine the effect of institutional activity upon the securities market. The study report was published in eight volumes in March 1971. The fifth volume provides an analysis of restricted securities and deals with such items as the characteristics of the restricted securities purchasers and issuers, the size of transactions (dollars and shares), the marketability discounts on different trading markets, and the resale provisions. This research project provides some guidance for measuring the discount in that it contains information, based on the actual experience of the marketplace, showing that, during the period surveyed (January 1, 1966, through June 30, 1969), the amount of discount allowed for restricted securities from the trading price of the unrestricted securities was generally related to the following four factors:

(a) *Earnings.* Earnings and sales consistently have a significant influence on the size of restricted securities discounts according to the study. Earnings played the major part in establishing the ultimate discounts at which these stocks were sold from the current market price. Apparently earnings patterns, rather than sales patterns, determine the degree of risk of an investment.

(b) *Sales.* The dollar amount of sales of issuers' securities also has a major influence on the amount of discount at which restricted securities sell from the current market price. The results of the study generally indicate that the companies with the lowest dollar amount of sales during the test period accounted for most of the transactions involving the highest discount rates, while they accounted for only a small portion of all transactions involving the lowest discount rates.

Exhibit 27–3 (concluded)

(c) *Trading Market.* The market in which publicly held securities are traded also reflects variances in the amount of discount that is applied to restricted securities purchases. According to the study, discount rates were greatest on restricted stocks with unrestricted counterparts traded over-the-counter, followed by those with unrestricted counterparts listed on the American Stock Exchange, while the discount rates for those stocks with unrestricted counterparts listed on the New York Stock Exchange were the smallest.

(d) *Resale Agreement Provisions.* Resale agreement provisions often affect the size of the discount. The discount from the market price provides the main incentive for a potential buyer to acquire restricted securities. In judging the opportunity cost of freezing funds, the purchaser is analyzing two separate factors. The first factor is the risk that underlying value of the stock will change in a way that, absent the restrictive provisions, would have prompted a decision to sell. The second factor is the risk that the contemplated means of legally disposing of the stock may not materialize. From the seller's point of view, a discount is justified where the seller is relieved of the expenses of registration and public distribution, as well as of the risk that the market will adversely change before the offering is completed. The ultimate agreement between buyer and seller is a reflection of these and other considerations. Relative bargaining strengths of the parties to the agreement are major considerations that influence the resale terms and consequently the size of discounts in restricted securities transactions. Certain provisions are often found in agreements between buyers and sellers that affect the size of discounts at which restricted stocks are sold. Several such provisions follow, all of which, other than number (3), would tend to reduce the size of the discount:

(1) A provision giving they buyer an option to "piggyback", that is, to register restricted stock with the next registration statement, if any, filed by the issuer with the SEC;

(2) A provision giving the buyer an option to require registration at the seller's expense;

(3) A provision giving the buyer an option to require registration, but only at the buyer's own expense;

(4) A provision giving the buyer a right to receive continuous disclosure of information about the issuer from the seller;

(5) A provision giving the buyer a right to select one or more directors of the issuer;

(6) A provision giving the buyer an option to purchase additional shares of the issuer's stock; and

(7) A provision giving the buyer the right to have a greater voice in operations of the issuer, if the issuer does not meet previously agreed upon operating standards.

Institutional buyers can and often do obtain many of these rights and options from the sellers of restricted securities, and naturally, the more rights the buyer can acquire, the lower the buyer's risk is going to be, thereby reducing the buyer's discount as well. Small buyers may not be able to negotiate the large discounts or the rights and options that volume buyers are able to negotiate.

.03 *Summary.* A variety of methods have been used by the securities industry to value restricted securities. The SEC rejects all automatic or mechanical solutions to the valuation of restricted securities, and prefers, in the case of the valuation of investment company portfolio stocks, to rely upon good faith valuations by the board of directors of each company. The study made by the SEC found that restricted securities generally are issued at a discount from the market value of freely tradable securities.

SEC. 5. FACTS AND CIRCUMSTANCES MATERIAL TO VALUATION OF RESTRICTED SECURITIES.

.01 Frequently, a company has a class of stock that cannot be traded publicly. The reason such stock cannot be traded may arise from the securities statutes, as in the case of an "investment letter" restriction; it may arise from a corporate charter restriction, or perhaps from a trust agreement restriction. In such cases, certain documents and facts should be obtained for analysis.

.02 The following documents and facts, when used in conjunction with those discussed in Section 4 of Rev. Rul. 59-60, will be useful in the valuation of restricted securities:

(a) A copy of any declaration of trust, trust agreement, and any other agreements relating to the shares of restricted stock;

(b) A copy of any document showing any offers to buy or sell or indications of interest in buying or selling the restricted shares;

(c) The latest prospectus of the company;

(d) Annual reports of the company for 3 to 5 years preceding the valuation date;

(e) The trading prices and trading volume of the related class of traded securities 1 month preceding the valuation date, if they are traded on a stock exchange (if traded over-the-counter, prices may be obtained from the National Quotations Bureau, the National Association of Securities Dealers Automated Quotations (NASDAQ), or sometimes from broker-dealers making markets in the shares);

(f) The relationship of the parties to the agreements concerning the restricted stock, such as whether they are members of the immediate family or perhaps whether they are officers or directors of the company; and

(g) Whether the interest being valued represents a majority or minority ownership.

SEC. 6. WEIGHING FACTS AND CIRCUMSTANCES MATERIAL TO RESTRICTED STOCK VALUATION.

All relevant facts and circumstances that bear upon the worth of restricted stock, including those set forth above in the preceding Sections 4 and 5, and those set forth in Section 4 of Rev. Rul. 59-60, must be taken into account in arriving at the fair market value of such securities. Depending on the circumstances of each case, certain factors may carry more weight than others. To illustrate:

.01 Earnings, net assets, and net sales must be given primary consideration in arriving at an appropriate discount for restricted securities from the freely traded shares. These are the elements of value that are always used by investors in making investment decisions. In some cases, one element may be more important than in other cases. In the case of manufacturing, producing, or distributing companies, primary weight must be accorded earnings and net sales; but in the case of investment or holding companies, primary weight must be given to the net assets of the company underlying the stock. In the former type of companies, value is more closely linked to past, present, and future earnings while in the latter type of companies, value is more closely linked to the existing net assets of the company. See the discussion in Section 5 of Rev. Rul. 59-60.

.02 Resale provisions found in the restriction agreements must be scrutinized and weighted to determine the amount of discount to apply to the preliminary fair market value of the company. The two elements of time and expense bear upon this discount; the longer the buyer of the shares must wait to liquidate the shares, the greater the discount. Moreover, if the provisions make it necessary for the buyer to bear the expense of registration, the greater the discount. However, if the provisions of the restricted stock agreement make it possible for the buyer to "piggyback" shares at the next offering, the discount would be smaller.

.03 The relative negotiation strengths of the buyer and seller of restricted stock may have a profound effect on the amount of discount. For example, a tight money situation may cause the buyer to have the greater balance of negotiation strength in a transaction. However, in some cases the relative strengths may tend to cancel each other out.

.04 The market experience of freely tradable securities of the same class as the restricted securities is also significant in determining the amount of discount. Whether the shares are privately held or publicly traded affects the worth of the shares to the holder. Securities traded on a public market generally are worth more to investors than those that are not traded on a public market. Moreover, the type of public market in which the unrestricted securities are traded is to be given consideration.

SEC. 7. EFFECT ON OTHER DOCUMENTS.

Rev. Rul. 59-60, as modified by Rev. Rul. 65-193, is amplified.

SOURCE: Rev. Rul. 77-287, 1977-2, C.B. 319.

Exhibit 27–4

Revenue Ruling 93-12

Issue

If a donor transfers shares in a corporation to each of the donor's children, is the factor of corporate control in the family to be considered in valuing each transferred interest, for purposes of section 2512 of the Internal Revenue Code?

Facts

P owned all of the single outstanding class of stock of *X* corporation. *P* transferred all of *P*'s shares by making simultaneous gifts of 20 percent of the shares to each of *P*'s five children, *A, B, C, D,* and *E.*

Law and Analysis

Section 2512(a) of the Code provides that the value of the property at the date of the gift shall be considered the amount of the gift.

Section 25.2512-1 of the Gift Tax Regulations provides that, if a gift is made in property, its value at the date of the gift shall be considered the amount of the gift. The value of the property is the price at which the property would change hands between a willing buyer and a willing seller, neither being under any compulsion to buy or to sell, and both having reasonable knowledge of relevant facts.

Section 25.2512-2(a) of the regulations provides that the value of stocks and bonds is the fair market value per share or bond on the date of the gift. Section 25.2512-2(f) provides that the degree of control of the business represented by the block of stock to be valued is among the factors to be considered in valuing stock where there are no sales prices or bona fide bid or asked prices.

Rev. Rul. 81-253, 1981-1C.B. 187, holds that, ordinarily, no minority shareholder discount is allowed with respect to transfers of shares of stock between family members if, based upon a composite of the family members' interest at the time of the transfer, control (either majority voting control or de facto control through family relationships) of the corporation exists in the family unit. The ruling also states that the Service will not follow the decision of the Fifth Circuit in *Estate of Bright v. United States,* 658 F.2d 999 (5th Cir. 1981).

In *Bright,* the decedent's undivided community property interest in shares of stock, together with the corresponding undivided community property interest of the decedent's surviving spouse, constituted a control block of 55 percent of the shares of a corporation. The court held that, because the community-held shares were subject to a right of partition,

SOURCE: Rev. Rul. 93-12, 1993-1, C.B. 202.

the decedent's own interest was equivalent to 27.5 percent of the outstanding shares and, therefore, should be valued as a minority interest, even though the shares were to be held by the decedent's surviving spouse as trustee of a testamentary trust. *See also, Propstra v. United States,* 680 F.2d 1248 (9th Cir. 1982). In addition, *Estate of Andrews v. Commissioner,* 79 T.C. 938 (1982), and *Estate of Lee v. Commissioner,* 69 T.C. 860 (1978), *nonacq.,* 1980-2C.B. 2, held that the corporation shares owned by other family members cannot be attributed to an individual family member for determining whether the individual family member's share should be valued as the controlling interest of the corporation.

After further consideration of the position taken in Rev. Rul. 81-253, and in light of the cases noted above, the Service has concluded that, in the case of a corporation with a single class of stock, notwithstanding the family relationship of the donor, the donee, and other shareholders, the shares of other family members will not be aggregated with the transferred shares to determine whether the transferred shares should be valued as part of a controlling interest.

In the present case, the minority interests transferred to *A, B, C, D,* and *E* should be valued for gift tax purposes without regard to the family relationship of the parties.

Holding

If a donor transfers shares in a corporation to each of the donor's children, the factor of corporate control in the family is not considered in valuing each transferred interest for purposes of section 2512 of the Code. For estate and gift tax valuation purposes, the Service will follow *Bright, Propstra, Andrews,* and *Lee* in not assuming that all voting power held by family members may be aggregated for purposes of determining whether the transferred shares should be valued as part of a controlling interest. Consequently, a minority discount will not be disallowed solely because a transferred interest, when aggregated with interest held by family members, would be a part of a controlling interest. This would be the case whether the donor held 100 percent or some lesser percentage of the stock immediately before the gift.

Effect on Other Documents

Rev. Rul. 81-253 is revoked. Acquiescence in issue one of *Lee,* 1980-2 C.B. 2.

Section 4.02(h) reemphasizes that the prices of stocks of publicly traded companies in the same or similar lines of business should be considered and the greatest care possible taken in analyzing the companies to select the ones that are most comparative to the subject securities. Chapter 10 discusses the identification and selection of guideline publicly traded stocks.

Weight to Be Accorded Various Factors

Section 5, "Weight to Be Accorded Various Factors," essentially makes the point that earnings should be accorded the most weight in valuing operating companies and asset values the most weight in valuing holding companies.

The section also notes that assets should be adjusted to market values if they are a factor in an operating company. For family-held investment companies, comparisons of per share value to underlying asset value can then be made on the basis of the multiples of market value to net asset value for closed-end investment companies, since such companies report the values of their assets at market on a regular basis. For closely held real estate holding companies, deriving a per share value by reference to publicly traded real estate holding companies is not quite as easy, since most real estate companies do not report their assets' market values. However, in the last few years quite a few real estate investment trusts (REITs) have started reporting market values. There now are enough reporting such market values that a table of REITs with the multiples of market prices to adjusted asset values can be constructed to provide guidance in valuing closely held real estate holding company shares.

Capitalization Rates

Section 6, "Capitalization Rates," makes further reference to publicly traded shares and notes that appropriate capitalization rates vary considerably both among companies and over time due to economic conditions.

Average of Factors

Section 7, "Average of Factors," is the section referred to in Chapter 16 that discourages use of a mathematical weighting of various factors. The reason is that "such a process excludes active consideration of other pertinent factors." However, as noted in Chapter 16 and in the examples presented in Chapter 16, mathematical weighting frequently is used in practice, even by government representatives, and relied on in court decisions despite the wording of this section.

Restrictive Agreements

Section 8, "Restrictive Agreements," makes the point that to be binding for estate tax valuation purposes, a price fixed under a buy–sell agreement must be binding during the life as well as at the death of the stockholder and not "a device to pass the decedent's shares to the natural objects of his bounty for less than adequate and full consideration in money or money's worth." See Chapter 28, "Buy–Sell Agreements," for additional discussion.

Summary of Guidelines

Although Revenue Ruling 59-60 was written over 35 years ago, it still offers considerable insight into the basic criteria and processes for valuing closely held common stocks. With minor modifications and amplification, it has stood the test of time.

Nevertheless, the nature of the process necessarily leaves much room for subjectivity and disagreement. Interpretations by IRS agents and courts have been somewhat less than consistent. It is not a subject that lends itself to such sharp definition of criteria that gray areas can be eliminated.

Chapter 14 Special Valuation Guidelines

Aside from the basic guidelines that have evolved over the years for valuing closely held securities for federal estate and gift taxes, in 1990 Congress passed a series of special valuation rules listed under a newly created Chapter 14 of the Internal Revenue Code. Chapter 14 was enacted to stem what the IRS convinced Congress to be certain abusive practices that involved valuation issues. Each of the four sections of Chapter 14, Sections 2701 through 2704, addresses a different series of issues and is discussed below. Because of limitations on the size of this book, we can only address the major topics with which a business appraiser is likely to deal under Chapter 14.

These special valuation rules potentially apply to all transactions (or modifications to prior existing arrangements) that occur after October 8, 1990, the effective date of the Chapter 14 statute.

It is very important to note that, if the Chapter 14 special valuation rules do not apply, the basic guidelines discussed in the previous section of this chapter, and other generally accepted techniques used to determine fair market value, will apply. The special valuation rules themselves are designed to modify the generally accepted appraisal guidelines for gift and estate tax valuation. Consequently, the structure of the special valuation rules clearly shows that Congress did not intend to eliminate consideration of discounts for lack of control for minority interest transfers or discounts for lack of marketability for estate and gift tax issues, even when family members as a group own control of an enterprise.

Valuing Recapitalizations and Senior Equity Interests under Section 2701

Section 2701 of Chapter 14 sets forth special valuation rules utilized for lifetime gifts when a junior equity interest (corporate, partnership, or limited liability company) is transferred from one family member to another and the transferor retains a senior equity interest in the company. In other words, Section 2701 deals with the classic preferred estate "freeze."

Triggering the Special Valuation Rules. To fall under the rules of Section 2701, the following characteristics must be present in a transaction:

- The retained security must be of a class senior to the transferred junior security.
- The subject securities (both the retained senior preferred and transferred junior securities) must be nonpublicly traded.
- The transaction must result in a transfer (directly or indirectly) between members of the family.[3]
- Immediately before the transfer, the transferor and applicable family members[4] in the aggregate have 50 percent or more (by vote or value) control of the corporate stock, or of the capital or profits interests in a partnership or

---

[3]*Member of the family* is defined as the transferor's spouse, the transferor's (or the spouse's) lineal descendants (and their spouses). In other words, any natural or adopted children or offspring of the children of the transferor and all associated spouses. Notice that such transfers do not apply to transfers from uncles and aunts to nieces and nephews.

[4]*Applicable family member* is defined differently than "member of the family." An applicable family member includes (1) The transferor and spouse, (2) the transferor's (or spouse's) ancestors (or their ancestors' spouses). For purposes of measuring control, the transferor's brothers, sisters, or other lineal descendants of the parents of the transferor (or spouse) are also included as part of the measuring group of interest holders. Indirect applicable family member holdings through corporations, partnerships, and trusts are also included. Some background in genealogy is thus required as part of the due diligence for estate and gift tax valuation under Chapter 14.

limited liability company. Or, the transferor and the applicable family members must own any general partnership interest in a limited partnership.

- The transfer is not a proportionate transfer of all senior and junior equity interests and, as mentioned, the transferor must retain a senior equity interest.

If the transfer has these characteristics, then certain retained rights of the "applicable retained interest" (as the preferred senior security is called in Section 2701) must be ignored, and a special subtraction method of valuation must be followed, in estimating fair market value for federal gift tax purposes.

Section 2701 basically requires that all rights and features of the preferred senior security that have any optional features in terms of payment amounts or timing that can potentially be manipulated by the controlling family be ignored or valued in a manner that results in the lowest possible value for the preferred senior interest.

As a result, all noncumulative distribution rights (such as dividends) are valued at zero. Similarly, any extraordinary payment right, such as a put, call, conversion, liquidation right, or option to acquire equity interests, is valued at zero—with certain exceptions described below.

The practical effect of these rules, from an appraisal standpoint, is that only a few features will provide a basis for attributing value to the applicable retained senior securities. These include:

- *Cumulative dividends or distribution rights.* These can be either fixed in amount or variable if linked by a fixed ratio to a public market interest rate. These are called qualified distribution rights. The taxpayer may make a permanent election to treat any noncumulative distribution right as a cumulative, qualified distribution right.[5] Therefore, the appraiser should check with the client or the client's tax advisors to see if such an election has been made or will be made. If such qualified distributions are not actually made within four years of their scheduled payment date, then these unpaid distributions are treated as gifts and compounded forward for ultimate payment when the holder dies or transfers his or her interest.
- *Voting rights.* In valuing voting rights, however, any of the extraordinary payment rights discussed above are assumed either not to exist or are exercised under the "lower of" rule discussed below.
- *Mandatory redemption rights.* This category of redemption rights must require the retained preferred senior interest to receive a specific amount at a specific date. Optional extraordinary payment redemption rights that can be voluntarily exercised by either the holder or the company do not count.
- *Nonlapsing conversion rights.* Conversion rights that add value under Section 2701 must require that the senior interests be convertible into a stated number of shares or percentage of the same class as the transferred interest. Obviously, this will tend to make the preferred interest increase in value with the underlying junior equity securities, and thus frustrate a freeze of the senior preferred interest. The timing of conversion can be optional.

There is also an additional "lower of" valuation rule that requires the appraiser to determine if any of the extraordinary payment rights, if exercised in

---

[5]The taxpayer also can elect not to treat a cumulative dividend right as a qualified distribution right. This would be rather unusual, as the distribution right is then valued at zero for gift tax purposes. This may make sense when the subject company cannot be certain that distributions can be made consistently within the four-year grace period for payment under Section 2701(d).

conjunction with any qualified distribution right, would lower the total value of the preferred security. If so, then the lower of the values must be used as the value of the applicable retained interest in the preferred securities.

As an example of this "lower of" rule, if a preferred stock had a high fixed, cumulative dividend yield that would cause it to be valued in excess of par value, but the preferred stock also had a put right or right to compel liquidation at par value, then the value utilized for the preferred interest would be par value—the lower of the two values.

Applying the Subtraction Method. Once it is established that the transaction falls under the special valuation rules of Section 2701, and that certain rights and features of the applicable retained interest in the senior preferred securities either do or do not add value under Section 2701, then the value of the transferred junior equity interest is estimated under the Section 2701 subtraction method. The value is estimated by following a four-step process:

Step 1. Estimate the fair market value of all the capital securities of the subject company held by: the transferor (or spouse), any applicable family members, and any lineal descendants of the parents of the transferor (or spouse), utilizing standard business interest valuation procedures. Under Section 2701, the appraiser must assume that all these family-held interests are owned by one person, using a consistent set of assumptions. At this point it is also appropriate to determine what percentage of each class of the senior and junior equity interests the transferor and applicable family members own in the aggregate, as this information will be used in Step 2. In many cases Step 1 may require the valuation of the entire company on a control basis, under either a going concern or a liquidation valuation premise, when the family owns 100 percent of the securities.

Step 2. From this value estimate subtract:
1. The fair market value of all family-held senior equity interests, other than those of the transferor and applicable family members. Also, as discussed immediately below in number 2, any percentage of the retained senior equity interests owned by the transferor and applicable family members in excess of the maximum percentage of junior equity interest classes held by the same transferor and applicable family member group is added back at this point in Step 2. These senior equity interests are valued utilizing standard business interest valuation procedures (see Revenue Ruling 83-120 and Chapter 21 on valuing preferred stock). In most family-owned businesses this calculation will not come into play, as all family member interest holders will be included in number 2 below.
2. The value estimated under the Section 2701 special valuation rules of the transferor's and applicable family members' retained senior equity interests. As noted above, this amount is further adjusted by reducing this amount so it does not exceed the largest percentage interest owned by the transferor and applicable family members of any of the junior classes of equity interests.

   As an example, if the transferor and applicable family members owned 100 percent of the preferred stock in a recapitalized company, but only owned 90 percent of the common class of stock (the rest being held by nonfamily member employees), then the number of preferred shares valued under the special valuation rules of Section 2701 would be 90 percent of the preferred share class. The remaining preferred shares would be valued using standard business interest valuation procedures, as noted immediately above in number 1.

This procedure recognizes that any advantage in not exercising the nonqualified distribution and extraordinary payment rights of the senior securities may benefit all junior equity holders, not just the immediate members of the family.

Step 3. Allocate the remaining value to the family-held junior equity securities. If there is more than one class of junior equity securities, then the allocation must start with the class of junior equity securities with the greatest preference over the other junior equity classes. The allocation of the remaining value is made by continuing with the same set of assumptions utilized for valuing the entire family-held equity in Step 1 and the senior equity in Step 2 (i.e., using the "lower of" rule and zero value rules).

A final special "minimum value" rule under Section 2701 provides that the total allocated value to the junior equity interests can never be less than 10 percent of the sum of (1) the total value of *all* the enterprise's equity interests plus (2) the total amount of any indebtedness owed to the transferor and any applicable family members.

Step 4. Determine the amount of the gift. The allocated values of the transferred junior equity interests are typically adjusted for discounts for minority interest (lack of control) and lack of marketability. In the IRS Final Regulations,[6] the IRS provides some examples that do not include such discounts for some situations in which appraisers (and existing case law) would ordinarily allow discounts. We assume that since these final regulations predate Revenue Ruling 93-12, the examples would be altered to show such discounts if they were issued currently.

The final regulations also suggest that the total reduction to the allocated value, for lack of control and lack of marketability discounts, should not cause the value of the transferred junior equity interests to be less than their fair market value utilizing standard business interest valuation procedures.

Also, any consideration paid to the transferor by the transferee would also require a reduction adjustment to the allocated value at this point in the process before determining the value of the gift under Section 2701. If this consideration is additional preferred stock, for example, swapped by the transferee to the transferor for common stock, the value of the preferred stock consideration is the value estimated under the special valuation rules of Section 2701 (and not fair market value).

Lastly, any value estimated under Section 2702 (regarding retained life, annuity, or unitrust interests in trust) is also subtracted during this step.

The remaining adjusted value allocated to the transferred junior equity shares is the deemed amount of the gift.

The discussion in the final regulations regarding the "minimum value" rule in Step 3 and the maximum reduction for discounts in Step 4 suggests that an additional iteration is also part of the subtraction process under Section 2701. We believe the appraiser also needs to estimate the fair market value of the applicable

---

[6]Treasury Decision 8395 (RIN: 1545-AP44), effective January 28, 1992.

retained senior equity interests and the junior transferred equity interests, without regard to the Section 2701 special valuation rules, in order to check these results against the results of the special valuation calculations.

Because value is assigned under Section 2701 only to payment of cumulative dividends on preferred stock, much of the current recapitalization activity is focused on partnerships and limited liability companies. Such entities do not have the income tax problem of having to pay taxes at the entity level before preferred interest payments are distributed.

However, the convoluted nature of the special valuation rules under Section 2701 has encouraged most estate planners to avoid transactions requiring its use. Consequently, the use of the traditional preferred stock estate freeze has greatly declined in popularity. However, there are still a number of private businesses with old pre-Chapter 14 preferred stock estate freezes outstanding that may require additional gifting of common stock after October 8, 1990. These new transactions will fall under the rules of Section 2701. We urge all appraisers who may become involved with an appraisal under the special valuation rules of Section 2701 to read the statute language, final regulations, technical corrections, subsequent clarifying revenue rulings and private letter rulings, and court cases on this subject carefully.

Valuation Issues under Section 2702

Because Section 2702 deals with retained life, annuity, and unitrust interests transferred via trusts for lifetime gift tax purposes, there are no special valuation rules included in this section that directly relate to closely held business interests.

Closely held business interests are often placed into various grantor retained annuity trusts (GRATs) and grantor retained unitrusts (GRUTs), or charitable remainder annuity trusts (CRATs), or charitable lead trusts (CRUTs). But the primary valuation issue in these cases is the application of the IRS annuity and life expectancy tables.

Buy–Sell Agreements or Sale of Options under Section 2703

Chapter 28 discusses buy–sell agreements in detail. For now, let us note the four factors that determine whether the buy–sell agreement is conclusively binding for estate tax purposes:

1. The agreement must restrict the transfer of the securities to the buy–sell price during the owner's life as well as at death.
2. There must be a valid business purpose for establishing the agreement.
3. The value established in the agreement must have been an adequate and fair price at the time the agreement was executed.
4. The value must reflect those typical of arm's-length transactions in the subject company's industry.

Thus, a properly drawn, "grandfathered" buy–sell agreement (i.e., one that predates Chapter 14) with a fixed transfer price may, over time, have provided a way to freeze the value of family members' shares at a value perhaps less than fair market value as of a subsequent date of death. Since October 9, 1990, this technique is unworkable from an estate tax standpoint for newly created or substantially modified buy–sell agreements due to the passage of Section 2703 of Chapter 14.

Valuation Rules for Lapsing Rights and Other Restrictions under Section 2704

This section of Chapter 14 addresses two basic areas of valuation issues. Subsection (a) of Section 2704 treats certain lapsed voting or liquidation rights in a family-controlled corporation, partnership, or limited liability company as a deemed transfer subject to gift or estate tax. Subsection (b) requires the appraiser to ignore certain restrictions on liquidation rights of business interests when valuing a transfer of an interest in a family-controlled enterprise.

Lapse of Certain Rights.   Section 2704(a) will come into play under the following set of circumstances:

- The holder of the lapsed voting or liquidation power and any applicable family members own, in the aggregate, a controlling interest in the subject company. *Applicable family member* and *control* are defined in the same manner as in Section 2701, discussed above.[7]
- Whenever a lapse of a voting right or liquidation right occurs.[8] If it occurs during life, it is treated as a gift; at death it is considered an estate tax issue. A lapse is defined as occurring at the time a presently exercisable right is restricted or eliminated. The sale or transfer of a voting or liquidation right is not included under this section, as these types of transactions are valued under the existing gift and income tax statutes.

Section 2704(a) does not apply if the transfer was already valued under the special valuation rules of Section 2701, to prevent double taxation. Also, if there is a change in a state law that causes the lapse, then Section 2704(a) does not apply. Of course, if the family does not have control over the unilateral capacity to liquidate, then Section 2704(a) does not apply. As an example, for a company requiring unanimous consent of all interest holders to liquidate, the presence of nonfamily member interest holders causes Section 2704(a) not to apply.

The practical effect of Section 2704(a) is to create the potential for additional gift or estate tax value only when the holder's interest has its highest fair market value under a premise of liquidation on a controlling interest basis. This most often tends to affect companies in asset-intensive industries like heavy manufacturing, farming and ranching, and real estate development, in addition to holding companies.

Disregarding Applicable Restrictions.   Under subsection 2704(b) an appraiser must disregard an applicable restriction on the ability to liquidate a company (in whole or in part) if the following conditions apply:

---

[7]The IRS's use of a 50 percent ownership level as the threshold for control in this context is curious and not supported by financial valuation theory or legal rights theory, as a 50 percent voting interest cannot unilaterally vote to compel a liquidation.

[8]The Treasury is also given the right under this statute to determine if other lapsing rights should be added to this list.

- If an interest is transferred to or for the benefit of a member of the transferor's family (either directly or indirectly).
- If the transferor and members of the transferor's family control the company immediately before the transfer. The definition of *control* is the same as in Section 2701, discussed above. However, the definition of *member of the family* is slightly different from that contained in Section 2701 and echoes the more inclusive definition utilized in Section 2702 and for determining family control under Section 2701. Under Section 2704, a member of the family for any individual includes (1) the individual's spouse, (2) any ancestor of the individual and spouse, (3) any lineal descendant of the individual and spouse, (4) any brother or sister (and their spouses) of the individual.
- The applicable restriction is more restrictive than the limitations that would apply under the state law generally applicable to the entity in the absence of the restriction.
- And the restriction either lapses after such a transfer or the transferor and member of the transferor's family have the right, either individually or as a group, to remove (in whole or in part) such a restriction.

Section 2704(b) does not apply in the case of a restriction on liquidation that is imposed under federal or state law. Thus, the basic default statutes of the state laws under which a company was formed can have a significant impact on the degree to which an appraiser must consider the liquidation values of the company in valuing an individual interest.

In addition, Section 2704(b) does not apply if a restriction on liquidation arises as part of the company's financing and is a commercially reasonable restriction imposed by an unrelated arm's-length third party. A typical example of this is the restriction on distributing asset sale proceeds to shareholders, while a loan is outstanding, contained in standard bank loan covenants.

An option or other agreement that is subject to Section 2703 regarding buy–sell agreements is not regarded as an applicable restriction. This provision avoids double coverage of the same issue under Chapter 14.

Section 2704(b) concerns itself primarily with restrictions that are more onerous than the basic rights contained in state statutes—that could be conveniently applied and then removed by the controlling family at appropriate times. Like Section 2704(a), the practical effect of Section 2704(b) is to create the potential for additional gift or estate tax value only when the holder's interest has its highest fair market value under a premise of liquidation on a controlling interest basis. This most often tends to affect companies in asset-intensive industries like heavy manufacturing, farming and ranching, and real estate development, in addition to holding companies.

Valuation Issues in Estate and Gift Tax Planning

Placing Family Assets in Corporate, Limited Liability Company, or Partnership Form

It may be worthwhile to consider incorporating various family assets into a family-controlled holding company before transferring interests to heirs. Aside from the business purposes of such transfers, such as centralization of supervision, reduction of potential personal exposure to creditors, assurance of smoother management succession, and prevention of the assets' waste by inexperienced heirs, there may also be estate planning advantages. The assets could be almost anything, such as marketable securities, real estate, art, coins, or any kind of collectibles. Since publicly traded securities of companies holding such assets (such as closed-end investment companies and REITs) tend to sell at a discount from underlying net asset value, so should shares of family-controlled corporations. Interests in this type of closely held company also are valued at a further discount for lack of marketability.

Of course, in making the decision to incorporate a family holding company to execute a portion of the family estate plan in this manner, one must realize that the justification for the discounted values is real, not contrived; that is, the heir who receives a gift of a minority interest of a family holding company or limited partnership representing an undivided interest in a portfolio of assets will not have control over those assets. Owning 15 percent of the assets and owning 15 percent of the stock of the company that owns them are two different things. The power to liquidate, transfer assets, declare dividends, and exercise all the other various elements of control will not go to the donee. There also may be income tax considerations, so such a move should not be undertaken without the aid of competent tax counsel. If the donor understands and is satisfied with the various implications, the creation of a family-owned holding company could be a tax-saving feature of the total estate plan.

An extension of this technique has been placement of family assets in S corporations and limited partnerships, which allows pass-through of most types of income generated by the underlying assets without being subjected to income tax at the corporate level (see Chapter 22, "Pass-Through Entities"). This technique has become more important with the repeal of the *General Utilities* doctrine in the Tax Reform Act of 1986. Under the *General Utilities* doctrine, a corporation selling its assets to another corporation, as in an acquisition, generally was allowed to liquidate within one year of sale without having to recognize gain on the assets' sale at the corporate level.[9]

Family assets also have been placed in partnerships or limited liability companies to facilitate the estate planning techniques described in the next two sections on minority interest transfers and recapitalizations.

Minimizing Taxes by a Series of Timely Minority Interest Transfers

In general, estate planning techniques for minimizing transfer taxes revolve around timing transfers when the value of the stock is relatively low and structuring them such that they have the least possible value.

The more rapidly a company is growing in value, the more important it is to effect stock transfers to heirs early rather than later, after the value has increased. However, if the business is cyclical, it may be possible to time transfers at a cyclical trough in the company's value.

For structure, the best technique usually is to plan transfers as a series of small minority interests. To begin, a married couple can give up to $20,000 ($10,000 per donor) in value to each of as many persons as they wish each year without paying federal gift tax. More important for transfers of substantial size,

---

[9]Mitchell M. Gans, "The Repeal of *General Utilities*: Estate Tax Implications," *Trusts & Estates,* July 1987, pp. 43–48.

however, is that, at least under the law and court rulings at this writing, minority interests are subject to substantial discounts in value per share compared with the per share value of a controlling interest. Minority interests are further discussed in Chapter 14.

Discounts for lack of marketability are discussed in Chapter 15. Minority shares in closely held companies can be valued for tax purposes by estimating their potential market value as publicly traded stock and then discounting them for lack of marketability. In general, the smaller the minority interest, the greater the extent to which this procedure can be applied. The net result may be that transfers of shares of closely held companies can be made at quite large discounts below the undiscounted control value of the entire company.

Although the IRS has conceded in Revenue Ruling 93-12 that family relationships will not be the sole reason to challenge minority interest transfers when a family owns control of an enterprise, the service remains sensitive to this issue. Appraisers should review all the facts and circumstances of each gift in a series of gifts for companies in which a single family owns control, as, infrequently, some minority interests deserve lesser discounts for relative lack of control and lack of marketability. This could be due to some factor relating to the relative distribution of ownership (a so-called swing vote issue)[10] or the ability to unilaterally elect one or more directors to the board, and thereby influence the policies of the company.

Loss of Key Person

Often the appraiser faces the valuation of closely held stock in the estate of the president, founder, or other key executive of a business. In this circumstance, it is reasonable to investigate the possibility that the value of the company—and, thus, of its securities—has been impaired due to the loss of the services of a key person in the business's management.

Whether such decline in value actually has occurred depends on the case. The following are the elements to be investigated in establishing any discount or diminution from the loss of a key person.

First, the appraiser determines the deceased executive's actual duties and areas of active involvement. A key person may contribute value to a company in both day-to-day management duties and from strategic judgment responsibilities based on long-standing contacts and reputation within an industry.

Second, the appraiser assesses the ability of existing successor management to move up the organizational ladder and take over the duties of the vacated position. Ideally, a strong and stable corporate organization will provide this capability. This assumes a succession plan actually exists. All too often, however, private business owners create "spider web" organization structures with themselves at the center—that is, all management decisions are made by the key executive-owner. The extent of organizational damage may also be related to the suddenness of the key manager's death.

---

[10]The IRS addressed the swing vote issue in a National Office Technical Advice Memorandum (Letter Ruling 9436005, May 26, 1994). We find swing vote issues a relative rarity as real-world willing buyers, even those already owning shares in a company, are rarely willing to bid much in excess of the amount a potential investor without existing ownership would pay for an interest. There is also an issue of whether a swing vote assumption is improperly based on the notion that the willing buyer possesses a special relationship with the seller that is not typical of the hypothetical willing seller–willing buyer standard of fair market value for estate and gift tax matters.

Third, the appraiser calculates the amount of compensation necessary for replacing the key executive or filling the positions vacated or created when successors move up.

Fourth, to this quantitative calculation the appraiser adds the damages arising from risks to the company in bringing in replacement executives who may be unfamiliar with the company's operations. These risks can be compounded by the appraiser's assessment of the complexity or precariousness of the company's competitive or financial position. This is especially true if the deceased was personal guarantor of the company's debts, as often is the case with closely held business loans. Sometimes these risks can be quantified as estimates of sales losses or profit margin declines over estimated future periods.

There are at least two offsets to these potential losses. One is the compensation, net of any continuing obligations, that the company ceases to pay to the deceased executive. The other is any insurance on the key person's life that is payable to the company and not earmarked for other purposes, such as repurchase of the deceased's stock in the company.

The estimates of key person losses can be directly incorporated into the valuation methods appropriate for the particular case. This may be accomplished by adjusting normalized earnings or price-to-earnings multiples or as reductions in estimated future cash flows to be discounted. Otherwise, the loss can be subtracted from the company's indicated value as a separate item, much like the discount for lack of marketability.

Evidence for the amount of the loss from the key person's death from securities' values in the public market shows that the magnitude of the decline varies with the circumstances. Generally, public companies have larger and more flexible professional management teams and thus can better absorb the shock of the loss of any one key person. An instructive example of a catastrophic loss of key executives, however, was the tragic death of most of the top management of Arrow Electronics in a hotel fire in December 1980. Arrow's New York Stock Exchange listed common stock fell approximately 20 percent after the announcement of the news.

Other Estate Planning Situations Requiring Valuations

Strictly speaking, the two techniques reviewed below do not require consideration of any valuation factors different from those mandated under Revenue Ruling 59-60. But an appraiser ought to be aware of these techniques, as he or she may be called on to prepare a valuation of a closely held business that will be used in this fashion.

Sale of Remainder Interest.   In this technique, the owner of a closely held business security sells to an heir a remainder interest in the security and retains a life interest in the current enjoyment of income and the security's voting rights. The *remainder interest* is valued by taking the security's appraised fair market value and discounting it to a present value under the IRS actuarial tables based on the seller's projected remaining life. At this writing, the present value interest factor of the actuarial tables is 10 percent. Thus, the present value of the remainder interest can be a small fraction of the security's current fair market value if the seller is relatively young. On the seller's death, the life interest terminates, leaving the security, including any appreciation after the sale, to pass, untaxed, to the heir outside the seller's gross estate.

Valuation is crucial to this technique, because if the sale transaction is not for full and adequate consideration, the asset's entire value will be brought back into the seller's estate at fair market value as of the date of death.

Sale for a Private Annuity or a Self-Canceling Note.   The business owner uses this technique to sell the entire business to an heir in exchange for a *private annuity*—a fixed periodic payment made to the seller for the rest of his or her life.

A *self-canceling note* is similar to an annuity but has the additional advantage that part of the periodic payment of principal and interest due from the heir can be forgiven (waived) by the seller under the annual $10,000 gift tax exclusion. One of the key issues in the structure of this technique is the correct valuation of the closely held business interest sold and the terms of the annuity or note received so as to avoid gift taxes on the initial sale and estate taxes at the seller's death.

Other Estate and Gift Valuation Issues

There are four other issues regarding valuation for estate and gift taxes of which an appraiser should be aware.

In Revenue Ruling 85-75, 1985-1 C.B. 376, the IRS has held that it will not necessarily be bound by values that it accepted for estate tax purposes as the correct cost basis for determining depreciation deductions or income taxes on capital gains from an asset's subsequent sale.

In a similar manner, in Private Letter Ruling 8447005 (July 26, 1984), the IRS states it may revalue gifts made in previous years, even if the values were not fraudulent and the filings exceed the statute of limitations, for the purpose of increasing the tax bracket applicable to taxable transfers reported on a business owner's subsequent gift or estate tax return.

On the other hand, it may be possible to use one value for calculating the gross estate value of a block of closely held stock and a different value for calculating the value of a portion of the block of stock that will be exempted from estate taxes as a marital deduction (i.e., the portion of the estate transferred to a spouse).[11]

The final valuation issue is the lower value for closely held business stock that may result if real estate used in a family-owned trade or business is valued for estate tax purposes for actively involved family members under the provisions of Section 2032A, "Special-Use Valuation." A detailed discussion of this section is beyond the scope of this book. Here simply note that closely held company valuation methods based on net asset values may be lower if an appraisal of the underlying operating real property follows the guidelines of this section. This issue is particularly relevant for family-owned farming or other agricultural business securities.

Summary

The entire area of estate and gift tax valuation can be a constantly shifting minefield of laws, regulations, and court decisions. Because of this, it is important that the appraiser be able to function as a knowledgeable contributor to the client's team of estate planning professionals.

---

[11]See *Estate of Chenoweth*, 88 T.C. 90 (1987).

With the top federal transfer tax rate at 55 percent, the tax implications of estate planning and gift and estate tax valuations can be huge. Inclusion of additional values into an estate that were originally thought to be gifted or transferred away via estate planning transactions can also create tremendous problems. The tax implications are exacerbated by the penalties that may be imposed on taxpayers for undervaluation for gift and estate tax purposes and overvaluation for charitable contribution purposes. Appraisers are also subject to significant penalties.

It is essential that valuations involving federal tax implications be performed in accordance with guidelines discussed in this chapter, as clarified and modified by ever-evolving case law.

Bibliography

Abbin, Byrle M. "IRS Valuation Process Receives a Billion Dollar Setback." *Journal of Taxation,* May 1990, pp. 260–65.

Adams, Roy M., and David A. Herpe. "Getting Familiar with Proposed Chapter 14 Regs." *Trusts & Estates*, August 1991, pp. 48–49.

Adams, Roy M.,; David A. Herpe,; and Thomas W. Abendroth. "Highlights of the Chapter 14 Final Regulations." *Trusts & Estates,* April 1992, pp. 35–49.

Alerding, R. James, Jr. "IRS Valuation Methods Lag behind Business Practice." *Taxation for Accountants,* July 1992, pp. 4–9.

Aucutt, Ronald D. "Fourteen Tips and Traps in Dealing with Chapter 14." *Estate Planning,* September/October 1993, pp. 259–66.

Beehler, John M. "Corporate Estate Freeze Valuation Rules under the Proposed Section 2701 Regulations." *Taxes,* January 1992, pp. 12–19.

Blatt, William S. "The Effect of Sec. 2701 on Preferred Interest Freezes." *Trusts & Estates,* March 1991, pp. 8–14.

Blattmachr, Jonathan G. "Don't Be Driven by Tax-Driven Formula Clauses." *Probate & Property,* September/October 1991, pp. 34–38.

Caudill, William H., and James T. Budyak. "New IRS Position on Valuation May Result in Reduced Marital and Charitable Deductions." *Journal of Taxation,* September 1993, pp. 176–79.

Chandler, William F., and Harold Dubroff. "Funding GRATs with S Stock, Partnership or LLC Interests." *Estate Planning,* November/December 1994, pp. 331–39.

Cooper Scott J. "A Guide through the Estate Freeze Maze." *Journal of Taxation of Estates and Trusts,* Winter 1992, pp. 5–10.

Dees, Richard L. "Now that the Monster Is Dead, Can You Avoid the Hot Seat?: The Cold Facts of Partnership Freezes under Chapter 14." *Taxes,* December 1993, pp. 902–21.

————. "The Slaying of Frankenstein's Monster: The Repeal and Replacement of Section 2036(c)." *Taxes,* March 1991, pp. 151–66.

DenHollander, Darlene. "Minority Discounts and the Effect of the Section 2704 Regulations." *Tax Lawyer,* Spring 1992, pp. 877–87.

Eastland, S. Stacy, and Margaret W. Brown. "New Attack on Family Business." *Trusts & Estates,* March 1991, pp. 48–56.

Eastland, S. Stacy, and Stephen L. Christian. "Proposed Valuation Regulations Provide Harsh Results under Adjustment and Lapse Rules." *Journal of Taxation,* December 1992, pp. 364–72.

Englebrecht, Ted D., and James M. Turner. "Alternate Valuation Election Has Side Effects." *Estate Planning*, May/June 1994, pp. 154–61.

Fiala, David M. "Business Success Planning." *National Public Accountant,* August 1991, pp. 22–27.

Fiore, Owen G. "Chapter 14 Special Valuation Renewed Estate Tax Savings Opportunities via Inter-Vivos Family Wealth Planning." USC Institute on Federal Taxation, January 29, 1992.

Freeman, Todd I.; John D. Fullmer; and Michael J. Smith. "The Progeny of Sec. 2036(c): The Valuation of Retained Interests." *Tax Adviser,* December 1991, pp. 767–71 ff.

Gardner, John H. "Estate Freezes 1990 and Beyond: The Story of the Repeal of Section 2036(c) and the Valuation Rules That Took Its Place." *Taxes,* January 1991, pp. 3–12.

————. "Planning with Chapter 14 and GST Interaction." *Estate Planning,* May/June 1994, pp. 146–53.

Gingiss, Randall J. "The Gift of Opportunity." *DePaul Law Review,* Winter 1992, pp. 395–429.

Goodman, Kenneth D. "Keeping It in the Family." *Trusts & Estates,* December 1988, pp. 37–40.

Harris, Richard W., and Edith E. Silvestri. "Estate Tax Valuation of Contingent Claims." *Trusts & Estates,* December 1993, pp. 29–32 ff.

Harrison, Louis S., and Heather Smith. "Prop. Regs. Address Adjustments and Lapsing Rights." *Estate Planning,* January/February 1992, pp. 3–9.

Hitchner, James R. "Valuation of Closely Held Businesses: Estate and Gift Tax Issues." *Tax Adviser,* July 1992, pp. 471–79.

Hitchner, James R., and Kevin J. Rudd. "The Use of Discounts in Estate and Gift Tax Valuations." *Trusts & Estates,* August 1992, pp. 49–56, 60.

Jurinski, James John, and W. Ron Singleton. "New Estate Freeze Rules Require Heating up of Planning Tactics." *Practical Accountant,* May 1991, pp. 21–33.

Keligian, David L. "Appraisal Issues Now Require Greater Attention for Tax Planning to Be Effective." *Journal of Taxation,* February 1994, pp. 98–103.

Kimball, Curtis R., and Robert F. Reilly. "Kinder, Gentler Gift and Estate Tax Valuation Rules Offer Planning Possibilities." *Journal of Taxation of Estates and Trusts,* Fall 1991, pp. 27–33.

King, Hamlin C. "Final Estate Freeze Rules Simplify Subtraction Method." *Taxes,* July 1992, pp. 460–90.

Kuenster, Richard A. "Estate Planning, Family Businesses and Divorce." *FAIR$HARE The Matrimonial Law Monthly,* October 1991, pp. 7–9

Leimberg, Stephan R.; Eric Johnson; and Robert J. Doyle, Jr. "The King Is Dead: Long Live the King! A First Glance at the Repeal of IRC 2036(c) and Its Replacement." *Tax Management Financial Planning Journal,* January 15, 1991, pp. 3–16.

Leimberg, Stephan R.; Ted Kurlowicz; and Robert J. Doyle, Jr. "GRATs, GRUTs, and GRITs after the Final Regulations." Parts I and II. *Journal of the American Society of CLU & ChFC,* January and March 1993, pp. 66–79; 74–87.

Mezzullo, Louis A. "A Guided Tour through Chapter 14." *Probate & Property,* May/June 1991, pp. 28–31.

————. "New Estate Freeze Rules Replacing 2036(c) Expand Planning Potential." *Journal of Taxation,* January 1991, pp. 4–12.

Monippallil, Matthew M. "New Estate Freeze Approach Uses Old Valuation Rules." *Taxation for Accountants,* March 1991, pp. 142–49.

Mulligan, Michael D. "Estate Freeze Rules Eased by New Tax Law but Other Restrictions Are Imposed." *Estate Planning,* January/February 1991, pp. 2–7.

Mulligan, Michael D., and Angela Fick Braly. "Family Limited Partnerships Can Create Discounts." *Estate Planning,* July/August 1994, pp. 195–204.

Murray, John V. "Securities Law Considerations in Valuing Stock for Tax Purposes." *Trusts & Estates,* December 1992, pp. 40–45.

Nager, Ross W. "Estate Freeze Rules Repealed, but Uncertainty Remains." *Journal of Taxation of Estates and Trusts,* Winter 1991, pp. 4–7.

_____. "IRS Reverses Valuation Position." *Family Business Advisor,* June 1993, pp. 2, 6.

Nager, Ross W.; Byrle M. Abbin; and David K. Carlson. "Significant Recent Development in Estate Planning." Parts I, II, and III. *Tax Adviser,* October, November, December 1994, pp. 587–605; 698–709; and 723–730.

Painter, Andrew D., and Jonathan G. Blattmachr. "How the Final Chapter 14 Anti-Freeze Regulations Affect Estate Planning Strategies." *Journal of Taxation of Estates and Trusts,* Spring 1992, pp. 5–14.

Pennell, Jeffrey N. "2036(c) Is Only a Skirmish: The War Involves Valuation." *Trusts & Estates,* January 1990, pp. 22,; 69.

Plaine, Lloyd Leva, and Pam H. Schneider. "Prop. Regs. on Valuing Rights and Restrictions Focus on Exceptions." *Journal of Taxation,* October 1991, pp. 204–6.

_____. "Proposed Valuation Regulations Provide Workable Exceptions for Transfers in Trust." *Journal of Taxation,* September 1991, pp. 142–49.

Rebane, Kirk A. "Living with Chapter 14: An Appraiser's View." *Tax Management: Estates, Gifts & Trusts Journal,* November 12, 1992, pp. 178–87.

Rothberg, Richard S. "Valuation of Interests in Family Businesses after Newhouse." *Journal of Taxation of Investments,* Winter 1991, pp. 161–65.

Schindel, Donald M. "Various Methods Exist for Establishing a Sustainable Value for Estate Assets." *Estate Planning,* September/October 1990, pp. 258–64.

Schlenger, Jacques T.; Robert E. Madden; and Lisa H. R. Hayes. "Blocks of Stock Are Aggregated when Determining Estate Tax Values." *Estate Planning,* May/June 1994, pp. 176–78.

Schneider, Pam H., and Lloyd Leva Plaine. "Proposed Valuation Regulations Flesh Out Operation of the Subtraction Method." *Journal of Taxation,* August 1991, pp. 82–90.

Shayne, Mark. "Valuation Issues under Chapter 14." *Tax Management: Estates, Gifts & Trusts Journal,* September 9, 1993, pp. 146–52.

Shore, H. Allen, and Howard D. Rosen. "Beyond Chapter 14—A Tale of Two (New) Freezes." *Taxes,* February 1993, pp. 97–104.

Stapper, Erik J. "Valuation of Real Estate for Estate Tax Purposes: A Personal and Practical Approach." *Tax Management: Estates, Gifts & Trusts Journal,* May 13, 1993, pp. 90–97.

Strauss, Benton C., and James K. Shaw. "Final Chapter 14 Regs. Clarify GRATs, Business Planning." *Estate Planning,* September/October 1992, pp. 259–66.

_____. "Final Chapter 14 Regulations Refine Estate Freeze Rules." *Estate Planning,* July/August 1992, pp. 195–202.

Switzer, Ralph V. Jr., and Douglas E. Chestnut. "Evolution of Estate Freeze." *National Public Accountant,* January 1994, pp. 20–25 ff.

Szabo, Joan C. "Congress Thaws the Estate Freeze." *Nation's Business,* February 1991, pp. 23–25.

Vaughan, Patrick J., and Donna Esposito Fincher. "Saving Estate and Gift Taxes with Intrafamily Discounts." *Journal of Financial Planning,* January 1994, pp. 32–34.

Wallace, John A. "Now You See It, Now You Don't—Valuation Conundrums in Estate Planning." In *1990 Institute on Estate Planning* (Miami: University of Miami, Heckerling Institute), pp. 8-1–8-59.

Ward, Burke T., and Malcolm L. Cowen. "Should the Service Have Two Opportunities to Revalue Gifts?" *Trusts & Estates,* November 1994, pp. 40–43.

Ward, Robert E. "An Old Problem, A New Statute." Parts 1 and 2, *Practical Lawyer,* March and April, 1991, pp. 13–28; 79–91.

Warnken, Wayne L., and Pamela R. Champine. "Anti-Estate Freeze Rules Can Have Wide Scope." *Estate Planning,* July/August 1993, pp. 220–25.

Weber, Richard P. "The Chapter 14 Maze." *Tax Adviser,* February 1995, pp. 104–5 ff.

Yuhas, Michael A., and Carl C. Radom. "Valuation of Stock in a Closely Held Corporation: Estate of Murphy—Should the Decision be Discounted?" *Review of Taxation of Individuals,* Autumn 1991, pp. 291–301.

Zaritsky, Howard M. "The Year in Review: An Estate Planner's Perspective of Tax Developments." *Tax Management: Estates, Gifts & Trusts Journal,* January 14, 1993, pp. 3–36.

Chapter 28

Buy–Sell Agreements

A buy–sell agreement can effectively prevent many potential problems regarding the disposition of stock or a partnership interest of a departing or deceased stockholder or partner. The buy–sell agreement can accomplish the following objectives:

1. Provide a mechanism with which the departing owner or the estate can liquidate the ownership interest.
2. Set a price or provide a mechanism for determining a price for the ownership interest.
3. Under some circumstances, set a price that will determine a binding value for estate and gift tax purposes.
4. Prevent the ownership interest from being sold or otherwise transferred to any party not acceptable to the other owners.
5. Provide a mechanism for pricing and liquidating the interest of a departing spouse in the event of a divorce.[1]
6. Provide a payment scheme that is affordable in the least disruptive manner to the subject company.
7. Provide a basis for valuation of the entire business or fractional interest for sale, initial public offering, or collateralization purposes.

Types of Buy–Sell Agreements

Buy–sell agreements used in closely held corporations or partnerships to provide for liquidation of the interest of a withdrawing or deceased shareholder or partner fall into one of three categories:

1. *Repurchase agreements* (also called *entity purchase agreements* or *redemption agreements*), in which the issuing corporation or partnership buys the interest from the withdrawing party or from the estate of the deceased party.
2. *Cross-purchase agreements*, in which one or more other individuals or entities buys the interest from the withdrawing party or from the estate of the deceased party.
3. *Hybrid agreements* (also called *wait-and-see agreements*), in which the issuer buys a portion of the interest and other stockholders or partners buy a portion. Such agreements can be drafted to allow both the company and the other shareholders the opportunity to wait until after the date of death to determine which is in the better tax and liquidity condition to purchase the shares.

Each type of agreement may be either mandatory—that is, binding on both parties—or optional on the part of one of the parties, usually the purchaser. Sometimes agreements are written with one set of buyout options during an owner's lifetime and with another set of options for a decedent's estate.

It is not necessary that the same agreement apply to all the owners of a particular entity. One or a few owners may be subject to an agreement while others

---

[1]For a discussion of the use of buy–sell agreements for divorce planning, see Wendy L. Hunkele Martinez, "Buy/Sell Agreements: From a Spouse's Perspective," *Texas Bar Journal,* October 1992, pp. 932–34.

are not, or different owners may be subject to different agreements. For example, it is common to find minority owners of an enterprise subject to a buy–sell agreement while the controlling owner is not. In limited partnerships, provisions applicable to limited partners normally differ from those applicable to general partners.

The provisions of any buy–sell agreement should be designed to best carry out the objectives of all the parties. From a seller's viewpoint, an important objective is to provide liquidity in the event of withdrawal from the business or death. From a purchaser's viewpoint, an important objective typically is to provide continuity of ownership and management without possible interference from outside parties. From the viewpoints of both seller and purchaser, an additional purpose is to establish the circumstances under which the agreement will become effective and a means of determining the price and terms of the transaction. As one experienced attorney aptly put it:

> The particular method selected by the parties for the determination of the price to be paid for the interest will, of course, depend on their attitudes toward each other and their objectives with respect to survivors, their beneficiaries, and the business entity.[2]

One consideration in the choice between the cross-purchase versus redemption form of buy–sell agreement is the number of shareholders or partners involved. The more there are, the more complicated the cross-purchase plan becomes relative to the redemption. In the cross-purchase arrangement, the number of party-to-party relationships, life insurance policies required if so funded, and so on rise exponentially with the number of parties involved. Also, the transfer of life insurance policies on other parties held in a decedent's estate could give rise to a taxable incident. One solution to these problems is to create an insurance trust agreement, but this would require drafting another complicated agreement. In the redemption type of agreement, the corporation owns the life insurance policies, so there are not administrative or tax problems arising from the necessity to transfer policies at the death of one party.

Naturally, the tax implications will be a major consideration in deciding which type of agreement to use. The tax implications, which are complicated and often subject to change, are beyond the scope of this book. Several references on tax implications appear in the bibliography at the end of this chapter, as well as in the bibliography at the end of Chapter 27 on estate planning.[3]

Valuation Provisions of the Buy–Sell Agreement

The provision for valuation is a critical element of the buy–sell agreement. The parties have a great deal of flexibility in structuring this provision, but often it is neglected or done hastily and thus eventually turns out to be unfair to one or the other party.

---

[2]J. D. Hartwig, "Valuing an Interest in a Closely-Held Business for the Purpose of Buy–Sell Agreements for Death Tax Purposes," *University of Southern California Institute on Federal Taxation* (Los Angeles: University of Southern California Law Center, 1974), p. 237.

[3]For a specific discussion of tax considerations involved in the choice between a cross-purchase agreement and a repurchase agreement, with extensive legal citations, see F. Hodge O'Neal and Robert B. Thompson, *O'Neal's Close Corporations,* 3rd ed. (Deerfield, IL: Clark Boardman Callaghan, 1987), pp. 172–94, §7.39. Reprinted with permission from *O'Neal's Close Corporations,* 3rd. ed., published by Clark Boardman Callaghan, 155 Pfingsten Road, Deerfield, IL 60015, (800) 221 9428.

Need for Clear Direction

The importance of having the valuation provisions of the buy–sell agreement thought through thoroughly by someone who understands valuation, and understood by all parties, before the agreement is signed cannot be overemphasized. Attitudes and relationships change, and one cannot assume that any ambiguity in the buy–sell agreement will be resolved amicably when the time comes to consummate a transaction pursuant to the agreement. Time and time again, most disputes relating to buy–sell agreements arise because one or several of the details of the agreement either were inadequately defined or were misunderstood by one or more of the parties.

For example, we are aware of an expert testifying in an arbitration case over the value of a business interest under a buy–sell agreement in which the document was so ambiguous about the applicable valuation date that the attorney required the expert to analyze and testify to the valuation of the interest for four different dates that the arbitration panel could conceivably select as being applicable in the circumstances. The value differences on the various dates were considerable, because the business was undergoing significant and somewhat unpredictable changes during the relevant time period. The ambiguity as to the applicable valuation date substantially increased the time and cost involved for the analysis as well as the uncertainty of the outcome of the arbitration.

J. D. Hartwig, attorney, lecturer, and author, points out the typical lack of adequate definition even when the valuation criterion for the buy–sell agreement is simply book value:

> Rarely do the agreements define book value; identify whether the books kept for tax purposes or for business purposes are intended; or whether such book value shall be computed as of the date of death, as of the end of the month preceding death, as of the end of the last regular accounting period of the entity, as of the end of the fiscal year of the entity nearest the date of death, or as of some other date.[4]

Chapters 3 and 14 discussed the fact that the fair market value of a minority interest usually is less than a pro rata share of the value of the entire enterprise. Many parties to buy–sell agreements have been unpleasantly surprised to learn that the fair market value of their interest (the standard of value specified in the agreement that they hastily read and signed) was less than a proportionate share of the total enterprise value. Robert Blum, a CPA knowledgeable about both buy–sell agreements and closely held business valuations, notes the "sum of the parts doesn't always equal the whole" and offers the following strong statement on this point:

> When stock ownership is divided among a number of shareholders, each being in a less than controlling ownership position, the application of a minority interest discount should be addressed in the agreement. Is each shareholder entitled to the proportionate value of the entire entity or is each interest to be reduced by the discount commonly applied to minority interests? Failure to address this question in the agreement will ensure litigation in the future.[5]

Buy–sell agreements may specify that the shares be valued strictly at their fair market value as minority interests, at a proportionate share of the enterprise value with no minority discount, or at a specified percentage discount (we have seen all the way from 10 percent to 50 percent) from a proportionate share of total enterprise value.

---

[4]Hartwig, "Valuing an Interest," pp. 238–39.

[5]Robert Blum, *Common Pitfalls to Avoid in Buy–Sell Agreements* (Milwaukee: CPA Services, 1985), p. 6.

We suggest that the reader contemplating a buy–sell agreement read Chapter 2 carefully and be sure the agreement covers all the relevant points. In addition, the terms of payment should be specified. The payment terms may differ under various circumstances, and the agreement may allow the company some flexibility, making allowance for the company's ability to pay. *The key point to keep in mind is that the buy–sell agreement is a legal document that will have to stand on its own at the time a triggering event occurs.*

One unique aspect of the price-fixing mechanism in a buy–sell agreement, as opposed to other valuation problems, is the extreme uncertainty concerning when a future event that triggers a transaction under the agreement will occur. This is a key reason there is no single approach to the problem of establishing the price for a buy–sell agreement that one can recommend as completely satisfactory for all situations. The valuation provision can be the same under all triggering events or it can differ in various circumstances, such as the owner's death or voluntary or involuntary termination of employment.

Most of the mechanisms for setting prices in buy–sell agreements generally fall into one or a combination of three categories:

1.   Some type of formula based on the financial statements, such as book value, some type of adjusted book value, capitalization of earnings, or some combination of such variables.
2.   Negotiation among the parties.
3.   Independent outside appraisal.

Certain other approaches occasionally found in buy–sell agreements are in general disfavor with attorneys and other professionals who frequently are involved with buy–sell agreements. Some agreements call for the value established for estate tax purposes to determine the transaction price. This is exactly the opposite of the more typical logic, which would seek to establish a desired transaction price that is also determinative for estate and inheritance tax purposes. Besides, having the estate tax value determine the price has the obvious disadvantage of encouraging an upward bias in the negotiations between the executor and the IRS in setting the price, with the result that both the estate and the government will collect more money.

Another approach that is sometimes used but often disparaged in the literature written by practitioners is to have one party make an offer in an attempt to buy out the other with the provision that if the other party rejects it, the latter must buy out the offering party on the same terms. While some like this approach, others claim it does not seem to work well in practice and may even be unfair because each party probably lacks equal financial capability for buyout of the other.

Formula Approaches

We are generally opposed to formula approaches for setting the price in a buy–sell agreement because the result usually turns out to be unfair to one party or the other when the transaction eventually occurs. As this book indicates, the valuation process should reflect a complex set of factors—usually too complex to be adequately embodied in a formula. A formula that might produce an appropriate value in one year might not do so in another year when circumstances in the company and the economy differ. For example, in the case of *St. Louis County Bank* v. *United States,* the court refused to honor for estate tax purposes an agreement that gave a corporation the right to purchase the decedent's stock under a formula that produced a zero value, even though the formula may have originally produced an acceptable value.[6] Having made this point, we will consider some of the most common formulas for fixing the price in a buy–sell agreement.

The most popular basis for a formula approach is to use book value or some type of adjusted book value. Earlier chapters made the point that book value equals the fair market value (or any other standard of value) of a business or business interest only by coincidence. Book value tends to come closest to fair market value in a business that has a very high proportion of its total assets in current assets, such as receivables and inventories that can be liquidated at or near face value with little or no goodwill value.

One of the obvious attractions of using book value is its simplicity. Even so, however, it must be well defined. Some buy–sell agreements call for book value with certain adjustments, such as adding back the LIFO inventory reserve or adjusting certain assets to current market value. Unless extremely carefully defined, such adjustments can be subjects of dispute among the parties. Some agreements specify that an independent appraiser or accountant make the adjustments to avoid disputes among the parties.

Of course, if a business is on a cash basis, it is almost always necessary to make some adjustments to book value to reach a price that more nearly approximates an accrual basis book value, at least recognizing the receivables and payables.

If a net asset value approach is used in a repurchase agreement funded by life insurance, one must keep in mind that the company's net asset value will increase by the proceeds of the policy on the stockholder's death, a fact the value should reflect.

If a capitalization of earnings formula is used, it seems almost essential to base it on an average or weighted average of several years' earnings to avoid aberrations in the result that could occur from one or two exceptionally good or poor years. However, we would not be opposed to formula valuations that rely heavily on the most recent earnings (or even projected earnings) if such earnings better represent the analyst's perception of the current earnings capacity of the company applicable to the interest being valued. This is often more appropriate in a growing company or one that is undergoing changes compared to recent historical results. Of course, as discussed elsewhere in this book, earnings should be adjusted to eliminate extraordinary items, although again such adjustments could be a source of disputes. The capitalization rate or multiplier is a critical variable, and a multiplier that is appropriate one year might not be so for another year because of changing economic conditions.

One common criticism of formula approaches that are based on the balance sheet or the income statement or both is that closely held companies have considerable latitude in reporting figures within the boundaries of generally accepted accounting principles, as well as control over such important variables as paying compensation to owner-employees versus retaining earnings. For this reason, controlling stockholders have the power to make decisions that could be detrimental to the minority stockholder whose value will be determined by a formula approach.

---

[6]*St. Louis County Bank v. United States,* 674 F.2d 1207 (8th Cir. 1982).

Negotiation among the Parties

Many practitioners believe that negotiation among the parties—usually annually—is the best approach to setting the buy–sell agreement price. The parties themselves usually have the most intimate knowledge of their own estate objectives as well as of their attitudes toward one another. They also may have a better idea than anyone else about how much the business is worth; in most cases, however, owners would benefit from professional outside guidance on that point.

The problems with this approach arise when the annual valuation is neglected or when the parties cannot agree. In our experience, the annual valuations seem to be neglected more often than not. The buy–sell agreement must provide for dealing with both of these eventualities.

The most common method of handling potential neglect of the annual valuation is to stipulate that if the price is not set annually on a timely basis, after some period (typically 12 to 24 months following the last price agreement) the price-fixing mechanism automatically reverts to either a formula approach or an independent appraisal. In the latter case, it is necessary to either name the appraisal firm or specify the method by which the appraiser will be selected. If a firm or person is named, provision must be made for an alternative selection procedure if the named appraiser is unable to serve.

O'Neal and Thompson offer the following guidance regarding provision for selecting appraisers in the buy–sell agreement. This guidance would apply whether appraisers are to be used in any case or to be used only in the event of inability to agree through negotiation:

> If the price of shares is to be fixed by appraisal, the names of the appraisers or a method of choosing them must be specified and a statement should be made that the decision of a majority of the appraisers will be binding. A typical appraisal provision states that the optionee or purchaser, as the case may be, shall select one appraiser, the offeror or vendor a second, and that the two appraisers shall choose a third. Occasionally an independent third party, such as a corporate fiduciary, is given the power to appoint the third appraiser; or the third appraiser is designated by office: e.g., the cashier of the bank with which the company does business may be named the third appraiser. Sometimes the appraisers are selected in advance and designated by name. If that is done, provision must be made for a method of appointing substitutes should the designated appraisers die, become incapacitated, or refuse to serve.[7]

Some buy–sell agreements provide for two or three appraisers to submit reports to an arbitration panel, which will make the final determination in case of a dispute, but this can get quite expensive.

One suggestion for avoiding the problem of neglecting the annual valuation is to ask one of the company's professional advisors, such as the attorney, accountant, insurance agent, or appraiser, to put a memo in his or her tickler file to remind the company to make its annual valuation.

Reversion to formula or outside appraisal approaches is also the most common type of provision for dealing with circumstances in which the parties cannot agree on a value through negotiation.

Exhibit 28–1 is a sample valuation article for a buy–sell agreement, providing for negotiation and for the price to be determined by an arbitration panel if negotiation fails.

---

[7] O'Neal and Thompson, *Close Corporations*, Chapter 7 p. 155.

Exhibit 28–1

Sample Valuation Provision for Buy–Sell Agreement
(Corporation Stock Redemption Example)

As soon as practical after the end of each fiscal year, the stockholders shall agree on the value per share of the stock that is applicable to this agreement. Such value will be set forth in Schedule A, which shall be dated, signed by each stockholder, and attached hereto. Such value shall be binding on both the corporation and the estate of any deceased stockholder whose date of death is within one year of the last dated and signed Schedule A.

If more than a year has elapsed between the date when Schedule A was last signed and the date of death of a deceased stockholder, then the value per share shall be determined, as of the date of death of the stockholder, by mutual agreement between the surviving stockholders and the personal representative or administrator of the deceased stockholder's estate.

If the surviving stockholders and the personal representative of the deceased stockholder's estate are unable to agree upon such a value within 90 days after such personal representative or administrator has qualified to administer the estate of the deceased stockholder, then such value shall be determined by binding arbitration. Either party may give written notice of such binding arbitration pursuant to this agreement to the other party. Within 30 days of such notice of arbitration, each party shall appoint one arbitrator. Within 30 days of the appointment of the two arbitrators, the arbitrators so appointed will select a third arbitrator. The first two arbitrators will have sole discretion in the selection of the third arbitrator, except that he must be an individual or qualified representative of a firm that regularly engages, as a primary occupation, in the professional appraisal of businesses or business interests. In the event that the first two arbitrators are

unable to agree on a third arbitrator within 30 days of their appointment, the Executive Director of the ABC Trade Association shall appoint the third arbitrator.

The standard of value to be used by the arbitrators shall be fair market value of the shares being valued as of the date of death, under the assumption that the stockholder is deceased and the corporation has collected the proceeds, if any, of insurance on the life of the deceased stockholder payable to the corporation.

Each arbitrator shall use his sole discretion in determining the amount of investigation he considers necessary in arriving at a determination of the value of the shares. The corporation shall make available on a timely basis all books and records requested by any arbitrator, and all material made available to any one arbitrator shall be made available to all arbitrators.

Concurrence by at least two of the three arbitrators shall constitute a binding determination of value. The value concluded by the arbitrators shall be reported to the corporation and to the personal representative or administrator of the estate of the deceased in writing, signed by the arbitrators concurring as to the concluded value, within 90 days of the appointment of the third arbitrator unless an extension of time has been agreed upon between the corporation and the personal representatives of the estate.

The corporation and the estate shall each be responsible for the fees and expenses of the arbitrators they appoint. The fees and expenses of the third arbitrator shall be divided equally between the corporation and the estate.

Buy–sell agreements with negotiation-based pricing for enterprises in which a family group holds 50 percent or greater controlling ownership interests will not be regarded by the IRS as binding for estate and gift tax filings, due to the presumption that the family members have a donative intent toward each other that prevents impartial arm's-length transactions.

Independent Outside Appraisal

An experienced business appraiser presents a nine-point case for the advantage of having a formal, independent outside appraisal, kept current with periodic updates:

1. The courts give great emphasis to formal appraisals and opinions of expert witnesses as to the valuation of interests in closely held businesses.
2. A professionally done, formal appraisal allows and promotes proper estate planning.
3. A buy–sell agreement containing a professionally prepared formal appraisal may avoid costly litigation in the case of a dispute between owners of the stock or, for example, in a divorce action.
4. A formal, professionally prepared appraisal is more likely to assure fair treatment to all concerned.

5. Just as preventive medicine and preventive maintenance on machinery is usually less costly than emergency treatment or repairs, and is more effective (less downtime), so is an appraisal prepared for a buy–sell agreement likely to be better prepared and less costly than one done in an emergency atmosphere of a death, a divorce, etc.

6. As periodic updates are made, the appraiser becomes increasingly knowledgeable as to the economics of the individual business and the industry of which it is a part.

7. A professional appraisal provides not only an opinion as to the value of a closely held business, but also an analysis of that business from a management consultant's point of view.

8. Knowing the value of a closely held business allows proper planning of mergers, acquisitions, reorganizations, a sale of the business, a stock option plan, etc.

9. The underwriters generally have the last word as to the price at which a previously closely held stock will be offered to the public. In planning a public offering, however, it cannot fail to be helpful to the owners of a corporation to know the worth of their stock.[8]

The obvious disadvantage of the formal appraisal with regular updates is the cost. However, the appraisal does not necessarily have to result in quite as lengthy and detailed a report as an ESOP valuation, since there usually are fewer beneficiaries to be satisfied and the appraiser and the directors need not be concerned with meeting ERISA requirements.

Whether or not a full, written appraisal report is prepared when pricing the buy–sell agreement, some degree of guidance from an independent professional business appraiser usually is helpful in arriving at a value that will be equitable to all parties and will forestall subsequent disputes.

Understanding an Agreement's Pricing Philosophy

Since business valuations rarely can be made with undisputable precision, there usually will be some relevant range of reasonable prices that will be acceptable to the IRS and, possibly, to all the parties. In other words, as Jeffrey Matsen, a principal in a law firm and professor of law, gently states it, "In light of several available methods of valuing closely held shares and the notable subjectivity involved in such valuations, some flexibility in setting the price is possible."[9]

Appraisers of real estate, equipment, or other tangible property sometimes include statements that their appraisals are accurate to within plus or minus 10 percent. However, few business interests can be appraised within such tolerances. Just look at how widely the prices of many publicly traded stocks fluctuate over relatively short periods. For many closely held businesses, it is not unreasonable for the high end of a value range to be 50 percent above the low end. For highly dynamic or speculative businesses, the reasonable range may be even wider.

Considering this flexibility, if the buy–sell agreement price is to be determined by an independent outside appraiser for unrelated parties, the appraiser can present the parties with a relevant price range, and they can make a decision

---

[8]Orville B. Lefko, "Buy–Sell Agreements and Appraisals," *Michigan State Bar Journal,* February 1976, pp. 120–24.
[9]Jeffrey R. Matsen, "A New Look at Business Buy-Out Agreements," *Practical Lawyer,* July 1979, p. 57.

based on their wishes. Of course, it is not uncommon for the various parties to the agreement to have differing circumstances and objectives that motivate them toward opposite pricing philosophies. In general, in arm's-length bargaining one would expect parties who anticipate withdrawing earlier to opt for a higher value and parties who expect to survive in the business the longest to choose a lower value. If the decision is left to the outside appraiser, it is incumbent on the appraiser to balance these conflicting self-interests in the fairest possible manner. For estate and gift tax valuations, the fair market value standard requires the appraiser to consider only those motives typical of hypothetical, arm's-length willing buyers and willing sellers.

The consensus among the many articles that address this subject leans from the middle of the range to a somewhat conservative valuation when setting up a buy–sell agreement, whether the value standard is one of fair market value or some other standard. There are several valid arguments for inclining toward a conservative value. One is that recognizing that the valuation is an imprecise matter, the parties tend to believe they will enhance their favorable working relationship by leaning over backwards (a little) to be fair to one another. We have encountered some feeling that if some benefit is to be gained in the pricing by one party or another, it most properly should accrue to those who will remain with the business. This attitude is based on a recognition that none of the parties knows exactly when or for which owner a buy–sell agreement transaction may first be necessary, but the surviving parties will bear the dual burden of carrying off the financing and payment of the transaction and of carrying on the management of the company during this process.

In a very close family situation, it is common to find the desire to minimize the price so as to lessen estate tax consequences. In these instances, it is especially important to have thoroughly documented justification of the price or basis selected, since the combination of a low price and a non–arm's-length family situation certainly will invite the scrutiny of the IRS and the state taxing authorities.

Terms and Funding

Two decisions that necessarily are integrally related in creating the buy–sell agreement are the provisions for payment terms and for funding.

Terms can run anywhere from immediate cash to payments spread out over several years, usually with interest. Funding can come from life insurance, corporate funds in the case of a redemption, or personal assets in the case of a cross-purchase. In some cases, borrowings may be used to fund either a redemption or a cross-purchase. For a buy–sell agreement to work, funding adequate for carrying out its terms must be available one way or another. Thus, provision for funding is an essential ingredient for a viable buy–sell agreement.

Term Payment Provisions

From the purchaser's viewpoint, the typical reason for preferring a term payment program to cash is to ease the funding burden. From the seller's viewpoint, the attraction of an installment payment program is the spreading out of the tax on the seller's gain over several of the seller's tax years.

If a term payment plan is used, careful consideration must be given to establishing the interest rate, because this is an integral part of the pricing decision. Attention also should be given to the matter of collateral or other protection to ensure the seller will receive the contractual payments in the full amount and on a timely basis.

As discussed elsewhere in this book, if the interest rate on a term contract is below the market interest rate for similar instruments at the time of the event that triggers the transaction, then the cash equivalent value the seller receives will be less than the contract's face value. Similarly, if the interest rate is above the relevant market rate, then the cash equivalent value will be greater than the face value. The arithmetic for computing the present value of a contract bearing interest above or below a comparable market rate is presented in Chapter 9, "Income Approach: Discounted Economic Income Methods" (see Exhibit 9–1).

However, in setting the interest rate in the buy–sell agreement, we face the problem that market interest rates fluctuate considerably over time, and we have no way of knowing at what time in the future the buy–sell transaction will be triggered nor what the market level of interest rates will be at that time. There are several possible approaches to dealing with this dilemma.

One procedure is simply to agree on an interest rate despite these uncertainties and hope it does not prove grossly off the mark in the future. If the price under the buy–sell agreement is set by annual negotiation or appraisal, the interest rate could be reviewed and adjusted annually at the same time. Another alternative is to set the interest rate by tying it to some index of interest rates at the time of the transaction. The interest rate index used should represent intermediate- to long-term rates, since such rates fluctuate less than short-term rates and would be more appropriate for a term payment contract. The yield on *Barron's* intermediate grade bonds or *Moody's* BBB bonds could provide appropriate guidelines for setting the interest rate. The agreement could specify that the index rate or some specified amount above or below it be used depending on the credit of the company involved, the degree of security provided, and the desires of the parties to the agreement.

It might be appropriate to use an interest rate index that represents securities whose maturities coincide with the payout terms of the buy–sell agreement. For example, an index representing five-year maturities can be used if the payout term is five years. The *Federal Reserve Bulletin* gives indexes of interest rates on U.S. Treasury bonds maturing in 1, 2, 3, 5, 7, 10, 20, and 30 years.

Income tax considerations could suggest the desirability of some trade-off between the price and the interest rate. The portion of the contract payments designated as interest will be a deductible expense to the buyer and income to the seller. The portion of the contract payments designated as principal will not be deductible to the buyer (unless there is an ESOP involved) and will be taxed as capital gains to the seller to the extent that they exceed the seller's basis. Thus, if the seller is in a low tax bracket and the buyer in a high one, it may be advantageous to structure the program to increase the interest rate and lower the price. Conversely, if the seller is in a high tax bracket and the buyer in a low one, it may be advantageous to lower the interest rate and increase the price.

Minimum interest rates based on U.S. Treasury rates are required for transactions among family members, and such applicable federal rates are published monthly by the IRS in a revenue ruling.

The buy–sell agreement should also provide for adequate collateral or security for the seller in a term payment agreement. Security could take the form of a mortgage or lien on physical assets, such as real estate or equipment. It is also common to require that certain financial criteria, such as some minimum level of working capital, specified minimum current ratio, and specified maximum debt-to-equity ratio, be met. A typical sanction for enforcing such protective standards would be to provide that the entire amount become due and payable immediately if any of the standards are violated. These are the types of protections that a bank would require in making a loan, and many people believe a seller of a business interest should be no less protected.

Funding the Buy–Sell Agreement with Life Insurance

Life insurance can serve as an important source of funding for stock purchase agreements pertaining to deceased shareholders. The advantages of using life insurance for this purpose are several. First, deceased shareholders' estates get paid in cash, eliminating their need to rely on the corporation's continuing prosperity. Second, the corporation's investment in the cash value of an ordinary life policy is a business asset. Third, any excess insurance the corporation carries over and above the value of the stock purchase agreement can be retained as earned surplus.

In general, the use of life insurance can fulfill three basic needs:

1. Liquidation of the stock of a departed or disabled stockholder, either by the corporation or by other stockholders.
2. Payment of estate taxes.
3. Provision for continuity of the business after loss of a key person.

The owner should constantly monitor the value of the business to know how much life insurance is needed to fulfill these needs and update the coverage accordingly. The owner should periodically consult with a professional who knows how to apply life insurance to businesses, especially the tax implications of the many types of policies and the various configurations of ownership and beneficiaries.

For example, under current tax laws, the receipt of life insurance proceeds from a policy owned by a corporation can give rise to additional corporate taxable income under the alternative minimum tax calculations.

Liquidation of Departed or Disabled Owner's Stock.   The beneficiary of life insurance purchased to acquire a departed owner's stock is logically determined by the buy–sell agreement: the corporation is the beneficiary in connection with a repurchase agreement, and the various stockholders are the beneficiaries in connection with a cross-purchase agreement. The repurchase agreement, with the corporation as the beneficiary of the life insurance policies, usually is simpler administratively if there are three or more stockholders involved, but tax and other considerations may outweigh this advantage.

Funding of the purchase of a stockholder's interest if the stockholder is terminated but not deceased can be accomplished through an annuity or through life insurance with a cash value feature. The matter of insurance for covering needs in the event of the stockholder's permanent disability often is overlooked, but such needs are common.

Payment of Estate Taxes. Estate taxes become a problem only to the extent that the estate's value exceeds the amounts exempted from estate taxes, under the unified credit, as discussed in the previous chapter. If the value exceeds the amount eligible for the unified credit exemption, the estate tax liability can be estimated from the estate and gift tax table in Chapter 27 (Exhibit 27–1). Provision for payment of the estimated amount of estate tax can be made with life insurance in that amount.

Providing for Business Continuity. Life insurance payable to the corporation also can provide funding to ensure continuity of the business following the loss of a key person. It is common to find a key person contributing far more to the business's annual cash flow than he or she is taking out in salary and benefits. The company can be protected against the financial impact of the loss of such a valuable person by estimating the potential earnings or cash flow shortfall to be compensated for until the key person can be replaced and the replacement brought up to speed. The company can then cover the estimated amount of that risk with life insurance on the key person.

Review of Prior Life Insurance Funding. If funding of the foregoing requirements has been provided for through life insurance taken out in prior years, that insurance should be reviewed as to both amount and type.

The necessary amounts of insurance can change for several reasons. One is inflation. Another likely reason is the increased value of the business due to its success. Still another could be changes in the makeup of the business's ownership. Finally, the value of a particular person in the role of a key person can change over time due to a variety of circumstances.

There has rarely, if ever, been as much change in the variety and costs of life insurance products as there has been during the last two decades, and important changes continue to occur at this writing. A review of the life insurance funding may reveal new products that are better suited to the owner's objectives and/or are more cost efficient.

Restrictions on Transfer

Most buy–sell agreements contain restrictions on the transfer of the shares. Generally, such restrictions require that before transferring shares to any outside party they first be offered to the corporation and/or to other stockholders. The price at which the shares must be offered to the company and/or other stockholders may be the price offered by the outside party. More often, however, the price is the one determined by the buy–sell agreement price-fixing mechanism. Such restrictions often are determinative of, or at least useful evidence of value for, other purposes, since they limit both the shares' marketability and the potential amount received for them.

In a case where there is more than one class of stock, the buy–sell agreement may provide that the shares automatically be converted from one class to another if transferred, such as from voting to nonvoting. One result of this may be to keep two classes of stock at equal or nearly equal values.

If the parties to a buy–sell agreement desire to have restrictive transfer provisions apply to involuntary transfers, such as in the cases of divorces or foreclosures when the securities have been hypothecated and a loan defaulted, such extensions of the restrictions should be spelled out in the agreement. Otherwise, courts may rule that the restrictions do not apply to such involuntary transfers.[10]

Buy–Sell Agreement Values for Estate and Gift Tax Valuation under Chapter 14

Generally, the price as determined by a buy–sell agreement will be binding on the Internal Revenue Service for estate tax purposes if the value falls within the range of what would be determined under Revenue Ruling 59-60 at the time of death. Of course, that value would be binding even in the absence of a buy–sell agreement, but it usually is easier to substantiate—or at least usually more readily acceptable to the IRS—in the presence of a buy–sell agreement, especially to the extent that the agreement value was established by arm's-length negotiation.

A review of the law, the literature, and the court cases indicates that the most important criterion is the extent to which the price was established on an arm's-length basis. Following is the complete text of Section 8 of Revenue Ruling 59-60, which addresses the effect of stockholder agreements on gift and estate tax values:

> Frequently in the valuation of closely held stock for estate and gift tax purposes, it will be found that the stock is subject to an agreement restricting its sale or transfer. Where shares of stock were acquired by a decedent subject to an option reserved by the issuing corporation to repurchase at a certain price, the option price is usually accepted as the fair market value for estate tax purposes. See Rev. Rul. 54-76, C.B. 1954-1, 194. However, in such case the option price is not determinative of fair market value for gift tax purposes. Where the option, or buy and sell agreement, is the result of voluntary action by the stockholders and is binding during the life as well as at the death of the stockholders, such agreement may or may not, depending upon the circumstances of each case, fix the value for estate tax purposes. However, such agreement is a factor to be considered, with other relevant factors, in determining fair market value. Where the stockholder is free to dispose of his shares during life and the option is to become effective only upon his death, the fair market value is not limited to the option price. It is always necessary to consider the relationship of the parties, the relative number of shares held by the decedent, and other material facts, to determine whether the agreement represents a bona fide business arrangement or is a device to pass the decedent's shares to the natural objects of his bounty for less than an adequate and full consideration in money or money's worth. In this connection, see Rev. Rul. 157, C.B. 1953-2, 255, and Rev. Rul. 189, C.B. 1953-2, 29.[11]

It also should be pointed out that a value fixed by a buy–sell agreement may be legally binding on the estate for transaction purposes even if it is not binding on the IRS for estate tax purposes. This could result in a situation where the estate ends up paying taxes on a value substantially higher than the price the estate actually receives.

---

[10]See, for example, *Castonguay* v. *Castonguay,* 306 N.W.2d 143 (Minn. 1981) and *Durkee* v. *Durkee Mower, Inc.,* 428 N.E.2d 139 (Mass. 1981).

[11]Revenue Ruling 59-60, 1959-1 C.B. 237, Section 8.

Valuation Requirements under Section 2703

The Chapter 14 special valuation rules are applied to all applicable transfers after October 8, 1990. As previously discussed in Chapter 27, Section 2703 of Chapter 14 deals with buy–sell agreements, options, and other similar influences on value for estate or gift tax transfers.

Section 2703 applies to any family-owned business in which the family members (defined in the regulations) control 50 percent or more of the vote or value of the company.[12] Any buy–sell agreement, restriction, or other similar factor relating to the right to use or sell the property will be ignored for estate, gift, and generation-skipping tax purposes unless the agreement meets all three of the following tests:

1. It is a bona fide business arrangement.
2. It must not be a device to transfer the property to the natural objects of the transferor's bounty (such as family members) for less than adequate and full consideration in money or money's worth.
3. Its terms must be comparable to similar arrangements entered into by persons in an arm's-length transaction.

The first two factors have long been part of the law regarding the effectiveness of buy–sell agreements for fixing values for estate and gift taxes. The third requirement is new with Section 2703.

Because of the effective date of the statute, many old buy–sell agreements will be grandfathered under the law, and transactions under these agreements need only follow the requirements in Revenue Ruling 59-60 and any court decisions involving similar fact patterns. The regulations for Section 2703, however, make it plain that any grandfathered agreement that is substantially modified after October 8, 1990, will thereafter be required to follow the rules under Section 2703. The IRS defines *substantial modification* as any change in the buy–sell agreement or other restriction that would alter (beyond a *de minimis* amount) the quality, timing, or amount of the rights of the parties to the agreement. Also, if any parties of a generation younger than those originally participating in the agreement as of October 8, 1990, are added by voluntary modification of the agreement (i.e., added as parties to the agreement by some discretionary method other than by a mandatory action such as inheritance), this will be considered a substantial modification.

Changes that are necessary to update the value of an agreement or restriction to make the value or terms of the agreement more nearly approximate fair market value are not to be considered material changes. An example of this would be a formula-based change in the earnings multiple used to calculate a value under the agreement. Failure to update an agreement requiring, say, an annual estimation of value constitutes a substantial modification.

What kind of formula-based value will work with buy–sell agreements under Section 2703? Under the pre-Chapter 14 rules, all that was basically necessary to make a buy–sell agreement (or other restriction) binding for estate and gift taxes was:

---

[12]We find the use of 50 percent as a threshold for control an odd choice. A 50 percent interest in a company is not per se a controlling interest, but merely a right to deadlock the company's decision-making process.

1. The agreement be binding during life as well as at death.
2. The agreement create a determinable value as of a specifically determinable date.
3. The agreement have at least some bona fide business purpose (this could include the promotion of orderly family ownership and management succession, so this was an easy test to meet).
4. The agreement resulted in a fair market value for the subject business interest when it was originally executed. Often, the buy–sell agreement value would generate future date of death or gift date values substantially below what the fair market value otherwise would have been for the subject interest—even though the value was reasonable when the agreement was made.

Now, the additional test to be met requires that the analyst search for comparable formulas or pricing methods for companies within the same or similar lines of business as the subject company. Effectively, this implies that buy–sell agreements established under Section 2703 will usually result in a value close to or at the standard of fair market value for the subject business interest that would have applied anyway as of the subsequent valuation date. As a result, Section 2703 limits the usefulness of buy–sell agreements to freeze the value of assets for estate planning purposes.

The use of a formula under this requirement will require research into the general commercial practices within the subject company's industry for buy–sell agreements and other restrictions between unrelated parties. In the regulations on this test, it was noted that this standard is not met by showing a few isolated comparables, but rather the general business practice in the industry. If several different valuation formulas are in general use, it is permissible to utilize only one.[13]

If more than one right or restriction is set forth in the buy–sell agreement, each is tested separately under the rules of Section 2703.

Summary

Buy–sell agreements can be very useful tools for controlling ownership and liquidating the interests of deceased or departed shareholders or partners. They may take the form of cross-purchase agreements (among owners), repurchase agreements (between owner and company), or some combination of the two. Agreements may be funded in any of several ways, most commonly with some type of life insurance and/or annuity product. Under some circumstances, the buy–sell agreement value may determine estate taxes.

A key provision in any buy–sell agreement, and one that often receives inadequate attention in its drafting, is the provision for valuation. Aspects of the valuation provision that are not addressed, addressed in an unclear manner, and/or not understood in the same way by all the parties can lead to irreconcilable divisiveness and protracted litigation. It is extremely important that the implications of every aspect of the valuation provision be understood and considered in detail by all the parties. If independent appraisal is being contemplated, the procedure

---

[13]Reg. Treas. Section 25.2702-1(b)(4).

for selecting the appraiser(s) should be precise and complete. The agreement should give clear direction to the appraisers on all aspects of the appraisal assignment, including the valuation date and a clear definition of the applicable standard of value.

Care should also be taken in the planning stage to avoid the potentially disastrous estate tax consequences of transfers among family members or with others at less than full and adequate consideration.

Bibliography

Abatemarco, Michael J., and Alfred Cavallaro. "The Importance of Buy–Sell Agreements for Closely Held Corporations." *CPA Journal,* February 1992, pp. 57–59.

Adams, Roy M.; David A. Herpe; and James R. Carey. "Buy–Sell Agreements after Chapter 14." *Trusts & Estates,* May 1993, pp. 22–32.

Bell, Lawrence L. "Valuation of Buy–Sell Agreements under Chapter 14 of the Internal Revenue Code." *Journal of the American Society of CLU & ChFC,* September 1992, pp. 48–53.

Birnbaum, Bruce L. "Practitioners Have Several Ways of Using Buy–Sell Agreements." *Taxation for Accountants,* April 1994, pp. 220–26.

Corelli, Julia D. "How to Draft Buy–Sell Agreements for S Corporations." *Practical Tax Lawyer,* Winter 1994, pp. 65–90.

Drake, Dwight J.; Kent Whiteley; and Timothy J. McDevitt. "The Ten Most Common Mistakes of Buy–Sell Agreements." *Journal of Financial Planning,* July 1992, pp. 104–12.

Etkind, Steven M. "How a Professional Practice Can Be Sold Effectively." *Estate Planning,* May/June 1994, pp. 162–68.

Fife, James D. "Structuring Buy–Sell Agreements to Fix Estate Tax Value." *Estate Planning,* March/April 1995, pp. 67–74.

Gamble, E. James. "How Do We Handle Buy–Sell Agreements under Chapter 14?" *Trusts & Estates,* March 1991, pp. 38–46.

_____. "Tax Law Notes: Buy–Sell Agreements, Section 2703, and the Final Regulations." *Michigan Bar Journal,* July 1992, pp. 664–66.

Geer, Carolyn Torcellini. "Prenuptial for Business Partner (Buy–Sell Agreements)." *Forbes,* December 5, 1994, pp. 166–67.

Gerchak, Yigal, and J. David Fuller. "Optimal Value Declaration in Buy–Sell Situations." *Management Science,* January 1992, pp. 48–56.

Grassi, Sebastian V., Jr. "Business Problems and Planning—Shareholder Buy–Sell Agreements and the Revenue Reconciliation Act of 1990." *Michigan Bar Journal*, May 1991, pp. 447–49.

_____. "Interim Guidance for Buy–Sell Agreements after the New Law." *Journal of Taxation of Estates and Trusts,* Spring 1991, pp. 4–6.

Hales, Robert E. "To Buy–Sell or Not to Buy–Sell." *Practical Tax Lawyer,* Fall 1994, pp. 31–38.

Hunkele-Martinez, Wendy L. "Buy/Sell Agreements from a Spouse's Perspective." *Texas Bar Journal,* October 1992, pp. 932–34.

Hunsberger, Donald A. "Owners and Estates: A Buy–Sell Primer." *Journal of the American Society of CLU & ChFC,* September 1991, pp. 48–52.

Johnson, Linda M., and Brian R. Greenstein. "Using Buy–Sell Agreements to Establish the Value of a Closely Held Business." *Journal of Taxation,* December 1994, pp. 362–68.

Kasner, Jerry A. "The IRS Loses One in the Buy–Sell Valuation Battle." *Tax Notes,* April 12, 1993, pp. 231–32.

Kelly, James P., III. "Waiving Rights under Buy–Sell Agreement Affects Stock Value." *Estate Planning,* September/October 1991, pp. 284–91.

Kramer, Harry. "Buy–Sell Agreements Need Not Restrict Corporate Carryovers. *Taxation for Accountants,* September 1992, pp. 168–73.

Louden, Ian K. "Practitioners Wary of Transfer Tax Potential in Buy–Sell Agreements." *Tax Notes,* September 21, 1992, pp. 1526–27.

Marcus, Fred J., and Douglas K. Freeman. "Valuation of Closely-Held Stock." *Journal of the American Society of CLU & ChFC,* September 1993, pp. 24–25.

Mezzullo, Louis A. "Buy–Sell Agreements after Chapter 14." *Trusts & Estates,* June 1994, pp. 49–59.

O'Connell, John J. "Net Gifts at Death and New Buy–Sell Agreement Problems." *Journal of the American Society of CLU & ChFC,* January 1994, pp. 72–76.

————. "The Triple Tax Traps in Family Firm Buy–Sell Plans." *National Underwriter (Life & Health/Financial Services Edition),* August 30, 1993, p. 7.

Peterson, James. "Ducking the Cross Fire: Avoiding Disputes in Buy–Sell Agreements." *Journal of Accountancy,* January 1991, pp. 65–69,; 71.

Reilly, Robert F., and Robert P. Schweihs. "How the Buy/Sell Agreement Smooths a Shift in Control." *Mergers & Acquisitions,* January/February 1991, pp. 52–57.

————. "Stock Valuation for a Buy–Sell Agreement Must Resist Scrutiny." *Small Business Taxation,* July/August 1990, pp. 363–67.

————. "Valuation Aspects of Buy/Sell Agreements Subsequent to the Repeal of Section 2036(c)." *Ohio CPA Journal,* Spring 1991, pp. 38–43.

Robbins, Valerie C. "Buy–Sell Agreement with a Twist." *Tax Adviser,* August 1992, pp. 524–25.

Rowland, Mary. "The Importance of Buy/Sell Agreements." *Nation's Business,* March 1995, pp. 57–58.

Segal, Mark A. "Buy–Sell Agreements—A Valuable Estate Planning Tool." *National Public Accountant,* February 1990, pp. 14–17.

Stoneman, Christopher. "Buy–Sell Agreements: Accomplishing Planning Objectives with Optimal Tax Consequences." *Tax Management: Estates, Gifts & Trusts Journal,* December 15, 1992, pp. 423–36.

Strouse, Jonathan E. "Redemption and Cross-Purchase Buy–Sell Agreements: A Comparison." *Practical Accountant,* October 1991, pp. 44–53 ff.

Switzer, Ralph V., and Edward D. Jones. "Orchestrating a Continuation Provision." *National Public Accountant,* December 1992, pp. 30–37.

Wagner, William J. "Questions about Trusteed Buy–Sells." *National Underwriter (Life & Health/Financial Services Edition),* April 25, 1994, pp. 7 ff.

Willens, Robert. "Buy–Sell Agreements: Constructive Dividend Dangers Lurk." *Journal of Accountancy,* February 1992, pp. 49–52.

Wise, Richard M. "Buy–Sell Valuation." *Canadian Tax Highlights,* June 22, 1993, pp. 44–45.

Chapter 29

Taxation Planning and Compliance—Ad Valorem

Introduction

This chapter will present many of the reasons to conduct a valuation analysis for purposes of ad valorem property taxation. These purposes include property tax compliance (i.e., the annual administrative filing of property tax renditions), property tax assessment administrative appeal, and property tax valuation and equalization litigation (including expert witness testimony).

First, we will define certain terminology that is specific to the ad valorem taxation assessment and appeal process. Second, we will introduce the basic principles of the property tax valuation process. Third, we will introduce the basic principles of the property tax equalization process. Fourth, we will introduce the basic principles of the property tax appeal process. Fifth, we will discuss the general functions that appraisers perform in the ad valorem taxation planning and compliance process. Sixth, we will present several special topics related to specific analyses that business appraisers can perform to assist taxpayers in the property taxation assessment, appeal, and litigation process. These special topics include the identification and quantification of external (or economic) obsolescence, the identification and valuation of intangible assets for taxpayers assessed under the unitary method of valuation, and the identification and application of appropriate income approach methods for ad valorem unitary valuation.

Definitions of Ad Valorem Taxation Terminology

The following brief definitions are set forth to acquaint the reader with some general terms that are used regularly in the ad valorem taxation planning and compliance process.

These definitions are consistent with, but not necessarily identical to, those presented in *Property Taxation,* 2nd edition, published by the Institute of Property Taxation in 1993. The Institute of Property Taxation is a major organization of professionals involved in the ad valorem taxation process.

- **Assess**—to make an appraisal of the property in connection with a listing of the property liable to ad valorem taxation. It implies the exercise of discretion on the part of the public officials charged with the duty of property assessment, including the listing—or inventory—of the property involved and the conclusion of an appropriate, defined value on that property. The word *assess* is sometimes used interchangeably with the word *levy*.
- **Assessor**—a public official elected or appointed to discover, list, and appraise privately owned property for ad valorem property tax purposes.
- **Assessed valuation**—the value placed on each taxable unit by the assessor, which provides the basis to which the applicable property tax rate is applied to determine the amount to be paid by the property owner as property taxes.
- **Assessment roll**—a list, or roll, of all privately owned taxable property within a taxing authority jurisdiction completed, verified, and deposited by the local assessor.
- **Tax rate**—typically developed by dividing the total cost of the local government's annual budget by the total assessed value on the tax roll (i.e., all privately owned property within the local taxing jurisdiction). An example of the way taxing authorities set the property tax rate in their jurisdiction follows:

Formula 29–1

$$\frac{\text{Annual municipal budget}}{\text{Total assessed value of private property per the tax roll}} = \frac{\$2{,}000{,}000}{\$100{,}000{,}000} = \begin{array}{l}\textit{a tax rate of 20 mills (\$2 per}\\ \textit{\$100 or \$20 per \$1,000 of}\\ \textit{assessed property valuation}\end{array}$$

- **Equal and uniform taxation**—ad valorem taxes are considered to be equal and uniform when no taxpayer or class of taxpayers in the taxing district— whether it be a state, county, city, town, or village—is taxed at a rate different from other taxpayers in the same taxing district upon the same value or the same type of property. The concept of equal and uniform taxation is a basic statutory and judicial goal of ad valorem property taxation. The departure of this standard by a taxing authority is one of the principal justifications for a taxpayer's assessment appeal.
- **Equalization ratio**—the percentage of market value at which a property is assessed. The equalization ratio is often simply called the ratio.
- **Ratio study**—generally the comprehensive comparison of actual property sales or of appraised values of selected parcels to the taxing jurisdiction's assessments in order to determine the effective equalization rate or ratio.
- **Ad valorem**—literally, this phrase means "according to value." The term *ad valorem tax* means a tax or duty on the value of the property subject to taxation. Such property could include tangible personal property, a parcel of tangible real estate, or a mass collection of income-producing assets (as in the case of a business subject to the unitary property assessment method).
- **Certiorari**—the name of a writ of review or inquiry. In ad valorem property tax practice, it brings the taxpayer's assessment appeal into a superior court, based on the record of the administrative tribunal (e.g., a board of tax review) or of an inferior judicial tribunal.

Market Value as the General Basis of Property Assessment

The most common basis for assessing real estate and personal property in the United States is market value. This market-derived property assessment basis is often referred to in state statutes, in judicial opinions, and in the property tax literature by such terms as fair cash value, fair value, cash value, true value, true cost value, economic value, and other similar terminology.

Notwithstanding these local statutory phrases, all these definitions have generally come to mean the most likely price at which a property will sell from a willing seller to a willing buyer, both cognizant of all pertinent facts and neither being under duress.

However, this classic "willing buyer–willing seller" definition must sometimes be tempered when there are no comparable sales transactions in the appropriate competitive market. This is often the situation in the case of special purpose properties such as mining operations, certain chemical processing operations, timber or other special agricultural businesses, or any other properties that are special purpose to fairly unique businesses. In these instances, a form of the cost approach to property valuation is often the most appropriate appraisal approach when recent market data regarding property sale transactions are not available.

Nonetheless, when either a cost approach or an income approach is used to value special purpose assessable property—because a lack of recent transactional data regarding such special purpose properties does not allow the effective use of the market approach—the objective of the analysis is still to estimate the market value of the subject property.

The Property Tax Valuation Process

As with the valuation of tangible and intangible properties for any purpose, there are three basic approaches to the valuation of privately owned property for ad valorem taxation purposes: the cost approach, the income approach, and the sales comparison (or market) approach.

In the cost approach to property valuation, four basic steps are involved:

1. The subject land (if any) is valued as if vacant and unimproved.
2. The reproduction or replacement cost of the building, site improvements, or personal property is estimated at current prices.
3. Allowances for physical depreciation, functional obsolescence, technological obsolescence, and external (including location and economic) obsolescence are subtracted.
4. The land value (if any) is added to this estimate of the depreciated replacement cost of the improvements and the personal property.

In the income approach to property valuation, the value of the property is based on its ability to produce either a net operating income or a net rental income. A capitalization rate is then divided into this economic income stream to convert it into an estimate of the taxable property's current value.

In the sales comparison or market approach, actual sales of similar properties are analyzed and a value is estimated for the subject property by a process of comparison.

Each of these three valuation approaches is described in greater detail in Chapter 12, which discusses the asset-based approach to business valuation.

The Property Tax Equalization Process

In determining the equalized valuations required by state statutes, local property tax assessment authorities often make and issue comprehensive assessment ratio studies. These assessment ratio studies analyze the average level of assessment, the degrees of assessment, uniformity, and the overall compliance with the assessment and classification requirements for each major class of property in each jurisdiction. These assessment ratio studies are performed to indicate (1) the degree of compliance with the law and rules and regulations of the assessment jurisdiction and (2) the proper classification of property in each assessment jurisdiction.

To ensure the equalization of the assessment process, assessment authorities typically collect and tabulate information relative to the sales of properties within their jurisdiction. They also cause appraisals to be made of properties of various classes in their jurisdiction (selected on a basis of random sampling or otherwise) to (1) confirm the assessment ratio derived from property sale prices, (2) assist in determining the appropriate assessment ratio when the number of actual property sales is insufficient to represent a specific class of properties in the jurisdiction, (3) provide a substitute for the actual sale prices of properties of a unique character or that are sold at infrequent intervals, and (4) establish an assessment ratio for the tangible personal property (as opposed to the tangible real estate) assessed in their jurisdiction.

Assessment Ratio Studies

Assessment ratio studies, designed to compare the assessed value to the market value of property, are performed principally for evaluating the accuracy of the assessment process and for ensuring valuation equalization in the assessment process. Property tax assessment authorities often use assessment ratio studies: (1) to establish the necessity for general reappraisals, (2) to identify any problems with their appraisal procedures, (3) to "trend" property appraisals between general reappraisal dates, (4) to adjust actual property sale prices for time, and (5) to develop property depreciation factors. Tax equalization officials also use assessment ratio studies to estimate the total market value of taxable property in their jurisdiction. This estimation is made, in part, to bring centrally assessed properties in line with locally assessed properties, from an assessment fairness perspective.

Use of Assessment Ratio Studies in Administrative Appeals and Litigation

An assessment ratio study is a means of testing the fairness of the property assessment procedure in a given jurisdiction. Property tax assessment authorities are generally required by law to assess all property in an assessing district uniformly. Only through an assessment ratio study can one determine whether the assessor meets this statutory requirement.

After reviewing some basic tax equalization concepts, the following section will discuss how to determine whether an assessment ratio study is justified, how to conduct one, and how to use it in property tax assessment negotiations. To understand how to use an assessment ratio study, taxpayers and their valuation advisors should understand the following basic concepts in ad valorem taxation: uniformity, changing values and their impact on uniformity, market values, and the assessment ratio.

Uniformity. The concept of uniformity in property tax assessment equalization is related to the most basic principle of ad valorem taxes. As mentioned above, ad valorem means "according to value." In very practical terms, this means that each dollar of property value is to be assessed so it will contribute the same amount of tax revenue to operate the local government. A $1 million personal residence should be assessed so the owner's tax burden will equal exactly the owner's tax burden that will result from a $1 million assessment on a retail commercial property, or a $1 million multifamily apartment house, or a $1 million parcel of vacant land, or a $1 million industrial building, or any other type of property in the assessment jurisdiction having a $1 million value on the same date.

A logical extension of this concept is that, as of a given date, the value of each separate property on an assessment roll in the taxing jurisdiction will be established for assessment purposes. This value will presumably relate to market value. The assessor then assesses each property in proportion to its market value. The assessment may be at 100 percent of market value (i.e., full value assessment), or, if the statute permits, the assessment may be at some fraction of market value (i.e., uniform assessment). So long as each property is treated equally, the assessment process has been equalized, and the ad valorem tax burden has been equalized.

Changing Values.   Changing property values may create the need for an assessment ratio study. Even if the assessment roll was properly assembled and represented an equalized distribution of assessments at a given date, over time, the values of the various properties will typically change at different rates. Some types of property (for example, retail commercial property) may increase in value at a greater rate than other types of property. Within a comparatively short time period, therefore, the assessment roll (which may have been uniform when it was assembled) is no longer equalized. The longer this situation continues without correction, the more inequitable the assessment roll becomes. If the assessments on these properties are not adjusted—that is, equalized—to reflect the varying rates of change in property value that occur over time, then the assessments no longer represent either (1) a full value assessment or (2) a uniform assessment.

Market Value.   The definition of market value in the assessment process is no different from the definition of market value generally. In estimating market value, the appraiser considers all the usual marketplace factors involved in and affecting the value of property. Among other criteria, appraisers consider income potential, typical financing patterns, zoning, development capacity, street frontage, land area and/or plottage, neighborhood characteristics and influences, availability and sufficiency of municipal utilities and services, functional utility of the structural and site improvements, convenience of and proximity to transportation facilities, marketability, and all other factors usual and necessary to the formulation of an opinion of value.

The Assessment Ratio.   The assessor begins with market value in assessing property for ad valorem tax purposes. Market value is generally the basis on which any assessment equalization is made. When an assessment roll is no longer uniform or equalized, one of the two items necessary to prove an inequitable or discriminatory property tax assessment is the market value of the subject property. The other item is the assessment ratio—that is, the ratio of the property's assessment to the property's market value—and whether the assessment ratio for the individual property exceeds the assessment ratio applicable to all other property on the same assessment roll as of the same date.

The Property Tax Unitary Valuation Process

Estimating the fair market value of an individual property such as an office building or an apartment complex is relatively straightforward. The taxable location of the property is readily ascertainable, and its value can be directly obtained by analyzing comparable sales, market-derived rental rates, and replacement or reproduction cost.

Many properties, however, are components of interrelated and interdependent operating business systems that span numerous taxing jurisdictions. Examples of such operating business systems include: traditional utilities, such as electric power generating companies; partially regulated but highly competitive businesses, such as long distance telecommunications companies, railroads and airlines; and businesses in transition, such as telephone companies.

The reason for the unitary valuation concept is the recognition that it is not possible to accurately value, for property tax purposes, the property of (for example) a railroad in one taxing jurisdiction simply by analyzing that property in isolation. Rather, it is more practical to value the entire operating system and then apportion some of that value to each taxing jurisdiction. This is the basic concept of unit value, sometimes referred to as unitary value or as system value.

This approach to valuing an entire system of operating assets has been extended to value business enterprise types other than railroads. This extension logically covers other interstate, capital-intensive businesses that employ operating systems of interdependent interrelated assets in multiple taxing jurisdictions. Historically (although much less so today), these companies were almost always publicly regulated utilities.

One issue that is implicitly present in the unit valuation process is that the going-concern value of the entire operating business is being estimated rather than the market value of the taxpayer's tangible property only. In other words, a fundamental question of the unitary valuation process is: Does this process value the overall business enterprise or does it value only the assessable assets of a taxpayer (albeit on a collective basis)?

The Property Tax Appeal Process

When assessment and millage rate formulas are consistently applied, the ad valorem assessment and taxation process is inherently fair and equitable. Disputes regarding valuation and/or equalization are inevitable, however.

Such disagreements usually arise when property owners believe that the market value placed on their property is excessive or overstated (either in absolute terms or in comparison with other properties in the same taxing jurisdiction).

For this reason, ad valorem assessments of property values are often vigorously contested and appealed. Such disputes are often resolved (at varying points in the administrative or judicial appeal process) through soundly reasoned, rigorously prepared, and comprehensively documented independent appraisals.

The ad valorem property tax assessment appeal process encompasses systematic procedures employed to answer specific questions regarding the value of real estate and tangible personal property. This process starts with the identification of the appraisal problem and ends with a reporting on the appraisal results.

For each ad valorem assessment appeal appraisal, the analytical and quantitative procedures depend on the nature of the assignment, the type of properties appraised, the purpose and objective of the appraisal, and the quantity and quality of available data.

Steps in an Appraisal

All ad valorem assessment appeal appraisals generally follow the process below:

1. Definition of the scope, objective, and purpose of the appraisal.
2. Identification, inspection, and inventory of the assets subject to appraisal.
3. Market research and analysis of all available valuation data.
4. Contemplation of the three generally accepted approaches to property appraisal.
5. Selection of the quantitative and qualitative appraisal methods and procedures to be used in the instant appraisal.
6. Performance of the selected appraisal methods and procedures.
7. Integration and synthesis of the results of the various appraisal methods and procedures.
8. Reporting of the final conclusion of property value.

The Assessing Authority's Objective

The objective of the property tax assessing authorities in setting ad valorem taxes is to estimate the value of all taxable properties within a given jurisdiction fairly and equitably—yet also efficiently and economically. Assessing authorities are supposed to treat owners of similar properties fairly and equally.

The Property Owner's Objective

The objective of a property owner is to ascertain the correct market value of his or her property and to file a property tax return reflecting that value. If an initial assessment is overstated or if the assessing authority does not accept a property owner's value for the property, extensive administrative and judicial appeal processes are available.

The Independent Appraiser's Objective

The objective of the independent appraiser is to prepare the most soundly reasoned and thoroughly documented appraisal possible. The appraiser must also remain independent and objective during the ad valorem assessment appeal process. While appraisers can perform certain advisory and consultative services—and act as intermediaries on behalf of their taxpayer clients—independent appraisers *cannot* become advocates or perform advocacy functions with regard to valuation or equalization appeals.

Preliminary Negotiations

During preliminary negotiations on initial assessments or a reassessment of property, the property owner typically deals directly with the local assessing authority.

During these preliminary negotiations, the property owner presents all evidence regarding the value of the property, and the assessor presents all his or her evidence. A compromise is frequently reached at this stage of the assessment process. If so, a revised property assessment is recorded and accepted by both parties. It is often useful for an independent appraiser to assist property owners even in these preliminary negotiations with taxing authorities.

Administrative Appeals

If preliminary negotiations are unsuccessful, then the property owner has various administrative assessment appeal remedies available; and, at this point, the property owner should retain competent legal counsel and a professional appraiser.

The assessment appeal procedures vary by taxing jurisdiction. However, most jurisdictions include quasi-judicial authorities in the administrative appeals process, such as county boards or state boards of equalization. The assessment appeal process before these administrative authorities is fairly formal, and the assessment appeal decisions of these administrative authorities may set an important precedent if the taxpayer pursues relief through judicial appeal.

Narrative Appraisal Reports

Property owners should typically come to the administrative appeal hearings with a fully documented narrative appraisal report. These appraisals should be prepared in accordance with generally accepted appraisal standards and in accordance with the definitions and the methods required by the statutory authority of the local taxing jurisdiction.

During the administrative appeal hearing, the taxpayer's appraiser may testify as an expert witness about the subject, content, and conclusions of his or her property appraisal. If either the taxpayer or the taxing authority is not satisfied with the decision of the administrative appeal authority, then judicial appeal remedies are available.

Judicial Appeals

The judicial appeal process involves formal legal proceedings in which the taxpayer typically will be represented by legal counsel. Before seeking judicial relief, the taxpayer's legal counsel works closely with both the taxpayer and the appraiser to assess the strengths and weaknesses of the particular assessment appeal case.

The legal counsel also works closely with the independent appraiser to prepare the appraiser for expert witness testimony at the trial. Simultaneously, the appraiser may perform various litigation-support and advisory services to prepare the attorney to deal with the property valuation and assessment equalization issues of the case.

Special Topics

In the next few sections of this chapter, we will explore several topics in which business appraisers may be particularly helpful to property owners in the ad valorem tax property valuation and equalization process—and in the ad valorem tax assessment appeal process.

Identification and Quantification of Functional Obsolescence

While functional obsolescence is most closely associated with the cost approach to property valuation, it is a consideration in the sales comparison and in the income approaches to property valuation as well. In the sales comparison approach, the appraiser attempts to select and analyze comparable properties with similar levels of functional obsolescence. In the income approach, the appraiser attempts to ensure that the subject property's economic income stream is properly adjusted for the economic detriments associated with the subject property's functional obsolescence.

Definition of Functional Obsolescence.   Functional obsolescence is an impairment of the functional utility of a property according to current market tastes and standards. To apply the concept properly—and it applies to all types of property—one needs to be aware that functional obsolescence can be curable or incurable. In addition, functional obsolescence represents more than practical usefulness—that is, it can take the form of superadequacies, as well as inadequacies.

A superadequacy is an excess in the capacity or quality of a property as compared with market standards. One example of a superadequacy is a warehouse with a ceiling height far greater than that required by the existing operations of the tenant or of the marketplace at large. An inadequacy is a characteristic of the subject property that is of a lower standard as compared with the marketplace. A three-bedroom apartment with only one bathroom might be an example of an inadequacy.

Sample Situations.   One could construct an endless list of examples of functional obsolescence. The following examples are intended only to be illustrative in nature:

- Commercial office buildings may have public spaces such as corridors that are abnormally wide or oversized.
- Some commercial amenities are considered standard in office complexes (e.g., express elevators, telecommunication hookups, inside parking, and retail space); the lack of these amenities may indicate the existence of functional obsolescence.
- Shopping centers that are nonenclosed or with an inappropriate floor plan (e.g., one with an unsuccessful skating rink in the center).
- Instances of inadequate lighting, heating, or air-conditioning typically represent functional obsolescence. These instances occur mostly in older buildings. They may also occur in cases in which facilities are currently being used for a purpose other than that for which they were constructed. Instances of excessive (and therefore partially unused) lighting, heating, or air-conditioning can also represent functional obsolescence.
- A manufacturing or processing plant that is too large to accommodate the current or planned levels of business operations; in other words, there is significant excess capacity. Or the manufacturing or processing plant that is too small to accommodate the current level of business operations, so there are operating inefficiencies and a paucity of capacity.
- For the particular type of production or processing operation in the facility, the plant ceilings may be too low—or too high. Likewise, for the particular type of production or processing operating in the facility, the plant floors may be too thin—or too thick.

- There may be excess construction costs in an older plant because the walls are too thick (as compared with modern construction techniques and materials). Likewise, in older plants, the walls may be too thin to allow for the current production or processing operations to occur on higher floors. In addition, in many older plants, concrete or other types of load-bearing columns consume excessive plant floor area or disrupt an otherwise efficient materials or production flow.

- Other than the load-bearing columns mentioned previously, there may be numerous examples of structural or physical impediments to material-processing flow or product-manufacturing flow. Inefficient layout or design, related both to real estate and to tangible personal property, are among the most common examples of functional obsolescence.

Identification of Functional Obsolescence. Many property owners realize that their existing properties are experiencing functional obsolescence only after they have purchased or constructed new properties. When the input, output, or operations of the older properties are compared with those of the newer properties, instances of functional obsolescence become clearly evident. In some cases, the property owner may identify functional obsolescence not by comparison of the subject properties with new properties, but rather by comparison of the subject properties with competitors' properties. When competitors have purchased new assets or constructed new facilities, these new properties provide a basis for comparison with the subject properties. Such a comparison can indicate instances of functional obsolescence.

Proper Applications. Functional obsolescence enters the property valuation process in any of the three traditional approaches to property value.

Income Approach. Assessors arrive at a fair market value indication using the income approach by projecting a prospective economic income stream and then capitalizing it. This simple approach may ignore the future costs to be incurred to make necessary corrections of design deficiencies (e.g., the costs involved in eliminating excess office space in an office/warehouse). Because of this design deficiency, the prospective economic income may not be stable. Furthermore, the comparable properties used to estimate the appropriate capitalization rate may not be suffering from the same amount of functional obsolescence as the subject property is subject to.

Sales Comparison Approach. Any sales comparison approach to analysis depends on the degree of comparability of the "comparable" property sales considered. Adjustments to comparable properties are made to account for, among other things, the functional deficiencies of the subject property—as compared with the functional deficiencies experienced by the comparable properties.

Cost Approach. Property tax assessors often use some version of the cost approach. Original costs are often increased based on indexing factors that adjust for property inflation factors and are then adjusted downward in an attempt to adjust for all forms of depreciation and obsolescence, including functional obsolescence. When used properly, the cost approach considers the various functional obsolescence factors impacting the subject property. To be curable, the cost of correcting the functional obsolescence must be the same or less than the anticipated increase in the subject property value. Functional obsolescence is curable if correcting it on the date of the appraisal is economically feasible; otherwise, it is incurable. Curable functional obsolescence is typically measured by the cost to correct the deficiency.

Quantification of Functional Obsolescence.   Clearly, after identifying and documenting significant instances of functional obsolescence, the next step in the ad valorem property tax appraisal process is the quantification of functional obsolescence. Although many individual procedures and techniques are available to quantify specific instances of functional obsolescence, all these procedures and techniques are often categorized into one or two methods.

The first method of quantifying functional obsolescence involves calculating the difference between the reproduction cost new and the replacement cost new of the subject property. The second method of quantifying functional obsolescence involves the capitalization of excess operating expenses (i.e., the costs of materials, labor, and overhead) associated with the operation of the subject property.

Reproduction versus Replacement Cost New.   This method is particularly useful when estimating incurable functional obsolescence associated with special purpose real estate and tangible personal property. In fact, the principal difference between the reproduction cost and the replacement cost of the subject property is the amount of incurable functional obsolescence. Those elements of functional obsolescence that are incurable should be eliminated before the estimation of replacement cost new (i.e., the cost to purchase or construct a new state-of-the-art productive asset or property).

Although it is a complex engineering and appraisal process to estimate both the reproduction cost new and the replacement cost new for the subject property, it is relatively easy to estimate the associated functional obsolescence. Once both the reproduction cost and the replacement cost have been estimated, the amount of incurable functional obsolescence is typically the mathematical difference between the two cost estimations.

Capitalization of Excess Operating Expenses.   This method typically quantifies the amount of curable functional obsolescence associated with the subject property. The approach quantifies the economic penalty associated with operating the subject property (given all its elements of functional obsolescence) instead of curing the subject property (and thereby eliminating the excess operating costs).

As mentioned previously, excess operating expenses include the material, labor, and overhead associated with operating the subject property. In the appraisal of tangible personal property, for example, excess material expenses should include the expense of carrying excess raw material and work-in-process inventory, as well as the excess expense of waste and scrappage due to a functionally obsolete machine or process. Excess labor expenses should include the costs of employee fringe benefits and employment taxes, as well as the direct expenses of excess machine operators, material handlers, etc. Excess overhead expenses should include the costs of excess electricity, gas, water, property and casualty insurance, rent, security, and property tax expense associated with operating the functionally obsolete property.

It is somewhat more difficult to quantify the amount of curable functional obsolescence associated with the capitalized excess operating expense method than with the replacement cost versus reproduction cost method. First, the excess expenses have to be identified and documented. This requires an estimation of what a normal level of operating expenses would be. Normal operating expenses may mean industry norms, expense data from specific competitors, expense data from other facilities operated by the same property owner, or historical operating expense data related to the subject property. Next, these excess operating expenses must be projected over the remaining useful life of the subject property. For the purposes of this projection, the remaining useful life typically means the lowest of the subject property's physical life or economic life.

The projection of excess operating expenses must be quantified as a present value, using an appropriate present value discount rate. This discount rate should reflect the property owner's cost of capital, the time value of money, and the risk associated with property ownership. Accordingly, the quantification of functional obsolescence using the capitalized excess operating expense method requires the appraiser to perform several detailed analyses.

Summary of Functional Obsolescence Issues.   Functional obsolescence is an impairment (inadequate or superadequate) of the functional utility of a property according to current market tastes and standards. It can be curable or incurable. The cost to correct incurable functional obsolescence exceeds the resulting increase in value.

Using the income approach to property valuation, functional obsolescence is quantified indirectly. That is because a property with functional obsolescence will generate less economic income to be capitalized in the income approach analysis. In the sales comparison approach to property valuation, functional obsolescence will also be quantified indirectly. That is because the appraiser will be required to make a number of adjustments to allow for the noncomparability of less functionally obsolete properties in the market data comparison base. In the cost approach to property valuation, functional obsolescence is specifically identified and quantified. This direct approach to the quantification of functional obsolescence requires the application of appraisal procedures to the financial and operational results caused by the elements of functional obsolescence.

In many ad valorem property assessments, functional obsolescence is not adequately identified or quantified by either the property owner or the assessing authority. However, a competent and comprehensive ad valorem property tax appraisal will both identify and quantify all elements of functional obsolescence—and thus properly estimate the fair market value of the subject property.

Identification and Quantification of External (or Economic) Obsolescence

There are two components to external obsolescence: (1) locational obsolescence and (2) economic obsolescence. Both of these components can directly impact the valuation of properties for ad valorem assessment purposes.

Locational obsolescence is a decrement in the value of a property due to changes in the physical environment in which the property operates. An example of locational obsolescence would be the construction of a nuclear power plant next to a luxury hotel; presumably the value of the hotel would decrease. Another example would be the construction of a high-rise office building between the subject office building and the lakefront; without its current lakefront views, the rental rates of the subject office building will decline and the value of the subject office property will decrease.

Economic obsolescence is the decrement in the value of a property due to changes in the economic condition of the industry in which that property operates. For example, as the trucking industry proves to be a cost-effective substitute to the railroad industry (and railroad industry profit margins decline due to the effect of the competition), then the value of our special purpose properties used in the railroad industry will decrease.

Locational obsolescence is a topic that may more fully be explored in a text related to real estate appraisal. In this section, we will further discuss economic obsolescence and its effect on the value of properties for ad valorem assessment purposes.

Definition of Economic Obsolescence.   Economic obsolescence is a reduction in the value of real estate and of tangible personal property due to the impact of events or conditions that are external to and not controlled by the physical nature or the structural or mechanical operation of the property.

Due to the dual characteristics of being (1) beyond the control of the property owners and (2) physically separate from the property, economic obsolescence is considered to be a form of external obsolescence. Although economic obsolescence manifests itself externally to the subject property, its valuation impact is as real and quantifiable as any other form of obsolescence.

Identification of Economic Obsolescence.   Of all the forms of obsolescence, economic obsolescence is, arguably, the most difficult to identify and quantify. In fact, economic obsolescence is often best evidenced by a reduction in the value of property that cannot be explained by any of the other forms of obsolescence.

With respect to special purpose properties, the following conditions may indicate the existence of economic obsolescence:

- Changes in zoning or zoning requirements.
- A significant increase in the number of comparable properties on the market.
- Changes in pedestrian or other traffic flow patterns around the subject property.
- The plan for or the erection of unsightly or incongruous-use properties near the subject property.
- A sudden or gradual decrease in the maintenance of properties in the subject locale (e.g., the deterioration of an older residential neighborhood).
- Otherwise unexplained decreases in occupancy or rental rates and increases in tenant turnover.
- Increases in local or regional unemployment, local or regional interest rates, or local or regional utility rates.
- Changes in local or regional government policies regarding economic development and local or regional industry mix.

Forms of Economic Obsolescence.   There are two significant categories or forms of economic obsolescence. The first category deals with curability; the second deals with universality. Curability relates to whether the economic obsolescence is curable or incurable. Universality relates to whether the economic obsolescence is local, regional, or national.

Curable economic obsolescence means the events or conditions that caused the obsolescence can be cured (i.e., fixed, repaired, or terminated) as the result of some expenditure of time, effort, or money. Incurable economic obsolescence means the events or conditions that caused the obsolescence cannot be changed, at least not by the owner of the property, regardless of the amount of expenditure of time, effort, or money.

Because economic obsolescence is caused by factors external to the physical structure of the property, most economic obsolescence is considered to be incurable. That is, the owner of the property cannot change the events or conditions that are causing the decrease in the value of the subject property. However, as there are not absolutes in valuation science, it is erroneous to assume all economic obsolescence is incurable.

For example, a real estate developer may construct a luxury hotel. Shortly after the hotel's construction, the neighborhood zoning is changed to allow a garbage dump to be operated next to the new hotel. Clearly, as occupancy rates dwindle, the otherwise luxurious hotel will experience substantial economic obsolescence. However, such economic obsolescence may be curable. It is conceivable, and perhaps economically astute, for the real estate developer to purchase the garbage dump site and turn it into an appealing, verdant park. In this example, the curative expenditure was not made on the subject property, yet the substantial economic obsolescence was cured.

However, it is true that most economic obsolescence is incurable. For example, suppose the same real estate developer constructed his luxury hotel at what was to be a major exit of a planned limited-access interstate highway. After the hotel is built, federal funds are canceled and the highway is never constructed. Clearly, this luxury hotel will experience prodigious economic obsolescence. Without the powers of eminent domain, it would be impossible, if not otherwise impractical and uneconomical, for the real estate developer to complete the highway. Thus, this hypothetical situation illustrates incurable economic obsolescence.

Universality.   The universality of economic obsolescence relates to its geographic impact. The degree of the impact of universality on the value of a property is a function of two factors. First, the special purpose versus general purpose nature of the property determines the impact of universality. Second, the breadth and scope of the secondary market for that property type determine the level of influence on universality.

Local economic obsolescence affects the value of properties located only within a locally defined geographic vicinity. For example, changes in zoning affect only those properties within a certain business district. Regional economic obsolescence affects the value of properties on a regional, statewide, or multistate basis. For example, when the semiconductor industry becomes depressed, real estate up and down the Silicon Valley will experience some economic obsolescence. Of course, national economic obsolescence affects all properties used in a certain industry, or in some other global category, on a nationwide basis. For example, when spot oil prices drop below $10 per barrel, the secondary market values for oil well drilling equipment decrease materially, due to economic obsolescence, on a nationwide basis.

Typically, properties that are very general purpose in nature are affected more by local economic obsolescence. Properties that are very special purpose in nature are affected more by national economic obsolescence. For example, the value of a general purpose commercial office building would be affected by local zoning requirements, local economic conditions, local interest rates, and local supply and demand for leased office space. A special purpose sulfuric acid processing plant would be affected by national economic trends, national and international trends in the sulfuric acid industry, and the supply and demand from both plant inputs and outputs on a global basis.

Properties that sell in specialized local secondary markets are affected more by local economic obsolescence. Properties that sell in broad general secondary markets are affected more by national economic obsolescence.

Quantification of Economic Obsolescence.   On a local level, economic obsolescence affects real estate to a greater extent than tangible personal property. Each of the traditional appraisal approaches to the valuation of real estate encompasses procedures to quantify economic obsolescence.

Multiple regression analyses—or other quantitative procedures—are often used in the sales comparison approach. These procedures allow for the identification and quantification of the impact of several independent variables on the value of the dependent variable (i.e., the value of the subject property). The actual independent variable elements that are used in the analysis will vary, based on the quality and quantity of available data, the kind of property appraised, and the judgment and experience of the appraiser. However, independent variables such as interest rates, time adjustments (i.e., elapsed time while the property was listed on the market before sale), and rental rates, or changes in rental rates, are not uncommon. Such independent variables encompass measures of local economic obsolescence.

The income approach to property appraisal requires both current analyses of—and prospective projections of—rental income, vacancy and collection losses, tenant renewal rates, operating expenses, and capitalization rates. Clearly, projections that encompass lower rental rates, higher vacancy and collection losses, lower renewal rates, higher operating expenses, and higher capitalization rates have included implicitly, if not explicitly, a quantification of local economic obsolescence.

The specific identification and quantification of economic obsolescence are most closely associated with the cost approach to property appraisal. The cost approach requires an estimate of either the replacement cost or the reproduction cost of the subject real property. From this estimate, allowances are subtracted for all forms of accrued depreciation and obsolescence—including economic obsolescence.

Using the cost approach, there are several commonly used methods for quantifying local economic obsolescence. One method involves estimating the reduction in annual net operating income associated with the specific economic obsolescence factors. This reduction in annual net operating income is capitalized to estimate the total amount of local economic obsolescence.

As with local economic obsolescence, there are several methods for quantifying national or industrywide economic obsolescence. For the most part, these methods all involve factors that are relatively macroeconomic and affect an industry on a global basis. Also, these methods typically involve an analysis of the relative change in these factors—for example, a specific macroeconomic factor today compared to the five-year average value for that factor.

One element frequently associated with industrywide economic obsolescence is the change in product selling prices. Typically, if average product selling prices across the industry decline materially, and with some anticipated level of permanence, then economic obsolescence occurs with respect to the special purpose real property and tangible personal property used in that industry. For example, a general and prolonged reduction in the price of a barrel of crude oil will cause economic obsolescence to occur in the assets used in the oil and gas exploration industry.

A general and prolonged reduction in the number of units produced, on an industrywide basis, is also indicative of industrywide obsolescence. This is true if there is relatively low price elasticity of demand for the products produced in the subject industry. A reduction of the total number of units produced in an industry could be the result of changes in consumer demand and preference or changes in competition, production quotas, or import or export quotas. For example, an industry that has historically produced 1 million units per year and now produces only 700,000 units per year, where there is little or no product price elasticity, will experience economic obsolescence associated with the properties used in that industry.

A current and sustained reduction in the level of investor returns, compared to historical industry averages, also indicates economic obsolescence on an industrywide basis. Appropriate measures of investor returns would include return on net assets, return on total assets, return on investment, return on equity, and return on tangible assets.

When rates of investor return are reduced industrywide, property owners cannot afford to replace worn-out productive properties with either new or used properties. If the property owners are earning an inadequate rate of return on their investments in the productive properties, they will not expect to earn an adequate rate of return on investment in new or replacement properties. Since the "return" portion of the formula is controlled by macroeconomic events, the "investment" portion of the formula will be affected by the property owners. That is, the property owners will continue to bid down or reduce the value of the subject properties until their level of investment in the subject properties is low enough to allow them to earn a fair return on investment. For example, as across-the-board rates of investor return declined in the steel industry a few years ago, the value of properties employed in the steel industry correspondingly declined, due to industrywide economic obsolescence.

Associated with rates of investor return, current and sustained reductions in the levels of profit margins may also be indicative of industrywide economic obsolescence. For example, in an industry that has historically earned a 10 percent net profit margin (e.g., return on sales) and now earns only 6 percent, industrywide economic obsolescence associated with the special purpose real estate and tangible personal property will become evident.

A general and sustained increase in present value discount rates or income capitalization rates for an industry, when compared to historical industry norms, may also be indicative of economic obsolescence. Such discount rates or capitalization rates are derived from the cost of capital components—both debt and equity—available to property owners in the industry. As with increases in the costs of labor and materials, increases in the costs of capital components have a deleterious effect on the value of the properties employed in the business. Accordingly, increases in the discount rates or capitalization rates that property owners require may cause a decrease in the value of the properties employed in the subject industry, due to economic obsolescence.

One method that may be used to quantify both company-specific (nonsystematic) economic obsolescence and industrywide (systematic) economic obsolescence involves the estimation of a company's business enterprise value. The business enterprise valuation encompasses the going-concern value of all the company's assets, including financial assets, real estate, tangible personal property, and intangible personal property. To determine the existence of economic obsolescence, the business enterprise value is compared to the depreciated replacement cost of the company's productive assets. If the business enterprise value is less than the depreciated replacement cost of the company's assets, then economic obsolescence typically exists.

Summary of External Obsolescence.   The identification and quantification of economic obsolescence is an important part of the valuation of properties for ad valorem assessment purposes. In this section, we have discussed several factors to look for in the identification of economic obsolescence and several methods to use in the quantification of economic obsolescence.

Identification and Valuation of Intangible Assets in the Unitary Method of Assessment

Using the unitary method of property tax assessment, the indicated values derived from the income approach (using either the direct capitalization method or the yield capitalization method) and from the market approach (using the stock and debt method) represent the total value of the assets of the subject taxpayer business enterprise, including all tangible and all intangible assets. However, in most taxing jurisdictions, intangible personal property assets are not subject to ad valorem taxation. Therefore, in jurisdictions in which they are not subject to property taxation, the value of the intangible personal property assets must be identified and deducted from the indicated total asset value of the unit (derived from either the income approach or the market approach) to arrive at the residual value of the taxpayer's assessable tangible assets.

Types of Intangible Assets and Intellectual Properties.   Generally, as presented in greater detail in Chapter 23, appraisers categorize individual intangible assets into several distinct categories for property tax assessment purposes. The intangible assets in each category are generally similar in nature and in function. Also, intangible assets are grouped in the same category when similar valuation and remaining useful life methods apply to that group of assets.

Several common categories of intangible assets include:

- Technology-related (e.g., engineering drawings).
- Customer-related (c.g., customer lists).
- Contract-related (e.g., favorable supplier contracts).
- Data processing-related (e.g., computer software).
- Human capital-related (e.g., a trained and assembled work force).
- Marketing-related (e.g., trademarks and trade names).

- Location-related (e.g., leasehold interests).
- Goodwill-related (e.g., going-concern value).

A specialized classification of intangible assets is called intellectual properties. Intellectual properties manifest all of the legal existence and economic value attributes of other intangible assets. However, because of their special status, intellectual properties enjoy special legal recognition and protection.

Like other intangible assets, intellectual properties are generally grouped into like categories. The intellectual properties in each category are generally similar in nature, feature, method of creation, and legal protection. Likewise, similar valuation methods would apply to the intellectual properties in each category.

Common categories of intellectual properties include creative (e.g., copyrights) and innovative (e.g., patents).

Valuing Intangible Assets for Ad Valorem Assessment Purposes. Like the traditional appraisal of real estate and tangible personal property, three generally accepted approaches are used in estimating the market value of intangible assets: the cost approach, the market approach, and the income approach.

Using the cost approach, several methods are used in quantifying the cost to re-create intangible asset utility: depreciated replacement cost, depreciated reproduction cost, re-creation cost, creation cost, and cost savings or avoidance. All the related methods share a common objective: to quantify the cost in current dollars to generate a perfect substitute to the subject intangible assets in terms of functionality, utility, usefulness, and remaining life.

Using the market approach, the value of the intangible assets is based on an analysis of actual arm's-length sales or license transactions regarding guideline, or similar, intangible assets. First, the appraiser selects objective criteria for assessing the degree of comparability of the intangible assets involved in an arm's-length sale or license transactions to the subject intangibles. These criteria may include: type of the intangible, use of the intangible, industry in which the intangible is used, size of the company, term of the license agreement, de novo versus seasoned agreement, de novo versus seasoned asset, and so on. Second, the appraiser surveys the appropriate secondary market and, using the objective criteria, selects for analysis a sample of guideline sale or license transactions. These agreements should all be arm's-length transactions between independent parties, involving comparative assets and/or license agreements to the subject assets. Third, the appraiser estimates the most appropriate value for the subject intan-gibles after rigorous review and comprehensive analysis of the arm's-length guideline transactions.

Using the income approach, the value of the intangible assets is based on some measure of the economic income earned by the subject company associated with the specific use of the subject intangible assets. Several measures of economic income are used, depending on the type of intangible asset, the type of company, and the nature of the industry. Some common measures of economic income include: operating profit margin (gross or net), return on investment (with investment measured as total assets, net assets, or owners' equity), and net cash flow (which may be before tax or after tax, before debt service or after debt service). The selected measure of economic income is capitalized (either through direct capitalization or yield capitalization) by an appropriate capitalization rate to estimate the value of the intangible assets.

Ideally, the final intangible asset value estimate will be based on a synthesis of two or three of the valuation approaches. However, depending on the quantity and quality of available data, it may be acceptable to rely on one valuation approach in the final estimation of the value of the taxpayer's intangible assets for ad valorem assessment purposes.

Estimating the Useful Lives of Intangible Assets.   Estimating the expected remaining useful life of an intangible asset will obviously impact the results of any of the three valuation approaches. For example, an intangible asset with an expected remaining life of three years will have a lower depreciated replacement cost than the same intangible with an expected remaining life of 15 years, all other factors held equal. The shorter-lived intangible asset will also generally result in a lower market-derived sale transaction price or license royalty rate, and it will produce economic income for a shorter time period (than a longer-lived intangible asset).

There are numerous ways to estimate the expected remaining life of intangible assets. Some of these measures include:

- Physical life.
- Functional life.
- Technological life.
- Economic life.
- Contract life.
- Statutory/judicial life.
- Legal/regulatory life.
- Actuarial mortality life.

Generally, the shortest of these remaining useful life measures is used in estimating the value of intangible assets for property taxation purposes.

Examples of Intangibles Commonly Found in the Assessable Unit.   Numerous examples of intangible personal property assets are commonly found in the business enterprise unit. Intangible personal property assets are identifiable, separable, and capable of systematic valuation and may include, for example, the following: trademarks and trade names, a trained and assembled workforce, computer software and systems, customer relationships, patents, supplier contracts, and royalty agreements.

Summary of Identification and Valuation of Intangible Assets.   The unitary method is a recognized method for quantifying the value of a taxpayer's assets subject to ad valorem property taxation. The unitary method is an indirect valuation method. In this method, first, the value of the taxpayer's overall business enterprise is estimated. Second, all the assets not subject to ad valorem taxation are identified and their values are quantified. And, third, the values of all the nontaxable assets are subtracted from the overall business enterprise value to estimate the value of the taxpayer's assets that are subject to ad valorem taxation.

In most jurisdictions, intangible personal property assets (and often intangible real property assets) are not subject to ad valorem property taxation. Therefore, an essential step in the unitary assessment method is the identification and valuation of nontaxable intangible assets. This section presented an introductory discussion of the identification, valuation, and remaining-life analysis (an important part of the valuation process) of intangible assets typically encountered in the unitary method of property tax assessment.

Identification and Application of Appropriate Income Approach Methods for Ad Valorem Unitary Valuation

Modern investment theory, including security analysis and portfolio management theory, emerged in the early 1900s as a result of increased interest in the business consolidations and mergers of that period. Modern investment theory analyzed the corporation from the economic viewpoint of an outside investor, such as a credit lender or an equity investor. Capital rationing, asset allocation, risk/return matrix analysis, and present value analysis became integral parts of this applied economics discipline—to allow for decision making with regard to the optimal allocation of the limited capital resources within the corporation.

The capital asset pricing model (CAPM) was developed by William F. Sharpe in the 1960s in the course of his study of the valuation of investment securities and of the mechanics of capital markets and efficient portfolio theory. Sharpe won the 1990 Nobel Prize in economics for his research and development of the CAPM, along with his other work in investment analysis and portfolio management.

While CAPM is, arguably, the most important univariate model to describe rational investment decision making during the last 30 years, this section will focus on the practical limitations and conceptual weaknesses of using modern investment theory, especially CAPM, for the ad valorem property tax valuation of operating properties.

In particular, we will consider the use (and misuse) of CAPM to quantify the required rate of return on operating property subject to ad valorem property taxation. And we will consider the use of CAPM to estimate a required capitalization rate (for the direct income capitalization method) or a required discount rate (for the yield income capitalization method).

For purposes of this discussion, we will assume the operating property subject to ad valorem taxation is a centrally assessed unit—that is, a property that is centrally assessed as an income-producing collection of real estate and tangible personal property.

Background.   CAPM is one method (and some would argue it is the most widely accepted method) of estimating the cost of equity capital component of an overall income capitalization rate (or of an overall yield capitalization rate—or present value discount rate).

The classic CAPM univariate formula is presented as follows:

Formula 29–2

$$k_e = R_f + B[E(R_m) - R_f]$$

where:

k_e = Cost of equity capital (or required rate of return on an equity instrument)

R_f = Risk-free rate of return

B = Beta coefficient for the particular investment subject to analysis

$E(R_m)$ = Expected overall long-term rate of return for the market portfolio of investments

For ad valorem property tax assessment purposes, the cost of equity capital is a critical factor in both the direct capitalization valuation method and the yield capitalization valuation method. And both the direct capitalization and, more commonly, the yield capitalization methods are often adopted for property tax purposes when the taxpayer is assessed under the unitary or centrally assessed method of property valuation.

The unitary method of property valuation is based on the concept that the value of an integrated set of assets is a function of the interaction of the various constituent components of the income-producing unit. By inference, the going-concern value of all the real estate and tangible personal property assets subject to property taxation is captured by the unitary method of property valuation.

Hence, the theory of CAPM is often adopted to estimate the cost of equity capital when applying either the direct capitalization or, more commonly, the yield capitalization method of arriving at the unit's overall value for property tax assessment purposes.

Portfolio management theory tells us that the risk of an investment in an individual asset should not be judged on the basis of possible deviations from its expected rate of return but rather in relation to its marginal contribution to the overall risk of a diversified portfolio of investment assets.

Sharpe's CAPM suggests that much of the nonsystematic (or security-specific) risk of a particular company is not relevant to the investors in the company's equity securities, as this risk could be diversified away in the well-managed, diversified portfolio of investments that the prudent investor may hold.

In market equilibrium, a security will be expected to provide a rate of return commensurate with its level of unavoidable or systematic risk. This is simply the type of risk that cannot be avoided by portfolio diversification. The greater the unavoidable systematic risk of a particular security, then the greater the rate of return investors will expect from the security. The relationship between the expected rate of return and unavoidable risk, and the valuation of the investment securities that follows, is the essence of CAPM.

As with any economic model, a number of assumptions must be made with CAPM.

First, CAPM assumes (1) that capital markets are highly efficient, (2) that investors are well informed, (3) that transaction costs are zero, (4) that there are negligible restrictions on investment, (5) that there are no taxes, and (6) that no investor is large enough to affect the market price of the stock.

Second, CAPM also assumes investors are in general agreement about the likely performance and risk of individual securities and their return expectations are based on a common investment time holding period (or investment horizon) of, say, one year.

The more the instant valuation case varies from this set of hypothetical assumptions, the more important are the specific, or nonsystematic, risks of an investment in an individual company. Remember, CAPM assumes this investment-specific risk can be diversified away. If, in fact, it cannot be diversified away, then certain conceptual and practical implications of the CAPM model do not hold up under analytical scrutiny.

Weaknesses of Using CAPM.   One of the major conceptual and practical weaknesses of using CAPM to estimate a capitalization rate for property tax purposes is whether, fundamentally, a theory developed for understanding the value of investment securities within a diversified capital market portfolio is applicable to the understanding of the value of illiquid assets operating within an individual going-concern company.

CAPM was designed to estimate the fair rate of return on capital market (i.e., marketable and negotiable) investment securities not the capitalization rate on the controlling interest in illiquid asset components of individual corporations. Since different investment assets are subject to different degrees of risk, clearly, they should have different expected rates of investment return.

For example, cash or cash equivalents, such as marketable securities, change hands regularly in well-established money markets, which are generally recognized as being highly efficient. Thus, these types of investment assets have rates of return that are closely monitored by investors.

Tangible operating assets, such as income-producing real estate and tangible personal property, are fundamentally different types of investments than marketable securities.

For one thing, the market for exchanging ownership of operating real estate or of tangible personal property is not nearly as efficient as either the established money markets or the capital markets for exchanging investment securities.

The following paragraphs discuss several of the differences in the market for securities exchange transactions and the market for real estate/tangible personal property exchange transactions. These differences in marketplace mechanics—particularly with regard to marketplace efficiency—explain, in part, why CAPM is more effective for estimating an investor's required rate of return on security investments than it is for estimating an investor's required rate of return for real estate/personal property investments.

Marketplace Differences between Securities Exchange Markets and Real Estate/Personal Property Exchange Markets. Table 29–1 presents some of the more salient differences between the typically efficient and organized markets in which capital market investment securities transact and the typically inefficient and unorganized markets in which real estate/personal property operating assets transact.

Table 29–1

Differences between Securities Markets and Real Estate/Personal Property Markets

Securities Transaction Market	Real Estate/Personal Property Transaction Market
1. Generally homogeneous properties competing for investment funds	1. Substantially heterogeneous properties competing for investment funds
2. Large number of buyers and sellers	2. Few buyers and sellers in any one price range at any one location (this is particularly true for special purpose assets)
3. Relatively uniform, stable, and low transaction prices	3. Relatively high and fluctuating transaction prices
4. Low cost of individual transactions (including brokerage, information, title transfer, and other fees)	4. High cost of individual transactions (including brokerage, information, title transfer, and other fees)
5. Relatively few government restrictions on secondary market transactions	5. Secondary market transaction subject to regulations, registration, and legislation at all levels
6. Supply and demand of properties never far out of balance	6. Volatile demand for and sluggish supply of properties
7. Reasonably knowledgeable and generally informed buyers and sellers	7. Potentially uninformed buyers and sellers who interact infrequently
8. Public disclosure of substantial financial and operational information regarding properties	8. Restricted disclosure of limited information (if any disclosure at all) regarding properties
9. Organized market mechanism, allowing for rapid consummation and confirmation of transaction	9. Small, fragmented, overlapping market segments causing delayed consummation and confirmation of transaction
10. Readily "consumed," quickly supplied, and easily transported properties	10. Durable, relatively immobile, and illiquid properties

The table provides a listing of some reasons the efficient and organized securities markets are fundamentally dissimilar from the inefficient and unorganized markets for real estate/personal property transactions. This is why an economic model that works well for estimating the investors' nondiversified risk and required rate of return in one market may not work well for estimating these risk and required return variables in a fundamentally different market.

Fundamental Investment Difference between Investment Securities and Real Estate/Tangible Personal Property. Table 29–2 summarizes some of the intrinsic differences between capital market securities (whether debt or equity instruments) and real estate and tangible personal property (either individual assets or going-concern assemblages of assets) as investment alternatives.

Table 29–2

Investment Differences between Securities and Real Estate/Personal Property

Securities (Debt or Equity Instruments)	Real Estate/Personal Property (Individually or as a Mass Assemblage)
1. Liquid, marketable investments	1. Illiquid investments
2. Noncontrolling interest in income production and distribution	2. Controlling interest in income production and distribution
3. Small, absolute dollar investment required	3. Large, absolute dollar investment required
4. Small percentage of overall wealth committed to this investment	4. Large percentage of overall wealth committed to this investment
5. Diversified portfolio of investments	5. Nondiversified portfolio of investments
6. Short-term investment time horizon	6. Long-term investment time horizon
7. Does not require re-investment to maintain investment base	7. Requires "replenishment" investment to maintain investment base
8. Investments expected to appreciate over time	8. Investments expected to depreciate over time
9. Income typically subject to only individual tax (from investor's perspective)	9. Income typically subject to both corporate and individual tax (from investor's perspective)
10. Portfolios can be created in limitless combinations of risky securities and risk-free securities	10. Portfolio limited to the particular combination of real estate and personal property that operate the subject business

As the table indicates, there are fundamental investment risk and return differences between (1) marketable, minority interests in debt and equity securities and (2) nonmarketable, controlling interests in operating real estate and tangible personal property. Due to these differences, and for other reasons, it is unlikely that an economic model that correlates nondiversified risk and expected return for one type of investment will effectively serve the same function for such a different type of investment.

Beta Measurement Problems. Another major weakness of using CAPM for ad valorem tax property valuation purposes is the same weakness of using CAPM for its original purpose of understanding the value of capital market securities in a diversified investment portfolio: the measurement of the various components of the CAPM equation. In particular, there is no single accepted source of data or method for measuring the beta coefficient component of the model. Several of these beta measurement problems are described on the next page.

First, different financial reporting services provide different estimates of beta—for the same industry and even for the same individual security. And there are at least a dozen reputable financial reporting services that analysts may refer to in order to obtain a beta for a particular security.

Second, different market indexes provide different estimates of the "market risk premium" component of CAPM. Some financial reporting services use the Standard & Poor's 500 as their benchmark market index; some use the Value Line index; some use the Russell 1000, 2000, or 3000 index; and so forth.

Third, different time frames for beta estimates, obviously, can provide different estimates of the subject beta. To compare the subject security prices to the guideline market index, some financial reporting services use weekly observations, some use monthly observations, some make their observations on the last trading day of each, some make their observations on the last Friday of each month (or on the Friday of each week), and so on. These differences in data collection—particularly the differences between weekly observation and monthly observation—can have a material impact on the estimation of beta for the same security.

Fourth, betas are typically measured infrequently; therefore, they can be out of date as of the particular valuation date. It is common that the most recent betas reported in reputable financial reporting services may have been estimated several months before the publication date of the financial service. And most financial reporting services do not estimate individual betas on a real-time basis. Rather, they will estimate the beta for an individual security periodically—typically only a few times each year.

Fifth, betas are not available for many securities. For example, betas are not generally available for infrequently traded securities. And there are thousands of publicly listed securities that are not followed by the financial reporting services, so published betas are not readily available for those securities.

Therefore, with all these beta measurement problems, the analyst is often uncertain as to:

1. What is the correct beta for the selected guideline companies used in the subject valuation analysis?
2. What is the correct beta for the subject company (whether or not a "published" beta is estimated directly or a beta based on guideline companies is estimated indirectly)?

CAPM Includes the Value of Assets Not in Place as of the Assessment Date. Another problem with the use of the CAPM to estimate the cost of equity capital for ad valorem valuation analysis is that the associated valuation model—and the resulting valuation conclusion—generally includes the value of assets not yet in place as of the property tax assessment date.

Since CAPM implicitly incorporates investors' expectation of security appreciation—that is, growth—it will impart a value to the returns from expected future investments in both tangible assets and intangible assets—assets not in existence on the assessment date.

Since the empirical data elements used in a CAPM analysis are market-derived, they indicate a consensus of investors' expectations regarding the prospective performance of the subject investment and/or the guideline investments. If the subject business is successful, these investor expectations will include the present value of future returns for two types of business assets that may not be subject to ad valorem taxation: (1) goodwill and (2) expected future capital expenditures in real estate and tangible personal property.

Goodwill is sometimes defined as the present value of future income from future customers. According to this definition, future customers are unidentified customers that the subject business may serve at some point in the future—as opposed to the expected recurring income for the current, identified repeat customers of the subject business.

While investors' expectation of future income from new customers is an important component of a going-concern business enterprise, the associated goodwill represents the intangible value of business relationships that do not exist (and are not subject to specific identification) as of the property tax assessment date.

In their security pricing decisions, investors will also assign a value to the positive net present value of the future capital expenditures of the subject business. (A positive net present value occurs when the business expects to earn a rate of return on its investment greater than its cost of capital.) Investors' expectation of future capital expenditures may, themselves, have two components: (1) future merger and acquisition activity at the subject company, and (2) future investments in plant, property, and equipment at the subject company.

It is reasonable for investors to expect that the component management of the subject business will continue to make new net investments (i.e., expenditures greater than that required to simply replace worn-out assets) in order to expand the business in new locations, new product lines, new services, and so on.

While these investor expectations are reasonable, valuation analyses that incorporate these expectations (through CAPM or otherwise) will include the present value of capital expenditures for tangible assets (and/or mergers and acquisitions) that do not physically exist as of the property tax assessment date.

CAPM Is Difficult to Adjust for Measures of Economic Income Other Than Net Cash Flow.

Practically, it is difficult to adjust CAPM to estimate required rates of return commensurate with measures of economic income other than net cash flow available to investors.

For example, it is difficult to adjust CAPM to accommodate pretax net income, operating income, operating cash flow or other economic income streams other than net cash flow available for distribution to stockholders.

Applying Guideline Company Betas to Subject Company Valuation.

There are also numerous, and difficult, adjustments that have to be made when applying betas estimated from guideline publicly traded companies to the valuation of a closely held company (i.e., the company subject to ad valorem taxation), including:

1. Different degrees of leverage between the guideline companies (or the industry average) and the subject company.
2. Different degrees of diversification that occur if the guideline companies are diversified "portfolio" type corporations and the taxpayer subject to assessment (whether a stand-alone company or a division or subsidiary of a larger corporation) is a single product line company.

3. Differences between the closely held nature of the subject company and the publicly traded nature of the guideline companies. This difference is particularly significant if the subject taxpayer entity is closely held or if it is a closely held division or subsidiary of a public corporation.
4. Difficulties that arise when the subject company is in one line of business only and the best available guideline companies are not "pure play" companies (i.e., companies with only one product line).
5. Difficulties that arise when the best (or any) guideline companies are substantially larger—and better capitalized— than the subject company.

Other Measures of the Cost of Equity Capital. There are several alternatives to the use of CAPM for estimating the cost of equity capital in either a direct capitalization or a yield capitalization valuation analysis. For identifying these alternatives only, the following methods are often used for estimating the cost of equity capital:

1. The cost of debt of the subject company plus an equity risk premium.
2. The sum of the dividend yield plus the capital gain yield for selected guideline companies.
3. The arbitrage pricing theory.

All these alternative cost of equity capital estimation methods have certain strengths and weaknesses. However, none of these methods "corrects" for all the problems encountered with the use of CAPM.

Using Income Approach Methods in Unitary Valuation. The conceptual and practical problems with the use of modern investment theory to estimate capitalization rates are greater—in the valuation of properties subject to ad valorem taxation—when using a standard yield capitalization method on a discounted net cash flow basis.

The conceptual and practical problems with the use of modern investment theory to estimate capitalization rates are lesser—in the valuation of properties subject to ad valorem taxation—when using the following alternative valuation methods:

1. An asset accumulation method, including the aggregate appraisal of all tangible real estate and tangible personal property (typically using either market approach or cost approach methods) and including the aggregate appraisal of all of the intangible value of the subject operating business in the form of going-concern value and goodwill. Typically, this intangible goodwill valuation should be based on a direct income capitalization method, but it should be based on the capitalization of historical—and not prospective—economic income.
2. A yield capitalization method, but without projecting any future growth in economic earnings; the implicit premise in the use of this valuation method is either:
   a. The level of capital expenditures equals the annual level of depreciation expense (so that there is only direct asset replacement in the valuation model), or

      b. Incremental (new) capital expenditures yield exactly the subject company's WACC (so that there is no increase in the subject company's unit value due to these incremental capital expenditures).

3. A direct capitalization method, but without projecting any prospective growth in economic earnings; the implicit premise in the use of this valuation method is that the annual level of depreciation expense exactly equals the prospective level of capital expenditures, so that there is a stable business enterprise asset base in the valuation model. In addition, the following factors should be considered in the use of a direct capitalization method for this purpose:

      a. The naive use of E/P, or earnings/price, ratios (i.e., the reciprocal of P/E, or price/earnings, multiples) is generally inappropriate in the estimation of a capitalization rate for property taxation direct capitalization analyses; this is because E/P ratios encompass both the current income yield and the expected capital appreciation for the subject investment. Accordingly, the use of E/P ratios will typically subject the taxpayer's unitary valuation to the inclusion of assets not yet in existence as of the property tax assessment date.

      b. Security investors demand both a return of and a return on their investment. They plan to sell their investment after a defined investment holding period, and they expect to enjoy appreciation in the value of their investment during that holding period. This investment appreciation typically does not occur with regard to the types of operating properties subject to ad valorem taxation.

      c. Operating property investors' yields must be materially adjusted in comparison to the yields earned by security investors. This is because operating businesses do not sell their portfolio of operating real estate and personal properties after a defined investment holding period, and they do not generally enjoy investment appreciation in these types of operating properties.

The Correct Application of the Income Approach to Unitary Valuation. The value of an operating business on a unitary valuation basis depends on the future economic income that will accrue to it, with the value of the future economic income discounted back to a present value at an appropriate present value discount rate. The theoretically correct application of this approach is to:

1. Project the future economic income associated with the subject operating properties in existence—and subject to ad valorem taxation—as of the assessment date.

2. Discount the projected economic income stream to a present value, at a discount rate appropriate for the expected risk of the ownership of the subject operating properties.

Use of the income approach for valuing operating properties for property taxation valuation purposes should not be confused with use of the income approach for valuing operating equities for federal gift, estate, or income taxation valuation purposes or for virtually any other valuation purpose. In the case of property taxation, the appraisal objective is to estimate the value of only those properties subject to ad valorem taxation. Accordingly, only the income from the properties subject to ad valorem taxation should be included in the appraisal. In the case of other appraisal purposes, the objective of the appraisal is to estimate the value of an entire going-concern business enterprise.

No matter how the analyst measures the prospective economic income associated with the future performance of the subject operating property, it is essential that the economic income stream that is projected is clearly defined and that a discount rate appropriate for that definition of economic income be used in the analysis.

In its most basic form, this income approach valuation model has only two variables:

1. The amounts of the expected prospective economic income in each period.
2. The required rate of return (or yield capitalization rate) by which each of the expected prospective economic income receipts should be discounted.

Expected Prospective Economic Income.   The answer to the question of "income associated with what?" depends on the answer to the question: "What exactly is the unit of operating properties that we are valuing?"

We are interested in projecting the economic income associated with operating properties subject to ad valorem assessment (e.g., income-producing real estate). We should include only the operating properties in place as of the assessment date, since these are the only assets subject to property taxation. Properties not yet in place as of the assessment date are to be specifically excluded from our projection of economic income.

Obviously, the economic income to be measured should be that level of income that is associated with—and generated by—whatever unit of operating properties is being assessed.

The Present Value Discount Rate.   The present value discount rate is the cost of capital for that particular unit of operating properties subject to assessment. The discount rate is determined by market conditions as of the valuation date, as these conditions apply to specific investment risk and expected return investment characteristics of the subject unit of operating properties.

The derivation of the appropriate present value discount rate is driven by the definition of economic income used in the valuation model. The discount rate used in the analysis must be appropriate for the definition of the economic income in the numerator of the income capitalization model and for the class of operating property to which it applies.

Discounting, for which a present value discount rate is used, is applied to one or a series of specific expected income amounts as of a specified time or times in the future, to convert those expected amounts to an estimate of present value. The discount rate is applied to all the expected future economic income related to the unit of operating properties subject to assessment.

Capitalizing, for which a direct capitalization rate is used, is applied to an amount representing some measure of economic income for a single period, to convert that economic income amount into an estimate of present value. Capitalization procedures can be used with expected, current, historical, or "normalized" or "stabilized" measures of economic income.

Components of the Present Value Discount Rate. Disaggregated into its simplest components, the present value discount rate, or the rate of return that investors require, incorporates the following elements:

1. A "riskless rate" (the amount an investor feels certain of realizing over the investment holding period). This includes:
    a. A "rental rate" for forgoing the use of funds over the holding period.
    b. The expected rate of inflation over the holding period.
2. A premium for risk. This investment risk premium includes:
    a. Systematic risk (that risk that relates to movements in returns on the investment market in general).
    b. Nonsystematic risk (that risk that is specific to the subject unit of operating properties).

Other important investment characteristics that sometimes are incorporated into the discount rate are:

1. The degree of minority ownership versus control ownership position represented by the ownership of the subject operating properties.
2. The degree of ready marketability or lack of marketability of the subject operating properties.
3. Other risk factors that differentiate an investment in operating properties from an investment in marketable securities.

The risk-free rate generally used is that rate available on investments considered to have virtually no possibility of default, such as U.S. Treasury obligations. As noted above, such instruments compensate the holder for renting out his or her money and for the expected loss of purchasing power (inflation) during the holding period.

In estimating the cost of capital for investments in operating properties, the short-term Treasury bill has an important shortcoming in that its maturity does not match the anticipated long-term holding period of most operating property investors. Its rate is much more volatile than longer-term rates, and the yield may not reflect longer-term inflation expectations.

Ownership of an operating industrial manufacturing plant, for example, is not a diversified investment portfolio to the extent to which investors diversify their holdings of publicly traded investment instruments. Thus, since the nonsystematic portion of total risk is likely to be diversified away to the same extent as in the case for a portfolio of publicly traded securities, it is necessary to reflect some part of nonsystematic risk, as well as systematic risk, in estimating an appropriate expected rate of return on an investment in operating properties.

An analysis that draws valuation conclusions based only on an aggregation of information from publicly traded stock prices erroneously ignores nonsystematic risk factors that are unique to a particular operating company.

The next step in estimating the appropriate direct capitalization rate or yield capitalization (discount) rate is to estimate the appropriate risk premium—that is, the amount of property-specific required rate of return above the risk-free rate.

The risk premium will be specific to the type of property subject to appraisal. And it will be a function of the definition of the unit subject to ad valorem tax assessment in the particular jurisdiction.

For example, if the unit subject to assessment is real estate only, then a real estate-specific risk premium should be estimated. If the unit subject to assessment is real estate and tangible personal property only, then a risk premium specific to that bundle of properties should be estimated. If the unit subject to assessment includes real estate, tangible personal property, and intangible assets, then a risk premium specific to this enlarged bundle of properties should be estimated. And if the subject of the appraisal is the entire business enterprise (which may include numerous assets that may not be part of the assessable unit), then a risk premium specific to an overall business enterprise should be estimated.

Finally, the overall capitalization or discount rate is estimated as the sum of the risk-free rates plus a risk premium that is specific to the types of properties included in the unit subject to ad valorem taxation.

Summary of Income Approach Methods for Ad Valorem Taxation Purposes. The objective of this section was to consider the identification and application of the appropriate income approach methods—and income capitalization rates—for ad valorem taxation unitary valuation purposes.

There are two fundamental valuation objectives that analysts should keep in mind when attempting to use the income approach for property tax unitary valuation purposes:

1. They are valuing operating real estate and personal properties (either collectively or individually) and not marketable debt or equity security instruments.
2. They are valuing the operating real estate and personal property in place on the assessment date only and not the present value of the prospective income to be generated by future properties not yet in existence as of the assessment date.

One conclusion is obvious, however: analysts should carefully consider all the implications before using income approach methods for the valuation of operating properties—either individually or on a unitary basis—for ad valorem property tax valuation purposes.

Summary

This chapter presented many of the reasons to conduct a valuation analysis for ad valorem property tax assessment purposes. These purposes include: initial assessments for newly constructed properties, re-assessments for properties that have transferred ownership, periodic property tax compliance (i.e., filing) purposes, and ad valorem property tax assessment appeal purposes. The basis of such an appeal could be either on grounds of property valuation (i.e., an overassessment) or on grounds of assessment equalization (i.e., an unfair assessment). In either case, a valuation analysis is required.

In addition to general topics related to ad valorem property tax terminology and procedural methodology, we discussed several special topics of particular interest to business appraisers, including: the identification and quantification of functional obsolescence, the identification and quantification of economic obsolescence, the identification and valuation of intangible assets under the unitary assessment method, and the identification and application of appropriate income approach methods for ad valorem unitary valuation purposes.

Bibliography

Bowman, John H.; George E. Hoffer; and Michael D. Pratt. "Current Patterns and Trends in State and Local Intangibles Taxation." *National Tax Journal,* December 1990, pp. 439–50.

Cook, Cline G. "The Appraiser's Role in the Tax Appeal Process." *Real Estate Appraiser,* August 1991, pp. 17–20.

Davis, Joseph M., and John R. Cesta. "The Valuation of Operating Leased Property in the Unitary Method." *ASA Valuation,* August 1994, pp. 42–56.

Dickerson, F. Gregg. "The Appraisal of Public Utilities and Railroads for Ad Valorem Taxation: Application of the Unit Rule." *Property Tax Journal,* June 1988, pp. 145–55.

Fletcher, Gregory G. "Significant Court Cases Concerning Ad Valorem Taxation of Public Utility and Railroad Property." *Assessment Journal,* January/February 1994, pp. 43–55.

Goodacre, Kenneth R. "Appealing Ad Valorem Taxes: The Income Approach." *Journal of Property Management,* July/August 1987, pp. 80–81.

Grissom, Terry V., and J. R. Kimball. "Using a Loaded Capitalization Rate to Estimate Property Taxes in Various Income Models." *Appraisal Journal,* July 1989, pp. 406–12.

Heaton, Hal B. "On the Stock and Debt Approach to Valuation of Utility Property." *Public Utilities Fortnightly,* August 3, 1989, pp. 13–17.

Hellerstein, Walter. "State and Local Taxation of Intangibles Generates Increasing Controversy." *Journal of Taxation,* May 1994, pp. 296–302.

Matonis, Stephen J., and Daniel R. DeRango. "The Determination of Hotel Value Components for Ad Valorem Tax Assessment." *Appraisal Journal,* July 1993, pp. 342–47.

Osborne, Kent. "Is the Goodwill of a Business Subject to Ad Valorem Taxation?" *Journal of Technical Valuation,* December 1991, pp. 11–15.

Rabe, James G., and Robert F. Reilly. "Valuation of Intangible Assets for Property Tax Purposes." *National Public Accountant,* April 1994, pp. 26–28 ff.

————. "Valuing Intangible Assets as Part of a Unitary Assessment." *Journal of Property Tax Management,* Winter 1994, pp. 12–20.

Reilly, Robert F. "Property Tax Valuation Services." *Banking Law Journal,* May/June 1989, pp. 229–45.

————. "What You Need to Know about Property Tax Valuation Services." *Practical Real Estate Lawyer,* January 1989, pp. 81–94.

Rife, Knute. "Appealing Property Tax Assessments." *Practical Real Estate Lawyer,* January 1991, pp. 69–88.

Schweihs, Robert P. "The Use and Misuse of CAPM in Property Tax Valuation." *Journal of Property Tax Management,* Fall 1994, pp. 51–60.

Walters, Lawrence C.; Gary C. Cornia; David W. Shank; Charles Gerschefske; Kenneth C. Uhrich; and Mark Freeman. "Measuring Obsolescence in Regulated Firms: Enhancements to the Cost Approach." *Assessment Journal,* May/June 1994, pp. 47–58.

Chapter 30

Employee Stock Ownership Plans

The mid-1990s has seen a number of trends with regard to ESOP formation, ESOP financing and refinancing, and ESOP employer corporation restructuring. These recent trends have both direct and indirect impacts on ESOP employer security valuation analysis and ESOP valuation practitioners. These trends are summarized below:

1. Smaller, less leveraged ESOP formation transactions as compared to the larger, highly leveraged transactions of the late 1980s.
2. More seller-provided financing in the ESOP purchase transaction in exchange for the favorable Section 1042 rollover provisions to the seller.
3. A significant number of refinancings and restructurings of the highly leveraged transactions of the late 1980s.
4. Greater recognition of the enhanced competitive position associated with employee-owned companies.
5. Increased awareness of the economic and legal liability associated with the stock repurchase obligation in ESOP-owned, closely held corporations.
6. Enhanced awareness of employee ownership-related corporate governance issues, particularly in cases where the ESOP has a controlling ownership interest in the employer corporation.
7. Augmented recognition of the need for all parties to an ESOP ownership transaction to comply with the ERISA-mandated fiduciary rules, particularly in light of a number of milestone judicial decisions and of the recent willingness of the U.S. Department of Labor to vigorously pursue apparent fiduciary obligation violations.
8. Increased union awareness of, and support of, ESOP ownership—both with regard to financially healthy unionized companies and financially distressed unionized companies.

The topics presented in this chapter should be read and considered in light of these recent trends with respect to employee corporate ownership and to ESOP formations and restructurings.

Introduction to ESOPs

The Employee Retirement Income Security Act of 1974 (ERISA) classified employee stock ownership plans (ESOPs) as statutorily defined employee pension benefit plans. According to ERISA, an *ESOP* is defined as a qualified retirement plan designed to invest primarily in the employer's securities, thus providing a means for employees to have an ownership interest in the company for which they work.

There are numerous taxation, financing, and organizational benefits to ESOP corporate ownership. The primary economic and organizational benefits of ESOP corporate ownership include the following:

1. ESOPs provide a means for employees to share in the direct ownership of the employer corporation.
2. ESOPs provide liquidity for closely held corporation stockholders and for their beneficiaries.

3. ESOPs are an effective vehicle for corporate financing and refinancing:
   a. For raising new capital.
   b. For financing a leveraged buyout (involving either the sale of the entire company or of a partial interest in the company).
4. ESOPs involve numerous income tax advantages to the corporate security sellers, to the ESOP security owners, and to certain sources of financing for leveraged ESOP transactions.
5. ESOPs have been demonstrated to promote improved employee relations and employee productivity.

Basic Features of an ESOP

Under ERISA, an ESOP is a qualified employee benefit plan designed to invest primarily in employer securities. However, neither the ERISA nor the Treasury regulations adequately define the term *primarily*. While most ESOPs are invested entirely in the employer corporation securities, various interpretations have suggested the plan may need to only be invested over 50 percent in such employer corporation securities.

Eligible Employer Securities.   The eligible employer corporation securities can be either (1) common stock or (2) preferred stock that is convertible into common stock. While most ESOPs are invested in common stock, there are certain income tax advantages to the ESOP ownership of convertible preferred stock.

Contributions in Cash and/or in Stock.   The ESOP can be used either separately or with other employee benefit plans. As with other such employee benefit plans, there must be a nondiscriminatory definition of the group of employees who will be eligible to participate—along with a minimum vesting schedule similar to that required in other employee benefit plans.

The periodic employer deductible contribution to the ESOP can be made either in cash or in employer corporation securities; it can also be some combination of these two options. If the employer contribution is made all in cash, then all or part of the contribution may be used to purchase employer corporation stock from existing shareholders or—in the case of a leveraged ESOP—to make payments on ESOP stock acquisition debt.

Both the cash contributions and the stock contributions are a tax-deductible expense to the employer corporation. If the contribution is made in securities, then the value of the employer corporation securities as of the contribution date is the amount considered to be a tax-deductible expense.

As with other employee benefit plans, the employer corporation can usually contribute up to 15 percent of the eligible payroll to the ESOP plan as a tax-deductible expense. In certain circumstances, however, the tax-deductible contribution can be as high as 25 percent of the eligible payroll amount.

Voting Rights.   In closely held corporations, the voting rights that accrue to the ESOP-owned shares normally are exercised by the ESOP trustees. Under ERISA, voting rights need to be "passed through" to the ESOP beneficiaries only on matters that, by either law or by corporate articles, require more than a majority stockholder vote. In publicly owned corporations, voting rights are typically passed through directly to the plan participants.

Required Put Option Creates the ESOP Repurchase Liability

Distribution of Stock.   In general, unless the employee participant elects otherwise, an ESOP must distribute any vested shares of stock to an employee plan participant within one year after the end of the plan year during which the participant's retirement, death, or disability occurred, or within one year after the end of the fifth plan year following the participant's employment termination for any other reason.

Right of First Refusal.   Under ERISA, ESOP shares can be subject to a right of first refusal in favor of the ESOP itself or of the issuing employer corporation, but not in favor of any other shareholder or of any third party. The right of first refusal must lapse no later than 14 days after the security holder has given notice of a third-party offer to purchase the employer corporation securities.

Put Option.   An ESOP participant who receives a distribution of stock in a closely held corporation must be given an option to sell the stock to the employer corporation. Such put option rights are required for some limited time period depending on the language of the plan documentation. The employer corporation may redeem the stock for cash, or the plan may allow payments over a period of up to five years with a reasonable interest rate.

ESOP Repurchase Liability.   This mandatory distribution of the vested employer corporation stock, along with the attendant put option, obviously creates an economic and a legal liability on the part of the employer corporation. The employer corporation's ability to meet that liability is an important aspect of the financial feasibility of any ESOP formation. It is noteworthy that the diversification of investment regulations discussed in a subsequent section also adds to the employer corporation's obligation to repurchase the employer stock. The corporation's financial strength with respect to meeting its repurchase obligation may also bear on whether or not the value of the employer corporation securities sold or contributed to the ESOP should reflect a valuation discount for lack of marketability (which will be discussed later in the chapter).

Funding the Repurchase Liability with Insurance.   The employer contributions to the ESOP—but not any loan proceeds that it receives—may be used to purchase key-person life insurance. The general ERISA and taxation rules that apply to the ESOP's purchase of key-person life insurance are similar to those rules applicable to other qualified employee benefit plans.

The insurance proceeds normally may be used to purchase employer corporation stock for the ESOP from the estate of a deceased shareholder. Under ERISA, the shareholder's estate may be contractually bound to offer the securities to the ESOP. However, the ESOP may not be contractually bound to buy the employer corporation securities.

Recently, the insurance industry has developed several special annuity type products designed to fund the repurchase of the employer corporation securities of retired or terminated ESOP participants.

Diversification of Investments

The Tax Reform Act of 1986 included a provision to allow ESOP participants the opportunity to diversify their investments as they approach retirement age. Any employee who has attained age 55 and completed 10 years of service with the employer corporation may elect to diversify up to 25 percent of his or her plan account into investments other than the employer corporation securities. The amount of the account so diversified increases to up to 50 percent after the employee reaches age 60.

Since the plan participant normally would exercise the option to sell shares of the employer corporation back to the employer to obtain funds with which to satisfy the diversification requirement, this requirement, in effect, accelerates the corporation's repurchase liability—to the extent that older employees elect to exercise their option to diversify.

ESOP Tax Incentives

Under the Internal Revenue Code, as currently legislated, several attractive taxation incentives are available to both employer corporations and to selling stockholders in connection with ESOP formations and financing. The primary ESOP-related income taxation incentives are as follows (these points are discussed in more detail below):

1. Periodic contributions to the ESOP are a tax-deductible expense to the employer corporation, whether they are made in cash or in stock.
2. Selling stockholders can roll over proceeds of sales of stock to the ESOP tax free, deferring the income or capital gains tax on the sale until the securities purchased with the ESOP purchase proceeds are ultimately sold; this is often called the Section 1042 rollover.
3. Dividends paid on ESOP-owned employer securities can be tax deductible to the paying employer corporation.
4. Under certain conditions, certain lenders recognize only half the interest received on an ESOP securities acquisition loan as taxable income, which normally results in below-market interest loans on ESOP employer security acquisitions.

Periodic Contributions to the Plan Are Tax Deductible

Employer corporation contributions to an ESOP are a tax-deductible expense to the corporation, regardless of whether the contributions are made in cash or in stock.

Cash contributions can be used to buy employer corporation stock from existing stockholders or, in the case of a leveraged ESOP, to make payments on ESOP stock acquisition debt. In the latter case, the economic effect is that the acquisition loan principal repayments, as well as the loan interest, become tax-deductible expenses to the employer corporation.

If the contribution to the ESOP is made in employer corporation stock (either treasury stock or authorized but unissued shares), then there is some dilution to the existing stockholders, but the effect on cash flow generally is positive. As the ESOP contribution is a deduction from taxable income, it usually results in a lower employer corporation income tax expense with no corresponding cash outlay.

The annual employer contribution normally can be 15 percent of eligible employer payroll, but in some cases it may be as high as 25 percent of employer corporation annual payroll.

Tax-Free Rollover on the Sale of Stock to an ESOP

An employer corporation shareholder selling stock to an ESOP can reinvest the proceeds on a tax-free rollover basis if the ESOP owns at least 30 percent of the corporation's stock immediately after the sale. To qualify for the tax-free rollover, the shareholder must invest the proceeds in stock, debt, or options of one or more domestic operating corporations within a 15-month period beginning three months before the date of the sale. Further, notice of the Section 1042 election must be filed on the appropriate form during the taxable year of the sale.

As long as the ESOP maintains its 30 percent ownership of the outstanding stock, additional sales of stock to the ESOP, in any amounts, are eligible for the Section 1042 tax-free rollover treatment.

Dividends Tax Deductible to Employer Corporation

Dividends Paid to Participants.   Dividends paid on the stock held by an ESOP are a tax-deductible expense to the employer corporation either if they are paid directly to the plan participants or if they are paid to the ESOP and then distributed to the plan participants or their beneficiaries no later than 90 days after the close of the plan year.

Dividends Used for Debt Service.   Dividend distributions also qualify as a tax-deductible expense if the dividends are used to make the debt service payments of principal and/or interest on the loan that was used by the ESOP to acquire the employer corporation stock. This tax attribute, of course, greatly enhances the stock acquisition ability of leveraged ESOPs, since such tax-deductible dividends can be paid in addition to the maximum contributions allowed on the basis of a percentage of eligible payroll. Also, the ability to use tax-deductible dividends to service ESOP stock acquisition debt enhances the attractiveness of using convertible preferred stock (which normally would carry a slightly higher dividend rate than common stock) instead of using common stock as the equity security in an ESOP.

ESOP Loan Interest Excluded from Taxable Income

Under certain circumstances involving the purchase of a controlling interest in the employer corporation by an ESOP, commercial lenders, such as banks, insurance companies, and regulated investment companies, may exclude from their taxable income 50 percent of the interest they receive on ESOP loans. Such loans may be made either directly to the ESOP or to the employer corporation, which in turn lends the loan proceeds directly to the ESOP.

As a result of this tax attribute, some financial institutions are more inclined to seek ESOP loan business. In addition, ESOP loans are often available as a tool for either leveraged buyouts or for raising capital for the employer corporation at interest rates below those the ESOP would otherwise have to pay for debt financing.

Leveraged ESOPs

A leveraged ESOP may be used to acquire all the equity of the employer corporation or any portion of the total equity ownership of the corporation. A leveraged ESOP may also be used to raise capital for the retirement of outstanding corporate debt, for corporate expansion purposes, or other legitimate corporate purposes.

A Typical Leveraged ESOP Transaction

The fundamental characteristic of the basic leveraged ESOP transaction is that the ESOP borrows money to buy employer corporation securities either from a selling stockholder(s) or from the employer corporation itself. The employer corporation typically guarantees the ESOP loan, because the only collateral the ESOP is permitted to provide, even if it owns other assets, is the employer corporation securities. The employer corporation then makes annual cash contributions to the ESOP (either as payroll-based contributions or as dividends on the ESOP-owned stock) in an amount sufficient to amortize the stock acquisition loan.

Normally, a vesting schedule is established so employer corporation stock is allocated to individual employee accounts on approximately the same schedule by which the ESOP loan is amortized and by which the employer securities pledged as collateral are released.

As mentioned above, the cash contributions used to amortize the ESOP stock acquisition must be based on the applicable percentage of eligible payroll. However, as discussed above, the employer corporation may supplement the percentage of payroll-based contributions in the form of dividends paid on the ESOP-owned stock to ensure that enough cash is available to amortize the ESOP loan. Both the payroll-based contributions and the dividends on ESOP-owned stock are treated as tax-deductible expenses from the employer corporation's perspective.

An Illustrative Example of a Typical Leveraged ESOP Transaction

The Alpha, Beta, Gamma Engineering Company has three shareholders: Messrs. Alpha, Beta, and Gamma. These three founding shareholders want to retire and make their personal estates more liquid. While they will accept the highest offer they receive for their engineering firm, the three founders would prefer that their loyal employees buy the company from them. A committee of employees is formed to consider the purchase of the entire firm, possibly through a leveraged

ESOP. Alpha, Beta, Gamma Engineering Company has funded the committee's retention of an attorney, an administrative advisor, and a financial advisor, all of whom will analyze the financial and legal feasibility of a leveraged ESOP buyout.

After careful analysis, the financial advisor believes the fair market value of all the outstanding equity of Alpha, Beta, Gamma Engineering Company is $11 million. This value estimate is confirmed by expressions of interest offered by several corporate acquirers who are interested in bidding for control of Alpha, Beta, Gamma Engineering Company.

Nonetheless, because of the tax-free rollover advantages available to them under Section 1042, the founders have agreed to accept an offer from the ESOP to buy the company for $10 million. Accordingly, because of this Section 1042 tax attribute available to the three selling stockholders, the ESOP is able to outbid the corporate acquirers at a lower offer price.

To finance this transaction, a commercial lender has made a commitment for the required $10 million financing on a seven-year net level-payment amortization basis. Because the ESOP will own over 50 percent of the stock of the employer corporation, the interest income on the ESOP debt will be tax advantaged to the lender. Therefore, the lender is willing to offer a slightly lower than normal interest rate on the ESOP stock acquisition debt.

Table 30–1 presents a summary of the salient facts regarding the ESOP's leveraged acquisition of the outstanding stock of Alpha, Beta, Gamma Engineering Company:

Table 30–1
Alpha, Beta, Gamma Engineering Company
Hypothetical Fact Set

Annual revenues	$20 million
Earnings before interest and taxes (EBIT)	3 million
Payroll eligible for ESOP contributions	6 million
Combined federal and state income tax rate	40%
Loan interest rate without ESOP	10%
Loan interest rate to the ESOP	8.5%

Exhibit 30–1 presents the projected income statement for Alpha, Beta, Gamma Engineering Company assuming both conventional acquisition financing and acquisition financing through an ESOP. Exhibit 30–1 also presents the loan amortization schedule and the after-tax cost to the company of servicing the stock acquisition loan assuming: (1) conventional acquisition financing and (2) acquisition financing through an ESOP.

The ESOP committee's administrative advisor has analyzed the potential cash requirements of the liability to repurchase the stock of the ESOP participants under the mandatory put option associated with employee retirements and with participants' elections to diversify investments after age 55. The administrative advisor has estimated that the $628,000 cash available annually—after debt service—should be adequate to cover the estimated repurchase liability.

The ESOP advisors have determined the company could make tax-deductible contributions of up to 25 percent of the eligible payroll. Based on projected annual payroll expense of $10 million, the maximum allowable annual deduction

Exhibit 30–1
Alpha, Beta, Gamma Engineering Company
Conventional Acquisition Financing versus ESOP Acquisition Financing
(in $000s)

Projected Income Statements

Conventionally Financed Acquisition		Leveraged ESOP Acquisition	
Company revenues	$20,000	Company revenues	$20,000
Operating profit (EBIT)	3,000	Operating profit (EBIT)	3,000
Interest	1,000	ESOP contribution	1,954
Taxable income	2,000	Taxable income	1,046
Income taxes	800	Income taxes	418
Net income	1,200	Net income	628
Nondeductible portion of debt service	1,054	Nondeductible portion of debt service	0
Cash available after debt service	$ 146	Cash available after debt service	$ 628

Acquisition Loan Amortization

	Conventionally Financed Acquisition					Leveraged ESOP Acquisition				
Year	Total Payment	Principal	Interest	Value of Deductions	After-Tax Cost	Total Payment	Principal	Interest	Value of Deductions	After-Tax Cost
1	2,054	1,054	1,000	400	1,654	1,954	1,104	850	782	1,172
2	2,054	1,159	895	358	1,696	1,954	1,197	757	782	1,172
3	2,054	1,275	779	311	1,743	1,954	1,299	655	782	1,172
4	2,054	1,403	651	260	1,794	1,954	1,410	544	782	1,172
5	2,054	1,543	511	204	1,850	1,954	1,529	425	782	1,172
6	2,054	1,698	356	143	1,911	1,954	1,660	294	782	1,172
7	2,054	1,868	186	75	1,979	1,954	1,801	153	782	1,172
Total	14,378	10,000	4,378	1,751	12,627	13,678	10,000	3,678	5,474	8,204

Analytical projections:
1. The $10 million acquisitive loan is amortized over seven years, with net level payments.
2. A 10% interest rate is available with conventional financing.
3. An 8.5% interest rate is available on the ESOP financing.
4. A 40% combined federal and state income tax rate is appropriate.

of $2.5 million is more than adequate to cover the $1,954,000 annual ESOP contribution required to amortize the ESOP stock acquisition debt.

A comparison of a conventionally financed acquisition and the ESOP-financed acquisition reveals that the use of an ESOP provided the following benefits:

1. Messrs. Alpha, Beta, and Gamma received a tax-free rollover by selling their stock to the ESOP and reinvesting the proceeds in a diversified securities portfolio.
2. Because the commercial lending institution could exclude 50 percent of the interest it received on the ESOP loan from its taxable income, the ESOP obtained the acquisition loan at an 8.5 percent interest rate, rather than at a 10 percent interest rate, resulting in a $100,000 per year saving in annual debt service (principal and interest).
3. Because the annual contributions to the ESOP are tax deductible, both principal and interest on the ESOP loan payment are paid with pretax dollars.
4. Because of the tax advantages available to the selling shareholders, the employees were able to purchase the Alpha, Beta, Gamma Engineering Company at a price that was $1 million less than the bids that were being contemplated by other corporate acquirers.

In this case, the ESOP not only facilitated the acquisitive transaction, but it also made it feasible for the employees to purchase the company. As is often typical in such cases, financing of the acquisitive transaction without the benefits of an ESOP would have been extremely difficult.

Multiple Investor Leveraged ESOPs

Often, companies using ESOPs for leveraged acquisitions must create several different classes of securities to attract and satisfy all the diverse parties to the transaction. These parties often include the party supplying the bulk of the acquisition financing, a management group, and the ESOP itself.

Based on a fair allocation of the total business value among the different securities classes and based on ERISA regulations regarding the securities eligible for ESOP ownership, the structure of such securities is bounded only by the financial creativity of the parties involved in the ESOP, the company, other participants, and their respective financial advisors. Permissible securities can include one or more classes of common stock, traditional and/or convertible debt or preferred stock, stock options, and various junior classes of securities. Voting rights may also be assigned to the various classes of securities in a number of ways.

Various chapters of this book address the valuation of classes of securities other than common stock, including debt securities (Chapter 20) and preferred stock (Chapter 21). A convertible debt or preferred security is, in essence, a combination of a traditional debt instrument or a preferred stock and an option. In many cases, it is difficult to find convertible securities in the public market that are adequately comparable in terms of economic characteristics to the convertible securities created for use in leveraged ESOP acquisitions. Therefore, for valuation purposes, it may be useful to desegregate these convertible securities into their financial components—that is, traditional debt or preferred stock plus a common stock option—and to value each component separately, with the guidance provided in the respective chapters of this book.

Criteria for Establishing an ESOP

As discussed above, an ESOP can often provide substantial tax, liquidity, and other economic advantages for an employer corporation and its stockholders. However, these economic advantages typically are not sufficient incentives to establish an ESOP unless the company's stockholders have a genuine desire to have broad ownership of the company's securities by employees, since the "eligibility to participate" criterion must be nondiscriminatory.

If there is a genuine desire for employee ownership, the decision criteria then involve weighing the economic costs versus the economic benefits. The primary costs are legal, administrative, and valuation. Most of the legal cost is related to the legal due diligence associated with establishing the plan and to the crafting of the plan documentation. These legal costs can run anywhere from a few thousand dollars for a small, simple plan up to six figures for a large, complicated ESOP.

The administrative costs involve both the initial and the ongoing recordkeeping associated with determining which employees are eligible to participate and to what extent, as well as to compute vested and forfeited interests and schedules of payments to those who have tendered stock to the company. Such administrative costs are similar to those incurred in other employee benefit plans. Another important administrative task involves the analysis and estimation of the ESOP repurchase liability. The analysis of the repurchase liability may be performed either by the firm providing ESOP administrative services or by a company specializing in ESOP repurchase liability analysis.

If a leveraged ESOP is contemplated, then an ESOP investment banker would typically be retained to arrange for the acquisition financing, and the investment banker would typically be compensated based on performance.

ESOP practitioners often suggest that a company should have at least $500,000 in eligible payroll to make the ESOP economically feasible; however, many ESOPs have been established with less than that amount of annual payroll expense. In addition, ESOP practitioners generally suggest that a company should be reasonably well established before an ESOP is contemplated, since the potential for employee disappointment or even total company failure certainly is greater with start-up companies.

Special Issues in the Valuation of ESOP Stock

ERISA requires ESOPs to pay no more than "adequate consideration" when investing in qualifying employer corporation securities. This means plan trustees and fiduciaries must estimate, in good faith, the fair market value of employer securities, pursuant to the terms of the plan and in accordance with regulations issued by the secretary of labor and the Internal Revenue Service. On May 17, 1988, the Department of Labor (DOL) issued the "Proposed Regulation Relating to the Definition of Adequate Consideration." As published in the *Federal Register* on May 8, 1995, the DOL withdrew the 1988 proposed regulation, effective February 1, 1995. This withdrawal was made without explanatory comment by the DOL. Nonetheless, while the DOL has withdrawn the 1988 proposed regulation, most ESOP practitioners still consider it carefully in discharging their responsibilities. Therefore, we will describe the valuation implications of this withdrawn proposed regulation in some detail in the next few pages.

As a reference source, the Valuation Advisory Committee of the ESOP Association has provided important guidance with respect to the valuation of ESOP securities to be considered by ESOP fiduciaries, sponsoring corporations, and professionals rendering advice to these plans. This guidance is in the form of a publication, *Valuing ESOP Shares,* which was updated in 1994 and covers the following topics:

1. The DOL proposed regulation and its implications for valuation.
2. Commonly accepted practices for estimating the fair market value of closely held stock for ESOP purposes.
3. Four special valuation positions adopted by the Valuation Advisory Committee: discount for lack of marketability, repurchase liability, premium for control, and effects of leverage.

Reference to this published resource, *Valuing ESOP Shares,* and to other published positions of the ESOP Association Valuation Advisory Committee, is highly recommended.

ESOP Stock Valuation Factors

The DOL proposed regulation defines *fair market value* as:

> The price at which an asset would change hands between a willing buyer and a willing seller when the former is not under any compulsion to buy and the latter is not under any compulsion to sell, and both parties are able, as well as willing, to trade and are well informed about the asset and the market for such asset.[1]

The DOL proposed regulation requires the fair market value of a security: (1) to be estimated as of the date of the transaction involving the asset, (2) to be estimated without considering transactions resulting from other than arm's-length negotiations, such as distressed sales, (3) to reflect the application of "sound business principles of evaluation," and (4) to be recorded in a document meeting the requirements of the proposed regulation.

This definition and requirements, with the exception of the requirement for written documentation, follow the established guidelines for estimating fair market value found in Revenue Ruling 59-60, which is discussed in detail in Chapter 27.

When the security being valued is the stock of a closely held employer corporation, the DOL proposed regulation requires that the written document include an assessment of all "relevant factors" plus an assessment of the following factors:

(A) The nature of the business and the history of the enterprise from its inception;

(B) The economic outlook in general, and the condition and outlook of the specific industry in particular;

(C) The book value of the securities and the financial condition of the business;

(D) The earnings capacity of the company;

(E) The dividend-paying capacity of the company;

(F) Whether or not the enterprise has goodwill or other intangible value;

(G) The market price of securities of corporations engaged in the same or a similar line of business, which are actively traded in a free and open market, either on an exchange or over-the-counter;

(H) The marketability, or lack thereof, of the securities. Where the plan is the purchaser of securities that are subject to "put" rights and such rights are taken into account in reducing the discount for lack of marketability, such assessment shall include consideration of the extent to which such rights are enforceable, as well as the company's ability to meet its obligations with respect to the "put" rights (taking into account the company's financial strength and liquidity);

(I) Whether or not the seller would be able to obtain a control premium from an unrelated third party with regard to the block of securities being valued, provided that in cases where a control premium is taken into account:

    (1) Actual control (both in form and in substance) is passed to the purchaser with the sale, or will pass to the purchaser within a reasonable time pursuant to a binding agreement in effect at the time of the sale, and

---

[1]Proposed Regulation Relating to the Definition of Adequate Consideration, 53 Fed. Reg. 17632 (1988), p. 17634.

(2) It is reasonable to assume that the purchaser's control will not be dissipated within a short period of time subsequent to acquisition.[2]

The requirement to assess factors (A) through (G) as well as all "relevant factors," such as the definition of fair market value, is clearly consistent with Revenue Ruling 59-60. Factors (H) and (I) are additional factors with specific application to ESOP-owned securities.

Requirement of Independent Annual Stock Appraisal

The Tax Reform Act of 1986 mandated that ESOP-owned employer securities that are not readily traded on organized exchanges must be appraised annually by a qualified, independent appraiser. A form stating the appraised value, signed by the independent appraiser, must be filed with the IRS.

The DOL regulation-providing guidelines as to what constitutes "adequate consideration," says that for plan fiduciaries to meet the requirement of estimating fair market value in good faith, the valuation must be performed by someone who is independent of all parties to the transaction. The DOL proposed regulation also requires a written valuation report and specifies its minimum content.

An appraisal of ESOP-owned stock is required:

1. When the ESOP makes its first acquisition of employer corporation stock.
2. At least annually thereafter (although some companies routinely have their stock appraisals updated semiannually or quarterly).
3. Whenever there is a stock sale transaction with a controlling stockholder or member of a control group.
4. If the ESOP sells out its stock position.

With regard to who qualifies as an independent appraiser, the DOL notes that under Internal Revenue Code Section 401(a)(28)(C), ESOP fiduciaries must employ an independent appraiser meeting requirements similar to Regulation 1.170A-13(c)(5) which relates to independent appraisals of donations to charitable organizations. A qualified appraiser, according to these regulations, is a person who, among other qualifications:

1. Is not a party to the transaction, is not related to any party to the transaction, is not married to any person with a relationship to the transaction, is not regularly used by any of the parties to the transaction, and does not perform a majority of appraisals for these persons.
2. Holds himself to the public as an appraiser or performs appraisals on a regular basis.
3. Is qualified to make appraisals of the type of property being valued including, by background, experience, education, and memberships, if any, in professional associations.
4. Understands that an intentionally false or fraudulent overstatement of value may subject the valuation practitioner to a civil penalty.
5. Receives an appraisal fee that is not based on a percentage of the appraised value of the property.

---

[2]Ibid., pp. 17637–38.

As stated in the DOL proposed regulation, each valuation report prepared in compliance with the fair market value requirement must contain the following information:

(A) A summary of the qualifications to evaluate assets of the type being valued of the person making the valuation;

(B) A statement of asset's value, a statement of methods used in determining that value, and the reasons for the valuation in light of those methods;

(C) A full description of the asset being valued;

(D) The factors taken into account in making the valuation, including any restrictions, understandings, agreements, or obligations limiting the use or disposition of the property;

(E) The purpose for which valuation was made;

(F) The relevance or significance accorded to the valuation methodologies taken into account;

(G) The effective date of valuation; and

(H) In cases where a valuation report has been prepared, the signature of person making valuation and date the report was signed.[3]

Accounting for Equity Dilution

When the contribution to the ESOP is made in the form of shares of stock, more shares of employer corporation stock will be outstanding. This, of course, will affect the value per share. After the issuance of additional treasury stock or of authorized (but previously unissued) shares, the per share value will automatically decrease. This is because additional shares of stock will be outstanding, and no increase in the company's value will have occurred. This phenomenon should be considered in estimating the value per share. The following formula will indicate the appropriate value per share:

Formula 30–1

$$\frac{Aggregate\ value\ of\ company\ stock\ -\ ESOP\ contribution}{Number\ of\ shares\ outstanding\ before\ contribution}$$

The next step is to divide the price per share derived by this formula into the dollar amount of the contribution to determine the number of shares to be contributed to the ESOP. As an example, assume there are 600,000 shares of stock outstanding before the ESOP contribution and the appraiser has estimated the value of the stock at $10 per share. Then, the aggregate value of the stock outstanding is $6 million (600,000 shares × $10 per share = $6,000,000).

Since the issuance of additional shares will not increase the aggregate value of the shares outstanding (i.e., of the total employer corporation business enterprise), then it will dilute, or reduce, the value per share. If we assume the value of the ESOP contribution is to be $300,000, the calculation for estimating the value per share after the ESOP contribution is as follows:

Formula 30–2

$$\frac{\$6,000,000\ -\ \$300,000}{600,000} = \$9.50\ per\ share$$

---

[3]Ibid., p. 17638.

Accordingly, the number of new shares to be issued for purposes of the ESOP contribution is then calculated as follows:

Formula 30–3

$$\frac{\$300,000}{\$9.50} = 31,579 \; shares$$

This will, of course, result in a new total of 631,579 shares outstanding. As a verification of this, multiplying the new number of shares outstanding by the new value per share results in the same aggregate value of the total shares outstanding as before the ESOP contribution transaction (i.e., 631,579 x \$9.50 per share = \$6,000,000).

Sometimes the appraiser's report must be rendered before the employer corporation has determined whether or how much new stock may be issued. In such a case, it would be proper for the employer corporation to adjust the appraiser's per share value in accordance with the above formula once the determination has been made. However, most ESOP valuation practitioners agree that if the percentage dilution is quite small, then the employer corporation may omit the adjustment on the basis that the amount is immaterial.

Effect of the ESOP on the Economic Income to Capitalize

One of the more controversial issues in ESOP share valuation is the treatment of the ESOP contribution itself as it affects the measurement of the employer corporation's economic income when a capitalization of economic income method is used in the ESOP valuation.

Cash Contribution. If a cash contribution is made to the ESOP and if the cash is used to buy stock from an existing stockholder, then the cash goes out of the employer corporation and into another stockholder's pocket. Accordingly, it would seem that no part of that contribution should be added back in estimating the employer corporation's economic income. In some situations, however, there could be justification for adjusting the amount of the cash contribution expense to the ESOP. For example, if the cash contribution is unusually large compared to what it is expected to be in future years, then it may be appropriate to adjust the difference as appraisers would normally adjust any nonrecurring expense item. For some employer corporations, the cash contribution simply is an effective and legitimate way to distribute to the owners the amount of company profits that a non-ESOP company might distribute as dividends.

One procedure for deciding whether or not to make an adjustment to ESOP cash contribution expense is to compare it, plus any other company employee benefit plan expenses, to the aggregate employee benefit plan expenses of guideline publicly traded companies or other companies for which data are available. The comparisons may be made as a percentage of revenues or pretax, prebenefit profit, and an adjustment may be made to the economic income to the extent that the contributions exceed guideline company averages.

For some small companies that are managed such that most of the pretax earnings are paid into the ESOP, then the choice of how to treat the ESOP contribution can make a material difference in the economic income subject to capitalization. There is no clear-cut answer on how to deal with this problem.

Stock Contribution.   If the ESOP contribution is made in the form of stock, then its value really remains within the employer corporation. The cash that would have been paid out stays in the cash account or is spent on other assets, and the capital account is increased by the stock's value. Thus, it would seem appropriate that the "expense" deducted as a result of this ESOP contribution be added back into net earnings in computing the amount of economic income subject to capitalization. (Of course, the economic effect of this will be offset, at least partially, by the effect of dilution, discussed in the previous section.)

An argument against this reasoning would be that without the ESOP, the pre-ESOP earnings would be fully taxable and a corporate buyer would consider only a fully taxed level of economic income (without the ESOP) in deliberations concerning the price to pay for an acquisition. This argument would suggest that we add back to the economic income base the amount of the ESOP contribution, less the amount of income taxes that otherwise would have to be paid were there no ESOP contribution.

The argument becomes moot, of course, if either cash flow or pretax earnings measures—rather than after-tax earnings measures—are capitalized. However, it is still important to develop capitalization rates based on comparable measures of publicly traded companies' economic income.

Control versus Minority Basis for Valuation

Appraisers generally agree that the basis for the ESOP valuation will differ depending on whether or not the block of stock subject to appraisal carries elements of control. Generally, a buyer of a controlling ownership interest will pay more for the stock because the buyer expects to make changes that enhance the income-generating aspects of the business or in some other way improve the economic situation for the business. This additional value is evidenced by a higher price relative to what would be paid for a minority interest position in the business.

However, appraisers often differ in their application of a control premium to a block of stock being purchased by an ESOP. Most appraisers agree that an ESOP should be able to pay whatever a hypothetical third-party buyer would pay for the block of stock being purchased. In other words, most appraisers recognize that fair market value is not influenced solely by arbitrary percentage limitations (e.g., greater than 50 percent ownership) but instead is estimated by what a willing buyer would pay to a willing seller.

In estimating what a hypothetical third-party buyer would pay, some appraisers believe we should give recognition to the facts and circumstances of the case, including any limitations that may be imposed on the ESOP as the buyer of the stock. Many of the unusual aspects of ESOPs—where elements of control may be present—result from the fact that the ESOP does not generally represent an active investor who is willing or able to make certain changes that could maximize the value of the stock. This condition may exist because the ESOP is represented by a fiduciary, and this fiduciary may be directed by an administrative committee made up of company management or employees.

For example, employer corporation management may be taking excessive compensation or maintaining certain perquisites that a third-party buyer purchasing control of the company might eliminate. The ESOP, represented by its fiduciary, may choose not to force such changes. Therefore, the value of its stock would be negatively affected accordingly. If the appraiser recognized the unlikelihood of the ESOP forcing such changes, then the level of the control premium paid for the purchase of such stock would likely be lower than what would be paid by the hypothetical third-party buyer.

Alternatively, some appraisers believe the ESOP should pay a control premium reflecting what a hypothetical third-party buyer would pay, without considering practical limitations applicable to the ESOP as the buyer. If, by virtue of holding the block of stock, the ESOP—in aggregate—has the ability to affect corporate transactions through electing board members, then the value of stock at the time of the purchase by the ESOP can reflect those changes. This is because, on obtaining control, the ESOP could sell the block of stock to a synergistic buyer (or to a buyer who could fully realize the benefits of control) or it could cause a liquidation, if such a sale or liquidation would result in the highest value.

Notwithstanding these differences of opinion among ESOP appraisers, certain general guidance may be offered regarding factors to consider when valuing an ESOP-owned controlling ownership interest. In addition to all other considerations that are otherwise relevant when estimating the value of a subject block of stock, the following are some factors to consider when estimating the appropriate control premium if any:

1.   The elements of control inherent in the particular block of stock.
2.   The degree of control—effective, operating, and absolute.
3.   The aggregate percentage interest purchased or held by the ESOP regardless of whether the sellers constituted minority or controlling interests.
4.   The potential for control, such as binding agreements with other shareholders that result in the passing of control to the ESOP.
5.   The distribution of the total stock ownership.
6.   Any empirical evidence of control premiums actually paid in similar transactions.
7.   Any value enhancements that may result from the passing of control (e.g., effective use of leverage, elimination of excess compensation paid to selling shareholders, sale of undervalued assets, etc.).
8.   Any value enhancement due to a put right.
9.   The rights and obligations under the employer corporation's articles of incorporation and state law.

Discount for Lack of Marketability

Another controversy in ESOP share valuation is whether, or the extent to which, some valuation discount should be applied for lack of marketability.

Certainly, the fair market value of ESOP-owned employer corporation stock depends, in part, on its marketability. Marketability is the ability of the stock to be sold and turned into cash quickly. On one end of the marketability spectrum, there are relatively few potential buyers for shares in most closely held companies (especially of minority ownership interests). It may take months to market these shares and receive payment. On the other end of the marketability spectrum, shares in publicly traded corporations have almost instant marketability on an organized exchange and high liquidity as the seller can receive cash within three business days.

In many ESOP appraisals, the market value estimate is based on market comparisons with publicly traded guideline companies. The value conclusion obtained from this appraisal method is on a marketable, minority ownership basis, sometimes referred to as an "as if freely traded value" or a "publicly traded equivalent value." If this is the preliminary basis of value, then a discount for lack of marketability may be appropriate to estimate the fair market value of shares in a closely held company. Nonetheless, other generally accepted valuation methods may implicitly incorporate the consideration of lack of marketability. ESOP appraisers, therefore, should not apply some standard discount for lack of marketability without fully understanding how marketability was considered in the initial conclusion of value.

The economic factor that generally distinguishes ESOP shares from non-ESOP shares in a closely held corporation is the put option associated with the ESOP shares. A put option requires the employer corporation to repurchase the distributed employer securities, unless the ESOP distributes benefits in cash, or unless the ESOP repurchases the distributed shares. Under Code Section 409(h)(1)(B), employer corporation securities that are acquired by an ESOP after December 31, 1979, must be subject to a put option if the securities are not readily tradable on an organized market at the time of distribution to the plan participants. Employer corporation securities acquired with the proceeds of an ESOP loan after September 30, 1976, must also be subject to a put option, if the shares are not readily tradable on distribution. For employer corporation securities not subject to these mandatory put option requirements, a voluntary put option may be provided by the employer corporation.

In the DOL proposed regulation, a written assessment of the marketability of shares held by the ESOP is required. The proposed regulation states the following with respect to a discount for lack of marketability:

> Where the plan is the purchaser of securities that are subject to "put" rights and such rights are taken into account in reducing the discount for lack of marketability, such assessment shall include consideration of the extent to which such rights are enforceable, as well as the company's ability to meet its obligation with respect to the "put" rights (taking into account the company's financial strength and liquidity).

The effect of the ESOP put option is to generally enhance the marketability and liquidity of the plan participant's ownership interest and, hence, to reduce (or perhaps to eliminate) the appropriate discount for lack of marketability. ESOP appraisers must evaluate the features of the subject put option, including payment terms, as well as the employer corporation's record in redeeming shares. Ultimately, the estimation of the appropriate amount of the discount to be used, if any, is a function of the ESOP appraiser's professional judgment.

Another economic feature unique to an ESOP is the repurchase liability that stems from the ESOP put option. The repurchase liability tends to increase over time as shares vest and as the value of employer securities increases. The repurchase liability arising from the terms of the ESOP is normally not considered to significantly affect the discount for lack of marketability, unless the ability to repurchase the stock is impaired or the employer corporation's ability to honor the put option is in question. The DOL proposed guidelines make it clear, however, that the employer corporation's financial ability to meet its put obligations must be considered when assessing an appropriate discount for lack of marketability.

The financial position of the ESOP trust must also be considered with regard to this lack of marketability issue. If the ESOP trust has excess cash, then it may repurchase the shares distributed to participants rather than having the shares repurchased by the employer corporation.

In summary, the principal economic factors that influence the discount for lack of marketability with regard to ESOP-owned employer corporation securities are summarized below:

1. The provisions of the ESOP plan documents, including the put rights.
2. The financial strength and solvency of the employer corporation.
3. The size of the share block owned by the ESOP.
4. The degree of liquidity.
5. The borrowing capacity of the employer corporation.
6. The repurchase liability and the funding thereof.
7. Any past repurchase experience of ESOP shares by the employer corporation.
8. The form and timing of the payment by the employer corporation to the selling shareholders.
9. The overall priority of acknowledged and contingent financial claims that may conflict with achieving liquidity for plan participants over time.

Valuations in Leveraged ESOPs

The impact of the ESOP debt on the employer corporation stock is often explicitly considered by the ESOP appraiser, and such debt naturally tends to reduce the value of the employer corporation equity. Whether using guideline publicly traded company or discounted economic income valuation methods, the valuations of the employer corporation following the formation of the ESOP must reflect the reduction in cash flow due to the repayment of the ESOP debt. Several valuation procedures can be taken to account for this, of which the most common include:

1. Valuing the overall business, using either the discounted economic income or the guideline public company approach, on a debt-free basis, and then subtracting the tax-adjusted value of the ESOP debt.
2. Inserting the specific debt service requirements into the economic income projection of the company on a pretax basis, thus accounting for the associated income tax savings. This valuation procedure is easiest to apply in a discounted economic income valuation analysis, and it accounts for the temporary nature of the ESOP debt service.

ESOP leverage also increases the risk of the employer corporation by increasing its fixed cash flow obligations—which increases the possibility that fluctuations in the company's operating results could cause financial distress. Leverage may also force the employer corporation management to focus primarily on current cash flow, rather than on longer-term economic benefits, thereby restricting discretionary investments in capital equipment, marketing, research and development, or other areas that require up-front cash outlays. These issues should be considered in the valuation of leveraged ESOP-owned companies.

Summary

This chapter explained how the use of employee stock ownership plans can provide financial incentives for employer corporations and stockholders. However, to achieve these economic benefits, companies must follow strict and complex rules to protect the interests of the employee participants and their beneficiaries. This chapter focused on the valuation aspects of compliance, particularly those peculiar to ESOPs.

The employer corporation stock valuation is one of the most critical aspects of ESOP compliance and the source of a large proportion of ESOP compliance problems. Most ESOP stock valuation problems have arisen because the appraisal was lacking in independence, objectivity, understanding of appraisal principles and/or regulatory or legal guidelines, or adequate written documentation of the appraisal process and conclusion. It is hoped the valuation principles and practices discussed in this book will allow many companies to enjoy a successful ESOP experience based on sound valuation criteria.

Often, appraisal firms are engaged by the ESOP trust, administrative committee, or trustee to act as a financial advisor to the ESOP trust. This financial advisory role encompasses responsibilities and expertise beyond that solely of business valuation. Such responsibilities may include expressing opinions as to the fairness of a proposed acquisitive transaction from a financial point of view as to the adequacy of consideration, and as to capital adequacy. In addition, the financial advisor may be expected to represent the ESOP trust's best interests in any negotiations among prospective investors in the transaction. This financial advisory activity, while within the capabilities of many business valuation experts, embodies responsibilities and representations beyond the intended purpose of this book.

Bibliography

Articles

Abrams, Jay B. "An Iterative Procedure to Value Leveraged ESOPs." *ASA Valuation*, January 1993, pp. 76–103.

Ackerman, David. "Innovative Uses of Employee Stock Ownership Plans for Private Companies." *DePaul Business Law Journal*, Spring 1990, pp. 227–54.

Ackerman, David, and Idelle A. Howitt. "Tax-Favored Planning for Ownership Succession via ESOPs." *Estate Planning*, November/December 1992, pp. 331–37.

Akresh, Murray S., and Barry I. Cosloy. "New Math for ESOPs." *Financial Executive*, May/June 1994, pp. 45–48.

Berkery, Peter M., Jr. "High Court OKs Retroactive Amendment of Estate Tax ESOP Deduction." *Accounting Today*, July 11, 1994, p. 8.

Blasi, Joseph R., and Douglas L. Kruse. "Employee Ownership and Participation: Trends, Problems, and Policy Options." *Journal of Employee Ownership Law and Finance*, Spring 1993, pp. 41–73.

Block, Stanley B. "The Advantages and Disadvantages of ESOPs: A Long-Range Analysis." *Journal of Small Business Management*, January 1991, pp. 15–21.

Braun, Richard S. "The ESOP Lifecycle." *ESOP Report* (official newsletter of The ESOP Association), December 1991, pp. 4–5.

Brockhardt, James, and Robert Reilly. "Employee Stock Ownership Plans after the 1989 Tax Law: Valuation Issues." *Compensation and Benefits Review,* September–October 1990, pp. 29–36.

————. "ESOPs Are Becoming Popular Corporate Financial Tools." *Trusts & Estates,* February 1990, pp. 40–43.

Bromberg, Alan R. "The Employee Investor: ESOPs and Other Employee Benefit Plans as Securities." *Securities Regulation Law Journal,* Winter 1992, pp. 325–40.

Brown, Karen W. "Payment of Control Premiums by ESOPs." *ESOP Report,* (November/December 1993, pp. 6–8

Buxton, Dickson C. "ESOP and Business Perpetuation Plans." *Journal of the American Society of CLU & ChFC,* November 1990, pp. 34–44.

Cahill, Kathleen. "Accounting for ESOPs." *CFO: The Magazine for Senior Financial Executives,* February 1993, p. 12.

Cefali, Sheryl L., and Sandra M. Wimsat. "An ESOP Valuation Case Study." *Journal of Employee Ownership Law and Finance,* Winter 1995, pp. 67–88.

Chaplinsky, S., and G. Niehaus. "Leveraged ESOP Financing and Risk." *Financial Analysts Journal,* March–April 1990, pp. 10–13.

Curtis, John E., Jr. "Use of 'Enterprise Value' When an ESOP Purchases Less than a 'Majority' of a Company's Outstanding Stock." *Tax Management Compensation Planning Journal,* June 5, 1992, pp. 126–28.

Curtis, John E., and Gregory K. Brown. "Avoiding Problems with IRC Sections 409(n) and 4979A in IRC Section 1042 Multi-Investor ESOP LBOs." *Tax Management Compensation Planning Journal,* March 5, 1993, pp. 43–45.

Dema, Robert J., and Duncan Harwood. "Tapping the Financial Benefits of an ESOP." *Journal of Accountancy,* April 1991, pp. 27–28 ff.

Elgin, Peggie R. "Accounting Change Removes Advantages of Leveraged ESOPs." *Corporate Cashflow,* April 1994, pp. 12–14.

"Employee Ownership (Special Report)." *Employee Benefit Plan Review,* July 1992, pp. 14–26.

Flesher, Dale L. "Using ESOPs to Solve Succession Problems." *Journal of Accountancy,* May 1994, pp. 45–48.

Freiman, Howard A. "Understanding the Economics of Leveraged ESOPs." *Financial Analysts Journal,* March–April 1990, pp. 51–67.

Garber, Steven. "A Proposed Methodology for Estimating the Lack of Marketability Discount Related to ESOP Repurchase Liability." *Business Valuation Review,* December 1993, pp. 172–81.

Gilbert, Ronald J. "Considerations for Initial Public Offerings Involving Employee Stock Ownership Plans." *Journal of Employee Ownership Law and Finance,* Fall 1992, pp. 77–84.

Gross, Robert J. "ESOP Valuation Issues." *Journal of Employee Ownership Law and Finance,* Winter 1991, pp. 53–62.

Heermance, Paul F. "A Valuation Approach for ESOP Convertible Stock." *ESOP Report,* February 1992, pp. 4–6.

Hill, R. Bradley. "Why Stock Ownership Is a Better Incentive than Stock Options." *Journal of Compensation & Benefits,* November–December 1992, pp. 24–27.

Huffaker, John B. "Retroactive Change for Stock Sales to ESOPs Upheld." *Journal of Taxation,* August 1994, p. 119.

Lannon, Allan L. R. "Valuing Non-ESOP Shares in ESOP Companies—Some Empirical Evidence." *Business Valuation Review,* March 1994, pp. 19–21.

Levitske, John, Jr. "ESOP Valuation: The 'Quality' of All Earnings is Not the Same." *Journal of Pension Planning & Compliance,* Fall 1994, pp. 76–85.

Lint, Ron J. "ESOP Power." *Management Accounting,* November 1992, pp. 38–41.

Maldonado, Kirk F. "Special Issues Affecting Termination of ESOPs." *Tax Management Memorandum,* August 23, 1993, pp. 247–56.

Mano, Ronald M.; E. DeVon Deppe; and Jerry L. Jorgensen. "The ESOP Fable: ESOPs and Pre-ERISA Problems." *Ohio CPA Journal,* February 1993, pp. 9–12.

May, Richard C.; Robert L. McDonald; and Brad Van Horn. "Valuation Issues in Leveraged ESOPs." *Journal of Employee Ownership Law and Finance,* Summer 1994, pp. 61–82.

McBreen, Maura Ann. "Retirement Plan Investments in Company Stock." *Journal of Corporate Taxation,* Spring 1993, pp. 87–93.

Mueller, Susan L., and Judith C. Gehr. "Valuation Issues in Multi-Investor ESOP LBOs." *Journal of Employee Ownership Law and Finance,* Winter 1995, pp. 27–46.

Murphy, John W., and John P. Murphy. "An Introduction to ESOP Valuation." *Journal of Employee Ownership Law and Finance,* Winter 1995, pp. 3–26.

Paone, Louis A., and Donna J. Walker. "ESOP Case Law—Valuation." *Journal of Employee Ownership Law and Finance,* Spring 1992, pp. 37–60.

Pratt, Shannon P. "Court Cases Involving ESOP Valuation Issues." *Journal of Pension Planning & Compliance,* Fall 1990, pp. 245–60.

Reilly, Robert F. "ESOPs are Becoming Popular Financial Planning Tools." *Trusts & Estates,* February 1990, pp. 22–24.

————. "Performing ESOP Valuations that Meet Tough Tests." *Mergers & Acquisitions,* March/April 1994, pp. 27–33.

————. "An Overview of ESOP Case Law." *Journal of Employee Ownership Law and Finance,* Spring 1992, pp. 3–10.

Rosen, Corey. "A Primer on Leveraged ESOPs." *Journal of Employee Ownership Law and Finance,* Summer 1994, pp. 3–22.

Ryterband, Daniel J. "The Decision to Implement an ESOP: Strategies and Economic Considerations." *Employee Benefits Journal,* December 1991, pp. 19–25.

Searfoss, D. Gerald, and Dionne D. NcNamee. "Employers' Accounting for Employee Stock Ownership Plans." *Journal of Accountancy,* February 1993, pp. 53–60.

Szabo, Joan C. "Using ESOPs to Sell Your Firm." *Nation's Business,* January 1991, pp. 59–60.

Theisen, Barbara A., and Robert T. Kleiman. "Employee Stock Ownership Plans: The Right Choice for Closely Held Corporations?" *Tax Adviser,* January 1991, pp. 40–49.

Thomas, Paula B., and Barbara Sutton. "The AICPA Tackles ESOP Accounting: What You Need to Examine." *Journal of Corporate Accounting & Finance,* Winter 1993/1994, pp. 255–63.

Urcinoli, Arthur. "A Piece of the Pie." *Executive Female,* May–June 1991, p. 72.

Vosti, Curtis. "The Haunting Side of ESOPs." *Pensions & Investments,* March 2, 1992, p. 30.

Wagner, William J. "ESOPs and Chapter 14 Valuation Rules." *Taxline,* April 1993, pp. 5–6.

Walter, Ira S. "Using Incentive Compensation to Create Shareholder Value." *Journal of Compensation & Benefits,* January–February 1992, pp. 40–45.

"What's It Worth?" *Employee Ownership Report* (official newsletter of the National Center for Employee Ownership), March/April 1991, p. 9.

Willens, Robert W. "ESOPs Provide Unique Tax Benefits." *Journal of Accountancy,* June 1994, pp. 28–29.

Wise, Richard M.; Line Racette; and Perry Phillips. "ESOPs Change the Rules." *CA Magazine,* September 1992, pp. 28–33.

Wood, Robert W. "ESOP Stock Sales May Incur Gift Tax Liability." *Taxation of Mergers & Acquisitions,* February 1992, pp. 24–27.

Wynne, Kevin C. "The Forgotten Fiduciary Duty of ESOP Trustees." *Journal of Compensation & Benefits,* September–October 1991, pp. 34–40.

Books

Blasi, Joseph R. *Employee Ownership: Revolution or Ripoff?* Cambridge, MA: Ballinger, 1988.

Blasi, Joseph Raphael, and Douglas Lynn Kruse. *The New Owners: The Mass Emergence of Employee Ownership in Public Companies and What It Means to American Business.* New York: HarperCollins, 1991.

Braun, Warren L. *On the Way to Successful Employee Stock Ownership.* Harrisonburg, VA: Dr. Warren L. Braun, P.E., 1992.

Employee Benefit Plans in Mergers and Acquisitions. Chicago: American Bar Association, 1987.

Frisch, Robert A. *The ESOP Handbook: Practical Strategies for Achieving Corporate Financing Goals.* New York: John Wiley & Sons, 1995.

————. *The Magic of ESOPs and LBOs.* New York: Farnsworth Publishing Co., 1985.

Kalish, Gerald I., ed. *ESOPs: The Handbook of Employee Stock Ownership Plans.* Burr Ridge, IL: Richard D. Irwin, 1989.

Kaplan, Jared; John E. Curtis, Jr.; and Gregory K. Brown. *ESOPs (Tax Management Portfolio).* Washington, DC: Tax Management Inc., 1991.

Manson, Veronica. *International Employee Stock Ownership Plans (ESOPs) for Multinational Corporations.* Oakland, CA: National Center for Employee Ownership, 1993.

McWhirter, Darien A. *Sharing Ownership: The Business Manager's Guide to ESOPs & Other Ownership Incentive Plans.* New York: John Wiley & Sons, 1993.

Quarrey, Michael. *Employee Ownership and Corporate Performance.* Oakland, CA: National Center for Employee Ownership, 1986.

Quarrey, Michael; Joseph R. Blasi; and Corey Rosen. *Taking Stock: Employee Ownership at Work.* Cambridge, MA: Harper Business Publications, 1986.

Rosen, Corey; Katherine J. Klein; and Karen M. Young. *Employee Ownership in America: The Equity Solution.* Lexington, MA: Lexington Books, 1986.

Smiley, Robert W., Jr., and Ronald J. Gilbert, eds. *Employee Stock Ownership Plans: Business Planning, Implementation, and Law and Taxation.* Englewood Cliffs, NJ: Maxwell MacMillan/Rosenfeld Launer, 1991. (Now published by Warren, Gorham & Lamont and updated annually.)

Valuing ESOP Shares, rev. ed. Washington, DC: The ESOP Association, 1994.

Young, Karen M., ed. *The Expanding Role of ESOPs in Public Companies.* New York: Quorum Books, 1990.

Part VIII

Litigation Support

Chapter 31

Litigation Support Services

Frequently, commercial, taxation, or family law litigation involves a controversy over the value of assets, properties, or business interests. Appraisals performed within a litigation environment require that the analyst understand the legal context within which the appraisal is being made. The analyst should tailor the valuation work to address the facts and circumstances of the case, while considering all relevant statutory authority, judicial precedent, and administrative rulings. Prevailing statutory, judicial, or administrative law often varies considerably from one valuation purpose to another and from one jurisdiction to another.

This chapter precedes the chapter on expert witness testimony, deliberately separating that of general litigation support from that of expert testimony. In this chapter, we discuss several valuation consulting, economic analysis, and financial advisory services within the context of litigation support and controversy resolution.

Valuation-Related Controversy Matters

Most valuation-related disputes can be resolved, and the odds of a favorable resolution are substantially increased when clients work closely from the beginning with an appraiser who is experienced in litigation and dispute resolution matters. An experienced appraiser can be very helpful in assessing the merits of the case, both in estimating a reasonable range of values and in weighing the risks involved in going to court. If the case cannot be resolved outside the courtroom, then the decision to go to court will be based on a sound assessment of the situation from a valuation viewpoint. And the preparation for the litigation may be more orderly and thorough.

When clients or their counsel assess valuation-related litigation issues without the assistance of an experienced appraiser, then the interests of the client are not best served. These situations usually arise when principals or their counsel attempt to minimize the expert's fees, when they do not know how to locate an appraiser experienced in controversy matters, or when they do not fully understand the best way to utilize the appraiser's experience and expertise. In any event, when contacted late, the appraiser's ability to provide the best advice may be constrained.

It is also important to integrate expert witness testimony with other litigation support services. To support or refute a plaintiff's claim of damages, expertise in several areas is often required in order to assess the significant factors affecting the plaintiff's likely activities (absent the alleged wrongful action) and to ascertain whether the defendant's actions were indeed the principal cause for the harm to the plaintiff. Damage cases in which significant dollar amounts are at stake may require that numerous experts, including industry, accounting, finance, and economics experts, be retained by both the plaintiff and the defendant to adequately address the specific questions relating to their areas of expertise.

An appraiser can sometimes help select and supervise other experts. Specialized experts may be needed to address certain elements that may impact the value of an asset, property, or business interest, such as industry experts or experts in specific types of property. Appraisers often maintain files of such advisors because they need to call on them from time to time for informational or other purposes. For various reasons, the attorney may call in more than one appraisal expert: (1) to get more than one expert's opinion; (2) to have an expert address in depth certain especially controversial or critical aspects of the case, such as the appropriateness of a certain method or the quantification of some premium or discount; or (3) to have one expert for rebuttal and another for the case in chief.

One valuable litigation support service of an experienced appraiser is to review and critique materials and expert reports prepared by other experts on the same side of the case. In some situations, for a variety of reasons, such a review can be part of the input an attorney needs to decide whether to call in a particular expert to testify. In other cases, the review may help focus and buttress the testimony to be presented by a particular expert.

An independent appraiser is an advocate for his or her position only, and not an advocate for the client. The independent appraiser may assist both the client and the lawyer in preparing the best possible case. However, when it comes to the independent expert's opinion, the expert must present an unbiased, nonadvocative position on all substantive issues on which he or she has been asked for an opinion. The independent expert must remain free from both actual bias and the appearance of bias. If the attorney believes that any litigation support functions the independent expert otherwise might logically perform would create the perception of a bias, then the attorney might wish to have these services performed by other professionals.

The vast majority of valuation-related controversy matters never reach the stage of requiring expert testimony before a judge, jury, or tribunal. Accordingly, thoroughly documented appraisals can contribute significantly to successful settlements of valuation-related controversies. The same level of analytical rigor and appraisal documentation that leads to successful settlements can also provide the underpinnings for proper trial preparation. It is often said the best way to facilitate a successful settlement is to begin preparing from the outset as if the case were going to court.

Types of Litigation

Commercial litigation claims typically involve the determination of the occurrence of an action, the causation of an action, and the amount of damages that relate to the action. Appraisers and economists are frequently called on to assist attorneys in evaluating these claims—and especially in estimating the existence of, and the amount of, commercial damages. In many instances, the appraisers and economists are also asked to provide expert testimony as to the damage issues.

The following paragraphs summarize some common reasons parties become involved in litigation concerning the valuation of assets, properties, and business interests.

Contract Disputes

Breach of contract or warranty involves all types of products or services. The Uniform Commercial Code generally describes the laws of damages regarding breaches of contract. Different remedies are prescribed, depending on the breaching party. For instance, only buyers may claim consequential damages (i.e., losses resulting from an act or a breach that are not direct or immediate) under certain circumstances.

Commercial Torts

These involve claims of negligence or intentional torts that include interference with business, unfair competition, fraud, or interference with a contract. Damages are often measured by lost earnings; and in some cases, damages are measured by the lost profits resulting from negligence and from intentional torts.

Business Interruption Claims

Businesses organized to make a profit can suffer contract or tort claims that may be measured in terms of lost profits. Some business interruptions are also caused by casualty. Business interruption insurance can cover either the loss of earnings caused by the casualty or the loss of income sustained and any expenses incurred to resume normal business operations. This category of business interruption insurance may sometimes cover events related to eminent domain, condemnation, and expropriation issues.

Antitrust Claims

Examples of these claims are predatory pricing, price fixing, and other anticompetitive actions. Damages are frequently measured by estimating the difference between the inflated anticompetitive price and the normal competitive price—or by estimating the amount of lost profits that resulted from the anticompetitive practices of another company or companies.

Securities Litigation

These legal actions result from disputes involving the value of corporate or other securities including, for instance, corporate and partnership dissolution, buy–sell agreements, minority shareholder rights, and going public or going private transactions. Also included in this category of litigation are damages that occur in cases involving securities fraud. In such cases, damages are often measured as the difference between the true or intrinsic value of the securities involved and the actual price at which shares were exchanged.

Marital Dissolution

The valuation of a closely held business is often a contested issue in the division of property (i.e., the marital estate) between spouses involved in a marital dissolution. The value of the family-owned business on several valuation dates (e.g., date of the marriage, date of the filing of the dissolution action, etc.) is often a matter of controversy between the spouses.

Personal Injury or Wrongful Termination Cases

A party injured or wrongfully terminated often requires the estimation of lost employment earnings that were suffered as a result of the wrongful action. In the case of a self-employed individual involved in a personal injury matter, for example, the lost profits of the individual's business are sometimes used as a measure of the individual's earnings.

Estate, Gift, and Income Taxes

In these cases, the taxpayer is opposed by the federal government—usually the Internal Revenue Service. These cases may include, for example, the allocation of the purchase price paid for a bundle of assets, gift and estate tax claims, employee compensation issues such as employee incentive stock options grants, debt forgiveness in restructurings, corporate reorganizations of entities, recapitalizations, charitable contributions, abandonment losses, property contribution issues, intercompany transfer pricing issues (of tangible and intangible assets), use of NOL carryforwards, and S corporation built-in gains tax. See Chapters 26 and 27 for further discussion on income tax–related valuation matters.

State and Local Property Taxes

Special purpose properties and income-producing properties subject to state and local property taxes are often the subject of valuation controversies. Such properties include, for example, cable and broadcast television properties, mining operations, timberland and forestry operations, chemical processing plants, gas and electric utilities and power generation plants, data processing and telecommunications facilities, high-technology properties, railroads and regulated industries, farmland and agricultural properties, hotels and motels, strip and enclosed shopping malls, and mixed-use properties. In such valuation controversies, it is often important to separately identify and appraise nontaxable intangible personal property (or other nonassessable) assets. See Chapter 29 for further discussion on the topic of ad valorem taxation–related valuation matters.

Bankruptcy/Insolvency/Reorganization Situations

The appraiser may be called on to independently create or assess a reorganization plan, to analyze debt and equity capital restructuring proposals, to review financial forecasts and projections, to value various classes of collateral, to test the going-concern versus liquidation presumptions of alternative plans of reorganization or liquidation, to identify spin-off opportunities, to prepare fraudulent conveyance analyses, or to express a solvency or insolvency opinion—to name a few typical financial advisory services.

Intellectual Property Rights Infringement

An increasingly common concern in the information age, claims of intellectual property rights infringement involve trademarks, trade names, copyrights, patents, proprietary technology, computer software, and many other intangible assets and intellectual properties.

Engaging the Appraiser

An appraiser providing expertise in a litigated valuation case serves as a forensic economist in that the appraiser is using expertise in the applied microeconomic analysis of property valuation. It is important to retain appraisers who can not only use their education and experience to develop and support a sound position but who can also communicate that position in terms that a judge and/or jury can understand. It is important to evaluate appraisers' abilities through the examination of their credentials and experience, their reputations, their references, and/or personal interviews.

Qualifications

Courts are often reluctant to deny the right to testify to almost anyone offered as an expert in a field, regardless of how meager or tangential his or her qualifications may seem. Unfortunately, the result has been a plethora of self-made but ill-qualified "experts" who provide litigation support and expert testimony in valuation and economic analysis matters—often to the detriment of the client's interests.

Although previous litigation experience is helpful, it is also important for the appraiser to have experience in performing analyses for the purpose of actual purchase, sale, and/or license decisions—and, thus, to have the benefit of real-world transactional experience along with the experience of doing battle in a courtroom.

Valuation issues are affected by a wide variety of legal mandates and precedents. Such mandates and precedents differ significantly in their application to various valuation purposes. Even for valuations for similar purposes, both statutory authority and judicial precedent are subject to considerable variation from one jurisdiction to another. Many statutes and court decisions contain vague or ambiguous wording, so that an understanding of different interpretations from one jurisdiction to another may require study of several cases. Ignorance of these variations can result in misdirection in litigation-related valuation work. Of course, the attorney must finally decide any legal matter; nevertheless, such decisions can be greatly enhanced by appraisers who have a good working knowledge of the valuation-related aspects of the law.

The research capabilities and other professional resources of the appraiser's firm are often an essential component of the appraiser's ability to successfully perform litigation support and dispute resolution services. Accordingly, the appraiser should have a collegial staff with appropriate qualifications, with the inclination to meet the required deadlines, and of a size necessary to carry out the research and analytical requirements of the case. Library and other research resources are time consuming and expensive to develop. Even in this age of on-line services, a crucial task in the controversy process is to index and organize documents, articles, statistical data, published court cases, and miscellaneous economic, industry, and corporate reports. Having the relevant research material is critical to the appraiser involved in a controversy matter, but so is having that material well organized, indexed, and easily accessible.

Active involvement in professional organizations and activities may increase an appraiser's ability to provide effective litigation support. These activities include attending seminars sponsored by leading professional appraisal organizations and by specific industry trade associations, speaking at such programs, and writing for well-recognized professional publications. These activities help to keep the appraiser current on the thinking and developments in the mainstream of the profession and to expose the appraiser's own thinking to peer scrutiny.

To establish whether there is a concurrence of valuation philosophy, the attorney may wish to approach the prospective witness with a hypothetical scenario. In this way, the attorney can get some idea of the methods and procedures the witness would use in reaching the value conclusion without revealing the client's name or identifying the actual asset, property, or business interest to be valued. One of the nuances of this exercise is that the credibility of the potential witness is maintained if it can be established that he or she was hired to ascertain a value independently, and not to testify to some value predetermined by the interested party.

This comparison of valuation philosophies is as important to the appraiser as it is to the client, since no reputable appraiser wants to be under pressure to testify to a conclusion that cannot be professionally supported. Usually, a brief dialogue between an experienced attorney and an experienced appraiser is all that is necessary to determine whether the appraiser can be useful as a witness on the specific case.

Conflicts of Interest

The appraiser should be independent of the parties on both sides of the case. Very early in the proceedings, the attorney must disclose the names of all the parties in the case to the prospective witness to ascertain that there is no conflict of interest. Apart from having already been retained by the opposing party, the most common conflict of interest would be having a financial or investment interest that would introduce the appearance of a conflict of interest. Potential conflicts should be promptly disclosed to the client and/or the client's attorney, because the appearance of a conflict can discredit a witness (whether the witness considers it a conflict or not).

In general, it is not a disqualifying conflict for the appraiser to have performed services for the opposing party. It is never a disqualifying conflict that the appraiser has been retained on unrelated assignments by the opposing party's law firm. To the contrary, that may be viewed as a sign of professional integrity and independence. For example, our firm has performed a number of income taxation–related valuation and economic analysis assignments both for the Internal Revenue Service and for corporate and individual taxpayers.

One common problem is the appraiser who is interviewed by one side and not retained and then is contacted by the other side. A potential problem can be avoided if the appraiser makes it clear to the attorney in initial interviews that no confidential information or analysis should be shared until after the appraiser has been formally retained.

Engagement Agreement

In many cases, engagement agreements for litigation support services give very little detail, often because the attorneys have not yet determined exactly what services they will need from the appraiser. It is not uncommon for the appraiser to assist the attorney at various points in the case with regard to focusing the issues, gathering the data, and developing the scope of the assignment. While it is important to include as many of the elements of the assignment as possible, the engagement agreement may become discoverable by the other side, along with drafts and modifications to the agreement. Since the legal strategy of the case may change after the engagement has commenced—and since attorneys don't want their legal strategies to be discovered—standardized, nondescriptive engagement letters are often used for litigation support projects.

If the appraiser knows enough about the property to be analyzed to estimate the time required, the assignment may be performed for a fixed fee or within a narrowly estimated fee range. Otherwise, an agreement fee based on hourly billing rates is usually adopted.

Often, litigation cases can be structured in advance around specific tasks and a specific work product. For example, the first phase, at a predetermined budgeted amount, could include an assessment of the case, some preliminary consultation with the attorney regarding the apparent merits of the case, and a brief critique of the opponent's work product. Subsequent phases might include a detailed valuation work plan, a review of material provided in response to a document request, a preliminary range of value conclusions, an analysis of the benefits and costs of pursuing litigation, a full narrative valuation opinion report, and so forth.

The amount of time to be spent in depositions, preparation with attorneys for court, observation and testifying in court, and other aspects of litigation support are normally beyond the appraiser's control. For that reason, the compensation for these services usually is made on an hourly basis, at a specific hourly rate. The attorney and the appraiser often cooperate in order to structure the compensation to be flexible enough to accommodate the many uncertainties involved in litigation but rigid enough that the expert will not become a party at interest to the outcome of the case.

> Make sure you receive the check for your airfare, estimated hotel expenses and three days of your time before you leave home for a trial ... If it comes out in court that you have not been paid lately, the jury may think the outcome of the case is very important to you. Your objectivity may be suspect ...
>
> Q: *Does your client owe you any money?*
>
> A: *No. My bills have been paid to date and my expenses for this trip were paid in advance. My being paid does not depend on the outcome of this case.*[1]

Assessing the Case

Matters such as the applicable standard of value and the relevant valuation date or dates are not always obvious. In many controversy cases, there is no statutorily defined standard of value or applicable valuation date. Sometimes the relative rights of various parties are very complex and careful definition of the property and its relevant rights and restrictions is a crucial prerequisite to the assignment itself. Ultimately, the attorney must decide the question or questions to ask the appraiser to address. Often the appraiser's knowledge and experience can be helpful in focusing the relevant questions, in defining the case to the client's advantage, and to achieving a successful outcome.

Once the basic work plan is framed, the appraiser may be asked to do some preliminary work to suggest a reasonable range of value within which the final value conclusion might be expected to fall. Often, it is possible to provide such information on a preliminary basis. The preliminary range of values can help the attorney decide on the litigation posture. Sometimes the most valuable service an

---

[1] Daniel F. Poynter, *Expert Witness Handbook* (Santa Barbara, CA: Para Publishing, 1987).

appraiser can perform for clients is to tell them what they don't want to hear—that the value is not what they suspected and, at least from a monetary standpoint, the case is not what it appeared to be. Heading off financially unproductive litigation can save the client tens of thousands of dollars. When each side is provided with an opinion as to a reasonable range of value from a genuinely competent appraiser, the groundwork for a settlement is often laid. On the other hand, if a settlement cannot be reached, the preliminary range of value the appraiser provides lends some confidence to a decision to proceed with litigation.

Often the appraiser can facilitate the identification and quantification of areas of financial uncertainty so the attorney can better assess the risks of litigation. Sometimes reasonable people will reach different conclusions because of different assessments of the economic or other exogenous factors affecting the subject asset, property, or business interest. Sometimes there may be contingent assets or liabilities that may have a substantial impact on the appraiser's estimation of value. It often helps to try to quantify the risk that arises from various uncertainties. For example, if the preliminary range of value is between $8 million and $12 million, the litigation posture could be significantly different than if the preliminary range of value is between $0 and $20 million.

After the valuation issues have been framed and a preliminary range of value has been estimated, the attorney is in a better position to assess the relationship between the litigation's potential benefits and costs. In making this analysis, the attorney may ask the appraiser to estimate some range of likely or possible costs to complete the case, including preparation for testimony, depositions, direct and cross examination at trial, and the preparation of posttrial briefs. Possibly the most important of all these fees are those related to pretrial preparation between the appraiser and his or her attorney. Also, in the heat of litigation, costs tend to run over expectations more often than under. Appraisers, attorneys, and clients should fully consider the difficulty of controlling deposition and court time and, especially, the costs of responding to possible unknown material the opposition may present.

Critique of the Opposition

In many valuation-related litigations, critiquing the opposition's position is as important to reaching a satisfactory resolution as preparing the valuation case in chief—or even more so. After all, if the opposition's position is found to be unsound and indefensible, there probably will be no case.

The critique of an opposing expert's report or presentation may occur at any time from the outset of possible litigation throughout the trial itself. If an expert's report is available at the beginning stage of assessing the case, it is important to review it then. It may be a sound piece of work, and an early review may result in a recommendation to accept it or possibly to negotiate some minor modifications, thus forestalling thousands of dollars of futile litigation costs.

If the opposition's expert is off base, it is good to know why as soon as possible. The more sophisticated the expert on the other side, the more likely it is that a settlement can be reached through narrowing and compromising on the valuation issues that are genuinely arguable. If the other side has used an inexperienced expert, then it is usually much more difficult to engage in a constructive exchange leading to a resolution short of the courtroom. In any case, the appraiser must provide the attorney with an understanding of the strengths and weaknesses of the opposing expert's position.

Expert Testimony

Obviously, one of the most important litigation support services available from appraisers and economists is expert witness testimony. Deposition and court testimony are the subjects of the next chapter.

Rebuttal

The type of rebuttal needed largely depends on what is wrong with the other expert's work. If the expert has made a mathematical error, that should be brought to the court's attention, along with its impact on the conclusion. If the expert has taken a position unsupported by the preponderance of authority on an issue, evidence as to the preponderance of authority must be researched and developed. For example, if the opposition takes the position that there should be no discount from enterprise value when estimating the fair market value of a minority stock interest, then the rebuttal should cite authoritative regulations, texts, articles, and other sources that make it clear such a discount should be taken. If the expert's approaches are basically sound, but the expert has reached a poor conclusion because of inadequate and/or erroneous data, then the best rebuttal approach may be to recalculate the results with his or her own methodology, but using complete and accurate data.

Assistance in Preparing Briefs

Appraisers who have testified and either listened to or read the testimony of an opposing expert tend to have a sharp sense of the difference between their and their opponents' positions on the important valuation issues. Briefs in a case are enriched by a good expert's insights. The appraiser can help bring these differences into sharp focus, particularly as they apply to issues that have the greatest monetary impact, and can express clear, concise reasons why his or her position is superior. The attorney may want to take advantage of the appraiser's insights by discussing the briefs before preparing them or by having the appraiser review the briefs in draft form.

Similarly, the appraiser often can provide a special understanding of the opponent's briefs. One thing to look for is any mischaracterization of the appraiser's own evidence or testimony; another is any unjustifiable conclusions or implications made on the basis of the opposing expert's testimony. Sometimes the appraiser reviewing the opposing briefs will notice a clearly erroneous factual statement on some valuation matter that the attorney reading the brief might not realize is an error. A review by the appraiser is a good safety check for ensuring that any unwarranted contentions do not go unnoticed but are treated with a firm and convincing reply.

Discovery

Within the area of litigation, one of the most important tasks that can be performed by the appraiser or economist is assisting the attorney with discovery. Unfortunately, many appraisers concentrate on selecting the correct valuation procedures, which are then applied to either meaningless or unreliable financial information. It is extremely important that the appraiser be brought into the early stages of a case to assure that the necessary information is gathered before the actual valuation is started.

In most cases, the more cooperative and less formalized the discovery process, the better both parties are served. If all parties are willing to cooperate, it is often easiest for experts to gather sufficient information for a thorough understanding by directly contacting the information sources rather than by working through the attorneys. It is not unusual for an unconstrained discovery process to uncover previously misinterpreted facts, leading to a settlement of the case.

When the parties are unwilling to cooperate, the experts must rely on the attorneys to enforce discovery of the necessary information. If the information is delayed or documents do not arrive on a timely basis, then the attorneys must follow up immediately and vigorously. Further, it is up to the experts to keep the attorneys informed about whether the requested information is arriving in a timely manner. Keeping the attorneys apprised in this way will facilitate their follow-up and make it possible for them to accurately report to the court about the receipt of information.

In virtually all valuation cases, a standard set of documents is needed for the business valuation. These documents will usually include historical and (if available) prospective operating statements, income tax returns, ownership lists, prior transaction information, and documentation of the ownership of the subject assets, properties, and business interests (for an example of a document request list, see Exhibit 4–1).

The appraiser should compose a data and document request list tailored as specifically as possible to the particular situation, given what is known about it at the time, and provide for one or more follow-up requests. This is because it is usually impossible to know what every relevant document will be until the appraiser has reviewed the initial batch of data and knows more about the appraisal subject.

If the appraiser can expect to receive the parties' cooperation, then the initial documents request need cover only the known essentials, and the expert can inspect additional documents during a field visit and/or include them in a supplementary request as necessary. If the parties refuse to cooperate, then the initial documents list must be as complete as possible. Even so, lists that demand voluminous material of little or no direct relevance serve no useful purpose and often delay discovery on the grounds that the demand is unreasonably burdensome. The appraiser's experience and judgment can help generate a reasonable and manageable documents list for the specific circumstances.

Business Appraisal Discovery

A business valuation is heavily influenced by the company's financial condition and its operations, so it is important for the appraiser to have the necessary and meaningful financial data regarding the subject company. Many times this data comes from outside the company and from atypical places.

Permanent Files

Documents that may provide meaningful information are the company's permanent files, such as the stock register, articles of incorporation, bylaws, shareholder and/or board of director meeting minutes, and other legal documents. The originals of these documents are sometimes maintained by the company's corporate counsel. These documents often will contain financial projections, buy–sell agreements, evidence of prior sales of interests in the company, and so on.

Accountant's Files

The company's independent accounting firm is often a source of information. These files contain working copies of the historical financial statements and tax returns and will also contain supporting documents, legal documents, accountant's notes, correspondence with the company, and other data that are not necessarily part of the company's records. When reviewing these records, the appraiser should understand the accountant's materiality standard. The materiality standard adopted by the accountant for financial statement reporting purposes may not be consistent with the materiality standard required for the subject litigation. For example, the company's capital expenditure practices and fixed-asset recordkeeping practices may be summarized by the accountant for financial statement reporting purposes but may contain details that would be extremely relevant to the litigation. Another example is when employee stock option grants are not required to be reported on financial statements but would be critical to accurately report the per share valuation conclusion. An offer to buy or sell the company may be in the accountant's files, too.

Many times, the accountant's working papers will resolve questions that the appraiser may have, thus saving the time and expense of the appraiser replicating the already completed work. For example, the accountant's papers may explain why certain expense categories increased or decreased from normal levels during a single accounting period or may disclose unusual or nonrecurring income or expenses of the business.

Bank Files

If the company has an operating line of credit or has used bank financing to finance the purchase of business assets, then the bank that provides the financing will maintain a loan file on the company. This bank loan file may contain many documents that are relevant to the subject valuation, including the following:

1. The loan application and financial worth statement of the company and/or the company's owner.

2. Prior financial statements of the company.
3. Memorandums from the loan officer that disclose additional information on the company or the financial statements that may not be apparent from a review of those statements.
4. Articles and other data on the company and on the industry in which the company participates.

Invoices

A review of selected company invoices may be necessary. For example, if the company is being valued because of a marital dissolution and if the appraiser notices that the legal and accounting expenses for the business have increased substantially in the most recent financial statements, a review of the paid invoices may be in order. A review may disclose that the fees were not for business purposes but were primarily related to the owner's own personal legal and accounting problems. Also, payments near year-end may be prepayments of future expenses even though they were classified as payments for goods or services already rendered.

Interrogatories

Interrogatories are far more cumbersome than interactive questions and answers. For one thing, the next logical question often depends on the answer to the prior question. Moreover, in an interactive situation, the respondent has the opportunity to clarify and perhaps narrow the scope of a broad inquiry, which may save considerable time and expense in complying with the inquiry. As with the documents request list, the burden of the initial interrogatories can be eased for both parties if they provide for follow-up interrogatories. In developing suggested questions, the appraiser must keep in mind both the scope of the inquiry and the clarity of wording to elicit what is intended and relevant. Also, as with the document request list, the appraiser's experience and judgment can be invaluable in developing relevant and incisive interrogatories.

Depositions

Information can be gathered from depositions of fact witnesses and from other expert witnesses. The appraiser can help the attorney prepare for both categories of deposition. The appraiser can suggest areas of questioning that will enhance the information on which to base his or her expert opinion. The purpose of deposing the fact witness is to get information and to ensure the witness is as committed as far as possible to whatever the factual testimony will be.

The purpose of deposing opposing experts usually is to understand what they have done, what they have concluded, and the basis for their conclusions. In some cases, where settlement is the object, the deposition can be a powerful tool of persuasion by exposing the weaknesses in the expert's analysis. Attorneys can widen their perspective by calling on their own experts for some guidance in deposing opposing experts.

The attorney may have his or her own expert, or a member of the expert's staff, on hand when deposing the opponent's experts. The appraiser can thus point out lines of questioning that might elude the attorney but are perfectly logical to one with specific knowledge of information sources, various valuation techniques, and all the calculations and jargon current in the valuation profession. A meaningful deposition prevents experts from going into court still wondering exactly what the opposing experts did in developing their opinions. In many cases, information and insights gained through an incisive deposition can lead the parties to a settlement.

Research

Appraisers and their staffs can support litigation by providing research on such topics as economic and industry data, guideline company data, comparative transaction data, authority for positions on valuation issues, and many others. Specific research assignments may be tailored to the needs of a particular case. The results of this research may eventually be incorporated into expert testimony or brought into evidence in other ways. Such information may also be used by attorneys in cross-examination, arguments, and briefs.

Calculating the Amount of Damages

Although the burden of proof regarding damages rests with the plaintiff, and at times may appear to represent a near monumental task, defendants assume significant risk when they rely on a plaintiff's inability to calculate exact damages. This is because the court may merely require that the plaintiff's presentation be reasonable. It is essential that defendants provide expert evidence as to the actual amount of damages (or lack of damages). Otherwise, a defendant may end up facing a significant liability at the conclusion of the trial, regardless of how weak the plaintiff's presentation may have been, because that presentation was the only proof provided.

Though the circumstances surrounding different damage claims will determine the specific type of claim filed (e.g., breach of contract, antitrust, lost business opportunity), the methods used to calculate claims are fairly standard. With the exception of breach of contract, which is often covered by liquidated damages and other provisions within the contract itself, most damage claims can be calculated by administering one or more of the following methods:

1. Before and after.
2. Yardstick (comparable).
3. Sales projection ("but for").

The Before-and-After Method

Using the before-and-after method, economic income is estimated during the damage period based on results (1) attained before the alleged damaging acts, and/or (2) after the effects of the alleged acts have subsided. Either or both of these is compared to results during the period of the effect of the alleged acts. The success of this method depends on the ability of the expert to establish and support a proven historical financial record for the subject property so that operations preceding and succeeding the event are able to serve as "damage bookends," clearly illustrating the effects of the interruption or the violation period. Ideally, operations before and after the damage period will show similar trends, thereby enabling the expert to estimate the subject property's performance during the damage period using either pre- or postdamage operations as a performance standard with comparable damage amounts resulting. In many cases, only the before period or the after period is available to use to predict the "but for" performance during the damage period.

The Yardstick (Comparable) Method

The yardstick, or comparable, method requires the expert to identify companies or industries that are generally comparable to the plaintiff's company and plot the performance of the plaintiff's company along the lines of the comparable companies' or industry's performances. This method requires that the expert not only satisfy the often difficult task of identifying similar companies or industries, but also that the companies or industries selected by the expert be, themselves, unaffected by the alleged damaging acts of the defendant. Applying as a proxy the performance of another company or a particular industry to project the performance of the subject company, absent the alleged damaging actions of the defendant, is a straightforward, understandable method in estimating losses. Once again, the key lies in carefully identifying the most appropriate guideline companies or industry. In some instances, a comparable but unaffected branch or division of the subject company may provide the needed yardstick.

Sales Projections ("But For") Method

The sales projections, or "but for," method entails the creation of a performance model for the subject company, complete with growth and return estimates. Using the model, operations for the subject company are projected during the damage period absent (i.e., "but for") the alleged effects of the defendant's actions. The returns suggested by the model are then compared with the actual results realized by the company during the period.

Of these three methods, probably the most common is some variation of the sales projection method. Typically, most business operators are in a position to provide sales projections for their businesses and fit within one of a countless number of industries subject to annual, semiannual, or even quarterly forecasts by a variety of both public and private data sources. Such circumstances lend themselves to the development of simulation models designed specifically for the subject business. However, a key factor to keep in mind when developing a sales projection and the resulting profits is that courts tend to prefer projections based on historical track records, even in light of numerous concurring industry forecasts and other published financial data regarding normal growth and returns for participants within the relevant industry.

Regardless of the method undertaken, the extent that projected results exceed actual results represents the plaintiff's loss. This loss often not only represents profits lost during the damage period, but also can, and often does, represent a decrease in overall business value separate from lost profits. Whatever is represented by the total damage claim, all concerned parties should bear in mind that the sum total of combined lost profits and any decrease in overall business value is limited to the present value of total future profits anticipated by the business before the alleged damaging acts. The value of any business is the present (discounted) value of all expected future economic profits. Intuitively, this should serve as a recurring reasonableness check throughout the calculation process.

Mitigation

The principle of mitigation suggests that even victims of contract breaches have a duty to mitigate damages—that is, to keep them as low as possible—and that damages are not recoverable for losses that the injured party could have avoided without undue risk, burden, or humiliation. Even in fraud situations, courts have long held that once a plaintiff learns of the fraud, alleged damages that accrue thereafter are not caused by the fraud, but rather by the plaintiff's decision to continue its relationship with the defendant irrespective of his or her knowledge of the fraud.

With regard to buyers and sellers of goods or services, the buyer is required by the principle of mitigation to "cover" by making reasonable efforts to find replacement goods or services to purchase, while a breached seller is obligated to make reasonable efforts to find an alternative purchaser for the breached goods or services. Excess costs incurred by the buyer in acquiring replacement goods, differences between the contract price and the resale price incurred by the seller, and incidental damages such as expenses incurred in stopping the manufacture of goods, inspecting, transporting, receiving, or storing goods that resulted from the breach are normally recoverable.

Summary of Damages

In general, damage cases require a creative, but realistic, approach to calculating hypothetical values absent the alleged effects of the damaging party's actions. A thorough understanding of the damaged party's industry is important in any damage calculation, and, if available, a historical record of the damaged party's operations should be beneficial. Knowledge of case law will provide the expert with important guidance regarding approaches and methods that the courts will or will not accept in the calculation of damages in the specific legal context in question.

Work Product

Reports that the expert may provide can range from an oral expression of the analysis and conclusions, a single letter addressing a single fact or conclusion, to a detailed narrative report.

Affidavits

The purpose of an affidavit is to put a sworn statement before the court without the author's physical presence. Affidavits are most commonly used in connection with pretrial matters, but sometimes they are introduced as evidence in a trial. The subject matter of an affidavit can be anything from scheduling information, such as the days on which an expert is and is not available for testimony, to a statement of an expert's opinion with a summary of the supporting reasons.

Written Reports

For valuation cases in some jurisdictions, it is mandatory for the opposing parties to exchange written reports no later than 30 days before the call of the trial docket. In U.S. Tax Court, for example, the expert report typically serves as the appraiser's direct testimony. In other jurisdictions, the manner in which expert opinion is expressed is a critical component of the litigation strategy and is left to the attorney's discretion. In such jurisdictions, some attorneys insist on a written report; others decide whether to have a written report on a case-by-case basis. Some attorneys believe a written report or even knowledge that a written report is available detracts from the court's attention to the expert's testimony during the trial. If a written report is to be prepared for litigation purposes, then it normally will follow the guidelines discussed in Chapter 17.

Summary

This chapter presented a brief discussion of many of the important litigation support services that an appraiser or economist can provide in addition to expert testimony. It is beneficial to engage the expert's assistance early in the litigation proceedings so such services, particularly as they relate to the discovery process, can be fully integrated with the anticipated expert testimony. Very often, the expert's services may facilitate a settlement rather than culminate in expert testimony in court.

Although the appraiser may be of great assistance in many ways in preparing and administrating the case, it is essential that the attorney and the client fully respect the appraiser's independence in arriving at any opinion. The appraiser should not only avoid bias in fact, but the appraiser should also avoid the appearance of bias. For this reason, it may be preferable to have certain litigation support services performed by another appraiser. In any case, the effective use of the appraiser's expertise in providing litigation support services can facilitate an expeditious and satisfactory outcome in many controversy cases.

Bibliography

Bjorklund, Paul R. "Calculating Lost Earnings for Damage Awards." *Practical Accountant,* June 1991, pp. 62–70.

Cromley, J. Timothy. "Patent Infringement Damages and Business Valuations." *Business Valuation Review,* September 1994, pp. 120–22.

Fournier, Gary M., and Thomas W. Zuehlke. "Litigation and Settlement: An Empirical Approach." *Review of Economics and Statistics,* May 1989, pp. 189–95.

Lansche, James M. "Business Damages: What Are They Worth?" *Washington State Bar Association Business Law Newsletter,* October 1990, pp. 1–3.

Lanzillotti, R. F., and A. K. Esquibel. "Measuring Damages in Commercial Litigation: Present Value of Lost Opportunities." *Journal of Accounting, Auditing & Finance,* Winter 1990, pp. 125–44.

Love, Vincent J., and Steven Alan Reiss. "Guidelines for Calculating Damages." *CPA Journal,* October 1990, pp. 36 ff.

O'Brien, Vincent E., and Joan K. Meyer. "A Guide to Calculating Lost Profits." *National Law Journal,* January 29, 1990, pp. 17–19.

Paulsen, Jon. "Valuation of Patent Infringement Damages." *ASA Valuation,* March 1994, pp. 18–22.

Reilly, Robert F. "Tackling a Common Appraisal Problem." *Journal of Accountancy,* October 1992, pp. 86–92.

_____. "Valuation Factors Regarding Deprivation Analyses." *National Public Accountant,* November 1992, pp. 32–36.

Sherman, Andrew J., and Deborah E. Bouchoux. "Litigation and Its Alternatives." *Business Age,* August 1989, pp. 22–28.

Smith, Carlton M. "Innovative Settlement Techniques Can Reduce Litigation Costs." *Journal of Taxation,* February 1993, pp. 76–80.

Wagner, Michael J. "How Do You Measure Damages? Lost Income or Lost Cash Flow?" *Journal of Accountancy,* February 1990, pp. 28–31 ff.

_____. "The Accountant's Role in the Process of Damage Measurement." *Practical Accountant,* July 1990, pp. 52–60 ff.

Wagner, Michael J., and Bruce L. MacFarlane. "Opportunities in Litigation Services." *Journal of Accountancy,* June 1992, pp. 70–73.

Chapter 32

Expert Witness Testimony

"Give your evidence," said the King; "and don't be nervous, or I'll have you executed on the spot."[1]

Court testimony challenges an expert witness because it is part of an adversary proceeding. If the opposite side were willing to accept the witness's valuation, there probably would be a settlement instead of a trial. Indeed, most valuation cases settle before they reach the courtroom, especially if the witness has prepared the case thoroughly and the attorney has drawn on the expert's research in negotiating with the opposition. Thus, if the case goes to court, it's because of sharp disagreement. Competent, thorough preparation must culminate in a clear and convincing presentation.

It is essential that an analyst be objective and unbiased when legal testimony is involved. One school of thought holds that since courts in some situations tend to split the difference between opposing positions, an analyst must take an extreme position, because that is the only strategy that will lead to a fair court result. However, in order to be effective, the expert witness should arrive at a conclusion that he or she expects to present and defend without compromise on cross-examination. Usually, a rigorously prepared, convincingly presented, objective case will prevail over an extreme position, which a competent judge will tend to discredit. The only reasonable expectation is that courts will adopt the well-supported position of one side of a case without compromise.[2]

As it relates to damage cases, this chapter focuses on the damages calculations and not on the liability or causation portions of such cases.

Background Preparation

When legal controversy is involved, there is no substitute for thorough homework and preparation. The expert witness virtually must prepare not only his or her own case, but the other side's as well. The expert valuation witness must attempt to anticipate any apparent weaknesses the opposing attorney may seize on in cross-examination and be prepared to defend against attacks on them. Also, the expert witness should be prepared to critique the case the opposing side presents.

Basic Preparation and Documentation

The basic research itself should follow the principles and procedures previously outlined in this book. In legal testimony, one must rely as much as possible on facts, not on conjecture. Documentation is the undergirding of every step. It makes no difference how thoroughly the witness is personally convinced of the validity of the facts and conclusions if he or she is unable to convince the court.

---

[1] Lewis Carroll, *Alice's Adventures in Wonderland* (Middlesex, England: Puffin Books, Penguin Books, Ltd., 1946).

[2] See, for example, *Estate of Saul R. Gilford*, 88 T.C. 38 (1987); *Estate of Albert L. Dougherty*, 59 T.C.M. 772 (1990); and *Estate of Eric Stroben*, T.C. Memo 1992-350 (June 22, 1992).

If the witness were presenting the company in question to a prospective buyer, it might be valid to presume the buyer knows something about the business or industry involved. However, an appraiser cannot presume that the court can have the prospective buyer's sophistication about every business brought before it. Every fact on which the witness intends to rely in reaching his or her conclusion must be presented, along with whatever supporting documentation is necessary for convincing the court that it should indeed rely on that fact.

Moreover, unlike presenting the company to a prospective buyer, in which the buyer would ask the analyst to research and provide supplementary information, the expert has no such chance in court. The analyst cannot take a couple of weeks to do additional homework and come back for another audience. The court, however concerned it may be with reaching an equitable decision, will make its determination based on the initial presentation, however inadequate. Thus, the research had better be thorough the first time.

Federal Rules of Civil Procedure

Rule 26 of the *Federal Rules of Civil Procedure* took effect December 1, 1993. Particularly relevant for expert witnesses are the requirements for disclosure of expert testimony:

(2)   Disclosure of Expert Testimony.

(A)   In addition to the disclosures required by paragraph (1), a party shall disclose to other parties the identity of any person who may be used at trial to present evidence under rules 702, 703, or 705 of the federal rules of evidence.

(B)   Except as otherwise stipulated or directed by the court, this disclosure shall, with respect to a witness, who is retained or specially employed to provide expert testimony in the case or whose duties as an employee of the party regularly involve giving expert testimony, be accompanied by a written report prepared and signed by the witness. The report shall contain a complete statement of all opinions to be expressed and the basis and reasons therefore; the data or other information considered by the witness in forming the opinions; any exhibits to be used as a summary of or support for the opinions; the qualifications of the witness, including a list of all publications authored by the witness within the preceding ten years; the compensation to be paid for the study and testimony; and a listing of any other cases in which the witness has testified as an expert at trial or by deposition within the preceding four years.

(C)   These disclosures shall be made at the times and in the sequence directed by the court. In the absence of other directions from the court or stipulation by the parties, the disclosures shall be made at least 90 days before the trial date or the date the case is to be ready for trial or, if the evidence is intended solely to contradict or rebut evidence on the same subject matter identified by another party under paragraph (2)(b), within 30 days after the disclosure made by the other party. The parties shall supplement these disclosures when required under subdivision (e)(1).[3]

---

[3]FED. R. CIV. P. (Rule 26).

Discovery

If the managers of the business being valued are unwilling to cooperate with the witness, they can make it difficult to get the information necessary for doing the job. The analyst must keep legal counsel apprised of what documents need to be reviewed, what facilities should be visited, and who needs to be interviewed. The expert witness must provide this information as early as possible so that if the opposition parties decide to drag their feet they will not prevent the analyst from completing a thorough valuation. As noted in the previous chapter, the expert witness also should keep the attorney informed of the timeliness and adequacy of the information received. That way, the attorney can follow up on missing data and report accurately to the court on how promptly and completely the information was supplied.

Reading Prior Cases and Articles

Part of the homework for testifying on a valuation or economic analysis issue is to become familiar, if possible, with relevant prior court cases. The full texts of the cases, rather than only the digests various services provide, often provide insight to the expert witness that has been overlooked by others. Although the digests help keep one abreast of day-to-day developments in the field, they are a weak substitute for the detail of the full text when addressing a specific case. It also can help to read articles by other experts analyzing particular cases or categories of cases.

Significant court cases on valuations for various purposes are cited throughout this book. These are not to be considered substitutes for fresh research.

Federal Rules of Evidence Regarding Expert Testimony

Rules 702 through 705 govern testimony by expert witnesses. These are reproduced as Exhibit 32–1.

Use of Hearsay Evidence

The opposing attorney probably will object to any testimony the expert witness offers that might be classified as hearsay. The term *hearsay* refers broadly to any information obtained from third parties without personal verification. The expert witness should not, however, avoid collecting information and opinions from other people if they are relevant. The judge has a great deal of latitude in deciding what evidence to consider and usually wants to hear anything that might help reach an equitable decision. Most judges are reluctant to disallow any potentially relevant testimony on technical grounds, especially if there is no jury. Once the witness has been qualified to testify as an expert before the court, judges tend to want to hear what he or she has to say. They want to know how the witness reached his or her opinion, even if portions of the testimony would be disallowed as hearsay in certain other legal proceedings. The judge can then determine what weight, if any, to accord any statements in the testimony. Rule 703 of the Federal Rules of Evidence states:

Exhibit 32–1
Federal Rules of Evidence Rules 702–705

Rule 702. Testimony by Experts

If scientific, technical, or other specialized knowledge will assist the trier of fact to understand the evidence or to determine a fact in issue, a witness qualified as an expert by knowledge, skill, experience, training, or education, may testify thereto in the form of an opinion or otherwise.

Section references, McCormick 4th ed.

§ 12, § 13, § 14, § 202, § 203

Note by Federal Judicial Center

The rule enacted by the Congress is the rule prescribed by the Supreme Court without change.

Advisory Committee's Note
56 F.R.D. 183, 282

An intelligent evaluation of facts is often difficult or impossible without the application of some scientific, technical, or other specialized knowledge. The most common source of this knowledge is the expert witness, although there are other techniques for supplying it.

Most of the literature assumes that experts testify only in the form of opinions. The assumption is logically unfounded. The rule accordingly recognizes that an expert on the stand may give a dissertation or exposition of scientific or other principles relevant to the case, leaving the trier of fact to apply them to the facts. Since much of the criticism of expert testimony has centered upon the hypothetical question, it seems wise to recognize that opinions are not indispensable and to encourage the use of expert testimony in nonopinion form when counsel believes the trier can itself draw the requisite inference. The use of opinions is not abolished by the rule, however. It will continue to be permissible for the expert to take the further step of suggesting the inference which should be drawn from applying the specialized knowledge to the facts. See Rules 703 to 705.

Whether the situation is a proper one for the use of expert testimony is to be determined on the basis of assisting the trier. "There is no more certain test for determining when experts may be sued than the common sense inquiry whether the untrained layman would be qualified to determine intelligently and to the best possible degree the particular issue without enlightenment from those having a specialized understanding of the subject involved in the dispute." Ladd, Expert Testimony, 5 Vand.L.Rev. 414, 418 (1952). When opinions are excluded, it is because they are unhelpful and therefore superfluous and a waste of time. 7 Wigmore § 1918.

The rule is broadly phrased. The fields of knowledge which may be drawn upon are not limited merely to the "scientific" and "technical" but extend to all "specialized" knowledge. Similarly, the expert is viewed, not in a narrow sense, but as a person qualified by "knowledge, skill, experience, training, or education." Thus within the scope of the rule are not only experts in the strictest sense of the word, e.g. physicians, physicists, and architects, but also the large group sometimes called "skilled" witnesses, such as bankers or landowners testifying to land values.

Rule 703. Bases of Opinion Testimony by Experts

The facts or data in the particular case upon which an expert bases an opinion or inference may be those perceived by or made known to the expert at or before the hearing. If of a type reasonably relied upon by experts in the particular field in forming opinions or inferences upon the subject, the facts or data need not be admissible in evidence.
(As amended Mar. 2, 1987, eff. Oct. 1, 1987.)

Section references, McCormick 4th ed.

§ 10, § 13, § 14, § 15, § 203, § 208, § 324.3

Note by Federal Judicial Center

The rule enacted by the Congress is the rule prescribed by the Supreme Court without change.

Advisory Committee's Note
56 F.R.D. 183, 283

Facts or data upon which expert opinions are based may, under the rule, be derived from three possible sources. The first is the firsthand observation of the witness, with opinions based thereon traditionally allowed. A treating physician affords an example. Rheingold, The Basis of Medical Testimony, 15 Vand.L.Rev. 473, 489 (1962). Whether he must first relate his observations is treated in Rule 705. The second source, presentation at the trial, also reflects existing practice. The technique may be the familiar hypothetical question or having the expert attend the trial and hear the testimony establishing the facts. Problems of determining what testimony the expert relied upon, when the latter technique is employed and the testimony is in conflict, may be resolved by resort to Rule 705. The third source contemplated by the rule consists of presentation of data to the expert outside of court and other than by his own perception. In this respect, the rule is designed to broaden the basis for expert opinions beyond that current in many jurisdictions and to bring the judicial practice into line with the practice of the experts themselves when not in court. Thus a physician in his own practice bases his diagnosis on information from numerous sources and of considerable variety, including statements by patients and relatives, reports and opinions from nurses, technicians and other doctors, hospital records, and X rays. Most of them are admissible in evidence, but only with the expenditure of substantial time in producing and examining various authenticating witnesses. The physician makes life-and-death decisions in reliance upon them. His validation, expertly performed and subject to cross-examination, ought to suffice for judicial purposes. Rheingold, supra, at 531; McCormick § 15. A similar provision is California Evidence Code § 801(b).

The rule also offers a more satisfactory basis for ruling upon the admissibility of public opinion poll evidence. Attention is directed to the validity of the techniques employed rather than to relatively fruitless inquiries whether Rogers Imports, Inc., 216 F.Supp. 670 (S.D.N.Y.1963). See also Blum et al., The Art of Opinion Research: A Lawyer's Appraisal of an Emerging Service, 24 U.Chi.L.Rev. 1 (1956); Bonynge, Trademark Surveys and Techniques and Their Use in Litigation, 48 A.B.A.J. 329 (1962); Zeisel, The Uniqueness of Survey Evidence, 45 Cornell L.Q. 322 (1960); Annot., 76 A.L.R.2d 919.

If it be feared that enlargement of permissible data may tend to break down the rules of exclusion unduly, notice should be taken that the rule requires that the facts or data "be of a type reasonably relied upon by experts in the particular field." The language would not warrant admitting in evidence the opinion of an "accidentologist" as to the point of impact in automobile collision based on statements of bystanders, since this requirement is not satisfied. See Comment, Cal.Law Rev.Comm'n, Recommendation Proposing an Evidence Code 148-150 (1965).

1987 Amendment

The amendment is technical. No substantive change is intended.

Rule 704. Opinion on Ultimate Issue

(a) Except as provided in subdivision (b), testimony in the form of an opinion or inference otherwise admissible is not objectionable because it embraces an ultimate issue to be decided by the trier of fact.

(b) No expert witness testifying with respect to the mental state or condition of a defendant in a criminal case may state an opinion or inference as to whether the defendant did or did not have the mental state or condition constituting an element of the crime charged or of a defense thereto. Such ultimate issues are matters for the trier of fact alone.
(As amended Pub.L. 98-473, Title II, § 406, Oct. 12, 1984, 98 Stat. 2067.)

Section references, McCormick 4th ed.

§ 12, § 14, § 206, § 313

Editorial Note

Subdivision (a) is the entire rule prescribed by the Supreme Court and enacted without change by the Congress when it enacted the Rules of Evidence in 1974, except for the addition of the matter preceding the comma, which was added by the Congress in 1984.

Subdivision (b) was added by the Congress in 1984 as a part of the Insanity Defense Reform Act of 1984. P.L. 98-473, Title II, ch. IV, § 406.

Advisory Committee's Note

56 F.R.D. 183, 284

Subdivision (a).

The basic approach to opinions, lay and expert, in these rules is to

Exhibit 32–1 (concluded)

admit them when helpful to the trier of fact. In order to render this approach fully effective and to allay any doubt on the subject, the so-called "ultimate issue" rule is specifically abolished by the instant rule.

The older cases often contained strictures against allowing witnesses to express opinions upon ultimate issues, as a particular aspect of the rule against opinions. The rule was unduly restrictive, difficult of application, and generally served only to deprive the trier of fact of useful information. 7 Wigmore §§ 1920, 1921; McCormick § 12. The basis usually assigned for the rule, to prevent the witness from "usurping the province of the jury," is aptly characterized as "empty rhetoric." 7 Wigmore § 1920, p. 17. Efforts to meet the felt needs of particular situations led to odd verbal circumlocutions which were said not to violate the rule. Thus a witness could express his estimate of the criminal responsibility of an accused in terms of sanity or insanity, but not in terms of ability to tell right from wrong or other more modern standard. And in cases of medical causation, witnesses were sometimes required to couch their opinions in cautious phrases of "might or could," rather than "did," though the result was to deprive many opinions of the positiveness to which they were entitled, accompanied by the hazard of a ruling of insufficiency to support a verdict. In other instances the rule was simply disregarded, and, as concessions to need, opinions were allowed upon such matters as intoxication, speed, handwriting, and value, although more precise coincidence with an ultimate issue would scarcely be possible.

Many modern decisions illustrate the trend to abandon the rule completely. People v. Wilson, 25 Cal.2d 341, 153 P.2d 720 (1944), whether abortion necessary to save life of patient; Clifford-Jacobs Forging Co. v. Industrial Comm., 19 Ill.2d 236, 166 N.E.2d 529 (1960), medical causation; Dowling v. L.H. Shattuck, Inc., 91 N.H. 234, 17 A.2d 529 (1941), proper method of shoring ditch; Schweiger v. Solbeck, 191 Or. 454, 230 P.2d 195 (1951), cause of landslide. In each instance the opinion was allowed.

The abolition of the ultimate issue rule does not lower the bars so as to admit all opinions. Under Rules 701 and 702, opinions must be helpful to the trier of fact, and Rule 403 provides for exclusion of evidence which wastes time. The provisions afford ample assurances against the admission of opinions which would merely tell the jury what result to reach, somewhat in the manner of the oath-helpers of an earlier day. They also stand ready to exclude opinions phrased in terms of inadequately explored legal criteria. Thus the question, "Did T have capacity to make a will?" would be excluded, while the question, "Did T have sufficient mental capacity to know the nature and extent of his property and the natural objects of his bounty and to formulate a rational scheme of distribution?" would be allowed. McCormick § 12.

For similar provisions see Uniform Rule 56(4); California Evidence Code § 805; Kansas Code of Civil Procedure § 60-456(d); New Jersey Evidence Rule 56(3).

Report on House Committee on the Judiciary

H.R. Report 98-1030, 98th Cong., 2d Sess., p. 230; 1984 U.S.Code Cong. & Ad.News 232 (Legislative History)

Subdivision (b).

The purpose of this amendment is to eliminate the confusing spectacle of competing expert witnesses testifying to directly contradictory conclusions as to the ultimate legal issue to be found by the trier of fact. Under this proposal, expert psychiatric testimony would be limited to presenting and explaining their diagnosis, such as whether the defendant had a severe mental disease or defect and what the characteristics of such a disease or defect, if any, may have been. ***

Rule 705. Disclosure of Facts or Data Underlying Expert Opinion

[Effective until Dec. 1, 1993. See, also, Rule 705, below.]

The expert may testify in terms of opinion or inference and give reasons therefor without prior disclosure of the underlying facts or data, unless the court requires otherwise. The expert may in any event be required to disclose the underlying facts or data on cross-examination.

Rule 705. Disclosure of Facts or Data Underlying Expert Opinion

[Effective Dec. 1, 1993. See, also, Rule 705, above.]

The expert may testify in terms of opinion or inference and give reasons therefor without first testifying to the underlying facts or data, unless

SOURCE: FED. R. EVID. (Rules 702–705).

the court requires otherwise. The expert may in any event be required to disclose the underlying facts or data on cross-examination.

(As amended Mar. 2, 1987, eff. Oct. 1, 1987; Apr. 22, 1993, eff. Dec. 1, 1993.)

Amendment

Congress may postpone the proposed amendment, effective December 1, 1993, may decline to approve such amendment, or may make changes to the amendment.

Section references, McCormick 4th ed.

§ 13, § 14, § 15, § 16, § 31, § 324.3

Note by Federal Judicial Center

The rule enacted by the Congress is the rule prescribed by the Supreme Court, amended only by substituting "court" in place of "judge."

Advisory Committee's Note
56 F.R.D. 183, 285

The hypothetical question has been the target of a great deal of criticism as encouraging partisan bias, affording an opportunity for summing up in the middle of the case, and as complex and time consuming. Ladd, Expert Testimony, 5 Vand.L.Rev. 414, 426-427 (1952). While the rule allows counsel to make disclosure of the underlying facts or data as a preliminary to the giving of an expert opinion, if he chooses, the instances in which he is required to do so are reduced. This is true whether the expert bases his opinion on data furnished him at secondhand or observed by him at firsthand.

The elimination of the requirement of preliminary disclosure at the trial of underlying facts or data has a long background of support. In 1937 the Commissioners on Uniform State Laws incorporated a provision to this effect in their Model Expert Testimony Act, which furnished the basis for Uniform Rules 57 and 58. Rule 4515, N.Y.CPLR (McKinney 1963), provides:

"Unless the court orders otherwise, questions calling for the opinion of an expert witness need not be hypothetical in form, and the witness may state his opinion and reasons without first specifying the data upon which it is based. Upon cross-examination, he may be required to specify the data … ."

See also California Evidence Code § 802; Kansas Code of Civil Procedure §§ 60-456, 60-457; New Jersey Evidence Rules 57, 58.

If the objection is made that leaving it to the cross-examiner to bring out the supporting data is essentially unfair, the answer is that he is under no compulsion to bring out any facts or data except those unfavorable to the opinion. The answer assumes that the cross-examiner has the advance knowledge which is essential for effective cross-examination. This advance knowledge has bee afforded, though imperfectly, by the traditional foundation requirement. Rule 26(b)(4) of the Rules of Civil Procedure, as revised, provides for substantial discovery in this area, obviating in large measure the obstacles which have been raised in some instances to discovery of findings, underlying data, and even the identity of the experts. Friedenthal, Discovery and Use of an Adverse Party's Expert Information, 14 Stan.L.Rev. 455 (1962).

These safeguards are reinforced by the discretionary power of the judge to require preliminary disclosure in any event.

1987 Amendment

The amendment is technical. No substantive change is intended.

1993 Amendment

This rule, which relates to the manner of presenting testimony at trial, is revised to avoid an arguable conflict with revised Rules 26(a)(2)(B) and 26(e)(1) of the Federal Rules of Civil Procedure or with revised Rule 16 of the Federal Rule of Criminal Procedure, which require disclosure in advance of trial of the basis and reasons for an expert's opinions.

If a serious question is raised under Rule 702 or 703 as to the admissibility of expert testimony, disclosure of the underlying facts or data on which opinions are based may, of course, be needed by the court before deciding whether, and to what extent, the person should be allowed to testify. This rule does not preclude such an inquiry.

The facts or data in the particular case upon which an expert bases an opinion or inference may be those perceived by or made known to the expert at or before the hearing. If of a type reasonably relied upon by experts in the particular field in forming opinions or inferences upon the subject, the facts or data need not be admissible in evidence.[4]

Correctly analyzed, it is the opinion of the expert that is the evidence, not the hearsay information that supports it. The key phrase in the above quotation from the Federal Rules is *"reasonably relied upon by experts in the particular field in forming opinions."* Particularly in business valuation, the expert often derives important portions of information from conversations with other people. The expert may conduct some interviews personally, and members of his or her project team may conduct others. If the use of such information may provoke controversy, the attorney should ask the expert a question, or a series of questions, on the stand to ensure that the court understands that analysts typically rely on such information in the course of valuing businesses.

Nevertheless, the witness runs the risk that anything that could be considered hearsay may be disallowed or accorded little or no weight in the court's deliberations. Therefore, the expert should take all feasible steps to make any research that might be considered hearsay both admissible and convincing. If the expert is surveying customers, suppliers, or competitors to obtain information on industry practices, the larger the sample, the better. Using specific names and companies to identify who said what will tend to make the testimony more acceptable than using confidential sources.

To be on the safe side, though, the expert should structure the research and conclusion so anything that could be considered hearsay is not essential to the conclusion even if it may lend considerable support to the conclusion if accepted.

Depositions

The term *depose* means to *state under oath but not in open court*. It is common for the opposing attorney to take an expert witness's deposition some time before the trial, for several reasons. One is to help the attorney assess the relative strengths of the opponent's case for guidance on whether to offer or accept a settlement and, if so, on what basis. Another reason is to try to learn enough about the witness and his or her testimony to prepare a cross-examination that will damage the testimony's credibility. Still another reason is that an attorney can sometimes embarrass or discredit a witness by bringing out inconsistencies between deposition testimony and trial testimony.

Scheduling Depositions

The time and place of the deposition is determined by the attorneys subject to the expert's availability. Some attorneys like to take depositions of experts well in advance of trial, but also expect the experts to complete trial preparation before the deposition. Obviously, a witness cannot disclose the results of research not

---

[4]FED. R. EVID. (Rule 703).

yet completed. Therefore, there is an inherent conflict between the desire for an early deposition and the desire for the work to be as complete as possible.

When scheduling the deposition, the expert should advise the attorney how complete the preparation can be expected to be as of various dates. If the attorney wants the expert to be thoroughly prepared at the deposition—perhaps because he or she considers a settlement possible—the need to finish the work should be considered when setting the schedule. The attorney should give the expert adequate notice and lead time and confirm the expert's ability to be prepared on time.

What to Take to the Deposition

The expert should ask the attorney what to take to the deposition, unless a subpoena with clear instructions has been served. The necessary materials will vary greatly from one situation to another. Instructions for depositions have varied all the way from taking absolutely nothing to taking every document and working paper in the file.

Keep in mind that everything taken to a deposition must be made available to opposing counsel if demanded. The Federal Rules (Rule 612) and many state rules also entitle the adverse party to demand production of any document used by a witness before a deposition or trial to refresh his or her memory for purposes of testimony. Federal Rule of Evidence 612 is presented in full in Exhibit 32–2.

If there is any question, the expert's attorney should advise the expert as to which items opposing counsel are entitled to see and which they are not. Obviously, before the deposition the attorney and the analyst should review all work papers, correspondence, memos, and any other material in the case file. By doing so, the attorney will gain a thorough knowledge of the information used and also get a chance to review the material for items, if any, that are not subject to discovery by the opposing attorney because of attorney–client privilege. The attorney should have this opportunity even when the deposition is pursuant to a subpoena that specifies what is to be brought.

Deposition Testimony

The witness will be sworn in, and the deposing attorney will introduce himself or herself and state a few basic ground rules, which include the witness's right to have any question repeated or clarified.

The opposing attorney will ask most, if not all, of the questions. The scope of allowable questions varies considerably from one situation to another, but often it is quite broad. It usually starts with the expert's background. Attorneys often ask about the expert's past valuation work, other testimony, and work on past cases of a similar nature in the hope of finding something that will appear to contradict the witness's positions in the current case.

The question of work done for other clients is sensitive, because much of the information may be confidential. According to the USPAP Ethics Provision, "An appraiser must protect the confidential nature of the appraiser–client relationship." The expert must advise the attorney that he or she cannot divulge confidential information without the client's permission. If uncertain about how to handle this or any other matter, the witness may request a recess to consult with his or her attorney.

Exhibit 32–2

Federal Rules of Evidence Rule 612

Rule 612. Writing Used to Refresh Memory

Except as otherwise provided in criminal proceedings by section 3500 of title 18, United States Code, if a witness uses a writing to refresh memory for the purpose of testifying, either—

(1) while testifying, or

(2) before testifying, if the court in its discretion determines it is necessary in the interests of justice,

an adverse party is entitled to have the writing produced at the hearing, to inspect it, to cross-examine the witness thereon, and to introduce in evidence those portions which relate to the testimony of the witness. If it is claimed that the writing contains matters not related to the subject matter of the testimony the court shall examine the writing in camera, excise any portions not so related, and order delivery of the remainder to the party entitled thereto. Any portion withheld over objections shall be preserved and made available to the appellate court in the event of an appeal. If a writing is not produced or delivered pursuant to order under this rule, the court shall make any order justice requires, except that in criminal cases when the prosecution elects not to comply, the order shall be one striking the testimony or, if the court in its discretion determines that the interests of justice so require, declaring a mistrial.

(As amended Mar. 2, 1987, eff. Oct. 1, 1987.)

Section references, McCormick 4th ed.

§ 9, § 93, § 97

Note by Federal Judicial Center

The rule enacted by the Congress is the rule prescribed by the Supreme Court, amended by substituting "court" in place of "judge," with appropriate pronominal change, and in the first sentence, by substituting "the writing" in place of "it" before "produced," and by substituting the phrase "(1) while testifying, or (2) before testifying if the court in its discretion determines it is necessary in the interest of justice" in place of "before or while testifying." The reasons for the latter amendment are stated in the Report of the House Committee on the Judiciary, set forth below.

Advisory Committee's Note
56 F.R.D. 183, 277

The treatment of writings used to refresh recollections while on the stand is in accord with settled doctrine. McCormick § 9, p. 15. The bulk of the case law has, however, denied the existence of any right to access by the opponent when the writing is used prior to taking the stand, though the judge may have discretion in the matter. Goldman v. United States, 316 U.S. 129 62 S.Ct. 993, 86 L.Ed. 1322 (1942); Needelman v. United States, 261 F.2d 802 (5th Cir.1958), cert. dismissed 362 U.S. 600, 80 S.Ct. 960, 4 L.ED.2d 980, rehearing denied 363 U.S. 858, 80 S.Ct. 1606, 4 L.Ed.2d 1739, Annot., 82 A.L.R.2d 473, 562 and 7 A.L.R.2d 473, 562 and 7 A.L.R.3d 181, 247. An increasing group of cases has repudiated the distinction, People v. Scott, 29 Ill.2d 97, 193 N.E.2d 814 (1963); State v. Mucci, 25 N.J. 423, 136 A.2d 761 (1957); State v. Hunt, 25 N.J. 514, 138 A.2d 1 (1958); State v. Deslovers, 40 R.I. 89, 100 A.64 (1917), and this position is believed to be correct. As Wigmore put it, "the risk of imposition and the need of safeguard is just as great" in both situation. 3 Wigmore § 762, p. 111. To the same effect is McCormick § 9, p. 17.

SOURCE: FED. R. EVID. (Rule 612).

The purpose of the phrase "for the purpose of testifying" is to safeguard against using the rule as a pretext for wholesale exploration of an opposing party's files and to insure that access is limited only to those writings which may fairly be said in fact to have an impact upon the testimony of the witness.

The purpose of the rule is the same as that of the *Jencks* statute, 18 U.S.C. § 3500: to promote the search of credibility and memory. The same sensitivity to disclosure of government files may be involved; hence the rule is expressly made subject to the statute, subdivision (a) of which provides: "In any criminal prosecution brought by the United States which was made by a Government witness or prospective Government witness (other than the defendant) shall be the subject of subpoena, discovery, or inspection until said witness has testified on direct examination in the trial of the case." Items falling within the purview of the statute are producible only as provided by its terms, Palermo v. United States, 360 U.S. 343, 351 (1959), and disclosure under the rule is limited similarly by the statutory conditions. With this limitation in mind, some differences of application may be noted. The *Jencks* statute applies only to statements of witnesses; the rule is not so limited. The statute applies only to criminal cases; the rule applies to all cases. The statute applies only to government witness; the rule applies to all witnesses. The statute contains no requirement that the statement be consulted for purposes of refreshment before or while testifying; the rule so requires. Since many writings would qualify under either statute or rule, a substantial overlap exists, but the identity of procedures makes this of no importance.

The consequences of nonproduction by the government in a criminal case are those of the *Jencks* statute, striking the testimony or in exceptional cases a mistrial. 18 U.S.C. § 3500(d). In other cases these alternatives are unduly limited, and such possibilities as contempt, dismissal, finding issues against the offender, and the like are available. See Rule 16(g) of the Federal Rules of Criminal Procedure and Rule 37(b) of the Federal Rules of Civil Procedure for appropriate sanctions.

Report of House Committee on the Judiciary
House Comm. on Judiciary, Fed. Rules of Evidence, H.R.Rep. No. 650, 93d Cong., 1st Sess., p. 13 (1973); 1974 U.S. Code Cong. & Ad.News 7075, 7086

As submitted to Congress, Rule 612 provided that except as set forth in 18 U.S.C. § 3500, if a witness uses a writing to refresh his memory for the purpose to testifying, "either before or while testifying," an adverse party is entitled to have the writing produced at the hearing, to inspect it, to cross-examine the witness on it, and to introduce in evidence those portions relating to the production of writings used by a witness while testifying, but to render the production of writings used by a witness to refresh his memory before testifying discretionary with the court in the interests of justice, as is the case under existing federal law. See Goldman v. United States, 316 U.S. 129 (1942). The Committee considered that permitting an adverse party to require the production of writings used before testifying could result in fishing expeditions among a multitude of papers which a witness may have used in preparing for trial.

The Committee intends that nothing in the Rule be construed as barring the assertion of a privilege with respect to writings used by a witness to refresh his memory.

1987 Amendment

The amendment is technical. No substantive change is intended.

For the most part, the general rules applicable to courtroom testimony, discussed later in this chapter, also apply in deposition testimony. The expert is not required to provide any more information than the question specifically calls for—and normally should not. The two worst faults of some expert witnesses are unresponsiveness and overresponsiveness, that is, giving answers beyond the scope of the question. Once certain that he or she understands the question, the expert should answer forthrightly, to the point, and as briefly as possible. It is not the witness's responsibility to assist examining counsel by rephrasing questions the way they should have been asked or to volunteer information, no matter how pertinent, that the question did not address.

The attorney often tries to fence in the witness with a question such as, "Is that *everything* you considered in forming your opinion?" The witness usually should insist on leaving the gate open with something like, "That's everything I can recall at this time."

The expert should remember that although the deposition results in a written transcript, pauses generally do not appear in the text. Before starting to talk, the witness should take time to frame a concise answer that will read well in the transcript. A good rule is to answer questions as though you were dictating your testimony, which will make you think before you speak.

After the Deposition

The witness has the right to receive, read, and make any corrections to the transcript of the deposition, or he or she may waive that right. Although court reporters generally are fast and accurate, they do make mistakes—and occasionally the mistakes can make a good point pointless or, at worst, change the meaning, such as by leaving out a *not*. Also, reading over the transcript of the deposition is a constructive exercise for the witness, because it helps call attention to any weakness or disorganization, which the witness can correct before the trial.

Further, the witness has the right to check and recheck data as thoroughly as desired. Any errors found at any time between the deposition date and the court date should be corrected. If the opposing attorney tries to embarrass the witness with the inconsistency in court, the witness should state frankly that the material was preliminary at the time of the deposition and that the process of checking the material disclosed an error that subsequently was corrected.

Outlining Courtroom Testimony

In preparing for courtroom testimony, it is important to know what the format of the trial will be. Legal counsel will be pursuing his or her "theme" for the case, and the format of the expert witness testimony should complement the case's legal strategy (in presentation format, not in opinion). Whether a judge or a jury will be making the decision can affect how detailed the testimony must be, the nature and size of exhibits, and much of the style of testimony. Most business valuation cases are tried before a judge without a jury. Even if the parties have a right to a jury trial, attorneys on both sides usually opt to waive that right in business valuation cases, partly because of the extra time and cost of dealing with a jury. Moreover, it is very difficult to educate laypeople about the complexities of business valuation within the tight time frame and structured format of a jury trial. Consequently, regardless of how conscientious and well-intentioned the jury may be, they could be hard-pressed to reach an equitable decision in a business valuation case.

Regardless of the format, the expert witness and the attorney must spend time together preparing the presentation. The witness should know what areas of questions to expect in order to prepare direct and complete answers. The attorney needs to know what evidence the expert witness has prepared to be sure of getting all of it presented. Some attorneys like to put the expert witness on the stand and ask one broad question, such as, "Will you please describe your investigation and findings as to the value of XYZ Company?" Most attorneys prefer to develop the case logically and point by point in a format of questions and short answers between the attorney and the witness.

In some instances, the judge issues a pretrial order requiring each side of the case to prepare and exchange formal, written reports and then find areas of agreement and disagreement among themselves, limiting the verbal testimony to the unresolved issues.

It is legal counsel's decision whether he or she or the witness should prepare the first draft of the question list. Either way, the direct testimony usually proceeds in more or less the following sequence:

1. Identification and qualifications of the witness.
2. Description of the assignment.
3. Conclusion.
4. Steps taken in carrying out the assignment.
5. Findings.
6. Restatement of the conclusion.

Qualifying the Witness

Qualifying the witness as an expert is an essential first step in establishing the witness's credibility in the court's eyes. This step usually establishes not only the witness's expertise on the subject of business valuation, but also his or her position and affiliations, making it clear the witness is independent of the company being valued and the parties to the suit.

Frequently, opposing counsel gratuitously offers to stipulate that the witness qualifies as an expert. This offer should be rejected. The attorney calling the expert wants to acquaint the judge and/or jury firsthand with the expert and his or her qualifications relevant to the forthcoming testimony. The extent of the qualifying process varies considerably from one case to another, but it usually proceeds approximately along the following sequence and format.

Education.   The qualifications usually start with academic degrees and relevant nondegree programs.

Professional Credentials.   Professional credentials are the expert's professional designations and affiliations. Since appraisal and financial analysis designations (such as ASA and CFA) are less known to most courts than accounting designations such as CPA, it often is appropriate to explain to the court the nature of these designations and the qualifications required for attaining them. Professional involvements such as holding office and/or serving on committees may also be covered at this point, as well as special honors or recognition.

Publications and Teaching. Books and/or articles written, appraisal courses taught, and a summary of relevant professional appraisal lectures given usually logically follow professional credentials.

Employment History. The focus should be on the portion of the witness's employment history that bears on his or her qualifications as an appraiser. It may focus on the scope of the appraisal work of the firm that employs the analyst and on the analyst's involvement in that work.

Experience Particularly Relevant to the Case at Bench. The expert's relevant experience may be past appraisal work on companies in the same industry and/or may focus on past experience with appraisals involving similar issues.

Description of the Assignment

The description of the assignment usually includes such information as when the witness was retained, by whom, and what the assignment was, including the standard of value to be used. This information is similar to that included in the description of the assignment section of a written report as discussed in Chapter 2, "Defining the Valuation Assignment."

The matter of the witness's compensation may or may not be raised, either by the attorney on direct examination or by the opposing attorney on cross-examination. Whether the compensation is a flat fee or on an hourly basis, it is a good idea for the witness to come to court prepared to answer the question of how many hours have been spent in preparation. If the witness has carried out all the steps in the valuation process suggested in this book, he or she will have spent many hours, and testimony to that effect will lend further support to the thoroughness of the preparation.

Summary of Conclusion

Once the witness has been qualified and the assignment defined, most attorneys ask the witness to state his or her valuation conclusion, before describing the research undertaken to reach it, very much as the introduction to a written appraisal report summarizes the ultimate conclusion. Some attorneys prefer to wait until the entire research project has been described before having the witness present the conclusion. In this, as in all other procedural matters in testimony, the attorney's judgment should prevail.

Description of Steps Taken

The description of the steps taken in reaching the valuation conclusion should include the sources of information, such as those that appear in the written report, plus brief statements of what was obtained from the various sources. For example, in listing persons interviewed, the witness might relate at this point in the testimony which subjects were discussed. In listing written information sources, the witness also might discuss which pieces of information were obtained from each source. On the other hand, the style of the testimony, as determined by legal counsel, may call for the expert witness to merely explain that information was gathered as was necessary to reach a reasonable conclusion.

Findings

Each written or oral business or intangible asset appraisal report must:
(a) clearly and accurately set forth the appraisal in a manner that will not be misleading;
(b) contain sufficient information to enable the intended user(s) to understand it. Any specific limiting conditions concerning information should be noted;
(c) clearly and accurately disclose any extraordinary assumption that directly affects the appraisal and indicate its impact on value.[5]

Even oral testimony about the research findings should cover the remainder of the information discussed in Chapter 17, "Writing an Appraisal Report." Findings include pertinent aspects of the economic outlook, the industry in which the company operates and the company's position in that industry, a description of the company, and the analysis leading to the valuation conclusion.

Final Conclusion

Even though in valuing the company the appraiser probably has used several valuation approaches and has come up with a reasonable range of possible values, the concluding statement usually should be a single figure and a restatement of the standard of value. The attorney probably will ask the witness to state the conclusion in a manner similar to this: "It is my opinion that the fair market value of the common stock of ABC Grocery Company, as of the valuation date, is $152 per share." The attorney usually will also ask whether all the procedures followed in the valuation have been in accordance with generally accepted business valuation principles and procedures, or, as is now more common, in conformance with USPAP.

Exhibits

Naturally, an important part of preparing for court testimony is creating exhibits that will help communicate the thoroughness and credibility of the valuation. Such exhibits usually include the witness's qualifications, in a format such as that used as an appendix to a written report, all the tabular statistical data for the written report, and any charts, pictures, or other supporting material that may assist the court in understanding the business and how it should be valued.

In courtroom testimony, the old adage, "A picture is worth a thousand words," is particularly true. The witness probably has seen and toured the company's facilities; the judge very likely has not. Since the court usually can't go to the facilities, the next best thing is to bring the facilities to the court. Through photographs, the witness can give a "walking tour" of the business, giving the court a better understanding of what is being valued and, one would hope, making the financial analysis more meaningful. The pictures used in the courtroom usually can be prints that the judge can see and that can be entered as official

---

[5]Standards Rule 10-1, *Uniform Standards of Professional Appraisal Practice*, 1995 edition (Washington, DC: The Appraisal Foundation, 1995), p. 55.

Exhibit 32–3

Typical List of Exhibits on Business Valuation
to Be Submitted with Court Testimony

Qualifications of witness	Five-year summary of the subject company's income statements
Pictures of business facilities	Subject company's financial ratios compared with industry norms
Latest five years' financial statements for the subject company	Market price data for guideline publicly traded companies
Five-year summary of the subject company's balance sheets	Summary statistics of valuation approaches used and conclusion

NOTE: The above list applies to a simple, basic case and should be expanded to include whatever additional material may be relevant in each specific case.

exhibits. If the proceeding is a jury trial, the attorney and witness may wish to present the pictures as slides so all parties in the courtroom can see the same thing while the witness is describing the company's operations. If slides are used, copies should be prepared for possible submission as exhibits.

For exhibits of a size and format that can be readily copied, such as 8½-by-11-inch, such as would be included in a written report, it is convenient to prepare an extra set for the judge in addition to the set to be labeled by the clerk and entered as the official exhibit in the court record. Doing so will make it convenient for the judge to look at the tables and other exhibits while the witness is discussing them in direct testimony, as well as during cross-examination. It is also a courtesy, and usually a requirement, to provide a set of copies for the opposing attorney.

The exhibits the witness proposes to use should be reviewed with the attorney who will conduct the examination to ensure that all are appropriate and are legally admissible. A sample list of exhibits appropriate for a simple, basic case is presented in Exhibit 32–3.

Preparation with the Attorney

Once the testimony outline and exhibits have been drafted, the attorney should review them thoroughly with the expert. The attorney should understand the significance of the major points in the expert's work to be able to phrase questions most meaningfully, spend the most time on the most salient points, and know what topics, if any, to revisit on redirect examination. The expert should be sure to understand any legal issues that bear on the testimony and how his or her testimony fits into the overall case. Even though the trial attorney is busy and under pressure, both he or she and the appraiser must understand how important it is to work together to prepare a well-focused and persuasive presentation of the expert's work. Too often the attorney fails to gain the full impact of the expert's knowledge and research because of inadequate preparation.

In the Courtroom

The expert should appear in court as rested, alert, and neatly groomed as possible. Whether a man or a woman, the expert should wear a business suit, perhaps one appropriate for an initial meeting with a new client.

What to Have on the Stand

In general, the witness should take what he or she expects to have to refer to, a calculator, perhaps a notepad, and no more. If asked questions about any document the witness has not brought along, the witness is entitled to request a copy of it and examine it. Documents should be sufficiently organized that the witness will have little trouble finding references.

The witness should not plan to read testimony except quotations from documents when it is important to have the record reflect the document's exact wording. An outline of testimony points might help ensure that the witness overlooks no important point. The expert should keep in mind, however, that opposing counsel may examine and copy all materials brought to or referred to on the witness stand.

General Guidelines for Testimony

Perhaps the most critical thing for the witness to keep in mind in the courtroom is the need to be objective and unbiased, not an advocate. An advocate is defined as "one who pleads the cause of another" or "one who supports something as a cause." Pleading and supporting the client's cause is the attorney's role. The expert witness's role is to present the facts as they are and to use his or her professional expertise to interpret those facts to reach an objective conclusion.

Another key responsibility on the witness stand is to respond to the questions asked. The witness first must pay attention to the question and be sure of understanding it and should pause long enough before answering to be *sure* that the answer will satisfy the question. If unsure whether he or she understands the question, the witness should ask for clarification.

Although answers should be concise but complete, how far to go is a matter of judgment. However, the witness definitely should avoid introducing material or ideas irrelevant to the question. Nevertheless, there is a fine line of judgment. A question may be worded such that a direct answer without clarification could leave a misleading impression. Naturally, in such cases the witness should volunteer the necessary clarification. (Of course, such questions are more likely to come from the opposing attorney during cross-examination, because he or she either doesn't understand the material or wishes to lead the witness into creating a false impression.)

The witness should speak distinctly and slowly enough for the judge and attorneys to understand the ideas and for the court reporter to type the words into the record. If it is necessary to use proper names or esoteric terminology, the appraiser should spell them so the court reporter can enter them into the record correctly.

The witness should make enough eye contact with the judge and/or jury to ensure that they are following the testimony and understanding the ideas. If not sure whether the judge and/or jury understands, the witness should pause and rephrase the point more clearly. The key point is that the person one is trying to communicate to is the trier of fact, either judge or jury, *not* the client's counsel or opposing counsel.

In general, the expert witness should avoid technical language and jargon. Usually there is no reason to believe the judge and/or jurors are trained in the very technical discipline of business valuation or in the specifics of the industry in which the subject business operates. If a technical term is necessary for making a point, it should be defined or explained in terms intelligible to a layperson.

In referring to an exhibit, the witness should say something like, "I direct your attention to Exhibit 10" and give the judge time to find Exhibit 10 before proceeding.

The witness should avoid distracting mannerisms and utterances such as "well," "ummm," and "uhhh." Unconscious habits, such as clicking a ballpoint pen or tapping a pencil, should be eliminated.

Otherwise, the witness should be his or her natural self, exuding competence and confidence but never arrogance.

Direct Examination

The expert witness must be careful not to omit any material facts, even (or especially) if their implications do not support the client's case. One should always assume the opposing attorney and expert witness are properly prepared (even if one suspects they are not) and will not allow any adverse facts to be overlooked. If the expert witness omits material facts, whether because of incompetence or of advocacy, his or her credibility with the court will be in question. It is also essential that the expert witness not distort any facts or their interpretations. *Straightforward* is a good key word to go by.

Whether the expert enters all exhibits in one batch at the beginning of the testimony or one by one as they become relevant is a matter of preference. Many attorneys think the latter approach helps keep the court's attention focused on the subject at hand. After the oral qualification of the expert witness, his or her written credentials may be entered as an exhibit. From that point forward, each exhibit can be introduced immediately before the witness discusses it so the judge can view it as the witness describes and interprets it.

Exhibits are numbered by the court as they are entered, and usually other exhibits have been entered earlier in the case; therefore, the witness's Table II may be the court's Exhibit 15, for example. As the exhibits are entered, the witness should write the court's exhibit number at the top of his or her own copy, since that usually is how the exhibit will be identified when the witness is called to discuss it on cross-examination.

The witness should not be surprised if the opposing attorney raises frequent objections. He or she may object to the form or substance of a question, an answer given by a witness, or the introduction of an exhibit. When an objection is raised, the witness must pause while the attorneys argue it out, then proceed when so instructed by the judge or by the attorney conducting the examination.

Cross-Examination

It is the opposing attorney's job to expose to the court any weaknesses in the expert witness's testimony. The witness should not take it personally. The attorney may attempt to discredit the witness in various ways, such as asking questions designed to attack the witness's competence to present expert testimony on the valuation issue at hand or to bring out possible conflicts of interest that would impugn the witness's independence. If the witness has testified in previous cases, he or she should assume the opposing attorney has read the transcripts of such cases and will ask questions to bring out any apparent inconsistencies between previous and present testimony. The witness also should assume the attorney has reviewed all the books and articles that he or she has written.

As discussed earlier, in preparing for direct testimony the witness also must prepare for cross-examination. If the witness did not use a particular approach that may seem reasonable on the surface, he or she should be prepared to explain why. If the witness did not use a company as a guideline, he or she should be prepared to explain why the company was disqualified. (This particular problem will be taken care of almost automatically if the procedures outlined in Chapter 10 are followed and documented.)

Some attorneys use a cross-examination technique of asking questions in a manner designed to leave the court with an impression that they might like to convey but that may be misleading. A favorite ploy is to carefully frame a complicated question so as to leave a certain impression and then demand a yes or no answer. The witness should realize that he or she cannot be compelled to limit the answer to yes or no if it would not be appropriate. The witness has the right to clarify the answer and should demand to be allowed to do so if failure to clarify would leave a misimpression. The witness should first answer yes or no if it is possible to do so and then give the clarification. If it is a compound question and the answer is yes to one or more parts and no to others, the witness should make clear to which part or parts each response refers. If the question simply cannot be answered yes or no, the witness should explain why. The witness also may request the attorney rephrase a question, either for clarification or to "unbundle" a compound question.

Another cross-examination ploy is to ask a question that contains a misleading presumption. In such a case, the witness must correct the false presumption in the answer; otherwise, he or she will risk leaving the impression of accepting the false premise.

It also is common for cross-examining attorneys to mischaracterize a witness's prior testimony, reading into it some impression that was never intended. In replying to such a misrepresentation, the witness may need to preface the answer with wording such as, "To put the answer to your question in proper context, I need to correct the misunderstanding of my prior testimony that was implied in your paraphrasing of it."

The hardest questions to deal with are those that are so abstruse that they are unintelligible. Usually the expert should not heroically attempt to interpret such questions but admit not understanding them and request clarification.

Through all of this, the witness should try to remain courteous. Nevertheless, he or she must also be firm and not feel intimidated by an overbearing attorney.

A witness must avoid attempting to bluff if he or she does not know an answer. Any suspicion of bluffing could cast doubt on the credibility of the witness's entire testimony. If the witness does not know the answer, he or she must say so. Also, if there is some error in the data, the witness should admit it and correct it, making whatever adjustment to the conclusion the correction would indicate.

If the expert witness has done his or her homework thoroughly, the cross-examination actually can help the case. With each answer explaining why a particular approach was rejected, for example, the opposition's expert witness testimony, which hasn't even been presented yet, could be discredited.

Redirect Examination

Even when the cross-examination has been completed, it is not time for the witness to breathe a sign of relief. The attorney who conducted the original examination usually will want to keep the witness on the stand to ask redirect examination questions. The general purpose of redirect is to expand any points brought out in the cross-examination that the attorney thinks need elaboration. It is the attorney's opportunity to counter possible misimpressions that might have been left with the court during the cross-examination and to reinforce any positions about which the cross-examination may have raised doubts.

If there is a recess between cross- and redirect examinations and the witness feels the need to clarify any points further, he or she should inform legal counsel so that counsel can ask the appropriate questions (provided the court hasn't prohibited discussion of the case). If the witness feels strongly that something should be brought out on redirect examination and there is no scheduled recess, he or she usually can request a conference with the attorney. The redirect and recross examinations can go back and forth indefinitely, limited only by the attorneys' restraint and the judge's patience.

The judge may break in at any time during the direct examination, cross-examination, or any part of the proceedings to ask questions. Some judges are more apt to do so than others. Questions from the judge usually are a good sign—at least the judge is paying attention, and judges often ask penetrating and perceptive questions. Also, the witness should prefer that the judge ask for clarification of something the witness has left unclear or omitted rather than just leaving the issue alone.

Rebuttal Testimony

Attorneys often ask experts to present testimony for the purpose of rebutting testimony presented by the opposition's expert. Such testimony can take a wide variety of forms. Rebuttal testimony is most often presented to correct factual errors or errors in appraisal procedure committed by the opposing expert. Of course, if factual errors are to be corrected, it is important to present complete documentation for the correction. If procedural errors are to be corrected, the appraiser must present as strong authority as is possible for the correct procedures.

In many cases, rebuttal testimony is at least as important as the basic testimony and it should be presented as constructively as possible. Often, when the errors are corrected, the different approaches of the opposing experts ultimately may lead to similar conclusions.

Exclusion of Witnesses

From time to time, the opposing attorney may move to have the expert witness excluded from the courtroom when testimony of the opposing expert is presented. The exclusion rule aims to keep fact witnesses from being influenced in their testimony by the testimony of other fact witnesses. It is often *very* important to have the expert in the courtroom to hear opposing expert testimony, sometimes to give the attorney technical advice about the testimony, especially for cross-examination, and sometimes so the expert can rebut testimony of an opposing expert. A witness cannot be excluded when that person's presence is essential to the presentation of the party's cause. Rarely, if ever, will a judge exclude an expert when this is called to the court's attention. Rule 615 of the *Federal Rules of Evidence* which covers this point, is reproduced as Exhibit 32–4.

Exhibit 32 4

Federal Rules of Evidence Rule 615

Rule 615. Exclusion of Witnesses

At the request of a party the court shall order witnesses excluded so that they cannot hear the testimony of other witnesses and it may make the order of its own motion. This rule does not authorize exclusion of (1) a party who is a natural person, or (2) an officer or employee of a party which is not a natural person designated as its representative by its attorney, or (3) a person whose presence is shown by a party to be essential to the presentation of the party's cause.

(As amended Mar. 2, 1987, eff. Oct. 1, 1987; Apr. 25, 1988; eff. Nov. 1, 1988; Nov. 18, 1988, Pub.L. 100-690, Title VII, § 7075(a), 102 Stat. 4405.)

Section references, McCormick 4th ed.

§ 50

Note by Federal Judicial Center

The rule enacted by the Congress is the rule prescribed by the Supreme Court, amended only substituting "court," in place of "judge," with conforming pronominal changes.

Advisory Committee's Note

56 F.R.D. 183, 280

The efficacy of excluding or sequestering witnesses has long been recognized as a means of discouraging and exposing fabrication, inaccuracy, and collusion. 6 Wigmore §§ 1837-1838. The authority of the judge is admitted, the only question being whether the matter is committed to his discretion or one of right. The rule takes the latter position. No time is specified for making the request.

Several categories of persons are excepted. (1) Exclusion of persons who are parties would raise serious problems of confrontation and due process. Under accepted practice they are not subject to exclusion. 6 Wigmore § 1842. (2) As the equivalent of the right of a natural-person party to be present, a party which is not a natural person is entitled to have a representative present. Most of the cases have involved allowing a police officer who has been in charge of an investigation to remain in court despite the fact that he will be a witness. United States v. Infanzon, 235 F.2d 318 (2d Cir.1956); Portomene v. United States, 221 F.2d 582 (5th Cir.1955); Powell v. United Sates, 208 F.2d 618 (6th Cir.1952); Jones v. United States, 252 F.Supp. 781 (W.D.Okl.1966). Designation of the representative by the attorney rather than by the client may at first glance appear to be an inversion of the

attorney-client relationship, but it may be assumed that the attorney will follow the wishes of the client, and the solution is simple and workable. See California Evidence Code § 777. (3) The category contemplates such persons as an agent who handled the transaction being litigated or an expert need to advise counsel in the management of the litigation. See 6 Wigmore § 1842, n. 4.

Report of Senate Committee on the Judiciary

Senate Comm. on Judiciary, Fed.Rules of Evidence, S.Rep. No. 127, 93d Cong., 2d Sess., p. 26 (1974); 1974 U.S.Code Cong. & Ad.News 7051, 7072

Many district courts permit government counsel to have an investigative agent at counsel table throughout the trial although the agent is or may be a witness. The practice is permitted as an exception to the rule of exclusion and compares with the situation defense counsel finds himself in—he always has the client with him to consult during the trial. The investigative agent's presence may be extremely important to government counsel, especially when the case is complex or involves some specialized subject matter. The agent, too, having lived with the case for a long time, may be able to assist in meeting trial surprises where the best-prepared counsel would otherwise have difficulty. Yet, it would not seem the government could often meet the burden under Rule 615 of showing that the agent's presence is essential. Furthermore, it could be dangerous to use the agent as a witness as early in the case as possible, so that he might then help counsel as a nonwitness, since the agent's testimony could be needed in rebuttal. Using another, nonwitness agency from the same investigative agency would not generally meet government counsel's needs.

This problem is solved if it is clear that investigative agents are within the group specified under the second exception made in the rule, for "an officer or employee of a party which is not a natural person designated as its representative by its attorney." It is our understanding that this was the intention of the House committee. It is certainly this committee's construction of the rule.

1987 Amendment

The amendment is technical. No substantive change is intended.

1988 Amendment

The amendment is technical. No substantive change is intended.

SOURCE: FED. R. EVID. (Rule 615).

Summary

Providing expert testimony in an adversarial proceeding is considered by most professional business analysts to be the most challenging aspect of the profession. By the time an adversarial proceeding reaches the courtroom, settlement efforts have been exhausted and the disagreements are razor sharp.

Many aspects of the courtroom drama are very much like theater in style, posturing, and pace. However, when legal controversy is involved, the expert witness has no substitute for thorough homework and preparation. The expert witness virtually prepares not only for his or her own case, but for the other side's as well.

Bibliography

Amsden, Ted T. "Cross-Examining an Opposing Expert at Trial." *For the Defense,* December 1989, pp. 17–20.

Arneson, George S. "Effects of Proposed Changes in Federal Rules of Civil Procedure and Evidence on Appraisers as Experts in Litigation." *ASA Valuation,* June 1992, pp. 2–8.

_____. "How Changes in Federal Rules Could Affect Management-Consultant Expert Witnesses." *Journal of Management Consulting,* Spring 1993, pp. 29–32 ff.

Broecker, Howard W. "Cross-Examination of a Business Valuation Expert Witness." *American Journal of Family Law,* Fall 1989, pp. 213–21.

Cheifetz, Carl B. "Direct Testimony of the Accounting Expert." *FAIR$HARE: The Matrimonial Law Monthly,* May 1990, pp. 3–5.

Crain, Michael A.; Dan L. Goldwasser; and Everett P. Harry. "Expert Witnesses—In Jeopardy?" *Journal of Accountancy,* December 1994, pp. 42–48.

Crimm, Nina J. "A Role for 'Expert Arbitrators' in Resolving Valuation Issues before the United States Tax Court: A Remedy to Plaguing Problems." *Indiana Law Review* 26 (1992), pp. 41–64.

Dennis, Stephen G. "Selecting and Using a Financial Expert in Dissolution Practice." *Family Law Quarterly,* Spring 1992, pp. 17–25.

Feder, Robert D. "Direct Examination of a Business Appraiser in a Divorce Action." *American Journal of Family Law,* Spring 1993, pp. 1–11.

Field, Harold G. "Direct Examination of a Business Valuator." *American Journal of Family Law,* Fall 1989, pp. 223–32.

Harris, Timothy J. "The Requirement of Expert Testimony in Appraisal Litigation." *Appraisal Journal,* January 1992, pp. 68–73.

Joseph, Gregory P. "A Complete Guide to Deposition Practice." *Practical Litigator,* January 1993, pp. 59–96.

Kendig, Robert E. "Discovery Issues in Valuation Cases." *American Journal of Family Law,* Spring 1992, pp. 55–74.

Lerch, Mary Ann. "Appraisal Practice before the U.S. Tax Court." *Business Valuation Review,* June 1989, pp. 65–67.

Mitchell, Marvin. "Cross-Examining an Opponent's Business Valuation Expert." *FAIR$HARE: The Matrimonial Law Monthly,* May 1990, pp. 13–19.

Oldenburg, Mark D. "Everything You Need to Know to Be a Good Expert Witness in a Civil Case." *Real Property Perspectives,* July 1994, pp. 16–28.

Orpett, Mitchell A., and H. Wesley Sunu. "Letter from the United States: Expert Reports Versus Depositions." *The Expert,* Autumn 1994, pp. 43–45.

Sattell, Milton. "How to Handle Yourself as an Expert Witness." *Practical Accountant,* November 1990, pp. 87–89.

Schweihs, Robert P. "Litigation Support, Valuation-Related Dispute Resolution, and Expert Witness Services." *ABI Journal,* November 1993, pp. 10, 19, 22.

Shayne, Mark. "The Role of the Business Valuator in Marital and Family Business Litigation." *American Journal of Family Law,* Fall 1991, pp. 239–49.

Sickler, Jay. "Appraisers as Expert Witnesses—Changes to FRCP 26." *Business Valuation Review,* September 1994, pp. 130–31.

Skoloff, Gary N. "Special Rules for Cross-Examining the Accountant." *FAIR$HARE: The Matrimonial Law Monthly,* May 1990, pp. 5–6.

Stone, Marvin L. "Proposed Changes in Federal Evidence Rules." *Journal of Accountancy,* February 1993, pp. 83–86.

Strohn, Gregor M. "Expert Witness Testimony." *Real Property Perspectives,* July 1994, pp. 1–6.

Wagner, Michael J. "Expert Problems." *Litigation,* Winter 1989, pp. 35–37;, 56.

Weinstein, Jeffrey P. "The Use and Abuse of Economic Experts in Divorce Litigation." *FAIR$HARE—The Matrimonial Law Monthly,* February 1995, pp. 3–6.

Winslow, Daniel B., and Richard J. Dennis, Sr. "The Appraiser Takes the Witness Stand." *Real Estate Appraiser & Analyst,* Winter 1990, pp. 74–77.

Zipp, Alan S. "Powerful Testimony Techniques (Pointers for Expert Witness CPAs Engaged in Business Appraisals)." *Journal of Accountancy,* December 1992, pp. 79–83.

Chapter 33

Arbitration

Clogged courts and escalating litigation costs have made arbitration as a solution for civil disputes and claims of conflict more necessary than ever before. Arbitration is a process by which a dispute is settled by an impartial, disinterested person or group who is authorized to render a decision that is legal, final, and binding. Arbitration is used as an alternative to litigation because it provides for an expeditious and inexpensive resolution of disputes by arbitrators having expert knowledge within a particular field, who act in an informal process that maintains the privacy of business transactions.[1]

One of the hottest things going in the mid-1990s, with clogged court calendars and escalating litigation costs, is "alternative dispute resolution" (ADR). However, most usage of this phrase refers to some form of mediation, the product of which is advisory rather than a binding conclusion.

The process of arbitration usually results in a binding conclusion, as noted in the quote above. Depending on the directive giving rise to the arbitration, the arbitrator(s)' conclusion may be contractually binding by itself, or it may be subject to limited review and confirmation by a court.

Business valuation disputes lend themselves exceedingly well to the arbitration process, partly because there normally is a single, unambiguous conclusion—that is, a value—and partly for several other good reasons outlined below. The authors have had extensive experience serving as arbitrators, expert witnesses before arbitrators, and consultants to attorneys contemplating or conducting an arbitration process. Whenever the arbitrators themselves are experts in the field, as suggested in the above quote, our experiences have been very positive with respect to the fairness of the conclusion and, in most cases, the expeditiousness of the process.

Advantages of Arbitration over Court Trial

The primary advantages of arbitration over a court trial are the following:

1. There is less likelihood of an outlandish result in favor of one side over the other, provided the arbitrators are qualified, professional business appraisers. In cases where the issue is a dispute over the value of a business or a business interest, an arbitrator, if properly chosen, is usually in a better position as a result of experience and knowledge to assess the value of a business or business interest than either a judge or jury.
2. Arbitration usually takes less elapsed time from start to finish.
3. Scheduling normally can be made more convenient for all parties involved.
4. Arbitration usually costs less. Attorneys' time and experts' fees frequently are considerably reduced. The appraisal process itself may not be less expensive than a court trial, but the amount of time required for preparing for cross-examination and rebuttal to an opposing expert in court can be substantial.
5. Arbitration usually is less formal and less taxing on all participants, especially the principals in the disputed issue.

---

[1] Jerome N. Block, "The Process of Arbitration," *The Appraisal Journal,* April 1993, pp. 234–38.

6. The hearings are private rather than public and in many cases are not recorded by a court reporter, a compelling advantage in many circumstances.

7. The award of the arbitrators in most situations is final and binding and can be confirmed in court on motion.

Situations Suitable for Arbitration

Almost any dispute over the value of a business or a partial interest in one can lend itself to resolution by arbitration instead of trial. If the parties in divorce and corporate or partnership dissolutions decide ahead of time to resolve any valuation issues by arbitration, they may never reach the point of dispute. The following have been the major categories in the authors' experience:

1. Corporate and partnership dissolutions—buyouts of minority interests.
2. Dissenting stockholder actions.
3. Damage cases.
4. Divorces.

Corporate and Partnership Dissolutions—Buyouts of Minority Interests

Like marriages, many business ownership relationships that appeared to be made in heaven end up with an agreement to disagree. Often the best solution is to sever the ownership relationship, preferably sooner rather than later.

Arbitrating the valuation issue usually is a far lesser distraction of management's focus on running the business than is going to court. Arbitration in this common situation also has all the other advantages listed above. Often especially relevant is the issue of fairness of the outcome, avoiding the tendency of judges and juries to become biased by the "good guy, bad buy" epithets that often characterize such court proceedings. Besides the issue of fairness, the arbitration process generally results in a far less rancorous parting of the ways than a court trial.

Arbitration also works well in those few states where a corporate or partnership dissolution occurs pursuant to a state corporate dissolution statute, such as California[2] and Rhode Island.[3]

Dissenting Stockholder Actions

A merger, sale, or other major corporate action can give rise to dissenting stockholders' appraisal rights under the statutes of all states except West Virginia. The expediency and lower cost make arbitration an attractive alternative to a trial for determination of the value under appraisal rights in such cases, especially smaller ones for which prolonged and expensive court proceedings can result in a no-win situation for everyone.

---

[2]Cal. Corp. Code §§1300 and 2000.
[3]R. I. Bus. Corp. Code §7-1.1-90.1.

Damage Cases

Damage cases, in which the valuation of a business or practice often is the central issue in determining the amount of relief, include the following:

1. Breach of contract.
2. Condemnation.
3. Antitrust.
4. Lost profits.
5. Lost business opportunity.
6. Amount of casualty insurance proceeds or allocation of proceeds among parties at interest.
7. Infringement of intellectual property.
8. Business torts.
9. Violation of securities laws.

We have observed that the risk of the court reaching an outlandish determination of value is greater in damage cases—especially those involving breach of contract and antitrust—than in any other major category of disputed valuation cases. One reason for such extreme decisions is that some juries or courts allow their view that there should be liability for damages to affect their objectivity about the valuation issue; similarly, they may be swayed by some sentiment toward the parties involved. This risk can be significantly reduced through the use of an arbitration process using qualified appraisers as arbitrators.

Plaintiffs may resist arbitration by qualified appraisers in favor of "rolling the dice" for a high award based on a jury's indignation over the defendants' egregious actions. However, witnesses testifying to extreme amounts may lack credibility (especially if faced with a strong rebuttal witness), and judges often have authority to vacate or substantially reduce jury awards. Furthermore, the costs of court trials often exceed the depths of plaintiffs' pockets when faced with unlimited resources of some defendants.

Divorces

Of all situations involving disputed valuations of businesses or professional practices, those arising from divorces often are the most difficult for the parties to resolve by amicable negotiation. Although marital dissolution matters may be a small part of a typical valuation practice, they account for a large proportion of the occasions on which appraisers prepare for, and appear on, the witness stand in court to present expert testimony.

Disputed valuation issues can become a major element in the already intense emotional strain accompanying divorce proceedings. Frequently, the valuation for the property settlement is the major, if not the only, disputed issue. Besides the time and cost advantages, arbitration spares the parties the tension and added antagonism of fighting it out in court.

We believe that the trend toward settling business valuation issues by arbitrating in marital property divisions will accelerate as more family law attorneys become familiar and comfortable with the arbitration process in this context.[4]

---

[4]For a very useful article on family law arbitration, see Allan R. Koritzinsky, Robert M. Welch Jr., and Stephen W. Schlissel, "The Benefits of Arbitration," *Family Advocate,* Spring 1992, pp. 45–47, 52.

The Arbitration Agreement

The arbitration agreement is critical because it is a document governing the arbitration that is binding on both the parties and the arbitrators. The arbitration agreement usually originates in one of the following ways:

1. An arbitration clause is included as part of a corporate document or contract among the parties, such as a buy–sell agreement. When such an agreement is triggered, it generally is desirable for the attorneys to draw up and for the parties to execute a supplemental agreement addressing details discussed below that may not have been covered in the general arbitration clause.
2. An arbitration agreement is created specifically for the situation at hand, sometimes with direction or assistance from a court.

In any case, the authors highly recommend that an appraiser experienced in arbitration be engaged to assist in the drafting of the arbitration clause or agreement.

The arbitration document must be clear, complete, and unambiguous. We have seen incredible amounts of unnecessary frustration and wasted time and energy expended as a result of parties' and arbitrators' disagreements as to the interpretation of the arbitration agreement.

We also highly recommend that all parties to the arbitration agreement read and understand it before they agree to become bound by it. For example, many buy–sell agreements specify the standard of value as the fair market value of the shares. Minority stockholders often are shocked when they learn they have been forced to sell under this clause at a price considerably lower than a pro rata portion of the enterprise as a whole.

Factors Specified in the Arbitration Agreement

Factors that should be mandated by the agreement include the following:

1. Procedure for selection of arbitrators.
2. Definition of the property to be appraised.
3. Date as of which the property is to be valued.
4. Standard of value to be used (as discussed in Chapter 2 and elsewhere in the book).
5. What constitutes a conclusion by the arbitrators, such as:
    a. Agreement by at least two out of three.
    b. Average of the two closest to each other.
    c. Conclusion of the third (neutral) arbitrator, such as in a "special master" situation.
6. Format and procedure for the arbitrators' rendering of their conclusion.
7. Terms of payment of the amount determined by the arbitrators, including interest, if any.
8. Time schedule for the various steps in the arbitration process, at least the selection of arbitrators and some outside time limit for the total process.

Failure to specify any of the above factors may leave the door open for costly and extensive legal battles.

The agreement may specify a reporting deadline, or a schedule may be worked out in conjunction with engaging the arbitrators. In our experience, reporting deadlines written into arbitration agreements often are too optimistic to allow for the time necessary to work out legal details, collection and transmission of all the information necessary for the arbitrators, and accommodation of the schedules of the arbitrators, attorneys, parties, and witnesses.

Factors Left to the Arbitrators' Discretion

Factors that can, and in most cases should, be left to the discretion of the arbitrators include the following:

1. Whether or not each arbitrator is expected or required to make a complete, independent appraisal, or the extent to which each arbitrator considers it necessary to do independent work, as opposed to relying on certain data or analyses furnished by other arbitrators and/or appraisers.
2. The obligation of the arbitrators to communicate with each other (writing, telephone calls, personal meetings), and the rules for sharing information.
3. Scheduling of the arbitrators' work and meetings, within the constraint of the agreed on reporting schedule.
4. The valuation approaches and criteria to be considered, within the constraints of any legally mandated criteria.
5. The facts, documents, and other data on which to rely (although the principals may agree to stipulate certain facts or assumptions, which could make the arbitrators' job easier with respect to some matters of possible factual uncertainty).

Other Factors to Address

Generally, the arbitration agreement may specify rules on various matters or, in the absence of specific rules, should contain some broad language giving the arbitrators authority to make rules on points not addressed in the agreement. An example would be rules regarding contacts between parties and the arbitrators. Often participants in arbitrations are given no rules as to whether ex parte contact is permitted, and arbitration statutes provide little or no guidance.

Another topic often not addressed is rules specifying whether the arbitrators are free to obtain property-specific information independent of that provided by the parties, or should they rely solely on information presented to them by the parties and their witnesses and made part of the arbitration record.

Selection of Arbitrators

Two factors need to be delineated regarding the selection of arbitrators: the criteria and the procedure for selection.

Criteria for Selection

The arbitration process produces the most equitable results for all parties if all the arbitrators (or the arbitrator) are experienced, qualified, professional appraisers of businesses, professional practices, intangible property, or whatever the subject property may be. If there are three arbitrators, it is most desirable that all three should be full-time professional appraisers, but two out of three are far better than only one or none at all.

In some cases, if the business or profession is highly specialized, it may be desirable to seek as arbitrators one or more appraisers who have experience in appraising the specific line of business or professional practice. It is generally *not* desirable to gain the desired industry expertise by using as an arbitrator someone who is an active or retired participant in the industry or profession involved, or who has done ancillary functions such as accounting or economic analysis work in the industry or profession, but who is not experienced in matters related directly to valuation. Many of these people lack the requisite training to deal professionally with the specific issue of valuation, and there is also the risk that such people's biases toward the industry or profession could prevent objective valuation. The expertise of industry experts can be gained through informal discussion with the arbitrator(s) or by formal testimony presented to the arbitrator(s). This is preferable to having them act as arbitrators themselves.

We have observed sound valuation conclusions reached by arbitration panels composed of industry people knowledgeable in finance, along with attorneys knowledgeable in both the industry and valuation matters. However, in these instances, costs were incurred not only for the three arbitrators, but also for expert testimony to be presented to the arbitration panel by at least two appraisers (one or more retained by each party) in each case. We have also seen nonprofessional panels reach conclusions that we do not believe a consensus of responsible professional appraisers would consider to be supportable within a reasonable range of value.

Obviously, one criterion for selection is the availability of the desired arbitrator(s) so that the arbitration can take place reasonably promptly.

Procedure for Selection

The most typical procedure is that each party selects one arbitrator and the two arbitrators select the third. It is preferable for the two arbitrators appointed by the parties to have complete authority to select the third, rather than having the selection of the third arbitrator subject to the approval of the principals. This avoids delays and dealing with pressures arising from the principals' biases, which are almost sure to be injected.

It is important that there be an alternative procedure for the selection of a third arbitrator in case of a deadlock. Plan this contingency procedure in advance or in conjunction with entering into the arbitration agreement. There should be a deadline, at which time the alternate selection process takes effect if the first two arbitrators have failed to reach agreement on a third arbitrator. In case of a deadlock, the procedure should call for the appointment of the third arbitrator, who is a qualified appraiser, by some predetermined entity, such as the American Society of Appraisers, the American Arbitration Association, a court, or some designated official in the industry or profession. This procedure will almost assure that at least two of the three arbitrators will be professional appraisers, if one side has already chosen one. If one side insists that the third arbitrator be a qualified professional appraiser and presents a list of appraisers who are independent of the principals involved, it is not likely that anyone charged with making such an appointment would select someone not so qualified over someone who is qualified.[5]

---

[5]A list of American Society of Appraisers accredited senior appraisers who are certified in business valuation may be obtained from the American Society of Appraisers, P.O. Box 17265, Washington, DC 20041, (800) ASA-VALU.

Another possibility is to establish the procedure so the two arbitrators attempt to reach agreement, bringing in the third arbitrator only if they are unable to do so. In that case, we recommend, based on our experiences, that the prospective third arbitrator be agreed on between the first two at the outset, before they get involved in other aspects of interaction with each other in the arbitration process.

American Arbitration Association Procedure

The American Arbitration Association (AAA) procedure for appointing arbitrators is different from that described in the foregoing section. When parties agree to submit a disputed matter to arbitration through the AAA, the association sends the parties a list of suggested arbitrators from the association's panel of arbitrators. Each party may veto nominees and indicate its preferences, but the final decision is made by the AAA.

In many AAA arbitrations, each party will retain its own expert appraiser who will present testimony before the arbitration panel, rather than having the expert actually participate as an arbitrator. In this sense, the preparation and presentation of expert testimony is similar to a court trial, although it is slightly less formal.

Engagement and Compensation of Arbitrators

Once the arbitrators have been appointed, the engagement should be committed to writing. The description of the engagement may take the form of a standard professional services agreement initiated by an appraiser serving as arbitrator, an engagement letter drafted by one of the attorneys or parties, or both. All aspects of the engagement should be adequately covered. Sometimes, addendums to the initial engagement document(s) may be necessary, since decisions on some items, such as schedules and some expenses, may be made or changed as the engagement progresses.

The engagement document(s) should include by reference the statute and/or document(s) giving rise to the arbitration (e.g., a buy–sell agreement) and should cover compensation of the arbitrator and all necessary instructions not addressed or not made clear in the arbitration document(s).

All documents relating to the engagement of an arbitrator should be signed by the arbitrator and whoever is responsible for compensating him or her. The most common compensation arrangement is that each party assumes responsibility for the compensation and expenses of the arbitrator it has nominated or appointed, with the parties equally sharing the compensation and expenses of the third arbitrator. Such arrangements vary, however, from case to case.

The amount of compensation is usually based on each arbitrator's normal professional hourly or daily billing rate (or some mutually agreed on rate) plus out-of-pocket expenses. It is much less common for an arbitrator's compensation to be based on a fixed fee, because it is very difficult to estimate in advance how much time the total appraisal and arbitration process will require. However, it is reasonable to expect to discuss some estimate of probable fees and the daily rate or other basis for the fees. Under the procedures of the American Arbitration

Association, these arrangements are carried out by a representative of that organization. If they are to be directed to appoint qualified business appraisers, they should also be directed to expect to pay the fees normally charged by such qualified appraisers.

The Arbitration Process

One of the major variables in the arbitration process is the extent to which each arbitrator is expected or required to carry out independent appraisal work. Some arbitration documents specify that each expert on the arbitration panel do a complete, independent appraisal. At the other extreme, some arbitration documents specify that the arbitrator(s) rely entirely on evidence presented by the parties or their witnesses. More commonly, however (and we think preferably in most cases), the extent of independent appraisal work to be done is left to the judgment of each individual arbitrator, or to the arbitration panel as a group. This subject should be discussed with the parties or their representatives before the arbitration commences. It would be useful to have this addressed in the arbitrators' engagement letter, preferably allowing them considerable discretion.

Review of Arbitration Document

Each arbitrator should begin with a careful review of the statute and/or document(s) giving rise to the arbitration. If there is any confusion or disagreement about any details of the assignment, such as the exact definition of the property, the effective date of the valuation, or the applicable standard of value, the arbitrators should seek clarification immediately. This should be done in writing to avoid any possible disputes later.

Initial Communication among Arbitrators

We recommend that the arbitrators establish communication among themselves at the earliest possible time after their appointment. A face-to-face meeting is ideal if geographic proximity to each other makes that feasible, but a conference call or a series of conference calls is usually sufficient, perhaps supplemented by correspondence. While each case is unique, the following is a generalized list of points to try to establish early:

1. Status of work already accomplished, if any (who has performed what work up to that point).
2. An agreement as to sharing of information. (Our preference is to agree that all information gathered or developed by one arbitrator will be shared with the other arbitrators as quickly as possible.)
3. An agreement, if possible, as to the relevant valuation approaches to consider. (Where this becomes an issue, it seems fair to allow the parties' representatives to be heard as to their preferences. However, in our experience, this often results in highly biased supplications by parties' representatives who have no technical knowledge of relevant valuation approaches.)

4. A list of documents and data needed, and assignment of responsibility for obtaining each and seeing that the necessary distribution to other arbitrators is made. (It should be agreed up front that any such documents in the possession of the parties will be provided as evidence to the arbitrators promptly and completely.)

5. Any other possible division of the research effort, such as searches for guideline transactions, development of economic and/or industry data, and routine financial statement analysis (spread sheets, ratio analysis, comparison with industry averages, and so on). Division of research effort, of course, must depend on each arbitrator's willingness to accept certain efforts of another, which must be based on a judgment of professional ability and unbiased presentation of data and analysis.

6. Scheduling.

Field Visit

In most cases, arbitrators will want to visit the operating premises and interview relevant principals and/or management. It works out best if the arbitrators can conduct this field trip together, if possible. Together, the arbitrators will see the same things at the same time, and all can benefit from hearing each other's questions and answers firsthand. A joint field trip also gives the arbitrators an opportunity to address any items not fully covered in their previous communications. Also, this gives arbitrators who did not know each other previously an opportunity to get to know each other and form a basis for working together.

Hearings

The arbitrators should offer each party the opportunity to present oral and written information and opinions if they so desire. It is frequently convenient to hold a meeting to accommodate such input in conjunction with the field trip.

The Valuation Meeting

Usually, the arbitrators will meet in person to reach the valuation conclusion. In some instances, this meeting may be replaced by a conference call. In either case, all should be as prepared as possible, having exchanged and assimilated as much information as possible before the meeting.

In the meeting, it is usually most productive to come to agreements issue by issue, identifying and keeping track of each point of agreement and disagreement. Good notes should be kept so it is clear exactly what points have been agreed on, and what the respective positions are on points that have been addressed but on which agreement has not been reached. Each arbitrator should be receptive to the others' information and viewpoints and attempt to reach compromises on points where reasonable judgments may differ.

It is most desirable to come to a conclusion that can be endorsed as fair by all members of the arbitration panel. This agreement can usually be achieved if all the arbitrators are qualified professional business appraisers. If unanimous agreement cannot be reached, the arbitrator in the minority position may render a dissenting opinion for the record if he or she so desires.

Reporting the Results of the Arbitration

The formal report of the valuation conclusion reached by the arbitrators is usually contained in a very brief letter that does no more than reference the arbitration agreement, state that the arbitrators have completed their assignment in accordance with the agreement, and state the conclusion reached. The letter is signed by the arbitrators concurring in the conclusion. In the parlance of arbitration, this is called an *award*. In some cases, the letter must be notarized as well as signed.

In a significant proportion of cases, the principals on both sides would like to have a brief report explaining how the valuation conclusion was reached. In arbitration parlance, this is called an *opinion*. In such situations, we suggest that such an advisory report be the sole responsibility of the third appraiser. To make such a report a joint task of two or more arbitrators, each of whom probably judged various factors a little bit differently—though they were able to agree on a conclusion—would usually be an unnecessarily complicated and costly exercise.

If the valuation conclusion is reached unilaterally by a special master, normally he or she would be the only one to sign the report. An explanation of the procedures and criteria used is usually included.

Summary: The Most Critical Elements

The two most critical elements for an expeditious and successful arbitration are:

1. *A definitive and unambiguous arbitration agreement that provides the arbitrators with unambiguous instructions on the key matters listed above and that all parties understand.*
2. *The appointment of independent arbitrators with a high degree of relevant valuation expertise who will be both fair and competent in reaching a conclusion about the value of the subject property.*

If these two elements are properly addressed, the arbitration process can be a very efficient and fair way of resolving business or professional practice valuation matters.

Bibliography

Block, Jerome N. "The Process of Arbitration." *The Appraisal Journal,* April 1993, pp. 234–38.

Carper, Donald L. "Remedies in Business Arbitration." *Arbitration Journal,* September 1991, pp. 49–58.

Koritzinsky, Allan R.; Robert M. Welch, Jr.; and Stephen W. Schlissel. "The Benefits of Arbitration." *Family Advocate,* Spring 1992, pp. 45–52.

Nicolaisen, Donald T., and Albert A. Vondra. "How Arbitration Can Reduce the Cost of Disputes." *CPA Journal,* September 1991, p. 10.

Pearson, Claude M. "Using Streamlined Arbitration to Resolve Valuation Disputes for an Accounting Partnership." *Practical Accountant,* September 1987, pp. 116–17.

Appendix A

Index to IRS Positions

Revenue Rulings contain a lot of useful valuation guidance, but it often is time consuming to find a reference or references regarding a certain point. This index covers the following Revenue Rulings:

59-60   Valuing closely held stock.

65-192   Extends 59-60 to all types of business interests and to income taxes as well as gift and estate taxes.

68-609   "Formula method" (excess earnings).

77-287   Use of restricted stock studies in quantifying discount for lack of marketability.

83-120   Valuing preferred stock.

93-12   Allows minority discounts when valuing minority interests of family members in family-controlled businesses.

The index also covers the *IRS Course Book on Valuation Training for Appeals Officers* (referred to in index as VT). The first number following VT is the lesson number. The second number or numbers refer to the page within that lesson.

Appendix B

Present Value Tables

Table 1

Present Value of One Dollar Due at the End of n Periods

$$PV = \frac{\$1}{(1+r)^n}$$

PV = present value; r = discount rate; n = number of periods until payment.

n	1%	2%	3%	4%	5%	6%	7%	8%	9%	10%	n
1	.99010	.98039	.97007	.96154	.95238	.94340	.93458	.92593	.91743	.90909	1
2	.98030	.96117	.94260	.92456	.90703	.89000	.87344	.85734	.84168	.82645	2
3	.97059	.94232	.91514	.88900	.86384	.83962	.81630	.79383	.77218	.75131	3
4	.96098	.92385	.88849	.85480	.82270	.79209	.76290	.73503	.70843	.68301	4
5	.95147	.90573	.86261	.82193	.78353	.74726	.71299	.68058	.64993	.62092	5
6	.94204	.88797	.83748	.79031	.74622	.70496	.66634	.63017	.59627	.56447	6
7	.93272	.87056	.81309	.75992	.71068	.66506	.62275	.58349	.54703	.51316	7
8	.92348	.85349	.78941	.73069	.67684	.62741	.58201	.54027	.50187	.46651	8
9	.91434	.83675	.76642	.70259	.64461	.59190	.54393	.50025	.46043	.42410	9
10	.90529	.82035	.74409	.67556	.61391	.55839	.50835	.46319	.42241	.38554	10
11	.89632	.80426	.72242	.64958	.58468	.52679	.47509	.42888	.38753	.35049	11
12	.88745	.78849	.70138	.62460	.55684	.49697	.44401	.39711	.35553	.31863	12
13	.87866	.77303	.68095	.60057	.53032	.46884	.41496	.36770	.32618	.28966	13
14	.86996	.75787	.66112	.57747	.50507	.44930	.38782	.34046	.29925	.26333	14
15	.86135	.74301	.64186	.55526	.48102	.41726	.36245	.31524	.27454	.23939	15
16	.85282	.72845	.62317	.53391	.45811	.39365	.33873	.29189	.25187	.21763	16
17	.84438	.71416	.60502	.51337	.43630	.37136	.31657	.27027	.23107	.19784	17
18	.83602	.70016	.58739	.49363	.41552	.35034	.29586	.25025	.21199	.17986	18
19	.82774	.68643	.57029	.47464	.39573	.33051	.27651	.23171	.19449	.16351	19
20	.81954	.67297	.55367	.45639	.37689	.31180	.25842	.21455	.17843	.14864	20
21	.81143	.65978	.53755	.43883	.35894	.29415	.24151	.19866	.16370	.13513	21
22	.80340	.64684	.52189	.42195	.34185	.27750	.22571	.18394	.15018	.12285	22
23	.79544	.63414	.50669	.40573	.32557	.26180	.21095	.17031	.13778	.11168	23
24	.78757	.62172	.49193	.39012	.31007	.24698	.19715	.15770	.12640	.10153	24
25	.77977	.60953	.47760	.37512	.29530	.23300	.18425	.14602	.11597	.09230	25

Table 1 (continued)
Present Value of One Dollar Due at the End of *n* Periods

n	11%	12%	13%	14%	15%	16%	17%	18%	19%	20%
1	.90090	.89286	.88496	.87719	.86957	.86207	.85470	.84746	.84034	.83333
2	.81162	.79719	.78315	.76947	.75614	.74316	.73051	.71818	.70616	.69444
3	.73119	.71178	.69305	.67497	.65752	.64066	.62437	.60863	.59342	.57870
4	.65873	.63552	.61332	.59208	.57175	.55229	.53365	.51579	.49867	.48225
5	.59345	.56743	.54276	.51937	.49718	.47611	.45611	.43711	.41905	.40188
6	.53464	.50663	.48032	.45559	.43233	.41044	.38984	.37043	.35214	.33490
7	.48166	.45235	.42506	.39964	.37594	.35383	.33320	.31392	.29592	.27908
8	.43393	.40388	.37616	.35056	.32690	.30503	.28478	.26604	.24867	.23257
9	.39092	.36061	.33288	.30751	.28426	.26295	.24340	.22546	.20897	.19381
10	.35218	.32197	.29459	.26974	.24718	.22668	.20804	.19106	.17560	.16151
11	.31728	.28748	.26070	.23662	.21494	.19542	.17781	.16192	.14756	.13459
12	.28584	.25667	.23071	.20756	.18691	.16846	.15197	.13722	.12400	.11216
13	.25751	.22917	.20416	.18207	.16253	.14523	.12989	.11629	.10420	.09346
14	.23199	.20462	.18068	.15971	.14133	.12520	.11102	.09855	.08757	.07789
15	.20900	.18270	.15989	.14010	.12289	.10793	.09489	.08352	.07359	.06491
16	.18829	.16312	.14150	.12289	.10686	.09304	.08110	.07078	.06184	.05409
17	.16963	.14564	.12522	.10780	.09293	.08021	.06932	.05998	.05196	.04507
18	.15282	.13004	.11081	.09456	.08080	.06914	.05925	.05083	.04367	.03756
19	.13768	.11611	.09806	.08295	.07026	.05961	.05064	.04308	.03669	.03130
20	.12403	.10367	.08678	.07276	.06110	.05139	.04328	.03651	.03084	.02608
21	.11174	.09256	.07680	.06383	.05313	.04430	.03699	.03094	.02591	.02174
22	.10067	.08264	.06796	.05599	.04620	.03819	.03162	.02622	.02178	.01811
23	.09069	.07379	.06014	.04911	.04017	.03292	.02702	.02222	.01830	.01509
24	.08170	.06588	.05322	.04308	.03493	.02833	.02310	.01883	.01538	.01258
25	.07361	.05882	.04710	.03779	.03038	.02447	.01974	.01596	.01292	.01048

Table 1 (concluded)
Present Value of One Dollar Due at the End of *n* Periods

n	21%	22%	23%	24%	25%	26%	27%	28%	29%	30%	n
1	.82645	.81967	.81301	.80645	.80000	.79365	.78740	.78125	.77519	.76923	1
2	.68301	.67186	.66098	.65036	.64000	.62988	.62000	.61035	.60093	.59172	2
3	.56447	.55071	.53738	.52449	.51200	.49991	.48819	.47684	.46583	.45517	3
4	.46651	.45140	.43690	.42297	.40960	.39675	.38440	.37253	.36111	.35013	4
5	.38554	.37000	.35520	.34111	.32768	.31488	.30268	.29104	.27993	.26933	5
6	.31863	.30328	.28878	.27509	.26214	.24991	.23833	.22737	.21700	.20718	6
7	.26333	.24859	.23478	.22184	.20972	.19834	.18766	.17764	.16822	.15937	7
8	.21763	.20376	.19088	.17891	.16777	.15741	.14776	.13878	.13040	.12259	8
9	.17986	.16702	.15519	.14428	.13422	.12493	.11635	.10842	.10109	.09430	9
10	.14864	.13690	.12617	.11635	.10737	.09915	.09161	.08470	.07836	.07254	10
11	.12285	.11221	.10258	.09383	.08590	.07869	.07214	.06617	.06075	.05580	11
12	.10153	.09198	.08339	.07567	.06872	.06245	.05680	.05170	.04709	.04292	12
13	.08391	.07539	.06780	.06103	.05498	.04957	.04472	.04039	.03650	.03302	13
14	.06934	.06180	.05512	.04921	.04398	.03934	.03522	.03155	.02830	.02540	14
15	.05731	.05065	.04481	.03969	.03518	.03122	.02773	.02465	.02194	.01954	15
16	.04736	.04152	.03643	.03201	.02815	.02478	.02183	.01926	.01700	.01503	16
17	.03914	.03403	.02962	.02581	.02252	.01967	.01719	.01505	.01318	.01156	17
18	.03235	.02789	.02408	.02082	.01801	.01561	.01354	.01175	.01022	.00889	18
19	.02673	.02286	.01958	.01679	.01441	.01239	.01066	.00918	.00792	.00684	19
20	.02209	.01874	.01592	.01354	.01153	.00983	.00839	.00717	.00614	.00526	20
21	.01826	.01536	.01294	.01092	.00922	.00780	.00661	.00561	.00476	.00405	21
22	.01509	.01259	.01052	.00880	.00738	.00619	.00520	.00438	.00369	.00311	22
23	.01247	.01032	.00855	.00710	.00590	.00491	.00410	.00342	.00286	.00239	23
24	.01031	.00846	.00695	.00573	.00472	.00390	.00323	.00267	.00222	.00184	24
25	.00852	.00693	.00565	.00462	.00378	.00310	.00254	.00209	.00172	.00142	25

Table 2
Present Value of an Annuity of One Dollar for *n* Periods

$$PV = \frac{\$1}{r} - \frac{\$1}{r(1+r)^n}$$

PV = present value; *r* = discount rate; *n* = number of periods until payment.

n	1%	2%	3%	4%	5%	6%	7%	8%	9%	10%
1	.9901	.9804	.9709	.9615	.9524	.9434	.9346	.9259	.9174	.9091
2	1.9704	1.9416	1.9135	1.8861	1.8594	1.8334	1.8080	1.7833	1.7591	1.7355
3	2.9410	2.8839	2.8286	2.7751	2.7232	2.6730	2.6243	2.5771	2.5313	2.4868
4	3.9020	3.8077	3.7171	3.6299	3.5459	3.4651	3.3872	3.3121	3.2397	3.1699
5	4.8535	4.7134	4.5797	4.4518	4.3295	4.2123	4.1002	3.9927	3.8896	3.7908
6	5.7955	5.6014	5.4172	5.2421	5.0757	4.9173	4.7665	4.6229	4.4859	4.3553
7	6.7282	6.4720	6.2302	6.0020	5.7863	5.5824	5.3893	5.2064	5.0329	4.8684
8	7.6517	7.3254	7.0196	6.7327	6.4632	6.2098	5.9713	5.7466	5.5348	5.3349
9	8.5661	8.1622	7.7861	7.4353	7.1078	6.8017	6.5152	6.2469	5.9852	5.7590
10	9.4714	8.9825	8.5302	8.1109	7.7217	7.3601	7.0236	6.7101	6.4176	6.1446
11	10.3677	9.7868	9.2526	8.7604	8.3064	7.8868	7.4987	7.1389	6.8052	6.4951
12	11.2552	10.5753	9.9539	9.3850	8.8632	8.3838	7.9427	7.5361	7.1607	6.8137
13	12.1338	11.3483	10.6349	9.9856	9.3935	8.8527	8.3576	7.9038	7.4869	7.1034
14	13.0038	12.1062	11.2960	10.5631	9.8986	9.2950	8.7454	8.2442	7.7861	7.3667
15	13.8651	12.8492	11.9379	11.1183	10.3796	9.7122	9.1079	8.5595	8.0607	7.6061
16	14.7180	13.5777	12.5610	11.6522	10.8377	10.1059	9.4466	8.8514	8.3125	7.8237
17	15.5624	14.2918	13.1660	12.1656	11.2740	10.4772	9.7632	9.1216	8.5436	8.0215
18	16.3984	14.9920	13.7534	12.6592	11.6895	10.8276	10.0591	9.3719	8.7556	8.2014
19	17.2261	15.6784	14.3237	13.1339	12.0853	11.1581	10.3356	9.6036	8.9501	8.3649
20	18.0457	16.3514	14.8774	13.5903	12.4622	11.4699	10.5940	9.8181	9.1285	8.5136
21	18.8571	17.0111	15.4149	14.0291	12.8211	11.7640	10.8355	10.0168	9.2922	8.6487
22	19.6605	17.6580	15.9368	14.4511	13.1630	12.0416	11.0612	10.2007	9.4424	8.7715
23	20.4559	18.2921	16.4435	14.8568	13.4885	12.3033	11.2722	10.3710	9.5302	8.8832
24	21.2435	18.9139	16.9355	15.2469	13.7986	12.5503	11.4693	10.5287	9.7066	8.9847
25	22.0233	19.5234	17.4131	15.6220	14.0939	12.7833	11.6536	10.6748	9.8226	9.0770

Table 2 (continued)
Present Value of an Annuity of One Dollar for *n* Periods

n	11%	12%	13%	14%	15%	16%	17%	18%	19%	20%
1	.9009	.8929	.8850	.3772	.8696	.8621	.8547	.8475	.8403	.8333
2	1.7125	1.6901	1.6681	1.6467	1.6257	1.6052	1.5852	1.5656	1.5465	1.5278
3	2.4437	2.4018	2.3612	2.3216	2.2832	2.2459	2.2096	2.1743	2.1399	2.1065
4	3.1024	3.0373	2.9745	2.9137	2.8550	2.7982	2.7432	2.6901	2.6386	2.5887
5	3.6959	3.6048	3.5172	3.4331	3.3522	3.2743	3.1993	3.1272	3.0576	2.9906
6	4.2305	4.1114	3.9976	3.8887	3.7845	3.6847	3.5892	3.4976	3.4098	3.3255
7	4.7122	3.5638	4.4226	4.2883	4.1604	4.0386	3.9224	3.8115	3.7057	3.6046
8	5.1461	4.9676	4.7988	4.6389	4.4873	4.3436	4.2072	4.0776	3.9544	3.8372
9	5.5370	5.3282	5.1317	4.9464	4.7716	4.6065	4.4506	4.3030	4.1633	4.0310
10	5.8892	5.6502	5.4262	5.2161	5.0188	4.8332	4.6586	4.4941	4.3389	4.1925
11	6.2065	5.9377	5.6869	5.4527	5.2337	5.0286	4.8364	4.6560	4.4865	4.3271
12	6.4924	6.1944	5.9176	5 6603	5.4206	5.1971	4.9884	4.7932	4.6105	4.4392
13	6.7499	6.4235	6.1218	5.8424	5.5831	5.3423	5.1183	4.9095	4.7147	4.5327
14	6.9819	6.6282	6.3025	6.0021	5.7245	5.4675	5.2293	5.0081	4.8023	4.6106
15	7.1909	6.8109	6.4624	6.1422	5.8474	5.5755	5.3242	5.0916	4.8759	4.6755
16	7.3792	6.9740	6.6039	6.2651	5.9542	5.6685	5.4053	5.1624	4.9377	4.7296
17	7.5488	7.1196	6.7291	6.3729	6.0472	5.7487	5.4746	5.2223	4.9897	4.7746
18	7.7016	7.2497	6.8399	6.4674	6.1280	5.8178	5.5339	5.2732	5.0333	4.8122
19	7.8393	7.3658	6.9380	6.5504	6.1982	5.8775	5.5845	5.3162	5.0700	4.8435
20	7.9633	7.4694	7.0248	6.6231	6.2593	5.9288	5.6278	5.3527	5.1009	4.8696
21	8.0751	7.5620	7.1016	6.6870	6.3125	5.9731	5.6648	5.3837	5.1268	4.8913
22	8.1757	7.6446	7.1695	6.7429	6.3587	6.0113	5.6964	5.4099	5.1486	4.9094
23	8.2664	7.7184	7.2297	6.7921	6.3988	6.0442	5.7234	5.4321	5.1668	4.9245
24	8.3481	7.7843	7.2829	6.8351	6.4338	6.0726	5.7465	5.4509	5.1822	4.9371
25	8.4217	7.8431	7.3300	6.8729	6.4641	6.0971	5.7662	5.4669	5.1951	4.9476

Table 2 (concluded)
Present Value of an Annuity of One Dollar for n Periods

n	21%	22%	23%	24%	25%	26%	27%	28%	29%	30%
1	.8264	.8197	.8130	.8065	.8000	.7937	.7874	.7813	.7752	.7692
2	1.5095	1.4915	1.4740	1.4568	1.4400	1.4235	1.4074	1.3916	1.3761	1.3609
3	2.0739	2.0422	2.0114	1.9813	1.9520	1.9234	1.8956	1.8684	1.8420	1.8161
4	2.5404	2.4936	2.4483	2.4043	2.3616	2.3202	2.2800	2.2410	2.2031	2.1662
5	2.9260	2.8636	2.8035	2.7454	2.6893	2.6351	2.5827	2.5320	2.4830	2.4356
6	3.2446	3.1669	3.0923	3.0205	2.9514	2.8850	2.8210	2.7594	2.7000	2.6427
7	3.5079	3.4155	3.3270	3.2423	3.1611	3.0833	3.0087	2.9370	2.8682	2.8021
8	3.7256	3.6193	3.5179	3.4212	3.3289	3.2407	3.1564	3.0758	2.9986	2.9247
9	3.9054	3.7863	3.6731	3.5655	3.4631	3.3657	3.2728	3.1842	3.0997	3.0190
10	4.0541	3.9232	3.7993	3.6819	3.5705	3.4648	3.3644	3.2689	3.1781	3.0915
11	4.1769	4.0354	3.9018	3.7757	3.6564	3.5435	3.4365	3.3351	3.2388	3.1473
12	4.2785	4.1274	3.9852	3.8514	3.7251	3.6060	3.4933	3.3868	3.2859	3.1903
13	4.3624	4.2028	4.0530	3.9124	3.7801	3.6555	3.5381	3.4272	3.3224	3.2233
14	4.4317	4.2646	4.1082	3.9616	3.8241	3.6949	3.5133	3.4587	3.3507	3.2487
15	4.4890	4.3152	4.1530	4.0013	3.8593	3.7261	3.6010	3.4834	3.3726	3.2682
16	4.5364	4.3567	4.1894	4.0333	3.8874	3.7509	3.6228	3.5026	3.3896	3.2832
17	4.5755	4.3908	4.2190	4.0591	3.9099	3.7705	3.6400	3.5177	3.4028	3.2948
18	4.6079	4.4187	4.2431	4.0799	3.9279	3.7861	3.6536	3.5294	3.4130	3.3037
19	4.6346	4.4415	4.2627	4.0967	3.9424	3.7985	3.6642	3.5386	3.4210	3.3105
20	4.6567	4.4603	4.2786	4.1103	3.9539	3.8083	3.6726	3.5458	3.4271	3.3158
21	4.6750	4.4756	4.2916	4.1212	3.9631	3.8161	3.6792	3.5514	3.4319	3.3198
22	4.6900	4.4882	4.3021	4.1300	3.9705	3.8223	3.6844	3.5558	3.4356	3.3230
23	4.7025	4.4985	4.3106	4.1371	3.9764	3.8273	3.6885	3.5592	3.4384	3.3254
24	4.7128	4.5070	4.3176	4.1428	3.9811	3.8312	3.6918	3.5619	3.4406	3.3272
25	4.7213	4.5139	4.3232	4.1474	3.9849	3.8342	3.6943	3.5640	3.4423	3.3286

Appendix C

American Society of Appraisers: Business Valuation Standards*

This release of the approved Business Valuation Standards of the American Society of Appraisers contains all standards approved through January 23, 1994, and is to be used in conjunction with the Uniform Standards of Professional Appraisal Practice (USPAP) of The Appraisal Foundation and the Principles of Appraisal Practice and Code of Ethics of the American Society of Appraisers.

It contains the following sections, with the effective approval date of each:

Preamble (September 1992, Revised January 1994)
Business Valuation Standards
Definitions (January 1989, Revised September 1992, Revised June 1993, Revised January 1994)
Statements on Business Valuation Standards
Procedural Guidelines and/or Advisory Opinions
To be issued when appropriate

Preamble

Approved by the ASA Board of Governors, September 1992

I.   To enhance and maintain the quality of business valuations for the benefit of the business valuation profession and users of business valuations, the American Society of Appraisers, through its Business Valuation Committee, has adopted these standards.

II. The American Society of Appraisers (in its Principles of Appraisal Practice and Code of Ethics) and The Appraisal Foundation (in its Uniform Standards of Professional Appraisal Practice) have established authoritative principles and a code of professional ethics. These standards include these requirements, either explicitly or by reference, and are designed to clarify and provide additional requirements specifically applicable to the valuation of businesses, business ownership interests or securities.

III. These standards incorporate, where appropriate, all relevant business valuation standards adopted by the American Society of Appraisers through its Business Valuation Committee.

IV. These standards provide minimum criteria to be followed by business appraisers in the valuation of businesses, business ownership interests or securities.

V.   If, in the opinion of the appraiser, circumstances of a specific business valuation assignment dictate a departure from any provisions of any Standard, such departure must be disclosed and will apply only to the specific departure.

VI. These Standards are designed to provide guidance to ASA Appraisers conducting business valuations and to provide a structure for regulating conduct of members of the ASA through Uniform Practices and Procedures. Deviations from the Standards are not designed or intended to be the basis of any civil liability; and should not create any presumption or evidence that a legal duty has been breached; or create any special relationship between the appraiser and any other person.

BVS-I: General Requirements For Developing A Business Valuation

I.   **Preamble**
     A. This standard is required to be followed in all valuations of businesses, business ownership interests, and securities by all members of the American Society of Appraisers, be they Candidates, Accredited Members (AM), Accredited Senior Appraisers (ASA), or Fellows (FASA).
     B. The purpose of this standard is to define and describe the general requirements for developing the valuation of businesses, business ownership interests, or securities.

C. This standard incorporates the general preamble to the Business Valuation Standards of the American Society of Appraisers.

II. **The Valuation Assignment shall be Appropriately Defined**

A. In developing a business valuation, an appraiser must identify and define the following:

1. The business, business ownership interest, or security to be valued
2. The effective date of the appraisal
3. The standard of value
4. The purpose and use of the valuation

B. The nature and scope of the assignment must be defined. Acceptable scopes of work would generally be of three types as delineated below. Other scopes of work should be explained and described.

1. Appraisal

   a. The objective of an appraisal is to express an unambiguous opinion as to the value of the business, business ownership interest, or security, which is supported by all procedures that the appraiser deems to be relevant to the valuation.

   b. An appraisal has the following qualities:

      (1) It is expressed as a single dollar amount or as a range.

      (2) It considers all relevant information as of the appraisal date available to the appraiser at the time of performance of the valuation.

      (3) The appraiser conducts appropriate procedures to collect and analyze all information expected to be relevant to the valuation.

      (4) The valuation is based upon consideration of all conceptual approaches deemed to be relevant by the appraiser.

2. Limited Appraisal

   a. The objective of a limited appraisal is to express an estimate as to the value of a business, business ownership interest, or security, which lacks the performance of additional procedures that are required in an appraisal.

   b. A limited appraisal has the following qualities:

      (1) It is expressed as a single dollar amount or as a range.

      (2) It is based upon consideration of limited relevant information.

      (3) The appraiser conducts only limited procedures to collect and analyze the information which such appraiser considers necessary to support the conclusion presented.

      (4) The valuation is based upon the conceptual approach(es) deemed by the appraiser to be most appropriate.

3. Calculations

   a. The objective of calculations is to provide an approximate indication of value based upon the performance of limited procedures agreed upon by the appraiser and the client.

   b. Calculations have the following qualities:

      (1) They may be expressed as a single dollar amount or as a range.

      (2) They may be based upon consideration of only limited relevant information.

       (3) The appraiser performs limited information collection and analysis procedures.

       (4) The calculations may be based upon conceptual approaches as agreed upon with the client.

III. Information Collection and Analysis

The appraiser shall gather, analyze, and adjust relevant information to perform the valuation as appropriate to the scope of work. Such information shall include the following:

A. Characteristics of the business, business ownership interest or security to be valued including rights, privileges and conditions, quantity, factors affecting control and agreements restricting sale or transfer.

B. Nature, history and outlook of the business.

C. Historical financial information for the business.

D. Assets and liabilities of the business.

E. Nature and conditions of the relevant industries which have an impact on the business.

F. Economic factors affecting the business.

G. Capital markets providing relevant information, e.g., available rates of return on alternative investments, relevant public stock transactions, and relevant mergers and acquisitions.

H. Prior transactions involving subject business, interest in the subject business, or its securities.

I. Other information deemed by the appraiser to be relevant.

IV. Approaches, Methods, and Procedures

A. The appraiser shall select and apply appropriate valuation approaches, methods, and procedures.

B. The appraiser shall develop a conclusion of value pursuant to the valuation assignment as defined, considering the relevant valuation approaches, methods, and procedures, and appropriate premiums and discounts, if any.

V. Documentation and Retention.

The appraiser shall appropriately document and retain all information and work product that were relied on in reaching the conclusion.

VI. Reporting

The appraiser shall report to the client the conclusion of value in an appropriate written or oral format. The report must meet the requirements of Standard 10 of The Uniform Standards of Professional Appraisal Practice. In the event the assignment results in a comprehensive written report, the report shall meet the requirements of BVS-VII.

BVS-II   Financial Statement Adjustments

I.   Preamble

A. This standard is required to be followed in all valuations of businesses, business ownership interests, and securities by all members of the American Society of Appraisers, be they Candidates, Accredited Members (AM), Accredited Senior Appraisers (ASA), or Fellows (FASA).

B. The purpose of this standard is to define and describe the requirements for making financial statement adjustments in valuation of businesses, business ownership interests, and securities.

C. This present standard is applicable to appraisals and may not necessarily be applicable to limited appraisals and calculations as defined in BVS-I, Section II.B.

D. This standard incorporates the general preamble to the Business Valuation Standards of the American Society of Appraisers.

II. **Conceptual Framework**

A. Financial statements should be analyzed and, if appropriate, adjusted as a procedure in the valuation process. Financial statements to be analyzed include those of the subject entity and any entities used as guideline companies.

B. Financial statement adjustments are modifications to reported financial information that are relevant and significant to the appraisal process. Adjustments may be necessary in order to make the financial statements more meaningful for the appraisal process. Adjustments may be appropriate for the following reasons, among others: (1) To present financial data of the subject and guideline companies on a consistent basis; (2) To adjust from reported values to current values; (3) To adjust revenues and expenses to levels which are reasonably representative of continuing results; and (4) To adjust for non-operating assets and liabilities and the related revenue and expenses.

C. Financial statement adjustments are made for the purpose of assisting the appraiser in reaching a valuation conclusion and for no other purpose.

III. **Documentation of Adjustments**

Adjustments made should be fully described and supported.

BVS-III   Asset Based Approach to Business Valuation

I. **Preamble**

A. This standard is required to be followed in all valuations of businesses, business ownership interests, and securities by all members of the American Society of Appraisers, be they Candidates, Accredited Members (AM), Accredited Senior Appraisers (ASA), or Fellows (FASA).

B. The purpose of this standard is to define and describe the requirements for the use of the Asset Based Approach to business valuation and the circumstances in which it is appropriate.

C. This present standard is applicable to appraisals and may not necessarily be applicable to limited appraisals and calculations as defined in BVS-I, Section II.B.

D. This standard incorporates the general preamble to the Business Valuation Standards of the American Society of Appraisers.

II. **The Asset Based Approach**

A. In business valuation the Asset Based Approach may be analogous to the Cost Approach of other disciplines.

B. Assets, liabilities and equity relate to a business that is an operating company, a holding company, or a combination thereof (mixed business).
   1. An operating company is a business which conducts an economic activity by generating and selling, or trading, in a product or service.
   2. A holding company is a business which derives its revenues by receiving returns on its assets which may include operating companies and/or other businesses.
C. The Asset Based Approach should be considered in valuations conducted at the total entity level and involving the following:
   1. An investment or real estate holding company.
   2. A business appraised on a basis other than as a going concern. Valuations of *particular ownership interests* in an entity may or may not require the use of the Asset Based Approach.
D. The Asset Based Approach should not be the sole appraisal approach used in assignments relating to operating companies appraised as going concerns unless it is customarily used by sellers and buyers. In such cases, the appraiser must support the selection of this approach.

BVS-IV Income Approach to Business Valuation

I. **Preamble**
   A. This standard is required to be followed in all valuations of businesses, business ownership interests, and securities by all members of the American Society of Appraisers, be they Candidates, Accredited Members (AM), Accredited Senior Appraisers (ASA), or Fellows (FASA).
   B. The purpose of this standard is to define and describe the requirements for use of the income approach in valuation of businesses, business ownership interests, and securities, but not the reporting therefor.
   C. This present standard is applicable to appraisals and may not necessarily be applicable to limited appraisals and calculations as defined in BVS-I, Section II.B.
   D. This standard incorporates the general preamble to the Business Valuation Standards of the American Society of Appraisers.

II. **The Income Approach**
   A. The income approach is a general way of determining a value indication of a business, business ownership interest or security using one or more methods wherein a value is determined by converting anticipated benefits.
   B. Both capitalization of benefits methods and discounted future benefits methods are acceptable. In capitalization of benefits methods, a representative benefit level is divided or multiplied by a capitalization factor to convert the benefit to value. In discounted future benefits methods, benefits are estimated for each of several future periods. These benefits are converted to value by the application of a discount rate using present value techniques.

III. Anticipated Benefits

A. Anticipated benefits, as used in the income approach, are expressed in monetary terms. Depending on the nature of the business, business ownership interest or security being appraised and other relevant factors, anticipated benefits may be reasonably represented by such items as net cash flow, dividends, and various forms of earnings.

B. Anticipated benefits should be estimated considering such items as the nature, capital structure, and historical performance of the related business entity, expected future outlook for the business entity and relevant industries, and relevant economic factors.

IV. Conversion of Anticipated Benefit

A. Anticipated benefits are converted to value using procedures which consider the expected growth and timing of the benefits, the risk profile of the benefits stream and the time value of money.

B. The conversion of anticipated benefits to value normally requires the determination of a capitalization rate or discount rate. In determining the appropriate rate, the appraiser should consider such factors as the level of interest rates, rates of return expected by investors on relevant investments, and the risk characteristics of the anticipated benefits.

C. In discounted future benefits methods, expected growth is considered in estimating the future stream of benefits. In capitalization of benefits methods, expected growth is incorporated in the capitalization rate.

D. The rate of return used (capitalization rate or discount rate) should be consistent with the type of anticipated benefits used. For example, pre-tax rates of return should be used with pre-tax benefits; common equity rates of return should be used with common equity benefits; and net cash flow rates should be used with net cash flow benefits.

BVS-V   Market Approach to Business Valuation

I. Preamble

A. This standard is required to be followed in all valuations of businesses, business ownership interests, and securities by all members of the American Society of Appraisers, be they Candidates, Accredited Members (AM), Accredited Senior Appraisers (ASA), or Fellows (FASA).

B. The purpose of this standard is to define and describe the requirements for use of the market approach in valuation of businesses, business ownership interests, and securities, but not the reporting therefor.

C. This present standard is applicable to appraisals and may not necessarily be applicable to limited appraisals and calculations as defined in BVS-I, Section II.B.

D. This standard incorporates the general preamble to the Business Valuation Standards of the American Society of Appraisers.

II. The Market Approach

A. The market approach is a general way of determining a value indication of a business, business ownership interest or security using one or more methods that compare the subject to similar businesses, business ownership interests and securities that have been sold.

    B. Examples of market approach methods include the Guideline Company method and analysis or prior transactions in the ownership of the subject company.

III. Reasonable Basis for Comparison

    A. The investment used for comparison must provide a reasonable basis for the comparison.

    B. Factors to be considered in judging whether a reasonable basis for comparison exists include:

        1. Sufficient similarity of qualitative and quantitative investment characteristics.

        2. Amount and verifiability of data known about the similar investment.

        3. Whether or not the price of the similar investment was obtained in an arms length transaction, or a forced or distress sale.

IV. Manner of Comparison

    A. The comparison must be made in meaningful manner and must not be misleading. Such comparisons are normally made through the use of valuation ratios. The computation and use of such ratios should provide meaningful insight about the pricing of the subject considering all relevant factors. Accordingly, care should be exercised in the following:

        1. Selection of underlying data used for the ratio.

        2. Selection of the time period and/or averaging method used for the underlying data.

        3. Manner of computing and comparing the subject's underlying data.

        4. The timing of the price data used in the ratio.

    B. In general, comparisons should be made using comparable definitions of the components of the valuation ratios. However, where appropriate, valuation ratios based on components which are reasonably representative of continuing results may be used.

V. Rules of Thumb

    A. Rules of thumb may provide insight on the value of a business, business ownership interest or security. However, value indications derived from the use of rules of thumb should not be given substantial weight unless supported by other valuation methods and it can be established that knowledgeable buyers and sellers place substantial reliance on them.

BVS-VI Reaching a Conclusion of Value

I. Preamble

    A. This standard is required to be followed in all valuations of businesses, business ownership interests, and securities by all members of the American Society of Appraisers, be they Candidates, Accredited Members (AM), Accredited Senior Appraisers (ASA), or Fellows (FASA).

    B. The purpose of this standard is to define and describe the requirements for reaching a final conclusion of value in valuation of businesses, business ownership interests, or securities.

C. This present standard is applicable to appraisals and may not necessarily be applicable to limited appraisals and calculations as defined in BVS-I, Section II.B.

D. This standard incorporates the general preamble to the Business Valuation Standards of the American Society of Appraisers.

II. **General**

A. The conclusion of value reached by the appraiser shall be based upon the applicable standard of value, the purpose and intended use of the valuation, and all relevant information obtained as of the appraisal date in carrying out the scope of the assignment.

B. The conclusion of value reached by the appraiser will be based on value indications resulting from one or more methods performed under one or more appraisal approaches.

III. **Selection and Weighing of Methods**

A. The selection of and reliance on the appropriate method and procedures depends on the judgment of the appraiser and not on the basis of any prescribed formula. One or more approaches may not be relevant to the particular situation. More than one method under an approach may be relevant to a particular situation.

B. The appraiser must use informed judgment when determining the relative weight to be accorded to indications of value reached on the basis of various methods or whether an indication of value from a single method should dominate. The appraiser's judgment may be presented either in general terms or in terms of mathematical weighting of the indicated values reflected in the conclusion. In any case, the appraiser should provide the rationale for the selection or weighting of the method or methods relied on in reaching the conclusion.

C. In formulating a judgment about the relative weights to be accorded to indications of value determined under each method or whether an indication of value from a single method should dominate, the appraiser should consider factors such as:

1. The applicable standard of value;
2. The purpose and intended use of the valuation;
3. Whether the subject is an operating company, a real estate or investment holding company, or a company with substantial non-operating or excess assets;
4. Quality and reliability of data underlying the indication of value;
5. Such other factors which, in the opinion of the appraiser, are appropriate for consideration.

IV. **Additional Factors to Consider**

As appropriate for the valuation assignment as defined, and if not considered in the process of determining and weighting the indications of value provided by various procedures, the appraiser should separately consider the following factors in reaching a final conclusion of value:

A. Marketability, or lack thereof, considering the nature of the business, business ownership interest or security, the effect of relevant contractual and legal restrictions, and the condition of the markets.

B. Ability of the appraised interest to control the operation, sale, or liquidation of the relevant business.

C. Such other factors which, in the opinion of the appraiser, are appropriate for consideration.

BVS-VII Comprehensive, Written Business Valuation Report

I. **Preamble**
   A. This standard is required to be followed in the preparation of comprehensive, written business valuation reports by all members of the American Society of Appraisers, be they Candidates, Accredited Members (AM), Accredited Senior Appraisers (ASA), or Fellows (FASA).
   B. The purpose of this standard is to define and describe the requirements for the written communication of the results of a business valuation, analysis or opinion, but not the conduct thereof.
   C. This standard incorporates the general preamble to the Business Valuation Standards of the American Society of Appraisers.

II. **Signature and Certification**
   A. An appraiser assumes responsibility for the statements made in the comprehensive, written report and indicates the acceptance of that responsibility by signing the report. To comply with this standard, a comprehensive, written report must be signed by the appraiser. For the purpose of this standard, the appraiser is the individual or entity under-taking the appraisal assignment under a contract with the client.
   B. Clearly, at least one individual is responsible for the valuation conclusion(s) expressed in the report. A report must contain a certification, as required by Standard 10 of the *Uniform Standards of Professional Appraisal Practice* of The Appraisal Foundation, in which the individuals responsible for the valuation conclusion(s) must be identified.

III. **Assumptions and Limiting Conditions**
   The following assumptions and/or limiting conditions must be stated:
   1. Pertaining to bias—a report must contain a statement that the appraiser has no interest in the asset appraised, or other conflict, which could cause a question as to the appraiser's independence or objectivity or if such an interest or conflict exists, it must be dis-closed.
   2. Pertaining to data used—where appropriate, a report must indicate that an appraiser relied on data supplied by others, without further verification by the appraiser, as well as the sources which were relied on.
   3. Pertaining to validity of the valuation—a report must contain a statement that a valuation is valid only for the valuation date indicated and for the purpose stated.

IV. **Definition of the Valuation Assignment**
   The precise definition of the valuation assignment is a key aspect of communication with users of the report. The following are key components of such a definition and must be included in the report:
   1. The business interest valued must be clearly defined, such as "100 shares of the Class A common stock of the XYZ Corporation" or "a 20% limited partnership interest in the ABC Limited Partnership." The existence, rights and/or restrictions of other classes of ownership in the business appraised must also be adequately described if they are relevant to the conclusion of value.

2. The purpose and use of the valuation must be clearly stated, such as "a determination of fair market value for ESOP purposes" or "a determination of fair value for dissenter's rights purposes." If a valuation is being done pursuant to a particular statute, the particular statute must be referenced.

3. The standard of value used in the valuation must be stated and defined. The premise of value, such as a valuation on a minority interest or a control basis, must be stated.

4. The appraisal date must be clearly defined. The date of the preparation of the report must be indicated.

V. Business Description

A comprehensive, written business valuation report must include a business description which covers all relevant factual areas, such as:

1. Form of organization (corporation, partnership, etc.)
2. History
3. Products and/or services and markets and customers
4. Management
5. Major assets, both tangible and intangible
6. Outlook for the economy, industry and company
7. Past transactional evidence of value
8. Sensitivity to seasonal or cyclical factors
9. Competition
10. Sources of information used

VI. Financial Analysis

A. An analysis and discussion of a firm's financial statements is an integral part of a business valuation and must be included. Exhibits summarizing balance sheets and income statements for a period of years sufficient to the purpose of the valuation and the nature of the subject company must be included in the valuation report.

B. Any adjustments made to the reported financial data must be fully explained.

C. If projections of balance sheets or income statements were utilized in the valuation, key assumptions underlying the projections must be included and discussed.

D. If appropriate, the company's financial results relative to those of its industry must be discussed.

VII. Valuation Methodology

A. The valuation method or methods selected, and the reasons for their selection, must be discussed. The steps followed in the application of the method or methods selected must be described and must lead to the valuation conclusion.

B. The report must include an explanation of how any variables such as discount rates, capitalization rates or valuation multiples were determined and used. The rationale and/or supporting data for any premiums or discounts must be clearly presented.

VIII. Comprehensive, Written Report Format

The comprehensive, written report format must provide a logical progression for clear communication of pertinent information, valuation methods and conclusions and must incorporate the other specific requirements of this standard, including the signature and certification provisions.

IX. Confidentiality of Report
No copies of the report will be furnished to persons other than the client without the client's specific permission or direction unless ordered by a court of competent jurisdiction.

Definitions

Adjusted book value	The book value which results after one or more asset or liability amounts are added, deleted or changed from the respective book amounts.
Appraisal	The act or process of determining value. It is synonymous with valuation.
Appraisal approach	A general way of determining value using one or more specific appraisal methods. (See *Asset based approach, Market approach* and *Income approach* definitions).
Appraisal method	Within approaches, a specific way to determine value.
Appraisal procedure	The act, manner and technique of performing the steps of an appraisal method.
Appraised value	The appraiser's opinion or determination of value.
Asset based approach	A general way of determining a value indication of a business's assets and/or equity interest using one or more methods based directly on the value of the assets of the business less liabilities.
Book value	1. With respect to assets, the capitalized cost of an asset less accumulated depreciation, depletion or amortization as it appears on the books of account of the enterprise.
	2. With respect to a business enterprise, the difference between total assets (net of depreciation, depletion and amortization) and total liabilities of an enterprise as they appear on the balance sheet. It is synonymous with net book value, net worth and shareholder's equity.
Business appraiser	A person, who by education, training and experience is qualified to make an appraisal of a business enterprise and/or its intangible assets.
Business enterprise	A commercial, industrial or service organization pursuing an economic activity.
Business valuation	The act or process of arriving at an opinion or determination of the value of a business or enterprise or an interest therein.
Capitalization	1. The conversion of income into value.
	2. The capital structure of a business enterprise.
	3. The recognition of an expenditure as a capital asset rather than a period expense.

Capitalization factor	Any multiple or divisor used to convert income into value.
Capitalization rate	Any divisor (usually expressed as a percentage) that is used to convert income into value.
Capital structure	The composition of the invested capital.
Cash flow	Net income plus depreciation and other non-cash charges.
Control	The power to direct the management and policies of an enterprise.
Control premium	The additional value inherent in the control interest as contrasted to a minority interest, that reflects its power of control.
Discount for lack of control	An amount or percentage deducted from a prorata share of the value of 100 percent of an equity interest in a business, to reflect the absence of some or all of the powers of control.
Discount rate	A rate of return used to convert a monetary sum, payable or receivable in the future, into present value.
Economic life	The period over which property may be profitably used.
Effective date	The data as of which the appraiser's opinion of value applies (also referred to as appraisal date, valuation date and/or as of date).
Enterprise	See *Business enterprise.*
Equity	The owner's interest in property after deduction of all liabilities.
Fair market value	The amount at which property would change hands between a willing seller and a willing buyer when neither is under compulsion to buy and when both have reasonable knowledge of the relevant facts.
Going concern	An operating business enterprise.
Going-concern value	1. The value of an enterprise, or an interest therein, as a going concern. 2. Intangible elements of value in a business enterprise resulting from factors such as: having a trained work force; an operational plant; and the necessary licenses, systems and procedures in place.
Goodwill	The intangible asset which arises as a result of name, reputation, customer patronage, location, products and similar factors that have not been separately identified and/or valued but which generate cconomic benefits.
Income approach	A general way of determining a value indication of a business, business ownership interest or security using one or more methods wherein a value is determined by converting anticipated benefits.

Invested capital	The sum of the debt and equity in an enterprise on a long term basis.
Majority interest	Ownership position greater than 50% of the voting interest in an enterprise.
Majority control	The degree of control provided by a majority position.
Market approach	A general way of determining a value indication of a business, business ownership interest or security using one or more methods that compare the subject to similar businesses, business ownership interests or securities that have been sold.
Marketability discount	An amount or percentage deducted from an equity interest to reflect lack of marketability.
Minority interest	Ownership position less than 50% of the voting interest in an enterprise.
Minority discount	A discount for lack of control applicable to a minority interest.
Net assets	Total assets less total liabilities.
Net income	Revenue less expenses, including taxes.
Rate of return	An amount of income (loss) and/or change in value realized or anticipated on an investment, expressed as a percentage of that investment.
Replacement cost new	The current cost of a similar new item having the nearest equivalent utility as item being appraised.
Report date	The date of the report. May be the same as or different from the appraisal date.
Reproduction cost new	The current cost of an identical new item.
Rule of thumb	A mathematical relationship between or among a number of variables based on experience, observation, hearsay, or a combination of these, usually applicable to a specific industry.
Valuation	See *Appraisal.*
Valuation ratio	A factor wherein a value or price serves as the numerator and financial, operating or physical data serve as the denominator.
Working capital	The amount by which current assets exceed current liabilities.

SBVS-1 The Guideline Company Valuation Method

I. Preamble

A. This statement is required to be followed in all valuation of businesses, business ownership interests, and securities by all members of the American Society of Appraisers, be they Candidates, Accredited Members (AM), Accredited Senior Appraisers (ASA), or Fellows (FASA).

B. The purpose of this statement is to define and describe the requirements for the use of guideline companies in the valuation of businesses, business ownership interests or securities.

C. This statement incorporates the general preamble to the Business Valuation Standards of the American Society of Appraisers.

II. Conceptual Framework

A. Market transactions in businesses, business ownership interests or securities can provide objective, empirical data for developing valuation ratios to apply in business valuation.

B. The development of valuation ratios from guideline companies should be considered for use in the valuation of businesses, business ownership interests or securities, to the extent that adequate information is available.

C. Guideline companies are companies that provide a reasonable basis for comparison to the investment characteristics of the company being valued. Ideal guideline companies are in the same industry as the company being valued; but if there is insufficient transaction evidence available in the same industry it may be necessary to select companies with an underlying similarity of relevant investment characteristics such as markets, products, growth, cyclical variability and other salient factors.

III. Search for Selection of Guideline Companies

A. A thorough, objective search for guideline companies is required to establish the credibility of the valuation analysis. The procedure must include criteria for screening and selecting guideline companies.

B. Empirical data from guideline companies can be found in transactions involving either minority or controlling interests in either publicly traded or closely held companies.

IV. Financial Data of the Guideline Companies

A. It is necessary to obtain and analyze financial and operating data on the guideline companies, as available.

B. Consideration should be given to adjustments to the financial data of the subject company and the guideline companies to minimize the difference in accounting treatments when such differences are significant. Unusual or nonrecurring items should be analyzed and adjusted as appropriate.

V. Comparative Analysis of Qualitative and Quantitative Factors

A comparative analysis of qualitative and quantitative similarities and differences between guideline companies and the subject company must be made to assess the investment attributes of the guideline companies relative to the subject company.

VI. Valuation Ratios Derived From Guideline Companies

A. Price information of the guidelines companies must be related to the appropriate underlying financial data of each guideline company in order to compute appropriate valuation ratios.

B. The valuation ratios for the guideline companies and comparative analysis of qualitative and quantitative factors should be used together to determine appropriate valuation ratios for application to the subject company.

C. Several valuation ratios may be selected for application of the subject company and several value indications may be obtained. The appraiser should consider the relative importance accorded to each of the value indications utilized in arriving at the valuation conclusion.

D. To the extent that adjustments for dissimilarities with respect to minority and control, or marketability, have not been made earlier, appropriate adjustments for these factors must be made, if applicable.

Appendix D

General Bibliography

Articles

Berkowitz, Richard K., and Joseph A. Blanco. "Putting a Price Tag on Your Company." *Nation's Business* (January 1992), pp. 29–31.

Bolotsky, Michael J. "Adjustments for Differences in Ownership Rights, Liquidity, Information Access, and Information Reliability: An Assessment of 'Prevailing Wisdom' versus the 'Nath Hypotheses.'" *Business Valuation Review* (September 1991), pp. 94–110.

Dukes, William P., and Oswald D. Bowlin. "Valuation of Closely-Held Firms." *Business Valuation Review* (December 1990), pp. 127–37.

Elgin, Peggie R. "Valuation Gains as Tool for Strategic Business Planning." *Corporate Cashflow* (March 1993), p. 14.

Emory, John D. "Why Business Valuation and Real Estate Appraisal Are Different." *Business Valuation News* (June 1990), pp. 5–8.

Englebrecht, Ted D., and Cathy H. Leeson. "Valuation of Closely Held Stock." *Tax Executive* (October 1978), pp. 57–64.

Field, Irving M. "A Review of the Principles of Valuation." *ASA Valuation* (June 1986), pp. 2–10.

Fodor, Gary, and Edward Mazza. "Business Valuation Fundamentals for Planners." *Journal of Financial Planning* (October 1992), pp. 170–79.

Friedman, Richard. "Business Valuation: Calculating It Right." *Practical Accountant* (October 1994), pp. 34–41.

Gregory, Michael A. "Why Appraisers Should Be Concerned with Standards." *Business Valuation Review* (March 1994), pp. 33–35.

Harper, Charles P., and Lawrence C. Rose. "Accuracy of Appraisers and Appraisal Methods of Closely Held Companies." *Entrepreneurship Theory & Practice* (Spring 1993), pp. 21–33.

Haynsworth, Harry J. "Valuation of Business Interests." *Mercer Law Review* (Winter 1982), pp. 457–517.

Hitchner, James R. "Valuation of Closely Held Businesses." *Tax Adviser* (July 1992), pp. 471–79.

Hochberg, R. Mark. "Valuing a Closely Held Business." *Financial World* (July 20, 1993), pp. 71–72.

Hoeppner, James B. "Closely Held Business Interests—Valuation Strategies." *Tax Adviser* (April 1990), pp. 218–20.

Howitt, Idelle A. "How to Appraise an Appraiser." *Journal of Employee Ownership Law and Finance* (Winter 1995), pp. 89–100.

————. "Valuing Closely Held Stock." *CPA Journal* (September 1993), pp. 44–45 ff.

Kaplan, Steven P., and Egon Fromm. "The Impact of Taxes on the Value of Close Corporations." *Estate Planning* (May/June 1992), pp. 137–42.

Kleeman, Robert E. "Valuing the Closely Held Business Entity: A Lawyer's Guide to Business Valuation." *American Journal of Family Law* (Winter 1990), pp. 385–96.

Labovitz, Irving D. "The Ongoing Development of 'Fair Market Value' Under Section 506." *Commercial Law Journal* (Spring 1993), pp. 162–78.

LeClair, Mark S. "Valuing the Closely-Held Corporation: The Validity and Performance of Established Valuation Procedures." *Accounting Horizons* (September 1990), pp. 31–42.

Ledereich, Leonard, and Joel G. Ledereich "What's a Business Worth? Valuation Methods for Accountants." *National Public Accountant* (February 1990), pp. 18–22.

Longenecker, Ruth R. "A Practical Guide to Valuation of Closely Held Stock." *Trusts & Estates* (January 1983), pp. 32–41.

Marcus, Fred J., and Douglas K. Freeman. "Valuation of Closely-Held Stock." *Journal of the American Society of CLU & ChFC* (September 1993), pp. 24–25.

Mard, Michael J. "The Business Valuation Process." *FAIR$HARE: The Matrimonial Law Monthly* (November 1991), pp. 25–26.

Meacham, Allen. "The Role of a Quality Control Checklist in Avoiding Appraisal Report Errors." *Appraisal Journal* (April 1993), pp. 261–66.

Murphy, John W. "Using an Appraiser to Value the Closely-Held Business." *FAIR$HARE: The Matrimonial Law Monthly* (March 1992), pp. 6–7.

Patton, Kenneth W. "What Is a Business Worth? A General Overview." *FAIR$HARE: The Matrimonial Law Monthly* (December 1994), pp. 7–8.

Reilly, Robert F. "Tackling a Common Appraisal Problem." *Journal of Accountancy* (October 1992), pp. 86–92.

————. "What Appraisers Need to Know about Deprivation Appraisals." *ASA Valuation* (January 1993), pp. 10–17.

————. "What Appraisers Need to Know about the Bankruptcy Valuation Process." *ASA Valuation* (June 1992), pp. 42–51.

————. "What Financial Advisors Need to Know about Business Valuation and Security Analysis Services." *Corporate Growth Report* (January 1992), pp. 11–14;, 18.

Richie, Sheldon E., and Jeff C. Lamberth. "The Valuation Process of Closely Held Corporate Stock." *Texas Bar Journal* (June 1991), pp. 548 ff.

Scharfstein, Alan J. "The Right Price for a Business." *CPA Journal* (January 1991), pp. 42–47.

Schilt, James H. "Comments on the IRS Valuation Guide." *Business Valuation Review* (March 1994), pp. 36–38.

Schreier, W. Terrance, and O. Maurice Joy. "Judicial Valuation of 'Close' Corporation Stock: Alice In Wonderland Revisited." *Oklahoma Law Review,* vol. 31 (1978), pp. 853-85.

Shambo, James, and Sheldon H. Eveloff. "Is It a Good Idea to Accredit Specialists?" *Journal of Accountancy* (April 1993), pp. 41–44.

Sherman, W. Richard. "Valuation of Closely-Held Businesses: Two Techniques." *Ohio CPA Journal* (June 1994), pp. 37–45.

Siciliano, Peter J., and Mark Jones. "Business Valuation for the Nonspecialist: Finding the Best Value." *Practical Accountant* (September 1991), pp. 70 ff.

Siegel, Joel G., and Mel Gavron. "Weighty Decisions: How Best to Price a Closely Held Business." *National Public Accountant* (April 1994), pp. 17–19.

Spencer, Leslie. "Valuing a Business." *Forbes* (April 11, 1994), pp. 98–99.

Thiewes, Ronald C. "Principles of Valuing Closely-Held Business Interests." *Journal of the Missouri Bar Association* (September 1992), pp. 437–43.

Tole, Thomas M.; Sammy O. McCord; and Charles P. Edmonds. "How Much Is the Business Worth?" *Real Estate Review* (Summer 1993), pp. 39–43.

Trugman, Gary R. "What Is Fair Market Value? Back to Basics." *FAIR$HARE: The Matrimonial Law Monthly* (June 1990), pp. 11–13.

Wall, Patricia S., and Lee Sarver. "Appraiser's Liability: An Overview." *National Public Accountant* (December 1992), pp. 42–46.

Young, S. David. "Business Valuation and the Privatization Process in Eastern Europe: Challenges, Issues, and Solutions." *Journal of Multinational Financial Management,* vol. 1, no. 4 (1991), pp. 47–65.

Books

Babcock, Henry A. *Appraisal Principles and Procedures.* Washington, D.C.: American Society of Appraisers, 1980.

Bodie, Zvi; Alex Kane; and Alan J. Marcus. *Investments,* 2nd ed. Burr Ridge, IL: Irwin Professional Publishing, 1993.

Bonbright, James C. *The Valuation of Property.* Charlottesville, VA: The Miche Company, 1965 (reprint of 1936 ed.).

Brealey, Richard A.; Stewart C. Myers; and Alan J. Marcus. *Fundamentals of Corporate Finance.* New York: McGraw-Hill, 1994.

Burke, Frank M. *Valuation and Valuation Planning for Closely Held Businesses.* Englewood Cliffs, NJ: Prentice Hall, 1981.

Cohen, Jerome B.; Edward D. Zinbarg; and Arthur Zeikel. *Investment Analysis and Portfolio Management,* 5th ed. Burr Ridge, IL: Irwin Professional Publishing, 1987.

Copeland, Thomas; Tim Koller; and Jack Murrin. *Valuation: Measuring and Managing the Value of Companies,* 2nd ed. New York: John Wiley & Sons, 1994.

Cottle, Sidney; Roger F. Murray; and Frank E. Block. *Graham and Dodd's Security Analysis,* 5th ed. New York: McGraw-Hill, 1988.

Dewing, Arthur Stone. *The Financial Policy of Corporations,* 5th ed., vols. 1 and 2. New York: Ronald Press, 1953.

Fishman, Jay E.; Shannon P. Pratt; J. Clifford Griffith; and D. Keith Wilson. *Guide to Business Valuations,* 5th ed. Fort Worth, TX: Practitioners Publishing Company, 1995.

Higgins, Robert C. *Analysis for Financial Management,* 3rd ed. Burr Ridge, IL: Irwin Professional Publishing, 1992.

Howitt, Idelle A., and Susan E. Schechter, eds. *Federal Tax Valuation Digest.* Boston: Warren Gorham & Lamont, annual.

IRS Valuation Guide for Income, Estate and Gift Taxes. Chicago: Commerce Clearing House, 1994.

Maginn, John L., and Donald L. Tuttle, eds. *Managing Investment Portfolios: A Dynamic Process,* 2nd ed. Charlottesville, VA: Institute of Chartered Financial Analysts, 1990.

McCarthy, George D., and Robert E. Healy. *Valuing a Company: Practices and Procedures.* New York: Ronald Press, 1971.

Mercer, Z. Christopher. *Valuing Financial Institutions.* Burr Ridge, IL: Irwin Professional Publishing, 1992.

Miles, Raymond C. *Basic Business Appraisal.* New York: John Wiley & Sons, 1984.

O'Neal, F. Hodge, and Robert B. Thompson. *O'Neal's Close Corporations: Law and Practice,* 3rd ed. Deerfield, IL: Clark Boardman Callaghan, 1995.

Pratt, Shannon P.; Robert F. Reilly; and Robert P. Schweihs. *Valuing Small Businesses and Professional Practices,* 2nd ed. Burr Ridge, IL: Irwin Professional Publishing, 1993.

Pratt, Shannon P.; Robert F. Reilly; Robert P. Schweihs; and Jay E. Fishman. *Business Valuation Videocourse* (videotape and course handbook). Jersey City, NJ: American Institute of Certified Public Accountants, 1993.

Reilly, Frank K. *Investment Analysis and Portfolio Management,* 4th ed. Orlando, FL: The Dryden Press, 1991.

Ross, Stephen A.; Randolph W. Westerfield; and Bradford D. Jordan. *Fundamentals of Corporate Finance,* 2nd ed. Burr Ridge, IL: Irwin Professional Publishing, 1993.

Schnepper, Jeff A. *The Professional Handbook of Business Valuation.* Reading, MS: Addison-Wesley Publishing, 1982.

Smith, Gordon V. *Corporate Valuation—A Business and Professional Guide.* New York: John Wiley & Sons, 1988.

Smith, Gordon V., and Russell L. Parr. *Valuation of Intellectual Property and Intangible Assets*, 2nd ed. New York: John Wiley & Sons, 1994.

Weil, Roman L; Michael J. Wagner; and Peter B. Frank. *Litigation Services Handbook: The Role of the Accountant as Expert,* 2nd ed. New York: John Wiley & Sons, 1995.

West, Thomas L., and Jeffrey D. Jones, eds. *Handbook of Business Valuation.* New York,: John Wiley & Sons, 1992.

White, Gerald I.; Ashwinpaul C. Sondhi; and Dov Fried. *The Analysis and Use of Financial Statements.* New York: John Wiley & Sons, 1994.

Woolery, Arlo, ed. *The Art of Valuation.* Lexington, MS: Lexington Books, 1978.

Zukin, James H., and John G. Mavredakis, eds. *Financial Valuation: Businesses and Business Interests.* New York: Maxwell Macmillan, 1990 (updated annually).

Index to Court Cases

General Index

A

Abandoned property, 627
Abandonment loss for nondepreciable business assets, 628
Abrams, Jay B., 326, 352n
Accelerated depreciation, 111–113
Accounting Principles Board Opinion No. 16, 541
Accounting Principles Board Opinion No. 17, 541
Accounting Principles Board Opinion No. 30, 119
Accounts receivable
  activity ratios, 131–132
  doubtful accounts, 107–108
Accredited Member (AM), 6
Accredited Senior Appraiser (ASA), 6
Accuracy-related penalties, 634
Acid-test ratio, 131
Acquisition multiple, 243-44
Acquisition premium, 300
Acquisition value, 544
ACRS (accelerated cost recovery system) depreciation method, 112
Activity ratios, 131–135
  in accounts receivable turnover, 131–132
  in inventory turnover, 132–133
  and sales to fixed assets and total assets, 134–135
  and sales to net working capital, 133–134
Adelman, Harvey E., 224n
Adelstein, Joel, 315
Adequate consideration, regulation relating to (DOL), 10, 727
Adjustable dividend rate of preferred stocks, 496
Adjusted book value, 256

Ad valorem taxes, 542, 686-716
  definitions of, 686-687
  and external obsolescence, 697-702
  and functional obsolescence, 694–697
  and market value as basis of property assessment, 687–688
  and property tax appeal process, 691–693
  and property tax equalization process, 688–690
  and property tax unitary process, 690–691
  and property tax valuation process, 688
  unitary method of assessment, 702–715
Ad valorem value, 544
A.E. Walbridge, 620n
Affidavits, 758–759
Affiliates, interest in, 118–119
Aged payables list, 60
Aged receivables list, 59–60
Aggregate consideration, 243
Albo, Wayne P., 251
The Alcar Group, Inc., 179
Alexander, G. J., 201
Alford, Andrew W., 237
Allowance for doubtful accounts, 107–108
Almanac of Business and Industrial Financial Ratios, 88, 90
Alternative dispute resolution, 783
Alternative valuation date, 22
Altman, Edward I., 284
American Arbitration Association (AAA), 788, 789
American Bankers Association, 4
American Institute of Certified Public Accountants (AICPA), 7–8, 55, 116

G

Gains, Mitchell M., 659n
Gale Research, 86
Gans, Mitchell M., 659n
Gasiorowski, John R., 124n
Geahigan, Priscilla Cheng, 98
Gelman, Milton, 332n, 338
Gelman study, 338
Generally accepted accounting
    principles (GAAP), 55
General Utilities, 659
Geometric mean (vs. arithmetic mean)
    equity risk premium, 174, 176
Gift and estate taxes
    debt securities, 481
    preferred stock, 494
    valuations, 643–651
Gilford, Saul, 360
Going-concern value versus liquidation
    value, 29–30, 210, 216, 242
Going-in capitalization rate, 269
Goodwill, 292–93
Government agencies and government
    publications, 87
Graham, Benjamin, 498
Graham, Michael D., 238
Grant, Mary McNierney, 103
Gregory. Michael A., 821
Griffith, J. Clifford, 823
Gross cash flow, 217
Gross domestic product (GDP), 81
Gross profit to sales, 140
Gross state product (GSP), 81
Growth, 226
Guideline company method, 204–238,
    415–17, 420, 422–28
    capitalization of dividends, 226–227
    central tendency and dispersion,
        224–225
    company tables, 218–223
    comparative ratio analysis, 221–222
    criteria for selection, 211–214
    excess assets or asset deficiencies,
        231
    going-concern value versus
        liquidation value, 210
    marginal operating real estate, 231
    market value data, 222

multi-line companies, 232
multiple of stock value to asset
    value, 228–230
multiples of earnings or cash flow,
    225–226
multiples of revenue, 227–228
nonoperating assets, 230–231
ownership characteristics, 209–210
portfolio effect, 232
public, 206–208
relationship to control premium,
    304–05
time period, 215
value measures, 216–218
*Guide to Special Issues and Indexes of
    Periodicals,* 87
Gustave Heckscher, 360

H

Hall, Lance S., 320n, 342n
Hall, Owen P., Jr., 224n
Halperin, Michael, 103
Hamada, Robert S., 169n
Hamilton, Mary T., 27n
*Handbook of Small Business Valuation
    Formulas and Rules of Thumb,*
    249
Harmonic mean, 222, 225
Harper, Charles P., 821
Harris, Don L., 322n
Hartwig, J.D., 669n, 670n
Haut, Arthur N., 313n
Haynsworth, Harry J., 821
Healy, Robert E., 823
Hearsay evidence, 764–67
Hempstead, Jean C., 603
Henderson, A. Randal, 251
H.H. Marshman, 620n
Hickman, Kent, 204n, 238
Higgins, Robert C., 823
Himstreet, William C., 391
Hitchner, James R., 821
HLHZ Control Premium Studies,
    318–19
Hochberg, R. Mark, 821
Hodges, John C., 392
Hoeppner, James B., 821
Holding companies, 216, 319–320

R